KU-635-722

# Introduction by Michael Howard

The twelve years which have passed since *The Struggle for Europe* was first published have not diminished the enthusiasm with which it was immediately and universally received. Now, as then, it stands out as one of those rare works of military history, such as Napier's *History of the War in the Peninsula*, which have enduring value both as an eyewitness account and as an authoritative survey of a large and complex campaign.

Wilmot had two advantages in tackling the immense task which he set himself in writing so general yet so authoritative a survey of the final years of the Second World War. The first was his experience as a professional war correspondent, which made him familiar with the conduct of war at every level from platoon to Army Group, and which enabled him to study at close quarters the commanders whose operations he was to describe. The second was his success in gaining rapid access to enemy archives which, but for the fortunes of war, might have remained sealed for a generation, and which might still, but for the requirements of the Nuremberg Trials, have taken years to sift. These advantages were not peculiar to Wilmot, but he exploited them with outstanding ability. Not all correspondents had his flair for the vital spot and the vital problem, while very few of those who had access to the mountains of captured documents had his capacity to winnow out the essentials. A further decade of sifting and editing by teams of scholars, British, American and German, has merely shown how little Wilmot missed in the few years that he had at his disposal to work on them.

The result of Wilmot's labours was a book which deserves to rank as highly as a journalistic scoop as it does as a work of history. Sir Winston Churchill's *Second World War* was still incomplete when *The Struggle for Europe* first appeared; so it fell to Wilmot to give the English-speaking world the first general survey, based on documents, of the manner in which strategy and grand tactics had been shaped on both sides of the hill, and of the bitter conflicts which lay behind the great decisions of the war. The Anglo-American differences over Grand Strategy; the conflicting views over the shaping of the Normandy campaign; the disputes over the course of operations in the late summer of 1944; the mounting suspicions between the Soviet Union and the Western Allies; above all, the friction between Hitler and his generals, culminating in the plot of July 20th 1944: all these conflicts were partially known to the general public, but it was Wilmot who first described them in full, showed their mutual interaction, and fitted them into a single narrative which bore the stamp of finality.

Yet every historian, however expert and objective, writes within the limitations imposed by his sources and by the values which he unconsciously absorbs from the surrounding society. Wilmot had no access to Russian source-material—a drawback for which not he but Soviet government policy must bear the blame; and he wrote his book during the culminating years of the 'Cold War' between 1947 and 1952, when it was almost impossible for anyone living in Western Europe to see the actions of the Soviet government in perspective. The first of these limitations made Wilmot's picture a very one-sided affair. The campaign in Russia, the greatest in the war, is given the briefest attention, and seen entirely through the eyes of the German High Command. The appalling sufferings which the Russian people endured at the hands of the German invaders are passed over in silence; and no attempt is made to assess the contribution of the Russian armies to the final victory. Had he lived, Wilmot, a man as generous as he was realistic, would surely have wished to revise his judgement that "the Western Allies, while gaining military victory, suffered political defeat." But for the Russians it is questionable whether there would have been any military victory for the West; and to see the resulting division of Europe into spheres of influence based on military occupation as a 'political defeat' indicates Western expectations of dominance in Eastern Europe which the British Government, at least, certainly did not share.

The same lack of perspective led Wilmot to make judgements about the place of the Balkans in Western strategy which now need revision. The documents do not bear out Wilmot's suggestion that as early as 1943 Mr. Churchill was seeking in the Mediterranean "to devise a plan of campaign which would not only bring military success, but would ensure that victory did not leave the democratic cause politically weaker in any vital sphere." In 1943 the Prime Minister and the Chiefs of Staff still had one overriding preoccupation: how best to deploy their forces so as to bring relief to a still hard-pressed Russia. This was the argument which they used at every Allied Conference during that year to persuade the Americans into continuing the fight in the Mediterranean: to turn the whole area into a heavy liability for the Germans which would distract them from the East as effectively as any Second Front. This was the consideration, also, that led the British Government, in 1943, to transfer their support in Yugoslavia from the politically "reliable" but militarily ineffective Mihailovitch to the avowedly Communist, Moscow-trained Tito. Rightly or wrongly, Britain's object in the Balkans was still to help the Russians; not to forestall them.

It was unfortunately this, the least soundly-based part of Wilmot's work, that made the greatest impact during the years of the Cold War, and his tragic death in 1954 prevented him from revising it in the light of fuller information and a more equable political climate. But the intrinsic worth of the book still remains. It will be many years before it is replaced as the best single-volume survey of the trials and triumphs of the Western Allies in the closing years of the Second World War.

# CHESTER WILMOT

# THE STRUGGLE
# FOR EUROPE

INTRODUCTION BY
MICHAEL HOWARD

*Professor of War Studies in the
University of London*


COLLINS
ST JAMES'S PLACE
LONDON

| FIRST IMPRESSION | JANUARY, 1952 |
| NINTH IMPRESSION | FEBRUARY, 1957 |
| REVISED EDITION | APRIL, 1965 |
| SECOND IMPRESSION | JANUARY, 1967 |
| THIRD IMPRESSION | 1971 |

CENTRAL RESOURCES
LIBRARY

HERTFORDSHIRE
COUNTY LIBRARY

940·53A

5357517

ISBN 0 00 211757 6

FIRST PUBLISHED 1952
COPYRIGHT RESERVED

PRINTED IN GREAT BRITAIN
COLLINS CLEAR-TYPE PRESS
LONDON AND GLASGOW

# Contents

# CONTENTS

# Maps

*Drawn by J. F. Trotter*

# MAPS

Oh, how comely it is and how reviving
To the Spirits of just men long opprest,
When God into the hands of their deliverer,
Puts invincible might.

*Samson Agonistes*

# PREFACE

TEN days before the end of the war in Europe, Mr. Churchill sent Marshal Stalin a personal letter in the course of which he said: " There is not much comfort in looking into a future where you and the countries you dominate plus the Communist parties in many other states are all drawn up on one side and those who rallied to the English-speaking nations and their associates or dominions are on the other. It is quite obvious that their quarrel would tear the world to pieces and all of us leading men on either side who had anything to do with that would be shamed before history. Even embarking on a long period of suspicion, of abuse and counter-abuse, and of opposing policies would be a disaster hampering the great development of world prosperity for the masses which is attainable only by our trinity."

We know how well founded were the fears that prompted this letter. The cleavage between East and West, then becoming apparent, has grown wider with the years until to-day it is difficult to foresee how the gap may be bridged. The ' Iron Curtain,' the ' Satellite State ' and the ' Cold War ' seem to have become permanent features of the political landscape of Europe, and the threat of another conflict which might indeed " tear the world to pieces " casts its shadow across the peoples so lately released from the scourge of the last. If we are seeking the origins of this situation, we must examine not the development of relations between Russia and the Western Powers since the war, but the course of their relations during the war and the impact that these had on both German and Allied strategy. We must discover, if we can, what caused the destruction of the European balance of power which Britain went to war to maintain and which she and those associated with her in the North Atlantic Treaty are now making such sacrifices to restore.

In this book, therefore, I have endeavoured to explain how the present situation came about; how and why the Western Allies, while gaining military victory, suffered political defeat; how and why, in the process of crushing Nazi Germany and liberating Western Europe, they allowed the Soviet Union to gain control of Eastern Europe and to prevent the application there of the principles of the Atlantic Charter for which they had fought. In considering the history of the war in the

West from the perspective of the 1950's, I have tried to show not only how Hitler was overthrown but also why Stalin emerged victorious; how Russia came to replace Germany as the dominant power on the Continent; and how Stalin succeeded in obtaining from Roosevelt and Churchill what he had failed to obtain from Hitler.

In seeking the answers to these questions, I have started with the situation on the eve of Dunkirk, when the struggle for Europe seemed to have been decided in Germany's favour. In the first part of the book, which is called *The Way Back*, I have considered the stages by which Hitler's power in Western Europe was weakened and Allied power was developed until it again became possible for a British Army to establish itself on the far shore of the Channel. During the four years between the evacuation of Dunkirk and the invasion of Normandy the problem of crossing the Channel, in one direction or the other, exerted a decisive influence on the conduct and development of the war. It was the refusal of the British to admit defeat and the frustration of the German invasion plan in 1940 that drove Hitler into attacking Russia. It was the necessity of defeating the Red Army before the Anglo-American forces could strike back across the Channel that led Hitler to seek in the East a quick victory which exhausted the Wehrmacht. When the question of cross-Channel invasion became identified with the Soviet demand for the opening of a Second Front it assumed a new significance. Accordingly, the Second Front controversy has been considered here not merely in the light of its influence on the defeat of Germany, but also as a political issue the outcome of which was that Anglo-American military power was employed in Western Europe, not in the Balkans.

In the second part, *The Battle of Normandy*, I have dealt with the actual operations in some detail, for the story of the invasion is intrinsically exciting, especially now that it can be told from the evidence of both adversaries. More important, this battle was the supreme test of the Anglo-American alliance in action and provided its greatest single victory. Since so much depends on that alliance to-day, it is profitable to consider how it worked in the field last time, and in particular to evaluate the achievements of the commanders, Eisenhower, Montgomery and Bradley, who have been the subject of so much controversy and who are again in positions of great responsibility. Finally, these operations provide a warning that, if another aggressor enjoying complete security on his eastern front were to advance to the Channel, the Anglo-Saxon Powers would have little chance of liberating Europe by invasion, except at terrible cost to themselves and to Western civilisation. The cross-Channel assault of 1944 would certainly have been defeated if the Germans had not been fighting with the Russians on their backs.

The last part, *The Road to Berlin*, deals with the operations and the strategic and diplomatic decisions which determined both the final course of the war and the shape of post-war Europe. The Anglo-American victory in Normandy placed Hitler's defeat beyond question and the evidence suggests that if this victory had been fully exploited the outcome of the war would have been very much more favourable to the democratic cause. In the summer of 1944 the Western Allies had it in their power, if not to end the war against Germany that year, at least to ensure that the great capitals of Central Europe—Berlin, Prague and Vienna— would be liberated from Nazi rule by the West, not the East. In this phase of the story, it was essential to take the broad view and to bring out the close inter-relation between strategy and diplomacy, between military events and their political consequences. To take only one example, the German offensive in the Ardennes in the winter of 1944 was military in origin, for it was Hitler's answer to the failure of the Allies to exploit their opportunity in the autumn. But it was political in purpose, since Hitler's object was to split the Grand Alliance, to make the Western Allies consider a compromise peace, and enable him to keep the Russians out of Germany. In this it failed, but its political impact was no less great. In order to assemble the forces for the Ardennes, Hitler took the risk of weakening the Eastern Front. Thus, while holding the Anglo-American armies well to the west of the Rhine, Hitler gave Stalin the chance of advancing from the Vistula to the Oder on the eve of Yalta. This strategic situation reacted directly on the diplomatic discussions of that historic conference, for Stalin, having overwhelmed his enemies in the field, was able to outmanœuvre his allies at the conference table.

I have not attempted to carry the story beyond the end of the war, for the map of post-war Europe was already drawn when Germany capitulated. The struggle for Europe then entered upon a new phase which is still in the process of unfolding.

In an Appendix entitled *A Note on Sources* I have given a survey of the documents and other material on which I have drawn in the preparation of this book, and I have expressed my gratitude to those who aided me in the collection and evaluation of the evidence. Here, however, I wish to acknowledge my indebtedness to those who have helped me more directly in research or in the preparation and correction of the text. Mr. E. T. Williams of Balliol College, Oxford, who was Field-Marshal Montgomery's chief Intelligence officer from the Battle of Alamein to the end of the war, has been a most helpful counsellor and frank critic throughout. Captain B. H. Liddell Hart not only gave me the benefit of his unrivalled knowledge of military history, but placed at my disposal a great deal of original material which he has collected, read my manuscript with a discerning eye and saved me from many errors of fact and judgment. The text was also read in whole or in part by F. T. Smith and Ronald Politzer, by Lt.-Col. Graham Jackson (of the War Cabinet Historian's Office) and by Col. C. P. Stacey (the chief Canadian War Historian). I appreciate the many valuable suggestions they made for its improvement. I am indebted also to Otto Giles, who spent many weeks translating the surviving fragments of Hitler's staff conferences; to J. F. Trotter, who worked with endless patience and uncommon skill on the preparation of the maps; to Mrs. Caspar Brooke, who helped with research; and to Laurence Gilliam, of the B.B.C., on whose behalf much of the documentary material used was originally collected.

Finally, I wish to record my particular appreciation of the great and generous assistance of those who worked most closely with me: Miss Therese Denny, and Mr. Graham Irwin of Clare College, Cambridge. Mr. Irwin carried out most of the original research for the chapters dealing with Anglo-American strategy and diplomacy, checked and corrected both the manuscript and the proofs, compiled the index and finally saw the book through the press during my absence in Australia. To him, and to Miss Denny, I am indebted more than I can say.

*September 1951*                              CHESTER WILMOT

*Part One*

★

THE WAY BACK

# CHAPTER I

## IF NECESSARY, ALONE

IN the summer of 1942 four hundred million people in Europe lay under the yoke of German rule. The empire of Adolf Hitler, then at its greatest extent, stretched from the Mediterranean to the Arctic, from the English Channel to the Black Sea and almost to the Caspian. Between the Pyrenees and the Ukrainian steppes there was no other sovereign state but Switzerland. Even Hitler's partner, Mussolini, had been reduced to the role of a puppet. In the ancient capitals of Europe—in Athens, Rome and Vienna, in Paris and Prague, Oslo and Warsaw—all other voices were drowned by the voice of Nazi Germany. The spearheads of Hitler's panzer armies had reached the Volga and were within striking distance of the Nile. Far to the west his U-boats had carried the German offensive to the Atlantic coast of North America and into the Caribbean. In the east his new ally, Japan, had engulfed the colonies of older empires, gained command of Asiatic waters and borne the Rising Sun into the Indian Ocean. The possibility that Germany and Japan might join forces east of Suez could no longer be disregarded. In three years of war Hitler had been denied victory only in the sky above London and in the snow outside Moscow.

Germany was now in conflict with a coalition of world powers, but of these only the Soviet Union was heavily engaged against her and it had already suffered grievous losses. In fifteen months the Red Army had incurred upwards of five million casualties. The great provinces of White Russia and the Ukraine had been over-run and with them the armament resources of the Dnieper Valley and the Donetz Basin had come into Hitler's grasp. In 1941 Leningrad and Moscow had withstood assault, but the renewed German offensive of 1942 had carried the Wehrmacht to Stalingrad and deep into the Caucasus, creating thereby a direct threat to Russia's richest oilfields and thus to her very ability to maintain the struggle.

While Russia burned and bled, there was little the United States or Britain could yet do to help her. Great though their potential strength was, they could not bring their armies into action on the Continent until they had contained the Japanese, had cleared the Axis forces from North Africa and had established command of the sea. They could not

17

comply with Stalin's demand for a 'Second Front' in the West that year, nor could they maintain the flow of convoys to Russia's Arctic ports. On both these counts Stalin had bitterly reproached the Western Allies, accusing them of a double breach of faith. In Washington and London there were many in high places who feared that Stalin might be compelled to negotiate a separate peace with Hitler, or at least that Soviet military and economic power would be crippled before the resources of Britain and the New World could be mobilised and brought to bear upon the mainland of Europe. In either event Hitler would be free to turn his main strength against the West, defy invasion and condemn the occupied countries to years of bondage under a régime which denied the most cherished values that European civilisation has painfully built up over three thousand years.

Hitler, it seemed, was at the pinnacle of his power, and the people of the United Nations could not yet tell how or when he might be brought down. Already, however, as early as 1940 the war had taken its decisive turn. That year of Hitler's greatest triumph was the year of his first great failure: a failure of far greater ultimate consequence than all his victories. It was Britain's refusal to yield or even to compromise that had driven Hitler into the fateful course of invading Russia. It was Britain's defiance that had roused and nourished the spirit of resistance in Occupied Europe and had compelled Hitler, when he turned to the East, to leave one quarter of his strength in the West guarding his conquests and keeping the subject peoples in subjection. If he had been able to conquer or neutralise Britain, Hitler would have had no cause to fear a 'Second Front', for there would not have been at the western gates of his empire the base from which the forces of freedom would one day set forth to break down the walls of his *Festung Europa*.

Germany's defeat and Europe's liberation began at Dunkirk. On May 25th, 1940, Hitler's plan for the destruction of the Allied armies in the West was on the point of fulfilment. The German corridor which had been driven down the Somme Valley to the Channel coast five days earlier had now been widened and strengthened by the capture of Arras and the isolation of Calais. Of the Channel ports, only Dunkirk and Ostend remained as avenues of escape for the Belgian, British and French armies that were being forced back to the sea. The plan of General Weygand, the Allied Commander-in-Chief, for a counter-attack from north and south against the flanks of the corridor had come to nought. The Anglo-French force, which had been preparing to strike southwards, had been diverted north to meet a new German thrust which not only threatened to divide the Belgians from their allies but menaced Dunkirk and was soon to capture Ostend.

That day King Leopold came to the inevitable conclusion that the Belgian Army could fight no longer. That night the British Expeditionary

Force, under General Lord Gort, began its withdrawal from the Lille area towards Dunkirk. The British and French were being squeezed into a shrinking pocket and the squeeze would be intensified as soon as the imminent Belgian surrender laid bare the northern flank. The fate of the B.E.F. appeared to lie in the hollow of Hitler's hand.

Across the Channel the Admiralty was mustering every craft it could, but the Prime Minister (Winston Churchill) and his closest advisers believed that at most " 20,000 or 30,000 men might be re-embarked." The ships and beaches were extremely vulnerable to air attack and they would shortly be under shell-fire. The troops were so closely locked in battle that it seemed impossible for more than a few thousand to disengage so long as the Germans maintained their pressure. Moreover, any powerful thrust with armour could split the pocket in twain, for the British had few anti-tank guns and fewer tanks. The Prime Minister feared that within a week it would be his " hard lot to announce the greatest military disaster in our long history."

In Flanders the infantry divisions of von Bock's Army Group B, attacking from the east, might be held long enough on the several water-lines between Ypres and the sea, but on the south-western flank the panzer divisions of von Rundstedt's Army Group A, now freed from any threat of counter-attack, were poised to deliver the *coup de grâce*. On this flank Gort had improvised a defensive position along the Gravelines–St. Omer–Béthune Canal, the last water obstacle before Dunkirk, but as yet that line was thinly manned and the enemy had already established three bridgeheads across it. Von Kleist's Panzer Group was far closer to Dunkirk than was the bulk of Gort's infantry.

The intention of the German Commander-in-Chief (von Brauchitsch) was that Kleist's armour should drive straight on to Dunkirk. The plan, as drafted by his Chief of Staff (Halder), called for " Army Group B by heavy frontal attacks merely to hold the enemy who is making a planned withdrawal, while Army Group A, dealing with an enemy already whipped, cuts into his rear and strikes the decisive blow."[1] On May 24th, however, just as this plan was about to be implemented, Hitler intervened.

As Supreme Commander of the Armed Forces, Hitler was supervising operations from his Field H.Q. at Münstereifel and he had already exercised a decisive influence on the campaign.[2] Against the advice of von Brauchitsch and Halder he had insisted on placing the *Schwerpunkt* of the offensive in the Ardennes and thus had created the opportunity for his panzer divisions to break through at Sedan. When this was achieved, however, Hitler was unnerved by his own success and was reluctant to drive on to the Channel until infantry had been brought up to cover the exposed flank. On the third day of the break-through Halder had written in his diary: " The Führer keeps worrying unaccountably about

[1]Halder's Diary, May 25th, 1940.
[2]For an outline of the structure of the German High Command see Appendix B.

the southern flank. He rages and screams that we are on the way to ruin the whole campaign." Although his fears had been unjustified, Hitler was now concerned lest the French should succeed in forming a new front along the Somme. His eye was fixed on Paris, the ultimate political goal, not on Dunkirk, the immediate military objective.

On the evening of the 24th, having discovered that von Rundstedt took the same view, Hitler summoned von Brauchitsch to Münstereifel. There the Führer announced that the Battle of Flanders was as good as won; they must concentrate forthwith on the Battle of France. Von Rundstedt's tanks were to stop, for there was no point, said Hitler, in involving armour in country honeycombed with canals. He had fought in Flanders in the last war and he knew from experience that panzer divisions could achieve no decisive success there. The armour must be halted and reorganised for the next phase, the advance against Paris. Von Rundstedt was to hold a blocking position along the line Gravelines–St. Omer–Béthune, and the task of crushing the Allies would be left to von Bock. He would be the hammer; von Rundstedt the anvil.

Von Brauchitsch protested that von Bock's nearest forces were 35 miles from Dunkirk; von Rundstedt, with his tanks barely 15 miles from the port, had the position and the power to close the trap; if they were to wait for von Bock the British would escape. Hitler replied that he would not be distracted from his main purpose: to defeat France. It was the French Army that mattered: destroy that and he was master of Europe.

That night von Brauchitsch issued fresh instructions, and Halder noted: " The left wing, which consists of armoured and motorised forces and has no enemy in front of it, will be stopped dead in its tracks upon direct orders from the Führer. The finishing off of the encircled enemy army is to be left to the Luftwaffe."[1] This order remained in force for forty-eight hours and, while von Rundstedt's armour stood " paralysed on the high ground between Béthune and St. Omer," von Bock pushed " slowly ahead, suffering heavy losses." By May 27th, when at last the panzer divisions were allowed to advance, the B.E.F. had had three days' respite in which to strengthen its southern flank. The German attack was thwarted. On the 30th Halder wrote: " Bad weather has grounded the Luftwaffe and now we must stand by and watch countless thousands of the enemy getting away to England right under our noses." By June 4th, 338,000 Allied troops (two-thirds of them British) had been lifted from the beaches and harbour of Dunkirk by the seamen of England. In Churchill's words, " the nucleus and structure upon which alone Britain could build her armies of the future " had been saved.

[1]Halder's Diary, May 24th, 1940. Mr. Churchill contends (*The Second World War*, Vol. II, p. 70) that " the armour was halted . . . on the initiative not of Hitler, but of Rundstedt." This contention is based on the evidence of certain entries in the war diary of von Rundstedt's H.Q., but it is not supported by the records kept by Halder or Jodl (the Chief of the Operations Staff at Supreme H.Q.) nor by the testimony of the German generals concerned. Indeed, von Rundstedt asserts that the full entry in his war diary shows that the ' halt order ' originated with Hitler.

The Dunkirk decision was Hitler's first great military mistake, but it was not so irrational and short-sighted as some German generals have asserted. Although Hitler was influenced by the lure of Paris, the goal of all German conquerors, a more important factor was his determination to avoid the costly mistakes of 1914. *He* would not falter and be stopped on the Somme, as von Moltke had been stopped on the Marne through excessive concern about the British on the flank and through failure to maintain the momentum of the right wing. He felt he could safely ignore the British for the moment, and he was soon to confide to von Kleist the opinion: " They will not come back in this war." Although he had often warned his military leaders that Britain was the more formidable enemy, his personal triumph at Munich had profoundly affected his judgment of British character. He was fond of declaring: " Our enemies are little worms; I saw them at Munich."[1] But there he had not met Churchill.

In concentrating on Paris and the French and disregarding Dunkirk and the British, however, Hitler was following not mere intuition, but a plan of campaign which he had outlined to his Commanders-in-Chief twelve months earlier. On May 23rd, 1939, he had told them:

> If Holland and Belgium are successfully occupied and if France is also defeated, the fundamental conditions for a successful war against England will have been secured. England can then be blockaded from Western France at close quarters by the Air Force, while the Navy with its U-boats can extend the range of the blockade. When that is done, England will not be able to fight on the Continent and daily attacks by the Air Force and Navy will cut her life-lines. The moment England's supply routes are severed, she will be forced to capitulate.[2]

Since this was still his belief, Hitler considered that any troops who escaped from Dunkirk would be imprisoned in the British Isles. The important task, therefore, was to gain quick and undisputed possession of the French coastline, as a rampart against further British interference in European affairs, and of the continental bases from which Britain could be bombed and starved into submission.

The last British ship sailed from Dunkirk just before dawn on June 4th. At noon Hitler conferred with his Naval Commander-in-Chief, Raeder, and told him that he planned " to reduce the size of the Army as soon as France has been overthrown and to release all older men and

[1]Speaking to his Commanders-in-Chief, August 22nd, 1939. (Nuremberg Document 789 PS.)
[2]The transcript of Hitler's speech on this occasion was presented in evidence at the Nuremberg Trial. (Document L 79.)

skilled workers." "The Air Force and the Navy," said Hitler, "will have top priority."[1] The invasion of England was not discussed.

That same afternoon the House of Commons rang with the first of the speeches by which Churchill was to rally the nation and rouse the world. Britain, he said, would fight on "if necessary for years, if necessary alone," but Hitler was convinced that this defiant mood would not outlive the fall of France. Consequently, when the Axis leaders met at Munich on June 18th to discuss the French request for an armistice, Hitler was ready to offer lenient terms and was particularly anxious to avoid provoking France lest her Government and her fleet might cross the Channel and encourage the British to further resistance.

Summing up Hitler's views, the Italian Foreign Minister, Count Ciano, wrote in his diary: "If London wants war it will be a total war, complete, pitiless. But Hitler makes many reservations on the desirability of demolishing the British Empire, which, he considers, even to-day, to be an important factor in world equilibrium."[2] Undeceived by this show of tolerance, Ciano added, "Hitler is now the gambler who has made a big scoop and would like to get up from the table risking nothing more."

There was, however, more than the gambler's instinct behind Hitler's desire for an understanding. He wanted to make Britain come to terms, but he did not wish to inflict on her a defeat of such magnitude that it would bring about the disintegration of the British Empire. "This," he told his Commanders-in-Chief, "would not be of any advantage to Germany. German blood would be shed to accomplish something which would benefit only Japan, the United States and others."[3] Although he had established his 'fundamental conditions for a successful war against Britain,' Hitler was not ready to challenge her world power. His armed forces had been developed and equipped only for a continental war. He knew that he could not conquer the British Commonwealth and Empire until he had built up his navy and air force for a world-wide struggle with a maritime adversary, and had secured the fuel resources to support the vast oil consumption of such a conflict.

When Hitler marched into Poland, he had reserve stocks of oil for less than six months of active operations. His total oil 'income' in the next twelve months, some seven and a half million tons, proved only just sufficient to meet the demand at home and in the field, even though half this period was that of the inactive 'twilight war.' A long-term plan[4] had been laid for increasing Germany's domestic output of synthetic and natural oil from the 1939 level of three million tons to eleven million by 1944, but this development would not yield sufficient fuel to maintain

[1]Führer Naval Conferences, June 4th, 1940. (For comments on this and other sources, see Appendix A.)
[2]Ciano, *Diary*, pp. 266-7.
[3]Halder's Diary, July 13th, 1940.
[4]Revised Economic Plan for the OKW, July 12th, 1938. In this year the output of crude oil totalled 164 million tons in the U.S.A. and 29 million tons in the U.S.S.R.

large-scale strategic bombing as well as intensive U-boat warfare until 1942. Nor would the air and naval forces be ready before then. In the meantime, Hitler's ambitions lay in the East, not only because his ultimate European objective was the subjection of the Slavs and the conquest of their lands, but because he could not embark with confidence on what he had called the ' life and death struggle with Britain ' until he had gained absolute security in Eastern Europe and had harnessed its economic resources to the German war machine. He had frequently assured his Commanders-in-Chief that he would not repeat the Kaiser's folly of becoming involved in a war on two fronts and so far he had succeeded. The Munich Agreement had provided the necessary safe-guard while he absorbed Czechoslovakia. The Non-Aggression Pact with the Soviet Union had covered his rear while he struck in the West, but he had never regarded this Pact as more than a short-term insurance and he was now concerned about Russia's intentions.

In June 1940, just when Hitler was dwelling upon his next step in the West, his attention was distracted to the East by Soviet moves which were to lead to the early annexation of territories on the Baltic and the Black Sea, which Russia had lost after the First World War. In secret protocols to the Non-Aggression Pact Germany had agreed that the Rumanian province of Bessarabia and the three Baltic Republics (with the exception of a small area in southern Lithuania) lay within the Soviet sphere of influence. When the Red Army marched into Lithuania in mid-June, however, it occupied the area which had been allocated to Germany and did not withdraw when Berlin protested. A week later Molotov informed the German ambassador in Moscow, von der Schulen-burg, that the Soviet Union was about to demand from Rumania not only Bessarabia but also Bukovina, which had not been covered by the protocol. Hitler forestalled an immediate crisis by urging Rumania to yield, but he showed his annoyance and anxiety by advising Moscow that henceforth Germany would guarantee the territorial integrity of both Rumania and Hungary.

These developments had an immediate influence on Hitler's attitude to Britain. With the Russians in Bessarabia, barely a hundred miles from his main external source of oil at Ploesti, he dared not commit himself to a prolonged struggle with the British Empire. Accordingly, Hitler became interested in concluding with Britain an agreement which would give him a free hand in the East and enable him to avoid the ' two-front war ' which the German people had good reason to dread. Just as he had wanted a pact with Moscow in 1939 to cover his rear while he attacked in the West, so he now needed a pact with London, and he believed he could get it. Britain, he thought, " should be inclined to make peace when she learns she can still get it now at relatively little cost."[1] He was prepared to be generous; he would demand nothing

[1] Memorandum on the Situation, June 30th, 1940. This was written by General Jodl, Chief of the Armed Forces Operations Staff, but it embodied Hitler's views.

more than the return of the former German colonies and the recognition of his dominion over Western Europe.

On this basis Hitler made devious approaches to Britain at the end of June, and, in spite of the eager recommendations of Goering and Raeder, he forbade the launching of an air offensive against British ports and cities, so anxious was he to encourage compromise by maintaining the pretence that he had no quarrel with Britain. When one of these overtures reached London through the agency of the Papal Nuncio in Berne, the spontaneous British response was expressed in the note which Churchill sent to the Foreign Secretary (Lord Halifax). It read:

I hope it will be made clear to the Nuncio that we do not desire to make any inquiries as to terms of peace with Hitler, and that all our agents are strictly forbidden to entertain any such suggestion.

The question whether to continue the struggle after the fall of France was never formally discussed by the British War Cabinet. At the start of the Dunkirk evacuation, when it had seemed almost certain that the B.E.F. would be destroyed and that Britain would be left to fight alone, Churchill had asked his military advisers to report on ' British Strategy in a Certain Eventuality.' The Chiefs of Staff replied: " Our conclusion is that *prima facie* Germany has most of the cards; but the real test is whether the morale of our fighting personnel and civil population will counter-balance the numerical and material advantages which Germany enjoys. We believe it will."[1]

This belief was not ill-founded. Once the first shock of the disaster in Flanders had passed, the people of Britain, with their strange capacity for seeing victory in defeat, drew encouragement from Dunkirk. The miraculous escape of 225,000 British troops from what had appeared to be certain destruction or capture came to be regarded as a divine deliverance which gave men and women throughout the land new faith in themselves and their destiny.

This was not the first time that a continental despot had stood on the shores of France and hurled threats across the Channel. Time and again in the past four hundred years England had fought to prevent the domination of Europe by a single power. Hitler was now faced with the same British stubbornness that had baulked Philip of Spain, Louis XIV, Napoleon and Kaiser Wilhelm II. When Hitler looked across the Channel from Cap Gris Nez in June, he saw only Britain's present material weakness; he did not appreciate the strength and courage her people drew instinctively from the past. Ignoring the warning of history, Hitler clung to the hope of another ' Munich,' or at least an ' Amiens,'

[1]Memorandum from the Chiefs of Staff Committee to the Prime Minister, May 27th, 1940.

but he was extravagantly optimistic in thinking that the traditional Balance-of-Power policy could be jettisoned by any British statesman in the summer of 1940, least of all by the descendant of its most renowned exponent, John Churchill, first Duke of Marlborough.

Due warning of the British temper began to reach Berlin early in July, but the Führer kept deferring his Victory Oration to the Reichstag in the hope that he might be able to make a simultaneous proclamation of peace.[1] When the British failed to respond to his overtures, Hitler persuaded himself—in defiance of all the evidence—that Stalin was " flirting with Britain to keep her in the war " and that it was only the hope of Russian intervention which explained " Britain's persistent unwillingness to make peace."[2]

Hitler would perhaps have clung with less persistence to the chance of compromise if he had had the means of enforcing his will by blockade, as he had once hoped. Germany had begun the war with only 57 U-boats, but Doenitz (then Flag-Officer, U-boats) had estimated, with accurate foresight, that a fleet of at least 300 would be needed before effective pressure could be brought to bear on Britain. By July 1940 seventeen ocean-going submarines had been lost and the force immediately available for Atlantic operations had been reduced to half a dozen.

The Luftwaffe too lacked the power of enforcing an economic stranglehold. It had been developed chiefly for direct support of the Army, as ' aerial artillery,' and it was prepared neither for strategic bombing nor for a war against shipping. Its Stukas were soon to drive overseas convoys from the Channel and the North Sea, but its long-range bombers could not patrol Britain's western approaches nor strike in force at the ports of the Mersey and the Clyde so long as R.A.F. Fighter Command stood undefeated in their path. As for night bombing of distant objectives, the Luftwaffe had neither the trained crews nor the technical equipment to obtain accurate results.

At best, blockade offered a long-term solution, but Hitler needed a means of bringing Britain to heel within the next six months so that he would be free to attack Russia in 1941. The only alternative was invasion, yet neither Hitler nor his service chiefs looked upon this expedient with enthusiasm. On July 2nd Keitel, the Chief of the Supreme Command of the Wehrmacht, issued a preliminary instruction for " a landing in England," but added the proviso: " All preparations must be undertaken on the basis that the invasion is still only a plan and has not yet been decided upon."

Until this time the German Supreme Command had made no preparations whatever for invasion. Since the previous November the Naval War Staff (independently and in secret) had been examining the problem, primarily it seems so that Raeder could have his objections well

---

[1]In his diary for July 8th Halder noted: " Postponement of the Reichstag session because of probable reshuffle in the British Cabinet."
[2]Ibid, July 13th, 1940.

documented if a sudden demand for a plan should be sprung upon him by his unpredictable Führer. The conclusions which Raeder reported to Hitler on July 11th were that no invasion fleet could put to sea until the Luftwaffe had destroyed the R.A.F. and had driven all British naval forces from the Channel. Hitler agreed with Raeder that air superiority was essential and that " invasion should be undertaken only as a last resort to force Britain to sue for peace."[1] The Army High Command endorsed this view. By tradition and training, it was essentially 'land-minded' and, lacking experience of amphibious operations, it shrank from the unfamiliar hazards of the sea.[2] It distrusted Goering and was sceptical, as was Raeder, of the Luftwaffe's ability to gain command of the air.

Hitler did not underestimate the difficulties, but in the absence of any other means of coercing Britain, he was compelled to turn to invasion. Accordingly on July 16th he issued 'War Directive No. 16,' which said (*inter alia*):

As England in spite of her hopeless military position has so far shown herself unwilling to come to any compromise, I have decided to begin preparations for and, if necessary, to carry out the invasion of England.

This operation is dictated by the necessity of eliminating Great Britain as a base from which the war against Germany can be fought. If necessary, the island will be occupied. . . .

I therefore issue the following orders:

1. The landing operation must be a surprise crossing on a broad front extending approximately from Ramsgate to a point west of the Isle of Wight. . . . The preparations . . . must be concluded by the middle of August.

2. The following preparations must be undertaken to make a landing in England possible:

(*a*) The English Air Force must be eliminated to such an extent that it will be incapable of putting up any substantial opposition to the invading troops.

(*b*) The sea routes must be cleared of mines.

(*c*) Both flanks, the Straits of Dover and the Western approaches to the Channel . . . must be so heavily mined as to be completely inaccessible.

(*d*) Heavy coastal guns must dominate and protect the entire coastal front area. . . .

3. The invasion will be referred to by the code-name ' SEALION.'

[1] Führer Naval Conferences, July 11th, 1940.

[2] How little the German Army understood the problem of cross-Channel invasion is apparent from the first detailed reference to it in Halder's diary. " Method," he wrote on July 3rd, " similar to large-scale river crossing." Hitler knew better than that.

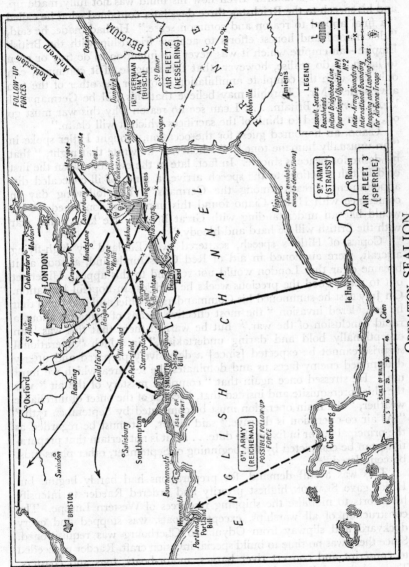

OPERATION SEALION

When Hitler issued this directive, six weeks of indecision had already slipped by since Dunkirk. Even now his mind was not fully made up, and his speech to the Reichstag three days later contained what he called " a final appeal to reason and common sense." He had made, he said, " determined and honest efforts to achieve friendship with the British Empire—an empire which it was never my intention to destroy or even to harm. I do realise, however, that this struggle, if it continues, can only end with the complete annihilation of one or the other of the two adversaries. Mr. Churchill may believe that this will be Germany; I know it will be Britain. . . . I can see no reason why this war must go on. I am grieved to think of the sacrifices which it will claim."

Ciano, an honoured guest for the occasion, thought Hitler spoke in " an unusually humane tone." " I believe," he wrote that night, " that his desire for peace is sincere. In fact, late in the evening, when the first cold British reactions to the speech arrive, a sense of ill-concealed disappointment spreads among the Germans." The following day in conference with Hitler, Ciano found this impression confirmed: " He would like an understanding with Great Britain. He knows that war with the British will be hard and bloody."[1]

Copies of Hitler's speech, scattered over England by high-flying aircraft, were auctioned in aid of Red Cross funds and, as soon as it became clear that London would not respond to this appeal, Hitler set out to make good the precious weeks he had lost in hopeful hesitation. On July 21st he summoned his Commanders-in-Chief and told them that he considered invasion " the most effective means of bringing about a rapid conclusion of the war." But he warned them that this was " an exceptionally bold and daring undertaking," in which " operational surprise cannot be expected [since] a defensively prepared and utterly determined enemy faces us and dominates the sea area which we must use." He stressed once again that " complete mastery of the air " was the chief prerequisite and insisted that, because of the onset of unreliable weather, " the main operation must be completed by September 15th." " As air co-operation is decisive," said Hitler, " it must be regarded as the principal factor in fixing the date. . . . If it is not certain that preparations can be completed by the beginning of September, other plans must be considered."[2]

This was a stiff demand, for preparations had barely begun, but Hitler gave SEALION highest priority and ordered Raeder to intensify his efforts to mobilise the shipping resources of Western Europe. The construction of all warships, except U-boats, was stopped and every dockyard and slipway from Gdynia to Cherbourg was requisitioned. Since there was no time to build special invasion craft, Raeder proceeded to conscript and convert river barges, motor-boats, tugs and coasters. To meet the minimum demands of the army, the Naval Staff estimated

[1]Ciano, op. cit., pp. 277-8.
[2]Führer Naval Conferences, July 21st, 1940.

that it would need 1,722 barges, 471 tugs, 1,161 motor-boats and 155 transports, but there was no certainty that such a force could be assembled, manned and made ready in time.

The more the Naval Staff studied the problem, the more formidable it seemed. " The task allotted to the Navy," they wrote,[1] " is out of all proportion to its strength." The embarkation harbours were either too small or too heavily damaged. The problems of weather, current and tides were likely to present " the greatest difficulties," especially as the initial landings would have to be made on an open coast. The ports, they believed, were too strongly defended to be directly assaulted, and, even if captured early, would almost certainly be mined and obstructed. The coastal waters were mined already and the sweeping of these could not begin until the Royal Navy had been driven from the Channel. " It cannot be assumed," said the Naval Staff, " that the Luftwaffe alone will succeed in keeping the enemy naval forces clear of our shipping, as its operations are very dependent upon weather conditions. Thus the possibility must be envisaged that, even if the first wave has been success-fully transported, the enemy will still be able to penetrate with resolute naval forces so as to place himself between the first wave, already landed, and the succeeding transports."

The most serious problem, however, arose from the demands of the Army regarding the scale and scope of the invasion. The Army High Command was convinced that it would have to make the initial assault with thirteen divisions on a broad front of more than 200 miles extending from Ramsgate to Weymouth and Lyme Bay; and that it would need to have these divisions established ashore and ready for mobile operations within two or three days. If that could not be achieved, the assault divisions would soon be pinned down in their bridgeheads.

To this demand the Navy replied that it could not hope to protect a crossing on so broad a front; in fact, an assault would be feasible only in the narrows of the Straits of Dover from Folkestone to Eastbourne. Moreover, while it might raise sufficient shipping to lift the first wave of 90,000 men and 650 tanks, as the Army plan required, it could not provide simultaneous transport for the second wave of 170,000 men plus 34,000 vehicles and 57,000 horses which they would need. This follow-up force would have to be ferried across " in four or five echelons at intervals of two or three days."

When this expectation was reported to Halder he replied sharply: " From the point of view of the Army, I regard this proposal as complete suicide. I might just as well put the troops that have landed straight through the sausage machine." Schniewind, the Naval Chief of Staff, was equally emphatic that any attempt to land on a broad front would mean the sacrificing of the assault wave before it even reached the shore.

This clash of opinion reflected the inevitable German dilemma. If the Navy should attempt to make the crossing on a front broad enough

[1] In an appreciation for Raeder dated July 19th.

to meet the Army's demands, the invasion fleet would almost certainly be destroyed at sea. On the other hand, if the assault were to be made on the narrow front which the Navy and the Air Force could protect, the Army would be given little chance of gaining success on land. The only hope seemed to lie in the Luftwaffe's securing such mastery of the air that the sea and land defences of Britain could be neutralised by aerial bombardment.

The supreme importance of air power was heavily underlined in the report which Raeder made to Hitler on the last day of July. The Grand Admiral then announced that preparations were in full swing, but would not be completed before September 15th and that this target date could be met only if the Luftwaffe could establish air superiority by the end of August. Given command of the air it might be possible to invade that autumn for, said Raeder, " the weather is generally good at the end of September and in the first half of October," and the most favourable period for moon and tide would fall between September 19th and 26th.

In all the circumstances, however, Raeder recommended that " the best time for the operation would be May 1941." Hitler was adamant. " An attempt must be made," he declared, " to prepare the crossing for September 15th. Whether or not the operation is to take place in September . . . will be decided after the Air Force has made concentrated attacks on Southern England for one week. If the effect of these attacks is such that the enemy air force, harbours and naval forces are heavily damaged, Operation SEALION will be carried out in 1940. Otherwise, it will be postponed until May 1941."[1]

The immediate result of this discussion was a fresh directive from Hitler, announcing his decision to " intensify air and naval warfare against England in order to bring about her final defeat. . . . The Luftwaffe with all available forces will destroy the English Air Force as soon as possible. . . . After the establishment of temporary or local air superiority, the air attacks will be continued on harbours . . . [but] in view of our own intended operations, attacks on harbours on the south coast must be kept to a minimum."

Thus the real responsibility for establishing the conditions in which SEALION could be ventured was placed on the Luftwaffe. It had to gain and hold command of the sea as well as the sky, for Germany's naval weakness could be made good only by the exercise of air power. Lacking the aid of naval gunfire, the assault divisions would have to rely on the Luftwaffe to neutralise the coast defences and provide close support until the Navy could land tanks and heavy artillery in sufficient strength. Moreover, the Air Force must provide auxiliary transport to compensate for the slow turn-around of shipping, since, as Raeder warned Hitler, " no traffic worth mentioning would be able to cross for several days until certain harbours could be utilised." If the balance of build-up was

[1]Führer Naval Conferences, July 31st, 1940.

to be swung in favour of the invaders during this critical phase, the Luftwaffe had to be able to provide rapid airborne reinforcements and to cripple the movement of British reserves by disrupting road and rail traffic in Southern England.

The Luftwaffe held the only keys which could open the defences of the British Isles for the rest of the Wehrmacht. Goering was confident of success, and well he might have been, for his air force had so far proved irresistible. On August 10th the Luftwaffe had 3,242 combat aircraft ready for action; that day the R.A.F. in Britain could have mustered barely 1,350.[1] In the fight for command of the air by day (the battle which promised to be decisive) the odds lay heavily with the Luftwaffe. Against the 1,392 bombers and 1,290 fighters which Goering could put in the air, the R.A.F. had 704 Hurricanes and Spitfires serviceable, backed by a fifty per cent reserve of aircraft, but with no reserve of pilots beyond the week-to-week output of the Flying Training Schools. Since these 700 fighters were necessarily deployed throughout the length of England there was every prospect that the Luftwaffe might secure a local advantage as great as ten to one, even over South-Eastern England where the main strength of Fighter Command was concentrated.

Nevertheless, the German Air Staff, chastened by the outcome of its first encounter with Spitfires over Dunkirk, was reluctant to join serious battle with the R.A.F. until the Luftwaffe had assembled its maximum strength on bases close to the Channel. Organised, as it had been, primarily for direct support of the Army, the Luftwaffe could not be pitched willy-nilly into a straight-out aerial battle with an opponent so formidable. Before the offensive could be launched substantial ground installations, technical services and stocks of fuel and bombs had to be moved up from the Reich. French, Dutch and Belgian airfields had to be extended and improved. Commands had to be reorganised, squadrons retrained and refitted. For a month after the fall of France these preparations proceeded with less urgency than the true situation demanded, for rumours of peace were in the air and there was no firm lead from the vacillating Führer or the dallying Reichsmarschall. Indeed, Goering had sent many squadrons back to Germany to rest and receive, on his behalf, the homage of an exultant nation.

At the start of August when Hitler at last gave the order for the air offensive to begin the Luftwaffe was still engrossed in preparations. With the launching of SEALION tentatively fixed for the third week in September, there was not a day to be lost, but it was August 6th before Goering summoned his senior commanders to Karinhall for a final review of the plans.

[1]These and all other figures of strengths and casualties in this chapter and the next are drawn from the files of the British and German Air Ministries. The overall strength of the Luftwaffe on August 10th was 4,295 combat aircraft, but the only fair basis of comparison on any particular day is the number of aircraft serviceable in the squadrons.

S.F.E.

B

The Luftwaffe's primary task, he declared, was " to eliminate the English Air Force both as a fighting force and in its ground organisation."[1] Next, it was " to strangle England's supply lines by destroying her ports and her shipping." The elimination of the R.A.F. was to be carried out in two phases. First, the fighter defences south of the line Chelmsford–Gloucester were to be overwhelmed by a massive and sustained assault against airfields and ground installations. This, said Goering, would take four days. In the second phase, the Luftwaffe was to carry its offensive by stages northward until the R.A.F. had been driven from its last base in England. That process, he explained, would take four weeks. Meantime, the destruction of the R.A.F.'s resources would be completed through the bombing of British aircraft factories by day and night. In a mood of high confidence Goering told his commanders that, weather permitting, the initial blow would be struck on August 10th, to which great occasion he had given the code-name EAGLE-DAY. By the exercise of air power, said Goering, Germany could counter the strategic advantages of Britain's island position. Once the R.A.F. had been annihilated, the way would be clear for the launching of SEALION—if that should still be necessary.

As soon as the conference was over, the operative code-word was carried by teleprinter, telegraph and radio to airfields and head-quarters throughout Western Europe. The following night in many a Luftwaffe mess from Brest to Berlin eager and confident German officers, like their fathers before them, raised their glasses to " Der Tag."

[1] No text of Goering's speech on this occasion has been discovered. This outline is based on his subsequent orders and on the interrogation of his air fleet commanders, Kesselring and Sperrle.

## CHAPTER II

# DAVID AND GOLIATH

TWENTY-FIVE tanks came back from France; 25 out of 704. Of the 400,000 men in the B.E.F. some 360,000 were saved, but only at the cost of sacrificing all their arms and equipment, except those weapons they carried home on their shoulders. For many weeks after Dunkirk, as Churchill was to tell the House in Secret Session, " an invading force of 150,000 picked men might have created mortal havoc in our midst." During those weeks, time was the most precious element in all Britain. At the end of June the Order of Battle of the Home Forces showed 27 divisions and 14 independent brigades: a substantial army— on paper. Twelve of these divisions were trained and had tasted battle in France, but they were now virtually unarmed. The rest were equipped for training, but, with four or five exceptions, were neither schooled nor armed for action. Some were only just learning to shoot.

As always in Britain's hour of peril thousands of civilians were rallying to defend their homes, with knives and shot-guns if they could get nothing better; but courage was no substitute for modern weapons. In the factories men and women were working without stint to re-arm the rescued battalions, but it would be two or three months before their efforts could make any substantial difference. Across the Atlantic, in the Ordnance Depots of the United States Army, weapons which had been stored in grease since the First World War were being packed for shipment to Britain: half a million rifles, 80,000 machine-guns, 900 field-guns, and appropriate ammunition. The first shipment had already reached Liverpool but the bulk of this windfall of armaments would not be in the hands of British troops until August, if then.

The Royal Navy, too, was in need of respite to bind its wounds and adjust itself to the changed conditions. Since the start of the Norwegian campaign in April the destroyer flotillas, which would have to carry the main burden of naval defence against invasion, had suffered severely. More than half the destroyers in home waters had been put out of action; 16 of them sunk and 42 damaged in less than two months, chiefly by the Luftwaffe. This was the most disturbing aspect, for the Admiralty had been inclined to belittle the effect of air attack on warships, until the operations off Norway and Dunkirk had shown that all but the most modern destroyers were extremely vulnerable. Belatedly the Admiralty ordered the installation of increased armament and heavier armour-plating, but the dockyards were so busy with repairs that there was no certainty that these modifications could be completed before the crisis of invasion came. In any event, it was now admitted that the Navy would run the risk of crippling losses if its destroyers were to operate in the Channel without substantial air protection.

Thus, for Britain, as for Germany, the outcome of the air battle was of supreme importance. While the Army was being trained and equipped, while the home defences were being organised and developed, while the Royal Navy was repairing and strengthening its destroyers, the task of holding the Wehrmacht off would fall first and foremost upon the R.A.F. If Britain could keep command of the air, her defences at sea and on land might never be put to the test of invasion; if not . . .

To the rest of Europe, and indeed to most of the world, it seemed that the odds were weighted overwhelmingly in favour of the Luftwaffe, but on the eve of Goering's ' Eagle-Day,' Britain was not altogether unready for the onslaught that was about to break upon her from the skies. That she was prepared at all was the result of the foresight and persistence of a small band of enlightened and progressive men who through the years of public complacency and political neglect had worked to give the country a scientific system of air defence. Their preparations had begun immediately after the Nazis walked out of the Disarmament Conference, and out of the League of Nations, in October 1933.

The following winter British agents in Germany reported that Hitler was re-arming in defiance of the Versailles Treaty and was concentrating much of his clandestine endeavour on the creation of an air force. In July 1934, the British Cabinet decided that in the next five years the Home Defence Air Force was to be increased from 42 squadrons to 75; 47 of them bomber squadrons and 28 fighter. This expansion had barely begun when the Foreign Secretary, Sir John Simon, at a conference with Hitler in March 1935, was startled by the blunt announcement that Germany had already achieved air parity with Britain and intended to go on building until she had an air force equal to those of Britain and France combined. This gratuitous warning jolted the Baldwin Cabinet into accepting a new plan for increasing the Home Defence Air Force to 121 squadrons with 1,512 first-line aircraft by April 1937. In this programme bombers were still given double priority over fighters, for the dominant opinion in the R.A.F. was in favour of offensive strategy and the Cabinet had been persuaded that the four-engined heavy bomber, already being planned, would provide a war-winning weapon.

This view continued to prevail but it was not universally accepted—least of all perhaps by Air Marshal Sir Hugh Dowding, who became C.-in-C., Fighter Command, on its foundation in July 1936. At a time when the War Office was doing its best to curtail the development of armoured forces and was shelving officers with advanced scientific ideas, the Air Ministry's appointment of Dowding stands out, in remarkable and fortunate contrast, almost as an act of genius.

Dour and rather professorial in manner—a man whose nickname, ' Stuffy,' seemed to suit his nature—Dowding was not the obvious choice for command of the most high-spirited and venturesome band of men in all His Majesty's Forces. What Fighter Command needed, however, was not popular leadership by personal inspiration and example, but scientific organisation of the highest order by a man of character, imagination, and great technical attainments. Dowding possessed the experience and the qualities. He had led a Fighter Wing in France in 1916. He had been Director of Training at the Air Ministry and had commanded the Fighter defences of the London area before becoming, in 1930, the Air Member responsible for Research and Development. In that capacity he had directed the technical progress of the R.A.F. with great energy and vision, and had done much to create the weapons and equipment for the defensive system which he was now to organise. Quick to appreciate scientific possibilities, restless in his search for perfection, courageous and outspoken in pleading his cause, he was determined to build up an incomparable fighting force, aided by all the services of Science, and to preserve it intact for what he foresaw was its historic mission.

Dowding realised that in the early stages of any conflict with Germany, the R.A.F. would be heavily outnumbered and would be forced on to the defensive. In 1937 and 1938, however, the star of offensive strategy was in the ascendant and the promised expansion of Fighter Command was delayed by the Treasury's reluctance to finance it. Simon, now Chancellor of the Exchequer, had evidently forgotten what he had learned as Foreign Secretary from Hitler's own mouth. By the time of the Munich crisis in September 1938, Dowding had only 406 aircraft in his 29 home defence squadrons, 160 in reserve and a monthly reinforcement from the factories of 35. This gave him less than two-thirds of the strength which he believed would be necessary to provide ' reasonable security.' He had only five squadrons of Hurricanes, none of Spitfires, and the Luftwaffe's fighter squadrons were already equipped with Messerschmitt 109s.

The Munich ' dress-rehearsal ' was followed by a searching inquest, as a result of which the Chamberlain Cabinet gave approval for Fighter Command to be increased to 50 squadrons (with 800 first-line aircraft) by April 1940. Even with this expansion it would have to accept numerical inferiority, for Germany's lead was too great. There was the chance, however, that Dowding might make good this disadvantage through the superior quality of his aircraft and of his scientific and technical equipment.

The foundation of this superiority had already been laid as a result of a series of inspired decisions dating back to 1934. At Dowding's instigation the Air Staff decided to order a fighter with a maximum speed of more than 300 m.p.h. and an armament of eight machine-guns. The outcome was the production of the Hurricane and the Spitfire, possessing far greater hitting-power than any foreign aircraft. But the Air Staff was well aware that the punch which these fighters could deliver would be of little avail unless it could be scientifically applied in the right place and at the right time. Warning and control were the keys to the air defence of Britain, for it was obviously impossible to provide standing patrols for all threatened areas. Until 1935 the only available means of warning were sonic and visual, but even the best sound-detectors had a reliable range of only 16 miles. If the defending fighters were to have a chance of intercepting the enemy before he dropped his bombs, they must be alerted when the raiders were still fifty miles out to sea.

The answer to this problem came from the National Physics Laboratory where a Scottish scientist, Robert Watson-Watt, had been experimenting with the use of radio waves for direction-finding and ranging in order to follow the movement of thunderstorms. At a demonstration in February 1935 a primitive form of radar equipment picked up an aircraft at a range of eight miles. With a quickness of appreciation and a foresight seldom encountered when a service ministry is offered a revolutionary idea, the Air Council gave Watson-Watt the support he needed, and the Treasury provided the money for research. In March 1936, he was able to report that aircraft were being detected 75 miles out to sea. With the magic eye of radar, the range, direction and approximate height of aircraft approaching over water could now be determined. Inland the raiders would still have to be picked up by the Observer Corps with sound-detectors and field-glasses, but the major problem of obtaining early warning had been solved. In 1936 work was begun on a chain of radar stations covering the southern and eastern coasts from the Isle of Wight to Dundee.

Having ensured this early warning, Fighter Command needed the means of distinguishing on the radar screen between friendly and hostile aircraft, and the means of tracking and controlling its own aircraft in flight so that it could direct them to intercept. Again the scientists provided the answers. They invented one electronic gadget which enabled British radar stations to tell friend from foe; another device, appropriately called ' Pip-Squeak,' by which fighters automatically reported their position to a control station on the ground; and finally, a Very High Frequency radio-telephone which provided clear, direct speech between pilot and ground-controller.

Under Dowding's direction, these and other inventions and improvements were incorporated into a scientific system of air defence with an elaborate network of communications and control-rooms, radar stations and Observer Corps posts. By September 1939 the essential structure was ready for operations, though some refinements were not yet installed.

The system was there, but the strength was still below the safety margin, and, in view of the continued expansion of the Luftwaffe, Dowding estimated that he would need 52 squadrons to hold the line of battle at home. He had 39, and of these, four went to France in the first week of war and another four were assigned to protect convoys on the East Coast and naval bases in the north.

Dowding asked for the formation of twelve more squadrons, but the output of the factories (only 93 Hurricanes and Spitfires in September) was not sufficient to maintain even the existing units in action. Priority in production was still being given to Bomber Command, which now had 55 squadrons and was being supplied with new aircraft at the rate of 250 a month. The Air Council was reluctant to curtail this production, for it was committed to the building up of a powerful bomber force as the R.A.F.'s main contribution to winning the war. Accordingly, it agreed to the formation of only two of the twelve squadrons that Dowding needed.

Following the swift collapse of Poland, with its dramatic demonstration of the strength and striking-power of the Luftwaffe, Dowding renewed his plea. On September 25th, 1939, in a letter to the Air Staff, he wrote: " The home defence organisation must not be regarded as co-equal with other commands, but it should receive priority over all other claims until it is firmly secured, since the continued existence of the nation and all its services depends upon the Royal Navy and Fighter Command."

These prescient words held more truth than Dowding knew at the time, but their logic even then was unquestionable for Hitler was free to turn his full attention to the West. In October the Air Council decided that Fighter Command should be increased to 60 squadrons within the next twelve months. By December, eighteen new units were in training, but none was equipped with modern aircraft. Between September and the end of the year the monthly output of single-engined fighters rose only from 93 to 122. This slow progress was a reflection of the mood of the country and the hesitancy of the Government.

At the outbreak of war the people had expected immediate and heavy air attacks. When these did not come, they relaxed into complacent lethargy from which Chamberlain's uncertain leadership could not rouse them. Food rationing did not begin until January and then it applied only to butter, sugar and bacon. The mobilisation of manpower was slow and at the start of 1940 a million men were still unemployed. The months of inaction on the Western Front encouraged a sense of false security at home and in this unreal atmosphere there was little drive behind the production programme, and no anticipation of the trial that lay ahead.

Hitler's invasion of the Low Countries and France on May 10th, 1940, confronted Fighter Command with a dilemma which Dowding had long feared. Its operational strength then stood at 53 squadrons, but six of these were on the Continent. The remainder, backed by very slender reserves, were, in Dowding's view, barely sufficient to hold the line at home, and yet in the first three days of the campaign he was called upon to send the equivalent of six additional squadrons to France and two to Norway. On May 14th when the French Premier, Paul Reynaud, appealed for ten more, the War Cabinet assented, but on the following day, at his own request, Dowding appeared before it.[1] He pleaded with fervour against the Cabinet's decision but made little apparent impression. When the argument seemed to have gone against him, Dowding rose from the long table and walked slowly towards Churchill's chair. He carried a piece of paper, and some of those present thought he was about to hand in his resignation, but what he placed in front of the Prime Minister was a graph showing that, if the present wastage of Hurricanes (then at the rate of 30 a day) were allowed to continue, the supply would be exhausted within six weeks. To Dowding's "inexpressible relief" the War Cabinet thereupon decided that no more fighters should be sent to France for the time being, and that bomber attacks should be made on the Ruhr in the hope of distracting part of the Luftwaffe from the land battle.

This decision was less than twenty-four hours old when news came of the German break-through at Sedan. On the morning of the 16th, the War Cabinet reluctantly agreed to send four more squadrons of fighters across the Channel. That afternoon Churchill flew to Paris and was so alarmed at what he learned from Reynaud that he asked the Cabinet to approve the urgent despatch of another six. This meant reducing Fighter Command at home to the strength it had had at the time of Munich.

When the War Cabinet met at eleven o'clock that night, it was faced with one of the gravest strategic decisions in history. Earlier in the day the issue had been put with convincing clarity by Dowding in a letter to Air Chief-Marshal Sir Cyril Newall, Chief of the Air Staff. Dowding wrote:

If an adequate fighter force is kept in this country, if the Fleet remains in being and if the Home Forces are suitably organised to meet invasion, we should be able to carry on the war single-handed for some time, if not indefinitely. But if the Home Defence Air Force is drained away in desperate attempts to remedy the situation in France, defeat in France will involve the final, complete and irremediable defeat of this country.

[1] In Volume II of *The Second World War* (p. 38), Mr. Churchill says that Air Chief-Marshal Dowding had told him that "with twenty-five squadrons he could defend the Island against the whole might of the German Air Force." Lord Dowding says that at no time did he make such a claim. The estimate of twenty-five squadrons, he says, was made by the Air Staff and was based on the assumption that the Luftwaffe would not have bases in the Low Countries and France. In any case, it was the absolute minimum.

This view was strongly presented to the meeting by Newall, who pointed out that in any case there were neither the airfields nor the ground organisation in France for ten additional British squadrons. He agreed that six Hurricane squadrons, based in England, should fly to France each day and operate from existing R.A.F. bases, but he declared then what he was to put in writing next day: " I do not believe that to throw in a few more fighter squadrons, whose loss might vitally weaken the fighter line at home, would make the difference between victory and defeat in France."[1]

This was the decisive argument, and within two days the swift and terrible march of events had endorsed it. By May 19th, when the vanguard of the panzer divisions was sweeping on from Amiens to Abbeville, there was a new and more pressing reason for husbanding Fighter Command. That day Churchill ordered: " No more squadrons of fighters will leave for France. If it becomes necessary to evacuate the B.E.F. a very strong covering operation will be necessary from English bases against German bombers who will certainly do their best to prevent embarkation."

A week later when the evacuation began Fighter Command was equal to the call, but it had no margin to spare. So many squadrons had been weakened or exhausted in supporting the B.E.F. that Dowding could not provide continuous cover in sufficient strength to parry every thrust. Yet the majority of the German raids were intercepted long before they reached the beaches and there were only two days on which the attacks were severe. If Hitler had concentrated the full striking power of the Luftwaffe against Dunkirk, as he might have done had his eye not been upon Paris, he must either have disrupted the evacuation or else have forced Fighter Command into a fierce defensive battle which would have made heavy inroads on its already depleted strength. As it was, however, the nine days of fighting over and around Dunkirk cost Dowding only 106 fighters and 75 pilots.

Nevertheless, the casualties of the whole campaign in France had imposed a considerable strain on Dowding's resources. Between May 10th and June 20th Fighter Command lost 463 aircraft and 284 pilots. At the time of the French collapse all the Hurricane and Spitfire squadrons were below strength and a third of them were unfit for battle. If the Luftwaffe had been able to take advantage of this situation, it might have gained the upper hand before the R.A.F. had recovered its breath. It was not until the second week of July, however, that the German attacks on Channel shipping and south coast ports began to demand intensive counter-action. By then Dowding had 51 squadrons operational and another eight in advanced stages of training or re-forming. He had been

---

[1]In Volume II of *The Second World War* (p. 46), Mr. Churchill gives the impression that the six extra squadrons were transferred to France. This is not borne out by the records of Fighter Command. Even the plan for these squadrons to operate from French bases was frustrated by the development of the situation.

able to make good his losses in aircraft without robbing reserves, for there had been a remarkable increase in fighter production. Under the spur of danger and the whip of Beaverbrook, who had taken charge of the newly-established Ministry of Aircraft Production on May 17th, the output of single-engined fighters rose from 325 in that month to 440 in June and 490 in July.

Men, not machines, were the difficulty now, and, when this became known, the Prime Minister addressed himself to the problem in his usual forthright manner. To the Secretary of State for Air (Sir Archibald Sinclair) he wrote: " The Cabinet were distressed to hear from you that you were now running short of pilots for fighters. . . . This is the first time that this particular admission of failure has been made by the Air Ministry. . . . Lord Beaverbrook has made a surprising improvement in the supply and repair of aeroplanes, and in clearing up the muddle and scandal of the aircraft production branch. I greatly hope that you will be able to do as much on the personnel side, for it will indeed be lamentable if we have machines standing idle for want of pilots to fly them."

Yet this problem could not be easily solved, for the turnover of the training schools could not suddenly or rapidly be increased. On July 7th Dowding had only 1,243 pilots trained and fit to fight, nearly 200 short of the number he required to bring his squadrons to full establishment. With these few and with the men—and women—who operated the system which had been created for their support, lay the prime responsibility for the fate of Britain.

By mid-July Fighter Command was better equipped than ever it had been to bear this responsibility, but the rapid recovery and expansion of its strength was largely offset by the greater burden placed upon it as a result of the German conquests. Not only was the Luftwaffe now free to concentrate its full effort against the British Isles, but from its new bases close to the Channel and the North Sea bombers could be escorted by single-engined fighters against any part of England south and east of a line running from Bristol to Hull. Far more serious, the area that could be threatened was broader as well as deeper. From airfields in Norway and Brittany, the Germans could strike at the south-west and the north-east, outflanking the existing chain of air defences which extended only from the Solent to the Forth.

As early as the previous February Dowding had asked for the extension of the signals network and technical installations to cover the coastal front from the Bristol Channel to Scapa Flow, but it was May 8th before his plans were approved and little was done to implement them until after Dunkirk. Only then was urgent priority given to the installation of the new radar stations and Observer Corps posts, airfields and sector stations, transmitters and signal lines, without which the fighters could not operate effectively. Through June and half July, while construction gangs and teams of engineers were toiling day and night to complete this expansion, the naval bases and ports west of the Solent were ill-protected, but with every week that Hitler waited they grew less vulnerable.

These weeks of comparative respite in the air were beyond price. They gave Fighter Command the chance not only to recover its strength and extend its chain of defences, but also to make good certain technical shortcomings which had been revealed in the battle over France. The Hurricanes and Spitfires were given higher performance by the fitting of constant-speed propellers, greater durability by the installation of self-sealing petrol tanks and stronger protective armour, better means of communication by the perfection of V.H.F. radio equipment. With these improvements there was reason to hope that, even though only the Spitfire could match the latest Messerschmitt 109 in high-altitude performance, Fighter Command would be able to retain the overall advantage of quality on which so much would depend in the battle that was expected to flare up at any moment to a fierce and sustained intensity.

The cauldron came slowly to the boil, for reasons that are apparent in the testimony of General Adolf Galland, who, as a major, led one of Goering's fighter wings that summer and was soon to become Commander-in-Chief of the Luftwaffe Fighter Arm. " The German commanders in the West," said Galland to Allied interrogators after the war, " were so chary about losing bombers that at first they gave the fighters the mission of going over alone and luring the R.A.F. into combat." When Fighter Command refused to be drawn, " something further had to be done to tempt opposition. . . . German fighter wings began to escort small formations of eight to twelve ' decoy bombers,' which attacked shipping and other targets along the south coast of England."

Fighter Command saw through this manœuvre very early. The Luftwaffe was clearly less interested in sinking ships than in bringing fighters to battle in conditions which favoured the attacker. In the case of operations over the Channel, radar could not always give sufficient warning to allow the British to climb to battle height; there was no chance of using anti-aircraft fire to break up enemy formations; and there was a smaller chance of saving damaged aircraft and baled-out pilots. Dowding was determined to avoid, so far as possible, pitting his small force against the mass of the Luftwaffe, except in circumstances which would enable his pilots to make full use of the technical services which had been developed for their support.

In the middle of July, therefore, the Admiralty closed the Channel to all except small coastal convoys, and at the end of the month even these were stopped until the ships had been equipped with barrage balloons as protection against dive-bombers. The Germans, seeking other objectives which the R.A.F. would be compelled to defend, turned their attention to Dover. On July 27th in a surprise attack by 120 aircraft one destroyer was sunk and two damaged. The same day the Luftwaffe sank another destroyer off the coast of Suffolk, and the Admiralty again applied the policy of withdrawing the target. Dover was abandoned as an advanced base for anti-invasion destroyers, and the immediate burden on Fighter Command was relieved. This meant, however, that the defence of the Straits now depended more than ever on the R.A.F.

For more than a month this probing and sparring went on with little satisfaction to the Germans. By August 12th, at a cost of 296 aircraft destroyed and 135 badly damaged, the Luftwaffe had sunk 18 small steamers and four destroyers, and had shot down 148 British fighters. For the R.A.F. on the other hand, these preliminary encounters provided the final tempering of Fighter Command's defensive weapons. During July it grew in strength and experience. The month's losses in aircraft were more than replaced by one week's output from the factories; the number of pilots reached a peak of 1,434 at the start of August, when Dowding had 55 squadrons in the line of battle and another six in training. More important still, the daily testing in action gave Fighter Command ample opportunity to try out its system of raid intelligence, its technique of interception and its battle tactics in conditions which did not overstrain its resources.

Experience brought fresh confidence, but as yet the defences had not been fully tried by mass raids or by direct attacks on the essential installations of the network of warning and control. Fighter Command was in daily apprehension that the Luftwaffe would turn against the radar stations, unmistakable targets with their steel masts, 360 feet high, rising like sentinels on the crests of coastal hills and headlands which had carried warning beacons of a different kind when Napoleon had stood in optimistic expectation on the far side of the Channel.

On August 12th Goering launched the type of attack which Fighter Command had most reason to fear. His bombers struck at five radar stations between Dover and the Isle of Wight. All suffered some damage, but only one was wrecked. On the same day there were sharp attacks on three forward airfields in Kent, and three major raids in quick succession against the Thames Estuary, Portsmouth and Dover, raids designed to divide and unbalance the defences. It was not known at Dowding's H.Q. that this was the overture to Goering's 'Eagle-Day,' which had twice been postponed on account of bad weather and was now fixed for the 13th. But the gathering intensity of the Luftwaffe's efforts was fully recognised and repair work on the four damaged radar stations continued throughout the night, for they protected the short approach to London.

Before dawn on August 13th, the radar defences were restored and gave early proof of their efficiency. At 5.30 a.m. two German formations began assembling over Amiens and were picked up at the remarkable range of 110 miles. A few minutes later two other large formations were plotted near Dieppe and north of Cherbourg. Every German move was watched and recorded, and from the H.Q. of No. 11 Group, commanding the air defences of South-East England, the fighter squadrons were directed into battle in good time. By 6.30 a.m. there were ten squadrons on patrol and the raiders were only just reaching the coast. For the first time the Luftwaffe was mounting simultaneous threats against two widely separated parts of the coast, the Thames Estuary and the Solent, but Fighter Command's technique of interception stood the test and every formation was turned back.

During the rest of the day there were three other heavy raids against southern ports and a series of attacks on airfields. The Germans were hoping to cripple Fighter Command on the ground, but their Intelligence was faulty. Of the eleven airfields which they chose as targets, only one was being used by fighters and that one they failed to hit. Yet they believed they had gained considerable success, for Halder, noting in his diary the Luftwaffe's confidential report, wrote: " Results very good . . . Eight major air bases have been virtually destroyed . . . Ratio of own to enemy losses, one to three." Goering's pilots were evidently making the wildest claims, for this day's battle had cost the Germans 47 aircraft; the R.A.F. had lost 13, a small return to the Luftwaffe for the commitment of 1,485 bombers and fighters.

The German effort would have been on a considerably greater scale, if Goering had not received at the last minute an unfavourable weather forecast which led him to send out another postponement order. His signal reached some units in time, but others were in the air before it arrived. As a result, in the early morning raids two formations of bombers attacked without escort and suffered heavily. The offensive went off at half-cock amid considerable confusion, and it was August 15th before Goering could reorganise his forces to carry out the grand assault he had planned for ' Eagle-Day.'

His intention was to smother the fighter defences in the south-east with four consecutive attacks, each by more than 200 aircraft, and to outflank these defences by a strong raid from Norway against the north-east coast. Goering expected to find this area ill-protected, for his Intelligence reported that many squadrons had been moved south to defend London. The cost of this mistaken appreciation was twenty-four bombers and one fighter destroyed without any loss to the R.A.F. The Luftwaffe made no further attacks from Norway. In the south on August 15th the day-long battle was much fiercer. Of the four attacks, two were effectively intercepted, but the others were not and in the evening the Germans were able to penetrate as far as Croydon. Five airfields and four aircraft factories were hit, and 34 fighters were destroyed, but the Germans paid severely for this success. Their losses for the day were the heaviest the Luftwaffe had ever suffered, 76 aircraft.

Fighter Command had been able to deal with such widespread and sustained attacks only because of radar, and yet on that very day in a special directive Goering declared: " It is doubtful whether there is any point in continuing the attacks on radar stations, since not one of those attacked has so far been put out of action."

This was Goering's first major mistake, and it was due primarily to the failure of the Luftwaffe to appreciate the supreme importance of radar in the British system of interception. Before the war the Germans had discovered the chain of stations on the English coast, but they had no idea how sensitive and accurate the British equipment was. Their own experiments, especially during the occupation of Czechoslovakia, had brought little success, and their scientists, fondly believing themselves to be the best in the world, scoffed at the suggestion that the British might have discovered some secret which had eluded them. Yet their own sets were primitive by comparison and their demonstrations made so little impression on Goering, the C.-in-C. of the Luftwaffe, that they could obtain no special resources for research from Goering, the Director of the Four-Year Plan.

At the outbreak of war the Luftwaffe was using an indifferent type of radar equipment to protect the naval bases in Northern Germany, but the employment of this in conjunction with offensive operations, which alone interested Goering, had not been developed. Nor had German science produced any high-frequency radio-telephone suitable for use by fighters in action. The ground-to-air control system which the R.A.F. had brought to a high degree of efficiency by 1939, was not adopted by the Luftwaffe until two years later! In 1940 it was outclassed in scientific knowledge and equipment.[1]

It was only after the Battle of Britain had begun that the Germans discovered the extent of their handicap. During July, says Galland, " we realised that R.A.F. fighter formations must be controlled from the ground by some new procedure, because we heard commands skilfully and accurately directing Spitfires and Hurricanes on to German formations. We had no radio fighter control at the time . . . and no way of knowing what the British were doing with their forces as each battle progressed. As a result, each German formation had to fly where it was ordered according to a carefully pre-arranged battle plan and had to depend on its own observations and initiative to assess the British reaction and take offensive measures. . . . The planning aimed at as much variety as possible to confuse Fighter Command, with the hope, too, that some successful strategy might be hit upon by chance."

Yet every German variation and manœuvre could be plotted by radar or spotted by the Observer Corps, traced on the map tables of the control-rooms, and passed by radio to the squadrons in the air. It was a battle of chance and force against science and skill. There was no shortage of courage on the German part, though their pilots lacked the zest of the British, but their confidence was undermined by the knowledge that in comparison with their opponents they were blind, deaf and dumb.

[1] This was freely admitted by General Martini, Director-General of Luftwaffe Signals, when interrogated after the war.

In these circumstances Goering's only answer was to seek the destruction of Fighter Command by sheer weight of effort. In an order of August 15th he said: " Operations are to be exclusively directed against the enemy Air Force, including the enemy aircraft industry. . . . For the moment other targets should be ignored." He also gave instructions that every squadron of dive-bombers was now to be escorted by three squadrons of fighters, but even this did not appreciably reduce their casualties. On August 18th in three major attacks on airfields, the Luftwaffe lost 71 aircraft, 37 of them bombers. Alarmed, Goering decided to withdraw his 300 remaining Stukas from the battle. Thus, by the mere threat of their intervention the Spitfires and Hurricanes were able to keep on the ground nearly a quarter of the German bomber strength.

Five days of bad weather brought a lull in operations until August 24th, when the Luftwaffe returned to the fight with renewed instructions from Goering: " Our first aim is to destroy all the enemy's fighters. If they no longer take the air, we shall attack them on the ground or force them into battle by directing bomber attacks against targets within range of our own fighters." He demanded more careful planning, for, he said: " Hurried orders and precipitate missions are impossible in the war against England; they can only lead to severe losses." Goering was already so concerned about his own casualties that he was not disclosing their full severity even to the Army High Command which was awaiting so anxiously the outcome of the air battle. Between August 8th and 26th, according to the Luftwaffe's own files, 602 German aircraft were destroyed, but the Air Staff admitted to Halder the loss of only 353. During this same period, when the R.A.F. in fact lost 259 fighters, Goering claimed, in private as in public, the destruction of 791. Believing this figure and assuming that he had now destroyed fifty per cent of Fighter Command, the Reichsmarschall was baffled by the continued strength and spirit of the British resistance. He gave orders, therefore, that " only half the [German] fighters are to be employed as direct escorts to our bombers. The aim must be to employ the strongest possible fighter force on free-lance operations, in which they can indirectly protect the bombers, and at the same time come to grips under favourable conditions with the enemy fighters."

This change in German tactics weighted the odds even more heavily against the Spitfires and Hurricanes. Squadrons of 10 or 12 found themselves engaging close formations of 20 to 40 bombers protected by more than 100 fighters. By main strength the Germans were frequently able to break through in spite of interception, and their efforts were much better directed. In the next two weeks there were thirty-three major attacks, and twenty-three of these were concentrated on the real nerve centres—the fighter airfields and sector stations of No. 11 Group, whose task it was to defend London and the South-East.

According to the Group commander, Air Vice-Marshal K. R. Park, " the enemy's bombing attacks by day did extensive damage to five of our forward aerodromes, and also to six of our seven sector stations. . . . By September 5th the damage was having a serious effect on fighting efficiency. . . . The absence of many telephone lines, the use of scratch equipment in emergency operations rooms and the general dislocation of ground organisation was seriously felt in the handling of squadrons."

On three days British losses were as heavy as those of the Luftwaffe and by September 6th the balance-sheet for the past fortnight showed how the margin of advantage had narrowed. The Germans had lost 378 aircraft; the British, 277. These severe casualties reduced the reserves of Hurricanes and Spitfires to the lowest point they had yet reached. When the losses through action and accident had been made good, the stock of fighters available for immediate issue had fallen to 125. The rate of loss during these two weeks had been greater than the capacity for production and repair.

Far more alarming, however, was the problem of pilots, for, as Dowding later reported: " By the beginning of September the incidence of casualties became so serious that a fresh squadron would become depleted and exhausted before any of the resting and re-forming squadrons were ready to take its place. Fighter pilots were no longer being produced in numbers sufficient to fill the gaps in the fighting ranks."

Pilots were transferred from the Fleet Air Arm and from Bomber and Coastal Commands after brief conversion courses. The final training of pilots was cut from a month to a fortnight, but even these extreme measures provided an output of only 65 trained pilots a week, and during this critical period Fighter Command was losing airmen—killed, wounded or exhausted—at double that rate. At the end of July its pilot strength had been 1,434: a month later it stood at 1,023. By September 6th there were no fresh squadrons to replace the battered units which had borne the brunt of the fight, and all the evidence from across the Channel indicated that the battle had not yet reached its climax.

By the first week of September, although Fighter Command was under heavy strain, ' the few ' had already gained for Britain what she needed most: time to build up an army which could face the menace of invasion with some confidence. There were now 16 divisions guarding ' invasion corner ' and the south coast and, while not at full strength in weapons, these formations had sufficient equipment to do themselves justice. Their most serious need was for anti-tank guns, but the shortage of armour was no longer acute. Since Dunkirk 350 tanks had come from the factories and the tank strength of the Home Forces stood at more than 800.[1]

[1] We know from Halder's Diary that the Germans would not have been able to land tanks in large numbers until they had captured and opened ports on the south-east coast. At the end of August the Wehrmacht had available for landing from the sea only 42 Mark IVs and 168 Mark IIIs.

This revival of Britain's military strength complicated Hitler's problem, since he could not count upon landing a force strong enough to defeat the new British Army unless the Luftwaffe could keep the Royal Navy out of the Channel. Nevertheless, Goering assured him that this could be done, for the R.A.F., so he thought, was nearly beaten. Accordingly, preparations for invasion were intensified, and Hitler told Ciano that he had " rejected an offer of mediation made by the King of Sweden."[1]

The invasion plans were ready; their execution awaited merely the final triumph of the Luftwaffe. The Navy's view that the landings must be concentrated on a narrow front had at last been accepted by Hitler; and von Rundstedt's Army Group, which was to lead the assault, had framed its orders accordingly. " Army Group Order No. 1 for the conduct of Operation SEALION," declared:

> The task of the Army is to land strong forces in southern England with the co-operation of the Navy and Air Force, to defeat the English Army and occupy London. Other areas of England will be occupied as opportunity permits. Army Group A with 16th and 9th Armies is entrusted with the execution of the Army's task.
>
> The task of Army Group A is first to occupy the south coast of England between Folkestone and Worthing, and then to form a broad connected bridgehead 20-30 km. deep.
>
> After the arrival of further reinforcements the Army Group will commence a determined offensive and occupy the line Thames Estuary–heights south of London–Portsmouth (Operational Objective No. 1). Mobile forces will be pushed forward west of London, first cutting off the capital from south and west and then continuing the attack until the line Maldon (N.E. of London)–Severn Estuary is won (Operational Objective No. 2).
>
> The task of 16th Army is to start from the line inclusive Rotterdam —inclusive Calais, and force a landing on the English coast in the sector Folkestone—inclusive St. Leonards. It will then form a broad bridgehead along the line Canterbury—line of the Great Stour–Ashford–Tenterden–Etchingham. . . .
>
> The task of 9th Army, which will start from the line Boulogne–Le Havre simultaneously with 16th Army, is to occupy the English coast between Bexhill and Worthing. In conjunction with 16th Army it will then press on to the line Hadlow Down–Burgess Hill–Storrington and farther west. . . .
>
> It is estimated that it will not be possible to pass over to the offensive from the bridgeheads to take Operational Objective No. 1 earlier than one week after the first landings. . . . If favourable circumstances allow for the speeding up of the operation, our highly mobile and versatile command will be able to adapt itself to the favourable situation as speedily as in former operations.

[1]Ciano, *Diary*, p. 287.

In the Army Group Order everything was clear-cut except the final all-important sentence:

The date of the first landing—*S-Tag*—remains to be fixed.

The fixing of this date depended on two inter-related factors beyond the control of the German Army: the Luftwaffe's victory and the completion of the naval preparations which were already behind schedule. Since mid-August the converted barges had been assembling in the estuaries of the Maas and the Scheldt. On September 1st the main body of invasion shipping began to move from north German ports to embarkation harbours between Rotterdam and Le Havre, but it was already obvious that the original target date, September 15th, could not be met. According to the Naval War Diary for August 30th, " The use of the sea-ways along the coast by barges in tow or steamers has so far been largely impossible, because of the danger from the air and also because of the threat of interference by enemy naval forces which cannot be eliminated by air power." It noted that mine-sweeping and mine-laying had also been delayed, and added, " The concentration of transports in the embarkation harbours is all that will be possible by September 15th, and then only if the development of the air war . . . is favourable. The earliest date on which the invasion fleet could put to sea is therefore September 20th."

This would still be time enough, for Raeder himself had declared that the most favourable period for tide and moon would fall between the 19th and 26th. Accordingly, on September 3rd Hitler fixed the tentative date for the landing as the 21st. His determination to invade, if he could, was not fully endorsed by Raeder, but the Grand Admiral was more confident now than he had been earlier, and on September 6th he reported to Hitler: " If air supremacy is increasingly established it will be possible to meet the new dead-line. The crossing itself will be very difficult; the Army cannot count upon keeping the divisions together. But, given favourable circumstances regarding air supremacy, weather, etc., the execution of Operation SEALION does appear possible."[1]

On the same day that Raeder made this report, the Luftwaffe was nearer to establishing air supremacy over the Channel than ever before. The fierce encounters and considerable losses and ground damage of the past four weeks had stretched the resources of Fighter Command almost to the limit. Of its one thousand pilots, only 840 were trained and fit for action. No one could tell how long they could keep the upper hand if the battle were to continue at its recent intensity and with the Luftwaffe concentrating nearly all its effort on the airfields and the network of control.

At this stage, however, a new factor began to exert its influence on the course of the battle. On the night of August 24th–25th the first bombs

[1] *Führer Naval Conferences*, September 6th 1940.

fell on Central London. The following day Churchill ordered an immediate retaliation raid on the German capital. That night 105 aircraft were sent to bomb Berlin. Only 29 found the city, but it was the promptness of the gesture which counted and during the next week there were four more raids on Berlin. Hitler demanded immediate reprisals and proclaimed in an hysterical broadcast: " If they attack our cities, we will rub out their cities from the map. The hour will come when one of us two will break, and it will not be Nazi Germany."

Goering responded eagerly to Hitler's demand, since he believed that the R.A.F. was sufficiently weakened for him to make mass daylight raids on London. At The Hague on September 3rd there was a critical conference between Goering and the commanders of the two main Air Fleets, Kesselring and Sperrle. Goering announced that the assault on London would begin on September 7th and is reported to have said that it would continue " day and night until the R.A.F. has destroyed itself in vain attempts to stop us, and until the people's will to resist is broken." Sperrle argued for continued attacks on airfields, insisting that " the English still have a thousand fighters available." But Kesselring thought " the English have next to nothing left," and claimed that " recently only the bad weather has prevented my bombers from reaching their targets." Schmid, Chief of Luftwaffe Intelligence, set the " absolute maximum figure " of British fighter strength at 350. (It was in fact 650.) Goering capped the argument by declaring that so far Fighter Command had saved itself from destruction only by withdrawing to airfields beyond the range of the Luftwaffe's single-engined fighters. Daylight attacks on London, he insisted, would compel the R.A.F. to throw in " its last reserves of Spitfires and Hurricanes."[1]

The Battle of London began late in the afternoon of Saturday, September 7th, when Goering sent over the largest force of bombers he could effectively escort, 372 bombers and 642 fighters, to make two concentrated assaults in quick succession. Expecting a major onslaught against London, Dowding had made provision for the rapid reinforcement of No. 11 Group by the groups on its flanks, and Park had issued special tactical instructions. His squadrons, he felt, had been patrolling too high and intercepting too late. They had been getting involved with the enemy's high-flying fighter screen and the German bombers had frequently penetrated to their targets undisturbed except by formations which were too small to stop them. His orders were, therefore, that the enemy's top-cover fighters were to be engaged only by *some* of the Spitfire squadrons. The remaining Spitfires, and all the Hurricanes, were to concentrate on the enemy bombers. " Whenever time permits," he declared, " squadrons are to be put into battle in pairs. . . . The enemy's main attack must be met in maximum strength between the coast and our line of sector aerodromes."

[1] No detailed record of this conference has been found, but Sperrle and others who were present have reported its main points.

On September 7th these plans were substantially successful. In the two hours that the battle lasted 23 fighter squadrons were sent up, 21 of them intercepted, but the attack was so sustained and prolonged that a continuous defence could not be maintained. By the time the second wave of raiders came over, the squadrons which had engaged the earlier formations were coming down to refuel. A large proportion of the bombers broke through to London and were only intercepted on their way home. In the East End there was great destruction. The docks were ablaze on both banks of the river for miles and provided an unmistakable beacon for the 255 bombers which attacked after dark.

A few hours before this daylight assault, the British Chiefs of Staff—weighing all the evidence from reconnaissance and secret intelligence, and from the arrest of four German spies who had landed from the sea—came to the conclusion that Hitler's preparations for invasion were so far advanced that he could strike at any time. The direct attack on London strengthened this impression and at eight o'clock that evening G.H.Q., Home Forces, issued to Eastern and Southern Commands the code-word CROMWELL, signifying 'Invasion Imminent.' All that night, as enemy bombers droned overhead on their way to London, the defenders kept a tense, unfailing vigil. In some areas the Home Guard was called out by the ringing of church bells, and rumour, travelling fast and far, reported that enemy parachutists had landed and that the armada was at sea.

On Sunday, September 8th, however, the Channel showed no stir, and, although columns of smoke rising above London could be seen far out to sea, the daylight bombers did not return. The enemy losses had not been heavy (24 fighters and 14 bombers destroyed), but the Germans had been surprised and unnerved by the strength of the fighter opposition and by their inability to cope with it. The R.A.F. had flown 817 sorties and had lost only 28 aircraft. The night bombers continued their attack on London, but the air superiority, which was now so urgently needed for SEALION, could only be won in daylight battles.

On the 9th Goering struck another blow by day at London and Fighter Command. This time the counter-measures were more successful. Nearly half the bomber formations were turned back and the rest were so broken up by interception and anti-aircraft fire that they were reduced to indiscriminate scatter-bombing. The switching of the attack from the airfields to London had proved the turning point in the battle, for with this change in German strategy Fighter Command was given the chance to recover its strength and efficiency.

This was Goering's second major mistake. Its effect on Operation SEALION was immediate. On September 10th, when Hitler was due to confirm his decision, he deferred it for another three days, but while he waited the situation became worse, not only in the air, but also at sea. Since the CROMWELL warning, the Royal Navy and Bomber Command had intensified their anti-invasion counter-measures, and on

September 12th the H.Q. of Naval Group West reported from Paris to Berlin:

> Interruptions caused by the enemy's air forces, long-range artillery and light naval forces have for the first time assumed major significance. The harbours at Ostend, Dunkirk, Calais and Boulogne cannot be used as night anchorages for shipping because of the danger of English bombing and shelling. Units of the British Fleet are now able to operate almost unmolested in the Channel. Owing to these difficulties, further delays are expected in the assembly of the invasion fleet.

When Raeder reported these facts on September 14th Hitler agreed that SEALION should " only be undertaken as a last resort," since " the degree of air supremacy necessary . . . has not yet been attained." The Führer insisted, however, that the air attacks had been " very effective and would have been more so if the weather had been favourable." He believed that British resistance might still be broken " if the pressure of the imminent landing were added to further air attacks."[1] He declared, says Halder: " Four or five more days of fine weather, and a decisive result will be achieved. . . . We have a good chance to force England to her knees. . . . Even though victory in the air should not be achieved before another ten or twelve days, Britain might yet be seized by mass hysteria."[2] Hitler decided that he would not cancel the invasion, but would endeavour to meet the target date of September 27th. Von Brauchitsch supported this decision, proposing, says Halder, " to make the Army independent of the dates set by the Navy and to execute the landing under protection of smoke screens " in the event of the Luftwaffe not being able to establish air supremacy. It was agreed, therefore, that the decision would be postponed for another three days and that in the meantime the Luftwaffe would make one further attempt to smash the R.A.F. in battle over London.

On Sunday, September 15th, Goering provided the strongest escort of the whole battle—five fighters for every bomber—in the hope of saturating the defences. Special trouble was taken to ensure their careful and close assembly, but this only served to give the British radar stations extra warning. Park had ample time to organise his squadrons into large formations and to call in reinforcements from the flanking groups. This was the decisive factor in the battle which raged over London and South-Eastern England for an hour in the middle of the day. The Germans were intercepted almost as soon as they crossed the coast and in many of the dog-fights that followed the British even had the advantage in numbers. Goering's formations were broken up, scattered and hunted

[1] Führer Naval Conferences, September 14th, 1940.
[2] Halder's Diary, September 14th, 1940.

home. In the early afternoon the story of the midday battle was repeated and Fighter Command clinched its victory.

This was the final proof of the defensive system. That night and the next the Germans in the Channel ports had a sharp reminder of the R.A.F.'s offensive strength as well. By the morning of the 17th some twelve per cent of the invasion barges and transports had been damaged or destroyed, and the German Navy was under no illusion about the fate of the remainder, if Hitler were to order them to put to sea. His decision, announced that afternoon, was recorded in the War Diary of the Naval Staff as follows:

> The enemy air force is still by no means defeated; on the contrary it shows increasing activity. The weather situation as a whole does not permit us to expect a period of calm. The Führer has therefore decided to postpone Operation SEALION indefinitely.

Two days later, on September 19th, at Hitler's instructions the great invasion fleet began dispersing to safer areas, without even attempting so much as a raid on the coast of Britain.

The air offensive against London was continued for another six weeks, but after the end of September it was maintained almost entirely by high-flying fighter-bombers. Goering persisted more in anger than in expectation of success, for September 15th had set the seal on the Luftwaffe's defeat. On this Sunday the British claimed the destruction of 185 enemy aircraft, but the Germans actually lost only 56.[1] Of these 56, however, 34 were bombers, and this was the significant fact. Goering had committed 679 fighters to protect 123 bombers, a fivefold escort, and yet one-third of the bombers had been shot down. These alarming losses at last convinced him that he could not neutralise Fighter Command, nor could he escort over Britain in daylight sufficient bombers to disrupt her economy or demoralise her people. That was the real lesson of September 15th and it decided the issue.

The severity of this lesson was largely due to the tactics which Goering compelled his pilots to employ. He had begun the battle with loose fighter formations and free-lance patrols, and by early September these tactics had brought him near to success, but, as his bomber losses mounted, he ordered the fighters to provide closer and closer escort. When the

[1]These figures like others quoted in this chapter, are drawn from the files of the German Air Ministry. The discrepancy between the contemporary claim of 185 and the actual loss of 56 aircraft caused some concern in Britain when it became known, but it is readily explained. This day's fighting was the fiercest, most confused and most widespread of the whole battle. The result was that many aircraft were claimed more than once. And, because the public was clamouring for the 'stumps score' immediately after the 'close of play,' there was no time for checking and cross-checking. It is worth noting, however, that in the less hectic phases of the battle the British claims were lower than the true German losses.

attack was switched to London, he carried these instructions to the point of absurdity. Galland says: " We had to fly straight-and-level with the slow unwieldy bomber stream and we were forbidden to engage British fighters unless we were attacked. By this order we were compelled to surrender to the Spitfires and Hurricanes the advantages of surprise, initiative, height, speed and, above all, the fighting spirit and aggressive attitude which marks all successful fighter squadrons."

Galland reports that when he protested against this order, Goering turned on him, and said " Well, Major, what kind of fighters would you like? "

" Reichsmarschall," he replied, " give me a squadron of Spitfires."

This remark became legendary in the Luftwaffe, but as an explanation of the German defeat it is a patent over-simplification. The Spitfire was only one factor, and not the most important, in the British victory, which was compounded of many elements, so closely fused that they cannot be fairly dissected: the selfless daring of the pilots, radar and the system of fighter control, the genius of the scientists and designers, the vision and resolution of Dowding, the boundless inspiration of Churchill, and the stout spirit of the people.

The defeat of the Germans was also due to grave shortcomings and failures on their own part. The basis of the Luftwaffe's theory of battle was the belief that the enemy's air force could be knocked out in the first days of any campaign by the destruction of its airfields and installations, and that his cities and armies could then be bombed at will in daylight.

The Germans were not prepared to fight it out in the air against a highly-organised and scientifically-directed antagonist. They had not enough first-class fighters, nor the technical equipment to use them to the best advantage, nor the production to replace heavy losses. Thwarted by day, they could not exert their full bomber effort by night because they had neither the technique nor the trained crews.

The Luftwaffe's greatest weaknesses in the matter of aircraft were the poor fire-power and vulnerability of its bombers and the short range of its single-engined fighters. In 1944-45 American daylight formations over Germany were made up of approximately equal numbers of bombers and fighters, but towards the end of the Battle of Britain Goering found it necessary to provide escorts of four and five to one. On September 15th, in spite of this, the British fighters actually had the advantage in numbers, thanks to early warning by radar and accurate direction of squadrons by radio. Had the Germans possessed similar scientific aids, they could have made far better use of their numbers and would not have been compelled to surrender the initiative. Since they could not tell what the Hurricanes and Spitfires were doing, until they saw them, the German fighters were instructed to concentrate on protecting their own bombers and had to curtail their roving, offensive patrols which were the only means of gaining them supremacy in the air.

Throughout the conflict the primary limitation on German operations was the shortage of single-engined fighters. The Luftwaffe was not even able to maintain its front-line strength and the rate of serviceability went steadily down as the battle progressed. Its own records show the decline:

| SINGLE-ENGINED FIGHTERS | | |
|---|---|---|
| | Front-Line Strength | Total Serviceable |
| August 10th | 1,085 | 933 |
| September 7th | 958 | 762 |
| September 28th | 957 | 741 |
| October 19th | 945 | 711 |

One cause of this decline lay in the failure of the German aircraft industry to increase its fighter production in the first twelve months of the war. It began with an output of 200 fighters in September 1939; a year later its average production was no higher, for Goering had given priority to bombers.[1] In the period from July 10th to September 30th the total German output of fighters did not exceed 600; their battle losses alone came to 623.

British operations, on the other hand, were never seriously restricted by lack of aircraft. Starting with an output of 93 Hurricanes and Spitfires in September 1939, the British increased their production to 157 in January 1940, to 256 in April, 325 in May, 440 in June and 490 in July. Even in the next three months, when the aircraft industry was under fire, the monthly output did not fall below 460.

Dowding's greatest problems were damage to his ground organisation and the shortage of pilots, but as soon as Goering switched the attack from the airfields to London the crisis passed and during the rest of September the battle moved more and more in favour of the R.A.F. Between September 7th and 30th, 435 German aircraft were destroyed, at a cost to the British of only 164. At the end of this month, when the danger of invasion had passed and serious daylight raiding was abandoned, the tally of casualties, since the start of the preliminary operations on July 10th, showed that the Germans had lost 1,408 aircraft and had succeeded in shooting down only 697 British fighters. This was the

[1] The relative production figures for 1940 are most revealing:

| | Bombers | Fighters | All Operational Aircraft |
|---|---|---|---|
| Britain .. .. | 3,710 | 4,283 | 9,924 |
| Germany .. .. | 3,954 | 2,424 | 8,070 |

These German figures are drawn from the files of the Ministry of Armaments and War Production. The *United States Strategic Bombing Survey* gives a higher figure for fighters, namely, 3,106, but this evidently includes 'ground attack' fighters. The figures I have given are those endorsed by the Minister, Albert Speer, himself.

measure of the British victory and the inner reason for it lay in the fact that the R.A.F. had prepared to fight the Battle of Britain long before the war began, but the Germans had not.

In 1917—in a report advocating the creation of an independent air force—a committee headed by General Jan Smuts, South Africa's Prime Minister, had given a warning which had not been ignored. The Smuts Committee declared: " We should not only secure air predominance, but secure it on a very large scale; and, having secured it in this war, we should make every effort and sacrifice to maintain it for the future. Air supremacy may in the long run become as important a factor in the defence of the Empire as sea supremacy."

This prophecy was fulfilled to the letter in the Battle of Britain. The defeat of the Luftwaffe was the final frustration of the SEALION Plan, the beginning of its own decline and the event which drove Hitler's armies eastward. These consequences were foreseen by Churchill even before the battle was joined. Within five days of Dunkirk he had cabled to Smuts: " I see only one sure way through now—to wit, that Hitler should attack this country and in so doing break his air weapon." Three weeks later, in another cable to his great friend, Churchill said: " If Hitler fails to beat us here he will probably recoil eastwards. Indeed, he may do this even without trying invasion."

## CHAPTER III

# THE VICTOR'S DILEMMA

ON July 31st, 1940, the Prime Minister cabled to President Roosevelt: " I am beginning to feel very hopeful about this war if we can get round the next three or four months. The air is holding well. We are hitting that man hard . . . but the loss of destroyers by air attack may well be so serious as to break down our defence of the food and trade routes across the Atlantic." Repeating in this cable a request he had made in May, Churchill said: " I am confident . . . that you will leave nothing undone to ensure that fifty or sixty of your oldest destroyers are sent to me at once." Within the next few weeks this appeal was to culminate in an agreement by which fifty over-age American destroyers were transferred to the Royal Navy in exchange for the granting to the United States of air and naval bases in Newfoundland, Bermuda and the West Indies.

That same day in Berlin Adolf Hitler addressed his Commanders-in-Chief. He knew nothing then of the impending ' Destroyers for Bases ' deal, but he was coming to realise that America was not prepared to stand idly by and see Britain overwhelmed. Accordingly, Hitler now declared: " In the event that invasion does not take place, our efforts must be directed to the elimination of all factors that let England hope for a change in the situation. . . . Britain's hope lies in Russia and the United States. If Russia drops out of the picture, America, too, is lost for Britain, because the elimination of Russia would greatly increase Japan's power in the Far East. . . . Decision: Russia's destruction must therefore be made a part of this struggle. . . . The sooner Russia is crushed the better. The attack will achieve its purpose only if the Russian State can be shattered to its roots with one blow. . . . If we start in May '41 we will have five months in which to finish the job."[1]

This was Hitler's solution to the dilemma in which he was placed by Britain's refusal to yield. The essence of his problem was that he could not gain the resources for a prolonged struggle with the Anglo-Saxon powers without involving himself in that ' war on two fronts ' which he had sworn to avoid. He could not inflict a crippling defeat on

[1] Halder's Diary, July 31st, 1940.

the British, let alone an Anglo-American combination, until he had greatly expanded his Navy and Air Force and was free to concentrate the main strength of his Army against the West. This he could not do so long as the threat of hostile Soviet action in the East compelled him to divide his forces and to allocate to the Army two-thirds of his mobilised manpower and of his armament production. Furthermore, he could not keep Occupied Europe fed and quiet during the conquest of Britain, nor could he wage the intensive air and naval warfare which alone could bring victory, unless he could be certain of two things: full control over the economy of the Balkans, and continued deliveries of grain and oil from the U.S.S.R. By the end of August, however, he was so alarmed at the possibility of further Russian encroachments that he dispatched twelve additional divisions to Southern Poland " to guarantee the protection of the Rumanian oilfields in the event of a sudden demand for intervention."

Hitler was not unaware of the dangers inherent in the course he was about to pursue, for he received repeated warnings from his Commanders-in-Chief, especially Raeder and Goering, who presented an alternative plan for expansion southward. Even before the postponement of SEALION, Raeder had been pleading the Mediterranean case, and on September 26th he told Hitler:

> The British have always considered the Mediterranean the pivot of their world empire. . . . While the air and submarine war is being fought out between Germany and Britain, Italy, surrounded by British power, is fast becoming the main target of attack. Britain always attempts to strangle the weaker enemy. The Italians have not yet realised the danger when they refuse our help. Germany, however, must wage war against Great Britain with all the means at her disposal and without delay, before the United States is able to intervene effectively. For this reason the Mediterranean question must be cleared up during the [coming] winter months.[1]

In support of this thesis, Raeder declared that " Britain with the help of ' de Gaulle France,' and possibly also of the U.S.A., wants to make North-West Africa a centre of resistance and to set up air bases for attack against Italy." He proposed, therefore, the seizure of Gibraltar, the dispatch of German forces to Dakar and the Canary Islands, and close co-operation with Vichy in order to forestall any Anglo-Saxon moves against the French colonies in North-West Africa. Having secured her western flank by these measures, Germany could support the Italians in a campaign to capture the Suez Canal and advance through Palestine and Syria to Turkey. " If we reach that point," said Raeder, " Turkey will be in our power. The Russian problem will then appear in a different light. Fundamentally Russia is afraid of Germany. It is doubtful whether an advance against Russia in the north will then be necessary."

[1] Führer Naval Conferences, September 26th, 1940.

Hitler agreed with Raeder's " general trend of thought," and said he would discuss the plan with Mussolini, but he pointed out that the Mediterranean was Italy's agreed sphere of influence and that the Duce was reluctant to accept German aid in the expansion of his ' new Roman Empire.' Moreover, the High Command of the German Army was unwilling to undertake any large-scale operations in the Eastern Mediterranean because it did not believe the Italian Navy could safeguard the communications of a German force strong enough to achieve substantial results. In Hitler's mind, however, the fundamental reservation was that he did not regard operations in the Mediterranean as an alternative to his plan for invading Russia, but only as a prelude, as one means of safeguarding himself against the possibility that Britain might open a ' Second Front ' in the West before he had crushed the Red Army.

Since Britain could not be defeated by direct action, Hitler decided that her power to intervene on the Continent must be curtailed by other means. On September 19th Ribbentrop arrived in Rome with " a surprise in his brief-case: a military alliance with Japan, to be signed within the next few days in Berlin." He told Ciano that this would have " a double advantage—against Russia and against America. Under the threat of the Japanese Fleet, America will not dare to move."[1]

This Tripartite Alliance was intended as a reply to the ' Destroyers for Bases ' deal, and as a reminder to the Russians that they should continue to turn a deaf ear to British overtures. By raising the spectre of war with Japan for both the United States and the Soviet Union, in the event of their joining with Britain, Hitler strove to put a premium on their neutrality and to discourage in London the expectation of substantial outside aid. At the same time he hoped that Britain might be kept on the defensive, not only by maintaining the threat of invasion, but also by arousing her anxieties about the safety of her imperial possessions in the Far East.

In further pursuit of insurance, Hitler endeavoured to form a *cordon sanitaire* in the west and south, by bringing Spain and Vichy France into the war on Germany's side and by encouraging the lesser powers of Central and South-Eastern Europe to join the Tripartite Alliance. In conformity with this plan Hitler had already laid a restraining hand on Mussolini's Balkan ambitions, issuing in August what Ciano describes as " a complete order to halt all along the line." Mussolini promptly replied: " The military measures we have taken on the Greek and Yugoslav frontiers are simply of a precautionary character " against two states, which are ready " to strike a dagger into the back of the Axis at the first opportunity."[2]

[1]Ciano, *Diary*, p. 291. Any historian of this period must draw heavily on Ciano's Diary. I have done so, but it would be tedious to give a detailed page reference for every extract quoted.

[2]Letter, Mussolini to Hitler, August 27th, 1940. The text of this and 25 other letters which passed between Hitler and Mussolini during the war were published in Paris in 1946 by Éditions du Pavois.

Nonetheless the Führer's order still stood, for Hitler was confident that he could gain control of the Balkans by political means through his well-tried technique of isolation and intimidation. Moreover, he wished for the moment to avoid any aggressive action which would either arouse Russian suspicions or aid the cause of those Americans who favoured increased aid for Britain. The American Presidential election was to be held in the first week of November, and although the Republican candidate, Wendell Wilkie, was as hostile to the Axis as was Roosevelt, neither could pursue a policy far in advance of public opinion. Accordingly, Hitler hoped that by rallying Spain, France and the Balkan states in support of his 'New Order,' he could represent to the world, and especially to the New World, that Europe was united and pacified under his hegemony and was being kept at war and in economic isolation only by Britain's irrational refusal to recognise the inevitable. Such a dramatic demonstration of the strength and solidarity of Axis Europe, he hoped, might encourage the Isolationists and delay the mobilisation of anti-German opinion in the United States.

If Hitler set his hopes too high so far as America was concerned, he had more substantial grounds for believing that nearer home his advances would be sympathetically received. In June, at the time of the French collapse, the Spanish Ambassador in Berlin had presented to Ribbentrop a memorandum in which General Franco declared himself " ready under certain conditions to enter the war on the side of Germany and Italy." The conditions were that the Axis powers should reward him with Gibraltar, French Morocco and Western Algeria, and should make available military and economic aid, particularly petrol and wheat. Hitler, however, felt no need of Spanish intervention yet; nor was he keen to have another mouth to feed at the peace table. Ribbentrop's reply was noncommittal, and the Spaniards received little encouragement beyond the dispatch of a German Military Mission to examine at close quarters the problem of capturing Gibraltar. In mid-September, therefore, Franco sent his brother-in-law and Minister of the Interior, Serrano Suñer, to Berlin to assure Hitler that " whenever Spain's supply of foodstuffs and war material was secure she could immediately enter the war."[1] Hitler was in a receptive mood, for Suñer's visit coincided with the realisation that the invasion of England could not be attempted that year. Franco's intervention was now worth bargaining for and Hitler promised that " Germany would do everything in her power to help Spain." In a letter to Franco next day, he agreed to " recognise the Spanish claim to Morocco with the one limitation of assuring Germany a share in the raw materials of this area ";[2] he promised military and economic

[1]The minutes of this meeting between Hitler and Suñer, together with a number of other documents concerning the relations between Franco and the Axis leaders, were published in 1946 by the U.S. State Department in a pamphlet entitled *The Spanish Government and the Axis.*

[2]No copy of Hitler's letter is available, but in his reply of September 23rd, 1940, Franco quoted certain passages.

aid " in the highest measure possible for Germany "; and suggested that he and the Caudillo should meet to settle the details.

Franco's response was prompt and compliant. " Your esteemed ideas," he wrote on September 22nd, " satisfy our wishes. . . . We believe ourselves to be in complete agreement. . . . I reply with the assurance of my unchallengeable and sincere adherence to you personally, to the German people and to the cause for which you fight. In defence of this cause, I hope to be able to renew the old bonds of comradeship between our armies." Among these soft words, however, there was no hard and fast promise, no mention of any date for Spain's entry into the war.

Nevertheless, the Axis powers seemed to be on the point of gaining another diplomatic victory of great military consequence when two extraneous factors began to disturb the calculations on which tentative agreement had been based. In Madrid on September 18th, the day after Suñer's interview with Hitler, a crisis which had been developing for some time came to a head. It concerned oil. In the first six months of 1940 exports of oil from the United States to Spain had risen steadily until in June they were more than double the pre-war monthly rate. In July at Britain's request the United States Government began to curtail the flow, and early in August Washington advised Madrid that in future it would permit the export of only so much oil as Britain would allow through the blockade. At first the British Government had to proceed warily, lest it should give Franco a popular pretext for intervention, but the R.A.F.'s spectacular victory over the Luftwaffe gave new strength to Britain's diplomatic arm. In mid-September Churchill was able to insist that the Royal Navy would not permit the passage of any oil beyond what was necessary to meet current consumption and to maintain stocks for two and a half months.[1] In these circumstances, unless Germany could guarantee Franco's oil supplies, Spain could not embark upon a struggle which was likely to last more than three months. He could obtain sufficient oil from Britain and America to stay at peace; could he extract from Hitler enough to go to war?

The second extraneous factor was the stout resistance offered by the Vichy French when General de Gaulle, with a Free French force and a British naval squadron, attempted on September 23rd to seize the West African base of Dakar. This incident led Hitler to take a kindlier view of the Vichy régime, since Marshal Pétain, forewarned of the attack, had sent strong reinforcements to Dakar, and had proceeded to bomb Gibraltar in retaliation. It seemed to Hitler, therefore, that further Gaullist and British intervention in North-West Africa could be thwarted only if Vichy would defend its own colonies, and that Pétain might even be persuaded to enter the war against Britain. Thus, when Ciano came

---

[1]The effect of these Anglo-American restrictions is shown by the fact that Spanish imports of oil from the United States, after rising from 2,131,000 barrels in the last half of 1939 to 2,678,000 in the next six months, fell to 1,324,000 barrels in the period July–December 1940. (U.S. Department of Commerce figures.)

to Berlin on September 28th, Hitler told him he wanted " to attract France into the anti-British coalition," and that he was " opposed to Spanish intervention, because it would cost more than it is worth." The Führer said he was " afraid that the agreement [with Spain] concerning Morocco would somehow become known to the French [who] might come to an agreement with the British if they knew that Morocco would be lost to them in any case after the war." On reflection, however, Hitler realised that the weakness of the Italian Navy made Spanish support indispensable. The Western Mediterranean could not be made secure without the co-operation of both powers: Spain for the conquest of Gibraltar, and France for the defence of the north-west corner of Africa. Consequently, he set himself to reconcile Spanish hopes and French fears.

On October 23rd Hitler met Franco at Hendaye, having already arranged to see Pétain at Montoire on the 24th. To Franco Hitler offered a Ten-Year Alliance and proposed a joint attack on Gibraltar early in the New Year. Franco replied that " Spain would gladly fight at Germany's side " as soon as her military and economic deficiencies had been made good and her political aspirations recognised.[1] He was less enthusiastic, however, after Hitler had told him that, because of the danger of revolt in French North Africa, Germany could make Spain no promises which might lessen the willingness of Vichy to defend its colonies. The Caudillo answered that he could not afford to accept an alliance which did not guarantee him French Morocco and part of Algeria. Hitler replied that Spain would receive " territorial compensation out of French North African possessions to the extent to which France could be indemnified out of British colonies." This did not entirely satisfy Franco and he would make no firm commitment. For nine long hours the Führer and the Caudillo haggled about honours and rewards. In the end even Hitler was exhausted. " Rather than go through that again," he reported to Mussolini, " I would prefer to have three or four teeth taken out."[2]

Nevertheless, it seemed likely that Spain might yet be induced to come in, provided that Hitler could persuade Vichy to accept his colonial formula. At Montoire on the following day, Hitler found Pétain, under the poisonous influence of Laval, willing to accept " collaboration in principle " and determined to defend the North African colonies against British intervention. Hitler assured him that, if France would aid Germany in hastening the defeat of Britain, she would obtain a final peace settlement sooner and on easier terms, for the Axis powers could then take their spoils from the British Empire. He suggested, says the official protocol, that after the war there should be " a re-partition of colonial possessions in Africa," and added that " the Axis Powers will

[1]No full account of this conference has been found, but we have a substantial fragment of the German minutes, and a personal account by Paul Schmidt, Hitler's interpreter. (See Schmidt, *Hitler's Interpreter*, pp. 194-7.)
[2]Ciano, *Diplomatic Papers*, p. 402.

undertake to see that France receives territorial compensations, and . . . retains in Africa a colonial domain essentially equivalent to what she possesses to-day."[1]

Pétain agreed to this formula, and thus allowed Hitler to confirm the offer to Franco, but the Marshal made no response to the suggestion that France should wage active war against her former ally. Hitler was piqued, but the door was not entirely shut on his hopes, for Pétain yielded to his suggestion that Laval should become Foreign Minister. With this traitor in power at Vichy, Hitler had reason to expect that collaboration, now accepted in principle, would bring substantial results in practice. That night Ribbentrop, telephoning from a station in France, told Ciano: "The programme of collaboration is heading towards concrete results."

If Hitler had not yet gained all he wanted, he believed he had established a basis for agreement with both Madrid and Vichy. At this delicate stage in the negotiations it was essential that nothing should disturb the international scene.

The illusion of a short war, which Hitler had been sedulously fostering, was broken overnight by the man, who, next to the Führer, had the closest interest in its maintenance—the Duce. His action, and still more the manner and cause of it, throw a revealing light on Axis politics and expose one of the fundamental flaws in the so-called ' Pact of Steel.' The two dictators were always at pains to present to the outside world a formidable façade of solidarity, but in reality there was little genuine consultation, less joint planning, and no common policy. However fraternal and grandiloquent the phrases in which they addressed each other, their relationship was eventually poisoned by mistrust, suspicion and a conflict of ambitions. In Mussolini's case jealousy and fear added their toxic influence. As the original Fascist tyrant, he resented the spectacular rise of the Austrian whom he had liked to regard as his protégé and to whom he had been accustomed to address fatherly homilies. " No one," he had once written to Hitler, " knows better than I, who have had some forty years of political experience. . . ."[2]

As events developed, Mussolini found himself ousted from the driving seat in the Axis chariot, and yet whirled along as a bewildered footman, now tempted to leap off and risk the lacerations when he feared it was heading for disaster, now clinging more firmly and leaning over to urge the driver on when prospects of quick and easy booty stretched ahead, and even seeking to take over one rein himself.

In August 1939, when he learned of Hitler's real purpose in Poland, he seriously discussed with Ciano the possibility of breaking altogether

[1] The text of this protocol was captured with the archives of the German Foreign Office.
[2] Letter, Mussolini to Hitler, January 4th, 1940.

with Germany. After the Polish campaign, he counselled Hitler to make peace. "For Mussolini," wrote Ciano, "the idea of Hitler waging war, and, worse still, winning it, is altogether unbearable. . . . He would be greatly pleased if Hitler were slowed down." Accordingly, when he learned of the Nazi plan to invade the Low Countries, Mussolini ordered his Foreign Minister to warn the Dutch and Belgian ambassadors.

Never suspecting the Duce, for whom at this time he had a genuine admiration and affection, modified only by his contempt for the Italian people, Hitler blamed King Victor Emmanuel for the betrayal of the secrets he had revealed to Rome. Thereafter, the Führer kept his intentions to himself and this made their fulfilment trebly galling to Mussolini. The Duce was jealous, because Hitler was able to bring off diplomatic and military coups which the weakness of Italy precluded him from attempting. "It is humiliating," he told Ciano, "to remain with our hands folded, while others write history." He was indignant, because each new German success was brought about either against his advice or without his knowledge. When they met, says Ciano, "Mussolini resented the fact that Hitler did all the talking. . . . He had to keep quiet most of the time, a thing which, as dictator, or rather the dean of dictators, he's not in the habit of doing." He was fearful, because he could not tell where he would be dragged by the violent and unpredictable ambitions of his colleague and yet, fascinated, he felt compelled to follow and, if possible, to emulate him.

Such was the background to the sequence of events which opened with a meeting between the Axis leaders at the Brenner Pass on October 4th, 1940. On this occasion, writes Ciano, "Hitler put at least some of his cards on the table and talked to us about his plans for the future." Britain, France, Spain, Russia were all discussed, but Hitler did not mention the arrangements he had already made for German troops to move into Rumania three days later. This unilateral decision infuriated Mussolini, the more so because only a few weeks earlier Hitler had 'ordered' him to make no move in the Balkans, and because Italy and Germany had jointly imposed upon Rumania a settlement of her frontier dispute with Hungary. "Hitler always faces me with a *fait accompli*," said Mussolini to Ciano. "This time I am going to pay him back in his own coin. He will find out from the papers that I have occupied Greece. In this way equilibrium will be re-established."

The attack was fixed for October 28th. On the 22nd Mussolini wrote to Hitler (back-dating his letter October 19th) and sent it to Berlin to await the Führer's return from France. The Duce referred to his impending action against Greece but indicated neither the form nor the date, lest he should provoke another restraining order. By telephone from Berlin late on the 24th Hitler was informed of the contents of this letter, and forthwith requested an immediate conference. Mussolini blandly suggested that the most suitable date would be the 28th. On that morning when Hitler stepped from his train at Florence, Mussolini

C

greeted him with the gleeful proclamation: "Führer, we are on the march!"[1]

Mussolini's rash and independent venture broke the fondly-nurtured illusion of 'a Continent at Peace,' and was soon to dispel the impression of Axis invincibility which the German triumphs had created. Hitler was incensed but he could hardly make any outright complaint, for he himself had established the practice of acting without notice. In any case, the Mediterranean was Italy's allotted sphere and Mussolini was already protesting against Hitler's flirtation with Laval. Accordingly, the Führer suppressed his indignation and gave an assurance of Germany's full support, but the Italian attack was regarded in Berlin as a " regrettable blunder,"[2] especially as it was launched with "entirely inadequate forces " (a mere three divisions) and was stopped short in the first week.

Hitler at once became alarmed about the general situation in the Mediterranean and the Balkans, for Churchill, enlightened and fortified by his deep understanding of history, was quick to seize the opportunity thus gratuitously presented to him. He would not repeat the folly of Addington, who had responded to the threat of Napoleonic invasion by keeping his forces at home and even weakening the garrisons of overseas bases as important as Malta. Like Pitt, Churchill saw that Britain's task was " not how to avoid defeat but how to inflict it," and that the place to inflict it was, as so often before, the Mediterranean. He was determined to take full advantage of the strategic bounty of Dunkirk. Grave though the defeat at Dunkirk had seemed at the time, it was, in fact, Britain's salvation. It rescued her from another disastrous war of attrition on the Western Front and released her strategy from the shackles of subordination to the land-bound doctrines of the French.

The influence of Britain in war has always been most effective when exerted, not in an effort to match the mass armies of the more populous European powers in continental warfare, but in the precise application through command of the sea of small yet highly-trained forces at vital or exposed points in the enemy's flank or rear. Used in close conjunction with the Royal Navy, British armies throughout modern times have been able to produce a strategic effect out of all proportion to their size.

In the First World War this lesson of experience was forgotten or ignored by most of her leaders, though not by Churchill, and the alliance with France resulted in the wanton out-pouring of the Empire's life-blood into the mud of Flanders. Britain had not yet recovered from this exhaustion of her manpower when she again found herself at war with Germany. Despite their recent warning against the 'strategy of immolation', the British became committed to it once more in 1939 as the

[1] Reported by Ribbentrop in evidence at Nuremberg, March 3rd, 1946. (*Nuremberg Trial Proceedings*, Part x, p. 194.)

[2] Minutes of conference between Jodl and Schniewind, November 4th, 1940. At this conference Jodl said: " On no occasion was authorisation for such an independent action given by the Führer to the Duce."

unavoidable price of French participation. At Dunkirk Hitler restored to Britain the strategic freedom of action which she had lost twenty-five years before.

Even while an autumn invasion still threatened, Churchill and the War Cabinet were preparing to send divisions from the Home Forces to the Mediterranean and the Middle East, and before the end of November an armoured division and the equivalent of two infantry divisions had been dispatched. At the same time the Admiralty maintained in the Mediterranean a fleet powerful enough to keep the Italians in or close to port. This was done regardless of the danger at home and the losses at sea, but the cost was heavy, for no less than 198,000 tons of merchant shipping were sunk by U-boats in the last week of October. As always in Britain's wars there was a conflict of opinion whether the primary task of the Navy should be the furthering of the main strategic purposes or the protection of merchant convoys. Experience spoke unfalteringly in favour of the former course, and like Marlborough and Nelson, Churchill pursued it. The reward came when Mussolini attacked Greece.

Had Britain not held command of the Mediterranean there is little doubt that the Greek Prime Minister, General Metaxas, would have had to yield, for the British Ambassador could not have given an immediate guarantee of British aid. Within a week a token force had landed on Greek soil, the Royal Navy had forestalled an Italian attempt to seize Crete, and the R.A.F., operating from Greek bases, had made its first raids on ports in Southern Italy. During this time most of the Italian battlefleet skulked in Taranto Harbour, but that was not to save it. On the night of November 11th–12th the Fleet Air Arm reached out to the Italian lair and sank or heavily damaged two cruisers and three of Mussolini's six battleships. For twenty-four hours Admiral Sir Andrew Cunningham trailed his coat off the heel of Italy, but the enemy did not accept the challenge.

This daring and dramatic stroke, in conjunction with the sturdy successes of the Greeks on land, transformed the Mediterranean scene, and bore witness to Vichy and Madrid that the war was unlikely to come to an early end. When Hitler received Ciano and Suñer at Berchtesgaden on November 18th, Suñer was openly critical of the German efforts to reach an understanding with France, and was unimpressed by the ' colonial formula ' which Hitler had induced Pétain to accept. It was clear that since the meeting at Hendaye Franco had raised his price.

" Hitler is pessimistic," wrote Ciano that night, " and considers the situation much compromised by what has happened in the Balkans. His criticism is open, definite and final." Two days later Hitler gave vent to his concern in a letter to Mussolini:

When I asked you to receive me in Florence, I set out with the hope of outlining my views to you before the beginning of the threatened conflict with Greece, of which I had only the vaguest information.

Above all I wanted to persuade you to delay this action a little, until a more favourable time, at any rate until after the American Presidential Election. . . . The situation, as it has now developed, will entail psychological and military consequences of the utmost gravity.

Hitler complained that the Italian fiasco in Greece had " accentuated the tendency of certain nations to avoid becoming entangled with us and to await the outcome of events." Hungary and Rumania were about to join the Tripartite Alliance, but Bulgaria and Yugoslavia had declined to do so and in France there had been " a decided strengthening of the position of those . . . who assert that in this war the last word has not yet been spoken." With regard to the military consequences, the Führer went on: " These, Duce, are extremely serious. Britain will have at her disposal a number of air bases within range of Ploesti. . . . If the petrol refineries are destroyed the damage will be irreparable. . . . I am determined, Duce, to react with decisive forces against any British attempt to establish a substantial air base in Thrace."

Turning to the question of counter-measures, Hitler declared: " Spain must be persuaded to enter the war forthwith. . . . If we encompass the fall of Gibraltar, we shall bolt the western door of the Mediterranean . . . and ensure the final establishment of the authority of Pétain over North Africa. . . . I continue to give No. 1 Priority in the Mediterranean to the expulsion of the British Navy. . . . By the judicious employment of our air forces the Mediterranean should become, in three or four months, the tomb of the British Fleet." This, he said, would be the " decisive prelude " to a spring campaign against Greece, for which they must secure the " positive collaboration " of Yugoslavia.

Mussolini's reply revealed him in a chastened mood. " Führer," he began, " I am sorry that my letter of October 19th did not reach you in time for you to give me your advice on the projected expedition against Greece, advice to which I should have strictly conformed, as on other occasions." He confessed that the Greeks had seized the initiative, but he could not curb his vanity for more than a few sentences and soon it began to strut across the page. Unable to admit that he was taking orders, he disguised his assent in the cloak of assertion, and wrote: " The Spanish trump can now be played. I am inclined to meet Franco myself and exert the necessary pressure to bring him into the war." He went on to repeat Hitler's main proposals as if they were his own, ending on the pompous note: " Those are the broad lines of the plan to which I am willing to give my consent." But here discretion made him quickly add, " I will give it also to all measures which you regard as necessary to restore the situation."

Hereafter the great Duce is unquestionably the lesser partner. Never again will he refer to his ' forty years of political experience.' Still bombastic yet ever compliant, he will tail along, summoned here, ordered there, until at last wounded pride will make him cry out: " I am sick and tired of being rung for."[1]

Even now Mussolini was given no hint of the relationship between Hitler's Mediterranean proposals and his overall strategy. Yet it is clear from contemporary German documents that the Mediterranean was essentially subordinate to Hitler's main purpose, the invasion of Russia. There was no question of a ' giant pincer movement ' directed against Suez, as the British feared at the time. Hitler had already decided to take " no action against Turkey for the purpose of breaking through to the Suez Canal via Syria," since this " would be a very lengthy operation and would involve very great difficulty."[2] In his letter of November 20th, he had told Mussolini: " I am convinced that an attack against the Nile Delta is out of the question before the autumn of next year." His plans did not go beyond the capture of Gibraltar, the banishment of the British Fleet, the closing of the Suez Canal by air attack, and the pacification of the Balkans—operations calculated to safeguard his flank and rear while he swept into Russia. Accordingly, he insisted to Mussolini, " the Mediterranean question must be liquidated this winter. . . . I must have my German forces back in the spring, not later than May 1st."

In his letter of November 20th, Hitler told Mussolini: " We should make every possible effort to turn Russia away from the Balkans and to direct her towards the Orient." It was with this purpose in view that Ribbentrop had invited Molotov to a conference in Berlin to discuss " the delimitation of their interests on a world-wide scale," a conference which was to have a profound bearing upon the course of the war. At their first meeting on November 12th the German Foreign Minister had assured his visitor that " England was beaten and that it would only be a question of time before she would finally admit defeat. . . . The Axis powers, therefore, were not considering how they might win the war, but rather how they could end the war which was already won."[3] If Russia would join in a political and economic alliance with the countries of the Tripartite Pact, she could take her share of the spoils when the British Empire was dismembered.

Ribbentrop proposed that they should " establish the spheres of influence between Russia, Germany, Italy and Japan along very broad lines," acting on the principle that the four powers should " normally direct the momentum of their *Lebensraum* expansion entirely southward." Germany, Italy and Japan were already looking in that direction and he

[1]Ciano, *Diary*, p. 351.
[2]Jodl to Schniewind, Führer Naval Conferences, November 4th, 1940.
[3]The German minutes of these discussions with Molotov were captured with the archives of the German Foreign Office and published by the U.S. State Department in 1948. (See *Nazi-Soviet Relations 1939-1941*, pp. 217-59.)

" wondered whether Russia would not also turn to the south for her natural outlet to the sea."

" Which sea? " said Molotov. That was the awkward question and Ribbentrop prefaced his reply with the jovial reminder that they had " done some good business together " in the past at the expense of Europe and could " continue to do good business together " at the expense of the British Empire. " The question was," he said, " whether in the long run the most advantageous access to the sea for Russia could not be found in the direction of the Persian Gulf and the Arabian Sea." With regard to the Black Sea Straits, Germany recognised that there should be a new convention securing " certain special privileges to Russia, [including] freer access to the Mediterranean." Molotov listened " with an impenetrable expression."[1] His reply was non-committal, but he revealed his acute awareness of the real issue when he said that " particular vigilance was needed in the delimitation of spheres of influence between Germany and Russia."

Ribbentrop's grandiose proposal for the division of the world was repeated by Hitler when he joined the discussions later that day. The Führer declared that " the question now was how much chance was there for these great countries (Germany, Russia and Italy) really to obtain free access to the ocean without in turn coming into conflict with each other over the matter." It was their responsibility, he said ominously, to " prevent this war from becoming the father of a new war."

Molotov replied that " he was also of the opinion that it would be in the interest of Germany and the Soviet Union if the two countries would collaborate and not fight each other. . . . The participation of Russia in the Tripartite Pact appeared to him entirely acceptable in principle, provided Russia was to be a partner and not a dummy. In that case he saw no difficulty . . . but the aim and the significance of the Pact must first be more closely defined. What was the meaning of the New Order in Europe and in Asia, and what role would the U.S.S.R. be given in it? . . . Moreover, there were issues to be clarified regarding Russia's Balkan and Black Sea interests with respect to Bulgaria and Rumania and Turkey."

The interpreters were amazed. " The questions hailed down upon Hitler," says Schmidt. " No foreign visitor had ever spoken to him in this way in my presence."[2] To Schmidt's surprise, Hitler was " meekly polite " and " avoided answering any more of Molotov's insistent questions by having recourse to the British." He suggested that it was time to adjourn, adding, " otherwise we shall get caught in the air-raid warning."

When the discussions were resumed next day, Hitler spoke of Germany's economic interest in Finland and reminded Molotov that

[1] Schmidt, op. cit., p. 212. Schmidt was present and kept the minutes, though he did not act as translator.
[2] Schmidt, op. cit., pp. 214-15.

" Germany had not occupied any territory which was within the Russian sphere," whereas the Soviet Union in both Lithuania and Bukovina had gone beyond the original Russo-German agreement. He gave warning that Russia " should not seek successes in territories in which Germany was interested for the duration of the war." He was anxious, he said, to prevent " any new conflict in the Baltic Sea," and he wanted to know " whether Russia intended to make [another] attack on Finland." According to the German minutes of the meeting, Molotov answered this question " somewhat evasively," but the implication was that Germany must acquiesce in the absorption of Finland by the Soviet Union. Hitler replied that, " if a general settlement were made, no German troops would remain in Finland," and warned Molotov that there must be no renewal of the Russo-Finnish conflict of the previous year.

In an attempt to escape from this impasse into the larger sphere of global plunder, Hitler suggested that " after the conquest of England the British Empire would be apportioned as a gigantic world-wide estate in bankruptcy [and that] from this bankrupt estate Russia would obtain access to ice-free waters." He pointed out, however, that " All the countries which could possibly be interested in the bankrupt estate would have to stop all controversies among themselves and concern themselves exclusively with the partition of the British Empire." For the achievement of this he wished to create " a world coalition of interested powers."

Molotov interrupted these flights of fancy by saying that " he wanted to discuss first a problem closer to Europe, that of Turkey." He protested that Rumania had accepted the guarantee of Germany and Italy without consulting the Soviet Union. He suggested that the guarantee should be revoked as being " aimed against the interests of Soviet Russia, if one might express oneself so bluntly." Furthermore, in view of Russia's interest in the Straits, he wanted to know " what Germany would say if Russia gave Bulgaria a guarantee under exactly the same conditions as Germany and Italy had given to Rumania." Hitler answered that Rumania had asked for the German guarantee. Had Bulgaria made any such request to Russia? He did not know of one and before he could reply he would need to consult the Duce. He would not give even the " provisional expression of opinion " for which Molotov asked, and he suggested that " in view of the possibility of English air attacks " they should adjourn for supper.

During the adjournment Hitler instructed Ribbentrop to drive a bargain by making a concrete and formal offer of alliance. Accordingly, late that evening when the two Foreign Ministers met in Ribbentrop's air-raid shelter, a draft agreement was submitted to Molotov. This provided for the expansion of the Three-Power Pact into a Four-Power Alliance, and Ribbentrop suggested that a secret protocol should define the territorial aspirations of the signatories. Germany's aspirations lay, he said, " in the Central African region," Italy's " in north and north-east Africa," Japan's " south of the Japanese home islands and Man-chukuo." " The focal points in the territorial aspirations of the Soviet Union," said Ribbentrop, " would presumably be centred south of the territory of the Soviet Union in the direction of the Indian Ocean."

This was even less attractive to Molotov than Ribbentrop's original offer of " access to the Persian Gulf and Arabian Sea." Although the Russian refused even to comment on the question of " an outlet to the Indian Ocean," his reply showed unmistakably that Russia's major interest was in the Black Sea and the Baltic. " Paper agreements," he pointed out, " would not suffice for the Soviet Union; rather she would have to insist on effective guarantees for her security." He said that " the fate of Rumania and Hungary could not be immaterial to the Soviet Union in any circumstances." He wanted to know further " what the Axis contemplated with regard to Yugoslavia and Greece? " Russia, he said, was also interested in German intentions in Poland, in the question of Swedish neutrality, and the exit from the Baltic.

There was no doubt in which direction Soviet ambitions lay and Ribbentrop complained that he was being " interrogated too closely." Once again he tried to escape from Molotov's pointed and particular questions, declaring he could " only repeat again and again that the decisive question was whether the Soviet Union was prepared . . . to co-operate with Germany in the great liquidation of the British Empire." Molotov was not to be fobbed off with distant promises. He remarked that " the Germans were assuming that the war against England had already been won. If, therefore, as the Führer had declared, Germany was waging ' a life and death struggle against England,' he could only construe this as meaning that Germany was fighting ' for life ' and England ' for death.' " And he added as a parting shot at Ribbentrop: " If England is in fact defeated and powerless, why have we been conducting this discussion in your air-raid shelter? "[1]

Two weeks later Molotov gave the German Ambassador in Moscow the Soviet Government's formal reply to Ribbentrop's proposal. This showed that Stalin was not prepared to move one inch from the stand his Foreign Minister had taken in Berlin, for it said:

The Soviet Government is prepared to accept the draft of the Four-Power Pact which the Reich Foreign Minister outlined in conversation on November 13th . . . subject to the following conditions:

1. Provided that German troops are immediately withdrawn from Finland. . . .

2. Provided that . . . the security of the Soviet Union in the Straits is ensured by the conclusion of a mutual assistance pact

[1] This last remark is not in the German minutes. It was reported by Molotov to Eden when the Foreign Secretary was in Moscow in December 1941.

between the Soviet Union and Bulgaria, and by the establishment of a base for land and naval forces of the U.S.S.R. within range of the Bosphorus and the Dardanelles by means of a long-term lease.

3. Provided that the area south of Batum and Baku in the general direction of the Persian Gulf is recognised as the centre of the aspirations of the Soviet Union.

4. Provided that Japan renounces her rights to concessions for coal and oil in northern Sakhalin.

In framing this reply Stalin's approach was strictly pragmatic and expedient. His immediate concern was the security of his own country. He had little sympathy for Britain's cause, but he was interested in her survival as an insurance against the concentration of the Wehrmacht's undivided strength against Russia. He would give Germany a free hand in the West, only if Hitler would first concede to the Soviet Union territories, bases and rights which would safeguard her against any ultimate threat of Nazi invasion. German troops must be withdrawn from Finland so that the Leningrad flank would be safe. Russia must have bases in Bulgaria and the Dardanelles to ensure her access to the Mediterranean, to protect her against a southern outflanking movement and to guarantee that she, not Germany, would control the oil of Iraq and Iran. These demands were a serious test of Hitler's good faith. If they were accepted, then Stalin could place some credence on the assertion that Germany wanted a long-term alliance and intended, after the conquest of the British Isles, to direct her aggressive energies southwards. If not, it was obvious that Hitler was merely trying to buy him off for the moment with promises which would never be fulfilled. Stalin wanted immediate guarantees, which would protect him against the day when the Führer changed his mind.

Hitler was not prepared to see the door to his Eastern ambitions thus bolted and barred; nor was he willing to place himself in the position of being permanently dependent on the good graces of the Soviet Union for the supplies of oil he needed for the conquest of Britain. In his plan the oil resources of the Persian Gulf area had been divided between the two powers. Stalin's counter-plan put them all within the Russian sphere. Exasperated at finding a bargainer tougher than himself, Hitler declared to Raeder: " Stalin is nothing but a cold-blooded blackmailer."[1] Even if Russia were to remain neutral, it was unlikely that she would continue to deliver oil, grain and raw materials in sufficient quantities, unless Hitler were to maintain in Eastern Europe an army large enough to compel compliance. That would require at least 100 divisions. He was resentful that the monopoly of blackmail was no longer his.

By this time Hitler was convinced that, in view of Roosevelt's re-election, the United States would eventually enter the war. Before then, he must either consolidate his position in the West by subduing Britain

[1] Führer Naval Conferences, January 8th, 1941.

or remove the threat in the East by defeating the Soviet Union. He could invade Russia with his existing war machine in 1941, but he could not invade Britain until he had fundamentally reorganised the Wehrmacht and the German war economy to place the predominant striking power in the hands of the Luftwaffe and the Navy, and this could not be accomplished so long as he was compelled to maintain a large army in Eastern Europe. Hitler believed that he could scotch the Russian menace before American aid would permit the British to assume the offensive in the West. Thus, by taking the short-term risk of a war on two fronts, he would free himself for many years to concentrate his own military power and all the resources of Europe from the Atlantic to the Urals for the defence of a single front against the Anglo-Saxons. There was even the possibility, which Ribbentrop told him was a strong probability, that the capitalist powers would change their attitude to Nazi Germany when once she appeared as the leader of Europe in an anti-Communist crusade.

Hitler's answer to Molotov's memorandum was sent not to Moscow, but to the German Commanders-in-Chief in a directive of December 18th which began: " The German Armed Forces must be prepared, even before the end of the war against England, to overthrow Soviet Russia in a rapid campaign (Operation BARBAROSSA)." The directive said that all preparations were to be completed by May 15th, 1941, and declared: " The goal of the operation is to set up a screen against Asiatic Russia along the general line Volga–Archangel."

Hitler was confident that Russia could be defeated in less than six months. " We have only to kick in the door," he told Jodl, " and the whole rotten structure will come crashing down." This optimism was not shared by his Commanders-in-Chief, but the leaders of the Army, von Brauchitsch and Halder, hardly dared to voice their criticism, and, although Goering protested strongly, his opinion carried less weight since the Luftwaffe's defeat in the Battle of Britain.

The most serious opposition came from Raeder, who saw more clearly than his colleagues the significance of the Mediterranean and the strategic consequences of the resounding defeat which General Wavell had inflicted on the Italians at Sidi Barrani in the second week of December. At a conference with Hitler, Keitel and Jodl two days after Christmas, Raeder summed up the results of this British victory.

> The threat to Egypt [said the Admiral] and thus to Britain's entire position in the Eastern Mediterranean, the Near East and the North African area, has been eliminated with one stroke. . . . The transfer of air units and army formations to the Greek Zone has already been observed. . . . It is no longer possible to drive the British Fleet from the Mediterranean . . . or to carry out in the Mediterranean the decisive action for which we had hoped.[1]

Raeder argued that Germany could not attack Russia without running

[1]Führer Naval Conferences, December 27th, 1940.

the risk of becoming involved in a war on two fronts, for Britain's power was still formidable and was being steadily reinforced by shipments from the United States. "Britain's ability to maintain her supply lines," he said, "is definitely the decisive factor for the outcome of the war." And yet, with the current allocations of manpower and materials, "the maximum monthly output of U-boats amounts to eighteen at the most, perhaps only to twelve." Arguing that "the greatest task of the hour is the concentration of all our power against the British," he went on to express "serious doubts concerning the advisability of launching Operation BARBAROSSA before the overthrow of Britain."

Hitler rejected this plea, insisting: "In view of Russia's inclination to interfere in Balkan affairs, we must at all costs eliminate the last remaining enemy on the Continent before coming to grips with Britain."

Natural optimism, fattened on spectacular success and profound faith in his own military genius, led Hitler to underestimate the difficulty of defeating Russia and to belittle the possibility of British interference in the West. Yet he agreed with Raeder that they must make further efforts to force Britain on to the defensive in the Mediterranean and the Far East and thus strengthen the overall strategic position of Germany before she invaded Russia. To this task the Nazi leaders bent their diplomatic and military energies in the six months between the issuing and the implementation of the BARBAROSSA Directive.

Appreciating full well the importance of blocking the western entrance to the Mediterranean, Hitler had attempted in December to force Franco's hand with a peremptory request that German troops should be allowed to march into Spain on January 10th for an early attack on Gibraltar. Franco had replied that this was impossible for many reasons, the chief of which was that he could not put the Spanish colonies in jeopardy so long as the British Fleet possessed freedom of action. Because of this, he "could not enter the war until Britain was on the point of collapse."[1]

During January Wavell's sweeping victory over the Italians in Cyrenaica made it inopportune for Hitler to renew his approach to Madrid, but on February 6th, when the British advance appeared to be coming to a halt, the Führer again addressed himself to the Caudillo. His tone now was harsher and harder. "The battle which Germany and Italy are fighting," he wrote, "is determining the destiny of Spain as well. Only in the case of our victory will your present régime continue to exist." Germany was ready to deliver grain and military supplies "to the greatest extent possible," but this, Hitler added, "remains contingent upon Spain's final decision to enter the war. For about one thing, Caudillo, there must be clarity; we are fighting a battle of life and death and cannot at this time make any gifts."

Unhappily for Hitler, this letter arrived in Madrid on the same day as the news that the British in Cyrenaica had destroyed the last of Marshal

[1] Führer Naval Conferences, January 8th, 1941.

Graziani's army south of Benghazi; that the Royal Navy had bombarded Genoa; and that the aircraft carrier, H.M.S. *Illustrious*, which the Luftwaffe claimed to have sunk, had sailed right through the Mediterranean from Gibraltar to Alexandria. It is little wonder, therefore, that on February 26th, Franco should have replied to Hitler that " the logical development of the facts has left the circumstances of October far behind," and that " the Protocol then agreed upon must now be considered outmoded." On receiving this letter, Hitler wrote to Mussolini: " The long and short of the tedious Spanish rigmarole is that Spain does not want to enter the war and will not enter it. This is extremely tiresome since it means that for the moment the possibility of striking at Britain in the simplest manner, in her Mediterranean possessions, is eliminated."

The final rebuff from Madrid was the climax of a winter of frustration for Hitler's diplomacy. He had been double-crossed by Mussolini, blackmailed by Stalin and jilted by Franco. Even Pétain had summoned up the courage to dismiss Laval.

Hitler turned his back on the Mediterranean in disgust and, in so doing, exemplified one of his gravest weaknesses, a tendency to minimise or ignore factors which he could not shape to his will. He had counted on Malta falling into his hands as a matter of course once he had closed the Suez Canal and the Straits of Gibraltar. During January, however, Malta had been reinforced and Hitler shrank from undertaking any independent operation against it. When Raeder advocated this, Hitler replied: " That operation is contemplated for the autumn of 1941, *after* the completion of BARBAROSSA." Thus, when Germany moved east, Britain still held the three most important strategic bases on her southern flank—Gibraltar, Malta and Alexandria.

While Hitler was trying, and failing, to build his Grand Alliance of continental powers, the Anglo-Saxon countries on either side of the Atlantic were drawing closer together. In December 1940, Roosevelt had called upon the American people to make the United States " the great arsenal of democracy." Responding to this call, Congress had proceeded to endorse the President's Lend-Lease Plan, which Churchill was to call " the most unsordid act in history." The Lend-Lease Bill was passed by the House of Representatives on February 8th, 1941. The timing could not have been more appropriate, for it coincided with the arrival in Madrid of that letter in which Hitler had said to Franco: " We are fighting a battle of life and death and cannot at this time make any gifts."

The hesitancy of Franco and the initiative of Roosevelt made Hitler the more anxious to persuade the Japanese to enter the war against Britain. " Thereby," said Hitler in a directive of March 5th, " strong British forces will be tied down and the centre of gravity of American interest will be diverted to the Pacific." At the end of this month, therefore, when the Japanese Foreign Minister (Matsuoka) came to Berlin at

Hitler's invitation, Ribbentrop urged him to bring about an early attack on Singapore and other British possessions in the Far East. Matsuoka replied that he himself was eager for war with Britain, but there were many in Tokyo who regarded him as " a dangerous man with dangerous thoughts." He doubted whether he could convince his Government, since it was afraid that the Russians would attack Japan in the rear as soon as she moved against Singapore. Matsuoka said that he hoped " to clarify the Soviet attitude " in Moscow on his return journey. This announcement was not at all to the liking of the Germans. It would not suit their plan if Russo-Japanese relations were to be improved on the eve of BARBAROSSA, for that would allow the Red Army to transfer divisions from the Manchurian border to Poland. Accordingly, Ribbentrop asked Matsuoka " not to carry the discussions in Moscow too far," and promised that " Germany would strike immediately should Russia ever attack Japan." He mentioned that " a conflict between Germany and Russia is within the realm of possibility," but he did not say anything about the BARBAROSSA Plan, since Hitler had given strict orders that the Japanese were not to be informed.

Matsuoka gave no promises and took no chances. Two weeks later the German Ambassador in Moscow telegraphed to Ribbentrop: " Matsuoka has just visited me in order to make his farewell call. He stated to me that a Japanese-Soviet Neutrality Pact had been arranged at the last moment and in all likelihood would be signed this afternoon."[1] Hitler did not relish the taste of his own medicine, but if, as he complained to Ribbentrop, he had been betrayed by his ally, this was the direct result of his own suspicion and deceit.

This miscarriage of Hitler's diplomacy was followed by a further miscarriage of plan in the realm of strategy. In January, with the object of maintaining Italian power in North Africa and thereby preventing Britain from sending additional forces to Greece, Hitler had persuaded Mussolini to accept German aid in the defence of Libya. Early in February Lieut.-General Erwin Rommel had arrived in Tripoli with the advance guard of the Africa Corps, and with the task of making himself a nuisance to the British. Hitler had no thought of invading Egypt that year, and in his orders to Rommel he expressly said: " For the time being the main task of the German Africa Corps is to defend the positions reached in Tripolitania and to hold down the largest possible British forces in North Africa." Rommel was told that, even when his entire force had arrived, he was not to undertake any extensive operations into Cyrenaica.[2]

Unaware that Hitler was sending German troops to North Africa and

[1]Telegram of April 13th, 1941. (See *Nazi-Soviet Relations 1939-1941*, p. 322.)
[2]Führer Directive of February 18th, 1941. Rommel was ordered to prepare a long-term plan for the re-conquest of Cyrenaica and to submit his plan by April 20th. Taking advantage of permission to " reconnoitre aggressively," Rommel invaded Cyrenaica at the end of March and by April 20th had re-conquered the whole of that province except Tobruk. Rommel then wanted to go on but, when he failed to take Tobruk at the start of May, he was forbidden to advance into Egypt " except for purposes of reconnaissance."

anticipating that he would soon come to Mussolini's aid in Greece, the British Government had already advised the Greeks of its willingness to transfer a large part of Wavell's forces from Libya. The Greek Prime Minister (General Papagos) accepted this offer with misgiving, for it seemed to him that, while the three or four divisions which Wavell could spare would not be sufficient to save Greece from German invasion, they might provoke it. Churchill and the British Chiefs of Staff believed, however, that Hitler's intervention was inevitable and that it could be checked only if all the Balkan countries stood firm and united against Nazi aggression. They argued that the arrival of British and Anzac troops in Greece would encourage Yugoslavia to resist and might bring Turkey into the war on the side of the Allies. In mid-February, therefore, in the hope of fostering Balkan resistance, Churchill sent the Foreign Secretary (Anthony Eden) and the C.I.G.S. (General Sir John Dill) to Athens and Ankara. Their mission was not unsuccessful.

Throughout February Yugoslavia declined Hitler's 'invitation' to join the Tripartite Alliance, but on the last day of that month German troops were given a free passage into Bulgaria, which then publicly proclaimed its adherence to the Axis cause. Thus almost enveloped, Yugoslavia gave way, but the *coup d'état* by a group of army officers who overthrew the Cvetkovic Government on March 27th created a situation which Hitler could not tolerate. Suspecting, rightly, that this revolt had been encouraged by the British, the Führer told his Commanders-in-Chief that, " without waiting for possible declarations of loyalty from the new government," he intended to " destroy Yugoslavia militarily and as a national unit." Thus committed to a much larger campaign than he had bargained for, Hitler announced: " The beginning of Operation BARBAROSSA will have to be postponed up to four weeks as a result of the Balkan operations."[1]

The German war machine moved remorselessly into action in the Balkans on April 6th, and before the end of the month all organised resistance had ceased in Yugoslavia and on the Greek mainland. Rapid though the victory was, the campaign involved Germany in a diversion of effort which she could ill afford at this juncture. Hitler's plan for the invasion of Russia required the mobilisation in the East of his full offensive power, for the German High Command calculated that between the Black Sea and the Baltic the Red Army could muster at least 155 divisions. The German forces on this front would amount to 110 front-line divisions, plus 16 divisions in reserve, and another 12 provided by Rumania: 138 in all.[2] Even allowing for the superior quality of the German troops

[1]Minutes of Conference between Hitler and his Commanders-in-Chief, March 27th, 1941. (Nuremberg Document 1746 PS.)

[2]These figures and those given below are taken from the Minutes of the Conference between Hitler and the Army High Command held on February 3rd, 1941, from Directive No. 25, issued on March 27th, 1941, and from the BARBAROSSA movement time-table dated June 6th, 1941. Before BARBAROSSA began, however, German Intelligence estimated that the Werhmacht would be opposed by 213 Russian divisions.

and equipment, therefore, Hitler had not the margin of advantage which past experience had shown was necessary for a successful offensive with objectives deep in enemy territory.

This was the prospect when it was thought that only a minor operation would be necessary against Greece, but, as soon as the Yugoslav crisis developed, Hitler increased the force for the Balkans Campaign from 18 to 28 divisions, 24 of which were already earmarked for BARBAROSSA, and these included seven of his nineteen panzer and three of his twelve motorised divisions. The result was that a third of the mobile formations, which were intended to be the spearheads of his deep thrusts and great encirclements in Russia, were diverted to the Southern Balkans just when they should have been moving to assembly areas in Poland.

It is evident now that Hitler might have overrun Greece and Yugo-slavia with half this force, but he could not afford to risk a stalemate or even a few weeks' delay. Speed called for strength and this meant postponing the attack on Russia, for it took more than two months to transport the 24 BARBAROSSA divisions from the Balkans to the Eastern Front over the inadequate and uncertain railways of South-Eastern Europe.[1]

What actual delay the Balkans Campaign imposed upon the launching of BARBAROSSA is difficult to appraise, because the weather was unfavour-able for offensive operations from Poland at least until the second week of June. The decision to postpone had been made, however, without taking the weather into consideration, and it is impossible now to tell whether Hitler would have tried to start on May 15th, as originally planned, if he had not been drawn into Yugoslavia and Greece. The opinion of Blumentritt, then Chief of Staff of the Fourth Army in Poland, and of Halder, is that " the friction in the Balkans and the excep-tional weather in 1941 caused the loss of four precious weeks." Those weeks were to be worth many months before the year ran out.

On June 2nd, 1941, when Hitler drove his armies into Russia, it was twelve months to the day since the signing of the French armistice. In that year he had extended his power to the Black Sea and the Mediter-ranean and had tightened his grip on Western and Northern Europe, but he had failed in his most important purpose; he had failed to subdue Britain. She had spurned his offer of peace; she had withstood his bombardment and blockade; she had thwarted his plan to unite all Europe under Nazi leadership; she had foiled his efforts to exclude her from the Mediterranean; she had dared to set foot again on the Continent at a time and place most awkward for him; and she had driven him at last into the desperate and hazardous expedient of attacking Russia as the only means of freeing or securing the military and economic resources necessary for him to wage effective war against her. When he

[1]According to von Thoma, who was Chief of Mobile Forces at the Army High Command, only 2,434 tanks were available for the Eastern Front in June 1941; of these more than 800 had to be moved back from the Balkans.

attacked in the West in 1940, he had been able to guard his eastern frontier with a Non-Aggression Pact and seven divisions; when he attacked in the East in 1941, he felt obliged to guard the Atlantic coastline against British intervention with 49 divisions.

If to some extent the frustration of Hitler's plans was due to the fact that he had been embarrassed and even betrayed by those who professed to be his friends, this in turn was the result partly of their justifiable mistrust of him, and partly to their not so justifiable fear of that British power which Churchill lost no opportunity of demonstrating, slight though his real resources were.

Militarily, during this year, Britain had been able to do little more than harass the fringes of the German Empire, but by bold use of the great flexibility which naval and air power gave her, she had been able to deny Hitler the strategic victories which would have made him safe from the danger of a war on two fronts. He was thus compelled to commit the Wehrmacht to an offensive in the East before he had secured his defences in the West and South.

At the time, although Hitler was piqued at the failure of his overall strategy, he was confident that his Continental Empire was inviolable and that Britain could do nothing to disturb the fulfilment of his plans. He was even deluded enough to retain the hope that Britain might come to terms and join his ' anti-Communist crusade,' once he had invaded Russia. " When BARBAROSSA begins," said Hitler to his generals, " the world will hold its breath and make no comment."[1] But on June 22nd, Churchill held neither his breath nor his tongue. Broadcasting from London that night the Prime Minister said:

We have but one aim and one single irrevocable purpose. We are resolved to destroy Hitler and every vestige of the Nazi régime. From this nothing will turn us—nothing. We will never parley, we will never negotiate with Hitler or any of his gang. . . . Any man or State who fights against Nazidom will have our aid. Any man or State who marches with Hitler is our foe. . . . It follows therefore that we shall give whatever help we can to Russia and the Russian people. We shall appeal to all our friends and allies in every part of the world to take this course and pursue it, as we shall, faithfully and steadfastly to the end.

This answer, which Roosevelt was soon to confirm as the answer of the Anglo-Saxon world, made it absolutely imperative that Hitler should gain in the East a victory that was swift and decisive.

[1]Minutes of Conference between Hitler and the Army High Command, February 3rd, 1941.

# CHAPTER IV

# INTUITION ON THE MARCH

" I DECLARE to-day—and I declare it without any reservation—
the enemy in the East has been struck down and will never rise
again." Those confident words were addressed by Adolf Hitler to the
German people on October 3rd, 1941, fifteen weeks after the start of
BARBAROSSA. On the previous day he had begun what he called " the
final drive for Moscow " and had sent his troops into action with the
assurance that this was " the beginning of the last great decisive battle
of this year." Convinced that he spoke the truth, Hitler was already
preparing for other years. In a directive issued as early as July 14th
he had said : " The military domination of Europe after the defeat of
Russia will enable the strength of the Army to be considerably reduced
in the near future. Naval armament must be restricted to those measures
which have a direct connection with the conduct of the war against
Britain and, if the case should arise, against America. The main effort
in armament will be shifted to the Air Force, which must be greatly
increased in strength."[1]

At the end of September, in execution of this policy, he had ordered
the Army High Command to disband 40 infantry divisions and return
their personnel to industry. He had also given orders for an immediate
decrease in production for the Army and an immediate increase in
armaments for the Air Force and Navy. During the development of the
air and sea-power necessary for the direct assault on the British Isles, the
Wehrmacht was to carry out early in 1942 a general offensive in the
Middle East : from Libya to the Nile and Suez, from Bulgaria through
Turkey to Syria and Palestine, and from the Caucasus to the oilfields of
the Persian Gulf area.[2]

The optimism which inspired these orders was not shared by the
German High Command. Von Brauchitsch and Halder had always
doubted the wisdom of invading Russia, and from the outset had been

[1]This Directive was presented in evidence at Nuremberg. (Document C 74.)
[2]This plan was outlined in a directive dealing with " The further conduct of the
war upon the termination of the campaign in the East," issued in August 1941. (Nuremberg Document C 57.)

opposed to the plan of campaign upon which Hitler had insisted. They had wanted to concentrate on a massive drive to Moscow, arguing that the primary task should be the destruction of the military power of the Red Army and that Moscow was the one city the Russians must defend.[1] Hitler, on the other hand, was more concerned with economic and political objectives. In the north he wished to gain possession of the Baltic coast and Leningrad and to join forces with the Finns as soon as possible; in the south his aim was to secure the wheatlands of the Ukraine and the industrial resources of the Lower Dnieper; Moscow could wait.

The plan which emerged was, to some extent, a compromise. It followed Hitler's concept in broad outline, but it did not preclude the subsequent development of the main offensive in the direction of Moscow, since it placed the *Schwerpunkt* of the initial attack north of the Pripet Marshes. Here Army Group Centre (von Bock) was to envelop and destroy the Soviet forces in White Russia with a series of pincer movements astride the main Warsaw–Moscow railway. Having reached Smolensk, however, von Bock was to pause and, if necessary, detach one of his two panzer groups to aid Army Group North (von Leeb) which had orders to advance " in the general direction of Leningrad [and] to annihilate the enemy forces fighting in the Baltic [States]." " Only then," said Hitler's directive, " *after* the accomplishment of this most important task, which must be followed by the occupation of Leningrad and Kronstadt, are the offensive operations aimed at the occupation of . . . Moscow to be pursued."[2]

While von Leeb was heading for the Gulf of Finland, von Rundstedt's Army Group South was to carry out a corresponding thrust to the Black Sea. He was to attack from Southern Poland " in the general direction of Kiev, in order to penetrate quickly with strong armoured units deep into the flank and rear of the Russian forces and then roll them up along the Dnieper River." After crossing the Lower Dnieper to the Sea of Azov von Rundstedt was to take the Crimea, but his operations were essentially separate from and subsidiary to the main drive in the north, which was designed to capture Moscow as soon as the Baltic flank had been made secure.

In his directive Hitler said: " The mass of the Russian Army in Western Russia is to be destroyed in daring operations by driving forward deep armoured wedges, and the retreat of units intact into the vast expanse of Russian territory is to be prevented." The application of these tactics brought immediate success, and on July 3rd Halder noted in his diary, " It is probably not an exaggeration to say that the campaign against Russia has been won in fourteen days." By the middle of August von Rundstedt had driven down the Dnieper Valley to the Black Sea;

---

[1] Not all the generals took this view. Von Rundstedt, for instance, thought that Hitler's plan for the initial phase was right.
[2] Führer Directive No. 21, December 18th, 1941.

von Leeb had cut off the Russian forces on the Baltic coast and was approaching Leningrad; von Bock had advanced 450 miles and captured Smolensk.

Remarkable though these advances were the German High Command was beginning to have misgivings about the course of the campaign, for it felt that Hitler's stubborn adherence to his original plan was leading, as Halder observed at the time, " to the dispersal of our forces and to stagnation in the decisive direction, Moscow."[1] Already, Hitler's refusal to give full priority to the central thrust had prevented von Bock from repeating at Smolensk the double enveloping movement he had executed at Minsk. East of Smolensk the Russians had succeeded in extricating half a million men to bar the road to Moscow. Moreover, the Germans now knew that the Red Army was very much stronger than they had thought. " We have underestimated Russia," wrote Halder on August 17th. " We reckoned with 200 divisions and we have already identified 360. On this broad expanse our front is too thin; it has no depth. In consequence the enemy counter-attacks often meet with success."

On the following day, disturbed by the capacity for recovery which the Red Army had shown, von Brauchitsch again urged Hitler to advance upon Moscow in maximum strength and without delay. " We knew," said Halder when interrogated after the war, " that the Russians were building fresh positions between Smolensk and Moscow and organising substantial new forces for the defence of the capital. The centre of gravity of the Red Army was therefore on von Bock's front and it was here that we wanted to make our main effort before the Russians had time to bring up any more reserves."

In the south at this time, although von Rundstedt's armour had crossed the Lower Dnieper, Kiev was still holding out and substantial Russian forces had evaded the German scythe and had withdrawn in good order to the east of that city. The prospect of trapping these armies in an enveloping movement more ambitious than anything he had yet attempted fired the Führer's imagination. On August 21st Hitler rejected von Brauchitsch's ' Moscow Plan,' and decided, says Halder, that " the strongest possible forces from Army Groups Centre and South were to be concentrated for a great pincer movement against the Soviet forces east of Kiev. . . . [Thus] the aim of defeating decisively the Russian armies in front of Moscow was subordinated to the desire to obtain a valuable industrial area and to advance in the direction of Russian oil. . . . Hitler now became obsessed with the idea of capturing both Leningrad and Stalingrad, for he persuaded himself that if these two ' holy cities of Communism ' were to fall, Russia would collapse."

Although Smolensk had been taken on August 7th, the capture and envelopment of Kiev was not completed until September 20th. At Kiev the Germans claimed to have taken 665,000 prisoners in what Hitler called " the greatest battle in the history of the world." It seemed to

[1]Halder's Diary, July 28th, 1941.

Halder, however, that it was " the greatest strategic blunder of the Eastern campaign," for in the six weeks between the fall of Smolensk and the taking of Kiev the opportunity of seizing Moscow was lost. In those six weeks the Russians were given time to organise the defence of their capital, German armoured strength was weakened by the wear and tear of cross-country movement, and before this victory had been won the first snow had fallen. In spite of this warning that the winter would be early, in spite of reports of gathering Russian strength, in spite of the approaching exhaustion of the panzer divisions whose losses had exceeded the output of the German tank factories, von Brauchitsch once more proposed, and Hitler now agreed, that Army Group Centre should be strongly reinforced for a concerted and powerful drive to Moscow " in the time available prior to the onset of winter weather." Although he accepted the principle of making the main effort against the Russian capital, Hitler did not accept von Brauchitsch's corollary that operations on other sectors of the front should be curtailed. He agreed that von Bock should be strengthened, but insisted that von Leeb's attack on Leningrad and von Rundstedt's advance to Rostov and the Caucasus must continue. Thus again Hitler committed the fatal mistake of failing to concentrate on the decisive objective.

In August von Bock might have succeeded in breaking through to Moscow but by October 2nd, when his offensive was eventually launched, it was already too late. Yet this was not immediately apparent, for within a fortnight the Germans had covered half the distance from Smolensk to Moscow in one bound and the panzer groups had completed two great envelopments, capturing, so they claimed, more than 600,000 men around Vyasma and Bryansk. By October 20th the leading armoured columns were only 40 miles from Moscow and even the sober Halder was ready to admit that, " given moderately correct leadership and moderately good weather the encirclement of Moscow must succeed." In the last ten days of October, however, there was heavy and almost incessant rain. Tanks and vehicles were stalled and the attack came to a standstill. By the end of the month snow lay thick upon the ground. Von Rundstedt, the wisest of Hitler's field commanders, now proposed that they should call a halt for the winter, but von Bock and von Brauchitsch, believing that Moscow was within their grasp, endorsed Hitler's determination to drive on in the hope of clinching their victory that year. On November 15th, as soon as the ground had frozen, the offensive was renewed. " One final heave," said Hitler to Jodl, " and we shall triumph "; and von Bock called upon his troops for a supreme effort, declaring, " the last battalion will decide the issue."

By December 2nd the leading elements of von Kluge's Fourth Army were within sight of the Kremlin, fighting in the western suburbs of Moscow, but there they were halted. Von Kluge was threatened with encirclement when the Red Army, equipped and prepared for winter campaigning, opened its counter-offensive a week later. The long arm which had reached out to Moscow was in danger of being cut off, but Hitler sent orders: " Fourth Army is not to retire a single step." Haunted by the terrible example of Napoleon's winter withdrawal, he feared that any retreat would become a rout. The order issued to Fourth Army was applied to the whole front. When he learned of Hitler's insistence that the troops must stand fast even though by-passed and even encircled, Halder commented: " Troops simply do not hold their ground when it's 22 degrees below zero."

This order brought about a further crisis between Hitler and the Army High Command. The outcome had far-reaching importance, but its full significance is apparent only when it is seen as the final act of the process by which Hitler, the one-time corporal, outmanœuvred the strongest general staff and gained absolute control of the most formidable military machine that the world had ever seen. In this there lay the seeds of Germany's ultimate defeat.

When Hitler became Chancellor in January 1933, Germany was still limited by the Treaty of Versailles to an army of 100,000 men, the Reichswehr. The titular Supreme Command of the Armed Forces was vested in President von Hindenburg by virtue of his office, the political direction of military affairs lay with the Reich Minister for Defence, von Blomberg, but the real centre of military power was the Army High Command (*Oberkommando des Heeres*, known as ' OKH '). Here the traditions and ambitions of the old *Grosse Generalstab* were staunchly maintained by officers who were politically conservative and who looked upon the new Chancellor as a demagogue and an upstart. The antagonism was mutual, for, says Halder, " Hitler, with the fervour of a revolutionary, hated the older type of officer as representative of an upper class which he regarded as rotten and incompetent." A product of the masses and a man of passion, whose chief experience of war had been as a battalion runner, Hitler spontaneously distrusted these ultra-rational, aristocratic professional soldiers. Yet he needed them, for they controlled the decisive force in the state; they alone could provide the foundations of Germany's military resurrection.

Unlike most of history's successful despots, Hitler had not come to power at the head of an army whose loyalty to his person had been won in battle. His own Brown Shirts, the *Sturmabteilung* (SA), however efficient in political street-fighting, were not capable of opposing the Reichswehr. Since the early days of the Party struggle, the leader of the SA, Roehm, had sought to convert his storm-troops into a militia, which would in time absorb and swamp the Reichswehr, thus providing Hitler with a thoroughly Nazified military instrument. Roehm wanted to take the citadel of the General Staff by direct assault; Hitler preferred the tactics of patient infiltration. He would slip in through the President's side door, as soon as death had claimed the ailing von Hindenburg.

In the meantime he sought to placate the Generals, for he realised that he could not succeed to supreme authority without the full backing of the Army. He therefore assured its leaders that " the Wehrmacht would be the sole bearer of arms and that its structure would remain unaltered." But the Army wanted a more practical guarantee. The price of its support was that Hitler should break the power of Roehm and the extremists in the Party, who were demanding a " second revolution " and a " people's army." For more than a year Hitler strove to avoid choosing between the SA and the Reichswehr, but in the summer of 1934 Roehm precipitated a crisis by openly demanding that the Brown Shirts should be made part of the Army. In the ' Blood Purge ' of June 30th, 1934, Hitler settled the issue with the murder of Roehm and his chief supporters and the forcible suppression of the SA.

By this drastic disowning of his own, Hitler seemed to have delivered himself into the hands of the Generals, but their victory was short-lived. On August 2nd, 1934, von Hindenburg died. Allegedly in execution of his will, and certain in any case of the Army's support, the Reich Cabinet forthwith merged the offices of President and Chancellor. That same morning von Blomberg and the heads of the three services were summoned to Hitler's study and ordered to swear an oath which he himself had drafted out on a short slip of paper: an oath of allegiance not to the Constitution, as hitherto, not to the Fatherland, but to the Führer personally. The following day every member of the German Armed Forces was likewise obliged to declare:

I swear by God this holy oath: that I will render unconditional obedience to the Führer of the German Reich and People, Adolf Hitler, the Supreme Commander of the Armed Forces, and will be ready, as a brave soldier, to stake my life at any time for this oath.

With that oath the Wehrmacht, and through it the German people, became bound body and soul to the person and the policies of Adolf Hitler. From that compact there was no divorce and little desertion until Hitler released the bond by taking his own life. That oath was to be the corner-stone of his power, the rock upon which every attempt at military opposition to the Nazi régime was broken. In obedience to it Germans in arms were to carry out manifold acts of aggression and spoliation, torture and murder throughout the length and breadth of Europe.

The personal oath was Hitler's first step along the road to absolute military power. He was determined to be ' Supreme Commander ' in fact as well as name, but he was not yet strong enough to challenge the Generals directly nor to establish his own creatures in office at OKH. Accordingly, in 1935 he created a new overall command, superior to that of the Army. Von Blomberg became both Minister for War and Commander-in-Chief of the Armed Forces, with Keitel, a pliant toady, as his Chief of Staff. To them, and to the new Combined Services General Staff, Hitler assigned the task of planning for war. There was a sound military justification for these innovations, but the inner purpose was political—Hitler's desire to curtail the authority of the Commander-in-Chief and the General Staff of the Army.

Its leaders certainly welcomed Hitler's revival of German nationalism and militarism, for, as von Blomberg has declared, " a war to wipe out the desecration involved in the creation of the Polish Corridor . . . was regarded by all officers and about ninety per cent of the German people as a sacred duty, though a sad necessity."[1] But the Generals resented being subordinated to what they regarded as a political command and they doubted whether Hitler could carry out rapid rearmament or aggressive expansion without provoking serious reprisals from Germany's neighbours. They were afraid that he would lead them into war before they were ready.

Hitler attributed the Generals' caution to lack of courage and feared that they would try to frustrate his plans and might even seek his overthrow. He was well aware that an army strong enough to realise his external ambitions might also be too strong for his internal security. Consequently, in February 1938, he dismissed both von Blomberg and the C.-in-C. of the Army, von Fritsch, allegedly on grounds of personal impropriety, but in reality because he needed to consolidate and extend his own authority before embarking upon his first serious act of aggression, the *Anschluss* with Austria.

No successor was appointed for von Blomberg. Hitler became his own War Minister and decreed: " Henceforth, command over the entire Armed Forces will be exercised directly by me personally." Thus the nominal Supreme Commander expanded the authority he had inherited from von Hindenburg and made himself the actual Commander-in-Chief. At the same time he declared that the High Command of the Armed Forces (*Oberkommando der Wehrmacht*, or ' OKW ') would be " directly under my command as my military staff." It became, in Halder's words, " the military executive of the revolutionary politician."

The Generals meekly accepted this transformation in the structure of command, even though it involved the victimisation of von Fritsch, the one man who had the position and prestige to challenge Hitler's usurpation of supreme military power. They approved the dismissal of von Blomberg, whom they distrusted as a ' political general ' and who had destroyed his own standing by his marriage to a former prostitute. But the case of von Fritsch was on an entirely different footing. A distinguished soldier of high character, he was revered throughout the Army. The preposterous charge of homosexuality, which Himmler brought against him, was shown (in the trial which cleared his name) to have been fabricated by the Gestapo.

This abject surrender by the Army High Command was a major

[1]In an affidavit presented at Nuremberg, April 1st, 1946.

victory for Hitler. Von Fritsch was succeeded by von Brauchitsch, a general less experienced, less influential and more pliable. Six months later another restraining influence disappeared, when the Army Chief of Staff, General Ludwig Beck, resigned in protest against Hitler's plan to attack Czechoslovakia. Beck hoped that his resignation would warn the people that they were being led into war, and would rouse the Army to act against Hitler. But in fact Beck played into the Führer's hands, for resignation is a useless weapon in a police state. Hitler thwarted Beck's design by keeping the news secret until the crisis had passed. Nevertheless, Beck succeeded in convincing his colleagues at OKH that the invasion of Czechoslovakia would bring about a world war, and persuaded them to formulate a plot for Hitler's overthrow. The Generals, led by Halder and von Witzleben, had already decided to arrest the Führer, when news came that Chamberlain was flying to Berchtesgaden.

Hitler's triumph of political judgment, military bluff and sheer force of personality at Munich rallied the nation behind him and won over to his side many doubters in the Army High Command. This was the third time that he had disregarded the counsel of his Generals and had gained a bloodless victory. There was now no stopping him, and in the following March when he occupied the rump of Czechoslovakia, OKH was not even consulted. The necessary orders were issued direct by Hitler from OKW to the field commanders concerned.

By this time none dared offer political objection to his strategic plans, but, when it came to the attack on Poland, the Army General Staff was hardly prepared to have him dictate to it on questions of tactics. Yet Hitler personally worked out to the last detail the plan for the attack on the key bridge at Dirschau, and he demanded a substantial increase in the general tempo of the attack. Von Brauchitsch and Halder, the new Chief of Staff, both regarded his timing as too venturesome and over-optimistic, but the battle went even better and faster than he had predicted. This confirmed his preconception that the Army High Command was a collection of ' hidebound pessimists ' who opposed his plans out of stubborn stupidity.

At the conclusion of the campaign Hitler called a conference of his senior generals and, says Halder, " in an excited and uncontrolled manner told them that they were the representatives of a spirit, the incompetence of which had been proved by the results of the World War. . . . He criticised them for having opposed all his successful actions instead of thanking him for having created a new Army, which alone had made possible the success of the Polish Campaign. He demanded whole-hearted acceptance of his ideas and unconditional obedience."

This outburst did not prevent von Brauchitsch and Halder from objecting when Hitler went on to demand the carrying out of an offensive in the West that autumn. Making the most of the unfavourable weather, they succeeded in having the operation postponed from week to week until Hitler's attention was distracted to Scandinavia. Their delaying action, however, so intensified Hitler's distrust that they were barely consulted about this next move. He merely announced that preparations for the occupation of Denmark and Norway would be " under my direct and personal guidance," and told OKH to make available certain forces " for special purposes . . . directly under my orders." Von Brauchitsch surrendered his troops to Hitler's personal command. With them he yielded what was left of his own independence.

The remarkable success of these operations enhanced Hitler's prestige to such an extent that OKH had to waive all objection when he adopted an even more ambitious plan for the invasion of France and the Low Countries. This was the crucial test between Hitler and the Generals. OKH had proposed to follow substantially the classical Schlieffen Plan, making a powerful left wheel through Belgium. Hitler, adopting the suggestion of von Manstein (Chief of Staff to von Rundstedt), insisted upon the *Schwerpunkt* being in the Ardennes. This plan was strongly opposed by the Army High Command, but Hitler demanded its execution and gained a triumph even beyond his own expectations. His position, and his decisions, were now unchallengeable. His critics had been so consistently wrong, first in their political protests and then in their military objections, that he was accepted by the mass of the people and the rank and file of the Wehrmacht at his own valuation, a political and military genius.

Had Hitler's plan in the West miscarried, or been only partially successful, the Army High Command might have been able to reassert its influence and exercise some restraint over him. But, as it was, he would no longer take advice even on the most technical matters and he insisted upon dealing personally and directly with an ever widening range of problems. Success made him more than ever convinced of his divine mission to turn the Continent into a German empire and in due course to challenge the world. It is perhaps not too much to say that Germany's eventual defeat was ensured when Hitler won the Battle of France, for, after that, there was nothing to stop his unbridled ambition from plunging Germany to ruin.

When the dreaded order for the invasion of Russia was issued, the Army High Command accepted it with little demur. The Generals knew by now that any opposition on their part would provoke violent outbursts of recrimination, and would prejudice their chances of modifying the plan later so as to keep its objectives within reach of the Wehrmacht's strength. Halder reports that these efforts were of no avail, for " Hitler's belief in his own infallibility and in the omnipotence of his will increased; so did his nervous irritability. His interference in the direction of the Army, even in small matters, increased too, and tense debates about strategic and even tactical questions, which were purely the responsibility of the C.-in-C., Army, became more and more frequent. Spoiled by the quick successes of the previous campaigns, he expected operations to be carried through in a space of time that completely ignored the conditions of terrain and roads in the East. The advance into Russian territory could never be fast enough for his impatience."

Even in the first months of victory in Russia, Hitler had begun to over-reach himself. The 150 German, Finnish and Rumanian divisions available at the start of BARBAROSSA were sufficient for the initial objectives, but they could not support a sustained and deep offensive on a rapidly expanding front. Advancing out of the comparatively narrow throat between the Black Sea and the Baltic, the German armies were soon swallowed up in the vastness of the steppes. The more desperately Hitler pressed the pursuit of the withdrawing Russians, the more dangerously he exposed himself to a counter-stroke as soon as winter brought campaigning conditions which favoured the Red Army. When the drive for Moscow was halted in December, von Brauchitsch proposed that the Army should pull back and assume the defensive for the winter, but, says Halder, "Hitler fought with fanatical rage against the idea of with-drawing to a winter line . . . and demanded that even in tactically impossible situations the troops must defend themselves to the last man wherever they stood."

Having protested against the senseless sacrifices of men and material which this involved, von Brauchitsch 'resigned.' Von Rundstedt had already retired; the other Army Group Commanders, von Bock and von Leeb, were soon relieved on grounds of ill health; and Halder was retained on sufferance only until September 1942. On December 19th, 1941, following the removal of von Brauchitsch, Hitler completed his destruction of the Army's independence by assuming the post of Commander-in-Chief himself. Thus the powers of the Head of State, the Minister for War, the Supreme Commander of the Armed Forces, and the C.-in-C., Army, were all vested in the Führer, to whom every German soldier, sailor and airman, every Government official and every member of the Nazi Party was personally bound by oath of allegiance. As if this were not sufficient, he demanded and received from the Reichstag the title of 'Supreme Law Lord' with absolute powers of punishment and dismissal.

This consolidation of command in Hitler's own hands was the more drastic in its effects because he had already halved the powers of both OKW and OKH. Until the start of BARBAROSSA, the Supreme Command of the Armed Forces, OKW, had planned and directed the strategy and exercised general control over the operations of all three services every-where; OKH had controlled the Army, directing its day-to-day operations on all fronts, its servicing and its training. In the middle of 1941, however, Hitler had decreed that, so far as operations were concerned, OKH should confine itself to the Russian front (excluding Finland) and that all other theatres were to be the preserve of OKW, which thus became little more than another General Staff for the Western, Southern and Northern theatres of war.

When this division of power was followed by the dismissal of von

Brauchitsch, Hitler's triumph over the Generals was complete. No individual general now commanded more than one Army Group. Hitler alone was in a position to issue orders to all elements of the Army on all fronts. There was no adequate command or staff responsible for the strategic planning and direction of the war as a whole. In fact the only co-ordinating link between the Eastern Front and the other theatres of war, between OKH and OKW, was Hitler and his own small personal staff. The separation of OKW and OKH was so strict that even the transfer of a regiment from the East to the West had to be referred to Hitler personally.

These changes in the structure of the High Command were designed not for more efficient prosecution of the war, but for more effective protection of Hitler's political position. He applied to the Army the policy of divide and rule which he had so successfully employed in dealing with his political opponents at home and abroad. He thus made it extremely difficult for any one general, or group of generals, to gain control of forces great enough to challenge his authority.

Hitler's campaign to weaken the power of the Army High Command did not stop at this reorganisation. Ever since the suppression of the SA in 1934, Hitler had been insuring himself against an Army putsch by the unobtrusive development of independent forces under the command of his two staunchest subordinates, Goering and Himmler. In 1935 all anti-aircraft units became part of the well-Nazified Luftwaffe. Thus Hitler ensured that there would be loyal cells of armed men throughout the Reich and that the Army would not have under its direct control any means of defending itself against the Air Force, if it ever became necessary for Goering to use the Luftwaffe to suppress a revolt by the Generals. In 1942 Hitler further strengthened the forces under Goering's control. Reinforcements were urgently needed for the Eastern Front and it was decided that surplus Air Force personnel, who had been recruited for the renewed assault upon Britain, should be retrained as soldiers. OKH wanted to draft these recruits into Army divisions, which were battle-worn, but experienced, thus blending new blood and old to the advantage of both. At Goering's suggestion, however, Hitler had formed them into Luftwaffe Field Divisions, some 20 in all, and, even though they fought under Army command, they remained part of the Luftwaffe.

Far more serious—militarily and politically—was the expansion of the *Waffen Schutzstaffel* (the Armed SS). The SS had originally been raised as Hitler's personal bodyguard but before the war it had been developed into a State Military Police Force with a strength, by 1940, equivalent to three divisions. During 1941 it was rapidly increased and was given priority in manpower and equipment to ensure that the SS divisions, eventually numbering more than 30, would be *élite* formations.

These developments divided the ground forces internally. The commander of an army or a corps often had under him, as well as his

Wehrmacht formations, SS and GAF Divisions which were not completely within his control. In the last resort they ' belonged ' respectively to the ' private armies ' of Himmler and Goering, to whom the divisional commanders could appeal direct if they disagreed with any ' Army decision.' The result was a perpetual conflict of jurisdiction and a general weakening in the structure of command, except at the top.

Whatever advantages this policy had for Hitler, personally and politically, it was militarily disastrous. According to Speer,[1] who understood him better than did most of his close associates, " Hitler's decision to assume command of the Army was the most unfortunate decision of the war, because in consequence the Army was left without a Commander-in Chief. A C.-in-C. is expected to defend the interests of his service and to have close contact with his troops; he must make endless specific rulings on matters of detail. Hitler had not the time for this and no expert knowledge and so in effect the post of C.-in-C., Army, was abolished."

It was abolished just when the German Army was more than ever in need of balanced and professional leadership, but Hitler's only answer to the grave problems which arose from the outbreak of war between Japan and the United States was to rely more and more on his own judgment and authority, less and less on that of the experts whom he distrusted. It was perhaps no accident that the extension of his personal power in December 1941 followed immediately upon the expansion of the war from a European conflict into a world struggle.

Since the start of BARBAROSSA one of the objectives of Hitler's overall strategy had been to ensure the belligerency of Japan and the neutrality of the United States. He wanted, to quote Jodl, " a strong new ally without a strong new enemy." Accordingly, whereas Raeder was told on June 21st, 1941, that the Navy was to " avoid absolutely any possibility of incidents with the U.S.A. until the development of BARBAROSSA becomes clearer,"[2] Ribbentrop was ordered to persuade the Japanese to enter the war forthwith and to direct their attack, not on Singapore as Hitler had formerly proposed, but on Vladivostock, thus closing one route by which Lend-Lease supplies could reach the Red Army.

On July 10th Ribbentrop cabled to his Ambassador in Tokyo: " I ask you to employ all available means in insisting further upon Japan's entry into the war against Russia at the soonest possible date, as I have mentioned in my note to Matsuoka. . . . The natural objective remains that we and Japan join hands on the Trans-Siberian railway before the winter starts."[3]

---

[1] Albert Speer came to the fore as Hitler's personal architect and during the last four years of the war was Minister of Armaments and War Production, in which post he revealed a brilliant talent for organisation and improvisation.

[2] Führer Naval Conferences, June 21st, 1941.

[3] Nuremberg Document 2896 PS.

The response in Tokyo was not encouraging; nor were the Japanese more amenable to a further approach in October. When a new cabinet was formed under General Tojo, the two key posts in the Ministry of Foreign Affairs were given to Togo and Nishi, both strong advocates of friendship with the Soviet Union. According to Keitel, this assurance of continued neutrality on Japan's part, allowed the Russians during the next few months to transfer 18 to 20 divisions from the Far East to help stem the German advance.[1]

The failure to enlist the aid of Japan against Russia made Hitler the more determined not to give the United States any pretext for intervention. In July 1941 American forces took over the defence of Iceland. In September, after a clash between a U-boat and an American destroyer, Roosevelt gave warning that " from now on, if German or Italian vessels of war enter the waters, the protection of which is necessary for American defence, they do so at their own peril." American warships would shoot first. When this order was announced Raeder and Doenitz at once asked for the removal of the restrictions which Hitler had placed on U-boat operations, but the Führer reaffirmed his desire " to avoid having the U.S.A. declare war while the Eastern campaign is still in progress." Accordingly he ordered that " care be taken to avoid any incidents in the war on merchant shipping before about the middle of October."[2]

When October failed to bring the decisive victory which Hitler needed in the East, he became increasingly concerned at the danger of finding himself at war with both the Anglo-Saxon powers before he had finished with Russia. At the end of this month the United States moved a step closer to open belligerency with the decision to amend the Neutrality Act and with the President's pronouncement that American merchant ships " armed to defend themselves against the rattlesnakes of the sea . . . must be free to carry our American goods into the harbours of our friends . . . protected by our American Navy," which had orders " to shoot on sight." " The forward march of Hitler and of Hitlerism," said Roosevelt, " can be stopped—and it will be stopped."

Two years earlier Hitler would not have let this pronouncement go unanswered, but now " in keeping with strategic necessity " he again confirmed the order to his U-boats to avoid incidents with American ships. He was not ready for a show-down, nor was he anxious to precipitate a conflict between the United States and Japan. He was afraid, however, that if the moderates in Tokyo were to prevail, the Japanese might reach an understanding with America, as they had with the Soviet Union, and thus permit the United States to enter the European war untroubled by any distraction in the Far East. Consequently, Ribbentrop encouraged the Japanese to be intransigent in the conversations which proceeded in Washington during November, and on the

[1] *Nuremberg Trial Proceedings*, Part xi, p. 20.
[2] Führer Naval Conferences, September 17th, 1941.

29th assured their ambassador in Berlin: "Should Japan become engaged in a war against the United States, Germany, of course, would join the war immediately."[1]

Nevertheless, there was no concerted action to a common plan. The Japanese Fleet was already en route to Pearl Harbour before Germany and Italy were even warned that the Washington negotiations had broken down. On December 3rd, 1941, the Japanese Government asked the Axis powers " to declare war on America immediately after the outbreak of hostilities," but it gave no indication when or how the first blow would be struck. In keeping with the established diplomatic procedure, as between Axis partners, neither Hitler nor Mussolini knew anything of the Japanese plan to attack Pearl Harbour until the news of this act of treachery broke upon the world. Two days earlier, however, the Axis powers had given Japan the guarantee she wanted, although, as Ciano noted, " the idea of provoking American intervention is less and less liked by the Germans."[2] The Japanese attack was indeed the final miscarriage of Hitler's overall strategy. In September 1939 he had entered upon a continental war in which he sought to encompass the destruction of his opponents one by one, thus avoiding any question of a war on two fronts. Now in December 1941 he became embroiled in a global struggle for which he was by no means prepared against a combination of world powers capable of striking at Germany from all sides.

Hitler was slow to realise the full strategic significance of the new situation, for the immediate advantages of Japan's action obscured the long-term dangers. On December 12th, when Raeder advised him that " the situation in the Atlantic will be eased by Japan's successful inter-vention," Hitler asked, almost rhetorically, " Is there any possibility that the United States and Britain will abandon East Asia for a time in order to crush Germany and Italy first? " Raeder replied, " It is improbable that the enemy will give up East Asia even temporarily; by so doing Britain would endanger India very seriously and the United States cannot withdraw her fleet from the Pacific so long as the Japanese Navy has the upper hand."[3]

On the basis of this estimate of Allied intentions, an estimate with which Hitler fully agreed, Raeder argued that, while Britain and America were preoccupied with the struggle in the Pacific, Germany should take the opportunity of seizing Malta, advancing to the Suez Canal and opening the way for a junction with the Japanese in the Indian Ocean. Throughout the winter Raeder pressed this view, asserting that " the favourable situation in the Mediterranean, so pronounced at the present time, will probably never occur again." Hitler ignored the opportunity. He was engrossed in the struggle with Russia and in so far as he concerned

[1] International Military Tribunal, Far East, Document No. 2593.
[2] Ciano, *Diary*, p. 406.
[3] Führer Naval Conferences, December 12th, 1941.

himself about the Western Powers he turned his eyes not to the Mediterranean, but to Norway.

In the week after Christmas 1941 British Commandos made two small raids on the Norwegian coast. On December 29th Hitler told Raeder that he was expecting the British to make " an all-out attack with their fleet and landing troops. . . . The German Navy must therefore use all its forces for the defence of Norway." The battleships *Scharnhorst* and *Gneisenau* and the cruiser *Prinz Eugen* must be transferred there from Brest as soon as possible. " This could best be accomplished," said Hitler, " if the vessels were to break through the Channel taking the enemy completely by surprise, i.e. without previous training movements and during bad weather which makes air operations impossible."[1] The Naval Staff replied that such an attempt could not be made with any hope of success, but on the Führer's insistence it was planned and carried out.

This bold sortie had an influence upon Hitler and his strategy far exceeding the intrinsic importance of the operation. It led him to underestimate Britain's offensive capacity and it replenished the fountain of his self-confidence. He had always believed that victory was a matter of will-power and that his professional advisers were lacking in resolution. In the past he had repeatedly overruled the objections of his generals and had carried to success plans which they had condemned. In naval affairs, however, he had never been so sure of himself and he had not previously had the chance of proving a theory at the expense of the admirals.

This reinforcement of his faith in his own military genius came at a time when Halder and the Army General Staff were doing all they dared to persuade him that Germany had not the resources to sustain another offensive in the East. They were advocating a policy of strategic defence, designed to exhaust the Red Army while conserving the strength of the Wehrmacht for the decisive battle in the West which they knew must come. Hitler treated this advice with contempt. He refused to take account of the heavy inroads which had been made upon the Army's strength as a result of his own insistence that the troops must hold their ground whatever the cost.[2] On the contrary, he regarded their substantially successful resistance to the Soviet winter offensive as further proof that his generals were incompetent, cowardly and defeatist. *His* will-power had stopped the winter withdrawal; *his* will-power would drive the spring offensive. He asserted that the Russian reserves had now been exhausted and that the German conquest of the Caucasian oilfields would bring the Soviet war machine to a standstill.

Thus Hitler set the Wehrmacht on the road to Stalingrad in a

[1] Führer Naval Conferences, December 29th, 1941.
[2] The official German records show that between June 22nd, 1941, and February 28th, 1942, the German losses on the Eastern Front were: Killed, 210,572; Wounded, 747,761; Missing, 47,303. The casualties due to frost-bite came to at least 112,627.

supreme effort to gain a verdict in Russia before Britain and the United States were ready to open another front in the West. He had gambled on a short war confined to the European continent, but if, as now seemed likely, he should have to engage in a prolonged struggle against an Anglo-American alliance, it was essential that he secure the oil of the Caucasus.

In 1941 his total supply of oil had amounted to 8,929,000 tons (compared with seven million tons in the last year before the war) and he had been able to carry on only by withdrawing 1,140,000 tons from his meagre reserves. By the end of the year the stocks held for all military and civil purposes, except the needs of the Navy, were only 797,000 tons, barely one month's supply.[1] This did not provide Hitler with a working margin, and he had not yet been forced to wage an intensive campaign on two fronts.

Hitler's existing sources could not provide him with more than twelve million tons of crude oil a year. Synthetic production, four million tons in 1941, was to be increased to six million by 1943, but this gain would be partly offset by the declining output of the Rumanian oilfields. Wear and tear had already reduced their yield from 8.7 million tons in 1937 to 5.5 million in 1941, and half this amount was needed by Rumania herself for the maintenance of her essential economy and of her forces fighting in Russia. Even if he were to assume the strategic defensive in the East, Hitler would not have enough oil to wage air and naval warfare against the Western Powers on a scale sufficient to encompass their defeat.

In 1941 the Luftwaffe had been forced to draw upon stocks for more than 25 per cent of its consumption, and any renewal of the air offensive in the West at the intensity of the Battle of Britain would require at least twice as much aviation spirit as German-controlled Europe was producing. The plight of the Navy was equally serious. On November 13th Raeder presented to Hitler the following eloquent table:[2]

| FUEL OIL | |
| --- | --- |
| Total stocks of the German and Italian Navies .. .. .. .. | 410,000 tons |
| Total monthly requirements of both Navies .. .. .. .. | 200,000 tons |
| Total monthly supplies .. .. | 84,000 tons |

U-boat operations were not yet affected, for supplies of diesel oil were adequate, but before the end of the year the shortage of fuel oil had compelled the German Navy to abandon Atlantic operations which had

[1] 'The Effects of Strategic Bombing on the German War Economy,' *United States Strategic Bombing Survey* (henceforth quoted as *U.S.S.B.S.*, ' Economic Report ') p. 75.
[2] *Führer Naval Conferences*, November 13th, 1941.

been planned for the *Tirpitz, Scharnhorst* and *Gneisenau.* On December 12th Raeder reported: " The oil situation is very critical. The Navy's requirements have been cut by 50 per cent; this has caused an intolerable restriction on the mobility of our vessels. . . . Rumanian exports to us and to Italy have ceased entirely." The Rumanians, Raeder said, were " demanding gold to back their currency." Hitler replied that the gold would be sent at once, but even this did not produce supplies in sufficient quantity. Deliveries of Rumanian fuel oil, which had stood at 46,000 tons a month in the middle of 1941, were only 8,000 tons in April 1942. For that month the allocation to the Axis Navies was 61,000 tons, enough to meet only one-third of their needs, and no more could be made available. In the past five months stocks had fallen from 380,000 tons to 150,000.

Diplomatic appeals by Ribbentrop to the Rumanian dictator, General Antonescu, brought the reply, " As for crude oil, Rumania has contributed the maximum which it is in her power to contribute; she can give no more. The only way out of the situation would be to seize territories rich in oil."[1] Hitler drew the same conclusion as Antonescu. In June 1942, on the eve of his summer offensive to the Caucasus, he told the senior officers of Army Group South, " If I do not get the oil of Maikop and Grozny, then I must end this war."[2]

Strategic defence in the East offered at best a prospect of stalemate leading to a compromise peace. But Hitler would not accept this solution. He knew that the world would not forgive Germany a second time. He knew that neither his personal power nor that of the Nazi Reich would survive a settlement by negotiation. Having submitted the future of his régime, and of Germany, to the gamble of war, he had to continue to the last throw in the hope that the winning numbers would turn up. Total Victory or Total Defeat: that was the essence of the nihilist philosophy which was the foundation of Nazism. He was determined to pursue without falter or scruple the policy which he had declared in secret to his Commanders-in-Chief on November 23rd, 1939:

I shall strike and not capitulate. The fate of the Reich depends on me alone. . . . Every hope of compromise is childish. It is Victory or Defeat. The question is not the fate of a National-Socialist Germany, but who is to dominate Europe in the future. . . . No one has ever achieved what I have achieved. My life is of no importance in all this. I have led the German people to a great height, even if the world does hate us now. I am setting all my achievement on a gamble. I have to choose between victory and destruction. I choose victory. . . .

Then he added prophetically:

[1] Minutes of meeting between Antonescu and Ribbentrop, February 12th, 1942. (*Nuremberg Trial Proceedings*, Part vi, p. 287.)
[2] Evidence of Field-Marshal Paulus. (*Nuremberg Trial Proceedings*, Part vi, p. 244.)

As long as I shall live, I shall think only of the victory of my people. I shall shrink from nothing and shall destroy everyone who is opposed to me. . . . I shall stand or fall in this struggle. I shall never survive the defeat of my people. There will be no capitulation to the powers outside, no revolution by the forces within.[1]

In this declaration Hitler restated almost to the word what he had said to Hermann Rauschning at Berchtesgaden seven years before: " We shall not capitulate—no, never! We may be destroyed, but if we are, we shall drag a world with us—a world in flames! "[2]

[1]Quoted from the minutes of this meeting. (Nuremberg Document 759 PS.)
[2]Rauschning, *Hitler Speaks*, p. 15.

# CHAPTER V

# SEARCH FOR A BLUEPRINT

TWELVE months before the start of BARBAROSSA, while the rest of
Europe stood awestruck at the fall of France, the British had taken the
first tentative step along the course that was to lead them back across the
Channel. The Franco-German Armistice was signed on June 22nd, 1940,
and with it, so Hitler declared, Britain had been "driven from the Continent
for ever." Unaware of the Führer's insistence upon this point, British
Commandos carried out a reconnaissance raid on the French coast near
Boulogne the following night. The raid was to have been made by 200 men,
but so strained were Britain's resources that suitable craft could be found for
only 120. Two boatloads landed on deserted sand-dunes; two others
engaged in brief skirmishes which yielded little information and no
prisoners, and the men of one party, returning by mistake to the wrong
port, were arrested by the Military Police as deserters. From that
inauspicious beginning the vast invasion force of 1944 was to develop.

Within the next month Churchill established a Combined Operations
Command to prepare the way for the eventual return to the Continent
and in the meantime to carry out a series of harassing and distracting
raids on the occupied coastline. On October 5th, 1940, when daylight
attacks on London were still in progress, he ordered the Joint Planning
Staff to study the possibility of offensive operations in Europe, including
the establishment of a bridgehead on the Cherbourg Peninsula.

So long as Britain stood alone, however, she could not seriously
challenge Hitler's power on continental soil. The advantage was overwhelmingly in favour of the defender, for the possibility of invasion was
fundamentally a question of the balance of strength. The prospects at
any particular time could be worked out by arithmetical calculation:
what forces could the British land and maintain on the far shore of the
Channel; what forces could Germany bring against them there? It was
a question of numbers, equipment and, above all, the means of transportation. No administrative improvisation, no strategic or tactical
ingenuity, no readiness for sacrifice could alter the verdict which statistics
told in advance. The answer was that there could be no cross-Channel
invasion until a large part of Germany's strength had been drawn off

to other fronts; until Britain's arm had been reinforced from sources outside the Commonwealth and Empire, and until she had established command of the Atlantic supply routes and of the air over Western Europe.

The first substantial shift in the balance of strength on either side of the Channel came in June 1941 when Hitler invaded the Soviet Union. Within a month of Russia's status changing from that of an unfriendly neutral to that of a needy ally, Stalin sent Churchill the first of a long series of messages urging the prompt creation of a Second Front in France. This was a request which Britain had not the power to fulfil, for even with 150 German divisions committed in the East, the Wehrmacht still kept nearly 50 divisions guarding the West and Norway, a garrison more than adequate in view of Britain's weakness. By September, however, the Soviet request had become almost a demand. In a personal message to Churchill on September 4th, Stalin said, "The Germans consider the danger in the West a bluff and are transferring all their forces to the East with impunity." And he added the unwarranted allegation that it was the British failure to act in France which had enabled Hitler to seize half the Ukraine and reach the gates of Leningrad. Next day, in a signal to the British Ambassador in Moscow (Sir Stafford Cripps) the Prime Minister put the issue in hard, military terms. "If it were possible," he said, "to make any successful diversion upon the French or Low Countries shore which would bring back German troops from Russia, we should order it even at the heaviest cost. All our generals are convinced that a bloody repulse is all that would be sustained, or, if small lodgments were effected, that they would have to be withdrawn after a few days . . . [for] the Germans still have more divisions in the West than we have in Great Britain . . . [and] the shipping available to transport a large army to the Continent does not exist." Summing up, Churchill said, "Nothing that we could do or could have done would affect the struggle on the Eastern Front." The Ambassador presented these facts in Moscow, but Stalin replied, "I can only reiterate that the absence of a Second Front simply favours the designs of our common enemy." When the Russian demands and reproaches continued, Churchill again cabled to Cripps, as follows:

> I fully sympathise with you in your difficult position, and also with Russia in her agony. They certainly have no right to reproach us. They brought their own fate upon themselves when, by their pact with Ribbentrop, they let Hitler loose on Poland and so started the war. They cut themselves off from an effective second front when they let the French Army be destroyed. If prior to June 22nd they had consulted with us beforehand, many arrangements could have been made to bring earlier the great help we are now sending them in munitions. We did not however know till Hitler attacked them whether they would fight, or what side they would be on. . . . We

have acted with absolute honesty.  We have done our very best to help them at the cost of deranging all our plans for rearmament and exposing ourselves to heavy risks when the spring invasion season comes.[1]

The Prime Minister cautioned Sir Stafford not to " rub all these salt truths into the Russian wounds," but to assure the Soviet Government of the " loyalty, integrity and courage of the British nation." Although Britain could do little to draw German forces away from Russia at this time she was already making plans, as Churchill had told Roosevelt in August, for " coming to the aid of the conquered populations by landing armies of liberation when the opportunity is ripe." In September Churchill had instructed the Joint Planning Staff " to complete as a matter of urgency their examination of the plan for operations on the Continent in the final phase, with particular reference to the requirements of all types of special craft and equipment both for the actual operations and for the training of the necessary forces." By December 1941, an outline plan had been produced in London for the invasion of France in the summer of 1943, and by the time this plan was ready the United States was in open alliance with Great Britain.  Thereafter, all plans and preparations for the eventual cross-Channel assault proceeded on an Anglo-American basis.

Two weeks after Pearl Harbour Roosevelt and Churchill, meeting in Washington with their Chiefs of Staff, reached two decisions of the greatest consequence.  The first was that the entire military and economic resources of the two nations should be pooled under the direction of a common command, the Combined Chiefs of Staff.  This was the root of Allied success, for, in the words of General George C. Marshall, the Chairman of the U.S. Joint Chiefs of Staff, it provided " the most complete unification of military effort ever achieved by two allied nations. Strategic direction of all the forces of both nations, the allocation of manpower and munitions, the co-ordination of communications, the control of military intelligence and the administration of captured areas all were accepted as joint responsibilities."[2]

Within the Combined Chiefs of Staff there were inevitably sharp differences of opinion, clashes of personality and conflicts of national interest and character, but these do not impair Marshall's general contention.  The divergences were, as Churchill once said, " of emphasis and priority rather than of principle." They were the result of honest convictions, frankly and freely expressed.  The Combined Chiefs of Staff, operating under the general direction of Roosevelt and Churchill, were a true exemplification of the democratic method, a committee in action. Perhaps the best measure of the ability and integrity of the men who

[1] This and the preceding messages are quoted in Churchill, op. cit., Vol. III, pp. 405, 409, 411 and 420.
[2] Marshall, *Biennial Report of the Chief of Staff of the United States Army, July 1, 1943 to June 30, 1945, to the Secretary of War*, p. 8.

formed it is the fact that, for all their differences, they were able to formulate agreed policies and to mobilise and weld together the human and material resources of both powers in successful execution of those policies. The Combined Chiefs of Staff provided leadership which was integrated, balanced and comprehensive and gave the Allies a vast and incalculable advantage over their enemies in the higher direction of the war.

The second great decision of this Washington meeting (which became known as the ARCADIA Conference) determined what the agenda called the " fundamental basis of joint strategy." This problem had been the subject of Anglo-American staff conversations in London in February 1941 and it had been agreed then that, in the event of the United States becoming involved in a war with both Germany and Japan, the main Allied effort would be directed first against the Germans. When they went to Washington after Pearl Harbour, however, Churchill and his colleagues were concerned lest the severity of the Japanese onslaught in the Pacific might result in an American request for a change in plan. The British were greatly relieved, therefore, when at the first meeting General Marshall presented a memorandum which said: " Notwithstanding the entry of Japan into the war, our view is that Germany is still the prime enemy and her defeat is the key to victory. Once Germany is defeated, the collapse of Italy and the defeat of Japan must follow."[1]

This proposal became the foundation of Anglo-American strategic policy. It was put forward on strictly military grounds, but Roosevelt's prompt endorsement of it was an act of great political courage, for he knew that the American people were impatient to gain their revenge on Japan. They had not been precipitated into the European war by any treacherous incident like the Pearl Harbour attack, nor did they feel that their ' vital interests ' were as much at stake in Europe as in the Pacific. When they look to the Far East, the people of the United States think as Americans, but inevitably when they turn towards Europe their national unity is impaired by the old loyalties and old enmities which they or their fathers brought from Europe with them. Consequently, they were not agreed in their attitude towards Germany and Italy as they were vis-à-vis Japan. When war came to them their anger and ardour were directed primarily against the Japanese and they had in the Pacific a commander, General MacArthur, whose ambition and egotism prevented him from seeing any theatre of war but his own, and who not only denounced the ' Hitler First ' strategy[2] but was to use every stratagem of political manœuvre to secure its abandonment.

The basic strategic decision was undoubtedly right. When the Allied leaders met, the Germans were on the outskirts of Leningrad and Moscow and no one could tell how long Russia could hold out. Her resistance

[1] Quoted in Sherwood, *Roosevelt and Hopkins*, p. 445.
[2] I say this advisedly, for, as a correspondent, I heard MacArthur make this denunciation at a press conference in Melbourne in June 1942.

had already far exceeded the expectations of the British and American Chiefs of Staff, and they feared that it might crack before the strength of the United States could be mobilised and brought to bear. The President therefore insisted that American troops must be engaged against Germany as early as possible in 1942 and accepted in principle a proposal by Churchill for an Anglo-American landing in Tunisia. From there an Allied force could drive into Tripolitania in conjunction with an offensive by the Eighth British Army which captured Benghazi on Christmas Eve.

On that day, however, the Australian Prime Minister, John Curtin, cabled a warning that the fall of Singapore was only a matter of weeks, and asked for immediate aid. In the next fortnight, while Churchill was still in America, the situation in the Far East deteriorated so rapidly and seriously that for the moment the dispatch of fresh forces to check the Japanese had to be given priority. The Americans could not provide the shipping to carry out their share of the Tunisia plan in addition to the reinforcement of the Pacific, and the diversion to the Far East of five British divisions, which were in or en route to the Middle East, ruled out the possibility of an early advance by the Eighth Army into Tripolitania.

In the first three months of 1942 the Japanese advance to New Guinea and into Burma threatened to force a revision in Anglo-American global strategy. In March, Admiral Pound, the First Sea Lord, summed up the changed situation when he wrote, " Although Germany still remains the prime enemy and her defeat is the key to victory, it has now become vital to stem the Japanese advance in order to enable us to defeat Germany." The basic assumption of the ARCADIA decision had been that Japan could be halted short of areas which were vital to the Allies and without the employment of resources, especially shipping, which were essential for operations against Germany. By April, however, with the Japanese in the Bay of Bengal and Hitler about to renew his drive to the Caucasus, there was grave danger that the Axis powers might effect a junction in the Indian Ocean.

Faced with this possibility, the British Chiefs of Staff concluded that the strategic centre of gravity lay in the Persian Gulf and its oilfields, for in that area the two wars were strategically linked. Accordingly, they argued that the most pressing tasks for 1942 must be: to halt the Japanese, to safeguard the Middle East and to gain command of the sea. Until these aims were achieved, they feared that sufficient forces could not be concentrated for any serious offensive against Germany.

The governing factor in all Anglo-American strategic calculations at this time, and for many months to come, was shipping. At the ARCADIA Conference, however, none of the Allied leaders had appreciated what a rapid and drastic decline there would soon be in Allied maritime power. Between September 1939 and December 1941 nearly ten million tons of merchant shipping had been destroyed and only one-third of this tonnage had been replaced, but it was assumed that American shipyards, which were aiming to produce eight million tons in 1942, would be able to make good the deficit and replace a large part of the fresh losses of merchantmen. The experience of the past year suggested that the British had the U-boat menace under control. In the first half of 1941 shipping losses had averaged 470,000 tons a month, but in the five months before Pearl Harbour the average had fallen to 170,000 tons in all waters. This substantial improvement had led to the optimistic conclusion that the Battle of the Atlantic was in a fair way to being won. At the Washington meeting, therefore, no particular decision was taken with regard to the U-boat war and no special priority was accorded it.

This optimism was soon dispelled, for the extension of the war to the Pacific and Indian Oceans brought about a vast increase in the demand for shipping at the very time when there was an alarming and unexpected rise in the losses at sea, particularly those caused by U-boats. Between the start of the war and Pearl Harbour the strength of the German submarine fleet had increased from 57 to 249, and with the entry of the United States into the war an entirely new sphere of operations was provided for Doenitz in the Western Atlantic which had previously been closed to him for political reasons. In his diary for December 9th, 1941, Doenitz wrote, " The whole American coast is now open for operations by U-boats . . . there will be the opportunity of intercepting enemy merchant ships in conditions which have ceased almost completely elsewhere. We must attempt to achieve a spectacular success." He did.

On the Atlantic coast of the United States, and later in the Caribbean and the Gulf of Mexico, in the first half of 1944, the Germans found rich and easy pickings. " My Navy," said Roosevelt to Churchill in a letter of March 18th, " has been definitely slack in preparing for this submarine war off our coast. As I need not tell you, most naval officers have declined in the past to think in terms of any vessel of less than two thousand tons. You learned the lesson two years ago. We still have to learn it."[1] No arrangements had been made for coastal shipping to travel in convoy, and few warships or aircraft were available for anti-submarine patrol. American merchantmen were not even armed, and it was five months before the waterfront communities on the Atlantic coast were required to dim their lights. According to the American naval historian, Professor Morison, " Miami and its luxurious suburbs threw up six miles of neon-light glow, against which the southbound shipping was silhouetted. Ships were sunk and seamen drowned in order that the citizenry might enjoy business and pleasure as usual."[2] From 196,243 tons in January Allied merchant shipping losses in American waters rose alarmingly to 354,489 tons in March and 452,000 tons in May. Nearly half the May losses were incurred in the Gulf of Mexico where 41 ships were sunk by half a dozen U-boats. " The sad thing is," says Morison, " that at least half these sinkings might have been prevented by the measures later adopted—coastal convoys for all merchantmen,

[1]This letter is quoted in Churchill, op. cit., Vol. IV, p. 178.
[2]Morison. *The Battle of the Atlantic*, p. 130.

and adequate air coverage."[1] During May, 95 per cent of the U-boat successes were gained in waters for which the United States Navy was responsible. That month, with the help of anti-submarine trawlers provided by Britain, the Americans at last organised their shipping in convoys, but by this time the heavy losses the U-boats had inflicted were threatening to undermine the foundations of Anglo-American strategy. No part of the huge deficit of the first two years had been made good and sinkings in all areas since Pearl Harbour had exceeded the output of the shipyards by more than two million tons.

Grave though the shipping situation was the President and his Chiefs of Staff continued to think in offensive terms. On March 9th Roosevelt cabled to Churchill, " I am becoming more and more interested in the establishment of a new front this summer on the European continent . . . and even though losses will doubtless be great, such losses will be compensated by at least equal German losses and by compelling Germans to divert large forces of all kinds from Russian fronts."[2] The Prime Minister gave a guarded reply to this proposal, but the Americans proceeded with their planning, and on April 8th Marshall and the President's personal representative, Harry Hopkins, arrived in London to advocate direct and early action in Europe. The British did not dispute Marshall's general thesis that " the final blow against Germany must be delivered across the English Channel and eastward through the plains of Western Europe," and they accepted his recommendation that they should begin preparations immediately for a large-scale cross-Channel invasion (code-named Operation ROUNDUP) to be launched in the spring of 1943. Churchill greeted this as a " momentous proposal " which he had " no hesitation in cordially accepting," but he made one broad and fundamental reservation, namely, that it was " essential to carry on the defence of India and the Middle East " in order to " prevent a junction of the Japanese and the Germans."

While they agreed with Marshall's long-term plan, the British Chiefs of Staff were alarmed at his further suggestion that the Allies should be prepared to make a landing in France in 1942 " as a sacrifice to avert an imminent collapse of Russian resistance." Marshall contemplated the establishment of a small bridgehead that autumn as a foothold for the major offensive in the spring of 1943. Yet he had to admit that the minimum requirements of troops and shipping could not be assembled before October, by which time the weather would be most unfavourable for an amphibious operation in the Channel. Even then, there would be sufficient transport to maintain ashore only nine divisions at the very most and such a meagre force, the British argued, could not embarrass the Germans even if it should succeed in holding throughout the winter.

[1]Morison, *The Battle of the Atlantic*, p. 142.
[2]Quoted in Churchill, op. cit., Vol. IV, pp. 175-6.

At a meeting on April 14th it was finally agreed that a landing in France should be attempted in 1942 only if some desperate measure should become necessary to save the Soviet Union from collapse. This plan was given the grandiloquent code-name SLEDGEHAMMER although it was realised—by the British at least—that it could provide no more than a minor diversion and might become a major disaster.

On April 11th, while the SLEDGEHAMMER plan was being discussed in London, but before any decision had been reached regarding its practicability, Roosevelt sent Stalin a cable in which he said: " I have in mind very important military proposal involving the utilisation of our armed forces in a manner to relieve your critical Western front. . . . I need your advice before we determine with finality the strategic course of our common military action."[1] Roosevelt suggested that Molotov and a military adviser should come to Washington to discuss the proposal.

Molotov did not hurry to Washington, but he came with an urgent demand. Arriving at the end of May—six weeks after the President's invitation—Molotov warned Roosevelt and Marshall that " Hitler might throw in such reinforcements in manpower and material that the Red Army might not be able to hold out." On the other hand, the prospect would be very different " if Great Britain and the United States . . . were to create a new front to draw off 40 German divisions."[2] Molotov said that he had discussed this question with the Prime Minister in London but had received " no positive answer." He would like " a straight answer " from the President.

According to the American minutes of this meeting, " The President then put to General Marshall the query whether developments were clear enough so that we could say to Mr. Stalin that we are preparing a Second Front. ' Yes,' replied the General. *The President then authorised Mr. Molotov to inform Mr. Stalin that we expect the formation of a Second Front this year.*[3] General Marshall added that . . . we had the troops, all adequately trained; we had the munitions, the aviation and armoured divisions. The difficulties lay in transport." In subsequent discussions the President pointed out that because of the shortage of shipping it would be difficult for the United States to carry out the double task of continuing the planned Lend-Lease shipments to Russia and of building up the necessary invasion forces in England. He proposed therefore that Lend-Lease tonnage to be shipped to Russia during the next twelve months should be reduced from 4,100,000 tons to 2,500,000 tons, but pointed out that this would not mean any curtailment in the volume of tanks, ammunition or any other supplies needed for the immediate battle. The President pointed out that the Russians could not " eat their cake and have it too."

" To this statement," say the American minutes, " Mr. Molotov

[1] Quoted in Sherwood, op. cit., p. 528.
[2] The text of the American minutes of these discussions with Molotov is reproduced at length in Sherwood, op. cit., pp. 557-77.
[3] (*The italics are mine.* C.W.)

retorted with some emphasis that the second front would be stronger if the first front still stood fast and inquired with what seemed deliberate sarcasm what would happen if the Soviets cut down their requirements and then no Second Front eventuated." Although he could not give any assurance that Russia would agree to a reduction in Lend-Lease supplies, Molotov continued to demand from the Americans a definite and public commitment that they would carry out a cross-Channel invasion that year. In pursuit of this commitment he drafted a communiqué which contained the words, " In the course of the conversations full understanding was reached with regard to the urgent task of creating a Second Front in Europe in 1942." When this draft was shown to Marshall he regretted the too ready assurance he had given and he advised the President that the words " in 1942 " should be omitted. But Molotov was not to be denied, and he arrived in London, en route for Moscow, having secured American approval for the release of a communiqué in the terms that he had laid down.

In London Churchill accepted Molotov's text, believing that such a public proclamation would alarm and mislead the Germans, but he privately assured him that the British Government could not guarantee to open a Second Front in France that year. Lest Molotov should be in any doubt about the British view, he was handed an *Aide Mémoire* which said:

> We are making preparations for a landing on the Continent in August or September 1942. . . . Clearly however it would not further either the Russian cause or that of the Allies as a whole if, for the sake of action at any price, we embarked on some operation which ended in disaster. . . . It is impossible to say in advance whether the situation will be such as to make this operation feasible when the time comes. *We can therefore give no promise in the matter.*[1]

Clear and precise though this *Aide Mémoire* was, it was the published communiqué that mattered to the Russians, and they were to insist that it represented a definite promise. The same view was taken by the peoples of Britain and the United States and, when no Second Front materialised in 1942, the public concern on both sides of the Atlantic was deep, widespread and justifiable. The ' Molotov Communiqué ' was to prove a grave embarrassment to the Western Allies, and especially to the President. For the next two years the assurance he had given lay uneasily on his conscience and left him at a moral disadvantage in his dealings with Stalin.

The more the British studied the problem the more certain they became that if any major amphibious operation was going to be carried out with Anglo-American forces in 1942 it should, and could, only be against French North Africa. In June, during further discussions in Washington this view was strongly presented by Churchill and General

[1]Quoted in Sherwood, op. cit., p. 577.

Sir Alan Brooke, the Chief of the Imperial General Staff. Roosevelt was receptive, but Marshall still hoped that SLEDGEHAMMER might be possible and was determined that nothing should interfere with Operation BOLERO, the build-up of American forces in Britain for a cross-Channel assault. While this question was still being debated, however, the battle in Libya turned in favour of the Germans. Tobruk fell and Rommel drove the Eighth Army headlong into Egypt. The Middle East appeared to be threatened by an enveloping movement through Suez and through the Caucasus, for the Germans in Russia were approaching the Don and seemed likely to break through to the Caspian. The British fear that the Germans and the Japanese might join forces in the Indian Ocean was revived and intensified.

Quick to appreciate this danger Roosevelt offered to send an American armoured division to Egypt, but Marshall strongly and openly dissented on the ground that this would seriously reduce the shipment of American troops and supplies to Britain for ROUNDUP. He proposed instead the sending of 300 Sherman tanks and 100 self-propelled guns. This proposal satisfied Brooke, since it was equipment, not men, which the Eighth Army needed, and the Sherman (unlike the British Crusader) promised to be a match for any tank that Rommel had in Africa. Beyond this, and the dispatch of aircraft, the American Chiefs of Staff were not prepared to go in pursuit of a Mediterranean strategy and they insisted that BOLERO should continue " full blast . . . until the first of September."[1] Churchill and Brooke accepted this with the greatest reluctance, for they considered that, so long as every ship was needed for the mere maintenance of the existing hard-pressed battlefronts, none should be diverted for a hazardous and desperate project like SLEDGEHAMMER. Yet they could not afford to condemn this project too strongly, lest the Americans should turn their main attention to the Pacific. Churchill's assent to the continuation of BOLERO was taken by Marshall to mean that the British were willing to carry out an invasion of France that year if the Russian situation should become critical, but no definite understanding had been reached when Rommel's advance to Alamein compelled Churchill and his advisers to return at once to London.

While Allied strategy was still being hammered out in Washington, Major-General Dwight D. Eisenhower arrived in London to take command of the U.S. Army in the European Theatre and to prepare it for a cross-Channel attack at the earliest opportunity. He soon found, however, that the British planning staffs were convinced that there could be no successful invasion of France in 1942 and that an abortive assault would do far more harm than good, because it would relieve Hitler of any serious threat in the West for months to come and would allow him to concentrate on annihilating the Red Army. On his return to Whitehall,

[1] Stimson, *On Active Service in Peace and War*, p. 424.

Churchill endorsed this opinion. As he saw it, the most urgent problem was to save the Middle East, where the strategic situation had gone from bad to worse since the discussions in Washington. It seemed to him and to the British Chiefs of Staff that the shipping allocated to BOLERO and SLEDGEHAMMER would be better employed for the reinforcement of Egypt and the invasion of French North Africa.

The shipping stranglehold was even more severe than it had been in the spring. Resolute and confident though he was, Marshall himself had become alarmed and on June 19th had written to Admiral Ernest King, the C.-in-C. of the United States Fleet, " The losses by submarines off our Atlantic seaboard and in the Caribbean now threaten our entire war effort. . . . Of the 74 ships allocated to the Army for July . . . 17 have already been sunk. . . . I am fearful that another month or two of this will so cripple our means of transport that we will be unable to bring sufficient men and planes to bear against the enemy in critical theatres to exercise a determining influence on the war."[1] This was no under-statement for June was the worst month so far in the entire war at sea. That month merchantmen were being sunk at the rate of one ship every four hours and the toll reached the staggering total of 825,310 tons. In July the casualty rate increased and on the 14th Churchill cabled to Roosevelt: " Allied shipping losses in the preceding seven days were close on 400,000 tons for this one week. This rate, unexampled in either this war or the last, will clearly be in excess of existing replacement plans if it is maintained."

By this time the tonnage of merchantmen lost in all waters since the start of the year exceeded four and a half million tons and was already greater than the total losses suffered in 1941. Nearly all this terrible destruction had been caused by the Germans at a cost to themselves of *only 21 U-boats in six months.* During this period they had built five U-boats for every one sunk; at the start of July Doenitz had a fleet of 331 of which 140 were operational, and there was little immediate prospect of their ravages being kept in check.

In these circumstances the British considered that it would be the greatest folly to attempt to carry out any cross-Channel attack that year. Eisenhower and the other American commanders now in London did not agree with this appreciation, and, when they reported the British view to Washington, the immediate reaction of the U.S. Chiefs of Staff was to advise Roosevelt that America should assume the defensive in the war against Germany and should concentrate on defeating Japan. The strongest advocate of this course was Admiral King.

At meetings of the Combined Chiefs of Staff, King consistently and frankly maintained the attitude that his war was against the Japanese. Nor is this surprising. The Pacific War was a maritime struggle in which the Navy was unquestionably the senior service applying the power of the other services in execution of its own strategy. King was a proud

[1]Quoted in Morison, op. cit., p. 309.

and ambitious man. In the Pacific his navy could win honour and glory on its own account, but in the Atlantic there was no enemy worthy of its steel. There it would be reduced to the menial role of escorting convoys and supporting the amphibious operations of the Army, which every American sailor had been brought up to regard with antagonism and contempt. Furthermore, in European waters American warships would almost certainly have to fight under the overall command of the Royal Navy, which King regarded as obsolete and incompetent. He is credited with having said, " I fought under the goddam British in the First World War and if I can help it, no ship of mine will fight under 'em again." Whether or not this remark reflected his considered views, it is beyond dispute that he consistently sought to restrict the employment of U.S. naval forces in the war against Germany. Because he took this stand, and because Roosevelt had justifiable confidence in his professional judgment and efficiency, King was to exert a powerful influence on the development of Anglo-American strategy during the next three years.

At this stage, moreover, King was not alone in wanting to turn to the Pacific. On July 10th, when Eisenhower's signal arrived, the Secretary for War, Henry Stimson, noted in his diary, " The British War Cabinet . . . are seeking now to reverse the decision which was so laboriously accomplished when Mr. Churchill was here a short time ago. . . . I found Marshall very stirred up and emphatic over it . . . and he proposed a showdown, which I cordially endorsed. As the British won't go through with what they agreed to, we will turn our backs on them and take up the war with Japan."[1]

On July 15th Marshall and King presented to Roosevelt an alternative plan for major operations in the South-West Pacific and Stimson suggested that this reversal of strategy should be used at least as a threat to bring the British round. This the President refused to countenance. On the contrary, he sent Marshall, King and Hopkins to London with orders to ensure that American ground forces were brought into action against Germany in 1942. They were to battle for SLEDGEHAMMER, but were to settle for the North African alternative if the British held to the view that there could be no successful invasion of France that year. In a directive to Marshall next day Roosevelt said, " I am opposed to an American all-out effort in the Pacific . . . it is of the utmost importance that we appreciate that defeat of Japan does not defeat Germany and that American concentration against Japan this year or in 1943 increases the chance of complete domination of Europe and Africa." Thus Roosevelt upheld the original ARCADIA decision and from this stand he never wavered.

The discussions which began in London on July 18th were exhaustive and prolonged, but the Americans were fighting a losing battle against facts which they sought to belittle but could not deny. The British insisted that the only cross-Channel assault which would seriously distract

[1]Stimson, op. cit., p. 424.

Hitler from Russia in 1942 would be one in substantial strength against the Pas de Calais. But this area was too strongly defended, too easy for the Germans to reinforce and too exposed to counter-attack. An invasion there would certainly be repulsed, for sufficient landing-craft were immediately available for only one division, and there was no chance of assembling adequate shipping before the inevitable onset of bad weather in October.

Accepting this analysis, Marshall then proposed a landing on the Cherbourg Peninsula. There the enemy was more vulnerable, but this advantage was offset by the slower turn-around of shipping and by the difficulty of providing air cover, for the long-range fighter had not yet been developed. The British added the argument that, even if a foothold could be gained near Cherbourg, it could not become the base for a major offensive, nor would it cause the diversion of a single German division from Russia, since the narrow neck of the Peninsula could be sealed off quickly and easily by the enemy forces already in France. Such a bridgehead would become a running sore throughout the winter, draining away the resources which would be needed for ROUNDUP. The mere threat of invasion was already keeping 40 German divisions idle in the West and this threat could be maintained by heavier Commando raids, increased air attacks and deceptive movements of shipping. The only way to divert additional German troops from the Russian front, they said, was to establish a totally new threat by invading French North Africa.

The Americans answered that an unsuccessful landing in France was better than none at all; that North Africa was too far away to affect the real issue, the fate of Russia; and that, if they were to become involved in the Mediterranean in 1942, they would not be able to carry out a cross-Channel invasion in 1943. This was the operation on which they had set their hearts. To Marshall, and indeed to most of America's military leaders, the problem of defeating Germany was one of production and organisation. He thought, as one of Churchill's staff put it, that " if sufficient driving power were put behind the transportation of American forces across the Atlantic, their momentum would carry them across the Straits of Dover." It was merely a matter of extending the production-line technique into the field of strategy. Marshall's eagerness for the offensive was also an expression of the abounding optimism and self-confidence which marks the American character. Neither Marshall nor King had any experience of amphibious operations or of German strength and they felt that the British had been led by the discouragement of successive defeats into exaggerating the difficulties and dangers of invasion. Whatever these were, they could surely be overcome by American enthusiasm, resource and drive.

Marshall was also influenced by a political factor. The United States was raising the largest army in its history and this could not be left idle in training camps. The American people, impatient by nature, were itching for revenge on the Japanese, and a holding campaign in the Pacific could be justified politically only if there was aggressive and effective action against Germany. He doubted whether the invasion of French North Africa would satisfy either the demands of American public opinion or the needs of Allied strategy.

Consequently the Americans were " unconvinced and deeply disappointed " when the British finally rejected the SLEDGEHAMMER plan on July 22nd. Eisenhower thought that this might come to be regarded as the " blackest day in history "[1] and it seems that Marshall and King would forthwith have turned their backs on Europe, but for two factors: Roosevelt's determination to uphold the ' Hitler First ' strategy; and Churchill's insistence that the North African invasion (now given the code-name TORCH) was the essential prelude to ROUNDUP, since the opening of the Mediterranean would set free at least a million tons of shipping which was currently absorbed in supplying the Middle East and India by the Cape route. The American Chiefs of Staff were inclined to keep the SLEDGEHAMMER Plan in being until September 15th in case the Russian situation were to become desperate, but on July 25th the President settled the issue with a cable which said that TORCH must take place " not later than October 30th."

After their return to Washington, Marshall and King endeavoured to persuade Roosevelt to change his mind, but their illusions about the feasibility of invading France that year must have been dispelled in August by the bitter outcome of the Dieppe Raid. Of the 5,000 Canadians who took part in this attack 3,369 became casualties, but their sacrifice was not in vain. This ' reconnaissance in force ' proved beyond doubt that no fortified Channel port could be taken by direct assault with the resources available in 1942, and provided experience which was to save hundreds of Allied lives within the next two years. It is now known that far from weakening the West, Hitler had reinforced it in response to the mere threat of invasion which the British created by raids and maintained by deception. That summer seven divisions (four of them armoured) were specially transferred from Russia to France. This made the total force in the West, including Norway, 45 divisions—nearly a quarter of the German field forces—just at the time when every fighting formation was needed for the drive to the Caucasus. In the case of the Luftwaffe the distraction was even greater. Barely half its strength was on the Eastern Front; the remainder was deployed in the Mediterranean and Western Europe. (On September 30th, 1942, according to the files of the German Air Ministry, there were 2,417 first-line aircraft in the East; 1,467 in the West and the Reich; and 754 in the Mediterranean.)

Meantime, early in August, believing that the North African venture

[1]Eisenhower made this comment to his aide, Captain Harry Butcher, who noted it in his diary. (See Butcher, *My Three Years With Eisenhower*, p. 29.) After the war, however, in his book, *Crusade in Europe* (p. 71), Eisenhower wrote, " Later developments have convinced me that those who held the SLEDGEHAMMER operation to be unwise at the moment were correct in their evaluation of the problem."

was firmly agreed, Churchill had gone to Egypt to reorganise the Middle East Command for an offensive from Alamein in conjunction with TORCH. From Cairo he flew on to Moscow to advise Stalin of the Allied plans. In the opening discussions at the Kremlin, the atmosphere was "bleak and sombre." Ignoring the written statement Churchill had given Molotov in June, Stalin alleged that the failure to open a Second Front in 1942 was a breach of faith, and accused the Western Powers of being "too much afraid of fighting Germans." Churchill answered these charges firmly and frankly and then revealed the plan for Operation TORCH. This revelation eased the tension, for Stalin promptly realised its strategic significance, but he was not completely satisfied and his Chief of Staff, Voroshilov, kept insisting to Churchill's military advisers that "a Second Front is essential and therefore must be possible." The Russians were confident, however, that they could hold the Caucasus once the snow came, and Stalin said that he had 25 divisions available for its defence. Beyond this, and the assertion that Russia was producing 2,000 tanks a month, Stalin revealed little of his plans or resources, but Churchill returned to London convinced that the Red Army would hold out and confirmed in his belief that TORCH was the right Allied plan. He was accordingly dismayed to find the Americans still doubtful about invading North Africa, and reluctant to attack there as soon or as boldly as the British Chiefs of Staff proposed.

The Anglo-American controversy which developed around this operation demands close scrutiny, because its course reveals basic differences in the strategic concepts of the two powers and its outcome had a profound influence on the war. Is it true, as some Americans have claimed, that TORCH and the Mediterranean campaign to which it led were an unnecessary diversion which delayed the opening of the real Second Front for a year and prolonged the war? Or was it the essential prelude to an attack across the Channel, an apt illustration of the old saw that 'the longest way round is the shortest way home'?

Throughout August the argument raged back and forth across the Atlantic as the Chiefs of Staff searched for a practical compromise. The roles were now reversed; the British eager, the Americans reluctant. The ultimate objective of the campaign, as conceived by Churchill, was to open the Mediterranean, strike at Italy and expose Germany's southern flank. To this end he wanted to clear the Axis forces out of North Africa by converging attacks from east and west, but this could bring quick success only if the Allies could forestall the probable German reaction, the establishment of a blocking force in Tunisia. The British Chiefs of Staff accordingly proposed that the attack should be made early in October, before the winter stalemate in Russia set free German reserves, and that the invasion forces should land well inside the Mediterranean, as near as possible to the Tunisian naval base of Bizerta.

This bold plan made little appeal to the Americans, for they felt that it would lead them into a prolonged Mediterranean campaign and a further postponement of the attack across the Channel. They did not believe that the Eighth Army could defeat Rommel in Egypt and they feared that German intervention through Spain would close the Straits of Gibraltar within a few days and cut the life-line of any forces landed inside the Mediterranean.

In the original draft directive for Eisenhower, who was to be Allied Commander-in-Chief, the British Chiefs of Staff had suggested landings at Casablanca, Oran, Algiers and at Bone, barely 120 miles by road from Bizerta. When it became apparent that the Anglo-American naval forces in Atlantic and European waters were not strong enough to protect such widespread assaults, the British proposed to cut out the landing at Casablanca. But the Americans insisted that a base must be secured outside the Mediterranean in order to guarantee an alternative supply route to the forces landed inside, in case the Straits should be closed. The breadth of the assault thus came to depend on obtaining additional support from the United States Navy. King, however, was interested in TORCH only as the means of preventing the Germans from obtaining U-boat bases at Dakar and Casablanca. He agreed to provide warships from the U.S. Atlantic Fleet to cover and support landings on the West coast of Africa, but he made it clear that unless ordered he would not transfer any naval forces from the Pacific for operations inside the Mediterranean. Admiral Halsey had already begun an offensive in the Solomons and King was anxious to exploit the success won there before Japanese resistance congealed. This offensive was not without its influence on the African campaign, because it reduced Japanese naval strength in the Indian Ocean to five submarines and four auxiliary cruisers, and made it impossible for Japan to meet Hitler's request for aggressive action against British convoys bound for the Middle East.[1] But this was a minor compensation to those who saw the possibility of a great victory in North Africa if only the Allies could amass the naval strength to take the boldest course.

Admiral Sir Andrew Cunningham, the Naval C.-in-C. for TORCH, was keen to strike straight for Bizerta regardless of the risk of air attack from Sicily and Sardinia. This plan was still under consideration in the second week of August when a strongly-escorted convoy for Malta began its perilous run through Tunisian waters. From Sardinia onwards it was under fire. As Churchill told the House of Commons, " Three or four hundred German and Italian shore-based bombers, torpedo planes and long-range fighters were launched against our armada—an enormous concourse of ships—and in the narrows, which were mined, it was attacked by E-boats and U-boats. Severe losses were suffered by both the convoy and the escorting fleet. One aircraft-carrier, the *Eagle*, two cruisers and one destroyer were sunk and others damaged." More

[1] Führer Naval Conferences, November 19th, 1942.

serious, but not publicly revealed at this stage, was the fact that only five out of fifteen merchantmen got through to Malta. This was sufficient to raise the siege of the island, but the price that had to be paid provided an almost unanswerable argument for those who opposed Cunningham's venturesome plan. No compromise solution had been reached when the Prime Minister returned from Moscow.

The U.S. Chiefs of Staff, who had been so eager to plunge across the Channel in September, were now unwilling to land east of Oran, and doubted whether they could undertake even this limited operation before November. Their caution was due partly to their dislike of the whole scheme and partly to the fact that they were finding out from experience what they had been reluctant to learn from their allies. On closer study of the practical problems of an amphibious operation, Marshall and his advisers had come to realise the great inherent difficulties and America's lack of appropriate resources and suitably-trained troops. The War Department Planning Staff decided that there was " less than a fifty per cent chance for success,"[1] and, though Marshall was not so pessimistic, he became over-concerned at the possibility of failure.

Fearing that these counsels of caution would undermine the plan, Churchill cabled to Roosevelt on August 26th:

> Risks and difficulties will be doubled by delay and will far outstrip any increase of our forces. Careful planning in every detail, safety first in every calculation, far-seeing provisions for a long-term campaign to meet every conceivable adverse contingency, however admirable in theory, will ruin the enterprise in fact. . . .
>
> In order to lighten the burden of responsibility on the military commanders, I am of opinion that you and I should lay down the political data and take the risk upon ourselves.

This signal brought forth the necessary intervention by the President. King agreed to provide extra warships and the U.S. Chiefs of Staff approved the extension of the assault frontage to include Algiers, but no initial landings were to be made farther east. The British accepted this compromise with some misgiving, because they feared that it would impose too great a handicap of distance on the invading forces in the race for Bizerta. Yet in the circumstances of the time the Americans could hardly be expected to pursue the bolder course. This was their first offensive operation against Germany; they did not altogether believe in it and they had before them the harsh and recent lesson of the Malta convoy. In that action, without knowing or intending it, Hitler secured his opportunity in Tunisia two months before that country came under attack. The victory which Hitler then achieved over the ' mind ' of the Anglo-American High Command, won for him an advantage which he could not have gained on the field of battle, for it caused the Allies to

[1]Butcher, op. cit., p. 55.

abandon plans and to shrink from actions which would unquestionably have been attended with success. In his subsequent report to the Combined Chiefs of Staff, Cunningham declared:

> It is a matter of lasting regret to me that the bolder conception for initial assault in that area [Bone] or even further eastward was not implemented. Had we been prepared to throw even a small force into the eastward ports, the Axis would have been forestalled in their first token occupation and success would have been complete. They were surprised and caught off balance. We failed to give the final push which would have tipped the scales.

Cunningham's view is undoubtedly right; Hitler could have been forestalled by greater boldness at the outset, for even by December 1st, more than three weeks after the Allied landings in Algeria and Morocco, he had moved only one German division into Tunisia.[1] But at the time when the strategic decision had to be made, the Combined Chiefs of Staff could not count upon the complete surprise which was achieved, nor upon the immobility of the Italian battlefleet through lack of oil. As it happened, their caution was unfortunate, for it doubled the length of the campaign, but this does not mean that their doubts were unjustified.

It is not easy to justify, however, the delay in launching the operation. The original decision about Torch was made on July 25th, but the plans necessary to implement it were not approved until six weeks later—and then only after Roosevelt had forced the issue with his own Chiefs of Staff. The rearguard action against the plan, fought primarily by King, prevented the early October landing which the British had proposed, and allowed little chance of gaining a decision before the winter rains. The consequent prolongation of the African campaign into the late spring of 1943 ruled out the possibility of any cross-Channel invasion that year. Allied strategy was never able to make good the months which were lost through the trans-Atlantic argument about Torch.

Nevertheless, the invasion of French North Africa did yield tremendous dividends. Hitler may have succeeded in delaying the assault on Southern Europe by several months, but the effort cost him 150,000 men from some of the best German divisions, and it reduced to breaking point the strength and spirit of Italy. Jodl subsequently claimed that the defence of Tunisia " won for us a certain gain in time which was worth every sacrifice "[2] but its outcome was recognised by the Army High Command as " a disaster second in magnitude only to Stalingrad."[3]

The campaign was even more important for the direct advancement it brought in the position and power of the Allies. The command of the

---

[1] Führer Conferences, Fragment 29, December 1st, 1942.
[2] In a speech to *Gauleiter*, November 7th, 1943. (Nuremberg Document L 172.)
[3] Reported by Speer.

whole North African shore released a million tons of shipping for fresh offensive purposes and doubled the area of Occupied Europe which the Allies could threaten. Moreover, TORCH provided an invaluable test for the technique and equipment of amphibious operations which had to be perfected before there could be any successful attack across the Channel. It revealed how ill-prepared and ill-trained the Allied forces really were for such an exacting task. It gave them and their commanders experience and confidence which could only be gained by battle in conditions which did not over-tax their resources or their skill.

The Americans drew particular profit from the North African campaign. If they had more to learn than had the British, they were quicker and more thorough in appreciating and applying the lessons of their own experience. The foundations of the great American armies which were to roll across Europe two years later were laid in North Africa. Here too the Americans showed that in ' Ike ' Eisenhower they had produced a great man, peculiarly fitted for the role of Allied Supreme Commander. North Africa was the proving ground for Eisenhower's conviction that it would be possible to create a closely-knit Anglo-American command organisation, inspired by a spirit of unity and common purpose which would override international prejudices and inter-service rivalries. This welding together of the Allied armies in the field was Eisenhower's unique contribution to victory. He may not have been one of the great captains, but he was a man to whom the great captains of his day gladly paid allegiance. Universally trusted, he evoked spontaneous affection, respect and loyalty from political and military leaders alike, from the people of America and Britain and from their troops in the field.

Eisenhower's success as Commander-in-Chief in North Africa was the more remarkable because, until the start of this campaign, he had no experience of battle or of high command. In the First World War he had been denied the chance of serving overseas and between the two wars he had been engaged almost exclusively in staff work. After a year at the War College in 1928 he had served for six years as a special assistant to the Assistant Secretary for War and to the Chief of Staff of the Army. There followed four years in the Philippine Islands as Chief of Staff to MacArthur, who was then engaged in building and training the Philippine Army. In 1940, after a brief tour of regimental duty, he had been successively Chief of Staff of a division, a corps and an army, holding each post for three or four months, but in the fourteen years before Pearl Harbour he had, to his great regret, spent only nine months in a command appointment and this was with an infantry regiment in training. Immediately after Pearl Harbour Marshall had transferred Eisenhower to the War Plans Division in Washington, set him to work out a plan for a cross-Channel invasion and then sent him to London to command the American forces which were to be assembled for this venture. Within the space of one year the Chief of Staff of an American army training in Texas became the Allied Commander-in-Chief of the greatest amphibious operation the world had yet seen.

In promoting Eisenhower and giving him a rapid grooming for high office, Marshall showed remarkable judgment, but the inevitable result was that there was no time for Eisenhower to go through the mill of command and gain battle experience. On the other hand, the ten years in Washington and Manila had given him intimate knowledge of politico-military problems on the highest level and a breadth of outlook unusual in a regular soldier. This training stood him in good stead when he rose to be Commander-in-Chief for Operation TORCH. In this post the personal and political integrity of the man was more important than the professional ability of the soldier. Others could—and did—provide expert and experienced leadership in the field, but nobody else revealed Eisenhower's remarkable capacity for integrating the efforts of different allies and rival services and for creating harmony between individuals with varied backgrounds and temperaments. From the outset he demanded " immediate and continuous loyalty to the concept of unity " and at the end of the campaign he could report to the Combined Chiefs of Staff the acceptance throughout his command of his own cardinal principle that " in such a venture the greatest patriot is the man who is most ready to meet his partner with consideration and respect, and to reach an objective solution to every problem without concerning himself with matters that he conceives to be in national self-interest." Because he remained true to this principle, Eisenhower was to become the most successful commander of allied forces in the history of war.

## CHAPTER VI

# THE GRAND DESIGN

IN December 1942, three weeks after TORCH had been lit, Roosevelt and Churchill suggested to Stalin that they should hold a Three-Power conference to consider the future course of Allied strategy. "We must decide," said the Prime Minister in his telegram, "at the earliest moment the best way of attacking Germany in Europe with all possible force in 1943." Stalin replied that he welcomed the idea of a meeting, but regretted that, owing to pressure of military business, he would not be "in a position to leave the Soviet Union . . . even for a day." The implication in the answer which Stalin sent to Roosevelt was that he was more interested in action than discussion. "Allow me to express my confidence," he said, "that the promises about the opening of a Second Front in Europe given by you, Mr. President, and by Mr. Churchill, in regard to 1942, and in any case in regard to the spring of 1943, will be fulfilled, and that a Second Front in Europe will be actually opened by the joint forces of Great Britain and the United States of America in the spring of next year."[1]

Both the President and the Prime Minister were most anxious to keep faith with Stalin and, since no detailed strategic plans had been made for the coming year, it was agreed that they and the Combined Chiefs of Staff must hold another conference, even though Stalin could not be present. This conference was held in January 1943 at Casablanca. Here the issue most earnestly debated at the military meetings was not, as is commonly supposed, whether in 1943 the main Anglo-American effort in Europe should be made in the Mediterranean or across the Channel, but whether the Allies should concentrate their offensive capacity during this year against Germany or Japan. It was recognised by the British and Americans alike that the Tunisian campaign was unlikely to be concluded before May. In that case no invasion could be launched from England until September and it would then be too late to achieve any real success before the winter. It was not now a matter of making a desperate diversion to relieve the Russians, but of landing in Northern France in such strength that the invading armies could liberate Western Europe and strike on into the heart of Germany.

[1] These telegrams are quoted in Churchill, op. cit., Vol. IV, pp. 596-8.

The Combined Chiefs of Staff took little time to decide that an operation of such magnitude could not be launched before the spring of 1944. It would demand the assembly in Britain of at least forty divisions before the assault, and the eventual employment of up to a hundred, by far the greater part of which would have to be provided by the United States. The intervening months would all be needed to complete the mobilisation of American resources, to secure the supply-line by which these could be moved across the Atlantic, and to gain command of the air over Europe. The Chiefs of Staff determined, therefore, to undertake an all-out offensive against the German sub-marines and to carry out a mounting campaign of bombardment against Germany's main industrial centres in order to reduce her internal capacity to wage war. In the meantime the detailed planning and prepa-ration for the invasion of France (soon to be renamed Operation OVER-LORD) was to be pressed forward in Britain by an Anglo-American staff.

This much was common ground between the two allies, but there was no such consensus on the immediate questions—where was the major strategic effort to be applied during 1943; what was to be done with Eisenhower's military and maritime resources after the conquest of Tunisia? The answer which Churchill gave to these questions had been set out in a cable to Roosevelt on the eve of the Casablanca meeting. The Prime Minister then said, " The paramount task before us is, first, to conquer the African shores of the Mediterranean and set up there the naval and air installations which are necessary to open an effective passage through it for military traffic; and, secondly, using the bases on the African shore, to strike at the under-belly of the Axis in effective strength and in the shortest time."[1]

The British view was that it was essential to keep the Germans fighting hard in the Mediterranean throughout the months which must elapse before the Allies could attack across the Channel. They proposed the invasion of Sicily as a stepping stone to the Italian mainland, hoping thereby to draw Hitler into a major campaign in the Mediterranean and compel him to reinforce the defences of Southern Europe, at the expense of the West, in order to guard against an Allied incursion from Italy into the Balkans or the South of France. An assault against Italy, they argued, would most probably bring about the fall of Mussolini, and the collapse of one Axis partner would have serious political repercussions for Hitler inside Germany and throughout the occupied countries. More-over, from bases in Southern Italy the Allied Air Forces could strike at German war factories beyond the reach of bombers based on Britain and, most important of all, at the Rumanian oilfields.

The desire to bring this vital and vulnerable target within bombing range was one consideration behind the further British proposal that Turkey should be induced to declare war on Germany by the offer of substantial aid. Her entry would have the added advantage of opening

[1] Quoted in Sherwood, op. cit., p. 674.

the short convoy route to Russia through the Bosphorus, thus saving the expensive detours to Murmansk or through Persia for Lend-Lease supplies. The development and maintenance of an active Mediterranean front offered new opportunities of weakening the Wehrmacht and of compelling Hitler to disperse his forces still more, thus exposing himself to a decisive blow in the West.

This strategy was resolutely opposed by the U.S. Chiefs of Staff. They did not share the British view that operations in the Mediterranean would contribute materially to the success of OVERLORD; on the contrary, Marshall feared " the creation in Italy of a vacuum into which the resources of the cross-Channel operation would be dissipated as the Germans had bled themselves in the North African campaign."[1] He and his colleagues felt that since the main offensive capacity of the Allies could not be used for a direct attack into France that year, it should be employed against Japan.

In suggesting this, the Americans were not intending to propose a complete reversal of the agreed overall strategy, but the events of the past six months in the Far East had made them extremely anxious to prevent the Japanese from consolidating their extensive gains in the Pacific islands and tightening their stranglehold on China.

Since the heavy defeats inflicted on the Japanese Navy in the battles of the Coral Sea and Midway in the middle of 1942 there was no longer any real danger of Japan's extending her conquests in the Pacific Islands, but the subsequent operations on Guadalcanal and in New Guinea had revealed a new and disturbing factor. There the Japanese had demonstrated in defence an endurance, tenacity and stoicism unto death surpassing anything in modern experience. With them the military cliché ' fighting to the last man and the last round' had become a literal reality. It was apparent that in obedience to the Emperor, whom he regarded as divine, the ordinary Japanese soldier would resist so long as he breathed. He was not susceptible to the mathematics of superior force which would induce European troops to lay down their arms when the struggle became hopeless. Devoutly believing that death in battle for the Emperor would speed his soul to heaven, the Japanese would gladly crash-dive his aircraft on to its target, or leap aboard an Allied tank with a chain of explosives tied to his waist.

The example of New Guinea and Guadalcanal raised a gruesome portent. The Japanese were in possession of all the strategic bases covering the approaches to their home islands. If they were given time to entrench themselves with ample stocks of food and ammunition, the bloody process of extermination would have to be carried from island to island. Some might be by-passed and ignored, but the major strongholds would have to be taken before a mortal blow could be struck at Japan herself. In this primitive warfare of jungle and swamp, where even the diseases favoured the enemy, the vast industrial superiority of the United

[1]Marshall, op. cit., p. 11.

States could not redress the balance because it could not be fully applied. It seemed that the Pacific War might drag on for years while the Japanese and the jungle took merciless and mammoth toll of American manhood.

Militarily, and politically, the problem was most alarming. The Americans had eagerly assumed the major burden of the war against Japan, and Churchill had accepted Roosevelt's view that " the whole operational responsibility for the Pacific area will rest on the United States." Admiral King had interpreted this to mean that the Pacific campaign was no concern of the Combined Chiefs of Staff. Having shouldered the responsibility and being anxious to discharge it, the Americans foresaw an exhausting, life-for-life struggle which their Army and people would not and could not stand.

At Casablanca, in the hope of allaying this concern and persuading the United States to apply a greater proportion of her immediate resources against Germany, Churchill promised that, as soon as Hitler had been defeated, " all the forces of the British Empire, land, sea and air, will be moved to the Far Eastern Theatre with the greatest possible speed, and that Great Britain will continue the war by the side of the United States with the utmost vigour until unconditional surrender has been enforced upon Japan." The Prime Minister offered to embody this assurance in a special treaty, but Roosevelt replied that Britain's word was enough. It was apparent, though unexpressed, that the Americans were eager, for reasons which became apparent later,[1] to win the Pacific War without British aid. In any case the human cost of a war of attrition would be no less harrowing if it were shared by Britain. It was not a question of manpower and resources, but of securing the bases from which to launch a decisive attack on Japan herself, especially from the air. The mere lopping off of the island branches of her empire would not suffice so long as the trunk and roots were unassailed.

Because they reasoned along these lines, the Americans were particularly disturbed at the possibility that Chinese resistance would collapse now that the loss of Burma had cut the land route to Chungking. If that were to happen, the Americans did not see how victory over Japan could be achieved. Hence they argued that in 1943 the major proportion of the resources available for amphibious attack should be employed in the Far East: to reopen the road to China by the reconquest of Burma, and to keep the Japanese unsettled in the Solomons by conducting further offensive operations there.[2] In retrospect, the American fears about the Pacific War may not appear so well founded as they seemed at the time, but they were genuine and profound and they were to have a decisive impact on Allied strategy in Europe.

[1] See Chapter XXXII.
[2] In a telegram to the War Cabinet on January 18th, the Prime Minister said, " Admiral King, of course, considers the Pacific should be a first charge on all resources and both American Army and Navy authorities are very keen on more vigorous action in Burma to help China." (See Churchill, op. cit., Vol. IV, p. 606.)

It was clear to Roosevelt, however, and eventually to his Chiefs of Staff, that the Western Powers could not adopt the defensive in Europe throughout 1943 and still expect to launch a successful offensive across the Channel in the following spring. The Russians might come to terms with Hitler if they should find themselves continuing to carry the burden of the European War almost unaided. They had come to terms with Hitler once before. In any event, if the Wehrmacht were not compelled to wage an active campaign in Western or Southern Europe, Hitler might be able to inflict a crippling defeat on the Red Army, and he would then be free to switch considerable reinforcements to the West before the spring of 1944.

These arguments eventually prevailed. The 'Hitler First' strategy was confirmed, and the statement of Anglo-American military decisions, drawn up on January 23rd, expressly said that although " operations in the Pacific shall continue with the object of maintaining pressure on Japan . . . these operations must be kept within such limits as will not, in the opinion of the Joint Chiefs of Staff, jeopardise the capacity of the United Nations to take advantage of any favourable opportunity for the decisive defeat of Germany in 1943." In this statement the vital phrase was " in the opinion of the *Joint* Chiefs of Staff " (not the *Combined* Chiefs), for that left the Americans free to determine the scope of Pacific operations. This was the more serious because Marshall and his colleagues remained sceptical of the value of the Mediterranean campaign. They agreed that the Prime Minister should make overtures to Turkey and that in July Eisenhower should invade Sicily (Operation Husky); they agreed in principle that pressure on Italy should be intensified in the hope of inducing her to capitulate; but no long term plan of campaign was made and no orders were issued to Eisenhower for operations following Husky. Marshall argued that Hitler would not attempt to defend Southern Italy once he had lost Sicily and that it would not be necessary for the Allies to make any major amphibious assault on the Italian mainland. Accordingly, the Americans laid their plans for the war against Japan on the assumption that Eisenhower would not require large numbers of landing craft after the conclusion of Husky. This was a most unfortunate assumption, as events were soon to prove.

Although the military discussions at Casablanca left many questions unanswered, there was one issue on which the Allied leaders committed themselves unreservedly and publicly. At a Press conference on the final day, January 24th, the President made an announcement which, for good or ill, was to have a profound influence on the war and, therefore, on the character of the post-war world. Roosevelt told the correspondents that the Allies were determined to demand the ' Unconditional Surrender ' of Germany, Italy and Japan, and added, says the correspondent of *The Times*, " as if it were a happy thought that had just entered his mind, that we might call this the ' Unconditional Surrender ' Meeting."

The President himself subsequently intimated to Hopkins that this phrase had ' popped into his mind ' while he was talking and that he had used it on the spur of the moment. This casual explanation is not accepted by Hopkins's biographer, Robert Sherwood, himself a member of Roosevelt's personal staff. Sherwood says, " This announcement of Unconditional Surrender was very deeply deliberated," and he insists that the President " had his eyes wide open when he made it."[1] This is undoubtedly true. In Washington, a week before the start of the Casablanca Conference, the American Chiefs of Staff discussed and approved " the President's Unconditional Surrender formula." On the third day at Casablanca Roosevelt brought out the phrase while lunching with Churchill and Hopkins. The Prime Minister immediately expressed his approval and on the following day (January 19th) cabled to the War Cabinet: " We propose to draw up a statement of the work of the conference for communication to the Press at the proper time. I should be glad to know what the War Cabinet would think of our including in this statement a declaration of the firm intention of the United States and the British Empire to continue the war relentlessly until we have brought about the ' unconditional surrender ' of Germany and Japan." He suggested that in order to speed Mussolini's downfall the formula should not be applied to Italy, but in their answer the War Cabinet said it was " unanimously of opinion that the balance of advantage lay against excluding Italy," and it endorsed the general proposal.

After receiving this reply, it appears that the Prime Minister did not discuss the matter again with the President and, when the official communiqué was being drafted by members of their staffs, no reference to ' Unconditional Surrender ' was included. Roosevelt evidently assumed, however, that his proposal had been fully approved, and before the Press conference he drafted the following notes:

> The President and the Prime Minister, after a complete survey of the world situation, are more than ever determined that peace can come to the world only by a total elimination of German and Japanese war power. This involves the simple formula of placing the objective of this war in terms of an unconditional surrender by Germany, Italy and Japan.[2]

The President had these notes in his hand when he spoke to the correspondents and he reminded them that in the American Civil War General Ulysses S. Grant had become known as ' Unconditional Surrender ' Grant—a nickname he had earned through demanding the ' Unconditional Surrender ' of the beleaguered garrison of Fort Donelson in Tennessee. This formula may have been appropriate in the case of an isolated fortress in a domestic conflict, but to apply it carte blanche to the contestants of a world struggle—contestants so varied in national character and martial ardour as Germany, Italy and Japan—seems to

[1]Sherwood, op. cit., pp. 696-7.
[2]Quoted in Sherwood, op. cit., p. 696.

have been both illogical and dangerous. Yet it appears that little consideration was given to the effect of this demand on enemy resistance. Certainly there was no preliminary examination by experts in psychological warfare of the probable impact of these two ominous words upon the German armed forces or the German people. The slogan was looked upon at the time as a vote of self-confidence, as a clarion call to the United Nations to rally for victory, and, above all, as an assurance to Stalin that the inability to open a Second Front in 1943 did not indicate any weakening in the resolution of the Western Allies. The effect upon post-war Europe of a fight to the finish seems to have been overlooked.

The Anglo-American decision to make this demand was the outward expression of new-found faith in their own strength and of their determination to ensure that never again would Germany threaten the peace of the world. Before Casablanca the British Government was publicly committed—by the Anglo-Soviet Agreement of July 1941—to make no separate peace with Germany, and Eden had then declared that Britain was " not in any circumstances prepared to negotiate with Hitler at any time on any subject."

This stand had subsequently been endorsed by the Americans, who were as determined as the British that this time they would carry the war into the heart of the German homeland. There would be no compromise with the devil nor would the German people escape unscathed and untaught, as in 1918. They would not give the Germans the chance to charge them with breaches of this war's ' Fourteen Points.' They would offer Germany no points at all. To those whose minds ran along these lines, ' Unconditional Surrender ' seemed to be the appropriate demand to make of an enemy who waged ' Total War.' This point of view was not unreasonable in the light of past experience, but it was one thing to form this resolve in secret for ultimate enforcement; it was quite another to proclaim it to the enemy in advance.

By doing this, the Anglo-Saxon powers denied themselves any freedom of diplomatic manœuvre and denied the German people any avenue of escape from Hitler. Ten months before Casablanca Goebbels had written in his diary, " The more the English prophesy a disgraceful peace for Germany, the easier it is for me to toughen and harden German resistance." After Casablanca Goebbels had delivered into his hands a propaganda weapon of incalculable power. The Nazis were now able to command conviction when they said to the Nation, " It is you, as well as we, that they want to destroy."

On the first stage of their long flight to Casablanca Roosevelt and Hopkins had landed at Trinidad on January 11th, 1943. From that port two weeks earlier a slow convoy of nine tankers, escorted by a destroyer and three corvettes, had started its trans-Atlantic journey bound for

Gibraltar with oil for the Allied forces in North Africa. In the course of its journey this convoy was intercepted first by a U-boat on patrol and then by one of Doenitz's ' wolf-packs.' Of the nine tankers which had left Trinidad, only two arrived at Gibraltar. By the time these survivors reached port the Casablanca Conference had begun.

On January 19th the Combined Chiefs of Staff decided that " the defeat of the U-boat must remain a first charge on the resources of the United Nations " and they recommended to the President and the Prime Minister that top priority must be given to " security of sea communications." It was agreed by the political and military chiefs alike that there could be no decisive invasion of Western Europe until the Battle of the Atlantic had been won.

The facts presented to the Combined Chiefs of Staff at Casablanca about the progress of the war at sea were most alarming. There was still a critical shortage of escort vessels, and the construction of anti-submarine craft had not yet been given priority in the U.S. Navy's construction yards. Adequate protection had been provided for the North African invasion only by reducing the shipments of food to Britain to 55 per cent of what they had been a year earlier and by stopping convoys to Murmansk altogether. Eisenhower's forces had reached Africa completely un-scathed, but the price of their safe passage was paid by ships on the North Atlantic trade routes, for the escorts there had to be reduced well below the safety margin. Doenitz exploited his opportunity with terrible efficiency and in November more than 600,000 tons of Allied shipping were sunk by submarine attack.

In the last week of the year, 20 U-boats fastened on to a single convoy in the North Atlantic and sank 14 ships in a three-day battle. This disaster was the final item in the account for 1942. It brought the tonnage of merchantmen destroyed in these twelve months by U-boats alone to more than six million, and Doenitz's expanding fleet now numbered 400. The comparative figures showed that for every U-boat sunk in 1942 the Allies had lost 60,000 tons of shipping. During the autumn, the output of Anglo-American shipyards had begun to exceed the rate of sinkings, but there was a vast leeway still to be made good and the balance sheet for the whole year showed a deficit of 1,318,000 tons. The bulk of these losses had been borne by Britain, since two out of every three ships sunk in 1942 had worn the ' Red Duster ' of the Merchant Navy.

Throughout that year, waging the anti-submarine war had been like fighting a forest fire. No sooner had the danger been ' damped down ' in one place than it flared up in another, for Allied resources in escort vessels and aircraft were not great enough to permit the provision of strong protection in all waters at the same time. Because of this, the Battle of the Atlantic remained for the Allies essentially a defensive war, since the U-boats had the supreme advantage of greater flexibility. Moving a ' wolf-pack ' from one part of the Atlantic to another could be effected if necessary, by a single radio message from Doenitz. Varying a complicated convoy schedule and changing the corresponding arrangements for air patrols and surface forces was not so easy to achieve. The Germans, moreover, had all the advantages of their guerilla type of warfare—surprise attack, the initiative in time and place, and, above all, the ability to vanish when the occasion demanded. This was a campaign in which the military aphorism ' Hit 'em where they ain't ' did not apply.

A week after Casablanca, Hitler indicated his determination to intensify the attack on Allied shipping. He dismissed Raeder, whom he regarded as a ' battleship admiral,' and promoted Doenitz from Flag-officer, U-boats, to Commander-in-Chief of the German Navy. Moreover, in the following month when Albert Speer was placed in charge of German war industry, he was ordered to give the highest priority to submarine production. This change in command opened a new phase in the Battle of the Atlantic and, in a review of the situation in February, the Admiralty wrote: " Never before has the enemy displayed such singleness of purpose in utilising his strength against one objective—the interruption of supplies from America to Great Britain. The tempo is quickening and the critical phase of the U-boat war cannot be long postponed."

The following month, March 1943, marked the peak of the struggle. In the middle of that month four consecutive trans-Atlantic convoys were attacked by a concentration of U-boats which numbered as many as 70 on some days. The maximum strength was being employed on both sides, and the outcome of the battle, which lasted four days, seemed to be heavily in favour of the Germans. Twenty-nine ships were sunk in convoy and eight stragglers were lost; the German casualties were only one U-boat destroyed and two seriously damaged. Yet there was a note of concern in the entry Doenitz made in his diary on March 19th: " Nearly all the boats were at some time either bombed or depth-charged."

In the Atlantic in March the U-boats destroyed 523,000 tons of shipping and at the end of the month the Admiralty reported: " A disconcerting feature is the large proportion of tonnage sunk in convoy—nearly 400,000 tons. . . . This is the highest monthly tonnage sunk in convoy since the war began." In the following month, however, the counter-measures decided upon at Casablanca began to take effect. More escort carriers were available to provide close protection throughout the Atlantic passage. Independent support groups of the Royal Navy roamed far and wide on the flanks of convoys hunting U-boats wherever they might be found. Most important of all, ' Very Long Range ' aircraft, operating from Newfoundland, Iceland and Ireland were at last able to cover ' The Gap ' in mid-Atlantic which had previously been unpatrolled from the air. Moreover, these aircraft, and those of R.A.F. Coastal Command patrolling the Bay of Biscay and the exits from the main

U-boat bases, were equipped with a new type of radar which enabled them to locate enemy submarines with great accuracy and without revealing their own approach. The result of these developments was that Allied losses in April were less than half what they had been in March. Fifteen trans-Atlantic convoys were attacked but lost only eleven ships altogether. At the end of the month the Admiralty was able to say, " For the first time U-boats have failed to press home the attack when favourably situated to do so."

The scientific advantage which the Allies had gained was a source of alarm and mystification to the Germans. On May 6th Doenitz wrote in his diary, " All responsible departments are working at high pressure to provide U-boats with equipment which will establish what kind of radar is being used against them." A week later, after an attack by 41 boats on a North Atlantic convoy had resulted in the destruction of as many submarines as merchantmen (six in each case), Doenitz reported to Hitler, " We are at present passing through the greatest crisis in U-boat warfare, since the enemy, by means of new [radar] location devices for the first time makes it impossible to carry on the fight and is causing us heavy losses."

In the last half of May Doenitz made one more major onslaught against a trans-Atlantic convoy, but this time he lost four U-boats without sinking a single ship. Following this bitter experience, Doenitz wrote, " Losses, even heavy losses, must be borne when they are accompanied by corresponding sinkings. But in May in the Atlantic the destruction of every 10,000 tons was paid for by the loss of one U-boat. . . . The losses have therefore reached an unbearable height."[1]

At Berchtesgaden on the last day of May Doenitz reported to Hitler on the dramatic transformation which had taken place in the Battle of the Atlantic. He said:

> The substantial increase in the enemy air force is the cause of the present crisis in U-boat warfare. . . . As many planes now patrol the narrows between Iceland and the Faroes in one day as only recently appeared in the course of a week. In addition aircraft-carriers are being used in conjunction with North Atlantic convoys, so that all convoy routes are now under enemy air protection. . . . However, the determining factor is the new device by means of which aircraft are now able to locate U-boats. This device is also evidently used by surface vessels.[2]

Doenitz told Hitler that his most urgent need was for " an efficient radar interception set . . . which will show the frequency used by the

[1] Because the U-boat captains over-estimated their successes, the ratio was in fact even more strongly in favour of the Allies. In May, only 187,000 tons of Allied shipping were torpedoed and sunk in the Atlantic at a cost to Doenitz of 41 U-boats. Thus for each submarine lost only 4,500 tons of Allied shipping were destroyed, compared with 60,000 tons a year earlier.
[2] Führer Naval Conferences, May 31st, 1943.

radar-equipped planes and will warn the U-boats of impending attack." Then he admitted, " We do not have such a set. We do not even know on what wave-length the enemy locates us. Neither do we know whether high-frequency or other location devices are being employed." As an immediate counter-measure, he had " withdrawn from the North Atlantic to the area west of the Azores in the hope of encountering less air reconnaissance there," and he added, " We must conserve our strength, otherwise we will play into the hands of the enemy." He told Hitler that U-boat warfare should be continued, but that he " could not foretell to what extent it would again become effective."

Hitler replied, " There can be no talk of a let-up in the U-boat campaign. The Atlantic is my first line of defence in the West and, even if I have to fight a defensive battle there, that is preferable to waiting to defend myself on the coast of Europe."

By this time, however, the initiative had already passed to the Allies, and Doenitz's only recourse was to confirm his decision to withdraw his U-boats from the North Atlantic. June 1943, as Churchill told the House of Commons, " was the best month from every point of view we have ever known in the whole forty-six months of the war [at sea]." At the time he could not disclose the figures which justified his confidence, but in fact the number of merchantmen sunk in the Atlantic had fallen from ninety in March, to forty in May, and to six in June.

This remarkable improvement in the situation at sea, and especially in the North Atlantic, in the spring of 1943 was reflected in the decisions reached at the next meeting of the Anglo-American High Command, held in Washington at the end of May. At this conference, known by the code-name TRIDENT, the Combined Chiefs of Staff were sufficiently confident about the course of the war to decide that the target date for the cross-Channel invasion should be May 1st, 1944. By sharing this decision the British Chiefs of Staff committed themselves to Operation OVERLORD, and to the building up in Britain of the forces necessary for it, but they continued to believe that during the rest of 1943 the Mediterranean offensive should be prosecuted with the greatest vigour.

By this time, having visited the Turkish President in Ankara, Churchill and Brooke knew that Turkey would not yet enter the war and that consequently there was no chance of conducting any major operations in the Eastern Mediterranean. But this made them the more eager to carry the offensive into Italy, not as an alternative to OVERLORD, but in preparation for it.

The severity of the Axis defeat in North Africa had exceeded all earlier expectations and the British proposed that Eisenhower should be given sufficient resources to enable him to invade Italy without delay at the end of the Sicilian campaign. Marshall and his colleagues would not commit themselves. They wanted to go from Sicily to Sardinia and no farther, and the most they would agree to was an instruction that Eisenhower should " mount such operations in exploitation of the attack on Sicily as might be calculated to eliminate Italy from the war." They insisted that he must not act on this authority without further reference to the Combined Chiefs and they severely restricted his scope of decision by curtailing his resources. Eisenhower was told that four groups of heavy bombers were to return to England at the conclusion of HUSKY, and that a considerable proportion of his naval forces and amphibious equipment must then begin moving to the Far East and the United Kingdom. Moreover, seven of his divisions, four American and three British, would be required for OVERLORD and must be ready to move on November 1st.

These restrictive orders resulted from the grave and growing anxiety of the United States Chiefs of Staff about Burma and the Pacific. They felt that any campaign in Italy could be maintained only at the expense of the planned operations against the Japanese or of the build-up for OVERLORD, and they were not prepared to interfere with either. Roosevelt shared their concern and he was also embarrassed by a political factor which even he, for all his great courage, could not ignore—the powerful and persistent agitation of MacArthur's friends in Washington for increased allocations to the South-West Pacific. The Presidential election was only eighteen months away and MacArthur was a potential Republican candidate who did not let his personal and political antagonism to Roosevelt go unexpressed.

In the formulation of strategy democratic leaders must be most sensitive to domestic political opinion, and this is particularly true in the case of the United States. It was a considerable achievement on the part of Roosevelt and Marshall to maintain the ' Hitler First ' strategy as resolutely as they did, but the price of doing so was that they had to make some concessions to those who advocated priority for the war against Japan, and they had to be careful not to provide ammunition for the oft-repeated charge that they were employing American forces to advance British political purposes in Africa and Europe.

The argument over Mediterranean strategy brought out in sharp relief certain basic differences between the respective attitudes of the two allies towards the war and its conduct. The Americans were militarily unsophisticated and blunt. Germany was the major enemy; therefore strike at her first by the most direct means—across the Channel. If the Germans were too strong in France, they argued, then the Allies should keep on building up their forces in Britain until they had amassed there the necessary margin of power. They proceeded on the theory that, if they made their military machine big enough, they could drive it where they willed. Only a people with a surplus, actual or potential, and with vast resources and vast self-confidence could afford to pursue such a course.

The British, on the other hand, have never been numerically strong enough in war to proceed on the basis of riding rough-shod over the enemy. They have had to win their campaigns by manœuvre, not by mass. Instinctively therefore they were averse to a head-on assault against the enemy's strongest rampart, and they favoured a strategy of indirect approach. They were reconciled to the eventual necessity of a cross-Channel assault, since it was unlikely that sufficient force could be applied—elsewhere or by other means—to inflict a decisive defeat on Germany. Yet they were resolved not to attempt it until they had employed every alternative artifice of strategy to weaken the enemy's resistance in France. They knew from long experience of European wars that would-be invaders must first exploit the great mobility which sea-power (and now air-power) gave them, in order to keep the enemy dispersed and to counter his natural advantage of being able to move on interior lines. This was the reason for their eagerness to extract the greatest advantage from the Mediterranean before venturing upon OVERLORD.

The Americans regarded this oblique approach as waste of time. The British conception of making the enemy contribute to his own defeat called for a subtlety and skill in strategy which the Americans did not naturally possess and were slow to appreciate. They preferred to out-produce Hitler rather than to outmanœuvre him, and they were sure they could do so. Industrially they were accustomed to solving big problems in a big way, and they knew the capacity of their economic machine and were certain that it could provide them with the resources the Allies needed. Although they were not inclined to take advice or warning from the British, whom they regarded with some justification as over-cautious and unimaginative, they were quick to profit from their own experience and they ruthlessly applied the lessons of their own mistakes. They felt, therefore, that many of the difficulties which seemed so great to the British could be solved quickly and simply by American ingenuity and enthusiasm. War had rekindled the frontier spirit in them and they had a deep sense of physical and industrial superiority. This optimism was their strength and their weakness, for, while it gave them great assurance, it led them to over-simplify problems and to under-estimate the strength, as well as the degree of detailed planning, required for a gigantic undertaking like OVERLORD.

Their general belief in the direct assault was reinforced by profound faith in their own men—a faith that was in the long run to be justified—and by their willingness to accept heavy casualties. They had not suffered the terrible losses which had so maimed the British people in the First World War, and they had the advantage of being a nation that was still thriving and expanding biologically. On the other hand, Britain's political and military leaders were not at all sure how far their troops had recovered from the gruelling defeats of the early years and they were reluctant to impose too heavy demands upon them. They knew that Britain could not afford another 'Pyrrhic Victory' and they were quite prepared for the war to take a little longer if thereby it might cost less and achieve more. They were not affected by the time factor which spurred on their allies. The Americans were eager to 'get the war over and get the boys home,' even if it meant that fewer would come back. This was partly the result of a national inclination to impatience, partly of the knowledge that the people of the United States would pass open judgment on the conduct of the war in the Presidential election of 1944. American strategic decisions had to be taken in a turbulent and uncertain political atmosphere which had an influence, unconscious perhaps but inevitable, even upon minds that moved on a strictly military plane.

The U.S. Chiefs of Staff had such confidence in their power to carry out the cross-Channel attack, that they suspected the British of advocating a Mediterranean strategy for purely political reasons. The Americans liked to suggest that they were 'only concerned with the winning of the war,' as if war was merely an international tournament fought to decide who was the best exponent of the military art. But war is waged for political and economic objectives which must always be kept in view by the directors of grand strategy. Otherwise, as has so often happened, the war may be won but the peace will be lost.

At no time did the Prime Minister or his Chiefs of Staff suggest that the major offensive against Germany could, or should, be launched through Southern Europe, but Churchill did believe that limited diversionary operations in support of the Turks or of Greek and Yugoslav guerillas would contribute substantially to the winning of the war (by distracting German divisions from the Channel) and would enhance the prospects of winning the peace. Whatever strategic road to Berlin the Western Allies were to take, France, the Low Countries and Scandinavia would remain within the democratic camp; but it was by no means certain that the Balkan countries would be inclined or permitted to show such allegiance if they should be liberated by the Red Army. The interests of Britain, and in the long run of the United States, demanded the restoration of democratic influence in Central and South-Eastern Europe. During 1943, although he was still primarily interested in the problem of destroying Hitler's power, Churchill became increasingly concerned about the necessity of restraining Stalin's ambitions. Accordingly, while continuing to put the defeat of Hitler first, the Prime Minister sought to devise a plan of campaign which would not only bring military success, but would ensure that victory did not leave the democratic cause politically weaker in any vital sphere.

The Americans had no such apprehensions or designs. The U.S. Chiefs of Staff felt that they could justify to their own people the presence of American forces in Europe only if these were used for the strictly military purpose of defeating Germany by the most direct and speedy means. Accordingly, they took the view that in making strategic decisions the Allies should not be influenced by political considerations of the kind which influenced Churchill.

Roosevelt and his Chiefs of Staff felt alike on this matter. In fact, the President was so anxious to avoid the suggestion that his strategy was affected by political factors that he deliberately refrained from discussing military affairs in any detail with the State Department. Before Pearl Harbour his Secretary of State (Cordell Hull) had been a member of Roosevelt's War Council. After Pearl Harbour he was never invited to attend any meetings which concerned military matters. Hull himself says: " The question of where the armies would land and what routes they would take across the Continent in the grand military movement to conquer Hitler was a subject never discussed with me by the President or any of his top military advisers."[1]

To some extent this American attitude was the product of an innate distrust of European politicians. There is in the United States a traditional belief that American diplomats, honest but ingenuous, are easily beguiled and misled by the suave and scheming statesmen of Europe. Although the American Chiefs of Staff greatly admired Churchill, they doubted his strategic judgment and suspected his political motives. They fully appreciated his capacity to drive and inspire, but they wondered where it would lead them. They never really understood how his mind worked and they were appalled at the extravagant ideas which he would suddenly spring upon them. New plans and projects tumbled over each other in his restless and fertile brain and he kept his own Chiefs of Staff in constant anxiety about what he would propose next. They were forever placing the curb of facts upon the wild gallop of his imagination but they learned to sense when he was in earnest and when he was merely working an idea out of his system.

At a meeting or over dinner he was prone to toss an outlandish proposal into the stream of conversation, sometimes merely to provoke a battle of wits and words, but for the most part because he was eager to goad his audience into presenting every possible objection. The President realised this and would lead Churchill on, confident that he could hold his own in argument. But Marshall, King and Arnold seldom distinguished between serious advocacy and mere kite-flying on the Prime Minister's part. They were reluctant to be drawn into open debate with him, for they knew they would be outmatched in oratory and dialectics. So they tended to follow the precept, " Don't argue, just say ' No.' " But what Churchill wanted was open criticism, not silent opposition. He surrounded himself with men of strong character and high professional attainments and he expected them to be outspoken. He never forgot that he was the servant of Parliament and he was most punctilious about seeking the advice and authority of the War Cabinet and the Chiefs of Staff for the decisions and actions which he planned. But to the Americans he seemed both unpredictable and uncontrollable.

[1]Hull, *Memoirs*, p. 1,110.

They were determined not to fall under the spell of his brilliance and they were inclined to oppose from him suggestions which they would have been willing to accept from a more restrained and less captivating personality.

Churchill was undaunted by the many-sided American reluctance to continue the campaign into Italy, and so late in May, with Marshall and Brooke, he flew to Algiers, determined to make the most of the little freedom of decision which the Combined Chiefs of Staff had left to Eisenhower. The Prime Minister sought to convince Eisenhower that " nothing less than the capture of Rome could satisfy the requirements of the year's campaign " and that this would be " the best possible preparation for OVERLORD." Hardly more amenable than Marshall, Eisenhower replied that he could make no decision until he had tested the opposition in Sicily, which was to be assaulted on July 10th.

This operation progressed so favourably that within a week Eisenhower had decided that Italy should be invaded. On July 20th the American members of the Combined Chiefs of Staff gave their belated approval but they still required that after the conquest of Sicily the transfer of air and naval forces from the Mediterranean to other theatres must proceed as planned. Their British colleagues were appalled at this short-sighted policy. It seemed to them that a great victory was within Eisenhower's grasp, but he was being denied the power to seize it.

The Prime Minister was ardent for bold and aggressive action, arguing, " Why crawl up the leg like a harvest bug from the ankle upwards? Let us rather strike at the knee! " With Churchill's encouragement, Eisenhower proposed to land at Salerno near Naples provided the necessary resources could be found. Accordingly, the British Chiefs of Staff, on their own account, issued a temporary standstill instruction to all aircraft and shipping which were under orders to leave the Mediterranean. This produced an outburst in Washington, where Marshall and King insisted on July 24th that the original movement orders must be carried out. Within twenty-four hours, however, news came from Rome that Mussolini had been driven from office. The opportunity which the British had been predicting for six months had now been thrust upon the Allies.

Invasion of the mainland in strength was imperative and urgent, but Eisenhower's forces were deeply committed in Sicily and to his dismay he discovered that with the shipping allocated to him he could make no large-scale landings before the first week of September. Even his capacity to strike from the air, and delay the movement of the German divisions into Italy, was curtailed by Marshall's confirmation on August 2nd of the order that four groups of Liberators must return to England forthwith in accordance with the TRIDENT decision.

Since he could not strike a quick blow to hasten Italy's collapse,

Eisenhower sought to encourage her disintegration by offering an armistice on reasonable terms and proclaiming a temporary cessation of bombing, but there was no response from the new Government of Marshal Badoglio. At the time, and later, this silence was attributed to the discouraging influence of the demand for 'Unconditional Surrender,' which was expressly reaffirmed by Churchill and Roosevelt. It is now clear, however, that this consideration weighed little with Badoglio. The decisive factor was lack of power to make a capitulation effective. He had only twelve weak divisions in the whole peninsula; the Germans had eight, four of them armoured, and a strong air force. Badoglio could surrender only to an authority which could protect his Government, for as he himself has written, "A unilateral declaration by Italy of her intention to make peace would have meant handing ourselves over to the Germans bound hand and foot. . . . I appreciated the necessity of temporizing with the Germans as far as possible and at the same time doing everything in my power to get in touch with the British and Americans. . . . I was sure that, if I could get into touch with the Allies, I could obtain better terms than the 'unconditional surrender' on which the English continued to insist."[1]

The problem was to establish contact. He could not act through the British or American Ministers at the Vatican because, through a deplorable lack of foresight, they possessed no secret code which the Germans could not crack! He was thus compelled to wait until mid-August, when an opportunity arose for sending an emissary to Lisbon disguised as a member of a mission of welcome to the Italian Ambassador returning from Chile. In the meantime, while maintaining a pretence of loyalty to the Germans, Badoglio could do nothing to hinder their occupation of his country.

There was no such procrastination on the German side, for Hitler had been expecting a political crisis in Italy ever since the Tunisian collapse and had begun to assemble in Austria and Northern Italy a reserve army under Rommel as a safeguard against Italian defection or an Allied invasion of Southern Europe. On July 25th the Führer was actually in conference with his staff, discussing the reinforcement of Rommel, when the news arrived of Mussolini's downfall.

Hitler's first inclination was to isolate Rome with airborne forces and to send a panzer grenadier division to " drive without any ado into Rome and arrest the Government, the King—the whole bag of them— especially the Crown Prince and Badoglio."[2] He decided, however, to hold his hand until he had consolidated his position in Northern Italy. At this stage he was prepared to give up the south, including Rome, and he gave orders that the withdrawal of the 70,000 German troops in Sicily should begin at once. It did not really matter, he said, if Rommel could not hold ' the Boot.' The important thing was to form a front

[1]Badoglio, *Italy in the Second World War*, pp. 49 and 56.
[2]Führer Conferences, Fragment 14, July 25th, 1943.

which could be held in the North, from Pisa across the Appenines to Rimini. Divisions to defend this line were to be drawn from Russia even if this should involve giving ground on the Eastern Front. The result was that there were fifteen German divisions on Italian soil and another four en route there before Badoglio's envoy even reached Lisbon. By then it was clear that, whatever the outcome of the diplomatic negotiations, the Allies would have to fight for Southern Italy, since Hitler, having taken full advantage of the respite, was now resolved to defend what he had previously been prepared to abandon.

The news that the Italians were ready to capitulate as soon as the Allies had landed in strength upon the mainland coincided with the start of another 'historic conference' (QUADRANT) between Churchill, Roosevelt and their Chiefs of Staff at Quebec. On August 18th they ordered Eisenhower " to accept the unconditional surrender of Italy and to obtain the greatest possible military advantage from it . . . to seize Sardinia and Corsica and attempt the establishment of air bases in the Rome area and northward, if feasible, maintaining unrelenting pressure on German forces in Northern Italy."

These instructions meant less than they said, because Eisenhower was not given the strength to carry them out. The transfer of resources from the Mediterranean for operations against the Japanese and for the build-up in Britain was to continue in compliance with the TRIDENT Plan. The withdrawal of the seven divisions earmarked for OVERLORD was unquestionably necessary, but to strip Eisenhower's command further at this moment of opportunity for the benefit of the war in the Far East seems to have been strategically unsound. Eisenhower was allowed to delay the departure to the Indian Ocean of 18 LSTs (Landing-Ships, Tank) until the Fifth Army had landed at Salerno early in September, but so strictly was he rationed for this operation that the assault was very nearly thrown back into the sea.

By the time of the Quebec Conference, however, it was too late to extract the full advantage from the Italian situation. The Allies should have been prepared to send a force into Italy at the moment of Mussolini's downfall, but this had been rendered impossible by the decisions of the TRIDENT Conference in May, when—at the insistence of the American Chiefs of Staff—the Pacific and Burma had been given priority over the Mediterranean for the last half of 1943. At the time of the Italian surrender there were thirteen American divisions operating in the Pacific; in the United Kingdom and the Mediterranean there were ten. Of these ten, only four were available for operations in Italy, and they could not be used to full effect because of the shortage of shipping. As a result of this maldistribution of resources, the Allies were to take a year to drive the Germans back to the Pisa–Rimini line, which Hitler had originally been content to hold until he saw that his opponents were not ready to exploit the overthrow of Mussolini.

Nevertheless, the campaign in Italy did bring substantial advantages which could not have been gained elsewhere and which were vital to the success of OVERLORD. The capture early in October of the Foggia airfields provided bases from which heavy bombers could raid the Rumanian oilfields and the fighter aircraft factories in Southern Germany and Austria. These were priority targets in the battle against the Luftwaffe, which had to be considerably weakened before there could be any cross-Channel invasion. Moreover, the Italian front proved to be a far greater drain on Germany than on the Allies. In October Eisenhower's eleven divisions were holding down a German force double that size in Italy alone. By his decision to fight south of Naples, Hitler gave himself a long sea flank exposed to further assault. As a safeguard against the threat of a landing between Rome and Genoa, he was compelled to keep ten divisions idle in Northern Italy—" and this," as Jodl admitted, " at a time when the Eastern Front, subjected to severe assault, was begging for reserves more urgently than ever."[1]

While the Mediterranean campaign was in full swing, the preparations for OVERLORD were proceeding in London under the direction of Lieut.-General F. E. Morgan and Brigadier-General R. W. Barker. At Casablanca, Morgan had been appointed ' Chief of Staff to the Supreme Allied Commander (Designate) '—a tongue-twisting title which he had shortened to ' COSSAC '—and had been ordered to set up an Anglo-American headquarters for the eventual Supreme Commander and to prepare an outline plan for the invasion of North-West Europe from the United Kingdom.

The COSSAC Plan, as presented to the QUADRANT Conference at Quebec, proposed the invasion of Normandy with three seaborne divisions and two airborne brigades in the assault and two more divisions, pre-loaded in landing-craft, for the immediate follow-up. After securing a foothold between Caen and Carentan, the Anglo-American forces were to concentrate on the capture of Cherbourg, but, realising that it would take some weeks to clear the harbour of mines and obstructions, the COSSAC planners proposed to supply and strengthen the bridgehead through two artificial harbours, which would be prefabricated in England and towed across the Channel. They expected to land eighteen divisions in the first fourteen days, at the end of which, they envisaged, the bridgehead would include Cherbourg and Western Normandy as far as the line Mont St. Michel–Alençon–Trouville. Into this area the main strength of the American Army would be shipped direct from the United States until the Allies had assembled up to 100 divisions for the invasion of the Reich itself.

By this plan the Allies would in due course establish powerful armies on French soil, but the crucial factor was the scale of the first assault, which was to be delivered in less strength than had been required for

[1]Jodl, Speech to *Gauleiter*, November 7th, 1943.

the invasion of Sicily. It was thus limited because Morgan had been closely restricted with regard to landing-craft and transport-planes, and accordingly he stipulated that this plan could succeed only on the condition that " not more than twelve reserve, mobile field divisions should be available to the Germans in France, and that in the Caen area they should not have more than three [of these divisions] on D-Day, five by D plus 2 and nine by D plus 8."

Although the prospective margin between success and failure was admittedly narrow in the COSSAC Plan, the Combined Chiefs of Staff adopted it and confirmed May 1st, 1944, as the target date. It was American enthusiasm which carried the decision, for the British feared that there would not be sufficient strength in the initial attack to break through the formidable defences of the Atlantic Wall which Hitler had built. Churchill urged that the weight of assault should be increased by 25 per cent, but this was not accepted, for the Americans, who would have to provide the additional shipping, argued that none could be spared except at the expense of operations in the Pacific which they were not prepared to curtail.

As an alternative to this overall increase, Marshall proposed that the amphibious resources available in the Mediterranean should be used for an invasion of Southern France, thereby " to establish a lodgment in the Toulon–Marseilles area and to exploit northwards in order to create a diversion in connection with OVERLORD." This operation (to be known as ANVIL) was accepted by the Prime Minister with some reserve. He thought that the German divisions in this area could be pinned down by the mere threat of invasion and that the forces which would be needed for ANVIL could be better employed for a landing in Northern Italy or in support of the Yugoslav guerillas.

The Quebec decision that France should be invaded from north and south in the spring of '44 was conveyed to the Russians in October when the Foreign Ministers of the three major allies conferred in Moscow. Molotov was suspicious and sceptical, for Generals Ismay and Deane[1] (representing the Combined Chiefs of Staff) had to make it clear that they could give no unconditional assurance, since OVERLORD would be certain to fail if the Germans were able to withdraw large forces from the Eastern Front. When they pointed to the COSSAC proviso that the Germans should not have more than twelve mobile reserve divisions in the West on D-Day, Molotov inquired tersely, " And what if there are thirteen? " Ismay assured him that this was only a rough yardstick but Molotov evidently regarded it as an escape-clause and continued to demand firm guarantees and a definite date, which, for security reasons alone, Ismay could not give him.

Molotov was so emphatic about the importance of OVERLORD that his visitors were taken aback when he went on to propose that the Allies

[1]General Sir Hastings Ismay, Chief of Staff to Churchill in his capacity as Minister of Defence; Major-General J. R. Deane, Head of the U.S. Military Mission in Moscow.

should try to bring both Sweden and Turkey into the war. He did not press the Swedish question strongly, but he was so insistent on the need for Turkish intervention and the opening of the Dardanelles, that Eden agreed to make another approach to the Turks on his way back to London. The moment was hardly opportune, for British forces had just been expelled from certain of the Dodecanese Islands on which they had gained a foothold. The Turks reaffirmed their neutrality.

In spite of this, the Russian proposal acted as a spur to Churchill's search for new ways of striking at the Germans in the Mediterranean. Since Quebec his doubts concerning the practicability of the COSSAC Plan had deepened. The remarkable tenacity of German resistance in Italy and the powerful fighter strength which the Luftwaffe was able to display over Germany roused in him the anxiety that an attempt to invade France—*with the resources which the Americans were prepared to make available for* OVERLORD—would lead to a repetition of the sacrificial stalemate of 1914-18. He was not a man to shrink from the costs and hazards of war so long as they were necessary and unavoidable but, gravely disturbed, as he so often said, by " the prospect of corpses floating in the Channel," he was determined that British troops should not be pitted against the Atlantic Wall without adequate support. At Salerno, in conditions rather more favourable than those which might be expected in Normandy, Eisenhower's forces, assaulting on a front of three divisions, had narrowly escaped disaster. The risks implicit in OVERLORD were considerably greater, yet there was no sign that the warning of Salerno had been appreciated in Washington.

This analysis of the prospects led Churchill and his Chiefs of Staff to the conclusion that the COSSAC Plan, as approved at Quebec, could not secure any decisive success in the West in view of the enemy's defensive power. The root of the British anxiety was the extent to which the Americans were committed in the Far East. This concern was intensified in November when the Allied leaders met in Cairo to settle their joint plans before proceeding to Teheran for discussions with Stalin. When the Prime Minister arrived in Cairo he was surprised to find that Generalissimo and Madame Chiang Kai-Shek were already there (at the President's invitation), and that they had come to discuss an American plan for major operations in Burma. This plan, designed to open a land route for the movement of supplies to China, called for the launching of a large-scale invasion of Burma in the summer of 1944 by ground troops from India and China, and by amphibious forces from the Bay of Bengal. In putting forward this plan, the U.S. Chiefs of Staff were giving expression to their fear that, unless substantial and early relief could be brought to China, she might be obliged to come to terms with Japan or would at least be militarily crippled. In either event the United States would be denied the opportunity of striking at the Japanese home islands from a base on the mainland of Asia. Churchill and the British Chiefs of Staff did not share the American anxiety about the outcome of the

Pacific War. They were convinced that once Germany was defeated Japan could be persuaded to capitulate. Consequently, they opposed the Burma plan and protested against the readiness with which the President assured Chiang that it could be carried out.

At Quebec, when Churchill had advocated the allocation to OVERLORD of 25 per cent more landing-craft, Marshall and King had refused to commit themselves, arguing that the necessary amphibious forces were not available, but now these very resources were to be found and diverted to the Indian Ocean. The British were seriously alarmed by the American determination to persist with the invasion of Burma. They had committed themselves to OVERLORD on the assumption that the U.S. Joint Chiefs of Staff would make available, even at the expense of operations against Japan, the landing-craft, warships and merchantmen necessary to ensure its success, but these, it seemed, were not to be provided. At Cairo, therefore, Churchill and Brooke advanced the argument that if the OVERLORD assault could not be strengthened then it should not be launched until the Wehrmacht in France had been sufficiently weakened to turn the balance of advantage in favour of the invasion forces. This could be achieved, they said, only if Hitler was obliged to move substantial forces from the West in order to meet a fresh attack from the South.

In the course of the Cairo discussions, Roosevelt found that he could not meet both the Far Eastern plans of his own Chiefs of Staff and the British objections to OVERLORD. He was inclined, therefore, to fall in with Churchill's proposal that they should carry out further offensive operations in the Mediterranean until the German garrison in the West had been so reduced as to make the COSSAC Plan feasible. In coming round to this view, the President was swayed by the fact that in October the Russians themselves had suggested that the Western Powers should endeavour to bring about the intervention of Turkey. Before leaving Cairo, therefore, Roosevelt and Churchill agreed that the final decision on Anglo-American strategy for 1944 should be delayed until after their conference with Stalin. There was no such doubt, however, in the minds of the U.S. Chiefs of Staff. They left Cairo, says Sherwood, having " prepared themselves for battles at Teheran in which the Americans and the Russians would form a united front."[1]

When he arrived in Teheran Roosevelt had no doubt of his ability to deal with Stalin. This was an opportunity he had long been awaiting, for as early as March 1942 he had written to Churchill: " I know you will not mind my being brutally frank when I tell you that I think I can handle Stalin personally better than either your Foreign Office or my State Department. Stalin hates the guts of all your top people. He thinks he likes me better and I hope he will continue to do so."[2] Later, but before the Teheran Conference, Roosevelt said to William Bullitt,

[1] Sherwood, op. cit., p. 776.
[2] Quoted in Churchill, op. cit., Vol. IV, p. 177.

who had been the American Ambassador in Moscow: "I have just a hunch that Stalin doesn't want anything but security for his country, and I think that if I give him everything I possibly can and ask nothing from him in return, *noblesse oblige*, he won't try to annex anything and will work for a world of democracy and peace."[1]

Roosevelt's confidence in his own skill as a diplomat and his trust in Stalin's intentions were to have a marked effect on the outcome of the discussions which began at Teheran on November 28th. The first meeting was a private one attended only by Roosevelt, Stalin and their interpreters. Here, the two leaders discussed the world situation at large and the President made it clear that he had ideas about the conduct of the war and the structure of the peace which did not entirely square with those of the British Prime Minister. Sensing a desire on Roosevelt's part to appear independent of Churchill's influence, Stalin proceeded to stimulate it. At the beginning of the conference he proposed that Roosevelt should act as chairman at all sessions, and that evening invited him to move from the American Legation to the Soviet Embassy. Stalin suggested that this was a necessary security precaution, since there were rumours of a German plot to assassinate the President. As a further considerate gesture, Stalin gave up his own quarters in the Embassy and moved to a small cottage in the grounds.

At the first formal meeting Roosevelt welcomed the Russians as " new members of the family circle," and went on to give a detailed review of the war from the standpoint of the Western Allies, laying particular stress on the demands of the war against Japan in relation to the campaign against Germany. He then explained that it was the shortage of shipping, and above all of landing-craft, which had prevented the British and American forces from making a cross-Channel attack in 1943, but he assured Stalin that their chief objective for 1944 was to carry out whatever plans would best relieve the pressure on the Russian front. They intended to launch OVERLORD about May 1st, and would be reluctant to see it delayed on account of any other operations. The President said, however, that he and the Prime Minister had been considering the desirability of conducting a further offensive in the Mediterranean as a prelude to the invasion of France, but that they wished first to ascertain the Marshal's views.

Stalin replied, in effect, that what he wanted was OVERLORD and the sooner the better. He indicated that he placed little importance on the campaign in Italy, that the Balkans were far from the heart of Germany and that the only direct way of striking at that heart was through France. He assured the President that the United States need not be unduly concerned about the Pacific, since the Soviet Union would throw her strength into the war against Japan as soon as possible after the defeat of Hitler. " Then," he said, " by our common effort we shall win."

[1]William C. Bullitt, ' How We Won the War and Lost the Peace ', *Life*, August 30th, 1948.

Although this statement was not altogether unexpected (for Cordell Hull had been given a similar assurance in Moscow a month earlier) it brought about a marked change in the American attitude towards the war in Europe. The President now had, from the lips of Stalin himself, a formal guarantee that if the Western Powers would concentrate on defeating Germany, he would come to their aid in defeating Japan. This relieved the American fear that the Japanese war might be indefinitely prolonged and exorbitantly expensive, for the Russians would be able to deal with the powerful Kwantung Army in Manchuria and could provide bases near Vladivostock for the aerial bombardment of Japanese war industry. Roosevelt now had an effective answer to King and others who had been arguing that nothing should be diverted from the Pacific for OVERLORD.

The Russian announcement brought more satisfaction to the Americans than to the British and, at a subsequent session, when Churchill continued to urge the claims of the Mediterranean, Stalin inquired bluntly whether he really believed in OVERLORD or was " only thinking about it to please the Soviet Union." The Prime Minister replied that there was no question of shelving OVERLORD. The problem was to decide what should be done with the forces in the Mediterranean in the next five months before the cross-Channel assault could be undertaken. Stalin said he favoured the invasion of Southern France, but Churchill proposed that the Allies should land in Northern Italy in order to gain airfields in the Po Valley; that they should bring aid to Tito's partisans in Yugoslavia; and should retake the Dodecanese and the Greek Islands in conjunction with Turkey, if she would enter the war as the Russians themselves had proposed in October.

None of these projects interested Stalin and he pressed for an assurance that the amphibious resources in the Mediterranean would be used in Southern France, and not in the Balkans. It was clear that the Russians had changed their minds about Turkey, for they now felt confident of their own capacity to deal with the German armies on the Eastern Front, which had already been weakened by the diversion to Italy of fifteen first-class divisions. It was apparent—to Churchill at any rate—that Stalin did not want any Anglo-American forces in the Balkan countries which he was bent upon ' liberating.' There was a long-term political strategy behind the Russian desire for the Allies to concentrate on Western Europe and the Western Mediterranean.

Stalin suggested that there would be no need for any diversionary operations by Anglo-American forces in South-Eastern Europe, for the Red Army would launch an offensive in sympathy with OVERLORD and thus keep the Germans fully occupied in the East. This led him to ask for a firm date for the invasion. Churchill and Roosevelt repeated that May was the month, but that they could not give the actual day. In search of further assurance, Stalin inquired who would command the invasion and, when he was told that the appointment had still to be made, he said softly, " Don't you think you'd better decide? The time is getting rather short." He requested that the name of the Supreme Commander should be publicly announced before the end of the year, and Roosevelt assured him that this would be done.

By the time the Conference ended the President believed that he had established a workable personal relationship with Stalin, and after his return to Washington he spoke of him in the warmest terms, saying, " I believe that we are going to get along very well with him and the Russian people—very well indeed." This public statement represented his sincere conviction and he privately related to Frances Perkins, his Secretary of Labour, how he had broken down Stalin's reserve. " For the first three days," he told her, " I made absolutely no progress. I couldn't get any personal connection with Stalin, although I had done everything he asked me to do. . . . He was correct, stiff, solemn, not smiling, nothing human to get hold of. . . . I felt pretty discouraged because I thought I was making no personal headway." The President went on to tell Miss Perkins that on the third day of the conference he had tried a different approach: " As soon as I sat down at the conference table, I began to tease Churchill about his Britishness, about John Bull, about his cigars, about his habits. It began to register with Stalin. Winston got red and scowled, and the more he did so, the more Stalin smiled. Finally Stalin broke out into a deep, hearty guffaw and for the first time in three days I saw light. I kept it up until Stalin was laughing with me and it was then that I called him ' Uncle Joe.' . . . From that time on our relations were personal. . . . The ice was broken and we talked like men and brothers."[1] The belief that he had won Stalin's friendship exercised a most important influence on the policy which Roosevelt pursued between Teheran and his next meeting with Stalin at Yalta.

The President was not alone in believing that the results of the Teheran Conference were favourable to the Western Powers. The promised Russian support for OVERLORD and for the war against Japan removed many doubts in the minds of the American and British Chiefs of Staff. They had always been agreed upon the ultimate necessity for an assault across the Channel, and had differed only on the questions of time and strength. Brooke and his colleagues had been strong advocates of the campaign against Italy, but they had never been enthusiastic about the Prime Minister's Balkan and Aegean projects, and they were relieved to have a firm political decision that OVERLORD was to be launched.

The more remote political consequences were not immediately evident to the Americans or to the British, with the exception of Churchill, and it is doubtful whether even he appreciated at the time the full extent of Stalin's victory. Pushed by the Russians and pulled by the Americans,

[1]Frances Perkins, *The Roosevelt I Knew*, pp. 70-1. It is only fair to the President to add that before this particular meeting he had said to the Prime Minister, " Winston, I hope you won't be sore at me for what I am going to do."

the overall strategy of the Western Powers had been diverted away from the area of Soviet aspirations. Even before Teheran it was inevitable that the enforcement of 'Unconditional Surrender' upon Germany would leave the U.S.S.R. the dominant power in Eastern Europe, but it was by no means inevitable that Russian influence would extend deep into Central Europe and the Balkans. After Teheran, it became almost a certainty that this would happen. Thus the Teheran Conference not only determined the military strategy for 1944, but adjusted the political balance of post-war Europe in favour of the Soviet Union.

These possibilities lay beyond the horizon, unseen by the Combined Chiefs of Staff, who were naturally preoccupied with winning the war. Early in December they resumed their discussions in Cairo committed almost irrevocably to OVERLORD and to the invasion of Southern France (Operation ANVIL). The planned target date was barely five months away and they had not yet found the full resources necessary even for the COSSAC Plan. Nevertheless, it was only after prolonged argument, and as a result of a personal appeal from the Prime Minister to the President himself, that the American Chiefs of Staff agreed to postpone the invasion of Burma and to allocate to OVERLORD landing-craft for one extra division. This did not fully meet Churchill's request for a 25 per cent increase in the weight of assault, but no final decision on this point could be made until the plan had been appraised by Eisenhower, who was appointed Supreme Commander on December 6th.

That day the Combined Chiefs of Staff decided that OVERLORD and ANVIL would be " the supreme operations for 1944. . . . They must be carried out during May. Nothing must be undertaken in any part of the world which hazards the success of these two operations." Eisenhower's appointment and its purpose were publicly announced on Christmas Eve and the directive, which he subsequently received from the Combined Chiefs of Staff, defined his task in these words:

You will enter the continent of Europe and, in conjunction with the other Allied Nations, undertake operations aimed at the heart of Germany and the destruction of her armed forces.

## CHAPTER VII

# THE POWER OF THE WEHRMACHT

IN December 1943, following the Teheran Conference, the information reaching Berlin by clandestine channels made it clear that the Western Allies were firmly committed to opening a Second Front in France in the spring of 1944. To Hitler this information was not unwelcome, for the experience of the past two years in Russia had shown that he could not defeat the Soviet Union so long as he was obliged to deploy one-third of his army and two-thirds of his Air Force to defend Europe against the Western Powers and to keep the occupied countries in subjection. On the other hand, once the cross-Channel invasion had been repulsed—as Hitler was sure it must be—he would be free to withdraw substantial forces from the West and with their aid could win a great, perhaps a decisive, victory in the East. In the meantime, having expelled the Allied armies from Western Europe, he would drive the British and Americans on to the defensive by bringing to bear against them new naval and aerial weapons which would transform the situation: electro-U-boats of revolutionary design and performance, jet aircraft, flying-bombs and long-range rockets. With these weapons Hitler expected to regain the initiative in the air and at sea, and to secure a respite from land attack in the West until he had established at least a stalemate in the East and South. Then, so he hoped, his adversaries would have no alternative but to accept his conquests.

The very foundation of this plan was the Führer's assumption that the cross-Channel attack could be repulsed. On December 20th, in a discussion with his staff about the invasion problem, Hitler spoke in contemptuous terms of the Anglo-American forces. " I am firmly convinced," he said, " that they are incapable of solving this problem." Their Mediterranean landings had succeeded " only with the help of traitors." There would be no traitors in the West, nor any sector of the coast unguarded. The Allies, he insisted, would be employing " entirely inexperienced units " against German troops who had been tested in battle, and against fortifications which had been made almost impregnable. Those at Dieppe were " a thousand times stronger " than they had been in 1942, and he himself was " constantly thinking out new

143

ways to improve the defences" and was devising "the most diverse devilries." The assault would be broken at the Atlantic Wall.[1]

Hitler's confident appreciation was readily accepted by his immediate entourage with the notable exception of Jodl who, as Chief of the Operations Staff at OKW, was responsible for all theatres of war except the Russian. Six weeks earlier, addressing a meeting of *Gauleiter*, the District Leaders of the Nazi Party, Jodl had spoken with unusual frankness about the threat from the West. "On the Eastern Front," he said, "things are getting warm, but no success gained by the enemy there can be directly disastrous unless we should lose the Rumanian oilfields. On the other hand, the High Command cannot close its eyes to the fact that in the West the brand is now held in readiness to start a conflagration which, if not extinguished then and there, will get out of control."[2] Warning the *Gauleiter* of the difficulty of defending the entire Atlantic coast, Jodl said, "Along a front of 2,600 kilometres it is impossible to reinforce the coastal front with a system of fortifications in depth at all points. . . . Hence it is essential to have strong, mobile and specially well equipped reserves in the West for the purpose of forming *Schwerpunkte*. Any weakening of these tactical reserves will involve a risk acutely endangering the overall situation."

In this passage Jodl stated the crux of the problem as the General Staff saw it; reserves were more important than fortifications, since the mobility and flexibility resulting from command of the air and sea would give the Allied forces the power to strike almost anywhere from Northern Norway to the Spanish border. It seemed to Jodl that this advantage could be countered, not by an attempt to hold every mile of coastline, but by the creation of a strong central reserve which could be readily directed to whatever area the Western Powers chose to assault. In the first two years of the war Germany had acquired what Jodl called "a capital sum of space on which we are now living," but the holding of this "capital sum" was absorbing nearly all Germany's military income. Hitler was fast becoming the prisoner of his own conquests. By this time the total of German divisions in the field was half as great again as the number she had deployed at the start of the Russian campaign and yet these were all fully occupied. Of the 320 divisions outside the Reich in November 1943, the Red Army was engaging 206;[3] 24 were in the Balkans; 22 in Italy; 50 in France and the Low Countries; and 18 in Denmark and Norway. Inside Germany there were another 15 divisions in the process of being formed or re-formed, but there was no strategic reserve.

[1]*Führer Conferences*, Fragment 35, December 20th, 1943. The transcript of this conference is very badly damaged, but the general trend of Hitler's thinking emerges clearly.

[2]Nuremberg Document L 172. This contains the text of Jodl's speech and the detailed staff reports on which it was based.

[3]Ibid. In addition to these German forces, Hitler had at his disposal in the East 30 satellite divisions: 14 Finnish, 10 Rumanian and 6 Hungarian.

In the spring of 1943 Hitler had begun to form a central reserve, but this had been committed on the Eastern Front in the summer and, when re-formed in the autumn, had been drawn into Italy. The High Command was planning to build up a new reserve of more than twenty divisions during the winter, but this could not be assembled until a stable line had been established in the East. There, following the catastrophe at Stalingrad where Hitler had lost 300,000 men, the Wehrmacht had made a skilful withdrawal from the Caucasus and, by retaking Kharkov in March 1943, had gained a breathing space which had lasted into mid-summer. Hitler might then have held the Ukraine and White Russia if he had not attempted another offensive. His original plan for this operation—against the Kursk salient north of Kharkov—was supported by Zeitzler, who had succeeded Halder as Chief of the Army General Staff, and by von Kluge and von Manstein, the commanders of Army Groups Centre and South respectively. They proposed that it should be launched in May as a 'spoiling attack' designed to disrupt the Red Army's preparations for a summer offensive. Not content with this limited objective, Hitler decided—on the advice of one of his army commanders, Model—to wait until he had accumulated greater tank strength. When the Kursk attack was finally made in mid-July, Hitler threw in 17 panzer divisions, half his total armoured strength, but by this time the Russians were ready and he suffered a severe defeat.

Having committed all his mobile reserves here, Hitler had nothing in hand to meet the crisis brought about by the overthrow of Mussolini on July 25th. To prevent the immediate defection of the Badoglio Government and to defend Italy against invasion, he was obliged to transfer half a dozen of his best divisions from Russia. This transfer might have been accomplished without creating a further crisis in Russia, if there had been already prepared a reserve line to which Hitler's armies could withdraw. After Stalingrad Zeitzler had proposed the immediate preparation of such a position along the Dnieper, but Hitler had refused since he believed that as soon as his generals knew there was a fortified line behind them they would be inclined to retreat to it. No move to fortify the Dnieper was made until the summer and before this new position, known as the Hagen Line, was ready, Hitler ordered von Manstein and von Kluge to make a rapid withdrawal to it so that they could release forces for Italy.

At a conference on July 26th von Kluge protested that he could not " fall back to a position which is practically non-existent," that he would have to continue operations east of the Dnieper while the Hagen Line was being completed, and that until he had reached the protection of this line he could not spare any divisions. Von Kluge said, " The earliest time for occupying the Hagen Line would be in about four weeks "; to which Hitler answered, " Well, we just can't wait as long as that. We must free troops before then."[1] The divisions Hitler wanted

[1]Führer Conferences, Fragment 16, July 26th, 1943.

were made available and the withdrawal began, but on August 3rd the Russians launched their summer offensive. During the next seven weeks the Germans fell back under heavy pressure and the Red Army followed up so closely and strongly that von Kluge and von Manstein had no time to establish their troops in the Hagen Line before it, too, was assaulted and broken.

Having forced the Dnieper in the autumn, the Russians continued their offensive into the winter, and by driving westward from Kiev in December, threatened to outflank and envelop Army Group South in the great bend of the Lower Dnieper. By Christmas von Manstein's position was so critical that he suggested he should withdraw entirely from the Dnieper Bend, thereby shortening his front and creating a reserve with which to meet any further Russian penetration west of Kiev. At a conference on December 27th Zeitzler strongly supported this proposal, arguing that the Dnieper salient was " becoming untenable anyway," and that they could not check the Soviet offensive unless they could find additional troops quickly. Hitler replied that a withdrawal by von Manstein would mean losing the Crimea. This, he said, would have a most serious effect on the attitude of the Turks, who were already under pressure to enter the war on the Allied side, and would have " catastrophic consequences " in Rumania, since it would expose the Ploesti oilfields to attack by the Red Air Force. Hitler insisted that by now the Russians must be nearly exhausted. " They are bound to wear themselves out," he said. " After all, there's no reason to think that they're like the mythical giant who grew stronger every time he was struck down."[1] He was confident that the Red Army could be halted without his having to yield more territory. " Just wait and see," he said. " We've lived through a couple of these situations in which everybody said that things were beyond repair. Later it always turned out that they could be brought under control after all."

At the Führer's H.Q. the argument about von Manstein's proposal continued into the New Year and ranged far beyond the question of giving up the Dnieper Bend. The issue that emerged was no less than the question whether Hitler would agree to carry out a further substantial withdrawal in the East during the winter in order to make certain of defeating the invasion in the West in the spring. When Jodl joined the discussion, he urged Hitler to withdraw not only from the Ukraine but also from the little Baltic states, and to concentrate on holding the shortest line between the Black Sea and the Baltic. Jodl considered that this might save more than twenty divisions and provide for the West such powerful forces that the cross-Channel assault the Allies were planning would be foredoomed to failure. Once again, however, the Führer refused to give way. He agreed to make some adjustment on the northern sector of the Russian front, thereby saving eight divisions, but he would not abandon the Baltic States. He feared that if he were to

[1]Führer Conferences, Fragment 7, December 27th, 1943.

do so, the Soviet Navy would be able to interrupt the summer movement of iron ore from Northern Sweden. Moreover, as Doenitz reminded him at a further conference on January 1st, they had to hold the eastern shore of the Baltic if they were to protect their only safe U-boat training area. Following this discussion, Doenitz wrote, " The Führer remains firm in his determination not to yield an inch if he can help it."[1]

Hitler's confidence that he could both hold the front in the East and repulse the cross-Channel invasion was stimulated and sustained by the knowledge that during the past two years, although the offensive strength of the Wehrmacht had declined, the economic power behind the German war machine had developed at a remarkable rate and was still rising, in spite of Allied bombing. In 1943 the total supply (from production and imports) of steel, coal, oil and other basic materials was the highest in German history and the output of arms and munitions reached unprecedented levels, as this table indicates:

|  | 1940 | 1941 | 1942 | 1943 |
|---|---|---|---|---|
| Ammunition |  |  |  |  |
| (in metric tons) | 865,000 | 540,000 | 1,270,000 | 2,258,000 |
| Automatic Weapons | 170,880 | 324,800 | 316,691 | 435,400 |
| Artillery  ..      .. | 5,499 | 7,082 | 11,988 | 26,904 |
| Armour  ..      .. | 1,359 | 2,875 | 5,573 | 11,897 |
| Aircraft  ..      .. | 8,070 | 9,540 | 12,950 | 22,050 |

The source of this table is a 'Comprehensive Survey of German War Production, 1940-44,' drawn up by the German Ministry of Armaments and War Production. The figures quoted differ in some cases from those accepted by the *United States Strategic Bombing Survey*, but the differences are not important and this table provides a fair basis for a year-to-year comparison.

In this table 'Artillery' includes field, anti-tank and anti-aircraft guns; 'Armour' includes all heavy and medium tanks, assault-guns and self-propelled guns; and 'Aircraft' includes all operational types.

If this increase in production could be attributed to the efforts of any one man, that man was Albert Speer, who had been appointed Minister of Arms and Munitions in February 1942 at the age of thirty-six. An architect by profession, Speer knew little about industrial production, but he had a flexible and brilliant mind, great energy and an exceptional talent for improvisation. As the Führer's personal architect, Speer had directed the construction of most of the Nazi Party buildings at Nuremberg, Munich and elsewhere, and, since his relationship with Hitler had been that of one artist to another, he had gained a most favoured

[1] Führer Naval Conferences, January 1st, 1944.

standing. It appears that he alone of the leading Nazis was given freedom to speak frankly, a freedom which he had the courage to exercise.

Outside Germany it was commonly believed that Hitler's Reich, as a Totalitarian State, was a regimented society in which all man-power and all economic resources were harnessed to a war machine that was driven according to a master plan. Prior to the appointment of Speer, however, there had been no attempt to mobilise the resources of the Reich or the occupied countries for Total War. Between September 1939 and February 1942, according to the *United States Strategic Bombing Survey*, " the bulk of the economy was permitted to operate in a leisurely, semi-peacetime fashion under the loose supervision of Funk's Economic Ministry. . . . Production of surplus civilian goods continued and scarce materials were allocated to non-essential programs."[1] There was little increase in the length of the working week or in the number of workers engaged in war production, and there was only a minor rise in the output of arms and munitions, for Hitler's plans had been based on the assumption that the war would be of short duration and limited scope. This assumption had been strongly challenged by the economic planning staff at OKW, but the experience of the first two years appeared to confirm it. Each campaign was won much more cheaply than had been expected, and the Wehrmacht had not called for any marked expansion of armament production. No plans had been prepared for a long war or for the development of Germany's economic potential to fit her for a global struggle against an alliance of world powers. Indeed, in the autumn of 1941, Hitler had been so confident of victory that he had ordered OKW to divert production resources from the Army to the Luftwaffe and the Navy. This had been done and during the winter that followed, while the Wehrmacht in Russia was suffering its first defeats and losing substantial quantities of equipment, factories in the Reich were being busily converted from the manufacture of those very armaments which were soon to be desperately needed.

In September 1939 Germany's war production had far exceeded that of Britain, but in the next two and a half years Hitler had cast his advantage away. During this period Britain, by mobilising her resources more rapidly and more drastically and by demanding a considerable reduction in the standard of living of her people, had achieved an output of aircraft, tanks and munitions which in 1941 and 1942 was much greater than that of Germany. In these years of adversity Churchill was able to call upon the British people to make efforts and sacrifices which Hitler dared not demand of the Germans, since the Führer's popularity was built, not on the promise of " blood, tears, toil and sweat," but on the assurance of early victory in the field and continued prosperity at home.[2]

[1] *U.S.S.B.S.*, ' Economic Report,' p. 24.

[2] Even in May 1943, Goebbels noted in his diary, " The Führer simply won't approve a 100-gram reduction in the meat ration. Yet it is so necessary." When this reduction proved to be unavoidable, Goebbels observed that it had had "a very serious psychological effect." See Goebbels, *Diaries*, pp. 285 and 303.

The phase of wasted opportunity did not end immediately upon the appointment of Speer. " Neither the intensity of the war effort nor the way in which it was organised were, as yet, seriously questioned," says the *United States Strategic Bombing Survey*.[1] There was still no central planning of the whole economy, no real control over industry. Throughout 1942 Speer encountered strong opposition from the civil ministries which resisted his efforts to curtail domestic production, and from the services, which were jealous of their independence. Nevertheless, by taking advantage of industrial capacity hitherto untapped and by making more efficient use of existing resources of plant, labour and materials, Speer doubled the monthly output during his first year.

Except in the general sense that Hitler had driven his forces beyond their strength, the disaster at Stalingrad in the winter of 1942-43 was not due to any shortage in armament production. In 1942, thanks to the development brought about by Speer, output exceeded ' expenditure ' in all the main categories of arms, armour and ammunition. While keeping pace with demands, however, Speer was not able to build up any substantial stocks, and the losses of the Stalingrad campaign made serious inroads on what meagre stocks there were. The records of the Army High Command show that at Stalingrad the Wehrmacht lost the equivalent of six months' production of armour and vehicles, three to four months' production of artillery, and two months' production of small arms and mortars.

After this disaster Hitler at last admitted the need for an immediate and considerable expansion in the output of arms and munitions. Speer now became Minister for Armaments and War Production with authority over almost every phase of economic life, civil and military, with the exception of the aircraft industry. Hitler continued to intervene in the fixing of production targets and priorities, and even in the determination of complex technical questions, but by this time Speer had learned how to translate the Führer's extravagant, and often conflicting, demands into practical programmes. With Speer in command there was a belated attempt to plan and control the German economy. He established a Central Planning Board to allocate plant and materials, and he set up for each industry ' shock-committees,' headed not by civil servants or business men but by ' technocrats,' experts in industrial management. Through these committees Speer ruthlessly reorganised the less efficient factories, introducing mass-production methods and assembly-line techniques which had hitherto been neglected. By drastic rationalisation large savings were made in production time and raw materials, and by the conscription of another huge draft of foreigners the number of workers engaged in war industry was increased during 1943 by one and a half millions.

The result was a further remarkable rise in the general level of

[1] *U.S.S.B.S.*, ' Economic Report,' p. 24.

armament production. By December 1943 the rate of output of arms and ammunition was 150 per cent higher than it had been in February of the previous year. " In general," says the *Survey* already quoted, " despite the retreats and consequent losses in the latter part of 1943, the German army was better equipped with weapons at the beginning of 1944 than at the start of the Russian War."[1] This was specially true of the armoured formations, for the manufacture of tanks, assault-guns, and self-propelled guns had been trebled since Speer took charge, and the ' panzer strength ' of the army had increased from 4,512 tanks, etc., on January 1st, 1942, to nearly 11,000 two years later. Moreover, this period had seen the rearming of the panzer divisions with heavier and more powerful equipment. The light tanks of the early years had all but disappeared; ' mediums ' now predominated and the Wehrmacht was well supplied with heavy Panthers and Tigers, which were more formidable than any Allied tanks except the Joseph Stalins. At the start of 1943 it had only 72 Tigers and Panthers, but by the end of the year there were 1,823 in the hands of units, and another 375 were coming from the factories every month.

Although the expansion of German war production in 1942 and 1943 was spectacular after the negligible progress of the first two years, the total output was not great enough to support prolonged and intensive operations on more than one major front. Germany had not the resources to win a war of attrition. In December 1943 Speer launched a new production drive designed to bring another industrial rise in the first half of 1944 but he knew, if Hitler did not, that the German war economy was approaching the limit of its capacity, and that, because of the shortage of steel, this capacity could not be much further expanded.

This limitation was one of the legacies of Hitler's ' short-war ' theory. In 1938 General Thomas, the head of the economic planning staff at OKW, had warned Hitler that Germany's steel production, then less than two million tons a month, could not meet the demands of the prolonged and bitter struggle which the General Staff feared would develop. Thomas advocated the construction of new blast furnaces and foundries in order to broaden Germany's industrial base, and thereby to increase her military potential. This long-term development plan was

---

[1]*U.S.S.B.S.*, 'Economic Report,' p. 187. The pattern of development of German war production before and after the advent of Speer is indicated by the following figures of monthly output:

|  | June '40 | June '41 | Dec. '41 | Dec. '42 | Dec. '43 | July '44 |
|---|---|---|---|---|---|---|
| Rifles      .. | 106,400 | 102,280 | 52,865 | 96,415 | 190,809 | 249,080 |
| Machine-guns  .. | 4,400 | 7,770 | 3,424 | 10,716 | 15,704 | 24,141 |
| Mortars[1].. | 1,165 | 1,073 | 207 | 2,360 | 1,290 | 2,225 |
| Artillery[2]    .. | 294 | 317 | 103 | 523 | 962 | 1,554 |
| Armour (all types) | 121 | 310 | 378 | 760 | 1,229 | 1,669 |
| Aircraft (Operational) | 675 | 1,040 | 978 | 1,548 | 1,734 | 4,219 |

[1]The decline in the output of these single mortars in 1943 was due to the development of the multiple mortar, the *nebelwerfer*.

[2]Includes only field and medium artillery.

rejected by Hitler who insisted that the steel available for war production must be devoted to securing the maximum immediate output of arms and ammunition. This was done and again it seemed that Hitler had been right. With the occupation of Czechoslovakia and the conquest of France and the Low Countries, Germany acquired sufficient productive capacity to increase her output of crude steel by nearly 50 per cent. The need for the construction of new furnaces and foundries seemed to have disappeared, and even in 1941, when Germany had steel capacity to spare, none were built.

By the time Speer came to office, it was too late to initiate the large-scale capital construction programme that would have been needed to bring any major increase in Germany's steel resources. In 1942, and still more in 1943, the cry was for immediate supply. One tank to-day was worth two tanks to-morrow. By working the available plant to capacity Speer managed to raise the monthly output from 2.4 million tons to 2.9 millions within a year. During 1943 Germany and the occupied countries provided Hitler with 34,644,000 tons of crude steel, but this was the peak and it was less than one-fifth of the combined production of Germany's adversaries.

In the long run Germany's relative industrial weakness was to prove one of the main causes of her defeat, but at the end of 1943 the Wehrmacht had sufficient weapons and equipment to meet the threat from the West with confidence. Nor was it unreasonable for Hitler to believe that he might yet emerge triumphant provided that he could defeat the Allied invasion quickly and thus avoid becoming involved in a fresh campaign on a new front. Moreover, it seemed that the restrictions imposed on Germany's military power by the limitations of her industrial potential might soon be removed by the achievement of her scientists, who had developed new weapons of aerial and naval warfare.

At the Führer's H.Q. on July 8th, 1943, Doenitz advised Hitler that two new types of submarine had been designed and that these would revolutionise the war at sea. The most remarkable characteristic of these U-boats was their ability to travel as fast under water as on the surface and to operate submerged for prolonged periods without having to come up to charge their batteries. Doenitz said: " Entirely new possibilities are introduced by permitting U-boats to approach a convoy quickly and also to take swift evasive action under water instead of being obliged to surface. This will make the enemy's present anti-submarine defence entirely ineffectual." Doenitz reported that he was " well satisfied with the models," and recommended that they should be " built with the greatest possible speed."[1]

Hitler immediately ordered Speer to grant top priority to the construction of these U-boats. Before this conference the Naval Staff had

[1] Führer Naval Conferences, July 8th, 1943.

estimated that none could be completed in less than 17 months, but Speer proposed to reduce this time by half. He suggested that they should not wait for prototypes to be built and tested; that the new models should be put into production as soon as the detailed drawings and specifications were ready; and that, in order to avoid delays caused by Allied air attacks on the established contruction yards, they should be prefabricated in sections which would be brought to the slipways only for assembly. Radical and risky though this plan was, Doenitz accepted it in the interests of speed. By December 1943 a full-scale 'mock-up' of each type had been built, and Speer was able to report that the first electro-U-boats would be ready in the spring of 1944.

In the meantime, Doenitz was obliged to continue the Battle of the Atlantic with the conventional submarines that had already been defeated. In September, having provided his U-boats with better defensive radar, heavier anti-aircraft armament and a new torpedo, acoustically-guided, Doenitz again attempted to raid the North Atlantic convoy routes. As in the previous April and May, however, his losses were severe and his successes meagre. The Royal Navy had anticipated the development of the acoustic torpedo and had an effective counter already prepared. The new German radar equipment was no more effective than the old in detecting the approach of hostile aircraft and the mystery of the equipment the Allies were using remained unsolved. On November 12th a note of despair appeared in Doenitz's diary when he wrote: " The enemy holds every trump card, covering all areas with long-range air patrols and using location methods against which we still have no warning. . . . The enemy knows all our secrets and we know none of his."

In the previous year, when the Allies were losing more than six hundred thousand tons of merchant shipping every month, Doenitz had believed that he could win ' the tonnage war ' with his existing U-boat fleet, but he now knew that this belief was vain. During 1943, in all waters, the Allies had lost less than three hundred thousand tons a month, and for every ship sunk they had built four. Convoys were now crossing the Atlantic in steadily increasing volume, unchecked, indeed almost unopposed, by the U-boats they had once dreaded. Hitler's " first line of defence in the West " had gone, and it could not be restored until the new submarines were brought into action.

The eclipse of the German Navy, and the inability of its U-boats to hinder the build-up of the Allied invasion forces in Britain, made it the more important that Hitler should quickly complete his preparations for the bombardment of the invasion base, and especially London, with his new *Vergeltungswaffen,* ' weapons of revenge ': the flying-bomb (V.1) and the rocket (V.2). Plans for the production of these pilotless projectiles had been put forward by Speer during 1942,[1] but Hitler had been sceptical of their value until, on Christmas Eve that year, an experimental V.1 was successfully launched on the island of Peenemunde in the Baltic. Elaborate precautions were taken to keep the project secret, but by the following April British agents, with the help of the Polish Underground, had learned enough to give the War Cabinet in London a general warning of the danger. In May 1943, a Royal Air Force reconnaissance plane located the Peenemunde research station and air photographs subsequently revealed that the Germans were conducting experiments there with pilotless jet-propelled aircraft. The secret was out, but the question was, where and when would they be used?

The decision on this point was taken that summer after the first long-range test in which a V.1 made a flight of 243 kilometres without deviating more than one kilometre from its course. This dispelled Hitler's doubts about its accuracy, and on July 10th, 1943, he ordered Speer to devote special attention to the production of flying-bombs. Launching sites were to be constructed along the Channel coast, mainly in the Pas de Calais, and were to be directed on London and on the Southampton–Portsmouth area. Ninety-six sites were to be ready before December 15th, by which time production was to have reached 5,000 a month and a stock of 5,000 was to be available to start the offensive.

In August 40,000 conscript workers began to construct the launching sites and supply centres, and in mid-November it seemed likely that these would all be ready by Christmas. Before the end of November, however, 63 sites had been discovered by Allied air reconnaissance. At first there were in the Air Ministry and at Eighth U.S. Air Force H.Q. some sceptics, who thought the preparations were a hoax designed to draw the strategic bombers away from targets in Germany, but the counsel of those who took the menace seriously prevailed, and on December 5th Allied bombers began attacking the launching sites. Neither bad weather nor good camouflage afforded the Germans any protection. Using the latest radar aids for navigation and bomb-aiming, British and American aircraft were able to strike at these extremely small targets with a degree of accuracy previously unattainable.

After five weeks of this onslaught the Germans were driven to the conclusion that " if the attacks continue on the present scale for another 14 days every site will have been destroyed."[2] This gloomy prediction was not fulfilled, for Allied bombers had to turn to other targets of greater urgency. Nevertheless, by February, 73 of the 96 sites had been so severely damaged that they were not worth repairing, and the Germans decided to abandon the entire system. They were back where they had been eight months earlier and they now set about constructing launching

[1]Halder (*Hitler as War Lord*, p. 16) says that plans for the development of long-range rockets had been presented to Hitler by von Brauchitsch in 1939, but had been rejected.
[2]War Diary of Flak Regiment 155, January, 7th, 1944.

sites of a new type, less efficient but simpler to build and so thoroughly camouflaged that aerial reconnaissance could not detect them.

In the hope of preventing the Allies from locating these sites through agents on the ground, security measures were more stringently enforced. ' Unreliable ' foreign workers were combed out of the construction gangs, and Flak Regiment 155, which was to carry out the launching operations, was purged of all non-German elements. ' Security ' became such an obsession with the regimental commander, Wachtel, that he adopted the name of Wolf and sought to disguise himself with a false beard. His H.Q. changed its location and took on the title and garb of a labour unit of the Organisation Todt. For some reason which the records of the regiment do not explain, this sartorial metamorphosis was accomplished —at least so far as the officers were concerned—one dark February night in taxis in the streets of Paris!

A precaution of greater operational significance, however, was the decision of the Luftwaffe High Command that the new sites should neither be stocked with bombs nor equipped with launching tackle and ramps until the offensive was about to begin. During the spring 64 of these sites were completed as nearly as this security order would allow, but a further delay was now caused by a miscarriage in production plans. In August 1943 the R.A.F. had inflicted serious damage on installations at Peenemünde and had disorganised research there just when the design of the flying-bomb was being perfected. At this time some faults in the prototype had still to be eradicated, but Hitler, in his anxiety to bring the V.1 into operation, gave orders that mass production was to begin without waiting for the results of further trials. The outcome was that, when the first series came to be tested, the majority crashed, and it was found that successful flights could only be made after extensive modification and adjustment of each individual bomb. The first three months' production was consigned to the scrap heap.

In December, instead of five thousand, the output was less than one thousand and it was the following March before an adequate stock had been accumulated. Even then, however, with the monthly production only just reaching two thousand, there was not sufficient flow from the factory to sustain a serious offensive. Accordingly, Hitler decided to hold his hand and husband his stocks until the start of the invasion should provide an appropriate opportunity for initiating his V-weapon campaign. Then, so he hoped, the Allied Air Forces would be too busy supporting the assault to take effective counter-action against the launching-sites. Thus the first five months of 1944 were to go by with the flying-bomb offensive still hanging fire long after it should have started and would have started but for the intervention of Allied air power.[1]

[1]This survey is based on the records of Flak Regiment 155; on the interrogation of its chief engineer, Eberhardt, and of Speer; and on the minutes of Speer's meetings with Hitler.

These setbacks deprived Hitler of the immediate means of carrying out the campaign of retaliation which he regarded as the best answer to the Allied bombardment of Germany. Up to the end of 1943, however, he was not unduly alarmed about the Anglo-American air offensive. At Casablanca the Combined Chiefs of Staff had decided that the object of this offensive should be " the progressive destruction and dislocation of the German military, industrial and economic system, and the undermining of the morale of the German people to a point where their capacity for armed resistance is fatally weakened." During the rest of this year little progress had been made towards the achievement of either of these objectives. The United States Strategic Air Forces, operating from the Mediterranean and from Britain, had joined Bomber Command in the assault against the Reich and the weight of attack had been four times greater than in 1942. Yet there had been no proportionate increase in the damage inflicted on German war industry. Reporting on the year's operations, Speer's Ministry said that although bombing had " resulted in some reduction in the output of raw materials and armaments," this had been " held within tolerable limits by energetic repair work."[1]

By far the greater part of the tonnage dropped in 1943 had been delivered by the R.A.F. in area raids at night. These attacks had caused vast physical destruction and heavy civilian casualties, especially in the Ruhr and at Hamburg, but they had not seriously disrupted the output of armaments. There had been local dislocations and temporary delays, but these had soon been made good because there was as yet no shortage of man-power, factory space or industrial equipment. More than six million foreign workers and prisoners of war had already been conscripted into the German economy and their presence had made it unnecessary for Hitler to call up any large number of women or to extend the length of the working week. With few exceptions German armament factories were working shorter hours in 1943 than in 1941 and were still operating on a single-shift basis. Because there was thus a substantial ' cushion ' of reserve capacity to absorb the initial impact of the Allied offensive, Speer was able to maintain—and increase—the output of arms and munitions even in the heavily damaged cities. From Hitler's point of view the indiscriminate British bombing had certain advantages, because it awakened in the German people an urgent sense of national danger and a readiness to make sacrifices which hitherto he had been reluctant to demand.

Although Speer foresaw that Allied bombing was likely to become more severe and more effective in the months ahead, he found it difficult to convince Hitler or Goering that the danger was really serious. In

[1]*Bericht zur Deutschen Wirtschaftslage, 1943-44,* a report prepared by the Planning Department of the Ministry of Armaments and War Production. This report estimated that the ' Incidence of damage ' was greatest in the case of crude steel production and that this would have been 6.4 per cent higher if there had been no bombing.

August 1943, immediately after the devastating R.A.F. raids on Hamburg, Hitler told Doenitz: " The new defensive weapons which technology is providing will make the air raids too costly and will cause them to be discontinued."[1] In November, when the R.A.F. began attacking Berlin in strength, Goering assured a meeting of aircraft manufacturers that the raids on the capital " though heavy, cannot be termed disastrous and are not likely to become so."[2]

The Nazis leaders were encouraged to be complacent not only by the inaccuracy of the British night raids, but also by the limited range of the American daylight penetrations. In October 1943, the Eighth U.S. Air Force had sent its heavy bombers without fighter escort to attack the heart of the German ball-bearing industry at Schweinfurt in Bavaria. Of the 228 bombers engaged, 62 were destroyed and 138 damaged; even more serious, 599 American airmen lost their lives. After this bitter experience the Eighth Air Force decided to abandon all unescorted daylight operations until its fighters had been given greater range. Believing that the Americans could not produce a fighter capable of making deeper penetrations, Goering assured Hitler that German industry had little to fear from air attack by day. The Reichsmarschall continued to hold this belief until he himself narrowly escaped destruction by American fighters which intercepted his private aircraft over Hanover and pursued it to Berlin.

Prior to this chastening experience, Goering had remained sanguine. The comparative failure of the Allied air offensive during 1943 gave the Germans a false sense of security, which led them to underestimate the need for any radical revision of the Luftwaffe's strategy or any great increase in its defensive strength. Yet the German Air Force, and especially its Fighter Arm, was now about to suffer the consequences of the years when too much had been demanded of it and too little had been done to prepare it for the supreme test it would have to face in 1944.

Between the Battle of Britain and the Battle of Stalingrad there had been no serious attempt to expand the Luftwaffe and Hitler had used it mercilessly in his efforts to force a decision in Russia. Thus, although the monthly output of aircraft had been doubled during this period, the losses on the Eastern Front and in the Mediterranean had been so severe that the Luftwaffe's front-line strength was lower at the end of 1942 than it had been two years earlier. Moreover, throughout these years, in tune with Hitler's offensive strategy, priority had been given to the production of bombers and this policy was maintained until the spring of 1943. The preference which Hitler then grudgingly accorded to fighters had led to output being increased from 962 in March to 1,263 in July, but this progress had been interrupted by Allied bombing. This bombing was not heavy, but it was sufficiently accurate to compel the Germans to

[1]Führer Naval Conferences, August 9th, 1943.
[2]Minutes of a meeting between the Reichsmarschall and leaders of the aircraft industry, November 24th, 1943.

carry out a dispersal programme which interrupted both current manufacture and planned expansion. December yielded only 687 new fighters and the year ended with the Fighter Arm weaker than it had been in the summer. This situation could easily have been avoided if prompt use had been made of the reserve productive capacity that was unquestionably available, but Speer had no control over the aircraft industry, Goering was slothful, and Hitler was more interested in the development of V-weapons and jet-aircraft than in the production of conventional fighters.

The case of the 'jets' provides yet another example of the opportunities which Hitler sacrificed to his belief in a short war. As early as 1940 the Luftwaffe General Staff had put forward plans for the production of jet-fighters, but these had been shelved because, according to Galland, who became C.-in-C. of the Fighter Arm, "Hitler thought the war was nearly over." It was not until late in 1942 that the production of 'jets' was undertaken and then it became involved in palace politics. Through his personal influence with the Führer, Willi Messerschmitt obtained priority for the development of a single-jet fighter, a freak aircraft known as the Me 163. General Milch, the Director-General of Aircraft Production, opposed its acceptance for the excellent reasons that it required a highly specialised fuel which was very scarce, that it could carry sufficient of this fuel for only *seven* minutes flying, and that it needed exceptionally long runways. Hitler swept these arguments aside and, at the expense of development of other 'jets,' the output of Me 163s reached 80 a month by the autumn of 1943. The production of fuel, however, could not keep pace and Galland received enough to train only ten pilots a month. This problem had almost been mastered when, in a raid on Hamburg in November of that year, the R.A.F. destroyed a chemical plant which was the sole producer of an indispensable component of the fuel. No substitute could be found and the project had to be abandoned. The lead in jet-propulsion which German science had gained was thus frittered away in two years of neglect and another year of fruitless experiment. Messerschmitt now turned to the production of a twin-jet fighter—the Me 262—with far greater endurance than the '163' and a 'thirst' which could be satisfied with less specialised fuel, but there was little likelihood that this could be produced in large numbers before the Allied invasion of the West.

With the failure of the 'jet' programme and the falling off in the output of conventional fighters in the last quarter of 1943, the Luftwaffe found itself in a most critical position. The number of operational aircraft produced had risen from 12,950 in 1942 to 22,050 in 1943, but even this substantial total barely covered the year's losses, and it represented only one-fifth of the number produced by the United States and Britain. In December Goering was compelled to recognise the need for a vast and rapid expansion of the Fighter Arm. This expansion had barely begun when, on February 19th, 1944, the Allied Air Forces launched a fresh onslaught against German aircraft factories, the Americans attacking by day and the British by night. During the next week a series of telling blows were struck at the main centres of fighter production in Central and Southern Germany which had previously been beyond the range of daylight attack.

The effect on fighter output was immediate and considerable, but the exact extent of the losses inflicted may never be known, for there is reason to believe that factory and departmental records were falsified—apparently with the connivance of Goering and Milch—so that the full scale of the disaster might be hidden from Hitler. A careful cross-check of various sets of German figures indicates, however, that these attacks deprived Hitler of at least 2,500 fighters; 500 destroyed in the air during the offensive, 1,000 destroyed at the factories and another 1,000 lost through the breakdown of production.[1]

Serious though the damage was, the Germans made a remarkable recovery. On March 1st all fighter production was brought under Speer's control and he promptly set about reorganising the industry. Within a month he had restored output to the January level, and in April for the first time the total number of fighters (single and twin-engined) produced was greater than two thousand. Yet this was achieved only at the cost of concentrating on the manufacture of existing models and enforcing such rigid standardisation that no further improvements could be carried out. This was particularly serious so far as the single-engined daylight fighters were concerned for the two main types, the FW 190s and Me 109s, were already out of date by comparison with their American and British opponents.

Because they were obliged to continue using inferior machines, the day fighter squadrons suffered heavy casualties in their efforts to protect the Reich against American attack.[2] The development of long-range escorts, and of new radar equipment for ' blind ' bombing, enabled the Americans to maintain throughout the spring of 1944 a scale of effort which the Luftwaffe had not expected and could not match. At the start of the year Galland had been planning to build up a reserve of a thousand fighters as an ' anti-invasion striking force,' but this plan was endangered as the squadrons he was training and the aircraft he was hoping to save for the Battle of France were drawn into the Battle of Germany.

The overall result of these developments—in the air and at sea, on

---

[1] The Eighth U.S. Air Force claimed the destruction of 692 German fighters in the air during the week. The records of OKL, however, show the loss of only 688 single-engined fighters in action during the month. The estimate of those destroyed at the factories may be too low, for it is known that 465 Me 110s were wiped out and nearly all the American attacks were directed at factories making other types.

[2] The Luftwaffe's records show that in March, April and May 2,442 single-engined fighters were destroyed in action and that at least another 1,500 were lost through accidents and other causes. During the same period the number delivered from the factories was 3,918.

the land battlefronts of the East and South, and within the Reich itself—
was that during the winter of 1943-4 the balance of strength in the West
was swinging in favour of the Allies. As yet, however, the shift in the
balance had done no more than create the preliminary conditions in
which the invasion of France could be undertaken. The triumph of this
assault was by no means assured and, unless it should succeed, there
seemed to be no means by which the United Nations could enforce their
demand for ' Unconditional Surrender.' Hitler's power was still unbroken
and his success in containing the bridgehead which the Allies established
at Anzio in Italy in January 1944, gave him further confidence in his
ability to repulse the cross-Channel assault. He was convinced that if
he could defeat this invasion and then bring his V-weapons and new
U-boats into play, he would remain master of Europe.

## CHAPTER VIII

# FÜHRER PRINZIP IN PRACTICE

WHEN he addressed the *Gauleiter* in November 1943, Jodl concluded with a declaration of his faith in the Führer and a statement of his reasons for believing that Germany would triumph. " My most profound conviction," he said, " is based on the fact that at the head of Germany there stands a man who . . . can only have been destined by Fate to lead our people into a brighter future. . . . In defiance of all views to the contrary, I must testify that he is the soul not only of the political but also of the military conduct of the war, and that the force of his will-power and the creative riches of his thought animate and hold together the whole of the Wehrmacht."

There were not many senior German generals who would have endorsed this appraisal of the Führer's military prowess, but none could deny that he was the driving force behind the German war machine. His early victories, and his defensive success during the first bitter winter in Russia, had strengthened his faith in his own infallibility and his conviction that war was primarily a question of will. " In Hitler's opinion," says Speer, " military leadership was a matter of intellect, tenacity and nerves of iron. He felt that he possessed these qualities to a much higher degree than any of his generals. He felt that he alone was tough and inflexible enough to withstand the blows of Fate."[1] Hitler believed that success in battle was merely a question of having the courage to be more ruthless and more brutal than the enemy. Readiness to hazard all in attack, refusal to yield a yard in defence; these he thought were the supreme military qualities which would bring victory regardless of the material balance of power. In addition he had a remarkable sense of strategic opportunity and a flair for the unorthodox and the unexpected, but he had no idea how to fight a battle for position —an operation requiring professional skill in the tactical handling of armies.

Because Hitler lacked this skill, his generals were all too ready to dismiss him as a ' facile amateur ' or a ' jumped-up corporal.' But, in

---

[1] All quotations from Speer in this chapter have been taken from a paper he wrote on Hitler for the Field Intelligence Agency (Technical) of the U.S. Army in 1945.

fact, he had studied far more thoroughly and widely than most of his
officers the works of the outstanding German commanders and military
writers from Frederick the Great and Clausewitz to Moltke, Schlieffen
and Seeckt. He continued to read voraciously throughout the early years
of the war and he acquired an exceptional grasp of technical detail.
According to Speer, " On matters of Army equipment his knowledge
was far superior to that of his military staff. He was better informed
than they about the characteristics of specific weapons and tanks, types
of ammunition and armament innovations. Actually, he knew more
than was good for a man in his exalted position."

To a great extent Hitler's wide military reading and his extraordinary
memory for detail made good his lack of professional training, and in
one respect this deficiency was a decided advantage so long as Germany
held the initiative. He possessed a radical approach to almost every
problem and his military thinking was untrammelled by the conventional
ideas, standing regulations and established procedures which cramped
the mind and limited the imagination of the regular German staff officer.
Because of his very unorthodoxy, Hitler exerted a decisive influence on
the campaigns of the first two years of the war. Germany's successes
then were due not only to her superior strength in men and weapons,
but to the boldness and originality of Hitler's strategy.

" War has been erected into a secret science and surrounded with
momentous solemnity," said Hitler to Hermann Rauschning in 1933,
" but war is the most natural, the most everyday matter . . . War is life."[1]
To the conduct of war Hitler applied those methods which had brought
him success in the political sphere. There, he had always been a
revolutionary and an authoritarian. He had never understood the
democratic process of reasoned discussion leading to a solution which will
fit the facts. For him the political forum had been the place for declama-
tion, not debate. During his rise to power he had dealt with his opponents
by shouting them down, by breaking up their meetings with his storm-
troops, by passionate assertion of his own viewpoint and an equally
passionate denunciation of any other. Within the Reich he became so
powerful that he had only to express his will and his orders were carried
out. The reality of absolute power at home gave him the illusion of
absolute power abroad, and this illusion gained an appearance of reality
through his early triumphs, which he attributed almost entirely to his
own genius, determination and intuition. Thereafter, his entourage—
and especially the ever-present Martin Bormann, ' the Führer's Brown
Shadow,' who combined the offices of private secretary and Head of the
Party Chancery—fostered this illusion by endeavouring to keep from
him any facts which might undermine his faith in himself and his mission.
Their object was, says Speer, to maintain Hitler's *nachtwandlerische
Sicherheit*, his ' sleepwalker's sense of security.'

From the time he assumed direct command of the Army in December

[1]Rauschning, op. cit., p. 16.

1941, Hitler seldom visited either Berlin or the battlefronts. Apart from occasional sojourns at Berchtesgaden, he immured himself in his Field H.Q., first at Vinnitsa in the Ukraine and then at Rastenburg in East Prussia. "The Führer's H.Q.," said Jodl at Nuremberg, "was a mixture of cloister and concentration camp. . . . Apart from reports on the situation, very little news from the outer world penetrated into this holy of holies."[1] Even that news was carefully censored before distribution and was allowed a very limited circulation. By Hitler's order, Foreign Office intelligence was not supplied to the General Staff, nor was military intelligence made available to the Wilhelmstrasse. The records of the Führer Naval Conferences show that even Doenitz had to apply to Hitler for " permission to see the Foreign Office reports regarding the enemy." This was given, but, say the minutes, " the Führer . . . emphasises that the reports are exlusively for the personal information of the Commander-in-Chief, Navy."[2]

During the war the Reich Cabinet never met, except to ' rubber-stamp ' decisions Hitler had already made. His political, economic and military advisers were called to joint conferences only on the rarest occasions and then they were summoned to listen or to provide information, not to advise or to take part in a round-table discussion. At Nuremberg Keitel reported that, when Hitler did seek advice, " Ministers or special plenipotentiaries visited headquarters according to a plan which seldom required the simultaneous presence of several of them. . . . Hitler dealt with each of these officials and functionaries separately, gave him his orders and dismissed him."[3] There is no reason to doubt Keitel's assertion that " no one was told more than the Führer wanted him to know," or the statement of Doenitz that " only the Führer had an overall picture."

The restriction Hitler imposed on the information available to his subordinates was an essential feature of his exercise of power, for it meant that no one could argue with him on a basis of equal knowledge. If Jodl were to oppose a particular decision on military grounds, he could be answered with a political explanation, the validity of which he could not contest. Similarly, a protest from Speer, based on economic considerations, could be silenced by resort to strategic calculations of which he knew nothing. Thus, by curtailing the knowledge of those around him, Hitler curtailed their power and proportionately enhanced his own. This, in turn, made them the more dependent on him. After a long private session with Hitler in August 1943, Doenitz wrote, " The enormous strength which the Führer radiates, his unwavering confidence and his far-sighted appraisal of the Italian situation have made it clear that in these days we are all very insignificant in comparison with the Führer, and that our knowledge and the picture we get from our limited

[1] *Nuremberg Trial Proceedings*, Part xv, p. 283.
[2] *Führer Naval Conferences*, July 8th, 1943.
[3] *Nuremberg Trial Proceedings*, Part x, pp. 318-19.

vantage-point are fragmentary. Anyone who believes that he can do better than the Führer is stupid."[1]

Men of real character and independence did not survive long in his intimate circle, yet it would be an oversimplification to dismiss all his associates as 'yes-men' like Ribbentrop, or sycophants like Keitel, or time-servers like Bormann. Even men of considerable ability in their own departments, such as Speer, Doenitz and Jodl, who had the intelligence to see the consequences of his policy and the courage to speak out, came under the spell of his personality.

Speer says, " All his associates who had worked closely with him for a long time were entirely dependent on and obedient to him. However forceful their behaviour in their own sphere, in his presence they were insignificant and timid. Cowardice alone does not account for this. As a result of their long co-operation, they not only developed an uncanny faith in him but also fell completely under his influence. They were in his spell, blindly subservient to him and with no will of their own. I noticed that being in his presence for any length of time made me exhausted and void." Doenitz, who was regarded by his subordinates in the Navy as a hard and inflexible commander, makes a similar confession: " I purposely went very seldom to his H.Q., for I had the feeling that I would thus best preserve my power of initiative, and also because after several days there I always had the feeling that I must disengage myself from his power of suggestion."[2]

Jodl, who was subjected to this power more persistently perhaps than anyone else and who witnessed its repeated application to others, declared at Nuremberg: " Hitler's knowledge and his intellect, his rhetoric and his will-power triumphed in the end in every spiritual conflict over every adversary."[3] That is the universal verdict of the men who came into close contact with Hitler. Those who submitted came to regard him as a genius, but Halder, who managed to preserve some detachment, says, " A man who for twelve years set not only Central Europe but the whole world in commotion, must have been more than life sized, but I never found genius in him, only the diabolical."[4]

Although Hitler's power was absolute and unchallengeable, his exercise of it was vitiated by temperamental instability and lack of experience in the operational direction of armies. His shortcomings were more and more apparent once he had lost the strategic initiative, for he discovered, as he said in December 1942, that " It's a thousand times easier to storm forward with an army and gain victories, than to bring

---

[1]*Führer Naval Conferences*, August 9th, 1943.
[2]*Nuremberg Trial Proceedings*, Part xiii, pp. 243-4.
[3]Ibid., Part xv, pp. 287-8.
[4]U.S. Army Interrogation.

an army back in an orderly condition after a reverse or a defeat."[1] The circumstances of 1943 demanded a professional skill which Hitler did not possess, but he continued to insist that even detailed tactical decisions must be referred to him as C.-in-C. of the Army. During the first winter in Russia, convinced that the Wehrmacht's only weakness was lack of resolution on the part of its senior officers, he had given instructions that in future no commander was to order even a minor tactical withdrawal without his permission. This order was so rigidly enforced that it was a common quip among officers on the Eastern Front that a battalion commander dared not move a sentry from the window to the door. At his staff conferences, held twice daily, Hitler would demand information and issue orders about the movement of particular battalions and the capture or defence of minor objectives. The result was that strategic planning, which should have been the concern of the Supreme Command, was neglected, while tactical operations, which should not, were interfered with more and more.

The excessive concentration of power in Hitler's hands, and his refusal to allow his field commanders any discretion, imposed upon his armies a system of control which was both rigid and unpredictable. Sometimes there was a reckless abandon when his intuition ran wild and he provided answers to complex questions by relying on his infallibility or by gambling on his good luck. At other times there was paralysis at the top and, says Speer, " Important decisions would hang over his head for months without his being able to make up his mind even though it was imperative that he should do so." Speer felt that this was mainly due to overwork. " As the predicaments brought about by the situation in the field grew more serious," he says, " Hitler's suspicions of his military entourage intensified, prompting him continually to enlarge his own volume of work and making his condition of overstrain worse and increasingly pathological. . . . He forced himself to become a diligent, methodical worker and this neither suited his personality nor benefited his decisions. . . . He lost his gift for working intuitively which had been his main asset. . . . Yet, when he tried to work rationally and logically, he was often incapable of coming to a decision."

As the tide of war turned against him, his procrastination became more serious, for it was accentuated by his refusal to admit the truth. " Strategic problems," says Halder, " were not tackled in accordance with any long-term plan, nor even in the light of a full and rational examination of the facts. Hitler lived in a world of self-deception and overconfidence which prevented him from distinguishing the possible from the impossible. At his H.Q. intuition prevailed over reason, improvisation over planning. In fact, after October 1942, no long-range planning studies were made because these could only have reached conclusions which Hitler would not accept."

The disastrous consequences of Hitler's method of command were

[1]Führer Conferences, Fragment 8, December 12th, 1942.

appreciated by many, if not most, of his senior generals, but the habit of obedience was so ingrained in them that they accepted his tyrannical and erratic control with little demur. They complained bitterly to each other, but they seldom challenged his decisions to his face and they shrank from taking any direct action against him. They were deterred by their oath, and by the fear that another ' stab-in-the-back ' legend would grow up, with the guilt this time on the officer corps. Moreover, they knew that the rank and file of the Wehrmacht and the mass of civilians still had great faith in the Führer's leadership and that his authority on the home front had been strengthened, not weakened, by the threat of Communist invasion and the reality of Allied bombing. During 1943, awakened at last to the realisation that their security and their future were directly challenged, the German people, instead of turning against Hitler, were roused to give him greater support.

While this was broadly true, there was during this year a steady increase in the strength and extent of anti-Nazi feeling within the Reich. When he spoke to the *Gauleiter* in November, Jodl said, " Up and down the country the devil of subversion strides. All the cowards are seeking a way out, or—as they call it—a political solution. They say that we must negotiate while there is something in hand. . . . They attack the people's natural instinct that in this war there can only be a fight to a finish. Capitulation is the end of the Nation, the end of Germany."

The development of opposition to Hitler had been a slow and dangerous process. Long before the outbreak of war the Nazis had destroyed the old centres of resistance—the political parties and the trade unions of the Weimar Republic. The sending of a quarter of a million Germans to concentration camps in ten years was testimony of Himmler's ruthless counter-measures. Once the rule of the Gestapo had been established, the revival of organised opposition on a nation-wide scale had become almost impossible, and during the early years of the war the enemies of the Nazi régime could do little more than keep the spirit of resistance alive in local or sectional groups. The loose alliance between these groups was not a coalition of parties, representing a national resistance movement, as in France, but rather an association of individuals whose motives and aims were as varied as their political and social backgrounds. The sole unifying force was the desire to over-throw Hitler and to end the war. The only common link was their recognition of the leadership of General Ludwig Beck, the former Chief of the Army General Staff, who had resigned on the eve of the Munich crisis, and had been unfaltering in his opposition to Hitler ever since. Beck's moral stature was unquestioned, but he had little political under-standing and he did not play any active part in the organisation of the actual conspiracy.

If Beck was the ' head ' of the Opposition, the ' heart ' was Dr. Karl Goerdeler, a former Burgomeister of Leipzig. Goerdeler's zeal and energy were boundless, but his excessive optimism and his lack of discretion discouraged many who were sympathetic to his cause. Politically, Goerdeler was a conservative and his closest associates were former members of right-wing parties or officials who had no party affiliations but were anxious to see the rule of law re-established. What Beck, Goerdeler and their friends wanted was a political revolt, not an economic and social revolution. Accordingly, it was difficult for them to gain support from the Left, except among the more moderate Social Democrats, such as Julius Leber and Adolf Reichwein, who believed that the supreme considerations were the removal of Hitler and the cessation of hostilities, and who realised that no *putsch* could succeed unless it were carried through with the aid of the Army. The revolt would have to come from above.

The slow development of the conspirators' plans for the overthrow of the Nazi régime was a reflection of the inherent difficulty of organising a successful revolt in a police state at war. Their first problem was to find or create the opportunity of assassinating Hitler, for so long as he lived the members of the officer corps and the civil service would remain bound to him by their oath of loyalty. Moreover, if Germany was to be saved from internal chaos and from being left helpless at the mercy of her external enemies, it was essential that the conspirators should be able not merely to set up a government of their own, but also to maintain the battlefronts intact while they were negotiating with the Allies for an armistice.

The only power capable of challenging Hitler's authority from within lay in the Army, but in the early years of the war the Opposition had gained little encouragement from this quarter. Few of the generals were prepared to forego the opportunity of taking part in the conquest of Europe even under Hitler's leadership. They resented his usurpation of supreme military power and his violent outbursts against the officer class, but for the most part it was military defeat, not moral scruple, which turned them against him. The Stalingrad crisis greatly strengthened the influence of the Opposition, and in January 1943 there was a strong move among the leading generals on the Eastern Front to denounce Hitler's military leadership and to demand that he should appoint a soldier of high standing as C.-in-C., Army. This move did not mature and, when the Allies proclaimed their demand for ' Unconditional Surrender,' even commanders like von Kluge and von Manstein, who foresaw where Hitler's policy was leading Germany, refused to act against him. Since it seemed that the Allies were determined to destroy the German military caste, the generals were prepared to give Hitler another chance to bring off a miracle and secure a victory which would enable Germany to make ' peace with honour,' that is, a peace which would ensure their own survival.

This was a grave disappointment to Beck and Goerdeler, and during 1943 their plans suffered two further setbacks. The first was the failure of an attempt on Hitler's life. This was planned by a group of officers at von Kluge's H.Q., but it miscarried because a time-bomb, placed in the Führer's aircraft on March 13th when he was returning from one of his rare visits to the front, failed to explode. The second setback was the collapse of the organisation which the conspirators had established through the Abwehr, the Counter-Intelligence Service of OKW. The chief of the Abwehr, Admiral Wilhelm Canaris, was an anti-Nazi by conviction but he preferred to play a lone hand against Hitler and he did not actively join the ranks of the Opposition. Nevertheless, he shielded and aided its members and turned a blind eye to the treasonable activities of his principal assistant, Major-General Hans Oster. Exploiting the secrecy which naturally surrounds espionage, Oster had become the chief executive of the conspiracy and had developed a network of communications between the various underground groups. In the spring of 1943, however, one of Oster's staff, Hans Dohnanyi, was arrested by the Gestapo and later in the year Oster himself was driven from office. With his disappearance the plotters had to set about rebuilding the organisation by which they planned to seize power as soon as Hitler had been killed. This task was entrusted to a young colonel, Count Klaus von Stauffenberg, who after being badly wounded in North Africa had been posted to Berlin as Chief of Staff to General Friedrich Olbricht, the deputy commander of the Home Army.

Olbricht was a leading member of the conspiracy and with his help the plotters had already made plans for using Home Army units to seize control of the capital and the principal cities, and Home Army communications—the only network not under Himmler's control—to bring about the transfer of power. Stauffenberg, a man of deep Christian faith and strong moral conviction, brought to his task both fervour and courage, but his first attempt to strike at Hitler, in December 1943, was frustrated by the last-minute cancellation of the conference at which he had intended to set off a bomb in a brief-case. After this no further opportunity developed during the winter, and with the coming of spring and the expectation of invasion in the West the conspirators were in doubt whether they should endeavour to strike before the Allies landed or should wait to see the outcome. It seemed that if the invasion were to fail or to prove very costly, the Western Allies might be prepared to grant Germany reasonable terms. On the other hand, if it were to succeed, the war would be irretrievably lost and the conspirators might at least count upon greater support from the Army and the people. In any event, their position would be stronger, either at home or abroad, after the invasion had been launched. Within the Opposition there was much disagreement, but the prevailing opinion was that they should stay their hands for the moment. Thus, even though the opposition to the Nazis was to increase during the first half of 1944, the régime was safe from serious political challenge at least until the Allies had made their long-awaited attack in the West.

## CHAPTER IX

# FROM COSSAC TO SHAEF

ON the last day of 1943 Winston Churchill sat in the sun at Marrakech, in French Morocco, recovering from a severe bout of pneumonia. The year that was just ending had been one of almost unbroken success for Allied arms against Germany. At sea, the U-boat had been heavily defeated, and the Mediterranean had been reopened. In the air the Western Powers were now dominant and the strategic bombardment of Germany had reached a new peak with the introduction of the long-range American fighter, which made it possible for the Allies to attack any target in the Reich with a thousand bombers by day as well as by night. On land the severe defeats in Russia and the Mediterranean had cost Hitler more than a million men killed or captured in the past twelve months. The fatal casualties of the German Army now exceeded the total for the war of 1914-18. The Wehrmacht had been stretched, as well as bled, for the Anglo-American offensive in the Mediterranean, and the consequent collapse of Italy and inflammation of Yugoslavia, had compelled Hitler to dispose as many divisions in Southern Europe as he had in the West.

In spite of destruction at home and disaster and dispersion abroad, Nazi Germany was still far from defeat. There was no indication that the German war machine was running down, that civilian morale was about to crack or that there was any resistance movement strong enough to challenge Hitler's authority. There was still a large cushion of occupied territory around the heart of Germany. The Red Army had driven the Wehrmacht back from the Volga to the Dnieper, but it was still nearly five hundred miles from the borders of Germany proper. In Italy the Allied advance had been brought to a standstill for the moment by mountains and mud, and by skilful and determined defence which provided stern warning of the continued fighting spirit of the ordinary German soldier. Along the Western coast of Europe the Nazis still stood firm and every week saw an increase in the strength of their Atlantic Wall which blocked the short road to the Reich and the Ruhr.

The German armament industry had not only reached an unprecedented level of output but was rightly believed to be producing weapons which could give it a marked qualitative superiority in aerial and naval warfare. There were rumours of new U-boats and jet-propelled aircraft and, so far as Allied scientists could tell, it was not beyond the bounds of possibility that the Germans were successfully developing an atomic bomb. In any event, there was ample evidence from the Pas de Calais of preparations for the launching of rockets and other secret weapons at which Goebbels was hinting. It was clear now that this grave threat could not be removed, nor could the final defeat of Germany be brought about until Anglo-American armies had broken into the Nazi Fortress from the West.

The invasion of France was the major task for the year ahead, but Churchill still had grave doubts about its accomplishment. The target date which he and the President had named to Stalin was only four months away, but the Supreme Commander had not yet taken over, the final plan was not settled, and the detailed preparations were proceeding on the basis of the original COSSAC proposal. No provision had been made for the 25 per cent increase in the weight of assault which the Prime Minister had suggested at Quebec; in fact, the Combined Chiefs of Staff had not yet allocated sufficient shipping even for the requirements of the COSSAC Plan.

In drawing up this plan Morgan and Barker had been handicapped, as already mentioned, by the strict limitation of the shipping allocated to them, and by the atmosphere of doubt which prevailed in Britain about the whole OVERLORD project. They had inherited from the Combined Commanders[1] a series of planning studies (detailed and thorough but pessimistic in tone) which led to the conclusion that a cross-Channel attack could not be attempted until there was assault shipping for ten divisions. The COSSAC planners had been given sufficient for five. When Morgan took office, Brooke, the C.I.G.S., outlined to him the problem and the resources available, and then added, " Well, there it is. It won't work but you must bloody well make it."

With this as his motto Morgan began planning in March 1943. He started by gathering round him British and American officers who believed that the operation was possible, but it was an uphill battle. The shadow of Dunkirk, Norway and Greece still hung over the army which was being trained in England, and few of its senior officers believed that any cross-Channel invasion could succeed except at a ghastly price. The Combined Commanders had come to regard it as a desperate venture, which would lead at best to a battle of attrition in the '14-'18 style, fought along a narrow coastal strip. They had been so preoccupied with the problems of getting and staying ashore that they had hardly turned their minds to the extensive operations which must be developed if the invasion was going to yield any real dividend.

Morgan had been ordered by the Combined Chiefs of Staff not only

[1]This was the title of the inter-service committee appointed by Churchill in 1942 to study the problem of cross-Channel invasion and prepare tentative plans.

to draw up a plan of assault, but to prepare for a campaign which would deliver a vital blow at the heart of Germany with a force of 100 divisions. Their directive to him declared that the object of OVERLORD was:

> To mount and carry out an operation, with forces and equipment established in the United Kingdom and with target date 1 May, 1944, to secure a lodgment on the Continent from which further offensive operations could be developed. The lodgment area must contain sufficient port facilities to maintain a force of some twenty-six to thirty divisions and enable that force to be augmented by follow-up shipments from the United States or elsewhere of additional divisions and supporting units at the rate of three to five divisions per month.

COSSAC's first problem was: where to attack? The Nazis held three thousand miles of coastline in Western Europe, but the area of possible assault was narrowed to the 300-mile stretch between Flushing and Cherbourg, since this was the only sector which could be adequately covered by fighter aircraft based on Great Britain.[1] Next, the area chosen must include harbours capable of handling the vast build-up, and ample beaches across which the assault forces could be reinforced during the weeks before ports could be captured and cleared. These factors restricted the possible areas of assault to two: the Pas de Calais, between Dunkirk and the mouth of the Somme, and Western Normandy, between Caen and the Cotentin Peninsula.

> The Pas de Calais [the planners reported] has many obvious advantages such as that good air support and quick turn-around for our shipping can be achieved. On the other hand, it is a focal point of the enemy fighters disposed for defence and the maximum air activity can be brought to bear over this area with the minimum movement of his Air Forces. Moreover, the Pas de Calais is the most strongly defended area of the whole French coast. . . . Further this area does not offer good opportunities for expansion. It would be necessary to develop the bridgehead to include either the Belgian ports as far as Antwerp, or the Channel ports westward to include Le Havre and Rouen. But both an advance to Antwerp across the numerous water-obstacles, and a long flank march of some 120 miles to the Seine ports must be considered unsound operations of war unless the German forces are in a state not far short of final collapse.

Normandy had fewer drawbacks. The turn-around of shipping would be slower, but this, Morgan's staff decided, should be counteracted by the fact that :

[1]The basic factor in considering air cover was the range of the Spitfire, for, although American fighters were soon to have almost double its range, approximately half the fighter cover would have to be provided by Spitfires of the R.A.F. (See Morgan, *Overture to Overlord*, p. 51.)

the Caen sector is weakly held; the defences are relatively light and the beaches are of high capacity and sheltered from the prevailing winds. Inland the terrian is suitable for airfield development and for the consolidation of the initial bridgehead; and much of it is unfavourable for counter-attacks by panzer divisions. Maximum enemy air opposition can only be brought to bear at the expense of the air defence screen covering the approaches to Germany; and the limited number of enemy airfields within range of the Caen area facilitates the local neutralisation of the German fighter force. The sector suffers from the disadvantage that considerable efforts will be required to provide adequate air support for our assault forces and some time must elapse before the capture of a major port.

In order to speed up the capture of Cherbourg they considered the possibility of landing on the Cotentin as well as on the Caen beaches, but decided that this was " unsound [because] it would entail dividing our limited forces by the low-lying marshy ground and the intricate river system at the neck of the Cotentin Peninsula, thus exposing them to defeat in detail. . . . In the light of these factors it is considered that our initial landing on the Continent should be effected in the Caen area with a view to the eventual seizure of a lodgment area comprising the Cherbourg–Brittany group of ports."[1]

COSSAC's next problem was to settle the weight of the attack, but in this its discretion was strictly limited. Morgan's orders had stated that craft would be provided for an assault from the sea with five divisions and from the air with two more, but, when he came to examine his actual resources, he found that he could lift only two airborne brigades and three seaborne divisions. The original over-estimate, it seems, was the result of a fundamental error in Washington, on the part of the planners who had advised the Combined Chiefs of Staff. They had failed to make due allowance for the fact that in an assault, when a landing-craft is a ' weapon' as well as a vessel, it cannot be loaded to its full nominal capacity. A certain type of LST (Landing-Ship, Tank) may be able to carry 30 tanks closely packed for convoy travel, but it may be impossible to land from it more than 25 tanks at one time on a particular beach. Hence its *unloading* capacity, not its *carrying* capacity, is the decisive factor. This was the first of a series of planning miscalculations which Morgan, and later Eisenhower, had to fight against before they could extract from Washington the shipping they required.

This shortage of landing-craft reduced the scale of the assault, as COSSAC had to plan it, to a level which prejudiced success except in the most favourable circumstances. Consequently, Morgan had to stipulate that the operation could be carried out only if the enemy had no more than twelve mobile divisions in reserve in France at the time of the

---

[1] As the assault phase of OVERLORD was given the code-name NEPTUNE, the Caen–Cherbourg area became known as the ' NEPTUNE area.'

invasion, and if there were no more than three of these divisions in the Caen area on D-Day, no more than five by D plus 2, and no more than nine by D plus 8.

The inclusion of these provisos was taken by some American critics of the plan as evidence of British faint-heartedness, but Morgan had to cut his pattern to his cloth. All he did was to lay down the ratio necessary for victory and it can hardly be alleged that he demanded over-insurance. The great contribution of the COSSAC staff to OVERLORD was not that they devised a final or even a feasible plan for invasion, but that they determined the basic considerations which would govern success and overcame most of the practical difficulties which had seemed insurmountable to earlier planners.

The weaknesses of the COSSAC Plan might have been remedied in good time if the Supreme Commander (and his Commanders-in-Chief) had been appointed at Quebec in August 1943, when Morgan's draft proposals were approved. At this conference Churchill warmly accepted Roosevelt's suggestion that the Supreme Commander for OVERLORD should be Marshall, but no formal decision was recorded. When this proposal became known in Washington, it was strongly criticised not only by Roosevelt's enemies but by many who sincerely felt that Marshall was indispensable as Chief of Staff. Among the latter were Marshall's own colleagues on the U.S. Joint Chiefs of Staff, who felt, as King said, that they " should not break up a winning combination." General J. J. Pershing, who had commanded the A.E.F. in the First World War, was of the same opinion. When Pershing, on September 16th, protested that " the suggested transfer of General Marshall would be a . . . very grave error in our military policy," the President wrote in reply: " I think it is only a fair thing to give George a chance in the field. . . . I want him to be the Pershing of the Second World War."[1]

Meanwhile, the public outcry against the President's plan reached serious proportions, for, says his Secretary of War (Henry Stimson), " persons eager to discredit the administration claimed that it was a British plot to remove his [Marshall's] influence from the central direction of the war."[2] In the hope of disarming these critics by giving Marshall an appointment which would unquestionably enhance his authority and prestige, Stimson proposed that he should take over the direction of all operations against Germany: OVERLORD, the Mediterranean campaign and strategic bombing. This idea was not acceptable to the British, who argued that such an omnibus command would be militarily unworkable and would render the Combined Chiefs of Staff almost superfluous. At the first Cairo Conference in November Churchill reaffirmed his eager-

[1] These letters are quoted in full by Mrs. George C. Marshall in her book, *Together*, p. 120.
[2] Stimson, op. cit., p. 440.

ness to have Marshall take charge of the cross-Channel invasion, but he found that the President had not yet made up his mind. Roosevelt might have reached a decision more easily and earlier if Marshall's natural reserve and selflessness had not inhibited him from indicating his own preference. Under pressure he admitted to Stimson that " any soldier would prefer a field command," but he would make no such admission to Roosevelt. His sense of duty was stronger than his ambition. He knew that his place was in Washington, but he was too modest to suggest that he could not be spared. Stimson says that before Teheran he " begged Marshall not to sacrifice what I considered the interests of the country to the undue sensitiveness of his own conscience in seeming to seek a post."[1] But after Teheran, when Roosevelt as good as offered him the OVERLORD crown, Marshall insisted that the President must make the choice. Roosevelt interpreted this reluctance as a tacit confession that Marshall wanted to remain as Chief of Staff, and in his heart he wanted this too, for he said to Marshall, " I could not sleep at night with you out of the country."[2] The President decided therefore that Marshall should remain in Washington and that Eisenhower should lead the invasion.

This was undoubtedly the right decision, for Marshall's grasp of political and administrative factors at home and of the military complexities of global war, made him irreplaceable as Chief of Staff. But it was most unfortunate that the settlement of the OVERLORD command was deferred so long, since it meant a delay of three or four months in the development of the COSSAC Plan. This remained in a tentative and unsatisfactory form until there was a Supreme Commander who could bang the table and demand sufficient resources to make it practicable.

As finally settled the pattern of command was this:[3] at SHAEF (Supreme Headquarters, Allied Expeditionary Force) Air Chief Marshal Sir Arthur Tedder became Deputy to Eisenhower, who had Lieut.-General W. Bedell Smith as his Chief of Staff; Admiral Sir Bertram Ramsay and Air Chief Marshal Sir Trafford Leigh-Mallory had been appointed earlier as the Commanders-in-Chief of the Allied Naval and Air Forces respectively, but there was no corresponding appointment of a C.-in-C., Allied Land Forces; General Sir Bernard Montgomery, who came from the Eighth Army to take over the British 21st Army Group was given operational control over all land forces in the assault phase, but it was understood that Eisenhower would assume direct command of land operations himself when an American Army Group took the field under Lieut.-General Omar Bradley. In the meantime, Bradley would lead the American assault forces as Commanding General, First U.S. Army.

Stimson, op. cit., p. 442. Here Stimson quotes the entry he made in his diary at the time.

[2] Marshall himself reported the President's comment to Sherwood. See Sherwood, op. cit., p. 803.

[3] See Appendix B for a chart of the OVERLORD Command Organisation.

As soon as they could lay down their Mediterranean responsibilities, Eisenhower set out for Washington and Montgomery for London, both travelling via Marrakech in order to confer with the Prime Minister. There on New Year's Eve Churchill produced for them a copy of the COSSAC Plan. This was the first time Montgomery had seen it, but Eisenhower had perused it unofficially in October and had then commented that the assault would have to be launched " in greater weight and on a broader front " with the particular object of ensuring the early capture of Cherbourg. At that time his interest had been academic, but he now repeated this criticism, which Montgomery emphatically endorsed. Next day Eisenhower left for the United States after instructing Montgomery to make his first task in London the revision of the plan in conjunction with Ramsay, Leigh-Mallory and Bedell Smith.

The COSSAC Plan provided that the assault should be made by one army on a frontage of one corps with three divisions, and that three other corps, each with three or four divisions, should be landed behind the assault formations as rapidly as possible and should leap-frog through them. To Montgomery's orderly and incisive mind this was " simply not an operation of war." In a memorandum to Churchill on January 1st he suggested what the outcome would be. " By D plus 12," he wrote, " a total of twelve divisions have been landed on the same beaches as were used for the initial landings. This would lead to the most appalling confusion on the beaches and the smooth development of the land battle would be made extremely difficult, if not impossible. Further divisions come pouring in, all over the same beaches . . . the confusion instead of getting better, would rapidly get worse."

He declared that the " initial landings must be made on the widest possible front "; that " one British Army [should] land on a front of two, or possibly three, Corps. One American Army similarly "; and that during the assault phase " Corps must be able to develop their operations from their own beaches and other Corps must not land through those beaches."

In this criticism Montgomery put his finger on planning weaknesses which would have seriously handicapped the tactical and logistic[1] development of the assault. He was convinced that an adequate bridgehead must be secured at the very start in order to provide a base firm enough and large enough for exploitation. Otherwise the invaders would be unable to outstrip the enemy's build-up and his " reserve formations might succeed in containing us within a shallow covering position with our beaches under continual artillery fire."

After discussions in London in the first fortnight of January, Montgomery suggested that the frontage of assault should be widened to include the beaches at the mouth of the Orne and on the east coast of the Cotentin Peninsula at the head of which stands Cherbourg. In

---

[1]Logistics is the branch of military science dealing with the movement and supply of armed forces.

his view the existence of the flooded area across the base of the Peninsula made it absolutely imperative that a strong force should be landed on the Cotentin so as to turn—and indeed to make use of—the water-barrier which would otherwise block the road to the only good port in the invasion area. But, since the flooding also obstructed the exits from the only suitable beaches on this coast, Montgomery intended that the necessary strength should be ensured by dropping airborne divisions beyond the inundations. This operation was firmly opposed by Leigh-Mallory, who declared that the flak defences of this area were so strong and the terrain so unsuitable for the landing of gliders and parachutists that the losses in personnel and aircraft might run as high as 75 or 80 per cent. Montgomery regarded this estimate as unduly pessimistic, and he persisted in his recommendation, for he and Bradley believed that only the employment of powerful airborne forces could guarantee the early capture of Cherbourg.

In addition, Montgomery wanted to give more power to the main assault against the beaches between the Orne and the Vire. He felt that the COSSAC planners had been too sanguine in their calculations that the bridgehead could be expanded to the line Mont St. Michel–Alençon–Trouville by D plus 14; that they had made too little allowance for bad weather, which could be expected to interfere seriously with unloading and disembarkation on one day in four; and that, even if all were to go well, the COSSAC rate of build-up could not provide sufficient strength ashore to meet the concentrated counter-attack with armour which could be expected about D plus 4.

Accordingly, Montgomery proposed that the invasion should be launched by two, and if possible three, airborne divisions (not two brigades) followed within a few hours by an assault from the sea by five divisions (not three) with two more divisions, pre-loaded in landing-craft, for the immediate follow-up. This meant extending the frontage of the assault from 25 miles to 50, and increasing the weight of the initial landings from the sea by 40 per cent and from the air by 200 per cent.

It was easier to plan these increases than to find the means of implementing them. Ramsay strongly favoured the revision, but he had to report that the Admiralty did not yet know whether it could meet even the COSSAC requirements: 3,323 landing-craft,[1] 467 warships and 150 minesweepers. He would now need nearly double this number of minesweepers, an additional 240 warships and a further thousand landing-craft. It was soon evident that these deficiencies could not be made good by May 1st. Ramsay and Montgomery therefore proposed that the invasion should not be launched until early June, thus gaining another month's production from the shipyards; that landing-craft should be borrowed from the Mediterranean, even if this should mean that ANVIL could not be undertaken at the same time as OVERLORD; and that the

[1]Here and elsewhere, unless the sense indicates otherwise, the term 'landing-craft' is used generically and includes 'landing-ships.'

U.S. Navy should be asked to provide a Task Force for escort and bombardment.

On January 21st Eisenhower endorsed these proposals and over-ruled Leigh-Mallory's objections to the airborne operation on the Cotentin. As it turned out, this postponement was to prove most un-fortunate for the Anglo-Saxon cause, but, by the time Eisenhower and Montgomery took up their appointments, it was already too late to complete the, preparations by May 1st. The responsibility for this must be laid at the door of the Combined Chiefs of Staff and particularly its American members. In August 1943, they had accepted the COSSAC Plan and fixed the target date, but they did not make then and there the decisions necessary to ensure its success. They rejected Churchill's suggestion for strengthening the assault and, as late as the Cairo confer-ence in December, had confirmed their original decision that all the warships for OVERLORD and two-thirds of the landing-craft should be provided by the navies of Great Britain, the Dominions and the European Allies. So little did the Americans appreciate the seriousness of the shipping situation, that late in 1943 the U.S. Navy transferred landing-craft from the Mediterranean to the Pacific.

These difficulties might have been more easily solved if the Supreme Commander and his Commanders-in-Chief had been appointed at Quebec. In that case Eisenhower, Montgomery and Ramsay could have been released from their responsibilities in the Mediterranean after the fall of Naples on October 1st, could then have revised the COSSAC Plan and presented before the end of October the recommendations which they now made three months later. Had this been done OVERLORD's landing-craft problems could have been solved with comparative ease, since the crux of the problem was not, as has been supposed, the ' bottleneck of production.'

During 1943, by remarkable energy and organisation, the tonnage of landing-craft produced in the United States was trebled and 19,482 craft (not counting amphibious vehicles) came from American slipways that year. In May 1943, however, when the Combined Chiefs of Staff made their detailed allocation of shipping for the COSSAC Planners, all that could be provided for the invasion which was to be launched in twelve months' time were 3,323 landing-craft and of these the United States Navy agreed to contribute only 1,024, five per cent of the strength it was to have at the end of that year. This decision was endorsed at Cairo in December. According to Marshall, the problem was the " acute shortage of landing-craft . . . the Mediterranean theater could be bled no further . . . the shipyards broke all records . . . but there were still not enough landing-craft in sight."[1] All this is true, but the shortage of craft was relative, not absolute. The problem was allocation, not production. The

[1]Marshall, op. cit., pp. 27 and 30.

difficulty was to extract the craft from the tight-fisted hand of Admiral Ernest King. On May 1st, 1944, King had at his disposal 31,123 landing-craft of which he had allocated to OVERLORD no more than 2,493,[1] and these reluctantly.

American shipyards producing landing-craft were under the direct supervision of the United States Navy and, although the War Production Board could and did speed up the rate of output through its control of labour and materials, the Navy guarded most jealously its right to determine how and where its income should be spent. In theory the strategic deployment of American war matériel was decided by the U.S. Joint Chiefs of Staff, but, as Stimson has made clear, this body " was incapable of enforcing a decision against the will of any one of its members . . . any officer, in a minority of one, could employ a rigorous insistence on unanimity as a means of defending the interests of his own service. . . . Only the President was in a position to settle disagreements by a definite and final ruling, and Mr. Roosevelt's general position was that disagreements should be adjusted without forcing him to act as judge."[2]

In London, similar clashes of inter-service opinion and interest did not create the same problem. Churchill, as Minister for Defence, was never reluctant to arbitrate, and in the last resort the conflict could usually be resolved by the War Cabinet, which, because of its direct and collective responsibility to the House of Commons, was in a much stronger position than the American executive. It is true that Air Chief Marshal Sir Arthur Harris and Bomber Command were allowed to conduct a more or less independent war (often at the expense of the overall needs of British strategy) but the extent and influence of Harris's ' private empire ' was not to be compared with that of Admiral King.

Because of his close association with the Navy in the First World War, Roosevelt tended to favour its interests, and he very seldom intervened to restrain his Naval C.-in-C. Consequently, the verdict of King generally determined the number of warships and landing-craft which the American members of the Combined Chiefs of Staff were able to offer for a particular operation. Whenever he was questioned closely about his resources and how he was employing them, King took the stand, as he once put it, that " what operations are or are not conducted in the Pacific is no affair of the Combined Chiefs of Staff since this theater is exclusively American." Although the British Chiefs of Staff never recognised this extreme view, they had to accept American statements as to what shipping could be spared for the war against Germany, since they could not examine these estimates in the light of the full facts.

The outcome was, therefore, that at the end of 1943, when the Combined Chiefs of Staff decided that OVERLORD and ANVIL were to be " the supreme operations for 1944," by far the greater part of the U.S.

[1] King, *U.S. Navy at War, 1941-1945*, p. 137.
[2] Stimson, op. cit., pp. 515-16.

Navy's landing-craft was in the Pacific. During that winter the War Production Board carried out an aggressive drive for a greater output of landing-craft in the shipyards of the Atlantic coast and the Gulf of Mexico, and achieved spectacular results, but even so the increased requirements of the new OVERLORD Plan could not be met by May 1st. On the other hand, if the full extent of Eisenhower's requirements had been known in November, as they might have been, landing-craft could have been brought round from the Pacific in good time. By the end of January it was too late to solve the problem by re-allocation and re-distribution.

Nor was it possible to make up the deficiency by increasing the output of British shipyards. They were so fully engaged in the production of the pre-fabricated harbours and in repairing ships and craft damaged in action and training that they were turning out only 150 new landing-craft a month. The additional vessels had to come from the United States and these could not be available in time for an invasion in May.

Quite apart from the question of shipping, there were other factors supporting the case for postponement. The increase in the size and scope of the assault would call for the training of several thousand additional crews for landing-craft, troop-carriers and gliders, and of two more assault divisions plus all the engineer and beach-operating personnel required for their support. The delay would also give the strategic bombers greater opportunities for weakening German war industry and communications and would provide another month of good flying weather for pin-point attacks on bridges and railway facilities which had to be knocked out if the movement of German armoured reserves to the invasion area were to be effectively disrupted. Moreover, by early June the weather on the Eastern Front would be more likely to favour the commencement of a large-scale Russian offensive in conjunction with OVERLORD, and there was the additional consideration that the extra weeks would give General Alexander the chance to deliver a crippling blow in Italy, thus firmly pinning down the German armies there.

Although he would have preferred to launch the invasion of Normandy in May, " in order to obtain the longest campaigning season," Eisenhower felt obliged to ask the Combined Chiefs of Staff that it should be delayed by a month and that ANVIL should be temporarily reduced to a threat so that OVERLORD could be carried out on a frontage of five divisions, instead of three. " Nothing less," he cabled on January 23rd, " will give us an adequate margin to ensure success."

The Combined Chiefs of Staff agreed to the postponement, but the American members would not countenance any interference with ANVIL. They regarded this operation not as a mere diversion, but as the means of opening up a major port of entry for the French Army which was training in North Africa and for American divisions which would be ready to sail direct from the United States in the middle of the year. They were also determined to make quite sure that the amphibious resources of the Mediterranean Command should not be used in Italy or the Balkans.

It was argued by the planning staffs in Washington that the additional month's production would be adequate. " On the basis of the planning data available to them," says Eisenhower, " they stated that sufficient craft would be on hand to mount an OVERLORD assault of seven divisions (including the two follow-up divisions) and an ANVIL of two divisions. These figures did not coincide with those of my own planners."[1]

The Washington calculations were based on the experience of operations in the Pacific islands. These were no real guide, however, for there the assault forces required no engineers to clear beach obstacles or demolish concrete defences; they had little chance of using armour, no call for anti-tank guns and far less need for anti-aircraft defence. The two problems were in no way comparable and yet the United States Navy continued to challenge Eisenhower's estimates until he sent over Bedell Smith to make it plain that a division assaulting the Atlantic Wall would have to be built up to a strength of approximately a division and a half, so that it could take with it the essential engineer, armoured, anti-tank and anti-aircraft units, and the whole organisation of beach control. Without these it would be impossible to ensure the smooth and rapid build-up of reinforcements in time to meet the armoured counter-attack which could be expected within the first week, a factor which had hardly to be considered in the Pacific. The amphibious assaults which MacArthur and Nimitz had so far carried out were small ventures compared with the operations which now confronted Eisenhower. On the first two days of the invasion he was planning to land 176,475 men and 20,111 vehicles, including 3,000 guns, 1,500 tanks, and 5,000 other armoured vehicles.

Although Eisenhower's case was unchallengeable, the argument about landing-craft went on for two months. At last on March 24th the American Chiefs of Staff consented to the target date for ANVIL being postponed to the middle of July, so that the bulk of the shipping necessary for the southern assault could first be used for the invasion of Normandy, yet the postponement of ANVIL need not have been necessary, for King could have found sufficient craft to carry out both invasions simultaneously if he had faced the issue in time. Of the 6,047 landing-craft available for OVERLORD less than half were provided by the U.S. Navy and its contribution represented only a small proportion of its total resources, as the table on page 180 shows.

It took Washington even longer to agree to the allocation of the American warships which Ramsay so urgently needed to protect and support the enlarged operation. The result of this prolonged hesitation was, to quote Ramsay's own dispatch, that " for some months we were planning without being certain that our full demands would be met.

[1]Eisenhower, *Report to the Combined Chiefs of Staff*, p. 15. (Hereafter quoted as ' Eisenhower, *Report.*')

## LANDING-CRAFT: U.S. NAVY, 1944

|  | LST | LCT | LCI | LCM | LCVP |
|---|---|---|---|---|---|
| On strength May 1st | 409 | 687 | 478 | 5,058 | 9,950 |
| Allocated to OVERLORD | 188[1] | 279 | 124 | 315 | 1,382 |

(Figures supplied by Bureau of Ships, U.S.N.)

This table covers all the main classes of landing-craft used in the OVERLORD assault: LST (Landing-ship, Tank), LCT (Landing-craft, tank), LCI (Landing-craft, Infantry), LCM (Landing-craft, Mechanised) and LCVP (Landing-craft, Vehicle and Personnel).

[1] The most serious shipping problem for the OVERLORD Planners was the shortage of LSTs. In the end 233 were available; all were American built but only 188 were provided by the U.S. Navy. At the same time in the Pacific the American force invading the small island of Saipan, garrisoned by *one* Japanese division, was provided with 87 LSTs.

This uncertainty was a constant anxiety and was only removed at the eleventh hour." It was in fact April 15th—with D-Day only seven weeks away—before King could be persuaded to provide a Task Force of three battleships, three cruisers and forty destroyers from the United States Navy.[1]

These delays would have been disastrous if Eisenhower had not proceeded on the assumption that his demands would be met, and if he had not been able to inspire such remarkable enthusiasm and co-operation in his own H.Q. and throughout his command. As winter turned to spring much of the lost ground was made good and with the knowledge

[1] The total number of major warships eventually engaged in the bombardment, escort and covering forces was:

|  | ROYAL NAVY AND ROYAL CANADIAN NAVY | U.S. NAVY | ALLIED NAVIES |
|---|---|---|---|
| Battleships - - - | 4 | 3 | — |
| Monitors - - - | 2 | — | — |
| Cruisers - - - | 21 | 3 | 3 |
| Destroyers - - - | 116 | 40 | 8 |
|  | 143 | 46 | 11 |

The remaining 553 warships (sloops, frigates, corvettes, patrol craft, gun-boats, anti-submarine trawlers, motor torpedo boats, etc.) were all provided by the Royal Navy, or the Royal Canadian Navy, except for 129 vessels which were American.

that sufficient resources would be provided there came a steady rise in confidence.

The broadening and strengthening of the assault was only part of the answer to the complex problem of breaching the German defences and ensuring that the Allies would be able to gain the advantage in build-up. Fortunately the COSSAC planners, and the War Office, had paid good heed to the lessons of the Dieppe Raid and had devised equipment and technique which were to revolutionise the conduct of amphibious operations. The first of these lessons was the need for stronger and closer support for the assaulting troops. Dieppe had shown that preliminary attacks by aircraft and warships could not completely neutralise the defenders and that they revived quickly when the bombardment lifted from the beaches as the landing-craft drew near the shore. If the craft were not to be most perilously exposed at this critical juncture, it was essential to maintain drenching fire from close-support weapons. COSSAC suggested that the solution might be found if the assault infantry were accompanied by their own floating artillery—guns, mortars and batteries of rockets mounted in small craft. Montgomery developed this idea by ordering that the artillery, anti-tank guns and tanks which would be brought in on the heels of the infantry should be so loaded that a proportion of those on each landing-craft could fire while waiting to land. Thus it was hoped to saturate the beaches with point-blank fire until the moment of touchdown, and thereafter to maintain this close bombardment on targets which the warships could not shell without endangering the troops on shore.

Next, it was decided that the fire of floating artillery should be reinforced by the power of amphibious armour. As a result of Dieppe, Brooke had concluded that the Atlantic Wall could not be stormed at bearable cost unless the infantry were given tank support from the very moment of landing. In March 1943, therefore, he had converted the 79th Armoured Division into an experimental formation and had ordered its commander, Major-General Sir Percy Hobart, to devise and develop specialised armour and equipment for the cross-Channel invasion.

Hobart was one of the great pioneers of armour, but his ideas had been far too advanced for the 'conservatives' in the War Office, and his outspoken intolerance of fools had been a goad to his opponents. As the commander of the original tank brigade, created in 1934, Hobart had worked out tactics and doctrines of tank warfare which the Germans had promptly applied in the development of their armoured formations. In Britain, however, the 'die-hard' generals had been determined to curb, if they could not cripple, the growth of tank forces. Accordingly, when an armoured division was formed, its command had been given first to a gunner and then to a cavalryman. In 1938, when Hobart's claims to advancement could no longer be denied, he was shunted off to Egypt. There, out of a scratch formation, he created the famous 7th Armoured Division, but in the process so outraged the orthodox thinkers that he was recalled before he could test his theories in action. Driven into premature retirement in 1940, he became a corporal in the Home Guard. He was rescued from oblivion only by the personal intervention of Churchill, but it was not until 1943 that he was given a real opportunity to employ his exceptional talent for ingenious and imaginative invention.

Working on the principle that the troops who would have to deal with each feature of the German fortifications should be carried into battle behind armour and should be given mechanical means for accomplishing their tasks, Hobart and his staff prepared for the British forces a remarkable variety of armoured vehicles which no other army possessed. Before D-Day British inventiveness and industry were to produce bulldozer tanks to clear away beach obstacles; ' flail tanks ' to beat pathways through minefields; tanks which could hurl explosive charges against concrete fortifications; turretless tanks which were in effect self-propelled ramps, over which other tanks could scale sea-walls; tanks carrying bridges to span craters and ditches; flame-throwing tanks to deal with pill-boxes and, most important of all, amphibious or DD (Duplex-Drive) tanks which could swim ashore under their own power.

Some of these, such as the ' flails ' and DD tanks, had been devised before Hobart began his experiments, but they were only in the first stages of development. The DD tank was the invention of a Hungarian-born engineer, Nicholas Straussler, who had succeeded in selling the idea to the War Office in spite of the Admiralty's scorn. Naval experts had declared that these tanks would never be able to swim in the open sea, and could not be launched from landing-craft. Even after Straussler had refuted this criticism with convincing demonstrations, the Navy continued to regard the ' DD ' as unseaworthy, primarily, it seems, because it did not have a rudder!

The five DD tanks which Hobart took over were obsolete Valentines, but he was able to adapt the equipment to the American Sherman, the principal tank in the Allied armoury. In July 1943, Brooke placed orders for the conversion of 900 Shermans, but the Ministry of Supply was reluctant to divert manpower and materials to the production of experimental equipment which was condemned by the Navy. The output was so small that six months later Hobart doubted whether these tanks would be available in sufficient numbers to permit their mass employment on D-Day, as Montgomery proposed immediately he saw them. The problem was solved only by enlisting the production genius of the Americans. On January 27th the DD tank was demonstrated to Eisenhower for the first time. The following day he sent a British engineer by air to Washington with the blue-prints. Within a week American factories were hard at work on the project and within two months 300 Shermans had been converted and were on their way to England.

The third lesson of the Dieppe raid was that no major port could be captured quickly or intact. Accordingly, the COSSAC Planners had made their preparations on the assumption that, even if Cherbourg could be seized within the first two weeks, the clearing of mines and repairing of demolitions would take at least two months. During this time the OVERLORD forces would have to be supplied across open beaches, unless some means could be found of protecting the anchorages. This was no new problem and Churchill had applied his mind to it many years before, when devising a very different plan for a landing on German territory. At this time he had suggested the construction of " a number of flat-bottomed barges or caissons, made not of steel but of concrete, which would float when empty of water and thus could be towed across " to the far shore. " On arrival," he had written, " sea cocks would be opened and [the caissons] would settle on the bottom. . . . By this means a torpedo and weather-proof harbour would be created in the open sea." This proposal had been made by Churchill in a plan for the occupation of the Frisian Islands, drafted " without expert assistance,"[1] as he points out, on July 17th, 1917. In the same plan Churchill had suggested the construction of landing-craft for tanks!

Twenty-five years later, when the loss of Singapore deprived Britain of her main naval base in the Far East, Churchill ordered his Chief of Combined Operations (Admiral Lord Louis Mountbatten) to explore the possibility of building an artificial harbour at an island in the Indian Ocean. Reverting to this question, in a minute to Mountbatten on May 30th, 1942, the Prime Minister turned to another aspect, and wrote:

Piers for use on beaches: They must float up and down with the tide. The anchor problem must be mastered. . . . Let me have the best solution worked out. Don't argue the matter. The difficulties will argue for themselves.

These two ideas—concrete caissons and floating piers—were worked on by Mountbatten's experts and, although the Indian Ocean project did not materialise, the results of their researches were applied to Normandy. The outcome was the production of two prefabricated harbours, known by their code-name as MULBERRY A and MULBERRY B.[2] Each harbour was to be roughly the size of Dover and was to consist of an outer floating breakwater, an inner fixed breakwater made of concrete caissons, and four floating piers running out from the beaches to ' spud pierheads.' At these pierheads small coasters and landing-ships

---

[1]Churchill, *The Second World War*, Vol. II, p. 215.

[2]Speaking of the MULBERRY harbours, Morgan (op. cit., pp. 261-2) says that in his opinion " the credit for the entire concept belongs to Commodore John Hughes-Hallett," the Senior Naval Officer at COSSAC H.Q. Morgan relates that in the summer of 1943, when the question of ports was being discussed, Hughes-Hallett remarked: " Well, all I can say is, if we can't capture a port we must take one with us." There is no doubt that this was said, but it was not an original suggestion. Mountbatten, evidently inspired by Churchill's proposals, had made a similar remark to Eisenhower a year earlier. (See Eisenhower, *Crusade in Europe*, p. 235.)

would unload direct into army lorries, while Liberty ships and other vessels could dump their cargoes into barges and ferries. The components of these two harbours were to be made in England, towed across the Channel and sunk or moored off the Normandy coast north-west and north-east of Bayeux. It was estimated that it would take three or four weeks to complete the assembling of the harbours and in this interval shelter was to be provided for the unloading craft by sinking lines of obsolete ships to form breakwaters at each of the five main assault sectors. As a further means of countering the enemy's destruction of port facilities, COSSAC made provision for laying an oil pipe-line under the Channel to Cherbourg, and later to Boulogne.[1]

Even with the aid of these ingenious and novel facilities, it was by no means certain that the Allies could outstrip the build-up of the Germans, who could move their reinforcements over the best road and rail network in Europe. Eisenhower's staff estimated that it would be at least seven weeks before he could bring into action on the Continent the 37 divisions which would be at his disposal in England by June 1st. The maximum scale of assault and rate of build-up was fixed by the availability of shipping and aircraft. Eight divisions could be landed from air and sea on D-Day, another two by the evening of D plus 1. By the fifth day 15 divisions might be ashore, but after that the maintenance of the current battle would absorb so much shipping that further divisions could not be landed at the same rate. The planners reckoned that the invasion force could be built up to:

18 divisions by D plus 10,
24 divisions by D plus 20,
30 divisions by D plus 35.

On the other hand, when the revised Allied plan was drawn up in February, it seemed that there would be five or six German divisions in position to oppose the landings on D-Day and at least twelve by D plus 4, and that thereafter the enemy strength would increase to:

25 divisions by D plus 10,
30 divisions by D plus 20,
$37\frac{1}{2}$ divisions by D plus 35.

These estimates indicated that, unless the potentially unfavourable balance could be redressed, the fate of the whole enterprise might be determined by the mere factor of weight, for this would dominate all other considerations in the first few weeks of the invasion. The enemy's natural advantage could be countered only if continued pressure on the Russian and Italian fronts precluded any substantial strengthening of the

[1] Since these were to be 'Pipe-Lines Under The Ocean,' they were known by the code-name, 'PLUTO.'

German forces in the West, if these forces could be kept widely dispersed by the maintenance of threats against the Pas de Calais and Southern France, and if the movement of German reserves could be seriously impeded by the bombing of railways and bridges. It was to these major strategic preliminaries that Eisenhower directed his primary attention as soon as the revision of the plan had been completed.

He anticipated that, although the Germans would fight strongly in Normandy, they would make their main stand in France along the line of the Seine, and that when this had been forced the real battle for Germany would begin. Eisenhower hoped that the issue might be decided before the end of the year, but when he outlined the revised plan to the Prime Minister, Churchill said to him: " If by the winter you have a bridgehead from the mouth of the Seine to Cherbourg and the Brittany Peninsula, and if you have 36 divisions ashore, I'll consider it a victory; and if you have Le Havre as well I'll regard it as decisive."

" By Christmas," replied Eisenhower, " we shall be on the Rhine."

## CHAPTER X

# PRELUDE TO OVERLORD

BETWEEN Eisenhower and the Rhine lay the task of launching the greatest amphibious operation in history against the most strongly defended coastline that any force had ever tried to assault. The Germans had had nearly four years in which to build their Atlantic Wall and as early as August 1942 the Dieppe Raid had yielded bloody warning of its strength.[1] At that time, however, the enemy had done little more than fortify the main ports and set up long-range guns in the Pas de Calais. A week before this raid, Hitler had ordered the general fortification of the western coast and this project was given fresh impetus when Germany was forced on to the strategic defensive in 1943. Then, however, the work was interrupted, indirectly, by the Allied Air Forces. In the spring 50,000 labourers were transferred from the Atlantic Wall to the Ruhr to help repair the damage caused by British bombs.[2] Later there was a further diversion of manpower, steel and concrete, first to strengthen the submarine pens in the Biscay ports, and subsequently to build—and then re-build—the launching-sites for flying-bombs in the Pas de Calais.

By the end of the year, although a quarter of a million garrison troops and as many conscript workers were toiling at the construction of the Atlantic Wall, it was approaching completion, according to the existing plan, only in the sector between Le Havre and Antwerp. The progress might have been greater if the C.-in-C., West, Field-Marshal Karl von Rundstedt, had had any faith in fortifications. But it was he who had outflanked the Maginot Line in 1940 and broken through to the Channel. He had seen then the danger of having too many divisions bottled up in fixed defences and too few available as mobile reserves to deal with any penetration or outflanking movement. Now that he had a defensive task, he was resolved to avoid the mistake the French had

---

[1]At Dieppe the Canadians alone suffered 3,369 casualties, including 907 men killed or died of wounds; the total German casualties in all three services were, their records show, fewer than 600.

[2]Evidence of Speer.

made. "We Germans," he said to a correspondent early in 1944, "do not indulge in the tired Maginot Spirit."

The basis of von Rundstedt's plan for countering the invasion was his belief that the actual landings could not be prevented. Committed, as he was, to defending 1,700 miles of coastline on the Atlantic and another 300 in the Mediterranean, he could not hope to parry every blow. Like Jodl, he believed that the great strategic flexibility which the Allies possessed could not be countered by a static defensive system like the Atlantic Wall. He planned, therefore, to hold strongly only the most vulnerable sections of the coast—the Pas de Calais, the mouths of the Somme and the Seine, Cherbourg and Brest—and to make the major ports impregnable against direct attack so that he could deny them to the Allies by protracted defence and thorough demolition. Thus he hoped to delay the Anglo-American build-up to such an extent that his counter-attacking forces could drive back into the sea any small bridgeheads which might be established between the main ports.

The success of this plan depended on his having sufficient armoured divisions and mobile infantry in reserve to deliver the counter-stroke once he knew which was the main Allied attack. It depended too on his having sufficient fighter squadrons to cover the movement of this force to the threatened area. In January 1944, however, von Rundstedt had only 50 divisions and 26 of these were absorbed—by Hitler's direct order —in manning the Atlantic Wall. Of the rest, a dozen were either newly-formed training divisions or exhausted skeletons from the Russian front, and the others were being steadily milked to provide drafts for the East.

During the winter of '43-'44 von Rundstedt appealed repeatedly to OKW for reinforcements: for fighting divisions to strengthen his reserves, not for foreign labour battalions of the Organisation Todt. He appealed in vain. The strategic dispositions of the Wehrmacht were determined by Hitler alone and he was pre-occupied with the immediate crises created by the landing at Anzio and, more particularly, by the Russian winter offensive which showed no sign of abating short of the spring thaw. Hitler did not doubt that the cross-Channel invasion was coming, but his defensive success in Italy made him confident that the assault from the West could be broken. His optimism sprang partly from bad intelligence, partly from a grave misinterpretation of the importance of the Dieppe Raid.

Goebbels had naturally portrayed the Dieppe Raid to the world as a " vain attempt at invasion." This was good propaganda, but there was no military justification for making—as did von Rundstedt's Chief of Staff, Zeitzler—an official report to Hitler representing the raid in this distorted light. Captured documents and other evidence produced by his Intelligence officers clearly indicated that it had been only a ' reconnaissance in force.' Nevertheless, the fiction became the accepted opinion at the Führer's H.Q. and Zeitzler's diligence in confirming Hitler's wishful thinking was soon rewarded. In September 1942, he was appointed Chief of the Army General Staff in succession to Halder, and thus he became responsible for operations against the Russians. This gave him a special interest in maintaining his interpretation of the Dieppe Raid and in belittling the extent of the invasion danger. Zeitzler's false counsel served to reinforce Hitler's natural disinclination to look beyond his present problem.

At the Führer's H.Q. the truth was further obscured by spurious intelligence reports—by-products of the growing conflict between the Party and the Wehrmacht, between Himmler's Security Service (the SD) and the Abwehr run by Admiral Canaris for OKW. Himmler was determined to bring all intelligence agencies of the Reich under his own control, for he had good reason to believe that the Abwehr was being used to organise underground resistance. His campaign was aided by the inefficiency of the Abwehr, which had failed to give any warning of the invasions of North Africa or Sicily, and had been repeatedly outwitted by the British Secret Service. This was particularly the case before the invasion of Sicily when British agents managed to pass into the hands of the Abwehr documents which convinced Hitler that the Allied landings would be made on Sardinia and the Peloponnese. In the succeeding months, when Hitler was most in need of reliable and unbiased intelligence, Himmler sought to discredit the Abwehr by challenging its reports and presenting direct to Hitler conflicting information allegedly received from the SD's own agents abroad. Knowing that Hitler wanted reassurance, not truth, the SD consistently painted an optimistic picture of the situation in the West and flagrantly misrepresented the strength and preparedness of the Anglo-American forces.

To counter this optimism, the branch of Army Intelligence which dealt with ' Foreign Armies, West,' had ' created ' some thirty fictitious British and American divisions and late in 1943 it listed these among the forces being assembled in England for the invasion. The chief of this branch, Colonel von Roenne, justified this falsification to his staff on the ground that by the time the SD had gone through its usual process of scaling down his estimates, its appreciation might be somewhere near the truth.[1] By the end of the winter this subterfuge had achieved its immediate purpose of stimulating a more realistic approach, but it was to prove easier to get these fictitious divisions on the Order of Battle maps than to get them off again. They were to bedevil the German High Command's appreciation of operations in the West for months after D-Day.

Hitler's first reaction to von Rundstedt's appeal for reinforcements was to send to the West the erstwhile hero of North Africa, Field-Marshal Erwin Rommel, who was at this time, November 1943, in Northern Italy commanding Army Group B, the H.Q. of the strategic reserve which

[1]The originator of this idea was von Roenne's deputy (Michael). See ' File on Colonel M,' British Army of the Rhine Intelligence Review, March 4th, 1946.

Hitler was planning to form. Initially Rommel was ordered merely to inspect the Western defences from Denmark to the Spanish border, but in January 1944, when he proposed to Hitler that radical changes should be made in von Rundstedt's anti-invasion plans, he asked for and was given command of the two armies holding the most important sector of the invasion coast from the Zuider Zee to the River Loire. Von Rundstedt remained C.-in-C., West, but his command was reorganised into two Army Groups:

*Army Group B* (Rommel) comprising:

| 88 Corps | Holland, |
|---|---|
| 15th Army | Antwerp to the Orne, |
| 7th Army | The Orne to the Loire. |

*Army Group G* (Blaskowitz) comprising:

| 1st Army | Biscay Coast, |
|---|---|
| 19th Army | Mediterranean Coast. |

This reorganisation placed the primary responsibility for repulsing the invasion upon the younger Field-Marshal, whose favoured standing with the Führer gave him substantial independence. It was a rebuff for von Rundstedt, but at the age of sixty-nine position was more important to him than power. He had served too long under Hitler's Supreme Command to retain any illusion about the amount of authority which he or any other Field-Marshal might exercise when the real battle began. " As C.-in-C., West," he said later, " my sole prerogative was to change the guard in front of my gate ": a humiliating position for the man who had won Germany's most striking victories in the first two years of the war. As an Army Group Commander he had directed the envelopment of the Polish Forces south of Warsaw in 1939, the break-through to the Channel in the following year and the drive across the Ukraine to the Crimea and Rostov in 1941. But now he was to be little more than a figurehead, a role which he accepted because his sense of patriotic duty outweighed his professional pride.

From Hitler's point of view, von Rundstedt as a figurehead was a decided asset. He was the doyen of the Officer Corps, the only Field-Marshal who had never lost a battle. He had not been involved in the reverses on the Eastern Front, since he had been retired at his own request in November 1941, after protesting against Hitler's plan for a winter campaign. This retirement had enhanced his prestige and brought him a reputation for independence and moral courage. He was now living on that reputation, even though he had virtually ' sold out ' to Hitler in July 1942, when he had agreed to emerge from retirement and become C.-in-C., West. To the army at large he represented military soundness and integrity, but to Hitler his value lay in his willingness to lend the endorsement of his presence to the carrying out of policies with which he disagreed.

The truth was that von Rundstedt had lost his grip. He was old and tired and his once active brain was gradually becoming addled, for he had great difficulty in sleeping without the soporific aid of alcohol. For eighteen months he had lived in ease, seldom leaving his H.Q. at St. Germain, near Paris, and had grown accustomed to delegating almost everything to his energetic Chief of Staff, Blumentritt. Nevertheless, he still looked the part of Commander-in-Chief. The son of an aristocratic, military family, he had developed an austere but impressive dignity which contrasted sharply with Rommel's confident swagger. Cold, reserved and not easily ruffled, von Rundstedt was far removed in temperament from the eager, impetuous Württemberger who now came under his command.

Von Rundstedt's approach to military problems was along the firm straight road of his general staff training. He was inclined to prejudge situations and to apply orthodox text-book solutions, but in his prime his application of these had been so expert and efficient that success had been ensured. The inflexibility of purpose which Prussian military training sought to create in commanders tended to develop in them inflexibility of mind as well, and in von Rundstedt's case this was so. He lacked imagination and because his own approach was conventional and direct he presumed that his opponents would think similarly. In 1940 when he was planning the invasion of England, he had been compelled by the weakness of his air and naval support to prepare for a frontal assault across the narrowest part of the Channel. Three years later, applying his own plan in reverse, he assumed that the Allies would inevitably make their main effort in the Pas de Calais.

Rommel's first appreciation was that the Allies would land at the mouth of the Somme with the object of seizing Le Havre from the rear, but his real disagreement with his superior concerned the detailed measures by which the invasion should be met. Rommel produced imaginative and unorthodox proposals which shocked von Rundstedt and most of his senior commanders. The Wehrmacht generals had always been sceptical of Rommel's ability and jealous of the publicity which Goebbels had lavished on him. To them he was a political general, a military upstart and an ambitious showman, who had risen from Colonel to Field-Marshal in three years only because of his standing with the Party. In this they did him less than justice. He may not have been a great strategist, but he had an original mind, a keen practical sense, a flair for personal leadership and a remarkable capacity for exploiting a tactical opportunity, and for extricating his troops from the precarious situations in which his over-eagerness occasionally landed them. He was the type of commander who appealed to the Führer, for he acted more from instinct than reason. Originally, moreover, there had been a peculiar bond between Hitler and Rommel. The military capacity of both had been belittled by the General Staff, and yet both had triumphed in the field.

In Africa Rommel had been at his best when the battle was fluid, for he was a master of movement. His early successes in the Western Desert had been due in part, of course, to the superior quality of his tanks and anti-tank guns, and to the shortcomings of successive British commanders—Beresford Peirse, Cunningham and Ritchie—whose minds moved at the infantryman's pace. Nevertheless, the decisive factor had been the speed and daring with which Rommel had manœuvred his armour. This had thrown his opponents off balance and enabled him to strike at the weak spots thus exposed. It was not until Montgomery arrived that Rommel met an opponent who would not be unbalanced no matter how dramatically the panzer divisions were flung about. It is generally believed, however, that Montgomery triumphed over him only when the advantage of strength had swung unquestionably in favour of the Eighth Army. This is not so. Rommel's most significant defeat occurred at Alam Halfa, seven weeks before the main battle of Alamein and at a time when Montgomery's forces were inferior in firepower and armour.

The Rommel who came to France had learnt much since Alam Halfa. His courage was as high as ever, but his confidence had waned with the growth of Allied air power and he was convinced that this would be the most important single factor in the coming battle. Rommel argued that Montgomery would attempt to assault only within range of strong air support, and that therefore the main landings would be made somewhere between Dunkirk and Cherbourg. He predicted that Allied aircraft would frustrate the movement of von Rundstedt's central reserve; that if a bridgehead were established the invaders could build up such material superiority, even without capturing a port, that eventually they would break out; and finally that once it became a war of manœuvre the Wehrmacht would face certain defeat because of the Luftwaffe's weakness. Command of the air, he said, would give the Allies such an advantage in tactical mobility once they were firmly ashore, that Germany's only hope lay in forcing her adversaries to fight the decisive battle at the Atlantic Wall, where, with most of their strength still at sea, they could be caught at the greatest disadvantage. It would not be sufficient to make the ports impregnable; the invasion must be defeated on the beaches if it was to be defeated at all.

In his orders he declared: " In the short time left before the great offensive starts, we must succeed in bringing all defences to such a standard that they will hold up against the strongest attacks. Never in history was there a defence of such an extent with such an obstacle as the sea. The enemy must be annihilated before he reaches our main battlefield. . . . We must stop him in the water, not only delaying him but destroying all his equipment while it is still afloat."[1]

Rommel proposed, therefore, that every man and weapon should be

---

[1] Letter of Instructions to Army Commanders, April 22nd, 1944. This letter re-stated earlier orders issued in February.

G

packed into the Atlantic Wall, or held in very close reserve behind it. " The high-water line," he declared, " must be the main fighting line." As this agreed with Hitler's order that not a yard of territory must be yielded, Rommel was given authority to modify von Rundstedt's plan accordingly. He began in February by devising an elaborate and ingenious scheme for obstructing the coastline with underwater obstacles. Sharp tetrahedra, jagged hedgehogs, concrete dragon's teeth and stout logs loaded with spikes and mines would, he hoped, take severe toll of landing-craft even before they reached the minefields on the beaches. To hinder airborne landings, all open areas within seven miles of the coast were to be obstructed with heavy posts, bedded firmly in the ground and tipped with shells which would be set off by trip-wires running from one post to the next. Low-lying areas were to be flooded and gaps between the inundations were to be heavily mined.

On Rommel's orders coastal and anti-tank artillery positions were to be roofed and walled with concrete as a protection against bombardment, even though this might limit their arcs of fire. New pill-boxes, new minefields, new belts of wire were to make the network of defences increasingly thicker, particularly north of the Seine, but also in the area between Le Havre and Cherbourg which had previously been neglected.

As Rommel planned it, heavy coastal batteries immune from air attack would engage Allied shipping off-shore and landing-craft on the run-in. As they neared the beach, the assault waves would come under direct fire from machine-guns and anti-tank guns established in concrete pill-boxes and fortified houses, and under indirect concentrations from mortars and artillery farther inland. Those craft which survived this fire and the maze of under-water obstacles, would, he hoped, be wrecked on the mined beaches. Additional minefields and barbed wire on the dunes and along the waterfront, and flame-throwers fed from pipelines behind the dunes would make the progress inland slow and costly. Gaps in the sea-walls would be blocked with concrete, and other exits from the foreshore would be closed with minefields and anti-tank ditches, so that the invading armour and transport would be locked on the narrow beaches and there destroyed as they had been at Dieppe.

To provide the manpower for these defences Rommel was prepared to sacrifice depth. He reduced the sectors of the coastal divisions by moving to the beaches some of the mobile infantry which von Rundstedt had held in reserve. He gave orders that all forward units should entrench every single man, including batmen, bakers and clerks, in fire-positions on or near the beaches. Immediately behind this narrow coastal belt he proposed to deploy all the armoured divisions, with their guns and tanks far enough forward to bring down fire on the foreshore almost immediately. " It is more important," he said, " to have one panzer division in the assaulted sector on D-Day, than to have three there by D plus 3."

This unconventional plan drew spirited opposition, especially from Geyr von Schweppenburg, who, as commander of 'Panzer Group, West,' controlled all von Rundstedt's armoured forces. Geyr was appalled at the proposal to put everything in the shop window. Rommel replied that this was no ordinary military problem. The conventional argument in favour of defence in depth did not apply, since problems of unloading and supply would prevent the Allies from making a rapid and deep penetration in the first few days, as the Wehrmacht had done in 1940. Reserves need not be held well back from the coast to meet such a penetration and, if they were, they would never be able to move in time against the bridgehead in the face of Allied air power. In any case, he argued, it would be hardly more difficult to switch reserves from a coastal sector which was not attacked, than it would be to move them from inland assembly areas. The over-riding consideration in his mind was that the maximum force must oppose the invasion on the very day of the landings. " The first twenty-four hours," said Rommel, " will be decisive."

Irked by Geyr's opposition, Rommel appealed first to von Rundstedt, and then to the Führer, who produced an illogical compromise. Hitler divided the control of the armoured forces, with the result that there was neither a strong tactical reserve, nor a strong strategic reserve. This solution satisfied neither Rommel nor Geyr and until the very eve of the invasion each continued to plead his own cause.

Throughout the spring of 1944 the Atlantic Wall grew in strength as Rommel stumped the coast examining the defences and haranguing the garrisons. Before his appointment the work of fortification had been carried on without any real plan or conviction, except at the major ports. Von Rundstedt's opinion that the landings could not be stopped had penetrated to his troops, who thus had little confidence in their defences and less inclination to improve them. In a few weeks Rommel transformed the situation by his drive and enthusiasm, his own originality and his eagerness for new ideas. According to Admiral Ruge, his naval adviser and confidant, " Rommel brought a new impulse to the preparations. He fundamentally altered the underlying idea, thus changing the atmosphere of despondency and vague hope to one of hard work and clear plans. He was untiring in his efforts to instil his ideas into his men and they took them up eagerly because they appreciated his personality, his experience and his common sense."

By temperament Rommel was an improviser and in battle he was inclined to be impetuous. But his close and accurate study of the Allied technique of invasion and the practical counter-measures which he ordered reveal abilities in the spheres of planning and organisation for which he has been given too little credit by either his fellow generals or his opponents. It was fortunate for the Allies that Rommel had not begun his task six months earlier and that his plans were not wholeheartedly endorsed by his superiors nor thoroughly carried out by his subordinates, for even as it was the problem of invasion became more formidable and more hazardous with every week that passed.[1]

Command of the sea and air enabled the Allied planners to follow Rommel's intensive preparations step by step and to take counter-measures and precautions accordingly. Reconnaissance planes mapped the German progress with aerial photographs which were taken, in some cases, almost from sea level. Naval survey parties in midget submarines and small craft charted coastline, sea-bed and minefields off-shore. Commandos landed by night to examine beaches and fortifications. Inland a close watch on German dispositions and defences was kept by agents parachuted into France and by men and women of the French Resistance.

Of all Rommel's innovations, none caused so much concern to the Allies as the under-water obstacles. Their appearance at the end of February silenced those who were urging Ramsay to land under cover of darkness, and thus ended one controversy, but they necessitated certain changes of plan which reveal the extraordinary complexity and delicacy of the calculations which had to be made. At this time Montgomery had not yet obtained sufficient landing-craft for the assault infantry and their supporting weapons, but, as the belt of obstacles thickened, it became clear that special demolition squads would have to be landed hard on the heels of the infantry. The problem of finding the craft for these engineers was to worry the planners until the very eve of the invasion.

Far more serious was the danger that if the first assault waves were to touch-down at high-tide, as had been planned, large numbers of landing-craft would be wrecked. On the other hand, if the landings were to be made at low-tide, thus leaving the maximum time for clearing the obstructions, the infantry would have to cross several hundred yards of open, fire-swept beach and might have to wade through deep runnels before they could reach dry land. In either case the casualties were likely to be severe. Montgomery decided upon a compromise which demanded the most precise timing: the first troops would land short of the main belt of obstacles at half-tide, or earlier, if necessary, three or four hours before high-water. This, he hoped, would greatly reduce the danger to the assault-craft and would give the engineers time to clear lanes for the follow-up craft before the incoming sea interrupted their work.

This solution meant, however, that the infantry would be exposed to considerable fire before they could bring their own weapons to bear against the defences. To meet this hazard, Montgomery adopted a suggestion of Hobart's for placing armour in the vanguard of the assault.

[1] This account of the German plans and preparations is based mainly on the interrogations of von Rundstedt, Geyr and Blumentritt, on a detailed statement of Rommel's views and actions prepared by Admiral Ruge and on Rommel's Letter of Instructions issued on April 22nd, 1944. (See also the account by Rommel's Chief of Staff, Speidel, *We Defended Normandy*, Chapters iii, vii-ix.)

He decided to land the DD tanks in the first wave, the specialised armour in the next and the infantry in the third.

This decision revolutionised the technique of invasion but it raised an unexpected difficulty. Because the beaches were mined, Hobart proposed to use 'flails' to clear the way for the DD tanks and other armoured devices, but the planners were warned that on some of the assault beaches there were treacherous patches of soft clay below high-water mark. This information came from one of Montgomery's scientific advisers who had spent a holiday on the Bay of the Seine before the war and had noted the presence of clay. The patches were located from aerial photographs and commandos brought back samples which showed that the warning was well-founded.[1] At Brancaster in Norfolk geologists discovered a beach with similar patches, and when tanks were tested there they became bogged.

Refusing to admit defeat, Hobart produced a device by which a tank could lay a carpet of matting in its own path and leave it there as a roadway across the clay for others to follow. These tanks became known as 'bobbins' and the loading tables were so adjusted that in every LCT which was due to touch-down opposite a clay patch, the first tank out would be a 'bobbin.'

This solution had barely been perfected when a fresh complication arose. On April 23rd in an air attack against a coastal battery one bomb fell wide among the under-water obstacles. The instantaneous photograph of the bomb-fall showed fourteen explosions—sympathetic detonations which told the planners that the Germans had now laid mines below high-water mark. The presence of these mines in some of the clay patches made it necessary to avoid those areas in choosing landing-places for the assault armour. It was hoped, however, that elsewhere the combination of 'bobbins' and 'flails' would open the way for the DD tanks and the other British inventions, and allow Montgomery to carry out his plan for screening the approach of the infantry and overwhelming Rommel's new fortifications by sheer weight of armour.

While the planners wrestled with the final details of loading-tables and landing-craft, the attention of Eisenhower and his Commanders-in-Chief was focused on the question of the overall balance of strength. In spite of the improvements and additions to the plan, there was still no guarantee that the Allies would be able to match the enemy's build-up in Normandy. From their Intelligence officers they sought the answer to four questions in particular: How many German divisions would there be in the West on D-Day? How would these be disposed? How many of them could be pinned down by diversionary threats against areas remote from Normandy? How effectively could the battlefield be isolated

[1]An official of the British Museum made a valuable contribution to the solution of this problem by discovering in a French journal a most detailed description of a clay patch on the beach at Luc-sur-Mer, near Caen. This information was obtained from an unexpected source, the *Bulletin de la Société Préhistorique Française*, Vol. XXXV, 1938.

and the movement of German reserves be frustrated or delayed by bombing and sabotage?

The answer to the first of these questions depended primarily on Hitler's ability to stabilise the Russian front. During February the Soviet winter offensive continued unchecked but (as von Manstein had predicted it would when Hitler forbade his withdrawal from the Dnieper Bend) the number of divisions in von Rundstedt's command was increased from 50 to 53. It became apparent, however, that unless there was an early thaw, the Wehrmacht could halt the Red Army only by bringing 20 or 25 divisions from other fronts, or by making a general and orderly withdrawal to the narrow 'throat' between the Baltic and the Black Sea. Ignoring the advice of Zeitzler and Manstein, Hitler chose to gamble on the weather. The thaw was late and the Red Army rolled on, driving all before it on the sector south of the Pripet Marshes. By the middle of March the Russians had established a vast salient extending to the Dniester and the frontier of Poland, and even threatening the passes which led to the Rumanian oilfields. This advance compelled Hitler's weakened forces to defend a front longer than the Leningrad–Rostov line which they had been unable to hold eight months earlier.

From the Balkans, Scandinavia and the Reich itself, OKW scraped up a dozen divisions, but none was taken from the West or from Italy, where all Hitler's reserves had been drawn into the battle by the timely Allied landing at Anzio. While disaster followed disaster in the Ukraine, von Rundstedt continued to receive reinforcements and by the end of March his strength had risen to 57 divisions. " For the moment it would seem," wrote Montgomery's Chief Intelligence Officer (Brigadier E. T. Williams), " that the enemy is courting further and deepening disaster in the East to retain a good chance in the West; a strange gamble militarily, made intelligent politically by the prospect of a compromise peace if the Western decision bore fruit: in short, more and more Stalingrads in the hope of one Dunkirk."[1]

As the situation in the East grew more serious, the Western Allies kept close watch on France for any sign of movement and in the last week of March it came. While Berlin Radio was insisting that " the strategic conception of the German High Command has not been forced to undergo any decisive change as a result of the Russian advance," four of von Rundstedt's best divisions (9th and 10th SS Panzer, Panzer Lehr,[2] and 349th Infantry) were heading East for Poland. This sudden switch of power and change of plan—on what the Germans then thought was

[1] 21st Army Group Intelligence Review, April 2nd, 1944.

[2] *Lehr* means 'training,' but this was no training formation. It had been formed early in 1944 from demonstration units of the panzer training schools and had been specially equipped for an anti-invasion role. On June 6th, 1944, it was the most powerful panzer division in the Wehrmacht, for it had 190 tanks, 40 assault guns, and 612 half-tracks—double the normal complement—for the rapid movement of its infantry.

the eve of invasion—revealed the extent of the disaster in the East and reinforced the British and American belief that Hitler had no central strategic reserve and no spare offensive divisions on any other front. He could no longer keep one antagonist quiet, while he dealt with the other. The several fronts had become irrevocably one war.

" The Allies," wrote Williams at the time, " benefit by the inter-dependence of their assaults. A break-through towards Lwow affects a division at Lisieux (10th SS); the supply line of the divisions moving back into the Galatz Gap is bombed from Foggia. The Russian advances were made possible by the Allied bombing of Germany, by Lend-Lease, by the containing actions in the Mediterranean and by the imminence of invasion in the West. Two-thirds of the German Air Force and 100 German divisions were kept preoccupied. Thus was the Red Army given opportunity. They grasped it with both mighty hands. Making the weather their ally, first they divided the Southern German Sector from the Centre and the North; next they rent it in twain; now they tear these twain in pieces. So, in their doughty turn, the Russians make OVERLORD more possible."

The loss of three of his seven armoured divisions left von Rundstedt's reserves weaker than at any time since the middle of 1943. In the second week of April, however, the thaw came on the Eastern Front. The Russian offensive was halted in the mud and Hitler could hope, with some justification, that there could be no renewal of the Red Army's attack before June. There was still time to restore von Rundstedt's armies to their March strength, and by the third week of May this had been done, nominally at least. The divisional total stood at 60, the highest yet, but ten short of the number which von Rundstedt had demanded as " the absolute minimum for security " and which he might have received had it not been for the Russian victory, and, be it said, the Anglo-American landing at Anzio, which led Hitler to send reinforce-ments to Italy.

Even after the thaw, 9th and 10th SS remained in Southern Poland, but Panzer Lehr came back and with it the remnants of four armoured divisions which the Russians had mauled. The best of these—1st SS Panzer, the ' Adolf Hitler Division '—began rebuilding in Belgium with the priority naturally accorded to the Führer's bodyguard, but the old wine of the others was poured into the new bottles of von Rundstedt's three panzer training divisions. This was essentially a short-term policy, for it jeopardised the replacement system, but Hitler was only concerned to tide over the next crisis. Thus on the map—on *his* map anyway—the forces available to meet the invasion appeared to be considerably stronger, but with the Russians quietened only for the moment and with the Italian front about to flare up again there was little chance of von Rundstedt's receiving any further substantial reinforcement before midsummer.

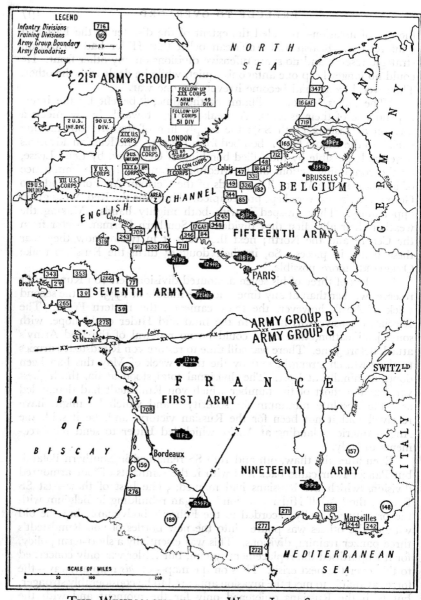

THE WEHRMACHT IN THE WEST, JUNE 6TH, 1944

The limitation thus imposed on the strength of the garrison in the West, reduced, but did not remove, the possibility that the enemy's rate of reinforcement to Normandy might exceed that of the Allies. With 60 divisions von Rundstedt had a considerable margin in his favour, for all the 37 divisions under Eisenhower's command in Britain could not be brought into action until seven weeks after D-Day. To some extent this numerical advantage was counter-balanced by the indifferent quality and limited mobility of some German divisions and by the Allied command of the sea and air, which enabled Eisenhower to threaten the invasion of almost any sector of the enemy coastline. The German forces were consequently strung out from the Mediterranean to the Zuider Zee. Nevertheless, if von Rundstedt were to learn or to guess correctly the time and place of invasion he might still be able to concentrate sufficient forces to ensure its defeat. Thus at all costs by secrecy and deception the Allies had to gain surprise.

As D-Day approached the security ring around Britain was tightened. In February all civilian travel between the United Kingdom and Eire was stopped, in order to reduce the leakage of information to Dublin where German diplomats maintained a fertile centre of espionage, apparently unhindered by the Irish Government. In April a coastal belt, ten miles deep, from the Wash to Land's End and on either side of the Firth of Forth, was closed to all visitors, and unprecedented restrictions were imposed upon foreign diplomats. Neither they nor their couriers were permitted to enter or leave the country and their mail was subjected to censorship.

The public announcement of these orders aroused considerable interest, and irritation, in the enemy camp and produced an outburst from Hitler at a staff conference on April 6th. " Frankly," he declared, " this English performance seems to me farcical: the latest reports of these prohibitive regulations, these restrictive measures and so on. Normally that sort of thing isn't done when one plans an operation like this. . . . I can't help feeling that after all this may be nothing but insolent posturing. . . . It's all so unnecessary. They can assemble their forces there, embark them and ship them across to here, and we can't find out what they're up to. I'm inclined to think that this is sheer impudent bluff."[1]

There was no element of bluff in these restrictions, though they were intended to contribute incidentally to the war of nerves. All the guile and ingenuity of British Intelligence were being turned to the devising of a scheme of strategic deception, far more subtle in technique, far more sinister in design. The object of this plan, which carried the code-name FORTITUDE, was to convince the German High Command *before D-Day* that the assault would come in the Pas de Calais, and *after D-Day* that the Normandy landing was a preliminary and diversionary operation, intended to draw German reserves away from the area north of the Seine

[1] Führer Conferences, Fragment 40, April 6th, 1944.

so that the main Allied attack might be delivered there at a later date. By this bluff it was hoped that an army of a quarter of a million men might be kept, idle but expectant, between Le Havre and Antwerp until the Battle of Normandy had been won.

The seed of deception was sown in fertile ground, for von Rundstedt, and the General Staff at OKW, had already concluded that the Pas de Calais was the place most likely to be attacked. It contained the main launching sites for V-weapons. Through it lay the easiest route to the Rhine and the Ruhr, and any successful landing there would probably mean the loss of all France. To the Germans the Pas de Calais was of vital importance and they made the common German mistake of assuming that it must therefore bulk equally large in the eyes of their adversaries. In working to strengthen these preconceptions, the British played upon the notorious tendency of German Intelligence Officers to approach problems with a card-index mind, indefatigable in collecting information, but incompetent in assessing it.

The primary weapon for the carrying out of FORTITUDE was air power, and the aerial plan was shaped accordingly. For every reconnaissance mission over Normandy, two were flown over the Pas de Calais. For every ton of bombs dropped on coastal batteries west of Le Havre, two tons were put down on batteries north of it. In the bombing of railways 95 per cent of the effort was directed against targets north and east of the Seine.

The impression created by these operations was confirmed by information which came from the English side of the Channel—from air reconnaissance, wireless interception, and the reports of spies who were surreptitiously provided with appropriate data. The deception of enemy pilots and agents had been begun by COSSAC in 1943, as part of its attempt to threaten invasion that year. An elaborate combined operations H.Q. had been built at Dover, and the pumping-head for one of the PLUTO's had been ostentatiously set into the cliffs facing Boulogne. New staging camps and depots, new roads and railway sidings, additional port facilities and ' hards,'[1] had been constructed in the south-east then, and good use was made of them now. Divisions which could not be landed early in the assault were concentrated opposite the Pas de Calais. Dummy landing-craft were assembled in the Thames Estuary and in south-eastern ports; dummy gliders were set up on airfields in Kent and East Anglia.

These and other preparations in the south-east were discreetly revealed, but those being made in the south-west were hidden as carefully as possible. In this deception the Luftwaffe gave gratuitous help. Because it was easier to make ' snap and run ' flights over Kent and Sussex than over Devon and Cornwall, German air reconnaissance provided von Rundstedt's Intelligence branch with more effective photographic

---

[1] ' Hards ' are stretches of open beach specially paved with concrete or stone, so that tanks and vehicles can back straight into the ' open mouths ' of beached landing-craft.

cover of the area on which the Allies wished its attention to be concentrated.

The presumption that the main invasion forces were assembled in the south-east was reinforced by deceptive wireless traffic. Although Montgomery's H.Q. was close to Portsmouth, its radio signals were conveyed by landline to Kent and transmitted from there.[1] By another radio subterfuge the idea was conveyed that the two follow-up armies (First Canadian and Third American) were in fact an assault force destined to land in the Pas de Calais. The Germans were allowed to learn that this Army Group was under the command of Lieut.-General George S. Patton, who was an ideal bogey. In Sicily he had shown himself to be the outstanding American field commander and, as he was considerably senior to Bradley, this set-up carried conviction to the logical German mind.

Through February, March and April all the evidence from France pointed to the success of this deception scheme. The Fifteenth German Army, north of the Seine, continued to receive priority in reinforcements. During these three months its infantry strength increased from 10 divisions to 15, and here alone, in the sector between Le Havre and Calais, was the enemy able to establish defence in depth with a second line of infantry divisions in close support of those holding the coast. There was no indication that the German command seriously contemplated a landing between Le Havre and Cherbourg. Reinforcements were spared for the Mediterranean coast in March and for Brittany in April, but none went to Normandy.

To Allied Intelligence officers, studying the enemy's Order of Battle, it seemed almost too good to be true, but in mid-April there was a sudden alarm when air photographs of the Orne Valley revealed that the enemy was erecting stout posts as ' anti-air landing obstacles ' in the very fields where the British gliders were due to land. Had the enemy got wind of the plan? Reconnaissance aircraft were dispatched to other sectors and their photographs showed that similar obstructions were being set up right along the Channel coast, and particularly between Calais and Dieppe.

Anxiety was allayed, but only for the moment. In the first week of May there was exceptionally heavy rail traffic in the area between the Seine and the Loire. Aerial reconnaissance and agents' reports indicated that a drastic re-arrangement of enemy reserves was in progress, and that the focal point was Normandy. It was soon known that the 21st Panzer Division had moved from Rennes in Brittany to the Caen–Falaise area, hard by the beaches which Second British Army was to assault, and that Panzer Lehr, returning from Hungary, had gone not to its old location around Verdun, but to the region of Chartres–Le Mans–Châteaudun,

[1]This was duly noted by the enemy. In his weekly report to C.-in-C., West, dated May 21st, Rommel declared: " The formation of the Allied *Schwerpunkt* in Southern and South-Eastern England is again confirmed by the location of Montgomery's H.Q. south of London."

NORMANDY, APRIL 1944

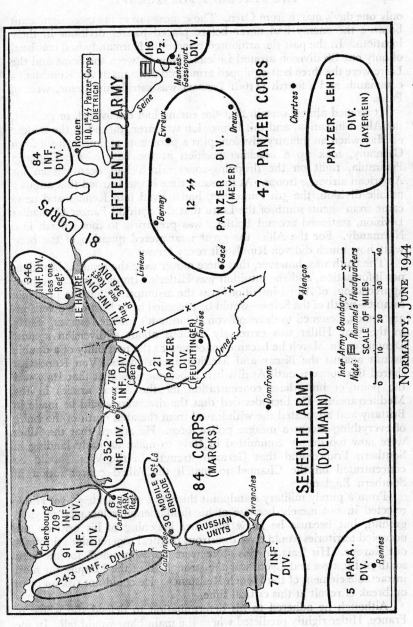

**NORMANDY, JUNE 1944**

**FIFTEENTH ARMY**

116 Pz. DIV.

H.Q. 1st SS Panzer Corps (DIETRICH)

Rouen

Seine

84 INF. DIV.

Mantes-Gassicourt

Evreux

Bernay

Breux

Chartres

**47 PANZER CORPS**

12 SS PANZER DIV. (MEYER)

Gacé

**81 CORPS**

346 INF. DIV. less one Regt.

LE HAVRE

711 INF. DIV. plus 346 INF. DIV. Regt.

Lisieux

Falaise

Alençon

**PANZER LEHR DIV. (BAYERLEIN)**

716 INF. DIV.

21 PANZER DIV. (FEUCHTINGER)

Caen

Orne

Bayeux

352 INF. DIV.

Domfront

**SEVENTH ARMY (DOLLMANN)**

St Lô

**84 CORPS (MARCKS)**

Carentan

6 PARA. Regt.

Coutances

30 MOBILE BRIGADE

Cherbourg

709 INF. DIV.

91 INF. DIV.

243 INF. DIV.

Avranches

**RUSSIAN UNITS**

77 INF. DIV.

5 PARA. DIV.

Rennes

*Inter Army Boundary* ——×——

*Note:* ▥ *Rommel's Headquarters*

**SCALE OF MILES**

0  10  20  30  40

Note: On D-Day the commander of 12th SS was de Witt, but Meyer succeeded him on June 12th only one day's march from Caen. Those moves were the more significant because the enemy had never before placed panzer divisions in these locations. In the past the armoured reserves in Normandy had consisted of only one SS division around Lisieux. Now between the Seine and the Loire were the three best-equipped armoured divisions in von Rundstedt's command, and a fourth (116th Panzer) was astride the Seine, west of Paris.

It seemed almost certain that the enemy had discovered, or guessed, the Allied intention, and this impression was strengthened in the middle of May when an infantry division, plus a parachute regiment, fresh from Germany, took up a blocking position at the base of the Cotentin Peninsula, right on the dropping-zones which had been chosen for American airborne troops. At the same time it was learned that another mobile division, the 5th Parachute, had moved into Rennes and news came from agents south of the Loire that the 17th SS Panzer Grenadier Division, stationed around Poitiers, was preparing to move north into Normandy. For the Allies the great unanswered question of the hour was: how much did von Rundstedt really know?

The truth was, however, that these moves were the result of intuition, not information, and the intuition was Hitler's. Implicit in the German appreciations of Allied intentions was the assumption that the principle assault—north of the Seine—would be preceded by at least one diversionary attack, designed to draw off von Rundstedt's mobile reserves. Early in the year Hitler was extremely anxious about a diversion against Denmark. In March he became concerned at the possibility of a double assault against the Biscay and Mediterranean coasts. Von Rundstedt shared this concern until April when it became apparent that Italy was the point of immediate concentration for the Allied armies in the Mediterranean. He then decided that the diversion would be made in Brittany and advocated the withdrawal from the area south of the Loire of everything except a meagre police force. He argued that the Allies were now too deeply committed in Italy to make an early landing in Southern France and that German strength in the West should be concentrated on the Channel to match the Allied concentration in Southern England.

From a purely military standpoint this was sound strategy, yet Hitler rejected it, not merely because of his fundamental reluctance to yield ground, but because he knew that any loosening of his grip on the occupied territories would have disastrous political repercussions throughout Europe. His fears on this score were not unjustified, for the area south of Limoges and Lyons was the stronghold of the Maquis, the most intractable element of the French Resistance. He could not risk an open outbreak of revolt at this critical time.

Although he adhered to his determination to defend the whole of France, Hitler rightly predicted where the main blow would fall. In the last week of April, when the Allied assault shipping began to assemble in the embarkation ports, German reconnaissance aircraft noted the heavy concentrations in harbours west of the Isle of Wight and the absence of any marked increase in the forces in Dover and Folkestone. On May 2nd, in the light of this evidence, Hitler proclaimed to his staff the belief that the *Schwerpunkt* of the Allied landings would be in Normandy, and he ordered the immediate reinforcement of the sector between the Seine and the Loire.

Von Rundstedt carried out these orders reluctantly, since Admiral Krancke, commanding Naval Group West, assured him that it was " almost impossible " for large-scale landings to be made between Caen and Cherbourg on account of the dangerous outcrops of rock off-shore.[1] In addition, von Rundstedt's chief engineer insisted that the flooding around Carentan would discourage any major assault on the Cotentin Peninsula. Accordingly, C.-in-C., West, remained true to his original conviction that the initial blow would fall between Fécamp and Le Tréport (i.e. around Dieppe) and the chief assault north of the Somme. He, and his staff, decided that the shipping concentrations in Devon and Cornwall must be part of a deception plan designed to distract their attention from the Pas de Calais. When their night reconnaissance aircraft reported that road convoys driving to ports in South-Western England were using their lights they presumed that this ' breach of security ' was deliberately designed to deceive.

Rommel's appreciation fell half-way between the views of Hitler and von Rundstedt. He continued to believe that the major landings would be made at the mouth of the Somme, but he now expected a strong diversion in Western Normandy. Accordingly, in May he intensified the fortification of the sector between Cherbourg and Le Havre, strengthened the static garrisons and redistributed his reserves, moving them closer to the coast. He suggested further that 12th SS, one of the panzer divisions held back in Hitler's strategic reserve, should be moved to the area St. Lô–Carentan—to the immediate vicinity, in fact, of the chosen American assault beaches. Von Rundstedt opposed this and for once Hitler did not force the issue in Rommel's favour.

The Allied commanders knew nothing of these arguments and estimates, but they learned enough to realise that the character and strength of the enemy forces in the NEPTUNE area had altered drastically and dangerously during May. To them the only reassuring fact was that none of these changes had been made at the expense of the Pas de Calais, which was still the most strongly defended zone, nor was there any sign that the enemy felt free to weaken his garrison in Southern France.

At the end of May, as far as the Allies knew, von Rundstedt's strength was still widely dispersed, for his 60 divisions were deployed as follows:

[1]The information in this paragraph is based on the evidence of Blumentritt and Ruge. (See also Speidel, op. cit., p. 46.)

|  | INFANTRY | ARMOURED | TOTAL |
|---|---|---|---|
| Holland - - - | 4 | 1[1] | 5 |
| Between the Scheldt and the Seine - | 16 | 3 | 19 |
| Between the Seine and the Loire - - | 15 | 3 | 18 |
| Channel Islands - | 1 | – | 1 |
| Biscay Sector (South of the Loire) - - | 4 | 2[2] | 6 |
| Mediterranean Sector | 9 | 2 | 11 |
|  | 49 | 11 | 60 |

[1]This was only the rump of a division (19th Panzer) which had returned from Russia to refit and was not yet ready for serious operations.

[2]One of these was a panzer grenadier division (17th SS) containing as its armoured element only one battalion of assault guns, instead of the two tank battalions of a panzer division.

This dispersion was the inevitable result of the Allied command of the sea and air and of Hitler's insistence that the whole of France must be defended. It gave an initial advantage to the invaders, but the strengthening of the coast defences and the last-minute reinforcement of Normandy kept the overall balance of ground strength weighted against them. When the revised OVERLORD Plan was approved in February, it was estimated by Williams that the Allies would meet not more than six divisions on D-Day. By mid-May, however, it seemed likely that at least eight divisions, two of them armoured, would be able to oppose the landings on the first day and that three other armoured or mechanised divisions and an additional infantry division could be in action against the bridge-head by the morning of D plus 2, instead of D plus 4 as originally estimated. It was now apparent that Rommel was seeking to defeat the invasion on the beaches and that the critical phase would be the first week or ten days. During this period there was the possibility that the comparative rate of build-up would be as follows:

| BY THE EVENING OF | D-DAY | D+1 | D+3 | D+7 | D+10 |
|---|---|---|---|---|---|
| Allied Divisions | 8 | 10 | 13 | 16 | 18 |
| German Divisions | 8 | 12 | 15 | 22 | 27 |

This prospect heightened the importance of the campaign of disruption and deception which the Allied Air Forces had been waging against German defences and communications since February.

The air supremacy, which the Allies had established from the Atlantic and Mediterranean coasts to Berlin and Vienna by March 1944, enabled Eisenhower to make full use of the flexible weapon of aerial power in support of OVERLORD, but his plan for its employment was settled only after a prolonged and acute controversy. This revolved chiefly around the question whether the primary target for the Strategic Air Forces in the months preceding the invasion should be the railway system of Northern France and the Low Countries or the synthetic oil refineries and other industrial targets in Germany.

Eisenhower insisted that he could not outstrip the German build-up unless the rail communications leading to the invasion area were paralysed, and this, he urged, could be assured only if rail targets were subjected to a prolonged and intensive campaign of bombardment, not only by the ' mediums ' of the Allied Expeditionary Air Force, but by the ' heavies ' which were not under his jurisdiction. The U.S. Strategic Air Forces and R.A.F. Bomber Command were directly responsible to the Combined Chiefs of Staff and their commanders, Spaatz and Harris respectively, were most reluctant to be diverted from their appointed task of crippling German industry just when they believed they were about to achieve decisive success. They were both convinced that Germany could be bombed into impotence, if not submission, provided that their attacks were maintained without respite; any slackening or pause would give the enemy the opportunity to patch up existing scars and carry through his programme of dispersal.

Harris's reluctance was due primarily to his doubt whether he could " achieve the extraordinary precision needed if the project was to succeed," for experience had shown that railways were " extraordinarily difficult and unrewarding targets for air attack."[1] Bomber Command had been concerned almost exclusively with attacks on large industrial areas, and, says Harris, " there was little reason to think that the whole force could be rapidly switched to the destruction of small targets."

The chief opposition came, however, from Spaatz, for his Fortresses and Liberators were about to launch an offensive against the synthetic oil plants, which provided the life-blood of the German war machine and had become increasingly important in view of the growing Soviet threat to the Rumanian oilfields. The attack on German oil was to be the culmination of the American campaign in the air, for now at last they had the air supremacy, the range and above all the radar equipment to strike accurately through cloud or smoke screen even at such small targets as refineries. Like Harris, Spaatz was ready to harness his forces

[1]Harris, *Bomber Offensive*, pp. 196-7.

to the OVERLORD plan for the weeks immediately before and after the landing, but both were opposed to any premature diversion of their strength for the sustained bombardment of rail targets. Spaatz suggested that enemy communications could be sufficiently disrupted by direct attacks on the main lines and junctions in the immediate NEPTUNE area on the eve of invasion.

This proposal was rejected by Eisenhower, who was advised by Tedder and Leigh-Mallory that nothing less than the saturation of the repair and maintenance facilities of the French railways would produce the necessary paralysis. Accordingly he demanded that all air resources be employed to ensure the success of the main Allied effort, OVERLORD. The bombing of oil refineries, even if successful, would not affect the strength of the Wehrmacht in the field in time to assist the over-riding task of getting the troops ashore in Normandy. The railway bombing plan did promise to do so.

Eisenhower's view prevailed and in March the Combined Chiefs of Staff agreed to place the Strategic Air Forces under his ' operational control.' He in turn delegated to Tedder the intricate task of co-ordinating the efforts of the British and American heavy bombers and of Leigh-Mallory's A.E.A.F. Thus Tedder exercised the authority of the Supreme Commander in respect of air operations. This was a wise move. The Americans were reluctant to follow Leigh-Mallory's direction, but they accepted Tedder in the role of co-ordinator because he spoke for Eisenhower.

A successful commander of fighters in the defence of Britain and the Dieppe Raid, Leigh-Mallory had risen to become A.O.C.-in-C., Fighter Command, but he was not experienced in bomber operations and he lacked Tedder's strategic sense and diplomatic touch. In directing operations Leigh-Mallory was resolute and aggressive, but in planning he was inclined to take counsel of his fears. He had very strong opinions about the use of air power, and many of his original ideas were to be proved correct by events, but he was obstinate and blunt in presenting his views and extremely hot-tempered when crossed. He inspired great loyalty and confidence in his staff and his fighting squadrons, but he was not so successful in his dealings with other services, or with the Americans who resented his dogmatic manner. He did not possess the knack of easy association essential for an Allied commander-in-chief in a combined operation. Admittedly, he had a difficult task, for successful air commanders tend to become temperamental personalities, and the Americans were unwilling to accept anything more than nominal control.

Tedder, on the other hand, had exactly the qualities and the experience to play the role of referee. In Africa and the Mediterranean he had directed the Allied Air Forces with a brilliant hand. The Americans liked and respected him and he understood what the Army needed. Of all the British commanders serving under Eisenhower, he was undoubtedly the best fitted to resolve inter-service and inter-Allied difficulties. Even Tedder's appointment, however, did not entirely eradicate the weakness of the Air Command. He had no staff and there was no Supreme Air Headquarters. Tedder had to co-ordinate as best he could the efforts of three separate Air Forces, each with its own Commander-in-Chief and each jealous of its own position. Out of this complex and unwieldy arrangement even his deft direction could not evolve a fully integrated air plan.

The decision regarding the control of the heavy bombers did not end the argument about targets. The plan to bomb the French railways evoked repeated protests from the Prime Minister and from General Pierre Koenig, the Commander of the F.F.I. (*Les Forces Françaises de l'Intérieur*), who were alarmed at the casualties which might be inflicted upon civilians. Koenig offered to achieve equal dislocation of the railways by sabotage. " You name the targets," he said to Eisenhower's Chief of Staff, Bedell Smith, " and we will see that they're destroyed." This gallant offer had to be refused, for the scope and character of the plan was such that its fulfilment could not be left to the hazard of sabotage.

In Sicily and Italy Tedder had learned how difficult it was to cripple enemy rail communications by the conventional methods of line-cutting and bridge-busting, but he had also discovered that a whole railway system could be paralysed if the attacks were concentrated on the centres of maintenance and repair. His primary targets, therefore, were railway workshops and locomotive sheds, the destruction of which would cause long-term and widespread dislocation which the enemy could not rapidly make good. Since most of these centres were alongside major junctions and marshalling yards they provided dual-purpose targets and it was possible to strike simultaneously at both the current traffic and capital equipment of the railways. When this process of attrition was well advanced, Tedder planned to switch the main attack to locomotives, lines and bridges, paying special attention in the final week to the road and rail bridges over the Seine and, he hoped, inflicting damage so severe that the enemy's already weakened repair services could not cope with it.

Although the primary purpose of the rail offensive was to reduce the enemy's capacity for moving reserves, it was important that it should also contribute to the deception plan. By a fortunate accident of geography a single bombardment programme could achieve both objects. The chief German supply routes to Western Normandy were either extensions of, or offshoots from, lines which served the Pas de Calais or the Le Havre–Amiens area. They ran either through Paris or across the Seine west of the capital. Thus the bombing of repair-shops and junctions between the Seine and the Meuse could disrupt German communications with Normandy almost as effectively as attacks directed at the zone between the Seine and the Loire. Moreover, the general paralysis of the railway system could best be achieved by attacks on targets in the *Région Nord*, for it was here that the principal maintenance facilities were located. Nor would the bombing of the Seine bridges betray the Allied

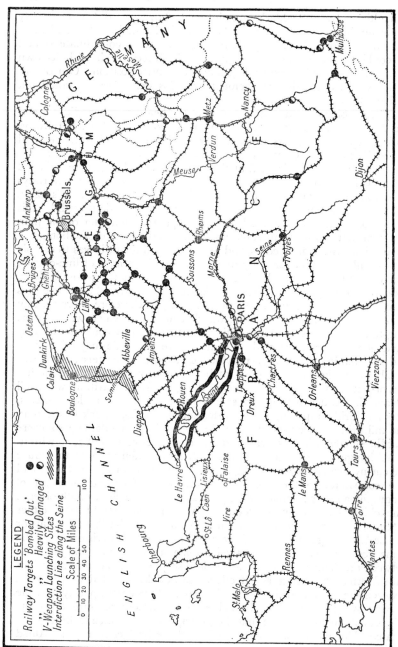

PRE-INVASION BOMBING

intention, since this would appear as the last act in an attempt to isolate the Pas de Calais.

For the execution of this plan a team of railway experts chose 80 key targets in Northern France and Belgium, 39 of which were to be dealt with by Bomber Command. The offensive opened on the night of March 6th-7th with a raid by the R.A.F. on Trappes, 20 miles west of Paris. There the engine shed was wrecked and 190 direct hits were scored on the tracks; the marshalling yard was still under repair at the end of April. Bomber Command exceeded all expectations in the accuracy of its attacks; the Eighth U.S. Air Force was equally successful, and, once the ' heavies ' had devastated a particular target, the ' mediums ' kept the scars open with stoking raids, and fighter-bombers harassed the reconstruction gangs.

At the end of March the bombed lines were usually repaired within forty-eight hours, but before the end of April it was taking more than a week to get them open and by the middle of May the accumulation of wreckage was so vast that even important routes were closed for ten to twelve days after an average attack. By this time 15 major marshalling yards and 40 large depots for the servicing of locomotives had been wrecked, and little could be done to restore them owing to the serious shortage of cranes.

Early in May Colonel Hoeffner, who was in charge of all rail trans-portation for von Rundstedt, reported to OKW that the situation was critical. To maintain the Wehrmacht in France, he said, required 100 trains a day from Germany; the daily average for April had been 60 and this had now fallen to 32. Of these, nearly half were coal trains from the Saar, for he could no longer supply the French railways with coal from Belgium. Consequently he was only just able to meet the current needs of the forces north and north-west of Paris. He could not maintain supplies for work on the Atlantic Wall nor could he carry out the planned stocking-up of ammunition and petrol dumps near the coast. More than 50,000 Germans and foreigners had been brought in to keep the railways running but more would be needed, because it was becoming increasingly difficult to find Frenchmen to operate the trains or repair the lines west and north of Paris.

When Hoeffner made that report the offensive had not yet entered its most intensive phase. This began on May 21st when the policy of strategic attrition was supplemented by tactical interdiction and disloca-tion, by attacks on bridges, viaducts and locomotives and by straight-out line-cutting. Although the raids were more widespread, the deceptive purpose was maintained and the Germans recorded 246 attacks on targets north of the Seine and only 33 south of it during the next week. By the end of the following week 430 locomotives had been wrecked by Allied aircraft; of the 2,000 engines in *Région Nord*, 1,500 were now immobilised by direct air attacks or lack of maintenance; and traffic had fallen to 13 per cent of the January level. At the H.Q. of *Région Nord* in Brussels the Germans kept an elaborate wall chart showing the weekly state of traffic, lines and rolling stock. On this chart from the end of March the graphs went steadily down until at last on May 28th the Germans abandoned the attempt to keep account of the damage and destruction. In the three months before D-Day only four of the 80 special rail targets escaped serious damage, and traffic over the whole of France declined by 70 per cent.

The final blow in the preparatory campaign against enemy communications was the attack on bridges over the Seine, the Oise and the Meuse. The technique for these attacks was worked out by the Ninth U.S. Air Force, which used fighters as dive-bombers with spectacular success. By June 5th, of the 24 road and rail bridges over the Seine between Paris and the sea, 18 had been destroyed, three were closed for repair and the remaining three were under such threat of air attack that they could not be used for any large-scale movement in daylight.

This successful interdiction counteracted to a very large degree the increase in strength which the May reinforcements had brought to the Seventh German Army in Normandy and made it likely that the early battle would have to be fought out by the divisions already deployed between the Seine and the Loire. In the immediate area of the invasion there were now six, possibly seven, infantry divisions and one panzer division, with two other panzer divisions at close call and capable of intervening within twenty-four hours, unless their attention could be distracted to another quarter.

While the Allied Air Forces were developing their assault against the enemy's communications and coastal defences, there was little opposition or counter-action from the Luftwaffe. Even daylight raids on vital installations were seldom resisted by German fighters and the anticipated onslaught against the harbours of Southern England by V-weapons and conventional aircraft did not materialise. In February and March London had nine night raids—ironically dubbed ' the Little Blitz '— but these were merely token reprisals for the bombing of Berlin. On moonless nights during April and May there was some minelaying and scatter-bombing along the south coast, but it never reached serious proportions. The failure of the Germans to launch their promised offensive with V-weapons was amply explained by the persistent bombing of the launching sites, but the limited activity of the Luftwaffe, even during the most ostentatious exercises in the Channel, seemed accountable only on the ground that Goering was husbanding his resources until the armada put to sea. In the final weeks every enemy airfield within 130 miles of the Channel coast was heavily bombed, yet it was by no means certain that the degree of air superiority which the Allies enjoyed during May would prevail in the first critical weeks after D-Day.

While the air offensive developed in power and scope, the final plan for the NEPTUNE assault was approved by Eisenhower, though Leigh-Mallory continued to express his fears about the employment of airborne troops in the Cotentin Peninsula. The Army plan provided for the operation to begin with the dropping of three airborne divisions behind the Atlantic Wall during the night immediately preceding the main invasion from the sea. These divisions—the 6th British in the Orne Valley and the 82nd and 101st American at the base of the Cotentin—were to secure the flanks of the bridgehead and weaken the beach defences at keypoints by attacks from the rear. Their landing was to be followed soon after daybreak by the seaborne assault, for which the Order of Battle was:

FIRST U.S. ARMY (Lieut.-General Omar Bradley) to land North and East of the Vire Estuary:

*Right:* VII U.S. Corps (Major-General J. Lawton Collins).
UTAH Beach—4th U.S. Infantry Division assaulting, followed by the 90th, 9th and 79th Divisions.

*Left:* V U.S. Corps (Major-General L. T. Gerow).
OMAHA Beach—1st U.S. Infantry Division, with part of the 29th Infantry Division under command, and the rest of the 29th, plus the 2nd Infantry Division, to follow up.

SECOND BRITISH ARMY (Lieut.-General M. C. Dempsey) to land between Bayeux and Caen:

*Right:* XXX British Corps (Lieut.-General G. C. Bucknall).
GOLD Beach—50th Northumbrian Division and 8th Armoured Brigade, followed by the 7th Armoured Division and the 49th Infantry Division.

*Left:* I British Corps (Lieut.-General J. T. Crocker).
JUNO Beach—3rd Canadian Infantry Division and 2nd Canadian Armoured Brigade followed by Commandos of 4th Special Service Brigade.
SWORD Beach—3rd British Infantry Division and 27th Armoured Brigade, followed by 1st Special Service Brigade, the 51st Highland Division and 4th Armoured Brigade.[1]

The immediate task which Montgomery had given to these forces was to form two bridgeheads on D-Day: one between the Rivers Vire and Orne, including Isigny, Bayeux and Caen; the other on the coast of the Cotentin, north of the Vire, extending to the line of the Carentan

[1] Four U.S. tank battalions were to land with the American assault divisions, and all the British units were to be preceded by special assault teams of the 79th Armoured Division.

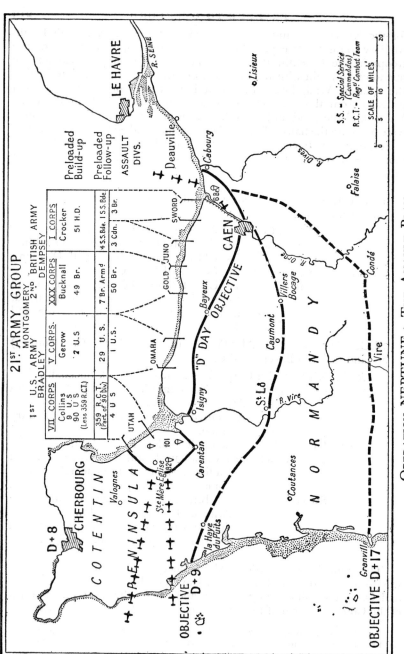

OPERATION NEPTUNE: THE ASSAULT PLAN

Canal and beyond the River Merderet. It was not expected that these two bridgeheads could be linked up before D plus 1 at the earliest, for Carentan was strongly held and there was no likelihood that it could be attacked on the first day.

Montgomery intended that in the next week this foothold should be expanded north-west, west and south, but not appreciably east or south-east. On the left flank the role of I British Corps was to hold Caen and the open ground immediately south of the city as a pivot and as a bastion, which must at all costs withstand the counter-attack of the enemy's main panzer reserves stationed in the area Chartres–Paris–Amiens–Rouen. From the centre of the bridgehead V U.S. Corps and XXX British Corps would attack south to secure by D plus 9 the high ground along the line St. Lô–Caumont–Villers–Bocage, thus gaining sufficient depth to protect the MULBERRY harbours from direct fire. Meantime VII U.S. Corps was to strike west and seal off the base of the Cotentin and north to capture Cherbourg—by D plus 8 if all were to go well, though Bradley did not believe that this could be achieved before D plus 15.

With Cherbourg taken, Bradley's full strength would be concentrated for a southward drive to expand the bridgehead into a substantial lodgement area. Montgomery hoped that by D plus 50 his forces—including the First Canadian and Third U.S. Armies—would hold an area including the Brittany ports and extending south to the Loire and east to the line Deauville–Tours. If the battle were to follow the plan, the Allied armies (strengthened by divisions brought direct from the United States to Cherbourg and possibly to Brest) would be established along the Seine, across the Paris–Orléans gap and down the valley of the Loire to the sea by D plus 90.[1]

This statement of the probable course of events is taken direct from the notes Montgomery used on May 15th when he spoke at a Final Presentation of Plans in the presence of the King and the Prime Minister. Confident and resolute, Montgomery talked " without pretension or bombast," to quote the opinion of Brereton, who commanded the Ninth U.S. Air Force.[2] His survey was masterful and prescient, and when he turned to speak of the enemy he revealed how thoroughly he understood his opponent's mind.

" Last February," he said, " Rommel took command from Holland to the Loire. It is now clear that his intention is to deny any penetration: OVERLORD is to be defeated on the beaches." He then went on to state in detail what changes Rommel had made, and he continued, " Rommel is an energetic and determined commander; he has made a world of

[1] " These phase lines," says the U.S. War Department in an historical study, " were set with the most favourable possible development of the operations in mind. They insured readiness for the maximum progress but represented neither a hard-and-fast schedule nor an optimistic forecast." (*OMAHA Beach-head*, p. 5.)

[2] Brereton, *Diaries*, p. 264.

difference since he took over. He is best at the spoiling attack; his *forte* is disruption; he is too impulsive for a set-piece battle. He will do his level best to ' Dunkirk ' us—not to fight the armoured battle on ground of his own choosing, but to avoid it altogether by preventing our tanks from landing by using his own tanks well forward. On D-Day he will try to force us from the beaches and secure Caen, Bayeux, Carentan. . . . Thereafter he will continue his counter-attacks. But, as time goes on, he will combine them with a roping-off policy and he must then hold firm on the important ground which dominates and controls the road axes in the bocage country."

Montgomery then propounded his solution: " We must blast our way on shore and get a good lodgement before the enemy can bring up sufficient reserves to turn us out. Armoured columns must penetrate deep inland, and quickly, on D-Day; this will upset the enemy's plans and tend to hold him off while we build up strength. We must gain space rapidly and peg out claims well inland. . . . Once we get control of the main enemy lateral Granville–Vire–Argentan–Falaise–Caen and have the area enclosed in it firmly in our possession, then we will have the lodgement area we want and can begin to expand."

He concluded with this injunction: " We shall have to send the soldiers into this party ' seeing red.' They must see red. We must get them completely on their toes, having absolute faith in the plan; and imbued with infectious optimism and offensive eagerness. Nothing must stop them. Nothing. If we send them into battle in this way—then we shall succeed."

To the inculcation of this fiery spirit in his troops Montgomery bent all his energy and ardour in the weeks that remained before they set forth upon their great crusade.

## CHAPTER XI

# FORECAST AND FORTITUDE

THROUGHOUT May the Germans in France lived in almost daily expectation of invasion, for they had become alarmed after detecting the assembly of assault shipping in the South Coast ports at the end of April. But when Eisenhower made no attempt to take advantage of the long spell of perfect weather in May, Hitler, von Rundstedt and Rommel were all inclined to believe that there would be no invasion until after the start of the Red Army's summer offensive, and they knew that the lateness of the thaw in Poland would not permit this to begin before the middle of June.

In trying to estimate Allied intentions, the German High Command was working under a serious handicap, for its Foreign Intelligence Service, now in Himmler's sinister control, was producing information of the most doubtful character. Himmler's absorption of the Abwehr in March could not have come at a less opportune time. Inefficient though Canaris's organisation was, it did exist, and Himmler had no adequate substitute. For the most part the Gestapo types whom he sent abroad were gauche thugs, ignorant and inept. Their big ears picked up every canard which British agents spread abroad in neutral capitals, and in the weeks immediately preceding the invasion Himmler's men were deliberately swamped with ' secret information ' which they had neither the time nor the wit to sift and appraise. The German Intelligence machine became clogged, and the material sent in by Abwehr agents who were still in the field was lost among the rubbish. After the war in the records of the German Admiralty the Allies found a dossier containing some 250 individual reports from agents dealing with the time and place of invasion. Of these only one, from a French colonel in Algiers, was correct, but this had been filed away unheeded with the dross. The majority opinion gave July as the month and the Pas de Calais as the place.

German Intelligence was no better served by the Luftwaffe, for its reconnaissance aircraft were seldom able to pierce the formidable defences. On May 21st in his weekly report to von Rundstedt, Rommel complained: " There are *no* results of air reconnaissance of the island for the entire period." In the following week the Luftwaffe reconnoitred three of the seventeen harbours in which Ramsay's assault forces were assembled, but it failed to make a comprehensive survey of the South Coast and none of its aircraft succeeded in penetrating by day into the area of greatest concentration around the Isle of Wight. It did observe, however, that there were still "only a small number of landing-craft at Folkestone and Dover." At the H.Q. of both von Rundstedt and Rommel this fact was given undue importance, because the two Field-Marshals were the victims of their own obsession about the area north of the Seine, an obsession which led them to expect that the final warning would be the assembly of landing-craft in the harbours of Kent.

The German High Command was incapable of assessing correctly even the evidence which was presented to it by the character and course of Allied operations. On May 30th in an estimate of the situation for Hitler, von Rundstedt declared: "It is true that the hour of invasion draws nearer, but the scale of the enemy air attacks does not indicate that it is immediately imminent."

While the Germans were reaching this conclusion the invasion armies sweated to complete their last-minute preparations in the wired and guarded camps of the marshalling areas. In the first days of May they had concluded their final rehearsals, designed to test out the machinery of movement and embarkation, and through the ensuing sunlit weeks they waited with mounting impatience. 'Any day now,' they hoped, for the tedium of waiting heightened the suspense and left men's minds free to dwell upon the unknown hazards which lay beyond the sea. Reassured by Montgomery's vibrant faith, their confidence in themselves and in him was high, but inevitably there had been communicated to them something of the deep, unspoken dread with which the people of Britain faced the coming assault upon the Atlantic Wall. The people had hardened themselves to endure what must be endured. There would be no shrinking from sacrifice, since their resolution was far stronger than their fear, but they could not altogether dispel from their hearts the memories of Passchendaele, Dunkirk and Dieppe.

For the men in the leading divisions these weeks were the severest test of morale. The listless air of uncertainty hung heavily over the camps and each day seemed longer than the one before. Uneasiness grew with inactivity. After the middle of the month most of the assault troops had little to do but await the movement of the inexorable machine which had them in its grip. In its own good time the machine would move them down to the ships, across the Channel and on to the beaches. But which beaches? When?

These doubts and anxieties remained unresolved till the last week of the month when the camps were sealed and the men were gradually let into the secret. For the British troops, the first hint was the issuing of French money and of a booklet which began: "A new B.E.F., which includes you, is going to France. You are to assist personally in pushing the Germans out of France and back where they belong."

This note of personal responsibility was emphasised in the next few days of intensive instruction. Inside the closely guarded ' briefing-huts,' each man saw spread out before him the extent and significance of his unit's task and that of his division. Aerial photographs, taken almost from the wave-top, gave him a picture of the shore as he would first see it. Other photographs, taken from various heights and angles, revealed the German defences in every detail: pill-boxes, minefields, road-blocks, machine-gun nests, anti-tank emplacements, battery positions. Large-scale models, maps and sketches amplified the story so that he could follow the unfolding of the plan step by step. " You will land here," the briefing officer would say, " you will go there, you will take this, you will do that. These minefields will be gapped by ' flails '; those pill-boxes will be dealt with by DD tanks. This battery position will be neutralised by the Navy; that one by fighter-bombers." And so he went on—through the full ramifications of the plan.

The men could see for themselves that the ' strong-point ' which they had ' taken ' so often in rehearsal was indeed an exact replica of the enemy position which they could now pick out on the scale model as their own objective. They could see where the model matched the map and how the map was confirmed by air photographs. They drew encouragement from the extent and detail of the intelligence information on which the plan was based. Here the strength and the weaknesses of the Atlantic Wall were laid bare, and it seemed less formidable now that they knew exactly what they had to tackle. It was no longer a question of plunging into the dark unknown.

For the briefing of British glider pilots and air-crews a most ingenious device was used. The Army constructed a detailed model of the Orne Valley, correct even to the height of the trees and the size of the houses. From this model the R.A.F. made a film, which gave the impression that one was flying over the actual coast of France, following the precise route the gliders, tugs and troop-carriers would be flying. This was far more instructive than the study of conventional air photographs for, as they watched the film, the pilots saw features and landmarks coming into view and learned what to look for. After they had seen the film several times with normal lighting it was screened again through a blue filter, which gave a faithful representation of moonlight conditions. The crews, knowing the landmarks, were then able to see which were most likely to be visible at night.

The trust and care which characterised the briefing of the assault divisions enhanced the confidence of the men in themselves, their leaders and the plan. Once they had been briefed, the men of the invading armies knew that nothing had been left to chance. Knowledge drove out anxiety and, though each man retained some personal apprehension about his own fate, none doubted that the invasion would succeed.

Aware of the plan, they became the more impatient to see it launched, but the plan was geared to elements which were beyond human power to govern or prescribe—the tide, the moon and the weather.

The fixing of the hour and the day was the result of balancing many factors. In the Mediterranean all the major landings had been made under cover of darkness, but for NEPTUNE Eisenhower's three Commanders-in-Chief[1] decided to invade in daylight, in order to facilitate the identification of the beaches, the navigation of the mass of small craft and the observation of shore targets for air and naval bombardment. For this ' softening-up ' Ramsay and Leigh-Mallory needed at least an hour of daylight and this consideration outweighed the Army's desire to attack at dawn, but it was essential that the initial landings be made on the earliest possible high-tide so that the follow-up forces could be brought in on a second tide before nightfall.

These calculations were complicated by the appearance of the underwater obstacles. To avoid them and to give the demolition squads time to deal with them dryshod, it was decided, as we have seen, that the first assault echelons should touch down three hours before high-water. Because of the flow of the tide up the English Channel, however, it would be high-water on the most westerly beach, UTAH, 40 minutes earlier than on the easternmost beach, SWORD. Between these two extremes there were local difficulties due to outcrops of rock and the extent of the obstructions, which in some places were emplaced below the half-tide mark. Consequently each of the main beaches had to have its own H-Hour. This staggering of the touch-down time made it necessary to reduce the period for the observed bombardment of UTAH beach to the bare minimum of 40 minutes, and even this meant that the force on the eastern flank would be exposed in daylight to enemy fire for more than an hour before it could begin to land. It meant also that the second tide would not come until late in the evening.

The final consideration was that D-Day should fall at a time when there was a late-rising full moon, so that aircraft carrying the airborne forces could approach their objectives before it rose and yet have moonlight to help them identify their dropping zones. The ultimate formula, on which the Commanders-in-Chief agreed, was that the invasion should be launched on a day when it would be half-tide on the east coast of the Cotentin Peninsula (UTAH Beach) 40 minutes after first light, following a night when a full moon rose between one and two a.m. The necessity of meeting these varied requirements limited the suitable days in any month to *three*.

On May 17th, after a special photographic survey had been made

---

[1] Although Montgomery was not designated ' C-in-C., Land Forces,' he acted as such. Thus the phrase ' three Commanders-in-Chief,' while not strictly accurate, is a fair statement of the command organisation.

of the under-water obstacles, Eisenhower selected Monday, June 5th, as the tentative D-Day, but the final decision depended on the weather. The minimum conditions acceptable to all three services were that D-Day itself must be quiet, followed by three quiet days: surface winds not exceeding Force 3 (8-12 m.p.h.) on shore, nor Force 4 (13-18 m.p.h.) off-shore; cloud base above three thousand feet and cloud no thicker than 5/10ths; visibility at least three miles; half moonlight for the airborne landings. The records for the past century showed that the chances of Normandy having weather in June which met all these requirements was thirteen to one against.

Most of May the weather was ideal, a succession of soft spring days with the Channel smooth and sunlit. Weather for poets. Twice a week Eisenhower conferred with his meteorologists and, on the strength of their predictions, made ' test-runs,' deciding for or against a notional invasion thirty-six hours ahead. Thus he schooled himself to weigh the many factors involved and tested the reliability of the forecasts and of the men who made them. The chief of these was Group-Captain J. M. Stagg of the R.A.F.—a tall, gaunt Lowlander, a scientist to his bones with all the scientist's refined capacity to pass unimpassioned judgment on the evidence, a man of sharp mind and soft speech, detached, resolute, courageous. In these trial forecasts Eisenhower learned that the man whose opinion and nerve he could trust in the hour of decision was Stagg.

In May there were 18 days which met all the weather requirements and the month went out in a blaze of sunshine, but on the last day the high pressure area over the Azores—the guarantor of the good weather so far—was showing signs of weakness. Thursday, June 1st, dawned dull and grey and Stagg noted in his diary,[1] " Fairly optimistic, but obviously a very marginal and difficult situation." The following day, when the experts reported to Eisenhower and his three Commanders-in-Chief at Southwick House, near Portsmouth, " the situation," Stagg noted, " was not what we hoped for." He reported that " the whole development was sluggish and slow to show its hand, but on the whole still mainly favourable from wind point of view though very uncertain about cloud. Supreme Commander questioned about Tuesday and Wednesday; I said no worse than Sunday and Monday. Nothing really bad in respect of gales, but cloud continuing poor." The prospect was hardly encouraging for the start of the most elaborate operation in the history of war, and as the weather men went out, Ramsay's Chief of Staff, Admiral Creasy, commented—" Six feet two of Stagg, and six feet one of gloom."

In spite of the uncertainty, some of the bombarding forces had to

[1] I am greatly indebted to Dr. Stagg for permission to draw upon the diary which he kept throughout this period. The entries written—sometimes in ink, sometimes in pencil, on a dozen sheets of foolscap—were jotted down after each conference. Here Stagg noted his own feelings, the reactions of his colleagues and of those he was advising, and the development of the most important weather situation which any meteorologist ever had to appraise.

begin moving south from Scapa, Belfast and the Clyde that night if they were to reach the Channel for invasion on Monday, the 5th. They sailed, but next morning (Saturday) the situation was still uncertain and two of the forecasting stations presented diametrically opposed interpretations of its probable development. That evening, however, at the Supreme Commander's conference, Stagg declared that his fears were confirmed. The high pressure area over the Azores was " rapidly giving way " and a series of depressions, three in all, were bringing unfriendly weather into the Channel. From early on Sunday until late on Wednesday—over the only three June days when the tide and moon would be suitable—they could expect high winds, thick low cloud and some fog over the Normandy beaches.

" When I had presented the main picture," wrote Stagg in his diary, " there was a grave gloom over the place. The Supreme Commander said, ' You were a bit more optimistic last night. Isn't there a chance that you may be a bit more optimistic to-morrow? '

" ' No, sir; as I hoped you realised I was very unhappy about the position yesterday morning, the whole picture was extremely finely balanced. Last night there was a slight tip in the balance on the favourable side but the tip to-night on the unfavourable side is too big to be counterbalanced overnight.' "

Postponement was almost inevitable, but Eisenhower decided that the American assault forces assembled in the ports of South Devon should sail, as planned, in case there should be some unexpected improvement. There was still an element of doubt. The reports from one of the weather ships in the Western Atlantic conflicted sharply with evidence from other sources, and the several forecasting stations, on which Stagg and his colleagues had to rely, were not even agreed upon the facts. " This synoptic situation," wrote Stagg that night, " is the worst and most uncertain during the whole time in 1944 that I've been in this job. . . . The lack of complete certainty and unanimity is very disconcerting. It is better to have to make the decision oneself and take the whole blame."

When they met again in the library of Southwick House at 4.15 a.m. on Sunday, June 4th, the main body of the assault forces was due to sail within two hours. Stagg began: " We see no reason for substantial change from the evening's conference, except that the cold front (over Nova Scotia and New England) then expected to clear our area of low cloud on late Wednesday is now expected earlier on Wednesday. Winds the same : Force 5 (19-24 m.p.h.) on the English coast from today; less on the French coasts. 10/10ths cloud along the Channel; base 500-1,000 feet. No difference between Sunday, Monday and Tuesday."

This forecast of rising wind and thicker, lower cloud was in such contrast to the weather prevailing outside that Ramsay asked, " When will this cloud appear? It is practically a clear sky with the wind calm at the moment."

" By 8 or 9 a.m.," replied Stagg, " four or five hours from now."

Montgomery was prepared to go ahead in defiance of the weather, but Ramsay was most dubious and Leigh-Mallory gave warning that the Air Forces could carry out only a fraction of their programme in the conditions predicted. This was the determining factor, because, said Eisenhower, " the operation in its present form and with our present strength is feasible only because of our very great air superiority."

Stagg continues, " The Supreme Commander then said, ' It looks as if we must call off the sailing of the last Forces—S and J—and take the necessary steps to recall the forces now at sea. Are there any dissentient voices? '

" There was none. He instructed his Chief of Staff to inform the Combined Chiefs of Staff that the assault had been postponed by one day . . .

" When we went out into the quiet, still, almost cloudless night, the enormity of the decision was borne in upon us. If the high winds and clouds don't show here by the morning, we needn't show ourselves. . . . There is still an element of doubt in what we have done."

Stagg slept from sheer exhaustion until ten, and then: " Awake to see bright sky and not too much wind. Heavens! What can be done now? The sky should be 10/10ths and wind up to Force 4 by now. Before I get up the cloud has come over and wind risen. By 10.30 or 10.45 cloud is 8/10ths and the trees overhead are swayed in a good Force 4, I should say Force 5. It looks as if the first stage of our forecast is partly justified and we can go over to ANCXF[1] with impunity."

At 11 a.m. the Admiralty issued a gale warning to all shipping in the Irish Sea. The question was: how long would this bad weather last? How quickly would the clearing front from Nova Scotia and New England cross the Atlantic? It was not expected to reach the Channel until Wednesday and by then it would be too late, for the convoys that had already sailed would not have sufficient fuel to stay at sea till then.

As Sunday, the 4th, dragged on, the storm gathered in fury, and it seemed that all the months of preparation would be nullified by the one factor which could not be harnessed to the plan. A surging wind drove white breakers against the fog-bound beaches of Normandy. A couple of miles off-shore two of the Royal Navy's midget submarines lay on the restless sea-bed, waiting to guide in the invasion fleet and ignorant as yet of the postponement. Out in the Channel the recalled convoys, punching into a head sea, strove to reach the shelter of Weymouth Bay, and one convoy had a particularly severe buffeting, for it had been half-way to France before a seaplane turned it back. In the crowded harbours from Falmouth to Harwich the rest of the armada tossed uneasily and tugged at its anchors. Many of the hundred thousand troops

---

[1]A.N.C.X.F.—Allied Naval Commander-in-Chief, Expeditionary Force. Ramsay's H.Q. was Southwick House. The library, where the weather meetings were held, was his Mess.

who were packed in the ships had already needed their anti-sea-sickness pills. They had been on board for more than a day, some for three or four days, and the strain of waiting—and watching the weather worsen —was searing the nerves of even the most hardened. The rain came in squalls and overhead the protective screen of barrage balloons danced to the tune of an irresponsible wind. On shore that wind howled through the pine trees around Southwick House where Eisenhower and his Commanders-in-Chief and their Chiefs of Staff gathered at 9 p.m. to hear the forecast on which the decision must be based.

" As on the preceding nights," says Stagg's diary, " they're all in easy-chairs and sofas, not formally round the table. . . . I start, ' Gentlemen, since the presentation yesterday evening there have been some rapid and unexpected developments in the situation over the Atlantic. A front from one of the depressions has swept farther south than expected and will come through the Eastern Channel areas to-night; it is nearly over Portsmouth now. When that front has passed, there will be a period of fair conditions—less than 5/10ths cloud, base 2,000–3,000 feet and reduced winds; this will last till at least dawn on Tuesday. After that, cloud will increase to 8/10ths–10/10ths from the West during Tuesday afternoon for a short period lasting overnight Tuesday. Then variable skies with considerable fair periods till Friday. . . .'

" Then the questions started. Supreme Commander: ' Can you say anything about conditions beyond Friday? ' ' No, sir. The general conditions must continue to be regarded as disturbed . . . but there is good reason for expecting a trend to improvement.'

" Tedder asked a question about confidence in the forecast. I explained that ' Lows ' had been careering along at a speed and rate of development appropriate to midwinter; our confidence was not yet high that the situation would settle immediately, but there was a good chance that the Azores High might get a chance to build up again.

" Leigh-Mallory asked if I had compared notes with his met. advisers. I said I had and they had agreed to the picture: almost perfect visual bombing weather from evening Monday to early forenoon Tuesday. Then periods of good bombing intermixed with poor periods from Tuesday afternoon till Friday.

" Eisenhower then started to discuss whether the assault should be laid on again and we withdrew."

The discussion continued under the pressure of urgency, for Ramsay pointed out that Admiral Kirk (commanding the U.S. Naval Forces) " must be told within the next half-hour if OVERLORD is to take place on Tuesday."[1] The trend of debate swung towards acceptance of the slender

[1]For the details of those discussions which Stagg did not hear, I have drawn on the record written at the time by Air Marshal J. M. Robb, Tedder's Chief of Staff. His record is confirmed by the notes kept by Ramsay's Chief of Staff, Rear-Admiral G. E. Creasy.

chance that Stagg had forecast. " It looks to me," said Bedell Smith,
" that we've gotten a break we could hardly hope for. . . . It's a helluva
gamble but it's the best possible gamble." Others felt likewise, but Leigh-
Mallory was concerned lest German night bombers might be able to
operate while Allied night fighters were grounded. He was worried too
about the conditions for the heavy bombers, whose second mission, if
not their first, was likely to be prejudiced by low cloud.

Eisenhower did not discount this danger, but he felt that, if the rest
of the air plan could be fulfilled, they might succeed. " After all," he
said, " we have a great force of fighter-bombers." Then, turning to
Montgomery he asked, " Do you see any reason for not going on
Tuesday? " Montgomery replied, " I would say—Go! "

Ramsay agreed, and Eisenhower went on, " The alternatives are too
chancy. The question is—just how long can you hang this operation
on the end of a limb and let it hang there? The air will certainly be
handicapped, but if we don't give the instructions now, we can't do it
on Tuesday."

No one needed to be reminded that if they did not invade on that
Tuesday, they would have to wait another fortnight for a suitable tide,
and then they would not have the moonlight they needed. Wednesday,
the 7th, was ruled out because some warships and convoys would have
to refuel. The Thursday would be too late, for the second high tide on
that day would not come till it was almost dark and that would disrupt
the fine balance of the build-up time-table.

The issue was clear-cut: take a chance on the Tuesday, or wait for
two weeks. But such a postponement was almost out of the question.
The troops had been briefed; they could not now be told that this was
another rehearsal. They could not be kept cooped up in the ships nor
could they easily be drafted back into their marshalling camps, because
these were already being taken over by the build-up divisions. The whole
gigantic machine had been set in motion; it could be stopped for twenty-
four or even forty-eight hours, but it could not be put into reverse without
serious risk of disorganisation and loss of security. Already an idle girl,
playing with a teletype machine in the London office of the Associated
Press, had inadvertently sent out the flash, " Eisenhower's forces have
landed in France," and American radio stations had repeated the ' news,'
before it could be ' killed.' What would the Russians say to postponement? Stalin had been promised " the first week in June," and the Red
Army had agreed to open its summer offensive in co-ordination with the
attack from the West.

The dangers of postponement were palpably greater than the hazards
implicit in Stagg's forecast—if it was right—and Eisenhower summed up
the common conclusion when he said, " Well, boys, there it is; I don't
see how we can possibly do anything else. I'm quite positive we must
give the order. The only question is whether we should meet again in
the morning? "

Ramsay was prepared to take this as the final decision, but Leigh-Mallory asked that they should meet again, for he was not yet convinced that the weather would allow him to carry out the air programme. He felt it might still be necessary to cancel the sailing instructions which Ramsay was now about to send to those American forces that needed early warning. It was agreed, therefore, that this tentative order would depend upon confirmation of the forecast when the meteorologists reported again at 4.15 a.m. As yet they were banking only on a trend, seeking to exploit a short and unexpected break in an otherwise unfavourable sky.

Outside the library Eisenhower walked across to Stagg and said, " We've put it on again. For heaven's sake hold the weather to what you've forecast for us. Don't bring us any more bad news."

It was still raining heavily when the conference adjourned, but by the time they reassembled for the final and irrevocable decision it was beginning to clear. " I started again," says Stagg, " and told them that there was really no substantial change from the previous presentation but what there was was in the direction of optimism. The fair interval, which had now set in here at Portsmouth and which would clear all Southern England during the night, would probably last into the late forenoon or afternoon of Tuesday. . . . It was a joy to see the relief caused by this statement. Immediately I had made it the tension fell and the S.C. and C.-in-C.s became informal. . . . There were a few questions. Tedder asked what really had happened to clear the warm air so quickly. I said that a front, which twenty-four hours or so before had turned westward into the next depression off Nova Scotia and Newfoundland, had suddenly cut away down south and swept through Ireland and was now sweeping through Southern England.

" To another question (I forget expressly from whom) I said there was a good chance now of all further depressions from the Western Atlantic moving more slowly and taking a north-easterly track, allowing the Azores High to build up and protect our areas. The S.C. then turned to Ramsay and asked what further instructions were necessary. We then came out. Other high-ranking Navy, Army and Air Force officers were standing about in little knots outside, not so much talking as waiting, just waiting to hear what had been decided."

They did not have to wait long. Inside the library the discussion quickly died away. None now doubted that the tentative decision of the previous evening should stand. Even Leigh-Mallory agreed that the chance, slender though it was, must be taken. Eisenhower listened to their final comments, he paused a moment, and then confirmed what he had said the night before: " O.K. We'll go."

Within two hours of this decision the invasion convoys were slipping out to sea, into the stormy Channel on the far side of which lay the

long-awaited ' Second Front.' The wind came in fierce gusts, the waves
were five to six feet high and the clouds were low and threatening. In
the uneasy ships those who knew their history recalled that the last
invasion armada to sail the English Channel had come to grief in a
south-westerly gale—356 years before. Some of the minor landing-craft
were driven back to port but throughout the day the concourse grew as
more and more ships sailed out from Falmouth, Fowey, Plymouth,
Salcombe, Dartmouth, Brixham, Torbay, Portland, Weymouth, Poole,
Southampton, Solent, Spithead, Shoreham, Newhaven, Harwich and
the Nore. By mid-afternoon 3,000 landing-craft and more than 500 warships were moving towards the start of the swept Channel which began
south of the Isle of Wight at a point officially designated ' Area Z,' but
known to the Navy as ' Piccadilly Circus.'

Here was the fulfilment of Britain's destiny at sea. It was the full
turn of the wheel. Four years earlier, almost to the day, the Royal Navy
under the direction of Ramsay as Vice-Admiral, Dover, had rescued the
B.E.F. from the beaches of Dunkirk. Since then under his command
other expeditionary forces had been successfully landed in North Africa,
in Sicily and Italy, but none of these could compare in power or purpose
with the vast armada that now sailed in full flood of strength and
confidence back to France.

Above the convoys swarms of fighters wove a protective screen. On
the flanks aircraft of R.A.F. Coastal Command, and British and American
warships patrolled far and wide searching for U-boats and E-boats,
reinforcing the protection afforded by the minefields which they had
already laid. Early that afternoon flotillas of mine-sweepers began
sweeping ten clear channels from ' Piccadilly Circus ' south to the Bay
of the Seine. They encountered fewer mines than they expected, though
at that time they did not know the reason. The coastal waters from Le
Havre to Dunkirk had been heavily mined early in the spring, but the
German Navy's plan to lay a special barrage of mines between Cherbourg
and Le Havre had been foiled by Allied air and naval power. The bombing of French railways had delayed the arrival of the mines, and, when
at last in May there were sufficient stocks available at Le Havre, a mine-
laying flotilla had been dispatched from Brest to carry out the plan.
Coastal Command and the Royal Navy intercepted the ships, only one
got through, and the barrage was never laid.[1]

Because of this, Ramsay's minesweepers made faster progress than
had been expected, and the leading flotilla arrived in sight of the
Normandy coast at 7.57 p.m., three hours before dark. For the last hour
of daylight it was close enough to the shore for the crews to pick out
with the naked eye buildings on the waterfront west of OMAHA Beach.
Before nightfall two flotillas were in full view, but no gun opened up
against them. The crews presumed that the enemy was deliberately

[1]These facts were reported by Admiral Krancke, the Commander of Naval Group,
West. (See *British Army of the Rhine Intelligence Review*, December 17th, 1945, p. 28.)

holding his fire, for it seemed impossible that they had not been sighted and reported.

In the meantime Operation FORTITUDE was distracting enemy attention far from Normandy. Since June 1st Allied aircraft had been attacking with increasing vigour tactical targets between Calais and Le Havre, striking not only at the coastal guns but at the actual beach defences. It had been planned that these deceptive attacks should be abandoned and that the full weight of the Allied Air Forces should be directed against Normandy on D minus 1 if there was any sign that the Germans anticipated where the blow would fall. But on the morning of June 5th there was no such indication and the attacks on the Pas de Calais continued.

That evening after dark the impression created by this bombing was reinforced by other measures. The OVERLORD planners had presumed that by this time on D minus 1 the enemy would certainly have discovered the invasion fleet at sea, and would have noticed that, although a few ships were sailing south towards the Bay of the Seine, the main force was still moving eastwards up the Channel. This force was not due to reach ' Piccadilly Circus,' the start of its southward run, until darkness had fallen and it was essential that the change of direction should be hidden from the enemy. This could be done by scientific deception directed against the enemy's warning system on the Channel coast. Accordingly, the plan required that those radar stations still operating between Cherbourg and Le Havre should be put out of action by jamming, and that the radar stations between Le Havre and Calais should be led to believe that the fleet was heading towards this sector of the coast.

The execution of this plan was entrusted to 105 aircraft of the R.A.F. and 34 small ships of the Royal Navy. Soon after dark 18 of these ships steamed towards Cap d'Antifer, just north of Le Havre, towing barrage balloons so as to produce ' big ship echoes ' on the enemy radar tubes. Above this ' fleet ' a squadron of heavy bombers flew round and round dropping every minute bundles of ' window,' strips of metalised paper which would produce false readings on the German radar sets. The aircraft flew in a continuous orbit, moving gradually nearer the French coast to give the impression of a large convoy sailing across the Channel. Similar deception was practised by ships and aircraft off Boulogne, while other bombers patrolling the Channel represented themselves as an airborne invasion in flight. The men who planned FORTITUDE did not expect that the enemy could be completely misled, but they hoped that these stratagems might leave him uncertain and confused about the real Allied intention. Throughout the night radio and radar stations in Southern England kept close and constant watch for the first sign of German reaction.

The break in the fine weather at the start of June confirmed the

German assumption that invasion was not " immediately imminent."
On June 4th at the H.Q. of Air Fleet III in Paris, its chief meteorologist,
Major Lettau, drew encouragement from the synoptic situation which
was causing such grave anxiety to Stagg and his colleagues. The forecast
which Lettau issued indicated that there could be no invasion within
the next fortnight, and he added the comment, " The enemy has not
already made use of three periods of fine weather for his invasion and
further periods of fine weather in the coming weeks cannot be reckoned
with more accurately." On the strength of this report, Rommel left Paris
next morning for his home near Ulm, intending to spend the Monday
with his family and then proceed on Tuesday, the 6th, to Berchtesgaden.
He wanted to make a personal plea to Hitler for more troops and for
permission to move the 12th SS Panzer Division to the St. Lô–Carentan
area. At this juncture, however, Hitler's main concern lay elsewhere.
On June 4th at his orders, an infantry division from the Pas de Calais
set out for Italy to help in preventing further disaster following the
imminent fall of Rome.

On the morning of June 5th Rommel's weekly situation report was
dispatched to von Rundstedt. It began: " *Estimate of Overall Situation.*
Systematic continuation and intensification of enemy air-raids and more
intensive mine-laying in own harbours . . . indicates an advance in
enemy's preparations for invasion. Concentration of air attacks on coastal
defences between Dunkirk and Dieppe and on Seine–Oise Bridges confirms presumption as to *Schwerpunkt* of large-scale landing. . . . Since
1.6.44 increased transmissions on enemy radio of warning messages to
French Resistance organisations, [but] judging from experience to date,
[this is] not explicable as an indication of invasion being imminent. . . .
Air reconnaissance showed no great increase of landing-craft in Dover
area. Other harbours of England's south coast NOT visited by reconnaissance aircraft."

The report declared, " Survey urgently needed of harbour moorings
on the entire English south coast by air reconnaissance," but on this
critical day bad weather kept the Luftwaffe on the ground. It flew only
one reconnaissance mission in the West, and this off the coast of Holland!
Nor did the Navy report anything untoward, for all its patrols had been
driven into harbour by the storm.

In the late afternoon at the H.Q. of 716th Infantry Division in Caen,
General Richter held his usual weekly conference with his regimental
commanders. He outlined the training programme for the next week
and discussed the difficulty they were having in preventing the strong
tides and rough seas from carrying away the underwater obstacles. He
remarked in passing that he had received from higher authority a
warning that the invasion would come " between the 3rd and the 10th,"
but added with a touch of irony that they had received similar warnings
" every full moon and every no moon period " since April. The meeting
broke up about 7 o'clock. Within the next hour the first British mine-

sweeper sighted the French coast on this division's front but, if any German look-out spotted them, General Richter was not informed.

At 9.15 p.m. on the French Service of the B.B.C., 'The Voice of SHAEF' began broadcasting the usual session of coded messages for the Resistance. Normally this 'programme' lasted five to ten minutes but on this night it ran on for twenty, and during it the spokesman declared, " To-day the Supreme Commander directs me to say this: In due course instructions of great importance will be given to you through this channel, but it will not be possible always to give these instructions at a previously announced time. Therefore you must get into the habit of listening at all hours."

When this was monitored at von Rundstedt's H.Q. it put the Germans on the alert and their suspicions were soon sharpened. From 10 p.m. onwards radar stations between Cherbourg and Le Havre reported that they were being jammed, while other stations from Fécamp to Calais reported abnormally heavy movements of shipping in the Channel. Between 10 and 11 p.m. Luftwaffe Signals Intelligence discovered that meteorological reconnaissance aircraft for American heavy and medium bombers were broadcasting weather information. Since these aircraft had never been detected operating at this time before, German night fighter units were alerted. In spite of this mounting evidence, von Rundstedt's Chief of Staff, Blumentritt, scouted the suggestion that this was the start of the invasion and no special precautions were ordered by C.-in-C., West.

At Rommel's H.Q., however, this evidence had already produced action. At 10 p.m. a 'Most Urgent' signal went out for all troops to stand-to ready for action, but this alarm was directed to the Fifteenth Army alone—to the divisions between the Orne and the Scheldt. To the Seventh German Army, guarding the coast towards which the Allied invasion fleet was then heading in earnest, Rommel's H.Q. gave no warning at all.

*Part Two*

★

# THE
# BATTLE OF NORMANDY

# CHAPTER XII

# ASSAULT FROM THE SKY

ON the evening of June 5th, 1944, as the last glow of twilight was fading from the western sky, six R.A.F. Albemarles were drawn up on the runway of Harwell airfield. Gathered around them, drinking tea and smoking cigarettes, were 60 men of the 22nd Independent Parachute Company, pathfinders who were to guide the 6th British Airborne Division to its landfall behind the Atlantic Wall near Caen. Their faces and equipment were smeared with brown, black and green paint, and over their uniforms they wore camouflaged jumping smocks. Every man was a walking arsenal. They had crammed so much ammunition into their pockets and pouches, so many weapons into their webbing, that they had found it difficult to hitch on their parachute harnesses. Grenades were festooned about them; they had fighting knives in their gaiters and clips of cartridges in the linings of their steel helmets. No man was carrying less than 85 lbs.; some more than a hundred, and in addition each had strapped to his leg a 60-lb. kitbag containing lights and radar-beacons with which to mark the dropping and landing-zones for the rest of the division.

These men were the torchbearers of liberation. Like all paratroops they were volunteers, and they had been specially picked and trained for this responsible task, but otherwise there was little to distinguish them from the rest of Montgomery's force. Beside the leading aircraft were the ten men who were due to land first, at the point of the invasion spearhead, a Berkshire hod-carrier and a toolmaker from Kent, a brick-layer from Edinburgh, a Worcestershire kennelman and a lorry driver from Dumfries, two 'regulars,' a deserter from the 'army' of the Irish Free State and a refugee from Austria, led by a young lieutenant, who, when war began, had been in the chorus of a West End musical comedy. Three of them had been at Dunkirk, one had fought in Africa, but the rest were going into battle for the first time.

These pathfinders were the vanguard of the force that had the most vital role in the NEPTUNE plan—that of seizing and holding the left flank of the bridgehead—the open flank, against which the main weight of German counter-attack was likely to fall as the panzer divisions moved

233

in from their garrison areas south-east and east of Caen. If 6th Airborne were to fail, the whole bridgehead might be rolled up from this wing before the seaborne divisions could become firmly established.

The nearest of these divisions, 3rd British, was to land on SWORD beach just west of the Orne. This river and the canal which runs parallel to it from the sea to Caen, eight miles inland, provided a naturally strong flank position. Montgomery wanted not merely to secure the line of these water obstacles but to hold east of them a base from which to expand the Allied bridgehead south-east beyond Caen into open ground where Rommel's panzer divisions might be profitably engaged. The seizure of this base was the responsibility entrusted to the commander of 6th Airborne, Major-General Richard Gale. Tall, spare and ramrod-straight, with ruddy face, bristling moustache and bushy eyebrows, Gale looked a 'Poona colonel' every inch, but this first impression was misleading. When he spoke, the power of his blunt but lucid words revealed a man who could both devise a plan of daring originality and imbue his men with the confidence and courage to carry it out.

The orders Gale received were that between midnight and dawn of D-Day he must capture, intact if possible, the bridges on the only through-road over the Orne and the canal between Caen and the sea; he must destroy a coastal battery capable of firing on to SWORD beach from Merville, near the mouth of the river; and he must protect this flank by demolishing five bridges in the flooded valley of the River Dives, some six miles east of the Orne, and by gaining command of the high wooded ground between the two rivers. These initial objectives were to be secured by two brigades of parachutists and a small glider-borne force, but, for the defence of this area, he was to be reinforced about the middle of D-Day by Commandos of the 1st Special Service Brigade, who should by then have fought their way through from SWORD beach, and in the evening by the rest of his own division, the 6th Air-Landing Brigade, which would arrive in 250 gliders just before sunset.

The accomplishment of this task was as difficult as it was important, and the difficulty had increased as D-Day approached. The movement of the 21st Panzer Division into the area between Caen and Falaise made it almost certain that the airborne troops would have to face an armoured counter-attack within a few hours of dawn. It was thus essential to land anti-tank guns by glider during the night. But the erection of the anti-air-landing obstacles and posts—known to the troops as 'Rommel's asparagus'—made it too hazardous to bring in these gliders until the landing-zones had been cleared.

For the assault upon the two main bridges, this hazard had to be faced. These were garrisoned and prepared for demolition; their defenders must be overwhelmed by a swift, surprise assault before they could set off the charges. Confronted with this problem, Gale decided upon a plan which was bold, imaginative and worthy of the occasion, for this attack would be the first blow struck upon the soil of France for the liberation of Europe.

At twenty minutes past midnight on D-Day, some six hours before H-Hour, infantry and engineers, carried in six gliders, would crash-land against the very defences of the bridges and seize them by *coup de main*. This force of less than 200 men might take the bridges but would not be able to hold them unless speedily reinforced. Accordingly, Gale planned that the pathfinders would come in at the same time and would set up their signals so that his two parachute brigades could start dropping half an hour later, at ten minutes to one. Of these two brigades, the 3rd was given the role of silencing the Merville battery, destroying the bridges in the Dives valley and seizing the ridge between the rivers; the 5th was ordered to take over the defence of the Orne and canal bridges and to clear the enemy and his obstructions from the landing-zone north of the village of Ranville so that 72 gliders carrying guns, transport and heavy equipment could land at 3.30 a.m., two hours before first light.

If all were to go well, the left flank of the invasion would be protected before the seaborne landing began, but it was clear that the execution of this plan would be a race against time. The pathfinders and the gliders with the *coup de main* force could not take off before dark lest their departure be detected. It would take the pathfinders at least half an hour to set up their navigation aids, and the paratroops would need two hours to clear the landing-zones for the gliders. Once these were down there would be barely sufficient time to get the anti-tank guns into position before 21st Panzer was ready to counter-attack.

This was the plan. The keys to its success lay with the 60 chosen men who now stood talking to Gale beside the Albemarles. At ten to eleven the aircrews went aboard. The pathfinders drained their tea-mugs, adjusted their harness, stubbed out their cigarettes and clambered aboard. The door slammed behind them. The engines spoke up. A signal flashed from the control tender and the six Albemarles roared down the runway in quick succession, lifted, circled and headed south for France and invasion. The hopes of every man in the division rose into the sky with them. The drone of the engines faded away, but another and greater sound welled up in its place. The throb of aircraft soon filled the night as eleven hundred transports took off from a score of airfields, carrying British and American paratroops. The planes climbed above the sleeping, unsuspecting countryside, their red and green navigation lights twinkling like fireflies. Soon after 11.30 the swarm of lights moved in formation over our heads and faded into the distance.[1]

Two hours later the gliders are following the same course. Riding behind an Albemarle tug we are scudding through clouds which shroud

[1]At this time I was a war correspondent for the B.B.C. and on its behalf accompanied the 6th Airborne Division to Normandy, as the narrative now reveals.

moon and ground alike. There is soft rain on the perspex of the cockpit and all we can see is the guiding light in the tail of the tug, until a break in the clouds gives us a brief glimpse of the south coast from which the invasion fleet has long since sailed. Half-way across the Channel it clears again, and we can see the dark, stormy water, flecked with the wake of countless ships. More cloud, and we are flying blind again at 2,500 feet. The glider begins to pitch and bucket in the gusty wind that threatens to sunder the tow-rope and leave us drifting helpless in the sky. But this is a minor worry compared with those that lie ahead.

Does the enemy know we are coming? What will the flak be like? Are there mines and booby-traps as well as obstructions on the landing-zone? Will the paratroops have had time to clear it? Will a battle be raging there already as we come in to land? Will the pilots ever find it in this weather?

If these thoughts are also running through the minds of the other 26 officers and men sitting in the dark fuselage of the glider, they show no sign of it. Above the steady roar of the wind beating on the glider's wooden surface, you can hear a snatch of song or a gust of laughter.

Three o'clock: half an hour to go. The clouds clear for a minute and we are warned of the closeness of the coast—and of another tug and glider which has cut across our bow, perilously near. Away to our left the R.A.F. is bombing enemy batteries near Le Havre and the sky is lit by the burst of bombs and flash of guns until the clouds shut us in again. Now when we need a clear sky, it is thicker than ever and at times we lose sight even of the tug's tail light. Suddenly the darkness is stabbed with streaks of light, red and yellow tracer from the flak guns on the coast. There are four sharp flashes between us and the tug and then another that seems to be inside the glider itself. It is, but we don't realise at first that we have been hit, for the shell has burst harmlessly well aft beyond the farthest seats. The tug begins to weave but it can't take violent evasive action lest the towrope should snap.

Over the coast we run out of the cloud and there below us is the white curving strand of France and, mirrored in the dim moonlight, the twin ribbons of water we are looking for—the Orne and the Canal. The tug has taken us right to the target, but we can't pick out the lights which are to mark the landing-zone. There is so much flak firing from the ground that it's hard to tell what the flashes are, and before the pilots can identify any landmarks we are into the cloud again.

Soon one of them turns and calls back to us—" I'm letting go, hold tight." As it leaves the tug the glider seems to stall and to hover like a hawk about to strike. The roar of the wind on the wooden skin drops to a murmur with the loss of speed and there is a strange and sudden silence. We are floating in a sky of fathomless uncertainty—in suspense between peace and war. We are through the flak-belt and gliding so smoothly that the fire and turmoil of battle seem to belong to another world.

We are jerked back to reality by a sharp, banking turn and we are diving steeply, plunging down into the darkness. As the ground rises up to meet us, the pilots catch a glimpse of the pathfinders' lights and the white dusty road and the square Norman church-tower beside the landing-zone. The stick comes back and we pull out of the dive with sinking stomachs and bursting ears. The glider is skimming the ground now with plenty of speed on and is about to land when out of the night another glider comes straight for us. We ' take-off ' again, lift sharply and it sweeps under our nose. The soil of France rushes past beneath us and we touch-down with a jolt on a ploughed field. It is rough and soft, but the glider careers on with grinding brakes and creaking timbers, mowing down ' Rommel's asparagus ' and snapping off five stout posts in its path. There is an ominous sound of splitting wood and rending fabric and we brace ourselves for the shock as the glider goes lurching and bumping until with a violent swerve to starboard it finally comes to rest scarred but intact, within a hundred yards of its intended landing place.

It is 3.32 a.m. We are two minutes late. Shouts and cheers echo down the glider, and a voice from the dark interior cries out, " This is it, chum. I told yer we wouldn't 'av ter swim."

We scramble out into a cornfield which is the graveyard of many gliders. Some have buried their noses in the soft soil, others have lost a wing, a wheel or a complete undercarriage, several have broken their backs, one has crashed into a house and two have crashed into each other. Few have come through with as little damage as ours and all around us the twisted wrecks make grotesque silhouettes against the sky, now lit by a burst of flame as the petrol tanks of a crashing aircraft explode.

The wreckage seems to signify the failure of the daring plan to land the gliders by night, but in fact, though we don't yet know it, 49 of the 72 destined for this field have landed accurately and, despite the chaos and the damage, the casualties to men and weapons are comparatively few. Indeed as we move off towards the rendezvous near Ranville church, men are climbing out of the broken wrecks, dragging their equipment and slashing away the splintered fuselages to set free jeeps and guns. Ten of the eighteen anti-tank guns have survived and soon they are moving to their appointed positions.

The flak guns are still firing spasmodically into an empty sky, but otherwise there is little sight or sound of fighting. It seems unreal to be walking about behind the Atlantic Wall unhindered by the enemy, and every moment we expect to hear a shot or challenge ring out of the darkness. In the absence of noise of nearby battle every sound is magnified. The rustle of troops moving through high corn, the muttered curse from a stumbling man, the crash of an axe on flimsy wood, the roar of a jeep engine, the rumble of a gun-carriage, carry far in the night, but the expected crack and thunder of guns is missing. The only challenge is from our own paratroops dug in on the edge of the landing-zone. To their call of " V for," we quickly add the other half of the password— " Victory."

That is all, until we reach the road near Ranville church, from which there comes an outburst of fire and counter-fire, followed by the sound of German voices, the roar of a departing car, a burst from a tommy-gun and then silence. The column of men on the road moves smartly to the cover of a hedgerow, expecting any minute to make contact with a German patrol. We lie there quiet and alert, picturing the enemy moving stealthily towards us from the direction of the church. But the sound that splits the silence is an unmistakable voice, booming out: " Don't you dare to argue with me—Richard Gale. Get on, I say, get on."

In the faint half-light we can now make out a halted column of jeeps and guns close by on a side-road with Gale himself urging them on. And, walking a little fractiously beside the column, shepherded by the General's aide-de-camp, is a handsome chestnut horse which had been grazing on the landing-zone.

" Take care of that animal, Tommy! " says Gale, " It's a fine morning for a ride."

In the next few hours, however, there were other matters for Gale's attention and foremost among these was the fate of Major R. J. Howard and the six platoons of the 2nd Battalion of the Oxfordshire and Buckinghamshire Light Infantry, the famous 52nd Foot, to whom he had entrusted the capture of the bridges.

Fifteen minutes after midnight, 5,000 feet above the mouth of the Orne, five of the six gliders carrying the *coup de main* force slipped their towropes and circled slowly down while their Halifax tugs went on to bomb Caen. As the flak-guns were engaging the bombers, the gliders swooped unheralded and undetected towards the bridges. At a thousand feet the pilot of the leading glider, bound for the canal, called a warning to the troops and dived straight for his objective. The wheels hit the ground fifty yards from the eastern end of the bridge and the glider lurched on, bowling over a cow, as the pilot steered it to a standstill in the barbed wire entanglement in front of the enemy trenches. The nose telescoped, blocking the door, which had been opened for quick exit, and the troops had to smash their way out through the battered cockpit. As they leapt to the ground, they heard two other gliders crash-landing a few yards behind them, but from the enemy defences there was neither sound nor movement. Most of the Germans were still taking shelter from the bombing, but as the first platoon dashed across the bridge a machine-gun felled its commander. Scorning this fire, the men raced on to overwhelm the defenders on the far side of the bridge, while the other platoons in a brisk skirmish cleared a pill-box and the network of trenches on the near bank and the engineers made certain that the prize could not be blown.

Meantime at the bridge over the Orne, half a mile east of the canal, the glider landings had not been so accurate—in fact one of the three had come down in the valley of the Dives—but two platoons made quick time to their objective, only to find that the defenders had fled. Surprise and speed had brought their reward. Both bridges had been made ready for demolition, but the garrisons had orders not to place the charges until they received the invasion ' alert ' and no such warning had come.

While this glider-borne force was securing the bridges, the path-finders, who had parachuted down near Ranville, were hastening to mark out the DZ (Dropping-Zone) for the 2,200 men of Brigadier J. H. N. Poett's 5th Parachute Brigade who were due at ten to one. Unfortunately the high wind had scattered the pathfinders, carrying them to the east of the DZ and in the short time available they had no alternative but to put out the navigation lights and beacons where they were. Because of this, the main body of parachutists were dropped wide of the mark and were carried wider still, partly by the wind and partly on account of the difficulty the men had in jumping from weaving, rocking aircraft with a 60-lb. kitbag strapped to one leg. Once they hit the ground many were dragged by their parachutes before they could disentangle themselves, and others had to hunt for kitbags which had broken loose during the descent. By this time the enemy was alert and the DZ was under fire from machine-guns which the advance parties had not had time to silence.

For these reasons the rallying was slow. By two o'clock the 7th Parachute Battalion, which mustered its men by bugle call, had assembled only 200 out of 620, but it could not afford to wait any longer, for sounds of heavy firing came from the direction of the canal bridge. By the time the paratroops reached there, however, the ' Ox and Bucks ' had dealt with the immediate threat and the tumult of battle which the 7th had heard proved to have been the exploding ammunition of a knocked-out German tank.

East of the Orne, the rest of Poett's Brigade cleared most of the main LZ (Landing-Zone) before the gliders came in at 3.30 a.m., and then proceeded to drive the enemy from the village of Ranville which screened the south-eastern approach to the river bridge. This was potentially the most vulnerable sector of the divisional front. Accordingly, as soon as the anti-tank guns had been rescued from the gliders, they were hurried through Ranville and sited to cover the open ground across which the tanks of 21st Panzer were expected to counter-attack.

The guns were moving into place soon after dawn, by which time Gale had set up his H.Q. in a chateau at Ranville. In the grounds the chestnut horse and a dozen sleek cows cropped the rich grass, somewhat disturbed by explosions on all sides as the airborne troops blew slit-trenches for themselves with plastic charges. These made such a noise that the occasional whine of a sniper's bullet or the crump of a mortar-bomb passed almost unheeded. But the predominant note in this medley was the gobbling of a flock of turkeys which had taken refuge in a large tree and felt constrained to give throat in answer to each explosion.

Into this bedlam rode Gale in a jeep, fresh from a visit to the captured bridges. At the top of the front steps he paused and looked around his newly-won domain, across the fields strewn with parachutes of many colours, and across the glider landing-zone to the wooded ridge where already, he hoped, the 3rd Parachute Brigade was established. As he turned in through the door, he muttered, half to himself,

> " *And gentlemen in England now a-bed*
> *Shall think themselves accurs'd they were not here.*"

Compared with Poett's concentrated task of securing the bridges, the 3rd Parachute Brigade, commanded by Brigadier S. J. L. Hill, had a ranging mission. Its objectives were spread over a wide area broken by woods and swamps and extending from the Merville battery near the coast to the bridge at Troarn, seven miles inland. The dispersal thus involved was accentuated by the wildness of the night. The pilots had difficulty in distinguishing the Dives from the Orne and many of them made their dropping-runs too high and too fast. The parachute battalions were scattered for miles. Hundreds of men came down in the flooded wastes of the Dives or in the treetops of the Bois de Bavent.

In spite of these mishaps four of the five target bridges in the Dives valley were blown up without great difficulty, but the fifth and most important—the one at Troarn—would have remained intact had it not been for the impudent daring of a major and seven sappers. Although their glider landed north of the Bois de Bavent, several miles from their proper LZ, they set forth by jeep without ado. On the outskirts of Troarn they crashed into a barbed wire entanglement, but managed to hold off the enemy for twenty minutes while they cut their vehicle free. Then, with engine roaring and sten-guns blazing, they shot their way through the town to the bridge beyond, blew it, abandoned their jeep and found their way on foot to Hill's H.Q. The blowing of these bridges gave the airborne force invaluable hours of immunity against counter-attack from the east and protected the rear of the 9th Parachute Battalion while it carried out the brigade's chief task—the capture of the Merville battery.

When he was entrusted with this mission, the Battalion Commander (Lt.-Col. T. H. B. Otway) found that the battery was thought to consist of four 150 mm guns. These, he was told, must be silenced half an hour before first light so that the invasion fleet and the beaches immediately west of the Orne should be protected. The guns were housed in bomb-proof concrete emplacements and defended by a garrison of about 180 men entrenched with some ten machine-guns covering two

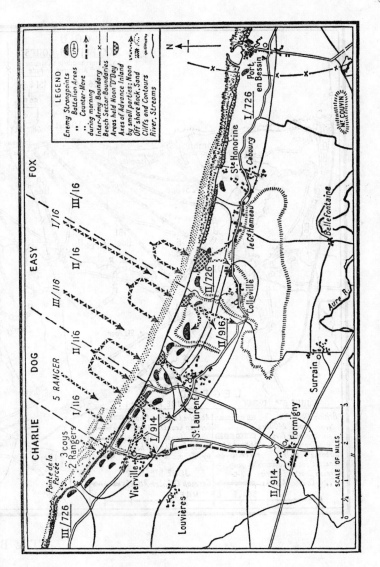

OMAHA : THE ASSAULT

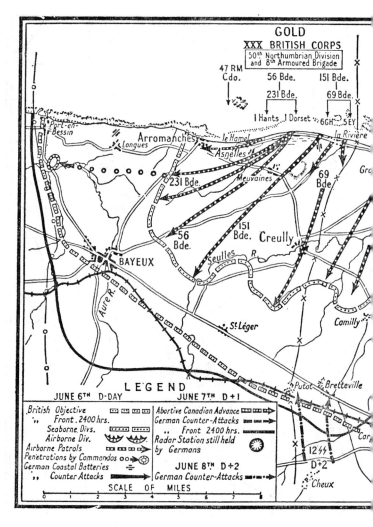

GOLD

XXX BRITISH CORPS

50th Northumbrian Division
and 8th Armoured Brigade

47 RM
Cdo.

56 Bde.        151 Bde.

231 Bde.        69 Bde.

1 Hants    1 Dorset    6 GH   SEY

Port-en-
Bessin

Arromanches    le Hamel    la Rivière

Longues

Asnelles    Gra

231 Bde.    Meuvaines    69
Bde.

151
Bde.    Creully

56
Bde.

Seulles R.

BAYEUX

Aure R.

St. Léger    Camilly

Putot   Bretteville

**LEGEND**

| | | |
|---|---|---|
| JUNE 6TH  D-DAY | | JUNE 7TH  D+1 |

British Objective
Front . 2400 hrs.
Seaborne. Divs.
Airborne Div.
Airborne Patrols
Penetrations by Commandos
German Coastal Batteries
Counter Attacks

Abortive Canadian Advance
German Counter-Attacks
Front  2400 hrs.
Radar Station still held
by Germans

JUNE 8TH  D+2

German Counter-Attacks

Cheux    12 44

D+2    Car

SCALE  OF  MILES

0    1    2    3    4    5    6    7    8

THE BR

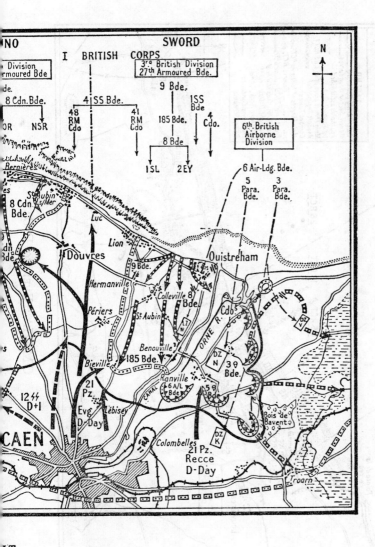

NO

I BRITISH CORPS

SWORD

3rd British Division
27th Armoured Bde.

Division
rmoured Bde
de.
8 Cdn.Bde.

OR    NSR

4 SS Bde.

48
RM
Cdo

41
RM
Cdo

9 Bde.

1SS
Bde

185 Bde.

4
Cdo.

8 Bde

6th. British
Airborne
Division

1SL    2EY

6 Air-Ldg. Bde.

5
Para.
Bde.

3
Para.
Bde.

Bernières

St Aubin
s/Mer

8 Cdn
Bde.

dn
Bde.

Luc

Lion

Douvres

9 Bde.

Hermanville

Colleville 8

Bde.

Ouistreham

Périers

St Aubin

Benouville

185 Bde.

Bieville

12 SS
D+1

21
Pz.

Evg
D Day

Lébisey

CAEN

ORNE R.

Cdo

DZ
N

3 Bde.

Ranville
6 A/L
Bde.

5 Bde.

DZ
K

Bois de
Bavent

Colombelles

21 Pz.
Recce
D-Day

Troarn

N

LT

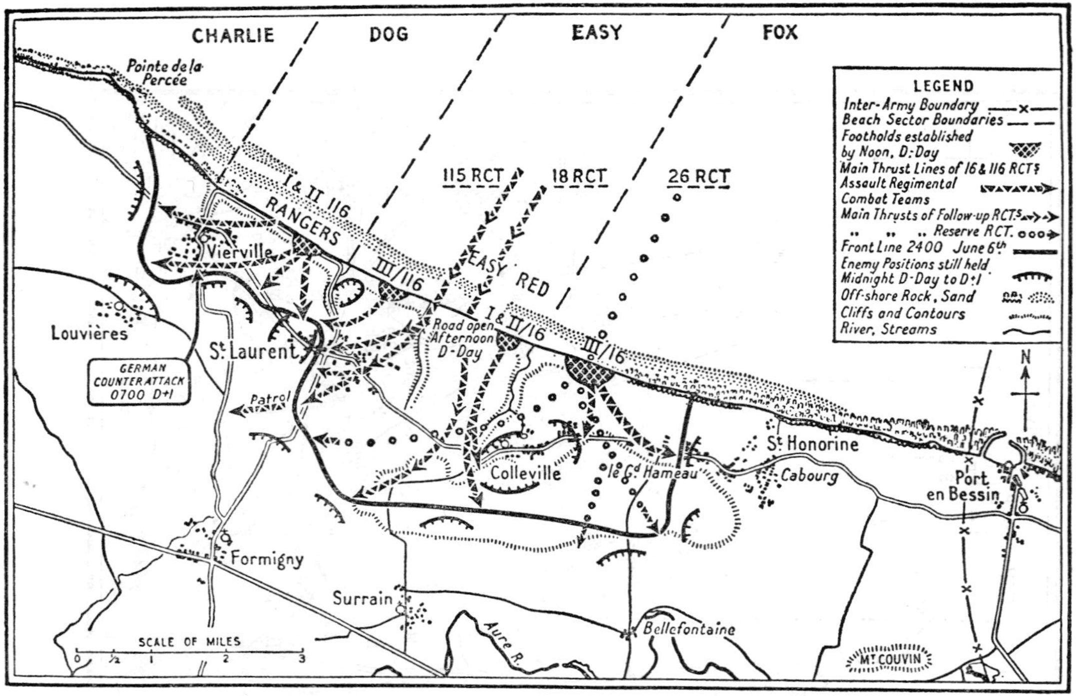

OMAHA : EVENING D-DAY

LEGEND

Inter-Army Boundary
Beach Sector Boundaries
Footholds established
by Noon, D-Day
Main Thrust Lines of 16 & 116 RCTs
Assault Regimental
Combat Teams
Main Thrusts of Follow-up RCTs
Reserve RCT.
Front Line 2400 June 6th
Enemy Positions still held
Midnight D-Day to D+1
Offshore Rock, Sand
Cliffs and Contours
River, Streams

CHARLIE   DOG   EASY   FOX

26 RCT
18 RCT
115 RCT

EASY RED

III/16
I & II/16

III/16
I & II/116

RANGERS

Road open
afternoon
D-Day

Pointe de la Percée

Vierville

St Laurent

Patrol

GERMAN
COUNTER ATTACK
0100 D+1

Louvières

Formigny

Surrain

Colleville

Le Grand Hameau

St Honorine

Cabourg

Port en Bessin

MT COUVIN

Bellefontaine

Aure R.

N

SCALE OF MILES
0   ½   1   2   3

belts of barbed wire which surrounded the position and enclosed a minefield 100 yards deep. This formidable stronghold had to be stormed by his lightly-equipped battalion without any support except a preliminary bombardment by 100 Lancasters.

Realising that paratroops alone could not be sure of cracking these strong defences in time, Otway decided upon the almost suicidal expedient of crash-landing three gliders, laden with troops, inside the defences and almost atop the casemates at the critical moment when his ground attack began. Although this meant that the gliders would plunge into a maelstrom of fire from both sides, the battalion volunteered to a man for this mission.

The operation was rehearsed in every particular, except the bombing, on a specially constructed replica near Newbury. After five rehearsals by day and four by night, all with live ammunition, Otway was confident of success, but he could not anticipate what the weather would do to his plan. The Lancasters' bombs fell more than half a mile from the target, narrowly missing the reconnaissance party which was then en route to the battery position. Five gliders, carrying the battalion's anti-tank guns, jeeps and explosives, broke their towropes in a squall and plunged into the Channel. The drop was little short of disastrous. Nearly half the battalion landed in or beyond the flooded swamps of the Dives. One ' stick ' was dropped 30 miles away and Otway's own party came down beside the H.Q. of a German battalion and he was lucky to reach the rendezvous at all.

There by ten minutes to three, two hours after the drop, Otway had only 150 men, one machine-gun and barely enough explosives to destroy the guns even if he could force an entry. There were no mortars, no anti-tank guns, no jeeps, no heavy assault equipment, no mine-detectors, no engineers, no doctors. His men were still searching the cornfields and orchards and the fringes of the swamp for weapons, explosives and equipment which had been dropped by parachute, but Otway could delay no longer. The gliders were due at 4.30 a.m. and he still had to march a mile and a half to the battery through an area where the Germans were now thoroughly aroused. He determined to move at once.

On the way Otway met Major George Smith, of the reconnaissance party, who reported that he had cut the outer wire and crawled through the anti-tank minefield to the inner entanglement and lain there for half an hour within a few yards of the German machine-gun posts, listening to snatches of conversation, and verifying the lay-out of the defences. Smith brought the good news that he had found no booby-traps or anti-personnel mines and that the barbed wire was much less formidable than had been feared. He reported too that the ' taping-party ' which was to make clear lanes through the minefield had arrived without any tape but had managed to mark the routes by kicking trails in the dust.

As they approached the battery the depleted battalion came under considerable fire, but this was ill-directed and before 4.30 a.m. Otway had his troops organised for the assault. Just as he was ready, flak-guns on the coast opened fire again, and two of the three gliders, which were to crash-land on the battery, circled low overhead. The pilots were obviously looking for the pre-arranged signal, but none could be given, for all the flares and mortars had been lost in the drop. One glider scudded over the battery, only 150 feet up, and, seeing it go on to a forced landing near the coast, Otway decided in desperation to attack with the meagre force he had.

Soon after 4.30 Bangalore torpedoes blew the barbed wire in two places and through the dust and smoke of the explosions two assault parties dashed across the minefield and through the gaps regardless of the machine-gun fire. Inside the wire one party became heavily engaged in hand-to-hand fighting through the network of German trenches, but the other went straight for the guns. The ground had been badly cratered by earlier bombing in May, but the parachutists fought their way forward from crater to crater until they were only 30 yards from the steel doors of the concrete casemates. Two of the doors were open and through them the attackers poured such a torrent of fire that the crews were terrified into surrender. The guns—which proved to be only 75 mms for the Germans had not yet installed any heavier armament—were quickly destroyed. The rest of the garrison continued a pointless battle in the outer defences for a little longer, but the real task was done.

At 4.45 a.m., 15 minutes before the appointed time, Otway fired the agreed success signal to inform the ships off shore and dispatched a carrier-pigeon to England with the news. Of his gallant 150, nearly half were now killed or wounded, but they had achieved on time what many had thought to be beyond the powers of a full battalion, and by capturing the Merville battery had gained for 6th Airborne the last of its major objectives.

While Gale's division was securing the eastern flank of the bridgehead, the 82nd and 101st U.S. Airborne Divisions had landed in the south-east corner of the Cotentin Peninsula to carry out the same role for the western flank. There the parachutists had an assignment of great importance to the seaborne forces, because the Germans had flooded considerable areas close to UTAH beach, on which Collins's VII American Corps (with the 4th U.S. Infantry Division in the van) was due to land. Immediately behind the defences on the dunes there was now a mile-wide lagoon, crossed by only five narrow causeways. Ten miles to the west and south-west of UTAH, the inundations in the valleys of the Merderet and the Douve were more extensive; in fact, the Douve was so flooded that it prolonged almost to the west coast the substantial water barrier formed by the estuary of the Vire and the Carentan Canal.

There was thus a decided danger that the assault from the sea might be contained either on the coastal fringe or within the narrow-necked pocket formed by the wider flooding of the river valleys. Accordingly (despite Leigh-Mallory's objections), Montgomery had insisted that airborne troops must be used to secure the beach exits and river crossings, and he determined to turn the German inundations to his own advantage. He planned to drop the two American airborne divisions in depth across the neck of the peninsula in the hope of sealing it off at one blow and isolating Cherbourg by establishing a defensive line along the northern edge of the flood-waters.

Two weeks before D-Day, however, Allied Intelligence learned from good friends on the staff of the French Railways that Rommel had moved a fresh division into the very area of the 82nd Division's dropping-zones around St. Sauveur le Vicomte. This fortunate knowledge prevented almost certain disaster, for Bradley was able to modify the original ambitious design. The revised plan was:

101st Division: Two parachute regiments to drop just west of the coastal lagoon, silence a heavy battery and seize the western exits of the causeways leading from UTAH beach:

One parachute regiment to drop north of Carentan, destroy the main rail and road bridges over the Douve and hold the line of that river and the Carentan canal so as to protect the southern flank of the Corps.

82nd Division: To drop astride the Merderet River south and west of Ste. Mère Église, extend the flank protection westward by destroying two more bridges over the Douve, and secure the Merderet crossings, thus forestalling any attempt to contain the invasion forces behind the inundations and opening the way for an early drive to the west coast of the peninsula.

This modification avoided the dangerous dispersion of the earlier plan and brought the zones of both divisions within easy reach of the seaborne forces, but Leigh-Mallory's fears were not allayed. A week before D-Day he expressed them again in a letter to Eisenhower, warning him that losses of planes and gliders might run as high as 80 per cent. He pointed out that the troop-carriers and tugs would have to fly a steady course at 1,000 feet in moonlight over an area thick with flak-guns and search-lights, that the ground was heavily garrisoned and was unsuitable for large-scale landings from the air because of the flooding or obstruction of the only open areas and because of the close nature of the remaining country. Serious as these objections were, Eisenhower felt compelled to overrule them, and the airborne assault went in as planned.

Night-fighters swept the way clear and heavy cloud covered the approach of the pathfinders shortly after midnight. They and the first flight of troop-carriers got through without serious difficulty, but later formations lost cohesion in the clouds and many aircraft drifted off their courses. By the time they were clear of the cloudbank, the pilots were already approaching the dropping-zones in and beyond the Merderet Valley and it was too late for those who had gone astray to start searching for the pathfinders' beacons, some of which in any case had been set up in the wrong places. The flak was becoming more troublesome and the pilots began to take avoiding action. Consequently, when the parachutists were due to leap, " many planes were flying at excessive speeds and at altitudes higher than those ideal for jumping."[1]

The anti-aircraft fire was generally ineffective, for the German guns were not laid by radar, and out of 805 American troop-carriers, which were over the Cotentin Peninsula that night, only 20 were lost. Thus Leigh-Mallory's worst fears were not realised, but aircraft were saved only by the bad weather and the wild manœuvres of the pilots, which combined to prejudice most gravely the success of the mission which the troops were dropped to fulfil. According to Major-General Maxwell Taylor, commanding the 101st, the anti-aircraft fire " did have considerable volume and produced an unfortunate effect upon the pilots who had never seen action before."[2] Their evasive tactics " greatly increased the difficulty and hazard of jumping." Taylor's division was scattered over an area twenty-five miles by fifteen, with stray ' sticks ' even farther afield. By dawn only 1,100 of his 6,600 parachutists had reached their rendezvous, and twenty-four hours later he had collected less than 3,000. In his opinion, this inaccurate drop was partly due to " the inadequate briefing of many individual pilots who could not reach their objective by their own pilotage." Confused by the cloud, thrown off their course in evading the flak, they flew high and fast and spilled their troops out of weaving aircraft with little idea where they might come to earth.

The 82nd (Major-General M. B. Ridgway) was more fortunate. His leading regiment had the advantage of surprise and three-quarters of the men landed within three miles of the DZ. They rallied quickly and by 4 a.m., two hours after the main drop, had taken Ste. Mère Église, thus blocking the Cherbourg—Carentan road. But then their real difficulties began. Only 22 out of 52 gliders—carrying guns, transport and signals equipment—managed to find the LZ. The enemy forestalled their attempt to seize the bridges over the Merderet and so the division was split by an almost impassable belt of river and swamp.

West of the Merderet, only four per cent of the other two regiments were dropped accurately. The rest were scattered over the eastern half of the area garrisoned by the 91st German Infantry Division, which had been specially trained for anti-air-landing operations. By a stroke of luck one party of paratroops succeeded in ambushing and killing the German divisional commander, but the Americans were so heavily engaged in fighting for survival that they could not proceed to the execution of their principal tasks—the blowing of the Douve bridges and

[1]After-Action Report, 82nd Airborne Division, June 1944.
[2]After-Action Report, 101st Airborne Division, June 1944.

the establishment of a compact bridgehead west of the Merderet to protect its crossings. Almost a third of each regiment came down east of the river, but the remainder, fighting indomitably in small parties, prevented the 91st from carrying out its allotted role of counter-attacking any force landing on the coast. Thus the German reserves were compelled to give battle not upon the beaches, but in the orchards and swamps of the Merderet Valley.

The 101st Division, on the other hand, landing east and south-east of the 82nd, had the good fortune to strike an area which was not so strongly held, because it lay between the coast defences and the reserves. If this had not been so, Taylor's men might have been wiped out before they could assemble, for the pattern of parachutes was such that they seemed to have been sprinkled over the countryside from some giant salt-shaker. Hundreds of men found themselves entirely on their own far from their proper DZs in close country where every hedge-bound field and orchard looked the same. They had few landmarks to aid their assembly, but one apparently insignificant device saved many of them. Each man in the division carried down with him a toy snapper of a type which makes a sound like a cricket. The ' clic-clac ' in the crisp night air drew man to man and squad to squad, told friend from foe and led men to their rendezvous.

Before daylight Taylor had been reinforced by the accurate and timely landing of 50 gliders, but at 6 a.m. he had mustered only one-sixth of his paratroops. Nevertheless, he succeeded in capturing the western exits of all the causeways and taking possession of the battery position, which was found to have been abandoned following an attack by the R.A.F. a week earlier. Along the southern flank of the 101st's area, however, the opposition was more formidable, and the forces which could be rallied here were so meagre that the Americans were not able to destroy the bridges over the canal and the river.

Yet the gallantry of individuals and the aggressiveness of small parties infesting a wide area forced the enemy on to the defensive and provided an effective, though thin, screen protecting the inland exits from the beaches upon which the remainder of Collins's corps was to land. In spite of the losses and confusion of the airborne landings, the battle of UTAH had been placed almost beyond doubt by the parachutists before a single infantryman set foot on shore.

For the Allied airborne commanders, striving to collect their troops on the ground, the weather and the inaccurate drop seemed to threaten disaster, but for the assault as a whole there were unexpected compensations. Although the first pathfinders were dropped fifteen minutes after midnight, the 84th German Corps (holding the sector from Caen to the west coast of the Cotentin) did not issue the invasion alarm until eleven minutes past one, by which time the valleys of the Orne and the

Merderet were coloured with parachutes. At 1.20 a.m. 84th Corps reported to Seventh Army: " As from 0030 hours paratroop landings area east and north-west of Caen, St. Marcouf, Montebourg, both sides of the Vire and on east coast of the Cotentin."[1] At half-past one the general alarm was raised throughout the Seventh Army area.

At the same time the H.Q. of Naval Group West in Paris ordered a state of immediate readiness for all naval units stationed on the Channel coast, but, to quote the concurrent entry in its own Operations Log, " It is not considered here that this is a large-scale invasion; C.-in-C., West, and Air Fleet III are of the same opinion. Increased defensive patrols in the Bay of the Seine are not being ordered on account of the unfavourable tide conditions and the weather. No further signs of an enemy landing."

At a quarter-past two, however, Pemsel (Chief of Staff, Seventh Army) reported to Speidel at Rommel's H.Q.: " Engine noises audible from sea on east coast of Cotentin. Admiral, Channel Coast, reports ships located by radar off Cherbourg." The indications were, Pemsel said, that " the operation is of a large-scale character." Speidel would not accept this interpretation, nor would von Rundstedt, and at 2.40 a.m. Pemsel was advised that " C.-in-C., West, does not consider this to be a major operation." But ten minutes later the Admiral confirmed these reports and added the significant comment, " Details unknown because of breakdown of radar equipment."

This breakdown was of such proportions that it amounted to the collapse of the enemy's outer line of defence, his early warning system. The Germans, profiting by their unhappy experience in the Battle of Britain, had built up an elaborate chain of radar stations covering the entire Atlantic coastline from Kirkenes in Northern Norway to the Spanish border. Along the shores of Holland, Belgium and North-Western France there was a major station every ten miles, backed by an inland system not so dense, but still comprehensive. The Luftwaffe had developed this cover to a high pitch of efficiency as part of the air defence of the Reich, and the German Navy had strengthened it with an additional series of stations for the detection of shipping. In theory this screen could not be pierced, for the network was capable of picking up ships at a range of 25-30 miles offshore, and any sizeable force of aircraft south of the line Bristol Channel–the Wash.

The Germans were confident that they could not be surprised; the penetrating eye of radar would give them ample warning. But they reckoned without Allied counter-measures. Between Boulogne and Cherbourg there were six long-range reporting stations for the detection of aircraft over Southern England, and four major radio stations which were the nerve centres of Luftwaffe fighter control and wireless intelligence.

<hr />

[1]The Telephone Log of Seventh Army H.Q. was captured intact near Falaise in August 1944. Its clipped but authoritative entries give an hour by hour account of the German actions and reactions during D-Day and throughout the Battle of Normandy.

In the week before D-Day every one of these was heavily and accurately attacked by the R.A.F. During the night before H-Hour most of the remaining radar stations—designed for medium-range aircraft reporting, shipping detection, fighter control and the direction of coastal artillery —were jammed, though sufficient sets were left operating *north* of the Seine to enable the Germans to pick up the faked convoys. The results exceeded the most optimistic expectations. There was no sign of life from any of the ten major stations which had been bombed, and later Leigh-Mallory was able to report in his *Dispatch*:

> In the vital period between 0100 and 0400 hours when the assault Armada was nearing the beaches, only nine enemy Radar installations were in operation, and during the whole night, the number of stations active in the NEPTUNE area was only 18 out of a normal 92. No station between Le Havre and Barfleur [on the north-eastern tip of the Cotentin Peninsula] was heard operating.

Because the Germans were blinded to this extent, the airborne armada was not intercepted at all; the Luftwaffe sent its main force of night-fighters against the ' ghost-stream ' of bombers operating over Amiens and kept them searching there from one o'clock till four, throughout the entire period of the airborne landing; the invasion fleet was not detected until Force ' U ' reached its ' transport area,'[1] twelve miles off the east coast of the Cotentin at 2 a.m., and then it was located not by radar but by sound!

This was a scientific victory of the first magnitude. It was another hour before Naval Group West made any counter-move. At 3.09 a.m. it ordered E-boats and other light craft to patrol the Bay of the Seine and, in response to one of the FORTITUDE feints, the coast between Dieppe and Le Tréport. Gradually the picture of Allied activity grew more detailed and at half-past three 84th Corps reported to Seventh Army: " Series of large-scale glider landings since 0325 hours, area Bréville, east of Orne, and Grandcamp. Landing-craft at mouth of Orne. Heavy artillery fire from land to sea. Situation around Grandcamp still unclear. Landing-craft presumably there. Battle H.Q. of 91st Division attacked by enemy in battalion strength. Communications with Ste. Mère Église cut off. Battery at Riva Bella [north of Caen] partially damaged by air attack."

At von Rundstedt's H.Q. by this time there was more confusion than alarm. An airborne landing, more than any other form of attack, gives rise to false and ominous reports, especially at night. Although he hears the aircraft and sees the parachutes or gliders, the watcher on the ground has little chance of telling the strength in which they come and none

[1]This was the area where the assault troops were transhipped from their transports into small landing-craft—LCAs and LCVPs. Force ' U ' was that bound for UTAH beach.

of ascertaining quickly which is genuine and which deception, which is forced-landing or bale-out. The very nature of the attack tends to unnerve the defender and exaggeration springs quickly to his lips as he embellishes his first laconic warning, ' Parachutists.'

Thus on this night, as the messages poured into von Rundstedt's H.Q., there was no immediate opportunity of checking their reliability or gauging the strength of the individual landings. In the space of a couple of hours the situation map in the Operations Room broke out in a rash of red markings. The rash was angriest north-east of Caen and north of Carentan, but its threatening spots spread east of the Dives and even beyond the Seine, for landings were reported between Le Havre and Rouen, and it was not yet known that these had been made by ' dummies,' fitted with delayed-action crackers which gave off sounds like small arms fire. So widespread were the landings, as they appeared on the German maps, that they gave a false impression of the breadth of the assault, and they provided no clear answer to the questions that von Rundstedt and his staff were asking: Where is the *Schwerpunkt?* Where is the flank?

From the situation map of France, the German Intelligence officers turned to the Order of Battle map of Britain. They did not find much enlightenment. The map showed more than sixty American and British field divisions in the United Kingdom,[1] so disposed that the main threat appeared to be directed against the Le Havre–Dunkirk sector. This impression seemed to be confirmed by what radar reports were still coming in from coastal stations near Le Tréport and Boulogne.

At 4 a.m. while the situation was still obscure, Blumentritt spoke to Jodl at Berchtesgaden and asked for Hitler's authority to employ the 12th SS and Panzer Lehr Divisions against the Normandy landings. Jodl replied that the Führer did not wish to commit the strategic reserve prematurely and that these divisions should not be moved until daylight reconnaissance gave a clearer picture of Allied intentions. If the airborne landings were a feint and the principal assault was in fact coming north of the Seine, it would be madness to send the armour racing west with the bridgeless river behind it. Having given this edict, Hitler went to bed, soothed by a sleeping-draught from his physician, Dr. Morell.

Hitler's caution was a reflection of von Rundstedt's own confusion. According to the Operations Log of Naval Group West, *as late as five o'clock,* " Supreme Command, West—and apparently also Army Goup B —are uncertain what counter-measures to order as they do not know whether the enemy landing up to this time is a dummy landing, a diversionary manœuvre or the main landing."

[1]There were, in fact, fewer than fifty British and American divisions in the United Kingdom at this time, and of these only 37 were available for cross-Channel operations. Nearly all the rest were training formations. Nevertheless, before the end of June Rommel's H.Q. was estimating Allied strength on both sides of the Channel, including training formations, at 94 to 98 divisions. (Weekly Report, Rommel to von Rundstedt, June 26th, 1944.)

Even after the start of the naval bombardment, which 84th Corps reported at six o'clock, and the coming of daylight, the Germans were still in doubt and the morning situation report[1] from Seventh Army to Rommel's H.Q. declared: " Depth of enemy air landings in area Orne and South Cotentin indicates large-scale attack. Purpose of coastal bombardment not yet apparent. It appears to be a covering action in conjunction with attacks to be made at other points later. Air and naval reconnaissance since daybreak has yielded no fresh information."

When this signal was sent, the seaborne assault on UTAH beach had already started.

[1] 0645 hours.

## CHAPTER XIII

# ASSAULT FROM THE SEA: I

## UTAH AND OMAHA

A RISING, surging sea carried the invasion fleet uneasily into the night. To the men whose destiny lay beyond the black horizon, the voyage seemed lonely and interminable. Cold, stinging spray swept the decks, but it was better there than it was below, where the pitching and throbbing of the ships was magnified and the humid air reeked of sickness. Nausea accentuated the natural anxiety of expectation. They did not imagine that the enemy was ignorant of their approach and his failure to respond seemed to many not only surprising but sinister. The sense of anti-climax added to their qualms, and they were slow to draw reassurance from the German inactivity.

Because the voyage was uneventful, it took on an air of unreality, which still prevailed at 2 a.m. when Naval Force ' U ' (Rear-Admiral D. P. Moon, U.S.N.) began assembling undisturbed in its transport area off the Cotentin, 12 miles north-east of UTAH sector. Aboard its ships, nearly a thousand all told, were 30,000 men and 3,500 vehicles due to be landed that day on this beach alone.

Good fortune smoothed their way. The E-boats, which had been ordered out from Cherbourg to patrol the Bay of the Seine, turned back " on account of the bad weather " without making contact. The twin islands of St. Marcouf, lying athwart the line of approach, were found to be undefended. The coastal batteries were silent, for their radar was being jammed. Moreover, during the night they had been severely hammered by R.A.F. Lancasters and at first light they came under fresh onslaught from air and sea. At 5.20 a.m. 300 medium bombers of the Ninth U.S. Air Force flew in below the clouds to strike at these guns again and at strongpoints on UTAH beach, which was already shuddering under shellfire from two battleships, two cruisers and a dozen destroyers. The accuracy of this double bombardment was evident as the assault craft, carrying two battalions of the 4th U.S. Infantry Division, drove in-shore leaving great white wakes on the dark-green sea. Even then there was little response from the coastal artillery

and the beach defences were subdued by drenching fire from the
' mosquito fleet,' which moved in behind and on the flanks of the assault
craft to rake the shore with rockets, flak-guns and howitzers.

In the vanguard of the invasion were two squadrons of DD tanks.
These were to have been launched four miles off-shore, but because they
were delayed by the weather, the LCTs carried them more than two
miles closer before setting them to swim. By then they were under the
lee of the Peninsula, which gave them considerable protection from the
wind that was lashing the beaches farther east, and 28 out of 32
' DDs ' got safely ashore. At least a dozen of them touched down with
the first wave of infantry at 6.30 a.m. and began firing from the shallows
as the men leapt from their landing-craft.[1]

With the tide still well out, most of the craft came to rest short of the
belt of obstacles set up for their destruction and the troops had nearly
500 yards to run before they reached the long, low line of dunes. From
these there came not the expected torrent of fire, but fitful and erratic
spurts, for the defenders were numbed by the bombardment which
still rang in their ears. They were slow to realise that it had switched
to targets on the flanks and those Germans who did come up to man
their weapons found their fire answered at once by tanks on the water's
edge.

Although Rommel had given warning that the Allies would employ
" water-proofed and submersible tanks," his troops do not seem to
have taken his admonition seriously, for the appearance of the ' DDs '
unquestionably came as a shock to them. They had thought that they
would turn their guns against soft human targets advancing unprotected
over open beach, but now the Americans were covered by fire from
armour which had come up out of the sea. Nothing in war is more
unnerving than the unexpected. Surprise gave the DD tanks an influence
far beyond their fire-power, striking terror in the hearts of the Germans
and adding confidence to the resolution with which the Americans swept
ashore. By 9 a.m. the leading regiment and the tanks had broken the
crust of the Atlantic Wall on a two-mile front between the sea and the
coastal lagoon.

In this they were aided by a mistake which proved no misfortune.
Owing to the early swamping of two control vessels, a slight error was
made in navigation, with the result that the assault battalions were
landed nearly a mile south of the prescribed beach. This brought them
to a sector where a single battalion of doubtful quality was manning
defences less formidable than those the Americans would have encountered
farther north. The Germans had presumed that the double belt of
inundations in this extreme corner of the Peninsula would effectively

[1]The authors of *Utah Beach to Cherbourg*, a campaign study prepared by the Historical
Division of the U.S. Army, say (at p. 44) that " the 32 DD tanks played little part in
the assault " and that they " beached approximately 15 minutes after the first assault
wave." This view is supported neither by the commander of the leading American
regiment (Col. J. A. Van Fleet), nor by the reports of prisoners.

discourage any attempt at landing or at least render nugatory whatever foothold might be gained there.

In the wake of the assault waves came naval demolition units and special squads of army engineers to blow and bulldoze clear lanes through the beach obstacles, thus preparing the way for the rapid and early landing of the rest of the 4th Division. This clearing operation was doubly hazardous, for most of the obstacles were mined and the foreshore came under increasingly heavy shellfire from long-range guns now able to operate without the aid of radar. Nevertheless, adequate gaps were cleared by the time the main body of the follow-up regiment began landing at 10 a.m. The infantry moved quickly through the shellfire and swung north along the dunes to attack the sector where the landing should have been made. There they encountered determined opposition, and they were not able to reach the guns, which continued their harassing fire in spite of counter-battery bombardment by the Navy.

This enemy shelling did not seriously delay the landing and unloading, and a stream of men, tanks, guns and vehicles came in to consolidate the division's hold on the coastal strip and to strengthen its westward advance. In the middle of the morning the infantry set out across the causeways with amphibious tanks moving through the water in close support. A few enemy positions on the far shore of the lagoon were still active, but the tanks subdued them and by 1 p.m. the seaborne and airborne forces had met. Already the parachutists had seized the exits from four causeways, while a fifth was found to be undefended and unmined even though it linked the beach with the main road leading straight through to the Merderet Valley.

No junction had yet been made between the 101st and the 82nd Divisions, but it was clear that a strong grip had been established on the Peninsula. Shortly before midday, Moon signalled to Kirk, commanding the Western Task Force, " Initial waves made landings on exact beaches after accurate air and naval bombardment. Fifteen waves landed by 0945B.[1] Succeeding waves continue to land. Both beaches cleared of obstacles. Roads under construction and vehicles proceeding inland. Little opposition. Coastal batteries under control."

This signal idealised the situation beyond the facts, for no one who was on the beach that morning would have reported in such glowing terms. But the general impression it conveyed—that the battle was developing according to plan—was justified and it brought profound relief to Omar Bradley, the Army Commander, who was in Kirk's flagship, the U.S. cruiser *Augusta*. There throughout the morning Bradley had been receiving reports of a very different character from the other American sector, OMAHA, where Gerow's V Corps was still fighting for a foothold against what proved to be the fiercest and most sustained resistance of the day.

[1]That is, 9.45 a.m. British Double Summer Time.

OMAHA was a concave beach four miles long and dominated at either end by cliffs which rose almost sheer for more than 100 feet. Between these two bluffs the gently curving strand sloped up to a cultivated plateau which reached a height of 150 feet half a mile inland and commanded the whole foreshore. The escarpment of this plateau was indented at four points where small watercourses had cut their way to the sea and these narrow valleys provided the only exits for vehicles. On the beach itself the tidal flat, some 300 yards deep, was firm sand, but it ended in a bank of heavy, smooth shingle which sloped up rather sharply.

On the western third of OMAHA this shingle ran up to a sea-wall and a paved road, beyond which the escarpment soon rose at a steep angle. On the rest of the beach the shingle bank was backed by sand dunes which were impassable by vehicles, as was the shingle in many places. On the far side of this line of dunes was a broad stretch of sand which was marshy and tufted with coarse grass at the entrances to the valleys. Here the rough slope was less steep, but it could not be negotiated even by tracked vehicles except in a few places. Apart from the paved road under the lee of the western bluff, the routes running inland were little more than cart tracks and all led through thickly-wooded cuttings into the stout stone villages of Vierville, St. Laurent and Colleville, which thus commanded every exit.

The inherent strength of this sector had been well exploited by the Germans in designing their defences. On the tidal flat there were three belts of obstacles; the beach above the shingle, and parts of the slope, were mined and wired; all the natural exits were blocked by mines and by either concrete obstructions or anti-tank ditches. The main strong-points, consisting of entrenchments, pillboxes and bunkers equipped with machine-guns, anti-tank guns and light artillery, were concentrated on the bluffs at either end of the beach and at the mouths of the four valleys. There the fire positions were terraced up the slopes on either side and were echeloned inland, so that they were almost impregnable against head-on assault. From these the Germans could cover most of the beach with direct and flanking fire.

Between the exit valleys, however, the defences were less formidable. There were trenches and weapon pits along the crest of the escarpment and some minefields on the plateau, but the Germans relied on their reserves in the string of coastal villages to cut short any penetration between the main strongholds. These villages formed a second defensive chain and three miles inland the flooded valley of the River Aure provided a further barrier which the Americans would have to force in order to avoid being contained in the narrow coastal belt.

This stretch of beach, thus fortified, was hardly inviting, but it was the only part of the entire 20 miles between the mouth of the Vire and Arromanches, north-east of Bayeux, where a landing could be made in strength. Elsewhere in this zone sheer cliffs or outcrops of rock off-shore provided natural protection and allowed the Germans to concentrate on the defence of OMAHA.

When the American plan was made it was thought that this four-mile sector was manned by little more than a battalion of the 716th Division, which was then holding 45 miles of coastline from the Orne to the Vire. This was an indifferent formation, containing many foreign conscripts and equipped only for a static role, but a mobile division of good quality, the 352nd, was known to be in close reserve around St. Lô. In May British Intelligence had come to suspect that this division had moved up to strengthen the coastal crust by taking over the western half of the Orne–Vire sector, but the evidence of that move was slender and the Americans were disinclined to accept it. When some confirmation was received early in June, it was too late to pass the warning on to the assault troops who were already embarking. Consequently, they went into action believing that though OMAHA was strongly fortified it was not particularly heavily garrisoned.

The plan provided for the 1st U.S. Division (Major-General C. R. Huebner) to assault with two Regimental Combat Teams, each of three battalions, supported by two battalions of DD tanks and two special brigades of engineers. On the right the 116th Regiment (attached from the 29th Division) was to land between Vierville and St. Laurent, and on the left the 16th Regiment, between St. Laurent and Colleville. For the assault both these regiments were to be under Huebner's command, but once a foothold had been gained, the 29th Division (Major-General C. H. Gehrhardt) was to take over the western sector and clear the area between the coast and the Aure as far as Isigny. Meantime, the 1st Division would swing east to link up with Second British Army at Port-en-Bessin and drive south to secure a bridgehead over the Aure, east of Trévières. It was hoped—a little ambitiously perhaps—that by nightfall V U.S. Corps might have a beachhead 16 miles wide and five to six miles deep, but it was realised that whether or not this 'phase-line' could be reached depended primarily on the whereabouts of the 352nd Division.

Soon after 3 a.m. Naval Force 'O' (Rear-Admiral J. L. Hall, Jr., U.S.N.) began lowering the assault-craft from their 'mother-ships' into a rough and unfriendly sea twelve miles off-shore. Several craft were swamped within a few minutes of touching the water; others were kept afloat only by strenuous baling by troops who used their steel helmets as buckets. None but the most hardened stomachs were unmoved by the pitching and tossing and men became weak from sickness long before they began the run-in. Perhaps the most unpleasant experience was that suffered by a boatload of the 116th Infantry. " Major Dallas's command party," says the regimental account, "made their start under inauspicious circumstances. In lowering the boats from the davits of H.M.S. *Empire*

*Javelin,* the command boat became stuck for 30 minutes directly under the outlet of the ship's ' heads ' and could go neither up nor down. During this half-hour the ship's company made the most of an opportunity that Englishmen have sought since 1776."

The rough seas had more serious consequences in the case of the DD tanks. One battalion decided not to attempt any launchings; the other put 29 tanks into the water, but some sank like stones as soon as they left the LCTs, others were swamped on the run-in and only two reached the shore. The weather was the primary factor in this disaster, but the casualties might not have been so severe if the tanks had not been launched so far out (they were set to swim nearly four miles) and if the training and maintenance had been more thorough. But whatever the reason, the plan to land the DD tanks ahead of the infantry miscarried, and the men themselves approached the shore under the gravest disadvantages. As one report says, " Men who had been chilled by their wetting, cramped by immobility in the small and fully-loaded craft and weakened by sea-sickness were not in the best condition for strenuous action on landing."[1]

While the assault battalions were heading for the shore, warships and aircraft began the bombardment of the coast defences. Owing to low cloud, visibility was poor when the shelling began and after a few minutes the dust and smoke made it almost impossible to pinpoint targets on shore. The task of the bombers thus became extremely difficult and, fearful of hitting their own troops, they left a good safety margin. This was unquestionably wise, but it meant that most of the bombs fell behind, not upon, the beach defences. In addition, many rocket-firing craft, confused by the smoke and over-anxious about the coastal guns, loosed their salvos well out of range and the in-coming troops had the mortification of seeing most of the projectiles burst in the water short of the beach.

Batteries and strong points were still active when the bombardment lifted, and the assault craft came under heavy shelling and mortaring over the last half-mile before they touched down on a beach almost unscarred by friendly bomb or shell. The severest fire came from the bluff which commanded the western end of the beach and from the Vierville exit, directly in front of which the 1st Battalion of the 116th Regiment was due to land in column of companies.

At 6.30 a.m., as the leading company approached this beach, known by the code-name Dog Green,[2] one of its six craft foundered and another was sunk by a direct hit, but the rest went on till they ran aground on a

---

[1]*Omaha Beachhead,* p. 38. This authoritative account of the landing, prepared by the U.S. War Department's Historical Division, is admirably frank and comprehensive.

[2]Between the Vire and the Orne the Normandy coast was divided by the planners into beach sectors labelled alphabetically from the West. The three sectors of OMAHA —D, E and F—were known from their lettering as Dog, Easy and Fox, and sub-sectors were designated by colours. Thus the 116th Regiment landed on Dog Green, Dog White, Dog Red and Easy Green; 16th Regiment on Easy Red and Fox Green.

sandbar several hundred yards short of the sea wall. The ramps went down and the men leapt into water which was waist to shoulder deep. Then, says the battalion's own story:[1]

> As if this were the signal for which the enemy had waited, all boats came under criss-cross machine-gun fire. . . . As the first men jumped, they crumpled and flopped into the water. Then order was lost. It seemed to the men that the only way to get ashore was to dive head first in and swim clear of the fire that was striking the boats. But, as they hit the water, their heavy equipment dragged them down and soon they were struggling to keep afloat. Some were hit in the water and wounded. Some drowned then and there. . . . But some moved safely through the bullet-fire to the sand and then, finding they could not hold there, went back into the water and used it as cover, only their heads sticking out. Those who survived kept moving forward with the tide, sheltering at times behind under-water obstacles and in this way they finally made their landings.
>
> Within ten minutes of the ramps being lowered, A Company had become inert, leaderless and almost incapable of action. Every officer and sergeant had been killed or wounded. . . . It had become a struggle for survival and rescue. The men in the water pushed wounded men ashore ahead of them, and those who had reached the sands crawled back into the water pulling others to land to save them from drowning, in many cases only to see the rescued men wounded again or to be hit themselves. Within 20 minutes of striking the beach A Company had ceased to be an assault company and had become a forlorn little rescue party bent upon survival and the saving of lives.

The vanguard of the assault on this flank of OMAHA was still at the water's edge when the next company came in 25 minutes after H-Hour. Several boatloads, which landed on Dog Green, the same sector as the first wave, were riddled on the water's edge, but the others, carried farther east and farther inshore by the tide, touched down on a less heavily defended stretch of beach which was enveloped in smoke. This shielded them as they dashed for cover of the sea-wall and from there two groups, each less than twenty strong, struggled through the wire and minefields and up the ridge to Vierville, 700 yards inland, not stopping to deal with the fortifications but infiltrating between them as best they could.

Because of the drag of the wind and tide, all six boats of the following company came in east of the Dog Green death-trap, and moved across

[1]This account was prepared by the U.S. War Department's Historical Division after close interrogation of the survivors.

the foreshore and up the slope with less than a dozen casualties, for they found an unmined gap between the strongpoints which guarded the natural exits. Before 10 a.m. this company and part of 5th Ranger Battalion, which landed behind it, had joined the two earlier groups in Vierville, just in time to beat off a sharp counter-attack. There some 200 men stopped a thrust which would have carried through to the beach, where the remnants of the 1st Battalion lay almost helpless in their foxholes, lacking the support of armour or heavy weapons.

A mile to the east, the other two battalions of the 116th Regiment, landing in succession on either side of the Les Moulins exit, met less opposition on the beach, because the Germans were blinded by smoke from grass and buildings on the crest set afire by the naval bombardment. This unintentional smoke screen saved many lives, but it caused great confusion. Most companies came in farther east than had been planned and " officers, knowing they were to the left of their landing areas, were uncertain as to their course of action, and this hesitation prevented any chance of immediate assault action."[1] They were slow in rallying, slower still in advancing up the slope, since they tended to move in single file through the minefields, and those who did reach the crest soon lost cohesion and direction, for there the smoke was so thick that the troops had to put on their gas-masks.

There was little progress until someone discovered, east of Les Moulins, a sector where the minefields had been detonated by the bombardment, opening the way for elements of both battalions to infiltrate towards St. Laurent before the enemy closed the gap with shellfire. This accentuated the congestion on the beach, for supporting weapons and transport had begun to land before the engineers had cleared any exits and before the infantry had subdued the strongpoints which raked the foreshore with fire. Wrecked landing-craft, burning vehicles, exploding ammunition and intermittent shelling added to the confusion, making it extremely difficult for commanders to organise the scattered and bewildered groups who had taken shelter under the sea-wall or the shingle bank, and impossible for the follow-up regiment to come in as planned at 9.30 a.m.

Meantime, the counterpart of this battle had developed along the eastern half of OMAHA, where two battalions of the 16th Regiment had landed at half-past six. Here, too, the bombardment had missed the beach defences and the assault craft were dragged by the run of the wind and tide half a mile and more to the east of their appointed stations. The whole assault side-slipped with most unfortunate results. On Easy Red, where the enemy fire at first was relatively light, barely 100 men were set down during the first half-hour, but the best part of three companies made their landfall on Fox Green directly beneath the

[1] *Omaha Beachhead*, p. 47.

unscathed guns of formidable strong points which covered the exit leading to Colleville. The terrible story of Dog Green was repeated.

On Easy Red, where the 2nd Battalion should have landed, the first meagre assault forces were pinned to the beach until " a lieutenant and a wounded sergeant of divisional engineers stood up under fire and walked over to inspect the wire obstacles just beyond the embankment. The lieutenant came back and, hands on hips, looked down disgustedly at the men lying behind the shingle bank. ' Are you going to lay there and get killed, or get up and do something about it? ' Nobody stirred, so the sergeant and the officer got the materials and blew the wire."[1] This courageous gesture rallied the men and the lieutenant led them to the top of the ridge in single file along a narrow pathway which was under fire and sown with anti-personnel mines. By that route this platoon, followed by another company, got within striking distance of the strongpoints which had turned this sector into a slaughter-ground. One by one these were silenced but the hazard of the minefields remained. One false step and a man lost a foot or a leg, if not his life. The wounded lay where they fell, afraid to move lest they might set off another mine, and the men in the shuffling line stepped over them. Shells dropped close but none dared to go to ground, for every yard was lethal. When the reserve battalion tried to find its own pathway, the minefield claimed 47 victims in the leading company, but some 300 men finally got through and headed for Colleville. The gap thus opened became a funnel for movement off Easy Red during the rest of the morning, but that movement was slow and perilous.

On the extreme left, however, the 16th's other assault battalion was able to make reasonable progress, in spite of early mishaps which might have proved disastrous. Rough sea and bad navigation delayed the landing. Several craft were swamped, or sunk by direct hits, one assault company was an hour and a half late and the other came in half a mile too far to the east. This, in fact, proved an advantage, since the men were able to organise under the lee of the cliffs and, instead of trying, as intended, to force the strongly-guarded exit from Fox Green, they found their way up a steep but ill-defended gully farther east. The rest of the battalion followed and opened a clear breach in the defences with the aid of fire from destroyers and small craft operating close in on the flank. Here by 9.30 a.m. the Americans were moving slowly but steadily east along the cliff-top towards Port-en-Bessin, where they were due to link up with the British.

Elsewhere on OMAHA, however, the situation was still extremely grave. By half-past nine, according to the After-Action Report of V U.S. Corps, the assault units " were disorganised, had suffered heavy casualties and were handicapped by losses of valuable equipment. . . . They were pinned down along the beach by intense enemy fire. . . . Personnel and equipment were being piled ashore on Easy Red, Easy

[1] *Omaha Beachhead*, p. 58.

Green and Dog Red sectors where congested groups afforded good targets for the enemy. The engineers had not been able to clear sufficiently large gaps through the minefields with the result that companies attempting to move through them off the beach suffered considerable casualties. . . . Action in this early period was that of small, often isolated groups—a squad, a section or a platoon without much co-ordination. Attempts were made to organise units but . . . the beaches were too confused to permit it."

In this confusion the forces already ashore were powerless to break the deadlock, and the men, tanks and guns which were so urgently required could not be landed because the engineers had not been able to clear the underwater obstacles or the general wreckage on the foreshore. Even those tanks and vehicles which had been landed were still immobilised on the narrow strip of sand between the rising tide and the shingle bank through which as yet no gaps had been cleared. The assault regiments were clinging to barely a hundred yards of beach. A few small parties, which were to reach Vierville, St. Laurent and Colleville, had made minor penetrations, but these had been partially closed behind them by enemy fire. The Atlantic Wall was holding firm, and the Americans now knew that the OMAHA sector was held by units of both the 352nd and the 716th Divisions.

In May, during the general strengthening of Normandy following Hitler's intuitive inspiration and Rommel's policy of strengthening the coastal crust, the 352nd Division had moved up to garrison the Bayeux–Isigny sector. There it took under command the regiment of the 716th which was holding this extensive front, and proceeded to nose in three of its own six battalions to defend OMAHA and another likely beach at Arromanches on the British front. This left three battalions of the 352nd in close reserve behind OMAHA and by chance one of these was carrying out an exercise on that stretch of coast on June 5th–6th.

There were thus eight battalions in the area between Bayeux and Isigny, where the Americans had expected to find four, and the defences had some depth, provided moreover by troops of fair quality, equipped for something more than a static role. This meant that when the bombardment miscarried and the amphibious armour failed to arrive, the Americans entered an unequal struggle with every advantage of weather, position and armament against them. The presence of the 352nd Division in and close behind the beach made it a matter of the most vital consequence to break through the coastal defences before they could be further reinforced.

This was the prospect at 9.50 a.m. when a signal from the troops ashore told Huebner, "There are too many vehicles on the beach; send combat troops. 30 LCTs waiting off-shore; cannot come in because of shelling. Troops dug in on beaches, still under heavy fire."

Huebner acted promptly. He called on the Navy to engage German batteries and strongpoints regardless of the danger of hitting his own troops, and he ordered the 18th Regiment to land at once on Easy Red. Of that regiment, however, only one battalion was loaded in craft which could make what amounted to an assault landing. The others had to be transhipped from their LCIs into small craft, and it was early afternoon before they were ready to go ashore.

By that time, the situation had been improved by the landing of one battalion on Easy Red and another on Easy Green. Both battalions found the beaches still under fire, but they curbed it by capturing several pillboxes. In the attack upon these they were supported by DD tanks, which had been landed dry-shod, and by sustained and accurate shelling from destroyers standing only a thousand yards off-shore.

At noon a report from Easy Green said, " Fire support excellent. Germans leaving positions and surrendering." A few minutes later came another report, from Easy Red, " Troops previously pinned down on Easy and Fox now advancing inland."

Even more important, by this time the last enemy strongpoints at the main exit from Easy Red had been reduced and engineers had begun clearing the minefields. Thus after a six-hour battle the defences began to crumble and the foreshore was gradually freed of small arms fire, but the shelling of the beach continued, in spite of counter-battery bombard- ment by warships and fighter-bombers. There were still no exits for vehicles; most of the passages through the minefields were little more than single-file tracks; and the enemy was opposing most strenuously any attempt to deepen the penetration. The first crisis had passed, but the battle was by no means won.

In the early afternoon movement off the beach was limited and sluggish and the enemy had time to re-form his front roughly along the line of the road that ran through Colleville and St. Laurent. Within an hour and a half of landing part of the 18th Regiment, by a very remarkable effort, reached the northern edge of Colleville, a mile inland, where several weakened companies of the 16th Regiment were waging a house- to-house battle. But the enemy, too, had been reinforced and throughout the afternoon the Americans could do no more than hold on and hope that additional support in men and weapons would get through from the beach.

Unfortunately, movement inland was delayed, primarily because of the psychological supremacy of German mines over the American engineers and infantrymen. Even when the minefields were no longer under direct fire, the engineers were tardy in tackling them and the infantry were so ill-schooled in the art of ' de-lousing ' mines that they preferred to pick a dangerous passage through them rather than set boldly about the task of clearance. In mid-afternoon, for instance, one battalion was led slowly and painfully in single file up the ridge, stepping over the wounded who lay on the mined path. By resolute action the way could have been cleared in half the time it took to pass the battalion man by man along it. Yet no one would grasp the nettle.

It was 2 p.m. before the engineers succeeded in clearing any exit track. Another two hours elapsed before tanks and vehicles began moving off the beach, and then full use could not be made of the exit because of shelling. Late in the afternoon this became so severe that Huebner's third regiment did not finish landing until after seven o'clock and two battalions of artillery were even further delayed. Thus the infantry who had battled inland were left without adequate supporting fire until some time after 7 p.m., when a few tanks and tank-destroyers came to their aid as the fight for the coastal villages hung in the balance.

Even the possibilities of direct air support could not be fully exploited, mainly because so many of the leading companies and battalions had lost their radio sets in struggling ashore. No one in the H.Q. ships knew where the front line was, the troops on the ground were far too busy to put out visual signals, and the smoke and dust which overhung the beachhead made accurate identification of targets impossible. This obscurity also handicapped the warships, but their bombardment was the most effective aid the infantry received.

It was only at the end of the long day that the Americans forced the line of the coastal road, and this success was principally due to the unquenchable spirit and drive of the 1st Division. On the right the units of the 29th Division, fighting their first battle, made little progress after taking Vierville and reaching St. Laurent in the morning. In the face of aggressive German probing, it was all Gerhardt's troops could do to hold a beachhead 1,200 yards deep, for only two of his infantry regiments and one artillery battalion were landed during the day, and that battalion lost all but one of its 12 guns. At dark the situation was still confused and St. Laurent was not completely clear. The American grip on this stretch of OMAHA was by no means secure, and there was considerable anxiety about the danger of a counter-attack against the tired and weakened battalions during the night. The opportunity was there and the Germans could exploit it—if they were to commit their reserves in the right place.

For eight hours after the airborne assault began, the H.Q. of the German 84th Corps (Marcks) was handicapped by lack of reliable information. Reports of the main paratroop and glider landings were reasonably prompt and accurate, but the jamming of coastal radar prevented the enemy from gaining any indication of the strength and dispositions of the forces at sea until after daylight, and by that time the coast defences were under fire from aircraft and warships. Although this bombardment did not cause serious damage to the defences on OMAHA, it did disrupt communications, especially in the Cotentin area. The start of the naval shelling was duly reported by 84th Corps to Seventh

Army at 6 a.m., but Marcks received no word of the seaborne landings until two hours later, and it was nearly 11 o'clock before he learned that troops were landing from the sea on the Cotentin. This news, which came only from the German Navy, could not be confirmed, and at 11.45 a.m. 84th Corps signalled, " Regarding East coast [of Cotentin] no reports available since at the moment communications are severed."[1]

In the meantime, the news from the OMAHA sector, though scanty, was encouraging. At 9.25 a.m. Marcks's H.Q. reported, " The forward positions in the area of 352nd Division have been penetrated but the situation is not so critical as in the area of 716th Division," i.e. between Bayeux and Caen, and it was for this sector that he requested immediate counter-action by panzer divisions. This policy seemed justified when at 1.35 p.m. it was stated by the Chief of Staff of the 352nd that " the Division has thrown the invaders back into the sea; only near Colleville is there, in his opinion, a counter-attack still in progress." On the strength of this news Seventh Army informed Rommel's H.Q. that " the situation in the area of 352nd Division is now restored." There was no contrary report from this division until 6 p.m. and in the meantime all armoured reserves had been directed against the British with the object of preventing the fall of Caen. None were sent to the area west of Bayeux.

In any case the reinforcements which Marcks could have thrown into the OMAHA battle were not as great as Allied Intelligence had feared they might be. Around St. Lô there was only a mobile brigade, and its mobility was limited to the skill of its members as cyclists, for it had no motorised troop transport. Nevertheless, if it had intervened at OMAHA during the afternoon the consequences might have been serious, but at midday it was ordered to counter-attack the British east of Bayeux. Thus the only reserves which could be employed against OMAHA that day were three battalions of the 352nd, deployed in close reserve between Bayeux and Isigny. Before dawn in response to the airborne landings on the Cotentin two of these battalions were ordered to move west " to establish and maintain the link through Carentan." One had started moving before Marcks learned of the OMAHA assault and the other, which had been stationed around Bayeux, was drawn into battle with the British. This left only a single battalion in position to reinforce the OMAHA defences, and it was pitted against the American right flank at Vierville and St. Laurent. It was here that the Germans should have made their counter-stroke during the night with the battalion which had started for Carentan and been recalled, but they made the fatal mistake of looking over their shoulders at a landing which was not and could not have been any real threat.

Soon after seven o'clock that morning three companies of Rangers

[1] This, and the other messages that follow, are taken from the Telephone Log of Seventh German Army H.Q.

(the American counterpart of British Commandos) had landed three miles west of OMAHA at the base of Pointe du Hoe, an almost sheer cliff 100 feet high. Their primary task was to silence a powerful coastal battery capable of firing upon both UTAH and OMAHA beaches. The cliffs appeared to be unassailable, but the Rangers shot grappling hooks and rope ladders to the top with rocket charges and scaled the heights under covering fire from two destroyers. This fire drove the Germans into their dug-outs and the Rangers met little opposition as they moved to the battery position. They found it so cratered by bombs and shells that it looked like the face of the moon; the casemates were wrecked, and the guns had gone.

Patrols were sent inland and after going half a mile two men found the missing battery, camouflaged and intact. There were stacks of ammunition on the ground, the guns were ready to fire on UTAH, but there was no sign of the crews or of any recent firing. The battery was put out of action with explosive charges, but the mystery of the silent and deserted guns on Pointe du Hoe remains unsolved. Whatever the reason, the most dangerous battery in the American assault area was never used and was exposed to destruction by a two-man patrol!

As the day wore on the small Ranger force, numbering 130 men, drew increasing attention from the enemy. There were two counter-attacks in the afternoon and three more after dark, when the Germans pitted against the Rangers the reserves which should have been used for an attack against the western and most vulnerable sector of the OMAHA beachhead.

There was no such diversion to aid the 1st Division in the slogging battle which carried it across the Colleville–St. Laurent road in the last few hours before dark. The recovery Huebner's men had made since the middle of the morning was extraordinary. It had seemed then that the leading regiment was broken and beaten, but at the critical moment its survivors had responded to the intrepid leadership of its commander, Colonel G. A. Taylor, who became famous that morning for the rallying cry, " Two kinds of people are staying on this beach, the dead and those who are going to die—now let's get the hell out of here."

In that spirit the first small parties had made the break and the follow-up regiment had exploited this slender advantage with a thrust to Colleville and beyond, which ended by cracking the second German position. This village was the keystone of the defence once the coastal fortifications had begun to yield. At dark some Germans were still holding out in Colleville, but they were so hard pressed by infantry and tanks that the village had lost its tactical significance. Maintaining the pressure south and east so long as the light lasted, the 1st Division's own regiments extended their beachhead to an average depth of a mile to a mile and a half on a four-mile front by the end of the day. It was a slender enough footing, but it was held by men who had been ashore before in North Africa and in Sicily, and who could not be dismayed even by the most desperate situation. Had this sector of OMAHA been assigned to troops less experienced, less resolute or less ably commanded, the assault might never have penetrated beyond the beaches.

The near-disaster which befell the Americans at OMAHA was in some degree due to the weather, which led to the miscarriage of the preliminary bombardment and the mislanding of the assault units, but the sea off OMAHA was hardly, if at all, more hostile than it was on the more exposed British beaches farther east. In so far as they suffered more severely from the rough sea, this was chiefly due to the fact that the U.S. Navy, concerned about the fire of coastal batteries, insisted upon lowering the assault craft as much as twelve miles off-shore, whereas the British ' lowering areas ' were less than eight miles out. The longer passage not only added to the strain upon the assault infantry but greatly increased the danger of swamping and of faulty navigation. The leading assault craft had to start their run-in while it was still dark, and were excessively and unwarrantably exposed to the vagaries of wind and tide. On the other beaches very few mislandings were made on D-Day, but on OMAHA less than half the companies in the assault battalions were landed within 800 yards of their appointed sectors. The U.S. Navy's unwillingness to take advice from Ramsay was the start of the trouble.[1]

So far as operations, on shore are concerned, it is suggested by the War Department's historians that " the principal cause of the difficulties of V Corps on D-Day was the unexpected strength of the enemy on the assault beaches."[2] This is only a partial explanation, for there were grave defects inherent in the American plan. The first of these was the fruit of the American predilection for direct assault. The plan for OMAHA was a tactical application of the head-on strategy which Marshall had so consistently advocated in pressing the case for cross-Channel invasion. The Americans knew that the main enemy fortifications covered the natural exits, and yet they deliberately planned to make their heaviest landings directly in front of these strongpoints with the object of taking them by storm. They scorned the lessons of earlier amphibious operations, which had shown the wisdom of landing between the beach strongpoints, not opposite them, infiltrating and assaulting them from the flank and rear. The plan for Dog sector was typical. Dog Green and Dog Red were each known to be covered by powerful ' exit ' strongpoints. Between those Dog White was comparatively weakly defended. The American intention, however, was to land four companies in succession on each of the former during the first hour and only two companies on the latter where prospects of success were greatest. The results might have been anticipated. Two companies of the 2nd Rangers landed according to plan opposite the Vierville exit on Dog Green; only

---

[1] In his public comment on this Ramsay was tactfully restrained, for in his *Dispatch* (paragraph 40) he was content to say: " The longer passage inshore for the assault craft of the Western Task Force appeared to add appreciably to their difficulties."
[2] *Omaha Beachhead*, pp. 109-10.

62 men out of 130 reached the sea-wall. But 450 men of the 5th Rangers landing at the same time on Dog White between the strongpoints " got across the beach and up the sea-wall with the loss of only 5 or 6 men."[1]

There might have been some justification for the policy of direct assault if the Americans had accepted Montgomery's plan for landing armour *en masse* at the start of the attack, and for using the specialised equipment of Hobart's 79th Armoured Division to deal with the fortifications and the underwater obstacles. When Montgomery first saw this equipment he ordered Hobart to make one-third of it available to the Americans, and set himself to interest Eisenhower and Bradley in its revolutionary employment. Hobart's account of the reaction of the three generals is illuminating.[2]

" Montgomery," he says, " was most inquisitive. After thorough tests and searching questions he said in effect: ' I'll have this and this and this; but I don't want that or that.' Eisenhower was equally enthusiastic but not so discriminating. His response was, ' We'll take everything you can give us.' Bradley appeared to be interested but, when asked what he wanted, replied, ' I'll have to consult my staff.' "

Bradley and his staff eventually accepted the ' DDs ' but did not take up the offer of ' Crabs,' ' Crocodiles,' ' AVREs ' and the rest of Hobart's menagerie.[3] Their official reason was that there was no time to train American crews to handle the Churchill tanks in which most of the special British equipment was installed, but their fundamental scepticism about its value was shown when they rejected even the ' Crabs ' which offered few training difficulties, since the ' flail ' device was fitted to the standard American Sherman tank.

The terrible consequences of this short-sightedness were only too apparent on OMAHA on D-Day. The failure of the bombardment and the non-appearance of the DD tanks left the infantry at the mercy of the strongpoints which they were required to take by storm. Where tanks were available, landed direct from LCTs, they proved invaluable, but they were too few and too dispersed, and they found great difficulty in manœuvring because of the congestion of vehicles on the foreshore.

This congestion was chiefly due to the absence of specialised armour capable of dealing with the natural obstacles and fixed defences. The British had learned from the Dieppe Raid that engineers cannot consistently perform under fire the deliberate tasks required of them unless they are given armoured protection. No such protection was available on OMAHA. Apart from lightly armoured bulldozers the Americans had no mechanised equipment for dealing with the obstructions and fortifications. They were expected by their commanders to attack pillboxes

---

[1] *Omaha Beachhead*, p. 53.

[2] This account was given to me by General Hobart on November 10th, 1946.

[3] ' Crabs ' were ' flail-tanks ' and ' Crocodiles ' were flame-throwing tanks. ' AVRE ' stood for ' Armoured Vehicle, Royal Engineers;' ' AVREs ' were used in demolishing fortifications and surmounting obstacles.

with pole-charges and man-pack flame-throwers, to clear barbed wire entanglements and concrete walls with explosives manually placed and to lift mines by hand, all under fire. That they often failed is not surprising. Throughout the morning tanks, guns and vehicles were immobilised at the water's edge because the engineers could not clear gaps in the shingle bank, a comparatively minor obstacle. Throughout the afternoon, infantry were compelled to move across the beach in single file because the sappers had no mechanical means of dealing with mines and hand-clearance was too slow. At the Vierville exit the last strongpoints were reduced by 2 p.m., but it was another eight hours before the mines and obstructions had been cleared, for they had to be cleared by hand.

At dark only this road and one other were open for vehicles, and the full sweep of the beach was still under fire from artillery and mortars. The corps beachhead was six miles wide and less than two miles deep at the point of greatest penetration, and there was a grave shortage of tanks, anti-tank guns and of artillery generally. Most of the battalions were seriously weakened, for the day's fighting had cost 3,000 casualties. In short, although the Americans were ashore, they held an area barely large enough to be called a foothold, and were in no condition to withstand any large-scale counter-attack with armour during the next two critical days. But whether or not the Germans would, or could, develop such an attack depended on the course of events on the front of Dempsey's Second British Army.

## CHAPTER XIV

# ASSAULT FROM THE SEA: II

## BAYEUX AND CAEN

THE Second British Army which sailed for Normandy was the fulfilment of the pledge that Churchill had given to France and Europe while Britain stood alone. In a broadcast to the French people on October 2nd, 1940, he had declared: " Remember we shall never stop, never weary and never give in, and that our whole people and Empire have vowed themselves to the task of cleansing Europe from the Nazi pestilence and saving the world from the new Dark Ages. . . . Good night then; sleep to gather strength for the morning. For the morning will come." This was the morning.

Dempsey's force was officially to be designated the ' British Liberation Army,' and so it was, when judged by its purpose in Europe, but for the people of Britain it was in a sense an 'Army of Vindication.' In their approach to OVERLORD, there was, of course, an element of vengeance for Dunkirk, but, above and beyond this, it was their final proof to the world that Chamberlain and Appeasement had been a betrayal of their true spirit and tradition. From the Battle of Britain to Alamein and Anzio they had been demonstrating this, but the recrossing of the Channel was the supreme expression of the nation's refound faith in itself.

The fruits of four years' striving at home and abroad had gone to the making of Second Army and it went forth trained and equipped as no other force in British history for the greatest operation of war the country had ever undertaken. As organised for the assault, this Army was formed by the confluence of the two main streams of Britain's military endeavour since 1940. I Corps, the 3rd British and 3rd Canadian Divisions, the 49th (West Riding) and the Commandos represented those who had come undaunted from Norway and Dunkirk, and had spent the intervening years guarding the invasion base and its Atlantic life-line, raiding Hitler's Fortress and training for the return to France. XXX Corps, 7th Armoured, the 50th and the 51st, stood for those who had learned their craft in the renaissance of Alamein and the subsequent restoration of Britain's Mediterranean power. Through the years of waiting and preparing there had been many doubters, but now the magnitude of the force assembled, the thoroughness of the plan and its smooth unfolding filled all but the inveterate pessimists with confidence and conviction of success.

That was the background of the Army which Rear-Admiral Sir Philip Vian and the Eastern Task Force convoyed across the Channel on this squally June night. In the half-light before dawn eager eyes were strained towards the still invisible coast which Dempsey's divisions were to assault between Port-en-Bessin and the mouth of the Orne, a 25-mile sector, somewhat less difficult to attack than the beaches that confronted the Americans. There were no extensive inundations, as at UTAH, nor any sharp coastal ridges, as at OMAHA, but the advantage of this easier terrain was more than offset by the danger of early counter-attack by panzer divisions stationed east and south of Caen. The first shock of enemy armour would certainly fall on the British front. Thus it was the more important that Dempsey should secure very rapidly a bridgehead of sufficient depth to give real defensive strength, for it was his task " to protect the flank of the First U.S. Army while the latter capture Cherbourg and the Brittany ports."[1]

The position which Dempsey was ordered to gain by the evening of D-Day included Bayeux and Caen, the line of the main road between these cities and the ' airborne bridgehead ' east of the Orne. From this firm base armoured columns were to thrust aggressively southward, that day if possible, and stake out claims nearly 20 miles inland on high ground at Villers-Bocage and Evrécy. This bold, indeed impudent, aspect of the plan was included by Montgomery (and retained on his insistence even after the palpable strengthening of the German defences and reserves in Normandy during May) so that his troops would have a star to strive for, and would not miss opportunities of exploitation for lack of orders, as had happened at Gallipoli.

Of necessity Dempsey's mind was fixed upon the coast and its defences, upon the immediate problem of getting ashore and establishing his troops in the Bayeux–Caen area. The assault against the western half of this area was to be carried out by XXX Corps with the 50th Division[2] and the 8th Armoured Brigade. These troops were to land north-east of Bayeux on GOLD sector, a flat concave beach backed by a belt of marsh-land and bounded at either end by strongly fortified villages, Le Hamel and La Rivière. Here, DD tanks and specialised armour were to lead the assault, closely followed by two brigades of infantry; on the right, 231 Brigade was to land east of Le Hamel, clear that village and then drive west along the coast towards the Americans and Port-en-Bessin, which was to be taken from the rear by Commandos; on the left, 69

---

[1]Second Army Operation Order No. 1, April 21st, 1944, para. 10.
[2]The 50th Division (Major-General D. A. H. Graham) was reinforced for the occasion with the 56th Independent Infantry Brigade. The specialised armour on this and other British beaches was provided by Hobart's 79th Armoured Division.

Brigade, after landing west of La Rivière, was to strike south across the River Seulles to the Caen–Bayeux road around St. Léger, eight miles inland. The gap between these divergent thrusts was to be filled by the two reserve brigades (56 and 151) which were due to begin landing at 10 o'clock and were to advance south-west to Bayeux and the high ground just beyond it.

In preparation for this assault, warships of the Royal Navy began bombarding the defences forty minutes before sunrise, concentrating their fire on the coastal batteries which had already been attacked by Bomber Command during the night. On the XXX Corps front, the sole reply was from four six-inch guns at Longues, north of Bayeux. These had been accurately bombed, but had survived because they were heavily protected by the concrete casemates Rommel had insisted upon. With its first salvoes, however, this battery was tactless enough to straddle the ship which carried the Sector H.Q. and the Corps Commander. At once, the six-inch guns of H.M.S. *Ajax* were brought to bear and in twenty minutes the duel was won. Three of the four casemates received direct hits and had their guns silenced, two of them by shells which entered the narrow embrasures!

Once this battery had been quietened, the assembly of the assault force went on untroubled except by the weather which Vian described as " unexpectedly severe for the launching of an operation of this type." The troops had other words for it. A 15-knot wind whipped up waves four feet high and drove white breakers against the shore. Some of the small craft had already been turned back; others had been delayed because their engine-rooms became flooded; raft-like ' Rhino ' ferries for carrying motor transport ashore had broken their tow-lines. So rough was the sea that it was decided not to ' swim ' the DD tanks, but to land them direct on to the beach behind the infantry. So strong was the wind that the tide was being driven in-shore half an hour ahead of its proper time; a matter of some consequence for landing-craft intended to touch down outside the belt of mined obstacles.

The unfortunate infantry felt the full severity of the weather when they left the comparative calm of their landing-ships for the tossing assault craft. They had all been ordered to take their tablets of hyoscine hydrobromide, an anti-sea-sickness compound chosen by medical experts after exhaustive tests. The results, to quote the doctors' own report, were " not convincing." The men found themselves obliged to make liberal use of those items of army equipment which the War Office, callously frank, calls ' Bags, Vomit.' Long before they came in sight of the shore, most of the troops were weak and nauseated by sickness, cold and wet from waves which broke over the plunging bows.

Only the thorough training and steady nerve of the crews brought the first waves of landing-craft in with minor casualties. Behind them the tide rose quickly and within an hour the outer obstacles stood in seven to eight feet of water. Succeeding waves ran a perilous passage, but the skill of the crews carried them through. As Vian wrote: " Their spirit and seamanship alike rose to meet the greatness of the hour and they pressed forward and ashore, over and through mined obstacles in high heart and resolution; there was no faltering and many of the smaller landing-craft were driven on until they foundered."

Shortly before 7.30 a.m., the leading companies of the 1st Battalion, the Hampshire Regiment,[1] leapt out into two feet of water to find that the specialised armour, apart from the ' DDs,' was already ashore engaging the defences. The bombardment had had less material effect than expected and on the extreme right the stronghold of Le Hamel was almost untouched. It had been earmarked for severe treatment by bombers, destroyers and a regiment of artillery firing from landing-craft. The bombs had fallen wide, the artillery had been unable to engage the defences accurately, for the control craft carrying its Forward Observation Officer had broken down, and the fire of the destroyers had been ineffective, because the enemy gun positions were protected on their seaward side by concrete walls or earthen embankments. But in the strength and survival of Le Hamel lay one of the gravest weaknesses of the Atlantic Wall.

The Germans had bought this protection at the price of accepting severely restricted fields of fire, for those machine-guns and anti-tank guns which were shielded against naval bombardment could not shoot straight out to sea. Sited to cover the foreshore with enfilade fire, their role was to wither the flank of the men who struggled ashore after the underwater obstacles had taken toll of the landing-craft. This layout was based on two assumptions. First, the Germans believed that the landings would be made at or near high tide and that consequently the main torrent of direct fire should be concentrated on the zone between the high-water mark and the sea-wall or the dunes, whichever backed the particular beach. Secondly they thought that, if the strongpoints were protected against direct bombardment from the air and sea, the assault battalions would have no means of silencing the heavy German weapons in their concrete emplacements. Thus the infantry would be wiped out before any armour could be landed to support them.

These two assumptions were rendered false by Montgomery's decisions to land before half-tide and to bring in the specialised armour ahead of the infantry. And so when the 1st Hampshires touched down east of Le Hamel at H-Hour, they were not exposed to the full weight of the enemy's fire during the vulnerable minutes when the men were wading ashore. Many of the German guns could not be traversed far enough to reach them, and by the time the infantry had moved in 200 or 300 yards to the area, where—in German theory—they were due to be

[1]This battalion is here given its full title, but subsequent references to this and other units will be by the simpler nomenclature ' 1st Hampshires ' or ' 2nd East Yorkshire Battalion ' or even the colloquial ' 2nd Ox. and Bucks.'

annihilated, they had the fire-power of the armour to cover their movement and aid their attack.

Without this armoured support there might have been a repetition of the OMAHA crisis, for the fire from Le Hamel was accurate and intense. The first three ' Crabs ' (flail-tanks) which flogged their way through the minefields were either destroyed by anti-tank guns or became bogged in the marsh behind the dunes, but another, more fortunate than the rest, charged off the beach and through Le Hamel flailing and firing. Under its onslaught the main enemy stronghold in a sanatorium on the sea-front was quietened long enough for two companies of the Hampshires to move across the foreshore and work round behind Le Hamel to the village of Asnelles. But when this ' Crab ' was knocked out, the Germans struck back with fresh venom, making the western end of the beach almost impassable. It took the rest of the Hampshires all the morning to reduce the defences on the dunes and they could make no impression on the sanatorium.

The other assault battalion of 231 Brigade, the 1st Dorset, was more fortunate since it landed out of range of the Le Hamel defences and was able to deal swiftly with the opposition on its own front. Here the specialised armour operated almost according to the book, covering clay patches, clearing mines, smashing concrete obstructions and filling craters. Within an hour the armoured assault teams had cleared three exits and the Dorsets were moving inland, covered by guns of the ' Crabs ' which did double duty in the absence of the ' DDs.' Making the most of their opportunity, the infantry drove on with great dash and determination. Their main objective was a pronounced rise south of Arromanches, but they found it strongly held by elements of the 352nd Division, who were dislodged only after a combined assault with infantry and tanks in the afternoon.

At the eastern end of the 50th Division's front, the bombardment was generally more effective than it had been at Le Hamel. Small support craft followed the infantry of 69 Brigade almost to the touch-down, firing over their heads as they dashed ashore. Most of La Rivière was in ruins, but by some freak chance the western corner of the defences had escaped and from it there came withering fire as the 5th East Yorks raced for the protection of the sea-wall. An 88 mm firing from a massive pillbox knocked out two AVREs before a ' Crab,' taking advantage of the gun's limited traverse, moved in at a sharp angle to ' post a letter ' through the embrasure at a range of 100 yards. With this stronghold silenced, the defence began to crumble, but for another two hours the East Yorks had to fight a sticky battle from street to street.

Meantime, west of La Rivière, the 6th Green Howards had penetrated the defences without great difficulty. One company was checked at first by fire from two pillboxes and a fortified house, and from snipers behind the sea wall. The deadlock was broken by three AVREs of the 6th Assault Regiment, R.E. When they arrived, says the unit's account,

" one pillbox was reduced by petard fire and the other silenced by the infantry. But the Germans behind the wall continued to fire and throw grenades. By this time the troop commander's patience was exhausted, so, leaving his sergeant to petard the reinforced house, he led his and another AVRE up the beach, charged the wall, dropped four feet on to the roadway and shattered a number of German illusions. The enemy routed, the infantry advance continued." By 9.30 a.m. the Meuvaines Ridge, a mile inland, was in British hands, and the 7th Green Howards were moving up with tanks to carry on the attack.

The assault gained fresh power when the follow-up brigades (56 and 151) began landing about eleven o'clock. They were an hour late, but by this time several passages had been cleared through the underwater obstructions, seven exits were working and the beach groups had the traffic moving so well that both brigades were assembling inland by 12.30 p.m. The beachhead was then two and a half miles deep and three miles wide, but the stubborn garrison in Le Hamel still prevented any widening of the breach. On this flank the Atlantic Wall was held by a battalion of the 352nd Division and its troops proved as troublesome as those who defended OMAHA. Le Hamel was not clear until four o'clock, but then the Hampshires turned westward to roll up the coast defences. With destroyers and small support craft putting down a barrage ahead of them, the infantry and armour drove on with such vigour that by 9 p.m. they had overrun two miles of strongly fortified coast to take Arromanches, and had expelled the Germans from the cliff-top above the anchorage. With this in British hands the western flank of the Corps beachhead was protected and the site was secured for one of the MULBERRY harbours, which were about to be towed across the Channel.

Meanwhile, the main weight of the Corps attack had been directed south and south-west. During the afternoon and evening 56 Brigade advanced six miles and thwarted the enemy's efforts to re-form his line on the rising ground between the coast and Bayeux. The city was ripe for capture and Frenchmen peeping from behind their shutters saw the last of the enemy straggle through dark and deserted streets. The British might have occupied it that night, for 56 Brigade was able to send patrols into the north-eastern outskirts and 151 Brigade reached the Bayeux–Caen road three miles to the south-east. On its left, 69 Brigade, which had fought and marched almost without pause since early morning, ended the day six miles south of its assault beach, an achievement which bore witness to its experience and endurance.

At nightfall the ' Fifty Div.' beachhead measured roughly six miles by six. The leading battalions were some two to three miles short of their D-Day phase-line, but the Battle of Bayeux was already won and there was no chance of the enemy using this valuable road centre to move any counter-attack forces against the vulnerable OMAHA. Between that beach and GOLD there was a seven-mile stretch of unsubdued coast-line, but here the Germans were already feeling the squeeze, for No. 47

(Royal Marine) Commando was within sight of Port-en-Bessin, having carried out a fighting advance of nine miles behind the defences. On the eastern flank, however, firm contact had been established with the Canadians, the right wing of I British Corps.

The three assault divisions of I British Corps (commanded by Lieut.-General J. T. Crocker) had the most formidable and responsible D-Day task. While the 6th Airborne Division was establishing the left flank of the Allied bridgehead beyond the Orne, the 3rd British Division was to capture Caen and the 3rd Canadian was to make the deepest penetration of the day, to Carpiquet airfield, eleven miles inland. The objectives given to Crocker's seaborne divisions were decidedly ambitious, since his troops were to land last, on the most exposed beaches, with the farthest to go, against what was potentially the greatest opposition. Because of the flow of the tide and the presence of rocks off-shore, the 3rd Canadian and 3rd British Divisions could not begin to land until an hour and a half after dawn, during which time the enemy would have ample opportunity to prepare a welcome in a sector where his reserves were well placed to take advantage of any warning. Moreover, the outcrops of rock so divided the Corps front that the only suitable beaches for these two divisions were five miles apart.

As for the opposition, it was believed that the coastal defences between the Seulles and the Orne were held by two or three battalions of the 716th Division with several other battalions of unknown quality in close support.[1] But the real enemy strength lay in the 21st Panzer Division. Its exact dispositions were uncertain, but it was believed to be stationed south-east of Caen and its recent manœuvres, which had been plotted by the tank-tracks visible in aerial photographs, showed that the defence of this city would be its primary task. It might be distracted by the airborne landing, but it seemed certain that early on D-Day its main force would head straight for the rising ground between Caen and the beaches.

In this event, the British were likely to be forestalled, since Crocker could not bring into action during the first few hours of D-Day sufficient tanks to smash through a panzer division fighting on its own ground, and any attempt to do so might prove to be a ' Pyrrhic victory.' Crocker had to look beyond D-Day to his fundamental responsibility for safeguarding the left flank. If he were to expend his strength in a slogging match with 21st Panzer, he might leave himself exposed to a serious reverse at the hands of the 12th SS Panzer Division (stationed between Evreux and Gacé), which might be launched against his front on the afternoon of June 6th.

The proximity of these two armoured formations—with an estimated

[1] This sector of the coast was, in fact, held by three battalions of the 716th Division.

strength of 350 tanks[1] between them—meant that Caen could be captured on D-Day only by a stroke of luck. For Crocker the important question was: Could his assault break through the coastal crust rapidly enough to enable 3rd British to reach Caen ahead of 21st Panzer? The odds undoubtedly favoured the Germans. The airborne landing would give them at least six hours' warning and, even if their armoured and mechanised units were down near Falaise, they would have to travel (unopposed except by aircraft) barely twice the distance that the British troops must cover fighting and on foot or bicycle.

This much was apparent from the information available to Crocker, and so his Operation Order made allowance for the possibility that his troops might be forestalled. He instructed the 3rd British Division that before dark on D-Day, Caen should be " captured or effectively masked " by " brigade localities firmly established (i) North-West of Benouville. . . . (ii) North-West of Caen."

" Captured or effectively masked "; when Crocker wrote this in May he did not know that most of 21st Panzer, apart from its armour, was already established in and around Caen. On Rommel's orders its flak battalion was in the city; of its four motorised infantry battalions, one was on the western outskirts, another was covering the eastern approaches, while a third, together with the twenty-four 88 mm guns of the anti-tank battalion, was stationed on Périers Rise, only three miles inland from the very beach on which the 3rd British Division was to land. The presence of this battalion and these guns astride the main road to Caen greatly increased the importance of the weather. If Crocker was to have that city even ' effectively masked ' by dark on D-Day, his divisions needed smooth landings, maximum fire support and swift penetration of the Atlantic Wall.


The task of the 3rd Canadian Division[2] which was to land on Juno sector, astride the mouth of the River Seulles, was complicated by the presence of treacherous reefs off-shore. Because of these, the local H-Hour had to be delayed until the tide was so high that most of the landing-craft, even in the first wave, would have to touch down in the midst of obstacles designed for their destruction. This risk had to be accepted, but it was accordingly the more important that the landing should not be late. On the morning of June 6th, however, the weather carried the plan astray, for it was rather worse on the Canadian sector than it was elsewhere. Delayed by the choppy sea, the leading assault craft came in nearly half an hour later than originally intended, and as a result were borne by the tide for several hundred yards through the belt of

---

[1]On June 6th, according to the records of Rommel's H.Q., the 21st Panzer had 146 tanks and 51 assault-guns, and 12th SS had 177 tanks and 28 assault-guns.

[2]In this operation the 3rd Canadian Infantry Division (Major-General R. F. L. Keller) was supported by the 2nd Canadian Armoured Brigade.

heavily-mined obstacles. On the run-in the casualties were surprisingly few, but many craft were sunk or damaged as they sought to make their way out to sea again. In the case of one battalion, 20 out of 24 were wrecked.

Late though they were, most of the Canadian infantry arrived ahead of the armour which should have led them in, and, to make matters worse, they found that the defences had survived the bombardment almost unscathed. Owing to the bad visibility, the main weight of the bombing and shelling had fallen behind the coastal fortifications and, because of the late touch-down, the garrisons had had time to recover their morale and man their weapons.

In the attack upon the defences at the mouth of the Seulles the 7th Canadian Brigade was assisted by DD tanks which had been launched only 800 yards off-shore, but its engineer assault vehicles did not arrive until half an hour after the first touch-down. Accordingly, although the infantry, with superb dash and with bold support from the tanks, managed to overwhelm or neutralise the main strongpoints on the waterfront within an hour, there was some delay in preparing exits from the beaches. By mid-morning both the Royal Winnipeg Rifles and the Regina Rifles were two miles inland, but behind them the narrow beaches were choked with armour, guns and transport. It took the reserve battalion an hour and a half to get through the congestion and during this delay the attack lost some of its impetus.

Farther east the 8th Canadian Brigade landed a few minutes after the 7th, but without any DD tanks. It was too rough for these to be swum through the rocky shallows and they had to be disembarked well behind the infantry. At Bernières the fight was sharp while it lasted. The assault craft of the Queen's Own Rifles were carried so far in by the tide that the men had only 100 yards to run to the cover of the high sea-wall which backed the beach, but this 100 yards was the beaten-zone of the enemy's fire. One company lost half its strength in that dash for the wall, for it landed by error directly in front of a heavily-armed strongpoint, which was taken by storm only after a flak-ship brazenly ran inshore and almost aground to pour its fire into the German defences.

So fast did the Queen's Own move against this and other positions that when the Régiment de la Chaudière began to land behind them fifteen minutes later the only fire on the beach was coming from snipers. Already two exits had been made by the armour, and the assault troops were scouring the town. By half-past nine Bernières was reported clear and the French-Canadians began to move through it. On the southern outskirts, however, their advance was stopped by machine-guns and 88 mms firing straight down the road that led through orchards and cornfields to Bény-sur-Mer. It was two hours before this opposition could be overcome, and during this time the traffic jam in Bernières became acute, because the divisional commander, before he knew of the hold-up, had ordered the reserve brigade, the 9th, to land on this sector. Its three battalions were ashore by 12.30 p.m., but the beach and the streets were so packed with armour and transport that it was three o'clock before they could move southward. By this time the Chaudières had advanced three miles to Bény and were still going, but the valuable hours which had been lost in the middle of the day could not be made good.

By dark only one battalion of the reserve brigade had been committed. Nevertheless, the foremost Canadian troops were nearly seven miles inland. Some Canadian tanks had even penetrated to the Caen–Bayeux road, but had withdrawn because no infantry had been able to keep up with them. On the whole it was not so much the opposition in front as the congestion behind—on the beaches and in Bernières—that prevented the Canadians from reaching their final D-Day objective. But this congestion was the almost inevitable result of the weather, which delayed the landing, prevented the early clearance of underwater obstacles and piled up wrecked craft upon the narrow foreshore. In the circumstances it was remarkable that the Canadians made as much progress as they did: more progress, in fact, than any other division on D-Day. At nightfall they were within sight of Caen, and two battalions were only three miles from the city's north-western outskirts. On the right the 7th Brigade had linked up with the 50th Division, making the common beachhead twelve miles wide and six to seven miles deep. But on the left there was still a strip of enemy-held territory between 3rd Canadian and 3rd British.

On the morning of June 6th, as Naval Force ' S,' carrying the 3rd British Division and its supporting units, assembled off the mouth of the Orne, the chief concern of its commander (Rear-Admiral A. G. Talbot) was not the weather but the 16-inch and 11-inch guns at Le Havre. The anchorage was well within their range, but they remained silent. The heavier battery had, in fact, been out of action for some days, following a raid by Bomber Command, and the other, unable to use its radar for ranging, was blinded by a smoke-screen which Allied aircraft had laid before daylight. Out of this smoke, however, just as dawn was breaking, three E-boats emerged, loosed their torpedoes and turned tail. Two torpedoes passed between the battleships *Warspite* and *Ramillies*, another sank a Norwegian destroyer, while a fourth shot under the bow of Talbot's flagship, H.M.S. *Largs*, the Combined Command Centre for SWORD Sector.

The E-boats did not wait to observe results, and, when they had disappeared into the smoke-screen, the invasion fleet saw no more of the German Navy throughout the day. The War Diary of Naval Group West records that " similar attempts by other forces to get through also failed," and adds ruefully, " It was only to be expected that no effective blow could be struck at such a superior enemy force." The Allies had expected some suicide attacks, but Coastal Command patrols roving far and wide up the Channel and into the North Sea sighted neither surface-craft nor U-boats.

Untroubled by the enemy, the bombardment force continued to wreak havoc on the beaches west of the Orne and on heavy coastal batteries to the east. Soon after dawn Fortresses and Liberators joined in the attack, closely followed by medium bombers and by fighters which ranged up and down the coast seeking signs of movement. In two hours SWORD beach received the heaviest bombardment of the day, for all the supporting fire available to the 3rd Division was concentrated on the front of a single brigade, a strip of coast three miles wide and half a mile deep.

To the airborne troops at the Orne bridges, awaiting early reinforcement from the sea, the sound of the bombardment was sweet music. They were in the extraordinary position of being just beyond the 'receiving end,' three miles inland from the trembling shore. When the first bombers came over it was barely light, but fierce flashes lit up the countryside like day, and the ground shuddered underfoot. In the last few minutes before H-Hour the thunder and scream of gun and shell and the roar of rockets reached a crescendo and it seemed that the skies would crack.

Behind this screen of fire the 8th British Brigade began its assault with the 1st South Lancashire Battalion (on the right) heading for Queen White Beach, and the 2nd East Yorks for Queen Red. Ahead of them went the DD tanks of the 13th/18th Hussars and LCTs carrying armoured assault teams.

In the heavy sea and bad visibility the swimming tanks were nearly overtaken by disaster when a flotilla of LCTs came in across their bows a mile off-shore. Two were rammed and sunk and the losses might have been higher if a salvo of rockets had not fallen short in the midst of the *mêlée* and forced the LCTs to change course. No 'DDs' were hit by rockets, but it was only the crews' superb seamanship which brought safely ashore 21 of the 25 tanks launched. Despite their misadventures, the DD tanks and specialised armour touched-down ahead of the LCAs and were already wading ashore when the infantry broke from their landing-craft at 7.30 a.m.

Under covering fire from the armour, the South Lancs quickly cleared the foreshore and plunged into the network of fortifications along the dunes. Within an hour three exits were cleared for tanks, and the attacking troops moved rapidly inland for a mile and a half to capture Hermanville by 9.30 a.m. There they were within sight of their objective, the Périers Rise, but this was held by infantry and anti-tank guns of the 21st Panzer Division and, when the '88s' drove the British armour back into Hermanville, the infantry attack petered out. Meantime, on Queen Red the East Yorks were engaged in a bitter struggle from strongpoint to strongpoint and the beach was freed of small-arms fire only after No. 4 Commando had taken the western edge of Ouistreham.

While the assault battalions were clearing the dunes and working their way inland the armoured assault teams fought and strove to make exits from the beach, which became more crowded and narrower every minute as the wind carried the tide farther inshore than had been expected. It came in so fast that the engineers had little opportunity of carrying out the plan to demolish and remove the underwater obstacles before follow-up forces arrived. The most they could do was to make them less dangerous and, while the tide was in, men swam about ' delousing ' the mines and shells with which the obstacles were primed. This undoubtedly reduced the losses, but the craft still had to weave in as best they might through or over the obstructions and past the wrecks of landing-craft and armour which cluttered up the foreshore, avoiding, if they could, the self-propelled guns which were firing from the shallows.

When the congestion was at its worst, the Germans began shelling the beach with such accuracy that they were obviously ranging on the barrage balloons set up for protection against dive-bombers. At 11.30 the balloons were cut loose and thereafter the enemy fire was less effective, but by noon the traffic jam was so bad that further landings were stopped until it was cleared. By this time the follow-up brigade was well ashore, but the reserve brigade could not land until the middle of the afternoon.

The advance was delayed, however, not so much by the shortage of infantry, as by the absence of drive on the part of two of the three leading battalions. Long before noon there was a marked relaxation of the pressure. The men of the 3rd Division lacked the experience of those formations which had landed in Sicily and Italy, and for many of them the last contact with the Germans had been at Dunkirk. Since then on the home front they had shared with civilians all the anxieties and frustrations, the uncertainties and disappointments of the four years of waiting. For months these men had known that they would be part of an assault division in the invasion of Europe. With this prospect they had lived too long, studying every aspect of the enemy's defences and weapons, rehearsing interminably for the crucial moment of the landing. They had steeled themselves for this hour, but in all their training their attention had been fixed upon the strip of sand which would lie ahead when the landing-craft ramps went down. " Try as you would," says their historian,[1] " during the days of preparation you could never project your mind beyond the great assault." They had been told that as soon as the beaches had been taken, they would reorganise in the woods and orchards beyond, and then drive on to their final objectives, but what mattered to them was the fight on the foreshore. This would be the testing time, when a man's life would be at a premium. Survive that and then think of the next step.

In the event, however, it was much less terrible, much less costly than they had expected. The assault was almost an anticlimax after all they had been told and all they had imagined. Many of them were

[1] Norman Scarfe in his book, *Assault Division*, p. 93

through the beach defences almost before they realised it and, having got through, their inclination was to dig in, consolidate, and defend what they had gained against the counter-attack which would surely come in great strength now that the coastal crust had been so quickly cracked. In the circumstances it was not unnatural that in pausing to regroup and consolidate the 8th Brigade dropped the momentum of the attack before the follow-up battalions were ready to carry it on.

To some extent this defensive complex was a legacy of the 3rd Division's training. Its commander, Major-General T. G. Rennie, a dogged and able Scot, who had served with great distinction in the 51st Highland Division from Alamein to Sicily, was well fitted for the exacting task of planning and launching the assault. There was no doubt that his men would get ashore and hold what they had taken, but by temperament he was not inclined to spur them into quick development of any early advantage. The Brigade Commander (Brigadier E. E. E. Cass) was stolid to the point of being ponderous, a ' bulldog type ' who would get a grip and hang on, but was ill-cast for the role of pursuit. His troops tended to take their cue from his own measured gait. The personalities of these two men had inevitably made their mark upon the battalions, and in assault exercises they had shown the same tendency to dig in prematurely. When Crocker returned from North Africa to take over the Corps, he had done what he could to cure this characteristic, but it was too deeply rooted in the men and their commanders, and in the general training of the forces which had remained in Britain since Dunkirk.

Throughout the morning the East Yorks were heavily involved, but Cass's other two battalions appear to have been unduly cautious. The South Lancs, having captured Hermanville with little difficulty before ten o'clock, proceeded to dig in there instead of driving on to their objective, the Périers Rise, which was intended to be the jumping-off ground for 185 Brigade. The reserve battalion (1st Suffolk) made hesitant progress in its task of capturing Colleville and two nearby strong-points, known by the code-names *Morris* and *Hillman*. And yet the area of its early operations was not resolutely defended. When its supporting artillery began ranging on *Morris*, an enemy battery position, 67 Germans came out with their hands up. The area had been thoroughly hammered by aircraft and warships, and the defenders were still bewildered, so much so that late in the morning Commandos of the 1st Special Service Brigade, followed by an engineer bridging party, strode straight through Colleville and on to the Orne where they joined forces with 6th Airborne at 1.30 p.m. It was to be another eight hours, however, before any infantry of the 3rd Division managed to get through to Benouville and the relief of the paratroops.

East of the Orne the ' airborne bridgehead ' had been subjected to probing attacks throughout the morning. Armoured reconnaissance patrols had approached Ranville as early as seven o'clock but had been stopped by the screen of anti-tank guns south of the village. Nevertheless, Gale's battalions had been so weakened by losses in the drop that he could not afford to direct the Commandos to their planned task of mopping up the coast between the Orne and the Dives. It seemed likely that a more formidable counter-attack would be made by 21st Panzer as soon as it had had time to muster its forces. With the Commandos to help him, Gale was confident that he could hold the bridgehead east of the Orne, but the situation on its western bank, on Rennie's front, required prompt and aggressive action in the drive for Caen.

Rennie had assigned this task to 185 Brigade, and its intention was that the 2nd Battalion, the King's Shropshire Light Infantry, riding on tanks of the Staffordshire Yeomanry, should thrust down the main road from Hermanville to Caen, while the 2nd Warwicks (right) and the 1st Norfolks (left) mopped up the flanks and made the corridor to Caen secure. Before eleven o'clock all three battalions of this brigade were assembled in orchards north of Hermanville according to plan, but then came trouble. At noon the Yeomanry's tanks and the infantry's heavy weapons were still entangled in the traffic jam on the beach, the Warwicks were already involved with Germans on the flank of their assembly area, and the 8th Brigade had not yet attacked either the Périers Rise or the strong-point *Hillman*, which lay south-west of Colleville and between the lines of advance chosen for the K.S.L.I. and the Norfolks.

In these circumstances there was grave danger in proceeding without the tanks, and some time was lost while the brigade commander was deciding what to do. Eventually he gave orders for the Shropshires to start out on foot down the main road from Hermanville, for the tanks to overtake them as soon as possible, and for the Norfolks to advance on a parallel route as soon as the Suffolks had dealt with *Hillman*.

There was still an outside chance of taking Caen that day, for 21st Panzer had not yet appeared in strength. Elements of that division had been engaged against 6th Airborne on both sides of the Orne since early morning, but where was its main force of armour? At 9.45 a.m. air reconnaissance had located some 60 tanks south-east of Caen, but there was no sign of movement on their part. At 12.15 the R.A.F. reported tanks north of Caen, but gave no details. How many were there? What was 21st Panzer's plan? These were the questions of greatest concern to the K.S.L.I. as they struck out on their lonely and hazardous journey down the road to Caen.

## CHAPTER XV

# THE FIRST EVENING

SINCE the summer of 1942 the Germans had been preparing to meet and defeat an invasion across the Channel, and yet the arrival of D-Day found them with no clear and agreed plan of command or campaign, for the difference of opinion between Rommel and Geyr about the employment of the armoured reserves was still unsettled. In the sector of Army Group B, between the Loire and the Zuider Zee, there were six panzer divisions in reserve. For administration, supply and training, these were all controlled by Geyr's H.Q., Panzer Group West, but for operational purposes there was no such unity of command. Hitler had allotted three of these divisions to Rommel for deployment in a tactical role: the 21st around Caen, the 116th astride the Seine west of Paris and the 2nd near Abbeville. At the end of May a new H.Q., 47th Panzer Corps, had arrived to command these divisions and was in the process of taking over when the invasion began.

The rest of the armour north of the Loire—Panzer Lehr in the Chartres–Le Mans area, 12th SS near Evreux and 1st SS close to Antwerp —was under command of 1st SS Panzer Corps led by *Obergruppenführer* ' Sepp ' Dietrich, whose H.Q. was at Rouen. These three divisions were held by von Rundstedt in strategic reserve, but he had strict orders that they were not to be committed to battle without the sanction of OKW, in other words, Hitler.

By this division of authority and strength, Hitler deprived his forces in the West of an adequate reserve either tactical or strategic. In trying to compromise between two plans he gained the advantages of neither, and he left in the minds of subordinate commanders an unsettling uncertainty regarding the plan to be pursued when the hour came. Thus Feuchtinger, commanding 21st Panzer, did not know whether, in the event of invasion between the Seine and Cherbourg, his division would come under operational command of 84th Infantry Corps, 47th Panzer Corps or Panzer Group West. All he knew was that he must make no move without orders from Army Group B.

In Feuchtinger's case there was an added complication, which sprang from the attempt to make one force serve two purposes. His instructions were that, if the Allies were to land near the mouth of the Orne, certain elements of his division would be transferred immediately and automatically to other commands. His two forward infantry battalions and his anti-tank battalion would come under the 716th Division and his anti-aircraft battalion would go to the Caen Flak Command. Thus, even when he had found out the corps under which he was to operate, Feuchtinger would have only a truncated and unbalanced formation to employ, for his tanks would be deprived of adequate anti-aircraft protection and his infantry of full anti-tank support. The result was that just as the strategic reserves had been reduced in order to create tactical reserves, so these in their turn had been whittled away in an attempt to bolster the coast defences.

The absence of an agreed plan and an established chain of command for the armoured reserves was the more serious on the day, because three of the five senior German commanders most deeply concerned were away from their H.Q. when the invasion began, and the two who were on the spot were hamstrung by superior orders which condemned them to inaction. Rommel was at Heerlingen, near Ulm ; Dollmann, commanding Seventh Army, was at Rennes directing an exercise designed to repel an invasion of Brittany; and Dietrich was in Brussels. Von Rundstedt and Geyr alone were in the right place, but Geyr had no operational command and von Rundstedt had no authority to commit the strategic reserves without authority from OKW.

Such was the state of the German command in France, when a few minutes after 1 a.m. on June 6th Feuchtinger learned that parachutists were landing in the Troarn area. The news was flashed at once to Rommel's H.Q. and, in accordance with his standing orders, Feuchtinger instructed his two foremost infantry battalions to engage the airborne forces on both sides of the Orne. Before daylight he sent his reconnaissance unit to scour the area south of Caen, where further paratroops were reported to have landed, but during the hours of darkness when his tanks might have been moving unimpeded from Falaise to Caen they were immobilised because he had no orders from Army Group B regarding their employment. In Rommel's absence, Speidel was reluctant to start moving the panzer reserves until he had seen where the main seaborne assault was coming. Finally, at 6.45 a.m., after speaking by telephone to Rommel at Heerlingen, Speidel authorised Seventh Army to employ 21st Panzer in the Caen area, but, owing to a breakdown in communications, another two hours elapsed before Feuchtinger received any operational orders from Marcks of 84th Corps, under whose command he now came. In the meantime, on his own initiative, he had sent a battle-group, including tanks, against the British airborne troops east of the Orne. This force was already moving into action when the centre of German alarm was diverted farther west.

At 9.25 a.m. Marcks reported to the Chief of Staff, Seventh Army (Pemsel), " The situation on the left bank of the Orne is dangerous;

enemy tanks have reached the artillery positions; 84th Corps has no mobile reserves equipped with anti-tank weapons." He asked for 12th SS to be dispatched at once to the area west of Caen, since 21st Panzer was already committed to the east of the Orne. Pemsel's reply is not recorded in the Seventh Army Telephone Log, but 12th SS was, of course, still officially immobilised by Jodl's order to 'wait and see.' In partial defiance of that, von Rundstedt had already dispatched half this division to the coast north of Lisieux to deal with parachutists and a reported seaborne landing near Deauville. Deprived of adequate air reconnaissance, he did not know how far eastward the Allied threat extended, and the staggered times of the various assaults from west to east gave the impression that there were more to come nearer Le Havre, which was then being bombarded by British battleships.

Denied the support of 12th SS, Marcks had no alternative but to instruct 21st Panzer to break off its attack east of the Orne, cross the river and restore the rapidly crumbling front between Caen and Bayeux. This he did shortly after 10.30 a.m. and thus at last—nine hours after the original warning—Feuchtinger received his first orders about the employment of his armour, but they came too late for him to give them full compliance. Half his infantry and part of his reconnaissance and assault-gun battalions were too busy in the battle east of the Orne. They could not be switched. The best he could do was divert his main tank strength westward, but its movement was harassed by air attack and naval gunfire.

It was nearly three o'clock before Feuchtinger's panzer regiment was clear of Caen and advancing in two columns towards the beaches. Even then the scope of his counter-attack was limited by shortage of infantry. Of his two battalions which had been west of the Orne when the day began, one had been engaged against 6th Airborne at Benouville since early morning. His anti-tank battalion, which had been stationed with its 88 mms on Périers Rise providing a formidable barrier between the coast and Caen, had come under command of the 716th Division before dawn and had been ordered to move westward. Concentrated, as Feuchtinger had them, these guns might have halted 3rd British close to the beaches; dispersed, their strength was frittered away. Some of them had held up the Canadians, but of the original 24, only three were still in position on Périers Rise when the 2nd K.S.L.I. (Lt.-Col. F. J. Maurice) began its thrust for Caen soon after one o'clock.

Skirting the fire from this rise, Maurice's battalion and one squadron of tanks struck boldly southward, but when the remaining tanks tried to follow a little later, they came under heavy fire and Maurice had to divert a company to deal with some guns which were shelling the road. This it did with great efficiency, taking the battery from the rear, and by four o'clock the tanks and infantry were advancing through Bieville, five miles inland and only three from the northern edge of Caen.

Their hopes were running high, but as they advanced from Bieville, 24 German tanks moved against them from the west. There was a

K

spirited duel until the enemy thrust was parried by the Yeomanry and some self-propelled anti-tank guns. Five German tanks were knocked out and the rest driven off. Meantime Maurice, an intrepid leader, had driven his infantry on, but they had gone less than a mile when the leading company came under intense fire from Lebisey Wood, a thickly timbered ridge athwart the road. The company commander was killed, and it was soon clear that this position could not be forced by anything less than a battalion attack, which Maurice could not afford to make so long as there was the possibility of a renewed thrust by 21st Panzer against his western flank.

The K.S.L.I. were out on their own, for the Norfolks had been delayed by the inability of the Suffolks to capture *Hillman*. When their initial attack was repulsed early in the afternoon, the Suffolks had proceeded to prepare a thorough-going assault with ample fire support. At this juncture such preparations were a luxury which the invaders could not afford. The need of the hour was for speed and action, almost regardless of casualties. The way had to be cleared or the initiative would be lost and its regaining would cost more lives than those which might be saved by immediate caution. And yet the Suffolks spent most of the afternoon organising their attack and they do not appear to have proceeded with the urgency the occasion demanded. This may have been partly Rennie's fault, for he told the C.O. (Lt.-Col. R. E. Goodwin) merely that they "must capture the strongpoint before dark." It was 8.15 p.m. when the last resistance was overcome and, although Goodwin's own report says that "the garrison fought with such determination that in some instances they had to be blown from their emplacements by heavy explosive charges," the Suffolks' losses in the entire day's fighting were only seven killed and 25 wounded![1] But the defences of *Hillman* inflicted nearly 150 casualties on the Norfolks when they tried to by-pass it during the afternoon. By the time they got through it was too late for them to overtake the K.S.L.I. and so they were ordered to occupy a pronounced wooded rise north-east of Bieville. This they did, but there they could lend no aid to the advance of the Shropshires and the Germans were able to strengthen their grip on Lebisey Wood.

In the evening Maurice's force at Bieville consolidated its position. It had made a bold and dashing attempt to reach Caen, but the capture of the city on D-Day had only been an outside chance and the weather had weighted the odds even more decidedly in the enemy's favour. As it turned out, it was fortunate that the indecision of the German High Command more than counter-balanced the delays and difficulties on the beaches. The congestion there had prevented the early landing and rapid movement inland of the 9th Brigade, and its commitment was further held up by a chance mortar bomb, which wounded the Brigadier and made a shambles of his first operational conference. By the time its

[1]On the same day the East Yorks lost 72 killed and 141 wounded; the K.S.L.I.'s casualties were 113 killed, wounded or missing; those of the South Lancs totalled 107.

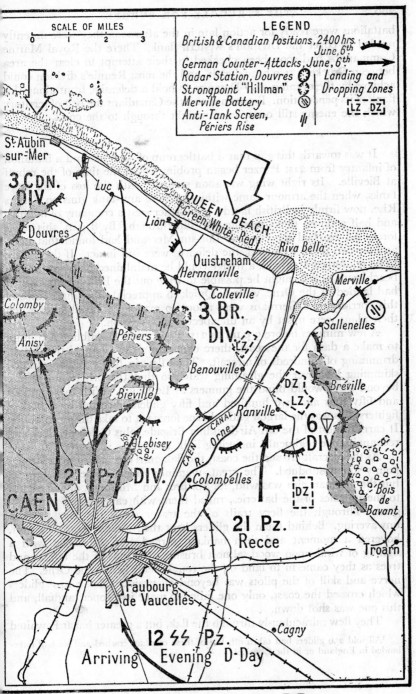

SCALE OF MILES
0 1 2 3

LEGEND
British & Canadian Positions, 2400 hrs.
June 6th
German Counter-Attacks, June 6th
Radar Station, Douvres
Strongpoint "Hillman"
Merville Battery
Anti-Tank Screen,
Périers Rise
Landing and
Dropping Zones
LZ  DZ

St. Aubin-sur-Mer

3 CDN. DIV.

Luc

Douvres

Lion

QUEEN BEACH
Green White Red

Riva Bella

Colomby

Ouistreham
Hermanville

Merville

Anisy

Colleville

3 BR. DIV.

LZ

Périers

Sallenelles

Benouville

DZ
LZ

Bréville

Bieville

Ranville
Orne

6 DIV.

CAEN CANAL
CAEN R.

Lebisey

21 Pz. DIV.

CAEN

Colombelles

Bois de Bavant

21 Pz. Recce

DZ

Troarn

Faubourg de Vaucelles

Cagny

12 Pz.
Arriving Evening D-Day

THE CAEN SECTOR: EVENING D-DAY

battalions were ready for action late in the afternoon they were urgently needed to cover the Division's western flank. There the Royal Marine Commandos had soon been checked in their attempt to clear the area between Crocker's two beachheads, and the most Rennie's division could achieve by the evening of D-Day was to hold a defensive front along this flank of its penetration. Between it and the Canadians the belt of territory which the enemy still occupied ran right through to the coast.

It was towards this gap that a battlegroup of 50 tanks and a battalion of infantry from 21st Panzer began probing about the time of the rebuff at Bieville. Its right wing was soon stopped, with the loss of six more tanks, when the armour came within range of anti-tank guns on Périers Rise, now firmly in British hands, but farther west a company of infantry and half a dozen tanks managed to slip through. By 8 p.m. this small force had reached the coast at Luc-sur-Mer and had found that here, and for two miles westward, the defences were still intact. If these were to be reinforced and held, a wedge could be maintained between the two beachheads and it might be possible to wipe out the British forces which had landed in the Orne Valley. Quick to appreciate the importance of this corridor, the Germans were about to exploit its possibilities when their plans were upset by an unexpected intervention.

A few minutes before 9 p.m. as 21st Panzer was assembling a column to make a dash for the coast, there came from the Channel the distant drumming of hundreds of aircraft. They flew in like a swarm of bees, skimming low over the gleaming water so that the bright sun setting beyond them would blind the gunners at Le Havre. With two hundred and fifty tugs and two hundred and fifty gliders, escorted by a host of fighters, this was the largest glider-borne force yet to take the air in battle. It carried most of the 6th Air-Landing Brigade, plus Gale's artillery and reconnaissance regiments, including light tanks.

As the aircraft crossed the coast, the flak-guns opened up from strongpoints still unsubdued. The great, ungainly gliders made easy targets, but the German aim was wild, for Spitfires and Mustangs, diving almost to the muzzles of the batteries, raked them with cannon and machine-gun. Through the fiery trails of the tracer shells the tugs flew on unwavering. Behind them the gliders kept their steady course, cast off, hovered a moment and then banked, turned and slid down with a sighing of wind upon wood, almost brushing the tops of the houses and trees as they came in to land on the rough fields beside the Orne. The nerve and skill of the pilots was beyond all praise. Of the 249[1] gliders which crossed the coast, only one failed to make its proper landfall, and this one was shot down.

They flew miraculously through the flak, but a greater hazard awaited

[1] All told 256 gliders had taken off, but of these one had crashed and six had force-landed in England or in the Channel.

them on the ground. After the first few had landed, the Germans began shelling and mortaring the LZs and several gliders caught fire as they were being unloaded, but troops and equipment were hurried away from the danger zone and the casualties were few. One ' Hamilcar,' carrying a tank, not only caught alight but buried its nose and jammed the exit. Undaunted, the driver started his engine and smashed his way out of the burning wreck like a moth bursting from its cocoon. The arrival of these reinforcements doubled the strength of 6th Airborne in one swift stroke and brought great relief to Gale's weary parachute battalions. There was little doubt now that the flank along the Orne could and would be held.

The success of this bold mass-landing of gliders in daylight was eloquent proof of Allied command of the air, and it had a most marked psychological influence on the land battle, for the Germans north of Caen were bewildered and overawed by the sight of the sky filled with gliders and parachutes.[1] The projected drive to the coast died in its tracks, for it appeared to Feuchtinger's troops that the airborne force had landed right across their path. By the time they had recovered from the surprise and shock, it was nearly dark, and the attack which then got under way was half-hearted and ill-directed. One column, advancing up the Caen–Courseulles road, ran into a Canadian ambush and withdrew bewildered and bloody.

All that night Crocker's divisions stood to, expecting a large-scale attack, while darkness gave the German army cover which the Luftwaffe could not provide. This was the time for a counter-stroke. The assault forces were tired and strung out in a series of hastily-prepared positions. The weather had so delayed the unloading that tanks, anti-tank guns and artillery had not been brought forward in the strength which had been planned. The line was thin and there were gaps which cried out for exploitation. But the Germans were not in a position to take advantage of the opportunity which was offered that night and that night alone. Too many hours had been wasted while the Supreme Command was making up its mind.

Hitler's 4 a.m. edict forbidding the employment of the strategic reserve of armour stood for nearly twelve hours. It was not reversed until his regular staff conference early in the afternoon and it was nearly 4 p.m. before Seventh Army learned that 12th SS and Panzer Lehr Divisions had been placed under its command. By that time it was too late for either to intervene that day in the battle around Caen. Nevertheless, shortly before five o'clock von Rundstedt's H.Q. warned Seventh Army of " the desire of OKW that the enemy in the bridgehead be annihilated by the evening of June 6th since there is a danger of fresh

---

[1] On these parachutes there were only containers of stores, not troops, but this was not realised by the Germans at the time.

landings by sea and air. According to General Jodl's orders, all available forces must be diverted to the point of penetration. . . . The bridgehead there must be cleaned up not later than to-night."[1] Pemsel replied that this was impossible.

It was easy for Jodl to issue this ambitious order, but, partly as a result of Hitler's own default, the bulk of the armoured reserves between the Seine and the Loire were still a day's journey or more from the main battlefield. When Pemsel pointed this out to Speidel a few minutes later, he was told: "The 21st Panzer Division must attack immediately with or without reinforcements. OKW has ordered that the bad weather conditions must be utilised to the full for bringing up reserves during the night of June 6th–7th."

Even by moving at night, however, the only additional force which could reach the Caen area by the morning of D plus 1 was that battle-group (led by Kurt Meyer) of 12th SS, which von Rundstedt had sent towards Lisieux in the middle of the morning. At 3 p.m. Meyer had been ordered to take his force at full speed to the area of Evrécy, nine miles south-west of Caen, and to "join forces with 21st Panzer Division and wipe out enemy forces which had penetrated west of the Orne." On the way Meyer's motorised and armoured columns were so repeatedly strafed from the air that they averaged barely four miles an hour. Although they had reached Evrécy, south-west of Caen, by midnight their fuel tanks had been almost drained by repeated diversions, slow running and frequent stops. Meyer had been expecting to draw fuel from a dump near Evrécy, but on arrival he found nothing but blackened and smoking drums. Allied aircraft had been there first.

The experience of 12th SS was typical of what the enemy suffered on this day as a result of Allied air supremacy. The Strategic and Tactical Air Forces flew 10,585 sorties in addition to the 1,730 flown by the Transport Commands in airborne operations. Of this vast force not a single aircraft was lost through the intervention of the Luftwaffe. For all the Allied navies and armies knew the German Air Force might hardly have existed. Throughout the day there was no sign of the Luftwaffe over the beaches and it was almost dark before British troops saw their first hostile aircraft. Then four Heinkels sneaked in and managed to scatter their bomb-loads near the Canadian beaches before a squadron of Spitfires pounced upon them. None got away.

By D-Day the Luftwaffe was a spent force. Its total bomber strength was lower than it had been in September 1939, and most of its machines were out of date. At the start of the Battle of Britain there had been 1,290 German bombers ready for action in the West; at the start of OVERLORD the number of serviceable bombers in Northern France and the Low Countries was 153. Since early in 1944, because of the strategic

[1]Seventh Army Telephone Log, June 6th, 1600 hours.

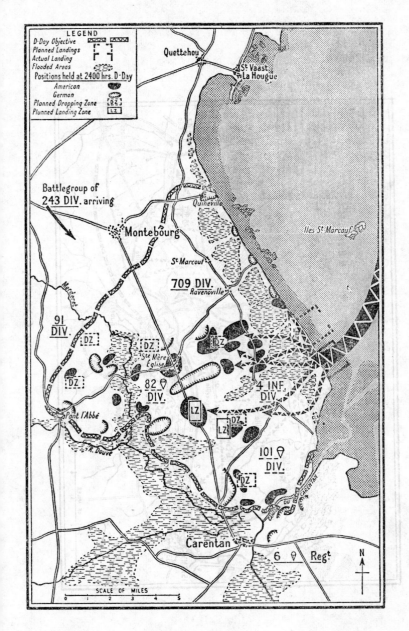

**LEGEND**
D-Day Objective
Planned Landings
Actual Landing
Flooded Areas
Positions held at 2400 hrs. D-Day
    American
    German
Planned Dropping Zone    DZ
Planned Landing Zone    LZ

Quettehou

St Vaast
La Hougue

Battlegroup of
**243 DIV.** arriving

Quineville

Iles St Marcouf

**Montebourg**

St Marcouf

**709 DIV.**
Ravenoville

**91 DIV.**

Merderet

DZ

DZ

DZ

Ste Mère Eglise

DZ

**82 DIV.**

**4 INF. DIV.**

LZ

Pont l'Abbé

LZ

DZ

R. Douve

**101 DIV.**

DZ

DU CARENTAN

**Carentan**

**6 Regt**

N

SCALE OF MILES
0  1  2  3  4  5

UTAH: D-DAY

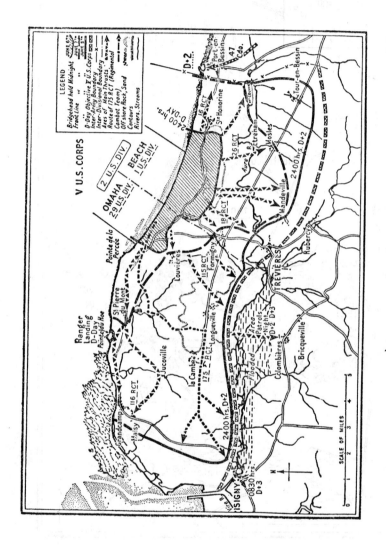

ADVANCE FROM OMAHA

bombardment of German war industry, overwhelming priority had been given to the production of fighters. On the eve of the invasion the output of single-engined fighters (1,523 in May) had never been higher and it was still rising, but the main types were obsolete and the front-line strength was lower than it had been a year earlier, for the losses in daylight battles over Germany had absorbed the increase in production. On June 1st, 1944, when the R.A.F. and the U.S.A.A.F. had more than 5,000 fighters operating from Britain, the total day-fighter strength of the Luftwaffe was 1,789 machines. On the Channel front there were 169, but only 119 of these were fit to fight.[1]

Goering had intended to transfer strong fighter forces from Germany to France as soon as it became apparent that the invasion was imminent, but during May when OKW expected the assault from day to day, no such transfer was possible because the commencement of the American offensive against the synthetic oil plants in the middle of the month made it imperative to concentrate the greatest possible strength for their defence. Two weeks before D-Day, Air Fleet III was compelled to send back to Germany six of its best fighter squadrons. At the start of June the Luftwaffe in the West was weaker than it had been at any time during the previous four years.

On June 6th, the Germans flew only 319 sorties over France and all but a few of these were driven back or shot down. Late in the evening Dollmann, telephoning to Rommel, complained bitterly of the Luftwaffe's absence, only to be told that "Luftwaffe units are just on the point of being moved." Their transfer had been delayed until this late hour by orders from OKW, faithful to its conviction that the first assault would be a feint. The reserves did not begin to move until the evening of June 7th and by then they had to move to airfields which had been heavily bombed. Thanks to this indecision, there was no chance of them intervening over the bridgehead before D plus 2 at the earliest. Thus Allied air supremacy was allowed to go unchallenged during the first forty-eight hours when, as Rommel knew, the Germans had to win the battle of the beaches if it were not to be lost irrevocably.

The value of this air supremacy can hardly be overrated. It was undoubtedly the most important single factor in the success of the invasion, for its influence penetrated to almost every aspect of the enemy's plans and operations. German strategy and tactics, fortifications and armament, logistics and psychology were all adversely affected by the dominance of Allied air power. It had played the decisive part in the campaign against the U-boat, the essential prelude to the concentration for OVERLORD; it had protected the invasion base from interference by the enemy's bombers or V-weapons and had denied him the opportunity of discovering through reconnaissance the state of Allied preparations or

[1]In addition there was an 'Operational Reserve' of 140 fighters in Southern France, but they were in the hands of units which were not fully trained, and on June 6th only 33 of these aircraft were serviceable.

the start of the cross-Channel movement. Through air power the Allies were able not only to surprise the enemy but to mislead him. The FORTITUDE plan could never have been carried through without the technique of radar deception and radio counter-measures, which Bomber Command had developed as part of its night bombing tactics, and the application of that technique succeeded only because of the superb navigational skill of the R.A.F. crews, trained in battle over Germany.

It is impossible to calculate how much stronger the Atlantic Wall would have been if the Germans could have carried out the improvements they planned. It would certainly have been as formidable in Normandy as it was in the Pas de Calais. (In its last situation report before D-Day, Rommel's H.Q. stated that the planned defences in the Fifteenth Army sector were 68 per cent completed, but that in the area of the Seventh Army only 18 per cent had been finished.) Since 1943, however, Hitler had been forced to divert labour and materials to the repairing of factories and communications in Germany, V.1 sites and railways in France and U-boat bases from St. Nazaire to Norway. Even after Rommel had brought fresh vigour and vision to the fortification of the Channel coast, his plans were only partly fulfilled owing to the destruction of French railways, which hindered the transport of reinforcements and supplies, and to the strategic attacks on the Reich, which led to the retention within Germany of the radar equipment and anti-aircraft guns which could have made the Allied airborne landings too costly to contemplate. The long arm of the strategic bomber left its fingerprints in unexpected places.

Finally, there was the successful interdiction of the Seine bridges, the threatened tactical isolation of the battlefield and the general undermining of German morale in France. Compared with all this, the actual bombing of the coast defences was perhaps the least important part of the air force contribution to the success of the landings. It is true that most of the heavy batteries were destroyed or temporarily put out of action by air attack before H-Hour and that 'mediums' of Ninth U.S. Air Force, bombing from below the clouds, hit the defences on UTAH with great precision, but elsewhere the bombing was generally rendered inaccurate by the weather or ineffective by the thickness of the concrete casemates and pillboxes.

Even the tremendous naval bombardment caused less material damage to the fortifications than had been hoped, and Eisenhower subsequently reported to the Combined Chiefs of Staff that " the coastal defences in general were not destroyed prior to the time when our men came ashore." A more detailed survey by Combined Operations H.Q. came to the conclusion that " except on SWORD beach, where the fire was of greatest density, the defences were generally in action when the fire-plan had been completed and the troops were landing. Any neutralisation during the run-in may have been due either to the moral effect of the bombardment or to the fact that, until the landing waves were close in-shore, the defences could not bring their fire to bear or had insufficient range."

In the battle on the beaches the predominant, and perhaps decisive, factor was the bold employment of specialised armour. On every beach where it was available, the assault went substantially according to plan in spite of the miscarriage of the preliminary bombardment and the grave difficulties caused by the weather. In Eisenhower's opinion, " Apart from the factor of tactical surprise, the comparatively light casualties which we sustained on all beaches, except OMAHA, were in large measure due to the success of the novel mechanical contrivances which we employed and to the staggering moral and material effect of the mass of armour landed in the leading waves of the assault. It is doubtful if the assault forces could have firmly established themselves without the assistance of these weapons."[1]

This judgment is fully confirmed by the comparison between the course which events took on OMAHA and the other beaches. As we have seen, the OMAHA defences proved to be so difficult and costly to crack largely because the American infantry did not have the necessary armoured support. Yet this support could have been available here, as it was elsewhere, if the Americans had been prepared to accept the advice and assistance of their more experienced allies.

At Bradley's H.Q., however, Montgomery's plan for armoured assault was regarded as just another example of British under-confidence and over-insurance, but if even some two dozen ' Crabs ' had been available on OMAHA, as they were on GOLD, to take the place of the ' DDs ' and to flail the exits, German guns and mines would not have taken such terrible toll of the unsupported infantry. It took 3,000 casualties on OMAHA to persuade the Americans that gallantry is not enough.

How many lives were saved on other sectors by the 79th Armoured Division nobody can tell, but if it had not been for the specialised armour and the policy of landing it as the spearhead of the assault, progress on the British beaches might have been almost as slow and expensive as it was on OMAHA. The day might have ended with the Allies holding such slender beachheads that the enemy counter-attacks could hardly have been resisted at all points.

The German defence was based on the theory that the Atlantic Wall would take the first shock and would contain the assault on or near the beaches long enough to enable the armoured reserves to move up and drive the invaders back into the sea before their anti-tank defences could be established. On OMAHA this theory might have proved correct, even in fine weather, if the 12th SS Panzer Division had been in close reserve as Rommel wanted. But on the front of Second British Army it turned out to be false, in spite of the proximity of 21st Panzer, because the

[1]Eisenhower, *Report*, p. 30.

specialised armour enabled Dempsey's divisions to break in rapidly. The delays caused by the weather were counter-balanced by the indecision of the German Supreme Command and at the close of D-Day Dempsey still held the initiative.

At the other end of the invasion front, in the Cotentin Peninsula, the DD tanks played a most important part in the rapid and economical breaching of the coast defences, but here the speed and depth of the penetration was primarily due to the courageous decision to land the two American airborne divisions regardless of the hazards. The achievement of these paratroops was remarkable, for they fulfilled their general role with less than a third of their strength.

At dark on D-Day the seaborne forces and the 82nd Division had not yet linked up, but the gap between them was less than a mile wide and VII Corps was in substantial control of the area between the coast and the Merderet River on a front of five miles north from the general line of the Carentan Canal. West of the Merderet, more than ten miles inland, several large groups from the 82nd had pegged out isolated claims to which the main force had yet to establish a firm title, and thus gave the beachhead far greater potential depth than had actually been secured.

On the right flank of the Corps beachhead, the 4th Division, which had directed its main drive northwards after crossing the coastal lagoon, had made less progress than expected and was still some three miles short of its D-Day phase-line. But the size of the area held was of small account compared with the fact that a landing had been made in strength where the Germans had thought none was possible. By flooding the base of the Peninsula, and stationing the 91st Division there, the enemy believed that he had closed the back door to Cherbourg, but the Americans had forced a cracksman's entry down the chimney and through the side window.

Between the Vire and the Orne the Allies by dark on June 6th had broken into Hitler's Fortress on a front of 30 miles. The enemy had been taken completely by surprise, his coast defences had been overwhelmed, his air force and navy had been rendered powerless and his armoured reserves had been unable to intervene effectively. But the battle was by no means over. The UTAH beachhead was isolated and no junction between the two American corps was likely for several days; the penetration at OMAHA was slight and insecure; there was still a gap seven miles wide between the two Allied Armies and another of three miles between the Canadians and 3rd British; none of the final D-Day objectives had been reached; the assault divisions were ashore in strength, but, because of the storm, the unloading was already eight to twelve hours behind schedule; there was the possibility that the enemy might yet deliver a counter-stroke which would cause a severe setback.

The unknown and almost unpredictable factor in the situation was the weather. On D-Day it had proved a less serious handicap than had been feared when Eisenhower made his fateful decision only thirty-six hours earlier; indeed, it had contributed substantially to the achievement of surprise. It had improved during the day and the evening was fair, but the meteorologists could give no assurance that it would hold. In the coming race for reinforcements the weather threatened to prove decisive. " That was the element," said Churchill later, " which certainly hung like a vulture poised in the sky over the thoughts of the most sanguine."

But that danger lay ahead. By the evening of June 6th the Allies had gained a striking victory at a cost of fewer than 2,500 lives,[1] and had accomplished the first phase of what Churchill rightly called " the most difficult and complicated operation that has ever taken place."

[1]The losses suffered by the assault armies on D-Day have not been accurately determined, and in the nature of things cannot be. It is safe to say that the total casualties did not exceed 11,000 of whom not more than 2,500 lost their lives. First U.S. Army subsequently reported that its casualties totalled 6,603, of whom 1,465 were killed, 3,184 wounded, and 1,954 missing. No comparable figure is available for Second British Army but, in view of the fact that its losses in killed and wounded were 5,259 in the first five days, the D-Day casualties can hardly have exceeded 4,000.

## CHAPTER XVI

# THE FIGHT FOR THE FOOTHOLD

AT the birth of OVERLORD the three military Graces—strategic deception, tactical surprise and technical ingenuity—were present in liberal mood to make good the natural disadvantages under which the Allies laboured and to lead the enemy into serious and fundamental misconceptions. On the evening of June 6th von Rundstedt was still in doubt regarding the scope and purpose of the Allied assault, for his reconnaissance aircraft had been swept from the skies and his communications had been disorganised by bombing, but his inflexible mind was wedded to the long-standing theory that there would be at least two landings and that the first would be a feint.

Hitler, von Rundstedt and Rommel found themselves, for once, in full agreement. This assault was a diversion to entice German reserves west of the Seine as a prelude to the main attack in the Pas de Calais. Carrying this analysis a step further, they concluded that the Cotentin landing was a diversion within a diversion, an attempt to threaten Cherbourg and thus distract German attention from the real danger spot, Caen, and the ultimate objective of the present operation, the Seine. There, they presumed, the forces now ashore in Normandy must be planning to link up with the greater invasion yet to come.

To meet that next blow, they were determined to keep Fifteenth Army intact north of the Seine to guard the V-weapon sites and the short road to the Ruhr. One of its divisions (346th Infantry, summoned from Le Havre to the Orne valley) had begun to cross the Seine on D-Day, but nothing else was to be moved, except a battalion of Tiger[1] tanks and a flak brigade. The Fifteenth's tactical reserves, five infantry and two panzer divisions with 300 tanks, were to stay where they were, idle and useless. Seventh Army must deal with the landings in Western Normandy from its own resources, strengthened by the five divisions in von Rundstedt's

---

[1]The 'Tiger' or Mark VI was the heaviest and most formidable German tank. The first series weighed 58 tons each; the second, 70 tons; but both these models were powered with the same engine as the 45-ton 'Panther' or Mark V. The main armament of the Tiger was an 88 mm gun. The Panther mounted a 75 mm. The Mark IV, a medium tank, was also armed with a '75.'

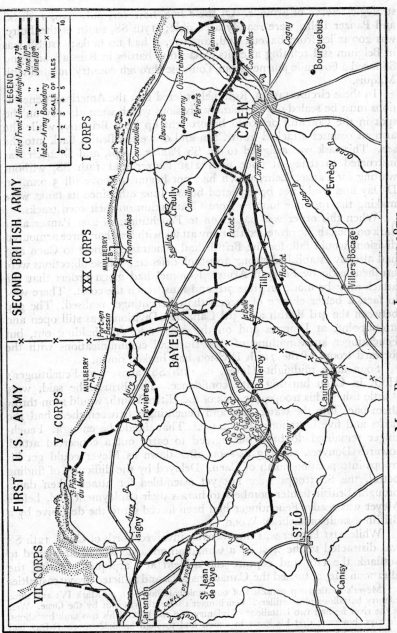

MAIN BRIDGEHEAD, JUNE 7TH–18TH

LEGEND

Allied Front-Line Midnight June 7th
" " " June 10th
" " " June 18th
Inter-Army Boundary

SCALE OF MILES
0 1 2 3 4 5

FIRST U.S. ARMY          SECOND BRITISH ARMY

VII CORPS    V CORPS    XXX CORPS    I CORPS

Bourguebus
Cagny
Colombelles
Ranville
Ouistreham
Anguerny
Periers
Douvres
Courseulles
CAEN
Carpiquet
Evrecy
Creully
Camilly
Putot
Tilly
Hottot
Villers Bocage
Seulles R.
Arromanches
MULBERRY B
Port-en-Bessin
la Belle Epine
Aure R.
MULBERRY A
Trevières
BAYEUX
Drome R.
Balleroy
Caumont
Berigny
ST. LÔ
Elle R.
St. Jean de Daye
CANAL DE VIRE
Route de Vire
Canisy
St. Pierre du Mont
Isigny
Aure R.
Carentan
Vire R.
Odon R.

strategic reserve of armour. Of these five, however, only two, 12th SS and Panzer Lehr, were readily accessible; 17th SS, south of the Loire, was 200 miles from Bayeux and, anyway, it had no tanks; 1st SS was in Belgium still refitting after its exhausting battles in Russia; and 2nd SS faced a 600-mile journey from Toulouse through country infested with Maquis.

In these circumstances, Rommel ordered that the American penetrations must be sealed off by infantry divisions which were already on the spot in the Cotentin or could be brought up from Brittany, while the armour counter-attacked from Caen and drove the British back into the sea. This task was assigned to 1st SS Panzer Corps, and Dietrich was instructed to strike at once with 21st Panzer and 12th SS, without waiting for Panzer Lehr, which had not begun to move till 5 p.m. on D-Day and could not be expected before June 8th, since its tanks were making the 130-mile journey from Châteaudun on their own tracks.

When this order was passed on to Feuchtinger of 21st Panzer after dark on the 6th, he protested that any attack with less than three armoured divisions would fail, for the British had penetrated almost to Caen and had already established strong anti-tank defences. These objections were brushed aside by Seventh Army. Rommel had given orders that the attack must be made on June 7th and must reach the coast. There was, in fact, a better chance of success than Feuchtinger realised. The gap between the 3rd British and 3rd Canadian Divisions was still open and strongpoints at Douvres and on the coast were still holding out, but Feuchtinger knew nothing of this, since all communications with the forward troops of the 716th Division had broken down.

Soon after midnight Meyer, of 12th SS, arrived at Feuchtinger's H.Q. in Caen bursting with confidence. The British, he said, were " little fish "; his troops, the pick of the Hitler Youth, would soon throw them back into the water. He and Feuchtinger between them had 160 tanks and five battalions of infantry.[1] That should be enough. Feuchtinger remained doubtful but agreed to carry out a concerted attack towards Douvres, starting as soon after dawn as Meyer could get his troops into position north of Caen. Delayed by the difficulty of finding petrol, the SS troops were not yet assembled for attack when dawn brought British fighter-bombers to harass their deployment and, before Meyer was ready, Feuchtinger had been forced on to the defensive by a British assault on Lebisey Wood.

While 21st Panzer was thus heavily involved north of Caen, 12th SS was distracted to the west by a Canadian advance which threatened to outflank the city and capture the airfield at Carpiquet. During the afternoon Meyer turned the Canadians back and inflicted heavy casualties

[1]Meyer's battlegroup consisted of one tank battalion with 90 Mark IVs and three infantry battalions plus artillery. Feuchtinger's strength was split by the Orne. West of the river he had two battalions of infantry and the bulk of his two tank battalions. He says, however, that his losses in action and through breakdowns on D-Day had reduced his total of ' runners ' to 70 on June 7th.

on them, but he was able to do so only by committing almost his entire battlegroup.

These encounters on both wings absorbed the bulk of the troops who were to have driven the British back into the sea. It was late in the day before Meyer managed to assemble a force to carry out the original plan of attacking through the gap towards Douvres, and then all he could muster from the resources which had seemed to him so imposing the previous night was one battalion of infantry and 17 tanks. By the time this force could set out the gap had been closed and the British and Canadian beachheads were firmly linked. The " little fish " were there to stay.[1]

Having committed his armoured reserves in defence of Caen, the enemy on June 7th could offer little resistance on the rest of Dempsey's front. By the middle of the day the people of Bayeux were celebrating an almost painless liberation, the 50th Division was digging in on the rising ground south and south-east of the city, and the Bayeux–Caen highway was in British or Canadian hands as far east as Bretteville l'Orgueilleuse.

These gains gave Second British Army a solid bridgehead 22 miles wide and five to ten miles deep by the night of D plus 1, a strong covering position in which Dempsey could confidently await heavier counter-attacks while gathering resources for a further advance by XXX Corps. This corps could certainly have made more progress that day, for there was little in its path except the reconnaissance battalion of 12th SS, but the build-up was already 12 hours behind schedule and was likely to fall farther in arrears. Dempsey may have been unduly cautious but, with the forecast still unfriendly, he considered that this was not the time to make premature advances which might unbalance the whole invasion force, particularly as the American foothold at OMAHA did not yet appear to be secure.

On this flank of Second Army the capture of Port-en-Bessin by Commandos before dawn on June 8th provided firm contact with the V U.S. Corps and brought into Allied hands a continuous stretch of coastline and Atlantic Wall 35 miles wide. All the previous day, however, American efforts to widen the OMAHA beachhead westward had been so heavily opposed that the 29th Division could make only minor advances. The beaches were still being mortared and shelled and were so cluttered up with wreckage that stores could be unloaded only from craft which could be beached. This fire abated during the day as the 1st Division gained ground to the south. The bitter fighting of D-Day had drastically

[1] At SHAEF there was an impression, subsequently recorded in Eisenhower's *Report to the Combined Chiefs of Staff* (p. 31) that the counter-attacks of June 7th " penetrated nearly to the coast." This is not so. The Canadians were forced to withdraw more than a mile, but neither they nor 3rd British lost any ground which they had taken on D-Day.

reduced the strength and spirit of the defence, and the Americans were able to establish a useful foothold across the River Aure. It was ironic that, on the section of the invasion front where the Atlantic Wall came nearest to fulfilling its purpose, there should have been no German reserves available to take advantage of the situation. By the evening of the 7th, although neither the troops on the spot nor the Allied command knew it, the issue at OMAHA was settled.

There was no such certainty in the Cotentin Peninsula, where the ease of the initial landing on UTAH proved no yard-stick of the opposition which lay farther inland. Here the enemy did have reinforcements close at hand and part of these had been automatically involved when American parachutists landed in their midst. The remaining reserves in the Cotentin were ordered into action soon after dawn on D-Day and the brunt of their attack fell upon 82nd Airborne. At dark this division, still isolated and dispersed, reported by radio, " Short 60 per cent infantry, 90 per cent artillery, combat efficiency excellent."[1] During the night, however, this efficiency was severely tried, for the Germans counter-attacked across the River Merderet in strength and were stopped only 400 yards from Ridgway's command post. Dawn found the Americans hard pressed and short of ammunition, but soon after seven o'clock reinforcements came in by glider and supplies were dropped by parachute. At 10 a.m. there was direct contact with the seaborne forces and by then the glider-infantry were in position along the Merderet. Against that line throughout the day the Germans attacked in vain. This successful defence, and a two-mile advance north-west by the 4th Division gave VII Corps a bridgehead eight miles deep and nine miles wide by dark on D plus 1.

There was still the possibility that the Americans might be hemmed in behind the inundations, but the enemy's chance of doing this depended upon the arrival of reinforcements from Brittany, and the start of their movement had been delayed. Until late in the afternoon of D-Day Seventh German Army H.Q. had believed that the landings in the Cotentin had been made only by airborne troops and that these could be dealt with by the forces already there.[2] It was nearly 11 p.m. before the Army Commander, Dollmann, ordered any large-scale withdrawal of reserves from Brittany. Thus one night of movement immune from air attack was lost and, when the German columns attempted to travel by day on the 7th, they were soon disrupted by Allied fighter-bombers. In addition, they were distracted by reports of further airborne landings north and west of Avranches. One report early on the 7th alleged that 300 aircraft

[1] After-Action Report, 82nd U.S. Airborne Division, June 1944.
[2] At 4.20 p.m. on June 6th, Pemsel told Speidel: " At the moment there is nothing operational to fear, as the enemy has not sufficient troops on the east coast of the Cotentin to cut it off from Normandy. It will probably be possible to clear the Cotentin with our own forces. It is to be noted that parachute troops have landed there without support from the sea." This was an extraordinary statement, for during the morning Seventh Army had received two reports of seaborne landings on the Cotentin.

had dropped paratroops in the Coutances–Lessay area west of St. Lô. This was, in fact, a feint carried out with dummies, but Rommel leaped to the conclusion that it was the prelude to a seaborne assault against the west coast of the Lower Cotentin and gave instructions that " all available troops be sent to that area." This order stood until the morning of the 8th and its countermanding was then delayed because Allied air attack had disrupted signal communications and the marching units were out of contact with Seventh Army.

These hesitations and misconceptions gave the Americans invaluable respite and they made good use of it, especially in the Cotentin. By the morning of June 9th, the 82nd and 101st had expanded the bridgehead west and south across the flood-lines and the enemy was in danger of losing his strongest defensive position. As yet, however, there was no link between VII Corps and V Corps, and Bradley decided that Carentan must be captured before he could proceed with his primary mission, the seizure of Cherbourg. The importance of Carentan was fully appreciated in both camps and Rommel gave orders that this wedge between the two bridgeheads must be " defended to the last man."

While the battle for Carentan was thus developing, the enemy's main offensive strength was being employed around Caen, for the fear of another landing still dominated his thinking,[1] and made it all the more important that a crippling blow should be delivered against the British before they became firmly established. But Meyer's experience on the 7th had shown how difficult it was to assemble any sizeable counter-attack force in the face of Allied air power, and no protection could be expected from the Luftwaffe, which reported that the forward concentration of its squadrons had been delayed by air attacks and could " only be effected in the next few days."

Nevertheless, early on June 8th Rommel ordered Dietrich to strike again between Bayeux and Caen using all three armoured divisions. But 21st Panzer was still locked in defensive battles on either side of the Orne; Panzer Lehr had not yet arrived, and though the rest of 12th SS had reached Caen it was so short of petrol that it could not throw in its full strength. Thus all Dietrich could do that day was to send Meyer, reinforced by fresh tanks and infantry, to attack the Canadians who had dug in astride the Caen–Bayeux road at Putôt-en-Bessin and Bretteville l'Orgueilleuse.

About 9.30 that morning the Royal Winnipeg Rifles in Putôt came under heavy fire, and soon caught sight of enemy infantry and tanks moving through the high corn south of the village. The Germans struck hard and, after a day-long battle in houses and orchards, the Canadians

[1]On the evening of the 9th Rommel told Dollmann that he did not expect any more airborne landings in the Cotentin since " OKW expects further large-scale landings on the Channel coast in the next few days." Seventh Army Telephone Log, June 9th, 1730 hrs.

were driven out. Having taken Putôt, the enemy turned against Bretteville and at last light a force of 20 tanks, whipped in by Meyer himself riding on the back of a Panther, broke into the Canadian positions. The Regina Rifles were overrun but they held their ground and maintained such steady fire that no German infantry could get through to support the armour. One Panther reached Battalion H.Q. before it was knocked out by a ' Piat ' and, when five others were destroyed, Meyer called off his tanks. This attempt to take Bretteville cost the Germans their hold on Putôt, which fell to a brilliantly executed counter-attack by 1st Canadian Scottish. Before dawn on the 9th the line had been restored.

This failure left the Hitler Youth decidedly chastened and fully occupied with the defensive task of holding a ten-mile front against repeated probing attacks by the British and Canadians. Nor was Panzer Lehr capable of offensive action when it straggled into Tilly-sur-Seulles, south of Bayeux, during the 8th. Its commander, Bayerlein, had learned in North Africa the meaning of Allied air superiority and had schooled his troops in camouflage discipline. But he was ordered by Dollmann to move in daylight and his columns were discovered almost as soon as they took to the road. Bayerlein says:[1]

> By noon on the 7th my men were calling the main road from Vire to Le Bény Bocage *Jabo-Rennstrecke*—' fighter-bomber racecourse.' Every vehicle was covered with branches of trees and moved along hedgerows and the fringes of woods . . . but by the end of the day I had lost 40 petrol wagons and 90 other trucks. Five of my tanks had been knocked out, as well as 84 half-tracks, prime-movers and S.P. guns. These losses were serious for a division not yet in action.

Even more serious was the disorganisation, and Bayerlein was given no respite in which to concentrate for attack. As his units arrived they were sucked into the battle piecemeal in response to a British thrust towards Tilly.

With all Dietrich's divisions now closely engaged, Rommel decided on the 9th that " there should be a return to the defensive in the sector between the Vire and the Orne and that the counter-attack should be postponed until all preparations have been completed."[2] He would await the arrival of the 2nd Parachute Corps (Meindl) from Brittany and then carry out a deliberate offensive against the main Anglo-American bridge-head.

[1]Seventh U.S. Army Interrogation. Bayerlein subsequently confirmed these facts in discussions with me, and emphasised the almost paralysing effect Allied air power had on the employment of German armour.

[2]Seventh Army Telephone Log, June 9th, 1730 hours. Unless otherwise indicated, all the German orders and messages quoted in this and subsequent chapters dealing with the Battle of Normandy have been taken from this captured Telephone Log.

The organisation of this attack was entrusted to Geyr von Schweppenburg and the H.Q. of Panzer Group West, for neither von Rundstedt nor Rommel had any faith in Dietrich's ability to handle a major operation. But it was apparent that Montgomery was also preparing for an offensive and the question was, Who would be ready first?

In the race for the initiative Second British Army had been severely handicapped by the weather, which had delayed the landing of the follow-up divisions and the unloading of ammunition, and which had given some protection to enemy reserves as they moved towards the front. Primarily because of this, the Germans had been able to forestall Montgomery at Caen and to foil his plan for sending armoured columns through to Villers-Bocage and Evrécy in the first forty-eight hours while the situation was still fluid. By D plus 2 the Germans had managed to set up a defensive screen in the close bocage country between Bayeux and Tilly.

Normandy south and south-west of the Caen–Bayeux road is an area of undulating hills broken by the steep-sided valleys of innumerable streams. The hills become more rugged and more heavily covered with woods and thickets as you move south-west along the few straight, tree-lined highways or the countless, tortuous side-roads. The slopes and valleys are rich with farms and orchards, famous for camembert and calvados. However inviting to the tourist, ' La Suisse Normande ' is no country for offensive warfare.

Its dominant characteristic is the hedgerow—a bank three or four feet high with a ditch on either side and topped by a line of thorny bushes whose deep roots bind the earth into a wall which will rebuff even bull-dozers. With these hedgerows bordering the fields and with stone walls enclosing the orchards, the country abounds in natural anti-tank obstacles and ready-made defensive positions for infantry, while its thick woods and copses provide secure cover for lurking tanks. Moreover, the villages with their stout stone buildings and narrow streets provide formidable strongholds astride the roads and they cannot easily be by-passed.

Through this maze of small fields and smaller orchards, there are few good straight roads and these, almost without exception, follow the run of the country south-*west*. Bucknall's XXX Corps, seeking to advance south-*east*, was forced to follow by-ways which straggle up and down against the contours. These by-ways were mostly sunken lanes, so narrow that a tank could not traverse its gun, still less turn round. There was no observation beyond the next field and the armour was seldom able to manoeuvre across country, for the hedgerows were effective barriers and any gaps could easily be closed with mines and fire. The bocage was made for the sniper and the man who lay in wait beside the road with a *panzerfaust*.[1]

On June 8th, before Panzer Lehr had settled in, a British armoured column cut through to the eastern outskirts of Tilly, but could not consoli-

---

[1]The *panzerfaust* was the German equivalent of the American ' bazooka,' which fired a short-range, rocket-propelled, anti-tank projectile.

date its gains without the help of infantry. Bucknall had none to spare. Until the Americans could advance south of the Aure, he had to keep one brigade of ' Fifty Div.' covering his western flank. Moreover, in accordance with Montgomery's order to " gain space rapidly and peg out claims well inland," Bucknall had landed the 7th Armoured Division in the immediate follow-up, instead of his other infantry division, and had brought in the tanks of 7th Armoured ahead of its infantry. Thus on June 9th, with the enemy rapidly thickening his defences around Tilly, XXX Corps was handicapped by having too many tanks ashore and too few troops.

Realising that Caen could not now be taken by direct assault and that his attempt to by-pass it to the west was in danger of being frustrated, Montgomery determined to keep the battle mobile. " If the Germans wish to be offensive," he wrote to his Chief of Staff, de Guingand,[1] on the 9th, " and drive in our lodgement area between Bayeux and Caen, the best way to defeat them is to be offensive ourselves." He intended, he said, that the 7th Armoured Division should strike through Tilly " to secure Villers-Bocage and Evrécy and then exploit south-east." Meantime, the 51st Highland Division would " attack southwards, east of Caen, towards Cagny." When these gains had been made, he planned " to put down the 1st Airborne Division somewhere south of Caen in a big ' air lock ' and to link up with it from Evrécy and Cagny," thus enveloping the city.

This was a bold and ambitious plan, in which the first essential was the capture of the Villers-Bocage ridge. Accordingly, Dempsey ordered 7th Armoured to crack the German defences at Tilly before they crystallised further and told the Canadians to seize the Cheux ridge south of the Caen–Tilly road so as to protect the flank of the 7th when it thrust on to Villers-Bocage.

On the morning of June 11th, however, Dempsey was warned by Intelligence sources that the Germans were concentrating for an attack from Caen. This seemed to be the major armoured counter-stroke which he had been expecting since D plus 1 and, as his primary task was to safeguard the Allied left flank, he postponed the airborne plan, called for aerial bombardment of Caen and ordered Crocker (the commander of I British Corps) to convert the Canadian attack into a ' spoiling operation ' and to dispose the rest of his forces defensively. In particular, he told Crocker to concentrate his armour on the rising ground south of Douvres. " This bit of ground," he said, " is the heart of the British Empire. Don't move your armour from there! " Dempsey's action was fully justified on the evidence available to him, for he did not know what had happened the previous evening within the German lines.

On June 10th the Battle H.Q. of Panzer Group West was located

[1]Montgomery had moved his small Tactical H.Q. to Normandy on D plus 1, leaving his Chief of Staff (Major-General F. W. de Guingand) ' in command ' at the Main H.Q. of 21st Army Group.

in an orchard at La Caine, 12 miles south of Caen. Here *General der Panzertruppen* Freiherr Geyr von Schweppenburg, son of the Master of the Horse to the King of Württemberg, was putting the finishing touches to his plan for the great offensive that was to split the invasion front in twain. Geyr had commanded an armoured corps with some success in Russia but he had never before taken the field against an opponent who held command of the air, and he did not trouble to camouflage his H.Q. At La Caine four large wireless trucks and several office caravans and tents stood in the open and, to leave the passing pilot in no doubt as to the importance of this array, Geyr himself and his General Staff officers, with resplendent red stripes down their trousers, came out with their field-glasses from time to time to watch the R.A.F. at work.

On the previous day British Intelligence had located Geyr's H.Q. and a reconnaissance aircraft had confirmed its position. That evening the R.A.F. bombed it so accurately that little was left of the H.Q. except its surprised and enraged commander. According to one eye-witness, " all the staff officers were killed or wounded, the wireless trucks were knocked out and so was most of the transport." It was twelve hours before Seventh Army learned of the disaster.[1]

Geyr's Chief of Staff and 17 others were buried in one of the bomb craters over which the Germans were to raise a huge cross of polished oak, emblazoned with eagle and swastika—an appropriately impressive memorial, for this was the graveyard not only of these men but of Rommel's hopes for a major counter-attack before it was too late. The wounded Geyr and his shattered H.Q. were withdrawn to Paris to recuperate. Dietrich again became the senior commander in the Caen sector and, mindful of his earlier experience, immediately shelved Geyr's aggressive plan. The events of June 11th seemed to justify this decision, for the defensive preparations which Dempsey had ordered assumed a different aspect when viewed from the German side of the line. The Canadian spoiling attack and the bombardment of Caen were regarded by Dietrich as evidence that Second Army was about to launch a large-scale assault against the city, and that evening he received a warning which appeared to be conclusive.

Behind the British lines one German strongpoint still held out, a radar station near Douvres. Just south of this, around Anguerny, lay ' the heart of the British Empire ' where Crocker concentrated his armour that afternoon. At 8.45 p.m. the Germans in the radar station wirelessed to Dietrich: " Urgent. In Anguerny area assembly of up to now 200 enemy tanks with transport echelon facing south."[2] Earlier in the day the radar station had signalled: " Continuous movement heavy and medium tanks towards south-east. More than 80 tanks counted within one hour." Dietrich needed no further evidence. The following

[1]This account is based upon the interrogations of Geyr and a member of his staff and upon my own subsequent examination of the spot.
[2]Wireless Log of Douvres Radar Station for June 11th.

morning Rommel's H.Q. was warned that " in view of reports of tank concentrations, it can be expected that the full-scale attack on Caen will begin in the middle of the day or at the latest this evening."

On the Caen front throughout June 11th Germans and British alike stood braced to meet the other's attack but, while Dietrich's attention was fixed on this sector (and well it might have been, since Caen was under almost continuous bombardment by British battleships)[1] Dempsey turned to exploit an opportunity which had developed on the western flank of Second Army.

Since the first two critical days V U.S. Corps had made remarkable progress from OMAHA and had given the enemy no opportunity of restoring his shattered defences. His last hope of making any stand on the line of the Aure disappeared on the night of June 8th–9th, when the 29th Division sent one regiment to wade a mile and a half through the inundations, and another to outflank them by opening the road through Isigny. These bold night moves took the enemy unawares and left him incapable of organising any serious delaying action. On the morning of the 9th Montgomery ordered Bradley to exploit rapidly soutwards to St. Lô and Caumont and thereby give flank support to Dempsey.[2] Bradley acted at once. That afternoon the 175th Regiment, which had had no sleep and little respite since it landed, covered nine miles in five hours marching and fighting in the direction of St. Lô. Next day the 2nd Division, now brought into the centre of the Corps front, advanced almost unopposed for ten miles through country ideal for defence. By the evening of the 11th both the 2nd Division and the 1st were 14 miles south of OMAHA and had drawn level with the British who were still battling hard to get Tilly.

This advance represented an amazing recovery. The Americans might well have proceeded with some caution after their heavy losses on OMAHA, particularly as their supply position was far from satisfactory. During the first five days only 24 per cent of the planned tonnage of ammunition and other stores was landed on OMAHA, but the advance was not held back on this account. Bradley could now afford to be venturesome with V Corps, for between D-Day and June 10th it was opposed by no fresh troops except two battalions of cyclists supported by half a dozen assault guns. The main enemy reserves were being committed against the British between the mouth of the Orne and Tilly, and against VII U.S. Corps in the Cotentin, and those reinforcements which had been earmarked to oppose V Corps were slow in arriving for a variety of reasons, most of which found their origin in Allied air power.

On D-Day the German High Command had ordered the movement

<hr>

[1]During the night June 12th–13th H.M.S. *Nelson* and H.M.S. *Ramillies* put a 15-inch or 16-inch shell into Caen every half minute.
[2]Bradley, *A Soldier's Story*, pp. 282-3.

to Western Normandy of 2nd SS Panzer from Toulouse, 17th SS from the Loire Valley, 77th Infantry from St. Malo, 3rd Parachute from near Brest and regimental battlegroups from three other Brittany divisions. But of these the SS formations alone were adequately motorised. The paratroops had motor transport enough for only one regiment; the other divisions were even less mobile and all soon found it impossible to move by day with Allied aircraft commanding the skies.

Some units were put into ancient French buses. Others were sent off on bicycle or foot with their equipment following in horse-drawn transport. One regiment, coming from Nantes, was rashly loaded into a train with all its transport and horses. On June 7th it was half-way to St. Lô when American bombers discovered it in Fougères station. The resulting chaos was more serious than the actual casualties, for the tail of the train, carrying the horses, was severed from the rest by a direct hit and rolled back four miles down the line. By the time the hapless Germans found it, the French had removed the contents and the battalion became involved in a horse-hunt before continuing its journey—on foot.

The 2nd SS Panzer Division encountered problems which were rather more serious and varied. Late on D-Day, it was ordered to start moving from the South of France by rail and road. But its armour had to wait four days for trains and the loading had barely begun at Montauban when the marshalling-yard was so heavily bombed that it took another week to load all its tanks. Before the road convoys could leave, patrols had to subdue the population, who were roused to a rebellious mood by the news of the invasion and the prospect of German departure. Picquets were sent ahead, for the route lay through the heart of the area where the Maquis were strongest, but even so the convoys were frequently halted by demolitions or guerrilla bands. Some battalions had to fight pitched battles before they could get through; others were held up by subtler means.

In the latter class was the 3rd Battalion of the 4th SS Panzer Grenadier Regiment. At midnight on June 8th, when its convoy was north of Limoges, it was discovered that the Colonel had disappeared. The battalion halted until dawn and then turned round in search of the missing link in its chain of command. At midday the Colonel's car was found parked in a village 40 miles back. There were no signs of sabotage or violence, not even a puncture. The village and the surrounding countryside were scoured in vain until the following morning. By then the battalion had lost two night's travelling at a time when it was most urgently needed at the battlefront.

The Maquis were equally effective in hindering the division's rail movement and, before its trains reached the Loire, Allied bombers had closed every railway bridge except one, and this was so badly damaged that the rolling stock had to be towed across wagon by wagon. As a result of delays and difficulties such as these, the infantry units of 2nd SS took from 10 to 14 days to cover the 450 miles from Toulouse to St.

Lô, and its armour took still longer, for it was held up by shortage of petrol.

In the early months of 1944 OKW had built up considerable stocks of fuel in the West, but most of these were held in the Fifteenth Army area, north of the Seine. Hitler's intuitive selection of Normandy came too late to permit any redistribution of stocks and the German High Command relied on being able to replenish its forward dumps with supplies brought up in railways tankers from the G.H.Q. reserve near Paris. This proved to be impossible once the invasion had begun, and road convoys, able to travel only at night, could not handle the necessary quantities. In the battle area local distribution was seriously hampered by Allied fighter-bombers which singled out for special attention anything which looked like a petrol wagon or an oil dump.

As early as June 10th Seventh Army was in serious straits for petrol. That day shortage of fuel was delaying the organisation of the counter-attack which Panzer Group West was to launch from Caen, and was holding up the arrival of the divisions which were to close the gap that grew ever wider as the Americans advanced towards Caumont. This was to be the task of Meindl's 2nd Parachute Corps, but it was stranded on the road from Brittany. That morning Meindl reported that " the 3rd Parachute Division must be brought up piecemeal owing to the shortage of fuel. . . . One regiment is east of St. Lô but the main body is still in Brittany." At midday Seventh Army was told: " The leading units of 17th SS are stuck in the St. Lô area because of the lack of fuel."

As the line gave way, both here and in the Cotentin, for sheer lack of men to hold it, Hitler sent one of his characteristic ' stand-fast ' orders: " There can be no question of fighting a rearguard action nor of retiring to a new line of resistance. Every man shall fight and fall where he stands."[1] Even the Führer's edict, however, could not fill the gaps which had already been opened, for it was no longer a question of holding more doggedly to ground that was occupied, but of finding troops to take their stand on ground which was not defended at all.

On this day the only fresh unit which Dollmann could send against V Corps was the reconnaissance battalion of 17th SS, and it could do little to stem the advance. Early the following morning (June 11th), Marcks reported to Seventh Army that the situation on the St. Lô–Caumont sector was critical. He had lost touch with the 352nd Division which, he said, " now has small combat value and the gap between it and its right-flank neighbour [i.e. Panzer Lehr] is constantly increasing." He was anxious to throw in " Engineer Battalion Angers " as a stop-gap, but this unit had " not yet been found."

It was another twenty-four hours before the rest of 17th SS was ready for action and then, on the morning of June 12th, just as it was about to move to Caumont, serious news came from Carentan. During the 11th the 101st Airborne Division had forced the outer defences of

[1]Seventh Army Telephone Log, June 10th, 1700 hours.

the town after a day of costly fighting down the causeway which led across the inundations and into the northern outskirts. By that evening the spirit and ammunition of the defenders were almost exhausted. They called for supplies to be dropped by air and, when these did not arrive, they withdrew. The fall of Carentan meant the removal of the wedge that had been dividing the two Allied bridgeheads and Rommel immediately diverted 17th SS to drive the wedge back.

This move left undefended, on the very day when the 1st U.S. Division had orders for its capture, the most important single feature between Caen and St. Lô–Caumont, which stands on a bold fist of a hill dominating the surrounding countryside. In a last-minute effort to improvise a temporary garrison, Marcks set out for Caumont himself, but he was killed on the road by American fighter-bombers. By the time his H.Q. discovered his fate, it was too late for further action. A five-mile advance that day brought Bradley's patrols into the town and by the next morning it was firmly held by the Americans.

It was the situation created by this American advance that Dempsey turned to exploit on the afternoon of June 12th. South of Bayeux two days of hard fighting had carried the British 7th Armoured Division (Major-General G. W. E. J. Erskine) forward only three miles and had left Panzer Lehr still holding firm along the main road running east and west through Tilly. These defences could not be penetrated by an armoured division, least of all the 7th. Apart from a brief campaign in Italy, it had done all its fighting in the desert in conditions of open, mobile warfare. Even its re-training for OVERLORD had been carried out in the flat fenlands and sandy heaths of Norfolk, which provided no foretaste of what it was to encounter in Normandy. The transition to the bocage afflicted the men with claustrophobia. Tank commanders who had always fought with their heads out, were sniped and killed as they drove along apparently peaceful lanes. Crews, who had been accustomed to engage the enemy at half a mile or more, found themselves facing hostile anti-tank guns at a range of 50 yards, or, worse still, dealing with boarding parties who leapt on to their tanks from the cover of hedgerows.

In the bocage the advantage lay overwhelmingly with the defender. Once the Germans had established themselves, it became a matter of fighting forward in bounds, 100 to 200 yards at a time, from one hedgerow to the next with tanks covering the infantry advance and sappers blowing gaps through which the armour could move up. For operations of this kind Erskine had neither sufficient infantry nor appropriate armour. His division was equipped primarily with Cromwell tanks, mounting the 6-pdr. gun which had been out of date in Italy the previous year. The Cromwell was essentially a cruiser, a cavalry-type tank, quite unsuited for operations in the hedgerows and villages of Normandy against the heavily-armed and heavily-armoured Germans.

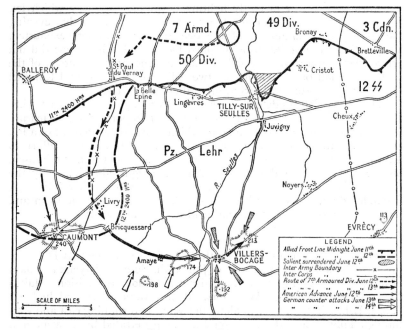

OPERATION PERCH

On the morning of June 12th, when Erskine was checked again, Dempsey ordered him to break off his direct attack on Tilly and carry out a right hook to Villers-Bocage. He was to start that afternoon and make a bold enveloping movement round Panzer Lehr's western flank, taking advantage of the gap the Americans had found and extended. Infantry of the 50th Division would follow up and consolidate his gains and, if the way was clear, he was to drive on to Evrécy. There, if necessary, he would be reinforced by the 1st Airborne Division, which was ready to be dropped on the first favourable occasion.

Here was an opportunity which might be made the turning point in the bridgehead battle. The enemy had built up a firm defence line east of the Orne and from the Orne across to the headwaters of the Aure, five miles west of Tilly. But beyond there his front was thin and fragmentary. If Second Army could outflank and undermine the section of the enemy's containing wall which had been built, he would have little chance of completing the rest which was still building. He might even be forced to withdraw behind the Orne.

Although the 22nd Armoured Brigade, which was to lead the way, received this plan with some misgiving, it was on the move by mid-afternoon and advanced twelve miles—six of them through enemy territory—before it was checked at Livry, north-east of Caumont. This opposition was cleared with nearly three hours of daylight to spare and the Brigade Commander (W. R. N. Hinde) was faced with the problem whether he should go on. He barely had time to secure Villers-Bocage before dark, even if he met no more trouble, and he was now due to turn east and that would disclose his intention. He decided to stop for the night near Caumont where his presence might be interpreted as part of the American drive southward.

Next morning a column of tanks and infantry moved at dawn. By 8.30 a.m. the armour had covered the five miles to Villers-Bocage unopposed and was entering the town to the cheers of the French and the consternation of two Germans, who made off at speed in a Volkswagen. Elated by this unexpected success, the leading tank squadron drove on towards its immediate objective, Point 213, half a mile to the north-east along the Caen highway.

In the meantime, the company of motorised infantry which was following passed through the town and halted its half-tracks along the edge of a tree-lined road. The troops had dismounted to stretch their legs while the tanks reconnoitred the way ahead, when the crack of a gun split the crisp morning air and the leading half-track burst into flames. Out of the woods to the north lumbered a Tiger tank, which drove on to the road and proceeded right down the line of half-tracks ' brewing up ' one vehicle after another. Behind these there was some incidental armour—a dozen tanks belonging to Regimental H.Q., the artillery observers and a reconnaissance troop. The Tiger destroyed them in quick succession, scorning the fire of one Cromwell, which saw its 75 mm shells bounce off the sides of the German tank even at the range of a few yards! Within a matter of minutes the road was an inferno with 25 armoured vehicles blazing—all the victims of this one lone Tiger.

Hinde, whose fearlessness had long since earned him the nickname ' Loony,' extricated his scout car from this imbroglio and vigorously organised the defence of the town. During the remainder of the morning there were no attacks on Villers-Bocage itself, but those of Hinde's tanks which had reached Point 213 were isolated and by early afternoon they had all been destroyed by a detachment of Tigers. Nevertheless, when the German armour turned against Villers-Bocage, it met stiffer opposition and by four o'clock its attacks had been beaten off with the loss, as Bayerlein reported, of " six Mark VIs and several Mark IVs."[1] The town remained in British hands.

By this time, however, the 7th Armoured Division was becoming dangerously strung out. It was deployed along a single road from Villers-Bocage to Livry, and late in the afternoon its positions came

---

[1]This was a costly rebuff, for at this time there were only 36 Tiger tanks on the entire Normandy front, but Bayerlein had been forced to expend his armour because he had no infantry available until late in the afternoon when two battalions of another division arrived.

under attack from troops of a fresh German division which had just arrived on the scene. Realising that before nightfall he must concentrate his strength, Hinde withdrew from Villers-Bocage to a knoll (Point 174) a mile to the west.

The Corps commander, Bucknall, now intended that Hinde's brigade should hold this high ground until the 50th Division advanced to relieve it. In making this plan Bucknall seems to have been rather optimistic. Throughout that day Panzer Lehr had continued its unyielding defence along the Tilly–La Belle Épine road. Far from weakening here in response to the thrust by the 7th Armoured Division, its opposition had become aggressive, and the British withdrawal from Villers-Bocage naturally encouraged Bayerlein to dig in his toes on the Tilly sector.

In these circumstances, Bucknall might have been expected to concentrate upon strengthening the threat provided by 7th Armoured; to reinforce success, not to persist in a line of approach which had already proved unprofitable. What Erskine needed was infantry and Bucknall had two brigades of infantry to spare. The opportunity had been opened and Bucknall had the resources to exploit it, but instead he gave 7th Armoured no further support and persisted in his head-on assault against the Tilly line.

In appraising the situation, however, Bucknall was influenced by two disconcerting factors. On his return from the Tactical H.Q. of 7th Armoured late in the afternoon, he announced that both his escort tanks had been " knocked out by a Tiger." As a result of this experience Bucknall concluded that Erskine's communications were endangered, and his concern grew in the evening when he learned that the infantry which was attacking Hinde's brigade belonged to the 2nd Panzer Division, the leading elements of which had made a rapid and undetected move from Amiens during the past three days.

While Hinde was thus left without reinforcement, the 50th Division renewed the direct assault on the Tilly line, this time with strong air support, but Panzer Lehr stood its ground. Bayerlein had the weaker position but the stronger nerve and that prevailed. At noon Bucknall decided to pull 7th Armoured back to Bricquessard, two miles east of Caumont, thus withdrawing the spear which he had plunged into the German flank. This manœuvre was certainly not forced upon him by the enemy[1] and, before it could be carried out, Hinde's brigade smashed a resolute counter-attack, thereby demonstrating most effectively its ability to hold. Nevertheless, the order for Hinde to withdraw still stood and during the night it was executed without further enemy interference.

Thus the fruits of the initial success, which might have been turned into a striking victory, were handed back to the enemy. Erskine's troops had suffered no defeat after the first costly encounter with the single

[1]That night the XXX Corps Intelligence Summary commented, " It seems surprising that at a moment when the enemy had the chance of dealing our troops around Villers a decisive blow, his attack should have been so half-hearted and ill-timed."

Tiger, and if Bucknall had reinforced and persisted with the attack by 7th Armoured, he would have provided a serious threat to the rear of Caen and would have forced Panzer Lehr to abandon the Tilly salient in order to help close the gap which the Americans had created at Caumont. This great opportunity of disrupting the enemy line and expanding the Allied bridgehead was lost not so much in the woods and orchards around Villers-Bocage, as in the Corps Commander's mind.

The failure of this operation, and the simultaneous repulse of the Highland Division's attempt to expand the bridgehead east of the Orne, led Dempsey to write at the time that there was " no chance now of a snap operation with airborne troops either to seize Caen or to deepen the bridgehead on XXX Corps front. It is clear now that Caen can be taken only by a set-piece assault and we do not have the men or ammunition for that at this time."

Nevertheless, while awaiting reinforcement, Dempsey had to continue his offensive tactics, which had already drawn into battle with Second Army all four panzer divisions that Rommel had in Normandy. It was essential that these should be pinned down between Caen and Caumont, lest they be withdrawn and reorganised for a deliberate counter-stroke. The foundation of the plan, which Montgomery had propounded long before D-Day was, as we have seen, that Second Army should " protect the flank of First U.S. Army while they capture Cherbourg and the Brittany ports." He had hoped that Dempsey would achieve this by gaining command of the Caen–Villers-Bocage–Caumont road during the first few days, thus interposing Second Army as a bulwark between the Americans and the German armoured reserves. By the premature commitment of his armour, Rommel had delayed the British advance, but in the process he had played into Montgomery's hands for, once the panzer divisions were locked in battle with Second Army, they could not be used for their proper offensive task.

Appreciating this only too well, Rommel on June 12th had advised Keitel at OKW: " For the present the Army Group must content itself with forming a connected front between the Orne and the Vire and allowing the foe to come on. . . . The Army Group is endeavouring to replace the panzer formations by infantry formations as soon as possible, and to re-form mobile reserves with them. The Army Group intends to switch its *Schwerpunkt* in the next few days to the area Carentan–Montebourg to annihilate the enemy there and avert the danger to Cherbourg. Only when this has been successfully done can the enemy between the Orne and the Vire be attacked."[1]

In anticipation of this enemy plan, Montgomery the day before had signalled to Brooke at the War Office: " My general policy is to pull the enemy on to Second Army so as to make it the easier for First Army

---

[1]Teleprinter message, Rommel to Keitel, June 12th, entitled " Appreciation of Situation on 11.6.1944." (Tempelhof Papers. For an explanation of the origin and content of these papers, see Appendix A.)

to expand and extend the quicker." This policy had always been implicit in his overall plan and it now became the guiding principle in his conduct of the battle. Since he could not use Second Army as a shield, he would make it a magnet. By threatening to break out south-east from Caen, he would compel Rommel to persist in the policy of concentrating the panzer divisions against the British.

By the end of the first week, although he had not captured either St. Lô or Caen, nor secured the depth he wanted, Montgomery had reason to be satisfied. In spite of the difficulties and delays caused by the weather, the Allied foothold had been consolidated by the linking up of the two bridgeheads. The immediate armoured counter-strokes, the attacks he had feared most, had been repulsed in every case but one, and the Germans had been forced to commit their armour defensively. Montgomery was now confident that he could deal with any German counter-attack, but if he was to thwart the attempt to contain the bridgehead in the bocage, the Allies must win what was now the crucial issue, the ' Battle of the Build-up.'

## CHAPTER XVII

# THE BATTLE OF THE BUILD-UP

IN his teleprinter signal to Keitel on June 12th Rommel summed up
the Normandy situation in these words: " The enemy is strengthening
himself visibly on land under cover of very strong aircraft formations.
Our own air force and navy are not in a position to offer him appreciable
opposition—especially by day. Thus the strength of the enemy on land
is increasing appreciably more quickly than our reserves can reach the
front. . . . Our position is becoming exceptionally difficult since the
enemy can cripple the movement of our formations throughout the day,
while he himself operates with quickly-moving formations and troops
landing from the air.

" Our own operations," said Rommel, " are rendered extraordinarily
difficult and in part impossible to carry out," owing primarily to " the
exceptionally strong, and in some respects overwhelming, superiority of
the enemy air force. The enemy has complete command of the air over
the battle zone and up to about 100 kilometres behind the front and
cuts off by day almost all traffic on roads or by-ways or in open country.
Manœuvre by our troops on the field of battle in daylight is thus almost
entirely prevented, while the enemy can operate freely. . . . Troops and
staffs have to hide by day in areas which afford some cover. . . . Neither
our flak nor the Luftwaffe seem capable of putting a stop to this crippling
and destructive operation of the enemy's aircraft. The troops protect
themselves as well as they can with the means available, but ammunition
is scarce and can be supplied only under the most difficult conditions."

In these circumstances, Rommel's only course, as Montgomery had
foretold in May, was to pursue a policy of ' roping-off ' and to exploit
the natural defensive strength of the bocage, where his troops might hold
their ground so long as they were not too heavily outnumbered. In view
of the impotence of the Luftwaffe, however, the success of this policy
depended chiefly on the ability of the German Navy to curtail the Allied
build-up and keep it within limits which the Wehrmacht could match.

The anti-invasion plan of Grand-Admiral Doenitz was based on the
realistic assumption that his surface forces could neither prevent a major
landing nor challenge the Allied command of the Channel. But in the

development of unconventional under-water weapons Germany was pre-eminent, and Doenitz hoped that the bold employment of the new devices which his scientists had designed would seriously delay, if not disrupt, the Allied build-up time-table. He expected that the new electro-U-boats (and even the latest orthodox models, fitted with the *Schnorkel*) would be able to operate with virtual impunity even in the shallow waters of the Channel; that the oyster, or pressure, mines would prove to be unsweep-able; and that his 'small battle units'—midget submarines, long-range circling torpedoes and one-man torpedoes—could infiltrate through the Allied naval screen which his main surface units could not expect to penetrate. In theory Doenitz's plan was ingenious and impressive, but, when D-Day came, the means of implementing it were not available.

By June 6th only two of the revolutionary electro-U-boats had been completed and the programme for their mass production was already three or four months behind schedule. This was due in part to the dislocation caused by Allied bombing. Reporting to Hitler in April, Doenitz had declared that " U-boat engines were not completed because too few construction workers were employed to repair bomb damage; and the completed hull sections could not be welded together because the engines were not ready."[1] Although alarmed at the delay, Hitler replied that priority must be given to the production of fighters and the repair of aircraft factories, since " otherwise industry might be destroyed still more and thus U-boat production would be halted completely." This was an unplanned and unexpected dividend from the Allied attacks on the German aircraft industry.

Perhaps the most important cause of delay, however, was the attempt to regain the scientific advantage in the war at sea by taking short-cuts in planning and production. The Germans were so hard pressed that, when the prototype of the larger submarine (Type XXI) was de-stroyed in an air raid on Kiel, they decided to continue mass pre-fabrication without waiting for another prototype to be finished and tested. Consequently, faults in design were not discovered until the components were assembled or, worse still, until trials were carried out at sea with models which were by this time in production. Even when the major 'snags' had been eradicated, the Germans found that in many cases the components could not be assembled without considerable modification. In the hope of saving time and escaping from bombing, the production of parts and sections had been farmed out to firms which had never been engaged in naval construction before and their workers lacked the necessary skill and precision. The gamble failed and Allied shipping was able to sail the Channel unhindered by the most formidable naval weapon which the Germans had ever devised.

Because of these delays, Doenitz was compelled to rely upon the orthodox U-boats which had already been roundly defeated the previous year. In the spring of 1944 he recalled his submarines from the Atlantic

[1] *Führer Naval Conferences*, April 12th–13th, 1944.

in order to equip them with the *Schnorkel*, which would at least permit them to recharge their batteries without coming to the surface. But here again he encountered numerous practical difficulties, and none of his U-boats had been successfully equipped with this breathing device when the concentration of Allied shipping at the end of April led him to the conclusion that invasion was imminent. In mid-May, therefore, he tried to transfer reinforcements from the Baltic and Norway to bases on the Bay of Biscay. Not being fitted with the *Schnorkel* these submarines were obliged to fight it out on the surface with aircraft of R.A.F. Coastal Command. For two weeks the Germans persisted in the effort to break through. A few succeeded; nine were sunk or badly damaged; the rest turned back.

This defeat left Doenitz with only 42 serviceable U-boats (barely a quarter of his operational fleet) in the Brittany and Biscay ports when the invasion began. By that time six of these had been equipped and tested with *Schnorkel* but they were not really battle-worthy. Nevertheless, on the afternoon of June 6th they set out from Brest and at dark the other 36 sailed from Biscay ports. These travelled on the surface, in the hope of making good the time lost by lack of warning, but during the night they were picked up by Allied air patrols. In the next few days 12 of the 36 were sunk or damaged too severely to proceed, and on June 12th the remainder were ordered back to port. Even the six which had been converted made slow progress up the Channel for their equipment was not reliable. Some were damaged by air attack; others developed technical faults; and not one reached the assault area in the first three weeks after D-Day. Nor was Doenitz able to employ his midget submarines and other ' small battle units.' A few had been completed and tried out in the Mediterranean, but none were available in the Channel during June and the Allied build-up proceeded undisturbed by submarine attack.[1]

German surface craft were similarly unsuccessful. Neither destroyers from St. Nazaire, nor torpedo-boats from Le Havre and Cherbourg, were able to evade the relentless patrols which screened the shipping corridor. The only German counter-measure which caused Ramsay any real anxiety was the laying of pressure mines in the anchorages. These mines were dropped by low-flying aircraft, which were extremely difficult to intercept because Allied radar could not give sufficient warning to the night fighters. " The enemy," wrote Ramsay later, " introduced two new types of mine, both of which were actuated by the reduction of pressure caused by a ship passing over them. One of these could not be swept under any conditions and the other only in certain weather."

[1]In the War Diary of Naval Group, West, on which this account of German counter-measures is primarily based, it is claimed that a U-boat (with *Schnorkel*) sank an Allied destroyer in the Channel on June 9th, but in the assault area no merchantman was lost to submarine attack until June 28th, when one ship was sunk. Another was torpedoed next day, but U-boats accounted for only one more merchant vessel in the invasion area during July.

Ramsay was surprised that these mines had not been dropped before D-Day in the harbours of Southern England, for there they could have wreaked havoc among the closely packed ships. Rommel had indeed asked that this should be done, but Doenitz had refused lest the secret should be discovered—and the device copied—by the British.[1] He feared that the use of this mine in the Baltic would close the only safe training and testing grounds still available for the new U-boats. Pressure mines were not even laid in advance on the German side of the Channel, because they had not been produced in sufficient numbers to cover all the threatened areas. When at last they were dropped in the Bay of the Seine on the third night of the invasion, the Luftwaffe pilots had strict orders that on no account should any of these mines be allowed to fall into Allied hands. On the morning of June 10th, however, several were found on shore intact. Within a few days Admiralty tests had shown that the pressure fuses would not be activated if shipping were to proceed slowly through the infected areas. By imposing speed restrictions, the Allies reduced the danger, but the Germans sewed the coastal waters not only with ' oysters ' but also with acoustic and magnetic mines of devilish ingenuity, and the build-up was maintained only because mine-sweepers and supply craft took risks which were, in Ramsay's opinion, " generally unacceptable." The unsweepable pressure mines would have caused the Allies considerably greater trouble if Doenitz had concentrated his entire effort upon the congested anchorages between the Orne and the Cotentin. But, accepting the general appreciation that there would be a further landing north of the Seine, he had proceeded to lay oyster mines off the main beaches and harbours between Le Havre and Ostend.

On June 12th, in the light of Rommel's pessimistic report, Doenitz, Keitel and Jodl in conference at Berchtesgaden reached the conclusion that " if the enemy succeeds in fighting his way out of the present bridge-head and gains freedom of action for mobile warfare, then all France is lost."[2] Since the Allies had already gained the lead in build-up, the only chance of avoiding this consequence seemed to them to lie in Eisenhower's attempting another landing—and failing. There was, they hoped, one stratagem which might " induce the enemy to attempt a second landing in Northern France," and that was the long-expected bombardment of London by flying-bombs, which were to be launched across the Channel for the first time that night.

On the afternoon of D-Day Flak Regiment 155, which was to conduct the V.1 operations, had received orders that the offensive must begin immediately. Following the destruction of the first series of bases, however, it had been decided that the final equipping and stocking-up of the launching sites should not be undertaken in advance lest this

[1]Führer Naval Conferences, May 4th–6th, 1944.
[2]Führer Naval Conferences, June 12th, 1944.

should lead to their being discovered by Allied aircraft. Wise though this precaution was, it had serious consequences, for Wachtel, the regimental commander, now reported that it would be ten days before the offensive could start. Most of the equipment and materials for completing the sites were still at depots well inland and so was much of the ammunition. Nearly 12,000 flying-bombs had been produced but, as a safeguard against air attack, they were dispersed in dumps scattered throughout Northern France, Belgium and Germany. Between these dumps and the launching sites almost every railway line was out of action. Regardless of these difficulties, Wachtel was instructed that operations must commence on the night of June 12th–13th.

His orders were that the onslaught was to begin just before midnight with a salvo of 64 bombs so timed in their launching that they would all strike the centre of London at the same moment, and in conjunction with a bombing raid by the Luftwaffe. An hour later the 64 sites were to send off another salvo and then carry on harassing fire until dawn. But these orders ignored the practical difficulty of completing the sites, and, when zero hour came on the 12th, only seven were ready for action. That night after several attempts to launch a salvo, the Germans were able to fire only ten harassing rounds and all that reached London was one lone bomb.[1]

During the next three days Wachtel's regiment completed 55 sites, and on the night of the 15th–16th the offensive began in earnest. In the first twenty-four hours 244 flying-bombs were launched, but they were not fired in devastating salvoes as had been planned, for the equipment was unreliable and the crews lacked experience. Thanks to the false start and the three days' respite, British fighter and anti-aircraft defences were amply warned and during the ensuing weeks they took increasing toll of the pilotless raiders.

As soon as the offensive started Allied bombers attacked the new launching sites, which could be located by radar now that they were in operation. By the end of June, according to the German records, these raids had put 24 sites out of action and had damaged 18 others. German operations were further embarrassed by attacks on supply centres and communications. Trains carrying flying-bombs in converted dining-cars and passenger coaches had to take slow, circuitous routes round bombed junctions and wrecked bridges. One train heavily laden with V.1's was held up at a damaged marshalling-yard near Paris long enough for French agents to advise London and call in Allied bombers to destroy the complete load.

The result was that during the last fortnight of June the Germans were able to launch only 2,000 flying-bombs. Of these 661 were brought down and barely a thousand reached London. Although the scale of this

[1] War Diary of Flak Regiment 155, June 1944. This document and the interrogation of Colonel Eberhardt, the chief engineer officer of this regiment, provided most of the material for this section.

bombardment was far less than even the most sanguine had predicted, the nervous strain was severe and many Londoners found it more gruelling than the orthodox bombing of 1940-1. On the other hand, the fatal casualties, amounting to only one person killed for every bomb launched, were small compared with those of the ' Blitz ' and the weapon was too inaccurate to be profitably employed against the south coast ports through which reinforcements and supplies continued to flow to Normandy. By the start of July it was clear that neither as a terror weapon, nor as a means of disturbing the Allied build-up, could the flying-bomb affect the issue. Nor did it succeed, as the German Supreme Command had hoped it might, in inducing the Allies to attempt a second landing. On June 18th Churchill assured Eisenhower that there must be no question of changing Anglo-American strategy for the purpose of accomplishing the early conquest of the V.1 bases. In the interests of the overall plan of campaign London would endure the bombardment so long as necessary.

The main influence of the flying-bomb offensive on the course of operations on the Continent was that it led to the retention in Britain of the fastest fighters and caused the distraction of a considerable proportion of the Allied Air Forces from the strategic bombing of Germany and the tactical support of the troops in Normandy. In the next two months R.A.F. Bomber Command was to divert half its effort to attacks on V-weapon installations, yet indirectly this counter-bombardment contributed to the battle in the bridgehead, because it helped to sustain the German conviction that there would be a further assault north of the Seine. This belief was strengthened by Allied deception, which now represented the Normandy landings as a diversion and kept reminding the Germans of the threat to the Pas de Calais. On June 19th Rommel reported to von Rundstedt: " Judging from the enemy's grouping of his forces, and from the tactical and technical possibilities, a large-scale landing is to be expected on the Channel front on both sides of Cap Gris Nez or between the Somme and Le Havre. This fresh landing may be timed to coincide with the general offensive from the Normandy bridgehead with the Paris area as the common, concentrated objective."[1]

Rommel was in a grave dilemma. The Normandy front was in desperate need of infantry to relieve the armoured divisions and free them for a counter-stroke in the Cotentin. And yet he could not draw upon his most convenient source of reinforcements (Fifteenth Army) since he did not dare to expose his Channel flank. Even the two divisions which had been brought from north of the Seine in the first few days were promptly replaced by new arrivals from Germany. Rommel's dilemma was accentuated by the Allied command of the air. The 18 divisions of

---

[1]Estimate of Overall Situation, June 19th, 1944. (Tempelhof Papers.) In view of this appreciation, no credence can be given to Speidel's post-war claim that by June 17th, " Rommel no longer believed that a second big landing would be made north of the Seine." (Speidel, op. cit., p. 107.)

Fifteenth Army were separated from the Normandy battlefront by the barrier of the Seine, because every road and rail bridge across the river between Paris and the sea had now been wrecked. Not having anticipated attacks of such accuracy, the Germans had made no provision for setting up pontoon bridges and the ferries they improvised could not handle any large volume of traffic. For these divisions the alternative route to the front involved a hazardous rail journey to Paris and then a march of 150 miles, for the few trains that still dared to run through the Paris–Orléans ' gap ' were filled with supplies of high priority.

The dislocation of the French railways was doubly serious for the Wehrmacht, since it had not the motor transport to make large-scale movements by road. The standard allocation of trucks to its divisions was based on the assumption that the infantry and artillery could be moved by rail. The Allied Air Forces rendered that assumption false, and by doing so not only disrupted the German supply system, but gravely curtailed the Wehrmacht's strategic mobility. Rommel knew that once a division was moved from the Pas de Calais to Western Normandy, it could not be moved back in time to meet a second landing. Consequently, after Brittany had been stripped of what amounted to four of its nine divisions, Rommel had to look to Holland and the South of France for further infantry reinforcements and these could not be expected to arrive until the end of the month.

In these circumstances, Rommel had to postpone his planned attack against the Americans, for he was compelled to continue using his panzer divisions to hold the line from Caen to Caumont, and (apart from 2nd SS Panzer, which was coming into reserve near St. Lô) no further armoured reinforcements were likely to reach him before the last week of June. The 1st SS Panzer Division was about to move from Belgium, and 9th and 10th SS were on their way back from Poland, but the hope that he might receive additional divisions from the East disappeared when the Russian summer offensive began, as Stalin had promised, two weeks after the start of the invasion.

By June 18th the Allies had gained a clear advantage in build-up, for Montgomery had 20 divisions ashore. Opposing him were elements of 18 divisions, but in fighting strength these were barely equal to 14. Between the Orne and the Vire Rommel's containing rope was under heavy strain, as the Americans kept thrusting for St. Lô and the British for Tilly-sur-Seulles. Two days earlier Dietrich had reported, " The last reserves of 1st SS Panzer Corps have been thrown in against tanks which have broken through at Longraye," west of Tilly, and he was able to close this gap only by filling the infantry line with sappers and signalmen, transport drivers and the crews of knocked-out tanks and guns. On the following day he protested to Rommel, " I am being bled white and am getting nowhere." When he was told that he must persist in the policy of counter-attacking every Allied gain, he demanded, " But with what? We need another eight or ten divisions in the next few days or we're finished!"[1] On the 20th, after the loss of Tilly, Dietrich warned Seventh Army, "If replacements do not come soon, the front cannot be held in the event of attack." The German situation was growing desperate, since no substantial reinforcements would become available for a week. If Montgomery could attack within this time, the rope would snap.

From the Allied side of the line, however, the extent of the German plight was not so evident, since the stubbornness of the defence gave it an appearance of far greater long-term strength than it really possessed. On the American sector the attempt to capture St. Lô had been most bloodily repulsed and Bradley had decided that it could not be renewed until his infantry and tanks had undergone a period of combined training for operations in the bocage. In the ten-day struggle for Tilly-sur-Seulles Panzer Lehr had fought with such skill and spirit that veterans in ' Fifty Div.' felt they were meeting a reincarnation of ' Ninety Light,' which they had fought so long in Africa.[2] After these slogging battles neither Dempsey nor Bradley had any divisions free for a major offensive action. There were certainly not the resources for a direct assault upon Caen, which was still powerfully held by 12th SS and 21st Panzer. On a semi-circular front of some 15 miles screening that city, these two divisions had 228 tanks and assault guns[3] backed by a formidable array of field and anti-tank guns, including more than 150 ' eighty-eights,' and by a brigade of heavy mortars. Accordingly, Montgomery planned to take Caen by envelopment, but this he could not do before the arrival of VIII British Corps (Lieut.-General Sir Richard O'Connor), for his plan required troops who were fresh and eager.

In pursuit of his declared intention " to pull the enemy on to Second Army so as to make it easier for First Army to expand and extend the quicker," Montgomery wanted O'Connor to cut through the German defences between Caen and Tilly, cross the Odon and the Orne and then establish his armour astride the Caen–Falaise road on the high ground between Bourguebus and Bretteville-sur-Laize. With VIII Corps there, Second Army would have outflanked and almost enveloped Caen, and would present a grave threat to Paris. That threat, Montgomery hoped, would draw in the German armour and keep it away from the St. Lô–Coutances area where the Americans were to make the main Allied effort. In preparation for this, and without waiting for the fall of Cherbourg, VIII U.S. Corps was to attack south from the flooded Douve valley, in order to gain sufficient room for Bradley to mount his break-out offensive.

[1] Canadian Army Interrogation.

[2] A captured ' Strength Return ' for June 25th, shows that by then Panzer Lehr had lost " 160 officers and 5,400 men," and that of the 190 tanks with which it had entered the battle only 66 were fit for action. The casualties inflicted, not the ground won, were the measure of the success of XXX Corps in the battle for Tilly.

[3] War Diary of Army Group B.

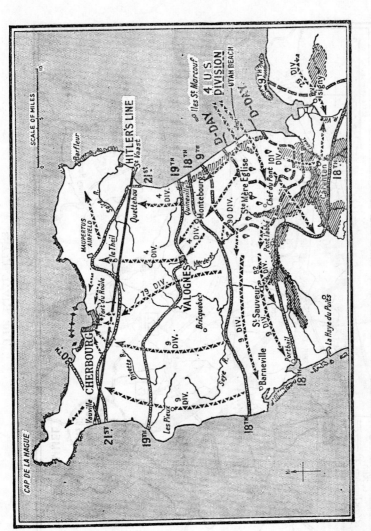

THE CHERBOURG CAMPAIGN

THE RIVAL PLANS

Montgomery had intended that the attack across the Odon should begin on the 18th, but on that day only one of O'Connor's three divisions was ashore, and Second Army had only meagre stocks of artillery ammunition beyond its 'bad weather reserve.' The ammunition situation had been a source of great anxiety since the start of the invasion, for the delays caused by the early bad weather had never been made good. The open beaches had proved extremely vulnerable and in the first four days the Americans had been able to unload less than a third of their planned tonnage of ammunition and stores. With the completion of the blockship shelters (known as GOOSEBERRIES) on D Plus 5, the rate of discharge improved, but the flow of supplies necessary to support large-scale offensive operations could not be reached until the MULBERRY harbours were working.

The first MULBERRY components had been towed across the Channel on D plus 1. A week later the outer floating breakwaters were in position and by June 18th most of the concrete caissons of the main breakwaters had been 'planted' and the floating piers were almost half finished. Both harbours were in use and the American unloading was now only 25 per cent behind schedule. Nevertheless, the slow turn-around of LSTs was still creating a most serious bottleneck. They were to have discharged their tanks and vehicles on to 'Rhino' ferries, but many of these proved unseaworthy and Ramsay had to order the LSTs to beach and dry out, even though this involved a delay of six hours until the next tide floated them off. But as soon as the MULBERRY piers were ready, an LST would be able to disgorge its 60 vehicles in 30 minutes, and this bottleneck would be broken.

The completion of these piers had been held up by the weather which had delayed the towing to Normandy of the seven miles of floating roadway, the least durable of the pre-fabricated parts. On June 17th, however, a friendly meteorological forecast encouraged Ramsay's H.Q. to dispatch on the following night more than two and a half miles of roadway, twenty-two sections instead of the usual five or six. In the early hours of June 19th these important links in the chain of supply were almost across the Channel when a gale sprang up, furious and unforecast. Every section was swallowed up by the storm within sight of the harbours, and this was only a fraction of the damage which wind and wave were to inflict upon the Allied cause in the next three days and nights. It seemed no coincidence that June 19th was D plus 13.

On the south coast of England convoys were driven back to port; in mid-Channel tows broke loose and were lost; off the beaches ships and craft dragged their anchors and were dashed ashore; beneath the turbulent waters dormant pressure mines were activated by the surge of the sea, and added to the losses caused by the storm. "By June 21st," Eisenhower subsequently reported,[1] "the MULBERRIES themselves began to disintegrate, particularly the U.S. installation, which was in an even

[1]Eisenhower, *Report*, p. 68.

more exposed position off St. Laurent than the British one at Arromanches. The Bombardons of the outer breakwaters broke adrift and sank; the Phoenix caissons shifted; and the angry seas poured through the gaps, pounding the ferry craft against the piers and smashing them to pieces. Only the blockships saved the situation from becoming one of complete disaster." Even as it was, the consequences were " so serious as to imperil our very foothold on the Continent."

The American MULBERRY was wrecked beyond repair and those parts of it which could be salvaged were used to make good the damage to the British harbour. Although the construction of the latter was not so far advanced, it suffered less, partly (as Eisenhower says) because it was less exposed, but primarily because it had been more slowly and more carefully assembled and ' planted.' But for the shelter which it provided, the loss of shipping would have been far more serious. When the storm abated 800 craft were stranded on the beaches and could not be floated off until the next spring tides in July. In the meantime there was an acute shortage of ferries, for the craft damaged or beached included nearly half the invaluable LCTs. In these three disastrous days the weather inflicted upon Allied shipping five times as much damage as the enemy had caused since D-Day.

The immediate result of the storm was to bring unloading virtually to a halt. The discharge of ammunition and stores had reached a peak of 24,412 tons on June 18th; on the 20th it was 4,560, and this was brought in almost entirely through the British MULBERRY at Arromanches. The impact of the gale upon operations ashore was direct and profound. The British attack across the Odon could not take place on the 22nd as planned, for neither the ammunition nor the men were available. When the weather broke, almost half O'Connor's troops were still in their ships, and there they had to stay until it cleared. The southward move of the Americans was also postponed, since Bradley was able to provide sufficient ammunition for operations against Cherbourg only by restricting expenditure on the rest of his front to one-third of the normal allowance, and by flying in some 1,500 tons. Before the storm abated the ammunition stocks of both the Allied armies were dangerously low.

This enforced lull in operations along the southern face of the bridgehead gave Rommel's tired and depleted divisions a respite in which to restore their defences. More important still, the storm allowed Rommel a second lease of life in Normandy, for it saved him from attack in the critical Caen–Tilly sector during the anxious week when he had no reserves whatever except the 2nd SS Panzer Division, which was west of St. Lô and not yet at full strength.

The destruction of the American MULBERRY gave added urgency to the campaign against Cherbourg, upon which VII U.S. Corps had been concentrating all its energies since the fall of Carentan and the firm junction of the two bridgeheads on June 12th. During the three preceding days Collins had expanded his foothold north to Montebourg and west across the Merderet River, thus forcing the first of the flood-belts behind which the Germans had sought to contain him. The enemy's line was already straining, and it must soon give way before the superior force which the Americans had amassed. Since D-Day both the airborne divisions had been reinforced with glider-infantry regiments and artillery, the 90th and 9th Divisions had been landed and the 79th was about to come ashore. The strength of Collins's corps had more than doubled, but the Germans had received virtually no reinforcements at all, and one of the three divisions which had been in the Peninsula at the outset, the 91st, had suffered 4,000 casualties in the first five days.[1]

Reserves from Brittany were still making their painful and arduous journey by bicycle and bus, foot and farm-cart along the much-bombed roads, and none were likely to arrive in time to stop the Americans from breaking out of their Cotentin bridgehead. In this situation Hitler's order of June 10th that " every man shall fight and fall where he stands " was an invitation to disaster. Yet this was not immediately apparent, for on the 12th and 13th the Germans had further defensive successes. Twice the 4th Division forced an entry into Montebourg, twice it was driven out; and the main American effort, the attack westward by the 90th Division with the object of cutting the Peninsula, made little headway.

On the morning of the 13th, however, Rommel's attention was distracted from this sector, for he discovered not only that 17th SS had failed to retake Carentan, but that seven miles to the west American troops had suddenly appeared south of the broad, flooded valley of the Douve and had built a bridge across it during the night. This move was regarded by Collins as a subsidiary operation, but to Rommel it seemed that the Americans were now trying to cut the Peninsula by a south-westerly thrust. Accordingly, early on the 14th, he gave orders that " everything is to be thrown into the gap . . . the neck must be kept open at all costs. " Every battalion the Germans could muster was committed on the Douve, but the new offensive which Collins launched that day was directed not south-west towards Lessay, but west to St. Sauveur le Vicomte.

Impatient at the slow progress of the 90th Division, which was in action for the first time, Collins had dismissed its commander and had leap-frogged through it the experienced 9th Division and the rest of the 82nd with orders to lose no time in reaching the west coast. This was typical of Collins's flexibility and drive, which were equally apparent in the way he suited his tactics to the terrain. The country through which this attack had to be made was bocage at its worst. The fields were smaller, the hedges thicker and the banks stouter than in most other

---

[1] Captured documents reveal that the 91st Division's strength was 10,555 on June 5th; 6,596 on June 10th.

parts of Normandy. It was difficult to deploy armour and almost impossible to get artillery observation. But this was no new experience for Collins. He had commanded an infantry division in the bitterly contested campaign which drove the Japanese from Guadalcanal in 1943. After jungle and coconut grove, the bocage seemed almost spacious. If some British commanders, schooled in the expanse of the African desert, felt tactically fettered when their tanks became road-bound, Collins was quite used to operating without benefit of roads or tanks. He had come to expect his infantry to advance through thick country relying almost entirely on the fire-power of the weapons they could carry themselves.

In the Cotentin Collins's answer to the bocage was to attack on very narrow fronts and to deliver a series of short, sharp thrusts astride two main roads. He had four regiments advancing in column of battalions, each regiment on a frontage of a thousand yards. He could afford to ignore his flanks, for the enemy had poor communications, small reserves and no tanks except obsolete French models manned by a training battalion. He drove his men hard in brief spells, relieving his leading battalions two or three times a day. In 48 hours the Americans advanced five miles and fought the enemy to a standstill.

On June 15th Dollmann reported to Rommel, " The situation now resembles a bow at breaking-point." Next morning the bow broke. The 82nd Division crossed the upper Douve at St. Sauveur and the 9th followed suit farther north, thus forcing the last natural defence line between the Americans and the coast.

By this time the German forces in the Peninsula had been organised into two battlegroups, named after their commanders, von Schlieben and Hellmich. The former, containing the 709th Division and part of the 77th, which had come up from Brittany, was charged with the defence of the direct route to Cherbourg. The latter, which included the remnants of the 91st and 243rd Divisions, had orders to stop the Americans reaching the west coast. But these two forces were split by the American advance and on the morning of the 16th Farmbacher, who had succeeded Marcks at 84th Corps, reported that Hellmich's Group was " completely exhausted both mentally and physically," and that " it can only be a matter of hours before resistance in this sector crumbles." No further reinforcement had arrived from Brittany and none was within call. It was thus impossible for a stand to be made at both Montebourg and St. Sauveur.

In these circumstances the only rational course for the Germans was to cut their losses and concentrate on the greater objective, the defence of Cherbourg, since the only purpose of continuing the campaign in the Cotentin was to deny the Allies the use of the port. But Farmbacher still had orders to " keep the neck open at all costs," and so he proposed

that von Schlieben should send his part of the 77th Division to aid
Hellmich and should start withdrawing the rest of his force at once
inside the short perimeter of the Cherbourg Fortress.

This course had no sooner been approved by Dollmann than an
order arrived from Hitler stating, " Movement towards Cherbourg is
forbidden; the present line must be held at all costs." But that line had
already been broken and a ' stand-fast ' order could serve only to make
a bad situation worse. This order, and the events which flowed from it,
faithfully recorded in the Seventh Army Telephone Log, provide a vivid
and typical example of Hitler's disastrous meddling in tactical matters
and its effect on his generals in the field. For the next twenty-four hours
the German commanders and staffs in France wrestled with the problem
posed by this order, trying to find an interpretation which would meet
the demands of the Führer and the needs of the situation.

Rommel, on the spot at the Battle H.Q. of 84th Corps, was inclined
to approve Farmbacher's plan, but from Berchtesgaden throughout the
afternoon there came reiterated injunctions against any retrograde
movement. When Farmbacher protested to Seventh Army that " the
Schlieben Group will have to move back on Cherbourg to avoid being
cut off," he was told, " According to the Führer's order, the Schlieben
group is to make a stand and then, if possible, break through." In other
words, it must commit military suicide at Montebourg, regardless of
the consequence—the exposing of Cherbourg to assault from another
quarter.

Telephoning to von Rundstedt that evening, Rommel protested
against this dangerous and stupid edict, and said:

If the Führer's order is interpreted literally, and all the forces in
the Peninsula remain in their present positions, then the enemy will
drive right on to Cherbourg along undefended roads behind our own
troops. . . . If we make a stand at our present line, without being able
to use mobile forces wherever they may be needed, the Cotentin will
be lost to us much more quickly than if we are allowed to operate
freely. It is essential that we should send something against the
Americans at St. Sauveur, otherwise there will be an immediate
collapse in the Cotentin, for there are no strong German forces either
in Cherbourg or south of the flooded areas.

Von Rundstedt agreed to refer the matter to Hitler again, but he
must have taken the view that in the meantime the Führer's order would
be treated as sacrosanct. In any case, the instructions which Rommel
issued immediately afterwards complied with it in spirit and letter. He
insisted that " there must be absolutely no question of a rearguard action;
on no account must the troops holding the present defences leave their
posts." The 77th Division was to send aid to Hellmich " to stop the
enemy forcing a way along the road [from St. Sauveur] to Cherbourg,"

but it was to move only reserves, not troops in the line. Since this division had no reserves, that part of the order was meaningless.

Twelve hours later, at 10.35 a.m. on the 17th, Seventh Army learned that the Führer had at last given partial recognition to the facts. His new order was: " The Fortress of Cherbourg must be held at all costs. Authorisation is given for the northern group [Schlieben] to make a fighting withdrawal under enemy pressure, but the action is not to be broken off."

This restored some tactical discretion to the commanders on the spot, but it still denied them the only course of action which offered any prospect of success—planned, orderly and immediate withdrawal inside the Cherbourg perimeter. Nor would Rommel connive at any liberal interpretation of the order. Von Schlieben must hold on until driven back, even though this would mean retreating with the enemy so close on his heels that there would be no chance of manning the Fortress defences in good order or good time.

Even this grant of limited freedom was begrudged by Hitler, and later in the day when he conferred again with his staff, he seemed inclined to re-impose his ' stand-fast ' order. When it was pointed out that there was no possibility of the existing positions being held, he shouted, " Very well then, if they won't hold there [meaning Monte-bourg], they must hold here," and, taking a red pencil, he slashed a line straight across the map from one side of the peninsula to the other just south of Cherbourg.[1]

With this enraged sweep of the hand, Hitler ensured Cherbourg's swift fall. Withdrawal, except under extreme pressure, was still forbidden but, if von Schlieben were forced back, then he must retreat no farther than the line " St. Vaast de la Hogue–Le Thiel–Vauville," which line, said the Führer in his favourite phrase, " must be held at all costs."

Thus von Schlieben was not to take up his final stand on the shortest and strongest line, the perimeter defences specially built to protect Cherbourg—the only line he had any chance of holding. When his force had been further weakened by prolonged defence of Montebourg, it was to be strung out across country on a 30-mile front as wide as the Peninsula, a front three times as broad as the sector to which he was now clinging only with the greatest difficulty. He was to treble his responsibilities without gaining any tactical or strategic advantage whatever.

The only satisfactory explanation of this preposterous order is that it came not from Hitler, the Supreme Commander, but from Hitler, the despot. He was venting upon his soldiers the fury of his own frustration, seeking to satisfy his craving for obedience, the visible proof of his exercise of that power which had once seemed boundless. Compared with this, the tactical needs of the local situation were of no account. He had

---

[1]This account is based on a personal interview with Major Friedl, who was liaison officer between OKW and the *Führerhauptquartier*, and one of the signatories of the armistice signed at Lüneburg in May 1945.

demanded that a line must be held; if not this line, then another line, some line, any line, just so long as his troops would obey and by their obedience prove that he, the Führer, still had the power to mould men and events to his will. But this was June 1944, not June 1940.

In Normandy von Rundstedt and Rommel bowed before this brain-storm and overrode the protests of their subordinates. In despair, or subservience, Rommel insisted upon literal compliance and gave no quarter to those who demurred. How submissive he was is apparent from the record of discussions between his H.Q. and Seventh Army that evening.

At ten minutes to ten Colonel Tempelhof, Rommel's *Ia* (Chief Operations Officer) rang his opposite number at Seventh Army, Colonel Helmdach. The conversation which ensued is recorded in the Telephone Log as follows:

*Tempelhof:* " The Naval Commander in Cherbourg has reported that General von Schlieben wishes to fall back on Cherbourg and has prepared the artillery on the west coast of the peninsula for demolition. . . . In no circumstances may this take place."

*Helmdach:* " But General von Schlieben was given a free hand this morning."

*Tempelhof:* " Only a delayed withdrawal was spoken of; not a wholesale retreat in one movement. Field-Marshal Rommel has ordered that only on his orders may the front be folded up and the two end-bulges[1] be relinquished."

*Helmdach:* " But if anything is to be held at all, the defender must attain his ultimate defensive line before the enemy has reached it."

*Tempelhof:* " The order is—to hold firm at all costs."[2]

At ten o'clock the burden of this conversation was passed on to 84th Corps, where Farmbacher, despite his earlier objections, was full of assurances that von Schlieben had " precise instructions in the spirit of the orders given." But at Rommel's H.Q. it was suspected that Farm-bacher was still lukewarm, and at 10.15 p.m. he was sacked.

After this drastic action, it must have been with some trepidation that Dollmann intervened an hour later and suggested to Rommel's Chief of Staff (Speidel) that perhaps the directive to von Schlieben might be framed to read that the line Hitler had indicated was " to be held as long as possible." Speidel's reply was brief and pointed. " That section of the directive," he declared, " was expressly decreed by the Führer himself. It cannot be changed." In that case, replied Dollmann, " the line will be broken through."

While the German commanders in the Cotentin were paralysed by

[1] I.e. the two promontories at the top of the Cotentin Peninsula on either side of Cherbourg.

[2] Seventh Army Telephone Log, June 17th, 2150 hours.

Hitler's Olympian edicts, the American 9th Division was driving hard for the west coast and on June 17th a six-mile advance brought it within sight of the sea. It had been able to maintain its progress only because of the speed with which Collins moved up fresh troops to cover its northern flank. The strength of this flank was tested on the night of the 17th–18th, when several columns of the Hellmich Group and the 77th Division tried to move into a blocking position between St. Sauveur and the west coast. The Germans thought that the roads were still clear, but the Americans arrested three of their military policemen and ambushed the columns which these M.Ps. were about to direct. Most of the German force was destroyed or dispersed but some twelve hundred men out of five or six thousand managed to slip through along the coast road before tanks and infantry of the 9th Division rode into Barneville early on June 18th, thus sealing off the base of the Peninsula.

Collins gave the Germans no chance to adjust themselves to the new situation. On the 18th, while the 9th Division was still moving westward, he regrouped in its wake so swiftly and smoothly that on the following morning he had three divisions—the 4th, 79th, and 9th—lined up ready to attack north, while the two airborne divisions and the 90th, now under VIII U.S. Corps, guarded the southern front along the inundations.

There was no hesitancy or humbug about ' Joe ' Collins. Enthusiastic, handsome, and looking far younger than his forty-eight years, he was known as ' the G.I.s' General.' He drove his commanders and his men hard and he had no compunction about removing those who failed him. His policy was to hit hard and keep the enemy on the run, but he was no ' smash-and-grab ' commander. Thorough in planning and flexible in direction, he was most adept at subtlety and surprise, quick to change his plan and seize a new opportunity, always ready to adapt his policy to the special needs of the terrain or the occasion.

Collins began his offensive northward with a surprise attack at Montebourg while enemy attention was still focused on the west coast. At 3 a.m. on June 19th, with no artillery preparation whatever, the 4th Division moved silently through the enemy's outpost line, and caught the Germans off guard and half asleep. By dawn they had overrun the defences on either side of Montebourg and had almost enveloped the town. By dark they had reached Valognes and had broken the enemy's main position. Heedless of the Führer's order, the Germans were in full retreat. West of Montebourg the opposition became progressively weaker, for the Germans there had thrown themselves into confusion by their abortive movement southward. That day the 9th Division advanced nearly 10 miles and by the following evening Collins's three divisions had reached the outer defences of Cherbourg and the other ' last stand ' positions which the Germans had taken up along Hitler's Line.

The fortifications of Cherbourg were formidable and had been specially strengthened against attack from the rear. But von Schlieben had not sufficient troops to man them effectively, because, in accordance with the Führer's order, nearly a third of his force was deployed outside the perimeter. He now felt most keenly the loss of those battalions which had ' broken out ' to the south, for he was left with the remnants of four battered divisions, plus an assortment of naval personnel and flak crews, marine gunners, and Todt workers from the V.1 sites: 21,000 men in all. Quoting that figure to Seventh Army, he added, " This doesn't mean anything, since the fighting ability can only be described as inferior, because of the shortage of officers and the inclusion of lower-grade troops who are capable of offering little resistance." Moreover, a fifth of his force were foreigners, and, as von Schlieben said later to his captors, " You can't expect Russians and Poles to fight for Germany against Americans in France."

According to one of his battalion commanders, Hoffman, " During the battle at Montebourg the men were completely worn out by the incessant naval bombardments and by air attacks. . . . The withdrawal to Cherbourg, which took place under extreme enemy pressure, drained the last ounce of their inner fortitude." By the time they reached the perimeter, " the units were too mixed up to allow a successful reorganisation in the time available. Even company commanders did not know how many men they had or where they were."[1]

The supply position was equally serious. During May the garrison of the Cotentin area had been almost doubled, but the Allied bombing of French railways had prevented any proportionate increase in the stocks of ammunition, fuel and food. It was June 16th, when the cutting of the Peninsula was imminent, before Seventh Army realised that the supplies in Cherbourg would not be sufficient for a prolonged siege. By then it was too late to make good the shortage. The German supply columns dared not use the roads by day and their very limited resources of motor transport could not carry the necessary quantities by night journeys alone. Because of this, the stocks of mortar and artillery ammunition stored in the Fortress had been drawn on to maintain the prolonged battle at Montebourg. The Luftwaffe tried to drop supplies by night, but at least one consignment landed on the Channel Islands, and others, according to Hoffman, contained " nothing but things which cannot be used."

On June 21st von Schlieben ignored a formal demand for surrender, but he can hardly have been encouraged by the report he received from Seventh Army Intelligence that six and a half American divisions were facing the Fortress. He had no means of telling that this estimate was 100 per cent wrong.

Collins paused for only a day and a half before launching his three divisions against the defences of the port, ignoring the rest of the extended German line which he watched with mechanised cavalry. The main Cherbourg defences were based on three ridges which commanded all lines of approach and had been heavily fortified. On the first day, June

[1]Seventh Army Telephone Log, June 24th, 1830 hours.

22nd, the Americans gained a foothold on each of these, but the defenders resisted most stubbornly and had to be blasted from every pillbox. The 79th in the centre made most progress and got to within two miles of the southern edge of the city by continuing its attack long after dark, but strong pockets still held out on its flanks.

Early in the afternoon of the 23rd von Schlieben reported to Seventh Army: " The enemy has broken through the land front and is advancing in four wedges. Hand-to-hand fighting is proceeding at some of our artillery positions and command posts. Positions which have not been destroyed are still holding out. Navy considers harbour has been destroyed for good."

This was a day of severe fighting and small but significant gains, especially on the left where the 9th Division advanced less than a mile but secured command of the south-western bastion, Mont du Roc. The Americans gradually crumbled the defences away, tackling the pillboxes one by one with a most effective technique. Dive-bombers and artillery drove the defenders in the outer entrenchments to seek the shelter of the concrete. Then the infantry, covered by a light bombardment, advanced rapidly until they were 300 to 400 yards from their objective. From there, machine-guns and anti-tanks guns directed intense fire into the embrasures while demolition squads worked round to the rear of the pillbox. Then they dashed in and blew down the steel door with ' beehives '[1] or ' bazookas,' thrust in pole-charges and phosphorus grenades and left the explosives and the choking smoke to do the rest. It was a slow process, but it was sure and comparatively inexpensive.

As the attack progressed, von Schlieben issued French weapons to clerks and cooks, sailors and signalmen and put them into the line to carry out the Führer's latest order that " the harbour and city must be defended to the last man." Hitler even demanded that reinforcements should try to get through from St. Malo by sea and was only dissuaded from making this sacrificial gesture when he learned that Cherbourg harbour was already sown with mines.

On June 24th, while von Schlieben was striving to bolster morale by handing out Iron Crosses dropped by parachute at his request, the 4th Division reached the coast three miles east of Cherbourg, but all attempts to penetrate into the city itself were thwarted. None came closer than the outskirts until the following day when the 4th and 9th Divisions worked along the coast from either flank. But in the centre, the 79th was involved all that day and the next in assaulting Fort du Roule, a massive stronghold on the crest of the precipitous bluff which towers above the city.

By the evening of the 26th all organised opposition in the city had collapsed and the Americans were swarming through the streets. Von Schlieben was captured in his underground H.Q., but refused to surrender the naval forts on the harbour mole or the chief surviving strongpoint, the Arsenal. As its massive walls could withstand almost any bombard-

[1] ' Beehives ' were special explosive charges that could be stuck on to their target.

ment, Collins next morning sent up a Psychological Warfare Unit with a sound truck. Before long the commander of the Arsenal, General Sattler, indicated through an emissary that he could not surrender to a verbal barrage, but, if the American tanks would fire a few rounds. . . . When this formality had been observed, Sattler and 400 men marched out, their honour satisfied and their bags packed ready for captivity. The harbour forts held out for another two days and the resistance of the German right wing, which had been driven back into the north-west corner of the Peninsula, continued until July 1st. By then the prisoners taken by VII Corps since D-Day numbered 39,042.[1]

Although the fall of Cherbourg was undoubtedly hastened by Hitler's intervention, its capture was a certainty from the moment Collins gained the lead in build-up. The foundation of his success was Eisenhower's determination to drop the two airborne divisions at the base of the Cotentin regardless of the risk. They provided Collins with an early advantage in strength and this was increased rapidly as other factors came into play. The maintenance of the threats to the Pas de Calais and Southern France governed the strategic distribution of German reserves in the West and limited the reinforcements that could be sent to Normandy; the Allied Air Forces—and, to a lesser extent, the Maquis —restricted severely the rate at which these reinforcements reached the front; and the British operations against Caen determined their tactical employment when at last they did arrive.

The German garrison in the Cotentin lay at the far end of this uncertain pipeline. Between D plus 1 and June 18th, when the Peninsula was cut, enemy reserves reaching Normandy were equivalent to nine divisions; of these only *one* was committed in the battle for Cherbourg and this (the 77th) was not at full strength. During this period the reinforcement of Collins was first priority in the Allied build-up plan, and he received thirty fresh battalions of infantry in twelve days while the Germans were strengthened to the extent of only six. Thus it became merely a matter of time before this superiority made itself felt. Hitler brought that time nearer, but this does not lessen the quality of the American achievement. As soon as the capture of Carentan freed his hand, Collins was ready. He never relaxed his pressure, and the speed with which he regrouped and changed direction after the 9th Division reached the west coast clinched the advantage that Hitler gave him.

The capture of Cherbourg in such a short time[2] was a considerable victory, even though the harbour was of little immediate value, and it

[1]As the Americans buried more than 4,000 German dead in the Cotentin, the enemy's total losses, including wounded, must have been well over 50,000. The American casualties amounted to less than half that number: 2,811 killed; 13,546 wounded; 5,744 missing or captured.

[2]The original COSSAC estimate that Cherbourg might be taken by D plus 8 was retained in SHAEF and 21st Army Group planning merely as a yardstick of maximum administrative needs. It became operationally unreal in May when the strength of the Cotentin garrison was almost doubled, and Bradley then reckoned that the port could not be taken before D plus 15.

had a profound psychological effect upon the German commanders in the West. Such faith as they had cherished had been based on the hope that at least they would be able to prevent the early capture of a port. Now they knew, as Rommel warned von Rundstedt, that the defences of their coastal fortresses were " not equal to the massed operations of the enemy air force and naval artillery. Even the strongest fortifications [at Cherbourg] were demolished section by section."[1]

With Cherbourg in Allied hands and the Normandy bridgehead thus consolidated almost beyond dispute, it seemed to von Rundstedt and Rommel that the stage was set for the second phase of the Allied plan, as they interpreted it—the landing north of the Seine. Their fears, and Hitler's, were fed by Allied deception and by their own Intelligence advisers, who were guilty of a staggering miscalculation. Before D-Day the German Naval Staff, astonishingly ignorant of the technique of amphibious operations, had warned Hitler that the Allies had sufficient shipping to land 25 divisions simultaneously.[2] Even the Wehrmacht commanders in the West expected that the invasion would be launched " on a front of 15 to 20 divisions."[3] Accordingly, when the Normandy landings were made with only six seaborne divisions, the Germans concluded that the rest of the armada was being held back for a second assault. This agreed with their assumption that the first landing would be a diversion, and it was supported by a gross overestimate of the number of divisions which Eisenhower still had in reserve.

By June 26th, when Cherbourg fell, there were 25 Allied divisions in the bridgehead, plus five independent armoured brigades which might have been mistaken for larger formations. In the United Kingdom there were 15 divisions awaiting shipment to Normandy, and half a dozen training divisions supplying reinforcements for the British Army on all fronts. Yet on this same day the best German Intelligence opinion was that " The enemy is employing 27 to 31 divisions in the bridgehead and a large number of G.H.Q. troops. . . . *In England another 67 major formations are standing to, of which 57 at the very least can be employed for a large-scale operation.*"[4]

The 42 non-existent divisions which German Intelligence placed in Eisenhower's reserve were the brain-children of British guile and German stupidity. Allied agents had had no difficulty in ' selling ' the Germans an absurdly inflated Anglo-American Order of Battle for, as already indicated, the Intelligence Branch at OKH had been eager to buy and in 1943 had even entered the business of manufacturing fictitious formations on its own account, so anxious was it to induce Hitler to take the threat of invasion seriously. Whatever their origin, these spurious

[1]Weekly Report of Army Group B, June 26th, 1944. (Tempelhof Papers.)
[2]Führer Conferences, Fragment 36, March 1944. (The exact date of this fragment is not known.)
[3]Minutes of Conference at H.Q., 84th Corps, May 11th, 1944.
[4]Weekly Report of Army Group B, June 26th, 1944. (Tempelhof Papers.) (The italics are mine. C.W.)

divisions clouded the judgment of the German High Command and helped to distort its strategy. When Cherbourg fell, there were more German divisions standing guard between the Seine and the Scheldt than there were engaging the Allies in Normandy.

On June 26th Rommel reported to von Rundstedt that all the evidence suggested that the Allies would soon make " a thrust from the area north and north-west of Caen towards Paris," in conjunction with " a large-scale landing between the Somme and Le Havre." In view of this double threat, he would have preferred to adjust his dispositions for defence, but such a course had already been vetoed by the Führer.

On June 17th Hitler had received the two Field-Marshals and their Chiefs of Staff at the specially-built Command Post at Margival near Soissons, from which he had intended personally to direct the invasion of England. There von Rundstedt warned Hitler that no successful offensive could be launched in the face of Allied air power and naval artillery, and Rommel expressed grave doubts of the Wehrmacht's ability even to contain the bridgehead unless the Luftwaffe could give greater protection to his supply lines, and unless he himself was allowed to conduct the battle in his own way. Rommel then proposed that they should gradually pull back to a new line, which would follow the strong natural barrier of the Orne as far south as Thury-Harcourt and then turn west through Mont Pinçon and the chain of heavily wooded hills that extended to the west coast near Granville. Along this line—still in the bocage but beyond the range of naval gunfire—the infantry might form a strong cordon and set the armour free to counter any break-out from the Normandy bridgehead or any fresh landing north of the Seine.

Blumentritt, who was present, says: " Hitler seemed to agree. He remained calm, but made no decision. To change the subject, he called for photographs of new types of aircraft and took charge of the talking. During the meal which followed, Hitler alone spoke and both Field-Marshals were disgruntled. After the meal, they tried to suggest a political solution—an approach to the West—but at this stage Hitler broke off the discussions brusquely."[1]

Later when the conversations were renewed Rommel again tried to make Hitler realise the necessity of coming to terms with the Western Allies. Hitler endeavoured to cut him short, but Rommel demanded, " My Führer, what do you really think of our chances of continuing the war? " Hardly able to suppress his anger, Hitler snapped back, " That is a question which is not your responsibility. You will have to leave that to me."[2]

Speidel says that in the course of the military discussions, " Rommel

[1] In reply to my written interrogation, August 19th, 1948. Speidel (op. cit., pp. 105-10) gives an account of this meeting which generally confirms that of Blumentritt.
[2] Jodl was evidently present during this discussion, for he quoted this interchange at Nuremberg on June 6th, 1946. (Nuremberg Trial Proceedings, Part xv, p. 354.)

did not mince his words in describing the inherent difficulties of the defence," and protested against the rigidity of the orders he had been receiving. Confronted with unpalatable facts, Hitler " took refuge in a strange mixture of cynicism and false intuition. . . . ' The V-weapons,' he said, ' would be decisive against Great Britain.' " He rejected a proposal that the V.1 offensive should be directed against the embarkation ports in England or against the bridgehead in Normandy and declared that the bombardment of London would " make it eager for peace."

Hitler may have believed this, but what happened after the Field-Marshals had left cannot have enhanced his confidence in the efficiency of his vaunted weapons of retaliation. An errant V.1 destined for London turned full circle and landed in the compound directly above the Führer's bunker. There were no casualties, but the incident so alarmed Hitler that he cancelled the visit he had agreed to make next day to Rommel's H.Q. for the purpose of hearing first-hand reports from front-line commanders.

Back at Berchtesgaden the Field-Marshals' suggestions smouldered in Hitler's mind. Their political solution he rejected out of hand, for he knew that, even if the Allies could be persuaded to compromise, they would certainly insist upon his own downfall and the destruction of the entire Nazi régime. He was now fighting not for Germany, nor even for the Party, but for himself. Nor would he allow his commanders in the field any operational discretion, since he believed more firmly than ever that only his nerve and will-power were strong enough to prevent disaster. Their ' mobile defence ' was nothing but a disguise for ' wanton retreat.' He would not even countenance a containing action, for nothing less than the annihilation of the invaders would give him the freedom to turn against the Red Army in strength.

On June 20th he ordered Rommel to launch another offensive immediately upon the arrival of the SS panzer divisions which were en route for Normandy. Where the Wehrmacht had failed, the SS—the *élite* Prætorian Guard—would succeed. So the Führer hoped. The Army might betray him, but the Party would show that his plans could be fulfilled. It was only a matter of faith and fortitude. The place to strike was between Caumont and St. Lô before the Americans could reinforce this sector with divisions from the Cotentin. The spearhead would be 2nd SS Panzer Corps (9th and 10th SS) which had been recalled from Poland. It would be reinforced by two other SS panzer divisions, the 2nd, now in reserve at St. Lô, and the 1st, which was coming from Belgium. Such a panzer phalanx could cleave a corridor to Bayeux and the coast, isolate the British and ' Dunkirk ' them. A repetition of that disaster, combined with the devastation caused by the V.1 and the threat of worse to come with the V.2, would soon make the British realise the futility of challenging Nazi Germany on the Continent.

Rommel accepted this edict for, if an offensive had to be launched, this plan[1] offered the best prospect of success. He did not believe that it could fulfil the Führer's extravagant hopes, but it might inflict upon the Allies a setback which would at least gain time, whatever the long-term consequences. But whether Hitler's order could be carried out depended not so much on Rommel as on Montgomery.

[1]At Margival Rommel had suggested such an offensive, but in his plan the essential prerequisite was that the German right flank should be withdrawn to the Orne and Mont Pinçon, so that the panzer divisions might be relieved and concentrated.

CHAPTER XVIII

# CAEN THE CRUCIBLE

FROM the walls of Montgomery's caravan at his Tactical H.Q. in Normandy photographic portraits of von Rundstedt and Rommel looked down upon the man who was planning their defeat. As he dwelt in solitude upon the development of the campaign and of his own plan, Montgomery studied the faces of the dispassionate Prussian and the volatile Württemberger whom he wished to subject to his will. He sought to project himself into their minds, to see the battle as they saw it and to gauge their reactions. He was determined to conduct his own operations in such a way that he could force his opponents into courses of action which would appear to them to provide logical and intelligent counter-strokes, but which would in fact contribute to their own undoing. This determination was the basis of his plan for threatening to break out with the British at Caen, while actually preparing to make his decisive effort with the Americans at St. Lô.

"This general plan," says Montgomery, "was given out by me to the General Officers of the field armies in London on the 7th April, 1944."[1] On the other hand, it has been suggested by Eisenhower and his Chief of Staff, Bedell Smith—as well as by other Americans less directly informed—that this plan was only devised following the failure of the British at Caen, some two weeks after D-Day. By then, to quote Bedell Smith, "changes were needed in the original tactical plan," because "the massing of opposition against our eastern flank made a break-out at that end of the line improbable."[2] When this became apparent, "our plans," says Eisenhower in his Report to the Combined Chiefs of Staff, "were sufficiently flexible that we could take advantage of this enemy reaction by directing that the American forces smash out of the lodgement area in the west, while the British and Canadians kept the Germans occupied in the east."[3]

Who is right? Was it ever intended, as Eisenhower states in his

[1] Dispatch to Secretary of State for War, June 1st, 1946.
[2] "Eisenhower's Six Great Decisions," No. 2, by Lieut.-General Walter Bedell Smith, *Saturday Evening Post*, June 15th, 1946.
[3] Eisenhower, *Report*, p. 41.

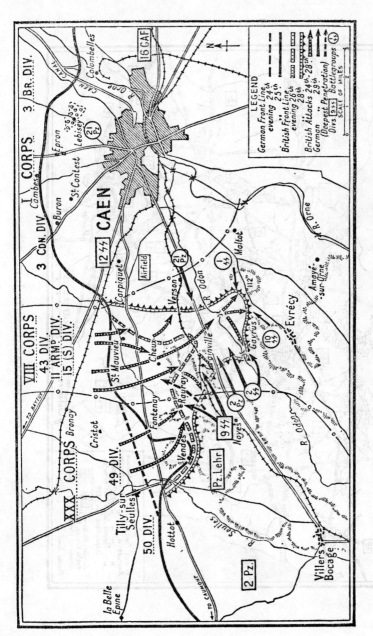

THE ODON OFFENSIVE, JUNE 25TH–29TH

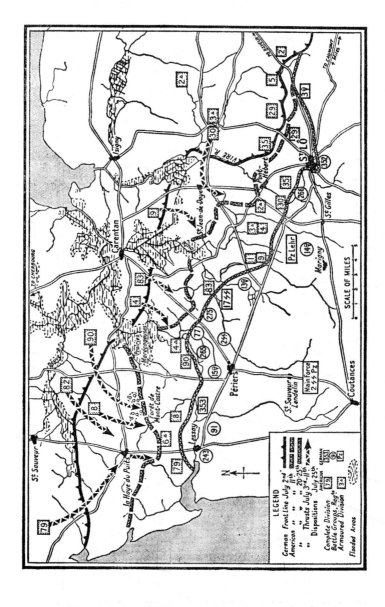

THE AMERICAN FRONT, JULY 3RD-25TH

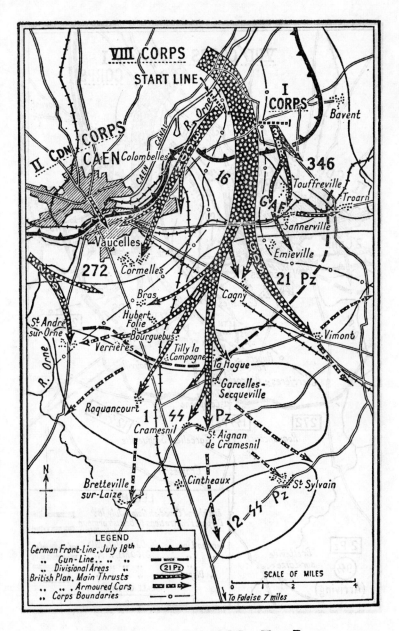

OPERATION GOODWOOD: THE PLAN

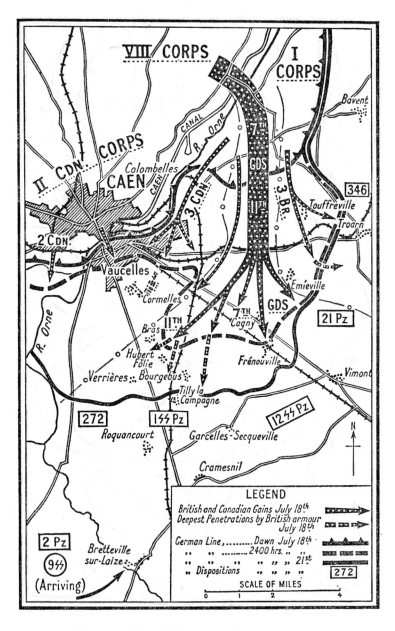

OPERATION GOODWOOD: THE BATTLE, JULY 18TH-22ND

Report, that the British should " break out towards the Seine "? Did Dempsey fail at Caen? Was Montgomery forced to change his plan? The answers must be sought, not in post-war dispatches and reflections, but in the orders and declarations issued by Montgomery before D-Day and during the first few weeks ashore.

In his survey of April 7th, two months before D-Day, Montgomery defined the British role in these words: " Second Army is to assault west of the River Orne and to develop operations to the south and south-east in order to secure airfield sites and to protect the eastern flank of First U.S. Army while the latter is capturing Cherbourg. In its subsequent operations the Second Army will pivot on its left and offer a strong front against enemy movement towards the lodgement area from the east." Commenting on the implications of this role, Montgomery added, " The administrative problem facing the United States forces is entirely different from that of the British. The operational plan envisages the British forces remaining in reasonable proximity to their advanced base, whereas the United States forces have first to make a rapid move to Cherbourg and then turn south to capture Nantes and the Loire ports."[1]

As Montgomery saw it, the assault upon the beaches would give him merely a foothold on the doorstep of France. He must still force the door —either by breaking it away at the hinge near Caen, or by hacking it down, or else by swinging it open through the scientific application of weight near the west coast of Normandy, which formed the jamb. He rejected the head-on assault which the first of these courses implied and the battle of attrition involved in the second. He chose the third, but he foresaw the danger that the Germans might provide a counter-weight, unless they could be induced to deploy the bulk of their strength close to the hinge while the main Allied pressure was being exerted against the outer edge. There he would not only gain the greatest purchase but, once the door was ajar, mobile forces could pour through the gap and sweep round to take in the rear those Germans who still had their shoulders to the door close to the hinge, and dare not let go for fear of being crushed if it were to swing violently back.

This plan for the development of the campaign was ' pure Montgomery ' and was radically different from what had been accepted before he took charge of the assault armies. The COSSAC planners, impressed by the difficulties of an offensive through the hilly bocage west of the Orne, had envisaged that the break-out should be made by the British into the Caen–Falaise plain. They had proposed that by the time the Americans reached Avranches and Domfront, the British and Canadians should have advanced to the line Trouville–Lisieux–Alençon. Montgomery considered that this plan carried the early development of the

---

[1]This extract is taken from the notes which Montgomery used when he spoke at this meeting. His plan did not require Second Army to take even Falaise until the Americans had reached the line Avranches–Domfront and were about to burst forth into Brittany and the Loire Valley.

bridgehead twenty to thirty miles too far eastwards. Accordingly, he re-drew the phase-line in question to run Avranches–Domfront–West of Falaise–Argences–Cabourg, thus deliberately disclaiming any intention of breaking out or even of gaining substantial ground on the eastern flank.

Nevertheless, the idea that this was—or should be—the intention was sedulously kept alive at SHAEF by Morgan (COSSAC himself) for, as Deputy Chief of Staff, he was well placed to continue the advocacy of his rejected plan. Morgan's admiration for Eisenhower (he was fond of saying, " There was a man sent from God and his name was Ike ") was matched only by his antipathy towards Montgomery. He regarded the ' pulling-in of the left flank ' as an example of what he called ' Montgomery's incurable defensive-mindedness ' and he harped on this theme at every opportunity.

Because of his paternal association with the original plan, Morgan was regarded at SHAEF as *the* expert on the operation, and he found a fellow-advocate of the ' break-out at Caen ' theory in the Deputy Supreme Commander. Tedder bore Montgomery no personal animosity, but he shared both Morgan's conviction that Montgomery was too cautious, and Leigh-Mallory's concern about the importance of gaining the airfield sites south-east of Caen. With the two senior British officers at SHAEF thinking along these lines, it is not surprising that Eisenhower and Bedell Smith came to consider that Caen was the proper place for the major offensive. From that, it was a short step to the belief that this was in fact what Montgomery intended.

Eisenhower accepted this view the more readily because it fitted into his own conception of war. His military thinking, like that of most American commanders, was essentially straightforward and aggressive, so much so that it might almost have been expressed in the simple formula, ' Everybody attacks all the time.'[1] He was uneasy if any substantial part of his force was not gaining ground. Like Marshall, he was an advocate of the direct approach and the straight punch. His faith lay in the sheer smashing power of superior force. The acquiring of that superiority was to him primarily a matter of logistics, of amassing resources of such magnitude that the enemy's counter-measures could be disregarded. When Caen was still untaken by the middle of June, Eisenhower feared that, because the rate of build-up seemed unlikely to provide this absolute superiority, there was grave danger of the Allies being locked in the bridgehead. His solution was to keep the Germans tactically unsettled by repeated attacks all along the front, thus gradually thinning and stretching their line until at last it would snap.

This policy of attrition was the antithesis of Montgomery's approach.

[1] Writing of the period in September, immediately after Eisenhower assumed direct command of the field armies, Bedell Smith says: " The Supreme Commander insisted on constant aggressive action everywhere." (*Saturday Evening Post*, June 22nd, 1946.) This was characteristic of Eisenhower's approach in Normandy also.

He was an equally firm believer in the employment of superior power; indeed he had become notorious for his refusal to commit his troops to the offensive without it. But he differed from Eisenhower about the method by which that superiority should be gained, and about the manner in which it should be employed. Montgomery's inclination was to manœuvre the Germans out of position and off-balance by compelling them either to disperse their forces defensively, or, better still, to concentrate them in the wrong place. The latter course involved the risk that they might use this concentration to disrupt his plan, unless an absolutely sound defence was maintained in any sector which they could threaten. It meant too that he must always hold sufficient strength there to keep the enemy unbalanced. Having gained the necessary relative superiority, his intention was to employ it not for a broad-fronted offensive, but for one concentrated blow; to cut the cordon, not to stretch it; to cut it with such force and momentum that there could be no question of the enemy's recovering and forming another line.

Montgomery was more concerned to make the Germans strategically unbalanced than to keep them tactically unsettled. What ground the Germans held, or how thoroughly they were dug in, was less important to him than the over-all disposition of their forces. He was not interested in driving them back to the Seine. He was determined to envelop them and destroy them in Normandy so that they should not be able to oppose his march into Germany.[1]

In pursuit of his main strategic purpose Montgomery never wavered, but he did modify and change the means by which he sought to achieve it. After the war, however, over-anxious to defend himself against American criticism, he asserted that " the operations developed in June, July and August exactly as planned." In making this claim, Montgomery does himself less than justice, for his real genius as a commander was shown in the way he varied his day to day policy to meet the unpredictable situations caused by bad weather, by Hitler's suicidal policy of fighting for every yard, and by tactical failure or slowness on the part of both British and American troops.

At the start of the invasion, Montgomery had believed that Second Army, in order to fulfil its role of ' protecting and threatening,' would have to secure the area south-east of Caen at the outset. In the first week, however, when Rommel had to commit his panzer divisions defensively, the capture of the Caen area became more difficult, but also less necessary, for the German armour was already pinned and contained there. Thus, although Montgomery on June 8th had ordered Dempsey

---

[1]It is surprising that Eisenhower did not appreciate Montgomery's purpose, for he was planning to carry out deliberately the strategic manœuvre which had unconsciously brought about the Union victory in the American Civil War. He intended to do to the Germans what Sherman had done to the Confederate Army in his march through Georgia in 1864. Perhaps the explanation is that in American military thinking the view still prevails that the decisive operation of the Civil War was fought not by Sherman but by Grant, the apostle of direct approach.

" to develop operations with all possible speed for the capture of Caen," he quickly modified this order when he saw that its fulfilment was likely to exhaust Dempsey's immediate resources. Montgomery was still anxious to get Caen, but not at the cost of so weakening Second Army that it would lose the power to maintain the threat to Paris.

In these circumstances, the only reason for hastening the capture of the ground south-east of Caen was to secure sites for more airfields. Upon this question Montgomery and the air commanders had never seen eye to eye. At a planning conference long before D-Day, Leigh-Mallory had urged most strongly that " Second Army should push east at an earlier stage than is envisaged in the present forecast of operations." De Guingand, replying on Montgomery's behalf, said, " The C.-in C. is not prepared to commit himself on this point as he has in mind the possibility that the enemy might concentrate his forces on this flank."[1]

The conversion of this possibility into a reality in the first week of the invasion brought about prematurely the strategic situation which Montgomery's plan required, and made it difficult, if not impossible, for him to meet Leigh-Mallory's request that Second Army should secure the Caen airfield zone without delay. Montgomery considered that from bases in England and from the fifteen airfields which would be operational in Normandy by June 21st the Tactical Air Forces could meet the Army's immediate requirements for protection and support. The scale of effort might not be quite as great as Leigh-Mallory had hoped, but then the Luftwaffe was far less active than had been feared. To Montgomery the Caen airfields were means, not ends. From the viewpoint of the land operations, the need for greater air support was not so pressing that he was prepared to distort his whole strategy in order to secure it.

This view was rejected and resented by Leigh-Mallory and by the Commander of the Second British Tactical Air Force, Air Marshal Sir Arthur Coningham. They tended to present their claims for more airfields almost as demands of right which Montgomery should be obliged to fulfil. This attitude sprang from a genuine eagerness to play their full part in the battle, but there were other factors involved. In spite of its own matchless achievements, the R.A.F. still suffered from a ' junior service ' complex, and was forever eager to assert its right to equality and independence. Accordingly, Montgomery's attitude to the Caen airfields was regarded by Coningham and other airmen as a further example of the Army's tendency to regard the Air Force as an ' auxiliary arm.'

This friction was accentuated by the personal conflict between Montgomery and Coningham. At Alamein they had worked in close association at a joint Army/Air H.Q., but this ' honeymoon ' had ended during the advance to Tripoli. Because the nature of the campaign made it necessary for him to be well forward at his Tactical H.Q. Montgomery left it largely to his staff to deal with the Air Force. Thus

[1]Minutes of Planning Meeting at H.Q. 21st Army Group, March 20th, 1944.

he appeared to treat the air commanders (Coningham and later Broadhurst)[1] as advisers, not equals. It was his battle. They were supporting him. This was resented, and so was the personal publicity which he deliberately courted as a means of enhancing the pride of the Eighth Army in itself. This resentment had grown more bitter after Montgomery's return to England in 1944. It was he who was publicly fêted and idolised, not Coningham. Public acclaim was directed almost entirely at the Eighth Army and its aggressive commander. There was little but a passing round of applause for Coningham and the Desert Air Force. The headlines stung. Speaking to war correspondents one day, Coningham burst out, " It's always ' Monty's Army,' ' Monty's Victory,' ' Monty Strikes Again.' You never say ' Coningham's Air Force.' "

Knowing how sensitive Coningham was, Montgomery would have been wise to humour him by due consultation. Instead, however, as soon as the broad plan had been settled, Montgomery went off on a ' morale-raising ' tour of camps and factories (a tour which the Air Force regarded as a personal publicity stunt), and nearly all the detailed negotiations with the airmen were handled by de Guingand, his Chief of Staff. Montgomery seldom attended conferences, and when he did deal direct with the Air Force, he turned to Leigh-Mallory. This was strictly correct, but it was tactless and it would have prejudiced the formulation of a joint plan, if de Guingand had not been so popular personally and so skilful in negotiation. Montgomery would have been a much more successful commander if he had spent as much effort in enlisting the co-operation of the Air Force as he did in winning the loyalty of his troops and the acclaim of the public.

These petty clashes of personality could be ignored if they had not impinged upon operations in Normandy. Coningham saw himself as an ' air general,' who would mould the shape of the land battle if only he was given the opportunity, and he regarded the failure to take the Caen airfield zone as a denial of his opportunity. Thus there persisted in Air Force circles and at SHAEF a powerful ' lobby ' which favoured the break-out at Caen policy, and which embarrassed Montgomery since it threatened to undermine his plan of campaign.

On the evening of June 23rd Hausser, commanding 2nd SS Panzer Corps, reported to Dollmann, the commander of Seventh Army. The two formidable divisions, 9th and 10th SS, with which he had halted the Red Army's offensive at Tarnopol in April, were back in France with orders from the Führer to drive the British into the sea. Their first trains, said Hausser, had left Poland on June 12th. Four days later they had reached Lorraine, but there they had stopped, because the lines farther

[1]Air Vice-Marshal Harry Broadhurst succeeded Coningham in command of the Desert Air Force and later commanded 83 Group, R.A.F., in Normandy.

west were too badly damaged to handle heavy traffic. The two divisions were now making a laborious 400-mile journey to Normandy by road, and they would not reach their assembly area around Alençon before the 25th. This was disturbing, for Dollmann knew that the lull imposed by the storm could not last much longer. The British were about to attack in the Caen sector and he had no reserves save those which Hitler had earmarked for the counter-stroke to Bayeux.

Time was running against Dollmann even faster than he feared. Allied Intelligence was already aware that 1st SS had passed through Paris, that 2nd SS had reached St. Lô, and that Hausser's Corps had detrained at Nancy and Bar-le-Duc and was moving by road. The weather might blind reconnaissance aircraft, but the Resistance and special Allied agents were watching every route to Normandy. Their reports left little doubt that Rommel was accumulating a substantial striking force. The smooth development of Montgomery's strategy demanded that Dempsey should draw this force into battle at Caen before Bradley attacked south from the base of the Cotentin at the end of the month. Consequently, although the weather was still unfriendly and the build-up of ammunition was five days behind schedule, the start of the Second Army offensive west of Caen was fixed for June 26th.

The plan was that VIII British Corps (O'Connor) should make the main thrust midway between Tilly and Caen. The 15th Scottish Division was to seize a bridgehead across the Odon and create a firm base on the broad ridge between that river and the Orne. Then, while the 43rd Division helped the Scotsmen to consolidate their gains, the 11th Armoured Division would attack south-east, cross the Orne and establish itself astride the Caen–Falaise road on the high ground between Bretteville-sur-Laize and Bourguebus. When Caen was thus threatened with envelopment, I Corps was to intensify the squeeze by taking Carpiquet airfield, west of the city, and by thrusting south from the ' airborne bridgehead' east of the Orne. In preparation for O'Connor's attack, the 49th Division (of XXX Corps) was to capture Rauray ridge on the previous day, and thus protect the right flank of 15th Scottish. Having taken Rauray, XXX Corps was to exploit southwards through Noyers to Aunay-sur-Odon.

The start was inauspicious. Delayed by a thick ground mist, the 49th Division was still a mile short of Rauray on the evening of June 25th. Heavy rain came during the night and before dawn O'Connor learned that the air forces based on Britain were grounded by bad weather. There would be no bombing to neutralise enemy strongholds on his left flank. Nevertheless the order to attack was confirmed, for if Rommel was to be forestalled, Montgomery could not afford to wait even another day.

Two hours after dawn on the 26th the 15th Scottish Division, with the 31st Armoured Brigade, moved into their first battle under a leaden and threatening sky. Ahead of them the barrage rolled across sodden cornfields and dripping hedges. A minefield checked the tanks but the infantry tramped stolidly on across the Caen–Tilly road and fought their way into the string of hamlets around Cheux, from which a mobile column of the 11th Armoured Division was to make a dash for the Odon bridges. Mines on the outskirts of Cheux, plus mortar-fire and wreckage in the village, delayed the armour, and gave the Germans a chance to recover from the bombardment. Southwards from Cheux the undulating fields were swept by fire from Rauray and from the villages and woods along the north bank of the Odon. The troops of 12th SS, who were holding this sector, fought with a tenacity and a ferocity seldom equalled and never excelled during the whole campaign. The armour was soon halted, and in the middle of the afternoon the reserve brigade of 15th Scottish went through to clear the way to the Odon. This attack started in the midst of a torrential downpour, and the routes through the minefield were soon troughs of mud which reduced the forward movement of supporting arms to a crawl. The right wing of the new attack was checked by opposition from Rauray, but on the left the Scotsmen splashed on to reach the Caen–Villers-Bocage railway at Colleville, some four miles south of the morning's start-line and one mile from the Odon.

This was the limit of the day's progress, but it was more than enough to set Dietrich clamouring for support. That evening he reported to Dollmann, " If further reinforcements are not sent up to-night a break-through on both sides of Cheux cannot be prevented." Two battalions of 1st SS had been promised to him, but they were immobilised near Thury Harcourt without fuel. On the 25th Dietrich had asked for help from 2nd SS Panzer Corps, but Rommel had insisted that its divisions must move that night to their concentration area south-west of Caumont in preparation for his great offensive to Bayeux. Now that the British onslaught had gathered momentum, Rommel relented. On the evening of the 26th he gave orders that " everything which can be assembled by General Hausser must be thrown into the fight."[1] Hausser's own troops were not to be committed, but the panzer divisions on the flanks of the break-through (the 2nd and 21st) must each furnish a tank battalion; 2nd SS would send a battlegroup from St. Lô and the two brigades of multiple-mortars would be switched from the American sector and from east of the Orne to provide supporting fire.

By the morning of June 27th, however, the German command, surprised that there had been no further British attack during the night, was congratulating itself on having gained " a good defensive victory." Dietrich reported that he was making " a counter-attack with 80 tanks

[1]Seventh Army Telephone Log, June 26th, 2100 hours. The records of Rommel's H.Q. show that the tank strength of 1st SS Panzer Corps on June 26th (in actual ' runners ' ready for action) was 114 Panthers and 200 Mark IVs. Since D-Day the panzer divisions engaged against the British had ' lost ' 232 tanks destroyed or put out of action. No panzer division had yet been engaged against the Americans.

in the direction of Cheux," and so Hausser was ordered not to move north of Aunay, and to be ready to carry out the original Bayeux plan. The Germans were premature in their optimism. Their armoured counter-attack, disorganised by heavy shelling, broke on the anti-tank screen which flanked the Scottish salient; it did not even prevent the 49th from capturing Rauray, nor did it distract O'Connor from his assault across the Odon. A bridge was captured intact, and by the morning of the 28th the main strength of the 11th Armoured Division was over the river and its tanks were probing southwards.

This advance created fresh consternation at Seventh Army H.Q. and early on the 28th the order went out that " 2nd SS Panzer Corps must move immediately to clean up the enemy penetrations south of Cheux." As only 9th SS had reached the forward area, Hausser proposed that he should fight a containing action during the next two days, while he assembled a force powerful enough to cut the British corridor by an attack from either flank. But Dollmann did not dare to wait. He was already panic-stricken, for Hitler had ordered a court-martial inquiry into the fall of Cherbourg and the verdict was not difficult to forecast. Overcome by anxiety, Dollmann collapsed and later that morning he died.[1] This created a command crisis, since von Rundstedt and Rommel by this time were on their way to Berchtesgaden for a conference with Hitler. Thus the German forces in Normandy were bereft of their three senior commanders just when they were most in need of strong and authoritative direction. There was no one there to countermand Dollmann's dying order that Hausser must strike without delay.

Hausser's endeavour to obey was frustrated by the British, who kept attacking to widen and deepen their corridor. South of the Odon a battalion of 15th Scottish captured a second bridge intact, but all attempts to link up with it from the north failed. The Germans gained some minor successes with local counter-attacks; yet they were not able to make any major riposte, even though elements of six panzer divisions were committed to battle during the day. By the evening Dempsey knew that the Germans had begun to dip into their strategic reserves, for both the 1st and 2nd SS Divisions had been identified. Moreover, Allied reconnaissance aircraft reported that on almost every road leading to the Odon Valley, motorised columns had been braving the daylight, protected far more heavily than usual by flak and fighters.

In these circumstances, Dempsey decided that O'Connor should not attempt to cross the Orne until he had consolidated his position north of the Odon. There the corridor was no more than a mile and a half wide and the only road by which he could supply the Odon bridgehead was under steady fire. The western flank was clearly the most vulnerable sector, for the ridge which ran past Rauray to Cheux provided a natural

---

[1]There is no suggestion from the German side that Dollmann committed suicide. His Chief of Staff, Pemsel, says he " died of heart failure in his bathroom."

approach. Here, therefore, O'Connor deployed his anti-tank guns, tanks and artillery in depth and awaited the German onslaught.

Hausser intended to begin with a holding attack against the Odon bridgehead by 10th SS (reinforced by a regiment of 1st SS); then, as soon as this diversion was under way, he would launch his main assault against the western flank of the salient, using the equivalent of two SS panzer divisions. This force would attack along the ridge to Cheux and link up with a subsidiary thrust from the east. In view of the narrowness of the corridor, there was a chance that this plan might succeed, if only the cloudy weather would continue. But dull or bright, the attack had to be launched early on June 29th. That was Hitler's order.

The fateful morning was fine and the R.A.F. was in action early. Before 10 o'clock Hausser was reporting, " The offensive cannot begin until the afternoon. Our concentrations are under continual artillery and air bombardment." But the afternoon brought no respite: " 1340 hours. The enemy is causing heavy losses by fighter-bomber attacks . . . the panzer divisions cannot bring up all their tanks owing to lack of fuel." It was 2.30 p.m. before the attack on the Odon bridgehead could begin, and by then it was too late. During the morning the 11th Armoured Division had gained possession of Hill 112, midway between the Odon and the Orne, and from this vantage point heavy and accurate shellfire was directed against all enemy movement. Even as a diversion this German attack miscarried, for on Rauray ridge that afternoon an officer of 9th SS was taken prisoner complete with a map and notebook which set out Hausser's plan. Thus forewarned, 15th Scottish was braced to meet the assault which materialised at six o'clock, but it came in with only half the planned strength, for artillery fire had disorganised the remainder. During the battle which raged from copse to hedgerow throughout the evening half a dozen tanks penetrated almost to Cheux, but the Scottish battalions stood firm and the German infantry which sought to follow the armour was driven back. Before dark the SS troops had been routed and the lonely tanks had been destroyed. Throughout the night the British gunners continued to shell the woods and villages in which the Germans were attempting to reassemble for a fresh move.

This shelling was so effective that no attack developed against the corridor during the 30th, but the Germans kept it under heavy fire, especially from mortars, and directed their offensive energies against the Odon bridgehead. There they were able to regain Hill 112 and the village of Gavrus, for the British armour had been withdrawn into reserve north of the Odon on Dempsey's order. But that evening Hausser (now in command of Seventh Army) acknowledged defeat when he told Rommel's H.Q., " The counter-offensive by 1st and 2nd SS Panzer Corps has had to be temporarily suspended in the face of intensive enemy artillery fire and supporting fire of unprecedented ferocity from naval units. . . . The tenacious enemy resistance will prevent our counter-offensive from having any appreciable effect."

Hausser, therefore, proposed that he should withdraw from Caen in order to " husband the resources of the panzer divisions and create a defensive line commensurate with our infantry strength." At midnight on June 30th Speidel telephoned to say that the evacuation of Caen would be ordered " as soon as authorisation is received from the Supreme Command." But the hope of obtaining any such authorisation had been scotched twenty-four hours earlier when Hitler ' conferred ' with von Rundstedt and Rommel.

At Berchtesgaden on June 29th, Rommel had proposed to Hitler that Seventh Army should fight a rearguard action back to the Seine, and that the armies in Southern France should be withdrawn to help create a new line along the Seine and across to Switzerland. The latest British offensive had been stopped only by committing his entire strategic reserve. If the Wehrmacht did not begin to withdraw from Normandy immediately, Seventh Army would be destroyed and Fifteenth Army would be powerless to repulse any second landing.

Neither fact nor logic could prevail upon Hitler. He admitted that " the overpowering aerial superiority of the enemy and his very effective naval artillery limit the possibilities of a large-scale attack on our part," but he still spoke hopefully of another offensive (" dependent on when troops and supplies can be brought up "). He would not hear of any withdrawal, not even of tactical adjustments of the line for better defence. He appeared to be encouraged by the outcome of the Odon Battle, regarding it as proof that the Allies could be prevented from breaking out. " We must not allow mobile warfare to develop," said Hitler, " since the enemy surpasses us by far in mobility. . . . Therefore every-thing depends on our confining him to his bridgehead, by building up a front to block him off, and then on fighting a war of attrition to wear him down and force him back."[1]

He proclaimed that he would outstrip the Allied build-up and win the battle of supply. Doenitz and Goering must intensify their attacks on Allied shipping " with every possible weapon." They must lay " more mines and still more mines in the Bay of the Seine with the tenacity of a bulldog." Seventh Army would be supplied by means of " several strong anti-aircraft highways, protected by a large number of flak emplacements and covered by fighter patrols." As usual Hitler's plans outran his resources. Doenitz replied that in the Channel area he had only twelve E-boats and eight *Schnorkel*-equipped U-boats. Sperrle, commanding Air Fleet III, pointed out that he would need " an additional 1,200 to 1,400 fighters" if the supply routes were to be

[1]Führer Naval Conferences, June 29th–30th, 1944. Doenitz was present at the latter part of this conference and recorded Hitler's views.

adequately protected. (The total day-fighter strength of the Luftwaffe on all fronts was only 1,523, and one-third of these were already in France.) Nevertheless, Hitler upheld his plan with promises about miraculous weapons and gave the customary injunction to " hold out in all circumstances."

The two Field-Marshals, says Blumentritt, returned to France " angry and disgruntled," but committed to a policy of aggressive and unyielding defence, the futility of which was made more than ever apparent on the very day of their return. On July 1st the Allied Air Forces were weather-bound. That day Hausser made one last attempt to cut off the Odon salient by a thrust from the west. His assault, by elements of four SS panzer divisions, was heavy and sustained, but it was broken by the stout resistance of 15th Scottish and the 49th, and by artillery fire which almost made up for the absence of air power.

That night von Rundstedt warned Keitel that this was the writing on the wall. " What shall we do? " cried the despairing Keitel. " What shall we do? "

" Make peace, you fools," said von Rundstedt, " what else can you do? "[1]

Keitel, the tell-tale toady, ran straight to Hitler, who happened to be conferring with Field-Marshal Gunther von Kluge at that very moment. Hitler's reaction was surprisingly mild. He merely wrote what von Rundstedt regarded as ' a nice letter,' telling him that von Kluge would take his place.

This appointment was not altogether fortuitous, for von Kluge had long been one of Hitler's favourites. In 1940-1 he had commanded Fourth Army in the break-through to the Channel and the drive to Moscow. In the next two years, as C.-in-C., Army Group Centre, he had gained a reputation (not wholly warranted) for ' victorious defence ' and had retained Hitler's confidence by accepting outrageous orders when others demurred. To this command he was about to return, after an absence of nine months following a motor accident, when Hitler sent him to succeed von Rundstedt.

Yet von Kluge was neither as resolute nor as loyal as Hitler believed. At Army Group Centre he had fallen under the spell of his Chief of Staff, von Tresckow, an ardent anti-Nazi, who had striven to induce the senior commanders on the Eastern Front to rise and denounce Hitler's strategy. Knowing that von Kluge had accepted a ' gratuity ' of RM 250,000 (£20,000)[2] tax free from the Führer's private purse, von Tresckow had endeavoured to shame his chief into supporting the insurrection. Several times he had led von Kluge to the point of open

---

[1]This incident was reported to Liddell Hart and to me by Blumentritt.

[2]Von Schlabrendorff, who was on von Kluge's staff, declares (*Revolt against Hitler*, p. 66) that he saw the cheque, and Hitler himself (Führer Conferences, Fragment 46, August 31st, 1944) said of von Kluge, " I myself gave him a large sum of money to settle him and a big increase in his Field-Marshal's pay."

revolt, but, whenever the time came for action, the Field-Marshal had faltered. Von Kluge had refused to be a party to the *Putsch* which members of his staff had planned in March 1943, but he had been prepared to join in overthrowing the Nazi régime, if the attempt to assassinate Hitler by blowing up his aircraft had succeeded. Intellectually von Kluge had long since joined the opposition and only his oath had kept him in uneasy allegiance to Hitler. When he arrived at St. Germain on July 4th, he seemed to Blumentritt to be " cheerful and confident . . . indeed almost gay about the prospects," but in his heart there was a ceaseless conflict between his pledge to Hitler and his duty to Germany.

The Battle of the Odon destroyed whatever chance the Germans had had of launching a counter-stroke to Bayeux, and accentuated the maldistribution of their forces. By his timely thrust Montgomery compelled them to commit their armoured reserves piecemeal and in haste; then by assuming the timely defensive he was able to inflict upon the SS Panzer divisions a costly defeat; and finally, by withdrawing his armour into reserve at the height of the battle, he re-created the threat of a major offensive in the Caen sector. At the end of June, of the eight panzer divisions in Normandy, seven and a half were engaged in halting the advance of Second Army. Although Rommel (in his Weekly Report of July 2nd) rightly anticipated that the Americans were about to make " a concentrated attack in the St. Lô–Coutances area," he did not dare to switch any armour there, except the battered rump of Panzer Lehr and the battlegroup of 2nd SS which had been involved at Rauray. The real danger zone was the Orne Valley, because, he said, " after taking possession of the area around Caen, the enemy's plan will be to advance on Paris."

Two days earlier, in a directive to Bradley and Dempsey, Montgomery had set out his plan. After restating his general intention of holding on the left and breaking out on the right, he wrote, " We must retain such balance and poise in our dispositions that there is never any need to react to enemy moves or thrusts; the enemy can do what he likes; we will proceed with our plan." Defining Bradley's task, he said, " First U.S. Army will pivot on the left in the Caumont area and swing southwards and eastwards to the general line Caumont–Vire–Mortain–Fougères." When this line was reached one American corps would turn round the corner into the Brittany Peninsula, and the remainder of the Army was to " direct a strong right wing, in a wide sweep south of the Bocage country towards successive objectives as follows: A. Laval–Mayenne, B. Le Mans–Alençon." These operations, which were due to begin on July 3rd, " should be carried out with the greatest drive and energy. There must be no pause until the Army has swung up on the line Caumont–Fougères. Thereafter the less delays the better."

The Americans now had four corps with fourteen divisions ranged along a 50-mile front which was held by six German divisions,[1] with another (2nd SS) in reserve. Thus Bradley had a marked advantage in numbers and fire-power, but his front was so constricted by natural obstacles that he could not bring his superiority to bear. On his left, he was blocked by the deep valley of the Vire and by the enemy's stubborn hold on St. Lô through which all the main roads ran. In the centre for fifteen miles his troops were confronted with the treacherous alluvial swamps of the lower Vire and the Taute. Across these inundations there was only one firm road—leading from Carentan to Périers—and this passed through a bottleneck of dry ground barely a mile and a half wide. On the Army's right flank, a bridgehead had been gained south of the flooded Douve in mid-June, but this foothold could not be exploited easily, since the way southward was barred by a group of steep and thickly wooded hills, clustered about the important road-junction of La Haye du Puits. Although the Germans were strongly entrenched on these hills, it seemed to Bradley that this was the only sector where he could bring any large force into action. He planned, therefore, that VIII U.S. Corps with four divisions should strike the first and major blow on this flank. He would then develop a general offensive with VII and XIX Corps: the former to thrust south from Carentan, and the latter to gain a bridgehead over the Vire and take St. Lô by envelopment.

From the start VIII Corps encountered the most stubborn opposition, for as usual the defence was stiffened by " a direct order from the Führer not to withdraw an inch."[2] This served to hold up the immediate American advance but at the cost of draining the long-term strength of the defenders. The terrain around La Haye was ideal for an economical delaying action, but Hitler compelled his troops to stand firm until they were destroyed by American fire or overrun. The cost was emphasised every day in the reports of 84th Corps to Seventh Army: " July 6th, 1905 hours. The enemy controls the air to such an extent that movement on the roads is impossible. . . . The enemy artillery, guided by aerial observation, is able to destroy our infantry in their defensive positions without exposing itself to any kind of retaliation. Thus we lose one and a half to two battalions every day."

No help was available from the Luftwaffe, for its primary effort was devoted to the protection of Hitler's ' anti-aircraft highways.' That evening Hausser urged Rommel to switch the Luftwaffe's centre of concentration to the American front; " otherwise the ground forces will be slaughtered." Rommel replied, " To-day there were 450 planes in the air and they simply could not get through."

[1] Seventh Army Telephone Log, July 4th, 1940 hours.
[2] There were three complete divisions (3rd Parachute, 17th SS and 353rd Infantry). The remnants of three divisions which had been in the Cotentin (the 77th, 91st and 243rd) had the strength of one. The 352nd was still fighting as a division, though it was barely a regiment strong; there were two regiments from the 266th Division, and one each from the 265th and 275th.

On July 7th the Germans gained some success with a counter-attack but that afternoon 84th Corps reported: " The troops are completely disorganised owing to severe losses. The principle of putting everything into the ' Main Line of Resistance ' causes units to be mixed up. Stragglers are picked up and pushed into the line anywhere. Several units have been merged and re-established. The heavy losses continue. . . . The struggle cannot be maintained with the present forces for any length of time."

Nevertheless, La Haye held out until July 8th. After seven days of severe fighting, the Germans had been driven back only five miles and they still held the hills south of the town. Meantime, VII Corps had found it even more difficult to break through the slender bottleneck on the Carentan–Périers road. Here there was no scope for local manœuvre and little room to deploy artillery. The way was barred by mines and felled trees, by paratroops and SS men. Daily gains of a few hundred yards were made only at heavy cost. After nine days the attack down this road was abandoned.

Farther east on July 7th there had been little immediate opposition when XIX Corps crossed the Vire seven miles north of St. Lô, but the extension of this bridgehead was restricted by inundations. When the Americans tried to exploit southwards, they were halted at Pont Hébert and they could not develop the western arm of the pincer movement which had been designed to squeeze the Germans out of St. Lô. By July 10th it was evident that First Army's offensive could not gain sufficient momentum to make an early break-out.

In sympathy with these American operations, Dempsey had maintained sufficient pressure from the Odon salient to prevent the withdrawal of 2nd SS Panzer Corps, and had redoubled his efforts to secure Caen. By the start of July all the German commanders from Dietrich to von Rundstedt were agreed that the city was untenable, but the personal intervention of Hitler denied the British the just military reward of the Odon battle. Thus, Dempsey was compelled to order a frontal attack on Caen, because, without command of this German pivot and the roads which led through it, he could not deploy sufficient strength to hold the German armour on the Second Army front.

The first move was an attack by the Canadians against Carpiquet on July 4th. The village was soon taken but on the airfield troops of 12th SS resisted every assault. The sustained tenacity of this defence led Dempsey to believe that the main assault on Caen could not be carried through rapidly and economically without the aid of Bomber Command. Harris agreed to ' turn on the heavies,' but rightly insisted that, in case some aircraft should bomb short, there must be a safety margin of 6,000 yards between the bomb-line and the foremost British troops. This meant that the target area could not cover the belt of fortified villages (some three miles from the northern edge of Caen), in which the Germans had been entrenched for the past month, but would be confined to the northern sector of the city itself where the Germans had no important defences. Dempsey accepted this, for he hoped the bombing of this zone would cut the enemy's forward troops off from reinforcements and supplies and so disorganise them that they would be incapable of waging a fight from street to street. But he was less interested in the destruction of enemy material than he was in gaining moral ascendency.

On the evening of July 7th, 467 Lancasters and Halifaxes dropped 2,560 tons of bombs on the northern outskirts of Caen.[1] At dawn next morning, greatly heartened by this massive display of air power, I Corps attacked with three divisions: 3rd British on the left, 59th British in the centre and 3rd Canadian on the right. These divisions were to converge on the city, clear it and seize crossings over the Orne. In the centre the opposition from 12th SS was as firm as ever and the 59th had to battle for every village. On the left, however, the defenders—part of a low-grade Luftwaffe division which had only recently arrived from Holland—were severely shaken, and by dark the leading brigade of 3rd British had reached the northern fringe of the built-up area. There, however, it was halted by craters and wreckage caused by the bombing. The older buildings of Caen are constructed of huge blocks of stone quarried in the Orne Valley. These blocks had been tossed about like lumps of sugar and the narrow streets were choked for hundreds of yards by mountains of rubble. The plan to send an armoured column through to rush the bridges had to be abandoned. The following morning patrols made their way on foot into the centre of the city, while bulldozers struggled to clear the blocked streets. In the meantime the Canadians, advancing astride the road from Bayeux, had come in from the west and reached the river, only to find that every bridge had been blown and that the far bank was strongly held. The city of Caen was in British hands, but by their continued defence of the suburbs and factories of Vaucelles beyond the river, the Germans were able to deny Montgomery the through routes he needed so that Second Army could maintain its threat to Paris.

By July 10th the situation in Normandy appeared to have reached a crisis. The American ' break-out ' offensive had bogged down. The enemy in the eastern half of Caen blocked the way to the Falaise plain. German infantry reinforcements from Southern France were now reaching Normandy in a steady flow. Cherbourg harbour was not yet open, and only one MULBERRY was working. The Allied Air Forces, handicapped

[1] It had been intended that the air bombardment should immediately precede the Army's dawn attack, but, because the forecast was unfavourable, the bombing was carried out on the previous evening. By the time this was known it was too late to change the Army plan, and thus the Germans were given six hours in which to recover. Harris was strongly critical of " the Army's failure to follow-up," but in the circumstances the delay was unavoidable. (See Harris, op. cit., pp. 211-12.)

by persistent bad weather over their English bases, were disgruntled because Second Army had not yet captured the ' Caen airfields.' At SHAEF Tedder and Morgan were openly critical of Montgomery's conduct of the battle and there were murmurs against him in Whitehall, where the Jeremiahs were already predicting a stalemate. Across the Atlantic the American press was impatient and the U.S. War Department was beginning to voice its concern at the slow development of operations. Even Eisenhower was affected by this uneasiness. Three days earlier he had written to Montgomery expressing the fear that the bridgehead was in danger of being sealed off and urging him to launch and maintain an all-out offensive. Because ground had not been gained as rapidly as Montgomery had forecast it might be, Eisenhower presumed that the plan had gone astray. He had not Montgomery's long and intimate experience in the daily conduct of operations, and he was not close enough to the current battle to see the steady unfolding of the basic strategy which Montgomery had proclaimed in April. One source of Eisenhower's concern was the knowledge that August would be a lean month for infantry reinforcements. No more British divisions would be available, and the American build-up would consist almost entirely of armoured divisions, for which there was limited scope in the bocage. Infantry divisions direct from the States would not begin to arrive until September, and he feared that, before these fresh forces could be brought to bear, the enemy would gather sufficient strength to contain the Allies throughout the winter, when air operations would be curtailed and the threat of a ' second landing ' north of the Seine could not be maintained.

Montgomery, on the other hand, drew encouragement from the very facts which alarmed Eisenhower. He knew that the tenacity of the defence was no yardstick of the enemy's continued power of resistance, for the German divisions were being steadily consumed in the fire of battle. He knew that the concentration of German armoured reserves against Second Army was ensuring the opportunity for First Army. Very soon they would need all the armour that Eisenhower could land.

At a conference on July 10th Bradley advised Montgomery that he could not make another major effort until he had restocked his ammunition dumps and had gained a firm jumping-off ground south of the swamps. He would first have to capture St. Lô and drive the Germans back to the St. Lô–Périers road. These preliminaries would take at least ten days. Montgomery accepted the delay, for he knew the difficulty of the terrain through which the Americans were fighting, and he was determined that the new attack should not go off at half-cock. On the other hand, the door of opportunity could not be kept open indefinitely. Montgomery had originally expected that the British and Canadian divisions would have to fight their holding action for no more than two or three weeks. This estimate had been upset by the bad weather of the first few days and by the subsequent gale, but he had taken good care not to blunt the cutting edge of Second Army either by making a premature assault on Caen or by persisting in the thrust across the Odon after the SS panzer divisions had been committed there. Even as it was, Dempsey's resources were stretched and the War Office had given warning that the present flow of infantry replacements could not continue for more than a few weeks. How much longer could Second Army keep the German armour pinned down?

Within the past ten days four German infantry divisions had reached Normandy and three of these had been put into the line opposite the British, thus relieving panzer formations which had begun moving to the American front. At all costs this westward movement had to be halted by a swift, bold stroke which would establish British armour on Bourguebus Ridge, south of Caen, and thus re-establish the menace of an imminent and powerful break-out towards Paris.

The only possibility was to strike from the ' airborne bridgehead ' east of the Orne. But this area afforded so little room for assembly and so narrow a frontage for attack that a conventional operation was certain to be stopped long before infantry could cover the eight miles to Bourguebus Ridge. Accordingly, Montgomery and Dempsey devised a revolutionary plan. They would group the three British armoured divisions under O'Connor's VIII Corps and send them roaring out of the Orne bridge-head behind an aerial bombardment of unprecedented ferocity. They resolved to make such a demonstration of armour and air power on this flank that German attention, and therefore reserves, would be con-centrated east of the Orne, just when the Americans were ready to break out west of the Vire.

It was eventually decided that this attack (Operation GOODWOOD) would begin on July 18th, that it would be preceded by a feint from the Odon salient on the night of the 15th-16th, and would be followed by First Army's break-out offensive (Operation COBRA) on July 20th. These attacks, said Montgomery in a signal to Eisenhower, would " set the Normandy front aflame," and he asked for maximum support by strategic and tactical air forces for both GOODWOOD and COBRA. From this request Eisenhower and the staff at SHAEF seem to have assumed that the attacks by Dempsey and Bradley were similar in purpose. Giving his impression of the plan, Eisenhower says, " By July 18th both the First and Second Armies had taken up positions from which the break-through attacks could be started. . . . The main British-Canadian thrust was to take the form of a drive across the Orne from Caen towards the south and south-east, *exploiting in the direction of the Seine basin and Paris.*"[1]

One source of this misconception was the Operational Instruction issued on July 13th by Dempsey's Chief of Staff. This declared that VIII Corps would " attack southwards and establish an Armd. Div. in each of the following areas: Bretteville-sur-Laize, Vimont–Argences, Falaise." It was this instruction which staff officers of Second Army took to England when they went to present the case for air support. The

[1]Eisenhower, *Report*, pp. 44-5. (The italics are mine. C. W.)

naming of Falaise as one of the objectives inevitably gave the impression that this attack, as well as Bradley's, was intended to achieve a clean break-through.

On July 15th, when he saw the Second Army Instruction, Montgomery gave O'Connor a personal memorandum which made his intention clear beyond dispute. This note began:

1. *Object of this operation.*

To engage the German armour in battle and ' write it down ' to such an extent that it is of no further value to the Germans as a basis of the battle. To gain a good bridgehead over the Orne through Caen and thus to improve our positions on the eastern flank. Generally to destroy German equipment and personnel.

2. *Effect of this operation on the Allied policy.*

We require the whole of the Cherbourg and Brittany peninsulas. A victory on the eastern flank will help us to gain what we want on the western flank. But the eastern flank is a bastion on which the whole future of the campaign in North-West Europe depends; it must remain a firm bastion; if it were to become unstable, the operations on the western flank would cease.

Therefore, while taking advantage of every opportunity to destroy the enemy, we must be very careful to maintain our own balance and ensure a firm base.

Montgomery then defined the task of VIII Corps: " The three armoured divisions will be required to dominate the area Bourguebus–Vimont–Bretteville, and to fight and destroy the enemy. But armoured cars should push far to the south towards Falaise and spread despondency and alarm and discover ' the form '." While this was happening, II Canadian Corps, which had taken over the Caen city sector, must clear the suburbs and gain " a very firm bridgehead " covering the built-up area. Then—" but NOT before "—VIII Corps could " crack about as the situation demands."

During the next two days Second Army Intelligence reported a steady thickening of the German defences and reserves east of the Orne. On the 17th, therefore, Dempsey further curtailed the objectives of VIII Corps and told O'Connor to " establish Armd. Divs. in the areas Vimont, Garcelles-Secqueville, Hubert Folie–Verrières." These contemporary orders show precisely what this operation was designed to achieve. Unfortunately for Montgomery's reputation, however, they did not penetrate to SHAEF, where the impression prevailed that GOODWOOD was one prong of a two-pronged break-out.


South of the Orne bridgehead the open cornfields sloped gently down to the embanked railway lines running from Caen to Troarn and to Vimont; then the ground rose gradually to the ridge behind Bourguebus. Between the suburbs and factories of Caen on the west and the woods and marshes of the Dives to the east, the plain was dappled with small villages. There were few hedgerows and, except for certain parts of the second railway embankment, no natural obstacles to hinder the movement of armour. But the villages provided ready-made and mutually-supporting strongholds for infantry and anti-tank guns, and the ridge afforded the defending artillery good observation and wide fields of fire. The only clear exit from the bridgehead was a corridor some 1,500 yards wide, which ran for four miles between flanking hamlets from Escoville to Cagny on the Caen–Vimont road. Beyond this road there was a cluster of villages on the slope leading to Bourguebus and a thick belt of woods on the flank of the more open approach to Garcelles-Secqueville. This was the chosen battleground for Operation GOODWOOD.

The plan was that three armoured divisions, the tank regiments leading, should debouch in rapid succession from the Orne bridgehead, charge through the corridor to Cagny and then fan out: the 11th swinging south-west to the Bourguebus area; the Guards turning south-east for Vimont; and the 7th driving straight on to Garcelles-Secqueville. Meanwhile, the flanks of the corridor would be cleared by infantry. On the right, II Canadian Corps had orders to secure the area from Colombelles to Vaucelles: on the left, I British Corps was to clear the string of villages from Touffreville to Émieville and subsequently capture Troarn.

In view of the strength and depth of the enemy defences east of the Orne, the success of this plan depended on the degree of air support available, but Harris was disinclined to help, because he felt that the Army had failed to take full advantage of his contribution to the assault upon Caen. His reluctance was overcome only when he learned that Dempsey wanted anti-personnel, not high-explosive, bombs dropped in the path of the main advance, and that there would be no delay between the end of the bombing and the start of the ground attack. It was finally settled that Bomber Command would neutralise the German strongholds and gun positions on the flanks of the armoured thrust, using H.E. bombs, for here cratering was acceptable. The actual corridor up to and beyond the first railway was to be saturated with fragmentation bombs dropped by American 'mediums,' and Cagny, which stood at the parting of the ways of the 11th and the Guards, was to be obliterated by Bomber Command. The area south of the second railway was to be carpeted with fragmentation bombs laid by 'heavies' of the VIII U.S. Air Force, which was also to attack the gun area near Troarn. Outside the zone of this bombardment, fighter-bombers of Second T.A.F. would strafe areas which might harbour enemy reserves or artillery.

The air plan was impressive, but it had one recognised weakness. Sufficient aircraft were not available to bomb the guns on the ridge behind Bourguebus, and, since this ridge lay at the extreme range of the British artillery, O'Connor expected that " in this area the armour will meet considerable opposition which it will be difficult to neutralise."[1] The Tactical Air Forces offered to turn around and attack these guns in the afternoon, but Dempsey thought that by then his armour would have reached the ridge, if it was going to get through at all. He might not have been so sanguine had he realised the full extent of the enemy's strength and awareness.

Second Army Intelligence knew that VIII Corps would be opposed initially by the 16th German Air Force Division, and then by 21st Panzer. It believed, however, that the zone of fixed defences did not extend south of the second railway, and that in this area " 12th SS is the only reserve formation not committed and it is but a shell of its former self."[2] The only other possibility was 1st SS, but its infantry were thought to be in the line astride the Orne south of Caen and at least some of its tanks had been identified west of Caen. Consequently, Dempsey estimated that after his tanks had crossed the Caen–Vimont railway they would be able to deploy freely and take the Bourguebus gun area by storm. He realised that this would be costly, but he was, he said, " prepared to lose two or three hundred tanks " in the course of the battle. He had tanks enough and to spare, but he could not afford to sacrifice the infantry whom he would need to ensure that this eastern flank remained " a firm bastion."

The real enemy picture was very different. The area between the Orne and the Dives was far more heavily defended than any other sector of the Normandy front, for Rommel believed that by preventing a British break-out at Caen he was compelling Eisenhower to postpone the second landing. From ' no man's land ' the zone of prepared defences extended right back to the ridge behind Bourguebus for a depth of ten miles, not three or four as Second Army thought. Rommel had been able to afford such depth, primarily because, unknown to Second Army, the 272nd Division had arrived from Southern France and had relieved 1st SS astride the Orne.

By July 17th Rommel had established five belts of defences east of the Orne. First, the ' expendable infantry ' (16th G.A.F. and the 272nd) which were to take the shock of the air and artillery bombardment in Vaucelles and the area north of the first railway. Secondly, the immediate panzer reserve: the armour of 21st Panzer, reinforced by 36 Tigers, and the medium tank battalion of 1st SS. The third zone, astride the Caen–Vimont railway, was a ' cushion ' of twelve small villages, each garrisoned by an infantry company and three or four anti-tank guns. Next, there was the gun-line, which ran along the crest of Bourguebus Ridge as far as the Secqueville woods and then swung north-east across the Caen–Vimont railway and up to Troarn. Along this line

[1]Counter-Battery Appreciation by Brigadier A. G. Matthew for O'Connor, July 15th, 1944.
[2]Second Army Intelligence Summary, July 17th, 1944.

Rommel had 78 ' eighty-eights ' and 12 other heavy flak guns, all sited for anti-tank as well as anti-aircraft defence.[1] In addition, he had 194 field pieces and 272 *nebelwerfer* (six-barrelled mortars), the German weapon Allied infantry dreaded most. From these 1,632 barrels they could drench the whole area between the Orne and the Dives.

Nor was this all. Behind the gun-line a fifth defensive zone was organised around the villages on the ridge, held by the six infantry battalions of 1st SS which had been set free by the arrival of the 272nd. Finally in reserve, five miles farther back, were the 45 Panthers of 1st SS and two strong battlegroups of 12th SS, each with 40 tanks. With these forces, thus deployed in exceptional depth and well dug-in in anticipation of ' carpet bombing,' Rommel confidently awaited the blow he knew was coming.

Even though only one British armoured division crossed the Orne before H-Hour, it was impossible for Dempsey to conceal his intentions. From the Colombelles factories, the Germans had a commanding view over the cramped ' airborne bridgehead.' They saw new bridges going up, new tracks being cut. At night they heard the heavy rumble of tracks as 700 tanks moved across from Bayeux to assembly areas near the Orne bridges. The cavernous limestone of the Caen plain acted as a sounding board, and Dietrich says he detected the movement simply by putting his ear to the ground—a trick he had learnt in Russia. On the night of July 16th-17th Luftwaffe reconnaissance aircraft took 'flare-light' photographs of traffic crossing the Orne bridges. Next morning, undeceived by the feint across the Odon, Rommel's H.Q. reported to von Kluge: " The local attacks on July 15th between Maltot and Vendes may be the prelude to the large-scale attack which is expected from the evening of the 17th for making a break-through across the Orne." That day all units in the Caen sector were appropriately alerted and, in case the British should strike east as well as south, a battlegroup of 12th SS was ordered to move by night to Lisieux.

That afternoon Rommel made a final survey of his defensive dispositions. On the way back from the Battle H.Q. of Panzer Group West,[2] his escorted car was spotted by British aircraft. As the planes roared down to attack, Rommel shouted to the driver to race for shelter in the next village, but the fighters were too swift. His driver was struck down at the wheel, the car crashed into a tree, and Rommel sustained severe

[1]Colonel Möser, who commanded these dual-purposes ' 88s,' provided me with this detailed account of the German defences. The only element lacking, he said, was minefields. It would have been a comparatively simple task to mine the throat between the two rivers, but because of the dislocation of the railways the Germans were not able to move forward from Verdun the thousands of mines which were stored there. The figures of gun and *nebelwerfer* strength were extracted for me by Manfred Rommel from his father's papers.

[2]Now commanded by General Hans Eberbach, this H.Q. had returned to Normandy and had taken over the eastern half of the front, leaving Seventh Army responsible only for operations against the Americans. At the end of July Panzer Group West was re-named Fifth Panzer Army.

concussion when he was hurled on to the roadway. He was carried unconscious and gravely injured into a nearby village which bore the name, Ste. Foy de Montgommery.

For three hours after dawn on July 18th the ground between Caen and Troarn shuddered under the heaviest and most concentrated air attack in support of ground forces so far attempted. The bombs rained down first on the flanks of the VIII Corps corridor and then on the corridor itself. At 7.45 a.m. as the last of the ' mediums ' turned away, the 11th Armoured Division (Major-General G. P. B. Roberts) began moving south behind a rolling barrage. As the tanks were swallowed up in the smoke and dust, fresh waves of bombers swept in to strike at the villages beyond the Caen–Vimont railway. Advancing in column of regiments on a front of a thousand yards, the 29th Armoured Brigade drove untroubled to the second railway, for the fragmentation bombing and the barrage had neutralised all opposition. In the villages on either side the dazed defenders were still in their shelters when they found themselves attacked by the infantry who were clearing the flanks.

The first serious resistance to the advance of the armour developed about half-past nine, when the two leading regiments came under fire from Cagny as they were manœuvring to climb the steep embankment of the Caen–Vimont railway. In Cagny half a dozen ' 88s ' and some Tiger tanks had miraculously survived amid the rubble of the ruined village, and these were difficult to combat because of their greatly superior range. Leaving one regiment to cover this flank, the other two negotiated the embankment and at ten o'clock began advancing towards Bourguebus. Now, however, there was no barrage to help them and they soon encountered lively opposition from anti-tank guns concealed in villages south of the Caen–Vimont railway. One troop of tanks from each regiment managed to slip through to the Bourguebus Ridge, but the main advance was checked short of it soon after eleven.

All but one of these villages had been hit by fragmentation bombs, but by extraordinary chance a section of each village had been missed, and in every case it was the section which now faced towards the British line of advance that had escaped unscathed. Armour alone could not clear the infantry and anti-tank guns from these strongholds, but the motorised battalions of 11th Armoured were still busy clearing the villages on the western flank of the corridor. The first onslaught had lost its momentum, and, although 29th Armoured Brigade had advanced six miles in barely three hours, it had not yet broken through the enemy's prepared defences, and the leading regiments were now under long-range fire from the ' 88s ' on Bourguebus Ridge and from Panthers which had moved up from the south.

Meantime the follow-up divisions were in trouble. Some German strongpoints on the fringes of the corridor had come to life and at the southern exit Cagny still defied every attack. In the wake of 11th Armoured, the Guards ran the gauntlet without serious loss, but when they turned south-east towards Vimont their tanks came under heavy flanking fire from both Cagny and Émieville and, though they pressed on, they soon found the way barred by a screen of guns and tanks secluded in the orchards east of Frénouville. In the early afternoon, before 7th Armoured was in a position to reinforce the offensive, the Germans began to strike back.

Soon after the start of the bombing Dietrich had lost all contact with his forward troops. Alarmed at the exceptional depth of the bombardment, he had prepared to make his stand on Bourguebus Ridge and thither he ordered the Panther battalion of 1st SS. It reached there from the south shortly before noon, just as British tanks were approaching from the north, and it was able to reinforce the garrisons of the villages around Bourguebus at the critical moment. Thus the German tanks not only secured the high ground but had the protection of buildings and sunken lanes and the support of infantry and anti-tank guns. They also had the advantage of superior range. By fire alone, without ever exposing themselves, they were able to thwart every British manœuvre. It was impossible to drive these German tanks back with artillery, for they were beyond the range of the 25-pdrs and the medium guns could not bring down concentrations of sufficient density. The Panthers were repeatedly harried by rocket-firing Typhoons which blocked several offensive moves, but these air attacks could not be co-ordinated with operations on the ground, because the R.A.F. Control Post with the forward troops had been put out of action during the morning.

In these circumstances, O'Connor decided that his only chance of gaining the Bourguebus Ridge was to drive relentlessly on with his armoured regiments and accept heavy casualties. Shortly before two o'clock, at a conference in the midst of the mêlée, he told Roberts to make a further effort to reach the Caen–Falaise road, west of Bourguebus, and ordered Erskine (of 7th Armoured) to attack towards La Hogue and Garcelles-en-Secqueville with his armoured brigade. But its regiments were strung out all the way back to the Orne. They had been slow in crossing the bridges and they were now moving warily down the corridor. Erskine regarded the whole operation as a gross abuse of armour and seemed determined to keep his tanks out of the maelstrom as long as possible. In response to pleas from Roberts and exhortations from O'Connor, Erskine maintained that there was no room to get through between the 11th and the Guards. His leading regiment had begun to move down the corridor in the middle of the morning, but it did not cross the second railway and enter the battle until six o'clock. By then it was too late to affect the issue. Throughout the afternoon the left flank of the 29th Armoured Brigade had been exposed to repeated counter-thrusts by Tigers and Panthers, and Roberts could not develop a fresh attack towards the Caen–Falaise road. The Guards were similarly unsuccessful. In the evening they captured Cagny, but they could not penetrate the anti-tank screen which blocked the road to Vimont, and their efforts to get through cost them 60 tanks.

At dusk 11th Armoured, having lost 126 tanks[1] (more than half its strength), was forced to consolidate for the night north of the Caen–Vimont railway. South of this line the enemy was well established in all the villages except one, and on Bourguebus Ridge his defences, almost untouched by the bombing, were still intact.

Disappointing though this progress was by comparison with what had seemed likely in mid-morning, the day's fighting had broken the enemy's hold on the area between Troarn and Caen. After a battle which continued far into the night, the Canadians cleared the Colombelles factory area and gained a foothold in Vaucelles. During the night, while engineers were bridging the river, the Germans withdrew from the Caen suburbs to the western end of Bourguebus Ridge, leaving only small rearguards to contest the advance of the Canadians. On the other flank, enemy resistance varied in direct proportion to the effectiveness of the bombing. Touffreville, the first objective of the 3rd British Division, had escaped and it held out until late in the afternoon, but infantry riding on the back of tanks by-passed this village and soon cleared the ruins of two more, where " those Germans still conscious were far too dazed to offer any resistance."[2] Then a fresh attack eastwards reached the outskirts of Troarn, but an attempt to strike south was firmly blocked at Émieville by the force which had caused such trouble to the Guards all day.

During the night of July 18th–19th infantry of 1st SS were brought up from reserve to the villages around Bourguebus, relieving the exhausted troops of 21st Panzer. This new line might have been forced quickly, if another bomb carpet could have been laid in the path of the armour, but the heavy bombers were busy preparing to support the American offensive which was due to begin on the 20th. Thus, it was now a matter of taking these strongpoints one by one and the character of GOODWOOD changed entirely.

During the next two days, in a series of skilful local actions, Canadian and British troops drove the Germans from all the villages on the northern slope of Bourguebus Ridge, except La Hogue. In the meantime, however, the enemy was able to strengthen his positions along the crest and, before these could be assaulted, the weather turned in his favour. On the afternoon of July 20th a heavy thunderstorm drenched the battlefield and turned the sticky soil of the Caen plain into a quagmire. That night

---

[1]Some 40 of these were actually destroyed; as many more were knocked out, but recoverable, and the rest were out of action for mechanical or other causes. Casualties among the crews were not heavy; one regiment which lost 41 tanks during the day had only 17 men killed and 39 wounded.

[2]Scarfe, op. cit., p. 118.

Montgomery ordered his armoured divisions to withdraw into reserve. Canadian infantry kept up the pressure but GOODWOOD was over.

The storm which burst over Caen on July 20th was a minor squall compared with the tempest that raged at SHAEF and at Leigh-Mallory's H.Q. over what was regarded as Montgomery's ' failure.' Expecting a break-through to Falaise and the consequent seizure of their airfield sites south of Caen, the Air Forces were particularly bitter. They were, reports Butcher (Eisenhower's aide), " completely disgusted with the lack of progress,"[1] the more so because, late on the 18th, Montgomery himself had issued a special announcement which began, " Early this morning British and Canadian troops of the Second Army attacked and broke through into the area east of the Orne and south-east of Caen," and ended, " Heavy fighting continues. General Montgomery is well satisfied with the progress made in the first day's fighting of this battle."

This announcement was premature and indiscreet to say the least, for, when it was made, the advance had been halted, not on Montgomery's order, but by the sheer depth and strength of the German defences. It cannot be justified even as a device to fool the enemy, for Montgomery disclaims any such intention; it can be explained only if it is judged in relation to Montgomery's strictly limited objective, as defined to O'Connor on July 15th, to get command of Bourguebus Ridge. On the evening of the 18th it seemed to Montgomery that he was almost there, and he did not then know that 11th Armoured had been forced to pull back to the Caen–Vimont railway. In any case, however, it was a grave psychological mistake to use the word ' break-through,' for that (in conjunction with the news of the colossal air bombardment) naturally led Fleet Street to the conclusion that this was another and greater Alamein, and the headlines were written accordingly.

In these circumstances it is not surprising that the Air Forces were incensed when they found that there had been no general renewal of the attack until late in the afternoon of the 19th, and that then the gains had been small. That evening, says Butcher, " Tedder called Ike and said Monty had, in effect, stopped his armour from going farther. Ike was mad. Monty always wants to wait and draw up his ' administrative tail.' . . . Tedder, reflecting the disappointment of the air at the slowness on the ground, said that the British Chiefs of Staff would support any recommendation that Ike might care to make with respect to Monty for not going places with his big three-armoured-division push."[2]

Although the British Chiefs of Staff were not suggesting that a change

[1]Butcher, op. cit., p. 617.
[2]Butcher, op. cit., pp. 616-17. There were occasions when Montgomery could be rightly criticised for ' waiting to draw up his tail,' but this was not one of them. During the planning Dempsey, reflecting Montgomery's views, had told O'Connor, " Don't worry about your infantry or your sappers or field ambulances or any of your tail. Just get the tanks and motor battalions there."

in command should be made, there were many senior officers at SHAEF who wanted Eisenhower to take over direct control of the land battle himself. Eisenhower spurned this suggestion, but he was anxious about the slow development and gave a hint of his fears to Churchill, who was about to visit the bridgehead. On the 20th Eisenhower flew to Normandy and conferred with Bradley and Montgomery. He was deeply disappointed when he learned that the American offensive, set for the morrow, had been further postponed by bad weather, but he was amazed to find Montgomery quite satisfied with the results of GOODWOOD and full of confidence about COBRA. Because he did not really appreciate the importance of concentration, Eisenhower was disturbed by Montgomery's determination to rely upon a 'single, annihilating stroke,' instead of a general offensive. What Eisenhower wanted, says his Chief of Staff, Bedell Smith, was " an all-out co-ordinated attack by the entire Allied line, which would at last put our forces in decisive motion. He was up and down the line like a football coach, exhorting everyone to aggressive action."[1] But this was just what Montgomery was determined to avoid. If everybody was to attack, nobody would have the strength to make a decisive break-through or to exploit it.

On the following day, Montgomery soon persuaded the acute Churchill that his plan was sound, that it was indeed the same plan he had outlined in April, and that he was on the point of gaining a major victory. Back in England, Churchill sought to reassure Eisenhower, but he could not dispel all the Supreme Commander's doubts, for Tedder and the staff at SHAEF remained dubious and critical.

GOODWOOD was accounted a failure by SHAEF because Second Army had gained neither a strategic break-through nor all its tactical objectives. The fact that the operation had achieved Montgomery's major purpose was ignored, for this purpose was not understood. By July 20th, Second Army had secured the 'vital' communications through Caen and expanded its territory east of the Orne from a tiny foothold to a substantial bridgehead five miles by twelve.[2] The German armour had

---

[1]Bedell Smith, *Saturday Evening Post,* June 15th, 1946. Butcher's simile was even less flattering. On July 20th he noted in his diary (op. cit., p. 619), " Ike is like a blind dog in a meat house—he can smell it, but he can't find it."

[2]This considerable advance was made at a fraction of the cost which would have been incurred if a conventional infantry attack had been launched. The casualties (killed, wounded and missing) suffered by VIII Corps were:

|  | 11TH | GUARDS | 7TH | TOTAL |
|---|---|---|---|---|
| July 18th - - - | 336 | 137 | 48 | 521 |
| July 19th - - - | 399 | 33 | 67 | 499 |

By comparison, the losses of I Corps, which had an infantry division and a half attacking on the eastern flank, were much heavier: 651 on the 18th, and 541 on the 19th. Yet the value of the bombing is apparent, when these casualties are contrasted with those which I Corps sustained in the assault on the city of Caen: 3,817 in three days.

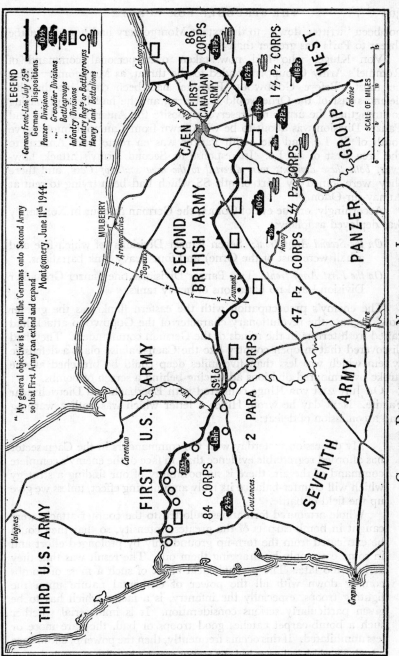

GERMAN DISPOSITIONS IN NORMANDY, JULY 25TH

LEGEND

German Front-line July 25th
German Dispositions
Panzer Divisions
Grenadier Divisions
Battlegroups
Infantry Divisions
Infantry Reg.ts or Battlegroups
Heavy Tank Battalions

" My general objective is to pull the Germans onto Second Army
so that First Army can extend and expand "

Montgomery. June 11th 1944.

not been ' written down ' to the extent Montgomery had hoped, but the threat to Paris was greater than ever.

Von Kluge, who had now taken over personal command of Rommel's Army Group, responded to the threat, as Montgomery knew he must. Before GOODWOOD Rommel had been confident that his defences east of the Orne would hold firm, and he had been preparing to strengthen the armoured reserves opposite the Americans. The 2nd Panzer Division was about to be withdrawn from Caumont into reserve south of St. Lô, and the 116th Panzer was en route from Amiens to the area west of St. Lô. In response to Second Army's attack, however, *both these divisions were diverted to the area south of Caen*, and there they were joined by part of 9th SS which had been trying to refit at Aunay-sur-Odon.

Accordingly, on the eve of COBRA, the German armour in Normandy was deployed as follows:

> *On the Second Army front:* Seven Panzer Divisions (of which five and a half were east of the Orne) and four heavy tank battalions.

> *On the First Army front:* Two Panzer Divisions, one Panzer Grenadier Division,[1] and no battalions of heavy tanks.

The enemy's preoccupation with the eastern flank was the greater now, because the revolutionary character of the GOODWOOD attack had raised fresh terrors in the minds of the German commanders. They had discovered that in open country like the Caen–Falaise plain a defensive system which was less than five miles deep could be breached at one stroke by armoured divisions advancing behind a screen of bombs.

On July 21st von Kluge conferred with Eberbach and Dietrich near Falaise. Next day he wrote Hitler a letter which was both a warning and a confession of defeat:

> My discussion yesterday with the commanders in the Caen sector has afforded regrettable evidence that, in face of the enemy's complete command of the air, there is no possibility of our finding a strategy which will counter-balance its truly annihilating effect, unless we give up the field of battle.
>
> Whole armoured formations, allotted to the counter-attack, were caught in bomb-carpets of the greatest intensity, so that they could be extricated from the torn-up ground only by prolonged effort and in some cases only by dragging them out. The result was that they arrived too late. The psychological effect of such a mass of bombs coming down with all the power of elemental nature upon the fighting troops, especially the infantry, is a factor which has to be given particularly serious consideration. It is immaterial whether such a bomb-carpet catches good troops or bad, they are more or less annihilated. If this occurs frequently, then the power of endurance

[1] 17th SS, which had never had any armour except a battalion of assault guns.

of the forces is put to the highest test; indeed it becomes dormant and dies.

I came here with the fixed determination of making effective your order to stand fast at any price. But when one has to see by experience that this price must be paid in the slow but sure annihilation of the force . . . anxiety about the immediate future of this front is only too well justified. . . . In spite of intense efforts, the moment has drawn near when this front, already so heavily strained, will break. And once the enemy is in open country, an orderly command will hardly be practicable in view of the insufficient mobility of our troops. I consider it my duty to bring these conclusions to your notice, my Führer, in good time.

## CHAPTER XIX

# ATTENTAT! ATTENTAT!

THE impact of the Wehrmacht's defeats on every front in the month
following the Normandy invasion shook the Nazi régime to its
foundations and brought the Underground Opposition inside the Reich
to the point of action.[1] During the first six months of 1944 there had
been no further attempt on Hitler's life, and many of the lesser members
of the Opposition had become discouraged by their leaders' failure to act.
There were various reasons for this failure and not the least was the
elaborate precautions taken to protect the Führer from assassination. He
lived at his heavily guarded H.Q. at Rastenburg in the midst of the East
Prussian lakes and there was virtually unapproachable. He seldom left
the shelter of his underground quarters, except to walk in the woods
with his Alsatian dog, Blondi, and the number of those who had access
to him was strictly limited and controlled. He never came to Berlin and
he refused to visit the front. On the few occasions when it was necessary
for him to inspect new weapons or equipment he adopted the practice
of altering the time and place at the last minute in order to upset any
calculated preparations. Early in April, thinking that the cross-Channel
invasion was imminent, he left Rastenburg for Berchtesgaden, but there
the checks and safeguards were equally strict.

Throughout these months Stauffenberg, who was now the mainspring
of the conspiracy though he acknowledged the general leadership of
Beck, had no chance of seeing Hitler himself or of arranging an *attentat*.
But these were not months of idleness. By the start of 1944 the Abwehr,
which had provided the plotters with a cloak for their seditious activities
and with an independent network of communications, had been purged
and was about to be absorbed by Himmler's Security Service, the SD.
It had been essential, therefore, for the conspirators to build up an
entirely new organisation capable of taking over the government as soon

[1]Many accounts of the ' Plot of July 20th ' have been written, but in the nature of
things there is very little documentary evidence available and the personal reports are,
for the most part, based on hearsay or conjecture. Few of these accounts agree, even
on the events of the vital day, and most of them contain self-contradictions. In this
chapter I have not attempted to discuss the merits of the various sources but have
presented what seems to me the narrative best supported by the evidence.

as Hitler was removed. To this task Stauffenberg devoted himself during the first half of 1944, in close association with his chief, Olbricht, who had been one of the early leaders of the Opposition. By June Stauffenberg and Olbricht had worked out the plans and mechanics for the transfer of power and had developed the necessary organisation at the H.Q. of the Home Army in Berlin's Bendlerstrasse, in the *Wehrkreise* and in the capitals of the Occupied Countries.

All this planning and organisation were officially disguised as military precautions against possible civil emergency created by internal revolt, an uprising of foreign workers or the landing of Allied airborne troops. The plans were formulated according to normal General Staff procedure and were set down as detailed operational instructions, for it was essential that they should be acted on at once and without question when the time came. Otherwise the *putsch* might be thwarted by the ' private armies ' of Himmler or Goering and the country might be plunged into anarchy or civil war. Moreover, unless the Army were to establish quick control of the situation at home and in the field, the battlefronts might give way and the new administration would then lose the power to bargain for a compromise peace.

These orders were drawn up during the spring and were sent out under seal to the commanders of the *Wehrkreise* and of the German Military Administrations abroad, who were thereby directed that, on receipt of the code-word WALKYRIE, they were to move troops into the more important cities and were to take possession of key installations such as telephone exchanges and radio, power and railway stations, pending further instructions from Berlin. The plotters' intention was that the WALKYRIE code-word should be transmitted as soon as Hitler had been killed, and that this should be followed by signals to the district commanders at home and the field commanders abroad advising them that the Führer was dead and that the Army had been empowered to form a new government with Beck at its head, von Witzleben as C.-in-C. of the Wehrmacht and Olbricht as his Chief of Staff. These commanders were then to arrest all *Gauleiter*, all senior officers of the SS and Police and other high Nazi officials.

To prevent these orders being countermanded by anyone at the Führer's H.Q. after his death, the radio transmitter and the telephone exchange there were to be put out of action by the only conspirator on Hitler's personal staff, his Signals Officer, General Erich Fellgiebel. Meantime, any counter-action by the Nazis in the capital was to be forestalled with the aid of the Chief of Police, von Helldorff, and the commandant of the Berlin garrison, von Hase, both of whom were privy to the plot. The Berlin Guard Battalion was to throw a cordon round the Government area, seize the H.Q. of the SS and the Gestapo, as well as the Propaganda Ministry, including Goebbels. It was also to secure the main radio station so that a proclamation of martial law could be broadcast to the German people as soon as the situation was under control. Yet this battalion would be the only force at the disposal of the plotters until the arrival of a panzer training regiment which was to move in from Krampnitz on receipt of the WALKYRIE signal.

By these measures the conspirators hoped to paralyse the Nazis and gain the power and the time to establish control of the State. After three or four days a civil government was to be set up by Beck with Goerdeler as Chancellor; Wilhelm Leuschner, the Social Democrat, as Vice-Chancellor; and Ulrich von Hassell, a former Ambassador in Rome, as Foreign Minister, thus proving to the world that what they had carried out was something more than a military coup. By this time Beck and Goerdeler expected to have made contact with the Western Allies through Stockholm and Madrid with the object of obtaining an early cessation of hostilities.

The essential prerequisite to the implementation of these plans was the assassination of Hitler, but the opportunity of striking at him could not easily be created. At the start of June, however, the C.-in-C., Home Army, General Fritz Fromm, appointed Stauffenberg to be his Chief of Staff. In this post Stauffenberg had official reasons for attending Hitler's staff conferences on those occasions when matters concerning the Home Army were to be discussed. Thus the man who had become the prime mover in the plot was placed in the position of being able to strike the blow which would set that plot in train. Yet Stauffenberg was not the assailant the conspirators would have chosen, for he had been seriously maimed in the Tunisian campaign when he had lost an eye, his right arm and two fingers of his left hand. There was no doubt that Stauffenberg was prepared to give his own life in order to kill Hitler, but Beck insisted that he was too valuable to be sacrificed. Stauffenberg had drawn up the WALKYRIE plans and it was essential to their smooth execution that he should be able to take charge in Berlin and direct the seizure of power. Accordingly, it was necessary to devise a plot which would enable him to play the double role first of assassin at the Führer's H.Q. and then of chief executive at the Bendlerstrasse.

This could be done only if Hitler's death were brought about in a manner which would allow Stauffenberg to escape from the conference and return post-haste to Berlin. The method he chose was that he would carry into one of Hitler's daily conferences a brief-case containing a time-bomb set to explode after he had left the Führer's presence. He would then fly at once to Berlin, leaving Fellgiebel to advise Olbricht of his success, so that the WALKYRIE signal could be sent without delay, and to destroy the communications at Hitler's H.Q. so that no surviving Nazi leader could send counter-signals of his own.

The development of this ' tactical ' opportunity coincided with the Anglo-American landings in Normandy, the Red Army's summer offensive in Poland, the heavy German defeat in Italy, and the realisation that the V.1 was no war-winning weapon. Of these events by far the most important was the success of the Allied invasion of France. Before this the Opposition had been divided and in doubt, for there were some who were prepared to give Hitler a last chance, not because they approved of the Nazi régime but because the repulse of the invasion would strengthen Germany's bargaining power vis-à-vis the Western Powers. By the end of June, however, even the waverers knew that there was no chance of stalemate, let alone victory, and that they could procrastinate no longer. Thus the success of the invasion strengthened the hands of the Beck–Goerdeler group, for they could now obtain from some of the leading field commanders, such as Rommel, assurances of support which had previously been withheld.

Their representative had approached Rommel as early as February and had gained the impression that the Field-Marshal would be prepared to become " a modern Hindenburg," as Goerdeler put it, if defeat became inevitable and Hitler refused to end the war. In May there had been further discussions in which Rommel was involved, either directly or through his Chief of Staff, but he had then made it clear that he thought Hitler should be arrested and brought to trial before a German court. When this view was contested by von Stülpnagel,[1] the Military Governor of France and the leading conspirator in the West, Rommel replied, " To kill Hitler would only make him a martyr." Rommel continued to hold this view but, after his meeting with Hitler at Margival on June 17th, he finally responded to the dictates of his conscience. He sent word to Beck that the front in Normandy was about to collapse and that, if any action was to be taken against Hitler, it must be taken at once.

Rommel's adherence to the conspiracy, late and guarded though it was, encouraged Beck and Goerdeler to believe that when Hitler had been removed they would be able to treat direct with the Western Allies on the military level. Although some members of the Opposition still believed that it would be easier and better to come to terms with the Russians, the prevailing view was that once they had gained power they must continue the battle in the East and open the Western Front so that the Anglo-American armies could advance rapidly into the Reich and prevent its occupation by the Russians. For the negotiations by which this might be brought about they knew now that they could rely on Rommel and they thought that when the time came von Kluge would act in concert with him. For more than a year von Kluge had hovered on the fringe of the Opposition but, when he came to the West at the start of July and discovered the gravity of the situation, he too indicated to Beck his readiness to support the conspiracy. Unlike Rommel, however, von Kluge stipulated that he would co-operate only if Hitler were dead.

In the first week of July Beck, Goerdeler and Stauffenberg knew that time was fast running out. They knew they must strike Hitler down before the Anglo-American forces in Normandy gained a victory so decisive that the Western Powers would no longer consider a compromise.

[1]General Count Heinrich von Stulpnagel.

They realised that Roosevelt and Churchill would demand ' Unconditional Surrender,' but they hoped that the offer of an unopposed advance to Berlin would be too tempting to be rejected. But this offer would be valueless once Eisenhower's armies had broken out of their bridgehead and were driving unchecked, as Rommel insisted they could, for the frontiers of the Reich.

While the rapid decline in Germany's military situation was driving the conspirators to act without further delay, another factor, directly affecting their own safety, provided an added spur to action. Early in July two Socialist members of the Opposition, Julius Leber and Adolf Reichwein, were arrested by the Gestapo. These two men had been endeavouring to enlist the support of the Communists and, according to some reports, had gone so far as to show the Central Communist Committee in Berlin a list of the proposed Government. A further meeting had been arranged, but before it could take place Leber and Reichwein were in the hands of the Gestapo. There was no means of the conspirators' knowing what information might have been extracted from them, nor of telling whether one of the alleged Communists might not have been a ' stool-pigeon ' for Himmler.

The first opportunity for action came on July 11th[1] when Stauffenberg represented Fromm at a Führer Conference at Berchtesgaden. He arrived with the bomb in his brief-case, but, when he found that Goering and Himmler were not there, he refrained from setting it off. In all their planning the conspirators had been agreed that it was necessary to assassinate the Reichsmarschall and the Reichsführer also, since they commanded military forces which owed them personal allegiance. It was evidently on this account that Stauffenberg held his hand.

Four days later, on the 15th, Stauffenberg made another journey by air to the *Führerhauptquartier*, which by this time had returned to its usual location at Rastenburg. On arrival there he drove from the airfield and left his car near the entrance to the inner compound within easy distance of the concrete bunker where the conference was to be held. Once more carrying the lethal brief-case, he entered the bunker. Hitler was there, Goering was there, but Himmler was not. When it came to his turn to report, Stauffenberg gave the information required of him, but he left untouched the bomb which, in that cramped space, would have blown Hitler, Goering and the rest to oblivion. As soon as he had finished his report, Stauffenberg hurried from the meeting and telephoned the Bendlerstrasse. He did not speak to Olbricht but what he learned from another of the conspirators made him decide to go ahead despite the absence of Himmler. When Stauffenberg reached the bunker, however,

---

[1]In evidence before the People's Court, General Stieff, who was close to Stauffenberg, said that the bomb was carried to a conference on July 6th also. This is not confirmed by other sources though none contradict it.

Hitler had already left and the conference was breaking up. Once again he flew back to Berlin with the bomb in his brief-case.

Stauffenberg's failure to act on this occasion is one of the mysteries of the plot. One of Beck's associates, Gisevius, reporting what was told to him by those who were at the Bendlerstrasse when Stauffenberg rang, says: " This dangerous as well as superfluous telephone call indicated that Stauffenberg had somewhat lost his head. Consequently, the melancholy conclusion was forced on us that Hitler had been saved not so much by a beneficent Providence as by Stauffenberg's psychological inhibitions. It seemed highly unlikely that he would succeed a third time where he had funked twice before."[1] This is a most unsatisfactory interpretation. There can be no doubting Stauffenberg's courage and, since he was the chief executive of the plot, there was no need for him to ask Olbricht for permission to act, or even for advice, when he found Himmler was absent. Why then did he telephone at all? The explanation appears to be that Stauffenberg and Olbricht had agreed that the WALKYRIE warning should be given to the regiment at Krampnitz at eleven o'clock that morning in order to ensure its early arrival in Berlin; that at one o'clock, when Stauffenberg rang to tell Olbricht the occasion was not opportune, he found this warning had in fact been issued, and accordingly decided that he must go through with the *attentat* if he could.

Whatever the explanation, the outcome was that Hitler had again been spared and the conspirators had compromised the security of their own plans by issuing the code-word before they were sure that the Führer was dead. Fromm and Keitel both discovered what had been done and Olbricht had difficulty in explaining it away as an exercise. This anticipatory warning could not be repeated, and it was agreed that on the next occasion they must not send out any alert until they knew that the attempt had succeeded. This meant that it would be at least three hours before the troops from Krampnitz could reinforce the Berlin Guard Battalion. The delay involved had to be accepted, for the pretence of legality could be maintained only if everything was done in accordance with standing orders. Thus, although this regiment was stationed only 15 miles from the Bendlerstrasse, it would take time to assemble, draw live ammunition and prepare for movement. Pending its arrival the conspirators would have to rely on the Berlin Guard Battalion and the readiness of its commander to obey their instructions.

The anxiety created by this false start among those implicated was intensified two days later when one of their number, Nebe (the Chief of Himmler's Criminal Department) warned Beck that the Gestapo had issued a warrant for the arrest of Goerdeler.

Realising that it was now or never Stauffenberg flew to Hitler's H.Q. on the morning of July 20th, determined to set off the bomb whatever the circumstances. These were not propitious. Neither Goering nor Himmler was present and, because the Führer's bunker was now being

[1]Gisevius, *To The Bitter End*, p. 520.

reinforced with extra concrete, the midday meeting was to be held in a lightly-built wooden hut nearby. About 12.30 a number of officers gathered outside the hut, waiting for the Führer: Keitel, Jodl, Warlimont (Jodl's Deputy), Heusinger (Chief of the Operations Staff at OKH), Brandt (Heusinger's Deputy), Korten (Chief of the Luftwaffe General Staff), Bodenschatz (Korten's Deputy), Assmann (Deputy Chief of the Naval Operations Staff), Puttkamer (a Naval Liaison Officer), Schmundt (Hitler's Adjutant), a stenographer named Berger and half a dozen others.

Stauffenberg stayed outside the inner compound until the Führer had appeared from his bunker and had led the way into the hut. Carrying maps and papers, his officers followed Hitler into a small bare room, and, because the day was hot, the windows were thrown open. In the centre of this room there was a massive oak table not borne by four legs but resting on a solid block several inches thick. The block carried the centre of the table and from each end of it equally stout beams ran off to the corners. Around this table Hitler and his officers ranged themselves while maps were spread out upon its broad surface. Except for the stenographer they all stood along the side of the table farthest from the door. On the extreme right was Assmann, next to him Bodenschatz, then closely grouped together Schmundt, Korten and Brandt, next to them Heusinger, then after a small gap, and almost half-way along this side of the table, stood Hitler, and beyond him Keitel, Jodl, Warlimont and the rest.[1]

The conference began with a review by Heusinger of the situation on the Eastern Front. Stauffenberg waited in his car until the meeting had been in progress for about five minutes. Then, so it seems, he opened his brief-case and, as he could not get a proper grip with his one maimed hand, bent forward and drew out the fuse-pin with his teeth.[2] This done, he snapped his brief-case shut and walked briskly across the inner compound and into the conference room. Heusinger was still speaking as Stauffenberg entered. He moved to the end of the table on Hitler's right, placed the brief-case on the floor, standing it against the heavy beam that ran up to one corner and, says Assmann, whispered to Brandt, " I must go and telephone. Keep an eye on my brief-case. It has secret papers in it."

Stauffenberg walked from the room and headed towards his car. He had gone about sixty yards when there was a fierce explosion. He looked round and saw the place where the hut had been, enveloped in dust, smoke and flying debris. Without waiting for further evidence of success, he ran to his car and drove smartly towards the exit from the outer compound. By the time he had travelled the four kilometres to the gate, the alarm had sounded, and the guards stopped him. Stauffenberg

[1]This account is based on the evidence given to Allied interrogators by Assmann and to the Nuremberg Tribunal by Bodenschatz.

[2]This explanation of the way in which Stauffenberg set the time mechanism in action is taken from the Gestapo report on the plot. It cannot be confirmed but appears reasonable.

walked to the telephone, rang the duty officer in the Guard Room and obtained permission to leave. In a few moments he was in his aircraft heading for Berlin, convinced that this time the bomb in the brief-case had done its job, and that before he reached the Bendlerstrasse his associates would have set in action the mechanism of the *putsch*.

Immediately after hearing the explosion, Fellgiebel had sent Olbricht the success signal, as planned, and had begun the task of sabotaging the Rastenburg communications. On receiving Fellgiebel's message, Olbricht went straight to Fromm, his C.-in-C., told him that Hitler had been assassinated, and said that he proposed to issue the code-word for internal disorder—WALKYRIE. Fromm was not a party to the plot, but his support, or at least acquiescence, was needed in order to preserve the fiction that legal action was being taken to deal with an emergency. Orders sent out under Fromm's name would be obeyed without question, but these orders he refused to give until he had personally confirmed Olbricht's report by telephoning Rastenburg. Believing that by this time the Führer's H.Q. was cut off from the outside world, Olbricht did not attempt to restrain Fromm. To his dismay, however, not only did Fromm get through to Rastenburg but he spoke to Keitel. The following conversation ensued:

> *Fromm:* What in the world is going on at H.Q.? Here in Berlin the wildest rumours are afloat.
> *Keitel:* What is supposed to be going on? Everything is all right.
> *Fromm:* I have just received a report that the Führer has been assassinated.
> *Keitel:* Nonsense! There was an attempt at assassination but fortunately it failed. The Führer is alive and received only superficial injuries. Where, by the way, is your Chief of Staff, Col. Stauffenberg?
> *Fromm:* Stauffenberg is not here yet.

The outcome of this telephone conversation[1] was that Fromm forbade Olbricht to send out the WALKYRIE signal and, since Olbricht himself was unnerved by the report that Hitler was still alive, he decided to take no action until Stauffenberg reached Berlin. Thus three hours were lost, for Stauffenberg did not arrive at Rangsdorf airfield until four o'clock. On landing he telephoned Olbricht's office and was dismayed to find that nothing had been done to implement their plans for seizing power. He assured Olbricht that Hitler was dead, ordered him to issue the operative code-word immediately, and himself drove at top speed to the Bendlerstrasse.

When Stauffenberg arrived, the still protesting Fromm was placed under arrest, and the conspirators took charge of the Home Army H.Q.

[1] The transcript of this conversation was presented in evidence before the People's Court.

The WALKYRIE signal had already gone out and it was now followed by the transmission of an announcement that the Führer was dead, that there was a state of emergency and that the Wehrmacht had taken over the protection of the Reich. Many of those who received these signals were in league with the plotters and therefore acted at once. In Breslau, Munich and Vienna, in Brussels, Paris and Athens, the agents of the conspirators gained control. In the French capital, for instance, von Stülpnagel arrested the representatives of the Gestapo and the SS, and telephoned the H.Q. of C.-in-C., West, with the object of persuading von Kluge to act on the sealed instructions which had been sent to him some days earlier. As von Kluge was away at the front and was going to the H.Q. of Army Group B at Laroche-Guyon, von Stülpnagel set out to meet him there, determined to force his hand.

While the seizure of power was proceeding smoothly in many places, there was doubt and confusion in certain of the H.Q. which had received the signals from Berlin, for some of these were signed by Olbricht, some by von Witzleben,[1] whom everybody knew was on the retired list, while others bore no signature except 'C.-in-C., Home Army.' Accordingly, those commanders who knew nothing of the plot refrained from acting until they had received confirmation, and in the late afternoon the Bendlerstrasse was bombarded with telephone calls from all over Europe. Stauffenberg, now in complete command, attempted to reassure the callers, but he was not always successful and the implementation of some orders was accordingly delayed. Nevertheless, it must have seemed to him that the *putsch* was on the point of success, for there had been no word from Rastenburg since Fromm's conversation with Keitel early in the afternoon, and no intervention on the part of anyone at the Führer's H.Q. Nor had Stauffenberg any reason to think that the process of securing the capital was not being carried out as planned.

By 4.30 the Berlin Guard Battalion had thrown a protective cordon round the Government quarter and had sent a small detachment to arrest Goebbels at the Propaganda Ministry. The commander of this battalion was a Major Remer and it so happened that on this day he had with him a National Socialist Guidance Officer, Lieut. Hagen, who had been lecturing to his troops. On learning what orders Remer had received, Hagen had become suspicious and had telephoned Goebbels, who, until this time, had heard nothing except that there had been an explosion at the Führer's H.Q. When Remer's detachment arrived to arrest Goebbels, they were 'received' by the Reichsminister himself who assured them, though he had no means of knowing, that Hitler was alive and that their orders had been issued by traitors. In the meantime Hagen had persuaded Remer to consult Goebbels before taking any

---

[1] Field-Marshal Erwin von Witzleben, Beck's choice for the post of Supreme Commander of the Wehrmacht, had been one of the leaders of the group which had planned to arrest Hitler on the eve of the Munich crisis. In 1942, when C.-in-C., West, he had been dismissed by Hitler and retired.

further action. When Remer reached the Propaganda Ministry, Goebbels put through a call to Rastenburg. It was some time before a connection could be established but, when it was, Goebbels spoke to the Führer himself. Hitler said that he had suffered only slight injuries—a fact which Stauffenberg would have discovered if he had waited another few moments before dashing off in his car.

That afternoon, when the bomb burst, Keitel rushed out with smoke-stained face and torn clothes screaming, " Attentat! Attentat! " Jodl was blown through the open window on to the ground outside; Puttkamer staggered from the room severely wounded, and Schmundt reeled out of the ruins minus a leg. Then came the Führer, leaning heavily on two officers, his left trouser leg torn away, his right shoulder hanging limp, but otherwise apparently unhurt.[1] The two officers helped Hitler across to his bunker, but half an hour later he reappeared in a fresh uniform and drove off to the nearby railway station to greet Mussolini, who was coming to inspect four Italian divisions trained for service on the Eastern Front.

As he grasped the Duce's hand, the Führer said, " I have just had the greatest piece of luck of my life," and then went on to tell how the bomb had burst within six feet of him, and how he had been saved because the meeting had been held in the flimsy wooden hut instead of the usual concrete bunker. Neither Hitler, nor his staff, however, were yet aware of the full implications of the attempt on his life, and the two dictators went through with their tour of inspection apparently ignorant of what was happening in Berlin. It was not until he returned from the inspection and spoke to Goebbels that Hitler realised the situation and began to act in his own defence.

He would have been both ignorant and powerless, however, if Fellgiebel had carried through the plan to put the Rastenburg communications out of action. After sending the message to Olbricht, Fellgiebel had begun his task, but had not completed it when he discovered that the bomb had not done its job. Then, it seems, he did nothing more, but the telephone exchange must have been incapable of handling outgoing calls for some hours, because no detailed news of the attempt on Hitler's life reached Berlin from Rastenburg until Goebbels telephoned the Führer about five o'clock.

Having talked to Goebbels, Hitler spoke to Major Remer, promoted him at once to the rank of Colonel and ordered him to round up the traitors, acting under Goebbels's direction to ensure the safety of the capital. Thus, the very troops upon whom Stauffenberg and Olbricht were relying to protect their H.Q. now had orders to put them under arrest.

Within the next few minutes Keitel was on the telephone to the Bendlerstrasse insisting that the Führer was alive and demanding to

[1]This description is taken from the evidence of the guard who was on duty outside the hut that afternoon.

speak to Fromm. On Stauffenberg's assurance, however, Keitel's assertion was dismissed by Beck and Olbricht as bluff but, even if it were true, there was still a chance for the *putsch* to succeed. The conspirators had at least an hour's start with the announcement that Hitler was dead and this news would be difficult to overtake, since they controlled the military signals network throughout Germany. The fate of the venture now depended on the outcome of the battle for communications, and the key to this was Berlin Radio.

No one realised that better than Goebbels. After speaking to Hitler he told Remer to carry out the instructions of the conspirators and to take possession of the Berlin radio station, but to hold it for *him*. At the same time, anticipating that the regiment from Krampnitz might also have orders to seize this objective, Goebbels sent out couriers to intercept it. When the regimental commander learned what the real situation was, he led his troops back to their barracks, leaving Remer in command of the radio station. Goebbels made good use of it and soon after six o'clock all German transmitters carried the announcement that there had been an attempt on the Führer's life, but that he had received " only slight burns and bruises but no other injuries."

This broadcast brought a fresh flood of telephone calls to the Bendlerstrasse from H.Q. all over Germany and the occupied countries. The callers declared that they were receiving orders from Rastenburg to ignore all instructions from Berlin and to obey only those that came from Keitel or Himmler, who, they were told, had been appointed C.-in-C., Home Army, in succession to Fromm. Stauffenberg endeavoured to insist that the Rastenburg signals and the Berlin broadcast were part of an attempt by Himmler and Goebbels to preserve the power of the Nazi régime; but by this time many of the doubting commanders had rung the Führer's H.Q. and had spoken to Hitler himself. Others who had begun to act on the sealed orders because they believed he was dead, and not because they were party to the plot, now played for time, anxious to make sure of the situation before they compromised themselves.

The course of events in Hamburg that evening was typical of what happened all over Germany. The *Wehrkreis* commander had received instructions, in Fromm's name, to arrest all senior officials of the SS, the Police and the Party. Accordingly, a number of these officials had been summoned by telephone to report to the *Wehrkreis* H.Q. at seven o'clock. Before they got there, however, the announcement of Hitler's escape had been broadcast and the commander was rather bewildered. While he was trying to make up his mind another teleprinter message arrived from the Bendlerstrasse, signed by Stauffenberg and stating, " All assertions that the Führer is not dead are false. Orders issued up till now are to be carried out with the utmost dispatch." Before any action had been taken on this message, another teleprint arrived, this time from Rastenburg, signed by one of Hitler's staff, Burgdorf. It said, " The Führer is alive. Orders from the Bendlerstrasse are not to be carried out." When the leading Hamburg Nazis reported to the *Wehrkreis* H.Q., therefore, they were not arrested and within a few minutes were on their way home again. In many other places similar scenes were enacted with the result that in city after city the plot fizzled out as the Nazis regained control of the essential communications.

In spite of all these miscarriages of plan at Rastenburg, in Berlin and throughout the Reich, the outcome might have been very different if there had been prompt and resolute action in the West at von Kluge's H.Q., since the conspirators could then have confronted the Nazis with a situation which it would have been extremely difficult to restore. The original intention of the plotters was that von Kluge and Rommel were to get in touch with the Allies on the Normandy front as soon as they learned of Hitler's death, and were to obtain a local armistice pending a wider settlement with the Western Allies. In the meantime, if the SS divisions refused to observe any armistice, they were to be disarmed by neighbouring Wehrmacht formations. Thus the 21st Panzer Division had been allotted the task of dealing with 12th SS, an unenviable assignment. All these instructions were contained in sealed orders delivered to agents of the conspirators at the H.Q. of Rommel at Laroche-Guyon, and of von Kluge at St. Germain.

By July 20th, however, Rommel was in hospital and von Kluge, who had taken over Rommel's appointment in addition to his own, was thus the only commander who could act. Von Stülpnagel had promised to ensure that he did so, and it was on this account that he had set out for Laroche-Guyon late in the afternoon after he had failed to reach von Kluge by telephone. Von Kluge arrived there before von Stülpnagel but in time to receive an urgent telephone call from Berlin.[1] The caller gave no name, but said to the Field-Marshal, " The Führer is dead. You must decide now what you intend to do." Von Kluge gave no reply. He merely replaced the receiver. A second call came from Berlin; the same voice with the same demand. Once again von Kluge replaced the receiver in silence.

Shortly after this incident von Kluge learned of the radio announcement put out by Goebbels, but this was followed almost at once by a teleprinter signal from Berlin, signed by von Witzleben. It began:

1. The Führer, Adolf Hitler, is dead. An unscrupulous clique of non-combatant Party leaders, utilising this situation, has attempted to stab our fighting forces in the back and seize power for their own purposes.

2. In this hour of extreme danger, the Government of the Reich, to maintain law and order, has decreed a military state of emergency and placed me in supreme command of the German Armed Forces . . .

[1]Gisevius, who was at the Bendlerstrasse that afternoon, says that it was Beck himself who made this call. Von Kluge's reaction was described to me by Blumentritt.

When this message came, von Kluge turned to Blumentritt and said, " This is an historic moment, you know. I would like to order a cessation of the V.1s immediately. If the Führer *is* dead we ought to get in touch with the people on the other side right away." Von Kluge was still in doubt, when the telephone rang again. It was Warlimont speaking from Rastenburg. He was soon able to convince the C.-in-C., West, that the plot had failed. Thus, when von Stülpnagel reached Laroche-Guyon, von Kluge told him, " Nothing more can be done. The Führer is alive." The last chance that the *attentat* might help to shorten the war had gone.

While von Kluge had been hesitating in France, Goebbels had taken strong action in Berlin. There, as elsewhere, the chief reason for the failure of the conspirators was that they did not command forces upon which they could rely absolutely. They had been so uncertain of support, even within the Army, that they had been compelled to issue guarded orders which indicated that the troops were maintaining law and order, not carrying out a *putsch*. In many instances, therefore, the recipients disregarded the conspirators' instructions as soon as they discovered the truth.

By early evening Remer's battalion and the SS had moved unopposed into the Bendlerstrasse in execution of Goebbels's orders. Inside the Home Army H.Q. Fromm had escaped from confinement and had begun to act against the conspirators in the hope of removing any suspicion from himself. Gathering a few other officers, equally keen to clear themselves by a display of loyalty, Fromm arrested Olbricht, Stauffenberg and three of their associates and had them taken into the courtyard and shot. Beck was handed a revolver and was given the opportunity to take his own life. When his attempt to do so miscarried, Fromm himself completed the task.

Well before midnight, therefore, the chief conspirators had been arrested or killed and the plot had been smashed, but it was still not known for certain what had happened to Hitler. Doubts on this score were not finally dispelled until 12.30 a.m. on July 21st when the Führer broadcast over all German stations. Hitler declared:

> If I speak to you to-day it is first in order that you should hear my voice, and should know that I am unhurt and well, and secondly that you should know of a crime unparalleled in German history. A very small clique of ambitious, irresponsible and at the same time senseless and very stupid officers had formed a plot to eliminate me and the command of the German Wehrmacht.

> The bomb was placed by Colonel Count von Stauffenberg. It exploded two metres to my right. One of those with me has died.[1]

[1]Four men were in fact killed by the explosion—Schmundt, Korten, Brandt and Berger.

A number of colleagues very dear to me were very severely injured. I myself sustained only some very minor scratches, bruises and burns. I regard this as a confirmation of the task imposed upon me by Providence . . .

The circle of these conspirators is very small and has nothing in common with the spirit of the German Wehrmacht and above all none with the German people. I therefore order now that no military authority, no leader of any unit, no private in the field is to obey any orders emanating from these groups of usurpers. I also order that it is everyone's duty to arrest, or if they resist, to kill at sight any one issuing or handling any such orders.

I am convinced that with the emergence of this quite tiny clique of traitors and saboteurs, there has at long last been created in our rear that atmosphere which the fighting front needs. . . . This time we shall get even with them in the way that we National Socialists are accustomed.

Hitler's speech was the start of a blood-bath far exceeding that of the Roehm purge in 1934. His declaration that " It is everyone's duty to arrest, or, if they resist, to kill at sight anyone issuing or handling " any instructions from the conspirators was liberally interpreted by Party officials as authority for liquidating any who were even vaguely suspected of hostility towards the régime. Under cover of this order many personal scores were settled and the Nazis vented their wrath on innocent and guilty alike as a double insurance against any further trouble.

The counter-measures started with the rounding-up of the major conspirators and especially the military members, but wholesale civilian arrests began when the Gestapo discovered the lists of names of those whom the conspirators had planned to place in administrative positions throughout the Reich. Most of these men had had nothing to do with the plot and had not even known of their ' selection ' for office, but this did not save them. The proceedings before the ' People's Court ' set up to try the conspirators were an even greater travesty of justice than the usual Nazi trials. How many were executed with or without trial will never be known exactly. One estimate, based on specific names, sets the number at 4,980, but at least another 10,000 were sent to Concentration Camps from which many never returned. In any case, it is certain that very few of those implicated managed to escape the purge, and that thousands of Liberals and Social Democrats who would have been invaluable in the reconstruction of post-war Germany were wiped out. The failure of the *putsch* meant not only the immediate strengthening of the Nazi Régime, but the emasculation of the forces of ultimate reconstruction.

The basic cause of the failure was the efficiency of Himmler's Security Service. It was this which made it extremely difficult to prepare an alternative means of dealing with Hitler if Stauffenberg's bomb were to

fail. It was this which prevented the conspirators from organising'
beforehand the strength to make sure that they could secure control of
Berlin Radio, the SS H.Q. and other keypoints in the capital. Moreover,
it rendered impossible the organisation of any mass action, such as a
general strike, to coincide with the attempt on Hitler's life. The fear of
the Gestapo and of Himmler's police was so strong that even among the
conspirators there were many who were not prepared to act until they
were sure that the *attentat* had been successful.

Nevertheless, the *putsch* would almost certainly have succeeded if
Hitler had not been saved by what can only be regarded as a miracle.
It was mere chance that on July 20th the midday conference should
have been held in a flimsy wooden hut and not in the usual concrete
bunker, where the explosion would have been deadly. It was equally
fortuitous that the table in the hut should have been so constructed that
the main force of the blast was taken by the solid understructure.[1] Even
as it was, three of the officers standing on Hitler's side of the table and
only a yard nearer the point of explosion lost their lives. Yet Hitler
himself survived.

The suppression of the conspiracy was followed by a series of measures
intended to bind the German people yet more firmly to the Nazi war
machine. A decree of July 25th appointed Goering to " adapt the whole
of public life to the requirements of total warfare in every respect," and
gave Goebbels the post of ' Reich Plenipotentiary for the Total War
Effort.' The result was a further drastic comb-out of manpower and
the delegation to the *Gauleiter* of complete freedom of action in dealing
with any workers suspected of slacking. Moreover Himmler's awesome
jurisdiction was extended to embrace almost every source of internal
power. In addition to being Minister of the Interior, Chief of Police
and Reichsführer SS, he became C.-in-C., Home Army. Thus he controlled both the police and the military forces within the Reich. He was
also given the task of raising and training the *Volksgrenadier* divisions
which were now to be formed, the final sacrifice of German manhood
in defence of Hitler's régime. Even when these divisions were sent to the
front they remained under Himmler's control for matters of ' discipline.'

As a result of these measures, any surviving spirit of resistance within
the Army was broken. In an effort to save the prestige of the Officer
Corps, Keitel, Jodl, von Rundstedt and Guderian formed a Court of
Honour, which discharged in disgrace the military members of the
conspiracy before handing them over to the People's Court. But this
did not prevent the Party from showing to German troops all over

[1]Some accounts suggest that Hitler was saved because he moved away from the table
to study a map on the wall just as the bomb went off. This is not so. The maps were
on the table, not the wall. The explanation I have given is supported by Assmann, who
saw where the brief-case was placed and who says that Hitler was standing at the table
when the explosion occurred.

Europe films of the trial and the hanging of the chief military participants. This parading of the degradation of German officers was bitterly resented throughout the Army, but it served as a sharp warning to others who might have contemplated acting against the régime. The Army's humiliation by the Party was final and complete, and it was marked by an order that henceforth all members of the Wehrmacht must give the Nazi salute.

Any possibility that further military disaster might bring about another anti-Nazi revolt disappeared when the Allies indicated after July 20th that Hitler's removal from power would not mean any modification in the demand for ' Unconditional Surrender.' In the months that followed, the fear of Russia dominated the German mind and gave Hitler's continuance of the war a popular acceptance—and even support—which would not otherwise have been forthcoming. Goebbels now played heavily upon the theme that the Führer had been preserved to save the German people from being " engulfed by Slavic Bolshevist hordes." Hitler himself had sounded the same note in his broadcast of July 21st, which concluded with the declaration: " It has again been granted to me that I should escape a fate which would have been terrible, not for me but for the German people, who see in this again the guiding hand of Providence directing that I must and will carry out my task."

Although Hitler survived this attempt on his life, his health was seriously impaired. For the past year he had been suffering from a nervous affliction which caused a slight tremor in his left arm and his left leg. After July 20th this disappeared for a while but then returned and was intensified. In addition he became partially deaf. The most marked change, however, was in his temperament. Guderian, who worked closely with him during the coming months as Chief of Staff at OKH, reports:

Hitler's mistrust now reached extremes and the miracle of his survival gave him greater faith than ever in his mission. He shut himself up in his bunker, engaged in no further private talks, and had every word of his conversations recorded. He lost himself more and more in a realm of the imagination which had no basis in reality. Every free expression of opinion and every objection to his frequently incomprehensible views evoked an outburst of rage on his part. He lost his capacity to listen to a report to the end. His criticisms became stronger, and his actions more drastic, with every passing day. He felt that he alone had the right to hold opinions upon which decisions would be based. He was convinced that he alone possessed clear perception concerning all fields of human activity. Accordingly, he condemned generals, staff officers, diplomats, government officials and towards the end even Party and SS Leaders as armchair strategists, weaklings and finally as criminals and traitors.[1]

[1] Seventh U.S. Army Interrogation.

In spite of this mental and physical deterioration, Hitler's power was now greater than ever. The Party Leaders knew that their fate was irrevocably bound to his and they not only continued to give him unquestioning support, but intensified their efforts to ensure the loyalty of the people. The mass of Germans saw defeat and ruin at the end of the road down which they were being marched, but none could turn off it. To the one side was the barbed wire of Nazi control; to the other the blank wall of the Allied demand for ' Unconditional Surrender.' They knew that the war was lost but they had no power to end it. Hitler's position was absolute and unchallengeable. His will, his faith in his mission and his blind refusal to yield to fate made him the driving force that would keep Germany at war regardless of defeat and disaster in the field, or of devastation and destruction at home. After July 20th, the ending of the war was not a question of crushing the German soldier in battle, nor of demoralising the German civilian by bombing, though these would contribute to the ultimate collapse. The will of one man and one man alone, maintained a continent at war. That man was Adolf Hitler, and his resolution to fight to the end was now fortified by the miracle of his deliverance on July 20th.

## CHAPTER XX

# THE BREAK-OUT

ON July 22nd von Kluge forwarded to Hitler the last report written by Rommel before his accident. " Within a measurable time," said Rommel, " the enemy will succeed in breaking through our thinly held front, especially that of Seventh Army, and in thrusting deep into France. . . . The force is fighting heroically everywhere, but the unequal struggle is nearing its end. In my opinion, it is necessary to draw the appropriate conclusion from this situation."[1] Rommel had already suggested what that conclusion should be but, by the time this report reached the Führer's H.Q., Hitler was even less inclined to take heed of the facts than he had been three weeks earlier at Berchtesgaden. He was now utterly intractable, and, in the light of the ' defensive success ' of Panzer Group West at Caen, he persuaded himself that Seventh Army too could hold its ground. The order to von Kluge was ' Starre Verteidigung.'

This reiterated ' stand fast ' order took no account of the complete miscarriage of the plans which Hitler had proclaimed at Berchtesgaden for winning the battle of supply and outstripping the Allied build-up. His ' anti-aircraft highways ' had never materialised, for the Luftwaffe had neither the fighters nor the flak to protect them. Although nearly 800 single-engined fighters were transferred from the Reich to the West in the first fortnight of the invasion, Air Fleet III was never able to challenge the Allied command of the air, for its numerical inferiority was accentuated by the disruption of its ground organisation. Galland, the C.-in-C. of the Luftwaffe Fighter Arm, reports that when the transfer began:

> Most of the carefully prepared and provisioned airfields had been bombed out and units had to land at hastily-chosen landing-grounds. The poor signals network broke down and this caused further confusion.[2] Because of the indifferent navigating ability of most of the

[1] Observations on the Situation, June 15th, 1944. (Tempelhof Papers.)

[2] The breakdown of line communications was a by-product of the Allied bombing of airfields and traffic centres. In addition, many underground cables were cut by French ' saboteurs.' An investigation by OKL revealed also that some of the faults which developed after D-Day had been ' built into ' the land-line network by the French technicians who had laid it for the Luftwaffe.

pilots (accustomed to flying under expert fighter control systems in Germany), many units came down in the wrong places. The alternative airfields were too few, poorly camouflaged and badly supplied. The main ground parties came by rail and in most cases arrived days or weeks late. The slightest exposure of activity sufficed to betray an airfield to alert Allied reconnaissance, and always resulted in prompt visits by low-flying fighters. Two weeks after the invasion began, many *Gruppen* were already wrecked and could barely put up two or three aircraft per day.

In these two weeks more than half the fighters sent to France were destroyed and the supply of replacements was drying up, for the Luftwaffe was now confronted with another danger which threatened its very survival.

In switching its main fighter strength to France, Goering had acted on the assumption that, while the bridgehead battle was raging, there would be few large-scale daylight raids on German industry. In the middle of June, however, Eighth U.S. Air Force resumed its campaign against the synthetic oil plants, upon which the Luftwaffe relied for 95 per cent of its fuel. During May American bombing had reduced the average daily output of aviation spirit from 5,850 tons to 2,800, mainly because production was completely interrupted at the two main refineries, Leuna and Pölitz. A week after D-Day the third largest plant, Gelsenkirchen, ceased operations following a night attack by R.A.F. Bomber Command. Despite this warning that the offensive against oil had been renewed, German fighters offered no resistance whatever when the Americans bombed the Schölven refinery on the 18th. Subsequent attacks were opposed, but with so little success that on June 22nd (three years to the day since Hitler had set forth to conquer Russian oil) the output of aviation spirit was 632 tons. Total production for June came to 53,000 tons (compared with 175,000 in April) and the month's consumption was met only by drawing 124,000 tons from the central reserve.[1]

On June 30th Speer warned Hitler: " If we do not succeed in protecting the synthetic plants and refineries better than in the past, then an unbridgeable gap will appear in the fuel supply of the Armed Forces and the homeland. . . . By September it will no longer be possible to cover the most urgent of the necessary supplies for the Wehrmacht." Speer advocated the strictest economy and a substantial increase in fighter, flak and smoke-screen protection for the oil installations.

Since the start of the invasion, the day-fighter strength of the Reich

[1] All these facts and figures, except the last, are quoted from the report which Speer presented to Hitler on June 30th, 1944. The amount drawn from reserve is taken from the interrogation of Milch, Inspector-General of the Luftwaffe, who also reveals that the total reserve of aviation spirit in May 1944 was 400,000 tons. From the German documents it is difficult to assess stocks exactly, for Hitler, OKW and OKL all kept a strategic reserve.

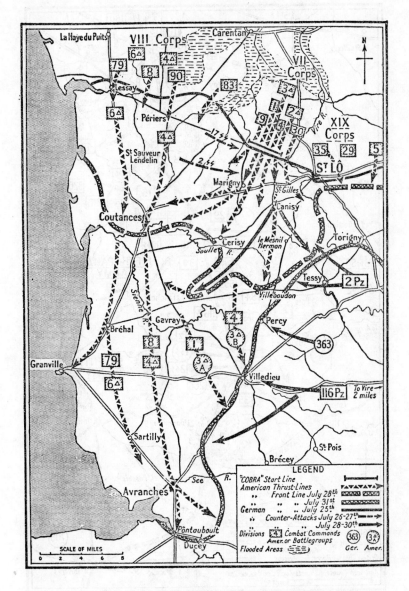

OPERATION COBRA, JULY 25TH–31ST

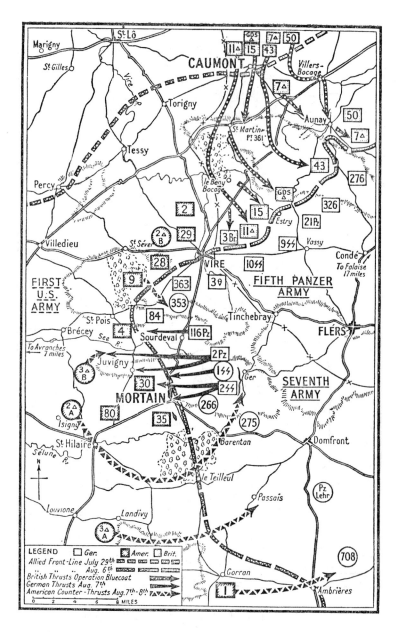

THE MORTAIN COUNTER-ATTACK, AUGUST 7TH-8TH

had fallen from 991 to 544, and it had been prevented from falling still farther only by the dangerous expedient of bringing instructional units into the line of battle. German fighter production was greater than ever and was continuing to rise, but it was not rising fast enough to keep pace with losses. In the three months ending June 30th, 4,545 single-engined fighters were delivered from German factories, but during the same period 5,527 were destroyed in action, in accidents or on the ground.[1] These severe casualties were an index both of the intensity of the air fighting, and of the deterioration in the quality of German aircraft and pilots.

To meet the fresh crisis on the ' oil front,' the Luftwaffe was compelled to curtail the westward flow of fighter replacements and to retain in the Reich eight *Gruppen*[2] which had come back to refit. These measures put an end to whatever chance there had been of establishing protected corridors for German supplies and troops moving to Normandy. Thus the strategic bombers helped to create for the rest of the Allied Air Forces the opportunity to roam almost unopposed over France and the Low Countries, ravaging and disrupting enemy supply lines and installations.

The campaign against railways, bridges and roads was pursued with unrelenting persistence over an ever-widening area. Having wrecked all rail bridges over the Seine below Paris, and over the Loire below Orléans, the Air Forces turned their onslaught against the lines passing through the ' Paris–Orléans gap.' From mid-June there were never more than two single tracks available for through traffic, and for the most part these could be worked only at night. Even then they were liable to be bombed by the light of flares. Several times the Germans managed to patch up rail crossings over the rivers, but their work was soon undone and they had to resort to ferries and pontoons. Between the Seine and the Loire fighters and fighter-bombers, patrolling every road and railway, forbade all daylight movement in clear weather, and during the short summer nights motorised convoys could seldom cover more than twenty miles, for there were frequent delays at bombed bridges and cratered crossroads. By July the dislocation of the railways was doubly serious for the excessive movement by road was rapidly depleting the German stocks of petrol, just when the bombing of the refineries had halved the output of motor spirit.

Had it not been for the recurrent bad weather in June and July, and the shortage of airfields in the bridgehead, the Allied Air Forces would have been able to blockade the battlefield still more closely. Even as it was, the reinforcement of Normandy was slow and painful, and the

---

[1] *Überblick über den Rustungsstand der Luftwaffe*, January 1st, 1945   This survey, a monthly Wehrmacht publication, gives the combat losses in this period as 2,545, but other OKL documents establish the full extent of the wastage.

[2] This left 15 *Gruppen* in the West and 21 in the Reich. A Fighter *Gruppe* had an establishment of 68 aircraft, but at this stage of the war few ever had a strength of more than 50 and the average was about 35.

Germans were given no chance of matching the Anglo-American build-up. In the first seven weeks they succeeded in bringing up some twenty divisions to support the eight which were in Western Normandy at the outset, and very few of these divisions arrived at full strength or in good condition. Most of them straggled up, a battalion or a regiment at a time, and were flung into battle in such haste and disorder that they suffered heavy casualties before they had time to settle down. In these seven weeks three divisions were wiped out and six others were so reduced that they could muster only two or three battalions each.

Reserves might arrive slowly, but replacements came hardly at all. Between June 6th and July 23rd Seventh Army and Panzer Group West lost 116,863 killed, wounded or missing, but only 10,078 men were sent up from the training depots.[1] The equipment situation was equally grave. Of the 250 tanks destroyed in the first six weeks, only 17 were replaced. Although the shortage of reinforcements was primarily due to the exhaustion of the general pool of trained manpower, the failure to make good the tank losses resulted directly from the Allied bombing of railways. At no time during the entire war was German tank production higher than in May, June and July of 1944. In these three months 2,313 tanks were ' accepted ' from the factories by OKH: in the same period the losses were 1,730.[2] The Wehrmacht had the tanks, but it could not transport them to the Western Front.

While the German forces west of the Seine were being steadily ground down, eighteen divisions kept idle guard on the Channel coast from Le Havre to Antwerp. The imminence of disaster in Normandy did not begin to outweigh the fear of another landing until the middle of July. Even then, only three divisions were taken from Fifteenth Army, and these reluctantly, for the general appreciation (as reported by Speidel from Army Group B on the 24th) was that " although a widely-spaced second landing operation is not very likely, the sector of the Fifteenth Army from north of the Somme to the Seine is particularly threatened." The fictitious divisions in Southern England were still distorting German calculations. Speidel declared that the Allies now had 40 divisions in the bridgehead and another 42 ready to cross the Channel.

The Germans were equally at fault in their estimate of Montgomery's intentions. Speidel anticipated that, while the American task was merely " the extension of the land base to the line Domfront–Avranches," the role of the British was " to secure a break-through in the direction of Falaise, thus creating the opportunity for a thrust towards Paris." This appreciation was reflected in the disposition of the forces containing the bridgehead. Thus on the eve of the American break-out offensive, von

[1]Weekly Report of Army Group B, July 24th, 1944. (Tempelhof Papers.) These 10,078 do not include those which the Luftwaffe sent to 2nd Parachute Corps. Its commander (Meindl) reported to Hausser on July 14th that he had received 10,000 replacements, of which " 6,800 had fallen out within a short time, through lack of experience."
[2]OKH Ordnance Directorate figures.

Kluge's armies—unprotected from the air, unbalanced on the ground, exhausted in battle and starved of reinforcements—were ripe for defeat.

The Germans were even less successful in attacking Allied supply lines than they were in protecting their own. Although Doenitz did all he could to implement the Führer's demands, the Anglo-American build-up was little hampered by U-boats or surface craft, or by the midget submarines and 'human-torpedoes,' which the Germans launched against the eastern anchorage in the first fortnight of July. Mines continued to be Ramsay's greatest anxiety, but constant and courageous sweeping kept this menace in check. In four weeks of Hitler's "offensive with every possible weapon," the number of Allied merchantmen sunk was five. The only serious hindrance which the Germans were able to impose on the flow of supplies to Normandy, resulted from their dislocation of the port of Cherbourg. Because of mines, obstructions and demolitions, no supply ships were able to enter that harbour until July 16th, and it was another three weeks before Liberty ships could tie up alongside the quays; two months before Cherbourg could handle in a day as much cargo as was unloaded over UTAH beach every twenty-four hours.

The delay in opening Cherbourg was a serious matter in view of the destruction of the American MULBERRY and the heavy loss of ferry-craft in the June gale. By mid-July more than 6,000 tons a day were coming ashore through the British MULBERRY and a few minor ports were working, but the bulk of the 54,000 tons that were landed daily came in over beaches, where the only protection was provided by the blockship breakwaters.[1] Long-range shelling curtailed, and in mid-July prevented, the use of the easternmost anchorage, but the capacity of the other beaches far exceeded all expectations, especially in the American sector.

Undismayed by the destruction of their artificial harbour, the Americans applied to the development of the OMAHA and UTAH anchorages their tremendous talent for invention and organisation. In defiance of orthodox opinion, they beached coasters and unloaded them direct into Army lorries at low tide. The booms of Liberty ships were regularly overloaded and sometimes they broke, but the general results fully justified the risks. Occasionally the Americans were too ingenious. On the OMAHA foreshore they scooped up the shingle to make a road-bed, only to find that, with the removal of the shingle bank, the waves came up and washed away the road. For the most part, however, their improvisations paid big dividends. The open roadstead and beach of OMAHA were so organised that during July the Americans here handled more than twice the tonnage which passed through the British MULBERRY.

This achievement has led to the suggestion that the vast expenditure

[1] The average daily tonnage of ammunition, petrol, supplies and other stores landed in July was made up as follows: OMAHA, 15,000; UTAH, 19,000; British beaches, 10,500; MULBERRY, 6,500; minor ports, 3,000.

of effort and materials on the artificial harbours was in fact unnecessary, and that the same build-up could have been achieved far more economically with a few hundred more landing-craft and ferries. From the viewpoint of pure logistics this case has some validity, but it ignores strategic and psychological factors of great importance. When the OVERLORD plan was drawn up, there was no shipping to spare and no evidence that a large-scale cross-Channel invasion could be maintained over open beaches. Strategically the ' possession ' of MULBERRY gave the planners freedom to choose a landing area well away from the heavily fortified major ports; psychologically it gave the Allied High Command a degree of confidence without which the venture, which seemed so hazardous, might never have been undertaken.

The Allied triumph in the battle of supply was such that in the first seven weeks one and a half million men were transported across the Channel with all their arms, equipment and supplies, an unparalleled achievement.[1] While the Germans were reinforcing Normandy with 20 divisions, the Allies landed 36, plus a vast number of supporting troops, air squadrons and service units. By July 20th the shallow bridgehead was filled to bursting point and the Americans were ready to break out.

Two days earlier First U.S. Army's persistence had been rewarded. Bradley's troops had reached the St. Lô–Périers road and had driven the Germans from the ruins of the town that had been a fortress in their path for six weeks. This slogging battle for St. Lô had cost the Americans ten thousand casualties in twelve days, and had heavily taxed the spirit and endurance of the riflemen upon whom the main burden of the hedgerow fighting fell. Nevertheless, it had secured for Bradley the firm ground from which to launch his new offensive, a four-mile stretch along the St. Lô–Périers road west of the Vire.

Of equal importance was the fact that, since July 3rd, the Americans, to use Montgomery's phrase, had " eaten the guts out of the German defence." Indeed von Choltitz, the commander of 84th Corps, reported to Seventh Army on the 15th: " The whole battle is one tremendous bloodbath, such as I have never seen in eleven years of war."[2] The German losses were the greater, because of Hitler's obdurate insistence upon standing fast, and when he did agree to a minor withdrawal he stipulated that it should be " from hedgerow to hedgerow only." By the time St. Lô fell the line was taut and thin. On the following day,

[1]The SHAEF build-up records showed that by July 29th the following had been landed:

|          | PERSONNEL | VEHICLES | STORES (tons) |
|----------|-----------|----------|---------------|
| American - - | 903,061 | 176,620 | 858,436 |
| British - - - | 663,295 | 156,025 | 744,540 |
| TOTAL - - | 1,566,356 | 332,645 | 1,602,976 |

[2]Seventh Army Telephone Log, July 15th, 2350 hours.

Hausser advised von Kluge that Seventh Army's sole reserve was three battalions of infantry. He asked in urgent terms for men and weapons, and especially for " a mobile formation of full fighting strength as Army reserve . . . and for one or two brigades of *nebelwerfer*."[1] Von Kluge replied that no armour could be spared, but that Panzer Lehr would be relieved in 14 days' time by an infantry division which was marching up from Belgium. As for *nebelwerfer*, the only three brigades of these in Normandy were " occupied in the main battle area at Caen," where, of course, seven of von Kluge's nine armoured divisions and his four heavy tank battalions were also concentrated.

It was not only in armour and mortars, however, that Panzer Group West had been given priority over Seventh Army. In the month following the fall of Cherbourg, eight German infantry divisions reached Normandy; six of these were put into the line opposite the British, and this during a period when the Caen sector was strengthened with four additional panzer divisions and two battalions of Tiger tanks.

On the eve of Operation COBRA, therefore, Dempsey's 14 divisions were pinning down 14 German divisions (with 600 tanks) and five of these divisions had been in the line for less than a fortnight. Bradley, on the other hand, with fifteen divisions of his own, and four of Patton's Third Army in reserve, was opposed by a hotchpotch of formations and battlegroups, amounting to nine divisions (with 110 tanks[2]), only one of which had been in action less than a month, and that one (5th Parachute) was regarded by Hausser as " completely untrained." The Germans had indeed been " pulled on to Second Army."

Bradley's plan for COBRA revealed how much he had profited from his recent experience. In his offensive of early July he had attacked along the entire front from St. Lô to the sea and, since this dispersal of his strength was accentuated by the nature of the country, he had been unable to gain a clear success anywhere. For COBRA, however, he accepted Montgomery's suggestion that he should concentrate a powerful striking force on a 6,000-yard front, five miles west of St. Lô. There, after a heavy air bombardment, he planned to breach the German defences with an infantry attack and then to drive armoured and motorised columns through to the west coast between Coutances and Bréhal, thus cutting off the German 84th Corps, which was holding the line of the St. Lô–Périers–Lessay road.

Seventh Army was particularly vulnerable to the kind of attack Bradley planned, for its left wing was deployed much too far forward. Consequently, the flank and rear of 84th Corps were gravely exposed to a thrust along the road from St. Lô to Coutances. Hausser wanted to pull back behind this road, but Hitler had forbidden any further with-

---

[1] Appreciation by Hausser for von Kluge, July 19th, 1944. (Tempelhof Papers.)
[2] The German records show that, on July 23rd, 2nd SS Panzer Division had 57 tanks ready for action. Bayerlein says that in Panzer Lehr he had " about 50 tanks and assault guns."

drawal and von Kluge did not dare even to suggest such a move. Since his defences had little depth and his reserves little mobility, Hausser decided to man his main infantry line very lightly and to concentrate upon holding the road junctions for a depth of three or four miles behind the front. The past month's fighting in the bocage had shown that tanks could not move far or fast across country, and that, if the road junctions were held, the speed of the American advance could be cut down to the pace of the infantry. Such dispositions, he hoped, would at least delay a break-through, but he did not know that the Americans had invented a hedge-cutting device to defeat such tactics.

This device, known as a ' Rhinoceros,' consisted of eight sharp steel teeth welded to the front of a Sherman tank about two feet above the ground. Equipped with this attachment, a tank could drive into a hedgerow at ten to fifteen miles an hour; the teeth would bite into the bank, loosen the earth and cut the roots; and the tank would plunge through with little loss of speed. Bradley quickly appreciated the value of the ' Rhino,' and through the middle of July his field workshops toiled night and day, forging and welding the means to break the deadlock of the bocage.

Bradley had originally hoped to attack on July 20th, but bad weather caused him to wait from day to day. This delay gave the Germans the chance to consolidate their defences and bring up supplies under cover of cloud and rain, but no fresh troops arrived to bolster the straining line. The operation was finally ordered for the 24th. Again, however, the weather closed in, but not before some of the bombers had taken off. The postponement signal reached them too late, and part of the air programme was carried out. Unable to identify their target visually, some aircraft dropped their bombs within the American lines. This false start was most unfortunate, for Hausser had been expecting that the Americans would attack on a broad front. Forewarned, he began to move his only mobile reserve (a battlegroup of 2nd SS) from St. Sauveur Lendelin, south of Périers, to the threatened area.

Although the Germans thought, and indeed announced, that Bradley's attack had begun, von Kluge continued to believe that an American advance in the bocage would have far less serious consequences than would a renewal of the British offensive in the open Caen plain. That night, therefore, the 2nd Panzer Division completed its transfer from the Caumont area to the Orne Valley, in anticipation of the attack which II Canadian Corps launched astride the Caen–Falaise road before dawn next day.[1]

On the morning of July 25th, while Panzer Group West was at grips

[1]This was essentially a ' holding attack ' with very limited objectives on the crest of Bourguebus Ridge. Montgomery's directive of July 21st repeated his familiar theme. Second Army was to " operate intensively " with the object of " leading the enemy to believe that we contemplate a major advance towards Falaise and Argentan," and thus inducing him to " build up his main strength to the east of the R. Orne, so that our affairs on the western flank can proceed with greater speed."

with the Canadians, the sky above St. Lô cleared at last and the weather
gave its blessing to Bradley's opportunity. The preliminary bombardment for COBRA began at 9.40 a.m. Fighter-bombers struck first, at the
German outpost line along the St. Lô–Périers road; then for an hour
Fortresses and Liberators saturated a rectangle four miles wide and a
mile and a half deep, covering the whole frontage of the ground attack
and the full depth of the German infantry defences. At eleven o'clock,
as the assault divisions of Collins's VII Corps moved forward, the ground
ahead of them was raked again by fighter bombers, and half an hour
later the 'mediums' laid deep barrages along the roads leading to St.
Gilles and Marigny. Once again some bombs fell short and, even though
the forward infantry had been withdrawn 1,500 yards, two of the leading
units suffered such severe casualties that reserve battalions had to take
their places.[1] This involved some delay in each case, but the rest of the
attack went in as planned, with the 9th Division on the right, the 4th
in the centre and the 30th on the left. Their general objective was the
Marigny–St. Gilles road; having reached that, the two flank divisions
were to swing outwards and hold open the gap for the exploitation
divisions, 1st Infantry (motorised for this battle), 2nd and 3rd Armoured.

The zone covered by the air bombardment corresponded almost
exactly with the sector held by Bayerlein's Panzer Lehr Division and a
regiment of paratroops. In accordance with Hausser's policy of holding
the main roads and junctions, Bayerlein had deployed his tanks in depth
down the two roads which ran along the backs of pronounced ridges to
Marigny and St. Gilles. Wherever possible he had secreted his tanks
in the 'mouths' of hedged lanes, but even these natural 'harbours' did
not save them. Bayerlein says:

> The planes kept coming over, as if on a conveyor belt, and the
> bomb carpets unrolled in great rectangles. My flak had hardly
> opened its mouth, when the batteries received direct hits which
> knocked out half the guns and silenced the rest. After an hour I had
> no communication with anybody, even by radio. By noon nothing
> was visible but dust and smoke. My front-lines looked like the face
> of the moon and at least 70 per cent of my troops were out of action
> —dead, wounded, crazed or numbed. All my forward tanks were
> knocked out, and the roads were practically impassable.[2]

[1]Bradley's request for air support for COBRA was made on the understanding that
the bombers would fly in from the west following the clear landmark of the Périers–
St. Lô Road, which ran parallel to the American front. On both the 24th and the 25th,
however, the American bombers came in from the north, at right angles to the front
and over the heads of the troops. " Had I known of air's intent to chance the per-
pendicular approach," says Bradley (op. cit., p. 347), " I would never have consented
to its plan."

[2]U.S. Army Interrogation. On July 28th, along two miles of the road to St. Gilles,
I counted 19 of Bayerlein's tanks, which had been knocked out by the bombing, or
abandoned. In St. Gilles there were three more. On this sector alone Panzer Lehr lost
half the 'runners' with which it began the day.

In the bombed area only a few isolated pockets of resistance remained when the Americans advanced across the St. Lô–Périers road in the middle of the day. The fields and hedgerows were cratered and blasted so severely that progress on foot was slow and even the tanks found the going difficult. By dark the Americans had gained less than two miles, but there was no sign of the opposition stiffening, except on the western flank, where 2nd and 17th SS had begun to intervene. Accordingly, Collins decided to unleash his armour next morning without waiting for the infantry to reach Marigny and St. Gilles.

Soon after dawn on July 26th medium bombers again laid ' carpets ' along the main roads leading south and in their wake the armoured and motorised columns went through. On the right, as the breach was not clear and the cratering was bad, the 1st Division (reinforced with a Combat Command[1] of 3rd Armoured) had to fight hard to reach Marigny, where the Germans held out until next morning. On the other flank, however, the 2nd Armoured Division punched straight through to St. Gilles and on to Canisy by dusk—a gain of three miles.

" That evening," says Bayerlein, " von Kluge sent word that the line along the St. Lô–Périers road must be held at all costs, but it was already broken. A new SS tank battalion, he said, was coming up with sixty tanks to drive to the Vire River and cut off the Americans. It arrived with five tanks, not sixty. That night I assembled the remnants of my division south-west of Canisy. I had fourteen tanks in all. We could do nothing but retreat."

The way was open and the Americans grasped their opportunity. During the night 2nd Armoured advanced another four miles to gain the high ground at Le Mesnil Herman, thus safeguarding the eastern flank of the columns which began thrusting south and south-west from the Marigny–St. Gilles gap on the morning of July 27th.

It had been thought that rapid exploitation through the bocage would be impossible, but the Americans had devised a tactical technique all their own. Early in the Normandy campaign Bradley had found that his troops were not adequately trained for the peculiar conditions of hedgerow fighting and, in the month between the fall of Cherbourg and the start of COBRA, First Army carried out behind the lines an intensive programme of experiment and re-training to improve the co-operation between tanks and infantry, and between armoured columns and fighter-bombers. The thoroughness of these preparations was soon apparent.

When the chance of exploitation came, fast-moving hard-hitting columns of tanks, infantry in armoured half-tracks, motorised artillery and engineers went into action. Now, however, they were not compelled to keep to the roads as they had been in the past. The ' Rhino ' gave the American tanks a freedom of manœuvre, which upset Hausser's plan for delaying the advance with road-blocks and demolitions. Whenever a

[1]A ' Combat Command ' in the U.S. Army was the equivalent of a British ' Brigade Group.'

column was checked by mines, craters or strongpoints, ' Rhino-Shermans ' and bulldozer tanks cut a by-pass through the hedgerows, and the armour swept on, while infantry or engineers dealt with the obstruction.

The German tanks and anti-tank guns had no such freedom. They had to remain on or close to the roads and there they were sitting targets for fighter-bombers. Each American combat command had two or three columns on the move simultaneously, and above each column flights of four Thunderbolts maintained a standing patrol in half-hour shifts. The columns identified themselves with bright fluorescent panels, which the pilots could pick out from a height of several thousand feet, and an air support control officer, riding with the foremost tanks, was in constant touch with the pilots by radio. Thus the fighter-bombers became ' aerial artillery ' directly controlled from the ground. Sometimes they spotted the opposition and dealt with it themselves or gave the column due warning. More often, because of the closeness of the country, resistance was discovered only when the troops on the ground bumped into it. Then the Thunderbolts were called in, the target area was marked with smoke-shells fired by the tanks, and the dive-bombers attacked. Occasionally they planted their bombs on tanks or strongpoints barely 100 yards ahead of their own troops. Such close and direct liaison between armour and aircraft had never been achieved before.

The decisive day was July 27th. While the 2nd Armoured Division directed its spearheads south towards the Bréhal–Tessy road, 1st Infantry and 3rd Armoured struck hard for Coutances, with the object of isolating 84th Corps which was now endeavouring to withdraw from the Périers–Lessay area. Reacting to this threat, 2nd and 17th SS, the only really mobile divisions, abandoned their attempt to cut the American corridor near its source, and moved west to head off the columns advancing on Coutances. On the morning of the 28th the two SS divisions succeeded in halting VII Corps two miles outside the town but, while parrying this blow from the east, the Germans exposed themselves to another from the north. That day the two armoured divisions of VIII U.S. Corps broke through from Périers and Lessay and swept down upon Coutances, which was captured during the afternoon. The remnants of half a dozen infantry divisions were cut to pieces.

By the evening of the 28th American columns were swarming down all the main roads between Coutances and the River Vire, and some had reached the Bréhal–Tessy road at several points 15 miles south of the COBRA start-line. West of the Vire that night there was no co-ordinated front, for 84th Corps had disintegrated and there were no reserves on hand to restore the line. Von Kluge had reacted slowly to the American offensive for, during the first two days of COBRA, the Canadians kept Panzer Group West so fully engaged that it could spare nothing to reinforce Seventh Army. On the night of the 26th–27th, the Canadian attack having been halted without any serious loss of ground, von Kluge sent the 2nd and 116th Panzer Divisions on a forced march from the Orne to the Vire. They were to strike at the eastern flank of the American break-through, in conjunction with an attack by 2nd and 17th SS from the west. On their journey across the front, however, the two ' relief ' divisions were repeatedly attacked from the air and, before they could intervene in strength, the area of 84th Corps (the base from which the SS divisions were to have attacked) had been overrun and First Army had broken out beyond recall.

In the first four days of COBRA the Americans gained a far greater victory than Bradley had expected. Always cautious about what he committed to writing, he had set his troops no distant objectives; indeed his plan stated that the exploitation by VII Corps to Coutances and Bréhal would be followed by a ' Consolidation Phase,' in which the other three corps of First Army would increase their pressure and engage in a general effort to force the Germans back. The concentrated thrust was to give way once more to the broad front. By July 28th, however, there was no question of consolidation. " Consequently," says Bradley in his official report,[1] " the ensuing period, which the plan had conceived would be a holding and mopping-up period, became a vigorous attack period."

Bradley now saw the possibility of carrying out the plan which had been outlined in Montgomery's directive of June 30th. Then, it will be remembered, Montgomery had said that, once First Army had begun its offensive, " there must be no pause " until it had driven south beyond Avranches and Mortain and had " swung up on to the line Caumont–Fougères." Then with the least delay it was to make a " wide sweep south of the bocage country . . . to Le Mans–Alençon." On this occasion it was not Montgomery who thought of ' pausing to consolidate.'

Bradley's orders of July 28th called for continued exploitation southwards by VII and VIII Corps, the latter under the tactical direction of Patton, whose Third Army was about to become operational. During the next two days, while VII Corps widened the area of the breakthrough by attacking south-east towards Mortain, Patton whipped VIII Corps through the gap between the German flank and the coast. The 4th Armoured Division, advancing 25 miles in thirty-six hours, reached Avranches at dusk on July 30th. By the following night it had fanned out from Avranches and gained a bridgehead over the River Selune at Pontaubault. The Americans were in Brittany.

Twelve hours after the fall of Avranches von Kluge, reporting from Seventh Army H.Q., warned Jodl: " As a result of the break-through of

[1]First United States Army, Report of Operations, November 20th, 1943–August 1st, 1944, p. 107. Bradley says that on the first evening of COBRA, gravely concerned about the effect of the short-bombing, he thought "there was little reason to believe we stood at the brink of a breakthrough. Rather, the attack looked as though it might have failed." (Bradley, op. cit., p. 349.)

the enemy armoured spearheads, the whole western front has been ripped open. . . . The left flank has collapsed." During the previous two days the 2nd and 116th Panzer Divisions and part of the 363rd Infantry had been attacking the American flank between Tessy and Villedieu in an effort to cut through to the coast at Granville. They had delayed the advance of VII Corps, but had gained no ground, and the two panzer divisions were now so closely involved that they could not be disengaged for a counter-stroke at Avranches. Seventh Army had no resources with which to rebuild its left wing, for its right wing was now in danger of collapsing.

On the second day of COBRA, when the Canadian attack on Bour-guebus Ridge was bloodily repulsed, Montgomery realised that for at least a week he would not be able to make another thrust in the Falaise Plain with sufficient strength to compel the Germans to retain the bulk of their armour east of the Orne. Accordingly, he ordered Second Army to develop on another sector an offensive powerful enough to prevent von Kluge from using his armoured divisions either to counter-attack the American flank or to head off the columns which had broken through. At the same time, with Seventh Army swinging its line back under American pressure, it became important to forestall any German attempt to use Mont Pinçon and Vire as pivots on which to execute a coherent withdrawal.

In support of Bradley's offensive, Dempsey had been planning to attack from Caumont with VIII British Corps on August 2nd, but the speed of the American advance and the movement of German armour westward made it essential that Second Army should strike without delay. On July 28th, therefore, Montgomery ordered Dempsey to transfer his armour rapidly from the Orne to Caumont and attack on the 30th, employing both VIII and XXX Corps with the object of seizing Hills 361 and 309 (the western half of the Mont Pinçon Ridge) and exploiting towards Vire. By this offensive (Operation BLUECOAT), Montgomery hoped not only to cover part of Bradley's flank and deprive the Germans of their natural pivot, but also to thrust in behind the new front which Seventh Army was trying to form along the River Vire. The success of this plan depended on Dempsey's ability to move and re-group more quickly than the enemy.[1]

Although there was no panzer division between Villers-Bocage and Caumont on July 30th, the task which faced Dempsey's troops was by no means easy. In spite of the amputation of the German left wing by the American break-through, there was no sign of the enemy's giving

[1]The British Order of Battle for BLUECOAT was as follows:
    VIII Corps: 15th Scottish Division, 6th Guards Tank Brigade, 11th and Guards
        Armoured Divisions.
    XXX Corps: 43rd and 50th Infantry Divisions, 8th Armoured Brigade, 7th
        Armoured Division.

way east of the Vire. Between Caumont and St. Lô V U.S. Corps had been attacking strongly since the 26th but had been able to drive the enemy back only three miles. Moreover, the area south of Caumont is the most rugged in the Normandy bocage and the Germans had been in undisturbed possession there for seven weeks. They had laid extensive minefields and had strongly entrenched themselves on the slopes and ridges north and west of Mont Pinçon.

Once again the enemy was favoured by the weather. On the morning of the 30th, when the preliminary air bombardment began, the clouds were low and threatening, and some 200 aircraft had to carry their bomb-loads home. But the rest, more than a thousand ' heavies ' and ' mediums,' made their attacks in defiance of the conditions and hit their targets with remarkable accuracy. When the ground attack went in, however, the 43rd Division, on the left, was halted almost at once by a dense minefield and a steep-sided stream which tanks could not cross. On the other flank, 11th Armoured also had trouble with mines during the morning, but in the centre 15th Scottish and the 6th Guards Tank Brigade soon overwhelmed the forward defences, and, after a further air attack in the afternoon, a tank battalion stormed the slopes of Hill 309. In the evening the infantry also gained the crest after a fighting advance of five miles since morning.

Next day, while the Scotsmen were consolidating their hold on the ridge and the 43rd were still in difficulties, an opportunity was created on the right flank and 11th Armoured exploited it brilliantly. During the night of the 30th–31st an infantry battalion moved in single file along an unguarded woodland trail to the outskirts of St. Martin des Besaces. Soon after dawn four armoured cars slipped past the village and through the Forêt L'Évêque to the River Souleuvre, five miles south of St. Martin. Finding a bridge intact, west of Le Bény Bocage, the troop leader called by radio for armour and infantry. Six reconnaissance tanks got through to him before the Germans stopped the gap, and nothing more could follow until St. Martin was cleared in the early afternoon.

By this time the R.A.F. had reported that a German mechanised column had crossed the Orne and was heading for Le Bény Bocage. The race was on, and in mid-afternoon an armoured regiment, with infantry riding on the backs of the tanks, drove hard for the bridge. This column came through from the north as the enemy approached from the east. The German force, a battlegroup of 21st Panzer, was caught in the woods beyond the river while assembling to attack. After a sharp engagement the Germans were put to flight and on the following morning (August 1st) there was little opposition when 11th Armoured advanced into Le Bény Bocage. That afternoon reconnaissance patrols, probing south towards Vire, encountered only slight resistance.

This second break-through in an unexpected sector caused consternation among the enemy, for the British had driven a deep wedge between Seventh Army and Fifth Panzer Army (as Panzer Group

West was now called) and the movement towards Vire threatened to precipitate the collapse of Hausser's right wing, just when he was striving to re-form his left. So far, although the Americans had broken through to Avranches, Seventh Army had been able to contain the flank of Bradley's corridor along the general line Tessy–Percy–Villedieu, but the hub of this defence was Vire, the most important traffic centre west of the Orne. The German divisions holding this line were twelve to fifteen miles west and north-west of Vire, but on the afternoon of August 1st the British armour was barely five miles from its northern outskirts, which were protected by an improvised and meagre force. That day everything Hausser could scrape together was moving towards Avranches, and the sole immediate reserve, 21st Panzer, was already committed. The 9th SS Panzer Division had begun to move from the Caen sector, but it could not intervene before the afternoon of August 2nd. In the meantime Vire was vulnerable and there was a gap ten kilometres wide between the two German armies.

On the night of August 1st–2nd British armoured cars found Vire almost deserted, but on the following morning Dempsey did not press the attack in this direction, for Vire lay on the American side of the boundary between First and Second Armies. It was one of Bradley's objectives, and accordingly Dempsey told VIII Corps to make its main drive south-east towards Flèrs, wheeling round behind Mont Pinçon, against which XXX Corps was to continue its attack with the utmost vigour. At the time this seemed to be a logical decision, for the general trend of the Allied advance was now running south-east, and the chief British task was to drive the Germans from Mont Pinçon quickly by direct assault and by the pressure of an outflanking movement. However logical the decision, the result was to give the Germans time to organise the defence of Vire and to extricate in fair order the divisions on the Tessy–Percy–Villedieu line.

On August 2nd when VIII Corps attacked towards Flèrs, it turned to meet the panzer reserves which were moving west from the Orne. Thus, although 11th Armoured made good progress to the Vire–Vassy road, the Guards (on its left) became heavily involved south-east of Le Bény Bocage. The Germans were not in great force, but they gave a false impression of their strength by operating most aggressively and shrewdly. Small battlegroups (each with two or three tanks, a company of infantry and a troop of *nebelwerfer*) infiltrated between the strung-out British columns and harried their flanks. By these means the enemy brought the Guards to a halt at Estry and forced 11th Armoured to check its advance at the Vire–Vassy road.

These tactics might have been effectively answered by counter-infiltration, by determined thrusts between the scattered centres of enemy resistance. The German battlegroups were extremely vulnerable, for they had no infantry at hand to form a co-ordinated front and no spare mobile forces to keep open their supply lines. Continued British attacks would have compelled the Germans to withdraw, for 9th SS, which provided the main opposition, had suffered severely during its march across the Orne. During the afternoon of August 2nd R.A.F. fighter-bombers and rocket-firing Typhoons had caught the main body of the division on the roads between Thury-Harcourt and Condé, and had caused considerable destruction and disorganisation.[1] By the morning of August 3rd, the Germans in front of VIII Corps were in no condition to withstand a further offensive. At this stage, however, the corps commander decided that he must halt his armour, until he could bring up infantry divisions to safeguard his eastern flank, which was extended and exposed because XXX Corps was still lagging well behind.

On the evening of August 1st the 43rd Division had captured Hill 361, two days behind schedule, but neither 7th Armoured nor ' Fifty Div.' had made any appreciable progress towards their objectives, Aunay and Villers-Bocage respectively. On the 2nd, after a stern warning from Dempsey to " get on or get out," Bucknall was dismissed, and next day, when Aunay was still untaken, Erskine was removed from command of the ' Desert Rats.'[2] Because of this unsatisfactory situation on the front of XXX Corps, Dempsey agreed that VIII Corps should pause and the opportunity of further exploitation towards Flèrs was lost.

Already, however, Operation BLUECOAT had amply fulfilled its purpose. By its swift advance to the Vire–Vassy road VIII Corps had intercepted the armoured reinforcements which had been destined for Seventh Army. By August 4th three panzer divisions and three battalions of heavy tanks were fighting to contain the British penetration. In the meantime, with Second Army threatening its rear and First Army attacking its front, Seventh Army had been compelled to abandon the Tessy–Percy–Villedieu line and had been driven back to Vire and Mortain. With each day the American corridor grew wider and more secure, and through it Third Army raced into Brittany untrammelled and unchecked.

On August 1st when Bradley assumed command of 12th U.S. Army Group,[3] he gave orders that, while First Army was seizing the area Vire-Mortain, Third Army should secure the line St. Hilaire–Fougères–Rennes in order to safeguard the Avranches exit, and should *then* turn westward

---

[1]Between 1430 hours and dusk 83 Group flew 923 sorties in this area. Its claims (10 tanks and 50 motor transport destroyed, 13 tanks and 76 MT damaged) are broadly substantiated by German sources.

[2]Brigadier Hinde was also relieved, as were the Commander, Royal Artillery, and the chief staff officer. This ' clean sweep ' was strongly resented within the division, and it failed to bring about any rejuvenation. Seventh Armoured had fought too long in the desert and was too set in its ways to adapt itself to the bocage. It did not recapture its former greatness until it reached the open plains of Northern Germany.

[3]Although there were now two Army Groups in the field, Montgomery, acting as ground forces commander, continued to direct the operations of both. At First Army Bradley was succeeded by Lieut.-General Courtney H. Hodges, who had been his Deputy.

into Brittany. Patton interpreted these instructions rather freely. On the evening of July 31st, when the 4th Armoured Division captured intact the bridge at Pontaubault, Patton ordered VIII Corps (Major-General T. H. Middleton) to drive deep into Brittany forthwith, sending one armoured and one infantry division down the centre of the Peninsula to Brest, and a similar force across it through Rennes to Quiberon Bay and Lorient. In the meantime, another corps was to move up to secure Fougères and Rennes.

Patton was always prepared to take a chance about his flanks and he knew that in Brittany there would be little opposition. This area had already been stripped of its mobile forces and the remaining units, remnants of four divisions, were nearly all engaged in manning the coast defences. The rest of the Peninsula, apart from the main road junctions, was virtually controlled by *Les Forces Françaises de l'Intérieur*, numbering 50,000 men in various groups, some of which had been organised by British and French paratroops of the Special Air Service and equipped with arms dropped by the R.A.F. The presence of these guerilla forces enabled Patton's armoured columns to drive hard for their objectives without pausing to deal with small pockets or even to round up prisoners.

The enemy's only serious counter-move was made by air against the most vulnerable point of Third Army's lifeline, the bridge at Avranches. At this vital crossing, Air Fleet III directed its entire bomber force. Between August 3rd and 7th this bridge was attacked repeatedly by day and by night, but it suffered only one glancing hit and the flow of traffic was never stopped. Patton did not wait to draw up movement plans or march tables. The bottleneck of the single road from Avranches to Pontaubault became a sheep-race. At the mouth senior officers herded units through in any order. At the exit each division was allocated one of the roads radiating from Pontaubault and, as its units came through the race, they were drafted down the appropriate route. While ack-ack guns and fighters thwarted the enemy's design, the corridor was packed with moving vehicles and marching men every hour of the twenty-four. Defying field regulations and text-book rules, Patton moved seven divisions down this one road in 72 hours.

By August 4th, Rennes had been captured and the 4th Armoured Division had raced across the Peninsula to the south coast at Vannes. Brittany was sealed off, but the main strategic prize was the port of Brest, and it lay 200 miles from Avranches. That day the 6th Armoured Division was already half-way there, but it had been halted since the previous afternoon by Middleton, who had ordered its commander (Major-General R. W. Grow) to send a combat command back to deal with a ' pocket ' at Dinan. Patton was furious when he found the column stationary at midday on the 4th and he told Grow, " Don't take any notice of this order, or any other order telling you to halt, unless it comes from me. Get going and keep going till you get to Brest." Although Grow thereupon advanced day and night, evading enemy rearguards with the help of French guides, he could not make good the twenty-four hours that had been lost. While he was covering the last hundred miles, the Germans had time to withdraw the coastal garrisons of Western Brittany inside the defences of the port. Reaching Brest on August 7th, Grow attacked at once, but the garrison managed to check his first spontaneous assault. Twenty-four hours earlier, however, the opposition would not have been so strong.[1]

While Third Army was sweeping almost unopposed through Brittany First Army continued its attacks east and south-east, to make the corridor secure against counter-attack. On the approaches to Vire the resistance was staunch and sustained, but to the south, on August 2nd, VII U.S. Corps captured Mortain and established a firm blocking position on the hills outside the town. With this area in American hands, Bradley had a hinge on which to swing his front, as Montgomery had said, " in a wide sweep . . . to Le Mans–Alençon." Accordingly, on August 3rd Bradley ordered Patton to leave the minimum forces in Brittany and to drive his main strength eastwards.[2] " Once a gap appears in the enemy front," said Montgomery in a directive next day, " we must press into it and through it and beyond it into the enemy's rear areas. Everyone must go all out all day and every day. The broad strategy of the Allied Armies is to swing the right flank towards Paris and to force the enemy back to the Seine."

The gap was already open and there was no organised opposition to the eastward advance which began on August 4th. In the next three days XV Corps bounded forward 75 miles, almost to Le Mans, cutting deep into the rear of von Kluge's armies. Unquestionably the time had come for a general withdrawal to the Seine, if the Germans in Normandy were not to be destroyed, but Hitler was not yet ready to admit that the battle was lost.

Late on August 2nd Warlimont, Jodl's deputy, arrived at von Kluge's H.Q. with orders from the Führer that the front must be restored. Before Warlimont's departure Hitler had admitted to him that a withdrawal might become necessary and that a new defensive position was

---

[1]Even on the 7th the Germans were surprised to find the Americans north of the city, and units from the coast defences were still moving into it. Brest did not fall, however, until September 18th, and then it was taken only after a ten-day assault by three infantry divisions.

[2]It was generally believed at Third Army H.Q.—and it is directly asserted by one of Patton's staff, Colonel Robert S. Allen (*Lucky Forward*, pp. 96-8)—that in launching this drive eastwards, Patton acted first and obtained Bradley's approval later. This claim is not substantiated by Third Army's own records. On the afternoon of August 2nd Bradley personally stopped the 79th Division, which was moving west on Patton's orders, and directed it south-east to Fougères. Bradley's instructions for the general advance to the east were issued next day, and XV Corps attacked on the 4th.

being prepared along the Somme–Marne–Saône line. But this was not to be mentioned to von Kluge for, said Hitler, " as soon as a line of defence is built behind the front line, my generals think of nothing but retreat."[1]

The following evening, however, von Kluge warned Warlimont that, in view of the American capture of Mortain and the British interception of 2nd SS Panzer Corps, there was no chance of closing the Avranches gap. The only rational policy was to withdraw to the Seine or farther. This might still be feasible, if his troops could begin their retreat at once. Fifth Panzer Army was holding firm in the Caen sector, and the British break-through from Caumont had been checked. Mont Pinçon and Vire were still in German hands. Seventh Army's front was intact from the Vire to Barentan and, though its southern flank was exposed, the Americans had not begun to sweep round it in the direction of Paris. Von Kluge proposed, therefore, that he should form a group of mobile divisions to cover this flank and hold the Americans in check, while the rest of his force carried out a deliberate withdrawal.

Hitler replied on the morning of the 4th with a categorical order that von Kluge must launch a counter-offensive from the Vire–Mortain area to the coast at Avranches. Eight of the nine panzer divisions in Normandy were to be employed and the Luftwaffe would throw in its entire reserve, including a thousand fighters. Both von Kluge and Hausser realised that this order was Seventh Army's death warrant, but they had long since learned the futility of protesting. They knew, however, that they dare not wait, as Hitler demanded, " until every tank, gun and plane was assembled."[2] They decided to strike on the night of August 6th–7th. If they were obliged to attack, then the less delay the better, for their general position was worsening every hour.

While von Kluge was preparing to carry out Hitler's order, the relentless Allied advance made its execution increasingly difficult. By the evening of August 6th Patton's troops were approaching Le Mans, and the 9th Panzer Division, newly arrived from Southern France, was diverted to check this eastward drive. Simultaneously, there was such severe and constant pressure on the northern front that, of the five panzer divisions engaged against the British, 1st SS alone could be released for the Avranches offensive. Thus, instead of the eight armoured divisions which Hitler had stipulated, von Kluge was able to assemble only four and these had no more than 250 tanks between them.

The German preparations could not be hidden from Allied air reconnaissance, and Bradley acted in good time to meet the threat. On a front of 18 miles between Vire, St. Pois and Mortain he deployed five infantry divisions with two armoured combat commands in reserve, and he held three of Patton's divisions in a ' back-stop ' position west of

---

[1] U.S. Army Interrogation. General Walter Warlimont was Deputy Chief of the Wehrmacht Operations Staff.

[2] According to Warlimont, Jodl repeated this injunction on the afternoon of the 6th and told von Kluge that he " should not worry about the extension of the American penetration, for the delay would mean cutting off so much more."

Mortain around St. Hilaire. Having thus covered the direct approaches to Avranches, Bradley proceeded to strike at the flanks of the salient where the Germans were assembling. While part of VII Corps held the Mortain area, its mobile forces moved round the enemy flank to Ambrières and Mayenne, where they linked up with Third Army. But Bradley's main forestalling action was directed against Vire, the bastion of Hausser's right flank.

Throughout August 6th the threat to Vire grew, as American and British thrusts converged upon the town. In the late afternoon the Germans counter-attacked and revealed the measure of their concern by throwing in part of the force which was due to strike for Avranches that night. Even this did not prevent the Americans from capturing Vire and overrunning a section of the enemy's chosen start-line east of St. Pois.

The German offensive was to begin soon after midnight, but at 10 p.m. von Funck, commanding the spearhead (47th Panzer Corps), reported to Hausser that the leading columns of 1st SS were still passing through Tinchebray; that 2nd Panzer had not received the Panther tanks, assault guns or motorised artillery, which had been promised; and that the commander of the 116th Panzer Division had " made a mess of things again " and should be relieved. " Consequently," said von Funck, " the attack on the right will probably be delayed for hours." Hausser replied, " This does not alter the fact that the operation must be carried out as ordered. I must admit that this is a bad start. Let us hope that the loss of time this evening can be made good by fog tomorrow morning."[1]

Under cover of darkness 2nd Panzer broke through between Mortain and Sourdeval and advanced seven miles towards Avranches before it was halted by a Combat Command of 3rd Armoured. South of this thrust the Germans retook Mortain, but they could not exploit their success, for the 30th U.S. Division remained in stubborn possession of the most important heights west and north-west of the town.[2] On the other flank of 2nd Panzer, the attack gained no ground at all, even though the Germans were favoured by a thick morning mist.

In the middle of the day, when the fog lifted, American Thunderbolts and R.A.F. Typhoons discovered German columns crowding the roads around Mortain. By 3 p.m. 47th Panzer Corps was protesting bitterly about the lack of air cover, and it warned Seventh Army: " The activities of the fighter-bombers are almost unbearable. The *Leibstandarte* [1st SS] reports that air attacks of such intensity have never before been experienced. Its attack has been stopped." At this time, the attack by 116th Panzer had not even started, for on its front the Americans were continuing to press forward.

[1]Seventh Army Telephone Log, August 6th, 2200 hours.
[2]One battalion of the 30th Division was isolated on a knoll east of Mortain but, supplied by air, this gallant little force repulsed every German attack until its relief five days later.

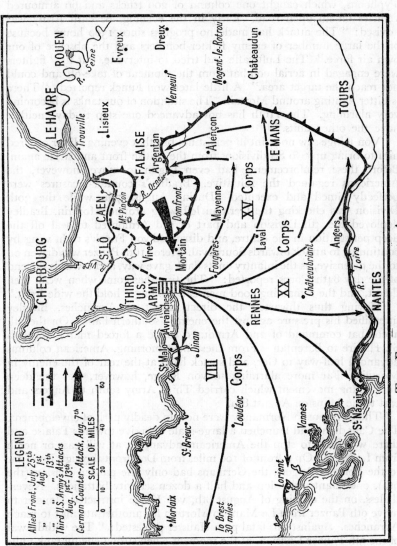

THE EXPLOITATION FROM AVRANCHES

LEGEND

Allied Front, July 25th
    "    "   Aug. 1st
    "    "   Aug. 13th
Third U.S. Army's Attacks
    Aug. 1st–13th
German Counter-Attack, Aug. 7th

SCALE OF MILES

0    10    20    40    60

Map locations:
ROUEN, R. Seine, Dreux, Evreux, Nogent-le-Rotrou, Châteaudun, LE HAVRE, Verneuil, TOURS, Lisieux, Trouville, Argentan, Alençon, LE MANS, FALAISE, XV Corps, R. Orne, CAEN, Mt. Pinçon, Domfront, Mayenne, Laval, Mortain, Fougères, Angers, ST. LÔ, Vire, R. Vire, THIRD U.S. ARMY, Châteaubriant, R. Loire, Avranches, XX Corps, RENNES, NANTES, St. Nazaire, CHERBOURG, St. Malo, Dinan, VIII Corps, Loudéac, Vannes, St. Brieuc, Lorient, Morlaix, To Brest 30 miles

As the afternoon wore on, the air attacks gathered intensity, and 2nd Panzer was mercilessly hammered, especially by rocket-firing Typhoons, which caught one column of 200 trucks and 60 armoured vehicles on an open road. Early in the evening, Seventh Army was advised: " The attack has made no progress since 1300 hours because of the large number of enemy fighter-bombers and the absence of our own air force." The Luftwaffe had tried to intervene, but its " fighters were engaged in aerial combat from the moment of take-off and could not reach the target area." A little later, von Funck reported: " There is bitter fighting around Mortain. The situation of our tanks is becoming very alarming. The 116th has not advanced one step to-day: neither have the other units."

Von Kluge saw no point in persisting, but that evening Hitler ordered him to bring up two SS divisions from the British front and strike again. Before these reinforcements had even begun to move, however, the Americans regained the initiative. Bradley's counter-measures were perfectly timed and executed. During August 7th, while the 30th Division was checking the German left wing around Mortain, Bradley deployed the 4th Division and part of 3rd Armoured to seal off the deep penetration in the centre, and disrupted von Funck's right wing by continuing to attack towards Sourdeval. Here 116th Panzer was driven on to the defensive, as the infantry on its flank gave way, and towards the end of the day 84th Corps reported: " The time has come when weak men desert, and the remaining good men can no longer hold the wide front."

Having thus thwarted the direct threat to Avranches, Bradley intensified his pressure against the enemy's southern flank. On the 7th a combat command of 2nd Armoured made a forced march through St. Hilaire to Barentan. From there next morning, American columns advanced half-way to Ger, and struck hard at the rear of the enemy in Mortain. Far more alarming to von Kluge, however, was the deep outflanking movement which carried Third Army south to Angers and east to Le Mans on August 8th.

The Germans in Normandy were now in deadly peril of envelopment. The Canadians had launched a large-scale offensive towards Falaise and there was little to stop the Americans advancing at will east or north from Le Mans. On a front of 100 miles from Domfront through Le Mans to the Loire at Angers, the Germans had only one panzer division (the 9th), one infantry division and half a dozen security battalions. Nevertheless, on the evening of August 8th, von Kluge instructed Hausser to move 9th Panzer from Le Mans to Mortain for another attempt to reach Avranches. Against this fatal plan Hausser protested: " The withdrawal of the 9th Panzer Division, at the moment when strong enemy tank units are thrusting into our flanks, would deal a death blow not only to Seventh Army but to the entire Wehrmacht in the West."[1] Von Kluge's only answer was: " It is the Führer's order."

[1] Seventh Army Telephone Log, August 8th, 1845 hours.

Hitler had demanded ' blind obedience ' from his generals and he would get it from von Kluge. The Field-Marshal was now excessively anxious to demonstrate his loyalty. The trial of those concerned in the Plot of July 20th had already begun. It might not be long before the Gestapo discovered some evidence to incriminate him. With this threat hanging over him, von Kluge was not prepared to provoke the Führer's wrath by challenging this order, even though he knew that it would mean the murder of an Army.

## CHAPTER XXI

# FALAISE AND PARIS

THE forty-eight hours, which began on the afternoon of August 6th, settled the fate of the German armies in Normandy. When they should have been withdrawing eastwards to the Seine, Hitler drove them westwards to destruction. While their southern flank was being rolled up, their northern front gave way, and the sides of the salient, from which von Kluge was striving to reach the coast, became the jaws of a trap. During these decisive days there appeared to be no relation whatever between the northern and southern sectors of the Normandy battlefield; they might have been different campaigns, so marked was the contrast between them.

From Avranches Patton's rampaging columns rode at will across the open farmlands and down the long, straight roads which led to the Loire and Le Mans. Occasionally a blown bridge or a mined road made them pause and detour. Here and there they found a town defended by a scratch force of supply troops and stragglers or, as at Le Mans, by a Luftwaffe security battalion which had been safeguarding Air Force installations against sabotage. Frequently they came upon villages which had liberated themselves. In one case, when they were greeted by neither hostile Germans nor delighted Frenchmen, the Americans advanced circumspectly into what seemed to be a deserted town, only to find the entire populace assembled in the market square where the local Resistance leaders were shaving the heads of women who had been unduly friendly to the Germans. There were neither natural obstacles, nor prepared defences, nor organised forces to staunch the flow of armoured and motorised troops who poured through the breach at Avranches and flooded the plain beyond.

On the other flank of the Mortain salient, however, the bocage provided a strong defensive framework and German resistance was coherent, skilful and determined. During August 4th and 5th Eberbach, the commander of Fifth Panzer Army, shortened his front by withdrawing from the area north of Mont Pinçon, abandoning the blasted ruins of Villers-Bocage, Aunay and Evrécy. The Germans extricated themselves in good order, covering their calculated retreat to the Orne with mines, booby-traps and demolitions. Eberbach now sought to hold fast along the line Bourguebus Ridge–the Orne–Thury Harcourt–Mont Pinçon–Vire, thus safeguarding the flank and rear of Seventh Army's counter-offensive. If Eberbach could not hold, Hausser could not strike with any prospect of success.

The capacity of Fifth Panzer Army to fulfil its protective role was seriously tested on August 6th, when the Americans (as already noted) captured Vire, and the British assaulted Mont Pinçon. Of all the local actions which shaped the pattern of the break-out battle, the attack upon Mont Pinçon was one of the most significant, not merely on account of its tactical consequences, but because of the qualities which it called forth in the men concerned. In many ways it was characteristic of the grim fighting in which American, British and Canadian troops had been engaged since they first set foot in Normandy.

It was not its height which made Mont Pinçon formidable, for its summit is less than 1,200 feet above the sea; it was the steepness and roughness of its slopes, especially the western, which rises 350 feet in half a mile. On August 5th the commander of the 43rd Division (Major-General G. I. Thomas) was planning to attack this hill from the south, and 129 Brigade had sent the 4th Wilts on a wide outflanking march to St. Jean le Blanc, while its other two battalions moved through the Bois du Goulet towards the western end of Pinçon. But at St. Jean the Wiltshires were stopped short, and Thomas revised his plan. He would make a feint from the north with 130 Brigade and strike from the west with 129. This meant assaulting the steepest rise, but there was no time to work troops round to the gentler northern slopes. The new Corps Commander (Lieut.-General B. G. Horrocks) was a man of fire and he had orders to capture Mont Pinçon without delay.

By midday on August 6th two battalions of 129 Brigade were ranged along the general line of the River Druance at the foot of the western escarpment, with tanks of the 13th/18th Hussars in support. The day was hot and sultry. The still air was laden with dust and the acrid smoke of explosives and the sickly stench of dead cattle bloated by the sun. Every moving vehicle stirred up more dust, and drew fire from the enemy and curses from the infantry, who lay in slit trenches awaiting word to move across the river and up the steep scarp. The valley was heavy with foreboding as it echoed the roll and crack of guns.

Shortly before three o'clock, under cover of smoke, pioneers lifted the mines from the bridge on the road to La Varinière and then the barrage came down on the far bank. Soon the barrage started to creep up the hill and immediately the 5th Wilts began wading the stream. They were still struggling across when the Germans came to life with machine-guns and mortars. In a matter of minutes the two leading companies were crippled and disorganised. The colonel went forward to rally them, but was killed almost at once, and the attack petered out. Half a mile to the north, the 4th Somersets suffered a similar fate. Their

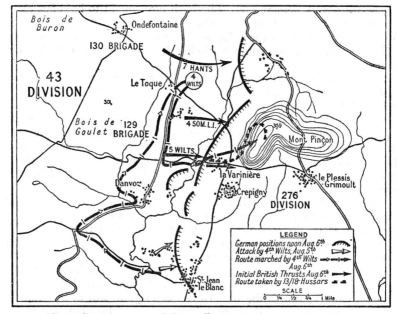

THE CAPTURE OF MONT PINÇON, AUGUST 5TH-6TH

tanks were stopped by mines and their men were pinned to the river bank.

The prospects were unpromising, but there was one small gleam of hope. The bridge on the road to La Varinière was clear and two of the Hussars' tanks had crossed it. The orchards south of the bridge were thick with Germans but, while these were blinded with mortar smoke and subdued with machine-guns by the support company, six more tanks rushed the bridge, followed by some sixty infantry, the only fit riflemen left in the entire battalion. With the tanks in close support, the Wiltshires covered the half-mile to La Varinière at the double and within twenty minutes had secured the crossroads.

Here the infantry had to halt but, when the Hussars found an unguarded track, which seemed to lead to the top of the hill, two troops of tanks were ordered to drive on and gain the summit. This armoured sortie began soon after six p.m. The track was narrow and tortuous, with a sheer bank on one side and a sharp drop on the other. Passing a quarry one tank side-slipped and overturned; another was hit by enemy fire, but the rest put down smoke and raced up the hill, reaching the top to the surprise and alarm of the few Germans who were guarding it.

The rapid and daring success of the Hussars was seen from the valley and the Brigade Commander promptly ordered his reserve, the 4th Wilts, to get to the crest with all speed. This battalion was already approaching exhaustion. It had fought a savage battle at St. Jean on the previous day, had withdrawn during the night and had marched seven miles to a reserve area, suffering some fifty casualties from shellfire on the way. The light was already fading when the Wiltshires began their ascent, moving in single file through the bewildered Germans who were still clinging to positions on the slope. Major A. D. Parsons, one of the company commanders who made the trek, describes it thus:

Enemy resistance was slight and the chief difficulty was the physical effort of climbing, for the slope soon became very steep and covered with scrub. It was a strange feeling, as we toiled up, heavily laden with weapons, ammunition, picks and shovels, expecting to find ourselves surrounded at any moment. The sergeant, commanding the leading platoon, very resourcefully told his men that they were not doing an attack, but were going up to relieve another unit already there. This materially helped the speed of the advance.

As we neared the top a thick fog came down. We could see no landmarks but we found the tanks. They were relieved to see us, for Germans could be heard shouting and digging in close by. We were as tired as any troops could be, and many of us fell asleep as we were digging positions in the rocky soil, falling headlong pick in hand into the half-dug trenches, dead to the ' wide.'

For us the Mont Pinçon operation was a bitter and fruitless day before St. Jean le Blanc, the withdrawal following it, and then an equally bitter battle to reach and hold the summit; not a battle against Germans, so much as against the burning sun, the choking dust, our parched throats and empty bellies, the craggy slopes and tangled thickets, the rocky earth and above all against our utterly weary bodies.

Such was the battle of Mont Pinçon; such was the Normandy campaign as many of the troops of First Army and Second Army had come to know it. The fight they had to wage for every field and village was the foundation of the victory which Third Army could exploit as it motored across France.

At Mont Pinçon the Germans had put in a wedge to stop their defensive door opening any farther, but that wedge was gone. On the same night that it took Mont Pinçon, Second Army forced a crossing over the Orne north of Thury-Harcourt. The door began to creak and the time had come for the Canadians on the Caen–Falaise road to strike at the hinge.

During the first week of August the continued movement of German armour westward across the Orne resulted in the removal of the strongest bolts from the Caen hinge. In place of the 1st and 9th SS, an infantry division (from Rouen) took over the defence of Bourguebus Ridge, and another was coming up to a reserve position north of Falaise. In quality of infantry and numbers of tanks, Dietrich's Corps was decidedly weaker than it had been in July, for now the only mobile reserve was 12th SS with 50 tanks. His anti-tank defences, however, were still intact, to the tune of more than a hundred ' 88s ' and ' 75s.' These guns possessed such range and the infantry were disposed in such depth that a rapid break-through was not easy to achieve. Yet the development of Montgomery's plan now required that the German hinge should be broken " decisively and quickly." If First Canadian Army[1] could break through to Falaise, while von Kluge had the bulk of his forces west of the Orne, there was every chance of precipitating a general collapse in Normandy.

This task was given to II Canadian Corps, commanded by Lieut.-General G. G. Simonds, a most able, forceful and original soldier.[2] Ambitious, reserved and ruthless, Simonds was not an easy man to serve, for he was intolerant of minds less capable than his own, but he certainly commanded confidence and respect. Like Montgomery, his approach to the problems of battle was that of a scientist. Both were military perfectionists but, whereas Montgomery was primarily the expert implementer, Simonds was a radical innovator, forever seeking new solutions. Simonds's originality was strikingly evident in the plan he devised for this operation, which was given the code-name TOTALIZE.

In GOODWOOD the difficulty had been that although the heavy air bombardment had opened a corridor for the armour, the advance had been halted at the enemy's second main defence zone, because infantry and artillery had not been able to move up fast enough and because a second bomb carpet could not be laid in time. In the next attack down the Caen–Falaise road (by the Canadians on the night of July 24th–25th) the infantry had been stopped by intense machine-gun and mortar fire before they could come to grips with the enemy's main strongpoints and, when daylight came, it had been impossible for the armour to get through the anti-tank screen. Since then three local attacks had been made by night with varying tactics against the fortified villages on Bourguebus Ridge and each had been sharply repulsed.

For Operation TOTALIZE, apart from the difficulty of achieving surprise, the most awkward problems were: first, to devise a means of getting infantry and tanks through the forward belt of defences quickly and economically, so that the enemy's second line could be assaulted before he could recover from the initial shock; and, secondly, to provide sufficient fire support, so that the armoured divisions could begin their exploitation without having to wait for artillery to move up.

Simonds decided to attack at night without any preliminary bombard-

[1]This Army, consisting of II Canadian and I British Corps and commanded by Lieut.-General H. D. G. Crerar, had taken over the sector east of the Orne at the end of July.

[2]Of all the Canadian commanders, Simonds was the most experienced, having commanded an infantry division in Sicily and an armoured division in Italy before taking over II Canadian Corps in January 1944 at the age of forty-one.

ment, and to penetrate between the forward German strong-points with compact columns of tanks, accompanied by infantry riding in heavily armoured carriers. (These were provided primarily by removing the 105 mm guns from the open tank chassis of ' Priests ' the self-propelled artillery with which the 3rd Canadian Division had been equipped for the D-Day assault.) Having penetrated some three miles the infantry would ' de-bus ' and attack the second belt of defences under cover of darkness. By these novel tactics, Simonds hoped to nullify the greatly superior range of the German machine-guns, mortars and, most important of all, the ' 88s,' which were accurate and deadly at two thousand yards.

During this phase, the ' break-in,' Simonds decided to employ only half the available air effort—the British night bombers, which were to saturate the defences on either side of the corridor and seal off its flanks. This would allow him to commit the American heavy and medium bombers early next afternoon in support of the ' break-out ' by the armoured divisions which were to exploit towards Falaise.

This daring plan, involving the tactical use of strategic bombers in close support of an armoured break-through at night, demanded the most accurate navigation by aircraft and tanks alike. Such a plan could not have been even contemplated but for the superb navigational skill of Harris's air crews and the target-marking technique which Bomber Command had developed. The Army, however, had little experience to draw upon. No such attack as Simonds planned had ever been attempted and the problem of keeping direction was considerable. Simonds decided to use a variety of aids. The thrust-lines for each column were fixed by survey, and the leading tanks were to move on a radio directional beam. Ahead the objectives were to be marked with green ' target-indicator ' shells; on the flanks Bofors A.A. guns were to fire bursts of tracer; and the light of the moon, which would rise just before midnight, was to be supplemented by searchlights. " We did not expect," says Simonds, " that any of these devices would be adequate, but we hoped that a combination of them all would enable direction to be kept."

The revolutionary nature of the plan and the incalculable scope of their opportunity fired the enthusiasm of the troops and their commanders. On the eve of the battle Crerar told a meeting of senior officers: " We have reached what very much appears to be the potentially decisive period of this five-year World War. I have no doubt that we shall make August 8th, 1944, an even blacker day for the German Army than that same date twenty-six years ago."[1] Crerar predicted that a large-scale victory in Normandy would " result in the crushing conviction to Germans that general defeat of their armies on all fronts has become an inescapable fact. A quick termination to the war will

[1] August 8th, 1918, marked the start of the great British offensive east of Amiens. After that war Ludendorff declared: " August 8th was the black day of the German Army in the history of the war."

follow." If this was over-optimistic, it was nonetheless the spirit in which First Canadian Army entered upon its first major offensive.

On the evening of August 7th the striking force (the 2nd Canadian and 51st Highland Divisions) assembled south of Caen in six long, narrow, tight columns of tanks and ' flails,' armoured infantry and SP anti-tank artillery. In each line the vehicles were packed nose to tail on a four-tank front and in this unique formation they were to advance. West of the Caen–Falaise road, and directed on the high ground north of Bretteville-sur-Laize, were two Canadian brigades (the 4th Infantry and the 2nd Armoured). East of the main road, and with the Cramesnil–St. Aignan area as their objective, were two British brigades (the 154th Highland and the 33rd Armoured). Meantime, the front was held by Canadian and Highland infantry who were to capture the by-passed strong-points.

An hour before midnight the bombing began on targets marked by flare shells. Half an hour later the compact columns moved forward on either side of the Falaise road and picked up the rolling barrage. The dust raised by the bombardment and by a thousand armoured vehicles, and a smoke screen laid by the enemy, soon blinded the navigators and bewildered the drivers who could see nothing but the dim tail-light of the vehicle ahead. There were many collisions. Some vehicles strayed from their course and were fired on by their friends or ran into strong-points they were meant to avoid. Some were knocked out and the blazing hulks quickly became aiming points for enemy artillery and mortars. Nevertheless, the general direction, if not the tempo, of the advance was maintained. It was soon obvious that the Germans were in even greater confusion and had no idea of the magnitude of the forces which were rolling through their lines.

The fortunes of one column, which advanced along the eastern side of the Falaise road, may be taken as typical. Within the first mile the three navigating tanks were ditched in deep bomb craters and, in trying to avoid these, the force behind soon lost cohesion and direction. " The chaos," says Lt.-Col. A. Jolly, who commanded the tank element of this column, " was indescribable. Everyone had been told to keep closed up and to follow the tank in front, but it was now obvious that the blind were leading the blind." Some semblance of order was restored only by officers dismounting and leading small groups of tanks on foot, and by Jolly firing Very lights and ordering the armour to follow the trail he was blazing. By these means the column was rallied and, though late, the infantry were set down within 200 yards of the planned ' debussing point.' Their objective, the village of Cramesnil, though strongly garrisoned, was quickly cleared.

By dawn British columns were firmly established according to plan three miles inside the German lines. Meantime, the Canadians had penetrated as far, but they had encountered stiff opposition on their western flank and had not reached their farthest objectives. Nevertheless, the enemy's second line had been cracked and a spectacular success had been won at a fraction of the cost which would have been involved in a conventional operation.[1] For several hours after dawn a thick ground mist delayed the Canadian advance and gave the enemy a chance to recover, but by the middle of the day the leading brigade had taken all but one of its objectives and the way seemed clear for the break-out.

On the enemy side, however, steps to check such exploitation had already been taken, primarily by one man, Meyer, the commander of 12th SS. Driving up the Falaise–Caen road immediately after the night bombing, Meyer had met parties of infantry streaming back in panic. Posting himself in the middle of the highway, Meyer challenged the stragglers and drove them back to the positions they had abandoned on the high ground around Cintheaux. Having re-established this blocking force astride the main road, Meyer reinforced it with armour and anti-tank guns, and directed his own two battlegroups to counter-attack the head of the Allied penetration north of Cintheaux.

This counter-attack was already in progress shortly after midday, when the Eighth U.S. Air Force began bombing the area Bretteville–Cintheaux–St. Sylvain in preparation for the ' break-out ' by the 4th Canadian and the 1st Polish Armoured Divisions. Since Meyer's forces were north of the bombing target area at the time, they suffered little from the bombardment and, although their own attack was repulsed, they were able to halt the Poles in the woods south of Cramesnil during the afternoon.

On the other side of the Falaise road, the Germans held Cintheaux until the evening and thus prevented the Canadian armour from exploiting rapidly. Neither the 4th Division nor the Poles had been in action before and, lacking experience, they did not thrust on aggressively as Simonds had ordered. They made little or no use of the fighter-bombers and medium artillery which were available to support them and, instead of by-passing opposition, they stopped to deal with it. The enemy was holding only a few key points and, if the superior range of the German anti-tank guns had been countered by smoke, the Canadians, if not the Poles, might have swept through. In the evening, when they should have been pressing on, both armoured divisions took up defensive positions for the night. The result was that between dawn and dark on August 8th the advance down the Falaise road gained only three miles and much of the advantage won by the bold ' break-in ' was lost.

Simonds sought to maintain the initiative by sending a mixed column under cover of darkness to seize Hill 195, west of the main road and half-way between Cintheaux and Falaise. This move miscarried, for the column lost its way during the night, and suffered heavily when a battery of ' 88s ' caught it on open ground east of the Falaise road soon after

---

[1] The armoured column, which by-passed Tilly in such confusion and went on to capture Cramesnil, lost only 12 men killed, but the Seaforth Highlanders, who took Tilly after an eight-hour fight, suffered 60 fatal casualties.

dawn. Throughout the day the Canadians made a desperate and gallant stand against repeated counter-attacks by 12th SS, but at dusk the survivors had to withdraw after losing 45 tanks.

During August 9th the Germans pulled back to their next defence line along the River Laison. By the next morning, although II Canadian Corps had taken Hill 195 and driven the enemy back nine miles, its leading troops were seven miles from Falaise and had not gained a clean break-through. The hinge was creaking, but it still held and the most the Canadians could claim was that they had thrust a crowbar between the door and the post. Another major wrench would be needed to break the hinge away.

There is little doubt that, if the armoured divisions had been more experienced and aggressive, the Canadian offensive would have been completely successful. On the evening of August 8th von Kluge had confessed to Hausser, " A break-through has occurred south of Caen, such as we have never seen."[1] On the following afternoon, however, the Field-Marshal told von Gersdorff, " I have just had a decisive conference with OKW. The situation south of Caen having been re-established, and not having had the much feared consequences, I propose to retain the idea of attacking again [at Mortain]. But now the attack must be prepared and executed deliberately; it must not be rushed."[2]

Although von Kluge expressed the decision as his own, it was in fact the Führer's. Hitler was convinced that the first offensive had failed only because his generals had not had the courage to wait until all preparations were complete, and he told Warlimont, " Von Kluge attacked too soon. He did that intentionally to show that my orders could not be carried out."

As in the case of the earlier effort, Hitler sent detailed tactical instructions. Six panzer divisions were to be employed and the *Schwerpunkt* was to be farther south than before. It was, in fact, to follow the course which von Funck had originally proposed, but now he was not to be in command. The attack was to be directed by Eberbach, who was to leave Fifth Panzer Army and improvise a new H.Q. for the occasion.[3]

At 9 a.m. on August 10th Eberbach telephoned to von Kluge's H.Q. giving his detailed requirements of troops and ammunition for the new offensive. At 9.15 Kuntzen, the Corps Commander on the southern

[1]Seventh Army Telephone Log, August 8th, 1845 hours.

[2]Seventh Army Telephone Log, August 9th, 1520 hours. Von Gersdorff was Hausser's Chief of Staff.

[3]The reason for this change lay far back in the history of the struggle between Hitler and the Generals. Warlimont says, " In 1940, after the Italian defeat, OKH sent von Funck to North Africa on a reconnaissance. On his return, von Funck reported to Hitler, who then realised, or discovered, that this officer had once been on the personal staff of von Fritsch, the former C.-in-C. Army. Thereupon von Funck was replaced by Rommel. In the case of the Avranches offensive, as soon as Hitler found out that von Funck was concerned he gave orders for Eberbach to take over."

flank, reported to Seventh Army, " The enemy has begun to push north
and north-east [from Le Mans]. With my present forces, four battalions,
I cannot even delay his advance. We must count upon Alençon being
in enemy hands to-morrow." This was a bombshell, for Alençon was
Seventh Army's main supply centre and the last report from Kuntzen
had indicated that the Americans were continuing to drive eastwards.

That had been the Allied plan, until the Germans counter-attacked
at Mortain on August 7th and invited envelopment. On the following
morning, when Eisenhower and Bradley conferred in Normandy, both
were fully alive to the magnitude of the opportunity now unexpectedly
and gratuitously presented to them. The Canadians appeared to have
broken through on the Falaise road and, if Third Army were to strike
north from Le Mans to Argentan, the Germans to the west might be
encircled and annihilated. There was a chance that von Kluge's armour
might yet cut through to the coast, but Eisenhower assured Bradley that
in this case the American divisions south of Avranches could be supplied
with 2,000 tons a day by air. The risk was small; the prospective gain
was incalculable.

At this time, Montgomery's plan[1] was, as he says in his Dispatch,
" to make a wide enveloping movement from the southern American
flank up to the Seine about Paris, and at the same time to drive the
centre and northern sectors of the Allied line straight for the river."
Accordingly, while accepting Bradley's suggestion that Third Army
should make a ' short hook ' to Argentan, Montgomery urged him to
continue the ' long hook ' to the Seine concurrently, or at least as soon
as the necessary forces could be released from the Mortain area. In view
of the situation around Mortain, where the battle was still raging fiercely,
Bradley could not continue the ' long hook ' at the moment, and the
orders he issued on the afternoon of the 8th declared: " Twelfth Army
Group will attack with the least practicable delay in the direction of
Argentan to isolate and destroy the German forces on our front." By
the 10th Patton had four divisions advancing in this direction to the
dismay of the German command.

Von Kluge was now in a terrible dilemma. The situation called for
prompt action, but he could make no counter-move without Hitler's
authority. He knew that the threat to Alençon and the vital supply
dumps could be met only if Seventh Army were to withdraw from the
Mortain–Sourdeval area, but that would have meant surrendering the

---

[1]There has been some controversy about the origin of this plan. Montgomery, in
his Dispatch, implies that it was his idea, but Bedell Smith (*Saturday Evening Post*, June
15th, 1946) says that, when Eisenhower and Bradley met, each was already contemplating
this encircling move to Argentan, and that Bradley then put it to Montgomery, who
endorsed the plan. Colonel Allen, expressing the Third Army view (op. cit., p. 102),
gives the credit to its commander, but on the day of the Eisenhower-Bradley meeting
Patton was busy in Brittany. " On the eighth," says Patton in *War As I Knew It*, p. 102,
" I drove to Dol, which is supposed to contain the largest phallic symbol in the world,
although I could not find it."

base from which he had been ordered to launch the new Avranches offensive. It would have been folly to have suggested such a withdrawal for even the suggestion would have been regarded by Hitler as an attempt to sabotage his orders.

The most von Kluge felt able to do that day was to seek permission for ' Panzer Group Eberbach ' to be " temporarily transferred from the Mortain area," so that it could be used to " destroy the enemy spearheads thrusting northwards," and thus " render possible the prosecution of the decisive offensive."[1] Hitler regarded even this proposal with deep suspicion and, although von Kluge was closely interrogated by telephone and teleprinter in the small hours of the morning, no decision was forthcoming from the Führer's H.Q.

While the German Command in the West was thus paralysed by lack of orders, the Allied armies pressed in on every side. During the morning of August 11th Seventh Army H.Q. was flooded with reports of further American advances. Mortain was lost, Sourdeval was threatened and the forces covering Alençon were driven back. At midday, with the crumbling edifice of German defence in Normandy about to crash around him, von Kluge summoned up courage to tell Jodl that " the offensive in the direction of Avranches is no longer practicable, since the enemy has brought up fresh forces. The thrust towards the sea will be a long, tough battle, to which the panzer troops are no longer equal."[2] Even now von Kluge was careful not to put this view forward as his own. He presented it as the opinion of SS General Hausser and of Eberbach, a staunch Nazi. " With their standpoint," said von Kluge, " I associate myself." This was symptomatic. Since July 20th every Wehrmacht general, every officer of the General Staff was suspect. Even a Field-Marshal of von Kluge's reputation could not speak with his own voice, on his own authority. He had to call in SS—and Party—Generals to substantiate his professional opinions. Galling though it must have been, von Kluge accepted the humiliation, for was not the ' July 20th Trial ' proceeding at the People's Court in Berlin?

That afternoon Hitler gave belated approval to the ' Alençon plan,' and appeared to accept its full implications, for he authorised Seventh Army to withdraw from the area between Sourdeval and Mortain. This movement had already begun, when a fresh directive arrived, insisting that " the purpose of resuming the offensive westward to the sea, after a success against the American XV Army Corps, must be adhered to."[3] This was madness, for it prevented von Kluge from freely disengaging the forces he needed to meet the threat to Alençon.

In the remote fastness of his H.Q. in East Prussia Hitler was living in a world of fantasy, sustained by optimism, ignorance and his un-

[1]Teleprinter Message, von Kluge to Jodl, August 10th, 1944. (Tempelhof Papers.)
[2]Teleprinter Message, von Kluge to Jodl, August 11th, 1944. (Tempelhof Papers.)
[3]This directive was quoted in full by von Kluge in a signal to his Army Commanders at 0730 hours on August 12th. (Tempelhof Papers.)

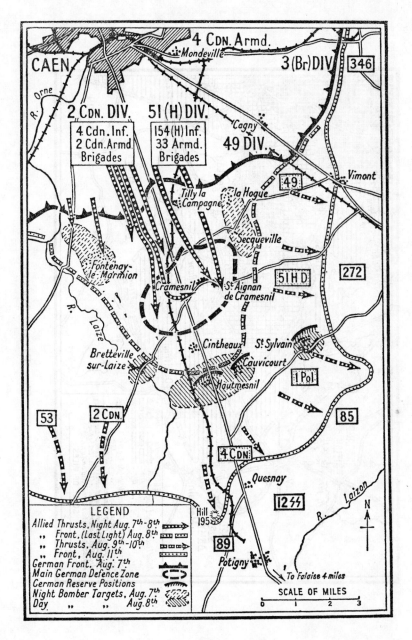

OPERATION TOTALIZE

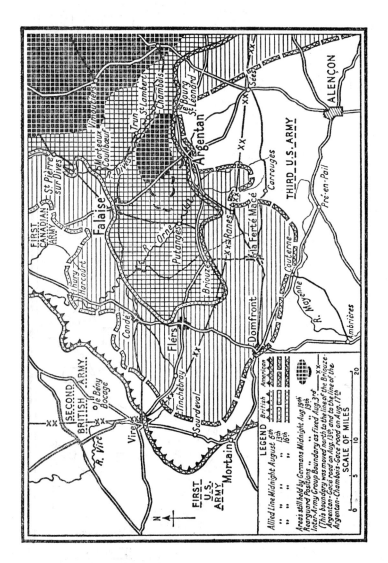

THE FALAISE POCKET

rivalled capacity for self-delusion. He took no account of the exhaustion of his divisions, the parlous state of their equipment, the shortage of supplies or the impossibility of making large-scale movements by day. Even if none of these conditions had applied, his demands would have been difficult enough to implement in face of the strength the Allies disposed, but Hitler did not understand that normal concepts of tactical time and space had been rendered invalid by Anglo-American air power and mechanisation. On the chess-board of his map, he continued to move pawns as if they were kings, and in defiance of the fact that von Kluge's armies were already in ' check.'

The more urgent the need for decision, the more insistent was Hitler that the decision must be made by him alone, and that he be sent the information on which to base it. This involved intolerable delays, for a decision could be obtained only at his midday and midnight conferences, and it usually took one conference to persuade him to accept an unpalatable situation and a second to extract any positive order. Thus the mere process of obtaining approval for an urgent tactical move might take twenty-four hours, and by the time the Führer's instructions reached the front, the facts upon which they were based had changed beyond recognition. In this case, not content with having prescribed the troops to be used, their assembly areas and objectives, Hitler proceeded to demand, " Plan of attack to be reported in detail. Likewise the proposed distribution of all armoured and assault-artillery units in the Army Group."

The disastrous consequences of this outrageous system of command, and of the orders which flowed from it, were apparent to every German general in France, and yet all accepted it. They knew that they were sending their armies to destruction, but they had been brought up to worship discipline and obedience above all else and to regard the voice of established authority as the voice of God. The price of disobedience was dismissal and disgrace (and, since July 20th, possibly death), and that price they were not prepared to pay. Even Sepp Dietrich, who stood as high as any man in the Führer's favour, would make no move, though many urged him to intercede in person and tell Hitler the truth. Dietrich's reply was, " If I want to get shot, that's the way to do it."[1]

Before von Kluge could act upon Hitler's directive and attack from Alençon, the rapid and inexorable progress of events turned it into waste paper. On August 12th the Americans captured Alençon and compelled Eberbach to commit in defence of Argentan the force he was assembling for attack. Even this was of little avail. In two days XV U.S. Corps advanced 35 miles and by the evening of the 13th it had an armoured division on either flank of Argentan, though the town was still in German hands. With the Americans established around Argentan, the gap between the northern and southern jaws of the Allied trap was barely 20 miles wide.

[1]Related by Schack, commander of the 272nd Division, to whom this remark was made.

That evening von Kluge warned Jodl, " The enemy seeks with all his power to encompass the encirclement of the bulk of Fifth Panzer Army and Seventh Army,"[1] and he implied that this encirclement was imminent, but even now he shrank from suggesting a general withdrawal. He merely proposed that Seventh Army should pull back from the western end of the pocket as far as Flèrs " in order to set free armoured forces " for the attack against XV Corps. Early on August 14th Hitler authorised this move, but within twelve hours the utter inadequacy of such a limited withdrawal was sharply revealed by developments on both flanks of the pocket. Shortly before midday Eberbach reported that he had not the strength to drive back the Americans at Argentan. At noon the Canadians launched another major attack towards Falaise.

Montgomery had ordered First Canadian Army to capture Falaise, exploit towards Argentan and close the gap. As before, the chief problem was the penetration of the screen of anti-tank guns, which covered the approaches to Falaise, and especially the direct approach down the road from Caen. Here the main enemy defences were in Quesnay Wood and on Potigny Ridge, and Simonds had already sent the 2nd Canadian Division to outflank these on the west. Since this movement had provoked considerable opposition, he decided to neutralise the Quesnay–Potigny area with a crushing air attack and to by-pass it to the east. This meant forcing the line of the Laison River. Once again he put his tanks in the van, mounted his infantry in ' unfrocked Priests ' and gave them strong air support. This time, however, he attacked under cover of a smoke-screen, not darkness, and adopted steam-roller tactics, instead of a policy of infiltration. His forces (the 2nd Armoured Brigade, the 3rd Infantry and 4th Armoured Divisions) were deployed for attack, not in long, narrow columns, but in solid phalanxes, each some 250 yards square.

While the German anti-tank gunners on the southern slope of the Laison Valley were blinded with smoke and subdued by bomb and shell, this great mass of armour rolled relentlessly to the river, the drivers steering for the sun, which showed through the angry haze like a great red disc. These tactics were unorthodox but effective. There was considerable confusion and some units lost formation and strayed too far eastward, but this confusion was nothing to the consternation of the German infantry, who suddenly found themselves overwhelmed by tanks which loomed up out of the dust.

The Canadians had some difficulty in crossing the river, but by late afternoon the armoured brigades had overrun the first gun line and were thrusting south, closely followed by the infantry. At dusk the leading troops of the 3rd Division were barely three miles from Falaise, but they

[1]Teleprinter Message, von Kluge to Jodl, August 13th, 1800 hrs. (Tempelhof Papers.) It was believed by Allied Intelligence at the time that the Germans must be unaware of the strength of Patton's forces on the southern flank, but the Tempelhof Papers show that von Kluge was most accurately informed about the Allied Order of Battle and told Jodl exactly what the American dispositions were.

were still meeting heavy anti-tank fire. Simonds had hoped that the Germans would be distracted to the north-west by the advance of the 2nd Division, but on the night of the 13th a Canadian scout car had run into the German lines. Inside it was a copy of some conference notes which gave Simonds's exact plan of attack. Thus forewarned, the Germans were able to concentrate their slender reserves to meet the danger. Throughout August 15th the rump of 12th SS (500 grenadiers and 15 tanks), plus a dozen '88s', checked the Canadian break-through on the last ridge before Falaise. There the Germans were still standing firm on the 16th, when troops of the 2nd Canadian Division broke into Falaise from the west. By the following evening the whole town, apart from the École Supérieure, was in Canadian hands and the gap between the closing jaws was only twelve miles wide.

While the Canadians were advancing to Falaise, the Americans on the southern flank were waging a fierce battle with Eberbach's Panzer Group. On the 12th, Major-General W. H. Haislip, commanding XV Corps, had been ordered by Patton to continue north to Falaise but, after reaching the Argentan area that day Haislip was halted on orders from Bradley, who was rightly concerned lest his troops might collide with the British advancing from Falaise. Patton strongly resented this order and he has asserted that his troops " could easily have entered Falaise and closed the gap. . . . We had reconnaissance parties near the town when we were ordered to pull back."[1]

This claim is not substantiated by the records of the units concerned but, even if it were, that would not mean that XV Corps could have followed in sufficient strength to close the gap and keep it closed. That day the Germans were still in Argentan, blocking the only through road. Eberbach had three panzer divisions on Haislip's western flank from Ranes to Argentan and another at Gacé. These divisions were only at half strength, but they were being reinforced with all the armour von Kluge could muster. This same day Haislip had only three divisions in the Ranes–Argentan–Sées triangle, for his fourth was east of Alençon. That force was sufficient to hold the southern jaw, but hardly strong enough to plug the mouth as well. Haislip could have carried out this double task only if reinforced, but that would have meant distracting Third Army from what Montgomery regarded as its main role—the wider envelopment up to the Seine.

Mongomery undoubtedly overestimated the speed with which the Canadians could advance from the north, but he was already looking far beyond Falaise. He wanted to trap those enemy divisions which had never been in the pocket, and to maintain the momentum of his offensive so that the Germans would have no chance of establishing a new line along the Seine or the Somme. There were times when Patton had to be

---

[1]Patton, op. cit., p. 105. Bradley reports that, after reaching Argentan, Patton telephoned him and said: "Let me go on to Falaise and we'll drive the British back into the sea for another Dunkirk." (Bradley, op. cit., p. 376.)

saved from himself, and this was one of them. Had he become more deeply involved between Argentan and Falaise, his attack towards Paris must have suffered. But because XV Corps was not required to continue north, Patton was able to send two of Haislip's divisions forthwith to Dreux. This strengthened by fifty per cent the eastward offensive which Third Army launched on August 15th, while the battle of the Falaise Pocket was still raging.

When the Canadians entered Falaise on August 16th, the bulk of the Seventh German Army was still west of the Orne, since no orders had been issued for a retreat from the pocket. Von Kluge, on his own initiative, had extricated 2nd SS Panzer Corps and had told Hausser to send out his administrative troops and motor transport, but he had hesitated to suggest to Hitler any more drastic withdrawal, for the tone of the signals from the Führer's H.Q. had been increasingly acid since the failure of the Mortain counter-attack. " The language of Hitler's orders," says Blumentritt, " was curt and even insulting. This naturally worried the Field-Marshal who was afraid that he would be arrested at any moment. He became more and more gloomy."[1]

The crisis which now developed, however, did not have its origin in the proceedings of the People's Court, for the first mention of von Kluge's complicity in the ' Plot of July 20th ' came in the evidence of his nephew two weeks later. It arose out of an incident which took place in Normandy on August 15th. That day, while driving from Laroche Guyon to the pocket, von Kluge was out of touch with his H.Q. for more than twelve hours. Arriving at Eberbach's H.Q. after dark " in a very shaken condition,"[2] von Kluge explained that he had been caught in a heavy artillery bombardment, that his radio car had been knocked out by fighter-bombers and that he had spent most of the day in a ditch. Eberbach and Blumentritt assert that this is true, but the Führer found another explanation for von Kluge's absence.

At a subsequent conference with Keitel and others, Hitler alleged that von Kluge had spent this day endeavouring to reach a rendezvous with the Allies. " Field-Marshal Kluge," said Hitler, " planned to lead the whole of the Western Army into capitulation and to go over himself to the enemy. . . . It seems that the plan miscarried owing to an enemy fighter-bomber attack. He had sent away his staff officer, British-American patrols advanced, but apparently no contact was made. . . . Nevertheless the British have reported being in contact with a German general."[3]

[1]Interrogation (Liddell Hart).
[2]Interrogation of Eberbach. (Second British Army.)
[3]Führer Conferences, Fragment 46, August 31st, 1944. Unfortunately the shorthand transcription of this conference is far from complete and there are many phrases missing even from the sections which were recovered. Neither Eisenhower nor Montgomery nor their Chief Intelligence Officers were cognisant of any such move by von Kluge.

From the Allied side there is no confirmation whatever of this charge. It is possible that von Kluge attempted to give himself up but, if this is so, the Allies were not aware of it, and there is no foundation for Hitler's claim that the British released a captured officer so that he could make contact with von Kluge. The source of Hitler's information is not yet known, but he did not hesitate to act upon it. Early on August 16th he summoned Model from the Russian front and ordered him to fly to France immediately and take over von Kluge's command.

In view of the situation in the pocket, there could hardly have been a less propitious moment for such a change but, because he believed that von Kluge had already tried to betray him, Hitler was obsessed with the fear that another, and successful, attempt would be made before Model could arrive. " August 15th," said Hitler later, " was the worst day of my life. It was due only to an accident that the plan was not carried out. The measures taken by the Army Group cannot be explained except in the light of this assumption."[1]

No warning of any change was sent to the West, beyond the ominous injunction: " Field-Marshal von Kluge will immediately leave the pocket and will direct operations from the H.Q. of Fifth Panzer Army."[2] From that H.Q. during the night August 15th–16th under strong pressure from his Army commanders, von Kluge telephoned to Jodl and at last ventured to propose an immediate withdrawal from the pocket. Hitler did not reply until the following day, and then the most he would agree was that Seventh Army should " withdraw across the Orne in two or three nights and establish a new front on the east bank of the river." Critical and urgent though the position was, he hoped that Model, the miracle-worker of the East, might be able to restore it without yielding further ground.

Thus it was that, while Model was journeying across Europe to take the helm, the stricken ship, instead of running before the storm, was anchored fast at Hitler's order with the waves breaking about her.

On August 17th V U.S. Corps took over Patton's divisions around Argentan and prepared to attack north towards Trun and Chambois, where it was to link up with II Canadian Corps. In spite of the danger that the converging Allied forces might become entangled in the mêlée, Montgomery had now decided that this risk must be taken, if Seventh Army was not to elude the trap. That day, while the Germans were still resisting in Falaise, the 4th Canadian and 1st Polish Armoured Divisions broke out across the River Dives in the Morteaux–Couliboeuf area and made a wide sweep to the south-east. Their orders were to capture Trun and Chambois " at all costs and as quickly as possible," and to establish a barrier along the Dives and on the ridge which flanks it to the north.

---

[1]Führer Conferences, Fragment 46, August 31st, 1944.
[2]Quoted by Blumentritt, when interrogated by Liddell Hart.

This move took the Germans by surprise, since they had concentrated their main blocking forces at Falaise and Argentan. By the evening of the 17th both the Canadians and the Poles were within two miles of Trun, and the capture of Bourg St. Léonard by the Americans had reduced the gap to six miles.

Under heavy pressure from American, British and Canadian Armies, Hausser's battered divisions had been squeezed into an area twenty miles wide and ten miles deep. Within this shrunken pocket, remorselessly pounded by bomb and shell, there were 100,000 German troops, the remnants of fifteen divisions with stragglers from a dozen more. Their only escape routes were the narrow roads which led through Chambois and St. Lambert and these were under fire from both sides and from the sky.

This was the desperate situation which confronted Model at the end of his first day as C-in-C., West. Without waiting to consult the Führer, he gave Hausser sole command of the forces in the pocket and ordered him to withdraw from the Orne and establish a new front along the Dives. Since this plan could succeed only if the Canadians could be driven back to Morteaux–Couliboeuf, Hausser ordered 2nd SS Panzer Corps to counter-attack from the east and cut off the Allied columns which had broken through to Trun.[1]

Throughout August 18th a fierce battle raged along the ridge north of Chambois. In the evening Polish tanks stood triumphant on the crest but the gap was still open, and many thousands of Germans escaped through it. Yet the process of escaping was perilous indeed, especially for the columns of transport which sought to move in daylight along the road through Chambois to Vimoutiers. There British and American aircraft found targets even more profitable than those of the past few days. Early in the afternoon one pilot reported: " 1,000 plus motor transport, tanks and horse-drawn transport in area . . . very little movement . . . facing east and south-east packed bumper to bumper. Much congested traffic moving east on road Vimoutiers–Orbec." Later a further signal from the air: " 1,000 repeat 1,000 motor transport Vimoutiers–Orbec now dispersed and static. Feeding main road from all side roads like herring bones." In the evening another pilot reported " whole are a burning."

Air power alone could not seal the exit, but within the pocket confusion and congestion grew more serious every hour, as the Allied armies closed in for the kill. While the Poles were fighting on the ridge, the Canadians in the valley of the Dives captured Trun and at nightfall were only two miles north-west of Chambois, which was closely threatened from the south by the 90th U.S. Division and 2nd French Armoured. Next day (August 19th) the lanes and by-ways between the roads Falaise–

---

[1]Hausser's Operation Order was captured by the Poles north of Chambois. Issued on the 18th, the order shows that Hausser hoped to complete the withdrawal to the Dives by August 21st.

Argentan and Falaise–Chambois were so choked with tanks, guns and transport that few vehicles could move, and only the smoke, which hung like a pall above this slaughter-ground, saved the Germans from the full fury of Allied air attack. In the evening, the Americans and the French joined forces with the Poles in Chambois and the Falaise Pocket was closed.

That night Hausser's armoured forces, the remnants of five panzer divisions, were ordered to breakout north-east and re-open an escape route for the infantry. The armour moved at dawn on the 20th, but the attacking columns were soon disorganised by a deluge of shellfire. On the approaches to Trun and Chambois the tanks were blocked as much by the wreckage and congestion, as by the barrage. The break-out forces themselves became enmeshed in the traffic jam and, as the shelling grew more intense, all order was lost in the holocaust of blazing vehicles and exploding ammunition. Men fled in terror, but there was no escape for the harnessed horses.

Between Trun and Chambois, however, remnants of the 2nd Panzer Division reached the Dives and an armoured column crashed through the thin Canadian line. For six hours the Germans kept open one road through the southern part of St. Lambert, but the northern half of this straggling village remained in Canadian hands. Here Major D. V. Currie,[1] of the 4th Armoured Division, with 175 men, 15 tanks, and four anti-tank guns resisted every assault. Several times, when the Germans seemed to be on the point of success, Currie ordered his men to take cover and called on the medium artillery to shell the entire village. Throughout the day he directed Canadian guns on to German columns crossing the Dives and their fire caused terrible carnage. They could not stop the armour getting through, but several close columns of horse-drawn transport were caught in bombardments as they approached the bridge. The horses stampeded. Careering through hedges and fences, the terrified animals plunged down the steep river bank, dragging their wagons and gun-carriages after them. Soon the ravine was choked with wreckage and with the bodies of men and horses, the dead and the wounded lying together in gruesome heaps.

Great though the slaughter was, many thousands of Germans escaped before the corridor through St. Lambert was closed again in the evening. During the night the enemy continued his frenzied efforts to break out and small parties managed to infiltrate through the Allied lines. Hausser, though badly wounded, rode out with a posse of tanks; Meindl, the commander of 2nd Parachute Corps, slipped through with a bodyguard of paratroops; and Meyer, of 12th SS, was led to safety by a French civilian. Whoever else was trapped, the generals for the most part made

---

[1]For his part in this action, Major Currie was awarded the Victoria Cross. The force under his command consisted of one squadron of the 29th Canadian Armoured Reconnaissance Regiment and one company of the Argyll and Sutherland Highlanders of Canada.

good their escape. Of the five corps commanders who were still in the pocket on August 17th all but one got away; of the fifteen divisional commanders only three failed to reach safety. Behind them they left some 50,000 men in captivity and another 10,000 dead, sacrificed on the altar of blind obedience to the Führer's command.

On August 21st a final attempt to relieve the forces in the pocket was made by 2nd SS Panzer Corps, which again endeavoured to dislodge the Polish Division from the ridge north of Chambois. For a while the Poles were isolated and they had to be supplied with ammunition by air, but they held fast. On the following day this panzer corps was ordered to join the rest of Model's forces in a general retreat. It was high time, for the Americans had already crossed the Seine on either side of Paris.

In the Mortain–Falaise Pocket, the Wehrmacht suffered its greatest disaster since Stalingrad, but on the Allied side there was considerable disappointment because more than a third of Seventh Army had eluded the trap. Many high-ranking Americans were extremely critical of what they regarded as Montgomery's slowness in closing the gap. So far as material losses were concerned, the delay was of small consequence, for most of the units which escaped from the pocket in the last few days, lost nearly all their tanks,[1] transport, guns and other heavy weapons. Moreover, of the equipment which was extricated, very little crossed the Seine. From the point of view of morale, however, the consequences of this defeat were not as great as they might have been.

At Stalingrad a complete German army was destroyed, and its commander and some twenty-five other generals were among those who capitulated. In Normandy there was no mass surrender and most of the generals escaped, as did the H.Q. of Seventh Army. There was no comparable capitulation, since there was no question of Hausser's Army having laid down its arms. Had the Allies been able to close the pocket by August 15th or 16th, Seventh Army and nine of the eleven panzer divisions in the West would have been trapped. Such a disaster, coming so soon after the *attentat* of July 20th, must have had a shattering moral impact upon the Wehrmacht and the German people. It was ironic that Hitler should have been spared the full consequences of his own folly.

Could the gap have been closed earlier? It seems that it could, for the evidence suggests that the thrust from the north was not pressed with sufficient speed and strength. In the final stages Montgomery had British divisions to spare, but Simonds was not reinforced. Nor was the Canadian attack as vigorous and venturesome as the occasion demanded. The opposition north of Falaise was admittedly strong, but in the attacks of

---

[1]After the battle a team of Allied investigators found 384 German tanks and assault guns which had been abandoned or destroyed between Mortain and Vimoutiers, but it was not able to comb every lane and field. Allowing for those missed, it was estimated that the Germans must have lost at least 500 tanks and assault guns in the pocket. (Report of No. 2 Operational Research Section.)

August 7th and 14th opportunities of exploitation were lost, and after the final drive to Chambois there was serious delay in ' thickening-up ' the barrier on the Dives. Crerar acknowledged this by relieving the commander of the 4th Canadian Armoured Division on August 20th, but by then the chance of extracting the maximum advantage from the enemy's plight had gone.

On the other hand, there is no reason to believe that XV U.S. Corps could have driven straight on from Argentan to Falaise on the 13th or 14th. Contrary to contemporary reports, the Americans did not capture Argentan until August 20th, the day after the link-up at Chambois. Patton's northward advance could have been maintained only at the expense of his offensive to the Seine, and this exploitation became the more demoralising, because it was carried out while the battle of Falaise was still in progress.

Third Army's offensive to the Seine began in earnest on August 15th. By the following night XII Corps on the right had captured Orléans; XX Corps in the centre was fighting in Chartres; and XV Corps had taken Dreux. On this northern flank, where the strongest opposition might have been expected, the 5th Armoured and 79th Infantry Divisions found the direct roads to Paris undamaged and almost undefended. On the 15th in eleven hours, the 79th Division motored from La Mêle-sur-Sarthe to Nogent-le-Roi, a distance of 60 miles. Although it was breaking new ground, the division was able to report " no contact with the enemy."[1]

Hitler had ordered Fifteenth Army to send three divisions to the Chartres area " to cover Paris and the rear of Army Group B," but he had no conception of the power which was rolling towards the Seine. He had blandly declared that anti-tank units were to " rush forward along the main roads leading west in order to obstruct enemy raids with individual armoured cars and tanks in the direction of Paris."[2] But his troops were now confronted, not with raids, but with an army on the march: three armoured and three motorised divisions advancing under the spur of the aggressive and venturesome Patton, a master of exploitation.

Both Hitler and the German Command in the West were gravely at fault in their estimate of American strength and skill. The High Command was contemptuous because the American Army had such a small professional core and so little military tradition or experience, but Hitler's scorn had a different source. " In assessing the military value of the Americans," says Speer, " Hitler always argued that they were not a tough people, not a closely-knit nation in the European sense. If put to the test, they would prove to be poor fighters." Hitler had learnt nothing since the Tunisian campaign, when he readily accepted the report by

[1] After-Action Report, 79th Division, August 1944.
[2] Führer Directive of August 11th, 1944. (Tempelhof Papers.)

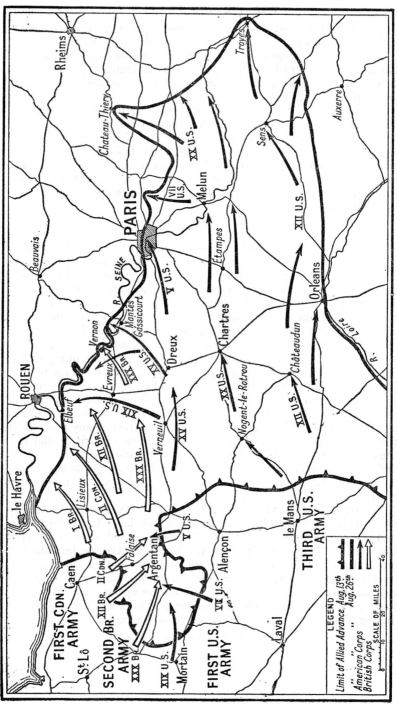

THE DRIVE TO THE SEINE

one of his entourage (Sonderführer von Neurath) that the American troops were " a shocking crowd." According to Neurath, who said he had been interrogating hundreds of American prisoners, " Most of them have come over to make money, or for adventure, or to see something new, to be in something exciting for once. Not one of them has a political opinion or a great ideal. They are 'rowdies' who quickly turn and run; they could not stand up to a crisis." When this was reported to him, Hitler commented: " America will never become the Rome of the future. Rome was a state of peasants."[1]

The Americans were not peasants: therefore they could not be tough; their armies could not have that deep inner fortitude which the dumb but staunch peasantry had always provided in the mass armies of the continental powers. To Hitler it was as simple as that. He did not realise that America's strength lay in this very absence of the 'peasant mentality,' with its narrow horizons, its acceptance of the established order, and its ignorance of machines. The basic German miscalculation was the failure to appreciate that America's military prowess was a logical consequence of her industrial power. The Germans learned by experience that this power had given the American forces boundless equipment, but they did not realise that it had also provided a vast reservoir of manpower skilled in the use of machines.

More than any other people, the Americans are mechanically-minded. In the United States the youth who cannot drive a car or has not operated a machine of some kind is a rarity. In their dealings with people, Americans are often unsure of themselves and betray their feeling of inferiority by their behaviour, which Europeans tend to regard as juvenile and even gauche. But in the realm of machines, the Americans possess a self-confidence, indeed a sense of mastery, which European peoples do not know. It was this technical understanding and experience which had enabled Marshall to build so rapidly a great army.

When the campaign became fluid, another factor assumed almost equal importance: the survival, or revival, of the frontier spirit. The Americans had in their blood a longing for adventure and an instinct for movement, which they inherited from those pioneers who had broken out across the Alleghanies and opened up the Middle West. To the American troops driving across France, distance meant nothing. They had no qualms about thrusting deep into the military unknown. This was not the case with the majority of the British forces. Apart from his armoured and airborne divisions, Dempsey had few units capable of rapid, offensive movement. He might transport his infantry in trucks, but he could not convert them psychologically into 'motorised divisions'; by nature the commanders and the men moved at a deliberate pace. In Bradley's command, on the other hand, as soon as the break-out had been achieved, every division, armoured and infantry alike, seemed to be capable of swift and bold exploitation.

[1]Führer Conferences, Fragment 39, March 5th, 1943.

This came as a tremendous shock to the German High Command. During operations in the Normandy bocage, reports from the front had consistently belittled the fighting quality of the Anglo-American forces, and had attributed all Allied successes to " overwhelming material superiority." The common opinion in the Wehrmacht was expressed by Bayerlein of Panzer Lehr, when he wrote in June: " A successful break-in by the enemy is never exploited to pursuit. . . . The fighting morale of the British infantry is not very high. They rely largely on artillery and air force support. . . . The enemy is extraordinarily nervous of close combat. . . . He strives therefore to occupy ground, rather than to fight over it."[1] Bayerlein acknowledged that British armoured units had " good offensive spirit," but the Germans considered that the Americans were, if anything, less aggressive and less formidable than the British. Reporting to C.-in-C., West, on American tactics in the battle for St. Lô, the 3rd Parachute Division declared that, " At the smallest resistance the infantry stops and retires, and a new artillery bombardment takes place in order to stamp out the remaining opposition. . . . In defence the enemy is a hard fighter only so long as he has good support from the artillery and mortar units. . . . So far his tank crews have not shown much enthusiasm for fights between tanks."

This view was bluntly contradicted when Bradley's divisions began to advance across France. Then the troops, who had seemed so hesitant in the bocage, suddenly became emboldened to the point of recklessness. Overnight infantry appeared to be imbued with the spirit and performance of mechanised cavalry. In their military conceit, the Germans had judged American capacity for movement by the yardstick of their own standards of mobility. During the *Blitzkrieg* campaigns the panzer and motorised divisions must have been highly efficient, but by 1944 the German standards of driving and maintenance were extraordinarily bad. The wear and tear on tanks and vehicles was excessive, for the ordinary German soldier, lacking the American's mechanical sense, tended to treat his machine with the same brutality which he applied to ' inferior races.' Moreover, the bulk of the Wehrmacht was still dependent upon horse-drawn artillery and transport, and its commanders had forgotten how fast a fully motorised army could advance. The German generals were as surprised as Hitler when Patton's columns covered fifty miles in a day.

From August 16th to 18th Third Army was halted on the line Orléans–Chartres–Dreux, partly for reasons of supply, but also because Bradley, after fighting so long and so hard in the bocage, did not fully appreciate the extent of the enemy's demoralisation. He wanted to make

[1]Report by Panzer Lehr Division to the Inspector-General of Panzer Troops for period June 6th–22nd. This report was a considered military judgment, not a vehicle for propaganda.

sure that Patton's extended northern flank was adequately covered by units of First Army, which were moving up from Mortain. Patton could have gone straight on from Dreux to the Seine, but it took three days of hard fighting to clear the Germans from Chartres, for the Americans made sparing use of artillery lest they should damage the majestic cathedral. On the 18th, however, the drive to the Seine was renewed, and by dark the 79th Division (Major-General I. T. Wyche) was only three miles from the river at Mantes-Gassicourt, west of Paris. Next day a patrol found a footbridge intact over a dam, which the Germans had only partially destroyed. Soon afterwards Patton arrived on the scene and, though greatly tempted to order Wyche to seize a bridgehead immediately, refrained from doing so, until he had flown back and consulted Bradley. The necessary authority did not reach Wyche until dark, but he acted at once. The 313th Regiment was roused from its blankets and soon after midnight in drenching rain troops began crossing the footbridge. Before dawn two battalions were over the river, and by the evening of the 20th Wyche had established a firm bridgehead without interference from the enemy.

The Seine was left unguarded at Mantes, because the divisions which should have held the river line had been sent by Hitler to guard the direct approach to Paris. At this stage, however, the Allies had no intention of forcing an entry into the French capital. They planned to envelop it and, accordingly, Patton was ordered to seize a second bridgehead over the Seine at Melun south-east of Paris. That task was accomplished by the 7th Armoured Division on August 23rd, but by this time events within the capital had brought about a change in Eisenhower's plans.

A week earlier almost the entire Paris police force had gone on strike, and on August 19th, 3,000 armed gendarmes had seized control of the Préfecture de Police, and turned the Île de la Cité into a fortress. This was the start of a general uprising by the forces of the F.F.I., and during the night of the 19th–20th they gained control of the heart of the city, occupying the Hôtel de Ville, the Palais de Justice, the Ministries of War and the Interior and a number of other government buildings. That night the German garrison made plans to suppress the insurrection, for it had direct orders from Hitler to " defend Paris to the last, destroy all bridges over the Seine and devastate the city."[1] Nevertheless, by the morning of the 20th the military commandant, von Choltitz, realised that the revolt had spread too far to be checked by force, and he asked for an immediate armistice to permit him to withdraw German troops from the western to the eastern sector of the city unmolested. In return, he offered to recognise members of the F.F.I. as belligerents, to leave them in possession of the centre of the city, and to allow the entry of French food convoys, which had been stopped in retaliation for sniping by the Resistance.

[1] Quoted by Eberbach, who saw the order. (British Army Interrogation.)

This was agreed. The armistice was to run until noon on August 23rd, but the boundaries were vague and the F.F.I. had not the means of controlling all their own troops. Some skirmishing and sniping continued, and on the night of the 20th the German-controlled Paris Radio broadcast a proclamation, declaring, " Irresponsible elements in Paris have taken up arms against the occupation authorities. The revolt will be rigorously suppressed." This warning may have been put out only for Hitler's benefit, but the Resistance leaders naturally regarded it as a breach of the armistice. Fighting flared up again, and spread over most of the city. On the following evening, when the Germans seemed likely to gain the upper hand, the F.F.I. sent envoys to warn the Americans of the plight of Paris.

On August 22nd, therefore, Bradley ordered Gerow's V Corps, with the 2nd French Armoured and the 4th U.S. Infantry Divisions, to enter the capital as soon as possible after the expiration of the ' armistice,' but to avoid heavy fighting. Throughout the 24th, Gerow's divisions were held up by rearguard parties and road-blocks on the outskirts of the city, but at dawn next day the French from the west and the Americans from the south began driving for the heart of Paris.

Under the combined impact of insurrection and assault the German defence collapsed. A few strong-points held out, but they were soon by-passed with the aid of local guides. All Paris surged out to meet the Allied columns and their advance was encumbered more by exultant and hysterical civilians than it was by the Germans. By 8.30 a.m. American cavalry stood before Notre Dame and French armour was riding in triumph down the Champs Élysées. North of the Seine the German garrison kept up a token resistance until mid-afternoon, but von Choltitz was waiting only for the opportunity of surrendering to the regular military forces and escaping the vengeance of the Resistance —old and new.

By dark all organised German opposition had ended, but the firing went on throughout the night as Resistance bands hunted down traitors and members of Darnand's hated militia. Paris was purging her own soul, and with the morning her people rose to breathe again after four years of agony and humiliation. Their joy and their pride were the greater because they had fought for their own freedom. And all Europe knew that with the liberation of Paris, as with her subjection four years earlier, the Battle of France was won.

## Part Three

★

## THE
## ROAD TO BERLIN

## CHAPTER XXII

# THE CLOSING JAWS

IN a directive to his Army Commanders two weeks after D-Day, Montgomery had declared that once Cherbourg and Caen were captured the Allies would have " a mighty chance to make the German Army come to our threat and to defeat it between the Seine and the Loire." It took Montgomery another five weeks to create the opportunity for inflicting the defeat he planned, but in those five weeks the course of the battle was such that the victory which followed was overwhelming. Moreover, the policy adopted by Hitler at Mortain and Falaise had now exposed the Wehrmacht to the threat of a second encirclement.

When the Americans reached the Seine at Mantes–Gassicourt (36 miles west of Paris) on August 18th, the remnants of Fifth Panzer Army and Seventh Army were squeezed into another pocket, bounded on two sides by the sea and the broad reaches of the Lower Seine, across which there were no bridges standing except one badly damaged rail bridge at Rouen. Bradley therefore proposed to cut off this line of retreat by sending an American corps down the left bank of the Seine while the British and Canadians were still reducing the Falaise Pocket. Montgomery agreed, and this wide enveloping movement started on August 20th when the 2nd U.S. Armoured Division struck north from Verneuil. In four days it advanced 60 miles into the flank of the retreating Germans, but at Elbeuf on the 24th it encountered strong opposition from armoured forces covering the escape route through Rouen and the numerous ferries farther downstream.

By holding Elbeuf for two days, and by fighting a skilful rearguard action against the British and Canadian forces closing in from the west, the German command prevented the retreat from becoming a rout. Bad weather made it difficult for the Allied Air Forces to maintain their onslaught against the Seine crossings, and allowed the enemy to make use of some sixty ferries and several pontoon bridges between Elbeuf and the sea. Some troops got away in small boats, some on rafts made of cider barrels taken from the cellars of farms and inns; others cut down trees, lashed them together with telephone wires and floated across with the current. Many had to swim.

Thousands of Germans were overtaken by Allied columns, thousands more were killed by Allied bombs, as they sheltered in the thickly wooded river bends waiting their turn to cross, but the majority of the men made good their escape. There was little else, however, that they could save. The Allies maintained such pressure on the ground and from the air that nearly all the heavy equipment—the tanks, guns, trucks and half-tracks —had to be left behind. " From the point of view of equipment abandoned," says Dietrich, who conducted the withdrawal, " the Seine crossing was almost as great a disaster as the Falaise Pocket."

These two disasters were the culmination of ten weeks' heavy fighting which had cost the Germans half a million casualties of whom 210,000 had been taken prisoners. The most serious aspect of these disasters was the destruction of the panzer forces. Some 2,300 German tanks and assault guns had been committed in Normandy; of these, says Blumentritt, " only 100 to 120 were brought back across the Seine."

On August 29th, as the last of his troops were crossing the river, Model reported to Hitler on the state of the Wehrmacht in the West. The average strength of the panzer and panzer grenadier divisions which had fought in Normandy was, he said, " five to ten tanks each." From these eleven divisions he might form eleven battlegroups of regimental strength, but could do this only if he were to receive prompt replacements of men and equipment. From the sixteen infantry divisions which had been brought back across the Lower Seine he could raise sufficient men to form four, but he could not equip them. These troops, he said, " have only a few heavy weapons and for the most part are equipped with nothing more than small arms. . . . The supply of replacements in men and material is utterly inadequate. . . . There is no reserve whatever of assault guns and other heavy anti-tank equipment."[1]

There was now no chance of the Germans making a stand on the Seine to cover the preparation of a new defence line along the Somme and the Marne. Since the fall of Paris the British and Canadians had established four bridgeheads over the Lower Seine, and the Americans had driven on east and north-east from the French capital. Accordingly, Model reported that Seventh Army was withdrawing at once to the Somme, and that the surviving mobile forces were being concentrated in the Rheims area " to ward off the swift and dangerous thrust " by the Americans against the rear of Army Group B.

These German moves were, in Model's opinion, merely " temporary expedients." Already, on August 24th, he had told Hitler that he would need to be reinforced by " at least 30 to 35 infantry divisions . . . and 12 panzer divisions," and had added the warning, " We must look ahead and build more rearward positions behind the Somme–Marne Line up to and including the West Wall." At this time there were no prepared defences on the Somme or any other river line in the West, for Hitler

[1]Teleprinter Message, Model to Jodl, August 29th, 2400 hours. (Tempelhof Papers.) In addition to the sixteen infantry divisions mentioned here, there were another seven, which had been wiped out in the Normandy fighting and were no longer included by Model in the German Order of Battle.

had forbidden the construction of ' rearward positions ' lest their existence should encourage his generals to retreat.

It was fortunate for the Germans that in Model they had, as C.-in-C., West, a man who was not afraid to stand up to Hitler, even though his rapid promotion to the rank of Field-Marshal at the early age of fifty-four was primarily due to the fact that he was one of the Führer's favourites. Model's career resembled Rommel's in many respects. He had no social graces, he did not belong to one of the traditional military families, and he would not normally have gained rapid promotion within the caste-bound Officer Corps. But Hitler, who hated and feared the old type of regular officer, was always on the look-out for ambitious and aggressive men who were ready to identify their fortunes with those of the régime.

As a staff officer in the training branch of the War Ministry, when the Wehrmacht was being rebuilt, Model impressed the Nazi leaders and, when war came, he amply justified Hitler's confidence by proving himself to be a most energetic and resourceful commander. In Russia in 1941 Model commanded a panzer division and led the drive to the Dnieper and beyond. Within six months Hitler appointed him to command an Army, and during the harsh winter of '41–'42 Model was as resolute in defence as he had been aggressive in attack. Thereafter, Hitler not only sought his advice but generally accepted it, and did not lose confidence in him even after the Kursk offensive in July 1943. On this occasion the German defeat was partly caused by Hitler's willingness to follow Model's plan against the more sober counsel of von Kluge and von Manstein.

Later that year Model was given command of Army Group North, and was so successful in checking the Red Army's winter offensive towards the Baltic States that in the spring of '44 Hitler brought him to Army Group South when Zhukov broke into Poland. Having restored the extremely critical situation at Lwow, Model was switched to Army Group Centre in July when the Russians were approaching Warsaw. Once again he brought their offensive to a halt. After these successes, Hitler called him ' the saviour of the Eastern Front ' and sent him to the West to work a similar miracle. Model was now rightly regarded as a master of improvisation and defensive strategy. Nor was there any doubt about his political reliability, for he had been the first commander of the Eastern Front to send a telegram reaffirming his allegiance after the attempt on Hitler's life.

Model's stocky, bustling figure was well known to his forward troops with whom he was very popular, but he was difficult to serve, since he expected his staff to match his own ruthless energy. Although critical of superiors and subordinates alike, he earned their respect by his efficiency. One of the best German tank commanders, Manteuffel, says of him, " Model was a very good tactician, and better in defence than attack. . . . His manner was rough, and his methods were not always acceptable in the higher quarters of the German Army, but they were both to the Führer's liking. Model stood up to Hitler in a way that hardly anyone else dared to do, and even refused to carry out orders with which he disagreed."[1]

This last characteristic was most marked in Model's handling of the crisis in the West. He had never been a ' yes-man,' and, unlike von Rundstedt and von Kluge, he did not hesitate to act first and ask permission afterwards, thereby forestalling the Führer's intervention. When the question arose of keeping a foothold west of the Seine, Model reported to Hitler, " The bridgehead will be withdrawn only when the advantages of holding it are outweighed by the disadvantages." When he suspected that Hitler's staff were censoring his reports before passing them on, he endorsed his more important signals, " For submission to the Führer *in the original.*"

If there was any German general who might restore the situation in the West, it was Model, who liked to call himself ' the Führer's fireman,' but even he could do little unless Hitler were to give him fresh and substantial reinforcements. Hitler's ability to provide these resources had already been gravely prejudiced by the development in the past ten days of yet another crisis on the Eastern Front.

By the middle of August the Russian summer offensive had carried the Red Army deep into the Baltic States, to the frontier of East Prussia and into Southern Poland as far as the Vistula and the Carpathian oilfields. All Hitler's mobile reserves had been committed between the Carpathians and the Baltic, and he was being compelled to hold a very much longer line than that which the Russians had broken in July. It was too late to create fresh reserves by yielding ground in the north, and thus shortening his front for, as he had told Doenitz, " we cannot withdraw during the summer because at this time the enemy can follow on an extended front across open country without depending on roads."[2]

In the spring Army Group North could have made a strategic withdrawal from the Baltic States to a line covering East Prussia. Had this been done, Hitler would have shortened his front by 300 miles and would have saved, for operations elsewhere, at least 30 of the 50 divisions which were now tied up in Esthonia, Latvia and Lithuania. He had rejected this policy because he agreed with the advice of Doenitz that, if the Russians were to gain free access to the Baltic, they could interrupt the movement of iron-ore from Sweden and the working-up of the new electro-U-boats on which they both set such store.

Hitler's refusal to give up the Baltic States left him with no adequate forces to meet the Soviet drive to the Vistula. On the approaches to Warsaw, however, the offensive began to lose momentum, for by this time the armies of Zhukov and Rokossovsky had advanced nearly

[1]Quoted by Liddell Hart, *The Other Side of the Hill*, pp. 101–2.
[2]Führer Naval Conferences, July 9th, 1944.

400 miles in little more than a month and were still dependent on supplies brought up from railheads east of the Dnieper. The railways in the western provinces of the Soviet Union had been converted to the standard European gauge behind the German advance and had been severely damaged by demolitions during their retreat. These lines had to be repaired and converted back to the broad Russian gauge before the Red Army could carry its offensive in Poland much farther.

Supply difficulties and the arrival of German reinforcements—especially the Hermann Goering Panzer Division from Italy—prevented the Russians breaking into Warsaw and joining forces with the Polish Underground, which had risen in revolt at the start of August. In their eagerness to gain control of the capital before the entry of the Red Army, the Poles had acted prematurely, but it is hardly likely that the Russians would have allowed themselves to be halted at the gates of the city if this insurrection had been raised by the Polish Communists and not by General Bor-Komorowski's Home Army, which was hostile to both Communism and the Soviet Union. In the circumstances, Stalin may well have been content to leave to his military opponents the task of wiping out his political enemies.

Be that as it may, there were cogent reasons of Soviet grand strategy which made it necessary for the Russians to pause on the Vistula. Now that Hitler's reserves had been absorbed in the north and the centre, the time had come for the Red Army to make the master-stroke of its summer campaign in the extreme south, between the Carpathians and the Black Sea. Here, on a sector of 300 miles held by 27 German and 20 Rumanian divisions, Hitler had no strategic reserve whatever and could not readily move reinforcements thither because the barrier of the Carpathians separated this sector from the rest of the Eastern Front. When the Russians attacked on August 20th, they quickly overran the unreliable Rumanians. Within three days they had crossed the River Pruth, captured Jassy and all but encircled the German armies opposing them. On the 23rd King Michael of Rumania arrested Marshal Antonescu and dismissed his Government. That night, in a broadcast from Bucharest, the King announced " the immediate cessation of hostilities " and the acceptance of " an armistice offered by the Soviet Union, Great Britain and the United States."

The German front collapsed and Malinovsky's motorised columns swept down upon the Ploesti oilfields before the Germans had time to destroy them. On August 31st the Russians entered Bucharest and next day reached the Danube at the frontier of Bulgaria, which had already declared her withdrawal from the war.[1] Finland made a similar declara-

---

[1] Bulgaria had only been at war with the Western Powers, not with the Soviet Union. She now endeavoured to proclaim her neutrality. The Russians could not tolerate this farcical situation, for German troops were still in Bulgaria and Bulgarian forces were occupying parts of Yugoslavia and Greece. On September 8th, therefore, the Red Army marched into Bulgaria and, a week later, occupied Sofia.

tion on September 2nd and asked for an armistice. Thus in barely two weeks the Russians had overwhelmed, and almost wiped out, two of Hitler's armies, had deprived him of three allies, captured what had been his main source of natural oil, reached the northern frontier of Yugoslavia, and gained control of the Lower Danube.

In this triumphant summer offensive the Russian High Command had applied—on a far grander scale, of course—much the same strategy which Montgomery had adopted in Normandy. In the first two months the Russians had exhausted the Germans on the northern and central sectors (as Montgomery had exhausted them at Caen) and had developed such a threat to Warsaw, and thus to Berlin, that Hitler had been compelled to concentrate the bulk of his armour north of the Carpathians. This was the counterpart of Montgomery's threat to Paris which the Germans had tried to meet by concentrating their armour opposite Caen. On the eve of the American break-out only two of the nine panzer divisions in Normandy were west of Mont Pinçon; on the eve of the final Russian break-through only two of the eighteen panzer divisions in the East were south of the Carpathians. In each case the Germans were worn down and unbalanced by having to meet a threat they could not ignore, and then the decisive blow was struck at their extreme flank which had thus been made vulnerable. In the East, as in the West, when that flank was broken and turned close to the sea, the Germans had not the resources to restore it.

On the Eastern Front the German catastrophe was aggravated by the defection of Rumania. Preparations for King Michael's *coup d'état* had been in train since the previous March, when his emissary, Prince Barbu Stirbey, began negotiations with the Allies in Cairo. These negotiations were aided by an assurance which Molotov broadcast from Moscow on April 2nd. "The Soviet Government," said Molotov, "declares that it does not pursue the aim of acquiring any part of Rumanian territory other than Bessarabia, or of altering the social structure of Rumania as it exists at present."

Before the Russian summer offensive began, it was understood that King Michael would endeavour to overthrow Antonescu as soon as the German armies on the Bessarabian sector were decisively defeated. Having seized power according to plan, the King proved his loyalty to the United Nations by declaring war against Germany on August 25th. With the active co-operation of the Rumanians, the Red Army was able to gain control of almost the entire country in the next two weeks. The Russians proceeded to exploit their victory by launching a fresh campaign up the Danube Basin directed on Belgrade and Budapest. They were able to do this with little delay because their attack, and the King's change of front, had been so swiftly executed that the Black Sea ports and the Rumanian railway network had fallen into their hands almost intact.

The Soviet High Command was thus able to maintain and reinforce its armies in Rumania by a new supply route across the Black Sea and up the valley of the Danube. By this route they could develop their offensive power in the Balkans at a time when they were still engaged in restoring their communications across the ravaged battlefields of White Russia and the Ukraine. This was a factor of supreme importance for the course of the war and the future of Europe. That autumn, because of the German strength in Poland and of their own supply difficulties, the Russians could not have continued their offensive beyond the Vistula in the direction of Berlin. Nor was that their primary intent. Stalin was determined to gain complete control of South-Western and Central Europe before the war ended. To him, therefore, Vienna was more important than Berlin.

The collapse of Rumania, and the loss of three-quarters of the German divisions which had been fighting there, presented Hitler with the urgent task of building up an entirely new front in the South-East. At the end of August he had ordered Army Group E to withdraw from Greece and Southern Yugoslavia, but this withdrawal was slow and difficult, since the German troops and their communications were constantly harassed by Greek guerillas, Yugoslav partisans and Allied aircraft. Hitler was able to improvise a fresh line covering the Hungarian frontier only by bringing divisions from Poland and Italy, for there was no central reserve on which he could draw. Nine months earlier, when his armies still stood well inside the western marches of the Soviet Union, he had been able to deploy 200 German and 16 satellite divisions on a front of 1,400 miles. Now, however, with only 120 German and 18 Hungarian divisions, he was endeavouring to hold an even longer front extending from the Gulf of Finland to the Iron Gate.[1] In these circumstances he did not dare to move a single division from the East to aid Model. Hitler was learning at last the bitter significance of having to wage war on two fronts.

The pressure of events had already compelled Hitler to consider making substantial withdrawals from Northern and Southern Europe so that he would be better able to meet the critical challenges from the East and the West. Before the Russian offensive in Rumania, he had asked Speer to report on the economic effect of such withdrawals. Speer worked on the assumption that all German forces would be evacuated from Finland and Norway, and from Southern Europe as far as the Alps in Italy, the River Sava in Yugoslavia and the River Tisza in Hungary. On September 5th he reported that, after giving up these areas, Germany

---

[1]The figures of the German strength in Russia at the end of 1943 are those given to Jodl by the Wehrmacht Operations Staff in November of that year (Nuremberg Document L 172) and do not include the Finnish Front or the Rumanian and Hungarian divisions that were then being formed or rebuilt. The figures for September 1944 are taken from the official records of OKH.

would have sufficient supplies or stocks of bauxite, copper, nickel and most other light or non-ferrous metals to maintain her war economy into 1946, but, he said, " through the loss of the chrome ore mines in the Southern Balkans and the stoppage of chrome supplies from Turkey, chromium has already become the biggest bottleneck . . . If present production of special steels is continued, chromium supplies will be exhausted by January 1st, 1945, and then armament production will come to a complete standstill." Even if the stocks of chrome could be made to last longer, Speer expected that a fresh crisis would soon develop since " crude steel production could be maintained in full only until September 1st, 1945."

Hitler was not prepared to accept such economic limitations, and his instinctive reluctance to surrender any occupied territory was reinforced by the fear of Allied air power. He knew that, as the German perimeter shrank, the air attacks on the Reich would be intensified and the Luftwaffe's ability to ward them off would be reduced. Already the strategic offensive against his oil supplies had gravely weakened his military and industrial power.

By the time the Red Army captured Ploesti, the Rumanian oilfields were contributing little to the German war machine. In the middle of 1943 (before the first American raid) Ploesti had been providing Germany with oil at the rate of 2,500,000 tons a year. Since, then, however, the Rumanian output had been reduced by American bombing, and the transportation of oil to Germany had been restricted by the mining of the Danube. The result was that by mid-summer of 1944 the amount of Rumanian oil reaching the Reich and the Wehrmacht was barely ten per cent of what it had been a year before.[1]

The cutting off of supplies from Rumania was specially serious because it coincided with a truly disastrous decline in the output of the synthetic refineries in the Reich. At the end of June, Speer had warned Hitler that unless these plants could be more adequately protected there would be, from September onwards, "an unbridgeable gap which must lead to tragic results." After this warning the flak defences and smoke protection of the refineries were greatly increased, but these were negative measures and the only effective safeguard was to prevent the Allied bombers reaching their targets. This the Luftwaffe had not the strength to do, even though German aircraft production was higher than ever.

---

[1]It is difficult to give exact figures, for the various German authorities are conflicting. The *United States Strategic Bombing Survey* (' Economic Report,' p. 75) says that German imports of oil products from Rumania and Hungary in 1943 amounted to 2,766,000 tons. This figure is based on the records of Speer's Ministry. However, a report prepared by Speer's planning department and dated June 30th, 1944 (*Bericht zur Deutschen Wirtschaftslage 1943-44*) gives approximately the same total of imports but says that of this 1,980,000 tons came from Rumania and 302,000 from Hungary. With regard to deliveries in 1944, the *Survey* (ibid., p. 79) says that imports from Rumania and Hungary declined from 200,000 tons in February to 40,000 tons in June and 11,000 in August.

By drafting more than 100,000 workers to repair, or rebuild elsewhere, the fighter factories which had been so heavily damaged in the spring, by simplifying production and by specialising in the manufacture of the Me 109 and the FW190, Speer was able to increase the output of single-engined fighters to a most remarkable degree during the summer of 1944, as the following figures show:[1]

| January | February | March | April | May | June | July | August |
|---------|----------|-------|-------|-----|------|------|--------|
| 1,248 | 892 | 1,050 | 1,345 | 1,523 | 1,677 | 2,001 | 2,036 |

Even these vast totals were not sufficient to make good the wastage. In July, when the Luftwaffe took delivery of 2,627 single-engined fighters (new or rebuilt) its battle losses were 1,476, but its overall casualties, counting both aircraft destroyed and those so badly damaged that they had to be rebuilt, were more than 3,000. The severity of these losses was in itself very largely due to the strategic bombardment of aircraft factories and oil refineries. Because of the crisis in fighter production, which had compelled Speer to concentrate on turning out the maximum number of existing types, the Luftwaffe had not been able to keep pace with the steady improvement in the performance of Allied aircraft. Because of the shortage in aviation spirit, the training of pilots and the testing of planes had been heavily curtailed. That summer German fighter pilots were sent into action after they had been given only one-quarter of the flying training hours of their American and British counterparts, and the final running-in time of aircraft engines was cut from two hours to half an hour. These were false economies, for the losses due to inexperience and mechanical failure were abnormally high, and so were the casualties in transit and training. During the first nine months of 1944 only half the fighters lost by the Luftwaffe were lost in action.

On July 28th Speer had reported to Hitler that " in spite of the high production figure for fighters, the number of planes ready for action or available has not risen but has gone down." He pointed out that at the start of June the day-fighter strength of the Reich defences was 991, but that by July 27th this had been reduced to 554.

In August, as in July, the Luftwaffe could do little to check the Allied onslaught, and there was a further fall in the yield of the synthetic plants, even though 150,000 workers were employed to make good the damage. These refineries had produced 542,000 tons of finished oil products in March, but in July their output was only 229,000 tons and in August

[1]These figures are drawn from a report prepared for the Luftwaffe High Command and dated January 30th, 1945 (*Überblick über den Rustungsstand der Luftwaffe*). The *United States Strategic Bombing Survey* (' Overall Report,' p. 18) gives ' acceptance ' figures which are even higher: e.g. June, 2,177; July, 2,627; August, 3,031. These figures are taken from Speer's files which are usually reliable, but I suspect that they include some fighters which had been rebuilt in the factories and were therefore not ' new deliveries.'

it was down to 184,000. The decline in the production of aviation spirit was even more serious, for this was the product of the last stage of the refining process and thus was always the last to be restored. Speer says it repeatedly happened that the attack on a plant was renewed as soon as Allied air reconnaissance showed it to be in production again, but before it had been sufficiently repaired to refine the high-grade petrol needed for aircraft.

In April, when the Luftwaffe had been conserving its strength to meet the invasion, it had consumed nearly all the 175,000 tons of aviation spirit produced that month. Thereafter, as the battle over the Reich and on the two main fronts grew more and more intense, the tonnage refined went steadily down:

| *May* | *June* | *July* | *August* |
|---|---|---|---|
| 156,000 | 52,000 | 35,000 | 17,000 |

The double disaster in Rumania and in the Reich created a situation which threatened to become catastrophic. In March, from natural and synthetic supplies, Hitler's refineries had provided 968,000 tons of finished oil products. In August the total was only 345,000 tons, of which, it should be repeated, only 17,000 were aviation spirit. To meet this crisis Speer had enforced the most drastic economies on the Home Front and in the Wehrmacht. In August even the Luftwaffe's allocation was cut by more than 30 per cent, compared with March, and its operations were maintained at this reduced level only by drawing heavily on reserves.

On August 30th Germany's total stocks of aviation spirit were so reduced that the Luftwaffe had only five weeks' supply at the rate of consumption prevailing before the air attacks began. That day, in a report to Hitler, Speer declared that the synthetic refineries were so badly damaged that they could not resume production until the middle of September; and that they could resume then only if their reconstruction had not been interrupted by further attack. Speer went on to suggest that the Luftwaffe could save itself from being immobilised through lack of fuel only if it could deliver one mighty, crippling blow against the American daylight bombers when next they ventured deep into Germany. " The Luftwaffe," he said, " must be ready for this last great gamble by the middle of September at the latest. It must employ its finest pilots, including its flying instructors, and its maximum strength in fighter aircraft. Not less than 1,200 of the most modern machines must be prepared for this venture. If this course is followed, it will mean the beginning of a new air force or the end of the existing Luftwaffe."

This plan was not new. Speer had already suggested it to Hitler at a conference on August 16th. At that time, although there had been no increase in the front-line strength of the Fighter Arm, its C.-in-C. (Galland) had built up a strategic reserve of 800 fighters and was busily training pilots to fly them. In agreement with Speer, he was preparing this force for what they called *Der Grosse Schlag*—' The Great Strike.' In the third week of August, however, as the Battle of Normandy approached its climax, Hitler demanded that this reserve must be thrown in to check the Allies in France. Galland and Speer protested violently, arguing, says Galland, that " while the reserve might be able to accomplish something under the fairly favourable conditions of defence in the Reich, it would soon be reduced to nothing in the bitter fighting in the West." Hitler spurned their reasoned arguments, and even talked of " reducing the Fighter Arm to a few squadrons and scrapping the rest in favour of a great expansion of flak." This wanton suggestion was characteristic; the Luftwaffe having failed him, Hitler would not hesitate to sacrifice it.

The order to transfer the fighter reserve to France was not finally given until the Allies had reached the Seine, and by then, as Galland says, the situation was already beyond repair. " The transfer of the reserve," he reports, " was accomplished in circumstances much worse than those of June. Units became lost, landed on fields already by-passed by Allied armour, found no fuel and had to destroy their aircraft." Many fighters were shot down during their transit flight, many more were destroyed on the ground and only a small proportion of this large force seems to have been able to engage in offensive action. The increase in the strength of the Luftwaffe in the West was hardly noticed by the Allied Air Forces and the extra opposition was soon swept aside. In Galland's opinion, " the entire 800 aircraft of the reserve did not destroy two dozen Allied planes."

The exact losses suffered by the German Fighter Arm in this futile venture are not known, but they were sufficiently heavy to rule out any chance of launching *Der Grosse Schlag* during September. In these circumstances, Hitler had to act on the assumption that the synthetic refineries would be successfully attacked again and that therefore his meagre reserves of aviation spirit must be made to last well into October. Accordingly, the petrol allocation to the Luftwaffe for September was cut to 60,000 tons, less than a third of the amount it had consumed in the last month before the invasion.

The only units of the Luftwaffe not affected by the oil crisis were those equipped with jet-aircraft, which operated on a low-grade fuel that was comparatively plentiful. For reasons already mentioned, however, the series production of the Me 262 had been delayed until 1944, and then the deliveries were so small that only 32 were available for operations at the end of August. Nor was the best use being made of these, for Hitler had insisted on employing the Me 262 as a bomber, thus depriving Galland of the only aircraft which was definitely superior to any fighter the Allies could use over Germany.

Hitler now knew that during the coming weeks, as the Allied Armies converged upon the Reich from east and west, the Luftwaffe would be powerless to check the onrush of the armour or the onslaught from the air. Even to him it must have been clear that, if the accuracy and intensity of the attack on his oil refineries were maintained, the Luftwaffe would be grounded by the end of October and the Wehrmacht immobilised before the winter.[1]

At the end of August Hitler received a letter which faced the facts. It had been written by von Kluge on August 18th after Model had arrived to succeed him. On the following day von Kluge had set off by car to return to Germany, but before the car reached Metz the Field-Marshal was dead. The doctor's report stated that he had died of cerebral hæmorrhage. Hitler ordered a State Funeral and called upon von Rundstedt to deliver the oration on his behalf. Those orders were cancelled as soon as the Führer had read von Kluge's letter.

" When you receive these lines," wrote von Kluge, " I shall be no more . . . I am dispatching myself where thousands of my comrades have already gone." The letter went on to explain why the Mortain counter-attack had failed and why the situation in the West had become desperate. " I do not know," he said, " whether Field-Marshal Model . . . will yet master the situation. From my heart I hope so but, if this should not be the case, and if your new, greatly desired weapons, especially those for the Luftwaffe, should not succeed, then, my Führer, make up your mind to end the war. The German people have borne such untold suffering that it is time to put an end to this frightfulness. There must be ways to obtain this object and above all to prevent the Reich from falling under the Bolshevist heel."

The contents of this letter were very much in Hitler's mind on August 31st when he interviewed Generals Westphal and Krebs, before sending them to the West to take the places of Blumentritt and Speidel respectively. He began by informing them of von Kluge's suicide and added that, in view of the evidence revealed in the People's Court on the previous day, the late Field-Marshal " might have been arrested immediately in any event if he had not taken his own life."[2] He then gave them his version of von Kluge's alleged attempt to surrender the armies in Normandy and assured them that he did not intend to capitulate.

Hitler told them: " The time is not yet ripe for a political decision. . . . I shall not let such an opportunity pass, but at a time of heavy military defeats it is quite childish and naïve to hope for a politically favourable moment to make a move. . . . The time will come when the tension between the Allies becomes so strong that, in spite of everything,

---

[1]The main sources used in the preparation of this section were: The *United States Strategic Bombing Survey* ('Economic Report'), pp. 73-83; Speer's unpublished reports to Hitler on the oil situation, dated June 30th, July 28th and August 30th, 1944; a special interrogation of Milch, Galland and Koller on Luftwaffe oil supplies; and the interrogation of Galland on the Luftwaffe's Fighter Arm.

[2]Führer Conferences, Fragment 46, August 31st, 1944.

the rupture occurs. History teaches us that all coalitions break up, but you must await the moment however difficult the waiting may be . . . I intend to continue fighting until there is a possibility of a decent peace which is bearable for Germany and secures the life of future generations. Then I shall make it . . . Whatever happens we shall carry on this struggle until, as Frederick the Great said, ' one of our damned enemies gives up in despair! ' "

## CHAPTER XXIII

# ROOSEVELT AND THE BALKANS

THE impending collapse of the Allied coalition now became one of Goebbels's favourite themes. On September 4th his spokesman told a press conference in Berlin, " The reports of Soviet victories in the Balkans will surely not be pleasant to the English. . . . With the apparent approach of victory for the Allies it is certain that the political conflicts will increase and will one day cause the edifice of our enemies to break irreparably." This expectation was not altogether illogical. Since the sixteenth century the abiding purpose of British foreign policy had been to maintain the balance of power in Europe. To prevent the domination of the Continent by one power or another, the British had fought half a dozen major wars, and in the last hundred years they had been almost equally determined to ensure that Russia did not gain control of the Black Sea Straits and the Bosphorus.

Both these dangers had arisen again, and acutely, with the Red Army's advance into Poland and Rumania, and it was becoming clearer every day that the annihilation of Germany would leave the Soviet Union in command of Central and South-Eastern Europe. Thus it was not unreasonable for Hitler and Goebbels to believe that this prospect would create friction between Russia and Britain, especially in the Balkans, and would weaken the British resolve to enforce the demand for Germany's unconditional surrender. The Germans were right in suspecting that Churchill was disturbed by the recent developments in Eastern Europe, but they did not realise the extent to which the strategy and diplomacy of the Western Allies were governed by Roosevelt's determination to keep out of the Balkans.

Before the Teheran Conference, as already noted, the President's attitude to all British proposals for operations against Southern Europe had been governed by his belief that the quickest and cheapest road to military victory lay through Western France. At the end of the first day in Teheran he had said to his son, Elliott, " I see no reason for putting the lives of American soldiers in jeopardy in order to protect real or fancied British interests on the European continent. We are at war and our job is to win it as fast as possible, and without adventures."[1]

[1] Elliott Roosevelt, *As He Saw It*, p. 186.

Operations in the Balkans, presumably, came under the heading of ' adventures.'

By the end of this conference Roosevelt had long-term reasons for wishing to keep out of South-Eastern Europe. He wanted to make certain of Russia's promised participation in the war against Japan and in the establishment of the United Nations. Accordingly, he was determined to avoid any action which might make Stalin suspicious of Anglo-American intentions, for he realised that the pursuit of an independent course by Russia would be as disastrous for the United Nations as American Isolation had been for the League. It is apparent from the Hopkins Papers and from Cordell Hull's Memoirs that Roosevelt became aware of Soviet ambitions, but hoped that, if Russia could be guaranteed security within the United Nations, she would not seek to protect herself by the creation of spheres of influence beyond her frontiers.

Far from being anxious, as was Churchill, to re-establish Western influence and prestige in Central and South-Eastern Europe, Roosevelt feared that any Anglo-American move in that direction would estrange the Russians and lead them to set up a *cordon sanitaire* of satellite states. Both Roosevelt and Hull were opposed in principle to all ' spheres of influence,' other than that of the United States in the Americas. Hull believed that " any creation of zones of influence would inevitably sow the seeds of future conflict . . . [and] could not but derogate from the overall authority of the international security organisation."[1] This doctrine may have been sound in theory, but it provided no answer to the practical danger that, unless some immediate limits were set by the Western Powers, Stalin would establish Russia's hegemony over much of Europe before the international security organisation could be established.

Churchill knew that there could be no stability or harmony on the Continent, if the advantage of power lay overwhelmingly with Russia, but Roosevelt believed that this problem could be solved by an extension of the ' Good Neighbour ' policy which he had applied with such success in the Western Hemisphere. His views appear to have been summed up in a memorandum prepared by the U.S. War Department before the Quebec Conference of August 1943. This paper said, " Since Russia is the decisive factor in the war, she must be given every assistance and every effort must be made to obtain her friendship. Since without question she will dominate Europe on the defeat of the Axis, it is even more essential to develop and maintain the most friendly relations with Russia."[2] Roosevelt apparently accepted almost with equanimity the prospect of Russia dominating the Continent, since he genuinely believed

---

[1] Hull, op. cit., p. 1,452.
[2] Quoted by Sherwood, op. cit., p. 748. Sherwood says that this memorandum, which Hopkins had with him at the conference, was identified only as " a very high level United States military strategic estimate," but he accepts it as an accurate reflection of the President's views.

that friendliness and frankness on his part would be met by an equally sympathetic response from Stalin.

Although the President's political objectives had a marked influence on the course of Allied strategy, the American Chiefs of Staff were equally determined, on strictly military grounds, to avoid commitments in South-Eastern Europe. The basic principle of the strategy which had been approved at Teheran and Cairo was that the main Anglo-American assault against Hitler's *Festung Europa*, and against Germany itself, should be made from the West through France, and that there should be no serious attempt, except by the air forces, to strike at the Reich from the south or at its sources of raw materials in the Balkans. Accordingly, the Americans had insisted that, in conjunction with OVERLORD, the Allied forces in the Mediterranean should invade Southern France (Operation ANVIL).

The British had accepted this strategic policy, but had continued to doubt whether decisive victory could be gained in the West, unless a powerful complementary offensive were maintained in Italy to provide a constant threat to Southern Germany and the Balkans. They feared that the Western Front would degenerate into trench warfare of the 1914–18 pattern, for the best military opinion was that, when the enemy saw he was beaten in Normandy, he would withdraw by stages to the Seine and the Siegfried Line, in order to retain a coherent front and a fair measure of tactical mobility. The Americans agreed with this appreciation of the enemy, but they were confident that the Western Allies could disrupt this ordered programme and avoid any stalemate, provided that the thirty-seven divisions Eisenhower would have in Britain by D-Day were reinforced by ten divisions from the Mediterranean and an additional forty or more which could be shipped direct from the United States as soon as deep-water ports in France had been captured and cleared. The American Chiefs of Staff saw no necessity for any strategic diversion into the Balkans or for waging more than a containing action in Italy once Rome was in Allied hands. They were not seeking victory by manœuvre; they were bent upon overwhelming the Wehrmacht by a frontal assault with a military steam-roller fashioned in the camps and factories of the United States. This became the President's philosophy also, and during the Teheran Conference he confided to his son, Elliott, " Our Chiefs of Staff are convinced of one thing. The way to kill the most Germans, with the least loss of American soldiers, is to mount one great big offensive and then slam 'em with everything we've got. It makes sense to me."[1]

To Churchill, however, this plan had never made sense and, when the Combined Chiefs of Staff met in London on June 11th (five days after the launching of OVERLORD), the British chiefs called for a re-examination of Allied strategy in the Mediterranean. This was the start of a debate which was to go on for two months and was to have a profound

[1]Elliott Roosevelt, op. cit., p. 185.

effect upon the military course of the war and upon the political shape of post-war Europe.

By this time Eisenhower's armies had gained a footing in Normandy and were encountering less opposition than had been expected. The mere threat of further assault was keeping ten German divisions idle on the Mediterranean coast of France, and it seemed to the British that Eisenhower would gain little extra advantage if this threat were converted into a reality. ANVIL had already been postponed once, because of the landing-craft problem, and the Supreme Commander in the Mediterranean (Maitland Wilson) now reported that this operation could not be launched before August 15th. By then it might not be necessary for the success of OVERLORD and would, in any case, be too late to have any major influence on the outcome of the summer fighting.

OVERLORD having been delayed until June, Eisenhower could not rely upon enjoying more than three months of good campaigning weather. In October, perhaps even in September, the weather would begin to favour the enemy, for the Western Allies could not maintain the threat of further large-scale landings, nor could they exert the full preponderance of their air power in support of the land battle or against German war industry and communications. It was thus likely that, if Hitler could avoid decisive defeat during the summer and early autumn, he would be able to prolong the war into the spring of 1945. Since this was the prospect, it was essential that during the short summer months of '44 all the Allies should maintain (by threat or action) the maximum pressure against Germany in those areas which were of such importance to her that Hitler could not afford to yield ground in order to gain time.

Italy was such an area and (in the opinion of Alexander, the commander on the spot) it now afforded " a golden opportunity of scoring a really decisive victory."[1] Rome had been captured on June 4th and the Allied Armies were hounding the routed Germans northwards to the Pisa–Rimini line, which ran east and west through Florence. Accordingly, the British Chiefs of Staff suggested that it would be more profitable to concentrate upon the exploitation of Alexander's victory than to divide Wilson's resources between Italy and Southern France. On the Italian front the offensive could be maintained without respite so long as the fine weather lasted.

Marshall, King and Arnold remained strongly in favour of ANVIL, but they accepted " the overriding necessity of completing the destruction of the German forces south of the Pisa–Rimini line."[2] Furthermore, they agreed to leave open for the time being the question where the amphibious resources of the Mediterranean Command should be employed. On

[1] Appreciation of June 7th, 1944. General Sir Harold Alexander was the Commander-in-Chief of the Allied Armies in Italy (Fifth U.S. Army and Eighth British Army). General Sir Henry Maitland Wilson was the Supreme Commander of all Allied forces in the Mediterranean Theatre.

[2] General Wilson's *Report to the Combined Chiefs of Staff on the Operations in Southern France*, p. 22.

June 14th Wilson was ordered to continue the offensive in Italy as far as the Pisa–Rimini line, and to prepare for subsequent assault operations against either Southern France, or Western France, or the head of the Adriatic, *the final choice of objective to await " the general development of the strategic situation."*

Three days later, at a conference with Marshall and Arnold in Italy, Wilson put forward a further possibility, namely " the allocation of existing and prospective resources to General Alexander for continuation of his offensive through the Pisa–Rimini line into the Po Valley, and, with the support of an amphibious operation against the Istrian Peninsula, for exploitation through the Ljubljana Gap into the plains of Hungary." He suggested that the development of a direct threat to the Upper Danube—the strategic centre of Europe—would compel the Germans to withdraw substantial forces from France. The help thus provided for Eisenhower would, said Wilson, " be less direct, but more effective."

Marshall replied that Eisenhower was insisting upon ANVIL because " the need for an additional major port was more pressing . . . than the diversion of enemy troops from Northern France."[1] There were, said Marshall, " some forty or fifty divisions in the United States ready for action," and these would be used " only in France where they could be deployed more rapidly and on a broader front, and that none would be sent to the Mediterranean other than as a possible build-up for an attack on Southern France." Whatever happened, " United States forces would not be used for a campaign in South-Eastern Europe."

The American preoccupation with the capture of ports in Southern France seemed to Wilson " to imply a strategy aimed at defeating Germany during the first half of 1945 at the cost of an opportunity of defeating her before the end of 1944." In a signal to the British Chiefs of Staff on June 19th Wilson stressed the importance of creating " a decisive threat to Southern Germany before the end of the year." In the past two weeks the Allied Armies in Italy had advanced a hundred miles, but they could not maintain the momentum of their attack if seven divisions were withdrawn, as planned, for ANVIL. Wilson gave warning that this diversion of a quarter of Alexander's land strength, and the complementary diversion of air power, would result in a pause of at least six weeks in offensive operations in the Mediterranean and would allow the Germans to establish themselves strongly in the Pisa–Rimini defences, the so-called 'Gothic Line.'

These arguments made little impression upon Marshall, who contended that the Germans, if hard-pressed, could " withdraw to the Alps without contesting the Po Valley " and that they had " nothing to lose in so doing." If Alexander were to continue his offensive, he would be left " beating at the air." This view defied the evidence and experience of the past year. The Germans had bitterly contested the Allied advance

[1]General Wilson's *Report to the Combined Chiefs of Staff on the Italian Campaign*, p. 34.

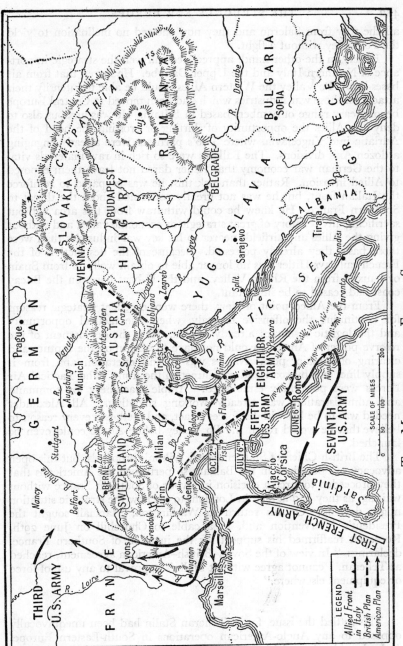

THE MEDITERRANEAN FRONT, SUMMER 1944

all the way from Salerno and they now showed no inclination to yield the Po Valley without a fight.

Hitler, on the other hand, appreciated full well the strategic importance of Northern Italy and the Upper Danube. He feared that from air bases in the Po Valley the Western Allies would be able to intensify their attacks on those war industries which had been moved to Central Europe beyond easy range of bombers based in Britain. He was anxious also to deny the Allies the opportunity of skirting or crossing the head of the Adriatic into Yugoslavia, where Tito's partisans were already engaging a dozen Axis divisions. The Balkans were so rich in raw materials vital to the German war economy that Hitler dared not leave them exposed to Allied invasion. Rather than risk this, he was prepared to reinforce the Italian front, but he was not greatly concerned about the threat to Southern France. He knew he could withdraw from this area without sacrificing any territory of great strategic or economic value, and without giving the Allies any airfields nearer to his key war industries than were those bases they already possessed. Because of the destruction of the French railways Hitler was no longer able to obtain wolfram from Spain or bauxite from the Rhône Valley, and the U-boat bases on the Biscay coast had ceased to be important.

From the Allied point of view, there were excellent strategic reasons for continuing the offensive in Italy, where the tactical opportunity and the logistic resources already existed. Here the deployment of the reserve power of America would not have to wait upon the capture and clearing of a major port. Naples was in full operation and from it supply lines ran by road and rail direct to the front. The Tactical Air Forces were powerfully established. Ample machinery for command and administration was already working smoothly. All Alexander needed was to be left with his forces intact, and there was every reason to believe that he would reach the Po Valley before ANVIL could even be launched.

The British Chiefs of Staff endorsed Wilson's proposals, but this open advocacy of operations in the Balkans so perturbed the Americans that they proceeded to force a decision in favour of Southern France without waiting, as they had agreed in London, to see how the strategic situation might develop. On his return to Washington, Marshall sought the President's intervention and, in a cable to Churchill on June 29th, Roosevelt reaffirmed his support for the invasion of Southern France, declaring: " In view of the Soviet–British–American agreement, reached at Teheran, I cannot agree without Stalin's approval to any use of force or equipment elsewhere."

This settled the issue, for at Teheran Stalin had been unequivocally opposed to any Anglo-American operations in South-Eastern Europe. Indeed, evidently anticipating that Churchill would reopen the question of a Balkan campaign once the Normandy invasion was successfully launched, Stalin had recommended that, if possible, "the attack on Southern France should precede OVERLORD by two months."[1]

Although his desire to preserve good relations with Stalin was the main political factor behind Roosevelt's insistence on ANVIL, he reminded Churchill that any Allied reverse in Normandy would have a serious effect on the November elections in the United States. Roosevelt was also aware that in election year he had to be particularly careful to avoid any action which would expose him to the charge of using American forces to serve British political ends. He knew that a campaign in the Balkans would be suspect on that score. Operations in Southern France, however, would evoke approval even from those who were eager to give priority to the war against Japan. Since 1776 there has been a strong sentimental link between France and the United States, and few would cavil at the employment of American troops to liberate the Sister Republic which had helped the thirteen colonies to liberate themselves. In January 1942 the first American propaganda leaflets, dropped over France, had carried the assurance, "To you who gave us liberty, we will restore liberty."

Whatever political justification there may have been for ANVIL, it was not upon this that Marshall and Eisenhower based their case. They regarded this operation as "an integral and necessary feature of the main invasion across the Channel." Early in 1942 Marshall had determined that France should be the decisive theatre and had approved Eisenhower's outline plan for a cross-Channel assault. Without Marshall's resolute and confident adherence to it, this plan might never have been brought to fruition, but his very single-mindedness had undoubted disadvantages. Eisenhower speaks with due admiration of his chief's ability to "reach a rocklike decision," but, having done so, it seems that Marshall tended to close his mind to other possibilities created by the turn of events. He appears to have believed, as Eisenhower undoubtedly did, that "the doctrine of opportunism, so often applicable in tactics, is a dangerous one to pursue in strategy."[2] Yet always to scorn 'opportunism' (in this sense) is often to spurn opportunity.

At this stage, it may be worth reiterating the defects of Marshall's virtues. In 1942 his prolonged advocacy of the plan to seize the Cherbourg Peninsula that summer so delayed the invasion of North Africa that the Allies were denied the chance of gaining a decisive victory in Tunisia before the winter. In 1943 his opposition to the invasion of Italy prevented the Allies from being ready to exploit Mussolini's downfall by making an immediate landing. Now, again, he refused to take advantage of a major strategic opening which did not fit into his preconceived plan.

[1]Stalin's Memorandum, presented November 29th, 1943. (Quoted by Sherwood, op. cit., p. 788.)
[2]The quotations in this paragraph are from Eisenhower, *Crusade*, pp. 231, 160 and 168.

Marshall was a military administrator rather than a strategist. In the sphere of organisation and especially in the mobilisation of America's manpower and resources, he was superb. His concepts were bold and clear; his decisions prompt and firm. By his integrity and diplomacy he gained from Congress a degree of support which even the President could not command. It was due to Marshall, more than to any other man, that the United States was able to develop so rapidly a vast army, well trained and magnificently equipped. This was his priceless contribution to the Allied cause. But, when the time came to employ these forces in the field, Marshall had neither the strategic insight nor the operational experience to guide his judgment. His ideas were simple and rigid. To him the application of military power was primarily a matter of logistics. In examining strategic problems he does not seem to have paid great attention to the enemy's point of view, for such an approach is foreign to the American Army which tends to concentrate upon the development of its own strength and, unlike the British Army, does not normally seek victory by playing upon its opponent's weaknesses.[1] Thus Marshall was preoccupied with the administrative problem of massing the greatest force on a single front. He had raised, trained and equipped sixty American divisions for OVERLORD; therefore space and opportunity must be created for their employment.

Eisenhower held the same beliefs on strategy. The need for a major port in Southern France was implicit in his plan of campaign, which was based on the assumption that the Allied advance to the German frontier and beyond should be on a broad front stretching unbroken from Switzerland to the North Sea. He was influenced also by the immediate fear that the Normandy bridgehead would be sealed off. By the end of June he was becoming both anxious and impatient, for he did not fully understand Montgomery's deliberate plan of unbalancing the enemy first and then breaking out with a ' single, annihilating stroke.' Accordingly, Eisenhower believed that the danger of a stalemate demanded an advance from Southern France against the flank and rear of the Germans in Normandy, and the destruction of forces which might otherwise directly oppose him. It is not without significance that Eisenhower was asserting this in a letter to Wilson on July 6th, and that on the following day he wrote to Montgomery urging him to " avoid having our forces sealed in the beachhead."[2]

The inevitable result of the American determination to carry out ANVIL was that Alexander could not exploit the splendid opportunity his troops had won by their victory. Not only did he lose seven divisions, but he received no replacement for divisions which had to be rested, and even the troops who remained in the line went short of supplies while

---

[1]Eisenhower (*Crusade*, p. 32) says that when the United States entered the war " a shocking deficiency that impeded all constructive planning existed in the field of Intelligence."

[2]Butcher, op. cit., p. 605.

priority on roads and railways was given to the southward movement of soldiers, airmen and equipment allotted to ANVIL.

The threat to the strategic centre of Europe from the south was thus relaxed just when it was assuming serious proportions. The decision to switch the Mediterranean *Schwerpunkt* from Italy to Southern France meant that from the start of July until the middle of August—during six irrecoverable weeks of summer campaigning, while the struggle in Normandy was at its height and while the Russian summer offensive was in full spate—the Allied assault along the whole southern flank of Europe was deliberately weakened and drastically curtailed. Hitler was spared the necessity of having to reinforce his southern front at the critical juncture when he was hard pressed to the point of desperation both in the West and in the East.

This judgment is not merely an expression of the British point of view; it is wholeheartedly endorsed by the American who had best reason to know the extent and the consequences of the opportunity that was lost—General Mark Clark, commander of the Fifth U.S. Army in Italy and later American High Commissioner in Austria. In his book, *Calculated Risk*, Clark says:

> A campaign that might have changed the whole history of relations between the Western world and the Soviet Union was permitted to fade away, not into nothing, but into much less than it could have been. . . . Not alone in my opinion, but in the opinion of a number of experts who were close to the problem, the weakening of the campaign in Italy in order to invade Southern France, instead of pushing on into the Balkans, was one of the outstanding political mistakes of the War. . . . Stalin knew exactly what he wanted in a political as well as a military way; and the thing he wanted most was to keep us out of the Balkans. . . . It is easy to see, therefore, why Stalin favoured ANVIL at Teheran . . . but I could never see why as conditions changed and as the war situation changed, the United States and Britain failed to sit down and take another look at the over-all picture. . . . There was no question that the Balkans were strongly in the British minds, but . . . the American top-level planners were not interested. . . . I later came to understand, in Austria, the tremendous advantages that we had lost by our failure to press on into the Balkans. . . . Had we been there before the Red Army, not only would the collapse of Germany have come sooner, but the influence of Soviet Russia would have been drastically reduced.[1]

This is not a case of ' hindsight ' on Clark's part. When Marshall was in Rome in June, Clark made a strong plea for the invasion of the Balkans, and, having failed, wrote in his diary, " The Boche is defeated, disorganised and demoralised. Now is the time to exploit our success.

[1]Clark, *Calculated Risk*, pp. 348-51.

Yet, in the middle of this success, I lose two corps headquarters and seven divisions. It just doesn't make sense."[1]

The preparations for the assault upon the French Riviera were already well advanced when the situation in the Normandy bridgehead was transformed by the American break-out into Brittany. The British Chiefs of Staff thereupon proposed to Wilson that the forces destined for Southern France might be diverted to Brittany where their entry was likely to be unopposed. On August 5th Churchill lunched at Eisenhower's H.Q. near Portsmouth and the whole problem was thrashed out again. The Prime Minister argued that the capture of Marseilles was no longer necessary, since the divisions from the United States would be able to come direct to deep-water ports in Brittany; that the invasion of Southern France would have no tactical influence on the development of the campaign in the north; and that the ANVIL forces would be better employed in Italy and in the Balkans where the underground forces were already in revolt.

Eisenhower replied that " the maintenance and administrative position would never be equal to the final conquest of Germany until we had secured Antwerp on the north and Marseille or equivalent port facilities on our right." He pointed out that " the distance from Brest to the Metz region was greater than the distance from Marseille to Metz,"[2] and that Brest was likely to be more heavily defended and more severely damaged. Churchill was supported by Cunningham, the First Sea Lord, and by Bedell Smith, Eisenhower's own Chief of Staff, but, says Butcher, " Ike said no, continued saying no all afternoon and ended by saying no in every form of the English language."[3]

Thus rebuffed, Churchill sought to reopen the question on the political level, but he knew it would be useless to advocate any operations in the Balkans, especially as de Gaulle had been assured that the seven French divisions, now in the Mediterranean, would be employed in France. Churchill therefore proposed to Hopkins that the ANVIL forces should be diverted to Brittany, but such a radical change in plan required Roosevelt's consent and he was far away in the North Pacific on a tour of inspection. This alternative might have been feasible if Wilson had been allowed to make preparations for it, as the British Chiefs of Staff had suggested in June. Now, however, the target date for the southern invasion was only a week away; the assault divisions could not undertake the longer and more exposed voyage without considerable unloading and reloading; and there was not sufficient shipping on hand to make up for the slower turn-around, since many of the American LSTs and LCTs, which had been available for the Normandy assault, were now on their way to the Pacific.

[1] Clark, *Calculated Risk*, p. 358.
[2] Eisenhower, *Crusade*, pp. 282-3. Eisenhower here quotes from his contemporary memorandum recording the gist of this discussion.
[3] Butcher, op. cit., p. 634.

It was already too late. The opportunity in Italy had been cast away in June, and the switch to Brittany would only have meant further delay in bringing back into the battle those divisions which had been withdrawn from the Italian front early in July. Alexander's troops entered Florence on August 13th, but their attacking power was almost spent and the Germans had been given time to man the Gothic Line from Pisa to Rimini. Two days later, when Seventh U.S. Army (Lieut.-General Alexander Patch) landed on the Côte d'Azur, Hitler ordered the immediate withdrawal of all German troops in Southern France, except the garrisons of Toulon and Marseilles. By the end of August the Allies had captured these deep-water ports for which so much had been sacrificed, but the American and French columns advancing up the Rhône Valley had not yet reached Lyons. The Nineteenth German Army was fighting such a skilful and resolute rearguard action that there was little chance of Patch's forces being able to cut off the First German Army which was withdrawing from the Biscay coast; or of providing " definite tactical and strategic support " for the Allied operations in Northern France, as Eisenhower had expected.

Indeed, the reverse was the case. Once the Allies had landed in Southern France, Hitler was no longer anxious about the Italian front and he promptly ordered Kesselring to send the Hermann Goering Panzer Division to Poland and his two strongest panzer grenadier divisions (the 3rd and 15th) to France. These two formed the core of the force which Hitler was organising to oppose the advance of Patton's Army on the Upper Meuse.

The invasion of Southern France came too late to contribute to the victory in Normandy, but it was to have a considerable effect on the exploitation of that victory. Having distorted Allied strategy in the Mediterranean, Operation ANVIL was now to contribute to the distortion of Allied strategy in the West; to the immediate benefit of Hitler and the ultimate advantage of Stalin.

## CHAPTER XXIV

# THE GREAT ARGUMENT

ON the day after the fall of Paris, the SHAEF Intelligence Summary, reviewing the situation in the West, declared: "Two and a half months of bitter fighting, culminating for the Germans in a blood-bath big enough even for their extravagant tastes, have brought the end of the war in Europe within sight, almost within reach. The strength of the German Armies in the West has been shattered, Paris belongs to France again, and the Allied Armies are streaming towards the frontiers of the Reich."

The end of the war in Europe was, indeed, "almost within reach." Between the beaches and the Seine the Allies had gained an overwhelming victory which could be made decisive if promptly and properly exploited. Before D-Day the Planning Staff at SHAEF had drawn up a 'long-term strategic concept' which Eisenhower had adopted as the basis of his operational plan.[1] In this he assumed that by D plus 90 the Germans would be driven back to the Seine, but that the Allies would not be able to force this river line until they had developed ports in Brittany for the reception of fresh divisions direct from the United States. Brest, which had been the main port of entry for American troops in the First World War, was the natural choice, but, because the Germans were likely to render it unusable, elaborate preparations had been made for the creation of a new port in the natural roadstead of Quiberon Bay on the south coast of the Brittany Peninsula. Having secured the necessary deep-water ports here (and, as a result of ANVIL, in Southern France also), the Allies would be able to drive the Germans back to the Siegfried Line, but Eisenhower did not expect that he could gain any decisive victory or make any deep penetration into Germany until he could deploy at least sixty divisions.

Eisenhower says that he intended, after crossing the Seine, "to push forward on a broad front with priority on the left." By making his main thrust north-eastward he would be able to open the Channel ports and Antwerp, clear the V-weapon bases and "directly threaten the Ruhr."

[1] For a detailed statement of this concept see Eisenhower, *Crusade*, pp. 225-9. All quotations in the next paragraph are taken from these pages.

In addition, however, he planned to send his right wing eastward with the aim of threatening the Saar Basin and making contact with the ANVIL forces after their advance up the Rhône Valley. " This linking-up of the whole front," he writes, " was mandatory," in order (*inter alia*) to " prevent the costliness of establishing long, defensive flanks along which our troops could have nothing but negative, static missions." Thus he would form a continuous front and could then compel the Germans to meet two major threats. Although he appreciated the importance of enveloping the Ruhr, he was bent upon " gaining the whole length of the Rhine before launching a final assault on interior Germany." " We wanted," says Eisenhower, " to bring all our strength against the enemy, all of it mobile and all of it contributing directly to the complete annihilation of his field forces."

This plan might have been appropriate if the outcome of the Normandy battle had not rendered its assumptions false. By his determination to fight for every hedgerow, Hitler had helped to create the conditions Montgomery had wanted for a complete break-through; by insisting on the counter-attack at Mortain and by staying too long at Falaise, Hitler had sacrificed the only divisions capable of holding the front together and covering a general withdrawal; and, finally, by sending the best part of Fifteenth Army west of the Seine at the ' thirteenth hour,' he had left himself with no organised force to guard the approaches to the Ruhr. In consequence, as Eisenhower says, " the enemy was momentarily helpless to present any continuous front against our advance."

Was this, then, the time for the Allies " to push forward on a broad front," advancing to the Rhine with four armies? Or was it the moment for a bold, concerted stroke at the heart of Germany's power to maintain the struggle—the Ruhr–Aachen area which was producing 51.7 per cent of her hard coal and 50.4 per cent of her crude steel? Without these basic resources the output of arms and ammunition would be drastically curtailed, if not crippled. The armies in the East might be supplied for a time from the mines and factories of Eastern Germany, Poland and Czechoslovakia, but these could not nourish a war on two fronts. If the Ruhr and the Rhineland could be captured or neutralised, it would matter little what armies Hitler might keep in the field in the West, since he would not be able to provide them with the means of continuing the fight.

The Ruhr was unquestionably vulnerable now, for the Wehrmacht had neither the reserves nor the mobility to counter a concentrated offensive. Because of their chronic shortage of oil, the Germans had never attempted to motorise their armies, as the Western Powers had done. Even during the *Blitzkrieg* phase, they had relied on railways for all major movement. Their panzer divisions were mechanised (though not on the same lavish scale as were the armoured formations of the Allies) but in the infantry divisions two-thirds of the vehicles and guns were drawn by horses. The Wehrmacht was essentially a marching army. This inherent lack of mobility had now been made acute by the impotence of the Luftwaffe, by the disruption of the railways in the West, by the destruction of at least 15,000 motor lorries in France since D-Day, and by the grave difficulty of finding fuel for the surviving vehicles.[1] In these circumstances Hitler was compelled to hold an extended front with his forces strung out all the way from the Swiss border to the North Sea. Lacking reserves, and unable to switch forces quickly from one sector to another, he dared not leave any part of the Reich frontier unguarded.

Eisenhower had no such defensive obligations *requiring* him to deploy his forces on a broad front. On the contrary, the situation demanded a deep advance on a narrow front, since that would accentuate the restricted mobility and enforced dispersion of the Wehrmacht and would enable the Allies to exploit their greatly superior capacity for concentration and movement. There was every likelihood that if he were to make a single, powerful thrust, he would cut through the stretched and straggling German armies to the Rhine. Such a course would involve no real risk. For the next month the enemy was likely to possess neither the mobility to launch a counter-attack nor the reserves to form a substantial counter-concentration of force.[2] Nor was there any reason for Eisenhower to be concerned about the southern flank; Patton had already demonstrated that this could be held by air power.

Even before the Allies had reached the Seine or closed the Falaise Pocket, the scope and nature of this unique opportunity had been foreseen by Montgomery. On August 17th he had suggested to Bradley that " after crossing the Seine, 12th and 21st Army Groups should keep together as a solid mass of forty divisions, which would be so strong that it need fear nothing. This force should advance northwards ": the Canadian and British armies directed on the Pas de Calais and Antwerp, the American armies on Brussels and Aachen " *with their right flank on the Ardennes.*" When this plan was first put to him, Bradley appeared to agree with it, but on the 19th he reported to Montgomery that Eisenhower intended " to split the force and send half of it west towards Nancy," in accordance with SHAEF's ' long-term strategic concept.'

It was vitally important that a firm and clear-cut decision should be

[1]According to the records of OKH, the number of lorries reported as lost by Army formations in June, July and August came to 34,614, compared with replacements numbering 15,278 received from the factories.

[2]Bradley says (op. cit., p. 400): " Beyond the Rhine, there was still a German Army. We were reminded of that . . . on December 16 in the Ardennes." This is a common misconception. The German records reveal that, of the divisions which took part in the Ardennes counter-offensive in December, very few were in existence as fighting formations during September. The training of the new *Volksgrenadier* divisions had only just begun, for the bulk of the troops who were drafted to them and to the depleted infantry units in the West during the autumn had been called up only in the last week of August. The spearhead of the Ardennes attack, Sixth SS Panzer Army, was not formed until September and its divisions were not fit for battle until November.

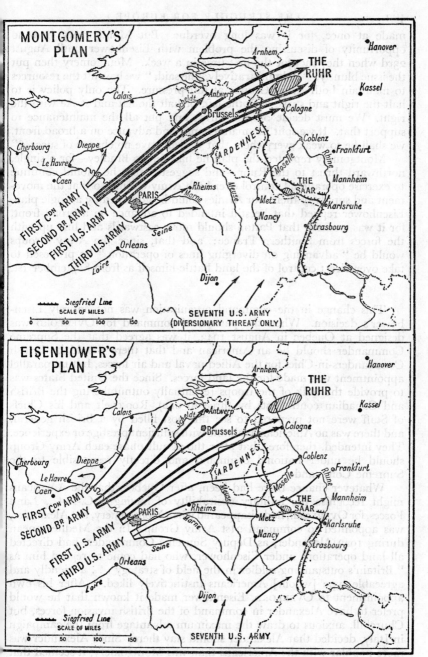

BROAD FRONT OR SINGLE THRUST?

made at once, for it was long overdue. But Montgomery had no opportunity of discussing the problem with Eisenhower until August 23rd when they met for the first time in a week. Montgomery then put the issue bluntly. " Administratively," he said, " we haven't the resources to maintain both Army Groups at full pressure. The only policy is to halt the right and strike with the left, or halt the left and strike with the right. We must decide on one thrust and put all the maintenance to support that. If we split the maintenance and advance on a broad front, we shall be so weak everywhere that we will have no chance of success."

Montgomery repeated the plan he had put to Bradley—for a single, northward thrust to the Ruhr—and suggested that he should continue to exercise operational control over both Army Groups so that the movement and supply of their four Armies could be governed by a single plan. Eisenhower replied that he still intended to advance on a broad front, for it was essential that Patton should move eastwards and link up with the forces from Southern France; and that, since the Army Groups would be " advancing on diverging lines of operation," he proposed to take over direct control of the land battle himself as from September 1st.

This change in the command organisation was not entirely Eisenhower's decision. When the pattern of command for OVERLORD was designed at Quebec in August 1943, it was agreed that the Supreme Commander should be an American and that there should be British Commanders-in-Chief for the Allied naval and air forces, but no parallel appointment was made for the land forces. Since the United States was to provide the bulk of the troops (eventually outnumbering the British and Canadian contingents by three to one), Roosevelt and his Chiefs of Staff were not prepared to see this post filled by a British general, and there was no American available with sufficient prestige or experience. They intended, therefore, that after the assault phase each Army Group should be under national command and directly responsible to the Supreme Commander.

Whatever chance there had been, after Quebec, that the Americans might recognise the military desirability of having a C.-in-C., Land Forces, for OVERLORD, had disappeared when Montgomery, not Alexander, was appointed to command 21st Army Group. In the Mediterranean during 1943 Alexander, as Deputy Supreme Commander, had directed all land operations under Eisenhower, who had come to regard him as " Britain's outstanding soldier in the field of strategy . . . a friendly and agreeable type [whom] Americans instinctively liked." After his own appointment to OVERLORD, Eisenhower made it known that he would prefer to have Alexander in command of the British invasion forces, but Churchill, anxious to draw the maximum advantage from the campaign in Italy, decided that Alexander should stay there. Since Alexander was more popular with the Americans than was Montgomery, it seemed that he might secure greater support from Marshall for those Mediterranean operations which the Prime Minister was so eager to develop. Accordingly, Churchill had appointed Montgomery: "a choice," says Eisenhower, "acceptable to me."[1] Eisenhower understood Montgomery better perhaps than did any other American but he was aware that few generals in the United States Army would serve happily for more than a short time under the victor of Alamein. Montgomery believed that strong direction and firm control from the top were the essential pre-requisites for victory, and so he liked to drive with a tight rein, a practice which was regarded by Americans as an unfair reflection on his subordinates and an unnecessary restraint on their initiative.

The uneasiness of the Americans became apparent at once when Eisenhower delegated to Montgomery full responsibility for the planning and direction of the opening phase of the invasion. At a meeting in London on January 12th, 1944, when Montgomery spoke in terms which suggested that he regarded himself as 'commanding' the assault forces of both armies, Bradley protested. Thereupon, says Brereton, who was then commanding Ninth U.S. Air Force, "General Montgomery made his position clear. He would command the British and Canadian troops, but he would suggest to General Bradley the scheme of maneuver or American troops."[2]

In practice, however, Montgomery's authority had extended far beyond mere suggestion, for the Normandy operations were, as Eisenhower insisted, "a single battle requiring the supervision of a single battleline commander,"[3] and Montgomery, by sheer clarity of mind and strength of personality, induced Bradley to follow his lead. It was clearly understood, however, that his authority was tactical and temporary, and that, when 12th U.S. Army Group became operational, Eisenhower would exercise direct control over all land forces. No time was fixed for this change over, but planning at SHAEF and at 21st Army Group H.Q. was based on the assumption that it would take place when the Allied Armies reached the Seine, which was expected to be about D plus 90.

Whatever professional respect the Americans had for Montgomery was tempered by personal suspicion, for his manner and methods aroused their traditional distrust of those who hold positions of great power. It was a matter not only of personality, but also of principle. The characteristic American resentment of authority, dating from the birth of the United States, has undoubtedly influenced command policy in their armed forces and has led to a considerable measure of independence and delegated responsibility at every level. "The American doctrine," says Eisenhower, "has always been to assign a Theater Commander a mission, provide him with a definite amount of force and then to interfere as little as possible with the execution of his plans."[4] Extending this principle

---

[1]Eisenhower, *Crusade*, p. 211.
[2]Brereton, *Diaries*, p. 236.
[3]Eisenhower, *Report*, p. 8.
[4]Eisenhower, *Crusade*, p. 369.

to the tactical sphere and objecting to the prescription of detailed geographical objectives, he writes: " A qualified commander should normally be assigned only a general mission, whether it be attack or defence, and then given the means to carry it out. In this way he is completely unfettered in achieving the general purpose of his superior."[1]

Bradley carried this doctrine even farther, for he believed: " You don't even tell a corps or division commander how to do his job when you have an army. You assign a mission and it's up to the fellow to carry it out. Of course, if you are in a position to have a look and talk it over with the guy you may make suggestions, but he doesn't have to take them."[2]

In the British services, on the other hand, command is very much more rigid and centralised. Orders tend to be more detailed and their execution more closely supervised than is generally the case within the American forces. In his dispatch on the Normandy assault, Admiral Ramsay reported that the U.S. naval commanders serving under him thought his orders " extended to too much detail " and " had to exercise considerable restraint in submitting " to the degree of control which he imposed.[3] On a higher level, Eisenhower says that he was shocked to find that " the British Chiefs of Staff in London maintained the closest kind of daily contact with their commanders in the field and insisted upon being constantly informed as to details . . . that in our service would only in exceptional circumstances go higher than a local army H.Q."[4] He and many other Americans were disturbed by this practice, not least because they believed it resulted in military plans being influenced by political pressure applied from Downing Street through the Chiefs of Staff.

The relative merits of these rival concepts of command need not concern us now, for what suits one nation may well be anathema to another. It is not surprising, however, that American generals found the British system irksome, especially as applied by Montgomery. To them his methods were the more objectionable because he was so clearly born to command and, even in his most tactful moments, he exercised his authority almost as a matter of right. Moreover, he was not as other men. He revealed no trace of ordinary human frailties and foibles. He shunned the company of women; he did not smoke or drink or play poker with ' the boys.' He could never be ' slapped on the back.' Because he lived in a small tactical H.Q. with a few aides and liaison officers, he was looked upon as setting himself apart from (and therefore above) his fellows. This impression seemed to be confirmed by his practice, resented as much by other British services as it was by the Americans, of sending his Chief of Staff, de Guingand, to represent him at conferences.

[1]Eisenhower, *Crusade*, p. 126.
[2]In an interview with A. J. Liebling, *The New Yorker*, March 10th, 1951.
[3]Ramsay, *The Assault Phase of the Normandy Landings*, Para. 4.
[4]Eisenhower, *Crusade*, pp. 369-70.

Unquestionably there was a marked element of professional vanity in Montgomery's make-up. He was not a man of snap judgments, but once he had made up his mind, he gave the impression of supreme confidence, in the rightness of his decision, and was frequently dogmatic in expounding his views because he had no time for cant, humbug or pomposity. The appearance of conceit was emphasised by his disregard for social graces when he was preoccupied with operations, but he was not so austere, aloof and unfriendly as many Americans thought. He was on closer and easier terms with his own troops than was any other British commander of his day, and he received unbounded loyalty from them. He was most approachable and informal with those who had operational reasons for seeing him and he freely sought expert advice in private discussion, but, he believed, as he once said to de Guingand, " You can't run a military operation with a committee of staff officers in command. It will be nonsense! "[1]

When Montgomery held a conference of his senior commanders and advisers, it was to ' tell them the form ' or to give out orders; not to collect ideas. In expounding a plan at this level, the clarity, directness and simplicity of his presentation was most convincing, but on other occasions he frequently gave the impression that he was ' talking down ' to his audience. This was the result of his habit of presenting every problem in the simplest terms with the deliberate intention of inspiring confidence in his solution by making it appear easier to accomplish. De Guingand writes: " When tackling a problem . . . [Montgomery] cuts away all the frills and gets down to those factors that really matter. He simplifies everything to an extent I have not met elsewhere. Some say he over-simplifies—this to some extent is true, but the resultant dividend is enormous."[2] Within the British Army this was certainly the case, but to many Americans who had not come into direct personal contact with him all this simplification seemed to be so much condescension.

The American attitude to Montgomery cannot be accounted for on grounds of national prejudice alone, although this was a contributing factor. His manner and methods would have been equally distasteful in an American. General Douglas MacArthur, who also exercised his authority with an autocratic hand, as though it were his by more than mortal dispensation, was heartily detested by many Americans, even by those who recognised his greatness in the field of strategy. On the other hand, Patton, whose eccentricities were as marked as MacArthur's or Montgomery's and far more flamboyant, did not provoke the same resentment. His behaviour made him unpopular in high places, but he was not suspect as an autocrat. The ' tough guy ' pose which he adopted in public (complete with pearl-handled revolver in open holster) was warm and familiar, in the best tradition of the ' Wild West.' Although

[1]De Guingand, *Operation Victory*, p. 158.
[2]Ibid, p. 173.

he liked to pretend that he was hard-boiled, he was in fact intensely emotional and soft-hearted. When deeply moved, he readily gave way to tears. Moreover, in all his posturing he conveyed the impression that he was showing off his personal toughness, rather than his professional authority. High-handed though his behaviour often was, he commanded in the American manner, debating his plans with his staff in daily conference as a 'democratic' general should, and abiding by the principle, "Never tell people *how* to do things, tell them *what* to do, and they will surprise you with their ingenuity."[1]

The Americans were prepared to accept Montgomery's leadership in the assault phase, because they recognised that he was, as Eisenhower says, "a master in the methodical preparation of forces for a formal, set-piece attack."[2] In Normandy Montgomery endeavoured to modify his method of command to make it more acceptable to the Americans. In this he was not unsuccessful, for Bradley says that Montgomery "exercised his Allied authority with wisdom, forbearance and restraint," and adds, "I could not have wanted a more tolerant or judicious commander."[3] Dempsey and other British officers considered that during the bridgehead battle Montgomery was "extremely tactful" in his dealings with Bradley, but the fact remained that it was Montgomery's plan which Bradley had to carry out.

During the weeks when Montgomery was drawing the German armour on to the British front in preparation for Bradley's break-out, the Americans became impatient. Montgomery's desire to keep the fighting to a minimum and to triumph by superior generalship was regarded as evidence of caution and timidity, and led to the belief that he would never be equal to the demands of exploitation and pursuit. Accordingly, as soon as the break-out had been achieved Bradley became increasingly eager to go his own way and to achieve full independence. About the same time the leading members of the staff at SHAEF (British and American alike) urged Eisenhower to take over from Montgomery without delay.

This private pressure developed into public demand when, on August 17th, newspapers in the United States revealed that although Bradley was now commanding an American Army Group he was still under Montgomery's 'operational control.' Marshall intervened immediately, warning Eisenhower that this news had provoked "severe editorial reaction," and urging him to "assume and exercise direct command of the ground forces." This determined the matter but, even if Marshall had not acted, Eisenhower could hardly have continued an arrangement which was no longer acceptable either to the American commanders and troops in the field or to the American people at home.

To a certain extent the new command organisation followed naturally

[1]Patton, op. cit., p. 357.
[2]Eisenhower, *Crusade*, p. 387.
[3]Bradley, op. cit., pp. 319-20.

from Eisenhower's decision to advance on a broad front. Since 21st and 12th Army Groups were now to pursue divergent courses, and since 6th Army group (from Southern France) was about to come under command of SHAEF, Eisenhower could hardly justify the delegation to Montgomery of even ' tactical co-ordination.' When Eisenhower raised this point, Montgomery suggested that Bradley should be appointed C.-in-C., Land Forces, and volunteered to serve under him. He argued that modern war moves so swiftly that land operations must be closely and continuously controlled by a single commander who can give his complete and undivided attention to the battle day by day, hour by hour. Eisenhower rejected this suggestion, partly, as he said, because the British people would not stand for the appointment of Bradley over Montgomery's head, and partly because the kind of control Montgomery advocated was quite foreign to American army practice. The inherent weakness of Eisenhower's alternative, however, is quite clear from his own statement that he intended that " each army group commander would be a ground commander in chief for his particular area; instead of one there would be three so-called commanders in chief for the ground."[1]

Although Eisenhower may have had no alternative but to take personal command of the land battle, his doing so was none the less unfortunate. In the role of Supreme Commander he had shown himself to be the military statesman rather than the generalissimo. In the past two years, except for one brief period early in the Tunisian Campaign, he had never attempted to exercise direct operational control over his armies. He had devoted himself to the task for which he was best qualified by temperament and training: the establishment of the political and logistic conditions necessary for the success of the operational plans devised and implemented by his service chiefs and field commanders. On issues that were purely strategic or tactical he had been content to determine broad objectives and policies and then to act as arbiter and co-ordinator. In Normandy, as in the Mediterranean, he had delegated to his army group commander full responsibility for the planning and direction of operations. This was sound policy since he had not the time to play the double role of Supreme Commander and Commander-in-Chief, Ground Forces.

Furthermore, being an honest and modest man, Eisenhower was conscious of his lack of experience in the tactical handling of armies, and this gave him a sense of professional inferiority in dealing with men like Montgomery and Patton who had been through the mill of command at every level. Because he had no philosophy of battle which he himself had tested in action, Eisenhower was reluctant to impose his own ideas, unless the decision was one which he, as Supreme Commander, had to

[1]Eisenhower, *Crusade*, p. 285. On August 31st, when Montgomery ceased to act as commander of all Eisenhower's land forces, he was promoted to the rank of Field-Marshal.

make. As a general rule, he tended to seek the opinions of all concerned and to work out the best compromise. When he could gather his commanders and advisers around the conference table, he had a remarkable capacity for distilling the counsel of many minds into a single solution, but, when his commanders were scattered over France, he was open to persuasion by the last strong man to whom he talked.

It seems fair to say that the very qualities which made Eisenhower a successful Supreme Commander prevented him at this time from becoming a successful commander in the field. His great talent lay in holding the Allied team together, and in reconciling the interests of different nations and services. In the situation which had now developed, however, Eisenhower's conscientious tolerance and inclination to compromise were liabilities. The occasion called for a man with a bold plan, a Commander-in-Chief who knew what was essential and had the will to impose his strategic ideas without regard for personalities or public opinion.

The plan which Montgomery presented to Eisenhower at their meeting on August 23rd was bold enough, but it meant halting Patton and confining Third Army to the defensive role of flank protection during the advance of the Second British and First American Armies to the Ruhr. Eisenhower's first reaction was that, even if it was militarily desirable (which he did not admit), it was politically impossible to stop Patton in full cry. " The American public," said Eisenhower, " would never stand for it; and public opinion wins war." To which Montgomery replied, " Victories win wars. Give people victory and they won't care who won it."

Montgomery may have been right so far as the British public were concerned, but Eisenhower knew that his troops in the field and his people at home would see the issue in simple terms, almost in terms of American football. Patton was ' carrying the ball,' and was making an ' end run ' with every American cheering him on. As Eisenhower saw it, there was no justification—in football or in battle—for taking the ball away from him. Patton had proved himself to be a master of exploitation and his troops were already across the Seine. Montgomery had no such reputation and his troops had not yet reached the Seine. Neither the British nor the Canadians had yet shown a capacity for advancing with the dash and drive the Americans had demonstrated so brilliantly since the break-out. It is not surprising, therefore, that Eisenhower should have doubted at this stage whether Montgomery had the troops or the commanders to carry the northward thrust through to the Ruhr before the Germans could re-establish a coherent front.

On the other hand, Eisenhower was most anxious to secure the Channel ports and Antwerp as soon as possible, and this could be achieved only if he were to give some measure of priority to Montgomery. He decided, therefore, that the British advance to Antwerp would be supported by First U.S. Army which was to " establish itself in the general area Brussels–Maastricht–Liége–Charleroi." Meanwhile, Third

Army was to continue east at any rate as far as Rheims and Châlons-sur-Marne. The outcome of this compromise was that although Patton was not to be stopped, two of Hodges's three corps were to march on Dempsey's flank from Paris to Brussels. Eisenhower said, however, that as soon as Montgomery had captured the V-weapon bases in the Pas de Calais and had seized Antwerp, Patton would continue eastwards to the Saar and join forces with 6th Army Group in the Vosges.

Montgomery had to be content with this, but he still feared that if Patton were allowed to go on, the northward offensive could not be fully exploited. In any case, it could not be launched immediately, for the British and American troops who had been engaged in the Falaise Pocket were still closing up to the Seine. Dempsey had only one small bridgehead, at Vernon, and none of his armoured divisions had even reached the river. Accordingly, Second Army was not able to begin its advance from the Seine until August 29th.

By that date Third Army had already crossed the Marne, captured Châlons and was approaching Rheims. So far, Patton had not been handicapped by lack of supplies, for the additional tonnage needed to sustain his advance had been provided by an air-lift which was delivering 500 tons a day to Orléans. This air-lift, however, could not be maintained because the transport aircraft were now needed to supply Paris with food and to prepare for an airborne operation in the Pas de Calais. On the 28th, therefore, Bradley had tried to insist that Third Army should pause at the Marne until First Army's northward move was well under way. " I had considerable difficulty," says Patton, " in persuading him to let me continue to the Meuse. He finally assented."[1]

Armed with this authority, Patton sent his Corps Commanders advancing east, but by August 30th Third Army's petrol reserves were almost exhausted. That day Patton received only 32,000 gallons of the 400,000 he had demanded, and when he met Bradley at Chartres he was warned that no extra petrol would be available for him before September 3rd. If Bradley thought that this would restrain Patton, he was wrong. When he returned to his own H.Q. that afternoon, Patton found that XII Corps had stopped at St. Dizier because its commander (Major-General Manton S. Eddy) had reported that if he were to go any farther he " would find his tanks without any gasoline." Patton promptly ordered him " to continue until the tanks stop and then get out and walk." Patton may not have realised that this order amounted to an act of defiance, but he must have known that if his armoured divisions were to advance until their tanks ran dry Bradley would have to provide him with petrol at the expense of the operations to which Eisenhower had given priority—the offensive into Belgium.

This offensive began on August 29th. By then VII U.S. Corps

[1] Patton, op. cit., p. 119.

(Collins), having crossed the Seine through Third Army's bridgehead at Melun, south-east of Paris, had driven north to Soissons. Here Collins was threatening to outflank the line of the Somme on which Model was endeavouring to make the next stand. Along this line, as we have observed, Model had only the meagre remnants of the infantry divisions which had been extricated from the Seine Pocket, for on the 28th he had ordered " the concentration of all available mobile troops in the area Châlons–Rheims–Soissons " in the hope of heading off Third Army. This meant that, just as the British were about to break out from the Vernon bridgehead, Patton was drawing to the east the only mobile forces capable of checking their advance.

In this advance Montgomery was determined to demonstrate beyond further argument his powers of exploitation. Mindful of the difficulty he had had with some of his commanders in the bridgehead, he gave orders that " any tendency to be ' sticky ' or cautious must be stamped on ruthlessly. . . . The proper tactics now are for strong armoured and mobile columns to by-pass enemy centres of resistance and to push boldly ahead creating alarm and despondency in enemy rear areas." Second Army's passage northward must be " swift and relentless."

In Horrocks, the new Commander of XXX Corps, Montgomery had a man with the drive and enthusiasm that the hour demanded. Horrocks had commanded a brigade in Montgomery's division before Dunkirk and, when Montgomery went to the Middle East, he had brought Horrocks out to command XIII Corps at Alamein. Later with X Corps, Horrocks had carried out the spectacular left hook which turned the Mareth Line and then, commanding IX Corps in the last North African battle, he had directed the break-through which brought about the capture of Tunis and precipitated the German capitulation. Before leaving North Africa, however, he had been seriously wounded during an air raid on Bizerta and for a year he had been in hospital. In June 1944 Horrocks was still convalescing in England and his doctors had told him that never again could he take command in the field, but early in August, when Montgomery needed a new commander for XXX Corps, Horrocks came at once. Within a few days his fresh and fiery spirit had transformed the Corps. A tall, lithe figure, with white hair, angular features, penetrating eyes and eloquent hands, he moved among his troops more like a prophet than a general.

By midday on August 30th the 11th Armoured Division was 40 miles from Amiens and was meeting only light opposition. That afternoon Horrocks ordered it to drive on by moonlight and " bounce the Germans out of Amiens before they can blow the bridges." That night the moon was obscured by heavy rain, but the advance went on and, as the long columns of tanks and guns, trucks and carriers wound through narrow village streets, men and women came out in night clothes, regardless of the rain, and cheered their progress. Several times the British columns ran into enemy convoys heading for what had been the German front line. Twice the leading tanks knocked out a German tank which tried to bar the way and by dawn the armour was rumbling down the cobbled streets of Amiens. The French who had gone to bed in an occupied city awoke to find themselves liberated. Three of the four bridges over the Somme, thanks to the French Resistance, were captured intact.

When the British tanks drove into Amiens that morning they passed within a mile of Seventh German Army H.Q. where Dietrich was in the act of handing over command of the Somme sector to Eberbach. Dietrich managed to slip away, but before Eberbach could move his newly-acquired command post it was overrun and he was taken prisoner as he tried to escape in a Volkswagen. In another car the British discovered a marked map, which revealed not only the Somme defences, but also the chaos which prevailed throughout the Wehrmacht in the West.

With the fall of Amiens, the capture of Eberbach and the rout of his H.Q., the line of the Somme was broken and Horrocks drove through the breach. The Guards came up fast on the eastern flank of 11th Armoured and by September 2nd British armoured cars had reached the Belgian border south-east of Lille. Farther east that day two American armoured divisions crossed into Belgium as far as the Lille–Mons road along which thousands of Germans from the Pas de Calais were endeavouring to escape. There were now three Allied Corps (XXX British, XIX and VII American) ranged along the Belgian frontier within one day's march of Brussels.

When the British reached Belgium they were still dependent on supplies brought by road from Bayeux, a distance of 250 miles. The Americans at Mons and Verdun were extended even farther, for their supply lines ran back in a wider sweep almost 400 miles through Paris to the Cotentin Peninsula. Le Havre was still in German hands and the Allies had no major port closer than Cherbourg. On September 1st the Canadians enjoyed the sweet revenge of capturing Dieppe before the Germans could destroy the harbour installations, but it was not to be working for another week and the crisis in supply was now.

There were ample stocks of all kinds ashore in Normandy but the problem was to move them forward in sufficient volume. Before the break-out the bridgehead had been so shallow and congested that there had not been room for large reserves of transport. Nor had it been anticipated that they would be needed. According to the Administrative History of 21st Army Group, " it had always been expected that somewhere a certain delay would be imposed which would have afforded an opportunity for the build-up of essential stores." Moreover, Montgomery's allocation of motor transport was based on the assumption that his forward troops would be operating within 200 miles of their railhead, but in the British sector there were no railways working even to the Seine. On August 30th the first train from the bridgehead reached Paris by a circuitous route, but it was clear that during the next vital fortnight only a fraction of the supplies the Allied armies needed could be brought up by rail. The destruction of the bridges over the Lower Seine, the devastation of the marshalling yards and the general disruption of the railway system—all the result of the air attacks which had contributed so greatly to the German defeat in Normandy—now saved the Wehrmacht from pursuit by the full strength of Eisenhower's forces.

In Second Army's advance through Northern France, XII Corps had been able to follow XXX only because VIII Corps and nearly all Montgomery's heavy, medium and anti-aircraft artillery had been grounded west of the Seine. By the start of September all the transport reserves of 21st Army Group were on the road. Imports were cut from 16,000 tons a day to 7,000 so that transport companies could be diverted from unloading ships to forward supply. This gain, however, was almost offset by the alarming discovery that the engines of 1,400 British-built three-tonners (and all the replacement engines for this particular model) had faulty pistons which rendered them useless.[1] These trucks could have delivered to the Belgian border another 800 tons a day, sufficient to maintain two divisions. By reducing the daily tonnage of First Canadian Army, by bringing in fresh transport companies from England, and by such expedients as welding strips of airfield track on the sides of tank-transporters to convert them for supply carrying, 21st Army Group was able to provide enough supplies to carry Dempsey's two forward corps into Belgium as far as Brussels and Antwerp, but with its own resources it could not go much farther.

Bradley's difficulties were even more acute. His supply lines were longer and he had the added burden of seeing that Paris was fed. Between the bridgehead and the French capital the Americans had already established a circular one-way traffic route from which all vehicles were banned except the trucks and trailers of the ' Red Ball Express '—an improvisation as characteristic as it was effective. By disregarding normal convoy procedure and by driving with lights on, the American supply services maintained the flow of traffic round the clock, and were able to deliver 7,000 tons of stores daily to Bradley's forces north of the Seine; yet this was only two-thirds of what he needed to keep both Armies advancing. Accordingly, in line with Eisenhower's plan that First Army should advance deep into Belgium, Bradley had given orders on September 1st that 5,000 tons a day should go to Hodges and 2,000 to Patton.

This plan was thoroughly debated next day when Bradley and Patton conferred with Eisenhower at Chartres. Eisenhower again declared that, because he needed ports quickly, priority would be given to operations in the Pas de Calais and Belgium until Antwerp was captured. Patton protested strongly, pointing out that, although his cavalry patrols had already reached the Moselle and entered Metz, his main force had been halted on the Meuse for two days through lack of gasoline. " My men,"

[1] See ' The Administrative History of the Operations of 21 Army Group,' p. 47.

he said, " can eat their belts, but my tanks have gotta have gas." Given the fuel, Third Army could quickly break through to the Rhine. Bradley supported Patton and urged that First Army should also turn eastward. This combined pressure again produced a compromise, for, says Patton: " We finally persuaded General Eisenhower to let V Corps of the First Army and the Third Army go on and attack the Siegfried Line as soon as the Calais area was stabilised."[1] Having extracted this concession, Patton says he went on to obtain " permission to secure crossings over the Moselle . . . whenever I could get the fuel to move." When he sought this concession, Patton did not reveal that one of his corps had just captured 110,000 gallons of petrol, sufficient to take it to the Moselle.[2]

This was an untimely concession. Once he had decided to give priority to the advance into Belgium, Eisenhower unwittingly endangered his own plan by giving Patton permission to move a yard beyond the Meuse. The farther Third Army advanced, the greater the tonnage it would need and the greater the possibility that it would become heavily involved and would then need extra supplies which could only be provided at the expense of First Army. This was not a remote possibility, for it was already apparent that the Germans were concentrating mobile forces to check Patton on the Moselle. Before the end of August his troops had identified the 3rd and 15th Panzer Grenadier Divisions fresh from Italy and two SS brigades from the Reich. Either Patton should have been given the resources to cut through this fresh opposition before it could establish a firm front, or else he should have been ordered not to become too deeply committed. As it was, he was given enough petrol to join the battle, but not enough to win it. To a commander of Patton's temperament this was most exasperating. He regarded Eisenhower's decision as " the most momentous error of the war,"[3] and refused to accept it as final.

On September 3rd, the day after Eisenhower's conference at Chartres, Hitler instructed Model to concentrate the most powerful armoured force he could on the Upper Moselle with the object of counter-attacking Patton's Army and striking into the American flank. By this means he hoped to delay the northward advance of the Allied armies which had reached the Belgian frontier, but, when these orders were issued, the British were already marching upon Brussels.

Montgomery had intended to open the way to the capital by dropping airborne troops to seize the crossings over the Scheldt at Tournai, but this was now clearly unnecessary and on the morning of Sunday the 3rd, the armoured divisions of XXX Corps drove into Belgium, the

---

[1]Patton, op. cit., p. 124.
[2]One of Patton's staff, Col. Robert S. Allen, says that this knowledge was " an ace secreted up his [Patton's] sleeve—a little secret he carefully had not divulged to Eisenhower." (Allen, op. cit., p. 136.)
[3]Patton, op. cit., p. 120.

Guards (on the right) heading for Brussels and the 11th for Antwerp. At dawn that day the Guards were 70 miles from Brussels, but once they had crossed the Scheldt on either side of Tournai there was nothing to stop them. The German resistance was scattered and incoherent and its collapse was accelerated by the Belgian Underground.

As the news of the British approach spread like a running fire from town to town, men—and women—of the Resistance unearthed hidden arms and harassed the fleeing Germans. They prevented the blowing of bridges and the erection of road-blocks, and when the enemy opposition was too strong for them to tackle unaided they went out to meet and forewarn the advancing armour. On the open road the columns raced along at 30 miles an hour, but in every town and village from the frontier to Brussels they had to crawl through crowds of cheering, laughing, shouting people. With wild delight in their voices and tears of joy in their eyes, the Belgians swarmed around the tanks and vehicles, thrusting into the hands of the embarrassed Tommies bottles of wine and beer, boxes of cigars and cigarettes, fruit, cakes and chocolate, flowers, flags and souvenirs.

By late afternoon the Guards were entering Brussels, and as they drove nearer the heart of the city the crowds thickened and the tumult grew. Only an hour earlier the streets had been bare and deserted, except for the last departing Germans. Now the buildings were plastered with flags, streamers and placards which the Belgians had prepared long since for this very day. In one square the tanks were halted by the throng and the Brussels police attempted to move the crowd back, but they could not restrain one little old woman who wore on her drab black dress her husband's medals from another war. She made a quick dart across to the nearest jeep, took the hand of the driver, kissed it, and said, "Je vous remercie, Tommy. Je vous remercie." And into his hand she pressed what was obviously all that she had—three cigarettes.

It was in this spirit that Belgium welcomed the Allies. Nowhere in France had the British troops been greeted with such great warmth and real gratitude. It had been difficult for the French, so proud of their military past, to admit that they owed their liberation to the Americans and British, whom they had always regarded as their inferiors in the art of warfare. The French had been thankful to be free but, even in Paris, they had not been able to bring themselves to show their appreciation with the enthusiastic spontaneity which the Belgians demonstrated in Brussels and in every hamlet.

Forewarned by the fall of Brussels, the German garrison in Antwerp should have been able to hold the city long enough to cover the demolition of the key points in the docks and port installations. On September 4th, however, the 11th Armoured Division, having skirted Brussels to the west, moved into Antwerp so boldly and swiftly that the leading tanks reached the docks by early afternoon and found them unguarded and almost unscathed. This was a tremendous stroke of fortune, for the sluice gates

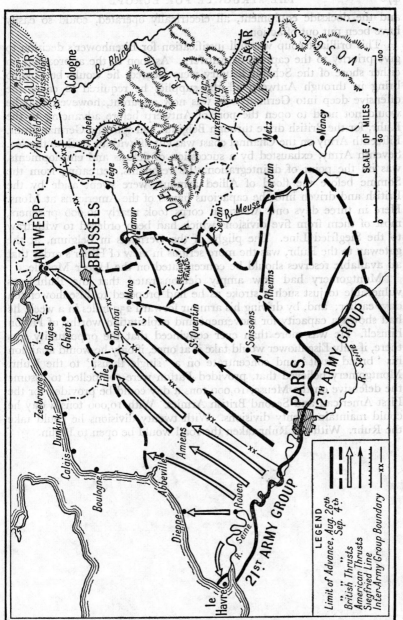

THE ADVANCE TO ANTWERP

LEGEND

Limit of Advance, Aug. 26th
"        "      Sep. 4th
British Thrusts
American Thrusts
Siegfried Line
Inter-Army Group Boundary ─xx─

SCALE OF MILES

100
50
0

and the dockside equipment, all electrically operated, could so easily have been put out of action.

This brilliant coup was full justification for Eisenhower's decision to give priority to the capture of Antwerp. As soon as the approaches on either shore of the Scheldt Estuary were cleared, he would be able to bring in through Antwerp all the supplies he required to carry the offensive deep into Germany. It was now apparent, however, that he would not need to open the port of Antwerp before advancing to the Ruhr, for the British drive through Belgium had split the German front. Fifteenth Army on the Channel coast was cut off with its back to the sea. Seventh Army, exhausted by a succession of defeats and envelopments, was on the point of disintegration. Its remnants, retreating from the Somme before the flood of Allied armour, were swept aside by the British and driven into the capacious hands of the Americans at Mons. Here in three days one American corps took nearly 30,000 prisoners, most of them from five divisions which had been ordered to withdraw to the Siegfried Line. The plight of the Germans in Belgium, at the gateway to the Ruhr, was the more serious in view of Hitler's order that all available reserves should be concentrated on the Upper Moselle.

Montgomery had now amply demonstrated that the Ruhr was vulnerable to just such a stroke as he had proposed to Eisenhower ten days earlier; and, by driving his armour forward 250 miles in a week, he had shown a capacity for movement and exploitation worthy of Patton himself. He was more than ever convinced that the opportunity was there, if only Eisenhower would take it at once, if only he would abandon his ' broad front ' and concentrate on a ' single thrust ' to the Ruhr. Montgomery believed that, provided Patton were compelled to assume the defensive on the Meuse, 10,000 tons a day could be provided for the First American and Second British Armies. With 10,000 tons a day he could maintain twenty divisions. With twenty divisions he could take the Ruhr. With the Ruhr taken the road would be open to Berlin.

## CHAPTER XXV

# THE TIDE OF FORTUNE

ON September 4th, the day that Antwerp fell, Hitler reinstated von Rundstedt as Commander-in-Chief in the West. Since his dismissal in July the aged Field-Marshal had shown his political reliability by presiding over the so-called Court of Honour, set up to expel from the Wehrmacht those officers who had been concerned in the Plot of July 20th. The recall of von Rundstedt was a belated attempt to reassure the Officer Corps and, perhaps, to provide a member of the ' Old Guard ' as a handy scapegoat in the event of further disaster. Meanwhile, the prime responsibility for preventing disaster was to remain with the energetic and ingenious Model, who, as Commander of Army Group B, continued to direct the critical battle for Belgium.[1]

The situation von Rundstedt inherited was infinitely more grave than that which had provoked his ' end the war ' outburst on July 1st. Then he had had 62 divisions in France and the Low Countries, 20 of them holding a 100-mile front in Normandy and the remainder either garrisoning the coast defences or moving to the battlefield. Since then 12 more divisions had been sent to the West, making 74 in all, and yet so many of these had been so severely mauled in the land battle and from the air that the total force now available to hold the 400-mile front from the North Sea to the Swiss border had the fighting strength, in Model's opinion, of only 25 divisions. In the last week the Allied armies had swept across the Somme and the Marne, through Flanders and the Argonne, over the very battlefields where the tide of the First World War had ebbed and flowed for four long, indecisive years. Moreover, the Allies, who had seemed so cautious in the Normandy bridgehead, had shown themselves to be proficient in that *Blitzkrieg* technique which the Wehrmacht had employed over this same ground in 1940.

Shocked by this abrupt disaster and disillusioned by the failure of the vaunted V-weapons, the German armed forces and the German people were sustained only by the fear of having to surrender unconditionally to East and West alike, and by the hope that the Western Allies might

[1]A chart showing the reorganisation of the German and Allied Commands in September 1944 is included in Appendix B.

yet be held on the Siegfried Line as they had been throughout the first winter of the war. This was Goebbels's boast and Hitler's plan. It was the Führer's intention to halt the Allies at the West Wall, on the Moselle, and in the Vosges, and to wait for the winter, when, as he said prophetically at a conference on September 1st, " fog, night and snow " would provide him with a " great opportunity."[1]

The Siegfried Line, however, was not yet ready for defence. Believing, as late as August 31st, that the Allies could be halted on the Somme–Marne Line, Hitler had taken no steps to garrison the West Wall. The concrete skeleton was there, but, since the campaign of 1940, it had lain militarily unoccupied and neglected. Nearly all the weapons and signal equipment, many of the belts of wire and mines had been removed, most of the field defences had been ploughed in and nothing had been done to modernise the fortifications in the light of experience gained in Russia or at the Atlantic Wall. Indeed, the concrete casemates, designed for the 37 mm anti-tank guns of 1939-40 could not house the ' 75s' and ' 88s' that were needed to deal with the armour of 1944. Many of the concrete bunkers and galleries were being used to shelter bombed-out families; others had been taken over to provide safe storage for precious war materials, and some of these were still locked. According to Warlimont, Jodl's deputy, there was considerable to-do at OKW while they were finding who had the keys!

More difficult and more urgent was the problem of collecting sufficient men to garrison the Line and to reinforce and rebuild the broken divisions which were streaming back to the frontiers of the Reich. On September 4th Model reported to Hitler's H.Q. that if Army Group B had to hold a line from Antwerp along the Albert Canal, the Meuse and the West Wall as far as the Franco-Luxemburg frontier, this line " must be manned by 25 fresh divisions with an adequate armoured reserve of five to six panzer divisions . . . otherwise the gateway into North-West Germany will be open."[2]

Model might as well have asked for the moon. In all Germany the Army High Command could not find even one ' fresh division.' There were training and demonstration units, but not one divisional formation fit to fight. In the last weeks of August, as we have seen, every division that could then be mustered, some seven in all, had been sent to the Upper Moselle to halt Patton. Within the Reich ten panzer brigades[3] were being formed from the remnants of armoured divisions which had been decimated on the Eastern Front, and Himmler, now in command

---

[1]Führer Conferences, Fragment 43, September 1st, 1944.

[2]Teleprinter Message, Model to Jodl, September 4th, 1944. (Tempelhof Papers.) That Model could have made this request shows that even Hitler's most trusted field commanders did not know the real gravity of Germany's plight.

[3]Most of these panzer brigades consisted of one panzer grenadier battalion, one panzer battalion (equipped with 33 Panthers and 11 assault guns), an engineer company and service troops; but some contained two panzer battalions (one with 48 Panthers and the other with 48 Mark IVs) and two panzer grenadier battalions.

of the Home Army, was endeavouring to raise forty new infantry formations with a much-reduced establishment—barely 10,000 men—and the
grandiloquent designation ' *Volksgrenadier* divisions.' Two of these had
already been sent to France, but only half a dozen more would become
available during September.

In this crisis Hitler once again resorted to improvisation. Garrisons
and fortress battalions, training regiments and schools of officer cadets
were converted overnight into operational units and dispatched to the
Siegfried Line. The four *Wehrkreise* (Military Districts) in Western
Germany were ordered to organise their depot staffs into divisional
H.Q. and to mobilise every man they could find: men on leave or
convalescing in hospital, men from ordnance depots and training
establishments, from engineer and signal units, from coastal and anti-
aircraft batteries, from the Navy, the police and the Organisation Todt.

By these, and other expedients equally desperate, Hitler and Himmler
succeeded in collecting 135,000 soldiers and Todt workers to garrison
and re-build the Western defences, but this force was regarded by von
Rundstedt as " totally inadequate." Moreover, these scratch battalions
and makeshift divisions were of little value outside the fixed defences of
the Siegfried Line or the fortifications at Metz, since they had neither the
fire-power nor the mobility to engage successfully in open warfare against
armoured and mechanised columns.

The British advance from the Belgian frontier to Brussels and
Antwerp in a day and a half had created a most critical problem for
Model. Isolated now in the lowlands of Flanders, Fifteenth Army could
escape only by sea across the estuary of the Scheldt to Walcheren, and,
even if this withdrawal could be accomplished without heavy losses in
men and equipment, it would take at least three weeks. The Seventh
German Army—or what was left of it—was being driven eastwards to
the Meuse and the Ardennes. Within three days the gap between these
two armies was to be 50 miles wide and the only forces available to close
it were one low-grade infantry division which had been guarding the
coast of Holland, one 'remnant' division from Normandy, one brigade of
Dutch SS and the garrison troops of the Netherlands Military District.
The Home Army could provide one depot division just formed from
convalescents and men who had been invalided out of the army. These
had been grouped into units according to the nature of their physical
disability. Thus there was a ' stomach battalion' for men with duodenal
ulcers; and an ' ear battalion ' for those with defective hearing.

At this critical juncture, when the Army's immediate resources were
exhausted, the Luftwaffe came to the rescue. On September 4th Goering
revealed, to the complete surprise of the Army General Staff, that he
had six parachute regiments in various stages of training or re-equipping,
and that he could raise two more regiments from paratroops in con-
valescent depots, making a force of 20,000 men altogether. To these he
could add as many as 10,000 from the Luftwaffe, air crews and ground

staff whose training or operations had been curtailed by the shortage of petrol. Few of these paratroops and none of the airmen were fully trained for fighting on the ground, but, as members of the German Air Force, they had all been thoroughly indoctrinated with National Socialism. Young, ardent and loyal, they could be relied upon to fight for Hitler to the end.

These troops formed the core of the First Parachute Army which was created on the afternoon of September 4th by orders telephoned from Hitler's H.Q. in East Prussia to Berlin—to General Kurt Student, the C.-in-C., Paratroops. Student, the founder of the German paratroop arm, had planned and led the assault on Rotterdam and the invasion of Crete, but never had he been confronted with such a desperate situation. First Parachute Army was ordered to close the gap in Northern Belgium by holding the line of the Albert Canal from Antwerp to Maastricht, a front of 60 miles. For this task, Student was given command of the forces already on the Dutch mainland, and of the parachute regiments and Luftwaffe battalions, but it would be at least a week before they could all be brought into the line.

Student's Parachute Army was the only substantial reinforcement that Hitler was able to offer von Rundstedt, but the Field-Marshal was ordered " to fight for time so that the West Wall can be prepared for defence." He was to stem the Allied advance on the water-line of the Albert Canal, the Meuse and the Upper Moselle, and " regardless of local losses, to advance deep into the American east flank, attacking in a north-westerly direction from the Épinal area "[1]: i.e. against the right flank of Third U.S. Army.

By September 6th, however (the day after von Rundstedt actually resumed command), the Allies had gained bridgeheads over the Albert Canal and the Meuse, and the line of the Upper Moselle was being held only by committing defensively the armoured forces which Model had been assembling for the Führer's counter-stroke. On the following day von Rundstedt reported that it would take six weeks to make the West Wall fit for defence.

" The whole organisation," he signalled, " takes time," but his forces had not the strength to gain that time. " All our own troops," he said, " are committed, are being heavily attacked and are becoming exhausted. There are no reserves worth mentioning." He reported that, whereas the Allies were advancing with some two thousand tanks (an accurate estimate), " Army Group B has about one hundred tanks fit for action." Then he added, " If I am to command with any possibility of success, I again request that, regardless of the consequences elsewhere, all available tanks be sent forward at once to protect the Rhine–Westphalia industrial area."

To make good the unrequited losses which his panzer divisions had suffered since D-Day, von Rundstedt needed at least 2,000 tanks and

[1]Teleprinter Message, Keitel to von Rundstedt, September 7th. (Tempelhof Papers.)

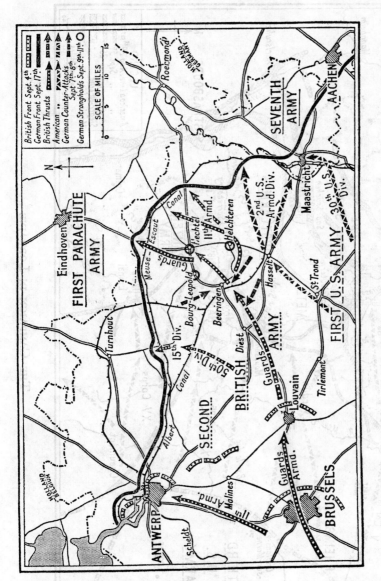

THE BATTLE FOR THE BELGIAN CANALS

THE CAMPAIGN IN LORRAINE

LEGEND
American Line. Aug 29th
  „    „    Sept. 5th
  „    „    „   25th
Siegfried Line
Maginot Line
Scale of Miles
0   5   10   20   40

Mannheim
Karlsruhe
STRASBOURG
RHINE
THE SAAR
Saarbrücken
Saarlautern
GERMANY
FRANCE
FIRST ARMY
Saverne
Sarrebourg
S
Colmar
V O S G E S
FIFTH PANZER ARMY
25th Sept.
19th Sept.
18th Sept.
R. Saare
Moselle
Thionville
METZ
Seille
13th Sept.
Arracourt
NANCY
Lunéville
Moselle
12th Sept.
Epinal
Luxembourg
8th Sept.
Verdun
Pont-à-Mousson
R.
XII Corps
Moselle
XV Corps
R. Meuse
V Corps
FIRST
THIRD
Bar-le duc
Marne
XX Corps
Chaumont
RHEIMS
Chalons-sur-Marne R.
THIRD U.S. ARMY
Troyes

assault guns, but there were no stocks of armour at Hitler's disposal.
In July, according to the records of the Army High Command, the
number of tanks and 75 mm assault guns destroyed on all fronts was
1,969, but only 1,256 replacements had been received from the factories,
and nearly all these had been sent to the Eastern Front before the Allied
break-out produced a crisis in the West. During August the number of
tank replacements received by the Army fell to 1,122, but at least twice
as many were lost.[1] Most of these were destroyed or abandoned in
France, but by the start of September the situation on the Eastern Front
was almost as desperate as that in the West and the need for armour
was even greater since there was no Siegfried Line, nor any water barrier
as formidable as the Rhine, in the path of the Red Army.

Before von Rundstedt's recall Hitler had given orders that " all
88 mm anti-tank guns, all Tiger IIs and all *Jagdpanthers*" were to go to
the West.[2] He had also allocated 200 Panthers (more than half the
August production) to equip the new panzer brigades which he had
promised Model, but he directed to the Eastern Front almost the entire
output of medium armour—the Mark IVs and the 75 mm assault guns,
the only armour which had the mobility to keep pace with the Shermans
in open warfare.

In these circumstances von Rundstedt could not create an armoured
reserve powerful enough or mobile enough to deal with another Allied
break-through. If the Allies were to advance on a broad front, he might
be able to check them, for he could seal off local penetrations, but if they
were to deliver a concentrated and powerful assault at any one point,
there was no doubt in his mind that they could breach the defences and
overwhelm the local reserves; and once the break-through had been
achieved, the Tigers and Panthers would be too slow and too few to halt
the Allied armour.

The outcome of the campaign seemed to rest, therefore, on von
Rundstedt's ability to prevent the battle again becoming fluid, and this
in turn depended on whether he could stave off the most immediate
threat—from First U.S. Army on the Meuse—long enough for the
Siegfried Line to be manned and made ready. By September 8th,
however, the line of the Meuse was gone, Liége had been captured and
the Americans had advanced through the Ardennes almost to Bastogne.
That day Model reported to von Rundstedt that " south of Liége as far
as the newly-prescribed Army boundary [on the line Trier–Thionville]

[1]The Inspectorate of Panzer Forces at OKH recorded the losses for August as 1,221
and those for September as 2,241. It seems, however, that nearly half the tanks and
75 mm assault guns included in the September total were in fact destroyed in August,
but were not reported then owing to the chaotic conditions in the West during the
retreat. All the figures quoted in this paragraph refer only to the types of armour which
were the main equipment of panzer divisions and the heavy tank battalions, namely,
Tigers, Panthers, Mark IVs and 75 mm assault guns.
[2]Führer Conferences, Fragment 43, September 1st, 1944. The *Jagdpanther* was a
mobile anti-tank gun, an 88 mm mounted on a Panther chassis.

there is only a very thin and totally inadequate defence line. Here the enemy enjoys almost complete freedom of movement as far as the West Wall, which is held—to the rear of the Seventh Army—*by only seven or eight battalions on a front of 120 kilometres.*"[1] It was a case, he said, of " now or never." Unless Seventh Army were substantially reinforced, " the strategic breach for which the enemy has been striving between the Meuse and the Moselle will be opened automatically, this time on the German frontier."

The crisis appeared to be approaching its climax. With a " strategic breach " developing on the Ardennes sector of the Siegfried Line and " the gateway into North-Western Germany" opening on the Albert Canal, von Rundstedt could look with confidence only to the Upper Moselle. Here the First German Army was being rebuilt to a strength of eight divisions and, while Patton's six divisions were halted on the Meuse in the first few days of the month, these fresh forces had established themselves on the Moselle from Thionville through Metz and Nancy to Épinal.

This was the only sector of the entire Western Front where von Rundstedt's troops could meet the Allies on more or less equal terms. Only here could he expect to hold the covering position while the Siegfried Line was prepared for defence. Elsewhere, he would have to rely for reinforcements on the fruits of Hitler's desperate improvisation, and, as these began to appear in the line, one British Intelligence officer dryly observed: " Both as regards quality and diversity, the enemy force opposing us shows the effects of the recent measures in Germany to step up the national effort. Paratroops and pilots, policemen and sailors, boys of 16 and men with duodenal ulcers—all of these have been through the Corps cage during the last few days. And now we have some deep-sea divers. The depths have indeed been plumbed."

The capture of Brussels and Antwerp presented the Allies with a strategic opportunity which had decisive possibilities. The reasons for concentrating on an all-out thrust in the north were now infinitely stronger than they had been when Montgomery advocated this course in August. With the isolation of the Fifteenth German Army and the rout of the Seventh, the road to the Ruhr lay for the moment almost unguarded. On this northern wing the Allies could bring to bear not only the strongest force of armour (they now had eight armoured divisions and two armoured brigades in Belgium or on the border) but also the greatest weight of air power. The forces in Belgium could be supported by tactical aircraft based in England without having to wait either for the preparation of new bases on the Continent or for the forward movement of the ground installations and supplies which could be brought up from Normandy

[1]Teleprinter Message, Model to von Rundstedt, September 8th, 1944. (Tempelhof Papers.) (The italics are mine. C. W.)

only by using road transport that was urgently needed to maintain the advance of the armies. Dieppe was about to open and as soon as the Scheldt Estuary was cleared, the supply lines for the northern sector of the Allied front would be very much shorter than those by which the southern wing could be maintained.

On the evening of September 4th, as soon as he learned of the capture of Antwerp, Montgomery sent a signal to Eisenhower suggesting that the time had come to make " one powerful and full-blooded thrust towards Berlin." He said that there was not sufficient transport to maintain two powerful thrusts and that the chosen line of advance must have absolute priority in supply. He suggested that the northern route (via the Ruhr) was likely to be the most profitable and might even prove to be decisive. Time, he said, was vital; a compromise solution would only prolong the war.

On the following evening Eisenhower replied that although he agreed with the idea of making " a powerful and full-blooded thrust towards Berlin," he did not think it should be launched at that moment at the expense of all other operations. He was still confident that his armies could capture both the Ruhr and the Saar; that they could overrun the Siegfried Line and cross the Rhine on a wide front before the Germans could recover; and that, while this broad advance was in progress, the ports of Antwerp and Le Havre could be opened in readiness for a final offensive into the heart of Germany. Within this overall plan, however, he still intended to give priority to the northern route of advance, but he did not believe that any redistribution of the existing supply resources would enable the Allies to maintain a thrust to Berlin.

To Montgomery this reply indicated that Eisenhower appreciated neither the tactical situation in Belgium nor the supply difficulties which had already brought a large proportion of the Allied forces to a standstill. This lack of appreciation resulted primarily from the fact that Eisenhower was not in touch with the battle. His field H.Q. was at Granville on the west coast of the Cherbourg Peninsula, nearly 400 miles from the front in Belgium. From Granville he could communicate with Montgomery and Bradley only by letter or by wireless telegraphy. There were no telephone lines, nor even a radiophone link, between his H.Q. and theirs. During the advance from the Seine he had made several journeys by air to see his Army Group commanders, but now he could not leave his H.Q. On September 2nd, returning from the conference with Bradley and Patton at Chartres, his aircraft had made a forced landing on the beach near Granville. In helping the pilot to pull the plane away from the water's edge, Eisenhower had wrenched his right knee so badly that his doctor was compelled to encase his leg in plaster and to keep him in bed.

Isolated in Granville, Eisenhower had little contact with his main H.Q. in London, and did not receive adequate information about the progress of operations. This would not have been such a serious matter if his only responsibility had been that of Supreme Commander, but at a time when the situation was developing rapidly, when fresh opportunities demanded fresh decisions promptly made in full knowledge of the latest facts, it was taking twenty-four hours for situation reports to reach him and another twenty-four hours for his instructions to get back to his commanders in the field. Meanwhile, Hitler was in instant contact with the H.Q. of von Rundstedt and Model by teleprinter.

The state of Eisenhower's communications was such that his ' Most Immediate ' signal, sent from Granville on the evening of September 5th in reply to Montgomery's proposal about Berlin, did not reach the Field-Marshal's H.Q. near Brussels until after breakfast on the 7th. Even then the signal was not complete and the missing paragraphs did not arrive for another two days!

On September 4th, before receiving this proposal, Eisenhower had issued a fresh directive, ordering the forces north-west of the Ardennes (21st Army Group and two corps of First U.S. Army) " to secure Antwerp, reach the sector of the Rhine covering the Ruhr and then seize the Ruhr." The forces south of the Ardennes (Third Army and one corps of First Army) were to " occupy the sector of the Siegfried Line covering the Saar and then seize Frankfurt." Referring to Patton's mission, Eisenhower said: " This operation should start as soon as possible, but the troops of the Central Group of Armies [Bradley] operating against the Ruhr north-west of the Ardennes *must first be adequately supported*."

Although this directive appeared to give continued priority to First Army, it was intended by Eisenhower, and interpreted by Bradley, as a reaffirmation of the ' broad front ' plan. In a memorandum which he dictated next day the Supreme Commander said, " I see no reason to change this conception. The defeat of the German armies is now complete and the only thing needed to realise the whole conception is speed . . . I now deem it important to get Patton moving once again so that we may be fully prepared to carry out the original conception for the final stages of this campaign."

Thus, in spite of Eisenhower's statement that operations against the Ruhr " must first be adequately supported," Bradley did not feel obliged to hold Patton back or to continue the arrangement by which First Army was receiving 5,000 tons of supplies a day and Third Army 2,000. On the 4th Bradley had decided that " the situation in the north having been stabilised " Third Army would get " half of the available supplies and could cross the Moselle and force the Siegfried Line."[1] Moreover, Patton's eastward drive was to be further reinforced. Already V Corps had been switched from the centre of First Army to the right flank so that it could cover Patton's northern wing as he drove for the Saar. His southern wing was now to be strengthened by the reconstitution of XV Corps with the 2nd French Armoured Division and the 79th U.S. Infantry Division which had been transferred to First Army before the fall of Paris.

These decisions seriously prejudiced the continuation of the drive

[1]Patton, op. cit., p. 126.

through Belgium to the Ruhr, for Hodges could not maintain his three corps with less than 4,500 tons a day, and his ability to advance in concert with the British was further reduced by the withdrawal of the 79th Division which was operating under XIX Corps on the left flank of First Army. This corps was already immobilised on the Belgian border through lack of petrol, and the transport which could have been sent back to bring fresh supplies from the dumps west of the Seine was now used to carry the 79th Division from the extreme left flank of the American front to the extreme right, from Tournai to Joinville, a lateral move of nearly 300 miles—and this at a time when every vehicle was needed to speed the forward advance.

With Bradley's blessing, Patton resumed his offensive on September 5th. By the 10th his troops had gained two small bridgeheads over the Moselle, south of Metz, but they were encountering heavy opposition from the fresh divisions which Hitler had thrown in, and it was clear that it would take a major effort to force the now strongly defended river line. Along Patton's southern flank, however, the situation was still fluid and on this day the 2nd French Armoured Division made contact with the 1st French Infantry Division near Dijon. Thus the forces of Over-lord and Anvil were linked and in the next few days an unbroken front was established from Switzerland to the Channel. But this excursion extended Patton's responsibilities southwards into an area of no strategic importance at a time when a major opportunity was developing in the north.

The German reinforcement of the Moselle front at the end of August had left the Belgian Meuse almost undefended and Hodges made good use of his opportunity. By September 10th his two leading corps were approaching the Siegfried Line on a broad front between Aachen and Trier, but XIX Corps, delayed by shortage of petrol and weakened by the loss of the 79th Division, was not able to advance with them. According to the revised supply plan, First U.S. Army was due to receive 3,500 tons a day, but throughout this week it averaged only 3,189 and a large share of this went to V Corps to enable it to keep up with Patton's rapid advance from the Meuse. Thus the result of giving Third Army sufficient petrol to carry it to the Moselle was that First Army had to drive forward on its right to cover Patton, instead of on its left to support Montgomery and the drive for the Ruhr.

These developments left Montgomery in a tantalising position. He knew that the Ruhr was vulnerable and yet he had not the strength to strike the vital blow. The Canadian Army (with six divisions) was about to assault Le Havre and the Pas de Calais ports, and to clear the Belgian coast. As for Second Army, VIII Corps (with two infantry divisions, two tank brigades and most of the Army's medium and heavy artillery) was still immobilised on the Seine; XII Corps, on the western flank, was engaged in driving Fifteenth Army back to the Scheldt Estuary; XXX Corps alone was in a position to continue the advance into Holland. Thus, of the fourteen divisions and seven armoured brigades in 21st Army Group, only the Guards and 11th Armoured were ready to maintain the offensive. This was the measure of Hitler's success in denying the Allies the Channel ports.

Nevertheless, Dempsey ordered Horrocks to strike on, with the Guards moving on the axis Louvain–Diest–Eindhoven–Nijmegen, and the 11th advancing from Antwerp through Tilburg to s'Hertogenbosch. At Antwerp, however, 11th Armoured had been so busy securing the docks intact that it had neglected to seize the bridges over the Albert Canal on the northern edge of the city. This was one unfortunate result of the confusion and conflict within the Allied High Command concerning future strategy. " Had any indication been given," says the Division's historian, " that a further advance north was envisaged, these bridges might have been seized within a few hours of our entry." Even in the absence of specific orders, however, it is strange that so astute a divisional commander as Roberts did not secure the bridges immediately as part of his general brief to capture Antwerp.

The cost of his failure to do so was soon evident. On September 6th a small bridgehead was established over the Albert Canal but it was so strongly counter-attacked that his troops could neither build a bridge nor ferry anti-tank guns across. On the 8th, therefore, Roberts was ordered to move his division to the right flank of XXX Corps where the Guards, having crossed the Albert Canal at Beeringen, were now heavily engaged with the vanguard of Student's paratroops and the rearguard of Seventh Army.

This flank was exposed because XIX U.S. Corps had not been able to keep pace with the British advance through Belgium. The 2nd Armoured Division (this corps' main striking force) had been halted for three days at the Belgian frontier because it had no petrol. When it was able to move—on the 6th—its operations were so restricted by supply difficulties that it took three days to reach Hasselt and another three days to gain a foothold beyond the Albert Canal.[1]

Between this water-barrier and the next (the Meuse–Escaut Canal) the terrain lent itself to defence, for it is sandy heath broken by small streams and patches of swamp. Here the Germans concentrated on holding the main crossroads, establishing themselves in stoutly-built villages which were difficult to by-pass and which could not be quickly taken by direct assault since the armoured divisions had not sufficient infantry or artillery. The defenders, mostly from parachute regiments, fought with fanatical bravery and were dislodged only when their village strongholds were demolished house by house. By September 10th the strength and persistence of this opposition was causing Dempsey some concern. His troops had now secured a second foothold across the

[1]After-Action Report, 2nd U. S. Armoured Division, September 1944.

Albert Canal, but the Germans in Bourg Leopold, Hechtel and Helchteren would not budge. Yet it was essential that Dempsey should crack this new front before it could congeal, since he could not launch another major offensive until he had secured a bridgehead over the Meuse–Escaut Canal.

On the afternoon of the 10th, the Household Cavalry, probing between Bourg Leopold and Hechtel, found an opening for the Irish Guards, who cut through the gap and, as darkness was falling, seized the canal bridge that Dempsey wanted.[1] During the night the Germans began withdrawing from Hechtel, and the Grenadiers joined the Irish Guards north of the Meuse–Escaut Canal, on the threshold of Holland, on the start-line for the great offensive which Montgomery had been discussing with Eisenhower in Brussels that very afternoon.

For the past month Montgomery had been seeking an opportunity for the mass employment of the Allied Airborne Army (which had been formed in August under command of Lieut.-General Lewis H. Brereton) either to cut off the enemy's retreat or else to clear the way for further exploitation by the Allied ground forces. Half a dozen plans had been made but each time the American and British armoured columns had overrun the chosen dropping-zones before the airborne divisions could be launched, and, much to Brereton's disappointment, the transport aircraft had been diverted to " their secondary job of carrying supplies."[2]

Early in September Eisenhower had proposed that the Airborne Army should be dropped in the Maastricht–Aachen area to make a gap through the Siegfried Line in front of First U.S. Army. This proposal was rejected by Bradley, who had little faith in airborne troops and preferred to continue using the Dakotas for air supply, since he was confident that so long as Patton had the petrol Third Army could continue motoring. Thereupon, in conformity with his plan for giving priority to the northern route, Eisenhower had ordered Brereton to " operate in support of the Northern Group of Armies [Montgomery] up to and including the crossing of the Rhine."[3]

Montgomery now proposed to use the Airborne Army for a bold and unorthodox stroke which, he hoped, would bring about a rapid break-through and a penetration deep enough to carry Second British Army across the Rhine in one bound. He would lay a carpet of airborne troops to seize the canal and river bridges ahead of Second Army and thus clear the way for the swift advance of its armour over the Maas and the Rhine. By this means he could outflank the Siegfried Line, which petered out north of Aachen, and establish a powerful armoured force on the edge of the North German Plain.

[1] This was a brilliant exploit and in honour of it the prize was named ' Joe's Bridge ' after Lt.-Col. ' Joe ' Vandelaer, the C.O. of 2nd Armoured Irish Guards.
[2] Brereton, op. cit., p. 339.
[3] Directive issued by Supreme Commander, September 4th, 1944.

There were two feasible routes of advance for Second Army. It could strike north-east across the Maas at Venlo and the Rhine at Wesel; or it could attack almost due north through Eindhoven, crossing the Maas at Grave, the Waal at Nijmegen and the Lower Rhine at Arnhem. The advantage of the Arnhem route was that, although it would require the capture of bridges over three major rivers and five minor waterways, the airborne divisions were likely to suffer less from fighters or flak during the landings, and the advance of the ground forces was likely to be more rapid. Moreover, there was the possibility that Second Army could continue the advance from Arnhem to the Zuider Zee, thus cutting off the Germans in Western Holland.

While this plan was under consideration, Dempsey learned from his Intelligence staff that " there is considerable railway activity at Arnhem and Nijmegen, and heavy and light flak in both places is increasing very considerably . . . Dutch Resistance sources report that battered panzer formations have been sent to Holland to refit, and mention Eindhoven and Nijmegen as the reception areas." This information, and the severity of the fighting on the Albert Canal, led Dempsey to doubt whether a rapid enough advance northward could be made by Second Army alone. During this advance he could expect no support on his right flank from the Americans, for they were heading almost due east. Accordingly, Dempsey was inclined to think that he would be wiser to hold a firm flank along the canals on the Dutch border, strike eastwards in conjunction with the Americans and cross the Rhine at Wesel.

On the morning of September 10th Dempsey arrived at Montgomery's Tactical H.Q. prepared to advocate this course. Montgomery greeted him with the news that a signal had just come from the War Office, suggesting that the first V.2s, which had landed on London on the 8th, were launched from bases in Western Holland near The Hague. The War Office inquired whether in the near future there was any chance of these bases being captured or at least cut off from their sources of supply in Germany. This news settled the issue,[1] since the Allied Air Forces had already warned Montgomery that the Wesel plan would involve heavy casualties because the unarmoured transport aircraft would have to fly through the thick flak defences covering the Ruhr. Accordingly, it was to be Arnhem —provided that the plan was approved by Eisenhower who was flying from Granville to meet Montgomery at Brussels airfield that afternoon.

They met in Eisenhower's aircraft and their meeting began inauspiciously, for Montgomery requested that Eisenhower's Chief Administrative Officer (Lieut.-General Sir Humphrey Gale) should not take part in the discussion but that his own (Major-General M. A. P.

---

[1]Montgomery says that he had decided on Arnhem before the arrival of this signal, and that the decisive argument against Wesel was the objection of the Air Forces. On the other hand, Dempsey asserts that he spoke to Montgomery by telephone shortly before the signal about the V.2s was received and that Montgomery then appeared to be still in doubt.

Graham) should stay. This request was hardly tactful, but Eisenhower granted it. Having got rid of Gale, Montgomery drew from his pocket a file of the signals which had passed between him and Eisenhower during the previous week, and proceeded to say—in language which was far from parliamentary—precisely what he thought of the policy outlined in them and what he believed would be the consequences.

A man of less generous nature might have reacted violently to this outburst but, as the tirade gathered fury, Eisenhower sat silent. At the first pause, however, he lent forward, put his hand on Montgomery's knee and said in a quiet but firm tone, " Steady, Monty! You can't speak to me like that. I'm your boss."

Montgomery bit back his next word and, responding to Eisenhower's forbearance, said, " I'm sorry, Ike." The rest of the discussion was freed from acrimony though the divergence of opinion was sharp. Montgomery went on to repeat his arguments in favour of a single powerful thrust to the Ruhr and beyond, but Eisenhower reaffirmed his intention of continuing the advance to the Rhine on a broad front. He approved Montgomery's plan for using the Airborne Army to secure the crossings over the Maas, Waal and Neder Rijn (Operation MARKET GARDEN) but, as he wrote later, he regarded this offensive as merely an " extension of our eastward rush to the line we needed for temporary security."[1]

Eisenhower's plan, as defined by him in a directive three days later, was to " drive forward through the enemy's western frontiers to suitable positions on which we can regroup while preparing the maintenance facilities that will sustain the great bulk of our forces on the drive into Germany." The basic assumptions in this plan were that with their existing resources for supply his armies could overrun the Siegfried Line, cross the Rhine and seize " the Ruhr, the Saar and the Frankfurt area," but that they could not strike any decisive blow at the heart of Germany until the port of Antwerp was working.

Montgomery challenged both these assumptions. He warned Eisenhower that the supply lines of all the Armies were already stretched to breaking point and that there could be no substantial advance *anywhere* unless at least one Army was halted. He asserted that, on the other hand, if the transport resources of Third U.S. Army and First Canadian Army, apart from what was needed to maintain them in defensive positions, were immediately made available to support the Second British and First American Armies, the 16 divisions which Dempsey and Hodges commanded, reinforced by the four divisions of the Airborne Army, would be able to capture the Ruhr. This, he argued, would cripple the German war machine and open the road to Berlin.

In suggesting that he could drive on to the German capital, Montgomery may have been over-bidding his hand. Yet, even if such a bold advance had been considered militarily (i.e. logistically) practicable, would it have been politically acceptable to the Americans? At a time

[1]Eisenhower, *Crusade*, p. 307.

when Third Army still appeared to be capable of advancing farther, Eisenhower felt that he could not tell Patton to stop in order that Montgomery might have the chance of inflicting the *coup de grâce*. This consideration, however, did not affect the validity of Montgomery's argument that the Ruhr could be captured only by a concentrated assault on a narrow front.

In his memoirs, Eisenhower says: " There was still a considerable reserve in the middle of the enemy country and I knew that any pencil-like thrust into the heart of Germany such as he [Montgomery] proposed would meet nothing but certain destruction."[1] In fact, however, Montgomery was not proposing a " pencil-like thrust." In his signal of September 4th he had advocated " one really powerful and full-blooded thrust," and he was now suggesting that this should be made by 20 divisions, at least six of them armoured. Nor is it correct for Eisenhower to suggest that SHAEF believed there was a " considerable reserve " in Germany. The advice given him at this time by his Chief Intelligence Officer (Major-General K. W. D. Strong) was summed up in the SHAEF Intelligence Summary of September 9th in these words: " The whole wreck of the Balkans and Finland may yield up perhaps half a dozen divisions. These will go no way to meet the crying need for more divisions to man the West Wall; moreover, a line in Transylvania will need to be manned. Where, then, are more divisions to be found? Not in Norway, withdrawal would take too long . . . Denmark might still supply one division, and a dozen or more may yet be formed in Germany, given time, from training units, remnants and so forth. The Italian and Russian fronts risk collapse if anything more is withdrawn from them. . . . In short, C.-in-C., West, may expect *not more than a dozen divisions within the next two months* to come from outside to the rescue."

SHAEF Intelligence had gone on to survey the immediate prospects on the Western Front and had concluded: " C.-in-C., West, will soon have the true equivalent of about fifteen divisions, including four panzer divisions, for the defence of the West Wall. A further five or six divisions may struggle up in the course of the month, making a total of about twenty. The West Wall cannot be held with this amount, even when supplemented by many oddments and large amounts of flak."

The point of view expressed in this appreciation was repeated by the Supreme Commander in Brussels on the 10th. It seems, therefore, that when he rejected Montgomery's plan, Eisenhower was influenced not by his concern about the enemy's reserves, but by his confidence that the Germans could not raise sufficient forces to hold the Siegfried Line. That afternoon he appeared to be confident of capturing both the Ruhr and the Saar without the unpalatable necessity of ordering either Patton or Montgomery to stop. This was certainly the impression he gave to Butcher next day. After a long discussion at Granville, Butcher noted

[1]Eisenhower, *Crusade*, p. 306.

in his diary, " Ike is thinking in terms of advancing on a wide front to take advantage of all existing lines of communication. He expects to go through the Aachen gap in the north and the Metz gap in the south and to bring the Southern Group of Armies (6th) to the Rhine south of Coblenz. Then he thinks he should use his airborne forces to seize crossings over the Rhine, to be in position to thrust deep into the Ruhr and to threaten Berlin itself. . . . Ike has decided that a northern thrust toward the Ruhr under Montgomery is not at the moment to have priority over other operations."[1]

At Brussels Montgomery had pressed hard for such priority, or at least for a supporting operation by First U.S. Army on Dempsey's right flank during MARKET GARDEN. These requests could be met only by stopping Third Army's offensive on the Moselle. The eight divisions of First Army were already stretched out over a front of nearly 150 miles covering the gap between the divergent axes of Dempsey and Patton. Accordingly, Hodges could not extend his front northwards to help Dempsey, unless Patton were to take over First Army's southern sector. Far from doing this, Patton was about to extend his front southwards by bringing in XV Corps on his right flank. Eisenhower was not prepared to countermand this move, because he wanted to establish a continuous front by making a firm junction with 6th Army Group which was due to come under his command on September 15th. The most Eisenhower would agree was that, in addition to the Airborne Army, he would provide Montgomery with extra supplies from American resources, though not at the expense of Patton's operations.

In these circumstances it was the more important that MARKET GARDEN should be launched quickly before the Germans had a chance to strengthen their forces in Holland any further. But Dempsey's difficulty was that, as First Army could provide neither protection nor diversion on his exposed eastern flank, he would have to bring VIII British Corps forward from the Seine to attack on the right of XXX Corps which was to make the main northward thrust. The bulk of the VIII Corps vehicles, however, had already been taken to supply the rest of Second Army, and it was now clear that, unless Eisenhower could provide considerably more transport than he had promised, Dempsey could not build up Second Army's stocks and move VIII Corps up to the Dutch border by September 17th, the target date for the Arnhem operation. On the 11th, therefore, Montgomery warned Eisenhower that he would not be able to attack before the 23rd at the earliest.

This warning produced immediate results. On the 12th Bedell Smith flew to Montgomery's H.Q. and, with Eisenhower's authority, promised to deliver 1,000 tons a day to Brussels by road or air.[2] That evening

[1]Butcher, op. cit., p. 661.
[2]On the following day it was decided at SHAEF that 500 tons a day would be carried from Bayeux to Brussels by ' Red Ball ' convoys, that another 500 tons would be delivered to Brussels by air transport, and that an additional air-lift would be provided by bombers which would fly petrol to Lille.

Montgomery believed that his view had triumphed, for Bedell Smith had told him that the drive to the Saar would be stopped, that the bulk of 12th Army Group's supply resources would be given to First Army, that this Army was to co-operate closely with him, and that three American divisions would be grounded and their transport used to maintain 21st Army Group. On the strength of these assurances, Montgomery fixed September 17th as D-Day for MARKET GARDEN and declared that he now hoped the war could be won " reasonably quickly."

While Bedell Smith and Montgomery were making these plans near Brussels, Bradley, Hodges and Patton were in conference at Rheims. Two days earlier Bradley had given orders that First and Third Armies were to advance " east to secure bridgeheads over the Rhine from Mannheim to Köln " (Cologne), i.e. on a front of 150 miles. If possible, he said, Patton was to cross the Rhine as far south as Karlsruhe, and, so that he would be free to concentrate on this eastward drive, the newly arrived Ninth U.S. Army (Lieut.-General W. H. Simpson) had already assumed command of operations in Brittany. With regard to supply, Bradley declared, " the Armies will have equal priority in supply *except that the capture of Brest will have first priority.*"[1]

The allocation of supplies on this basis could hardly be reconciled with Eisenhower's instruction that the forces operating against the Ruhr " must first be adequately supported," and it was the more surprising because on the previous day Bradley and Patton had agreed that " the taking of Brest at the time was useless because it was too far away and the harbour was too badly destroyed." " On the other hand," wrote Patton, " we agreed that, when the American Army had once put its hand to the plow, it should not let go. Therefore, it was necessary to take Brest."[2]

This was hardly the moment to give priority to prestige. The German garrison in Brest could be contained with comparatively small forces, because, having no armour and little transport, it lacked the mobility to threaten the main Allied supply lines which lay 150 miles to the east. Furthermore, the capture of Brest could not possibly relieve the immediate or long-term supply problem, for it was farther from the front than those Normandy ports and beaches which were already taking in more tonnage than the available trucks and trains could carry forward. The only harbours worth opening now lay north of the Seine, and yet Bradley was maintaining four divisions (some 80,000 troops)[3] in Brittany, and

[1] 12th Army Group, Letter of Instruction to Army Commanders, No. 8, September 10th, 1944. (The italics are mine. C. W.)
[2] Patton, op. cit., p. 128.
[3] *Conquer: The Story of the Ninth Army*, p. 52. There was a similar diversion of air power. Between August 26th and September 18th XIX Tactical Air Command, which usually supported Third Army, flew the majority of its missions against Brest on every day except three.

giving them 'first priority' while his armies on the Moselle and the Siegfried Line were running short of supplies. The actual tonnage diverted to Brittany by road was not great, but by persisting in active operations against Brest at this time, Bradley tied down truck companies which could have been used to maintain the advance towards Germany. Moreover, in the two weeks starting September 5th, 3,000 tons of ammunition a day were delivered to beaches near Brest by landing-craft which could more easily and more profitably have dumped their cargoes on the coast north of the Seine.

On September 12th Bradley advised Patton that the British plan for making the major effort in the north had been accepted by SHAEF and warned him that Third Army might have to " hold the west bank of the Moselle defensively." Patton thereupon proposed that he should get his troops so heavily involved beyond the Moselle that Eisenhower would not be able to call a halt. " I felt," Patton wrote later, " that could we force a crossing over the Moselle, this unfortunate situation could be prevented, and Bradley gave me until the night of the fourteenth to do it."[1]

In a new directive on September 15th Eisenhower reaffirmed his intention of advancing to the Rhine on a broad front, but he now admitted that the offensives to the Ruhr and to the Saar–Frankfurt area could not be supported simultaneously. In fulfilment of his assurance to Montgomery, he ordered that " all possible resources of the Central Group of Armies [Bradley] must be thrown in to support the drive of First U.S. Army to seize bridgeheads near Cologne and Bonn in preparation for assisting in the capture of the Ruhr. After the Northern Group of Armies [Montgomery] and First Army have seized bridgeheads over the Rhine, Third Army will advance through the Saar and establish bridgeheads across the Rhine." Regarding supply, Eisenhower wrote, "Operations on our left will, until the Rhine bridgeheads are won, take priority in all forms of logistical support," except in so far as supplies would be needed by the forces on the right for security, reconnaissance and the opening of ports.

These arrangements, however, were not to take effect until Third Army was established across the Moselle. In authorising this advance by Patton, Eisenhower intended that Bradley's Army Group should " push its right wing only far enough for the moment so as to hold adequate bridgeheads beyond the Moselle and thus create a constant threat . . . and prevent the enemy from reinforcing farther north by taking troops away from the Metz area." Justifiable as it may have been in strategic theory, this compromise was fatal, for it gave Patton the opportunity of running off at a tangent, regardless of Eisenhower's plan for striking first at the Ruhr.

When these orders were issued, Third Army had already secured five crossings in the Metz–Nancy area and, says Patton, " by the evening of

[1]Patton, op. cit., p. 130.

the fourteenth I had made good my promise to Bradley and had secured, in both his opinion and mine, a good bridgehead across the Moselle." His advance was being bitterly contested by the reconstituted First German Army, but he had two divisions about to attack Nancy and, once it was taken (as it was next day), he would have fulfilled Eisenhower's directive. Nevertheless, Patton says that he felt he " could still, with luck, keep edging towards the east," and, although Bradley was " quite depressed " by Eisenhower's decision, he, too, " thought that the Third Army could push on."[1] Patton appears to have reported Bradley's opinion correctly, for, in spite of Eisenhower's explicit instructions to the contrary, the supplies available to 12th Army Group north of the Seine were still divided equally between First and Third Armies.

Patton had little difficulty in finding an excuse for further offensive action. Eisenhower had given authority for " continuous reconnaissance by the forces on the right." That was all Patton needed, for he could, he says, " pretend to reconnoiter, then reinforce the reconnaissance, and finally put on an attack—all depending on what gasoline and ammunition we could secure."[2] Nor did he inquire too closely into the methods by which these supplies were secured. He records as a ' rumour ' what his staff were proud to acknowledge as a fact, that " some of our Ordnance people passed themselves off as members of the First Army and secured quite a bit of gasoline from one of the dumps of that unit." " This is not war," says Patton, " but is magnificent."

The outcome was that Patton did not stop, nor was any considerable quantity of supplies diverted from him to the armies north of the Ardennes. In his Report to the Combined Chiefs of Staff, Eisenhower says that " three United States divisions were completely immobilised in order to supply additional logistical support to the Northern Group [of Armies]," but these divisions were not in the line. They had only just arrived in Normandy and there was no transport to carry them forward or to maintain them there. With the help of truck companies from these divisions, ' Red Ball ' convoys began running from Bayeux to Brussels on September 16th, but the air-lift to Brussels was only slightly increased, from 400 tons a day to 500, and the plan for flying petrol in bombers to Lille did not materialise until the 21st.

Thus Montgomery was compelled to rely almost entirely on his own resources to carry out the build-up for MARKET GARDEN and he soon found that he could not bring forward both the necessary supplies and the divisions of VIII Corps in time to attack on the 17th. Since he had to make a choice, he chose tonnage rather than troops, fully realising that the inability of VIII Corps to attack in sympathy with XXX Corps would mean that the right flank of Second Army would be dangerously exposed. On the eve of MARKET GARDEN this danger became the greater because of the situation which developed on the front of First U.S. Army.

[1]Patton, op. cit., p. 131.
[2]Ibid, p. 125.

At five minutes past six on the evening of September 11th, an American reconnaissance patrol crossed the German frontier near Prüm. The invasion of the Reich had begun. Probing deeper next day, the Americans found that this sector of the Siegfried Line, opposite the Ardennes, was weakly garrisoned and that some of its fortifications were not manned at all. Because of supply difficulties, however, this opportunity could not be exploited at once and, before they were able to attack, German resistance had stiffened. On the 14th the Americans forced the first line of defences and advanced eight miles to the outskirts of Prüm, but here they were turned back.

Meanwhile, farther north, VII U.S. Corps had driven almost head-on into the defences of Aachen which, next to those of the Saar, were the strongest and deepest in the entire West Wall. This fact was fully appreciated by Allied Intelligence, but Hodges was so encouraged by the speed of his advance from the Seine that he hoped to overrun the Siegfried Line before the Germans could man it in strength. Immediately south of Aachen on September 13th and 14th, an American armoured division penetrated the first fortified zone to a depth of five miles only to be checked at the second line which ran parallel with the frontier, but east of the city. By this time Model had been able to bring in an infantry division which had just arrived from East Prussia, a panzer brigade and two armoured battlegroups.

In the next two days VII Corps could make little progress after penetrating the second line of defences. Beyond this lay a maze of coal-mines and factories around Stolberg and here its armour could not be used effectively. By the 17th the Americans were being counter-attacked and it was clear that it would take a major operation to capture Aachen. Before this could be launched XIX Corps would have to fight its way forward from Maastricht so that it could strike at Aachen from the north in conjunction with the VII Corps attack from the south.

In these circumstances there was no likelihood of First Army being able to conduct any offensive operations in support of MARKET GARDEN. By losing flexibility, First Army had lost the initiative, but this was not altogether the fault of Hodges. It was the direct result of Eisenhower's determination to move on a broad front, of his inability to restrain Patton and especially of his anxiety to bring about an early link up with the ANVIL forces. By his advance from the Marne to the Meuse and then from the Meuse to the Moselle, Patton had distorted the Allied Front and dragged it too far to the south. Third Army had become a magnet drawing forces and supplies away from what Eisenhower had declared should be the main drive. Because Patton's right flank had been extended south to Épinal, Hodges had been compelled to cover such a wide frontage that he could not concentrate at any one point sufficient strength to break through the Siegfried Line. Thus, far from being able to develop his own offensive " to seize bridgeheads near Cologne and Bonn," while Montgomery was advancing to Arnhem, Hodges now could not even keep up sufficient pressure at Aachen to maintain the threat of a break-through to the Rhine.

On September 16th, when Eisenhower realised this, he again instructed Bradley that priority in supply must be given to First Army and that Third Army must be stopped. Patton's reaction to this news was, to quote his own frank words, that " in order to avoid such an eventuality, it was evident that the Third Army should get deeply involved at once, so I asked Bradley not to call me until after dark on the nineteenth."[1]

True to his word, Patton launched a co-ordinated assault against Metz with the three divisions of XX Corps on the 17th and, when this was repulsed, " decided not to waste time capturing Metz but to contain it with as few troops as possible and drive for the Rhine." The spearhead of this drive was to be Eddy's XII Corps which he had sent advancing east from Nancy on the 18th. Its advance was checked by a sharp counter-attack at Lunéville, but, says Patton, " I was determined that the attack of the XII Corps on the Siegfried Line should go on in spite of what had happened at Lunéville "; and also, it seems, in spite of Eisenhower's orders.

By this time there was no chance of Patton's breaking through to the Rhine. The First German Army had a firm grip on Metz and was fighting stubbornly to regain the line of the Moselle north and south of that city. On the Nancy–Épinal sector Hitler had now brought in one of his ablest tank commanders, Manteuffel, who had arrived fresh from the Eastern Front where he had delivered a brilliant and successful counter-stroke against the Red Army in Latvia at the end of August. Thereupon, Manteuffel had been given command of the reconstituted Fifth Panzer Army and entrusted with the task of delivering the counter-offensive against Patton's southern flank.

The Americans were not yet aware of Manteuffel's arrival but they did know, as the SHAEF Intelligence Summary noted on September 16th, that the Moselle front " was receiving the highest priority for the allocation of both offensive and defensive type units." Patton also knew that six fresh or rebuilt divisions and four new panzer brigades had been identified on his front and that behind them lay the Maginot Line and the strongest sector of the Siegfried Line—the sector covering the Saar.

In his eagerness to maintain the advance of Third Army through the Saar to Frankfurt, Bradley had missed the opportunity of outflanking the Siegfried Line north of Aachen or of making a breach in its most vulnerable sector (between Aachen and Trier) where, as Model had reported on September 8th, " a very thin and totally inadequate defence line " was held by " only seven or eight battalions on a front of 120 kilometres." Instead, pursuing the direct approach, Bradley had endeavoured to drive First U.S. Army through the Aachen Gap, one of the traditional routes into Germany. Von Rundstedt had anticipated

[1]Patton, op. cit., p. 133.

this and, although Hitler had compelled him to send the bulk of his armour to the Moselle, he had strengthened the Aachen sector by giving it top priority in the allocation of infantry reinforcements. By September 17th this sector was holding firm and further reserves were en route there. The possibility of First U.S. Army gaining an early or significant success had gone.

Thus within three weeks of the fall of Paris and the overwhelming defeat of the German Armies in the Battle of France, the Wehrmacht had almost recovered its balance; at all events, it was no longer ' on the run.' The Germans were again holding a coherent line—admittedly thin and taut and with meagre reserves behind it—but a line nevertheless. And, because of their successful defence and demolition of the Channel ports and the approaches to Antwerp, they were denying to Eisenhower the supplies with which to maintain the full momentum of his advance. He, in turn, had unwittingly aided their recovery by his reluctance to concentrate the bulk of his logistic resources behind a single thrust at the Ruhr. Even when he had at last determined upon this course, he had not been able to give his northern armies the priority they required, for he had failed to impose his will on the evasive Bradley or the intransigent Patton.

When D-Day came for Operation MARKET GARDEN, although Eisenhower now had 52 divisions under his command, his sole chance of retaining the initiative, of recreating conditions of mobile warfare and of dealing a decisive blow at the Wehrmacht in the West that autumn rested with the three airborne divisions waiting at their airfields in England, and with the three divisions of XXX British Corps standing at the Dutch frontier. With them, though they could not know it, lay the last, slender chance of ending the German war in 1944.

## CHAPTER XXVI

# THE ROAD TO ARNHEM

SUNDAY, September 17th, was fine but overcast. There was little wind and the clouds were high, ideal weather for an airborne drop. By noon more than a thousand troop-carriers and nearly five hundred gliders were heading for Holland, for the greatest airborne operation ever undertaken. This aerial armada carried the best part of three divisions which were to be dropped along the line Eindhoven–Nijmegen–Arnhem with the task of capturing the road bridges over the Maas, the Waal and the Neder Rijn and over five other waterways, thus clearing a corridor for the armoured and motorised columns that were to drive north from the Meuse–Escaut Canal to the Zuider Zee. With this one sabre-stroke Montgomery intended to cut Holland in two, outflank the Siegfried Line and establish Second Army beyond the Rhine on the northern threshold of the Ruhr. If all were to go well, the armour would reach the Zuider Zee on the fourth or fifth day, but the hazards were great—especially for the airborne forces.

Because they were to form a corridor fifty miles long, the three divisions had to be landed in depth:

The 101st American (Major-General Maxwell Taylor) between Veghel and Zon, north of Eindhoven;

the 82nd American (Major-General James Gavin) between the Maas and the Waal, south of Nijmegen;

the 1st British (Major-General R. E. Urquhart) beyond the Neder Rijn, west of Arnhem.

The 1st and 82nd Divisions were to operate under command of H.Q. I British Airborne Corps (Lieut.-General F. A. M. Browning), which was also to land south of Nijmegen. A fourth division, 52nd Lowland, was available to be brought in by Dakota as soon as an airfield had been captured.

No such deep penetration, no such mass landing in daylight had ever been attempted. Holland was thick with flak. The Luftwaffe had ample bases within easy range, and its jet-aircraft had recently made their debut. The whole force might be crippled before it even landed. Blown bridges might check the relieving armour, or the slender corridor might be cut behind it, leaving the forward troops stranded. It was a gamble. The dividend could be high but the margin would be narrow.

The greatest danger was the weather, for there were not sufficient transport aircraft to carry the full strength of all three divisions in one ' lift.' With some five hundred aircraft (tugs and troop-carriers) available for each division, it was decided that on the first day both the 82nd and the 101st should land their three parachute regiments,[1] and that 1st Airborne should bring in one parachute brigade and the bulk of its air-landing brigade. When provision had been made for these, and for essential service troops, there was little room for either field or anti-tank artillery.

On D plus 1 and D plus 2 the Americans were to receive their glider-borne artillery and infantry, while two more parachute brigades (one British and one Polish) and the rest of the 1st Airborne Division were to be landed near Arnhem. It was vital, therefore, that there should be fair weather for at least two days so that the airborne divisions could be re-supplied and brought up to full strength.

This was a matter of particular concern to the British division for there was a fundamental weakness in its plan. The outstanding lesson of the Normandy operations was that airborne landings should be made on or hard by the objective, especially when that is a bridge. This had been amply proved by Gale, and the opinion of experienced Allied commanders, such as Gavin, was that " it is in general better to take landing losses and land on the objective than to have to fight after landing in order to reach the objective."[2]

In making the Arnhem plan this lesson was not observed, because the expert advice which Urquhart received was that heavy losses would be suffered if he attempted to make his initial landings south of the river close to the Arnhem bridge. The flak, it was said, would be intense, and the fenland here too soft for the landing of gliders. It was difficult for Urquhart to overrule this expert opinion, since he had no previous experience of airborne operations. Moreover, he had inherited a division which had suffered heavily in Sicily because its landings had been scattered and strongly opposed. Since then, the doctrine had grown up within the division that it was more important to land accurately and safely than to land close to the objective. Urquhart seems to have been influenced by this doctrine, for he accepted the view that the only feasible dropping and landing areas were north of the river, *six to eight miles west of the Arnhem road bridge which was his principal objective.*

The risk of frustration, inherent in landing so far away, was the greater because the whole division could not arrive in one ' lift.' Had

---

[1] An American parachute regiment was roughly the equivalent in strength of a British parachute brigade.

[2] James M. Gavin, *Airborne Warfare*, p. 81.

this been possible, Urquhart could have planned to move against the bridge with his force concentrated and then to seize a dropping-zone for re-supply south of the river. But, because his force was to arrive in three instalments, he decided that he must deploy the air-landing brigade outside Arnhem to protect the DZ-LZ area at least until the second ' lift ' came in on D plus 1. This meant that during the first critical afternoon he would be able to send to the Arnhem bridge only his lightly-armed parachute battalions and his reconnaissance squadron, and that another twenty-four hours must elapse before the main strength of the division would be available to reinforce the paratroops in the town. Thus the plan appeared to sacrifice the advantage of surprise and to expose Urquhart's divided force to the danger of destruction in detail. Consequently, the success of his operations seemed to rest, even more than did those of the American divisions, on continued fine weather and a slow enemy reaction.

There was a similar, though not so serious, weakness in the plan of the 82nd Division, but in this case it was unavoidable. Gavin had four major objectives: the bridges at Grave, at Nijmegen and over the Maas–Waal Canal, and the Groesbeek Ridge which runs along the German frontier dominating the area between the Maas and the Waal. These objectives were so widely separated that Gavin could not expect to secure them all with the forces which would be available to him in the first twenty-four hours. He decided, therefore, to concentrate his initial landings around Grave and Groesbeek, for Browning, the Corps Commander, had ordered him " not to attempt the seizure of the Nijmegen bridge until all other missions had been accomplished." This was sound, for that bridge would be of little use if Gavin failed to secure the bridges leading to it or the high ground that was essential to its defence.

Next to the weather, the greatest danger was that the relieving forces would not be able to advance rapidly enough to reinforce the airborne troops before they were counter-attacked by German units more heavily armed than themselves. Second Army now had three corps along the Meuse–Escaut Canal, but VIII Corps on the right was not yet ready to attack and XII Corps on the left was facing a belt of difficult, marshy country.[1] Moreover, there were sufficient supplies forward to maintain a deep penetration only by XXX Corps.

The relief of the airborne forces depended, therefore, on Horrocks's

[1]Once the airborne forces had landed, the Order of Battle of Second Army was to be:

| VIII CORPS | XXX CORPS | XII CORPS | I AIRBORNE CORPS |
|---|---|---|---|
| 11th Armd. Div. | Gds. Armd. Div. | 7th Armd. Div. | 1st Br. Airborne Div. |
| 3rd Inf. Div. | 43rd Inf. Div. | 15th Inf. Div. | 82nd U.S. |
| | 50th Inf. Div. | 53rd Inf. Div. | Airborne Div. |
| | 8th Armd. Bde. | 4th Armd. Bde. | 52nd Lowland Div. |
| | 101st U.S. | | (Air-portable) |
| | Airborne Div. | | |

three divisions and especially on Guards Armoured. From its bridgehead on the Meuse–Escaut Canal, however, there was only one clear route for the armour and there was every possibility that its advance would be checked, if not stopped, at one of the many water obstacles which lay athwart the road. In case some bridges should be blown, Horrocks had made elaborate preparations to bring forward columns of bridging material, DUKWs and assault-boats, but the task of moving these heavy columns and the necessary infantry and artillery along one road was indeed formidable. Since the Corps plan required the movement through the tenuous 'airborne corridor' of some twenty thousand vehicles, the success of the whole operation might well turn on the maintenance of the flow of transport by efficient traffic control and good driving.

For Browning, then, the vital questions were: Would the weather hold until his airborne reinforcements arrived? Would XXX Corps get through the corridor faster than the Germans could move against it?

These dangers were fully appreciated by Montgomery, but he hoped that the very violence and magnitude of the assault would leave the Germans so shaken and confused that they would not react with sufficient speed or strength. Second Army Intelligence estimated that the forces immediately opposing XXX Corps amounted to six infantry battalions supported by twenty tanks and twenty-five guns, including a dozen '88s'. The crust was expected to be hard but brittle, and behind it, so far as Second Army knew, there were only meagre reserves. Dutch Resistance sources reported that there were a half a dozen low-grade battalions in the Nijmegen area and that some battered panzer units from France were refitting north of Arnhem. It was suspected by British Intelligence that these might be the survivors of the 9th and 10th SS Panzer Divisions, which had not been identified by contact since the start of the month.[1] Even if this were so, it appeared to be unlikely that the two divisions together would amount to more than one motor brigade and one armoured brigade. Nevertheless, it was certain that the Germans would strike back with all the forces they could muster, for Southern Holland had to be held if they were to maintain their communications with the forces blocking the approaches to Antwerp and with the launching sites in The Hague, from which V.2s were already being fired on London.

The Allied air fleet flew into Holland protected by 1,240 fighters. The way was prepared for it by more than 1,000 bombers which struck at enemy anti-aircraft batteries along the route and around the dropping-zone. There was little sign of the Luftwaffe, except for 15 FW190s encountered over Wesel. Since the previous evening Bomber Command

[1]On September 15th the following message was received in London by radio from the Dutch Resistance: " SS Div. Hohenstrufl [sic] along Ijssel, sub-units observed between Arnhem and Zutphen and along Zutphen–Apeldoorn road. . . . Along Ijssel work on field fortifications in progress." This report, however, did not get through to the airborne forces in time to affect the plan.

and the Eighth Air Force had attacked the fighter bases from which the Germans could have intervened, but this was not the principal reason for the Luftwaffe's absence. The Allied air offensive against the synthetic oil refineries had been renewed during the past week, and the bulk of the German fighter force was concentrated in Central and Southern Germany. That afternoon not one British troop-carrying aircraft or glider was lost by enemy action, and the casualties suffered by the Americans (35 transports and 13 gliders) were almost entirely due to flak. Altogether, 4,600 aircraft of all kinds took part in the airborne operation on this day alone, and of these only 73 were shot down.[1] Both the Luftwaffe and the ground forces were taken by surprise.

If there was any German commander who should have foreseen this airborne assault, it was Student, whose First Parachute Army was holding the line of the Meuse–Escaut Canal. In his daily report to Model on the 16th, however, he had given no indication that he expected an airborne landing. He had merely said that " increased motor transport activity and confirmed armoured preparations strengthen the appreciation . . . that a heavy attack must be expected very shortly." On the 17th Student's H.Q. was in a cottage at Vught, only eight miles west of one of the American dropping-zones. " About noon," he says, " I was disturbed at my desk by a roaring in the air of such mounting intensity that I left my study and went on to the balcony. Wherever I looked I saw aircraft; troop-carriers and large aircraft towing gliders. An immense stream passed low over the house. I was greatly impressed but during these minutes I did not think of the danger of the situation."[2] He was moved more by envy than fear and, as he watched, he said to his Chief of Staff: " Oh, how I wish that I had ever had such powerful means at my disposal! " The wheel had gone full circle since Student himself had planned and led the airborne assault on Rotterdam four years earlier.

Student was not the only German commander who had a ' ringside seat ' for the airborne landing. Model was even closer, for his Tactical H.Q. was at Oosterbeek on the western edge of Arnhem. As the British parachutists floated down above and around him, Model did not wait

[1]The forces involved were the following:

| COMBAT AIRCRAFT | | | TRANSPORT AIRCRAFT | | |
| --- | --- | --- | --- | --- | --- |
| | U.S. | British | | Troop-carriers | Gliders |
| Bombers - - | 891 | 222 | 1st British - - | 155 | 358 |
| Fighters - - | 869 | 371 | 82nd U.S. - - | 482 | 50 |
| Fighter-Bombers | 212 | — | 101st U.S. - - | 436 | 70 |
| | | | Corps H.Q. - - | — | 13 |

(These figures do not include the aircraft of 2nd T.A.F. which, in support of the break-out by XXX Corps, flew 550 sorties.)

[2]Interrogation (Liddell Hart). The SS Commander in Holland, Rauter, reports that when he suggested to Model the possibility of an airborne landing the Field-Marshal replied: " Montgomery is a very cautious general, not inclined to plunge into mad adventures." (Netherlands War Ministry Interrogation.)

to watch. He drove post-haste into Arnhem and there, finding that the local garrison commander had been killed in an air raid, he took command himself, quickly restored order and called in reinforcements from the 9th SS Panzer Division which, as the Dutch had reported, was stationed north of Arnhem.

Thus it was that by a double twist of fortune the two Germans primarily responsible for the defence of Holland found themselves so placed that they could act at once to counter the advantage the Allies had won by gaining surprise. Nor was this all. The German reserves were slender, but Model and Student soon knew exactly where to use them. Early that afternoon an American glider was shot down close to Vught, and, says Student, " a few hours later the orders for the complete airborne operation were on my desk."[1]

By half-past one that afternoon the sky over Arnhem, Nijmegen and Veghel was filled with the throb of engines which drowned the soft sigh of gliders swooping in to land. In half a dozen towns and villages eager, grateful people rushed out to greet the airborne troops with flowers, and with food they could ill spare. But in most places the celebrations were cut short by the onset of battle and people fled from gay streets to anxious cellars.

West of Arnhem the paratroops and gliders of the 1st British Airborne Division landed accurately and with little interference from the enemy. Although none of Urquhart's 358 gliders were shot down, 38 failed to arrive. In nearly every case the reason was that the tow-rope broke—a common cause of mishaps in airborne operations—but it was particularly unfortunate that in the missing gliders were most of the armoured jeeps of the Reconnaissance Squadron which was to have rushed the road and rail bridges and seized them by *coup de main*. This was a bad start, but, while the 1st Air-Landing Brigade (Brigadier P. H. W. Hicks) organised the defence of the dropping-zones, the 1st Parachute Brigade (Brigadier G. W. Lathbury) assembled quickly and within an hour of landing was en route for Arnhem.

The drive for the bridges was led by Lt.-Col. J. D. Frost with the 2nd Parachute Battalion which moved smartly along the road that

[1] It was this series of mischances, not the betrayal of the plan, that accounted for the swift German reaction. In a series of articles in the London *Sunday Dispatch* in April and May 1950, however, Colonel O. Pinto (the wartime head of Dutch counter-espionage at SHAEF) alleged that the Germans were forewarned by a Dutchman, Christian Lindemans, who had been a Resistance Leader until he was suborned by the Abwehr in March 1944. It is true that Lindemans, after returning from Brussels on September 15th, warned the Chief of the Abwehr in Holland (Giskes) that the British were about to attack and would land airborne troops at Eindhoven on the 17th. Giskes has declared, however, that Lindemans " did not mention Arnhem . . . obviously because the objective of the planned air-ground offensive was not known to him." Nor did the Germans profit by such information as Lindemans provided, for Student has admitted that he was " completely surprised." The presence of 9th and 10th SS Panzer Divisions in the Arnhem–Nijmegen–Deventer area was the result of orders issued on September 8th, a week before Lindemans reported to Giskes.

followed the north bank of the Neder Rijn. Frost sent C Company to
seize the railway bridge, but just as his troops got there it was blown,
seeming, says one eyewitness, " to curl back on us." The other two
companies pressed on, but at Den Brink, less than two miles from the
road bridge, they encountered such strong opposition that Frost had to
detach B Company to deal with it.

While these operations were in progress, the road bridge lay unguarded.
During the afternoon its garrison, some twenty-five men of First War
vintage, had fled, and at 7.30 p.m. a Dutch policeman[1] found the defences

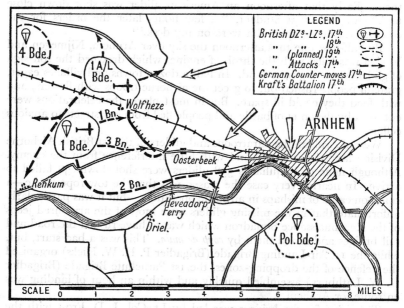

THE ARNHEM LANDING, SEPTEMBER 17TH

deserted. From his post at the northern end of the bridge he looked
anxiously westward for the first sign of the paratroops, but, even as they
appeared in the September dusk, a party of SS troops drove up from the
direction of Nijmegen and secured the southern end. Shortly after eight
o'clock Frost—with A Company, his H.Q. and some sappers—took
possession of the buildings around the northern approaches, but when
he sent a platoon to storm the German positions on the south side, it was
thwarted by fire from flak guns and an armoured car. Before long Frost
was joined by most of B Company and by part of Brigade H.Q., but,

[1]Constable van Kuijk. To him and other members of the Arnhem police force, and
to Charles Labouchère of the Dutch Resistance, I am indebted for information about the
condition and reaction of the Germans in Arnhem during the battle.

having only five hundred men and one anti-tank gun, he could do no more than hold his ground and wait for reinforcements. That night the great steel span was No-Man's-Land.

Meanwhile, the rest of the 1st Parachute Brigade, following on Frost's northern flank, had become heavily engaged within two miles of the DZ. SS Training Battalion Kraft (425 strong) which had arrived in the Oosterbeek–Wolfheze area only the day before, held up the advance of both the 1st and 3rd Parachute Battalions, and gave time for a battlegroup of 9th SS, dispatched by Model, to take up blocking positions north of Oosterbeek, and between that suburb and Arnhem. Since this battlegroup contained half a dozen tanks and some armoured cars, the paratroops could not drive it off. One company managed to slip through to the bridge after dark, but the rest of the brigade made little progress.

During the night Urquhart and Lathbury were stranded at the H.Q. of the 3rd Battalion, and so did not realise that the overall situation was already becoming precarious. The Germans, thanks to Model's personal intervention, had responded more quickly and more strongly than could reasonably have been anticipated. Because of this, the five hundred paratroops at the bridge were now isolated. Five miles to the west the other two parachute battalions, fighting separate battles, could not develop a concerted thrust. They were only a mile apart but, owing to a wireless failure, they had no communication with each other. Farther west, the air-landing brigade was widely dispersed in defence of the DZ–LZ area. Here Hicks had his own three battalions (less two companies which were coming with the second ' lift ') and a battalion of the Glider Pilot Regiment which was to prove in the course of the battle the value of the British policy of training glider crews to fight as infantry. If this brigade could have been committed that night it might have broken through to the bridge before the Germans could establish their blocking force, but Urquhart's plan required Hicks to stay where he was, awaiting the reinforcements that were due to arrive at ten o'clock next morning.

While the British were thus heavily involved at Arnhem, the Americans in the Nijmegen–Eindhoven stretch of the ' corridor,' finding less opposition, enjoyed more success. They met few Germans near the dropping-zones and most of these fled in panic. By dropping astride the Maas bridge at Grave, one battalion of the 82nd gained this vital objective within an hour of landing. Before dark Gavin's troops had secured the route into Nijmegen by capturing one of the bridges over the Maas–Waal Canal and establishing a cordon across the neck of the rivers along the Groesbeek ridge. Having secured his ' air-head,' Gavin sent the only battalion he could spare into Nijmegen to test out the defences of the massive bridge that spans the Waal. Four hundred yards from the southern end, however, the paratroops were checked, for the German garrison had already formed a tight perimeter to protect the bridge.

South of the Maas, the 101st Division had a rough passage through the flak defences around Eindhoven but, once on the ground, the Americans had a comparatively clear run. In Veghel they took all four bridges intact, but their southernmost objective, the bridge over the Wilhelmina Canal at Zon, was blown in their faces. Nevertheless, one parachute regiment scrambled across the canal during the night and by dawn was approaching Eindhoven, where it was due to link up with the armour advancing from the south.

At 1330 hours on the afternoon of the 17th, Horrocks was standing on a slag-heap beside the Meuse–Escaut Canal a few yards from 'Joe's Bridge.' He had just received word that the airborne drop was going ' according to plan,' and had therefore given orders for the ground attack to begin at 1435 hours. For some time his powerful field-glasses had been sweeping the northern skies but now they were trained along the straight white concrete road that led to Eindhoven. On this one road the success of his whole plan depended. Down this road the entire Corps had to move. Along this road the Guards Armoured Division had to break out.

Five hundred yards north of the Dutch border the Germans had set up a barricade across the road, but Horrocks calculated that because the road was concrete there would be no anti-tank mines embedded in its surface. He planned, therefore, to breach the German defences by the simple ruse of sending an armoured column straight down the road to blast and batter the barricade away and burst into Holland on a one-tank front. Behind the leading squadron were to come two more, carrying infantry on the backs of their tanks and in the wake of this spearhead the rest of the Guards were to follow in close order.

There was no other way north, nor was there any scope for armoured manœuvre, since the ground on either side was soft and swampy. The tanks would have to stay on the road and this would take them through a series of cypress plantations which provided natural cover for anti-tank guns and bazookas. There was no time to send infantry to clear these plantations. They would have to be neutralised by concentrations of fire from artillery and aircraft, concentrations so close and intense that the defenders on either side of the road would be driven from their weapons while the tanks went through. Such was the plan.

Ten minutes before H-Hour the guns of XXX Corps began putting down a rolling barrage one mile wide and five miles deep along the Eindhoven road. From the air a constant stream of Typhoons reinforced the barrage, skimming down to the tops of the trees before firing their rockets and machine-guns. Eight Typhoons from 83 Group arrived every five minutes and as each aircraft made several ' strikes ' it appeared to the onlooker that the stream was continuous. After the first half-hour a ' cab-rank ' of eight Typhoons was on call overhead all the time.

As the tanks of the Irish Guards rolled forward up the road, the

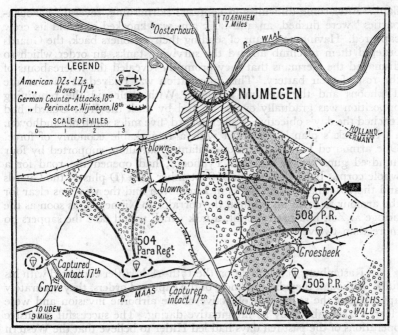

THE NIJMEGEN 'AIR-HEAD,' SEPTEMBER 17TH-18TH

Typhoon pilots were directed to their targets by radio from an armoured half-track, moving with the column. The white road, standing out against the dark pines, was easily identified, and all the tanks carried fluorescent orange screens which were plainly visible from the air and were soon to be hailed by the Dutch people as banners of liberation. The Typhoons were so efficiently directed that they were able to strike at targets within 200 yards of the tanks.

The Germans were so subdued by this onslaught that the leading squadron of Irish Guards, having shot its way through the barricade, was able to drive on beyond the first belt of woods without mishap. Nevertheless, the enemy (parachutists on one side of the road and SS troops on the other[1]) recovered quickly and, when the first of the squadrons carrying infantry tried to follow, it came under heavy fire, especially from bazookas. Eight of its tanks were quickly 'brewed up,' but the infantry jumped clear and began scouring the woods on either

[1]The Germans had concentrated five battalions to defend the road: two from the 6th Para. Regiment, one from 9th SS, one from 10th SS, and Penal Battalion No. 6—a unit in which convicts were given the opportunity of regaining their civil rights. Captured documents revealed that these units were organised into an *ad hoc* formation, 'Division Walther.'

flank. After some difficult and confused skirmishing, several 'bazooka-parties' were flushed, an anti-tank gun was knocked out and its crew captured. Having no means of sending their prisoners back, the Guards ordered them to climb aboard the surviving tanks, an order which so dismayed the Germans that they promptly revealed the whereabouts of the rest of their battery. This information was relayed at once to the Typhoons and the medium artillery. With their aid the remaining opposition was gradually overcome and by dusk the Irish Guards had reached the day's objective, Valkenswaard, five miles south of Eindhoven.

Horrocks's plan had worked with a remarkable economy of force. One armoured battalion and one infantry battalion, supported by four hundred guns and a hundred Typhoons, had opened the road for a whole corps. By the afternoon of September 18th (D plus 1) the Guards and the 101st had joined forces in Eindhoven and the way was clear for the armour to drive on through the corridor to Nijmegen, as soon as the bridge at Zon had been rebuilt, a task which would take the sappers no more than twelve hours.

In Rastenburg at midnight on the 17th–18th Hitler conferred with his staff. Although they did not know of the captured orders, they accurately appreciated the scope and objective of the airborne invasion and were clearly taken aback by its imaginative daring. The successful defensive operations of the past ten days had led Hitler to believe that the Western Allies had been halted, and that for the moment he could safely concentrate on repairing the breach in his Eastern Front caused by the collapse of Rumania. He was now faced with a situation which, he admitted, was "much more serious than that in the East," but it is apparent from the record[1] of this conference that there was not a single field division he could send at once to Holland. Jodl reported that the 59th Division, which had just been withdrawn across the Scheldt Estuary, was moving against the corridor from the west, and that the 107th Panzer Brigade, which was travelling by train from East Prussia to Aachen, had been re-routed to Venlo and would attack from the east. 'Emergency units' were being formed throughout Holland and Western Germany; two scratch divisions were already in the Reichswald–Venlo area south-east of Nijmegen; and in the course of a few days the Home Army would be able to provide two depot divisions, though these would be made up of low-grade troops.

The only fresh resources which Hitler could throw into the battle immediately were those of the Luftwaffe. On the 17th his jet-propelled fighter-bombers (Me 262s) had been unable to intervene because their airfields near Rheine had been severely bombed. Hitler was now informed, however, that these bases were being rapidly repaired, and that two fighter *Geschwader* had already been transferred from Berlin to

[1]Führer Conferences, Fragment 42, September 17th, 1944.

Western Germany and would be fit for action over Holland on the day that had just begun, September 18th.

That morning the aerial convoys which left England were much more vulnerable than those which had flown in the day before, for this second ' lift ' was made up almost entirely of tugs and gliders—slow, unwieldy combinations incapable of protecting themselves by violent evasive action. Nevertheless, their fighter screen was so vigilant and strong that of the 1,203 gliders which took off from England only 13 were shot down. It was the weather, not the Luftwaffe, that prevented the timely arrival of these reinforcements.

In England thick fog, lying heavy on the airfields, had delayed the departure of the gliders and transports. In Holland it was an anxious morning for the airborne troops on the ground. The Germans counter-attacked from the Reichswald and overran the landing-zones of the 82nd Division just before the gliders were due to arrive. There was no opportunity of warning or re-directing the pilots, and Gavin was unaware that his reinforcements had left England two hours late. Expecting the gliders to appear overhead any minute, the Americans counter-attacked in desperate fury and drove the Germans back with half an hour to spare. Even so, the gliders landed under fire and it took all the men Gavin could muster to hold the enemy off. The late arrival of the glider-borne troops saved them from heavy casualties, but it destroyed any chance there had been of capturing the Nijmegen bridge that day.

At Arnhem the delay, and its consequences, were yet more serious. Grounded even longer than the Americans had been, the British troop-carriers and gliders did not arrive until three o'clock, five hours late. By this time the two parachute battalions, which had been checked near Oosterbeek the night before, had forced an entry into Arnhem, but had been cut to pieces in a series of bitter actions around the Elizabeth Hospital, and their combined strength had been reduced to less than 250. They had neither the troops nor the ammunition to break through to the bridge, where Frost with no more than 600 men was still maintaining a gallant but precarious foothold at the northern end.

That morning his troops had effectively blocked the bridge by knocking out six armoured half-tracks which tried to rush through from the south. This road-block was covered by British fire from buildings beside the northern approach to the bridge, but late in the afternoon the Germans counter-attacked with infantry and tanks, and the para-troops had to yield ground when four of the houses they were holding were set alight. By the mere process of burning down the buildings, the Germans were bound to overpower the defenders before long unless substantial reinforcements could get through to them from Nijmegen or from the rest of their own division.

On the evening of this day (Monday, September 18th) the situation north of the Neder Rijn was extremely confused. In Arnhem itself the 1st Parachute Brigade, apart from Frost's battalion, was fast disintegrating. Early that morning Lathbury, the Brigade commander, and Urquhart had tried to reach the troops in the town, but had been cut off and compelled to take cover until the late afternoon. Then, as they sought to make their way back to Oosterbeek, Lathbury was wounded. Urquhart and another officer left him in the care of Dutch civilians, but were themselves forced to hide in the loft of a house. Even after dark, they could not escape, for there were Germans all around and an S.P. gun was stationed in the street outside.

In Urquhart's absence, Hicks (of the air-landing brigade) took command of the division, but he had no contact, even by radio, with Urquhart, Lathbury, Frost or any elements of 1st Parachute Brigade. This was partly due to the use of sets which would not work efficiently in a built-up area, and partly to the fact that a powerful British station was operating on the same frequency that had been allocated to the divisional command net. The frequency had to be changed, but the units isolated in Arnhem could not be advised, nor could they be heard on the old frequency. More serious still was the breakdown of communications with the outside world. Hicks urgently needed air support to deal with German tanks, but he could not call for it, as planned. The wireless link to the R.A.F. was not working, and he could not establish contact either with Airborne Base in England or with Browning's Corps H.Q. only 15 miles away.

For information about events in the town Hicks had to rely on reports from members of the Dutch Resistance who had seized the local telephone exchange. These reports cannot have revealed the full gravity of the situation in Arnhem, for Hicks continued to give prior consideration to the security of the ' air-head.' Into Arnhem he sent only two of his seven battalions, and he directed the newly-arrived 4th Parachute Brigade (Brigadier J. W. Hackett) to drive the Germans from the high ground north of Oosterbeek and thus strengthen the divisional perimeter. This attack proved to be a costly diversion of effort. The Germans were strongly entrenched in the woods and two parachute battalions lost half their strength in one day's fighting.

The battalions which headed for the bridge suffered even more heavily. It took them thirteen hours to cover three miles and, although they reached the Elizabeth Hospital and the survivors of 1st Parachute Brigade, they could advance no farther. Nor could any reinforcements get through to them. On the following day (Tuesday the 19th) this beleaguered force attacked and attacked in the hope of forcing a passage to the bridge, but German tanks and S.P. guns were covering every approach. When their anti-tank ammunition was exhausted, the airborne troops were driven back street by street through Oosterbeek to Hartenstein, where Urquhart, again in command, was forming a tight perimeter. There he hoped to stand his ground and conserve his strength until the arrival of XXX Corps.

The possibility of 1st Airborne being reinforced, or even re-supplied, by air was now remote, for it was not holding a large enough dropping area and the Germans had greatly increased their flak and fighter defences. That afternoon bad weather, and the appearance of more than five hundred enemy fighters, disrupted the reinforcement plan. Because of thick fog in the Midlands, the Polish Parachute Brigade and the glider infantry regiment of the 82nd Division were not able to leave their airfields. Some 655 troop-carriers and 431 gliders did take off from other bases, but only 60 per cent reached their destinations, and of those that failed to get through 112 gliders and 40 transports were lost. Worst of all, 390 tons of ammunition and food, dropped by parachute for 1st Airborne, fell almost entirely into enemy hands. The prearranged Supply Dropping Point was not located within the original landing area and the division had not been able to capture it. Urquhart had sent a signal suggesting a new dropping area but this had not been received in England.

The non-arrival of the Polish Brigade removed the last chance of any airborne forces coming to the rescue of the paratroops at the bridge in Arnhem. Since the previous morning, when a troop of anti-tank guns had broken through to him, Frost had been completely cut off. Nevertheless, he was still preventing the Germans from using the Arnhem bridge as a route for sending reinforcements to Nijmegen. But now, on the Tuesday evening, his situation was becoming desperate. His men were holding only a dozen houses and a school, and these were being heavily mortared and shelled. The cellars were filled with wounded. The surrounding houses were ablaze. The anti-tank ammunition was almost spent, and the four hundred men still fit to fight could no longer drive off the tanks which were systematically demolishing their positions. And yet they fought on, withdrawing only when the buildings they held were set afire; still hoping that help might come from Oosterbeek, and not knowing that this hope was gone, for they had been out of radio communication since the Sunday evening.

On the morning of Wednesday, September 20th, they regained contact with Divisional H.Q. through the Arnhem exchange, which was still being operated by Dutch patriots. Only then did Frost learn that there was no hope of rescue or relief unless he could hold out until the ground forces reached him from Nijmegen. There that day a combined attack was to be made upon the Waal bridge by the 82nd and the Guards who had strict instructions that the road to Arnhem must be opened at all costs.

On the morning of Tuesday, the 19th, the Grenadier Guards Group, the spearhead of their division, had driven rapidly through the corridor from Zon to the woods south of Nijmegen. There, however, they had found the Americans so hard pressed by attacks from the Reichswald that no move could be made against the Nijmegen bridges until mid-afternoon. Even then, Gavin could spare only one parachute battalion to operate with the Guards, for, as already mentioned, his glider infantry regiment had not been able to leave England. Since the road and rail bridges were both intact, a column was directed against each, but neither column could penetrate the defences which the Germans had had ample time to prepare.

All the approaches to the road bridge ran through some gardens, called Huner Park, which the Dutch had fortified before the war and had held for three days in 1940. The Germans in turn had strengthened the defences of the park, especially those of an old mediæval fort and a large wooded knoll, the Valkhof. At the southern edge of the Huner Park the Anglo-American attack was halted. Tanks which tried to rush the bridge were knocked out. Guardsmen and parachutists who tried to infiltrate through the defences were cut off. That night, as Allied troops waited within reach of this great prize, they expected to see it blown to destruction. They did not know that Model himself had given orders that the bridge was not to be blown. " Model," says Student, had " prohibited the demolition of the bridge in the belief that it could be successfully defended."

During the night of the 19th–20th, while a battlegroup of 10th SS was being ferried across the Neder Rijn to stiffen the Nijmegen garrison, Horrocks and Browning made a new plan, designed to give them full possession of the Nijmegen road bridge by simultaneous attacks from north and south. Next day an American parachute regiment (the 504th) was to cross the Waal a mile downstream and seize the northern end of the bridge in concert with an attack on the southern defences by the Grenadier Guards and a battalion of parachutists. First, however, the town of Nijmegen had to be cleared of Germans so that the assault troops could gain access to the south bank of the Waal.

This mopping-up took all the Wednesday morning and it was nearly three o'clock before the 504th were in position to launch their storm-boats into the fast-running river. The combined effect of the current and the severe enemy fire was such that only half the boats carrying the first wave reached the north bank. Undaunted, some two hundred men scrambled or swam ashore and established a slender foothold which was gradually reinforced and expanded as the afternoon wore on. This bold assault in clear daylight across a defended river, 400 yards wide, was a most brilliant and courageous feat of arms and was duly rewarded. By 6.30 the Americans had routed the opposition and were advancing towards the road bridge. En route, they secured the northern end of the railway bridge and there they raised the American flag.[1]

When this signal of success was seen by watchers on the southern bank, the Guards pressed home their attack. Here, in an afternoon of heavy fighting, while an American battalion was clearing the eastern

[1]When Dempsey saw Gavin after this exploit he said: " I am proud to meet the commander of the greatest division in the world to-day." That opinion was endorsed by many another British officer who saw the 82nd in action.

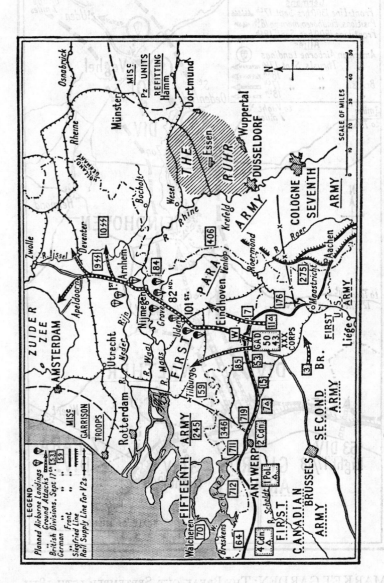

OPERATION MARKET GARDEN : THE PLAN

MARKET GARDEN: THE PLAN OF THE SEPTEMBER 17TH-18TH

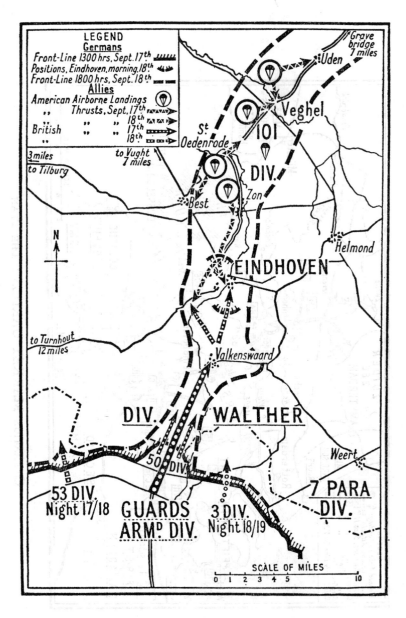

MARKET GARDEN: THE BREAK-OUT, SEPTEMBER 17TH-18TH

half of Huner Park, the Grenadiers had driven the Germans from the Valkhof and had taken the fort by storm. The capture of these two strongholds opened the way to the bridge. At dusk, shortly before seven o'clock, five British tanks drove through the park, paused to engage some '88s' shooting from the far bank, and then raced on with guns alive. Two tanks were hit by bazookas fired from the girders, but two others continued across the 600-yard length of the bridge, through the road-block at the northern end and beyond it to link up with the Americans who were just approaching from the west. The Nijmegen bridge was in Allied hands undamaged, and a straight red road ran north to Arnhem.

There by now the staunch defenders of the road bridge had been cut down from 600 to 140 and Frost himself had been wounded. His men were still fighting from half a dozen houses around the northern pylons, but they were no longer holding the school from which for nearly three days they had maintained their road-block, preventing the southward movement of armour and artillery. That afternoon, under point-blank fire from several tanks, the schoolhouse had collapsed in flames and its garrison had been driven into the open streets. Thus it was that three hours before the first British tank crossed the Nijmegen bridge, heading north, the first German tank crossed the Arnhem bridge, heading south.

During the night the Germans made good use of the bridge which had been denied them so long, and on the morning of Thursday, the 21st, R.A.F. reconnaissance reported that twenty tanks were moving south from Arnhem and that the Germans appeared to be establishing fresh defences between the Neder Rijn and the Waal astride the Arnhem–Nijmegen road. Nevertheless, Horrocks still hoped to secure a bridgehead over the Neder Rijn, link up with 1st Airborne and drive on to the Zuider Zee in fulfilment of the original plan. Owing to the breakdown of Urquhart's radio communications, however, Horrocks did not know how grave the situation really was.

At nine o'clock that morning, one of Horrocks's artillery units, the 64th Medium Regiment, had established radio contact with the airborne division and had obtained the first direct news from Arnhem since XXX Corps began its attack. Through this channel Urquhart, unaware that Frost's force had at last been overrun, reported:

> Enemy attacking main bridge in strength. Situation critical for slender force [there]. Enemy also attacking divisional position East from HEELSUM vicinity and West from ARNHEM. Situation serious but am forming close perimeter around HARTENSTEIN with remainder of division. Relief essential both areas earliest possible. Still retain control ferry-crossing HEVEADORP.

From this signal Horrocks naturally concluded that Urquhart had some troops at the bridge in Arnhem and had a foothold west of the town

large enough to be exploited, if quickly reinforced. He had already
ordered the Guards Armoured Division to strike north " as early as
possible and at maximum speed " along the main Arnhem road in the
hope of breaking through to the bridge before the enemy could organise
a new defence line. He now gave orders that, if the direct route were
blocked, the Guards should work round west of the main road and head
for the Heveadorp ferry. Arrangements had been made for dropping the
Polish Parachute Brigade that afternoon near Driel to secure the southern
end of the ferry, and it seemed that the Guards and the Poles together
should be able to secure a base from which infantry could cross the river
into Urquhart's perimeter. Then, with both banks in Allied hands, a
bridge could be built at the ferry-site.

The plan was clear but the resources to carry it out were not immediately available. North of the Maas, Horrocks had only two divisions,
the Guards and 82nd Airborne. Bad weather had so far prevented the
arrival of Gavin's glider infantry regiment, and the rest of the 82nd, with
the Coldstream Group in support, was fully engaged in defending the area
between the Maas and the Waal, where the Germans were making frequent
counter-attacks from the Reichswald flank.[1] In the Nijmegen bridgehead
Horrocks had one parachute regiment and two groups of Guards, but
the latter could not resume the offensive until they were relieved by
infantry of the 43rd Division which was only just crossing the Maas.

On the one road by which XXX Corps and the American airborne
divisions had to be reinforced and maintained traffic was moving slowly.
For most of the 45 miles between the Meuse–Escaut Canal and the River
Maas the roadway was narrow, and it passed through Eindhoven and
half a dozen villages and over two rebuilt bridges. Because this single
road was extremely vulnerable to air attack and artillery fire, the columns
were ordered to move with vehicles well spaced and, accordingly, it had
not been thought that they would be able to average more than ten
miles in the hour. This might have been adequate if a steady flow could
have been kept up, but an unexpected brake was imposed at the very
start of the corridor.

On the first evening two three-tonners, following the armour, had
been destroyed by mines which the Germans had laid in the grass verges
immediately beside their road-block. In passing through this, the two
trucks had gone off the concrete on to the grass and had been blown up.
Next morning the wreckage of these vehicles was seen by all drivers
moving north and, lest the warning should be disregarded, some over-
conscientious sapper had set up a notice: DON'T LET THIS HAPPEN TO
YOU. KEEP ON THE ROAD. VERGES NOT CLEARED OF MINES.

[1]Gavin was also handicapped by shortage of artillery ammunition, for the four
U.S. truck companies sent up from France to maintain the American airborne divisions
did not reach the Meuse–Escaut Canal until the 20th. It was then found that they were
loaded with the wrong type of 105 mm ammunition, and that some trucks had come up
empty!

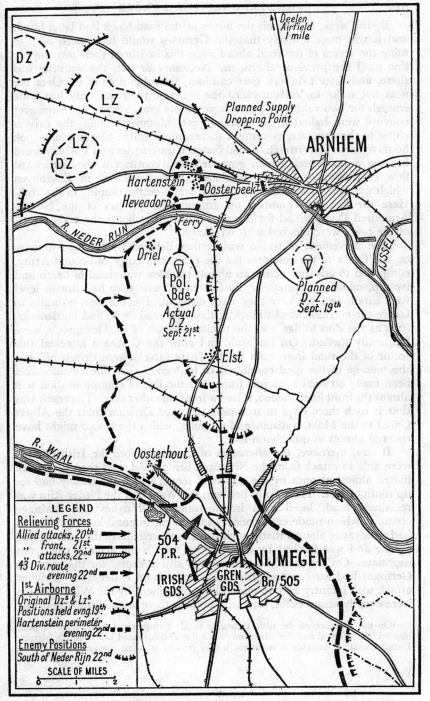

DZ

LZ

LZ

DZ

Deelen
Airfield
1 mile

Planned Supply
Dropping Point

**ARNHEM**

Hartenstein

Oosterbeek

Heveadorp

R. NEDER RIJN

Ferry

Driel

IJSSEL

Planned
D. Z.
Sept. 19th

Pol.
Bde.

Actual
D.Z.
Sept 21st

Elst

R. WAAL

Oosterhout

**LEGEND**

Relieving Forces
Allied attacks, 20th
    " front, 21st
    " attacks, 22nd
43 Div. route
    evening 22nd

1st Airborne
Original Dz.s & Lz.s
Positions held evng.19th
Hartenstein perimeter
    evening 22nd

Enemy Positions
South of Neder Rijn 22nd

SCALE OF MILES

0   1   2

504
P.R.

IRISH
GDS.

GREN.
GDS.

Bn/505

**NIJMEGEN**

THE ADVANCE TO THE NEDER RIJN, SEPTEMBER 20TH-25TH

By this time, in fact, all the mines at the road-block had been lifted, and it was most unlikely that the Germans would have been able to mine the verges of the road ahead since this had been their own supply line until the previous afternoon. Necessary or not, the warning was there, and British drivers, ever cautious, took due note of it. Over the next five miles to Valkenswaard the concrete road was only just wide enough for two vehicles. There were ample grass verges, but whenever convoys were halted to let more urgent columns through, the drivers clung to the concrete, creating a succession of traffic blocks which took hours to clear. The stretch of road between the frontier and Valkenswaard became a bottleneck which governed and constricted the northward flow of convoys.[1] Another bottleneck soon developed in Eindhoven which was heavily attacked by the Luftwaffe on the evening of the 19th. Here the Germans bombed an ammunition column of the Guards Armoured Division and for the next twenty-four hours the main streets of the town were blocked with wreckage.

The movement of traffic was further delayed by German activity on the flanks of the corridor, for the other two corps of Second Army, compelled to advance across an almost trackless wasteland of heath and swamp, made slow progress. By September 21st they had drawn level with Eindhoven but here they were checked. For the next 30 miles to Grave the corridor was little wider than the road itself, and bottlenecks, such as the Zon bridge and the tortuous streets of St. Oedenrode, were frequently shelled. On the 19th and 20th the Germans attacked this sector of the road from both sides. These attacks were driven off, but the passage of the road continued to be hazardous. The advance had been made on such a narrow front that the line of communication was almost the front line; indeed, it had a front on either side. The result was that it took three days to transport the 43rd Division from the Albert Canal to the Maas, a distance of 60 miles, which the troops might have covered almost as quickly on foot.

It was, therefore, the afternoon of the 21st before the Irish Guards were able to attack from the Nijmegen bridgehead, and then they were halted almost at once by the anti-tank screen which the enemy had set up south of Elst. The terrain between the Waal and the Neder Rijn was reclaimed land, laced with innumerable small dykes and drainage channels which made cross-country movement impossible. The Guards had to advance along a road which was raised well above the surrounding polder and was flanked by deep ditches which the armour could not negotiate. On the road the tanks were ' sitting shots ' for the guns the Germans had sited in orchards and farmyards on either side. A direct attack with infantry and an outflanking movement by the Welsh Guards were equally unsuccessful, primarily because there was so little supporting

---

[1] On the afternoon of the 18th, returning to file a dispatch, I found a traffic jam, two vehicles wide, almost the whole way from the Valkenswaard bridge to the Meuse-Escaut Canal. I was able to move south only by driving along the verge of the road.

fire. Owing to the shortage of ammunition, only one battery of artillery was available, and the Guards could not enlist the aid of the Typhoons as they had done so successfully on the first day. The aircraft were on call—in fact, they were overhead—but they could not be directed against the anti-tank guns, because the radio sets in the R.A.F. 'contact car' failed to work. This was a grave misfortune. Without the help of the Typhoons there was no chance of the tanks breaking through that afternoon to Arnhem.

While the Guards were halted in front of Elst, the Polish Parachute Brigade was dropped between Elst and Driel in the face of heavy opposition from flak and fighters. But, by the time the Poles reached the south bank of the Neder Rijn, the Heveadorp ferry had been sunk and the northern end of the ferry-site was in German hands. Urquhart's troops had been driven from it only two hours earlier.

On the previous day when Urquhart ordered his scattered and weakened battalions to withdraw inside the Hartenstein perimeter, some units, finding themselves cut off, had to fight their way in and lost heavily in the process. This was particularly the case with the 10th and 156th Parachute Battalions which had been trying to clear the woods north of Oosterbeek. When they reached the perimeter their combined strength was 135 men, fewer than ten per cent of those who had landed. Moreover, the Germans followed up so strongly that the 3,500 survivors of the division were compressed into an area 1,000 yards wide and 2,000 yards deep. This area was brought under heavy and continuous fire from three sides and was repeatedly attacked by infantry and armour. Thus, although some of the supplies dropped on the 21st fell inside the perimeter, it was almost impossible for the troops to collect them.

The only help that XXX Corps could give the airborne troops on this day came from the guns of the 64th Medium Regiment. Having established radio contact, the regiment was able to bring down considerable and accurate fire on German positions around the Hartenstein perimeter. This relieved the pressure, but that evening, with stocks of food and water almost exhausted and ammunition running low, Urquhart reported: "No knowledge elements of division in ARNHEM for twenty-four hours. Balance of division in very tight perimeter . . . our casualties heavy. Resources stretched to utmost. Relief within twenty-four hours vital."

Early on the morning of the 22nd Horrocks signalled, "43 Div. ordered to take all risks to effect relief today and are directed on ferry. If situation warrants you should withdraw to or cross ferry." Urquhart replied, "We shall be glad to see you."

Horrocks now abandoned the idea of breaking through to the Zuider Zee, but he still retained the hope that he might secure an adequate bridgehead beyond the Neder Rijn for subsequent exploitation when the corridor had been widened and fresh forces had been brought forward.

The plan for Friday, the 22nd, therefore, was that the 43rd Division (Major-General G. I. Thomas) should attack from the Nijmegen bridgehead at dawn with two brigades: one striking along the main road through Elst to Arnhem, and another, on its left, following a side road through Oosterhout to the Heveadorp ferry. As both these brigades had reached Nijmegen on the 21st, Horrocks assumed that, in execution of these orders, Thomas would move his troops across the Waal during the night so that they would be deployed to attack in strength at first light. This, however, was not done and the opportunity of surprising the enemy under cover of the early morning mist was lost. Taking advantage of that mist, armoured cars of the Household Cavalry drove through Oosterhout soon after seven o'clock and made contact with the Poles before Thomas's infantry had even begun their attack.

The mist had cleared when, at 8.30 a.m. on the 22nd, the 7th Somersets advanced towards Oosterhout supported by a squadron of tanks, a troop of 17-pounders, mortar and machine-gun platoons, a battery of self-propelled 25-pounders and a field regiment. An hour later, however, on reaching the outskirts of Oosterhout, the leading platoon was " held up by fire from a tank and some infantry "—to quote the battalion's own history.[1] The operation then proceeded according to the book, for Thomas had not told the C.O. " to take all risks." The platoon that had been halted was extricated under cover of smoke. Another company with a troop of tanks endeavoured to work round the village but was " held up by heavy mortar fire." These manœuvres occupied most of the morning.

In mid-afternoon, when a battalion attack was made, " resistance was not heavy and was quickly overcome. . . . By 1700 hours the village was clear." This was not surprising. The attack was supported by more than a hundred guns, and the garrison can hardly have been formidable, for Oosterhout yielded only " 139 prisoners, one quarter-master's store completely equipped, one Mark III tank, one 88 mm gun and five small A.A. guns." In the entire day's fighting, when the fate of the 1st Airborne Division and the saving of the whole operation were at stake, the Somerset's casualties amounted to " nineteen wounded."[2]

In fairness to the battalion, however, it must be said that they did no more than they had been trained to do. By nature Thomas was cautious and methodical and his troops followed his example. He was extremely thorough in the organisation of his attacks—so thorough that his battalions, like most of the infantry in Second Army, had come to believe that they could not advance without overwhelming fire support.[3]

[1]'The Story of the Seventh Battalion, the Somerset Light Infantry,' by Captain J. L. J. Meredith, p. 73.

[2]Ibid, p. 75.

[3]That evening, when I saw General Horrocks, he was inclined to excuse the 43rd's slowness, for he did not know how little opposition there had really been at Oosterhout. Thomas's chief of staff (Lt.-Col. David Meynell), however, said to me, " I rather think it is our fault. We have been slow."

There was considerable truth in the criticism the Germans had made in Normandy that British infantry sought " to occupy ground rather than to fight over it." The consequences of that policy were never more apparent than on this day at Oosterhout.

Near Driel that morning the Household Cavalry had picked up two officers sent back by Urquhart and had relayed the following message from him: " We are short of ammunition, men, food and medical supplies. DUKWs are essential, two or three would be sufficient. If supplies do not arrive tonight it may be too late." To this signal Horrocks replied, " Everything possible will be done to get the essentials through." Consequently, when he discovered that neither of Thomas's brigades had made any real progress, and that Elst was strongly held, he ordered him to concentrate on opening the road through Oosterhout. The moment the village was clear, Thomas was to dispatch to Heveadorp a strong mobile column carrying supplies for 1st Airborne. At 6 p.m. the column, made up of two infantry companies riding on tanks, carriers and DUKWs, drove through Oosterhout and went on to join the Poles in Driel. Moving nose to tail, the vehicles covered the ten miles in an hour, but darkness had fallen before they reached the river. It was then found that the banks were so steep and soft that the much-needed DUKWs could not be launched, and it was too late and too dark to reconnoitre firmer crossing places. No assault-boats were available and, although the troops toiled all night with improvised rafts, they were able to ferry across only fifty men of the Polish Brigade and a few small loads of food and ammunition.

It was now clear that a bridgehead could be established west of Arnhem only by a large-scale assault across the Neder Rijn, but the necessary troops and craft could not be brought forward immediately. Early that afternoon German tanks and infantry had cut the corridor between Veghel and Uden, thus isolating all forces north of the Maas. In consequence Horrocks was compelled to send the 32nd Guards Brigade back to reopen the road, a task which they, and American parachutists attacking from the south, were not able to accomplish until the following afternoon. This diversion of half the Guards Armoured Division to clear the corridor weakened the attack towards Arnhem. The direct road from Nijmegen was still blocked by the Germans in Elst and the minor route by which Thomas's troops had reached the Neder Rijn was under fire from Elst and was, in any case, unsuitable for heavy traffic.

On the evening of September 23rd, after ' aerial re-supply ' had again been thwarted by bad weather and enemy intervention, Urquhart signalled: " Morale still adequate but continued heavy mortaring and shelling is having obvious effects. We shall hold out but . . . hope for a brighter twenty-four hours ahead." That night, however, no major crossing of the Neder Rijn could be attempted, for 1st Airborne was so desperately in need of ammunition that the relieving forces had to concentrate on the ferrying of supplies. Between dusk and dawn only 250 Poles were able to cross the river and of these barely 150 reached the Hartenstein perimeter.

On Sunday the 24th—for the first time in the eight days since the start of MARKET GARDEN—the R.A.F. was able to provide strong air support for Urquhart's troops. Throughout the afternoon Typhoons struck at German positions around the perimeter and at enemy reinforcements moving towards it. This was the prelude to the assault-crossing, planned for that night, by Polish paratroops and the 4th Dorset. Inside the perimeter the writer of 1st Airborne's war diary noted, " Never was darkness more eagerly awaited." But darkness brought only disappointment. The attack was to have been launched at 10.30 p.m. but when the time came there were no assault boats available for the Poles and only four for the Dorsets. This was a direct consequence of the cutting of the road. After midnight, with these boats and five others that came up later, some 250 men crossed the river, a platoon at a time; but the swiftness of the current and the blackness of the night caused such disorganisation that the landings were widely spread and, before the Dorsets could find the airborne perimeter, the Germans closed in around them.

As dawn was breaking on the ninth day, Urquhart received a letter from Thomas advising him that Second Army had been obliged to abandon the attempt to establish a bridgehead and that 1st Airborne would have to be withdrawn. Urquhart replied that, if this was the plan, his troops must be withdrawn that night.

On the afternoon of the previous day (September 24th) Dempsey and Horrocks, meeting at St. Oedenrode, had decided that on the night of the 25–26th, they would make a final attempt to gain a bridgehead north of the Neder Rijn. Their ability to do this, however, depended on the road remaining open for the northward movement of ammunition, assault boats and bridging equipment. Horrocks left St. Oedenrode at 4.30 p.m., but, even as he was driving through Veghel a few minutes later, the Germans came in from the west behind him and cut the corridor again: this time in such strength that it was to remain closed for forty-eight hours. This counter-stroke, combined with information from air reconnaissance that German infantry were digging in on the north bank of the Neder Rijn and that panzer reinforcements were moving towards the only sector of the river where a crossing could be made, forced upon Horrocks and Dempsey the reluctant decision to withdraw the 1st Airborne Division.

Within the shrunken perimeter Urquhart now had only 2,500 men. For them, for the past five days, it had been, in the words of the division's own report, " a question of withstanding continuous attacks, mortaring and shelling. The force was dwindling steadily in numbers and strength . . and was becoming increasingly short of ammunition. Much patching by small parties and frequent minor adjustments of the perimeter were necessary but, except for the deliberate closing-in of the northern face of the perimeter, little or no ground was lost." That, in itself, is a measure of the steadfast endurance and abiding courage of Urquhart's men, for the enemy pressure against the perimeter had been relentless and sustained ever since the paratroops at the bridge had been overwhelmed. From the 22nd onwards, the survivors of the division were heavily out-numbered and heavily out-gunned, but they maintained such a resolute defence, even under attack by tanks and assault guns, that, by the afternoon of the 25th, the Germans were content to contain them.

During this afternoon the airborne troops prepared to make their withdrawal and, at Divisional H.Q. in the Hartenstein Hotel, a signals officer, Lieut. J. Hardy, set free the last of the carrier-pigeons they had brought from England. One of these pigeons reached the H.Q. of VIII British Corps in Belgium, carrying this message:

1. Have to release birds owing to shortage of food and water.

2. About eight tanks lying about in sub-unit areas, very untidy but not otherwise causing us any trouble.

3. Now using as many German weapons as we have British. MGs most effective when aiming towards Germany.

4. Dutch people grand but Dutch tobacco rather stringy.

5. Great beard growing competition on in our unit, but no time to check up on the winner.

They left that night in heavy rain and high wind. A barrage from the guns of XXX Corps screened their departure and kept the enemy quieter than usual. Through woods and gardens, streets and houses which had been their battleground for so many days, they slipped away silently in small parties, each man clinging to the hand or the jacket of the man ahead. At the river's edge boats were waiting for them, manned by British and Canadian sappers. All night the ferrying continued under spasmodic fire from mortars and artillery, but the Germans made no direct attempt to prevent the withdrawal, for they did not realise what was happening. The heavy shelling from the south bank, and a gallant diversion by the Dorsets from the narrow foothold they had gained down-stream, kept the Germans standing to in anticipation of another assault. Throughout the night the perimeter appeared to be manned, for wounded who could not be moved lay beside weapons and wireless sets and maintained the usual pattern of radio traffic and defensive fire. At day-break on September 26th the evacuation had to stop, for German machine-guns began sweeping the river. By then 2,163 men of the 1st Airborne Division and the Glider Pilot Regiment (together with 160 Poles and 75 Dorsets), had reached the safety of the south bank. Of the ten thousand who had landed north of the Neder Rijn only these few were rescued, and, as near as can be told, 1,130 airborne troops remained at Arnhem for ever. Three hundred wounded inside the perimeter, and another two hundred men of the 4th Dorset, were taken prisoner, bringing the total of those captured in and around Arnhem to more than six thousand, of whom nearly half were wounded before they fell into enemy hands.[1] Several hundred more remained at large, succoured and befriended by the Dutch. These were mostly men who had been cut off in the confused fighting of the past ten days or who, like Lathbury and Hackett, escaped from hospitals which the Germans captured. The majority eventually found their way back across the river, but another seven months were to elapse before British troops again set foot in Arnhem.

[1]The Germans, in a signal sent out by OKW on September 27th and recorded in the diary of the Naval War Staff, claimed that " 6,450 prisoners were taken," and gave their own losses as " 3,300 men," killed or wounded.

## CHAPTER XXVII

# THE LOST OPPORTUNITY

AS the exhausted survivors of the 1st Airborne Division were arriving in Nijmegen on the afternoon of September 26th, the road from the south was reopened. On the right flank of Second Army, VIII Corps reached the Maas at Boxmeer and compelled the Germans on this side to withdraw. The shaft of the Allied spear was now secure, but the point had already been blunted. Instead of a corridor running right through to the Zuider Zee, Second Army had to be content with a salient extending only to the south bank of the Neder Rijn. This salient, 60 miles deep, was of immense tactical value for the purpose of driving the Germans from the area south of the Maas and thus removing the threat of an immediate counter-stroke against Antwerp; strategically, however, it was in danger of becoming a blind alley, unless the bridgeheads over the Maas and the Waal could be quickly exploited. As soon as the autumn rains came to freshen the rivers, the Germans would be able to flood the polder, thereby blocking the northward route through Arnhem and making still narrower the neck between the Waal and the Maas, which was already constricted by the Reichswald. Thus, although Montgomery's troops were deployed beyond the northern end of the Siegfried Line, these defences had not been effectively outflanked. Moreover, the barrier of the Rhine remained and the threat to the Ruhr was neither as great nor as immediate as Montgomery had hoped.

Summing up the overall results of MARKET GARDEN, Montgomery subsequently claimed that " the battle of Arnhem was ninety per cent successful." This claim is difficult to support, unless the success of the operation is judged merely in terms of the number of bridges captured. Eight crossings were seized but the failure to secure the ninth, the bridge at Arnhem, meant the frustration of Montgomery's strategic purpose. His fundamental objective had been to drive Second Army beyond the Maas and the Rhine in one bound. " I was," he says, " deeply impressed with the magnitude of the military problems of fighting an opposed crossing over these great water barriers and wanted to avoid it at all costs."[1] His orders to Second Army were that it should " establish itself

[1]Montgomery, *Normandy to the Baltic*, p. 153.

523

in strength on the general line Zwolle–Deventer–Arnhem, facing East, with a deep bridgehead to the Eastern side of the Ijsel. From this position it will be prepared to advance Eastwards to the general line Rheine–Osnabrück–Hamm–Münster." Montgomery undoubtedly hoped that, if he could gain this position directly threatening the Ruhr, Eisenhower would realise the scope of the opportunity and give him the resources to exploit it.

Although the results of MARKET GARDEN fell so far short of what Montgomery wanted, this does not mean that the plan was over-ambitious or that the objectives were inevitably beyond his reach. If the operation had been as daring in tactical execution as it was in strategic conception, there is little doubt that it would have been a complete triumph. It was only at Arnhem that there was any serious miscarriage of Montgomery's plans, but, as this was decisive, its causes must be examined in some detail.

The basic reason for the failure at Arnhem was that the 1st Airborne Division landed too far from the bridge, and, having landed, devoted too much of its strength to securing a ' firm base,' too little to capturing its objective. In his official report on the lessons of Arnhem, Urquhart wrote:

> We must be prepared to take more risks during the initial stages of an airborne operation. It would have been a reasonable risk to have landed the Division much closer to the objective chosen, even in the face of some enemy flak. . . . Initial surprise was gained, but the effect was lost because it was four hours[1] before the troops could arrive at the bridge. A whole brigade dropped at the bridge would have made all the difference. . . . Both the Army and the R.A.F. were over-pessimistic about the flak. The forecast about the impossibility of landing gliders on the polder country was also wrong. Suitable DZs and LZs could have been found south of the bridge and near it.

The root of the trouble would appear to have been that Urquhart, as one of his staff said, was " over-concerned about a safe approach and a tidy drop." Many of Urquhart's officers considered that in 1st Airborne's planning there was a lack of bold and clear thinking. Even if it had been true, they felt, that the polder south of the Neder Rijn was unsuitable for the mass landing of gliders, there was no good reason why a small *coup de main* force should not have landed by glider and parachute at the southern end of the bridge on the first day. In Normandy, by doing just this, Gale had seized the Orne crossings in the face of much heavier flak. Nor is it clear why 4th Parachute Brigade (instead of dropping even farther west than its predecessor) should not have been put down on the south bank close to the bridge on D plus 1, for it was precisely here that Urquhart planned to drop the Polish Parachute Brigade on the following

[1] In fact, it was six hours.

day. It would have been reasonable for him to argue that, if the flak defences in this area were subdued by D plus 1, the risk would be small; and if they were not, it would mean that the bridge was not held and, therefore, it would be essential to take the risk of dropping a brigade there in order to ensure the capture of this vital objective.

All these solutions involved the acceptance of considerable risks, but Urquhart's parachute battalions were composed of men who had volunteered, and had been trained, to accept such risks. There were no finer troops in the British Army. That was shown by the way they fought at Arnhem, but they were never given the chance to earn the success that should have been the reward of the sacrifices they were willing to make—and did make, in full measure.

The price of a daring, direct assault upon the bridge could hardly have been greater than the cost of the vain endeavour to fight through to that bridge a force large enough to hold it. Although the Germans in the Arnhem area were much stronger than had been expected, they would not have been strong enough to overwhelm Urquhart's force if it had been concentrated. As it was, it took them more than three days to destroy the battalion at the bridge,[1] and, when the last three thousand were driven back into the Hartenstein perimeter, thrice that number of Germans could not subdue them. But the opportunity that was lost by initial caution could not be made good by subsequent courage.

The Arnhem story makes sad reading, but the real tragedy lies in the fact that with reasonably good fortune even this plan might have succeeded. If it had not been for the double mischance that the 9th SS Panzer Division and Model himself were in the Arnhem area on the 17th, a very much larger force would have reached the bridge that night. Once the advantage of surprise had been lost, the inherent weaknesses of the plan were accentuated by the speed and strength of the German reaction, by the sudden worsening of the weather, and by the virtual breakdown of radio communications.

Of these factors the most important by far, in the opinion of both Montgomery and Student, was the weather.[2] It was only on the first afternoon that the weather allowed the airborne landings to proceed according to plan. On D plus 1 Urquhart's second ' lift ' was five hours late. On D plus 2 the major element of the third ' lift ' could not leave its bases. On D plus 3 it was still grounded. On D plus 4 the aircraft took off, but less than half of them found the DZ. On D plus 5 the weather prevented any operations. By D plus 6 the situation at Arnhem was beyond redemption by airborne forces.

---

[1]In Gavin's opinion, the performance of Frost's force was " the outstanding independent parachute battalion action of the war." Frost's " tactical handling " was, says Gavin, " a model for parachute unit commanders." Gavin, op. cit., p. 120.

[2]Montgomery says that " Had good weather obtained, there was no doubt that we should have attained full success." (Op. cit., p. 186.) Student, when interrogated by Liddell Hart, did not go quite so far as this, but gave the weather as the main cause of the failure.

The decisive day was Tuesday, the 19th (D plus 2). By that morning there was little chance of Urquhart's main force breaking through to the bridge, but Frost's men were firmly established at the northern end, and it was reasonable to expect that they would soon be relieved either by the Poles, who were due to be dropped south of the bridge that afternoon, or by the Guards, who had reached Nijmegen that morning. Both these calculations were upset by the bad weather, which prevented the dispatch of the Poles and of Gavin's three glider infantry battalions. Without the aid of the Poles, Frost could not complete the capture of the Arnhem bridge. Without the glider-borne infantry, Gavin could not press home the attack on the Nijmegen bridge that night. By the time this bridge was taken the Germans had regained control of the Arnhem crossing and were able to delay the British advance to the Neder Rijn until the chance of making a successful assault across it had gone.

The crowning irony of this day of bitter frustration was that among the aircraft which could take off were 160 carrying supplies for 1st Airborne. In the face of heavy flak, they dropped their loads with daring precision at the prearranged point, but it was in enemy hands. This was the last day on which the division was holding an area large enough for accurate dropping or effective recovery. Thereafter, although the R.A.F. transport planes continued, as one of Urquhart's officers[1] put it, " to fly straight into a flaming hell," and suffered heavily (on one day 29 aircraft were lost out of 114) very little of the supplies they dropped reached the troops on the ground.

Nevertheless, the situation at Arnhem might yet have been saved if the weather had permitted the flying in of the Polish paratroops and the American gliders on Wednesday, the 20th—the day the Nijmegen bridge was captured—or if Horrocks and Browning had known then what the situation really was. That day Major-General E. Hakewill Smith, the commander of the 52nd Lowland Division (Browning's only reserve), offered to take one of his brigades by glider to Urquhart's rescue. Browning replied, " Thanks for your message but offer not repeat not required as situation better than you think."

Browning could not have sent this reply if he had been able to get first-hand information from 1st Airborne. But, as already noted, Urquhart had no radio contact with the force at the bridge or with Browning or with Airborne Base in England from the evening of the 17th until the morning of the 20th, and, when communications were restored, they were spasmodic and unreliable. If during these two days of silence Urquhart had been able to report even what he knew of the position in and around Arnhem, substantial glider-borne reinforcements might have been flown to him on the 20th and 21st. On both these days the airfields from which the R.A.F. transport groups operated were ' open ' and there were plenty of gliders in reserve.

[1] Lt.-Col. M. S. Packe, Commander of Urquhart's R.A.S.C. Of the 1,431 tons dropped by the R.A.F., Packe estimates that less than 200 tons were recovered.

Similarly it was a signals failure that was largely responsible for denying Urquhart the close support which the R.A.F. could have provided. On the 21st, communications were re-established through the 64th Medium Regiment, but during the next few days the air effort was curtailed by the weather. Throughout the operation, however, it was also curtailed by decisions of policy. On the one hand, the Americans insisted that 2nd T.A.F. should not operate during airborne missions, lest there should be a clash between American and British fighters. On the other hand, 2nd T.A.F. was reluctant to engage targets unless these could be very accurately pin-pointed. The pilots were naturally concerned about the danger of attacking friendly troops, but Browning was prepared to accept this risk. In a subsequent report he complained that of 95 requests made for air support during MARKET GARDEN, only 49 were accepted by the R.A.F.[1]

The other factor that must be considered is the inability of the ground forces to advance as quickly as was hoped. In a report to the U.S. Chiefs of Staff after the battle Brereton wrote: " It was the breakdown of the 2nd Army's timetable on the first day—their failure to reach Eindhoven in 6 to 8 hours as planned—that caused the delay in the taking of the Nijmegen bridge and the failure at Arnhem."[2]

Is this criticism justified? The Guards, breaking out along one road, met strong opposition nearly all the way to Eindhoven, and yet they drove their armour through these twelve bitterly contested miles in twenty-four hours. When they reached the southern end of the ' airborne corridor' on the evening of D plus 1, they were halted for the night by the blown bridge at Zon. This bridge might have been captured intact if the 101st Division had agreed to Montgomery's proposal that it should drop paratroops on either side of the objective, as was done at Grave. Finally, when the Guards reached Nijmegen on the morning of D plus 2 —remarkably early in the circumstances—the Waal bridge was firmly blocked by the Germans. Sufficient forces could not be mustered to seize it that day, because Gavin's eastern flank was under considerable pressure and his glider battalions did not arrive as planned.

Where the relieving forces did fail was not in the break-out or in the advance to Nijmegen, but in the drive from the Waal to the Neder Rijn on September 22nd. The reason for their failure lay in what was at this stage of the war the gravest shortcoming of the British Army: the reluctance of commanders at all levels to call upon their troops to press on regardless of losses, even in operations which were likely to shorten the war and thus save casualties in the long run. It was this which prevented the timely advance of the 43rd Division, just as it had led

[1]In this report Browning repeated the argument which the Army was seldom able to persuade the Air Force to accept: namely, that " If full value from air support is to be obtained, the R.A.F. must be prepared to take on area targets even though the results may, to them, appear disappointing. To the ground they forces are invaluable."

[2]Brereton, op. cit., pp. 360-1.

Urquhart to shrink from the cost which he feared would be incurred in a direct assault on the Arnhem bridge.

It was most unfortunate that the two major weaknesses of the Allied High Command—the British caution about casualties and the American reluctance to concentrate—should both have exerted their baneful influence on this operation, which should, and could, have been the decisive blow of the campaign in the West. This was no time to count the cost, or to consider the prestige of rival commanders. The prize at issue was no less than the chance of capturing the Ruhr and ending the war quickly with all that meant for the future of Europe.

When Eisenhower placed the Airborne Army at Montgomery's disposal on September 4th, he was committing his strategic reserve, the only major force he could throw in to clinch the victory that had been won in France. But he did not make available to Montgomery the supply resources necessary to ensure that the maximum advantage was drawn from the commitment of this precious reserve. Montgomery, it will be recalled, reached the Meuse–Escaut Canal, the start-line for MARKET GARDEN, on September 10th without any logistic help from Bradley or Eisenhower, apart from some five hundred tons a day which had been delivered by air during the previous week.[1] This help continued, but the American 'Red Ball' Express—carrying another five hundred tons daily from Bayeux to Brussels—did not begin until the 16th. Not one ton of these 'Red Ball' supplies reached Montgomery before the start of the Arnhem offensive, and even the truck companies sent up for the U.S. airborne divisions arrived three days after it began.

Additional resources were not provided for Montgomery, or for Hodges, because Eisenhower still thought in terms of advancing to the Rhine on a broad front with a succession of thrusts, of which Montgomery's was to be merely the first. On September 8th he wrote to Montgomery: " We must push up [to the Rhine] as soon as possible *all along the front* to cut off the retreating enemy and concentrate in preparation for the big final thrust."[2] Eisenhower's adherence to this policy (which he reaffirmed in another letter written only two days before the start of MARKET GARDEN) was due very largely to the consistently sanguine reports he received through Bradley from Patton.

Throughout the campaign the natural optimism of the Americans was

---

[1]It was commonly believed at Third Army H.Q. that Montgomery's advance through Belgium was largely maintained by supplies diverted from Patton. (See Butcher, op. cit., p. 667.) This is not true. The amount delivered by the 'air-lift' was sufficient to maintain only one division. No road transport was diverted to aid Montgomery until September 16th. On the other hand, three British transport companies, lent to the Americans on August 6th " for eight days," were not returned until September 4th.

[2]In italicising the words " all along the front," I have followed the example of Col. H. M. Cole, one of the official American historians, who quotes this extract in his volume, *The Lorraine Campaign*, at p. 56.

a source of great strength, but it became dangerous when, as at this time, it led commanders to represent the military situation too favourably. In some cases this optimism was a matter of policy as well as temperament. Ambitious American generals, like Patton and MacArthur, habitually represented their progress and prospects in the rosiest light, for they believed that they were then likely to be given greater resources. ' Reinforcing success ' is sound military practice, provided that the success is advancing the strategic plan, but, in war as in life, the Americans tend to value success for its own sake. Consequently, it was extremely difficult for an American commander to deny support to a subordinate like Patton who was being so successful. Already the fact that Montgomery had been given the Allied Airborne Army, had drawn from Patton's staff the jibe, " Eisenhower is the best general the British have! "

The political difficulty of restraining Patton, the universal optimism of the American High Command and the desire to form a coherent front from Switzerland to the North Sea—a front broad enough for the ultimate employment of the thirty divisions still waiting in the United States—were, it seems, the real factors behind Eisenhower's reluctance to provide Montgomery with sufficient resources to capture the Ruhr.

Since the war, however, Eisenhower has contended that the resources were not available. In *Crusade in Europe* he says that " a strong bridgehead definitely threatening the Ruhr " might have been established " had we stopped in late August all Allied movements elsewhere on the front . . . However, at no point could decisive success have been attained."[1] He insists that for this operation no more than " ten or a dozen divisions . . . could have been supported even temporarily."

At the start of September the Allied supply situation was certainly difficult, but it was not as serious as Eisenhower suggests, nor were the needs of his divisions as great as he asserts. Eisenhower says that " a reinforced division in active operation consumes 600 to 700 tons of supplies per day."[2] This figure he quotes not from his own personal experience in command but from the U.S. War Department's *Staff Officers' Field Manual*, and it includes all manner of ordnance and engineer stores which are normally carried but need not be immediately replaced in a short, swift campaign. It includes also ammunition for heavy and medium artillery, most of which was grounded in September because it was not needed so long as the momentum was maintained. At this time Allied divisions, and their supporting troops, could be, and were, adequately maintained in action and advancing with a daily supply of 500 tons. (The fact that he was receiving only 3,500 tons a day did not prevent Patton attacking with eight divisions on the Moselle.) In a defensive role Allied divisions needed only half this amount.

When Eisenhower and Montgomery met in Brussels on September

[1]Eisenhower, *Crusade*, p. 306.
[2]Ibid, p. 290. For the advance beyond the Rhine the planning of 21st Army Group was based on the yardstick of 400 tons a day per division.

10th, the Allied supply columns and transport aircraft could deliver from dumps in Normandy and bases in Britain to the front on the Moselle, the Meuse and the Dutch border some 10,000 tons a day for Patton, Hodges and Dempsey. The port of Dieppe was open and by the middle of the month had a daily intake of 3,000 tons, which was more than enough for First Canadian Army. In the last ten days of September with little help from air transport, the supply capacity was increased to 14,000 tons a day. Of this total ' lift,' 2,000 tons would have been ample to support Third Army if it had assumed the defensive. This would have left 12,000 tons a day to maintain the 20 British and American divisions with which Montgomery proposed to capture the Ruhr. Even on the basis of Eisenhower's inflated figure, this would have been sufficient, for in the wake of the advancing armies the supply facilities were being steadily improved. The petrol pipe-line from Cherbourg had reached Chartres by September 12th and was being laid at a rate of 25 miles a day. Rail communications were open from the Normandy bridgehead to Sommersous, 100 miles east of Paris, by September 7th, to Liége by the 18th, and to Eindhoven ten days later. At the end of September the port of Dieppe had a daily intake of 6,000 tons and by this time Ostend was also working.

Although the supply statistics of the period do not support Eisenhower's contention that no more than " ten or a dozen divisions could have been supported even temporarily " beyond the Rhine, this view has gained general acceptance, and is even endorsed by Montgomery's Chief of Staff, de Guingand. In his book, *Operation Victory*, de Guingand says: " If he [Eisenhower] had not taken the steps he did to link up at an early date with ANVIL and had held back Patton, and had diverted the administrative resources so released to the north, I think it possible that we might have obtained a bridgehead over the Rhine before the winter—but not more."[1]

De Guingand admits, however, that in expressing this opinion he is not speaking from first-hand experience, because, like Eisenhower, he was far from the front. During the first half of September he was, he says, " away sick in England " and so " was not in close touch with the existing situation."[2] He has accepted, apparently without question, the assurance of Bedell Smith and others at SHAEF that " Patton was getting very little during this period."[3] We now know that this was not the case, except during the first four days of September when Third Army was allocated only 2,000 tons a day. In the next three weeks the tonnage which Patton actually acquired, by one means or another, was greater than that delivered to Hodges.

When Patton was given authority to drive on from the Meuse to the

---

[1]De Guingand, op. cit., p. 413.
[2]Ibid, pp. 416-17.
[3]Ibid, p. 423. De Guingand says, " I have not sufficient information to be able to assess what such a diversion [of resources from Patton] might have meant in terms of daily tonnages."

Moselle and to sweep south to Épinal, he was amply supported. " On 4 September," says the official U.S. historian of Patton's campaign in Lorraine, " the gasoline drought started to break . . . and by 10 September the period of critical shortage was ended."[1] On the 11th air transport delivered to Patton a bonus issue of nearly a thousand tons of petrol. Next day, " adequate stocks of gasoline were available and all fuel tanks and auxiliary cans were full."[2] Moreover, " on 12 September the Third Army was given a special allocation of 3,554 long tons of Bailey bridging, and this was moved by separate bridge trains directly from Normandy to the front."[3] Throughout the week that began on September 10th, while Third Army was attacking in Lorraine with eight divisions, the critical supply situation in the north curtailed First Army's assault on the Siegfried Line and halted Second Army on the Meuse–Escaut Canal.

There was no question of Montgomery's waiting unnecessarily in order to build up a vast administrative reserve. He launched the offensive into Holland with nothing in hand at all, except what was immediately necessary to take XXX Corps to the Zuider Zee and to support limited advances by the corps on either flank. He was not able even to establish those corps in position to render the maximum assistance. Owing to the shortage of transport for troops and ammunition, XII Corps could secure only one small bridgehead beyond the Meuse–Escaut Canal before the 17th, and VIII Corps could not join the offensive until the 19th. Even then this corps had only two divisions, for the 51st Highland was grounded throughout the Arnhem operation so that its transport could be used to supply the forward troops. On the first two days of MARKET GARDEN Dempsey was able to employ offensively only three of the nine British divisions available, and, as already recorded, the actual break-out was made by two battalions advancing along one narrow road. This was the direct result of Eisenhower's policy. If he had kept Patton halted on the Meuse, and had given full logistic support to Hodges and Dempsey after the capture of Brussels, the operations in Holland could have been an overwhelming triumph, for First U.S. Army could have mounted a formidable diversion, if not a successful offensive, at Aachen, and Second British Army could have attacked sooner, on a wider front and in much greater strength.

The week's delay on the Dutch frontier gave Model and Student the opportunity of reorganising and strengthening the defences of Holland. During this week 2nd SS Panzer Corps was moved into the Arnhem–Apeldoorn–Deventer area; Corps Feldt (with two divisions) was deployed along the Maas from the Reichswald to Roermond; the scratch formations of paratroops, provided by Goering, were organised into divisions; and three divisions of Fifteenth Army were withdrawn from Flanders across

[1]Cole, op. cit., p. 52.
[2]Ibid, p. 70. In this passage Cole is referring only to XII Corps, but it is clear from his narrative that the other two Corps of Third Army were equally well supplied.
[3]Ibid, p. 85 n.

the Scheldt Estuary. Within this week, therefore, the strength of the German forces in the MARKET GARDEN area was more than doubled.

When the offensive was launched the 9th and 10th SS Panzer Divisions (each with the strength of a brigade plus some thirty tanks and assault guns)[1] were sent into action at once. In Arnhem 9th SS (Harzer) took under command the local garrison and two SS training battalions, and was reinforced from the Reich by a panzer grenadier regiment and a heavy tank battalion with 45 Tigers. With these additions Harzer's force was very much too powerful to be ' seen off ' by the dispersed and lightly-armed troops of 1st Airborne. Nevertheless, by holding the northern end of the Arnhem road bridge for three days, the paratroops imposed on 10th SS the laborious task of ferrying across the Neder Rijn the two battalions it sent to reinforce the Nijmegen garrison. On the eastern flank of the corridor, however, the Germans were able to build up their strength more quickly. Here, by the 22nd, First Parachute Army had been augmented by the arrival of the 6th Parachute Division from Cologne, two depot divisions from the Home Army, the 107th Panzer Brigade and a battlegroup of 10th SS. That day the defence of the western flank was taken over by Fifteenth Army which had now brought two more divisions safely across the Scheldt Estuary. Thus it was that on September 24th Second Army found itself opposed by fourteen German divisions,[2] a force very much larger than it would have had to engage if its momentum had been maintained or if the weather had allowed the Allied air forces to interfere with the movement of German reserves.

That day—one week after the start of the Allied offensive—Model reported to von Rundstedt: " The position of Army Group B in the northern sector has progressively deteriorated since the air-landings. . . . Our own reinforcements proved inadequate . . . [and] apart from firmly holding Arnhem the enemy's aims could not be obstructed." He said that he had tried to relieve the pressure on the " sorely-menaced front of First Parachute Army " by attacks against the corridor and at Nijmegen, but had not had the forces to make a lasting impression. He now feared that, as further airborne reinforcements had been landed south of Nijmegen on the previous day (these were Gavin's long-delayed glider battalions), the Allies had " the intention of effecting a penetration

---

[1] Von Rundstedt's Chief of Staff, Westphal, asserts that C.-in-C., West, was as surprised as the Allies to find that 11 SS Panzer Corps had so much armour. It appears that the SS Divisions, being directly responsible to Himmler, did not report their strength accurately to von Rundstedt or Model lest some of their tanks might be taken away.

[2] Few of these divisions had more than 5,000 or 6,000 troops of their own, but nearly all were reinforced by miscellaneous units and battlegroups. Schwalbe, who took command of the 719th Division at this time, told Canadian interrogators that this formation had only three of its own battalions but was " brought up to strength " with two Luftwaffe battalions (air-crews fighting as infantry), a railway security battalion, a local defence battalion, a battalion of Dutch SS and the " 36th Stomach Battalion." With these nine battalions, indifferent though they were, Schwalbe was able to put up considerable resistance so long as his troops were holding a canal line.

to the south-east between the Rhine and the Maas." "The threat to this area," said Model, "is particularly grave, since there are no permanent strongpoints in the presumed path of the enemy offensive. In view of the substantial reinforcements thrown in by the enemy, our own forces are not strong enough to hold up the threatened advance."[1]

Model was right. That was the plan, for Montgomery had no intention of surrendering the initiative just because he had been thwarted at Arnhem. He was determined to exploit the advantage he had gained to the very limit of his strength. He proposed, therefore, to drive through the Reichswald into the Rhineland before the Germans had time to recover from the onslaught that had so nearly overwhelmed them. His plan was that Second British Army should "develop a strong left hook against the Ruhr," in close conjunction with a right hook by First American Army. "It was my idea," he wrote later, "that as we progressed along the west bank of the Rhine we should take any opportunity afforded us of jumping the river; if enemy opposition made this impossible, the Allies would be in a position to undertake an opposed crossing operation once we had cleared the sector between Düsseldorf and Nijmegen."[2]

The execution of this plan depended on the acceptance by Eisenhower (and Bradley) of the proposals which Montgomery had repeatedly put forward during the past month: namely, that Patton must be compelled to assume the defensive; that the drive for the Ruhr must have complete priority in supply; that Hodges should shift his weight northwards and integrate his operations with those of Dempsey; and that one man should have direct operational control over both Second British and First U.S. Armies until the Ruhr was captured.

At Versailles on September 22nd this plan and its implications were examined in detail at the largest and most important conference that Eisenhower had held since D-Day. It was attended by twenty-three generals, admirals and air-marshals, including Eisenhower's deputy (Tedder), his Air and Naval Commanders-in-Chief (Leigh-Mallory and Ramsay), the commanders of the American Army Groups (Bradley and Devers) and of the U.S. Strategic Air Forces (Spaatz), Lee, the American supply chief, Bedell Smith and the senior staff officers at SHAEF (Gale, Strong, Morgan, Bull and Whiteley), de Guingand and Graham of 21st Army Group: everyone of importance, in fact, except the man whose name was uppermost in the minds of all—Montgomery.

The conference at Versailles on September 22nd was the culmination of a week of renewed argument between Eisenhower and Montgomery concerning strategy. On the 14th, Eisenhower, still isolated at Granville

---

[1]Teleprinter Message, Model to von Rundstedt, September 24th. (Tempelhof Papers.)
[2]Montgomery, op. cit., pp. 188-9.

on account of his injured knee, had received a very sanguine report from Bradley about Patton's progress. On the following day, therefore, he wrote Montgomery and Bradley a letter which began: " We shall soon, I hope, have achieved the objectives set forth in my last directive [of September 4th] and shall then be in possession of the Ruhr, the Saar and the Frankfurt area." Having gained these objectives, he said, he intended to move on Berlin with the forces of both Army Groups " all in one co-ordinated concentrated operation." The question was whether to advance via the Ruhr and Hanover, or through Frankfurt and Leipzig or by both routes.[1] What did they think?

Montgomery was amazed at Eisenhower's optimistic assumption that Patton and Hodges would soon reach the Rhine. His reply challenged this assumption and re-stated in the clearest terms the arguments he had been labouring since August 23rd. Time was the vital factor. There were not sufficient supplies to maintain the advance of all armies. One route must be chosen and given full priority. The northern route offered the best opportunity, but, if Eisenhower favoured the southern, he should give Bradley three armies and all the maintenance. Whatever the decision it must be made at once.

The burden of Eisenhower's next letter, written on the 20th, was that he completely agreed with Montgomery's idea of concentrating on the northern approach to Berlin, but that he did not intend to do this until Antwerp was open and the Allies had marshalled their strength along the western borders of Germany, if possible along the Rhine. This letter, and the degree of enemy opposition provoked by MARKET GARDEN, convinced Montgomery that the chance of making a deep penetration into Germany had gone. He hoped, however, that it might still be possible to capture the Ruhr that autumn, if only he could gain full support for the ' left hook ' plan which he now put forward in a signal to Eisenhower.

The conference at Versailles on September 22nd offered Montgomery the opportunity of presenting his plan in person and impressing his views by the very force and clarity of his presentation, as he had done so effectively before D-Day. Then, however, he had been stating his intentions, not pleading his case. Now he would have to appear as an advocate, almost as a suppliant—a role for which he knew he was ill-cast. He decided, therefore, to send de Guingand as his representative. This action caused considerable resentment among many of those present, who regarded it as an affront to Eisenhower, if not to themselves. But Montgomery's refusal to go to Versailles was not, as some thought, due to pique or arrogance; rather it was a tacit acknowledgment of his own limitations.

[1] The reference to an advance on Berlin via Frankfurt and Leipzig was perhaps included for Bradley's benefit. Only three days earlier the Combined Chiefs of Staff had sent a signal from Washington emphasising " the advantages of the Northern line of approach into Germany as opposed to the Southern." (Cole, op. cit., p. 210.)

The month-long argument about command and strategy had imposed a considerable strain upon him. On August 23rd he had believed he was on the point of gaining a victory which would end the war rapidly and save tens of thousands of lives. The chance of gaining that victory had been denied to him, and, since he was only human, this denial had been a bitter personal disappointment—the more so because of past criticism. He had so often been accused of being ' defensively-minded,' being too deliberate, preparing too diligently for his attacks and neglecting opportunities of exploitation. With his armies on the Seine, the time had come to prove that he had created the conditions for delivering the knock-out blow. With one bold stroke he would silence the critical and sceptical. This was the occasion for which he had trained and nursed his forces all the way from Alamein; the occasion for which he had given his life, schooling himself with rigorous devotion until he had become confident of his own mastery of the art and practice of war. But the cup of triumph had been dashed from his lips by men who, according to his standards, had hardly begun to understand the profession of arms. Now when all his warnings had been fulfilled, when the great opportunity that he had foreseen so clearly had been cast away, he did not trust himself to meet them at so ' public ' a gathering as this conference in Versailles. He feared that, if he did go, he might do more harm than good. On the other hand, de Guingand was a skilful diplomat, popular with the Americans and trusted by them. The plan, Montgomery thought, was more likely to be accepted if presented by his Chief of Staff.

It was accepted. The decision, as recorded in the minutes of the conference, was that " the envelopment of the Ruhr from the north by 21st Army Group, supported by the First Army, is the main effort of the present phase of operations." In addition, however, 21st Army Group was " to open the port of Antwerp as a matter of urgency," for Eisenhower insisted that " possession of an additional major port on the northern flank is an indispensable prerequisite for the final drive deep into Germany." " This," he said, " must be accepted by all." Bradley suggested that the attack on the Ruhr should be postponed until the Scheldt Estuary had been cleared and there were sufficient resources to support a general advance, but this proposal was rejected. Bradley was ordered to send two divisions to take over the southern sector of Dempsey's front and thus allow Second Army to concentrate greater strength north of the Maas. Hodges was to be " prepared to attack the Ruhr from the South in concert with 21st Army Group's attack from the North." The rest of 12th Army Group (the Third and Ninth Armies) would " take no more aggressive action." Moreover, Patton's southern corps was to be transferred to Seventh Army which was being maintained with supplies brought up from Marseilles.

That evening de Guingand signalled to Montgomery: " Excellent conference. Ike supported your plan one hundred per cent. Your thrust is main effort and gets full support." This signal brought the news for which Montgomery had waited so long, but the Battle of Arnhem was already lost. Eisenhower's decision had been made one month too late.

When the Battle of Arnhem ended the German forces guarding the Ruhr were extended to the point of exhaustion. On September 27th, the day after the British withdrawal across the Neder Rijn, Model reported to von Rundstedt on the critical condition of Army Group B, which was holding a line 300 miles long from the Scheldt Estuary through Arnhem and Aachen to Trier. On this front, now almost cleft in two by Montgomery's offensive, Model had 33 of the 52 divisions then in the West, but many of these were divisions in name only and, even though they were filled out with scratch units and sundry battlegroups, their average strength was considerably less than 10,000 men. Model gave warning that, although morale was "improving every day," his numbers were shrinking. "In the period from September 1st to 25th," he reported, "our casualties amounted to about 75,000 men; in the same period we received only 6,500 replacements."[1]

The crucial factor, however, was not man-power but fire-power. So many weapons had been lost and so few had been replaced that in his three armies Model had only " 239 tanks and assault guns " and " 821 light and heavy cannon," less armour and artillery than had been available in Britain after Dunkirk. Model had barely sufficient tanks to refit one armoured division; the Allies on his front alone had the equivalent of twelve armoured divisions.

Model reported these facts to von Rundstedt so that they could be brought " to the direct notice of the Führer," who kept in his own hands the control of all panzer replacements and reserves. On resuming command, von Rundstedt had proposed that, as new tanks arrived, they should be used to refit the panzer divisions which had fought in France, and that a reserve of armour should be built up in the Cologne Plain where it could best counter any break-through towards the Ruhr. Hitler insisted, however, that virtually all the 400 new Panthers and Mark IVs, which became available for the West during the first half of September, must be used offensively for the counter-stroke against Patton's southern flank. Moreover, instead of giving these tanks to the experienced though depleted divisions already in the West, he allocated them to the new panzer brigades which had been formed in Germany within the last six weeks.

This decision was characteristic of Hitler. At a time when the lack of replacements for men and equipment was leading, as Model said, " to the exhaustion of whole divisions," Hitler was desperately raising

---

[1]Teleprinter Message, Model to von Rundstedt, September 27th. (Tempelhof Papers.) In this total of replacements, Model was not including the 'new' divisions and battlegroups which had been made available to him during this period to replace (in part) the even heavier losses of the August fighting.

and equipping new formations. This frenzied policy sprang from personal, rather than military, considerations. By ' creating ' divisions as fast as they were consumed in the fire of battle, he persuaded himself that his power was not yet exhausted. To maintain the fiction of his invincibility he had given orders in August that no divisions would be ' written off.' Thus, even remnants with the fighting value of little more than a battalion continued to rank as ' divisions ' in the German Order of Battle and when the new formations were added the inflated figures sustained in him the illusion that the strength of the Wehrmacht was being expanded as the crisis grew more grave.

Hitler's original plan for the counter-offensive in Lorraine was that it should be delivered by Manteuffel's Fifth Panzer Army with three panzer grenadier divisions and at least four of the new panzer brigades. This plan was forestalled by Patton's advance from the Meuse in the second week of September. The three panzer grenadier divisions were pinned down on the Moselle, and Patton's forces, sweeping round their flank, reached the Lunéville–Épinal area before Manteuffel was ready to strike. In an effort to halt the American advance, two panzer brigades lost almost their entire strength before the real offensive began at Lunéville on September 18th.[1]

Although this offensive took Third Army by surprise, the Americans reacted so strongly that the Germans were thrown out of Lunéville the same day. Thereupon, Manteuffel sought to reach Nancy by outflanking Lunéville to the north. This manœuvre brought his tanks head on against the 4th U.S. Armoured Division, commanded by Major-General John S. Wood, a bold, aggressive and original soldier. In four days' fighting around Arracourt, north of Lunéville, Wood handled his armour brilliantly and dealt so severely with two of the new panzer brigades that by September 22nd these were both crippled. The 111th, having arrived in Lorraine with 98 tanks and two battalions of infantry, was now reduced to " seven tanks and eighty men." The 113th had suffered as heavily but its exact casualties are not known. These losses could not be explained away with the excuse that the Germans were outnumbered, for this damage was inflicted almost entirely by a single combat command which contained only one tank battalion. At small cost to themselves the Americans gained a resounding victory.[2]

It is not surprising that the panzer brigades were outfought. Although many of their officers and men had considerable experience on the

[1] The 106th Panzer Brigade (equipped with 33 Panthers and 11 assault guns) attacked Patton's northern flank on the night of September 8th–9th, but was so roughly handled that it came out of the fight with only nine tanks and assault guns. (See Cole, who quotes the German records, op. cit., p. 159.) Four days later, at Dompaire south of Lunéville, the 112th Panzer Brigade clashed with the 2nd French Armoured Division and lost 60 tanks during its first thirty-six hours in action. In ten days this brigade lost all its 98 tanks except " one Panther and six Mark IVs." (Cole, op. cit., p. 234.)

[2] In these four days the casualties suffered by CCA of 4th Armoured were: 25 men killed and 88 wounded; 14 Shermans and 7 light tanks totally destroyed. The two panzer brigades lost at least 150 tanks destroyed or badly damaged.

Eastern Front, they knew nothing of the entirely different conditions in the West, nor had their units had time to develop the cohesion that can come only with thorough training. The brigades had been hastily thrown together and equipped with tanks drawn direct from the factories. Many of these tanks had not even been run-in before they were committed to battle and a large proportion of the German casualties were the result of mechanical failures.

This defeat gave Hitler an excuse for dismissing the commander of Army Group G (Blaskowitz) who had long been politically suspect because he was personally independent. The command was given to General Hermann Balck, an experienced tank commander and a notorious optimist with a reputation for ruthless aggression. This appointment was not welcomed by von Rundstedt, for Balck had no experience of operations against the Western Powers. With Hitler, however, this was no doubt a point in his favour.

Balck arrived with instructions to renew the offensive against Third Army. Von Rundstedt protested at this order, arguing that the time for a counter-stroke in the south had gone and that the armour should be moved north to the Aachen sector which had become vulnerable because by far the greater part of Model's panzer reserves were of necessity being committed against the British in Holland. Hitler brushed this protest aside and ordered Manteuffel to continue the attack, reinforced by the 11th Panzer Division which had covered the withdrawal up the Rhône Valley.

On September 25th, when the attack was resumed, Fifth Panzer Army was stronger in infantry, but very much weaker in armour, than it had been seven days earlier. The American outposts were driven in, but the Germans made no real progress and by the 29th the back of their assault was broken. That day, evidently alarmed at the weakness of Model's armoured forces, Hitler gave orders that all the armour which could be spared should be concentrated to check the British drive for the Ruhr. Already, however, in the attempt to carry out Hitler's original instructions the panzer reserves in the south had been thrown away. Of the 350 Panthers and Mark IVs which he had sent to Lorraine since the start of September at least half had been totally destroyed and many of the remainder were in workshops. At the end of the month on the entire Western Front from the Swiss border to the North Sea von Rundstedt could not muster more than five hundred tanks and assault guns.[1]

The combined effect of Montgomery's offensive in the north and Hitler's counter-offensive in the south was that von Rundstedt was left with an even more extended front and with no adequate reserve to restore any major breach. Only a comparatively small proportion of Eisenhower's total strength had been engaged in Operation MARKET GARDEN and yet

[1]This is the figure given to me by von Rundstedt's Chief of Staff, Westphal. It may be too high.

it had been all Model could do to prevent Second Army reaching Arnhem and breaking through to the Zuider Zee. For a week the Allied corridor south of the Maas had been only a mile wide and yet Model could not keep it cut, nor had he been able to wipe out the meagre airborne forces north of the Neder Rijn.

Since the war von Rundstedt and other German generals who can speak with authority (Student, Westphal, Blumentritt, Speidel and others) have all declared that a concentrated thrust from Belgium in September must have succeeded. These generals are agreed that if even fifteen divisions had driven on after the capture of Brussels and Liége, as Montgomery proposed, the Wehrmacht would have been powerless to stop them overrunning the Lower Rhineland and seizing the Ruhr. Indeed Blumentritt says: " Such a break-through *en masse,* coupled with air domination, would have torn the weak German front to pieces and ended the war in the winter of 1944."[1]

In view of Hitler's unbroken resolve to continue the struggle even into the streets of Berlin regardless of the cost, there is reason to doubt whether the capture of the Ruhr and Rhineland alone would have brought the war to an end that year. It is quite certain, however, that the loss of these areas would have deprived Hitler of the means of carrying out the grandiose plan which was already forming in his mind for a winter offensive in the West.

[1] In reply to my written interrogation, December 7th, 1948.

## CHAPTER XXVIII

# THE GERMAN RECOVERY

THE opportunity of capturing the Ruhr remained open well into October, but Eisenhower could not take advantage of it. By September 22nd, when he finally decided that this would be the " main effort," he no longer possessed the ability to mass and maintain a force strong enough for the task. His lines of communication were so extended in so many directions that, as he subsequently wrote, " the life-blood of supply was running perilously thin through the forward extremities of the Army." It would not have been running so thin, however, if he had not gratuitously undertaken responsibilities beyond his resources. Having driven his right wing too far east and south, he had lost flexibility and was fast losing the initiative.

At the end of September he had 54 divisions on the Continent, but, as he says, " counting all types of divisions—infantry, armoured and airborne —we could, on the average, deploy less than one division to each ten miles of front ";[1] considerably less, in fact, for the line he had given his troops to hold was 600 miles long and eight of his divisions were immobilised in Normandy or on the Côte d'Azur waiting for transport to move them forward. Instead of having his armoured and airborne divisions free to make a fresh breach in the German front, he was now compelled to use them to hold his own. The result was that Eisenhower could neither concentrate enough strength for an offensive by Dempsey's Second Army and Hodges's First Army against the Ruhr, nor maintain sufficient pressure elsewhere to prevent the Germans massing additional forces to defend the Ruhr.

Before Hodges could develop operations in support of the British attack in the Rhineland, he had to capture Aachen, for he had not the resources to contain and outflank it. In the third week of September, while the Germans were still reeling back, VII U.S. Corps had made a quick breach in the main defences of the Siegfried Line south of Aachen

---

[1]Eisenhower, *Crusade*, p. 320. When the ' broad front ' concept was framed by the SHAEF Planning Staff, it was assumed that the Allies would not be deployed along the western border of Germany from Switzerland to the North Sea until 75 divisions were ashore and the Channel ports, including Antwerp, were open.

but had been checked in the industrial wilderness east of the city. During the last ten days of the month, while Patton was attacking and being counter-attacked on the Moselle, Hodges was so short of troops and ammunition that he could make little progress beyond advancing XIX U.S. Corps to the Siegfried Line north of Aachen. This respite gave the Germans time to seal off the breach in the Siegfried defences and to bring in two new infantry divisions to relieve the armoured formations which had checked the initial American thrust. On October 2nd, when Hodges, still short of ammunition, renewed the assault with both VII and XIX Corps, the Germans were braced to meet the blow. After two weeks of heavy fighting the Americans succeeded in encircling Aachen but the garrison in the heart of the city held out until the 21st. By this stubborn defence of Aachen Model blocked the southern approach to the Ruhr and kept First Army occupied for five weeks.

Meanwhile, two panzer divisions which had been withdrawn from the Aachen sector in the last few days of September and a panzer brigade from the Reich had joined 9th and 10th SS in Holland. With these fresh forces Model launched a series of counter-attacks from Arnhem and the Reichswald, and kept Second Army on the defensive. At the same time the Germans south of the Maas stood their ground on either flank of the British salient. Here, in accordance with the decisions of the meeting at Versailles, Bradley was to have taken over part of Montgomery's front, but this proved to be impossible because, as Eisenhower observed, " Bradley's forces are getting fearfully stretched south of Aachen " in the Ardennes, and " may get a nasty little ' Kasserine ' if the enemy chooses the right place to concentrate his strength."[1]

Without substantial help from the Americans, Montgomery could not carry out the double task which Eisenhower had given him on September 22nd—the capturing of the Ruhr and the clearing of the Scheldt Estuary. On October 7th, therefore, Montgomery reported that he would have to postpone his Rhineland offensive until he had driven the Germans from the Scheldt and from the area south of the Maas. This signal, and a gale which materially reduced the intake of supplies at Cherbourg and through the MULBERRY Harbour, made it clear that the opening of Antwerp must take priority over all other operations. On October 9th Eisenhower gave orders to this effect.

The Allies were now squarely confronted with the situation Montgomery had predicted on August 23rd. They were in the grip of a strategic strait-jacket. In his desire to seize both the Ruhr and the Saar–Frankfurt area, Eisenhower had lost the chance of capturing the Ruhr quickly. Then, in his anxiety to make good this mistake, he had authorised first MARKET GARDEN and then Montgomery's ' left hook ' plan, and thus had delayed the opening of Antwerp. The weakness of

[1]Butcher, op. cit., p. 676. Eisenhower used almost the same words in a letter to Montgomery on September 24th. Kasserine was where Rommel counter-attacked in February 1943 and inflicted on the Americans their first defeat in the Tunisian campaign.

Eisenhower's policy was that it was based on compromise and optimism. Because he was reluctant to make a definite choice between the rival plans, he had given limited approval to both, and had hoped that the necessary resources would be forthcoming to support them. The result was a double frustration. He had failed to capture the one objective in the West that the Germans could not afford to lose, and he had failed to secure the one port the Allies had to have if they were to maintain the broad front on which he had deployed his armies. He now had ample room for the many divisions which were trained and waiting in the United States, but he had not secured the ports through which these divisions could be landed and maintained. The question was therefore: could the Allies open Antwerp and amass the strength to reach the Rhine before the Wehrmacht had recovered from the disasters of the summer?

During September, while the main Allied forces were driving for the German frontier, General Crerar's First Canadian Army was the Cinderella of Eisenhower's forces. In the second week Crerar's six Canadian and British divisions were strung out along the Channel coast preparing to assault the fortresses of Le Havre, Boulogne, Calais and Dunkirk, and to clear the southern shore of the Scheldt Estuary where the remnants of Fifteenth German Army were holding a bridgehead covering Breskens. The Canadians had captured Dieppe and Ostend without a fight, but in each of the other Channel ports Hitler had left a garrison with roughly the strength of a division under strict orders to demolish the harbour facilities and fight to the last.

Although these ports were almost impregnable against assault from the sea, they had few permanent fortifications on the land side. The comparative weakness of these landward defences was not fully appreciated by Crerar who concluded that the ports could be taken only by deliberate ' set-piece ' attacks in which his infantry could be strongly supported by heavy bombers, artillery and special armoured equipment. Since his resources were limited, Crerar decided that he would have to take each fortress in turn.

In the event the defences were less formidable and the opposition less stubborn than had been expected. Le Havre, attacked by two British divisions on September 10th, was captured in forty-eight hours. At both Boulogne and Calais the German resistance lasted six days but in each case the Canadians were able to employ only two brigades. These ports, and the cross-Channel batteries at Cap Gris Nez, yielded 29,945 prisoners at a cost of fewer than 1,500 British and Canadian casualties. These operations were completed by October 1st, but the ports were so thoroughly mined and demolished by the Germans and so badly damaged by Allied bombing that it took three or four weeks to open them for shipping and then their capacity fell much below expectations.

The possession of these ports gradually relieved the supply difficulties of the Allied forces in the line, but, even though Le Havre was able to receive transatlantic Liberty ships by mid-October, there was no great increase in the rate at which the reserve divisions from the United States could be landed on the Continent. To save shipping space and loading time the heavy equipment and transport of these divisions had been packed in large crates, most of which could be lifted only by powerful dockside cranes. At Le Havre, as at Cherbourg, all such cranes had been put out of action by the enemy. Thus, until Antwerp was open, American divisions could not be routed direct to Northern Europe, and the progress of Eisenhower's build-up was governed by the fact that their boxed equipment had to be landed in Britain, unpacked and ferried across the Channel.[1]

Foreseeing this, Churchill proposed to Roosevelt that, rather than leave trained American divisions to stand idle in the United States throughout the autumn, some of them might be sent to Italy where they —and their boxed equipment—could be landed at Naples without delay. The Prime Minister argued that the Italian campaign was in danger of developing into a stalemate, but that if " two or possibly three American divisions " were sent to reinforce Fifth U.S. Army, the Allies could drive the Germans back to the Po and exploit the advantage they had gained by breaking the Gothic Line in September. They could thus prevent the enemy dispatching any further divisions from Italy to oppose Eisenhower in the West. This proposal was rejected by the U.S. Joint Chiefs of Staff primarily on the ground that the enemy was "free to transfer five or six divisions from Italy . . . whenever [he] considers such action more profitable than containing Allied forces south of the Po."[2]

The Americans were also influenced by their continued determination to keep out of the Balkans. In the first week of October British forces had landed in Greece and Churchill had conferred with Tito in Italy. These developments revived the American fear that, if the Mediterranean Command were reinforced, Churchill would take the opportunity of sending British divisions from Italy into Yugoslavia. This was, in fact, precisely what Hitler dreaded. He was maintaining the battle in Italy for the deliberate purpose of tying down there Allied forces which might otherwise be used to support the Yugoslav partisans, and deprive him of the bauxite, copper and other essential raw materials which he was still getting from the Balkans. By refusing to employ the American reserve divisions anywhere except in Western Europe, where they could not all be brought into action quickly, Marshall and his colleagues were failing to exploit the great strategic flexibility which the Allies enjoyed through their command of the sea.

[1] See ' The Influence of Logistics on Operations in North-West Europe, 1944-45,' by Brigadier C. Ravenhill, a member of Eisenhower's staff, *Royal United Services Institute Journal*, November 1946.
[2] In his diary for October 14th Butcher records the gist of the cables which passed between the Prime Minister and the President on this subject. (Butcher, op. cit., p. 686.)

During September little progress was made with the task of clearing the Scheldt Estuary, for Montgomery's eyes were fixed upon the Ruhr, and he gravely underestimated the time it would take him to open the approaches to Antwerp. As the crow flies, Antwerp is some fifty miles from the sea and, although the great port (with its potential intake of 40,000 tons a day) had been captured virtually intact on September 4th, the Germans continued to command the seaward approaches and to hold the northern suburb of Merxem which was within artillery range of the docks. At the mouth of the estuary—on the island of Walcheren and on the mainland shore between Breskens and Zeebrugge —the Germans had powerful coastal batteries which had to be silenced before any ship could enter Antwerp. Both these areas had been strongly fortified as part of the Atlantic Wall and were difficult to assault from the sea. Nor could they easily be taken by landward attack, once the Germans had recovered from the shock of the British advance through Belgium.

The only approach to Walcheren from the mainland is by the long, narrow isthmus and peninsula of South Beveland and then across a slender causeway on to the island. Much of Beveland and nearly the whole of Walcheren is reclaimed land (polder), which, lying below sea-level, could be readily flooded.

On the southern shore the Leopold Canal provided a natural perimeter for what became known as ' the Breskens Pocket.' Inside this perimeter Model left the 64th Division, a first-class field formation, 14,000 strong and made up primarily of men who had fought on the Russian front. These troops were well supplied with artillery and ammunition left behind by Fifteenth Army, and the nature of the country, much of it flooded, made their positions almost proof against attack by tanks. There were few places where the Canadians could attack with any hope of exploitation and the Germans were able to concentrate on the defence of these.

The capture of the Breskens Pocket and Walcheren was to involve the Canadian Army in a long and bloody campaign which might have been avoided if the necessity for it had been foreseen. Immediately after the capture of Antwerp, while the disorganised Fifteenth German Army was struggling to escape from Flanders, an amphibious force could have landed at the mouth of the Scheldt without great difficulty. The two German divisions, which had been holding this sector of the Atlantic Wall, had been sent south to check the British advance, leaving only a meagre garrison in the coast defences. At SHAEF, however, no provision had been made for taking advantage of such an opportunity. All its planning had been based on the assumption that any ports or pockets of resistance on the Channel coast would be taken from landward and no amphibious reserve had been kept in hand to exploit the Allied command of the sea. Once the Normandy bridgehead was firmly established, all the American landing-craft which were not needed to

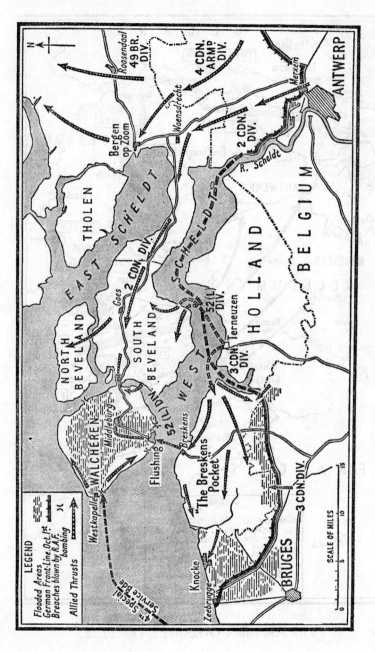

OPENING THE SCHELDT ESTUARY, OCTOBER–NOVEMBER, 1944

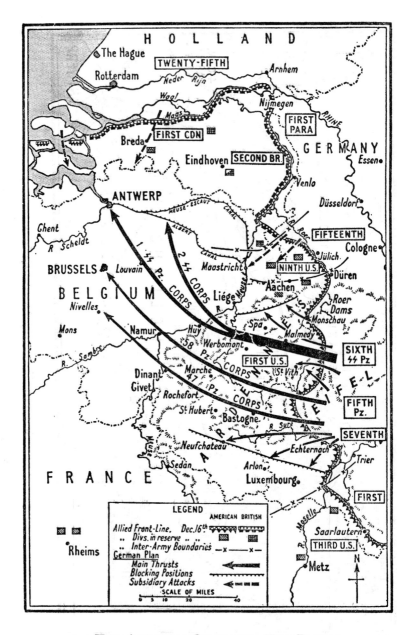

THE ARDENNES OFFENSIVE : THE PLAN

maintain the build-up, were sent to the Mediterranean (for ANVIL), or to the Far East which was receiving in addition almost the entire output of the American shipyards.

In the second half of September, when all the German reserves in Holland were absorbed in the MARKET GARDEN battle, Crerar could not take full advantage of the enemy's preoccupation. East of Antwerp he attacked across the Albert Canal with the object of sealing off the Beveland Peninsula and isolating Walcheren, but he could not make any serious inroad on the Breskens Pocket. For the reduction of this water-logged area he needed at least one infantry division but he had none available. From September 12th to 28th, while the Germans were consolidating their positions on the Leopold Canal, the 51st Highland Division, which could have been used to attack them, was grounded at Le Havre owing to lack of transport.

To some extent Crerar's inability to develop his full offensive strength during September was the result of the 'broad front' policy. While Eisenhower was reinforcing the Allied right wing—and even allowing Bradley to move an American infantry division from Belgium to Lorraine for this purpose—the left wing was allowed to languish. Patton's Moselle offensive was undertaken at the expense not only of the drive for the Ruhr but also of the operations to open Antwerp. Even so, these operations could have been undertaken earlier, if Montgomery had appreciated their importance. As it turned out, however, Antwerp was in Allied hands for a month before the Canadian Army was able to launch a concerted offensive against the German positions on either shore of the Scheldt Estuary.

The key to Antwerp lay in Walcheren. This island is shaped like a saucer. Around the rim natural dunes and man-made dykes hold back the driving waters of the North Sea which once engulfed the polder-land within. Very early in the planning Simonds, the commander of II Canadian Corps, foresaw that the Germans would flood the saucer sufficiently to saturate the polder and thus impose upon the Allies the almost impossible task of attacking along the few embanked roads and over the trackless dunes.[1] He suggested, therefore, that the R.A.F. should bomb the dykes and let in the sea. This, he said, would defeat the enemy's flooding tactics and enable the Allies to turn the flood-waters to their own advantage. The enemy would be denied the use of the roads for the movement of supplies and reserves, his strongpoints on the dunes would be isolated and, if wide breaches were made in the dykes, amphibious craft could sail inside the rim and strike at the German positions from the rear.

Simonds's radical and imaginative proposal, so characteristic of the man, was regarded by Crerar and his staff as "not a practical proposition,"

[1]The fact that there was so little firm, clear land on Walcheren made it impossible, in the opinion of Leigh-Mallory and Brereton, to use airborne troops in the assault upon the island.

but when Montgomery supported it, Bomber Command agreed to make an experimental attack. On October 3rd this was carried out by 243 Lancasters and was so successful that within a few hours the North Sea was pouring in through the Westkapelle Dyke. During the next week this gap was widened and breaches were made at three other points. By the middle of October three-quarters of the island was deep under water and the garrison (of some 8,000 men) was confined to three small strips of coast and to the towns of Flushing and Middelburg.

Walcheren was vulnerable, and Simonds (now acting as Army Commander, for Crerar was ill) intended to attack the island from the west and south with amphibious forces and from the east across the causeway. This triple assault could not be launched, however, until the seaborne task force had completed its training, and the Allies had gained possession of both South Beveland and Breskens. Simonds expected that operations against the Breskens Pocket would take " three or four days," but the defence was so determined and the terrain so difficult that it took four weeks.

On October 6th a brigade of the 3rd Canadian Division gained a precarious foothold across the Leopold Canal. Three nights later another brigade, ferried down the Scheldt from Terneuzen, was landed behind the German perimeter, but the defences did not crack. The determination of the Germans to fight until they were overpowered in their strongholds was fortified by the knowledge that any premature surrender would be treated as desertion and that, by order of the divisional commander, " in cases where the names of deserters are ascertained these will be made known to the civilian population at home and their next of kin will be looked upon as enemies of the German people."[1]

Two weeks of savage and arduous fighting from ditch to ditch carried the Canadians into the port of Breskens, but in the western half of the pocket the enemy continued to fight for every strongpoint, and the last of the coastal batteries was not taken until November 2nd. By then, in conditions which had taxed their courage and endurance to the utmost, the Canadians had taken 12,700 prisoners. " The credit for the victory," as the Canadian historian, Col. C. P. Stacey, so rightly observes, " lay, above all, with the infantry soldier whose dogged determination had carried him through mud, water and fire to dislodge the stubborn foe."[2]

Meanwhile, on the northern shore of the estuary, the infantry of the 2nd Canadian Division had triumphed over similar physical difficulties and equally stubborn resistance. In conjunction with another seaborne assault against the enemy's rear (this time by a British brigade), the Canadians had secured the Beveland Peninsula and reached the narrow causeway linking it with Walcheren. On October 31st the Canadians

[1]Order issued by General Eberding, the Commander of the 64th Infantry Division, on October 14th, 1944.
[2]C. P. Stacey, *The Canadian Army 1939-45*, p. 225.

attacked along the causeway and gained a shallow bridgehead. Next day, they were thrown back but, while the enemy was preoccupied with this attack, the main Allied assault came in from the sea.

On November 1st, under cover of darkness and of a barrage fired from the Breskens shore, Allied commandos[1] sailed into Flushing Harbour and gained a foothold on the waterfront before the garrison appreciated what was happening. Heavy fire greeted the second wave, for batteries on the western shore turned their guns southward, but by the middle of the morning half the town was cleared of Germans and the follow-up troops were streaming ashore. This landing distracted the enemy's attention from the naval task force which appeared off Westkapelle shortly after dawn, but it was soon clear that neither the flooding nor the R.A.F.'s preliminary bombing had seriously reduced the fire-power of the shore defences. H.M.S. *Warspite* and two monitors engaged the coastal guns, but the spotting planes, which were to have observed their fire, were grounded by fog at airfields in England and the warships could make little impression on the German batteries.

Undismayed by this miscarriage of plan, the support squadron (25 landing-craft, mounting rockets and light artillery) drove in-shore and joined unequal battle with the coast defences. Nine craft were sunk and eleven more were put out of action, but their sacrifice was not in vain. While these vessels and some R.A.F. Typhoons were engaging the enemy, commandos of the 4th Special Service Brigade landed almost unscathed on either shoulder of the Westkapelle Gap, where several craft of the support squadron had run ashore and were blasting the German positions at point-blank range. To the enemy's amazement some commandos sailed through the gap in amphibious 'Buffaloes' and took the village of Westkapelle by attack from the east.

Before nightfall the commandos had advanced along the western dunes to capture the two main coastal batteries, but on the eastern side of the island the Germans continued to block the causeway until November 4th, when a brigade of the 52nd Lowland Division, having crossed in assault boats from South Beveland, came in behind them. That day the Royal Navy began sweeping the estuary of the Scheldt. The battle for Antwerp was nearly over and, although it had been so long and so bitter, it ended on a lighter note.

On November 6th, in final execution of the Simonds plan, an amphibious force outflanked the defences of Middelburg and sailed into its western streets unopposed—to the great relief of the 37,000 Dutch civilians who had taken refuge in the upper stories of the flooded houses. A lieutenant of the Royal Scots then went in search of the German garrison commander, Lieut.-General Daser, who, while anxious to end the battle, was reluctant to surrender to so junior an officer. However, the immediate assumption by the subaltern of the 'local and temporary

[1]Although this attack was made by a British unit (No. 4 Commando) the term 'Allied' is rightly applied for it contained French and Dutch troops.

rank of lieutenant-colonel' satisfied the general's honour and he agreed to yield himself and the garrison of Middelburg.

The clearing of the 70-mile channel from the North Sea to Antwerp took more than three weeks and occupied a hundred mine-sweepers. It was November 28th before the first convoy could enter Antwerp. For 85 days the Germans had denied the Allies the use of this great port and, by so doing, had gained for Hitler time that he was soon to turn to good account.

The defensive victories which the Germans won at Arnhem, Aachen and Antwerp prolonged the war into the spring of 1945. These successes not only frustrated Eisenhower's strategic plans, but, coming as they did at the end of a summer of unrelieved defeat and disaster on all fronts, gave fresh heart to the Wehrmacht and the German people. They appeared to justify both Hitler's determination to maintain the struggle and Goebbels's boast that the Allies could be halted at the West Wall. Most important of all, they rallied the German people for the supreme effort which the Führer now demanded of them. The Germans responded the more readily because the first of these military successes coincided with the publication in New York of the outlines of an American plan for the post-war treatment of Germany.

This plan (which became known as the 'Morgenthau Plan' because it was fathered by Henry J. Morgenthau Jnr., the American Secretary of the Treasury) had been endorsed by Roosevelt and Churchill at Quebec on September 15th. The essence of the plan was that Germany should be dismembered and converted into "a country primarily agricultural and pastoral in its character."[1] In execution of this policy Morgenthau proposed that the Ruhr "should not only be stripped of all presently existing industries but so weakened and controlled that it cannot in the foreseeable future become an industrial area. . . . All industrial plans and equipment not destroyed by military action shall either be completely dismantled or removed from the area or completely destroyed, all equipment shall be removed from the mines and the mines shall be thoroughly wrecked."[2]

The Morgenthau Plan was strongly opposed by Henry Stimson, the Secretary of War, and Cordell Hull, the Secretary of State, who argued that this was "a plan of blind vengeance," through which Europe would suffer dearly, since "by completely wrecking the German industry it could not but partly wreck Europe's economy."[3] The news of this disagreement within the Cabinet soon leaked out. On September 24th the essential details of the Morgenthau Plan appeared in the American

[1] Stimson, op. cit., p. 577, quoting the memorandum approved by Roosevelt and Churchill on September 15th, 1944.

[2] Ibid, p. 574, quoting Morgenthau's proposal of September 6th, 1944.

[3] Hull, op. cit., p. 1606. Hull says (p. 1617) that he subsequently told the President that "only 60 per cent of the German population could support themselves on German land and that the other 40 per cent would die."

press to the discomfiture of Roosevelt, who was now inclined to reconsider his decision, and to the delight of Goebbels.

Throughout the summer Goebbels had been harping on the dire consequences of defeat, warning the Germans that their enemies intended to " pursue a plan of exterminating us root and branch as a nation and as a people."[1] The revelation of the Morgenthau Plan enabled him to produce incontrovertible evidence from Allied sources in support of his predictions. He had already instilled into the German people a profound dread of the Russians and it was not difficult now to convince them that they had as much to fear from the Anglo-Saxon powers. In the Wehrmacht and at home there had been many who favoured a policy of ' holding the East and letting in the West,' but Goebbels was able to undermine their influence by asserting, " It hardly matters whether the Bolshevists want to destroy the Reich in one fashion and the Anglo-Saxons propose to do it in another. They both agree on their aim: they wish to get rid of thirty to forty million Germans."[2]

The fact that Henry Morgenthau was a Jew gave powerful point to Goebbels's argument. " The Jew Morgenthau," said Berlin Radio, " sings the same tune as the Jews in the Kremlin." Even those Germans who had not been corrupted by years of anti-Semitic propaganda knew they had no right to expect mercy from the race which their own government had sought to destroy by persecution and pogrom in the most bestial campaign of genocide that Europe had ever known.

Goebbels was able to exploit the propaganda possibilities of the Morgenthau Plan the more effectively because the Allies could not deny that its broad purpose had been approved by the President and the Prime Minister. The situation was not materially altered when Roosevelt discussed the German problem in an election speech on October 21st. He used some reassuring phrases but his general tone was harsh. It could hardly have been otherwise. With the Presidential Election only two weeks away, any ' softness ' towards Germany would have been seized upon by his Republican opponents as evidence that his administration lacked the resolution and power to carry the war through to complete victory. Although by this time Hull and Stimson had convinced him that Morgenthau's proposal was irrational and dangerous, Roosevelt did not publicly disown it. He declared that " the German people are not going to be enslaved," but he gave no definition of ' Unconditional Surrender.' His silence on this point may have been due to his determination to avoid Wilson's mistake of making post-war commitments in the field of foreign policy,[3] but whatsoever the reason, the result was that it allowed Goebbels to continue his campaign almost unchallenged.

[1] *Das Reich*, June 30th, 1944.
[2] Ibid, October 21st, 1944.
[3] It is significant that on the day before this speech Roosevelt gave instructions that all specific planning for post-war Germany was to cease. In a memorandum to Hull that day he said, " I dislike making detailed plans for a country which we do not yet occupy." (Sherwood, op. cit., p. 819.)

For once Goebbels did not need to distort the truth. He could rightly claim that the Allies were proposing to turn the Reich into "a potato patch," and the *Völkischer Beobachter* was hardly overstating the case when it declared that the plan would mean "the destruction of German industry to such an extent that fifty per cent of the German population would be faced with starvation or would be forced to emigrate as working slaves . . . Germany has no illusions about what is in store for her people if they do not fight with all available means against an outcome that would make such plans possible. The Quebec decision will serve only to redouble German resistance." This was indeed its effect, as captured letters written by front-line troops were soon to show.

When this became apparent, Eisenhower himself appealed to the Combined Chiefs of Staff for some modification in the demand for 'Unconditional Surrender.' In Washington and London, however, the Allied leaders were agreed that the demand could not now be modified "without detriment to the prosecution of the war and the establishment of acceptable peace conditions."

By coupling the Morgenthau Plan with the demand for 'Unconditional Surrender,' Goebbels convinced the mass of the German people that their only hope of saving the Fatherland and themselves lay in giving unconditional obedience to the Führer and unconditional resistance to their enemies. Capitulation offered no escape, for they knew that Hitler would never surrender and there was no prospect of his being overthrown. The underground opposition, crippled and disrupted by the purge which followed the ill-fated *attentat* of July 20th, was powerless. The generals alone had the power but they were the more reluctant to act against Hitler now that invading armies stood on German soil. They were restrained not only by their solemn oath and by the fear of being accused of a 'stab in the back,' but also by the knowledge that the Allies were determined to destroy the German military class. Moreover, it was realised by soldiers and civilians alike that any internal revolution at this stage would only precipitate the engulfment of the Reich and its collapse in chaos. It was this fear of chaos that created a new community of interest between the Party, the Wehrmacht and the People.

The Germans had a double reason for dreading the breakdown of civil government. Within the Reich there were more than seven million foreigners working as slaves of the Nazi war machine. It was well known that the vast majority of these foreigners had been forcibly deported and brutally maltreated, and it was feared that at the moment of collapse they would seek their revenge. The dread of anarchy was accentuated by the desperate straits to which the bulk of the urban population had been reduced by Allied bombing. As the destruction and dislocation grew, the people became more dependent than ever on the State—and thus on the Party—for the very essentials of life. Instead of rising in revolt against the Nazi régime, as the Allies had hoped, they were obliged to support it as the only authority capable of preserving order and continuing the supply of food, clothing, fuel and other necessities. They could not sabotage the war effort without endangering their own already precarious existence.

Throughout the autumn of 1944, although the Allied bombing was heavier than ever before, the German people worked with unbroken vigour to repair the bomb damage and maintain the economy of total war. The indiscriminate area bombing of the main cities by the R.A.F., far from weakening the German will to resist, served to confirm Goebbels's contention that the Allies were anxious to destroy not only Germany's military power but the very livelihood of her people. This, he could proclaim, was the Morgenthau Plan in action. The issue was now simple. At all costs the flow of arms and munitions to the troops in the field must be maintained in the hope that the Western Powers, at any rate, would realise the futility of trying to crush Germany and would modify their demand for ' Unconditional Surrender.' Thus, as winter and the invading armies closed in upon them, the German people and their armed forces rallied to uphold the rule of the very man who had led them to the brink of ruin.

Having stabilised the battlefronts in the West and the East, and tightened his grip on the German people, Hitler's most urgent problem was to safeguard his shrinking stocks of oil. After the loss of Rumanian supplies, he had to rely more than ever on the synthetic refineries, and the extreme vulnerability of these had already been alarmingly revealed. At the end of August, as Speer had reported, the oil situation contained " all the portents of catastrophe." There were further attacks in the second week of September, just when the plants were about to resume the refining of petrol, and for nine days synthetic production ceased entirely. The month's output of aviation and motor spirit was only 57,400 tons, barely one-sixth of the amount consumed in August.[1] Stocks of petrol which had stood at more than a million tons in April were now reduced to 327,000—one month's supply at the rate of consumption prevailing before the oil campaign began. For September the petrol allocation to the German forces had been cut by fifty per cent and in October there was a further reduction. Thus, in spite of the delivery of 3,031 single-engined fighters in September (an all-time record for the Reich), the Luftwaffe was even less capable of defending the oil plants than it had been in the summer.

This was the moment for the Allied Air Forces to strike their own *Grosse Schlag.* Since the spring their main task had been to support the invading armies and the attack on oil had been rather a matter of ' private enterprise,' promoted by Spaatz, the commander of the U.S. Strategic Air Forces, with the reluctant though essential support of Harris's Bomber Command. In September, for the first time, the

[1]Report by Speer to Hitler, October 5th, 1944.

Combined Chiefs of Staff ordered Spaatz and Harris to make the oil refineries their top priority target.

That month and the next, however, less than ten per cent of the tonnage dropped on Germany was directed against oil targets, compared with more than twenty-five per cent in both July and August. This reduction of effort allowed the Germans to rebuild their refineries sufficiently to produce 96,000 tons of petrol in November. This was only a third of the output for April but, by enforcing the most stringent economies, Hitler was able to preserve his stocks and to postpone the day of reckoning into the new year.[1]

The slackening of the oil offensive was primarily due to bad weather, which came unexpectedly early and gave the key refineries in Eastern Germany and Czechoslovakia a degree of protection which the Luftwaffe could not provide. The summer raids on these plants had been made entirely by the Americans and, although their high-level formation-bombing had caused great damage, it had seldom resulted in a plant being put out of action for more than two or three weeks. The Americans had found that they needed to make repeated attacks if they were to keep the refineries idle, but the autumn weather did not allow them to do this.

When the weather began to curtail the daylight operations of the Americans, the Combined Chiefs of Staff suggested that the distant refineries should be attacked by Bomber Command which could deliver a much heavier and more concentrated blow. This proposal was not acceptable to Harris, who had been " altogether opposed " to the oil campaign at the outset and still doubted its value. He had always been suspicious of those who advocated attacks on specific industrial targets, because, in his opinion, " the arguments of the economic experts had invariably proved fallacious." He was subsequently to admit that the experts had been right about oil, but at the time he objected on principle to the bombing of what he called ' panacea targets,' and he persisted in the belief that he could do most damage to the enemy by intensifying his area attacks on industrial cities. Since Churchill supported this view, Harris was in a strong position.[2]

Harris's reluctance to attack the more remote oil plants was partly due to the fact that these lay beyond the range of the radar navigational aids which had enabled his bombers to strike so effectively at targets in the Ruhr. He argued, therefore, that refineries such as Leuna, Brüx and Pölitz could not be bombed accurately except in weather good enough for visual bombing, and such weather would favour the enemy. In spite of the petrol shortage, the Luftwaffe's night-fighter defences were

[1]In the active operations of the summer the Wehrmacht alone had needed well over 300,000 tons of aviation and motor spirit per month, but in the static warfare conditions of October the total consumption, in the field and at home, was only 97,000 tons. (*U.S.S.B.S.*, ' Economic Report,' pp. 80, 178 and 278.)

[2]See Harris, op. cit., p. 220.

still formidable and Harris believed that he would suffer very heavy losses if he sent his main force deep into Germany to attack objectives so obvious and vital as the synthetic plants. Since the chances of success appeared to him to be small, he was not prepared to take the risk until he had compelled the Luftwaffe to disperse its night fighters in defence of many widely-separated targets. He could compel such dispersion, he thought, only by resuming his mass raids on major cities. Thus it was not until December that he could be prevailed upon to attack Leuna and Pölitz.

In the meantime the main effort of Bomber Command was directed against the Ruhr and the Rhineland. In October the tonnage of bombs unloaded on German cities by the R.A.F. was twice as great as it had been in any previous month of the war, but the damage inflicted on the enemy's war industry did not rise proportionately. " Effective additional damage," says Harris, " could only be done to the already devastated cities . . . by an enormous expenditure of bombs, as much as four to five thousand tons in a single attack and sometimes up to 10,000 tons in two attacks in close succession." Even then the results were often disappointing. Bomber Command's most effective attacks had been those which caused great conflagrations, as at Hamburg in July 1943, but in cities like Cologne and Essen there was nothing left to burn, and the blast-bombs, which had caused great havoc when the buildings were intact, now did little more than convulse the rubble. Nor did these attacks bring about such disorganisation of labour as had the mass raids of 1943, for the majority of the workers were now living in bomb-proof shelters or reinforced cellars, or had been re-housed outside the main cities. In addition, nearly all the light industries—especially those making munitions, small arms, radio equipment and all manner of accessories and components for tanks, aircraft, vehicles and U-boats—had long since been dispersed in small towns or removed to Central and Eastern Germany. The Ruhr–Rhineland area was no longer the concentrated arsenal it had been in the first four years of the war, and so the immediate output of munitions and weapons, other than tanks, was not directly affected to any considerable extent by Bomber Command's renewed onslaught.

On the other hand, the heavy industries, which the Germans had not been able to ' transplant,' suffered severely. During the first nine months of 1944 the production of coal and steel had been maintained at a level little below the peak of the previous year, but from September onwards there was a sharp decline, as this table shows[1] (see p. 554).

Allied bombing was the principal cause of this decline but, in the case of steel at any rate, it " came too late to have a decisive effect upon the output of munitions."[2] In September most of the war industries outside the Ruhr had sufficient reserves of steel and coal to carry them through

[1] *U.S.S.B.S.*, ' Economic Report,' Table 60 and Appendix Table 73. In the case of crude steel ' All Germany ' includes Occupied Countries.
[2] *U.S.S.B.S.*, ' Economic Report,' p. 108.

the autumn, and although many factories could not carry out the usual stocking up for the winter, they were able to meet the immediate demands of the armaments programme. Moreover, in spite of the general reduction

| HARD COAL *(in millions of tons)* | | |
|---|---|---|
| 1944 | Ruhr | All Germany |
| 1st Quarter - - - | 32.1 | 71.1 |
| 4th Quarter - - - | 17.8 | 44.7 |

| CRUDE STEEL *(in millions of tons)* | | |
|---|---|---|
| 1944 | Ruhr | All Germany |
| 1st Quarter - - - | 3.4 | 9.2 |
| 4th Quarter - - - | 1.5 | 3.9 |

in output, the Ruhr continued to provide the essential heavy castings and forgings, high-grade electro-steel and special alloys which could not be produced in adequate quantities elsewhere. Area bombing alone could not stop this vital source of supply; it could be cut off only by the conquest of the Ruhr or by the complete disruption of its communications.

In their September directive the Combined Chiefs of Staff had ruled that, next to oil, the main target of the strategic air forces should be transportation, but it was November before a systematic plan for paralysing the railway and canal network of Western Germany was worked out. Through most of the autumn, as the *United States Strategic Bombing Survey* reports, the attacks on transportation, though fairly heavy, were largely tactical in character and were directed mainly against the railways which fed the Western Front. No serious attempt was made to isolate the Ruhr. Yet this could have been achieved if Bomber Command had concentrated on the precision bombing of key transportation targets (as it had done in France before D-Day) instead of on the area bombardment of cities.

The two main canals leading from the Ruhr, the Dortmund–Ems and the Mittelland, were, as Harris says, " a first-class panacea target," but he did not attack them until November. The flow of traffic along these waterways could have been stopped at least a month earlier. There was a similar delay in the development of the offensive against rail targets. The argument of those who opposed the bombing of marshalling yards and major junctions was that " purely military traffic was only a small proportion of the total traffic and that, even if the attacks . . . succeeded in reducing the railway system's capacity by two-thirds or three-quarters, this would cut only into non-military traffic and leave essential military communications unhindered."[1] This argument had already been disproved in the case of the French railways and it was even less valid when applied to Germany.

The bombing of cities in 1943 and the following winter had compelled the Germans to disperse their war industries and to resort to a policy of large-scale prefabrication. Components for tanks, aircraft, U-boats and other weapons were now produced in many different parts of the Reich and were brought together only when ready for assembly. Thus in the autumn of 1944 the most vulnerable points of the German war economy were not the great industrial cities, which Harris was bombing so thoroughly, but the network of communications which linked the dispersed factories with their sources of coal and raw materials on the one hand, and the assembly centres on the other. Even as it was, rail traffic declined by fifty per cent and water traffic by seventy-five per cent between August and December. It is quite apparent, however, from the records of the *Reichsbahn* and of Speer's Ministry that, if the attack on communications had been as heavy and as concentrated in October as it was in November, the Wehrmacht could not have been adequately rearmed for another offensive.

Although the strategic air forces did not succeed in bringing the Nazi war machine to a standstill in the autumn of 1944, they did compel Speer to resort to a series of desperate, short-term measures, which undermined the structure of the German economy and accelerated its eventual collapse. In September, October and November, Speer kept the munitions factories working at high pressure only by using up supplies of raw materials which were in the ' pipe-line,' by assembling stocks of components, by drastic rationalisation and by driving German and foreign workers alike to the point of exhaustion. By these expedients, and by reducing civilian production to the very minimum necessary for existence, Speer was able to maintain, and in some cases increase, the output of essential weapons and ammunition, as the following figures indicate:

| 1944 | Rifles | Machine-Guns | Anti-Tank Guns (75mm) | Mortars (80 mm) | Infantry Guns (75 mm and 150 mm) | Howitzers (105 mm and 150 mm) | Ammunition (in tons) |
|---|---|---|---|---|---|---|---|
| July | 249,080 | 24,141 | 1,000 | 2,225 | 335 | 1,154 | 306,000 |
| Aug. | 203,385 | 24,788 | 840 | 2,340 | 360 | 944 | 310,000 |
| Sept. | 169,023 | 26,629 | 928 | 2,250 | 356 | 946 | 321,000 |
| Oct. | 173,350 | 26,252 | 1,054 | 2,190 | 330 | 1,049 | 308,000 |
| Nov. | 213,342 | 25,741 | 1,025 | 2,320 | 387 | 824 | 294,000 |

[1] *U.S.S.B.S.*, ' Economic Report,' p. 5.

If it had not been for the Allied air attacks, the production of most of these armaments would have been even greater, but during the autumn of 1944 there was no serious decline in the output of any of the main weapons needed by the Army, except tanks. In June, July and August 2,438 Tigers, Panthers and Mark IVs came from the factories, but in the next three months the number produced fell to 1,764, and of these only 1,371 were delivered to the Wehrmacht.[1] The substantial difference between ' production ' and ' deliveries ' was itself due to the air offensive. Many tanks were destroyed when factories and railways were bombed, and many more developed mechanical defects which were the natural consequence of the chaotic conditions created by bombing. The most marked falling off was in the production of Tigers which declined from a monthly rate of 106 in the summer to 36 in the autumn, primarily as a result of a series of highly effective raids by the Eighth U.S. Air Force on the only factory producing these tanks, the Henschel works at Kassel. By the start of December these attacks, and the general dislocation caused by strategic bombing, had deprived the Germans of at least two hundred Tigers.

This decline in tank production—resulting in the ' loss ' of more than a thousand tanks of all kinds in three months—was partly offset by a phenomenal increase in the output of assault guns. Since most of the assault gun assembly plants were situated in Czechoslovakia, they suffered little direct interruption from bombing, and the manufacture of these weapons rose from 766 in August to 1,199 in November.[2] Thus, although Hitler could not replace more than half the tanks which his panzer divisions had lost in France, he was able to replenish their striking power with 75 mm assault guns. Not being mounted in turrets these '75s' were more effective in defence than attack, but at this stage of the war they were invaluable.

Remarkable though it was, the autumn rate of arms production was hardly sufficient to make good the current wastage on all fronts, let alone the vast losses of the summer. Nevertheless, Hitler continued to insist that by far the greater proportion of the new weapons should go, not to the hard-pressed troops in the line, but to the divisions which were being formed or re-formed in the Reich.[3] There, Himmler (C.-in-C., Home Army) was training and equipping twenty-five of the *Volksgrenadier* divisions which Hitler had ordered him to raise in September. These

[1]These figures are taken from the *U.S.S.B.S.*, ' Economic Report,' Appendix Table 104, and from the files of the Inspectorate of Panzer Troops at OKH.

[2]Ibid, Appendix Table 104. More assault guns were produced in the last three months of 1944 than in the whole of 1943.

[3]The records of OKH for September 1944 reveal the following extraordinary figures:

| | Losses in the Field | Distribution of Production | |
| | | Front-line Divisions | New Divisions |
| Machine-guns - - | 27,341 | 1,527 | 24,473 |
| Mortars (80 mm) - - | 2,090 | 303 | 1,947 |
| Field and Medium Artillery | 764 | 560 | 773 |

divisions had been created from ' burnt out ' formations which had been withdrawn from the Eastern and Western Fronts after the summer campaign to be rebuilt with the products—human and material—of Goebbels's drive for ' total mobilisation.'

By lowering the call-up age from seventeen and a half to sixteen years, by a thorough comb-out of industry and a general scouring of the Home Front, Goebbels had been able to provide Himmler with 300,000 men in August and a further 200,000 in both September and October. With these men, and with substantial drafts from the Luftwaffe and the Navy, the German Army received a blood transfusion of very much higher quality than any which had come to it during the past year. Most of those called up by Goebbels or transferred from the other services at this time were young men of good physique and thoroughly imbued with Nazi doctrines. The training of these recruits was entrusted to officers and N.C.O.s already experienced in battle, and it was so simplified and concentrated that a division capable of carrying out a defensive role could be produced in six to eight weeks.

Into the *Volksgrenadier* divisions Himmler drafted the last reserves of German manpower and, by doing so, prejudiced the maintenance of war production. In August, when Hitler decided to transfer a quarter of a million young men from industry to the Army, Speer protested that this would deprive him of many skilled workers who could not be replaced and would seriously affect the output of armaments before the end of the year. " Weapons," he argued, " are needed more desperately than soldiers." Hitler was deaf to this plea, for the effect on production would not be felt immediately and he was concerned only with the present emergency. The solution of this depended, he believed, on his capacity to rebuild his armies before the winter. The spring could take care of itself.

The German manpower crisis would not have been so acute if Speer had been able to bring in women workers to take the place of the men called to the colours. During the first five years of the war, for reasons of social policy, there had been no drastic mobilisation of German women for war work. In Britain the conscription of women was introduced in 1941; in Germany only in 1943 and even then it was not strictly enforced. The comparative statistics show that between May 1939 and May 1944 the number of women employed increased by only 182,000 in Germany but by 2,283,000 in Britain. In the Reich the number of women engaged in industry during this period actually decreased, while in Britain it rose by nearly fifty per cent. The Germans even maintained their pre-war rate of employment of domestic servants at a total of close on a million and a half, but the number of domestic servants in Britain declined from 1,200,000 in 1939 to less than half a million in 1944.[1]

In the autumn of 1944, when the Germans desperately needed to make use of their untapped reserve of ' woman-power,' it could not be

[1] *U.S.S.B.S.*, ' Economic Report,' Appendix Table 15.

mobilised. By this time the administrative machine was over-burdened with problems created by the air offensive; the re-housing of the bombed-out, the repairing of damaged factories, and the preservation of essential services and food supplies. It was now incapable of organising any large-scale transfer of women to industry. Nor could this have been done without disturbing still further the lives of those who were working. In the main cities normal domestic life had become so precarious that the mere task of maintaining their homes and caring for their children absorbed the energies of most of the women who were not already employed.

For the German people the most depressing aspect of their autumn ordeal was the Luftwaffe's apparent inability to offer more than token resistance to the daylight raiders. Even when a thousand American bombers, and as many fighters, flew deep into the Reich, as they often did, it was seldom that more than two hundred German aircraft rose to intercept them. In October the day-fighter strength of the Luftwaffe stood at the record figure of 3,100 machines, but the scale of its operations was limited both by the scarcity of petrol, and by Galland's determination to rebuild the Fighter Arm for *Der Grosse Schlag*, the operation he had been about to launch in August when Hitler had sacrificed the fighter reserve over France. After this debacle, Galland had convinced Goering that the Fighter Arm should not dissipate its energies in " day-to-day operations on a small scale," but should conserve its resources for " a series of mighty, concentrated blows."

Throughout October, therefore, operations were severely curtailed so that the bulk of the petrol allocation could be used to train fresh pilots and to school the fighter squadrons in new tactics of mass attack. In the past the Luftwaffe's interceptions had too often proved abortive because fighters mounting the heavy armament necessary to bring down the Fortresses and Liberators could not break through the American fighter screen; on the other hand, fighters possessing the speed and manœuvrability to engage the Mustangs and Thunderbolts successfully could not carry the fire-power to be sure of destroying the American bombers. Galland's solution was to attack the American formations with equally strong German formations containing a core of heavily-armed Focke-Wulfs, escorted by lighter and speedier Messerschmitts.

By the start of November Galland had trained and organised a fighter force far stronger, numerically, than Germany had ever possessed, and had accumulated sufficient petrol to allow him to commit 2,500 aircraft in a single operation. By attacking in such strength, he hoped, not unreasonably, that the American defences would be overwhelmed and that " between 400 and 500 bombers would be brought down for the loss of an equal number of German fighters and 150 pilots." He believed that such casualties—ten times greater than the average losses the Americans were suffering—would break their morale and certainly discourage them from attempting to reach the oil refineries again. He had no doubt that his airmen would rise to the occasion, for many had taken an oath " to shoot down or ram at least one bomber on each mission."

In preparation for the ' Great Strike,' Galland arranged a series of exercises designed to try out his new tactics and organisation. One of these was set down for November 2nd, but just as it was starting, a force of 680 American bombers and 750 fighters flew into Germany bound for Leuna. Willy-nilly the exercise became an operation. That day the Luftwaffe claimed the destruction of 50 American bombers at a cost to itself of 120 fighters, but this unpremeditated encounter was hardly a fair test of Galland's plan.[1] Only one-eighth of his potential force was engaged and there was no chance of swamping the raiders by weight of numbers. Nevertheless, two assault groups, with 62 heavy fighters, did break through the defensive screen and brought down 30 of the bombers that were destroyed.

If anything, the outcome was a vindication of Galland's tactics, but, when the reports reached Hitler, he ignored this achievement and seized on the fact that the 260 escorting fighters had claimed only 20 victims. That, he told his staff, was " a shocking performance." Arguing from this alone and applying a purely mathematical yardstick, he declared : " I send 260 fighters into action and I shoot down 20 bombers. If I employ 2,600 I will shoot down 200 . . . In other words, there is no hope of decimating the enemy with a mass assault. So it's madness to go on producing machines all the time just to enable the Luftwaffe to play about with figures."[2]

On the basis of this one incident—and his own illogical deductions from it—Hitler countermanded *Der Grosse Schlag*. There was to be no mass attack on the daylight raiders. Top priority would be given to the production of flak " without regard to any other consideration whatsoever."[3]

If Galland had been allowed to carry out his plan, it would have resulted in the fiercest and greatest aerial battle of the war and, almost certainly, in the final destruction of the Luftwaffe. It was the fear of this that made Hitler pause, for he now needed the Fighter Arm he had so often abused. He wanted to preserve it for a *Grosse Schlag* of his own, for a bigger and bolder blow not against the Allied air forces over the Reich, but against the Allied armies in the field.

Whatever the ultimate consequences of the autumn drive for maximum production and total mobilisation, the immediate result was to give

[1] In this operation the actual American losses were 38 bombers and 25 fighters.
[2] Führer Conferences, Fragment 2, November 6th, 1944.
[3] Minutes of a meeting between Hitler and Speer, November 4th, 1944.

Hitler the means of rebuilding his shattered armies and, for the first time since June, of creating a strategic reserve, the newly-formed Sixth SS Panzer Army. This remarkable recovery, and his strategic success in halting both the eastern and western invasions, convinced Hitler that he might yet obtain a compromise peace if only he could strike a crippling blow at one or other of his adversaries. But which? He soon realised that he had neither the forces to inflict a serious defeat on the Red Army, nor the petrol to maintain an advance deep enough to deprive Stalin of any essential resources. His best opportunity of regaining the initiative lay, he decided, in the West. Here with smaller forces and less petrol he might capture an objective of critical significance. In addition, it appeared to him that the Western Allies were more vulnerable and less tenacious than the Russians. He believed that the British were nearly exhausted and that the Americans had no real interest in the war against Germany. Lacking the toughness and the incentive of the Russians, American troops would quickly lose heart in adversity. Their victories had been won, so he thought, only by air-power, but, once winter deprived them of their customary air support, the Americans would collapse under the impact of a powerful assault.

The contemplation of an attack in the West led Hitler inevitably to the Ardennes, the scene of his greatest victory. For an offensive here, the attacking forces could be concentrated under cover of the thickly wooded Eifel, and could strike at the weakest part of the Allied front, the sector which lay between the American concentrations at Aachen and Metz. A strong, rapid drive through the Ardennes to the Meuse might open the road to Brussels and Antwerp before the Americans could move their reserves. If Antwerp were taken the Allies would lose the only major port they had captured intact, and, even more important, the Allied Armies north of the Ardennes would be trapped with their backs to the sea and with no major port by which to escape. Hitler had visions of another Dunkirk; but this time he would not allow his enemies to slip through his grasp.

Such a defeat, Hitler believed, would disrupt the Allied coalition, cripple the Western Powers and compel them to realise the futility of trying to crush Nazi Germany. Even if a compromise peace were not forthcoming at once, this offensive would dislocate the Allied plans for a winter campaign and would gain what Hitler most needed—Time. It would give him the opportunity to rebuild his bombed factories under the protection of winter weather, and to develop the production of jet-fighters for the defence of the Reich, of V-weapons for retaliation against the British, and of electro-U-boats to staunch the flow of American power across the Atlantic.

These extravagant hopes inspired the plan which Hitler and Jodl began preparing within a few days of the British withdrawal from Arnhem. On October 8th Jodl presented a draft plan for an offensive through the Ardennes to Antwerp to be launched at the end of November.

By then, he reported, they could assemble a force of thirty-two divisions: twelve panzer or panzer grenadier, two parachute and eighteen infantry. The latter, all of the *Volksgrenadier* class, were now being trained in the Reich. Six of the armoured formations were already being re-equipped east of the Rhine and the remainder could be withdrawn to refit during the next month. These divisions would provide the striking power for three armies: Sixth SS Panzer (Dietrich), Fifth Panzer (Manteuffel), and Seventh (Brandenberger), and their assault could be supported by a thousand fighters and four hundred bombers.

Jodl was instructed to proceed with plans and preparations in strictest secrecy. All the preliminary planning was to be carried out at the Führer's own H.Q. No one was to be told more than he needed to know sooner than he needed to know it, and then he must be required to sign a pledge of secrecy ' on pain of death.' No messages concerning the attack were to be sent by wireless or telephone. No couriers carrying orders were to travel by air, for such a courier had come down in Belgium in November '39. No reconnaissance was to be made until the last minute and, lest any unauthorised person should guess that preparations were being made for an offensive, the plan was given the code-name *Wacht am Rhein*.

Throughout October von Rundstedt maintained the front in the West without yielding any vital ground and without having to draw upon the reserves that Hitler was accumulating for the Ardennes. As yet, however, there had been no large-scale assault on the western defences, except at Aachen. Here the Americans had been checked, but would von Rundstedt be equally successful in November when the Allies resumed their offensive in greater strength, as surely they must? Would they then gain a break-through which would compel Hitler to commit his reserves? Would they, in any case, remain vulnerable in the Ardennes?

These questions stood unanswered, but Hitler was full of confidence and in his enthusiasm ignored his own security instructions. On October 28th he telephoned to Goebbels to wish him a ' Happy Birthday.' " After two minutes at the telephone," says one who was present,[1] " Goebbels came out of the next room with a beaming face. He said that Hitler wanted to speak with his wife as well. With her he spoke even longer. Frau Goebbels came back tremendously excited at what the Führer had said. She had tears in her eyes as she told us there were great hopes for the future. By Christmas the outlook would have changed completely. For Christmas the German people would receive the present of a great military triumph. Then the turn of the tide would come."

But whether this bold prophecy would ever reach fruition depended on the outcome of the battles to be fought in November.

[1]Rudolf Semmler, personal assistant to Goebbels, *Goebbels—the Man next to Hitler*, pp. 162-3.

## CHAPTER XXIX

# THE AUTUMN STALEMATE

THE rapid recovery of the Wehrmacht, the long delay in opening Antwerp and the early approach of winter, which gave such encouragement to Hitler, compelled Eisenhower to reconsider his strategic plans. In Brussels on October 18th he conferred with Bradley and Montgomery. They were agreed that another major effort must be made to reach the Rhine and gain a substantial bridgehead before the winter, but it was now evident that Antwerp would not be open much before the end of November and that any autumn offensive would have to be maintained from Normandy, Le Havre and the Channel ports. Montgomery therefore repeated his familiar arguments that they had not the resources for a general offensive and that they should concentrate on capturing the Ruhr. The essential condition of success was, he said, that there should be no offensive operations south of the Ardennes, except in so far as these could be sustained from Marseille.

Eisenhower did not accept this latter contention, but he agreed that the Ruhr was their primary objective and that the attack on the Saar should not be pressed until the armies north of the Ardennes had reached the Rhine. He agreed further that the capture of the Ruhr was a task for two armies under command of one man. He decided, however, that the armies should be American and that the man should be Bradley. This was a diplomatic decision. If Patton had to be restrained again, it was essential that the restraint should be imposed in the interests of an American, not a British plan, of Bradley, not Montgomery.

The plan which emerged from this conference was that the main drive to the Rhine should be made through the Aachen Gap by the First and Ninth U.S. Armies under Bradley's direction.[1] Their offensive would begin at the start of November and, once they had crossed the intermediate barrier of the Roer River, First Army would strike east to Cologne and Bonn, while Ninth Army wheeled north to Krefeld. In support of these operations, Second British Army, attacking from the Nijmegen area on or about November 10th, would clear the Reichswald

[1]The Ninth Army, commanded by Lieut.-General W. H. Simpson, had been brought up from Brittany at the end of September, and was now to take over the northern sector of First Army's front.

and advance south between the Maas and the Rhine so that the Germans could be squeezed out of the Lower Rhineland by converging thrusts. Thus, it was hoped, the Allies would gain the line of the river on a front of a hundred miles from Arnhem to Bonn. The Rhine would then be crossed by First Army south of Cologne and by Ninth Army north of Düsseldorf, and the Ruhr would be captured by a double enveloping movement.

At Brussels " no date was set for an attack by Patton's forces. The Third Army, it was agreed, would resume its advance ' when logistics permit.' "[1] Its operations, Eisenhower's directive expressly said, would be " subsidiary to " and " so timed as best to assist the main effort in the north."[2]

Bradley placed a liberal interpretation on these instructions, for, as he told Patton, he believed that " if all the armies . . . attacked simultaneously, it might well end the war."[3] Accordingly, the orders which Bradley issued on October 21st provided not for a concentrated offensive north of the Ardennes but for a general advance to the Rhine by his three armies: the First and Ninth to attack on November 5th and the Third five days later.

This was Bradley's intention when, on October 27th, the Germans launched a strong spoiling attack against an American armoured division which, on loan to Montgomery, was holding the southern sector of the British front east of Eindhoven. Although this attack was contained by the end of the month, it delayed the clearing of the area south of the Maas and prevented Second Army meeting the target date of November 10th for the attack on the Reichswald. It meant also that Montgomery could not immediately return the two American divisions which Bradley had lent him. These divisions were to have been available to First Army at the start of November and without them Hodges did not feel strong enough to begin his offensive.

In these circumstances a Supreme Commander exercising real control over the battle would have intervened to ensure that this setback did not disrupt his plan. He would have ordered Bradley to reinforce Hodges and assist Montgomery so that the primary task, the offensive in the Lower Rhineland, could be carried out as planned. Eisenhower made no such move. Nor did Bradley, for he realised that the necessary strength could be provided for Hodges only at the expense of Patton, and he had always been reluctant to make Third Army assume a subsidiary role. On November 2nd, therefore, finding that Patton was ready to " jump off on twenty-four hours' notice," Bradley authorised him to attack as soon as the weather allowed.

---

[1] Cole, op. cit., p. 299, quoting the minutes of the Brussels meeting.

[2] Since the SHAEF Directive, issued after the conference, is quite explicit on this point, it is surprising to read Bradley's post-war version of the Eisenhower plan. " In his plan," says Bradley (op. cit., p. 435), " 12th Army Group was to attack north of the Ardennes with the First and Ninth Armies, and south of that wooded barrier with the Third. All three were to push on to the Rhine and seize crossings if they could."

[3] Patton, op. cit., p. 156.

Bradley's eagerness to give Patton his head, and his inclination to rely more on him than on Hodges, reflected both his estimate of the two men and the history of his relations with them. Hodges was a competent but shy man who lived in the shadow of a frustrated past. He had once commanded Third U.S. Army but had been supplanted by Patton when this Army was sent to England for the invasion. Then, on Eisenhower's initiative, Hodges was appointed Deputy Commander of First Army with the intention that he should take over when Bradley went to 12th Army Group. After the Normandy break-out Hodges was nominally on an equal footing with Patton, but he had never held a field command before and he was eclipsed by Third Army's brilliant and forceful leader.

Hodges was at a further disadvantage *vis-à-vis* Patton, for he had been Bradley's deputy, whereas Patton had been Bradley's superior until the unfortunate occasion in Sicily when Patton slapped the face of a shell-shocked man in hospital. At that time Patton was commanding Seventh U.S. Army, in which Bradley had a corps, and was strongly favoured to lead the American forces in the cross-Channel assault. This appointment fell to Bradley, who was, says Eisenhower, " emotionally stable." Yet Bradley was forever conscious that Patton was not only his senior in rank, but also his superior in tactical skill and experience. Having great faith in the professional ability of his former chief, Bradley naturally reposed more trust in him than in Hodges. This was particularly the case when there was a possibility of exploitation. Hodges had been brought up with infantry, but Patton had all the dash and drive of the cavalryman who had been converted to armour.

Patton now assured Bradley that he could get to the Saar in three days and " easily breach the West Wall." With six infantry and three armoured divisions, plus two groups (i.e. brigades) of mechanised cavalry, Third Army numbered approximately a quarter of a million officers and men. Its opponents, the First German Army, had a total strength of only 86,000. Seven of the eight enemy divisions were strung out on a front of 75 miles and the only reserve was the 11th Panzer Division with 69 tanks. While the German formations were necessarily dispersed defensively, Patton, with command of the air and ample mobility on the ground, had the capacity to concentrate overwhelming force at any point he chose. Even on a basis of direct comparison he had an advantage of three to one in men, eight to one in tanks and a " tremendous superiority in the artillery arm."[1] By means which the records do not reveal, he had built up such substantial stocks of ammunition that his guns could put down treble the fire that was available to the Germans. With these advantages, and with the aid of an initial bombardment by 1,300 Fortresses and Liberators, Patton expected to achieve a quick, decisive break-through which would carry him to the Rhine. His plan was that XII Corps (Eddy) should make the main effort, attacking from

[1]Cole, op. cit., p. 317.

the Nancy sector and driving north-east to the Saar. Starting twenty-four hours later, XX Corps (Walker) was to envelop and capture Metz, thus clearing the way for Patton's left wing to advance to the Siegfried Line north of the Saar.

Patton decided to launch his offensive on November 8th at the latest, but throughout the three previous days it rained almost incessantly. By the 7th the rivers which ran athwart the front, already flooded by the October rains, were breaking their banks. Within two days " every bridge on the Moselle River, except one at Pont-à-Mousson, was cut, and the Seille River [in the XII Corps sector] had increased in width from two hundred to five hundred feet."[1] The fields were sodden and movement off the roads, even by tracked vehicles, was almost impossible. On the evening of the 7th Eddy urged Patton to " hold off the attack on account of bad weather and swollen rivers."[2] Patton asked him to name his successor. Eddy attacked next morning, but his troops went into action in a drenching downpour, with no support from the air until late in the afternoon and then very little.

That day the three infantry divisions of XII Corps, attacking on a thirty-mile front, gained their initial objectives, but their advance was slow and arduous and Eddy had no chance of unleashing his armour. On November 9th in rain and snow two armoured divisions endeavoured to drive through, but soon found that they could not manoeuvre across country and that on all possible avenues of exploitation the enemy had established road-blocks in depth. Mud and minefields restricted their progress and gave the enemy time to deploy his mobile reserves and head off the American columns while his infantry fell back to new positions already prepared.

The frustration of Patton's hope of a quick break-through was not entirely due to the weather. It was also the result of his failure to profit by the lesson of the campaign in Normandy. There in the first attempt to break out, the Americans had attacked all along the line and had succeeded at great cost merely in pushing the Germans back a few miles. Before the second attempt, Montgomery had persuaded Bradley to make a concentrated assault on a very narrow front at St. Lô. The break-through which resulted had been brilliantly exploited, but in the exaltation of success neither Bradley nor Patton appear to have remembered that the foundation of their victory was Montgomery's insistence on concentration.

In Lorraine Balck, the commander of Army Group G, anticipating that Patton would attack on all sectors, had laid his plans accordingly. The forward German positions were some forty miles west of the Siegfried Line, and this cushion of ' expendable territory ' allowed Balck to pursue a policy of elastic defence, as Ludendorff had done in 1917. The best answer to these tactics was not a co-ordinated advance along the entire front, but a concerted attack on a narrow sector, followed by a deep penetration. Once such a penetration had been made, the American armour could not have been checked by the slender reserves at Balck's disposal.

As it was, however, with every division trying to make a break-through, the artillery support was dispersed, and Eddy was able to gain only fifteen miles in eight days. The German line sagged, but did not break, for at no point was it subjected to an overpowering onslaught. Meanwhile, the enveloping attack against Metz, also made on a broad front, was similarly checked by skilful and stubborn defence. Even after a week of heavy fighting, the city was not encircled.

When the Third Army offensive began, Bradley hoped that this would attract to Lorraine German reserves which otherwise might be available to oppose First and Ninth Armies. This hope did not materialise. Knowing that he could afford to fall back to the Siegfried Line in the Saar sector and expecting that the main Allied effort would be made north of the Ardennes, von Rundstedt kept the bulk of his mobile forces concentrated to meet the attack from Aachen. He moved one infantry division south from the Ardennes, but, apart from this and an armoured battlegroup from OKW reserve, Balck had to rely on his own resources. Thus by November 16th, although Patton was still highly optimistic, he had gained no strategic success. But he had consumed vast quantities of ammunition which were soon to be needed by Hodges and Simpson.

In the protracted battle for Aachen First U.S. Army had drawn heavily on its stocks, and, says its Report of Operations, " ammunition became a matter of especial concern during the latter part of October."[1] By mid-November the position had improved, but neither First nor Ninth Armies was able to build up a reserve adequate to support a prolonged operation. This situation was due partly to the consistent delivery to Patton of his ' share ' of the available tonnage, regardless of Hodges's greater need; and partly to the excessive optimism of the late summer which had led to a slackening of production in the United States and of shipments to Europe. The ammunition crisis became so acute that Eisenhower himself broadcast a special appeal to the American people for increased output and more rapid dispatch. The restriction which this crisis imposed on the employment of their artillery made it the more important that Hodges and Simpson should not attack without maximum air support.

The plan was that the offensive should be launched by four divisions of First Army and four of Ninth Army on a 25-mile front between the Hürtgen Forest and Geilenkirchen. On this sector since the middle of September the Americans had eaten away the main fortifications of the

[1]First U.S. Army ' Report of Operations, 1 August 1944–22 February 1945,' p. 92.

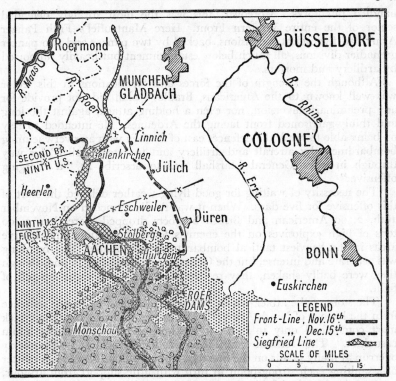

THE ATTACK TO THE RIVER ROER, NOVEMBER-DECEMBER 1944

Siegfried Line, but had not been able to make a clean breach and, by
holding Aachen for a month, the Germans had gained time to build a
new line east of that city. This line ran through the dense and hilly
Hürtgen Forest into a belt of factories and coal-mines around Stolberg
and then across open fields until it rejoined the West Wall proper at
Geilenkirchen. Some permanent fortifications were incorporated in this
line and it gained added strength from the forest in the south and the
tangled industrial area in the centre. Even in the more open northern
sector in front of Ninth Army, the compact stone villages provided ready-
made strongholds, for many of the houses had ' pill-box basements '
roofed with concrete and fitted with embrasures.

    In this constricted area there was little room for manœuvre and the
possibility of exploitation was further curtailed by a series of minefields,
heavily infested with new types of mines which, being mounted in
wooden or glass containers, could not be located by the electronic
detectors then in use. To locate these mines the Americans had to
resort to the hazardous expedient of prodding for them with long-

handled pitchforks. Moreover, this was the most strongly defended sector of the entire Western Front. Here Manteuffel's Fifth Panzer Army had five infantry divisions, backed by two panzer and two panzer grenadier divisions, all much below establishment but heavily supported by artillery and mortars.

Although the strength of the forces and fortifications in this sector was well known to the Americans, Bradley's plan did not provide for any preliminary diversion, nor even a holding attack, against the long and thinly-garrisoned front facing the Ardennes. He intended to rely on being able to crush the defences east of Aachen with an overwhelming bombardment by aircraft and artillery and to ' steam-roller ' his way through in what General Marshall was to describe as " a charging offensive."

The necessity of waiting for good flying weather delayed the start of this offensive for five days. When it was finally launched on November 16th, 2,500 American and British bombers dropped more than 9,400 tons of high explosives on the enemy's forward positions and reserve areas in the heaviest tactical bombardment ever made. The bombing was accurate and intense, but the Germans were well dug in and, though they were badly shaken, they recovered quickly and came up full of fight.

The story of the attack which followed is summed up in one sentence from the history of Ninth Army : " The enemy knowing how the attack must come, had only to block it head-on and inflict the maximum casualties." The German outpost line was lightly held and was quickly overrun at many points on the first day, but after that it became a matter of assaulting each strong-point in turn with little support from armour, because the drenched fields soon became quagmires, and with inadequate support from artillery because of the ammunition shortage. What might have been achieved with the aid of heavier and more concentrated artillery fire was apparent from the experience of the two divisions, one British and one American, which assaulted the intact defences of the Siegfried Line at Geilenkirchen, where Bradley's front joined Montgomery's. This attack gained rapid success, for American fire-power was reinforced by British guns which, as the Ninth Army's historian says, " had ample ammunition to permit artillery support on a far more lavish scale than American supply permitted."[1]

On the rest of the front, resolute defence, repeated counter-attacks and recurrent rain reduced the battle to infantry slogging of the nastiest kind. Daily gains were measured in yards. By the end of November Ninth Army had reached the Roer River from Jülich to Linnich, but it was another two weeks before First Army had closed up to the river opposite Düren.

Thus, after a bitter month which had taken heavy toll of his infantry, Bradley's troops were only eight miles deeper into Germany. Before them

[1]*Conquer*, p. 83.

lay the flooded Roer, on the east bank of which the Wehrmacht was manning a new line. The real strength of this line lay not in its prepared defences, but in the torrential floods which the Germans could release at will from seven dams on the upper reaches of the river. Bradley's engineers estimated, rightly, that if these dams were blown, the rush of water would sweep away all bridges downstream and make the river impassable for at least a week. Hodges had already made two attempts to capture these dams and the R.A.F. had tried to burst them with its heaviest bombs—all in vain. While the Germans held the headwaters, Bradley dared not send his armies across the Roer. The risk of their being cut off and destroyed was too great, particularly as the Germans had moved Sixth SS Panzer Army west of the Rhine at the end of November and had deployed it to counter any further advance towards Cologne and Düsseldorf.

On November 18th, two days after the start of the offensive from Aachen, Patton completed the isolation of Metz and renewed his attack towards the Saar with increased vigour. Next day, far to the south on the extreme right of the Allied front, where the Germans were holding the rugged line of the Vosges Mountains, the First French Army broke through the Belfort Gap and reached the Upper Rhine and the outskirts of Mulhouse after an advance of 25 miles in one day. The collapse of its southern hinge weakened the entire Vosges Line, the northern wing of which was already under heavy pressure from Seventh U.S. Army. On the 22nd Haislip's XV Corps forced the Saverne Gap and on the following day, with the 2nd French Armoured Division in the van, swept on almost unopposed to liberate Strasbourg. This brilliant stroke split the German front in two, for it fell at the junction of the First and Nineteenth Armies, and even the intervention of the rebuilt Panzer Lehr Division (released by Hitler from his strategic reserve) could not restore the breach.

The German situation in the Vosges was now extremely critical. Between the Seventh American Army at Strasbourg and the First French Army at Mulhouse the remnants of the Nineteenth German Army were compressed into what became known as the ' Colmar Pocket.' The Germans were still holding the main heights of the Vosges, but they were vulnerable to flank attacks from north and south along the Rhine Plain. If this pocket could be cleared, the Allies would be able to establish a strong defensive front along the Upper Rhine and thus set free considerable forces for offensive operations in areas of greater strategic importance. On the day after the fall of Strasbourg, therefore, Hitler gave orders that Nineteenth Army's bridgehead west of the Rhine must be held at all costs, and, to ensure that it was, gave command of this sector to Heinrich Himmler.

That same day Eisenhower and Bradley—en route to confer with Devers, the commander of 6th Army Group—called at the H.Q. of

Third Army. There Patton suggested to them that XV Corps should now turn north from the line Saverne–Strasbourg, instead of south against the Colmar Pocket, and should join his offensive against the Saar. Eisenhower was reluctant to agree to this plan, for he knew the importance of eliminating the pocket and securing the river line from Strasbourg to Basle. Later in the day, however, Eisenhower was assured by Devers that " the German Nineteenth [Army] has ceased to exist as a tactical force," and that the remnants could easily be dealt with by the French. In the light of this opinion Eisenhower agreed that *both* corps of Seventh Army should turn north in support of Patton.

The immediate result of this decision was that the Germans in the Colmar Pocket were obliged to meet attack from only one flank by an army whose strength was already spent. The Germans retained their bridgehead west of the Rhine and from it, as Eisenhower says, " later exerted a profound and adverse effect on our operations."[1]

When he decided to reinforce the drive against the Saar front, Eisenhower hoped that a combined offensive by the Third and Seventh Armies would " attract considerable German resources from the northern and central sectors " and might " resolve the impasse at the Roer."[2] That hope was not fulfilled, for this offensive was directed against the strongest sector of the West Wall and, as the pressure increased, the Germans fell back in fair order to the shelter of their fortifications. No reserves were diverted from the Roer. On the contrary, von Rundstedt was able to insist on the return of Panzer Lehr to reserve. By the start of December, although Patton was hammering at the Siegfried Line, west of Saarbrücken, he knew that he could not amass the resources, particularly the ammunition, to support any large-scale assault before the middle of the month.

On November 20th, when Eisenhower had asked the Combined Chiefs of Staff for a modification of ' Unconditional Surrender,' he had declared that there was " no sign of an early collapse of German morale in the west." On December 4th he wrote to Marshall that the enemy " should be able to maintain a strong defensive front for some time, assisted by weather, floods and muddy ground." From the Swiss border almost as far as Aachen the Allies were halted before the Siegfried Line, and in the Vosges the Germans still had a foothold on French soil. From the Upper Roer, east of Aachen, to the mouth of the Maas the Allies were held in check by rivers. It seemed now that the virtual stalemate of the late autumn would extend well into the winter.

The overall objective of Eisenhower's strategy throughout the autumn had been to gain the line of the Rhine or, failing that, to bring the reserves in Germany to battle west of the Rhine and to destroy them there, just as the reserves in France had been brought to battle west of the Seine and destroyed in Normandy. The first move in execution of this strategy,

[1]Eisenhower, *Report*, p. 90.
[2]Appreciation by SHAEF Planning Staff, November 28th, 1944.

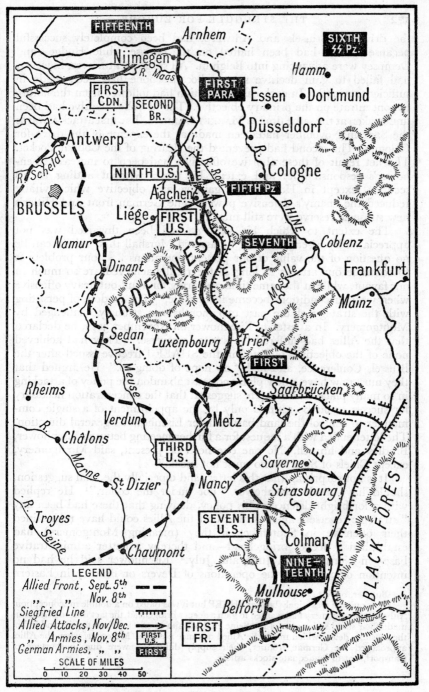

THE WESTERN FRONT, AUTUMN 1944

the drive for Brussels and Antwerp, had been completely successful because Patton had been halted on the Meuse while Hodges and Dempsey were advancing into Belgium. All subsequent moves, however, had failed to gain decisive success because none had been made in sufficient strength. In each case frustration had followed from the failure to concentrate on the primary objective. The Moselle offensive had been undertaken at the same time as MARKET GARDEN. The first attack towards the Saar in November had been made at the expense of the drive for Cologne. The second had prevented the clearing of the Colmar Pocket. The net result of these abortive offensives had been to increase Eisenhower's responsibilities and extend his forces without adding to his security, except in Holland, or gaining any objective which vitally reduced the enemy's defensive power. The German front and Hitler's new strategic reserve were still intact.

The extent to which his strategy had been thwarted was not appreciated by Eisenhower, for he assured Marshall that " there can be no question of the value of our present operations . . . our problem is to continue our attacks as long as the results achieved are so much in our favour, while at the same time preparing for a full-out heavy offensive when weather conditions become favourable." The wisdom of persisting with the strategy of the past two months was strongly challenged by Montgomery. In a letter to Eisenhower on November 30th, he declared that the Allies had suffered " a strategic reverse." They had achieved none of the objectives outlined in the SHAEF Directive issued after the Brussels Conference, and had " no hope of doing so." He argued that they must now have a new plan and must abandon the policy of attacking in so many places at once. He suggested that the concentration necessary for success could be assured only by the appointment of a single commander to control the land battle under Eisenhower's general direction. The letter ended with a request for a further meeting between Eisenhower, Bradley and himself. No one else need be present, said Montgomery, except Chiefs of Staff " who must not speak."

It is not surprising that this letter, and especially the final suggestion, should have made Eisenhower " hot under the collar."[1] He replied with a forthright defence of his policy, denying that there had been any " strategic reverse " and insisting that the Allies could have maintained their offensive in September if they (meaning Montgomery) had established a deeper bridgehead—and thereby a better administrative base—in Normandy in June and July.[2] Eisenhower said he had no intention of curtailing the operations of Devers or Bradley in Eastern

[1]Butcher, op. cit., p. 718.

[2]This opinion was widely held at SHAEF but it was based on a double misconception. Although Montgomery had wanted to gain a deeper bridgehead, the fact that the Germans made their stand so far west of the Seine enabled him to envelop their armies and inflict the crushing defeat which made the Allied advance possible. Moreover, when the Allies approached the German frontier, their supply difficulties were due to shortage of transport, not to inadequate stocks ashore.

France, because they were cleaning up the Allied right flank and providing him with what he called a " capability of concentration." Eisenhower agreed that there should be another conference, and added that he would bring his Chief of Staff who would be free to speak if he wished.

Before this meeting there was a further exchange in which each assured the other that more had been read into his letter than had been intended and each expressed anxiety lest any disagreement about the campaign should upset their close relationship. The strength of that relationship lay in their mutual frankness and, to use Montgomery's own phrase, in Eisenhower's " kindly forbearance."[1] However blunt the language of their wartime letters, they were written on the ' Dear Ike—Dear Monty ' basis throughout and their expressions of friendship were invariable and sincere. Some of Montgomery's letters and signals during these trying months might well have been regarded as insubordination by a superior who was less understanding. Eisenhower knew, however, that, although Montgomery would always press his case in the strongest terms down to the moment of decision, once the decision was firm he would carry out his orders to the letter and would never seek to gain his own way by intrigue. It was these personal qualities that Eisenhower valued and respected.

The meeting Montgomery had asked for was held on December 7th at Maastricht. There the plans and intentions of the Brussels Conference were reaffirmed. The lower Rhineland was to be cleared by converging offensives from the Roer and the Reichswald as soon as Bradley had captured the Roer dams. The target date was January 12th. Montgomery proposed that until then the Allies should husband their resources and undertake no large-scale offensive operations. Eisenhower argued, however, that they " could not afford to sit still and do nothing, while the German perfected his defences and the training of his troops." " My basic decision," he says, " was to continue the offensive to the extreme limit of our ability."[2] Accordingly, he authorised Patton to make one more effort to capture the Saar before Christmas.

On the way to Maastricht for this meeting Eisenhower drove through the Ardennes and noticed how thinly held this sector was. For miles behind the front he saw little sign of American troops, transport or installations. He had already questioned Bradley about the vulnerability of this sector where there were only four divisions on a front of seventy-five miles, and he now raised the matter again, though not in Mont-

---

[1]In a letter to Eisenhower at the end of the war Montgomery wrote: " I owe much to your wise guidance and kindly forbearance. I know my own faults very well and I do not suppose I am an easy subordinate; I like to go my own way. But you have kept me on the rails in difficult and stormy times and have taught me much. For all this I am very grateful. And I thank you for all you have done for me.

Your very devoted friend,

Monty."

[2]Eisenhower, *Crusade*, p. 340.

gomery's presence. Bradley replied that he could not make himself absolutely secure in the Ardennes without weakening his offensive concentrations on the Roer and in the Saar, and that if the Germans were to attack in the Ardennes they could be promptly counter-attacked from either flank and would be stopped before they reached the Meuse. He had taken the precaution, he said, of not placing in this area any supply installations of major importance.

None of the commanders who met at Maastricht that day believed that the Germans would attempt any large-scale counter-offensive. They feared that the enemy might be able to maintain a strong defensive front so long as the weather—the worst for fifty years—prevented the Allies from making full use of their air power and armour. They were disturbed by the revival of the enemy's morale and the capacity he had so far shown to find replacements for the infantry which, according to Allied estimates, were being destroyed at the rate of five or six divisions a week. The evidence of the past month, however, was that von Rundstedt's infantry resources were fast becoming exhausted, for rebuilt divisions had been appearing in the line with meagre equipment and only six weeks' training.

The problem of most concern to Eisenhower was his failure to compel the Germans to commit their new strategic reserves of armour. It was now known that the four divisions of Sixth SS Panzer Army had been re-equipped east of the Rhine and that another four, if not five, armoured divisions had also been withdrawn for refitting. On the other hand, the only panzer formation which had been engaged since it was rebuilt, Panzer Lehr, had " proved lamentably short of training and under-equipped with untested equipment."[1] There was no reason to believe that other refitted divisions were in better shape and in this case it was most unlikely that von Rundstedt would employ them prematurely. And the Field-Marshal, it seemed, was now in full command. The conduct of operations since his return in September had been so efficient and successful that the Allied Intelligence assumed von Rundstedt was no longer obliged to listen to ' intuitions from afar.'

At the start of December the great unanswered question was: How and where would von Rundstedt use Sixth SS Panzer Army? At Montgomery's H.Q. Williams, the chief Intelligence officer, had addressed himself to this question on December 3rd. His conclusion was:

> Von Rundstedt is unlikely to risk his strategic reserve until the Allies advance over the Roer . . . or until the Allies offer the enemy opportunity to take them off balance so that an abrupt counter-stroke could put paid to future Allied prospects for the winter. This latter is unlikely for it demands five elements not readily to be found

[1] SHAEF Intelligence Summary, December 3rd, 1944. When Panzer Lehr was committed on the Saar front for a few days at the end of November it had only 72 tanks, all new. On June 6th it had had 190.

together: First, vital ground, and there is nowhere obvious for him to go which would hurt us deeply. The bruited drive on Antwerp— a ' dash for the wire ' as of old—is just not within his potential. Secondly, he needs bad weather else our air superiority will disrupt his assembly; yet this very weather would clog his own intent. Third, he must find us tired and unbalanced. Fourth, he needs adequate fuel stocks. . . . Lastly, he needs more infantry and of better quality in better terrain and weather. . . . It seems more probable, then, if von Rundstedt continues to conduct operations unimpeded, that he will wait to smash our bridgeheads over the Roer, then hold his hand. He is sixty-nine.

Nevertheless, there were continued rumours of a great offensive designed to recapture Antwerp, and during the next fortnight the information reaching Allied Intelligence indicated that something special was afoot. A captured document revealed that Hitler himself had ordered "the formation of a special unit for employment on reconnaissance and special tasks on the Western Front." The personnel, it said, would be volunteers " fully trained in single combat " and must have " know-ledge of the English language and also the American dialect." For these special troops all units were to send in any " captured U.S. clothing, equipment, weapons and vehicles." Commenting on this order, First U.S. Army Intelligence said " it obviously presages special operations for sabotage, attacks on Command Posts and other vital installations by infiltrated and parachuted specialists."

By December 10th American Intelligence was aware that five German divisions had left Holland for destinations unknown; that the H.Q. of Fifteenth German Army had moved from Holland to the Roer sector where it was reported to have relieved Fifth Panzer Army; that this Army's new H.Q. was alleged to be at Coblenz; that between Coblenz and the Luxemburg frontier there were three of the refitted panzer divisions; and that several new *Volksgrenadier* divisions had arrived in the Eifel, the German end of the Ardennes.

All these straws in the wind gave portent of a coming storm but there was no evidence that Sixth SS Panzer Army was moving from the Cologne Plain into the Eifel, and Allied Intelligence continued to believe that the storm would not break until the Americans had crossed the Roer River. Von Rundstedt, they argued, was too good a soldier and too wise a man to cast away his strategic reserve in a gamble which was bound to fail. This was the basic miscalculation.[1] Allied Intelligence made the mistake of assuming that since the attack would be a military failure, therefore it would not be tried. But German strategy was no longer governed by purely military considerations. The decision lay not with the Field-Marshal but with the Führer.

[1] In his first Intelligence Review after the German offensive began, Williams frankly confessed his miscalculation, declaring simply, " We were wrong."

At the end of October when Hitler's Ardennes plan was presented to von Rundstedt and Model, they replied that the " forces available were much too weak for such far-reaching objectives."[1] They agreed that there should be an offensive in the West, but suggested that it should be designed merely to ' pinch out ' the Aachen Salient and to restore the Siegfried Line in this, the only sector where it had been breached. The most that could be achieved, they said, was to drive the Allies back from the Roer to the Meuse and capture Liége, the main American supply base. This proposal, which Model called the ' small solution,' was promptly rejected by Hitler. Such an operation, he believed, would merely postpone the day of reckoning; it would not compel the Western Powers to come to terms.

The plan which von Rundstedt and Model were eventually obliged to accept provided for an offensive in mid-December by three armies on a 75-mile front between Monschau and Echternach. The main effort was to be made in the northern Ardennes by Sixth SS Panzer Army (Dietrich) which was to cross the Meuse at Huy and Andenne and strike north-west for Antwerp. In the central Ardennes Fifth Panzer Army (Manteuffel) was to make a complementary thrust through Namur and Dinant to Brussels, while Seventh Army (Brandenberger) ran out a line of infantry divisions to cover the southern flank from Luxemburg to Givet.

This plan was delivered to von Rundstedt complete to the last detail —even to the timing of the artillery bombardment—and endorsed in the Führer's own handwriting ' NOT TO BE ALTERED.' Hitler gave strict instructions about the axes of advance and expressly declared that Dietrich was not to attack Liége. This city was to be by-passed to the south and crossings over the Meuse were to be secured for Dietrich by a special panzer brigade under command of Skorzeny, the man who had rescued Mussolini from captivity in 1943 and had carried out many desperate missions for the Führer. Skorzeny's force, wearing American uniforms and travelling in American tanks and vehicles, was to take the lead as soon as Dietrich had gained a break-through and, acting as a ' Trojan Horse,' was to rush on and seize the Meuse bridges between Liége and Namur. Meantime, sabotage parties, similarly disguised, were to infiltrate through the American lines and spread confusion in rear areas.

Ignoring the advice of his field commanders, who tried to make him realise the practical limitations of his power, Hitler planned to support his main offensive with three subsidiary operations:

On D plus three, an attack from the Lower Roer to retake Maastricht and prevent the movement of American reserves from the Aachen Salient;

[1]Although the attack in the Ardennes became known to the Allied world as ' the Rundstedt offensive,' the Field-Marshal had no part in its conception and showed his disapproval of it by taking only a formal interest in its execution.

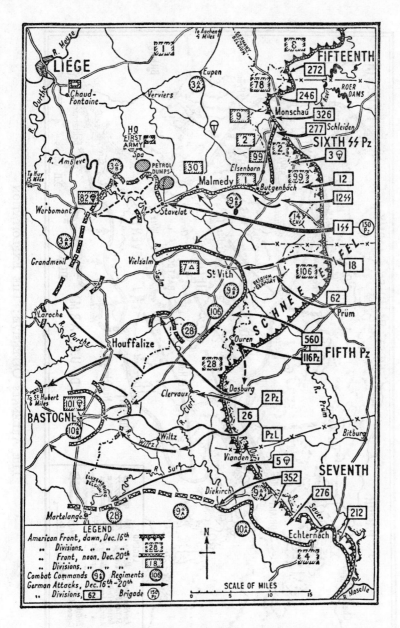

THE ARDENNES OFFENSIVE : THE ASSAULT

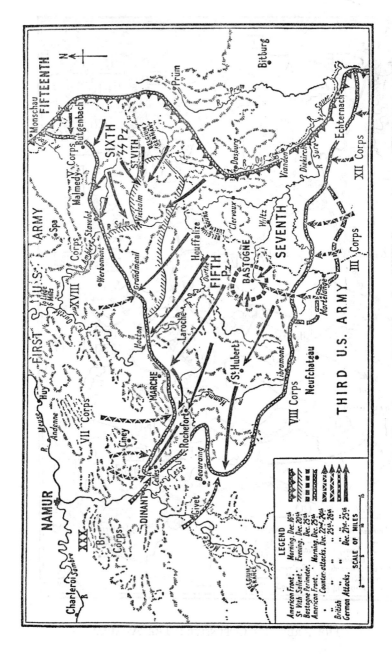

THE ARDENNES OFFENSIVE: THE EXPLOITATION

On D plus ten, an attack from Northern Holland to recapture Breda and pin down the British;

On D plus fifteen (or earlier if the forces were ready), a double attack from the Saar and from the Colmar Pocket to reconquer Northern Alsace and exploit the opportunity which would arise when the Americans transferred divisions from this area to the Ardennes.

In Berlin on December 2nd, at a final conference which von Rundstedt declined to attend, Model again argued for the ' small solution,' but his plea was dismissed by Hitler on the ground that they could always go over to this solution, if the larger plan were to miscarry. The course of events in November had strengthened the Führer's determination to carry the offensive through to Antwerp. His generals had doubted his ability to create any substantial reserve, but it had been created and armed. They had predicted that the western defences would collapse, if they were not strongly reinforced, but the front had been held without any considerable aid from the forces earmarked for the great offensive. Four of the *Volksgrenadier* divisions had been drawn into the battle during November and the refitting of four armoured divisions had been delayed. On the other hand, by inspired efforts in the factories and repair shops, 1,349 new or repaired tanks and assault guns had been sent to the West in November and nearly a thousand more would become available before Christmas.[1]

By the first week of December Hitler had accumulated twenty-eight divisions for the Ardennes and another six for the attack in Alsace. This was a far more formidable reserve than he had been able to concentrate on any active front during the past two years, yet it was much weaker than the force he had employed in the drive for the Meuse in 1940. Then von Rundstedt's Army Group, attacking between Aachen and Trier, had started with forty-four divisions and had been built up to seventy-one by the time it reached the Channel. Now in 1944 there would be no such possibility of reinforcing the assault, but there seemed to be an equally good chance of gaining surprise. During November, although Hitler had moved six of his new *Volksgrenadier* divisions into the line facing the Ardennes, the Americans had made no move to reinforce this vulnerable sector. It was held—as it had been in September when Hitler first sensed his opportunity—by no more than five divisions and behind these there appeared to be nothing in reserve.

On December 12th, four days before the offensive was due to begin, all the senior generals taking part were summoned to von Rundstedt's H.Q. " There," says Bayerlein, the commander of Panzer Lehr, " we were all stripped of our weapons and brief-cases and were then driven about the countryside in a bus for half an hour. When the bus stopped, we were led between a double row of SS troops into a deep bunker.

[1]According to the records of the Inspectorate of Panzer Troops at OKH, 950 tanks and assault guns were sent to the West in December.

Hitler came in with Keitel and Jodl. He looked old and broken and his hand shook as he read from a long, prepared manuscript."[1] Hitler spoke for two hours, during which time the generals sat stiffly to attention with an armed SS guard standing behind each man's chair and glowering so fiercely at them that Bayerlein, for one, was " afraid even to reach for a handkerchief."

In the course of this prolonged harangue, Hitler proclaimed the political motive behind his military plan. " Never in history," he said, " was there a coalition like that of our enemies, composed of such heterogeneous elements with such divergent aims. . . . Ultra-capitalist states on the one hand; ultra-Marxist states on the other. On the one hand a dying empire, Britain; on the other, a colony bent upon inheritance, the United States. . . . Each of the partners went into this coalition with the hope of realising his political ambitions. . . . America tries to become England's heir; Russia tries to gain the Balkans, the narrow seas, Iran and the Persian Gulf; England tries to hold her possessions and to strengthen herself in the Mediterranean. . . . Even now these states are at loggerheads, and he who, like a spider sitting in the middle of his web, can watch developments, observes how these antagonisms grow stronger and stronger from hour to hour. If now we can deliver a few more heavy blows, then at any moment this artificially-bolstered common front may suddenly collapse with a gigantic clap of thunder . . . provided always that there is no weakening on the part of Germany."

Hitler told them it was " essential to deprive the enemy of his belief that victory is certain," and this could be done only by a successful offensive. " Wars," he declared, " are finally decided by one side or the other recognising that they cannot be won. [Therefore] we must allow no moment to pass without showing the enemy that, whatever he does, he can never reckon on a capitulation. Never! Never! "[2]

None of the generals who listened to this tirade believed that Antwerp could be captured, if only because of the shortage of petrol. Although Hitler had promised that there would be ample supplies, they had received hardly enough to take them to the Meuse. They would have to bank heavily on capturing American dumps, but, owing to the Führer's ban on air reconnaissance, they had been unable to find out where the dumps were. Nevertheless, they were confident that they could reach the Meuse and inflict a severe defeat on the Americans provided that they could complete the concentration of their forces undetected. Summing up the reasons for his own optimism, Hitler had assured them that bad weather, forecast by one of his experts, would shroud their final

[1] The Generals did not know it at the time, but they had in fact been driven to the Führer's Battle H.Q. at Ziegenberg near Frankfurt. Although Bayerlein says that Hitler read his harangue, the stenographers present insist that there was no manuscript. Certainly the only record which has survived is the shorthand transcription and this is by no means complete.

[2] Führer Conferences, Fragment 28, December 12th, 1944.

movement. The conference over, the generals went out into the night, and it was raining.

On the next three days the weather favoured Hitler's plan. It curtailed Allied air reconnaissance, but it did not seriously hamper the nightly movement of German reserves to their assembly areas in the Eifel. In spite of this and the most stringent security precautions, some evidence of the German preparations reached the Americans, but its significance was not fully appreciated, for, as Hitler said later, " they lived exclusively in the thought of their own offensive."[1]

Late on the evening of December 15th at Spa in the Ardennes First U.S. Army Intelligence prepared this appreciation of the enemy's intentions: " Reinforcements for the West Wall between Düren and Trier continue to arrive. The identification of at least three or four newly-formed divisions along the Army front must be reckoned with during the next few days. . . . It is possible that a limited-scale offensive will be launched for the purpose of achieving a Christmas 'morale victory' for civilian consumption. Many P.W.s now speak of the coming attack between the 17th and 25th December while others relate promises of the recapture of Aachen as a Christmas present for the Führer."

Before this guarded warning had even been issued, Hitler's armies were marching into Belgium.

[1]Führer Conferences, Fragment 27, December 28th, 1944.

## CHAPTER XXX

# THE FÜHRER'S FINAL GAMBLE

ON the morning of Saturday, December 16th, Eisenhower received a letter from Montgomery reminding him of a bet he had made the previous year that the war against Germany would be over by Christmas 1944. Eisenhower replied that he would pay up on Christmas Day, but not before. " After all," he wrote, with a smile, " I still have nine days left." In the course of those nine days the prospect of victory which had once seemed so near was to recede across the dark horizon of the Ardennes. In those nine days the Western Armies were to be plunged into the gravest crisis they had known since 1940.

That December morning the thirty-one divisions of Omar Bradley's Army Group were ranged along the western marches of Germany on a front of 200 miles. They were deployed for attack. North of the Ardennes, on a 40-mile sector between Geilenkirchen and Monschau, he had sixteen divisions. South of the Ardennes, on a 60-mile sector facing the Saar, he had ten divisions. Between these two considerable concentrations, on a sector of 100 miles in the Ardennes itself, Bradley had five divisions. It was here that Hitler struck.

The Ardennes is rolling forested country broken by the steep and twisted valleys of mountain streams. There are many roads but few are good and most of these have to pass through narrow, awkward defiles where they cross the rivers. The best routes run south-west and, in seeking to drive west and north-west, the Germans would find themselves advancing against the grain of the country, taking for the most part secondary roads which follow the winding river valleys or straggle from village to village across the ridges and through the woods. Even in 1940, when they were virtually unopposed and were heading south-west in good spring weather, the Germans had taken three days to reach the Meuse.

Knowing this, Model realised that the campaign would become a battle for roads and, above all, for road junctions. He had no doubt that his armies would break through the American front, for he knew exactly what units were opposing him. " These units," wrote one of his Intelligence officers, " are capable of offering strong resistance against an energetic attack, only if the enemy succeeds in bringing south in a short time the operational reserves held in readiness for the Roer attack. In view of past experience, it can be assumed that the enemy will not quickly recover from his unexpected reverse."[1] It was on this that Model banked. Although sceptical about his chances of capturing Antwerp, he was sure he could reach the Meuse in strength before the Americans could move sufficient reserves to halt his armies or even to head them off.

In the north the immediate task of Dietrich's Sixth SS Panzer Army was to capture Monschau and Butgenbach and open the road leading north-west to Eupen and Verviers where three infantry divisions were to take up a blocking position on the northern flank of 1st SS Panzer Corps. Simultaneously two panzer divisions (1st and 12th SS) were to drive through the Butgenbach Gap to Malmedy and Stavelot. West of Stavelot the American tanks of Skorzeny's 'Trojan Horse' Brigade were to rush ahead to the Meuse bridges. Meantime, 2nd SS Panzer Corps (2nd and 9th SS) was to be held in reserve for exploitation or to ward off any American counter-attack from the north.

In the centre the key objectives of Manteuffel's Fifth Panzer Army were the important road junctions of St. Vith and Bastogne. East of St. Vith the Americans were entrenched in a sector of the Siegfried Line along the Schnee Eifel. This ridge was to be enveloped by two infantry divisions which were then to drive on to St. Vith. South of the Schnee Eifel the rival forces were lining the river Our which marks the boundary between Germany and Luxemburg. Here special assault teams of infantry and engineers, operating under cover of tanks, were to seize the river crossings and build bridges over which Manteuffel could pass his three armoured divisions. Taking the lead on the second day the armour was to strike westward for Houffalize and Bastogne and then on to the Meuse from Namur to Dinant.

In the south the four infantry divisions of Brandenberger's Seventh Army were to make assault crossings over the river line from Vianden to Echternach and establish a firm flank guard north of Luxemburg and Arlon. That was the plan. Its success depended primarily on surprise and speed creating confusion in the American High Command.

Since September the Ardennes sector had lain dormant and both sides had used it to 'break in' new divisions and to rest those that were tired. Bradley was so using it now. Middleton's VIII Corps, which was responsible for almost the entire sector, contained three infantry divisions (the 106th, which had been in the line only four days, the 4th and the 28th, which together had suffered nearly nine thousand casualties in the Hürtgen Forest) and one armoured division, the 9th, which was comparatively inexperienced. Along his 90-mile front Middleton's infantry was so extended that he had been obliged to commit in the line

[1]Intelligence Appreciation, 12th SS Panzer Division, December 14th, 1944. This appreciation was concerned only with the northern flank, but the same reasoning was applied with regard to the American reserves on the Saar front.

his reconnaissance cavalry and one combat command of 9th Armoured, thus leaving himself with little in reserve. The only part of the Ardennes that was more firmly held was the Monschau–Butgenbach sector from which two divisions of Gerow's V Corps were already striving to reach the Roer dams.

Before dawn on December 16th fourteen German infantry divisions moved through the misty forests of the Eifel towards the thinly-manned American line. The noise of the tanks, assault guns and transport moving with them was drowned by salvoes of V.1s which roared low overhead on their way across the Meuse to Liége and Antwerp, blazing in the night sky the trail which Model's armies would have to follow if they were to fulfil the Führer's plan. At 5.30 a.m. two thousand guns began shelling the American positions between Monschau and Echternach. Under cover of this bombardment the infantry advanced to attack and five panzer divisions moved up close behind them ready for quick exploitation.

In one of the waiting armoured columns an *Unterstürmführer* of the Hitler Youth Division (12th SS) set down his thoughts in a letter to his sister: " I write during one of the momentous hours before we attack, full of excitement and expectation of what the next days will bring. . . . Some believe in living but life is not everything! It is enough to know that we attack and will throw the enemy from our homeland. It is a holy task. Above me is the terrific noise of V.1s and artillery, the voice of war." On the back of the envelope he added a postscript: " Ruth! Ruth! Ruth! WE MARCH! "[1]

In this spirit of vengeful and patriotic exaltation the Germans, SS and Wehrmacht alike, fell upon their unsuspecting opponents as dawn was breaking from a leaden sky.

The bombardment had aroused the Americans, but few appreciated the significance of this unaccustomed activity until the German assault troops emerged from the morning mist. On the River Our sector the 28th Division, strung out on a front of nearly 30 miles, was assailed by five divisions and overwhelmed. That evening with the aid of searchlights, Manteuffel's armoured columns moved west across the Our with orders to continue advancing through the night. In the Schnee Eifel two raw regiments of the 106th Division were quickly outflanked and, though they held their ground, they were encircled early next morning. The way lay open to St. Vith. Thus Manteuffel's plan unfolded according to expectation.

On the southern flank, however, the 4th U.S. Division yielded little ground, and in the north V Corps gave Dietrich an anxious day. His right wing ran head-on into the American divisions making for the Roer dams. At Monschau his attack was stopped short. The drive for Butgenbach made small headway even though Dietrich threw in 12th SS

[1] This letter was captured, unposted, by the 1st U.S. Infantry Division. Many other captured letters struck the same note.

to reinforce his infantry assault. South of Butgenbach it was a different story. Here the 1st SS Panzer Division struck at a weak link—a cavalry group holding the junction between V and VIII Corps. Loosely deployed, the cavalry was soon overrun and by nightfall the vanguard of 1st SS (Battlegroup Peiper) had penetrated six miles.

Against this severe onslaught the Americans in the line defended bravely. On the VIII Corps front they were heavily outnumbered, but at no point on that first day did the Germans gain all their objectives. The American fighting troops did everything that could be expected of them; it was at certain higher H.Q. that the demands of the crisis were not fully appreciated.

Gerow, of V Corps, was the first to realise that this was ' something big.' In the middle of the day he asked First Army for permission to discontinue his own attack against the Roer dams and to withdraw in good time to the Butgenbach Ridge. Hodges refused both requests, for he did not appreciate the scale of the attack or the extent of the German penetrations farther south on Middleton's sector. The slow reaction of Hodges was primarily due to lack of information. Very early in the day most of the telephone lines immediately behind the front were cut by the German barrage or by infiltrated parties of saboteurs wearing American uniforms and travelling in jeeps. As a result, the reports reaching VIII Corps H.Q. in Bastogne were scanty and confused. By dark Middleton's few reserves were all committed, or about to be, but the German offensive had been in progress nearly twenty-four hours before any other reinforcements began moving to his aid.

Late on the afternoon of the 16th, when news of the enemy attack reached Versailles, Eisenhower and Bradley were conferring about the forthcoming American offensives. The report from First Army indicated " slight penetrations " at five points on a wide front, and Eisenhower " was immediately convinced that this was no local attack."[1] On the other hand Bradley at first concluded that it was " a spoiling attack . . . to force a halt on Patton's advance in the Saar,"[2] and this appreciation was to colour his thinking for the next two days. Nevertheless, as a precaution they decided to move two armoured divisions into the Ardennes at once, the 7th from Ninth Army and the 10th from Third Army.

Bradley expected that Patton would protest and he did—" very strongly "—but he sent 10th Armoured off at dawn next day. With his usual frankness, however, Patton admits that he " also directed Eddy to get 4th Armoured engaged " lest it too might be moved north by higher authority, and he adds, " the fact that I did this shows how little I appreciated the seriousness of the enemy attack on that date."[3] In this respect Patton was not alone. The SHAEF reserves (the 82nd

---

[1]Eisenhower, *Crusade*, p. 342.
[2]Bradley, op. cit., p. 455.
[3]Patton, op. cit., p. 189.

and 101st Airborne Divisions) were not even alerted for movement from Rheims to the battle area until the evening of the second day, the 17th.

By this time the spearhead of Sixth SS Panzer Army was 20 miles inside Belgium. That night, when Peiper's powerful battlegroup reached Stavelot, it was only eight miles from First Army H.Q. at Spa and even closer to two vast fuel dumps containing more than three million gallons of the petrol and oil the Germans were so anxious to capture. Elsewhere on the northern half of the front, however, it was a day of frustration. On Peiper's right flank the 2nd and 99th U.S. Divisions stood firm along the line Monschau–Elsenborn and were not unsettled by the descent of a parachute battalion behind them during the night of the 16th–17th. At Butgenbach 12th SS was again foiled, for a regiment of the stalwart 1st Division, moving south by night along the very road the German paratroops were intended to block, won the race for this commanding ridge and held it until the rest of their division came up next day.

At St. Vith too the Germans found themselves forestalled—this time by the 7th Armoured Division, led by Brigadier-General R. W. Hasbrouck, one of the great men of the Ardennes. Setting out before dawn from their ' rest area ' north of Aachen, one of his combat commands covered the 50 miles to St. Vith by early afternoon and the others by dark. This was a remarkable achievement, for Hasbrouck's convoys twice had to swing west to avoid the point of Peiper's lunging column,[1] and over the last part of their journey had to force a passage (occasionally with the threat of their guns) against the flood of service units and even combat troops retreating in dismay. That night Hasbrouck established his combat commands in a loose horseshoe around St. Vith. Into this horseshoe he gathered some remnants of the units which had taken the first shock and re-formed them to fight again.

Under Hasbrouck's leadership, St. Vith became a rock of defence on which the tide of assault broke and divided, flowing west in two channels. The northern channel which 1st SS had opened soon became a long, narrow salient, twenty miles deep, but nowhere more than five miles wide, and containing only one east-west road which followed the winding valley of the Amblève. By this road on December 18th Peiper's battle-group continued its advance but it had no room to manœuvre and three times it was diverted by blown bridges. Checked in his drive westward, Peiper turned north, probing for a way through, but each of his thrusts was parried by scratch forces which First Army had organised from headquarters troops. One thrust reached the edge of one of the great petrol dumps, but the Germans reeled back before a wall of flame as the Americans set up a road-block of blazing petrol drums and kept it burning. While Peiper was writhing in the confined river valley, the

[1]Part of one unit was trapped by Peiper's SS men. Some 160 Americans were taken prisoner and, as they were an ' embarrassment ' to the German tank crews, were lined up and machine-gunned. At least 142 were killed, but the rest, after feigning death, escaped by night to tell the grim story of the ' Malmedy Massacre.' Incensed by this outrage, the American reserves entered the fight thirsting for vengeance.

30th U.S. Division (transferred from the Roer sector) began to descend on his northern flank and that evening re-captured Stavelot. Peiper's supply line was cut and, with the Americans still holding Butgenbach and St. Vith, Dietrich could not rapidly bring forward sufficient reinforcements to relieve him or to maintain the momentum of the attack.

The German hope of a quick break-through to the Meuse was thus thwarted, but Hodges did not know this and he had already reacted to the threat created by Peiper's alarming advance. The psychological effect of this advance was the greater because its extent was not appreciated until after breakfast on the 18th, when Hodges discovered that the Germans had passed through Stavelot and had a column advancing on First Army H.Q. at Spa. There this news caused " considerable consternation," as Gavin (the Commander of 82nd Airborne) found when he reported for orders that morning. On seeing Hodges he learned that " the situation south and west of Stavelot was unknown except that the enemy had evidently overrun [the] front positions. There appeared to be a large force of U.S. troops centered on St. Vith,"[1] but on the Houffalize–Bastogne sector Hodges did not know what was happening.

It had been Hodges's intention to use 82nd Airborne at Houffalize to fill the gap between St. Vith and Bastogne. Now, however, having no troops in position to check the German column advancing west from Stavelot, Hodges ordered Gavin to establish his division around Werbomont. This Gavin did, thus blocking the exit from the northern channel, but the employment of 82nd Airborne here left the southern channel between St. Vith and Bastogne wide open.

South of St. Vith by the morning of December 18th Manteuffel had opened a breach twelve miles wide and through it he drove his three armoured divisions—the 116th for Houffalize, and the 2nd and Panzer Lehr for Bastogne, the two latter (with an infantry division) comprising von Lüttwitz's 47th Panzer Corps. In their path there was nothing but the remnants of the armour they had mauled the day before, one weak combat command. Von Lüttwitz was well aware of the need for speed because an American radio message, intercepted on the previous evening, had told him that American airborne divisions were moving up from Rheims. He presumed their destination to be Bastogne which lay only fifteen miles west of his leading columns.

In Bastogne that morning there were no American troops except Middleton's Corps H.Q. which had already been ordered to leave. Stragglers from the 28th Division, streaming back from the Our, brought, as one American historian says, " tragic tales [which] indicated a complete disintegration of regimental defenses."[2] Middleton had no

---

[1]Gavin's After-Action report to the U.S. War Department.
[2]Col. S. L. A. Marshall, *Bastogne, The First Eight Days*, p. 7. Marshall was 'Historian of European Theater of Operations.'

instructions to hold Bastogne and such was the state of American communications that he did not then known what, if any, reinforcements were moving to his aid. The nearest reserves which were in fact destined for the defence of Bastogne were the 101st Airborne Division at Rheims, 100 miles to the south-west, and Combat Command B (CCB)[1] of the 10th Armoured Division at Luxemburg, 40 miles to the south-east. That day, therefore, three forces were closing in from three directions on the town which contained the key to the defence of the southern Ardennes.

The first to get there was 10th Armoured's CCB which arrived at dusk—to Middleton's great relief, for German patrols were already reported (erroneously) on the eastern outskirts of Bastogne. Wasting no time, Middleton sent this force to block the three main roads leading into the town from the east and north-east in the hope of holding off the German armour until the arrival of the airborne division which he knew was on the way. Thus encouraged, but having no contact with First Army, Middleton proceeded to obtain direct from Bradley the authority to defend the town even at the risk of encirclement.

It was von Lüttwitz's intention to encircle Bastogne, unless he could capture it easily, and by ten o'clock that night his panzer divisions were barely five miles from it. The nearer, Panzer Lehr, had penetrated between two of the American blocking forces, and its commander (Bayerlein), who was with the leading column, decided that a quick thrust under cover of darkness might gain the prize. He might have succeeded, if he had not followed the advice of some civilians who were not perhaps as friendly as he thought. At their suggestion he tried a short-cut down a side road which proved to be a trough of mud. At dawn on the 19th Bayerlein was still two miles from Bastogne and he now knew not only that he had American armour on his flanks, but also that the town was held. The 101st Airborne Division had arrived during the night.[2] Soon after daybreak one of its regiments joined battle with Panzer Lehr.

Manteuffel had not expected the Americans to move so fast or to act so aggressively, but he was not deflected from his strategic purpose. Although checked at Bastogne throughout the 19th, his troops cleared the way for its early encirclement by capturing Wiltz and Houffalize on either flank. That evening on the entire southern sector from the St. Vith ' horseshoe ' to Diekirch, a distance of nearly 25 miles, the only

---

[1]Since armoured combat commands figure largely in this story, it may be noted that they usually contained, as did this one, a battalion of tanks, a battalion of infantry and supporting artillery. In the case of the 2nd and 3rd Armoured Divisions, which contained two armoured regiments instead of one, the combat commands normally had a much stronger tank element.

[2]The transfer of this whole division, 11,000 strong, from Rheims to Bastogne, 100 miles in well under twenty-four hours, was a remarkable feat of movement. It was accomplished so quickly only because the convoys which travelled by night drove with lights on as far as the Belgian border.

organised opposition was at Bastogne. How well organised its garrison was Manteuffel had yet to find out; for the moment he was bent on continuing westward. Accordingly, he instructed von Lüttwitz to contain Bastogne with infantry and to drive for the Meuse with his armour, and he appealed to Model for immediate reinforcement.

In drafting the original plan Hitler had placed the *Schwerpunkt* in the north with Sixth SS Panzer Army. This decision had governed the initial deployment of his armoured reserves: two SS divisions to exploit Dietrich's main thrust, and three Wehrmacht panzer or panzer grenadier divisions to strike at the Aachen salient from the north as soon as Dietrich had reached the Meuse. Model now suggested that, as Dietrich was checked, these five divisions should all be thrown in south of St. Vith to exploit Manteuffel's break-through. For political reasons, however, Hitler wanted the decisive blow to be struck by the SS. He insisted that the two SS divisions be committed in the north to give Dietrich another chance. The most he would agree to release to Manteuffel were the three Wehrmacht formations. Disappointed though he was, Model had good reason to expect that he would soon have advancing to the Meuse a far more powerful force of armour than that which the Americans had so far failed to check; and this force would strike, not against an organised line, but through the wide gap Manteuffel had already opened.

When the Ardennes offensive began, the reaction of the Allies was one of amazement and incredulity. They had become so used to thinking the Wehrmacht was on the point of collapse that they did not believe it capable of making an attack of the magnitude indicated by the first reports.[1] Then, when communications broke down, rumour took charge. German tanks were reported far behind the fighting line; German paratroops in a score of places though they had been dropped only at Monschau; German saboteurs in almost every town from the frontier to the Meuse. Conflicting reports from some areas and lack of any news from others soon produced doubt and confusion in rear areas, especially at First U.S. Army H.Q. On the evening of the 18th Hodges had to confess, " The enemy line cannot be well defined as the front is fluid and somewhat obscure."

One American historical officer (R. E. Merriam)[2] declares that " corps and higher commanders were unable to obtain sufficient information to put together the pieces of the puzzle. Retreating troops clogged the roads and blocked reinforcements on their way to the front.

[1]In an appreciation written on December 12th, Bradley's G-2 (Chief Intelligence Officer) Brigadier-General E. L. Sibert, declared, " the breaking point may develop suddenly and without warning." In a directive of December 15th Montgomery wrote, " His [the enemy's] situation is such that he cannot stage major offensive operations."
[2]In his book, *Dark December*, at p. 132. Merriam was with the 7th U.S. Armoured Division during the battle and later became Chief of the Ardennes Section of the Historical Division in the U.S. War Department.

At times complete panic gripped some units as rumours of approaching Germans were heard. . . . Much equipment was jettisoned in perfect working order."

It is undoubtedly true that there were cases of panic and that some service units, anxious to save their equipment, took to the roads in default of orders. Many others, however, organised their areas for defence and stayed to fight. It was, for instance, a small party of engineers engaged in operating sawmills, who halted Peiper's panzer column west of Stavelot and blew two bridges in his face. The delay imposed on the German advance by small groups of resolute officers and men, who demolished bridges or improvised road-blocks, cannot be calculated now, but it did much to account for the halting of 1st SS and for the comparatively slow progress of Manteuffel's armour in the race for Bastogne. Nevertheless, the German plan for spreading confusion and alarm behind the American lines succeeded even beyond Hitler's expectations.

Much of this confusion was created by Skorzeny's *Kommandos*. The ' Trojan Horse ' plan miscarried but more than forty jeep-loads of ' American-speaking ' Germans slipped through the crumbling front on the first two nights and some of them actually reached the Meuse before they were stopped. All except eight of these sabotage parties regained their own lines after cutting telephone wires, intercepting dispatch riders and liaison officers, shooting-up radio stations and killing military police-men posted to direct convoys. One brazen German even took over a pointsman's duty and turned an American regiment down the wrong road.

Skorzeny's plans were revealed (with some embellishments) by prisoners captured on the second day, but this knowledge did not lessen the impact of his operations. Indeed, the stricter security measures which the Americans introduced at once inevitably served the German purpose, for they extended the fear of infiltration and sabotage right back to Paris. There, because of a rumour that Skorzeny had sent a squad of thugs to assassinate the Supreme Commander, the Security Corps insisted, to his great annoyance, on providing Eisenhower with a special cordon of guards.

It was in this uncertain atmosphere, heavy with rumour and false report, that the Allied command had to devise its counter-measures. After making the initial moves, therefore, Bradley's policy was to wait and see how the situation developed. He did not order Patton to make any precautionary dispositions, and it was not until the third day (December 18th) that he became sufficiently alarmed to cancel Third Army's Saar offensive then planned to start on the 21st. So far Patton had been required to send only one armoured division to Hodges's aid; now Bradley asked him to intervene in strength. Patton replied that he would have three divisions moving north within twenty-four hours. There was no holding back on his part now. He was not losing divisions; he was being given a new chance to fight and there was nothing he liked better. Nor had he any equal on the Allied side in the rapid deployment of troops. Late that night Patton received a further order: to come to Verdun for a conference with Eisenhower, Bradley, Devers and others next morning. Patton arrived with outline plans already prepared for a counter-attack by four divisions of his own, plus those of VIII Corps, against the southern flank of the German penetration.

The keynote of the Verdun meeting was struck by Eisenhower who began by saying, " The present situation is to be regarded as one of opportunity for us and not of disaster. There will be only cheerful faces at this conference table." Patton thereupon proposed that they should " let the —— —— go all the way to Paris "; then they could " cut 'em off and chew 'em up." Eisenhower replied that the enemy must " never be allowed to cross the Meuse."[1]

As the main German effort appeared to be directed against Liége and Namur, Eisenhower's policy was " to plug the holes on the north and launch a co-ordinated counter-attack from the south "[2] in the direction of Bastogne. When could such an attack be made? Patton answered: " On the 22nd," a statement which, he says, " created a ripple of excitement." Patton then revealed that he had two divisions on the road already, and he outlined his plan which Eisenhower approved after cautioning him not to attack piecemeal or too soon. The advance was to be " methodical and sure." Eisenhower was most insistent on this point, since he felt that " Patton at first did not seem to comprehend the strength of the German assault."[3]

So that Patton could concentrate adequate forces for this attack, Eisenhower ordered Devers to take over the eastern sector of the Saar front. At this stage, however, 6th Army Group was not in a position to assume substantial fresh responsibilities. Devers was still plagued by the Colmar Pocket and, having advanced to the Siegfried Line in sympathy with Patton's drive for the Saar, he was already extended and vulnerable. Accordingly, Eisenhower authorised him to pull back to the Vosges if necessary, even at the cost of giving up Strasbourg. This ' permissive order ' brought a prompt and forthright protest from the French, and Eisenhower discovered how difficult it is politically for a liberating army to make a voluntary withdrawal from a major city.

When Eisenhower returned to Versailles on the evening of the 19th, he found that the situation had become very much more serious during the day. Although the northern and southern shoulders of the break-through appeared to be holding firm, the enemy on other sectors was advancing almost unchecked. The position at St. Vith was obscure, but it was obvious that the Germans had driven well beyond it on either flank. On the north their leading columns were barely 15 miles from

---

[1]Eisenhower, *Crusade*, p. 350, quoting the official record.
[2]Signal, Eisenhower to Montgomery, December 19th, 1944.
[3]Eisenhower, *Crusade*, p. 351.

Liége; on the south they had taken Houffalize and were alleged to be approaching Laroche, Marche and St. Hubert, 15 miles west of Bastogne. There were no American forces available to prevent the encirclement of Bastogne or to fill the 20-mile gap between the 101st Airborne Division here and the 82nd around Werbomont. Through this gap the Germans were advancing towards the Namur–Dinant–Givet sector of the Meuse which was virtually undefended. It seemed likely that the Germans would reach the river within the next twenty-four hours, and that the six panzer or panzer grenadier divisions not yet involved would be thrown in to exploit their break-through.

The gravity of the situation was accentuated by the fact that Bradley had no reserves whatever except the divisions which he was belatedly withdrawing from the Roer and Saar sectors, and these could not be fully deployed in the Ardennes for another two or three days. In SHAEF reserve there was nothing apart from an armoured division disembarking at Le Havre and two airborne divisions in England, none of which could be brought into action in time to affect the present crisis. Eisenhower accordingly gave orders that engineer and supply units were to be mobilised to guard the Meuse bridges, but he knew that these could not withstand any serious attack. If the Germans should cross the Meuse, the only reserves available to check them were the four divisions of XXX British Corps which Montgomery had been preparing for the Reichswald offensive. This corps, Eisenhower now learned, was being moved by Montgomery on his own initiative into the potential danger zone between the Meuse and Brussels.

Almost as serious as the lack of American reserves was the imminent breakdown of the structure of Bradley's command. The German penetration had split the American front in two and there was no direct contact between Bradley's Tactical H.Q. in the city of Luxemburg and Hodges's H.Q. now established at Chaudfontaine near Liége, nor between the severed parts of First Army. Such communications as were still operating were inadequate and uncertain, for the best telephone lines, those running through Bastogne, had been lost. Bradley had refused to move his command post to Verdun, arguing that he could not do so without adversely affecting military and civilian morale. Eisenhower did not press the point but he foresaw that in this case the remaining reliable links between Bradley and Hodges would soon be broken—as indeed they were[1]—and that from Luxemburg Bradley could not maintain effective control over the all-important battle on the northern flank of ' The Bulge.' Moreover, knowing that Antwerp was the enemy's objective, Eisenhower realised that the Germans would soon try to launch supporting attacks against the Allied front between Aachen and the mouth of the

[1]Normal radio communications were too slow and insecure, and the directional radio link depended on repeater stations sited within visual range of each other. The repeater chain was broken on December 23rd and the buried-cable telephone was cut the same day.

Maas and that, if these attacks were to materialise, the whole area north of the Ardennes would become one battle-zone.

At SHAEF late on the 19th Bedell Smith suggested to Eisenhower that the only logical solution would be to place all the forces north of the break-through under the command of one man and that Montgomery was the only man who had the reserves and the organisation to deal with the crisis. Eisenhower was inclined to agree and he gave Bedell Smith authority to warn both Montgomery and Bradley immediately that the change might be made. After breakfast next morning, Eisenhower confirmed this decision. " Then," says Strong, who was present, ·· Eisenhower himself telephoned to Bradley and a long and heated conversation ensued. We could not hear what Bradley was saying, but he was obviously protesting very strongly, for the conversation ended with Eisenhower saying, ' Well, Brad, those are my orders.' "[1]

This decision was prompted by sheer operational necessity and, when Eisenhower made it, he did not realise how strongly it would be resented by Bradley and his staff, and eventually by the American troops and their people at home.[2] Even if he had paused to consider the political implications, Eisenhower could not have afforded to allow these to affect his military judgment; nor would he have done so, for he knew what was at stake.

The reorganisation of the Allied command did not come a moment too soon, for the battle was already getting out of hand. Except on the northern and southern shoulders of the Bulge there was no coherent front, and the operations of First U.S. Army had developed into a series of individual delaying actions. The divisions which had been moved in to restore the broken line had not been deployed in accordance with any overall design, but had been caught up in the battle one by one as they arrived. It was sheer accident that had brought the 101st to Bastogne at the vital moment. It had been sent there, as Eisenhower says, " not in anticipation of the battle that developed in that area but merely because Bastogne was such an excellent road center "[3] from which to deploy. The movement of 7th Armoured to St. Vith was similarly fortuitous. It was the prompt decision of the local commanders which led to these two nodal points being defended. Here and elsewhere American divisions and regiments fought stubbornly and skilfully

[1]Bradley (op. cit., p. 477) says that " there was ample justification for the Army Group on the north taking temporary command of all Armies on that side of the penetration," but he also says that when Bedell Smith rang him on the evening of the 19th he replied: " Certainly if Monty's were an American command, I would agree with you entirely. It would be the logical thing to do."

[2]At Bradley's H.Q. it was believed that this change in command had been ' engineered' by Churchill. (See Top Secret, by Ralph Ingersoll, p. 264.) Eisenhower (Crusade, p. 356) makes it quite clear, however, that the Prime Minister knew nothing of the change until it had been decided.

[3]Eisenhower, Crusade, p. 357.

wherever they happened to be when the battle swept up to them, and they stood their ground even though ignorant of what was happening on their flanks or in their rear.

The situation was the more confused because Hodges had been left without clear directives. Since the German offensive began, he had seen neither Bradley nor any senior member of Bradley's staff and had received only the briefest orders, many of which were out of date by the time they reached him. Bradley's counter-measures had lagged far behind the tempo of the battle and by the evening of the 19th he had lost the power to control its course. In the south, when Patton was brought in, the unfortunate Middleton—still responsible for a sector of 90 miles—was valiantly but vainly endeavouring to command three distinct forces, those at St. Vith, at Bastogne and on the southern shoulder in the Ettelbrück–Echternach area. These forces had no contact with each other and little or none with Middleton. In the north Bradley had redistributed his forces but he had not reorganised his armies to enable Hodges to concentrate on the Ardennes. Ninth Army had been stripped down to a top-heavy skeleton with two corps controlling three divisions; the four corps of First Army were trying to manage twenty divisions on a wide and broken front.[1] While nominally responsible for the disintegrating southern flank of the Bulge, Hodges was striving to re-form the northern flank and to hold a defensive sector along the Roer. Such diverse and disjointed tasks were too much for any single Army H.Q.

Before Montgomery assumed command of the First and Ninth Armies on December 20th, he had made himself thoroughly familiar with the situation in the Ardennes by sending his own liaison officers to the American front on the two previous days. At noon on the 20th they reported to him again with first-hand information from all front-line sectors except St. Vith. Thus, when he reached First Army H.Q. an hour later, Montgomery was rather better informed about the battle than was Hodges himself.[2] He arrived, says de Guingand, " looking supremely cheerful and confident," but there was something more than confidence in his manner and it seemed to another of his officers that " the Field-Marshal strode into Hodges's H.Q. like Christ come to cleanse the temple."

It was perhaps too much to expect Montgomery to hide his feelings entirely. The wound was too deep. In the hour of triumph after Normandy the Americans, he felt, had spurned his leadership and had let slip the chance of gaining a decisive Allied victory. Now in defeat they had turned to him again to extricate them from a predicament which, he believed, would never have developed if he had been left in

[1] On the afternoon of December 19th XVIII Airborne Corps (Major-General Matthew B. Ridgway) had taken over the north-western sector of the First Army front, thus giving Hodges four corps.

[2] At First Army H.Q. that morning Brigadier-General A. R. Bolling (the commander of the 84th Division) which was moving across from Geilenkirchen, could obtain, so he said later, " no detailed information about the situation."

command of the ground forces. That afternoon Montgomery did not endear himself to his American audience, for his confident tone seemed to carry a note of censure.

Critical and confused though the situation was, Hodges and his staff were not lacking in resolution or aggressive spirit. They knew from captured documents that Sixth Panzer Army was making the main German effort and they believed that its plan was to cross the Meuse on both sides of Liége, thus enveloping the city. They expected, therefore, that the area of greatest danger lay between Monschau and Stavelot. Accordingly, they planned to hold this northern shoulder firmly and to attack from Werbomont towards Vielsalm and Houffalize, thereby striking the enemy in the flank, restoring the broken line and relieving the American force which was believed to be in St. Vith, although nothing had been heard from it for three days.

Montgomery too thought the Germans wanted Liége as their first step to Antwerp, but he believed that their immediate objective lay farther west. British Intelligence had discovered that the Luftwaffe had orders to bomb the bridges north of Liége, but not to attack those to the south. This information told Montgomery that Sixth Panzer Army hoped to cross the Meuse between Liége and Namur. If this were correct, the Americans must be prepared to meet a powerful attack north-west of Houffalize on either side of the River Ourthe. He admitted the danger to Liége, but he foresaw an equally serious threat developing to Huy and Namur.

Montgomery proposed, therefore, that Hodges should extend his defensive front west of Stavelot to Marche and should assemble a strong corps north-west of Marche for a counter-attack when the Germans were beginning to outrun their strength. So that First Army could shift its weight westward, he announced that Ninth Army would take over the entire Roer front, thus releasing VII U.S. Corps. This corps, commanded by Collins, would leave its divisions in the line east and south-east of Aachen and be re-formed. As Hodges had no reserves in hand, however, Montgomery suggested that First Army should withdraw from certain exposed positions on the northern shoulder, shorten its line and thus set free for attack divisions now tied down defensively.[1] This proposal was received with dismay. Hodges politely but firmly demurred and Montgomery did not press the point, for he sensed that, if he were to exert his authority in this regard, it might have a serious effect on American morale.

The unwillingness of Hodges to yield any ground was strengthened by the arrival at this juncture of a letter from Hasbrouck, of 7th Armoured, in St. Vith. From this Hodges learned for the first time that Hasbrouck

[1]Montgomery has been strongly criticised by American writers for suggesting such a course, but in this he had Eisenhower's backing. In a signal on December 20th Eisenhower asked him to report " on the possibility of giving up, if necessary, some ground in order to shorten our line and collect a strong reserve for the purpose of destroying the enemy in Belgium."

had not only his own division but also a combat command of 9th Armoured and two regiments of infantry, though these, he said, were " in bad shape." With this force he was holding a ' horseshoe line ' some twenty-five miles long around St. Vith but he had no contact with any other American units, nor any higher H.Q. " My right flank," wrote Hasbrouck, " is wide open. . . . Two German divisions . . . are just starting to attack north-west against it. . . . I can delay them the rest of to-day *maybe* but will be cut off to-morrow."

This letter determined the immediate policy. Montgomery agreed that the line should be straightened, not by pulling back, but by driving forward to Hasbrouck's relief. Accordingly, Hodges gave orders that Ridgway's XVIII Airborne Corps (now in the Werbomont–Grandmenil area) was to advance across the River Salm, " restore the line Malmedy–St. Vith–Houffalize . . . and gain contact with our units in Bastogne." Montgomery was doubtful of Ridgway's ability thus to close the gap, for the only troops available were the 82nd Airborne Division and one weak combat command of 3rd Armoured, but it was essential to extricate Hasbrouck's force and Montgomery hoped that an aggressive move by Ridgway would cover the assembly of Collins's corps for a more deliberate counter-stroke.

Ridgway wasted no time. That night 82nd Airborne closed up to the River Salm, clenched the ring around Peiper's embattled column and established contact with the western end of the St. Vith ' horseshoe.' Peiper's fate was now sealed,[1] but next morning (the 21st) Ridgway discovered that another German force, including the 116th Panzer Division, had turned his western flank by a rapid advance along the valley of the Ourthe. His own armour had been halted and the Germans were already attacking Hotton, 30 miles west of St. Vith and deep in his rear. Before this new threat could be dealt with, St. Vith had fallen and Ridgway found himself assailed by the full weight of 2nd SS Panzer Corps. Far from closing the gap, First Army was now set back on its heels by a swift succession of attacks more formidable than those which had broken its front six days earlier.

Twelve German divisions, seven of them armoured, delivered this fresh onslaught against First Army's extended front. The first of these new attacks was launched on the Malmedy–Butgenbach–Monschau sector in the early morning of December 21st and was maintained with reckless disregard of losses for forty-eight hours. The Germans gained no ground but it took the best part of six American divisions—half First Army's strength—to hold this northern shoulder at a time when Hodges was searching for reserves to rebuild his western flank.

[1]On December 23rd, after vainly trying to break out, Peiper and 800 of his original force of 2,000 worked their way through the American lines by night and escaped. But they left behind in the valley of the Amblève 39 tanks, 70 half-tracks, 33 guns and 30 supply-trucks.

The second attack, after driving the Americans from St. Vith late on the 21st, crushed in the sides of the 'horseshoe' and compelled Hasbrouck to withdraw across the Salm. This manœuvre was brilliantly executed but, by forcing a withdrawal, the Germans gained at last a clear route through St. Vith to Houffalize and St. Hubert, which was captured on the 23rd by forces which had by-passed Bastogne.

The third attack, made by the 2nd and 9th SS Panzer Divisions against the flanks of the Vielsalm salient which 82nd Airborne was now holding, obliged Montgomery to pull this division back from the Salm and gave the Germans control of the St. Vith–Vielsalm–Laroche road. The fourth attack, designed to extend this route through Marche to Namur, was thwarted, but south-west of Marche the 2nd Panzer Division, by-passing Rochefort, drove on to the last ridge before the Meuse. By the evening of December 23rd Manteuffel's armour was only four miles from Dinant.

As the fighting mounted in intensity, it seemed, says Merriam, that " the attempt to plug the gap had been converted to a struggle for survival, as every division sent to First Army in a counter-attacking role . . . was forced into the defensive fighting to prevent a new German break-out." Although the weather allowed them little air support, the American troops gave blow for blow wherever they met the enemy on anything like equal terms. But the strain was beginning to tell and Hodges had no reserves once he had brought VII Corps into position between the Ourthe and the Meuse, as he did on December 23rd. The Germans, however, still had something in hand. The question was, how much?

The answer given by First Army's chief Intelligence officer (Col. B. A. Dickson) was that the Germans had committed twenty-four divisions in the Ardennes and had thirteen more in close reserve, including four panzer divisions. Dickson said that another nine divisions were " reported in reserve but not confirmed " and that a further dozen might be brought up from Germany or from other battlefronts.[1] Although Hodges did not entirely accept this view, the knowledge that the Germans could readily commit at least another six divisions against First Army made him anxious to seal off the penetration at the earliest opportunity.

Throughout these days, when crisis followed crisis, Montgomery refused to be disconcerted by developments or predictions. The renewed attacks were heavier and more sustained than he had expected, but he was not worried about the Germans' gaining ground *so long as they were not advancing towards what he knew to be their main immediate objective:* the Liége-Namur sector of the Meuse, across which lay the direct route to Antwerp. He did not intend to waste his strength in trying to close the gap. He wanted first to head the Germans off, to turn them away from their strategic destination and so compel them to advance south-west where they could do no harm.

[1] First Army Intelligence Appreciation, December 22nd, 1944.

As Montgomery saw it, the situation would become dangerous only if the Germans should break through between Malmedy and Marche and thus open the roads leading north-west. In this sector First Army should hold the strongest and most economical blocking position and not worry about clinging to ground south of its main defensive line. He was unconcerned when the Germans gained control of the roads from St. Vith through Vielsalm to Laroche and through Houffalize to St. Hubert, for these roads led south-west, the way he wanted the Germans to go. The further they went, the more vulnerable they would become, and the less likely it was that they could concentrate the strength for a break-through to the north-west. Montgomery had no fear of their crossing the Meuse. As early as the evening of December 21st the bridges at Namur, Dinant and Givet were firmly held by British troops and XXX Corps was deployed west of the Meuse to deal with any forces which might cross the river or with any diversionary attack against the rest of the Army Group front north of Aachen. He was balanced and confident, he had only to be patient and the Germans would defeat themselves as they had at Alam Halfa and in Normandy.

Montgomery had the greatest difficulty in persuading Hodges to accept this policy and he never entirely succeeded. Its fulfilment demanded a degree of patience and restraint the Americans did not possess. Montgomery's approach was scientific; theirs was emotional. The German comeback in the Ardennes was the ' Pearl Harbour ' of the European war. Once they had recovered from the first shock, the American troops were out for vengeance. Far from wilting under the onslaught, as Hitler had predicted, they rebounded with all the vigour and indignation of a young people. Having suffered the ignominy of surprise and defeat, their instinctive reaction was to hold fast to whatever they were still holding and to strike back wherever they could as soon and as hard as possible. Only thus, they believed, could the Germans be halted and defeated. Faith and pride made them reluctant to execute any ' voluntary withdrawals '; to do so was ' un-American.' Every yard the Germans were allowed to gain was a reflection on American honour.

The first real clash of opinion on this issue came immediately after the fall of St. Vith. Early on December 22nd Ridgway ordered Hasbrouck to continue the fight east of the Salm River. If necessary, he was to form a defensive perimeter to be supplied by air. Hasbrouck answered that in this case there would soon be " no more 7th Armoured Division." Ridgway relieved him of his command. Before this order of dismissal could take effect, however, one of Montgomery's liaison officers arrived at Hasbrouck's H.Q. and immediately advised the Field-Marshal of the situation he had found. Hasbrouck was reinstated and, having been given permission to withdraw, brought his force safely back across the Salm.[1] Montgomery's intervention saved the gallant defenders of St.

[1]Ridgway's order relieving Hasbrouck was dated 0625 hours, December 22nd, and that reinstating him was dated 1853 hours the same day.

Vith from destruction, and provided Ridgway with a reserve to meet the
next crisis which arose on the 23rd when 82nd Airborne was assailed by
2nd SS Panzer Corps.

Once more there came a question of withdrawal. The airborne
division and an armoured combat command were holding a blunt-nosed
salient, protruding seven miles into enemy territory. Gavin, commanding
the 82nd, realised that " if a major German attack developed from the
south, threatening the right of the division, its continued occupation of
the salient . . . would be costly in life and to no advantage after the
extrication of the St. Vith force."[1] On December 23rd, when this force
had been extricated, Montgomery suggested that Gavin should pull back
to what was agreed to be an almost impregnable ridge south of Werbomont. Again Hodges and Ridgway demurred. That evening, however,
the 2nd SS Panzer Division, attacking along the main Bastogne–Liége
road, broke through the weak defences on Gavin's right flank. Montgomery now insisted upon withdrawal, but this move could not be
carried out until the following night. By then the Germans, exploiting
their success, had captured Grandmenil and it took all Ridgway's reserves
to contain them.

Montgomery considered that this crisis would never have come about
if the 82nd had been brought back to the main line in good time. To
him it was merely a tactical manœuvre; to Ridgway it was above all a
matter of the honour and the morale of his troops. Even Gavin, who
knew that it was tactically essential to give up the salient, was " greatly
concerned with the attitude of the troops . . . the Division never having
made a withdrawal in its combat history." His men, he says, carried out
the order, but "openly and frankly criticised it and failed to understand
the necessity for it." The stubborn determination to stand their ground
was a source of great defensive strength to the Americans, but sometimes,
as now, it resulted in a considerable sacrifice of tactical flexibility and
strategic balance.

This reluctance to shorten the line, except under enemy pressure, led
Hodges to deploy in defence of his western flank the divisions which had
been intended for counter-attack. On December 24th, therefore, Montgomery suggested that VII Corps should not be used to block the
Germans west of the Ourthe, but should swing back, if necessary as far
as the line Hotton–Andenne. That line, said Montgomery, must be
" held at all costs," but he did not want this counter-attack force to
become embroiled in the defensive battle. When Hodges replied that
such a refusal of his flank would uncover the Meuse and expose the
crossing from Namur to Givet, Montgomery assured him that these were
all firmly held by British troops. There was no danger at this extreme
western end of the enemy penetration. The Germans had command of
only two good east-west roads and, with the weather clearing, these were
being heavily attacked by Allied aircraft. The panzer columns reaching

[1]Gavin's After-Action Report to the U.S. War Department.

out to the Meuse were at the end of their tether owing to lack of fuel. On the previous evening the Americans had picked up a message sent by 2nd Panzer asking one of its units whether any petrol had been captured during the day. To Montgomery this was ' the writing on the wall.' The sector to watch, he said, was that between the Salm and the Ourthe where the Germans were clearly building up for a concerted attack in the hope of breaking through to the Meuse between Liége and Huy. To meet that attack there were at the moment no mobile reserves, except the 2nd Armoured Division, part of which was already sparring with the Germans west of Marche.

Hodges was most unwilling to restrain VII Corps. Under pressure he had agreed to ' voluntary withdrawals ' which had been galling to his commanders and troops alike. Now, he felt, he was being asked to ignore the gage which the Germans, by their advance almost to Dinant, had cast at Collins's feet. This was too much. Montgomery might call it ' refusing a flank '; Collins and his men would consider it ' refusing a fight.' Here again was the difference between the scientific and the emotional approach.

Officially Hodges told Collins to " roll with the punch," but he did not order him to refrain from attacking and privately encouraged him to do so. Collins did not hesitate to exercise his discretion, for he was presented with an opportunity he could not ignore, an opportunity which had its origin in the course that events had taken at Bastogne.

If the Germans had won the race for Bastogne, Manteuffel's armour would have had a clear run to Dinant and Namur on December 19th and 20th when there were no American forces between the Ourthe and the Meuse except two battalions of engineers and some light patrols of mechanised cavalry. As it was, however, the Bastogne garrison had acted so aggressively that Panzer Lehr and 2nd Panzer had taken three days to work round the town, and another armoured division (the 116th) had also been checked and diverted. This division had gone through the gap between Houffalize and Bastogne on the 19th, but Manteuffel had to pull it back east of the Ourthe again so that 2nd Panzer would have room to skirt the northern edge of the Bastogne defences. All this delay and disorganisation seriously reduced Manteuffel's momentum, and gave Hodges time to establish a defensive barrier astride the Ourthe as far west as Marche. This in turn compelled Manteuffel to take a wider westward sweep than he had intended and caused him further delay. It was then that he began to appreciate the importance of Bastogne.

Having failed to crush the Bastogne garrison by direct assault, the Germans set out to choke it and by the morning of the 21st the noose of encirclement had been cast around the town. When they sought to pull it tight, however, they soon found they were drawing against an iron ring. Probing for a weak spot to exploit, they made a series of piecemeal attacks which drove in the American outposts but could not penetrate the close perimeter. The garrison, commanded by Brigadier-General A. C. McAuliffe, stood fast and refused to consider itself contained. On the 22nd, when von Lüttwitz called upon the Americans to surrender, or suffer " total annihilation," McAuliffe sent his ultimatum bouncing back with the contemptuous answer, " Nuts! "

Before the Germans could make any further move against Bastogne, their southern flank came under heavy pressure from Third Army which attacked, as Patton had promised, that morning. Although the Germans were amazed at the speed with which Patton had disengaged divisions in the Saar and wheeled them northward, they received due warning of his movement by monitoring the radio net which controlled American traffic, and they were braced to meet his assault.[1] Patton had expected to cut straight through to Bastogne and drive on to St. Vith, but his troops soon discovered that on every approach the Germans had strong blocking forces which could not easily be by-passed because the intervening country was rugged and wooded. West of the Arlon–Bastogne road one armoured column came within five miles of the perimeter but was driven away by a sharp counter-attack. Elsewhere two days of hard fighting brought relief little nearer the beleaguered town.

Third Army's slow progress was a source of considerable anxiety to McAuliffe whose meagre supplies of ammunition were dwindling fast. On December 23rd his artillery battalions, with one exception, had in hand only ten rounds per gun and it was, says Marshall, " a neat question whether . . . relief would come before the ammunition ran out."[2] On this day, for the first time, the weather was good enough for supplies to be dropped from the air, and their arrival, though it did not end the ammunition crisis, put the garrison in fine spirit to meet the challenge which came that evening.

Making their heaviest attack so far, the Germans stove in the south-eastern corner of the perimeter and gained possession of a commanding height. Some tanks broke through into the streets of Bastogne itself but the Americans rallied quickly. The tanks were destroyed and their supporting infantry were hurled back. By morning the breach had been restored.

It was now the Germans' turn to become anxious about Bastogne, for Model and Manteuffel realised that its early capture was essential to the success of the revised plan which they put to Hitler on December 24th.

[1]Cole says (op. cit., p. 310): " The Americans themselves supplied German Intelligence with most of [its information] by extremely careless use of telephones and radios at the various traffic control points along the routes where troops were moving." This was written about the campaign in Lorraine but the same was true of operations in the Ardennes. Model's Chief Intelligence Officer (Colonel Roger Michael) subsequently testified: " As far as troop movements were concerned, we were not at all surprised—the First [American] Army traffic net was still working well for us." (See ' File on Colonel Michael,' British Army of the Rhine Intelligence Review, March 4th, 1946.)

[2]Col. Marshall, op. cit., p. 134.

By then their forces had advanced sixty miles into Belgium but they both knew they had no chance whatever of reaching Antwerp and little of crossing the Meuse. American resistance had been more stubborn and American reserves had moved more quickly than they had expected. They had been disappointed also in their hopes of capturing large quantities of American petrol, and without it their panzer divisions could not advance beyond the Meuse. Hitler had promised them sufficient fuel for three hundred miles of normal running, but in fact had given them enough for barely a third of that mileage, and most of this had been consumed in negotiating the tortuous side-roads which the armoured columns had been obliged to take. This was the price of the delay in capturing St. Vith and of the failure to secure Malmedy and Bastogne.

The revised plan was, in effect, the ' small solution ' which Hitler had already rejected. Model proposed that they should establish a firm western flank on the Meuse at Dinant and then drive north: Manteuffel (with four Wehrmacht panzer divisions) between the Meuse and the Ourthe heading for Huy; Dietrich (with four SS panzer divisions) between the Ourthe and the Salm in the direction of Liége. Having swept the east bank of the Meuse, they would drive on to Aachen. Meanwhile, an offensive force would be re-assembled on the Lower Roer for an attack southward to Maastricht. With these converging thrusts the Aachen salient could be wiped out. Model suggested that the necessary forces for this northern arm could be provided if the Führer would abandon his plan for the offensive in Alsace, due to start on New Year's Day.

Hitler rejected this last suggestion on the ground that his new offensive would compel Patton to transfer to Alsace the bulk of the forces which were now threatening to relieve Bastogne. The pressure on the southern flank of the Ardennes would thus be reduced, and Model would be free to concentrate on the drive to the north. Although Hitler was not prepared to accept Aachen, in place of Antwerp, as the ultimate objective, he endorsed the immediate plan, because he knew he could not strike at Antwerp until he had secured the Namur–Liége sector of the Meuse. He also agreed that before implementing this plan they must capture Bastogne.

For this new assault upon the besieged town Manteuffel brought in a fresh division, 15th Panzer Grenadier, and directed it to attack from the north-west where the defences had not been seriously tested.[1] By striking at the American ' back door ' he hoped to find a vulnerable quarter, but in fact he launched his troops against the strongest and freshest sector of the perimeter.

By Christmas Eve it was clear to the Americans in Bastogne that a major assault was coming. All day they had observed the steady build-

---

[1]The arrival of this division, and of two other infantry regiments, brought the strength of the forces investing Bastogne to the equivalent of three divisions. The garrison amounted to one and a half divisions.

up of forces to the north and north-west. That evening Bastogne was bombed twice. At midnight the front was ominously quiet and, says Marshall, " for the first time all around the perimeter men felt fearful. It seemed to them that the end was at hand. That night many of them shook hands with their comrades."[1] But whatever inner doubts or fears the Americans may have harboured, they revealed neither when the testing hour came.

The Germans attacked at three o'clock on Christmas morning and before dawn parties of infantry had penetrated the American line three miles north-west of Bastogne. At first light a further assault by armour and infantry opened another breach, but, when the German tanks drove on to exploit their break-through, they exposed themselves to flanking fire from American tank-destroyers well sited to deal with such an eventuality. McAuliffe had anticipated the German intention. Of the eighteen tanks which had broken through every one was knocked out; of their supporting infantry not a man escaped. By mid-morning the American line was again intact. Next day the Germans renewed their assault, but, before they could make any serious impression on the defences, Patton had driven a relief column through their containing ring in the south-west and the siege was raised.

To Manteuffel this was a severe defeat, for the wider consequences of his failure at Bastogne were already becoming apparent between Rochefort and the Meuse.

On Christmas morning the advance guard of the 2nd Panzer Division stood impatient on the ridge above Dinant waiting for petrol and reinforcement before making the final plunge down the western slope of the Ardennes to the gleaming Meuse below. This column had been waiting there for thirty-six hours while the rest of the division strove to capture Marche and Rochefort. Rochefort had now fallen (after being most gallantly defended for two nights and a day by a single American battalion) and the main body of 2nd Panzer was again advancing west. But it was advancing alone. On its left, Panzer Lehr, ' leg-roped ' to Bastogne where one of its regiments was engaged, could not advance in force beyond St. Hubert; on its right, the 116th Panzer Division had been abruptly halted between Marche and Hotton. Of the armoured reserves, which Hitler had promised Manteuffel, one division had been diverted to Butgenbach, another was involved at Bastogne, and the third, delayed by lack of petrol, was only just approaching Marche.

Nevertheless, Manteuffel's orders were that 2nd Panzer should press on without delay to Dinant. During the morning its reconnaissance battalion reported that there was a screen of British armour along the Meuse and already there had been some clashes with American tanks to the north near Ciney, but the Germans had no suspicion that the entire

[1]Col. Marshall, op. cit., p. 157.

2nd U.S. Armoured Division was bearing down upon their northern flank in overwhelming strength. General 'Joe' Collins was exercising his discretion.

In the middle of the day one American combat command struck straight for Rochefort and intercepted the reinforcement columns moving up; another enveloped the woods around Celles where the German advance guard was strongly entrenched. For two days the battle raged west of Rochefort, as the trapped force struggled to avoid annihilation, and the rest of the division, with help from Panzer Lehr and 9th Panzer, endeavoured in vain to break through to its relief. Short of petrol, the encircled Germans had to fight where they stood, but the Americans, manœuvring freely over ground now frozen hard, proceeded to beat the woods and scour the villages until all resistance had been crushed.[1]

By the evening of December 27th the forces which were to have taken Dinant were reeling back into Rochefort, and the spearhead of Manteuffel's Fifth Panzer Army lay broken in the snow. The Germans had looked upon the Meuse for the last time.

[1]After gaining possession of the battlefield, the 2nd Armoured Division reported that it had " destroyed or captured " 82 tanks, 16 other armoured vehicles, 83 guns and 280 motor vehicles. Not all these belonged to 2nd Panzer, but in this battle it did lose the vast majority of the 88 tanks and 28 assault guns with which it had begun the offensive.

## CHAPTER XXXI

# THE MEUSE AND THE VISTULA

CHRISTMAS in the Ardennes was cold and clear, and Hitler's armies, which had crossed the Belgian border burning with enthusiasm, now felt the chill breath of defeat. Over Christmas week-end the mist and cloud which had shielded the German advance during the first week lifted suddenly and gave Allied air power its opportunity. This abrupt improvement in the weather caught the Germans unawares and they paid heavily for having taken the risk of crowding the roads in daylight, and for having brought with them, as von Rundstedt admitted to Hitler, " a flood of superfluous motor vehicles taken along empty for loot."[1] Denied Malmedy and Bastogne, their supply convoys and reinforcement columns moving westward from St. Vith had only two good roads to follow and each of these passed through a crooked defile where it crossed the River Ourthe, the one at Laroche and the other at Houffalize. At these two bottlenecks and at St. Vith itself, as well as on the intervening roads, when the weather cleared, Allied airmen found concentrated targets such as they had not seen since the Falaise Pocket and the Seine crossing.

In four days the American and British air forces flew 15,000 sorties, striking not only at traffic in the Ardennes, but also at roads, railways and airfields throughout the Rhineland. The German ' railheads ' in the Eifel were soon rendered useless and Model's forces became dependent on supplies brought up by road from distant depots. For security reasons, Hitler had insisted that all the main dumps should be east of the Rhine, but the dislocation of railways and the destruction of road transport left him without the means of lifting the tonnage necessary to maintain the advance of his armies. He had neither the vehicles nor the petrol, nor could he use the roads by day, for the Luftwaffe was powerless to protect them. Commenting on this turn of events (and resorting to an outrageous pun) one of Montgomery's staff declared:[2] " The enemy is trying to get

[1]Führer Conferences, Fragment 41, December 28th, 1944.

[2]Williams, his chief Intelligence officer, at a press conference in Brussels on December 27th, 1944.

his second wind, but the Allied Air Forces are taking it out of his sails before he gets it."

Three days before Christmas, when the Germans were still advancing westward, Eisenhower had written in an Order of the Day: " By rushing out from his fixed defences the enemy may give us the chance to turn his great gamble into his worst defeat." Three days after Christmas it seemed that this chance had come. Defeat at Bastogne, disaster at Rochefort and devastation on the supply lines had taken the momentum out of the German offensive. Eager to exploit the enemy's embarrassment, Bradley proposed that the three divisions, now assembled in SHAEF reserve, should be used to reinforce Third Army's attack from the south and that First Army should make a large scale assault against the northern flank of the Bulge immediately.

This proposal was discussed by Eisenhower and Montgomery in Belgium on December 28th. The Field-Marshal's reaction was that First Army had not the strength to attack successfully so long as it was opposed, as it was then, by the enemy's main force, including seven, if not eight, panzer divisions. He argued that a premature counter-attack might give the Germans a chance of breaking through towards Liége and would certainly result in heavy American casualties, especially in the infantry units which were seriously short of replacements already. The Germans still had considerable reserves in hand and clearly " intended to make at least one more full-blooded attack " in the north. His policy was to defeat this attack and then to strike, when the enemy was exhausted. Montgomery said he was bringing British divisions east of the Meuse so that VII U.S. Corps could be brought into reserve " ready to follow in on the heels of the Germans as soon as they were repulsed."[1] Eisenhower agreed that " this plan would seize the best possible conditions under which to initiate a great counter-blow," but he was anxious not to wait too long. They decided, therefore, that, if there were no renewal of the German attack, First Army's counter-offensive would begin on January 3rd. In the meantime, the SHAEF reserve would be given to Patton so that pressure against the enemy's southern flank, particularly at Bastogne, could be intensified.

The decision to delay the attack in the north was strongly resented by Bradley and Patton, who felt that Montgomery was letting them do all the fighting and that he could take up the offensive at once if only he would use the four British divisions he had in reserve. Montgomery's reluctance to commit these divisions arose from his determination to hold a strong force in hand until the Germans had committed their reserves and from his desire to avoid the administrative complications which would have resulted from injecting a British corps into an American army in an area already congested. Moreover, Montgomery was looking far beyond the Ardennes. There were no new British divisions arriving, as there were American, and he was anxious to keep XXX Corps intact for the coming battle of the Rhineland.

<hr>

[1] Eisenhower, *Crusade*, p. 360.

The difference between the outlook and method of Patton and Montgomery came out very clearly in their attitude to reserves. Patton took the view that, since attack is the best method of defence, all the force at a commander's disposal should be employed in the line and, if possible, aggressively. During the battle following the relief of Bastogne, the local corps commander appealed to Third Army H.Q. for reinforcements and supported his plea with the statement that he had " only two battalions left in reserve." To this request Patton's Deputy Chief of Staff replied: " You'd better not let General Patton know you have two battalions. They are not only your reserve, but that's all the Army has in reserve. If the General hears you've got them, he'll commit them, sure as hell."[1] Montgomery, on the other hand, believed in Wellington's precept that reserves are the foundation of victory. His technique in the Ardennes, as in Normandy and at Alamein, was to allow the Germans to exhaust themselves in costly attacks and then to strike them with fresh forces concentrated in reserve. Subsequently, in reply to a question, " When did you know that the battle of Normandy was won? " Montgomery replied, " When I was able to withdraw three armoured divisions into reserve."[2]

While Eisenhower and Montgomery were meeting in Belgium, von Rundstedt was endeavouring to persuade Hitler that he should abandon all offensive operations and extricate his armies before the Allies could counter-attack in force. He reported that there was no possibility of carrying out even the ' small solution,' since the necessary supplies and reinforcements could not be brought forward with sufficient speed or strength. Accordingly he suggested that both Dietrich and Manteuffel should withdraw to a defensive line east of Bastogne and that their panzer divisions should be pulled back into reserve.

Hitler spurned this advice, for he was determined to renew the drive to the Meuse as soon as he had carried through the next phase of his overall plan, the attack in Alsace. On the 28th, addressing von Rundstedt and the commanders who were to direct this operation, Hitler said, " I am convinced that in the long run we could not maintain the defensive. . . . Only the offensive will enable us once more to give a successful turn to this war in the West."[3] He admitted that the attack in the Ardennes had " not resulted in the decisive success which might have been expected," but claimed that this was due to " delays caused by bad roads [and] the destruction of certain bridges which could not be repaired quickly." Nevertheless, he said, " a tremendous easing of the situation has come about. The enemy has had to abandon all his plans for attack. He has been obliged to regroup his forces. He has had to throw in again units which were fatigued. . . . He is severely criticised at home. . . . Already

[1]This incident is recounted by one of Patton's Intelligence staff, Col. Robert S. Allen (op. cit., p. 262).
[2]In a conversation with me, May 18th, 1946.
[3]Führer Conferences, Fragment 27, December 28th, 1944. The shorthand record of this speech has survived almost complete.

he has had to admit that there is no chance of the war being decided before August, perhaps not before the end of next year. This means a transformation in the situation such as nobody would have believed possible a fortnight ago."

Von Rundstedt and his field commanders, thankful at having gained so much, would have been content with this achievement, but Hitler's appetite for attack, so long starved, had now been whetted by success. The Americans, he told them, had been " forced to withdraw something like fifty per cent of the forces from their other fronts " to the Ardennes, with the result that their line in Alsace had become " extraordinarily thin." There, he said, " we shall find a situation which we could not wish to be better." The success of this new operation would " automatically bring about the collapse of the threat to the left of the main offensive," which could then be resumed with fresh prospect of success. Acting on this assumption, Hitler gave orders that Model should consolidate his hold on the Ardennes and reorganise his forces for yet another attempt to reach the Meuse. At the same time, he was to make a new and more powerful assault upon the Bastogne Salient. This assault, Hitler hoped, would keep Patton fully occupied while the German forces now concentrated in the Saar and in the Colmar Pocket were breaking out into Alsace.

On New Year's Day eight German divisions attacked southward from the Saar, but this time the Americans were not taken by surprise, widely extended though their forces were. West of the Vosges the main German thrust, towards the Saverne Gap, was halted before it had gone ten miles and the opportunity for exploitation with armour did not develop. East of the Vosges, where Devers had driven a salient into the Siegfried defences, Seventh Army—on Eisenhower's express instructions—made a deliberate and skilful withdrawal in face of the German advance. Thereupon, thinking he had his opponents on the run, Hitler switched his frustrated reserves to this sector, only to find that the Americans had re-formed their front at the Maginot Line. The attack from the Colmar Pocket was equally unprofitable, despite the personal intervention of Heinrich Himmler, who as commander of Army Group *Ober-Rhein*, discovered that the process of extermination was more difficult when the potential victim had the power to defend himself.

Himmler's sole success was the establishment of a small bridgehead over the Rhine north of Strasbourg, a move which caused the Americans to shorten their line by making a further withdrawal in the north-eastern corner of Alsace. At the start of the German offensive Eisenhower had been inclined to pull back to the Vosges, for he had no reserves whatever between the Ardennes and Switzerland. But this would have meant giving up Strasbourg, a city so prized by the French that its loss without a struggle would have created a grave political crisis. On de Gaulle's insistence, therefore, Devers was ordered to hold Strasbourg at all costs.    This he did, and brought the German offensive to a halt without requiring the diversion of any American forces from the main battle area.    Too late Hitler realised that the divisions he had expended in this abortive venture might have been used to better purpose elsewhere.

In the Ardennes at the start of January Patton had six divisions attacking from the south with the object of widening the Bastogne Salient and driving it deeper into the German flank.    This thorn in the enemy's side thus became a knife and, as Patton turned the knife in the wound, Hitler was forced to react more strongly than he had intended.    Three fresh infantry divisions were brought up from OKW reserve and four armoured divisions were transferred from Dietrich to Manteuffel with orders to capture Bastogne and establish an impregnable southern flank.

Throughout January 3rd and 4th the American positions around Bastogne were subjected to a succession of heavy and well co-ordinated attacks by elements of eight divisions.    The battle that developed was the fiercest of the entire Ardennes campaign, and the most costly, especially for the new and untried American divisions which Patton was obliged to commit west of Bastogne in order to relieve the pressure on the town. Although bad weather denied them air support, the defenders held fast and put down such concentrations of artillery that many attacks broke before they reached the American lines and none made any serious penetration.    On the 5th the German assault began to weaken and all idea of capturing Bastogne was abandoned, for the forces that had been entrusted with this task were now needed to ward off the Allied counter-offensive which Montgomery had launched against the northern flank of the Bulge two days earlier.

From the outset this attack was severely handicapped by atrocious weather which drastically limited Allied air operations and enabled the Germans to exploit the great defensive strength of the Ardennes.    The Americans attacking from the north and the British from the west found the enemy strongly entrenched on the timbered ridges, his positions camouflaged for him by a thick blanket of snow.    For this bitter winter fighting the Germans, with their long experience in Russia, were better trained and better equipped, and they made the attackers pay dearly for every yard gained.    Deep snowdrifts hampered the Allied infantry and ice-bound roads restricted the mobility of their armour, which was further curtailed by the cunning use of mines laid loose in the snow.    In five days the American drive for Houffalize gained only five miles, but this was enough to make Model demand permission to withdraw from the western Ardennes.

Beyond the Bastogne–Houffalize–Liége road Model still had seven of his ten armoured divisions and there was now only one good road by which these could be extricated.    That route, through Houffalize, was already under shell-fire, and although the Germans did not know it, the

Allies were using a new fuse operated by radar.[1] The use of this fuse enabled Allied artillery to fire air-burst shells with unprecedented accuracy and with deadly effect, especially when directed against a 'traffic target' such as the Houffalize bottleneck. On January 8th, no longer able to deny that most of his surviving armour was in danger of being trapped, Hitler authorised Model to give up the area west of Houffalize. With this reluctant and belated decision Hitler admitted that the Ardennes offensive had failed.

The fundamental reason for this failure was Hitler's assumption that the Wehrmacht had the power to repeat its performance of 1940. His plan had been based on a gross over-estimate of his own strength and an even grosser under-estimate of Allied strength and particularly of the American capacity to recover. He had made a further miscalculation in believing that it was air power which had decided the Battle of France in the summer and that, when winter weather reduced their air support, the American and British armies would be no match for the Wehrmacht. It was nothing new for Hitler to ignore the advice of his generals, but it is surprising that men of the calibre of von Rundstedt and Model should have submitted so meekly to his dictation at this crucial stage in German history.

With the achievement of the autumn to their credit the Field-Marshals had been in a strong position to insist that the planning and direction of the winter's operations should be left in their hands. They could not contest Hitler's right to determine political objectives and they agreed that an attack in the West should be made, but it was surely their duty to demand—even at the risk of their own lives—that the reserves which had been built up at such cost should not be cast away in a reckless gamble. They knew that Hitler's plan was foredoomed to failure, for he had neither the strength nor the petrol to recapture Antwerp, let alone to fulfil his boast that he would 'Dunkirk' the Allied Armies north of the Ardennes. They knew that the attempt to retake Antwerp would destroy the chance of recapturing Aachen and restoring the Siegfried Line. They knew that all they could gain in the Ardennes was Time, and this only at great cost. Hitler's suggestion that they could go over to the 'small solution' if the larger plan were to fail was military nonsense, for once the bulk of the reserves had been committed in the Ardennes they would not have the resources to strike at the Aachen salient in the north.

Of all the generals in the West, Manteuffel alone had the courage to

---

[1]The 'proximity fuse' was so called because shells in which it was fitted would explode as soon as they came in close proximity to the ground or to objects in the air. This fuse, invented in Britain and mass-produced in America, had played an important part in the defeat of the flying-bomb and was first used in ground operations during the Ardennes offensive. The invention of this fuse, the most important artillery development of the war, is yet another example of the superiority of Allied over German science.

challenge the ' NOT TO BE ALTERED ' Operation Orders handed down from the Führer's H.Q. When he did so, he says, his suggestions were " accepted without a murmur," but these were concerned only with points of tactical detail—the hour of attack, the timing of the artillery barrage and the deployment of the armour; they did not assail the strategic concept of the plan. Against this the Field-Marshals registered their objection but there is no evidence that they made it an issue. Von Rundstedt merely washed his hands of the whole affair; he did not carry his protest to the point of resignation as he had done in Russia in 1941. Perhaps it was that the shadow of July 20th clouded their counsel and weakened their will.

Although Antwerp was far beyond their grasp, the Germans should have been able to reach the Meuse once they had succeeded in gaining surprise and securing a clear break-through. In von Rundstedt's opinion their failure to do so was due primarily to Hitler's determination that the main thrust should be made by Dietrich's Sixth SS Panzer Army. The Field-Marshals had suggested that the *Schwerpunkt* of the attack should be placed in the central Ardennes where the roads were better and the defences weaker. This had been rejected by Hitler because he believed that only the SS divisions had the fanaticism to ensure success and, for the sake of Nazi prestige, he wanted them to win the glory of victory. These divisions could not be employed in the centre. The achievement of surprise depended on his ability to convince the Allies that Dietrich's Army was being held in reserve for a counter-attack on the Roer sector. To maintain this pretence, its move to the Eifel had to be delayed until the last three nights which meant that it could be committed only on the northern wing. Thus did politics, and the fear of Allied air reconnaissance, corrupt the plan. " This decision," said von Rundstedt later, " was a fundamental mistake that unbalanced the whole offensive,"[1] for neither Dietrich nor his troops had the ability to carry out the tasks the Führer gave them. This mistake was compounded when Hitler persisted in reinforcing the northern wing even after Manteuffel, not Dietrich, had created the opportunity for rapid exploitation.

That is one side of the story, but the frustration of the drive to the Meuse cannot be blamed entirely on Hitler and his strategic miscalculations, his tactical interference, and his refusal to recognise the limitations imposed by the shortage of petrol, by the indifferent training of the *Volksgrenadier* divisions and by lack of time and fuel to run in the tanks which were delivered direct from the factories. In his Operation Order at the start of the offensive Model wrote: " Quick exploitation of success on the first day will be decisive. The primary objective is to obtain freedom of movement for the mobile units." Although the Germans secured this freedom on Manteuffel's front, their exploitation of it was curtailed by the stubbornness of the American infantry who held the

---

[1] Canadian Army Interrogation.

shoulders of the break-through, by the resourcefulness of small rearguard parties who delayed the panzer columns and by the rapid movement of reserves to St. Vith and Bastogne. These were the factors that took the sting out of the initial attack, thwarted Dietrich and delayed Manteuffel. Moreover, the achievement of the American troops in the line gave the Allied High Command time to recover from the first shock of surprise. Before the Germans could re-group their forces and develop the momentum to take them to the Meuse, Montgomery had re-established the front in the north and Patton was counter-attacking from the south.

When Montgomery took command, the Germans still had a very good chance of reaching the Meuse in force, but this was soon eliminated by his strong and patient handling of the chaotic situation he had inherited. Bradley, Patton and other American generals thought that he was too patient and that his policy was unduly cautious. It may well be that Montgomery under-estimated the toughness and resilience of the American troops and did not appreciate their remarkable capacity to take up the offensive immediately after suffering a severe reverse. On the other hand, if Montgomery had allowed First Army to become engaged in a slogging match east of the River Ourthe, the Germans would have had a clear run between the Ourthe and the Meuse. Montgomery's contribution was that he converted a series of individual actions into a coherent battle fought in accordance with a clear plan. It was his early movement of XXX British Corps to the area between Liége and Brussels that restored the balance of the Allied armies and provided the depth which gave ultimate strength to the northern flank. It was his insistence on the withdrawal of First Army from its more exposed positions that enabled the Americans to establish a firm, defensive front blocking the road to Namur. It was his refusal to make piecemeal and premature counter-attacks that enabled the Americans to accumulate the reserves which thwarted the German attempts to penetrate and outflank this front.

Valuable though Montgomery's contribution was, the Allied cause would have been better served if he himself had not drawn attention to it. At a press conference on January 7th, however, the Field-Marshal surveyed the battle in terms which placed considerable emphasis on his own part in it. After describing how the Germans had created a situation which " looked as if it might become awkward," Montgomery said, " As soon as I saw what was happening, I took certain steps to ensure that if the Germans got to the Meuse they would certainly not get over that river . . . these were merely precautions, that is, I was thinking ahead." Continuing in this strain, he used some unhappy phrases. He said that, when the crisis came, " national considerations were thrown overboard," a statement which the Americans regarded as a suggestion that Eisenhower had called in the best man. Montgomery also declared that his first task had been to " tidy up the battlefield," and he spoke of the operation as " one of the most interesting and tricky I have ever handled." In the written statement which he issued to the correspondents, Montgomery paid warm and sincere tributes to Eisenhower and the American troops, but he made no mention of the name of Bradley. This omission may have been unwitting, but it was certainly unfortunate, and was bitterly resented.

Further resentment was caused by a statement which, taken out of context, gave an impression Montgomery certainly did not intend to convey. The offending statement was: " I employed the whole available power of the British Group of Armies; this power was brought into play very gradually and in such a way that it would not interfere with the American lines of communication. Finally it was put into battle with a bang and today British divisions are fighting hard on the right flank of First U.S. Army." Bradley regarded this statement as misleading and mischievous, and as an attempt to claim undue credit for the British Army. But when Montgomery said this, he was not claiming anything; he was defending himself against the charge that he had allowed the Americans to bear an unfair burden and he was explaining why he had not been able to bring the British into action sooner. He was not suggesting that they had saved the situation. On the contrary, he told the correspondents that the Germans had been halted before the British divisions were committed, and he expressly declared that the offensive had been stopped by " the good fighting qualities of the American soldier and by the teamwork of the Allies." Nevertheless, it was assumed at Bradley's H.Q. that Montgomery was claiming not only a personal triumph for himself but a national victory for the British.[1]

Commenting on this conference, Eisenhower says, " I doubt that Montgomery ever came to realise how deeply resentful some American commanders were. They believed he had belittled them—and they were not slow to voice reciprocal scorn and contempt."[2] None was more resentful than Bradley. Before this incident he had come to dislike Montgomery; henceforth he regarded him with feelings akin to hatred, but the full degree of his resentment was not revealed until six years later. Then, in his own account of the war, all the pent-up bitterness came out.

In his book, *A Soldier's Story*, Bradley belittles Montgomery's achievement in Normandy and, although he concedes that the Arnhem plan was " one of the most imaginative of the war," he makes this concession with a note of deprecation, commenting: " Had the pious teetotalling Montgomery wobbled into SHAEF with a hangover, I could not have

---

[1]Writing after the war, Bradley (op. cit., p. 485), said: " When Montgomery's statement reached us, via the B.B.C., my acutely sensitive staff exploded with indignation." Bradley correctly reports his staff's reaction, but he does not reveal the true source of its information. My dispatch to the B.B.C. was picked up in Germany, rewritten to give it an anti-American bias and then broadcast by Arnhem Radio, which was then in Goebbels's hands. Monitored at Bradley's H.Q., this broadcast was mistaken for a B.B.C. transmission and it was this twisted text that started the uproar. (See Ingersoll, op. cit., pp. 278-80.)

[2]Eisenhower, *Crusade*, p. 356.

been more astonished than I was by the daring adventure he proposed."[1] Discussing the Ardennes, Bradley is justifiably critical of Montgomery's contentious press conference and of those British newspapers which had depicted the Field-Marshal " as St. George come to save the American Command from disaster." Far from admitting that the situation was ever dangerous, Bradley claims not only that the American Command " had arrested the break-through . . . before Montgomery entered the picture," but also that it would have been able to " pinch off the enemy at the middle," if only Montgomery had not delayed First Army's counter-attack until he had " completed his primping."[2] These claims are hardly supported by the facts. The heaviest German attacks against the northern flank were delivered after the change of command and, if Eisenhower had required Montgomery to counter-attack before Christmas as Bradley wanted, the meagre offensive capacity then available to First U.S. Army would have been expended while the Germans were still strong.

At the time Bradley curbed his indignation in the interests of Allied unity, but in the interests of his troops he felt obliged to make a public answer. On January 9th he issued to the Press a firm and dignified statement, in which he acknowledged Montgomery's " notable contribution," justified his own conduct of the battle, and was at pains to defend the policy he had pursued before the German offensive began. After admitting that " the actual timing of the attack and its strength were somewhat of a surprise," Bradley said: " The build-up of German forces had been observed in the Cologne area for some weeks before the attack and the possibility of a German attack through the Ardennes was thoroughly studied by me and my staff. In leaving the Ardennes line lightly held we took a calculated risk to strengthen our Northern and Southern drives; in other words, instead of employing our surplus divisions in the quiet Ardennes we used them to attack in other sectors."

Since it was this policy that gave the Germans their opportunity, Bradley's claim must be closely examined. The calculations on which the Ardennes risk was taken were valid so long as Bradley's offensive concentrations were compelling the Germans to maintain defensive counter-concentrations. By the first week of December, however, the main American attack had come to a standstill. The enemy was thus free to employ his reserves offensively in the Ardennes, for he knew the Americans could not venture across the Roer River while the dams were in German hands. Both Bradley and Eisenhower have argued that the Ardennes sector could not have been held more strongly without gravely weakening the American drives on either flank. This was true with respect to Patton's attack, for it was due to be resumed before Christmas, but Bradley had no intention of launching his northern armies across the Roer until the second week in January. Thus the concentration of

[1]Bradley, op. cit., p. 416.
[2]Ibid., pp. 486, 480, 479.

American strength in the Aachen Salient in mid-December was serving no purpose tactical or strategic. It was certainly not necessary for the capture of the Roer dams. On December 16th there were four divisions in reserve around Aachen. Two of these could equally well have been resting in the Ardennes. Deployed there these divisions would have preserved the balance of Bradley's Army Group until he was ready to renew the drive to Cologne.

If Bradley really was taking a " calculated risk," it is strange that neither he nor Eisenhower nor any member of their staffs ever mentioned it to Montgomery; stranger still that Bradley should have had no plan ready to meet a German counter-stroke in the Ardennes, and should have reacted so slowly when the risk became a reality. While it is true that Bradley ordered the movement of two armoured divisions from the flanking armies on the first evening, the German attack had been in progress thirty-six hours before he called in the SHAEF Reserve which Eisenhower had given him; two days before he asked Patton to cancel his pending offensive in the Saar; three days before he began withdrawing divisions from the Roer front-line to reinforce the Ardennes; and even after four days he had produced no overall plan for bringing the situation under control.

Bradley was an able tactician, but he was less competent in the realm of strategy. In Normandy, commanding First U.S. Army, he had shown himself to be a resolute and resourceful leader, but neither then nor later did he seem to appreciate the importance of concentration and balance. He was successful in conducting operations so long as someone else was controlling the battle as a whole, preserving the balance of the force, manœuvring the enemy into a vulnerable position and then developing the concentration necessary for a decisive stroke. Bradley could deliver the stroke but he was less able to create the opportunity for it. The basic difference between Bradley and Montgomery was that, whereas Bradley moved at the dictates of the situation responding tactically, Montgomery endeavoured to mould situations to his will acting strategically.

Once he had passed from Montgomery's jurisdiction to command his own Army Group, Bradley lacked the assurance he had shown in Normandy. Although in the autumn of 1944 he had had at his disposal the most powerful single force on the Western Front—30 divisions in November—he had failed to inflict any serious reverse on the enemy, primarily because he had chosen the obvious, direct approaches and had dispersed his effort. Consequently, he had never been able to concentrate strength against weakness as he had done, under Montgomery's guidance, for the break-out from Normandy. The opportunity which Bradley's forces had exploited so brilliantly in the advance across France and Belgium had been created for them strategically by Montgomery . . . and by Hitler. Once he had outrun his resources, Bradley was unable to create another opportunity for himself until after the Germans had been exhausted in the Ardennes. Before this, however, the 'calculated risk' policy had given the enemy the chance of seizing the initiative, and Hitler had done so by taking an 'uncalculated risk.'

With characteristic magnanimity Eisenhower subsequently declared, " If giving him [the enemy] that chance is to be condemned by historians, their condemnation should be directed at me alone."[1] In writing this, Eisenhower takes too much blame upon himself. Eisenhower had sensed the danger in the Ardennes and had warned Bradley in good time, but, because it was not the custom of the American Army to impose firm control on commanders in the field, he had not asserted his authority.

From the start of the offensive, however, Eisenhower had shown a quicker and surer grasp of the situation than had any other American general and had intervened decisively. If Eisenhower had accepted Bradley's initial opinion that this was not an all-out attack, the application of Allied counter-measures, and especially the commitment of the SHAEF Reserve, would have been dangerously delayed. The choice of Bastogne as the concentration area for the 101st Airborne Division— perhaps the most important single decision of the whole battle—was made at Eisenhower's H.Q. When the front was split by the German break-through, he promptly appreciated the need to reorganise the command and bring in Montgomery; when other American commanders were advocating rigid defence, he authorised the yielding of ground in order to accumulate reserves; and, when Bradley and Patton were inclined to rush into counter-attack, he cautioned them to be patient and to make their advance " methodical and sure." In all his career as Supreme Commander there was perhaps no other time when Eisenhower revealed so clearly the greatness of his qualities.

The consequences of the costly German defeat in the Ardennes became apparent in the East sooner than in the West, for it was the Russians who reaped the immediate benefit of the Führer's reckless expenditure of his mobile reserves.

Since October the Red Army had made no major advances in Poland and the Germans had set up a new defensive front covering East Prussia and then following, broadly, the line of the Narew and the Vistula southward across the Polish Plain to the Carpathians.[2] Throughout the closing months of 1944 this vast front had lain quiescent, for Stalin could not continue his westward drive through Poland until he had repaired the railways of White Russia and the Ukraine; nor did he desire to do so before he had garnered the military and political fruits of the Rumanian

---

[1] Eisenhower, *Crusade*, p. 341.
[2] The only important development on the northern sector of the Eastern Front during the last three months of 1944 was the Russian advance through Lithuania to the Baltic. This advance isolated Memel and cut off 26 German divisions in Western Latvia, creating there the ' Courland Pocket.'

collapse, broken the German grip on South-Eastern Europe and established Soviet power in the Balkan capitals.

After securing Bucharest and Sofia in September, the Red Army had continued its offensive up the broad Danube Valley, entering Belgrade on October 20th at the same time as Tito's partisans. Meanwhile, Hitler had been endeavouring to extricate a dozen divisions from the Southern Balkans in order to hold the River Tisza in Hungary. This plan had been forestalled because Greek and Yugoslav guerrillas, nourished with Western supplies, had prevented a quick and orderly German withdrawal, and the Russians had broken the line of the Tisza before it could be adequately manned. By the first week of November the German front in Hungary had been forced back to the Danube, and Budapest had come under Soviet shellfire. In ten weeks since crossing the Dniester the Russians had swept round the flank of the main German front in the East, advanced 650 miles and created an entirely new threat to the German homeland.

Ranged along the Hungarian reach of the Danube, the Russians were within easy striking distance of objectives extremely important to the Luftwaffe and the whole German war economy. Hungarian bauxite mines, Hitler's main source of aluminium, were the very basis of the German aircraft industry, and, since the loss of Ploesti, Hungarian oil wells were providing one-third of Germany's natural oil; the only 'crude,' in fact, worth refining into aviation spirit and the more precious now because of the drastic decline in the output of synthetic plants. When the threat to these essential resources became critical, Guderian (the Chief of the Army General Staff) advocated the immediate dispatch to Hungary of certain divisions which were being prepared for the attack in the Ardennes.[1] Hitler rejected this suggestion, evidently believing that the Danube could not be quickly forced by Russian armies which had already carried out such a vast advance.

At the end of November, however, while the German forces in Hungary were preoccupied with the task of keeping Malinovsky out of Budapest, Tolbukhin's Army Group moved up from Belgrade and executed a brilliant crossing over the Danube near its confluence with the Drava. This crossing was made 120 miles south of Budapest in an area so swampy and so lacking in roads that the Germans had not anticipated any serious threat developing from it. Taking prompt advantage of the surprise he had gained, Tolbukhin drove rapidly north-west to Lake Balaton, loosened the entire front in Hungary and opened the way for the early envelopment of Budapest. By Christmas Eve—when the Germans in the Ardennes were but four miles from the Meuse—the Russians on the Danube had completed the encirclement of the Hungarian capital and, without waiting for its capture, had created for the liberated territory a government of their own persuasion.

That night Guderian again pleaded with Hitler to recognise the

[1]As there was no counterpart to von Rundstedt in the East, Guderian was responsible for co-ordinating the operations of the four army groups engaged against the Russians.

magnitude of the danger in the East. He proposed that they should abandon the offensive in the Ardennes and that the greater part of the panzer divisions involved there should be sent forthwith to the Eastern Front. Guderian argued that the drive to the Meuse had already gained them valuable respite in the West by disrupting the Allied plans, and that the most urgent task was to assemble strong mobile reserves in Poland before the Russians resumed their offensive on the Vistula. " I pointed out," says Guderian " that the Ruhr had already been paralysed by the Western Allies' bombing attacks . . . . [but that] the industrial area of Upper Silesia could still work at full pressure; the centre of gravity of the German armament industry was already in the East and the loss of Upper Silesia must lead to our defeat within a very few weeks. All this was of no avail."[1] Hitler refused to transfer forces from the West, and so far as he showed any concern about the Eastern Front, he was more interested in relieving the 150,000 men besieged in Budapest than in reinforcing the gravely threatened line in Poland. Without even consulting Guderian, he moved an SS panzer corps from the Warsaw area to Hungary. Thus, in the hope of gaining victory on the Meuse and recovery on the Danube, Hitler courted defeat on the Vistula.

Four days later, addressing von Rundstedt and other generals before the offensive in Alsace, Hitler said: " If at present things are not going well . . . in Hungary, you must realise that inevitably we cannot be strong everywhere. . . . Because of the treachery of our dear allies we have been forced to fall back to a narrower ring of barriers," but " we should not forget that even to-day we are defending an area . . . which is essentially larger than Germany has ever been, and that there is at our disposal an armed force which even to-day is unquestionably the most powerful on earth."[2]

When Hitler made this statement, he had more than seven million men in the Army alone.[3] Counting Wehrmacht and SS, he had 260 divisions in the field, twice as many as he had had in May 1940. Deployed in direct defence of the Reich these divisions could have offered prolonged, and perhaps successful, resistance to the invading armies which were pressing in on Germany. As it was, however, Hitler's divisions were so widely dispersed far beyond the German frontiers that neither in the West nor in the East could he amass forces with the striking power of those which had overwhelmed France in 1940 and invaded Russia in

---

[1]Guderian, *Erinnerungen eines Soldaten*, p. 347. The account of German strategy in this section is based on this book, on the Seventh U.S. Army's detailed interrogation of Guderian, and on the records of the Führer Conferences held on December 28th and 29th, 1944, and January 9th and 10th, 1945.

[2]Führer Conferences, Fragment 27, December 28th, 1944.

[3]The German records examined by the American historian, Col. Cole, show that the " total paper strength of the Wehrmacht " at the start of September 1944, was 10,165,303: of these, 7,536,946 were in the Army and the *Waffen-SS*; 1,925,291 in the Luftwaffe and 703,066 in the Navy. (Cole, op. cit., p. 30.)

1941. This dispersal was the direct result of his continued determination to cling to territories which weakened, rather than enhanced, his ability to prevent the invasion of the Reich. Hitler's stubbornness on this point was inspired not merely by the ' conqueror complex,' but also by the belief that the British and Americans might yet be forced to relax their demand for ' Unconditional Surrender,' provided that he could defeat their armies, or at least halt them at the Siegfried Line, and could then bring into powerful play the new air and naval weapons which, after so many frustrations and delays, were at last becoming available in sufficient volume to sustain his hopes. It was this that made him cling to the launching-sites in Western Holland from which V.2s were being directed against London and Antwerp; to the bauxite mines in Hungary and Croatia from which he was obtaining the aluminium for his jet-aircraft; and to the naval bases in Denmark and Norway from which the new electro-U-boats were about to begin operations against Allied shipping.

The importance Hitler attached to the holding of these U-boat bases reflected the rising power of Doenitz, who was fast becoming the most influential of his counsellors. In the past Hitler and Doenitz had conferred only two or three times a month, but from the start of 1945 they were to be in almost daily consultation. By this time Doenitz was the only high-ranking officer of real professional ability whose relationship with the Führer was still based on mutual trust and admiration, and this relationship was to exert a considerable influence on German strategy, especially in the East.

A stern and shrewd man, Doenitz was, as Goebbels observed, " a very cool and realistic calculator," but, like so many others, he had fallen under the spell of Hitler's magnetic personality and of what he once called " the enormous strength which the Führer radiates." Doenitz was not a member of the Party—as a serving officer he could not be—but he went further than any other senior commander in the Army or Navy in demanding that the armed forces must identify themselves with the Nazi movement. The generals, with few exceptions, had endeavoured to maintain the tradition that the regular officer must stand apart from politics; not so Doenitz. In one of his directives to the Navy he wrote: " The whole officer corps must be so indoctrinated that it feels itself co-responsible for the National Socialist State in its entirety. The officer is the exponent of the State. The idle chatter that the officer is non-political is sheer nonsense."[1] Even after the war Doenitz was ready to declare that he had " joyfully acknowledged . . . Adolf Hitler's high authority," and to claim that his former leader was a man of " extra-ordinary intelligence and a practically universal knowledge."[2]

For all his fervent loyalty, Doenitz was no sycophant, and he managed

[1]Directive of February 14th, 1944.
[2]In evidence at Nuremberg, May 9th, 1946. (*Nuremberg Trial Proceedings*, Part xiii, pp. 243-4.)

to preserve in his own sphere a degree of independence such as no contemporary German general enjoyed. On becoming Commander-in-Chief of the Navy in January 1943, Doenitz had dared to challenge Hitler on the very issue which had brought about the resignation of his predecessor, Raeder; namely, the Führer's petulant decision to scrap the High Seas Fleet because of its failure in an action against an Arctic convoy. Hitler had expected that Doenitz, as a U-boat man, would welcome this decision, but, on assuming overall command, the Grand-Admiral worked against it and, by tact and patience, secured its cancellation. Having gained his way on this occasion, Doenitz found that Hitler treated him " with decided respect," and the records of their conferences show that thereafter his advice was accepted not only on naval matters but also on wider questions of military and political strategy.[1] At times Doenitz openly disagreed with his master, but he expressed his disagreement in terms which did not challenge the Führer's authority or undermine his self-confidence.

Doenitz had been able to assert his independence because Hitler had long since recognised his professional efficiency and had been gratified to find in him the tenacity, ruthlessness and cunning which, he felt, was lacking in so many of his generals. Trusting Doenitz and knowing nothing of submarine warfare himself, Hitler had not attempted to interfere with the day to day conduct of U-boat operations, as he did in almost every other aspect of the war. Consequently, Doenitz never had to suffer the irrational and humiliating interventions which caused such bitter conflicts between Hitler and his field commanders. When they tried to make him appreciate the truth, they were usually cut short by outbursts of wrath and accusations of incompetence, if not sabotage; but, when Doenitz frankly reported the reasons for the repeated reverses his U-boats suffered in 1943, Hitler listened with surprising tolerance and accepted technical excuses for failures which would have brought about the downfall of less favoured commanders.

The influence which Doenitz continued to exert was the more remarkable because the standing of the individual members of Hitler's court tended to vary with the strength of their ' private empires ' and the extent of the contribution they could make to his power. During 1944, while the political authority of Goering was declining with the decline of the Luftwaffe, that of Doenitz was increasing, even though his U-boats were gaining fewer successes and suffering heavier losses than in any other period of the war.[2] The anomalous position Doenitz enjoyed was due

[1]Nuremberg *Trial Proceedings*, Part xiii, p. 244. In giving evidence at the Nuremberg Trial Doenitz said that he was never consulted on any matter which did not concern the Navy. This assertion is not confirmed by the minutes of the Führer Naval Conferences, especially those dealing with the Italian crisis in 1943. On that occasion it was the advice of Doenitz and Rommel which eventually prevailed.

[2]In the first year of the war, with a fleet which never exceeded 60, Doenitz had sunk 350 Allied merchantmen at a cost of 27 U-boats. In 1944, although his total strength reached 448 in May, the number of merchantmen he destroyed was only 132, and his own losses were 225.

primarily to the invention of the electro-U-boats which enabled him to offer Hitler the chance of regaining the initiative at sea with a revolutionary weapon.

The U-boat had always had a peculiar fascination for Hitler, perhaps because it satisfied his nihilistic lust for destruction, but this development gave it a new significance in his eyes. By nature Hitler was revolutionary and aggressive and it was the application of these qualities that had made him master of Europe. When confronted with defeat, therefore, he scorned the counsel of those who advocated strategic defence and political compromise, and he sought to avert his fate by revolutionary and aggressive expedients. In Doenitz he found a companion spirit.

Hitler maintained his faith in Doenitz in spite of the long delay in bringing the new U-boats into action. Far from having them ready before the cross-Channel invasion, as he had once hoped, Doenitz had none available for operations even at the start of 1945. By this time, because the production programme had been disorganised by Allied bombing, only 128 had been delivered, instead of 245 as planned, and since it took six months to commission and ' work up ' a new boat, there was no chance of any large-scale submarine offensive being launched before the spring. Nevertheless, the fact that he could hold out the hope of conducting any offensive whatever ensured for Doenitz a place of special favour. The Grand-Admiral can hardly have believed that at this late stage in the war his U-boats could bring about any decisive improvement in Germany's position, but to have admitted this would have been to undermine his own influence. There is no reason to believe that Doenitz saw himself as the Führer's eventual successor, but he was determined to preserve his own power and to do this he had to sustain in Hitler the hope that the Navy could still win a great victory, and this hope would exist only so long as Germany held the necessary shipyards, training waters and operational bases. This was the background of the conference which took place at Hitler's H.Q. on January 3rd, 1945.

Doenitz then reported that conventional U-boats, equipped with *Schnorkel*, were able to " achieve success even in waters where German U-boats were forced to cease operations more than three years ago," and especially in British home waters. He assured Hitler that very much greater successes would be won when the revolutionary types were brought into operation, since it was " difficult to combat these U-boats at sea because of their ability to remain submerged," and, of course, because their underwater speed (15 knots) was greater than that of most Allied merchantmen and escort vessels. " The difficulties," said Doenitz, " involved in the new U-boat offensive do not lie in operations at sea, but entirely in the threat to our home bases by the enemy air force."[1] He pointed out that the Allies were already taking counter-measures in advance, bombing the construction yards in North-West Germany and

[1]Führer Naval Conferences, January 3rd, 1945.

mining the shallow waters of the Western Baltic.[1] Consequently, the Eastern Baltic was now of decisive significance. It was more difficult for Allied aircraft to reach, and mines laid in its deeper waters were less dangerous. Doenitz suggested, therefore, that the Wehrmacht must continue to hold the Courland Pocket in Western Latvia as well as Memel, East Prussia and the Gulf of Danzig. The loss of these areas would " paralyse naval warfare and especially U-boat operations." Hitler " agreed entirely."

Three days before this conference Guderian had proposed that the forces in Courland and Memel should be evacuated by sea and that the Wehrmacht should also withdraw from the vulnerable bulge protecting East Prussia, so that it could concentrate on holding the shortest possible line between the Gulf of Danzig and the Carpathians, and could accumulate in Central Poland reserves to meet the Red Army's coming offensive. Hitler vetoed this proposal with the result that some forty German divisions (nearly one-third of the forces opposing the Red Army) continued to defend the shores of the Eastern Baltic from Königsberg north, contributing virtually nothing to the defence of the Reich and serving only to sustain the influence of Doenitz and the Führer's vain delusion.

The history of the Second World War affords no more striking example of the interplay of naval, air and land power, or of the inter-relation of the Eastern and Western Front or, for that matter, of the grotesque miscalculations and wild hopes that governed Hitler's strategy. Because the German Air Force was unable to protect the U-boat bases and training waters in the Western Baltic, the German Army was obliged to hold the Eastern Baltic against the Russians so that the German Navy might build up a new U-boat fleet capable of inflicting a severe defeat on the Western Allies, and especially on the hated British whose refusal to capitulate in 1940 had made inevitable that war on two fronts which had already destroyed most of Hitler's empire and was in the process of destroying the Third Reich.

On January 9th—the day after Hitler had authorised von Rundstedt to withdraw from the Western Ardennes—Guderian arrived at the Führer's H.Q. near Frankfurt, having just completed a tour of the Eastern Front. He reported, he says, that " the Russians had vast forces ready to attack and that the German troops in the East could not hold them." Once again he pleaded with Hitler to carry out a series of major strategic withdrawals, to abandon Italy and Norway, the Balkans and the Baltic, and to muster all possible reserves to keep the Russians out of Germany.

Guderian had good reason to be alarmed at the state of the forces

[1]British Naval Intelligence had learned that the Germans were developing these U-boats in 1943 and had kept abreast of Doenitz's plans.

opposing the Red Army, for these had received little reinforcement since the start of Hitler's preparations for the Ardennes offensive. During the last quarter of 1944 Hitler had raised 23 new infantry divisions of the *Volksgrenadier* class; of these 18 had been given to von Rundstedt. In the West a dozen panzer or panzer grenadier divisions had been substantially refitted, but the armoured formations in the East had not received sufficient replacements to make good current losses. In November and December of 1944, according to the records of OKH, 2,299 tanks and assault guns (new or refitted) had been sent to von Rundstedt, but only 921 had gone to Guderian for the Eastern Front and the majority of these had been light armour. The greater part of the Luftwaffe's strength was similarly directed westward. At the end of December more than two-thirds of its aircraft were deployed for action against the Anglo-American Air Forces.[1]

The Western Allies were now directly engaging 100 German divisions; 76 in the West and 24 in Italy. A further 27 were tied down in the outlying strategic areas, 10 in Yugoslavia and 17 in Scandinavia. Thus on the Eastern Front, where Hitler had been able to commit 157 German divisions when the Normandy invasion began, he now had only 133, barely half the total strength of his ground forces.[2] Nor were these so deployed that they could offer the most effective resistance to the main strength of the Red Army which Stalin had concentrated in Poland. On the northern flank in Courland and Memel there were 30 German divisions, cut off with their backs to the Baltic. On the southern wing, guarding the oil and bauxite of Hungary and blocking the way to Vienna, there were another 28 divisions, including half Guderian's armour.

Neither of these Army Groups was capable of influencing the decisive battle which was destined to be fought, as Guderian anticipated, between the Carpathians and the Baltic. Here in Poland and East Prussia, manning a line 600 miles long, the Wehrmacht had only 75 divisions with which to prevent the Red Army advancing from Warsaw to Berlin. Of all the fronts which Hitler was endeavouring to hold, this was the most vulnerable militarily and the most dangerous politically, and yet here the balance of strength was most clearly in favour of his enemies. Here he had fewer divisions than there were on a front of similar length

[1]The concentration of fighter forces against the West was even greater. The Luftwaffe's records show that on December 31st, 1944, 1,756 out of 2,276 day fighters, and 1,242 out of 1,289 night fighters were deployed in support of the Western Front or in defence of the Reich. Moreover, the protection of the German war economy against Anglo-American strategic bombing caused a vast diversion of manpower and productive capacity. The total strength of the Reich anti-aircraft command throughout 1944 was nearly 900,000 and one-third of all guns produced were flak. In addition, the *United States Strategic Bombing Survey* estimates that " the threat and the effect of strategic bombing reduced the labour force available for other purposes by at least 4.30 to 5.45 million persons." (*U.S.S.B.S.*, ' Economic Report,' p. 41.)

[2]In the last half of 1944 no fewer than 17 German divisions which were on the Eastern Front on June 6th were transferred to the West, either direct or after being re-formed. The remaining divisions which had disappeared from the Order of Battle in the East had been destroyed. (All the figures quoted here are from OKH records.)

between Switzerland and the North Sea, and these divisions were very much weaker than their counterparts in the West. Moreover, their line was not based on any system of permanent fortifications such as the Siegfried defences nor were there any natural obstacles as formidable as the Meuse and the Rhine in the path of the Red Army, for already in the autumn of '44 it had secured substantial bridgeheads west of the Vistula. Finally, the striking power of the Russian forces in Poland and East Prussia was at least twice as great as that of the Western Allies in France and the Low Countries.[1]

Hitler refused to heed these facts for, says Guderian, " he had a special picture of the world, and every fact had to fit into that fancied picture. As he believed, so the world must be; but, in fact, it was a picture of another world."[2] There were few now who dared to tell him the truth, and his mind was so distorted by fears and fantasies that he could not evaluate the truth even when he heard it. At a conference with his staff on January 9th he declared that the Wehrmacht had " three thousand tanks and assault guns in the East " and that the Russians did not possess " the necessary threefold superiority " to secure a break-through.[3] On the following day, after seeing Guderian, he announced that Sixth SS Panzer Army was to be extricated from the Ardennes and reorganised, but was to remain at von Rundstedt's disposal. " Priority," he declared, " must be given to the West so that we may keep the initiative there." The East would not be reinforced, nor would he countenance any further withdrawals anywhere. " I always get ' the horrors,' " said Hitler, " whenever I hear that somewhere or other we have had to disengage or withdraw in order to get ' operational freedom.' For two years now I have been hearing this and the results have always been disastrous."[4] But these results were to pale into insignificance by comparison with the disasters which were about to engulf him and which were to be made the more catastrophic by his refusal to yield space while there was yet time.

The Soviet offensive began on the frozen plains of Southern Poland on the morning of January 12th, when Konev's Army Group burst out of its bridgehead on the Upper Vistula between Cracow and Sandomir. The defences were thin, the reserves weak, and the Russians quickly gained a clear break-through. This was the first stroke in the greatest Soviet offensive of the war. For this attack Stalin had assembled in

[1]At this time Eisenhower had 78 divisions. The Red Army in Poland, according to the information Stalin supplied at the Yalta Conference, had 180 divisions, but these were smaller than those of the Western Allies and were less powerfully supported in the air. Guderian (op. cit., p. 345) says that before the Russian offensive began, OKH Intelligence had identified 225 infantry divisions, 22 tank corps, 29 other tank formations and three cavalry corps. Unless Stalin was deliberately under-stating his strength at Yalta, German Intelligence about the Eastern Front was no more reliable than its pre-D-Day estimates of the forces available to Eisenhower in the West.
[2]Seventh Army U.S. Interrogation.
[3]Führer Conferences, Fragment 9, January 9th, 1945.
[4]Führer Conferences, Fragment 33, January 10th, 1945.

Poland and East Prussia 180 divisions and at the points where he chose to strike his superiority in men and armour was not threefold but sixfold. Four days later Hitler returned to Berlin, to the ruins of the capital he was never to leave. There in the Chancellery he set up the command post from which he would direct the final battle for the defence of the Reich, pitting his will against the world.

Within the next few days, apparently still oblivious of the fate that was overtaking his armies in Poland, Hitler took the opportunity of going out to tea at the house of Doctor and Frau Goebbels, something he had not done for five years. Among those who watched him arrive was Goebbels's aide, Rudolf Semmler, who recorded in his diary an apt account of the occasion. Semmler wrote:

> At 4.30 Hitler's car arrived. Goebbels stood to attention with his arm stretched out as far as it would go. The children made their little curtsies and Hitler said how surprised he was at the way they had grown. He presented Frau Goebbels with a modest bunch of lily-of-the-valley, and explained that it was the best that could be found, as Doctor Goebbels had closed all the flower shops in Berlin!
>
> With the Führer were an adjutant, a servant, and six SS officers of the personal bodyguard. The servant was carrying Hitler's brief-case, which bore a large white F on it. From the pocket of the case a thermos flask could be seen sticking out. I realised that Hitler had brought his own tea and cakes.[1]

Semmler was not present at the tea party where the Führer became expansive as he described his plans for rebuilding Berlin after the war. "In the evening," wrote Semmler, "I heard from Frau Goebbels that Hitler had enjoyed the family atmosphere very much. . . . At supper Goebbels and his wife were very proud of the visit. 'He wouldn't have gone to the Goerings,' said Frau Goebbels."

The Russian winter offensive rapidly gathered momentum, as fresh armies took up the attack. Crossing the Vistula on either side of Warsaw, Zhukov isolated the Polish capital and on January 17th took it by an onslaught from the rear. Farther north, Rokossovsky broke the line of the Narew and drove north-west to the Gulf of Danzig. This time there was no Battle of Tannenberg, for, as Rokossovsky struck deep into the rear of the East Prussian defences, Cherniakovsky's Army Group overran them by direct assault. Within a week the whole front had become a seething battlefield and the Russian armour, plunging westward, had advanced nearly a hundred miles.

[1]Semmler, op. cit., pp. 174-5. Living now in constant fear of his life, Hitler would not eat or drink anything which was not prepared and tasted by his own chef. Semmler gives the date of this visit as January 12th, but he has evidently mistaken the day, for Guderian (op. cit., p. 356) makes it clear that Hitler did not return until the 16th.

Obliged by Hitler to pursue a policy of unyielding defence, the German forces were either overwhelmed where they stood or broken up into embattled fragments which sought survival in fortress towns that the Russians had by-passed. Guderian's reserves were incapable of checking so vast an offensive on so wide a front. The better part of his mobile reserves was already engaged in Hungary, in the vain attempt to relieve Budapest, and the twelve panzer divisions in Poland and East Prussia had not sufficient petrol to carry out aggressive counter-measures. Lacking even the fuel to conduct an effective delaying action, the armoured units had no chance of restoring a front breached in so many places.

On January 22nd, in a desperate endeavour to muster reserves, Hitler agreed to the evacuation of Memel, but he still refused to withdraw entirely from Courland, for Doenitz continued to remind him of " the great importance of the Gulf of Danzig, the only U-boat training area "[1] —as if that mattered at this stage. Now, when it was too late, Hitler ordered the immediate transfer of Sixth SS Panzer Army from the West, but even he was obliged to admit: " There is no point in hypnotising oneself into a state of mind by saying, ' I need something here, therefore it must materialise.' In the last resort I have to deal with things as they are. The deployment of really effective forces from the West cannot take place in less than six to eight weeks."[2]

By this time Germany had lost the advantage of her central position, for Allied air power had deprived the Wehrmacht of its strategic mobility. The German railways were now moving only one-third of the traffic they had been handling six months earlier.[3] The great *autobahn* which stretched unbroken across Germany from the Rhine to the Oder, was strategically useless, since there was no petrol for the large-scale movement of troops by road. It had been Hitler's boast that these military highways would enable Germany to exploit her interior lines of communication and, in such a crisis as this, to strike first at one adversary and then at the other. As it turned out, however, it was not the German armies, but those of the Allies, which found their movement facilitated by the *autobahn* network. Moreover, it was fortunate for the Allied cause that the concrete, steel and manpower employed in the construction of these roads had not been devoted to the building of another Siegfried Line on Germany's eastern frontier.

Throughout the second half of January the Russians advanced with giant strides. In the north Rokossovsky reached the Gulf of Danzig and the 25 German divisions in East Prussia were doomed. In the south, having taken Cracow, Konev broke into Upper Silesia and bore down upon Breslau. This advance carried the Russians into the only corner of Hitler's industrial domain on which Allied bombers had not set their

[1] Führer Naval Conferences, January 21st, 1945.
[2] Führer Conferences, Fragment 24, January 27th, 1945.
[3] Between June 1944 and January 1945 the ' daily availability ' of railway freight cars fell from 150,000 to 50,000.

THE EASTERN FRONT, 1945

stamp. Because of the decline in the output of the Ruhr, the Silesian coal mines had become Germany's main source of supply, providing in December 1944 60 per cent of her total production. The loss of these coal fields at a time when the railways, power plants and war factories had stocks for less than two weeks, created, as Speer told Hitler, " an unbearable situation." Speer reported that, following the loss of Upper Silesia, he would be able to provide only a quarter of the coal and a sixth of the steel which had been produced in January 1944.[1] Moreover, with the invasion of Silesia the Russians began over-running plants and factories which Hitler had moved from Western Germany in order to escape from Anglo-American bombing. Among these plants were three new synthetic oil refineries which were just starting production!

While Konev and Rokossovsky were crushing the German flanks, Zhukov drove at will through Central Poland advancing 220 miles in two weeks astride the road that runs from Warsaw to Berlin. By January 27th Zhukov had crossed the German frontier and was less than a hundred miles from Hitler's capital. That day the Berlin *Volkssturm*, Goebbels's Home Guard, were ordered to the Eastern Front, where Himmler, now in command of Army Group Vistula, was endeavouring to form a new line on the Oder.

On the evening of this day Hitler discussed with Goering and Jodl the political repercussions of the Soviet victory. When Hitler asked, " Do you think the English can be really enthusiastic about all the Russian developments? " Jodl replied, " No, certainly not. Their plans were quite different. Only later on perhaps will the full realisation of this come." Whereupon Goering said: " They had not counted on our defending ourselves step by step and holding them off in the West like madmen, while the Russians drive deeper and deeper into Germany."[2]

Hitler suggested that, if only the Russians would proclaim a National Government for Germany, the English would " really start to be scared." Then he went on, " I have given orders that a report be played into their hands to the effect that the Russians are organising 200,000 of our men led by German officers and completely infected with Communism, who will come marching into Germany. . . . That will make them feel as if someone has stuck a needle into them."

" They entered the war," said Goering, " to prevent us from going

---

[1]Report by Speer to Hitler, January 30th, 1945. The further curtailment in the output of steel was brought about more by the shortage of coking coal than by the loss of production facilities in Silesia. The extent of the decline is apparent from the following statistics taken from Speer's files:

|  | HARD COAL | CRUDE STEEL |
|---|---|---|
|  | *(in millions of tons)* | |
| March 1944 - - - | 24.7 | 3.1 |
| October 1944 - - - | 16.2 | 1.7 |
| February 1945 - - - | 7.0 | 0.5 |

[2]Führer Conferences, Fragment 24, January 27th, 1945.

into the East; not to have the East come to the Atlantic." There emerged from this discussion the strong belief that every step the Russians took towards Berlin would bring the Western Powers one step nearer compromise, and the Reichsmarschall expressed the hope that sustained them all when he said, " If this goes on we will get a telegram [from the West] in a few days."

When this conference took place, Roosevelt and Churchill were already on their way to meet Stalin at Yalta.

## CHAPTER XXXII

# STALIN'S GREATEST VICTORY

IT was not altogether fortuitous that the Yalta Conference coincided with the Red Army's spectacular victory in Poland, for the timing was determined by Stalin. The original initiative had come from Roosevelt, who had been eager to arrange a meeting of the Big Three at the first opportunity after his re-election as President. On his behalf, therefore, Hopkins had broached the subject with the Soviet Ambassador in Washington, Andrei Gromyko, early in November. When Gromyko had replied that Stalin could not leave the Soviet Union, since he was personally directing the military campaign, Hopkins had suggested that the conference might be held in the Crimea. Gromyko had passed this suggestion on, but no positive response had been forthcoming from Moscow.

The need for such a conference was unquestionable, not least because, as Hopkins later wrote, " there were no firm agreements as to what was to be done with Germany once she was defeated . . . [and] it was quite possible to visualise the collapse of Germany without any plans or agreements having been made."[1] There were other issues almost as pressing. Roosevelt was most anxious to secure a detailed understanding about the precise date and the extent of Soviet participation in the war against Japan, and to settle direct with Churchill and Stalin those problems concerning the proposed world peace organisation which had been left unsettled by the Four-Power Conference at Dumbarton Oaks in the autumn. The most important of these was the contentious question whether the Great Powers should have, as Russia claimed, an absolute right to exercise a veto in the Security Council. Furthermore, it was essential that the Allied leaders should come to an early agreement about the future of Poland.

By December this had become a matter of the greatest urgency, especially for Great Britain, since she had gone to war with Hitler in fulfilment of her guarantee to Poland. Churchill had publicly pledged himself to ensure " the re-creation of a strong, free, independent, sovereign

[1]In a memorandum written in October 1945 and quoted by Sherwood, op. cit., p. 843.

Poland," and with this in view had been striving for more than a year to bring about a reconciliation between the Soviet Union and the exiled Polish Government in London.[1] In the House of Commons on December 15th, 1944, however, the Prime Minister had announced that these negotiations had broken down, primarily because the Poles could not bring themselves to accept Stalin's demand that the future Russo-Polish frontier should follow the ' Curzon Line,' which had been adopted by the Supreme Allied Council in 1919 as a fair ethnographical boundary. In Churchill's opinion this demand did not go " beyond the limits of what is reasonable and just," for Russia had " the right of reassurance against future attacks from the West." If Poland would agree to yield her eastern territories, he said, she would gain " the whole of East Prussia west and south of the fortress of Koenigsberg," together with Danzig, and, he added, " the Poles are free, so far as Russia and Great Britain are concerned, to extend their territory, at the expense of Germany, to the West." Thus they would " find in Europe an abiding home and resting-place . . . not inferior in character and quality . . . to what they previously possessed."

The refusal of the London Poles to accept this territorial arrange-ment had already provided the Russians with a pretext for declining to re-establish relations with the exiled Government and for setting up in Lublin a ' National Committee of Liberation ' dominated by their own creatures. There was thus a grave danger that the future of Poland would be determined by the unilateral action of the Soviet Union for, once the Red Army was in possession of the whole country, the bargaining power of the legitimate Polish Government and the mediating influence of Britain and America would be seriously weakened. Realising this, Churchill now urged the Poles to " reach agreement with the Soviet Government about their disputed frontiers in the East before the march of the Russian armies through the main part of Poland takes place."

This appeal was in vain, for the last chance of securing a Russo-Polish agreement by direct negotiation had disappeared at the end of November with the resignation of the Polish Prime Minister, Stanislaw Mikolajczyk. After a stormy conference with Stalin and Churchill in Moscow in October, Mikolajczyk had been prepared to agree to the Curzon Line provided that it was modified in the south to leave within Poland the Carpathian oilfields and the ancient Polish city of Lwow. Unable to gain the support of his colleagues, however, Mikolajczyk had withdrawn from the government, leaving in power an intransigent group who would not compromise. Nevertheless, Churchill and Roosevelt, especially the latter, continued to hope that the impasse might yet be resolved by them in direct consultation with Stalin at their next meeting.

[1]The Soviet Union had severed diplomatic relations with Poland in April 1943 when the Polish Government had asked for an independent inquiry by the International Red Cross into the discovery at Katyn, near Smolensk, of mass graves containing the bodies of more than four thousand missing Polish officers.

The Prime Minister told the Commons that he and the Foreign Secretary were ready to " proceed to any place, at any time, under any conditions, where we can meet the heads of our two chief Allies." They had hoped that a conference might be held before Christmas, but so far, he said, " it has been impossible to arrange any meeting of the three Great Powers."

That statement was made on the day before the Germans attacked in the Ardennes. A week later, as Hitler's armies were driving hard for the Meuse, apparently unbrooked, a signal arrived in Washington stating that Marshal Stalin would be ready to meet the President and the Prime Minister at Yalta in the Crimea at the end of January.

There is no reason to believe that Stalin had anticipated Hitler's offensive in the West and had therefore delayed his reply to Roosevelt until the moment of greatest Allied embarrassment. On the other hand, the history of wartime and post-war diplomacy has made it clear that the Russians regard international conferences as opportunities for the recognition of situations which have already been created by the exercise of power, not as occasions for the negotiation of reasonable settlements mutually acceptable. Since he was more concerned with Power than Justice, Stalin was not interested in having another conference with the Western leaders until he had secured for himself the strongest military position his armies seemed capable of gaining.

In the autumn of 1944, when Roosevelt asked for a meeting, the Russians on the Vistula were farther from Berlin than were the Anglo-American armies in the Rhineland, and the Soviet High Command was extremely doubtful of its ability to continue the offensive through Poland. It was so concerned on this account that, when Churchill was in Moscow in October, Stalin had strongly advocated that the Allied Armies in Italy should cross the Adriatic and drive north through Yugoslavia in the direction of Vienna. Since Stalin had previously opposed every plan for Allied ground operations in the Balkans, this proposal can only have been dictated by the belief that the intervention of Anglo-American forces in Yugoslavia would tie down the German divisions which were being withdrawn from the Southern Balkans to Hungary, and might even attract reserves from Poland. Stalin would hardly have suggested this move unless he had believed that it would expedite his own advance to Vienna and Berlin.

In its summer offensive the Red Army had suffered such losses that by October Zhukov, at any rate, feared he had reached the limit of his westward advance. After the war Zhukov admitted; " When we reached Warsaw, we could not see how we could get beyond the Vistula unless the German forces on our front were considerably weakened."[1] There seemed little likelihood of this happening. On the contrary, the Soviet High Command (according to Zhukov) believed that Hitler, being so

[1] In a conversation with Brigadier John Spurling, of the 7th Armoured Division, in Berlin after the war.

fanatical in his hatred of Communism, would concentrate everything he could against the Red Army, whatever the cost on other fronts. They assumed that, when Hitler came to the point of having to choose, he would ' let in the West.' This was a logical assumption, not only because of the historic German fear of the Slav, but also because Eastern Germany was the stronghold of the Prussian military caste and had become, on account of Allied bombing, the centre of the German war economy. Having made this appreciation, the Russians were amazed and relieved when they learned of the German attack in the Ardennes.

This development transformed Russia's military and political prospects. The commitment of Hitler's entire strategic reserve in the West ensured the success of the Red Army's January offensive in Poland. Accordingly, when he cabled Roosevelt just before Christmas, Stalin had good reason to believe that by the start of the Yalta Conference he would be in possession of Warsaw and at least the greater part of Western Poland. Nevertheless, he proceeded to strengthen his position by a political manœuvre designed to present his Allies with a *fait accompli*. On December 30th Roosevelt and Churchill confirmed their willingness to come to Yalta early in February. On the following day, at the instigation of the Kremlin, the Lublin Committee proclaimed itself the ' Provisional Government of Liberated Democratic Poland ' and in the first week of the new year the Soviet Union extended to this puppet administration the diplomatic recognition it had refused to accord the legitimate Polish Government in London.

Even Stalin, however, can hardly have expected that the turn of events would swing the balance of power so quickly or so far in his favour. In the last fortnight of January, while the Russians were sweeping through Poland and into the Reich, driving before them a rabble of armies, the Americans in the Ardennes were meeting resistance as stubborn and as skilful as any they had encountered since D-Day. On January 16th the converging attacks of the First and Third U.S. Armies had met at Houffalize, but no substantial body of German troops had been cut off in the Western Ardennes, and the Wehrmacht had continued to fight a steady rearguard action back to the Siegfried defences. It was February before the Americans regained the line they had been holding six weeks earlier.

On February 4th the Americans captured the first of the Roer dams towards which they had been attacking when the Germans began their counter-offensive. The forces of the Western Powers were now ready to launch their long-delayed assault on the Rhineland, but they were no nearer Berlin than they had been in September 1944, or for that matter in September 1939. Except in the Roer River sector, the Siegfried Line was still intact; the Rhine had yet to be forced; and, since Eisenhower's engineers then believed that no large-scale crossing of the Lower Rhine could be carried out before May, there seemed little chance of Berlin being taken by attack from the West.

On the Eastern Front by this time Malinovsky, having thwarted the German attempts to relieve Budapest, was 80 miles from Vienna; Konev, having surrounded Breslau and secured several bridgeheads west of the Oder, was 120 miles from Prague; and Zhukov, having reached the Oder at Kuestrin north of Frankfurt, was 45 miles from Berlin. Thus the Soviet armies stood, with all the capitals of Eastern Europe already in their hands[1] and the three great capitals of Central Europe within their grasp.

At Yalta Stalin was to be in a doubly advantageous position, for the conference took place not only on the morrow of a severe Allied reverse and at the moment of the Red Army's greatest victory, but also at a time of Anglo-American suspicion and discord.

En route to the Crimea, Roosevelt and Churchill held a brief preliminary conference at Malta, where they discussed the Yalta agenda and those issues which had introduced a certain acrimony into their relationship since their last meeting at Quebec in September. From these discussions Churchill hoped that there would emerge a common policy which he and the President could then present to Stalin and by their unity offset the advantage of his strength. It was apparent, however, that Roosevelt was as anxious as ever to avoid making commitments or giving the Russians any reason to think that they were dealing with an Anglo-American alliance. He saw himself as ' the Good Neighbour of the World,' the independent arbiter whose task it was to preserve harmony between Churchill and Stalin and to prevent Anglo-Soviet rivalry from causing a breach in ' Big Three Unity.' In the course of the Malta meeting the British delegation were dismayed to find that their American colleagues were less suspicious of Russia's post-war intentions than they were of Britain's. The appreciation of this fact—astonishing though it may seem at this distance—is essential to the understanding of what happened at Yalta.

The roots of this suspicion lay deep in history. Ever since 1776 Americans have nurtured a profound prejudice against ' colonialism,' and have tended to presume that the independence which brought them such benefits must likewise transform the lives of peoples less fortunate than themselves. With little regard for the merits, or the difficulties, of particular cases, they have consistently favoured the early grant of self-government to all dependent peoples, and particularly to those still under the dominion of the British Crown, for to Americans—by virtue of their past—Britain has remained the symbol of all Imperialism. Although ready to concede that British colonial policies were more progressive and more humane than those of any other country, they persisted in the belief that Imperial rule contained such inherent evils that even good empires must be bad.

[1] The Red Army was not yet in full possession of Budapest, but the last German opposition here was overcome on February 14th, 1945.

This American belief did not imply any weakening of the traditional bonds of common heritage and mutual interest which preserved the essential unity of the English-speaking world, nor any lessening of the ties of almost filial affection which bound the United States to England. It was a case of the enlightened son seeking to reform the wayward father. In 1940, when Britain stood in danger of annihilation by a more sinister imperialism, the American people, under Roosevelt's leadership, gladly and generously came to her rescue, bringing material aid and moral encouragement not out of mere self-interest but from the realisation that, for all her shortcomings, Britain was the essential bulwark of freedom, the last unconquered trustee of Western civilisation in Europe. Yet there was always a reservation in the American readiness to help. Roosevelt was determined to prevent the destruction of England, but he was equally determined that American aid should not be used to bolster up the British Empire. With him the inborn American prejudice against Imperialism assumed the force of a principle, and he saw, in the fluidity of the world situation brought about by war, the opportunity for extending throughout the colonial world the revolution that had started in 1776.

Roosevelt's ' assault ' upon the colonial concept began with the Atlantic Charter. The first draft of this declaration was drawn up by Churchill, who endeavoured to set forth the principles which should guide the democratic nations in their struggle against German aggression and in the re-establishment of European peace. Reporting to the House of Commons on September 9th, 1941, the Prime Minister said: " At the Atlantic meeting we had in mind the restoration of the sovereignty . . . of the states . . . now under the Nazi yoke." This, he insisted, was " quite a separate problem from the progressive evolution of self-governing institutions in the regions and peoples that owe allegiance to the British Crown."

The President, on the other hand, had no such limited view. During the ' Atlantic Charter Conference ' he told Churchill: " I can't believe that we can fight a war against fascist slavery, and at the same time not work to free people all over the world from a backward colonial policy. . . . The peace cannot include any continued despotism. The structure of peace demands and will get equality of peoples. Equality of peoples involves the utmost freedom of competitive trade."[1] Thus, when he added to Churchill's draft the statement that he and the Prime Minister wished to " see sovereign rights and self-government restored to those who have been forcibly deprived of them," Roosevelt was thinking not only of the occupied countries of Europe but also of colonial peoples throughout the world. Furthermore, when he inserted an article declaring that they would endeavour " without discrimination to further

---

[1] Elliott Roosevelt, *As He Saw It*, p. 37. Some critics of this book have suggested that it misrepresents Franklin Roosevelt's ideas, but it is abundantly clear from the Memoirs of Cordell Hull, the Hopkins Papers and other first-hand American sources that Elliott was not an inaccurate reporter of the views his father held on the colonial question.

the enjoyment by all states, great or small, victor or vanquished, of access, on equal terms, to the trade and to the raw materials of the world," the President was avowedly aiming at the Ottawa Agreements, the foundation of Imperial Preference. Appreciating this, Churchill demanded that the words " without discrimination " should be replaced by the phrase " with due respect to their existing obligations," but this gained him only a brief respite from American pressure.

Five months later, when the master Lend-Lease Agreement was signed, Roosevelt insisted that, in return for American aid, Britain must agree to " the elimination of all forms of discriminatory treatment in international commerce and the reduction of tariffs and trade barriers " after the war. Cordell Hull, the prime advocate of this clause, reports that " a few Tory members of the British Cabinet . . . regarded the Lend-Lease Agreement . . . as an attempt to infringe on British Imperial sovereignty "[1]—which, of course, it was.

In his Memoirs Hull is quite frank about the President's purpose. " We had," he writes, " definite ideas with respect to the future of the British Colonial Empire, on which we differed with the British. It might be said that the future of that Empire was no business of ours; but we felt that unless dependent peoples were assisted toward ultimate self-government and were given it . . . they would provide kernels of conflict."[2] Neither Hull nor Roosevelt were content with the official British explanation that " self-government should be achieved within the British Commonwealth." On one occasion the President told his son, Elliott, " I've tried to make it clear to Winston—and the others—that, while we're their allies and in it to victory by their side, they must never get the idea that we're in it just to help them hang on to the archaic, medieval Empire ideas . . . Great Britain signed the Atlantic Charter. I hope they realize the United States government means to make them live up to it."[3]

Roosevelt's determination to make the Charter apply to colonial territories was reinforced by Japan's conquest of virtually all the British, Dutch and French colonies in the Far East. The failure of those powers to defend their possessions and the realisation that these would be liberated directly or indirectly by the military might of the United States greatly strengthened the President's hand. He saw the chance of insisting that these colonies would not be returned to their original owners, except in return for a guarantee that self-government, and eventually complete independence, would be granted to them.

There is no doubt that this was Roosevelt's policy. When Eden was in Washington in March 1943, " the President " (according to a memorandum written at the time by Hopkins) " made it clear that he did not want a commitment made in advance that all those colonies in the Far East should go back to the countries which owned or controlled

[1]Hull, op. cit., p. 1151.
[2]Ibid., pp. 1477-8.
[3]Elliott Roosevelt, op. cit., pp. 121-2.

them prior to the war." Hopkins also noted, " The President has once or twice urged the British to give up Hong Kong as a gesture of ' good will ' . . . Eden dryly remarked that he had not heard the President suggest any similar gestures on our own part."[1]

When Queen Wilhelmina saw Roosevelt later that year, he talked to her about the future of the Netherlands East Indies and, after reminding her that " it was American arms that would be liberating those colonies from the Japanese," he obtained a promise that the Indies would be granted " dominion status with the right of self-rule and equality."[2]

From Churchill, however, the President could extract no such assurance about British possessions, though he raised the question at nearly all their major meetings. In private Churchill replied, " Mr. President, I believe you are trying to do away with the British Empire," and in public he declared, " We mean to hold our own. I have not become the King's First Minister in order to preside over the liquidation of the British Empire." When Churchill made this statement—at the Mansion House on November 10th, 1942—few of his hearers realised that it was directed primarily at the man whom he was proud to acknowledge as " the greatest American friend we have ever known, and the greatest champion of freedom who has ever brought help and comfort from the new world to the old."

Undeterred by Churchill's defiant stand, Roosevelt continued to strive for the acceptance of his policy. Having set his heart on the establishment of an international organisation for the maintenance of peace, Roosevelt was the more determined to rid the world of ' colonialism.' He saw the issue in terms that were simple, almost naïve; and not always true. " The colonial system means war," he told Elliott. " Exploit the resources of an India, a Burma, a Java; take all the wealth out of those countries, but never put anything back into them, things like education, decent standards of living, minimum health requirements— all you're doing is storing up the kind of trouble that leads to war. All you're doing is negating the value of any kind of organisational structure for peace before it begins."[3]

Roosevelt's vision of the peace included not only the ending of the colonial system, but the abandonment of what he regarded as its essential concomitants, spheres of influence and regional balances of power. He expected, as Hull told Congress, that when the United Nations organisation was established there would " no longer be any need for spheres of influence, for alliances, for balance of power, or any other of the special arrangements through which, in the unhappy past, nations strove to safeguard their security or promote their interests."

This idealistic vision was not shared by Churchill who knew from long experience of European history that nations are less likely to succumb

[1]Quoted by Sherwood, op. cit., pp. 718-9.
[2]Elliott Roosevelt, op. cit., pp. 223-4.
[3]Ibid., p. 74. See also Hull, op. cit., pp. 1599-1601.

to the temptation of aggrandisement if their ambitions are restrained by a reasonable balance of power, and that such a balance could be preserved only by alliances and other ' special arrangements.' Churchill was by no means anti-Russian, but as early as October 1942 he had set down the view that " it would be a measureless disaster if Russian barbarism were to overlay the culture and independence of the ancient states of Europe."[1] After Teheran, while continuing to work for Hitler's defeat and Stalin's friendship, he had become alive to the danger that the war would leave the Soviet Union in a position of overwhelming power which could be counter-balanced only by a strong British Empire, a firm Anglo-American alliance and a United States of Europe.

The prospect of a Russian advance deep into Central and South-Eastern Europe dismayed Churchill, and was one of the main reasons for his unflagging advocacy of those Balkan operations which Roosevelt and the American Chiefs of Staff so persistently vetoed. Thwarted in his desire to forestall Russia militarily, Churchill endeavoured to restrain her by striking a political bargain direct with the Kremlin. In the early summer of 1944, before the Red Army had made any serious inroad on the Balkans, the Prime Minister proposed to Stalin (without the President's knowledge) that the ' controlling interest ' in Rumania and Bulgaria should be exercised by the Soviet Union, and in Greece and Yugoslavia by Britain. When news of this proposal reached Washington, the secretive British approach to Moscow was resented, and the plan was condemned by Hull on the ground that it amounted to " the division of the Balkans into spheres of influence." In reply Churchill argued that he was not proposing to carve up the Balkans, but that in the re-establishment of civil government " someone must play the hand " and that this should be done by the power responsible for military operations in each country. Roosevelt was not altogether satisfied, but he agreed to give the arrangement a three months' trial on the understanding that it would apply only to immediate problems and would not prejudice the post-war settlement. Nevertheless, the plan remained suspect in Washington, particularly as the President gave his consent to it without consulting, or even advising, his Secretary of State!

American suspicions were sharpened when Churchill, during his visit to Moscow in October 1944, " extended the arrangement still further, even reducing to percentages the relative degree of influence which Britain and Russia individually should have in specified Balkan countries."[2]

---

[1]The full text of the memorandum in which the Prime Minister wrote this has not been published, but extracts were quoted by Mr. Harold Macmillan to the European Assembly in Strasbourg on September 5th, 1949.

[2]Hull, op. cit., p. 1458. By this agreement the respective war-time interests of the Soviet Union and Great Britain were to be divided in the proportions 75 : 25 in Bulgaria, Rumania and Hungary; 50 : 50 in Yugoslavia; and 0 : 100 in Greece. How this peculiar agreement was to be carried out has never been explained, but the Russians certainly fulfilled their part of the bargain so far as Greece was concerned, permitting no agitation in favour of the Greek Communists during the crisis of December 1944.

Each of the major powers placed its own interpretation on this agreement. The Russians regarded it as a formal acknowledgment of their predominant role and interest in the Danube Basin. The British saw it as the recognition of the *fait accompli* in that region and were thankful to have preserved even a small voice in the affairs of the Danubian states and to have kept Russia out of Greece. In Churchill's opinion it was not a matter of dividing the Balkans between Britain and Russia, but of preventing the Soviet Union extending its sphere of influence over the whole peninsula. The Americans, on the other hand, considered the agreement a betrayal of the Atlantic Charter, a sinister scheme to further Britain's Imperial ambitions. In the State Department it was denounced as ' Churchiavellian.'

Before the close of the year a more severe strain was imposed on Anglo-American relations by developments in the Mediterranean, where, by Allied agreement, the chief political responsibility rested on Britain. In Italy, when the Bonomi Cabinet resigned at the end of November, the British Government let it be known that it could not endorse any new administration which included Count Sforza either as Prime Minister or Foreign Secretary. Although regarded by Churchill—with some justification—as an untrustworthy intriguer, Sforza had a long record of opposition to Fascism and was greatly respected in the United States where he had lived in exile throughout Mussolini's reign. When Churchill's disapproval of Sforza became known in Washington, there was a storm of protest in the press, and Edward Stettinius, who had just succeeded Hull as Secretary of State, felt obliged to dissociate himself publicly from the British policy. On December 5th he issued a statement in which he declared that " the composition of the Italian Government " was " purely an Italian affair " and should be settled " along democratic lines without influence from outside."

Churchill was incensed by this public admonition and he gave vent to his anger in an outspoken cable to Roosevelt. He was particularly irate at the criticism implied in Stettinius's statement that the principle of non-interference " would apply in an even more pronounced degree with regard to governments of the United Nations in their liberated territories." In London this was rightly taken as a thinly-veiled reference to Greece, where a most ugly situation had arisen following the employ-ment of British troops to prevent the recognised government being over-thrown by Communist partisans who had ' invaded ' Athens. Since the British in Greece were there, as Churchill reminded Parliament, " with American and Russian consent [and] at the invitation of the Govern-ment of all parties," they could not " leave Athens to anarchy and misery, followed by tyranny established on murder."

Nevertheless, the use of British forces against Greek Communists, who so recently had been fighting the Germans, caused grave heart-burning on both sides of the Atlantic, and Churchill came under the fiercest criticism, at home and abroad, that was directed at him during the entire war. It was assumed, even by men of goodwill, that his strictures on the Communists were unjustifiably severe, and he was accused of exploiting the crisis so that he could maintain in power a reactionary régime bent upon restoring an unpopular monarchy.

In Washington feeling ran so high that Admiral King—never a man to miss an opportunity of embarrassing his country's principal ally—gave orders to the commander of the U.S. naval forces in the Mediterranean that he was " not to permit any American LSTs to be used to transfer supplies to Greece." Fortunately Hopkins intervened to have the order countermanded, but not before it had come to Churchill's knowledge and roused him to a fresh pitch of righteous indignation. Further sharp exchanges passed across the Atlantic with the result, as Sherwood says, that " relations between the White House and Downing Street were more strained than they had ever been before."[1] It was considered in Washington that " Churchill's well-known predilection for constitutional monarchy was dictating policies which were against the people's will," and that, in defiance of the Atlantic Charter, he was determined to restore the " unsavory status quo ante in Europe."[2]

The tension was eased when Churchill, with Eden, flew to Athens on Christmas Day, brought about an armistice, arranged for Archbishop Damaskinos to act as regent, and gave an assurance that the King would not come back " unless a plebiscite of his people calls for his return." Churchill had good reason to be satisfied with this settlement, but he could not publicly reveal the true reason for his satisfaction, namely that he had saved Greece from becoming a Soviet satellite. When he saw Stettinius at Malta, however, the Prime Minister told him bluntly that " if the British had not had troops in Greece, the Greek Communists would have taken over the government " and that Britain had " a definite responsibility not to allow this to happen."[3] Stettinius does not appear to have been impressed by this argument, and the conviction remained among the American delegation that Churchill had interfered in the internal affairs of Greece in order to gain some selfish post-war advantage for the British Empire.

It was most tragic that such suspicion and discord should have developed on the eve of Yalta, for it seems to have led Roosevelt and some of his intimates to presume that the future threat to world peace and the independence of small nations would come not from Russia or international Communism, but from the old colonial powers, and particularly Britain. This peculiar aberration can be explained only if it is remembered that at this time Roosevelt did not believe that Stalin cherished any imperialistic aspirations.

[1] Sherwood, op. cit., p. 839.
[2] Ibid., p. 837. The fact that in both Italy and Greece the future of the Royal House was one of the points at issue made the Americans particularly suspicious of British policy. It is one of the traditional American political beliefs that monarchy is incompatible with democracy.
[3] Stettinius, *Roosevelt and the Russians*, p. 64.

Three days before he set out for Malta and the Crimea, Roosevelt took the oath for the fourth time as President of the United States, and, in the course of his inaugural address, declared, " We have learned to be citizens of the world, members of the human community. We have learned the simple truth, as Emerson said, ' the only way to have a friend is to be one.' "

This was the creed that Roosevelt carried to Yalta. There was, in his view, no fundamental conflict of national interest between the Soviet Union and the United States; the Russian and American peoples had so much in common that they would readily co-operate in the cause of peace and freedom if only there could be a real meeting of minds between their leaders. His trust in Stalin and his faith in his own ability to win the Soviet Union's lasting co-operation were still high, although the unhappy course of Russo-Polish relations during the past year might well have given him reason to doubt both his own personal influence and Russia's post-war intentions.

Three times since Teheran, Roosevelt had made a direct approach to Stalin in the hope of inducing him to reach a reasonable agreement with the Polish Government in London; each time he had been rebuffed and Stalin had shown no inclination whatever to allow the principles of the Atlantic Charter to apply to Poland. Nevertheless, Mikolajczyk reports—and there is no reason to disbelieve him—that, when he was in Washington in June 1944, Roosevelt told him, " Stalin is a realist, and we mustn't forget, when we judge Russian actions, that the Soviet régime has had only two years of experience in international relations. But of one thing I am certain, Stalin is not an Imperialist."[1] Roosevelt explained to Mikolajczyk that he had not been able to take a public stand on the Polish question because it was election year, but " eventually," he said, " I will act as moderator in this problem and effect a settlement." Believing, as he had said after Teheran, that Stalin was ' getatable,' Roosevelt felt sure that when they met again across the conference table there would be no problem they could not solve on a ' man-to-man ' basis.

Roosevelt was not alone in thinking that Diplomacy by Friendship would bring a sympathetic response from Stalin. The most influential of his advisers—military and political alike—were agreed, as Hull says, that they " must and could get along with the Soviet Government,"[2] and that this would be possible if they were " patient and forbearing." The idea that they could ' get along with ' the Russians came more easily to the American leaders than to the British, for the United States is the great melting pot and the American people have shown an unparalleled capacity for absorbing into their own society a multitude of nationalities.

Perhaps the best exposition of Roosevelt's idea is to be found in a memorandum which Hopkins wrote six months after Yalta. " We know

[1]Mikolajczyk, *The Pattern of Soviet Domination*, p. 65.
[2]Hull, op. cit., p. 1467.

or believe," he said, " that Russia's interests, so far as we can anticipate
them, do not afford an opportunity for a major difference with us in
foreign affairs. We believe we are mutually dependent upon each other
for economic reasons. We find the Russians as individuals easy to deal
with. The Russians undoubtedly like the American people. They like
the United States. They trust the United States more than they trust
any other power in the world . . . above all, they want to maintain
friendly relations with us. . . . They are a tenacious, determined people
who think and act just like you and I do."[1]

Eisenhower endorsed this view of the Russian people when he wrote,
" In his generous instincts, in his love of laughter, in his devotion to a
comrade, and in his healthy, direct outlook on the affairs of workaday
life, the ordinary Russian seems to me to bear a marked similarity to
what we call an ' average American.' "[2] Eisenhower believed too that
there was a special bond between the United States and the Soviet
Union, a bond that was inevitably lacking in the Anglo-American
association. He felt, he says, that " in the past relations of America and
Russia there was no cause to regard the future with pessimism."[3] On
the one hand, " the two peoples had maintained an unbroken friendship
that dated back to the birth of the United States as an independent
republic "[4]; on the other, " both were free from the stigma of colonial
empire building by force."

This remarkable statement stems straight from the Founding Fathers.
It was the American way of saying that politically both peoples were
free from original sin. That this was not true of either was irrelevant;
it was believed, not merely by Eisenhower but also by many Americans
who should have been better acquainted with their own history. This
belief was implicit in Roosevelt's approach to the problems which were
to be discussed at Yalta. In his eyes, Britain was an Imperial Power,
bearing the ' colonial stigma '; Russia was not. That assessment of his
allies was a decisive factor in Roosevelt's readiness to make concessions
to the Soviet Union both in Europe and Asia in order to ensure Stalin's
entry into the Pacific War.

Roosevelt's intimates give two reasons for his determination to enlist
the aid of Russia against Japan. His personal Chief of Staff, Admiral
Leahy, says that the President was actuated by the belief that " Soviet
participation in the Far East operation would insure Russia's sincere
co-operation in his dream of a united, peaceful world."[5] On the other
hand, his Secretary of State, Stettinius, reports that " immense pressure
[was] put on the President by our military leaders to bring Russia into

---

[1]This memorandum, written on August 1st, 1945, is quoted by Sherwood, op. cit.,
pp. 922-3.
[2]Eisenhower, *Crusade*, pp. 473-4.
[3]Ibid., p. 457.
[4]Ibid., p. 457. This is a reference to the fact that Russia was the first country to
accord the United States diplomatic recognition after the Declaration of Independence.
[5]Leahy *I Was There*, p. 10.

the Far Eastern War. At this time the atomic bomb was still an unknown quantity and our setback in the Battle of the Bulge was fresh in the minds of all. We had not as yet crossed the Rhine. No one knew how long the European War would last nor how great the casualties would be."[1] Stettinius adds that the American Chiefs of Staff had warned Roosevelt that "without Russia it might cost the United States a million casualties to conquer Japan"[2] and that the Pacific War might not end until 1947.

The chief advocate of this view was Marshall, but Roosevelt's military advisers were by no means unanimous in the belief that it would be necessary to invade the Japanese home islands. Leahy says that at Pearl Harbour, in July 1944, both MacArthur and Nimitz (the two commanders directly concerned) had told the President that "Japan could be forced to accept our terms of surrender by the use of sea and air powers without the invasion of the Japanese homeland."[3] Since then, at the Battle for Leyte Gulf in October, the Japanese Navy had suffered such a crushing defeat that well before Yalta Leahy considered that the war against Japan "had progressed to the point where her defeat was only a matter of time and attrition." This was also the opinion of Arnold, the Chief of the Air Staff, whose Super-Fortresses were already bombing Japan from island airfields. There was no longer any great need for air bases in the Maritime Provinces of the Soviet Union, and, after the unhappy experiment of 'shuttle-bombing' in Europe, Arnold did not set much store by any facilities he might be granted in Asia.[4] Nevertheless, the advice of Marshall and King prevailed.

The supporters of Russian intervention were considerably influenced by their estimate of the amount of help the United States would receive, or should accept, from Britain in the war against Japan. Here the colonial issue again entered American calculations. Virtually all the British and Imperial forces in the Far East were deployed in Admiral Lord Louis Mountbatten's South-East Asia Command (SEAC) for operations in Burma, and in due course Malaya and Sumatra. This deployment was dictated as much by geographical as political factors, but it was presumed in Washington that Churchill was more interested in regaining Britain's lost colonies than in bringing about the early defeat of Japan. Consequently, it came as a great surprise—to the British as much as to the American Chiefs of Staff—when at Quebec in September 1944 the Prime Minister suddenly offered to send a large part of R.A.F. Bomber Command and the main British Battle Fleet into the Central Pacific. This offer was promptly accepted by Roosevelt, but, when it was raised at the next meeting of the Combined Chiefs of Staff, "all hell broke

[1] Stettinius, op. cit., p. 89.
[2] Ibid., p. 269.
[3] Leahy, op. cit., p. 296.
[4] General Deane, the Head of the American Military Mission in Moscow writes (*The Strange Alliance* p. 107), "FRANTIC was the code-word selected for shuttle-bombing involving the use of Russian bases, and it was a masterpiece of understatement."

loose "—Arnold's phrase—and King " hotly refused to have anything to do with it." Cunningham, the First Sea Lord, reports that King was sharply called to order by Leahy and " eventually gave way; but with a very bad grace."[1]

Although there was no trace of King's Anglophobia in Marshall or Arnold, the American Chiefs of Staff had never allowed their British colleagues any voice in the conduct of the Pacific War, nor were they eager to have British forces play a major part in it lest this should give Britain the right to claim possession or trusteeship of some of the Japanese Empire. Further, they believed—and they so advised the President— that " in the interests of national defence, the Japanese mandated islands in the Pacific captured by our forces should be retained under the sovereignty of the United States and not delivered to the trusteeship of the United Nations."[2] True to his principles, Roosevelt rejected this proposal, but those same principles made him distrustful of the activities and intentions of the British and French in South-East Asia.

Roosevelt was determined that Indo-China should not go back to France and he had refused to agree to any French military mission being accredited to SEAC. He was prepared to allow the Dutch to return to the Netherlands East Indies, because Queen Wilhelmina had promised to give them self-government, but he intended that these islands should be liberated by American forces so that he would be in a position to enforce fulfilment of this promise.[3] Accordingly, the sole Dutch possession placed within the sphere of prospective British operations was Sumatra and this island only because of its geographical relation to Malaya. Moreover, the American Chiefs of Staff, on MacArthur's recommendation, decided that the British should not be allowed to take over the military control of the East Indies after their recapture. " The exact British intentions were not known," says Leahy, " but past experience indicated that if they did get control of some Dutch territory, it might be difficult to pry them loose."[4] This view appears to have been shared by Roosevelt, for he told Stettinius that " the British would take land anywhere in the world even if it were only rock or a sandbar."[5]

Roosevelt's eagerness to buy Stalin's aid in the war against Japan was principally due to his desire to save lives, but in the light of all the evidence it seems fair to say that he was also actuated by the hope that

[1]Cunningham, *A Sailor's Odyssey*, p. 612. Admiral Cunningham makes it clear, however, that " the attitude of the United States Navy in the Pacific was entirely different . . . the American fleet welcomed ours with open arms and gave us all the help in its power." (Ibid., p. 614.)

[2]Leahy, op. cit., p. 304.

[3]On this point see Hull, op. cit., pp. 1596-1601. In September 1944, Hull suggested to Roosevelt that Britain, France and Holland should be required forthwith to make public commitments giving " specific dates when independence or complete [dominion] self-government will be accorded."

[4]Leahy, op. cit., p. 300. It was not until July 1945 at Potsdam that the Netherlands East Indies were placed within the British sphere of operations.

[5]Stettinius, op. cit., p. 212.

Russia's intervention would enable the United States to strike the decisive blow at Japan, and compel her surrender, before the British, French or Dutch could regain possession of their colonies. The United States would thus be able to demand that the colonies which had been liberated from the Japanese should now be liberated from the dominion of their original owners.

In due course, as it turned out, the Americans were able to achieve this purpose without the intervention of Russia. When the Japanese announced their readiness to capitulate, MacArthur, who was acting as co-ordinator of all the surrender arrangements, forbade Mountbatten to accept any local surrender in South-East Asia or to send any relief or reoccupation forces into Japanese-held areas until the overall surrender had been signed in Tokyo. Since this ceremony was not to take place for another twelve days, Mountbatten ignored his orders so far as missions of mercy were concerned, because, as he says in his dispatch, " if relief stores and personnel had not been sent in at once, the delay of twelve days imposed on me would have resulted in many more deaths each day among the prisoners [of war]."[1]

The instructions regarding the movement of naval and military forces were observed, though these were already at sea, and the British were thus placed in the humiliating position of not being permitted to re-occupy their own colonies, until the Japanese High Command had formally acknowledged defeat to an American general on an American battleship in Tokyo Bay.

Although this particular manifestation of American anti-colonialism was not revealed until six months after Yalta, the attitude which inspired it was implicit in the policy Roosevelt pursued throughout the war.

The plenary sessions of the Yalta Conference[2] were held at Livadia Palace overlooking the Black Sea. The ownership of this palace had changed since it was built by the Romanoffs, but the aims and ambitions of the new owners differed little from those of its former masters. The only significant difference was that the men who now sought to fulfil Russia's imperial destiny were more ruthless and more powerful.

At the opening session on Sunday, February 4th, Stalin made a

[1] *Report to the Combined Chiefs of Staff by the Supreme Allied Commander, South East Asia, 1943-1945*, p. 184.

[2] No detailed official record of this conference was kept, but we have first-hand accounts from four of the chief American participants. Stettinius made copious notes and in his book, *Roosevelt and the Russians*, he published substantial extracts from them and gave the texts of nearly all the important documents which were under discussion. James F. Byrnes, who succeeded Stettinius as Secretary of State, took a shorthand record of the main discussions at the meetings he attended and reproduced part of his transcript in his book, *Speaking Frankly*. Admiral Leahy kept a diary, and Harry Hopkins took lengthy notes which Sherwood edited. I have drawn extensively on all these sources but do not propose to give detailed acknowledgment for each extract quoted.

gesture which was both tactful and tactical. He proposed, as he had at Teheran, that Roosevelt should take the chair, and thus once again he brought the President half-way to his side. Yet Stalin showed no early inclination to follow the chairman's lead, least of all with regard to the President's cherished plan for creating a world peace organisation based on the recognition of the sovereign rights of all nations. The first time the subject was raised, " Stalin made it quite plain," says Stettinius, " that the three Great Powers which had borne the brunt of the war should be the ones to preserve the peace." He declared, moreover, that he would " never agree to having any action of any of the Great Powers submitted to the judgment of the small powers." In reply to this argument Churchill spoke for all the Western World in saying, " The eagle should permit the small birds to sing and care not wherefor they sang." That evening, when Stettinius and Eden discussed the outlook, they agreed that " the trend . . . seemed to be more towards a three-power alliance than anything else."

Evidently sensing that the time was not opportune to pursue the question of the world peace organisation, Roosevelt, at the start of the second plenary meeting, turned the discussion to the future of Germany. At the Moscow Conference of Foreign Ministers in November 1943 it had been decided that Germany should be completely disarmed and should pay reparations for the physical damage she had inflicted on the Soviet Union and other Allied countries. Then, and at Teheran, the question of partitioning Germany had been debated without any conclusions being reached, but it had been assumed that in any case the three powers would occupy the country, and by November 1944 they had agreed upon the actual zones of occupation and upon their joint responsibility for Berlin. At Yalta the ' Big Three ' confirmed their determination to demand the ' Unconditional Surrender ' of Germany and, for the first time, there was detailed consideration by the Russian and Anglo-American Chiefs of Staff on the military measures necessary to bring about Hitler's final defeat. On the question of post-war Germany, however, there was no such unanimity and it was soon evident that there was a considerable divergence between the British and Russian attitudes, especially with regard to the principle of partition, the extent of reparations and the right of France to share in the occupation.

The Russian view was that there should be only three occupying powers; that they should decide at Yalta to partition the Reich into a number of separate states and to include a declaration to this effect in the surrender terms; and that Germany should be deprived of eighty per cent of her heavy industry and should pay reparations in kind to the value of twenty billion dollars, half of which should go to the Soviet Union.

Churchill was not slow to realise that, if these proposals were adopted, Germany would be rendered politically impotent and economically impoverished. Although determined to ensure that Germany should not again disturb the peace of Europe, he did not wish to see her entirely neutralised as a factor in the balance of power. Accordingly, he doubted the wisdom of partitioning the Reich unless the Soviet Union would agree to the creation of a strong Danubian Confederation—and this had already been rejected by both Stalin and Roosevelt. Moreover, he did not wish to make Germany pay such severe reparations that her economy would collapse unless it were sustained by the Western Powers as it had been after the First World War. Finally, the Prime Minister wanted the French to have an equal share in both the occupation and administration of Germany so that there would be a second European voice to support Britain's in the Allied Control Commission. He was the more emphatic on this point, for the President said that the American troops would be withdrawn from Europe in " two years at the outside." Whereupon Churchill commented, without indicating what threat he feared, " Great Britain alone will not be strong enough to guard the Western approaches to the Channel."

As the discussion developed—both in the plenary sessions and at meetings of the Foreign Ministers—Roosevelt and Stettinius endeavoured to take an intermediate stand on these issues. The result was that three distinct viewpoints emerged. With regard to partition, Stalin wanted a definite commitment both now and in the surrender terms; Churchill wished to make no commitments either way; and Roosevelt suggested that they should mention dismemberment in the terms without binding themselves to this policy. On the matter of reparations, Stalin demanded explicit acceptance in the Protocol of the overall figure of twenty billion dollars; Churchill opposed any mention of any figure even in a secret document; and Roosevelt inclined to the view that the Russian figure might be taken as " a basis for discussion." As for the occupation of Germany, Churchill insisted that France should have a seat on the Control Commission as well as a zone; Stalin argued against both suggestions; and Roosevelt proposed that France should have a zone but no seat.

On each of these questions the President was in fundamental agreement with the Prime Minister's stand (though not with all his reasons), but in public discussion Roosevelt played the mediator. He was not interested in upholding the balance of power concept, nor was he deeply concerned with the intrinsic merits of the German problem. To him Germany was not an issue in itself, but a bargaining point in the wider issue that was uppermost in his mind—the winning of Stalin's co-operation in the international peace organisation, and in the war against Japan.

To some extent the role of arbiter was thrust upon Roosevelt when he became chairman, but there is no doubt that he preferred it since he was thus able to preserve greater freedom of action and to avoid committing himself until he had heard the rival views. The results of the

President's determination to act as mediator were twofold. On the one hand, the assertion of what were in reality Anglo-American views and principles was frequently left to the British alone—much to Churchill's annoyance; and on the other, as one of Roosevelt's closest advisers says, " the Soviet leaders did over-estimate the ultimate extent of the President's generosity and his willingness to compromise on principles."[1]

The problem of Germany's future was still undecided when—at the third plenary session on February 6th—Roosevelt returned to the question of post-war peace and asked Stettinius to review the questions which had been in dispute at the Dumbarton Oaks Conference. There the Americans, British, Chinese and Russians had agreed on the principles and purposes of what was to become the United Nations, and had decided there should be a General Assembly, a Security Council and various other instrumentalities. The area of agreement had ended, however, when the Soviet Delegate, Gromyko, had proposed that all sixteen republics of the Soviet Union should have seats in the Assembly (a proposal which " left Stettinius and Cadogan breathless "[2]), and had demanded that in the Security Council the Great Powers should have the right to veto any proposals, except those which related to points of procedure.

It has been alleged by some of Roosevelt's critics that the establishment of the veto power in the Security Council was a concession made by him at Yalta to induce Stalin to join the United Nations. This is not so. The basic principle of the veto was never in dispute. None of the Great Powers was prepared to submit itself and its interests unreservedly to the jurisdiction of an international security organisation. All were agreed that there must be " unqualified unanimity of the permanent members of the Council on all major decisions relating to the preservation of peace, including all economic and military enforcement measures." This was inevitable. The President, haunted by the ghost of Wilson, insisted on the veto power because he knew that the United States Senate would not surrender to an international body the right to commit American forces to military action. Churchill was equally insistent on this point because, as he said at Yalta, he would " never consent to the fumbling fingers of forty or fifty nations prying into the life's existence of the British Empire."

Although both Britain and America felt obliged to retain the right to veto any international ' police action,' they had no desire to curtail discussion or to prevent any small power bringing a cause of grievance to the notice of the Security Council. At Dumbarton Oaks, however, Gromyko had refused to accept this view and had told Stettinius, " The Russian position on voting in the Council will never be departed from! " Nevertheless, on December 5th, 1944, Roosevelt had sent to Stalin and

[1]Byrnes, op. cit., p. 59.

[2]Hull, op. cit., p. 1679. Sir Alexander Cadogan was the British delegate at Dumbarton Oaks.

Churchill a compromise formula which, while recognising the need for unanimity on matters involving the application of sanctions, provided that on questions relating to the peaceful settlement of any dispute no member of the Council would cast its vote, or exercise its veto, if it were a party to that dispute.

Now, at Yalta, after Stettinius had re-stated this formula, Churchill declared Britain's acceptance of it, and added, " We see great advantage in the three Great Powers not assuming the position of rulers of all the rest of the world without even allowing them to state their case." When Stalin spoke, however, he again emphasised the importance of unanimity, declaring that the real problem was to preserve the unity of the Great Powers and to work out a covenant that would achieve this purpose. " The danger in the future," he said, " is the possibility of conflicts among ourselves." Apologising to the President, Stalin said that he was not yet ready to pass judgment on the voting formula, because he had had " no chance to study this question in detail." Yet he proceeded to give such a concise analysis of its implications that it was obvious he must have studied it rather carefully at some time during the two months since he had received Roosevelt's draft!

After this exchange Stettinius was more confident, believing that for the first time Stalin really understood the American point of view. Byrnes, on the other hand, felt that the Russians " could not be greatly interested in the United Nations organisation," and Leahy thought it " difficult to foresee on what grounds an agreement could be reached." This impression seemed to be confirmed when, at the next meeting of the Foreign Ministers, Molotov refused even to discuss the Security Council voting procedure.

Leaving this matter for the moment, Roosevelt brought up the Polish question. He announced his readiness to accept the Curzon Line, but proposed that Stalin might agree to leave within Poland the city of Lwow and the nearby oilfields. " He pointed out," says Stettinius, " that he was merely suggesting this for consideration rather than insisting on it." In fact, the main argument he advanced in its support was that " it would have a salutary effect on American public opinion," a consideration which was hardly likely to carry much weight with the Soviet dictator. Thus, although the President's expert advisers had warned him that these oilfields were essential to the Polish economy, he did not make an issue of it, so anxious was he to preserve the role of mediator, not only on the frontier question but also in the establishment of a new Polish government.

Churchill was already committed to the Curzon Line, but he declared that if Stalin were to accept the President's Lwow plan, it would be " a magnanimous gesture " which Britain would " admire and acclaim." The Prime Minister said, however, that he was more interested in the sovereignty and independence of Poland than in the matter of frontiers, and that he, like the President, wished to see established in Warsaw a

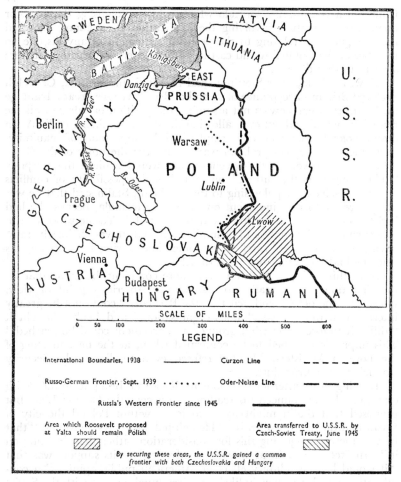

SCALE OF MILES

LEGEND

International Boundaries, 1938 ——————  Curzon Line —  —  —  —  —

Russo-German Frontier, Sept. 1939 . . . . . . .  Oder-Neisse Line —— —— ——

Russia's Western Frontier since 1945 ▬▬▬▬▬▬

Area which Roosevelt proposed
at Yalta should remain Polish

Area transferred to U.S.S.R. by
Czech-Soviet Treaty, June 1945

*By securing these areas, the U.S.S.R. gained a common
frontier with both Czechoslovakia and Hungary*

POLAND AND YALTA

"fully representative Polish government," pledged to the holding of free elections. For Britain, having risked so much in Poland's cause, this was a question of honour.

In reply, Stalin delivered an impassioned speech. "For the Russian people," he said, "Poland is not only a question of honour but also a question of security. Throughout history Poland has been the corridor through which the enemy has passed into Russia . . . It is in Russia's interests that Poland should be strong and powerful, in a position to shut the door of this corridor by her own force." Turning to the problem of frontiers, he said that the Soviet Union must have Lwow and could not accept anything but " the line of Curzon and Clemenceau." Stalin declared: " You would drive us into shame! What will be said by the White Russians and the Ukrainians? They will say that Stalin and Molotov are far less reliable defenders of Russia than are Curzon and Clemenceau . . . I prefer the war should continue a little longer . . . to give Poland compensation in the West at the expense of the Germans. . . . I am in favour of extending the Polish Western frontier to the Neisse River."[1]

Stalin was equally unresponsive to Roosevelt's suggestion that a new Polish Government should be formed from members of the five main political parties, including representatives of the Government in London. He stated that he did not trust the London Poles and would not recognise any administration except that already established in Lublin. " We demand order," he said, " and we do not want to be shot in the back."

Churchill joined issue vigorously with Stalin, declaring that Britain could not accept the Lublin Committee, since it did not represent more than a third of the nation; nor could he agree to extend Poland's western frontier to the River Neisse, thus giving her virtually all Silesia. " It would be a pity," he said, " to stuff the Polish goose so full of German food that he will die of indigestion." On that discordant note the meeting adjourned.

That evening Roosevelt sent Stalin a conciliatory letter, in which he reaffirmed the American opposition to the Lublin Committee, but added the assurance, " The United States will never lend its support in any way to any provisional government in Poland which would be inimical to your interests." Although he regarded this letter as an act of mediation, Roosevelt compromised his own independence by telling Stalin, " I am determined there shall be no breach between ourselves and the Soviet Union." With that statement he admitted that, if Stalin made an issue of Poland, the United States would give way.

When the Big Three met again next afternoon (February 7th) Stalin acknowledged receipt of the President's letter, but stated that his own reply was not yet ready as it was being typed; in the meantime he would like to discuss the international peace organisation. Roosevelt agreed, and Molotov proceeded to say that the Soviet Union was " happy to accept the entire American proposal " about voting in the Security Council, and would not press for all sixteen Soviet Republics to be members of the United Nations. It would be satisfactory if seats were granted to the Ukraine and White Russia. As it had already been agreed that Britain, the four Dominions and India should have individual representation in the General Assembly, Churchill could not oppose this request, and, although Roosevelt did not give his consent immediately, he told Stettinius that he " did not believe there was anything

[1]Byrnes, op. cit., pp. 30-2, quoting his contemporary shorthand note.

preposterous about the Russian proposal." Indeed, he regarded it as a small price to pay for Soviet co-operation.

The President and the Prime Minister were delighted at this manifestation of Stalin's willingness to join the United Nations and they felt he had made substantial concessions on two vital issues about which he had previously been intractable. They had feared that Stalin was interested only in securing a Three-Power Alliance, but now Roosevelt, at any rate, believed he had persuaded Stalin not only to recognise the sovereign rights of small nations, but also to act in friendly concert with the other great Powers in maintaining peace and extending the frontiers of freedom.

This belief was confirmed when Stalin agreed that the Soviet Union would take part in the United Nations Conference to be held in San Francisco in April, and would support there the right of the United States to have three votes in the General Assembly, if the President desired to make such a claim.[1] It seemed to Roosevelt that these concessions were an earnest of Stalin's good faith, for it could not be foreseen then that the Soviet Union would abuse the veto power, as it was to do in the years after the war, employing it to prevent discussion as well as decision and endeavouring to exercise it even on questions of procedure. That afternoon at Yalta it appeared that Anglo-American diplomacy had gained a considerable victory, and the President felt that the long and arduous journey had not been in vain.

During the brief adjournment which followed this discussion about the United Nations the prevailing opinion among the Western delegates was that the concessions Stalin had made represented a decided change of heart. Considered in relation to what followed, however, these concessions appear as a tactical manœuvre designed to make the Western delegations more receptive to the Soviet plan for Poland which Molotov put forward while the meeting still glowed with goodwill. This plan did little more than set out in formal terms the attitude Stalin had so forcibly proclaimed the day before. The only hint of any readiness to meet the Western view was contained in the statement that the present Provisional Government (i.e. the Lublin Committee) might be enlarged to include " some democratic leaders from Polish émigré circles." Since the Russians refused to regard even Mikolajczyk, the leader of the Peasant Party, as a ' democrat,' that concession meant nothing. The moral of this day's proceedings was that, while Russia was willing to join the United Nations, she was not prepared to rely on it entirely. She intended to safeguard her own security in any event by ensuring that she had subservient neighbours in Europe and a commanding position in Asia.

[1] This assurance was given by Stalin in writing on the last day of the Yalta Conference, but Roosevelt subsequently decided not to seek three votes for the United States.

Stalin's Asiatic ambitions were revealed on the following afternoon during a private discussion with Roosevelt about the Soviet Union's entry into the Japanese War. This discussion was conducted on a strictly Russo-American basis and in conditions of great secrecy. The only other persons present, apart from the two interpreters, were Molotov and Averell Harriman, the American Ambassador to the Soviet Union.

At the President's request, Churchill was not there and, when the negotiations were continued on the technical level by the Chiefs of Staff, the British did not take part. Even within his own entourage Roosevelt was most uncommunicative. Stettinius, though Secretary of State, was merely notified that talks were in progress. When he asked if the State Department should not be represented, Roosevelt replied that the problem was " primarily a military matter . . . and had best remain on a purely military level." This was a specious answer, for Stalin had long since committed himself on the basic military issue; the main point to be decided at Yalta was the political price of his participation.

It was in October 1943 that Stalin had first promised to join in the war against Japan after the defeat of Germany. He had made this offer to Cordell Hull, who says that it was " entirely unsolicited . . . and had no strings attached to it."[1] At Teheran a month later, Stalin had repeated this promise virtually as a *quid pro quo* for the Second Front and for Lend-Lease. Nevertheless, Roosevelt had then volunteered to restore Russia's rights in the Manchurian port of Dairen and to ensure her free access to warm waters. Finding that the President was a ' soft touch,' Stalin proceeded to make this gesture his price with the paradoxical result that Soviet demands grew as the American need for Russian assistance in the Eastern War declined. During Churchill's visit to Moscow in October 1944, the Marshal said that " the Soviet Union would take the offensive against Japan three months after Germany's defeat, provided the United States would assist in building up the necessary reserve supplies and *provided the political aspects of Russia's participation had been clarified*."[2] During this Moscow meeting, as on five other separate occasions in 1944, Stalin gave an assurance that Russian air and naval bases in the Maritime Provinces would be made available to American forces. In December, however, this assurance was withdrawn, presumably with a view to strengthening the bargaining position of the Soviet Union at Yalta.

The course of the fateful discussions which took place behind closed doors in Livadia Palace on the afternoon of February 8th is not known in detail, for none of those who took part have publicly revealed what was said and the accounts given by Leahy, Sherwood and Stettinius, though authoritative, are second-hand. What was decided, however, is revealed only too clearly in the terms of the agreement which was sub-

[1]Hull, op. cit., p. 1310.
[2]Deane, op. cit., p. 247. Deane was present when this was said. (The italics are mine. C.W.)

sequently signed by Stalin, Roosevelt and Churchill. This provided that " in two or three months after Germany has surrendered . . . the Soviet Union shall enter the war against Japan " on certain conditions: that " the status quo in Outer Mongolia " was to be preserved; that the Kurile Islands, north of Japan, were to be " handed over to the Soviet Union "; and that the rights Russia had lost after her defeat by Japan in 1904 were to be restored. Russia was thus to regain possession of Southern Sakhalin, the ' international port ' of Dairen and the naval base of Port Arthur. In addition, although China was to " retain full sovereignty in Manchuria," the principal Manchurian railways were to be " jointly operated by . . . a Soviet-Chinese Company " which was to safeguard " the pre-eminent interests of the Soviet Union." Apart from agreeing to enter the Pacific War, Stalin conceded nothing in writing. He promised Roosevelt that the United States could have bases in the Maritime Provinces, but this was not mentioned in the agreement, nor was there any reference to the one million tons of additional supplies that were to be provided by the Americans. These supplies were duly delivered, but the Russians made sure that the establishment of the bases never proceeded beyond discussions in Moscow.

The President's Chief of Staff (Admiral Leahy) says that, when the Russian terms were mentioned at a subsequent plenary session, there was " little discussion and no argument." It appears that Stalin blandly explained, " I only want to have returned to Russia what the Japanese have taken from my country "; and that Roosevelt replied, " That seems like a very reasonable suggestion from our ally. They only want to get back that which has been taken from them." Churchill must have listened a little incredulously to this exchange for he cannot have forgotten that Roosevelt had once said to him: " Winston . . . you have four hundred years of acquisitive instinct in your blood and you just don't understand how a country might not want to acquire land somewhere if they can get it. A new period has opened in the world's history and you will have to adjust yourself to it."[1]

The British should have known, if the Americans did not, that Stalin's justification could not by any means cover all the Soviet claims. The Kuriles had never formally belonged to Russia. The reclaimed ' rights ' in Manchuria were those which in the nineteenth century had enabled Russia to exercise in this province a degree of dominion which seriously impinged upon Chinese sovereignty. These ' rights ' rested on no more substantial foundations than those extra-territorial privileges which the United States, Britain and other countries had given up in 1943 at Roosevelt's own instigation and in fulfilment of his pledge to restore and

[1]Stettinius, op. cit., p. 212. Roosevelt made this remark to Churchill at Cairo in November 1943 when they were discussing the future of Indo-China. On this occasion, after talking to Chiang Kai-Shek, Roosevelt told Churchill, " China does not want Indo-China." Churchill replied, " Nonsense." It was this blunt answer that gave rise to Roosevelt's jibe. The President subsequently gave an account of this conversation to Stettinius who made a special record of it in his notes.

respect the independence of China. To accept the ' status quo ' in Outer Mongolia, which Moscow had been sedulously luring away from its allegiance to Chungking, was to acknowledge that the Soviet Union, not China, should enjoy political supremacy in that country. In short, by this agreement Russia was to become, with Anglo-American consent, the political heir of Japan in Manchuria, and thereby in North China.

No arrangement was made at Yalta with regard to the occupation of Korea and the post-war fate of that unhappy country appears to have been mentioned only incidentally. Stalin inquired whether it was to be occupied by any foreign troops. When Roosevelt replied that this was not intended, Stalin, no doubt thinking far into the future, " expressed his approval."[1]

Upon learning the full extent of the Soviet terms, some of Churchill's advisers were deeply concerned, for they discovered that, although Stalin had made no further commitments whatever and although the most important of his claims had to be met by their ally, China, not by Japan, the President and the Prime Minister were required to declare that " these claims of the Soviet Union shall be unquestionably fulfilled after Japan has been defeated." Moreover, Stalin was insisting that for security reasons the Chinese Government should not even be informed until the Soviet Union was ready to attack. Roosevelt had undertaken to secure Chiang Kai-Shek's compliance in due course but, as Sherwood says, " if China had refused to agree to any of the Soviet claims, presumably the U.S. and Britain would have been compelled to join in enforcing them." To some of the British delegation it seemed rather incongruous that, while urging Churchill to hand Hong Kong over to China as " a gesture of goodwill," Roosevelt was prepared to promise Stalin substantial concessions in Manchuria, and to do this without so much as consulting the Chinese. This point was appreciated by at least one of his staff, for Leahy reports that he warned Roosevelt, " Mr. President, you are going to lose out on Hong Kong if you agree to give the Russians half of Dairen "; and that Roosevelt replied, " Well, Bill, I can't help it."

Eden did all he could to dissuade the Prime Minister from setting his signature to the terms agreed upon by Roosevelt and Stalin. Churchill replied that he must sign, because he felt that " the whole position of the British Empire in the Far East might be at stake." The Prime Minister had good reason to fear that, since he had been excluded from the negotiations about the Japanese War, Britain might well be excluded from future discussions about the Far East if she did not stand by the United States now. Like Leahy, he may also have foreseen that, if these territorial concessions were made to Russia, Roosevelt would not be in a

---

[1]Sherwood, op. cit., p. 868. The agreement that the Russians should occupy Northern Korea was made later by American military authorities in order to expedite the disarming of the Japanese forces.

strong moral position to enforce his oft-repeated ' threat ' to reform the British Empire.

Of all the agreements reached at Yalta, this is the most controversial and would seem to be the least defensible. Yet it does not appear that the concessions, which Stalin obtained, were wrung from a reluctant Roosevelt. Sherwood records that the President had been " prepared even before the Teheran Conference . . . to agree to the legitimacy of most if not all of the Soviet claims in the Far East," although he expresses the opinion that " Roosevelt would not have agreed to the final firm commitment," if he had not been " tired and anxious to avoid further argument." Stettinius disagrees with this opinion and explains that " the Far Eastern agreement was carefully worked out and was not a snap decision made at Yalta." He endeavours to defend the concessions by asking: " What, with the possible exception of the Kuriles, did the Soviet Union receive at Yalta which she might not have taken without any agreement? "

That question does not pose the real issue which surely was: What did the Soviet Union receive at Yalta which she could not have taken without flagrantly violating the fundamental principles of the Atlantic Charter and the United Nations to which she had subscribed? The real issue for the world and for the future was not what Stalin would or could have taken but what he was given the right to take. This agreement provided Stalin with a moral cloak for his aggressive designs in Asia, and, more important, with almost a legal title enforceable at the Peace Conference to the territories and privileges which he demanded.

The President's surrender on this question is the more remarkable because it involved the sacrifice of those very principles which he had striven to uphold throughout his dealings with Churchill and Stalin. He had always insisted that he would not make any post-war commitments which would prejudice the peace treaties; he would recognise no spheres of influence, no territorial changes except those arrived at by mutual agreement, and no transfers of colonial territory except under conditions of international trusteeship. By making this agreement about the Japanese War, however, Roosevelt weakened both his mediating influence and his bargaining position in relation to problems arising out of the German War. He was not well placed to defend the sovereignty of Poland, once he had agreed to the infringement of China's sovereignty without her consent and in breach of the promise he had given to Chiang Kai-Shek at Cairo in 1943. He could not make any effective protest against the Russians' creating a sphere of influence in the Balkans, when he had acknowledged their sphere of influence in Mongolia and Manchuria. Having departed from his principles in Asia, he could not expect to be allowed to apply them in Europe; not against a realist like Stalin. Consequently, the President was now in a less favourable position than he had been at the start of the conference. Stalin's appetite had been whetted, not satisfied.

The records kept by those who were present at Yalta give the impression that the negotiations about Russia's part in the Pacific War on the Thursday afternoon marked the turning point in the week's discussions. If this was not realised by the Western delegations at the time, it seems to have been fully appreciated by Stalin. Thereafter, having gained the concessions which were to enable him to dominate China, he proceeded to consolidate politically the strategic advantages his armies had already secured in Europe. Stalin was better able to press his demands now, for he could play upon the sense of gratitude and co-operation he had built up in the Americans, and to a lesser extent in the British, by his agreement to help in the defeat of Japan and the creation of the international security organisation. The remaining negotiations were to prove the truth of the warning which had been sent to Washington two months earlier by the Head of the American Military Mission in Moscow (General Deane), an astute and not unsympathetic observer of the Soviet scene. In a letter to Marshall in December Deane had written, " We never make a request or proposal to the Soviets that is not viewed with suspicion. They simply cannot understand giving without taking, and as a result even our giving is viewed with suspicion. Gratitude cannot be banked in the Soviet Union. Each transaction is complete in itself without regard to past favours."[1]

When the discussions about Poland were continued, as they were at each session on the last four days, the Russians gained their way on almost every point. Nothing more was heard of the President's suggestion that Poland should keep the Lwow region. The Curzon Line was accepted and this fact was duly recorded in the Protocol. With regard to Poland's western frontier, however, Stalin did not press for the formal recognition of a specific line, since he realised that neither Roosevelt nor Churchill were prepared to go beyond the Oder. He readily consented to the suggestion that " the final delimitation of the western frontier should await the Peace Conference," for in the meantime that left him free to make his own arrangements about the German territory between the Oder and the Neisse.

The negotiations about the future government of Poland were very much more protracted and involved. The essence of the argument was that the Western Powers advocated the formation of an entirely new administration representing " all democratic and anti-Fascist forces," whereas the Russians proposed merely to enlarge the Lublin Committee, and to do this in such a way that the Polish Communists could retain control. Churchill and Eden fought for four days against this proposal, insisting that Great Britain could not withdraw her recognition of the London Government unless there was " a completely new start . . . on both sides on equal terms." The British also demanded that the new government should be provisional and should be pledged to hold " free and unfettered elections as soon as possible on the basis of universal

[1]Deane, op. cit., pp. 84-5.

suffrage and secret ballot," and that these elections should be conducted under the supervision of the American, British and Soviet Ambassadors. The Russians consented to the holding of free elections and Molotov told Roosevelt that these could be held " within a month." On the other hand, he bluntly rejected the supervision proposal, arguing that this would be " an affront to the pride and sovereignty of the independent people "! Eden endeavoured to insist on this safeguard, for he feared that any unsupervised elections would be a mockery, but at the final meeting of the Foreign Ministers Stettinius announced that " the President was anxious to reach agreement and that to expedite matters he was willing to make this concession."[1] With regard to the setting up of a new administration, the three Ministers eventually decided upon a compromise formula which read: " The Provisional Government which is now functioning in Poland should be reorganised on a broader democratic basis with the inclusion of democratic leaders from Poland itself and from Poles abroad." To this end various Polish leaders from all non-Fascist parties were to be brought together in Moscow for consultations with Molotov and the British and American Ambassadors.

When this formula was adopted at the plenary session on February 10th the Western delegates, with few exceptions, believed that they had reached, as Sherwood says, " an honourable and equitable solution." They were acting in good faith and they presumed that Stalin was equally sincere, for he also set his hand to a " Declaration on Liberated Europe " which reaffirmed the principles of the Atlantic Charter. By this Declaration the three Powers bound themselves " to build . . . a world order under law, dedicated to peace, security and freedom and the general well-being of all mankind," and agreed to act in concert " in assisting the peoples liberated from the dominion of Nazi Germany and the peoples of the former Axis satellite states of Europe . . . to create democratic institutions of their own choice."

These fine phrases were to prove less important than the terms of the Polish formula, which was so loosely worded that it left the Russians ample room to manœuvre. Roosevelt certainly entertained some doubts on this score, for he concurred when Leahy said to him, " Mr. President, this is so elastic that the Russians can stretch it all the way from Yalta to Washington without ever technically breaking it." The essential fact was that, while the British and Americans started by refusing to accord any recognition whatever to the Lublin Committee, they ended by allowing it to be described in the communiqué as " the present Provisional Government of Poland." Moreover, although they had originally insisted that an entirely fresh administration should be formed, they finally agreed to the words " the Provisional Government now functioning in Poland should be reorganised." The only real difference between that formula and what Stalin had initially demanded was a change in verb; " enlarged " had become " reorganised."

[1]Stettinius, op. cit., p. 225.

Having secured virtually all he wanted in Poland, Stalin made a conciliatory gesture with regard to the occupation of Germany. When the President announced that he now believed France should have a seat on the Control Commission as well as a zone of occupation, Stalin replied simply, " I agree." So far as he was concerned, this was a minor concession, for it did not require any material sacrifice on the part of the Soviet Union. Where her interests and assets were directly concerned, however, as in the matter of reparations, he was both stubborn and persistent. On the one hand, he refused altogether to discuss the Soviet Union's right to use German manpower; on the other, he demanded that a firm agreement should be reached at Yalta on the amount of ' reparations in kind ' that Germany should be required to pay. Again and again, one or other of the Soviet delegates returned to their original figure of ' 20 billion dollars ' arguing that, if this amount were accepted as " a basis for discussion," it " would not commit the Allies to that exact sum."

The Americans were inclined to accept that assurance, especially when it was repeated by Stalin, and to allow the figure to be mentioned in the Protocol. On this question, however, the British were absolutely adamant. Eden pointed out that they could not tell what Germany could afford to pay until they had discovered how much of the German economy survived the bombing and the general destruction of war. The settlement of the actual amount should be left to the Reparations Commission, which they had agreed to create. The Yalta Protocol should merely lay down principles to guide the Commission and should state that, " In establishing the amount of reparations account should be taken of arrangements made for the partitioning of Germany, the requirements of the occupying forces and Germany's need from time to time to acquire sufficient foreign currency from her export trade to pay for current imports." The British wanted it expressly stated that " Germany's industrial capacity would not be reduced to a point which would endanger the economic existence of the country." Eden argued that the Russians could not expect Germany to make large annual payments out of current production over a period of ten years, if German manufacturing capacity were reduced to the extent the Soviet Union demanded. These two objectives, he declared, were irreconcilable, as indeed they were to prove to be. " The British objective," said Eden, with marked prescience, " is to avoid a situation in which as a result of reparations we will have to finance and feed Germany." The logic of Eden's arguments was overwhelming and both Roosevelt and Stettinius agreed with it, but they did not think that the Soviet figure was unreasonable and they were strongly moved by sympathy for the terrible sufferings of the Russian people.

At the penultimate plenary session Stalin spoke with great emotion of the vast and wanton destruction which the Germans had caused in Russia and pleaded for due compensation. Churchill read a telegram

from the British War Cabinet protesting that reparations to the value
of 20 billion dollars was far more than Germany could afford. It seemed
that a deadlock had been reached. The Russians would not accept the
British principles, and the British would not accept the Russian figure,
not even as " a basis for discussion." Thereupon, Roosevelt suggested
that the whole problem should be left to the Reparations Commission
in Moscow. Churchill and Stalin agreed, but that was not the end of
the matter.

During this session Hopkins scribbled a note to Roosevelt saying,
" Mr. President, the Russians have given in so much at this Conference
that I do not think we should let them down. Let the British disagree
if they want to—and continue their disagreement at Moscow." That
night at a dinner given by the Prime Minister, Stalin tackled Churchill
again, saying that he did not like to have to go back to Moscow and
tell the Soviet people that owing to British opposition they would not
receive adequate reparations. The combined effect of Stalin's persistence
and Hopkins's intervention was that when the Protocol was signed next
morning it contained the statement that " the Soviet and American
delegations agreed " that the Reparations Commission " should take in
its initial studies as a basis for discussion the suggestion of the Soviet
Government that the total sum should be 20 billion dollars and that
50 per cent of it should go to the U.S.S.R." The British view that " no
figure should be mentioned " was also recorded, but this was of little
account. The figure was there—however hedged around with qualifying
phrases—and it was linked to the names of the Soviet Union and the
United States.

Although the very persistence of the Russians on this point might
well have served as a warning, it is doubtful whether any member of the
Western delegations foresaw then that, in spite of Stalin's repeated
assurances, the Russians would soon be claiming that to " take as a
basis for discussion " meant to " accept in principle." From this it was
a short step to the claim subsequently made by Molotov that " President
Roosevelt had agreed at Yalta that Soviet reparations should total at
least ten billion dollars."

On that final Sunday morning at Livadia Palace neither the
Americans nor the British suspected that the public communiqué and
the secret protocol, so solemnly signed and endorsed with such expressions of mutual trust and good-will, would soon be distorted and
violated by their Soviet Allies, and that this process of distortion and
violation would begin before the Prime Minister and the President had
been able to report to their respective legislatures on the conference at
which, they both asserted, the Great Powers were " more closely united
than ever before."

In the House of Commons on February 27th, the Prime Minister
declared: " The impression I brought back from the Crimea . . . is that
Marshal Stalin and the Soviet leaders wish to live in honourable friend-

ship and equality with the Western democracies. I feel also that their word is their bond. I decline absolutely to embark here on a discussion about Russian good faith." That evening in Bucharest—despite the Yalta Declaration on Liberated Europe—Molotov's deputy (Andrei Vishinsky) issued to King Michael a two-hour ultimatum, demanding the dismissal of the Rumanian Prime Minister, General Radescu, the leader of an all-party Government.

Four days later, addressing a joint session of Congress, the President said: " The Crimea Conference . . . spells—and it ought to spell—the end of the system of unilateral action, exclusive alliances, and spheres of influence, and balances of power and all the other expedients which have been tried for centuries and have always failed. . . . I am sure that—under the agreement reached at Yalta—there will be a more stable political Europe than ever before." That evening in Bucharest, without any reference whatever to the Allied Control Commission, Vishinsky issued to King Michael a second ultimatum, demanding that he should appoint as Prime Minister Petru Groza, the leader of the Rumanian Communists.

## CHAPTER XXXIII

# THE FINAL COLLAPSE

THE decision of the Three Powers at Yalta to persist in their demand for ' Unconditional Surrender ' made it certain that the war against Germany would not end until the Western and Eastern armies met in the heart of Europe. This could not be long delayed. On the Oder and on the Rhine the Wehrmacht might hold the closing jaws apart for a few weeks, or a few months, but Hitler's armies had almost reached the point of exhaustion. They might live for a while on the remaining stocks of weapons, ammunition and fuel, but they would receive little replenishment from a war economy already constricted by creeping paralysis. The better part of Upper Silesia was in Russian hands. The Ruhr lay in ruins. By February 1945 its production of coal and steel had been reduced to one-fifth of what it had been in the summer of 1944 and, owing to the dislocation of rail and water transport, a mere fraction of this meagre output could be moved to the hungry factories of Central and Southern Germany. The production of arms and munitions was being maintained at less than half the rate of the previous summer only by the assembly of components and the consumption of stocks. German war industry, having consumed its fat, was eating its tail.

The slender possibility that the new air and naval weapons might delay the verdict of the battle on the ground had now gone. Hitler was still telling Speer that the development of jet-fighters would have " a decisive influence on the whole course of the war," but the February production of Me 262s was only 283, and the airfields from which the jets operated were so easily identifiable—by reason of their exceptionally long runways—that they were heavily bombed as soon as they came into use. Nor, after all, were sufficient V-weapons being produced to affect the issue. Throughout the winter Hitler had been trying to neutralise the port of Antwerp and thus delay the Allied spring offensive, but with an output of only 1,500 V.1s and 600 V.2s a month the Germans could not maintain sufficient volume of fire to saturate the dock area; and nothing short of saturation could have prevented the working of the port. Even after 5,000 V-bombs had fallen on Antwerp and its environs, the total damage to docks and installations was no greater than might have been caused in one conventional raid by a hundred bombers.[1]

The prospect that the Allied build-up might be checked by a miracle at sea was equally remote. In mid-February, although 126 of the new electro-U-boats had been commissioned, only two had yet been sent out on operations and the chances of bringing the remainder into service had been considerably reduced by the advance of the Red Army to Memel and the Gulf of Danzig. New boats could still be 'worked up' in the Eastern Baltic but they would have to operate from bases which lay well within the range of Anglo-American air-power. Doenitz might continue to tell Hitler that " all equipment at present employed in naval warfare can now be circumvented and eliminated "[2] by the new U-boats; yet these would never be employed in sufficient strength to bring about the 'revolution at sea' which the Grand-Admiral had been promising as recently as January. Although there were 450 U-boats of all types in commission on February 15th (" the largest number," so Doenitz told Hitler,' " that Germany has ever possessed "), the war at sea was no longer of any strategic consequence. Nevertheless, such was the personal influence of Doenitz and such the lack of co-ordination and direction in the German war economy that there were under construction at this time no fewer than 114 U-boats—far more than the number for which the Navy could hope to provide trained crews or training facilities.

The difficulties the Germans were having in bringing their jet-fighters and electro-U-boats into operational use were not fully appreciated by the Allied High Command. It was considered to be more than likely that Hitler would regain the initiative in the air and at sea, at least temporarily, during the spring and would succeed in holding out on land until the autumn. There was one aspect of the scientific war, however, about which there was no anxiety. The Western Allies were already certain that the Germans were not on the track of the atom bomb.

In the summer of 1941 British scientists had warned the Prime Minister that there was " a reasonable chance that an atomic bomb could be produced before the end of the war." A year later, after further scientific progress, especially in Britain, Churchill and Roosevelt had decided to proceed with the development, and if possible the production, of an atomic bomb, for they knew, as Churchill later said, that they

---

[1]The bombardment of Antwerp revealed the limitations of the V.1 and V.2 as weapons of attack against military targets. When the bombardment came to an end in March 1945, 5,622 V.1s and 1,982 V.2s had fallen in North-Western Belgium and South-Western Holland. Of these 7,604 V-bombs only 242 had caused military damage or military casualties. Of the 5,960 which landed within an eight-mile radius of the centre of Antwerp only 302 fell inside the boundaries of the port. With these the Germans sank one ship and damaged sixteen others, and put one dry dock out of action for three weeks. It was the civilian population of Antwerp which suffered most heavily, for 3,470 Belgian civilians lost their lives, compared with the Allied death-roll of 682 servicemen.

[2]Führer Naval Conferences, February 17th, 1945.

" could not run the mortal risk of being outstripped in this awful sphere."

By the end of 1943 the Allies had good cause to fear that the Germans might outstrip them in this scientific race. The principle of atomic fission had been discovered by a German, Otto Hahn, and the first published statement of the theory of the chain-reacting pile had come from Germany. Accordingly, when the Americans succeeded in producing a chain-reaction in a uranium pile—as they did at the end of 1942— they, and their British colleagues, were convinced that German research must have advanced at least as far. This belief gave an added spur to the researches of Allied scientists and also to the inquiries of Allied agents in Germany.

No reliable evidence was forthcoming, however, about the state of German atomic development until August 1944, when Eisenhower's armies reached Paris. There an American scientific mission (known by the code-name ALSOS) picked up a valuable clue, namely, that a Professor Fleischmann, who was known to be one of Germany's leading nuclear physicists, had been working at Strasbourg University. A few weeks later, at the Philips works in Eindhoven, it was discovered that this University had recently ordered some new equipment for nuclear research. When the Allies liberated Nijmegen, therefore, three bottles of Rhine water were dispatched forthwith to Washington for analysis on the assumption that, if the Germans were using the Rhine or any of its tributaries for cooling a uranium pile, these waters might show some radio-activity. With the three bottles of Rhine water ALSOS sent back a bottle of French wine marked " Test this for activity too." The reply from Washington read, " Water negative. Wine shows activity. Send more. Action."

Although the test that mattered was negative, Strasbourg remained an objective of first scientific importance. In November 1944, when Strasbourg was finally captured by a swift and unexpected thrust, members of the ALSOS Mission followed in close behind the leading columns. At the University they found nothing, but then they discovered that the nuclear laboratory was in a wing of the Strasbourg Hospital and that the nuclear physicists they wanted were masquerading as medical officers.

Fleischmann and his associates were not very communicative but their laboratory yielded a rich haul of documents. The Professor, a meticulous taker of notes in the best German tradition, had kept a detailed record of his conversations with other German nuclear physicists and of the researches on which they were engaged. Thus at Strasbourg the ALSOS Mission gained sufficient evidence to report to Washington, " Germany has no atom bomb and is not likely to have one within any reasonable time." The scientific head of the mission (Professor Samuel Goudsmit) subsequently reported that " As far as the German scientists were concerned the whole thing was still on an academic scale . . . their pile work was still in a very early state. They had not yet succeeded in producing a chain reaction. . . . *In short, they were about as far as we were in* 1940, *before we had begun any large-scale efforts on the atom bomb at all.*"[1]

In February 1945, therefore, the possibility that a scientific miracle might save Germany from military defeat no longer existed. Nor was there any reason for Hitler to think, as he had thought on the eve of Yalta, that the Russian advance into Eastern Germany would incline the Western Allies to consider a separate peace. The likelihood of a split between East and West, and of a consequent political compromise with Germany, had all but disappeared. Nevertheless, Hitler still refused to consider capitulation. As an earnest of his inflexibility, he now contemplated denouncing the Geneva Convention " in order," so he said, " to make the enemy realise that we are determined to fight for our existence with all means at our disposal."[2] Such a course, he argued, would " induce the German people to resist to the utmost," and more important, might check the rapidly mounting numbers of surrenders in the field. " If I make it clear," he declared, " that I shall treat enemy prisoners of war ruthlessly and without regard for reprisals, then quite a few [Germans] will think twice before deserting."[3] When Doenitz counselled that " the disadvantages would outweigh the advantages," Hitler refrained from carrying out this threat, but the ruthlessness which inspired it continued to actuate his conduct of the struggle.

Hitler's refusal to yield was endorsed by the vast inarticulate mass of the German people, for the dread of Russian invasion was now added to the long-standing fear of the anarchy which would follow internal collapse. Although they accepted the inevitability of defeat, Germans were agreed that capitulation was out of the question with the Red Army on the Oder and the Western Allies at the Siegfried Line. They feared that, if the war were to come to an end with the Eastern and Western forces thus deployed, the greater part of the Reich would be overrun and plundered by the Russians. Germany could be saved from this fate only if the Red Army could be halted on the Oder until the Anglo-American forces had crossed the Rhine and advanced deep into the Reich.

Although Hitler was still thinking in terms of holding firm on both fronts, he was now compelled to give priority to the East. Responding to the immediate threat to Berlin, and believing that it would take the Western Allies at least two months to recover from the campaign in the Ardennes, Hitler had already stripped the West of more than half its panzer divisions and was directing to the Eastern Front virtually the entire output of his tank factories and repair shops. The movement of armour eastwards was so pronounced that in February 1,675 tanks and assault guns, new or repaired, were sent to formations engaging the

---

[1] Professor Samuel A. Goudsmit, *ALSOS*, p. 71. (The italics are mine. C. W.)
[2] Führer Naval Conferences, February 19th, 1945.
[3] Führer Conferences, Fragment 49. The precise date of this fragment is not known but the conference took place early in March 1945.

Russians. During that month the West received only 67. By this drastic redistribution of his armour Hitler hoped to stabilise his front along the Oder before the Anglo-American armies were ready to renew their offensive to the Rhine. Once again Hitler was guilty of underestimating the Americans.

The full extent to which Hitler would be compelled to weaken the West in order to restore the front in the East did not become apparent to the Allied High Command until February, but Eisenhower proceeded to plan on the assumption that " one more great campaign, aggressively conducted on a broad front, would give the death-blow to Hitler Germany."[1] Having repulsed the enemy's winter offensive, Eisenhower had no intention of waiting until the spring before resuming his own. Far from being still disorganised and dispirited by their initial reverse in the Ardennes, as Hitler believed, the American armies had emerged from their ordeal with renewed self-confidence and greater strength. The arrival of new divisions direct from the United States at the rate of one a week had made good the losses suffered in the Battle of the Bulge,[2] and there was no longer a shortage of ammunition as there had been in the autumn.

Eisenhower's plan for the Battle of the Rhineland was governed by the course he envisaged for the campaign beyond the Rhine. He intended that the main drive into the Reich should be made by Montgomery " from the Lower Rhine north of the Ruhr and into the North German Plain," because this route offered " the most suitable terrain for mobile operations . . . [and] . . . the quickest means of denying the Germans the vital Ruhr industries."[3] In addition, however, Bradley was to make a complementary attack from the Mainz–Frankfurt area north-east to Kassel, with the object of effecting " a massive double envelopment of the Ruhr to be followed by a great thrust to join up with the Russians." After the necessary forces had been provided for these two operations, a subsidiary effort was to be undertaken by Devers in Southern Germany, but, when the plan was made, it was not expected that this would be of any major significance.

For the campaign beyond the Rhine Eisenhower could count on being able to employ 85 divisions, two-thirds of them American. Of these he intended to commit 35 divisions in the main offensive north of the Ruhr and another 25 on the southern axis, Frankfurt–Kassel. This would leave him with a further 25 divisions to hold the Karlsruhe–Basle

---

[1]Eisenhower, *Crusade*, p. 369.
[2]According to SHAEF records, the casualties suffered by the First and Third U.S. Armies in the Ardennes were: Killed, 8,407; Wounded, 46,170; Missing, 20,905; Total, 75,482. No directly comparable German figures are available, but von Rundstedt's H.Q. estimated that the Wehrmacht's casualties came to " not less than 120,000," of which 12,652 were known to have been killed.
[3]Eisenhower, *Report*, p. 100.

and Bonn–Bingen sections of the Rhine which did not offer suitable opportunities for assault-crossings on a large scale. At SHAEF, however, the Planning Staff estimated that Eisenhower would not be able to concentrate the necessary force for the drive to Kassel, unless he were first to gain the line of the Rhine throughout its length. Its calculation was that, so long as the Germans were holding any substantial areas on the west bank the Allies would need to deploy more than half their strength defensively to contain them. Eisenhower concluded, therefore, that " before attempting any major operations east of the Rhine it was essential to destroy the main enemy armies west of the river."[1] Only when this was done would he be able to concentrate sufficient strength to carry out the envelopment of the Ruhr.

When this plan was reported to the British Chiefs of Staff early in January, before the start of the Russian offensive in Poland, the C.I.G.S. (Brooke) objected that Eisenhower would " never have enough strength to mount more than one full-blooded attack across the Rhine," and that, since the Combined Chiefs of Staff had agreed that the principal effort should be made north of the Ruhr, Eisenhower should concentrate on this thrust and should " pass to the defensive on all other parts of the line."[2] Brooke feared that the clearing of the entire west bank of the Rhine—involving, as it would, ousting the Germans from the main Siegfried fortifications in the Saar and the Eifel—would absorb so much of Eisenhower's forces that he would not be able to make any effective attack into the North German Plain.

This was the argument of the autumn once again—' single thrust or broad front? '—with the difference that this time events were to prove that Eisenhower's plan was sound and that the British fears were groundless. Brooke's criticism was not ill-founded when first put forward, but at the end of January, when the Combined Chiefs of Staff met at Malta, it no longer had the same validity. By then the Germans had been driven from the Ardennes and the Russians had reached the Oder. Nevertheless, the British continued to oppose Eisenhower's plan. Although they argued their case on strictly military grounds, the British had a political consideration very much in mind. They foresaw the possibility that the Red Army might sweep on from the Oder to the Elbe and the North Sea while the Anglo-American forces were still clearing the Rhineland. Accordingly, they were anxious to ensure that the Allies were well established across the Lower Rhine at the earliest opportunity, so that they would be in a position to reach the ports and naval bases of Northern Germany before the Russians. Henceforth, this was to be one of the principal objectives of British strategy in Germany, but in the atmosphere prevailing on the eve of Yalta the British could not openly advance this political plea without accentuating American suspicions.

[1]Eisenhower, *Report*, p. 104.
[2]Eisenhower, *Crusade*, p. 370.

At Malta Eisenhower's answer to the British criticism was given by his Chief of Staff, Bedell Smith, who pointed out that, on account of local logistic limitations, no more than 35 divisions could be maintained across the Lower Rhine and that a force of this strength could neither neutralise the Ruhr nor inflict a crushing defeat on the Wehrmacht. The southern attack from Frankfurt to Kassel, he said, was essential to the envelopment of the Ruhr, and this attack could not be carried out in adequate strength until the west bank of the Rhine was in Allied hands.

On the other hand, Bedell Smith assured the Combined Chiefs of Staff that Montgomery's Army Group would have top priority and would cross the Lower Rhine as soon as possible and without waiting until all the Rhineland had been cleared. The British were not satisfied with this assurance and the subsequent discussion produced, says Sherwood, " the most violent disagreements and disputes of the entire war."[1] Marshall finally clinched the issue, but only by going so far as to announce that, if the SHAEF Plan were not accepted by the British, he would " recommend to Eisenhower that he had no choice but to ask to be relieved of his command."

In endorsing Eisenhower's strategy the Combined Chiefs of Staff endorsed by implication his arrangements with regard to command. During the Ardennes campaign Brooke had revived the question of appointing a C.-in-C., Ground Forces, to direct the land battle under Eisenhower's general supervision. Both Marshall and Eisenhower had always opposed such an appointment, believing it to be unsound in principle, but, whatever theoretical justification there may have been for the British proposal, the issue was now clouded with questions of personality and prestige. The creation of a ground forces' commander at this juncture would certainly have been interpreted by the Allied press as a reflection on recent American leadership, and, if Montgomery had been appointed as Brooke suggested, there would almost as surely have been a ' revolt ' among Eisenhower's subordinates. Indeed, Bradley asserts that he threatened to resign rather than serve under Montgomery and that Patton would have resigned with him.[2]

Realising the strength of the American opposition, Brooke did not raise the question directly at Malta. Churchill, on the other hand, sought to achieve the British purpose by proposing that Alexander should succeed Tedder as Deputy Supreme Commander. In the Mediterranean in 1943, when Alexander had been his deputy, Eisenhower had delegated to him the task of commanding all ground forces and the two had worked in the closest harmony. Churchill assumed, therefore, that if Alexander were to become Deputy Supreme Commander at SHAEF, he would be well placed to influence the course of the land campaign along the lines advocated by the British Chiefs of Staff. Roosevelt at first agreed to this change but, when the full implications of Churchill's plan were

[1]Sherwood, op. cit., p. 848.
[2]See Bradley, op. cit., pp. 487-8.

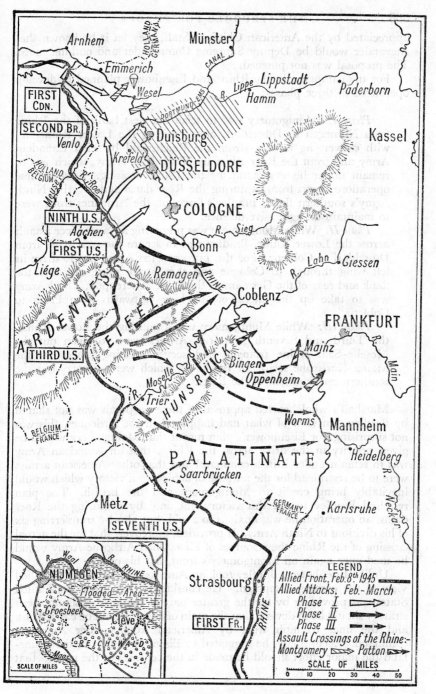

THE BATTLE OF THE RHINELAND

appreciated by the American Chiefs of Staff, they let it be known that Alexander would be Deputy Supreme Commander and nothing more. The proposal was not pursued.

For the campaign in the Rhineland Eisenhower planned to develop operations in three phases:

*Phase I:* Montgomery was to seize the west bank of the Rhine from Nijmegen to Düsseldorf, after clearing the Lower Rhineland with converging attacks—from the Reichswald by First Canadian Army and from the Roer River by Ninth U.S. Army, which was to remain under his command for the Rhine crossing. During these operations, apart from capturing the Roer dams and covering Ninth Army's southern flank, Bradley's forces on the Ardennes front were to maintain an aggressive defence.

*Phase II:* While Montgomery was preparing for a set-piece assault across the Lower Rhine, Bradley was to secure the west bank from Düsseldorf to Coblenz. For this purpose First Army was to drive its left wing through to Cologne and then strike south-east into the flank and rear of the Germans in the Eifel. Thereupon, Third Army was to take up the offensive, attacking eastwards from Prüm to Coblenz.

*Phase III:* While Montgomery was assaulting the Lower Rhine, the Third and Seventh American Armies were to clean out the Moselle–Saar–Rhine triangle, and secure crossing places on the Mainz–Karlsruhe sector for the forces which were to carry out the southern envelopment of the Ruhr.

Marshall's wholehearted approval of these proposals was not shared by Bradley. In view of what had happened in the Ardennes, this was not surprising, for Eisenhower's plan meant that Montgomery was to be given priority in the drive across the Rhine, that an American Army was to remain under British command and that other American armies were to be restrained for the purpose of achieving a victory which would inevitably bring credit to Montgomery and the British. The plan required Bradley to aid this victory not only by capturing the Roer dams, an operation he was anxious to avoid, but also by transferring six of his divisions to Ninth Army. It provided, moreover, that for the actual crossing of the Rhine the resources of First Allied Airborne Army would be used once again on Montgomery's front, not his own.

Unlike Eisenhower, Bradley took an American rather than an Allied view of the coming campaign. He considered that, since the United States was providing by far the greater part of the forces, Eisenhower's strategy should be so devised that the main offensive would be carried out, and the final triumph won, by American troops under American command. Accordingly, he suggested to Eisenhower that in the Rhineland the major effort should be made in the centre, not the north: that

Ninth Army should return to his command, and that First and Third Armies should drive straight on from the Ardennes through the Eifel keeping south of the Roer dams and advancing to the Cologne–Coblenz section of the Rhine. The long-term implication of this plan was that the offensive into Central Germany should be carried out by four American Armies (Ninth, First, Third and Seventh), leaving the Canadians, British and French merely to cover the flanks.

Bradley's proposal was open to the same objections that Eisenhower had raised against the Brooke-Montgomery plan for a single thrust in the north. There was the added objection that Bradley's alternative would bring the main Allied strength against the most rugged stretch of the Rhine valley, where there were few opportunities of crossing in the face of organised resistance, and this resistance was likely to be formidable if the Allies had not reached the river elsewhere. Furthermore, the communications on this sector were too limited to maintain a force strong enough to advance far beyond the Rhine, except in conjunction with powerful attacks from other sectors. Strategically there was little to commend Bradley's plan and tactically it would have involved a head-on attack against what was at this time the most strongly held sector of the Siegfried defences, for in the Eifel the Germans matched his strength division for division. It was only natural, however, that Bradley was reluctant to halt his armies just when they had given the Germans a thorough drubbing and were eager to put their claim to victory beyond dispute. This was not a matter of personal ambition; it was a question of giving his troops the chance to avenge completely the reverse they had suffered in the Ardennes. Upon being asked to give up forces which he wished to use for his own attack through the Eifel, Bradley told one of Eisenhower's staff that, if SHAEF wanted " to destroy the whole operation," they could " do so and be damned " and that " much more than a tactical operation was involved in that the prestige of the American Army was at stake."[1]

When this plan was rejected and the decision to leave Ninth Army with Montgomery was confirmed, Bradley explained to his army commanders that this arrangement had been imposed on Eisenhower by the Combined Chiefs of Staff and that the overall plan was a British concept fathered by Montgomery. Such was not the case. The plan was Eisenhower's and had been in almost its final form before being submitted to the Combined Chiefs at Malta. In his post-war account of the campaign, Bradley partially corrects himself by pointing out that at Malta Marshall " objected most strenuously to the Combined Chiefs issuing instructions to a field commander on how to accomplish his job."[2] He still blames Montgomery, however, and asserts that by demanding Ninth Army the Field-Marshal " put a crimp " in the American plan for continuing the attack through the Eifel. He also maintains, without

[1]Patton, op. cit., p. 225.
[2]Bradley, op. cit., p. 514.

explanation, that " Eisenhower had little choice but to accede to Monty's demand."[1] The truth is that the strategic plan for the destruction of the German armies west of the Rhine in three phases was drawn up at SHAEF under Eisenhower's direction. Montgomery's tactical plan for clearing the Lower Rhineland was accepted by Eisenhower only because it conformed to his own strategic policy. Nevertheless, Eisenhower did not escape the accusation that he had given in to the British and was allowing the Combined Chiefs of Staff to direct the campaign from Washington. Because this charge was freely made by Patton to his staff and his commanders, it gained a widespread currency and credence; so much so that there was perhaps no other time when Eisenhower was so severely criticised within the American Army.

If Eisenhower was disturbed by these rumblings of discontent, he did not allow them to influence his decision. He held to his plan, knowing that he had Marshall's full support and feeling more confident of his own authority than he had the previous year. In Normandy, as in the Mediterranean, he had left the direction of operations to the commander on the spot, and he had been so little in touch with the bridgehead battle that he had not fully appreciated Montgomery's design. In August, following the unexpected rout of the Wehrmacht, Eisenhower had been precipitated into assuming command of the ground forces at short notice and in a situation for which he was insufficiently prepared. Moreover, because of the injury which immobilised him within forty-eight hours of taking over from Montgomery, he had had no chance of gaining a grip on the battle, or on his field commanders, until the opportunity of winning a quick victory had gone. Nor had he possessed at that stage the experience and assurance to impose his own ideas on men as independent as Montgomery and Patton. Sanguine by nature, he had listened too readily to the confident predictions of his subordinates, inclining first to one plan then to another, and endeavouring to reconcile these with SHAEF's ' long-term strategic concept ' which was quite inapplicable to the situation that had developed. The result was the vacillation and frustration of the autumn; the strategy of compromise and optimism; the policy, as some said, of " Have a go, Joe." Between Paris and the Ardennes, Eisenhower had acted as the co-ordinator, rather than commander, of the ground forces and had maintained such light and loose control over his armies that the initiative had passed to the enemy.

A fortnight before the start of Hitler's great offensive, Eisenhower had unwittingly revealed the limitations of his strategic grasp. Replying to a critical letter from Montgomery he had written, " I do not agree that things have gone badly since Normandy merely because we have not gained all we hoped to gain. In fact, the situation now is somewhat analagous to that which existed in Normandy for so long." Yet the two situations could hardly have been more different. In June and July the

[1]Bradley, op. cit., pp. 496-7.

conditions had been created for an American break-through; in October and November the conditions had been created for a German break-through. In the summer the German panzer reserves had been kept in action and destroyed; in the autumn the German panzer reserves had been withdrawn from the battle and refitted.

In the Ardennes Eisenhower had learned the need for firm command to ensure concentration and for a central reserve to maintain flexibility. In the Rhineland campaign he applied these lessons. He produced a comprehensive and integrated plan for the entire front and laid down a time-table of action designed to bring about a succession of concentrated attacks each making a specific contribution to the whole. This plan was opposed and criticised by the most influential Americans in the field, but Eisenhower allowed no evasion. He rode out the storm of criticism, confident that the tide of battle would bring its own vindication.

The unfolding of Eisenhower's Rhineland plan began on February 8th when XXX British Corps, under command of First Canadian Army, attacked the Reichswald, debouching from the constricted neck between the Maas and the Rhine south-east of Nijmegen. This attack (Operation VERITABLE) was launched in overpowering strength after the most concentrated artillery bombardment of the war in the West. The preliminary barrage lasted five and a half hours and on the first day 1,034 guns put down more than half a million shells on a seven-mile front held by a single German division. Against this front the corps commander, Horrocks, hurled the best part of five infantry divisions, supported by three armoured brigades and eleven regiments of specialised armour, designed for breaching fortifications. Behind this massive punch, he held two more divisions in reserve for exploitation, but there were only two metalled roads by which they could be let loose and those roads ran through slender corridors between the Reichswald and the flooded valleys of the flanking rivers.

The original fortifications of the Siegfried Line did not extend as far north as the Reichswald, but the Germans had had five undisturbed months in which to develop the forest's natural defensive qualities and they had made the narrow neck narrower still by breaching the banks of the Rhine and inundating the polder. Beyond the Reichswald they had also fortified the towns of Goch and Cleve, and had deployed a mobile corps of three divisions farther south in readiness to meet an attack across the Roer or the Maas. The essence of Horrocks's problem was to drive his troops through the Reichswald and into the undulating sweep of the Lower Rhineland before the enemy could bring his reserves north to seal off the exit from the bottleneck.

When the plan was made, the ground was frozen and the going firm, but even as the divisions assembled for attack it started to thaw, and as they advanced into the Reichswald the forest rides became quagmires and the floodwaters began rising on their flanks. Nevertheless, while the Germans were still recovering from the fright and fury of the bombardment, the leading division (15th Scottish) drove through the northern fringe of the forest and on the afternoon of the second day reached the outskirts of Cleve. But Cleve had been bombed, and not with incendiaries as Horrocks had requested, but with 1,384 tons of high explosives. In the ruins of the town the attack came to a halt, for the streets were blocked with craters and rubble.

That evening, unaware of this, Horrocks ordered two mobile columns of the 43rd Division to move up from Nijmegen and exploit the breakthrough which he thought had been made. For these columns there was only one road, parts of it already two feet under water and the remainder jammed with tanks and transport which could not move off into the drenched fields. This order was a serious mistake, as Horrocks soon realised, for the Scottish division still had strength in hand (one of its brigades had not even been committed) and there was no room to deploy a fresh division. In attempting to pass the mobile columns through in darkness and rain, units of the two divisions became inextricably entangled. Congestion on the road and wreckage in Cleve caused such delay and confusion that the Germans were able to strengthen the garrison before the attacking troops could force a passage through the town or work their way round it. Cleve was not cleared until February 11th, nor the Reichswald until the 13th, and by this time the Germans had brought in two armoured and two parachute divisions to frustrate the break-out.

The German command was able to concentrate heavily against the attack from the Reichswald, because for the moment it had no fear of an assault by the Americans across the Roer River. In the hope of catching the enemy with his reserves on the move northward, Montgomery had intended that Ninth Army's offensive (Operation GRENADE) should begin on February 10th, forty-eight hours after the start of VERITABLE. On the 9th, however, as the Americans reached the last of the Roer dams, the Germans destroyed the discharge valves and thus ensured that the river would remain in flood for two more weeks. GRENADE was postponed, but the Americans now had the consolation of knowing that once the river had subsided the enemy could never again hold them in check on the Roer by the threat of flooding.

Since this was so, the prevailing opinion at SHAEF and other Allied H.Q. was that the Germans would withdraw behind the Rhine in good time and good order so that they could make the most of this formidable water barrier. In deciding to stand and fight west of the Rhine, the enemy was guilty, so Montgomery thought, of a " major blunder." For von Rundstedt, however, such a withdrawal was ruled out at this stage, not merely because of Hitler's insistence that every yard of German soil must be defended, but also because the Rhine waterway was the vital link between the Ruhr and the war industries of the rest of Germany.

The Siegfried Line, the Roer and the Maas provided an alternative to the Rhine as a defensive position, but there was no alternative to the Rhine as a supply route, in view of the state of the railways, nor to the Ruhr as a source of coal and processed steel, now that Upper Silesia was as good as gone. Thus did the Russian advance in the East and the Anglo-American bombing of the Reich itself determine Hitler's strategy in the West. It was the necessity of keeping the Rhine open which led the Wehrmacht to present such fierce and sustained opposition to the Reichswald attack.

Obliged to continue the battle alone for another fortnight, the British and Canadians gained ground slowly and became involved in a grim and gruelling struggle. As in Normandy, however, this bitter containing action was not in vain. While the First and Ninth American Armies were compelled to stand impatient behind the swollen Roer, nine German divisions were drawn into battle on a front which had been held by one. In this fortnight First Canadian Army absorbed the reserves which von Rundstedt had been endeavouring to build up in the Cologne Plain.[1]

Before dawn on February 23rd four divisions of Ninth Army and two of First Army began crossing the Roer. Since the flood had not yet fully subsided, they gained a measure of surprise by attacking while the Germans still laboured under a false sense of security. On the first day Simpson's four divisions lost fewer than a hundred men killed. By the evening of the second day his engineers had built nineteen bridges, seven of them fit for tanks. Rapid build-up enabled Simpson to maintain intensive pressure and on the last day of February his armour broke away. Two days later his right wing reached the Rhine south of Düsseldorf and on March 3rd his left made contact with the Canadian Army north of Venlo.

Fifteen German divisions were now caught in a vice and threatened with destruction west of the Rhine, unless they were promptly extricated. This Hitler forbade. He gave categorical orders that not a man, not a gun, was to be evacuated across the river without his permission. A bridgehead was to be held ' at all costs ' between Krefeld and Wesel to safeguard the continued movement of coal and steel from Duisburg to the Dortmund–Ems Canal and thence into Central Germany. Nor would the Führer permit any yielding in the Eifel or the Saar. When von Rundstedt tentatively suggested such a policy—in the hope of preserving his armies intact for the defence of the Rhine—Hitler told Jodl, " I want him to hang on to the West Wall as long as is humanly possible," since withdrawal would " merely mean moving the catastrophe from one place to another."[2] On the other hand, while every foothold

[1] The value of the battle in the north is apparent from the fact that in the clearing of the Lower Rhineland the Canadian and British casualties were more than double those suffered by the Americans: 15,634 compared with 7,478. The enemy losses cannot have been far short of 75,000, since 53,000 Germans were taken prisoner between February 8th and March 10th.

[2] Führer Conferences, Fragment 1. The exact date of this fragment is not known, but it is evident that the conference it records took place before March 6th, 1945.

west of the river was to be maintained till the last moment, if any bridge were to fall into Allied hands, the commander responsible would be shot. In the attempt to reconcile these conflicting orders there lay the possibility of disaster.

Opposite Düsseldorf on the night of March 2nd–3rd an American column, its tanks camouflaged to make them appear German, slipped through the disintegrating enemy lines and penetrated ten miles. Dawn found them in sight of the Rhine at Obercassel but it destroyed their disguise. The alarm was given, the town siren sounded and, as the tanks tried to rush the bridge, it crumpled into the water. A few hours later, at Uerdingen, another column was similarly frustrated, but this time the Germans were so late in acting that the American tanks were on the bridge before the charges were fired. Hitler was taking a grave risk.

While Montgomery was crushing the last resistance in the Lower Rhineland and securing the spring-board for his crossing north of the Ruhr, Bradley's attack gathered pace and power. On March 5th the northern corps of First Army reached Cologne and looked out across a bridgeless river. On the same day the rest of First Army wheeled south-east to strike into the flank and rear of the Germans in the Eifel, while Third Army fell upon them with a frontal attack. Under this combined assault the enemy defences collapsed. Patton's armour cut through the southern slopes of the Eifel, covering 56 miles in three days to reach the Rhine near its confluence with the Moselle. By this time (March 7th) a dozen bridges between Coblenz and Duisburg had gone crashing into the river and every attempt to seize a crossing by *coup de main* had been foiled.

That day, some twenty-five miles downstream, the 9th U.S. Armoured Division—one of the formations the Germans claimed to have destroyed in the Ardennes—was leading the advance of First Army along the northern edge of the Eifel. In its path lay the Rhine town of Remagen. The villages through which it passed were draped with white flags and the only forces it encountered were troops in flight from the all but encircled uplands of the Eifel. It was early afternoon when the leading Americans reached the last ridge above Remagen and saw to their amazement that the Ludendorff railway bridge was still intact. A motorised platoon raced down the hill and into a town crowded with stragglers. At a quarter past three a prisoner reported that the bridge was to be blown at four. At ten minutes to four the Americans reached the waterfront and dashed for the western end. While engineers cut every demolition cable they could see, infantry raced on across the standing span. One small charge went off and then a second. The bridge shuddered, but the detonator of the main charge failed to fire and, before another could be set, the defenders had been overpowered. Reinforcements poured across, cleared a shallow bridgehead and scaled the heights beyond to silence the flak defences. Before dark the line of the

Rhine was inviolate no longer. The Americans had breached the last barrier in the West.

Several hours later at his Tactical H.Q. in Namur, Bradley was conferring with Brigadier-General H. R. (' Pinky ') Bull, Eisenhower's Assistant Chief of Staff for Operations. They were discussing what Bradley regarded as a " larcenous proposal " that he should give up three, if not four, divisions to Devers for Seventh Army's attack in the Saar, the next step in Eisenhower's three-phase plan. The telephone rang. It was Hodges, the commander of First Army, announcing the capture of Remagen bridge.

With spontaneous exuberance, Bradley shouted down the phone, " Hot dog, Courtney, this will bust him wide open." Having instructed Hodges to reinforce the bridgehead strongly and at once, Bradley turned to Bull, and said, " There goes your ball game, Pink." While Bull was protesting, " You're not going anywhere down there at Remagen; it just doesn't fit in with the plan," Bradley telephoned to Eisenhower, who promptly replied, " Get across with whatever you need—but make certain you hold that bridgehead."

Next day, however, Bradley was ordered by SHAEF to commit no more than four divisions at Remagen. This order made him apprehensive lest the exploitation of First Army's success might yet be curtailed in the interests of the plan. Twelve American divisions (Ninth Army) had already been given to Montgomery, and another ten were earmarked for operations north of the Ruhr, since Eisenhower had told the Combined Chiefs of Staff that he would commit 35 divisions in the northern drive from the Rhine to the Elbe. Bradley realised that the majority of these additional divisions would have to be provided by him and, as he was already losing troops to Devers, he saw his armies being steadily whittled down. Although he knew Eisenhower planned to take the Ruhr by double envelopment and had tentatively allocated 25 divisions to the southern encircling thrust, Bradley feared that, after the demands of Montgomery and Devers had been met, his armies would not be strong enough to play the major role they deserved.

In accordance with the assurance Bedell Smith had given at Malta, the crossing in the north was to be carried out as soon as Montgomery was ready, and without waiting for the conquest of the entire Rhineland. Bradley knew that Montgomery would be ready on March 24th, and that the northern assault would be made with full benefit of airborne divisions, amphibious tanks, naval landing-craft and strategic bombers. There was no doubt that Montgomery would succeed and the chances were that American reserves would then be committed in exploitation of his success. In Bradley's opinion, this made it all the more important that he should establish further bridgeheads across the Rhine before Montgomery was in a position to call for the extra American divisions

Eisenhower intended to give him. He was afraid that Hodges would not be allowed to exploit the Remagen windfall until Patton had secured crossings in the Mainz–Mannheim area. Bradley revealed his concern to Patton and Hodges at a conference on March 9th. " We all felt," wrote Patton afterwards, " it was essential that the First and Third Armies should get themselves so involved that Montgomery's plan to use most of the divisions on the Western Front, British and American, under his command, for an attack on the Ruhr plains, could not come off and the First and Third Armies be left out on a limb."[1]

The approaches to the Mainz–Mannheim–Karlsruhe sector of the Rhine were guarded by the defences of the Saar and the Palatinate. According to the SHAEF Plan these defences were to be taken by direct assault, the main attack being made by Seventh U.S. Army northward from Alsace, in conjunction with a supporting thrust by one corps of Third Army eastward from Luxemburg. This plan still stood, but Patton's swift advance to the Rhine near Coblenz had uncovered the entire northern flank of the German First Army which was still holding the Siegfried Line on the Saar front and had been forbidden to withdraw. This flank was now protected only by the physical barriers of the River Moselle and the Hunsrück Mountains. Sensing their opportunity, Bradley and Patton decided that Third Army should attack not merely from Luxemburg but also across the Lower Moselle, biting deep into the enemy's communications. The Hunsrück were as rugged as the Eifel and had even fewer good roads, but, if Patton could fling his armour across these forbidding ridges too, he might reach the Rhine between Mainz and Mannheim, and perhaps cross it, before Montgomery could make his assault in the north. In that case, Bradley would be well placed to demand that no more American divisions should be given to Montgomery.

Although he had restrained Bradley from developing the Remagen bridgehead, Eisenhower had begun to doubt the wisdom of placing any more American troops under Montgomery's jurisdiction, for Ninth Army was already growing restive. In his initial planning directive (of January 21st) for the crossing of the Lower Rhine, Montgomery had declared that Dempsey's Second Army would command all the assault forces, including an American corps. On receiving this directive, " Ninth Army," says its historian, " was flabbergasted! The instruction of the Field-Marshal left General Simpson's command with no part to play in the assault."[2]

Ninth Army's indignation was fully warranted, for whatever technical justification there was for Montgomery's plan, the situation hardly required him to insist upon military orthodoxy and to do so was most impolitic. He might argue that to have two armies responsible for operations on a very narrow front was likely to lead to confusion in the early stages of the assault, but this was surely a minor consideration

[1]Patton, op. cit., p. 255.
[2]Conquer, p. 209.

compared with the resentment caused by his excluding the American Command from its place in the battle. Hyper-sensitive since the Ardennes, the Americans not unreasonably interpreted Montgomery's plan as a reflection on the competence of their senior commanders. Even more serious, they considered that Montgomery was attempting to make the Rhine crossing appear to the world as a British operation and thus a British victory. This criticism showed little appreciation of Montgomery's military character. His first inclination always was to pursue what he thought was the right military course without regard for national prestige —American or British. He was too jealous of his personal reputation, too proud a professional, to do otherwise. In a field commander this was a virtue; in an Allied leader, however, it was a serious handicap.

When Simpson protested, Montgomery issued a new directive, but the harm had been done and it was accentuated by a fresh controversy which arose early in March. After Ninth Army had broken through to the Rhine between Düsseldorf and Duisburg, Simpson suggested that he should make an impromptu crossing while the situation was still fluid. Although his troops had not been able to seize a bridge intact, their advance had been so rapid that the Germans had had no time to man the east bank of the river in strength. There is no doubt that Simpson could have crossed with ease between Duisburg and Düsseldorf, but this would have taken him into the middle of the Ruhr and Eisenhower's plan was that Montgomery should avoid becoming involved in this industrial wilderness which could quickly swallow up an entire army. For this reason Montgomery restrained Simpson, but in doing so revealed his failure to appreciate how near collapse the Germans were. Montgomery's insistence on tight control and balance had been invaluable in Normandy and the Ardennes when the enemy was still capable of striking back. Then his inflexible pursuit of his planned purpose had been a source of strength; now it was a weakness. The master of the set-piece assault and the ' tidy battle,' he did not appear to realise that American ' untidiness ' and improvisation, however dangerous when the enemy was strong, could now yield great dividends. An improvised crossing of the Rhine, even in the ' wrong ' place, might disturb his own plans, but it promised to disrupt and confound the enemy's.

The Americans could see no military justification for Montgomery's decision and at various of their H.Q., especially Patton's, it was freely alleged that Simpson had been curbed in order to deprive the U.S. Army of the credit of having crossed the Rhine first. It was argued further that under British command American initiative was unduly fettered. When Ninth Army's frustration was closely followed by First Army's brilliant coup at Remagen, the contrast gave fresh ammunition to Montgomery's critics and an added incentive to Bradley to act boldly and promptly in the Palatinate.

Patton crossed the Lower Moselle south-west of Coblenz on March 14th. Within two days his armoured columns had broken the back of the Hunsrück and had turned the corner of the Rhine into the rolling plain which led to Mainz and Mannheim. There was nothing in his path now except the remnants of one panzer division, for almost the entire First Army was locked in battle with Patch's Seventh Army. On the 19th, having broken a German counter-attack, Patton swept on again under the spur of a further warning from Bradley about the danger of his losing divisions to Montgomery if he did not secure a Rhine bridgehead quickly.[1] That night, with Montgomery due to cross in four days' time, Patton's spearheads were only ten miles from Mainz and only six from Worms. Hard on the heels of his armour came engineers with assault boats and bridging equipment, for Bradley had ordered him to " take the Rhine on the run."

By March 21st, the campaign in the Palatinate was almost over. Third Army had cleared the west bank from Coblenz to Mannheim, and the German divisions which might have fallen back to defend the river had been outflanked and cut off by Patton or overwhelmed by Patch. The rump of Hitler's First Army, driven at last from the Saar, was being crushed in a shrinking bridgehead west of Karlsruhe. Few would get back across the river before Patton was ready to strike again.

During the night of March 22nd–23rd six battalions of the 5th U.S. Infantry Division slipped across the Rhine at Oppenheim, south of Mainz, with little interference from the enemy. Their total casualties were eight men killed and twenty wounded. Having gained complete surprise, Patton asked Bradley to make no immediate announcement, lest the German High Command should be unduly roused. On the evening of the 23rd, however, with his infantry already holding a bridgehead six miles deep and seven miles wide and his armour already moving over on treadway bridges, Patton telephoned to Bradley and said, " I want the world to know Third Army made it before Monty starts across."

Later that night in Berlin the Führer and his staff discussed the new situation created by Patton's unexpected crossing. Hitler declared that he considered " this second bridgehead at Oppenheim as the greatest danger," since this section of the Rhine was virtually unguarded, and he asked, " Is there no panzer brigade or something like that which could be sent there? " One of his adjutants replied: " There are no units available. . . . At Sennelager there are five *Jagdtiger* which will be ready to-day or to-morrow. Everything else is committed . . . nothing more is at hand."[2] These five were destined for Remagen, but Hitler inquired how soon they could be sent to Oppenheim.

Such were the straits to which the once-mighty Wehrmacht had been reduced. The man whose panzer divisions had made Europe and Russia tremble was now obliged to concern himself with the fate of five disabled tank-destroyers in a repair shop at Sennelager.

[1] See Patton, op. cit., p. 264.
[2] Führer Conferences, Fragment 22, March 23rd, 1945. Sennelager was a tank depot east of the Ruhr.

Desperate though he was, Hitler was yet inflexible. No longer able to vent his passion for destruction and revenge on his enemies, he now turned it against his own people. " When he saw himself doomed," says Speer, " he consciously desired to annihilate the German people and to destroy the last foundations of their existence. He no longer knew any moral boundaries. To him the end of his own life meant the end of everything."

On March 18th, having learned that Hitler intended to proclaim a policy of ' Scorched Earth,' Speer risked his life by making an outspoken protest. In a memorandum to the Führer Speer said, " In four to eight weeks the final collapse of the German economy must be expected with certainty. After that collapse, the war cannot be continued even militarily. . . . [Accordingly], we must do everything to maintain, even if only in a most primitive manner, a basis of existence for the nation to the last. . . . We have no right at this stage of the war to carry out demolitions which might affect the life of the nation."[1] Unmoved by this appeal, Hitler issued a decree next day declaring that " the battle should be conducted without consideration for our own population." *Gauleiter* were ordered to destroy " everything . . . which could be of immediate or future use to the enemy for the continuation of the fight," and particularly " all industrial plants, all important electrical facilities, waterworks, gasworks . . . all food and clothing stores . . . all bridges, all railway installations, the postal system . . . also the waterways, all ships, all freight cars and all locomotives." The object was, said Hitler, " the creation of a traffic desert."

When Speer saw this monstrous order, he protested once again, only to be told by Hitler, " If the war is lost, the German nation will also perish. This fate is inevitable. There is no need to take into consideration the basic requirements of the people for continuing even a most primitive existence. . . . Those who will remain after the battle are those who are inferior; for the good will have fallen." Horrified by this brutal declaration of nihilism, Speer went straight to the Ruhr and induced Model and the leading industrialists to ignore Hitler's decree and to defy any Party officials who should endeavour to implement it. Returning to Berlin, Speer persuaded Hitler that this was an edict which not even he could enforce. The orders were modified in a way which allowed Speer to circumvent them, but Hitler's purpose was unchanged, and he was determined to achieve it by keeping the German people at war until the deluge of destruction swept over their homes.

The Germans were not unaware of the awful destiny that was about to overtake them, but, having surrendered to Hitler in the years of triumph, they had long since lost the power to protest. It was too late now to escape the consequences of their having delivered themselves into the hands of a man who was the incarnation of evil. " Helplessness combined with faith," says Speer, " gripped the nation when it saw its

[1] *Nuremberg Trial Proceedings*, Part **xvii**, pp. 34-6.

inexorable fate approaching. A paralysing fear preceded the ' twilight of the gods ' and cast its spell over almost everyone. There was a hopefulness with which many clung to the slightest chance, but also a fatalism and numbness to which many more were driven by the destruction of their cities, by lack of sleep and by fear of their very lives."

The task of averting further disaster in the West now devolved on Field-Marshal Albrecht Kesselring, who had succeeded von Rundstedt as C.-in-C., West, following the fiasco at Remagen. Kesselring was the man who had held the front in Italy so stubbornly and so long, but the new command he inherited on March 10th was already disintegrating. In the next fortnight, containing the Remagen bridgehead alone was to absorb all the reserves he could scrape together and there was nothing he could do to prevent the collapse in the Palatinate. By March 23rd Hitler had lost more than a third of the forces which had been guarding his western frontiers six weeks earlier, for 293,000 men had been taken prisoner and at least another 60,000 had been killed or seriously wounded since the start of the Reichswald offensive.

Eisenhower's three-phase plan for the Battle of the Rhineland had now produced a bountiful reward, as Brooke, its foremost critic, was the first to admit. When it had been won, he said to Eisenhower, " Thank God, Ike, you stuck to your plan. You were completely right and I'm sorry if my fear of dispersed effort added to your burdens."[1] Although Brooke made this generous acknowledgment, the tactical brilliance of Bradley and his field commanders in exploiting the opportunities which Eisenhower's plan had provided, has tended to obscure the fact that this plan was the real blueprint of the victory. Bradley's drive to the Rhine, which had failed in the autumn, succeeded in the spring not only because the enemy was much weaker but also because Eisenhower imposed a discipline which ensured the deliberate timing and concentration which had previously been lacking. In one sense, however, the concentration of Bradley's forces was due to Hitler, for it was the Ardennes offensive which had drawn Patton out of the Saar and had brought the bulk of Third Army north of the Moselle. In February Patton had wanted to go back to the Saar, perhaps because he was reluctant to admit that he could not get through its defences, but, as it turned out, this sector of the Siegfried Line withstood direct assault until it had been outflanked and attacked from the rear.

Although Patton's drive across the Lower Moselle and through the Hunsrück was a tactical improvisation, it was a direct dividend of Eisenhower's strategic plan. By making his initial effort in the north, while the main enemy strength was opposing Bradley in the centre, Eisenhower had caught the Germans off balance and had forced them to engage in what he rightly called " a bitter slugging match " which

[1]Eisenhower, *Crusade*, p. 372.

they could not afford. In the process virtually all the German armour remaining on the Western Front had been drawn into the Lower Rhineland. At the start of the second phase, Bradley's attack in the Eifel, six of von Rundstedt's eight armoured divisions were north of Cologne endeavouring to protect the Ruhr. Having moved their reserves to meet the immediate threat to their right, the Germans had made themselves vulnerable to a devastating blow against their left, such as they had suffered in Normandy. Patton's sweep through the Palatinate was the counterpart of his ' end run ' south of the bocage. Once again the German left flank was broken and turned and, as in France, there were no reserves to restore the line. Similarly the German right flank, firmly hinged on the coast, was still coherent and comparatively strong. The Allied objective now was to break that hinge by forcing the Lower Rhine and to open the way for another and vaster encirclement—this time not of an army, as at Falaise, but of a group of armies; not of a cluster of Normandy villages but of the greatest industrial complex in Europe, the original source of Germany's power to make war.

Montgomery's preparations for the assault across the Lower Rhine were elaborate. His armies were confronted with the greatest water obstacle in Western Europe (the river at Wesel was twice as wide as at Oppenheim) and their crossing was expected to require, as Eisenhower has said, " the largest and most difficult amphibious operation undertaken since the landings on the coast of Normandy." When his plans were laid in January and February Montgomery had to assume that, since this was the last obstacle before the Ruhr, it would be strongly defended and, as late as the first week of March, the unabated violence of the German opposition in the Lower Rhineland led him to believe that his assault might be a costly and difficult undertaking unless it were thoroughly prepared and strongly supported. He had also assumed that, when the Germans saw they were beaten west of the Rhine, they would retire to the east bank and would concentrate their main strength on his front. Accordingly, he had arranged that the Allied Air Forces should carry out a comprehensive programme of interdiction bombing designed to isolate the battlefield and prevent the movement of German reserves into the Westphalian Plain.

This air programme was most thoroughly carried out; too thoroughly, as it happened, for the reserves which might have moved against Montgomery were either committed to contain the Remagen bridgehead or destroyed in the Palatinate. Thus, the forces available to oppose him were very much weaker than had originally been expected. On the 30-mile front between Emmerich and the Ruhr in mid-March there were three parachute and three weak infantry divisions with two exhausted armoured divisions in reserve. In these circumstances, Montgomery might have attacked sooner than he did, but he saw no point in sending his troops across the Rhine until he had brought forward from west of the Meuse sufficient equipment to build the many bridges he would need to maintain a deep and rapid advance into Northern Germany. On his front the Rhine was running a stream five hundred yards wide and, as its flood plain was still sodden from the winter's heavy rain, the task of establishing communications across the river was most formidable. Since he would have to wait for bridges anyway, he preferred to wait west of the Rhine and save unnecessary casualties. He reasoned that, if he were to cross and then pause while the bridging equipment was being brought forward, he would merely give the Germans a chance to recover from the impact of his assault.

By March 23rd, through prodigious efforts on the part of British and American supply troops and engineers, more than 250,000 tons of ammunition, stores and bridging equipment had been transferred to dumps on the west bank of the Rhine. That night, with the weather set fair for an airborne drop next morning, the attack began. It was preceded, in the best Montgomery manner, by a crushing bombardment from 3,300 guns concentrated on a front of 25 miles, and by a heavy air attack on Wesel. Before this bombing a British commando brigade, crossing almost undetected, had infiltrated to the outskirts of that town and, by attacking while the defenders were still dazed, gained possession of most of it during the night. Meanwhile, on either side of Wesel, two British and two American divisions carried out their planned assaults without great difficulty.[1] By dawn the infantry were holding three firm bridge-heads and were moving inland supported by DD tanks which had swum the river. On the British front the only sustained opposition came from a battalion of parachutists in the riverside village of Rees which the Germans succeeded in holding for nearly three days.

On the morning of the 24th the assault was reinforced by two airborne divisions which descended in the enemy's midst, landing within artillery range of the river and thus at one blow both deepening the bridgehead and disrupting the defences. At the end of that day Montgomery's forces were six miles east of the Rhine. During the next forty-eight hours, while engineers were rapidly constructing bridges (there were twelve in operation by the evening of the 26th), the British and American bridge-heads were linked and expanded, and the German armour which attempted to counter-attack was thrown back. Montgomery's main problem now was to establish communications through Wesel which, despite the recent experience at Cleve, had been ' over-bombed.' At Wesel the Americans built two bridges at remarkable speed, but the flow of traffic across them was restricted by rubble and wreckage which had to be cleared with bulldozers, and this process was delayed by snipers who could not easily be winkled out of the ruins.

[1]The assault formations were: *Second Army*—51st Highland Division, 15th Scottish Division, 1st Commando Brigade; *Ninth Army*—30th and 79th Divisions. The airborne attack was made by the 6th British and 17th U.S. Airborne Divisions, under command of XVIII U.S. Airborne Corps. The degree of opposition is apparent from the fact that in the first twenty-four hours Ninth Army's casualties were 41 men killed, 7 missing and 450 wounded.

Montgomery, still inclined to overestimate the enemy's strength, had expected that it might be a fortnight before he could build up sufficient forces to break out, but the construction of bridges proceeded so rapidly and the enemy was so shaken by the power of the assault and so short of reserves that the opportunity developed after only five days. By the evening of March 28th the bridgehead, now 35 miles wide, had been extended to an average depth of 20 miles against weakening opposition. The German cordon was already thin and that night it snapped. During the day American airborne infantry working with a British tank brigade had made a sortie eastwards up the valley of the River Lippe. Meeting little resistance, the column continued its advance after dark and before dawn was 35 miles beyond the Rhine.

The Germans could no longer prevent Montgomery's armies from bursting forth into the Westphalian Plain and his armour would have broken clean away at once, if it had not been for the difficulty of negotiating passages through towns which had been bombed with unnecessary severity. In their enthusiasm to make sure of sealing off the battlefield the Allied Air Forces had put down on most of the interdiction targets three times the tonnage the army had asked for, and by doing so had aided the German rearguards. Yet these could not make any prolonged stand against the 20 divisions, with 1,500 tanks, which Montgomery had assembled east of the Rhine within a week of crossing. On his left the German garrison in Holland was still holding fast and the remnants of First Parachute Army were preparing to fall back from one water-line to the next in order to deny the allies the North German ports and naval bases; on his right Model's Army Group was standing firm in the Ruhr with orders to defend it as a fortress; but in the centre the way was open to the Elbe. Montgomery gave orders, therefore, that, while Crerar's Canadian Army turned north to cut off the Germans in Western Holland and to clear the Frisian coast, Dempsey and Simpson were " to drive hard for the line of the River Elbe so as to gain quick possession of the plains of Northern Germany." In the course of the advance Ninth Army was to seal the northern and eastern exits from the Ruhr and establish contact with First Army which was advancing rapidly from the south to close the trap.

In the third week of March, while Montgomery was preparing to cross the Rhine and Patton was racing through the Palatinate, Eisenhower had decided that the additional American divisions, originally intended for the northern thrust, should remain in the centre. He had also determined that as reserves became available, he would give them to 12th Army Group so that Bradley could rapidly complete the encirclement of the Ruhr and then drive east to meet the Russians. Accordingly, he had authorised Bradley to broaden the Remagen bridgehead and to move all three corps of First Army across the Rhine. By March 24th Hodges was holding the east bank from Bonn almost to Coblenz and had bridged the river in a dozen places. Next morning First Army broke the shackles of containment, striking not north towards the Ruhr as the Germans were expecting, but east along the valley of the River Sieg and south-east towards the Lahn, in order to link up with Third Army which had now extended its initial foothold south of Mainz and was in the process of establishing three more bridgeheads between Mainz and Coblenz. For three days Kesselring succeeded in imposing a measure of delay on the American exploitation, but on March 28th Patton and Hodges, having joined forces near Giessen, cut loose and drove in concert up the Frankfurt–Kassel corridor in a great enveloping sweep which would take them east of the Ruhr.

On the inside of this turning movement Collins's VII Corps which had been heading eastward now wheeled abruptly north into the unprotected rear of the forces which were still clinging to the Rhine between Cologne and Duisberg. That day American armoured columns covered 55 miles in the direction of Paderborn, the cradle of Hitler's panzer divisions. For forty-eight hours the famous training ground became a battlefield, as instructors and specialists, officer cadets and tank trainees put theory into practice, manning the guns and armour they had so often used in exercises. They fought with vigour and determination for the ground they were defending was sacred to the Wehrmacht and vital to Model. On April 1st, however, Paderborn was taken and the envelopment of the Ruhr was completed that afternoon by the junction of First and Ninth Armies at Lippstadt. Model's entire Army Group, nearly a quarter of a million strong, was trapped and with it were another hundred thousand troops of the Reich Flak Command.

The armament factories and oil plants within this huge pocket should have been more than capable of nourishing Model's forces, but the industry and transport of the Ruhr had been so dislocated by Allied bombing that the fuel and ammunition Model needed could not be produced. Because of this, he could neither fight his way out nor conduct a harassing campaign against Allied communications. He could not even maintain the Ruhr as a fortress. Under pressure the garrison gradually disintegrated, since the German troops were reluctant to prolong a battle which could only result in inflicting unnecessary hardship and destruction on the people of the Ruhr who had already borne so much. Model kept resistance alive for eighteen days, but, when the last opposition had been overcome, he committed suicide rather than join the 325,000 of his men who passed into Allied hands as prisoners of war in a capitulation greater than that of Stalingrad.

The mopping up of the Ruhr absorbed 18 American divisions, but it did not prevent the rest of Eisenhower's forces continuing without pause their drive for the Elbe. The Western Front was now wide open, for the encirclement of Model's armies had created a 200-mile breach which Kesselring had no chance of closing. He was able to maintain organised opposition only on the flanks and these were being driven relentlessly back into the southern mountains and the northern ports. Between Eisenhower and Berlin there were no prepared defences, nor any field armies; no physical barriers that could not be quickly broken, nor any resistance that could not be brusquely swept aside by the 60 divisions available for his next offensive. Moreover, those logistic difficulties, which had limited his progress through France and the Low Countries in the previous year, would not curtail to any appreciable degree his advance through Germany. There were huge stocks of petrol and stores well forward on the Rhine, and ample transport to move them eastward in the wake of his armies. Allied aircraft could deliver 2,000 tons of supplies a day to airfields east of the Rhine and within a week Allied trains would be crossing that river on a newly-built railway bridge at Wesel. Eisenhower's administrative resources were more than adequate to carry his armies to Berlin in irresistible strength.

Politically, too, the way was clear for, though the German capital lay in the centre of the area which was to be occupied by the Soviet Union after the war, it had never been suggested that the military forces of one power should not enter the occupation zone of another in pursuit of the common enemy. Nor was there any agreement that Berlin was to be captured by the Red Army. At Yalta this question had not even been discussed, perhaps because in the military circumstances then prevailing it had seemed academic.

Since Yalta the strategic situation on the two main battlefronts had been reversed. While the German armies in the West were being over-whelmed, those in the East had succeeded in setting up a new defence line along the Oder and its tributary, the Neisse. Here between the Baltic and the mountainous northern border of Czechoslovakia the Germans were standing fast on a comparatively narrow front which the Russians could not assault until they had established communications through devastated Poland. Similarly, on the southern sector of the Eastern Front the Germans had maintained a stable line in Hungary and, by holding the Bratislava Gap, were still blocking the only easy approach to Vienna. Thus, it was now by no means militarily impossible that Eisenhower's armies might reach Berlin and Prague, though hardly Vienna, before the Russians could breach the new front which the Germans were defending with a tenacity born of fear and desperation.

If military opportunity favoured a drive to Berlin from the West, political necessity made it most desirable that the American and British forces should advance as far as possible into Central Europe. Since the Yalta Conference a sinister trend had appeared in Soviet policy and behaviour, giving the Western Powers good cause to consider that Stalin was violating, or at least disregarding, the promises he had then made.

Following the imposition of Communist rule upon Rumania, it had become apparent that the Russians intended to dictate the composition of the Polish Government also. They had agreed at Yalta that the

Lublin Administration was to be " reorganised on a broader democratic basis " and that, in the formation of the new " Polish Provisional Government of National Unity," Molotov, Averell Harriman and Sir Archibald Clark Kerr (the British Ambassador in Moscow) should act as a commission of referees and should consult leading members of all democratic parties. On March 2nd, however, Harriman had reported to Roosevelt that Molotov was again insisting that the Lublin Committee should be merely enlarged, that the referees should not consult any Poles who were unacceptable to that committee and, in particular, that they should not invite Mikolajczyk, the outstanding moderate among the London Poles and one of the men most strongly commended to Stalin by the President and the Prime Minister. The Russian concept of the character of the new government was evident, Harriman indicated, from the fact that Molotov was prepared to accept only one of the London Poles proposed by the Western ambassadors. Since Molotov was quite adamant on these issues, the Moscow negotiations soon reached a deadlock.

At the end of March, therefore, when Churchill urged Roosevelt to make a direct appeal to Stalin, the President replied that he was " acutely aware of the dangers inherent in the present course of events," and would intervene. On April 1st, he sent Stalin a message in which he declared, " I cannot conceal the concern with which I view the lack of progress made in the carrying out . . . of the political decisions which we reached at Yalta, particularly those relating to the Polish question."[1] He challenged the interpretation Molotov had placed on the Protocol, and added that " any such solution which would result in a thinly disguised continuation of the present government would be entirely unacceptable and would cause our people to regard the Yalta Agreement as a failure."

Even this personal approach did not end the impasse; nor did it ease the tension created by other indications of Russia's determination to go her own way without regard to the undertakings she had given at Yalta. There the Soviet Union had made a detailed agreement giving Anglo-American missions the same rights of access to prisoner-of-war camps in Eastern Europe and the same facilities for the rescue and repatriation of liberated prisoners that had already been freely granted to Russian representatives in the West. This agreement had not been honoured. Only one American mission had been allowed to enter Poland, and it had not been permitted to visit any camp, to bring in medical aid and food supplies, or to use American aircraft to evacuate the sick, although all these points had been specifically agreed at Yalta. Notwithstanding a personal protest from Roosevelt to Stalin on March 18th, no other Allied officials were given permission to go farther west than

---

[1]The more important parts of this message, paraphrased for security reasons, is published in Byrnes, op. cit., p. 54. The paraphrasing in this and other telegrams quoted later involves only slight verbal changes.

Odessa and many hundreds of the American and British ex-prisoners who eventually reached there had to make their way on foot.

At Yalta, Stalin had personally promised Roosevelt that the United States could use certain airfields near Budapest, but, after American officers had made a survey, further facilities were refused. There was similar frustration with regard to the preparation of American bases in Russia's Maritime Provinces. Stalin had agreed that there should be " joint planning " on this and other operational problems associated with the Soviet Union's entry into the Far Eastern war, but early in March the American Military Mission in Moscow reported to Washington that this planning was " making no progress whatever."

There was no greater degree of co-operation in the advancement of the project which Roosevelt regarded as the most important achievement of the Yalta meeting—Stalin's assurance that the Soviet Union would play a leading role in the foundation of the world security organisation. In mid-March, Roosevelt learned that the Soviet delegation to the United Nations Conference in San Francisco in April would not be led by Molotov. On the 24th, in a cable to Stalin, Roosevelt expressed his profound disappointment at this decision, and said, " I am afraid Mr. Molotov's absence will be construed all over the world as a lack of comparable interest on the part of the Soviet Government in the great objectives of this conference." Once again, however, Stalin refused to be co-operative, and it now seemed to some members of Roosevelt's cabinet, such as Henry Stimson, that there had emerged in Russia " a spirit which bodes evil in the coming difficulties of the post-war scene."[1]

The difficulty of dealing with the Russians, now that they were no longer dependent on material aid from the West, became particularly apparent in the course of discussions about the independent surrender of the German armies in Italy. On March 10th, Alexander, who had succeeded Wilson as Supreme Commander in the Mediterranean, reported to the Combined Chiefs of Staff that General Karl Wolff, the Head of the SS in Italy, was ready to meet Allied representatives in Switzerland and to discuss the cessation of hostilities on the Italian front. Alexander asked for authority to send two staff officers (one British and one American) to meet Wolff in Berne and bring him to Allied H.Q. at Caserta for detailed negotiations. The American Chiefs of Staff were ready to agree at once but, on Churchill's suggestion, it was decided that no move should be made until the Russians had been consulted. Accordingly, Harriman was instructed to advise Molotov, who replied that the Soviet Government would have no objection to the proposed meeting at Berne, provided that three Russian officers could participate. This request raised an awkward problem for, if any Russians, let alone

[1]This comment was made by Stimson in his diary on March 17th, 1945, and is quoted by him in his Memoirs at p. 607. In response to a renewed request from President Truman after Roosevelt's death Stalin eventually agreed that Molotov should go to San Francisco.

three, were to go to Berne, it would be difficult to maintain security and the Germans might refuse to proceed with the discussions. In reply, therefore, the State Department pointed out that the meeting at Berne was merely for the purpose of arranging for German delegates to come to Alexander's H.Q., that all negotiations would take place there, and that Soviet representatives would be welcome at Caserta as observers.

This message produced a sharp rejoinder from Molotov. He declared that the American refusal to allow the Soviet representatives to go to Berne was "utterly unexpected and incomprehensible," and he added, "the Soviet Government insists that the negotiations already begun in Berne be broken off."[1] The asperity of this answer was no surprise to Harriman. Since Yalta he had found the Russians increasingly intractable and overbearing, and he now reported to Washington: "The arrogant language of Molotov's letter, I believe, brings out in the open a domineering attitude towards the United States which we have before only suspected. It has been my feeling that sooner or later this attitude would create a situation which would be intolerable to us."

Such a situation was fast arising, but Harriman was ordered to assure Molotov that, while contact had been established with Wolff in Switzerland, no 'negotiations' had taken place and that Wolff had refused to come to Caserta until he had consulted Kesselring who had just been transferred from Italy to the Western Front. This assurance drew from Molotov the direct accusation that the United States and Britain were "carrying on negotiations . . . behind the back of the Soviet Government."

On March 24th, the President, alarmed at the mounting tension, sent a firm but friendly cable to Stalin. In this Roosevelt said that, if there was a "possibility of forcing the surrender of enemy troops," it would be "completely unreasonable" for him "to permit any delay which might cause additional and avoidable loss of life in the American forces." Accordingly, he could "not agree to suspend investigations of the possibility" of such a local capitulation, since it involved "no political implications and no violation of our agreed principles of unconditional surrender."

When Stalin replied with an allegation that under cover of Allied negotiations the Germans had transferred three divisions from Italy to the East, Roosevelt pointed out that this transfer had begun weeks before any contact had been established with Wolff. The President gave his word that no negotiations for surrender had taken place at all, but Soviet suspicions were not to be allayed. In his next cable Stalin bluntly declared:

My military colleagues . . . do not have any doubts that the

---

[1] Since the original texts of the messages which passed between Washington and Moscow cannot be revealed without compromising codes, I have drawn on the paraphrased texts which Admiral Leahy quotes. (See Leahy, op. cit., pp. 386-93.)

negotiations have taken place and have ended in an agreement with the Germans on the basis of which the German commander on the Western Front—Marshal Kesselring—has agreed to open the front and permit the Anglo-American troops to advance to the east, and the Anglo-Americans have promised in return to ease for the Germans the peace terms. I think my colleagues are close to the truth. . . . As a result of this agreement, at the present moment the Germans on the Western Front in fact have ceased the war against England and the United States. At the same time, the Germans continue the war with Russia, the ally of England and the United States.

This cable amounted to an accusation of treachery, since it implied that the Western Powers were making a separate peace with Hitler. That this charge should have been levelled at Roosevelt of all men must have been most galling. The maintenance of Allied unity in war and peace had been the very cornerstone of his foreign policy. It was he who had nailed the United Nations flag to the mast by issuing the demand for ' Unconditional Surrender,' and who at Teheran and Yalta had laboured most earnestly to win Stalin's trust and friendship. On April 4th, although anxious as ever to preserve Allied unity, Roosevelt sent to Moscow a forthright denial of Stalin's charges, and declared, " Frankly, I cannot avoid a feeling of bitter resentment toward your informers, whoever they are, for such vile misrepresentations of my actions or those of my trusted subordinates."

The President's strong reply was fully endorsed by Churchill who dispatched his own protest to Stalin and cabled to Roosevelt:

I deem it of the highest importance that a firm and blunt stand should be made at this juncture by our two countries in order that the air may be cleared and they [the Russians] realise that there is a point beyond which we will not tolerate insult. I believe this is the best chance of saving the future. If they are convinced that we are afraid of them and can be bullied into submission, then indeed I should despair of the future relations with them and much else.

Before the end of March the Yalta Agreement had been broken or disregarded by the Russians in every important case which had so far been put to the test of action. It seemed to Churchill, therefore, that the Western Powers, in the formulation of their strategy, should pay more regard to these disturbing political developments, and that the Anglo-American armies should endeavour to advance to Berlin and thus secure a bargaining position from which to insist that the Soviet Union must honour the agreements she had made. He feared that, if they were not to act now, while they had the power and the opportunity, it would be too late.

In the last week of March, when Eisenhower was completing his plans for the final campaign in the West, he was quite unaware of the Soviet intransigence and hostility which were causing such concern in London and Washington. So far as he knew, inter-Allied relations were proceeding on a basis of friendly co-operation and, having received no political directive, he had taken into account nothing but military factors in shaping his strategic design. His sole aim was to encompass the defeat of Germany with the greatest speed and the least loss of life. Although the Wehrmacht had been decisively defeated in the field, a new military consideration now entered his calculations. " After the Ruhr was taken," says Eisenhower's Chief of Staff, " we were convinced there would be no surrender at all so long as Hitler lived. Our feeling then was that we should be forced to destroy the remnants of the German Army piece by piece, with the final possibility of a prolonged campaign in the rugged Alpine area of Western Austria and Southern Bavaria known as the National Redoubt."[1]

There was evidence to support the view that Hitler and the leading Nazis were planning to withdraw to a mountain stronghold around Berchtesgaden for a last, Wagnerian stand. " The main trend of German defence policy," said the SHAEF Intelligence Summary on March 11th, " does seem directed primarily to the safeguarding of the Alpine Zone." What else could explain the stubborn defence of Northern Italy and the dispatch of Sixth SS Panzer Army to the Danube Valley when it was so urgently needed on the Oder? " This area," the Summary continued, " is, by the very nature of the terrain, practically impenetrable. . . . The evidence indicates that considerable numbers of SS and specially chosen units are being systematically withdrawn to Austria . . . and that some of the most important ministries and personalities of the Nazi régime are already established in the Redoubt area."

Eisenhower's Intelligence staff painted a gloomy picture of the course events might take, if Hitler and his more fanatical followers were to entrench themselves in the Alpine fortress. " Here," they said, " defended both by nature and by the most efficient secret weapons yet invented, the powers that have hitherto guided Germany will survive to reorganise her resurrection; here armaments will be manufactured in bomb-proof factories, food and equipment will be stored in vast underground caverns and a specially selected corps of young men will be trained in guerilla warfare, so that a whole underground army can be fitted and directed to liberate Germany from the occupying forces."

In view of this appreciation, Eisenhower concluded that the National Redoubt was now of greater significance than Berlin. " Military factors," he says, " when the enemy was on the brink of final defeat, were more important in my eyes than the political considerations involved in an Allied capture of the capital," since this " no longer represented a

[1] ' Eisenhower's Six Great Decisions,' No. 5, by Lieut.-General Walter Bedell Smith, *Saturday Evening Post*, July 6th, 1946.

military objective of major importance."[1] In any case, as the Russians on the Oder were only 35 miles from the eastern outskirts of Berlin, it seemed almost certain that they would take the city long before the Western Allies could hope to do so.

Eisenhower decided, therefore, that after the neutralisation of the Ruhr, he would concentrate the mass of his forces under Bradley's command in the Kassel region and make a powerful thrust due east through the centre of Germany with the object of splitting the Reich in two and linking up with the Red Army in the Leipzig–Dresden area. This accomplished, he intended to drive his left wing north-east to Hamburg and the Baltic, and his right wing south-east to meet the Russians in the Danube Valley, west of Vienna, and seize the Redoubt before the Nazis could organise it for defence. In deciding to make the main effort with Bradley in the centre, not with Montgomery in the north, Eisenhower was directly influenced by his appraisal of the recent achievements of the two men. " Bradley," he told Butcher, " has never held back and never has ' paused to re-group ' when he saw an opportunity to advance."[2] He believed that Bradley by his brilliant tactical success in the Rhineland had shown himself bolder and more skilful in exploitation than Montgomery, and should therefore regain control of Ninth Army in order to lead the march to victory.

On March 28th, Eisenhower cabled the gist of his plan to Washington, London and Moscow, endorsing the last of these cables " Personal to Marshal Stalin." This plan, and Eisenhower's procedure in communicating it to the Russians before it had been endorsed by the Combined Chiefs of Staff, brought an immediate and emphatic protest from the Prime Minister. Eisenhower was taken aback by the vehemence of Churchill's reaction, for he considered that his message to Moscow was " a purely military move," covered by the instructions he had received from the Combined Chiefs of Staff after Yalta. He had then been authorised to communicate with the Soviet High Command on " matters exclusively military in character " in order to achieve " co-ordination of tactical operations," and in particular to arrange for the junction of the converging armies. Churchill considered, however, that Eisenhower's cable went far beyond tactical co-ordination, beyond strategy, into grand strategy, into the determination of objectives which were fundamentally political and which would govern the shape of post-war Europe. The Prime Minister, says Eisenhower, " was greatly disappointed and disturbed because my plan did not first throw Montgomery forward with all the strength I could give him from American forces in a desperate attempt to capture Berlin before the Russians."[3]

Making this protest by telephone on the 29th, Churchill stressed the political importance of the capture of Berlin by Allied forces in order

[1]Eisenhower, *Report*, p. 131.
[2]Butcher, op. cit., p. 793.
[3]Eisenhower, *Crusade*, p. 399.

to counter-balance the prestige the Red Army was about to gain by capturing Vienna and overrunning Austria  He pointed out that if the Russians were to secure Berlin as well, this double success would make it appear that the Soviet Union had gained the decisive victory. The Prime Minister implied that this would weaken the influence of the democratic forces in post-war Europe and enhance the power of the Communists. He had no doubt that the Russians fully appreciated the significance of Berlin. This was obvious from the unusual alacrity with which Stalin had approved Eisenhower's plan and had expressed his own willingness to make the main Russian thrust in the direction of Dresden. Churchill was not to be deluded by any assurances from Moscow that Stalin considered Berlin had " lost its political importance."

In communications to both Eisenhower and Marshall, Churchill insisted that the strategic plan approved by the Combined Chiefs of Staff at Malta had provided for the main effort to be made in the North German Plain by Montgomery, and he asked why this had been changed. Eisenhower replied that there had been " no change in basic strategy," and, in a cable to Marshall on March 30th, he justified this assertion by saying, " I have always insisted that the northern attack would be the principal effort in that phase of our operations that involves the isolation of the Ruhr, but from the very beginning, extending back before D-Day my plan . . . has been to link up the primary and secondary efforts in the Kassel area and then make one great thrust to the eastward." He was directing this thrust on the Leipzig–Dresden region because this contained " the greater part of the remaining German industrial capacity " and was the zone " to which the German Ministries are believed to be moving."

Churchill did not challenge these reasons but he considered them irrelevant. The war was won; it was the post-war balance of power that mattered now. Quite apart from the political advantage which the Russians would gain by capturing Berlin, Churchill feared that, if priority were given to Bradley's drive for Dresden, Montgomery would not have the resources to reach the Baltic quickly and thus prevent the Russians from ' liberating ' Denmark, seizing the North German ports and gaining an outlet to the Atlantic.

Under this barrage of arguments Eisenhower stood firm, staunchly supported by superiors and subordinates alike. Bradley advised him that it might cost the Western Allies " 100,000 casualties . . . to break through from the Elbe to Berlin," and this, Bradley thought, was " a pretty stiff price to pay for a prestige objective." Since the German armies in the West had been decisively defeated, this seems to have been an unduly pessimistic appreciation. In Bradley's mind, however, there were other considerations. If the Allies were to drive on to Berlin, this advance would be carried out by Montgomery, who would need Ninth U.S. Army and some extra American divisions as well as his own. In that case Bradley would have to halt Patton in the Leipzig area and would not be able to turn him southward as planned, against the National Redoubt. "We were less concerned," Bradley wrote later, "with post-war political alignments than destruction of what remained of the German Army. . . . As soldiers we looked naïvely on this British inclination to complicate the war with political foresight and non-military objectives."[1]

Bradley's reaction was also that of the American Chiefs of Staff, though they had much better reason to be aware of the magnitude of the issues at stake. They knew how seriously the political outlook had deteriorated since Yalta, and yet on March 31st Marshall advised the British Chiefs of Staff that he and his colleagues fully endorsed both Eisenhower's "strategic concept" and his "procedure in communicating with the Russians." "The battle of Germany," said Marshall, "is now at a point when it is up to the Field Commander to judge the measures which should be taken. . . . *The single objective should be quick and complete victory*."[2] In a later cable, on April 6th, Marshall was more specific, declaring, "Such psychological and political advantages as would result from the possible capture of Berlin ahead of the Russians should not override the imperative military consideration which, in our opinion, is the destruction and dismemberment of the German armed forces."

This declaration strengthened Eisenhower's hand, and on April 7th, in a cable to Marshall, he expressed the view that no drive for the German capital should be made until he had joined forces with the Russians in the centre, had reached the Baltic on the left and overrun the National Redoubt on the right. Nevertheless, Eisenhower went on to say: "I am the first to admit that war is waged in pursuance of political aims, and, if the Combined Chiefs of Staff should decide that the Allied effort to take Berlin outweighs purely military considerations in this theater, I would cheerfully readjust my plans and my thinking so as to carry out such an operation." On the following day, moreover, he told Montgomery, "If I get an opportunity to capture Berlin cheaply, I will take it."

By this time the Allied advance to the Elbe was well under way. Although Simpson and Hodges had detached half their strength to contain and mop up the Ruhr, they had swept unchecked across the Weser, and had drawn level with Patton's forces which had turned east from Kassel while First and Ninth Armies were completing the great encirclement. The American spearheads were now reporting "no opposition more serious than road blocks," and with 27 divisions deployed on a broad front between Hanover and Coburg, Bradley had ample strength for the drive that would divide the Reich.

On the evening of April 11th, after a triumphant advance of 57 miles since dawn, the armoured vanguard of Ninth Army reached the Elbe near Magdeburg and on the following day secured a bridgehead across it.

[1]Bradley, op. cit., pp. 528 and 536.
[2]The substance of this signal was repeated to Eisenhower by Marshall on March 31st. See Eisenhower, *Crusade*, p. 402. (The italics are mine. C. W.)

That night Bradley's troops were only 53 miles from the German capital, and the Elbe was lightly defended. "At that time," says Bradley, "we could probably have pushed on to Berlin had we been willing to take the casualties Berlin would have cost us. Zhukov had not yet crossed the Oder and Berlin now lay almost midway between our forces."[1]

When they reached the Elbe, the Americans were well inside what was to be the Soviet zone of occupation but there was still no political or military agreement to restrain them from advancing farther. No ' stop-line ' had yet been discussed with the Russians, and Eisenhower now advised Moscow that he considered " both armies should advance until contact is imminent." These favourable developments led Churchill and his Chiefs of Staff to redouble their efforts to impress upon Marshall the importance of Berlin. The Americans, however, were so alarmed at the danger of prolonged resistance in the National Redoubt that Marshall had even urged Eisenhower to direct the main American offensive on Munich, not Dresden. In any case, he was resolutely opposed to the issuing of any political directive, least of all one requiring Eisenhower to advance to the German capital. Yet it was Marshall himself who only a week earlier had helped to draft the ' vile misrepresentations ' signal which Roosevelt had sent to Stalin.

Since Marshall and his colleagues were quite adamant, Churchill realised that, if Eisenhower's strategic plan was to be changed for political reasons, the decision would have to be made, and made quickly, by the President. But Roosevelt was now tired and ill, for the long and arduous journey to Yalta and the strain of the conference had left him exhausted. At the end of March, on the insistence of his doctors, he had gone to Warm Springs in Georgia to rest and recuperate. There on April 1st he had received a personal message from Churchill about Berlin, but, even if he had been well, the President would have been reluctant to overrule his military advisers on a question about which they felt so strongly. Roosevelt was extremely distressed by the turn which political events had taken, and particularly by the hostile tone of the cables he had been receiving from Moscow with regard to the Polish Government and the German capitulation in Italy. Nevertheless, he was not prepared to make an issue of these controversies, especially as the discussions in Berne had proved abortive. He still hoped that if amity could be preserved until the United Nations Conference in San Francisco, due to begin on April 25th, the differences between the Western Powers and the Soviet Union might be ironed out.

At Warm Springs on the morning of April 12th—the day Ninth Army crossed the Elbe—Roosevelt drafted two cables.[2] The first was to Churchill who had consulted the President about what he should say to the House of Commons about Poland. In this cable Roosevelt said:

[1]Bradley, op. cit., p. 537.
[2]The paraphrased texts of these two cables are published respectively by Stettinius (op. cit., p. 278) and Leahy (op. cit., p. 393).

I would minimise the general Soviet problem as much as possible because these problems, in one form or another, seem to arise every day and most of them straighten out as in the case of the Berne meeting. We must be firm, however, and our course thus far is correct.

The second cable was to Harriman in Moscow. In this Roosevelt revealed once again his tolerance and his faith that he could carry into the peace the ' Great Power unity ' which, under his leadership, had brought them to the point of victory. To Harriman, Roosevelt said:

It is my desire to consider the Berne misunderstanding a minor incident.

This was the last message that came from Franklin Roosevelt's hand. An hour later, as he was sitting for an artist who was painting his portrait, he fainted in his chair. That afternoon he died.

On April 14th, two days after Roosevelt's death, Eisenhower reported to the Combined Chiefs of Staff, " The essence of my plan is to stop on the Elbe and clean up my flanks," explaining, in another signal next day, that this was necessary for logistic reasons. " While it is true," said Eisenhower, " that we have seized a small bridgehead over the Elbe, it must be remembered that only our spearheads are up to the river; our centre of gravity is well back of there." That same day, however, Simpson advised Bradley that he had the supply resources to go on to Berlin and could do so if he were given adequate reinforcement. Although three hastily-improvised German divisions had appeared on his front and had forced Ninth Army to give up one of its crossings, another bridgehead was being steadily expanded and Simpson believed he would soon be ready to break out.

The logistic difficulties, of which Eisenhower had spoken to Washington, were very largely of his own creation. He had proclaimed his intention of making a single major thrust, but once again he had allowed his armies to sprawl forward and had dissipated his strength. Bradley's forces were now spread out on a front 250 miles wide and, even if he had wanted to do so, he had lost the capacity to concentrate quickly the additional forces Simpson needed. Of the American divisions which had advanced eastward from the Rhine, only eight were deployed north of the Harz Mountains on the direct road to Berlin. South of these mountains, where an isolated German garrison was still standing fast, there were, counting Seventh Army, thirty-one American divisions and the majority of these were already swinging away south-east towards the Danube Valley and the National Redoubt. The striking power and the logistic capacity for a further substantial advance were available, but to Churchill and Brooke it seemed that they were in the wrong place and heading in the wrong direction.

In his signal to the Combined Chiefs of Staff announcing his intention to stop on the Elbe, except in the north where Montgomery was to advance to the Baltic, Eisenhower said, " If you agree, I propose to inform Marshal Stalin." The British did not agree but, since Roosevelt had rejected the argument that it was politically desirable for the Western Allies to reach Berlin before the Russians, there was no point in Churchill's reopening this question with the new President, Harry S. Truman. Precipitated into office by Roosevelt's tragic death, Truman could hardly be expected to reverse a policy which his illustrious predecessor had so recently endorsed and which his Chiefs of Staff still advocated. Accordingly, the Prime Minister adopted what was essentially an economic approach. It had become apparent since Yalta that the Russians intended to treat their occupation zone as a close preserve and that, as this zone included the most important food-producing areas of the Reich, Western Germany would be seriously short of food in the immediate post-war period unless the Russians would agree to the free movement of supplies across the zonal boundaries. On April 17th, therefore, Churchill suggested to Truman that Eisenhower's armies should continue advancing, if not to Berlin, at least as deep as possible into the Soviet zone and should not withdraw unless Stalin would agree to the pooling of all German food resources. Churchill foresaw that, if this were not done, the United States and Britain would have to undertake the heavy and unwelcome burden of saving the people of Western Germany from starvation.

In reply to this suggestion Truman took the stand that the Allies must fulfil their commitments despite the Soviet breaches of faith. " Our State Department," he said in a cable on April 21st, " believes that every effort should be made through the Allied Control Commission to obtain a fair interzonal distribution of food produced in Germany, but does not believe that the matter of retirement of our respective troops to our zonal frontiers should be used for such bargaining purposes." Upholding the Roosevelt-Marshall principle that strategy should be determined without regard to post-war political considerations, Truman said, " The question of tactical deployment of American troops in Germany is a military one. It is my belief that General Eisenhower should be given certain latitude and discretion."[1]

During this exchange of cables between Washington and London events on the Eastern Front had taken a new and dramatic turn. On April 16th the Russians had broken the German line on the Oder and the Neisse, and within five days Zhukov had reached the eastern outskirts of Berlin and Konev was approaching Dresden. These developments strengthened Eisenhower's determination not to advance any farther

[1]The text of this cable is published by Leahy (op. cit., p. 410).

This map shows the Russian and Anglo-American front-lines on April 16th, 1945. At this time the Red Army had not yet entered what was to be the Soviet Zone of Occupation; the Americans, on the other hand, were more than 100 miles inside that Zone.

### BERLIN : THE PRIZE

eastward. He had always been very much concerned about the danger that his armies might come into accidental conflict with the Russians, unless the converging forces could make their junction at a clearly defined geographical feature. The Elbe provided a natural meeting place and there was no other suitable line of demarcation east of that river.

On April 21st, therefore, in exercise of the discretion Truman had given him, Eisenhower advised the Soviet High Command that, apart from advancing to the Baltic near Lübeck, he was halting his armies on the general line of the Elbe, its tributary, the Mulde, and the mountainous western frontier of Czechoslovakia. He was halting, he said, " for logistic reasons," but it was not on this account nor through fear of clashing with the Red Army, that he was giving up the opportunity of liberating Prague. Although Patton had already reached the Czech frontier, Eisenhower's plan provided that Third Army should now strike south-east parallel with the border, advancing astride the Danube with Seventh U.S. Army on its flank and the National Redoubt as their common objective.

Next day Patton and Patch set forth on what proved to be a wild-goose chase.[1] Neither the Party nor the Wehrmacht had made any preparations for prolonged resistance in the so-called Alpine Fortress, and such plans as they had fashioned had been frustrated by the speed of the American advance to the Elbe and the Bohmerwald. The National Redoubt was a phantom. It was not here that Hitler would make his last stand.

In Berlin one evening early in April, Goebbels endeavoured to solace and encourage his Führer by reading aloud from their favourite book, Carlyle's *History of Frederick the Great*. The chapter he chose was one that Hitler never tired of hearing, or of commending to his entourage, for it told how in the bleakest hour of the Seven Years' War the King had decided that, if there was no change in his fortunes by February 15th, he would end his life by taking poison, and how on February 12th the Czarina had died, and by her death had brought about the Miracle of the House of Brandenburg. When they reached this point in the story, so Goebbels said later, " Tears stood in the Führer's eyes."

Recounting this incident to Schwerin von Krosigk, the Reich Minister of Finance, Goebbels revealed that, after he had finished reading to Hitler, they had sent for two horoscopes which Himmler had faithfully preserved: the Führer's, drawn up in 1933 on the day he became Chancellor, and that of the Republic, dated September 9th, 1918. " Both horoscopes," wrote Schwerin von Krosigk in his diary, " had agreed in predicting the outbreak of war in 1939, the victories till 1941, and then the series of defeats culminating in the worst disasters in the early months of 1945, especially the first half of April. Then there was to be an overwhelming victory for us in the second half of April, stagnation till August and in August peace. After the peace there would be a difficult time for Germany for three years; but from 1948 she would rise again to greatness."[2]

[1]Bradley says (op. cit., p. 536), " Not until after the campaign ended were we to learn that this Redoubt existed largely in the imaginations of a few fanatic Nazis. It grew into so exaggerated a scheme that I am astonished that we could have believed it as innocently as we did. But while it persisted, this legend of the Redoubt was too ominous a threat to ignore and in consequence it shaped our tactical thinking during the closing weeks of the war."

[2]Schwerin von Krosigk's Diary has not been published, but extracts from it are published by H. R. Trevor-Roper in his book, *The Last Days of Hitler*.

The confidence inspired by this astrological prediction led Goebbels, on April 6th, to issue to all German troops an appeal in which he said: " The Führer has declared to us that even in this very year a change of fortune shall come. And it will come even though we have to wait months for it. . . . The true quality of genius is its consciousness and its sure knowledge of coming change. The Führer knows the exact hour of its arrival. Destiny has sent us this man so that we, in this time of great external and internal distress, shall testify to the miracle. There is no solution except Adolf Hitler."

A week later, on the night of April 12th–13th, the R.A.F. raided Berlin, driving the presiding genius of the Reich to seek shelter in the *Führerbunker*. That night the Chancellery itself was hit and set ablaze, but about midnight, as the ' All Clear ' was sounding, the news arrived of the death of President Roosevelt. Half an hour later, Goebbels, who had just returned from a visit to the Eastern Front, telephoned to Hitler and said, " My Führer, I congratulate you. Fate has laid low your greatest enemy. God has not abandoned us. Death, which the enemy aimed at you in 1939 and 1944, has now struck down our most dangerous adversary. A miracle has happened." Hitler's reply is not recorded, but, when Goebbels put down the telephone, he turned in ecstasy to his staff and said, " This is the turning point. This is like the death of the Czarina in the Seven Years' War."[1]

Carried away by revived faith in his horoscope, Hitler was more than ever convinced that the Allied coalition was about to collapse. Several days earlier Kesselring had sent to the Führer's H.Q. a captured copy of the Allied plan for the occupation of the Reich. From this document Hitler had learned the layout of the occupation zones, as confirmed at Yalta, and in particular that the Soviet sphere was to extend west of the Elbe almost as far as Brunswick and Kassel. Encouraged by this knowledge, he had watched with relish the advance of the Americans to the Elbe, for this carried them into what was to be Soviet territory. On April 10th, he had decided that, if the Reich should be split in two, the Wehrmacht would continue the fight in the north under Doenitz and in the south under Kesselring. The troops of these two commands would, in effect, draw back and leave the way clear for the Russians and the Western Powers to meet head on, and, so Hitler hoped, squabble about their zones of occupation. In this he saw the possibility of a conflict which might yet disrupt the Grand Alliance.

This was the delusion of a desperate man in the final stages of physical and mental decline. Hitler had survived the strain of the last three months only by the force of his will and the almost hypnotic influence he exercised over those who were working closely with him. Without exception his associates speak of the power of fascination and compulsion which lay in his dull, blue-grey eyes, and made strong men amenable to

[1] This account is drawn from Semmler (op. cit., pp. 191-2) who was present and Trevor-Roper (op. cit., p. 110) who quotes the testimony of one of Goebbels's secretaries.

his whim. Yet to those who came into contact with him only casually at this time, he presented a pitiful figure. Such a one was Captain Gerhard Boldt, Guderian's adjutant, who had first met Hitler in February. Describing his presentation to the Führer on this occasion, Boldt says, " Guderian beckons and I approach Hitler. Slowly, heavily stooping, he takes a few shuffling steps in my direction. He extends his right hand and looks at me with a strangely penetrating look. His handshake is weak and soft. . . . His head wobbles slightly. . . . His left arm hangs slackly and his hand trembles a good deal. There is an indescribable, flickering glow in his eyes, creating a fearsome and totally unnatural effect. His face and the parts around his eyes give the impression of total exhaustion. All his movements are those of a senile man." In April, Boldt noted a further decline: " Now not only his body but also his brain showed more and more traces of complete disintegration. The wobbling of his head and the trembling of his left hand increased. He became hesitant and undecided."[1] Hitler now alternated between optimism and despair, between lethargy and frenzy, but whatever his mood or his behaviour he retained the capacity to command obedience.

On April 20th, the Führer's fifty-sixth birthday, the faithful and the self-seeking came to the bunker to pay their respects, and were assured that the Russians would suffer " their bloodiest defeat of all before Berlin." Next day, when it became apparent that the eastern and western allies were likely to make their first junction in the Dresden area, Hitler ordered the German forces on both sides of the Elbe between Dresden and Dessau to withdraw towards Berlin and thus accelerate the expected Soviet-American clash. On the 22nd, however, when Russian shells began falling in the Chancellery garden, he was again plunged in despair. A counter-attack he had ordered south of the capital had failed, and the Red Army had broken into the northern suburbs. He proclaimed that, since the Army and the Luftwaffe, the SS and the Party had all failed and betrayed him, he would not go to Berchtesgaden, as planned, but would stay in Berlin and direct its defence in person. Only thus could the capital be saved and if this failed, he would shoot himself.

" We all attempted to dissuade him," said Jodl to Koller, the Chief of the Air Staff, after the conference. " We even proposed bringing troops from the West to fight in the East. The Führer's answer to this was that everything was falling apart now, anyway, and he was no longer able to continue; that should be left to the Reichsmarschall. In answer to a remark that the troops would not fight for the Reichsmarschall, the Führer said, ' What do you mean, fight? There's not much more fighting to be done and, when it comes to negotiating, the Reichsmarschall can do better than I can.' "[2]

Next day Berlin Radio announced that Hitler and Goebbels were remaining in Berlin and would defend the capital to the last. This

[1]*Die Letzten Tage*, by Gerhard Boldt, pp. 15 and 37.
[2]Koller's Journal, April 16th–May 8th, 1945.

NORWAY

SWEDEN

NORTH SEA

BALTIC SEA

Courland

Memel

Königsberg

E. PRUSSIA

Danzig

DENMARK

Flensburg

Kiel

Rostock

Hamburg

Stettin

R. Elbe

Bremen

Hanover

BERLIN

POLAND

WARSAW

R. Vistula

HOLLAND

Wesel

RUHR

Cologne

Kassel

Leipzig

R. Oder

R. Neisse

Breslau

BELGIUM

R. Meuse

R. Rhine

Frankfurt

Cracow

Rheims

R. Moselle

SAAR

Nürnberg

CZECHO

PRAGUE

Pilsen

SLOVAKIA

Strasbourg

Stuttgart

R. Danube

VIENNA

FRANCE

Munich

AUSTRIA

BUDAPEST

HUNGARY

SWITZERLAND

R. Drava

R. Tisza

Geneva

R. Balaton

Milan

Venice

Trieste

Zagreb

R. Rhone

Turin

R. Po

Fiume

R. Sava

BELGRADE

Genoa

Bologna

YUGO-SLAVIA

Marseilles

Florence

ADRIATIC SEA

ITALY

ROME

LEGEND

German Front-Lines
Jan. 12th 1945

German Held Areas
April 28th 1945

Neutral Countries

SCALE OF MILES

0    50   100        200

THE FINAL PHASE

vainglorious gesture was directed at History, as a contribution to the legend of the Führer who sacrificed his empire and himself to save European civilisation from Bolshevism. Unconcerned with legends, most of those who had served him so long had now departed or were about to do so; Goering to Bavaria, Doenitz, Keitel and Jodl, Himmler, Ribbentrop and Speer by various routes to Schleswig-Holstein. There they would await the news of his inevitable end, which alone could release them from the oath that had held them fast for eleven years. By his refusal to leave Berlin for some other base whence he could direct operations and conduct affairs of state, Hitler had virtually abdicated; yet Goering, Doenitz and the rest, with the sole exception of Himmler, still felt themselves beholden to him. If any further evidence were needed of the power he exercised over those who had fallen under his spell, it was provided by the fact that even now, when he was reduced to a trembling spectre, when all hope had gone and only ruin lay ahead, he still retained his authority over them. So long as he lived, they could not assume the sovereignty that was slipping from his feeble hand. He had lost the power of decision but not the power to compel allegiance, isolated though he was in the doomed bunker. Since he would not make decisions, nothing was decided, for they had all become so reliant on him that without his leadership they were incapable of independent action.

Those who had left the bunker were now primarily interested not in the fate of the Führer or the Reich but in the question of succession, for they were so little aware of the realities of the situation that they believed there would be some power to inherit. The chief contestants for the heritage were Goering and Himmler. The Reichsmarschall was the successor-designate, and so, when he learned from Koller what had occurred in the bunker on April 22nd, he dispatched a telegram which began, " My Führer! In view of your decision to remain at your post in the fortress of Berlin, do you agree that I take over at once the total leadership of the Reich with full freedom of action at home and abroad, as your deputy, in accordance with your decree of June 29th, 1941? " Hitler's reaction was to denounce Goering as a traitor and to order his immediate arrest.

There is little doubt that Goering's proposal was made in good faith, and involved no breach of personal loyalty; the same cannot be said of the approach which Himmler made to Count Bernadotte, the Head of the Swedish Red Cross. On April 24th, anticipating Hitler's death and his own succession, the Reichsführer asked Bernadotte to advise the British and American Governments of his readiness to surrender unconditionally in the West while continuing the war in the East. This offer was summarily rejected, and on the 28th Churchill publicly stated, " It must be emphasised that only unconditional surrender to the three major Powers will be entertained and that the closest accord prevails between the three powers."

This announcement and the revelation of Himmler's independent overtures was a double blow to Hitler. Three days earlier the Russian and American armies had met at Torgau on the Elbe, and the first report to reach the *Führerbunker* (from a neutral source) stated, says Boldt, that " the Russians had accused the Americans of infringing in this area the agreements made at Yalta." This was not true but, in his eagerness to clutch at any straw, Hitler declared to those around him, " Here again is striking proof of the disunity of our enemies. Is it not still possible that any day—nay, any hour—war may break out between the Bolsheviks and the Anglo-Saxons over their prey, Germany? "

With Churchill's announcement, however, Hitler learned at last the vanity of this hope, but even more embittering was the realisation that Himmler (' Treuer Heinrich,' as he was fond of calling him) had also betrayed him. This was the final disillusionment; this was the act which determined the succession.

That night Hitler drew up his political testament. He began by disclaiming all responsibility for the war and blaming it " on the ruling political clique in England," the tool of " International Jewry." " Centuries will go by," he said, " but from the ruins of our cities and monuments, hatred of those ultimately responsible will always grow anew. . . . From the sacrifice of our soldiers and from my own comrade-ship with them unto death itself, the seed has been sown which will grow one day in the history of Germany to the glorious rebirth of the National Socialist Movement and thereby to the establishment of a truly united nation." He proclaimed his intention " to remain in Berlin and there to choose death voluntarily at the moment when . . . the residence of the Führer and Chancellor can no longer be held," but he called upon the German people " not to give up the struggle in any circumstances, but to carry it on wherever they may be against the enemies of the Fatherland."

Declaring that Goering and Himmler had " brought irreparable shame on the country and the whole nation by secretly negotiating with the enemy without my knowledge and against my will," Hitler expelled them from the Party and deprived them of all their rights and offices. With the ' traitors ' thus dismissed, Hitler proceeded to name his successor, announcing, " I appoint Grand Admiral Doenitz as President of the Reich and Supreme Commander of the Wehrmacht."

Having made this political decision, Hitler proceeded to another which was essentially personal. Early in the morning of April 29th, in the presence of Goebbels and Bormann, he married Eva Braun, " the woman who [so he said] after many years of true friendship came of her own free will to this city, already almost besieged, to share my fate." For twelve years Eva Braun had occupied a privileged, if undefined, position at his court. There she was the consolation of his leisure hours, sharing his relaxations, such as they were. There is no doubt that they were devoted to each other, for he had once told Speer that Eva Braun was the only friend who would remain faithful to him in his last decisive hour. Now that this was approaching, he was touched by the fidelity which stood in such sharp contrast to the treachery of his most trusted lieutenants, Goering and Himmler. There was little reward he could offer beyond ending the ambiguity of her position and granting her the privilege of sharing, as his wife, his sacrificial death. This intention was frankly proclaimed in his personal will which he dictated to his secretary, Frau Junge, as soon as the marriage ceremony had been performed.[1] It was not incongruous, therefore, that in the prevailing atmosphere of fatalism the wedding breakfast should have been enlivened by a dispassionate discussion of his plans for their suicide.

Thirty-six hours later, on the afternoon of April 30th, when Russian tanks were less than half a mile from the *Führerbunker*, these plans were duly carried out. In accordance with the instructions in Hitler's will, their bodies were burned in the garden of the Chancellery and no trace of them was ever found.

On the night before Hitler's suicide three couriers left the bunker, carrying copies of his personal and political testaments for his successors and for posterity. None of these was delivered and it was only through a telegram from Goebbels on the afternoon of May 1st that Doenitz learned of Hitler's death and his own succession.[2] That night Doenitz broadcast this news to the world and announced that he would " continue to wage war on the British and Americans in so far as and so long as they hinder me in the prosecution of the fight against Bolshevism." He realised that there was no hope of his negotiating a separate peace with the Western Powers alone, but his policy was to maintain the front in the East so that the greatest number of German troops could surrender to Eisenhower's forces and thus avoid passing into the hands of the Russians as prisoners of war.

The process of piecemeal capitulation had begun while Hitler was still alive. The first move was made in Italy, in acknowledgment of the crushing defeat which Alexander had inflicted on the Germans there during April. At Caserta, on the 29th, an armistice was signed by Wolff (the instigator of the ' Berne incident ') now acting as plenipotentiary for the C.-in-C., South-West, von Vietinghoff. Fighting on this front came to an end on May 2nd. Meanwhile, on April 30th, a German emissary had arrived in Stockholm to report that the C.-in-C., North-West (Busch) would surrender the forces in his command, as soon as the British had advanced from the Lower Elbe to the Baltic and thus sealed off Schleswig-Holstein and the Danish Peninsula from Soviet penetration.

[1] In the final paragraph of his personal testament, Hitler declared: " My wife and I choose to die in order to escape the shame of overthrow or capitulation. It is our wish that our bodies be burned immediately in the place where I have performed the greater part of my daily work during the course of my twelve years' service to my people."

[2] After sending this telegram Goebbels took his own life and those of his wife and six of his children. Bormann, the only other important Nazi in the bunker when Hitler died, was probably killed that night trying to escape from Berlin.

This military prerequisite was quickly fulfilled. Montgomery's troops had crossed the Elbe near Lüneburg on April 29th and in the first two days of May, British and American columns drove north to Lübeck and Wismar on the Baltic, forestalling the Red Army by a mere twenty-four hours.

On May 4th at Montgomery's Tactical H.Q. on Lüneburg Heath Admiral von Friedeburg and other representatives of the German High Command signed an armistice providing for the surrender, as from next morning, of all German forces in North-West Germany, Denmark and Holland, and, appropriately, at Dunkirk. This was the decisive act, for within the area covered by this capitulation, the new Führer and the Supreme Command of the Wehrmacht had established their last headquarters in the border town of Flensburg. The general and unconditional surrender of the Third Reich was now imminent, since the succession of Doenitz had provided at one stroke a Supreme Commander to whom the Wehrmacht could transfer its allegiance and a Head of State with whom the Allies could treat.

The remaining question of major significance for post-war Europe was how far the Red Army would be able to advance westward before the end came. On May 2nd the Russians had completed the capture of Berlin, and, as Vienna was already in their possession, Prague, alone of the capitals of Central Europe, had yet to be liberated. In his eagerness to overrun the National Redoubt, Eisenhower had given up the opportunity of advancing into Czechoslovakia and had told the Soviet High Command he would not do so. At the start of May, however, since he had substantial forces standing idle on the Czech border, Eisenhower advised Moscow that he would advance to Prague " if the situation required." There was no danger here of a clash between the American and Russian forces, for the Red Army had no troops within 70 miles of the Czech capital, and was opposed, moreover, by German armies which showed no sign of giving way. Nevertheless, Stalin promptly replied that Eisenhower's forces " should not advance beyond the line Karslbad–Pilsen–Budejovice."[1] There is no doubt that Patton could have reached Prague with ease, but on the evening of May 4th, when Eisenhower authorised Bradley to move into Czechoslovakia, he also ordered him to stop Third Army on the line Stalin had laid down. Next day, as the Americans poured across the border, the Czech Underground rose in revolt against the hated Germans and broadcast from Prague an appeal for Allied aid. In view of his agreement with Stalin, however, Eisenhower felt he could not go to their assistance. The liberation of the Czech capital—and all the political advantage which this was to

---

[1] General Deane, who transmitted Eisenhower's proposal to Antonov, the Red Army Chief of Staff, says that it produced " a violent protest. . . The fine hand of the Soviet Foreign Office could be seen in Antonov's attitude—Czechoslovakia was to be in the orbit of the Soviet Union and Czech gratitude to America for the liberation of her capital was not part of the program." (Op. cit., p. 159.)

bring—was left to the Russians. Even so, the Red Army was unable to penetrate the German defences in Eastern Bohemia until the general capitulation of the Wehrmacht had taken place.

This came about early on the morning of May 7th at Eisenhower's H.Q. in Rheims in the presence of representatives of the United States, Great Britain, the Soviet Union and France. There at last, Jodl and von Friedeburg, acting for Doenitz, signed an instrument which provided for the unconditional surrender of all German forces on all fronts.

Having signed, Jodl rose stiffly and said in English, " I want to say a word," and, proceeding in German, declared: " With this signature the German people and the German armed forces are for better or worse delivered into the victor's hands. . . . In this hour I can only express the hope that the victor will treat them with generosity." There was no reply.

The war in Europe ended at midnight on May 8th–9th. During the next few days, while the capitals and hamlets of the countries which had been locked so long in the struggle with Nazi Germany rang with the cheers of victory and the tumult of rejoicing, there was little thought for the future and what it held. Above the ferment the voice of wisdom and of foresight was hardly heard, for it proclaimed a warning which few were inclined to heed in the hour of triumph and relief. As so often before it was the voice of Winston Churchill. From London on May 13th, 1945, five years almost to the day since he became the King's First Minister, Churchill spoke of the task ahead. " On the continent of Europe," he said, " we have yet to make sure that the simple and honourable purposes for which we entered the war are not brushed aside or overlooked in the months following our success and that the words ' freedom,' ' democracy ' and ' liberation ' are not distorted from their true meaning as we have understood them. There would be little use in punishing the Hitlerites for their crimes, if law and justice did not rule, and if totalitarian or police governments were to take the place of the German invaders. . . . It is the victors who must search their hearts in their glowing hours, and be worthy by their nobility of the immense forces that they wield."

# CONCLUSION

ON September 3rd, 1939, when the British Government declared war on Germany, it acted in fulfilment of its pledge to Poland and in accordance with its traditional policy—temporarily abandoned a year earlier—of upholding the rights of small nations and maintaining the balance of power on the Continent. On May 8th, 1945, when the war in Europe ended, Poland was in the grip of another alien dictator and the balance of power was as dangerously distorted as it had been five years earlier, for Berlin, Prague and Vienna, as well as every capital in Eastern Europe, were again in the possession of a single power. As yet the full significance of this distortion was not widely appreciated by the people, or the governments, of the United States and the British Commonwealth, but there was a growing uneasiness about the future of Poland. Within the next few months the Polish question was to provide the test both of their ability to establish the kind of Europe they had fought for, and of Russia's readiness to co-operate with them in the settlement of post-war problems by international agreement.

Since the discussions in Moscow in March there had been no progress towards the reorganisation of the Provisional Polish Government " on a more democratic basis," as had been agreed at Yalta. Not only had Molotov persisted in his refusal to accept the nominees proposed by the British and American ambassadors, but, more disturbing, sixteen leaders of the Polish Underground, after being promised safe conduct to Moscow for consultation, had been arrested by the Soviet authorities in Poland on charges of espionage. When this became known in Washington, Truman sent Hopkins on a special mission to the Kremlin in the hope of ending the Polish impasse, but Stalin refused to release the arrested men and the most he would agree was that, of the eighteen or twenty posts in the Lublin Government, " four or five . . . could be given to representatives of other groups." When Hopkins asked that certain " fundamental rights," such as freedom of speech and assembly, should be granted to all non-Fascist parties in Poland, Stalin answered that these freedoms could " only be applied in full in peacetime and even then with certain limitations."[1] Although the compromise that Stalin agreed to

[1]Sherwood (op. cit., pp. 885 ff.) quotes the texts of Hopkins's reports on these discussions.

make hardly fulfilled the provisions of the Yalta Agreement, Britain and America carried out their part of the compact by granting the ' new ' government diplomatic recognition. Not content with this, Stalin carried his unilateral settlement of the Polish problem a stage further. When the ' Big Three ' met at Potsdam in mid-July to discuss the post-war settlement of Europe, Churchill and Truman were confronted with a *fait accompli* with regard to Poland's western frontier. Without so much as consulting London or Washington, Stalin had authorised the Polish Government to take over the administration of German territory as far as the rivers Oder and Neisse, the line which the President and the Prime Minister had always refused to recognise. At Potsdam the Western Powers were able to insist that Stalin must subscribe to a joint declaration that " the final delimitation of the western frontier of Poland should await the peace settlement," but the Poles remained in occupation. Moreover, with the aid of the Red Army they proceeded to expel most of the seven million Germans remaining in the disputed territory.

Thus the Polish question was ' settled ' by Stalin in his own way and to his own satisfaction, regardless of his solemn agreements. The pattern of Poland was repeated elsewhere in Eastern Europe as the states the Red Army had liberated were converted into Soviet satellites ruled by Communist minorities. The history of the next few years was to show that Communist Russia had become the heir of Nazi Germany in Central and Eastern Europe; that although one tyrannical régime had been overthrown, another—as oppressive and as formidable—had taken its place; and that the Western democracies, for all their sacrifices, had succeeded in rolling back the tide of totalitarianism only from the Rhine to the Elbe. The struggle for Europe was not yet over; it had merely entered on a new phase with a new protagonist, more dangerous perhaps than the old because less reckless and more calculating.

On December 4th, 1941, when the Germans were already in the western suburbs of Moscow, Stalin gave a lavish dinner at the Kremlin to the Polish Prime Minister, General Sikorski. " At the height of the party," says Mikolajczyk, " when Sikorski believed he had found some mellowness in the man, Stalin turned to him, and said: ' Now we will talk about the frontier between Poland and Russia.' "[1]

Thus, in defeat as in victory, Stalin kept his post-war political objectives steadily in view. As Russia's fortunes fluctuated, his tactics varied, but whether he was blunt or oblique, co-operative or intransigent, the long-term purpose of his grand strategy remained constant. The overwhelming verdict of the evidence is that from the outset he was determined to exploit the situation created by the Second World War in

[1]Mikolajczyk, op. cit., p. 25. Mikolajczyk was then a member of Sikorski's Cabinet.

order to advance Russia's imperial ambitions. Although the Soviet design for the domination of Eastern Europe did not find fulfilment until the end of the war, it was implicit in the discussions with Roosevelt and Churchill at Yalta in 1945, just as it had been in the negotiations with Hitler and Ribbentrop in Berlin in 1940. There is no reason to believe that the aggressive and acquisitive actions of the Russians in Europe immediately following the defeat of Germany were forced upon Stalin as reactions in self-defence, though he may well have regarded them as such. What had changed by this time was not Anglo-American policy or Russian aims, but the nature and scope of Stalin's opportunity. The outcome of the war gave him the position and the power to carry out designs of long standing, unrestrained by the obligations of his wartime alliance or, until 1948, by the fear of Western counter-measures.

During an after-dinner conversation at Yalta Stalin explained that he would not have entered into a Non-Aggression Pact with Hitler in 1939, if it had not been for the Munich Agreement of the previous year. This agreement, and Russia's exclusion from the discussions which led to it, were interpreted in the Kremlin as a deliberate attempt by Britain and France to turn Hitler eastward into conflict with the Soviet Union. In signing the Pact on the eve of war Stalin believed he had neatly turned the tables on Chamberlain and had ensured that Germany and the Western democracies would become locked in another war of attrition which would leave Europe so exhausted that it would be vulnerable to Communist penetration. When the sudden collapse of France rendered the Soviet calculations false, Stalin, having already acquired Eastern Poland, sought to make himself more secure by absorbing the little Baltic States and Rumania's northern provinces. These moves naturally provoked suspicion and hostility in Germany, but Stalin was not deterred. In November 1940, during Molotov's visit to Berlin, it became quite clear that Stalin had a great and abiding interest in the Balkans and that he would not acquiesce in the destruction of Britain unless the Soviet Union were guaranteed free access to the Mediterranean and undisputed control of Middle East oil. When he resisted Hitler's demands and set a high price on Soviet co-operation, Stalin must have known that he was courting war, yet he still hoped to avoid it and he spurned Churchill's friendly overtures.

By December 1941 the structure of Stalin's policy lay in ruins. The territory and the time he had gained by his Pact with Hitler had availed him little. If the Germans were within sight of the Kremlin and if Russia was now bearing almost the full onslaught of the Wehrmacht's power, Stalin had no one to blame but himself. Yet even in these straits he sought to turn his immediate military weakness to ultimate political advantage. He knew that both Britain and the United States were seriously concerned lest he should again come to terms with Germany and thus leave Hitler in indisputable command of Europe. Accordingly, when Eden visited Moscow that December to prepare the way for a treaty of alliance between Britain and the Soviet Union, he was confronted with a categorical demand that Britain should recognise Russia's frontiers as they had been at the start of the German invasion. Since this meant acknowledging Russia's title to parts of Finland, all the little Baltic States, Eastern Poland and Northern Rumania, Eden demurred and his stand was supported by both the Prime Minister and the President.

During the first three months of 1942, however, the serious decline in the world situation of the Allied Powers induced Churchill to modify his attitude. He advised Roosevelt that if the Soviet claims were not recognised, there was " no guarantee that Russia would not make a separate peace,"[1] and in a further message said: " The increasing gravity of the war has led me to feel that the principles of the Atlantic Charter ought not to be construed so as to deny Russia the frontiers she occupied when Germany attacked her."[2] The Prime Minister went on to ask the President to approve the proposed treaty, including the territorial clauses. Roosevelt refused and, though Molotov battled hard for these clauses when he came to London in May 1942, he eventually signed a treaty which contained no territorial provisions whatever. Thus the first Soviet attempt to obtain wartime acknowledgment of its post-war claims was foiled.

After this rebuff Stalin changed his tactics. During the next eighteen months these claims were never mentioned by Stalin or Molotov, though they let it be known through diplomatic channels that their views were unaltered. At the same time the threat of a separate peace was kept alive, with the particular object, it seems, of making sure that the Western Allies did not leave Russia and Germany to wage a campaign of mutual exhaustion. And, when no Second Front was opened in the West in 1943, Stalin showed his chagrin by recalling his ambassadors from London and Washington.[3]

At Teheran there was no discussion of Russia's territorial interests during any of the plenary sessions, and, when Churchill raised the issue one evening over dinner, Stalin answered, " There is no need to speak now about any Soviet desires, but when the time comes we will speak." Clearly, he did not intend to speak until he had strengthened his hand by action. His purpose at Teheran was not to seek from Roosevelt and

---

[1]Hull, op. cit., p. 1172.

[2]Churchill, op. cit., Vol. IV, p. 293. This message was sent on March 7th, 1942.

[3]This incident did not pass unnoticed by Hitler. On August 9th, 1943, after telling Doenitz of the withdrawal of Maisky and Litvinov, the Führer commented: " The war aims of Moscow . . . have caused the British to sit up and listen. . . . There is danger of an expansion of Russian power into the heart of Europe. . . . The British entered the war in order to preserve the ' balance of power ' in Europe but Russia has awakened and . . . developed into a great power which constitutes more of a menace than in the past." Conflict between the war aims of Britain and Russia was inevitable, and therefore, said Hitler, " even though to-day the Anglo-Saxons are still determined to annihilate us, favourable political developments are by no means impossible in the future." (Führer Naval Conferences.)

Churchill political recognition of his claims, but to create the strategic situation that would enable him to enforce those claims whether they liked it or not. He strove, therefore, to make certain that Anglo-American military power was so employed that it would contribute materially to Germany's defeat without interfering with the achievement of Russia's ambitions. This objective was gained when Stalin succeeded in insisting that the main offensive effort of the Western Allies should be directed through France and that they should undertake no major operations in the Balkans, the zone of Soviet aspirations.

By the time the ' Big Three ' met again at Yalta the Red Army was in command of all Eastern Europe except Greece. The fate of the Baltic states was not discussed. Stalin enforced his demand to Eastern Poland, including the Lwow Province, and when he could not secure his way about Poland's western frontiers he avoided any commitment and left that point to be settled by his own unilateral action. He accepted Roosevelt's resounding Declaration on Liberated Europe, but yielded nothing in doing so, since he could afford to ignore it now that his troops were in full possession of Rumania, Bulgaria and Hungary.

In strategy, as in diplomacy, Stalin's policy was always in tune with his post-war ambitions. Once military victory was assured, Stalin was less interested in bringing about Hitler's early downfall than he was in securing for the Soviet Union a commanding position in the heart of Europe. Although the timing of his various offensives in the last nine months of the war may have been governed very largely by tactical and logistic considerations, it is surprising how clearly these offensives fitted into the strategic pattern most likely to secure his political objectives. After reaching Warsaw, he concentrated on the drive up the Danube Valley through Bucharest and Belgrade to Budapest. Having thus gained control of the Balkans, he proceeded to complete the conquest of Poland by advancing from the Vistula to the Oder and then, though Berlin lay within his grasp, he turned his main attention to the capture of Vienna. The attack on the German capital was not resumed until it was in danger of being taken by the Americans. Finally, when the Red Army was unable to break through to Prague, Stalin bluffed Eisenhower into restraining the Allied advance so that Russia could enjoy the military honour and political advantage of liberating this capital also.[1]

When the Second World War ended, therefore, of all the major political objectives which Stalin had sought to gain in Europe—either from Hitler or from Roosevelt and Churchill—the only one which had been denied him was control of the Black Sea Straits. The failure to secure access to warm-water ports in the Mediterranean represented the thwarting of one of Russia's traditional aims, but this was more than offset by the tremendous territorial gains she had made in Central and

[1] It was nearly three years before Stalin was able to exploit this last advantage, but the triumph of the Czech Communists in the *coup* of February 1948 had its origin in the fact that Prague was liberated by the Russians not the Americans.

Eastern Europe. Since August 1939 the western frontiers of her power had been advanced 600 miles to the south-west, from the Dniester to the Adriatic, and 750 miles to the west, from the Pripet Marshes to the Thuringerwald, where the border of the Soviet Zone of Occupation ran within a hundred miles of the Rhine. With Germany destroyed, Britain and France exhausted, and the United States about to retire from active participation in European affairs, Russia could afford to go her own way, disregarding both the protests of her Allies and the provisions of the Yalta Agreement and the United Nations Charter.

There may have been a time when Stalin was prepared—as both Roosevelt and Churchill thought—to co-operate with the Western Allies on a friendly basis for the maintenance of post-war peace, but the records of the various conferences make it quite plain that the Soviet leaders never placed any great trust in international pacts or organisations. In November 1940, when Ribbentrop presented the Führer's offer of a Four-Power Alliance for the division of the world, Molotov replied that " paper agreements would not suffice for the Soviet Union; rather she would have to insist on effective guarantees for her security." By " effective guarantees " Molotov meant physical possession of strategic areas related to Russia's defence. At Yalta, although Stalin never expressed himself so bluntly, the same point was implied. He agreed to join the United Nations—very much on Roosevelt's terms—but at the same time he expected to be given a free hand in what he regarded as Russia's proper sphere of influence, and especially in Poland.

In Stalin's mind this became the test of Anglo-American sincerity. Roosevelt and Churchill had both declared that they would not tolerate the establishment in Poland, or any other country on Russia's borders, of a government hostile to the Soviet Union. But they had also insisted upon " free and unfettered elections " with a secret ballot and universal suffrage. Stalin knew that these two principles were mutually exclusive, since any free election in any of the states of Eastern Europe would be certain to result in the return of a non-Communist Government suspicious of, if not openly antagonistic to, the Soviet Union. Consequently, in the months following Yalta when the American and British Governments made an issue of " free elections " in the western sense, Stalin not unnaturally concluded that their real objective all along had been to set up a *cordon sanitaire* which would curtail his sphere of influence.

When the Polish question was discussed at Yalta, Potsdam and innumerable other conferences, Stalin persistently stressed the fact that Russia must have a ' friendly ' Government in Warsaw and that the Poles must be strong enough to hold the corridor by which the Germans had so often invaded Russia. While it was only natural that Stalin should be concerned about the security of his country, the treatment which Poland has received at the hands of the Soviet Union since the war indicates that Stalin's real concern was not security but expansion. For him Poland was the gateway *to* the West. Unless he were to control

Poland, he would not have free access to Central Europe, and he needed to dominate Central Europe, and especially the Bohemian Mountains in order to protect not the Soviet Union but her conquests in the Balkans. He was clearly determined to make certain that Russia secured for herself the fruits of victory. And why not? It was for these that she had fought.

In the triumph of the Soviet Union there was an element of the inevitable. Having become involved in war through German aggression twice in one generation, the peoples of Britain, America and Western Europe were resolved that Germany's military power must be broken for ever and that her people must be made to realise that ' agression does not pay.' This resolve was strengthened in the closing years of the war when it became known that throughout the Occupied Countries the Nazis had pursued a policy of plunder and murder. At the same time in the Anglo-Saxon countries there was a tremendous upsurge of sympathy and good-will towards the Soviet Union in recognition of the Red Army's heroic resistance. Stalin was trusted and admired (the appelation ' Uncle Joe ' was a mark of approval), for it was widely believed that, whatever the past excesses of his régime, he was genuinely on the side of progress and democracy in the struggle against reaction and tyranny. By and large Western opinion was almost as strongly 'pro-Russian as it was anti-German, with the result that, even if they had been inclined to do so, the British and American Governments could not have won public support for any policy which was designed to keep Russia in check or which provided for anything less than the extirpation of German militarism.

While this is true, it is difficult to escape the conclusion that the Casablanca demand for ' Unconditional Surrender ' was both unnecessary and unwise. Admittedly, Hitler always intended to fight on, as he once said, " until five past midnight," but the insistence on ' Unconditional Surrender '—coupled with the Morgenthau Plan and the indiscriminate bombing of cities—ensured that the Wehrmacht and the German people would fight on with him. The Casablanca decision would have been less harmful to the Allied cause if Roosevelt had followed Stalin's example and had drawn a clear distinction between the Nazis and the German people. This would have aided the activities of the anti-Nazi Opposition and might have enabled them to win such support that they could have achieved something more than an abortive *attentat*. In the event, however, the Western Powers gratuitously curtailed their own freedom of diplomatic action in relation both to their adversaries and their allies. Most important of all, the carrying out of Roosevelt's principle ensured that the war against Germany would continue beyond the stage of military decision to the point of political collapse, and would not end until the Russian and Anglo-American armies met in the heart of the Continent.

Although he subscribed to it publicly, Stalin privately doubted the wisdom of the President's policy, and he said so at Teheran; yet it turned out to his peculiar advantage in two ways. On the one hand, the added destruction necessary to enforce ' Unconditional Surrender ' increased the ' proletarianisation ' of the people of Germany and Central Europe and thus made them more susceptible to Communist influence. On the other, the process of continued enforcement by armies of occupation meant that the Red Army, having advanced to the Elbe, would have a lawful reason for staying there and for maintaining what would amount to occupation forces in the countries through which its supply lines ran.

The ' Unconditional Surrender ' formula, though the President's brain-child, was the natural result of the American determination to wage the war to absolute victory without regard to the political consequences. Roosevelt certainly had noble and unselfish political aims—the winning of Russia's friendship and the setting up of a United Nations Organisation which would preserve peace and enforce throughout the world the principles of the Atlantic Charter. Carried away by this idealistic vision and convinced of his own ability to ' handle ' Stalin, Roosevelt failed to foresee that the immediate political situation arising out of the war might thwart the fulfilment of his ultimate political dream. The success of his policy really depended on his ability to maintain by personal contact over the conference table the spirit of ' Big Three ' co-operation which, he believed, he had established at Teheran and maintained at Yalta. But Roosevelt seems to have made no allowance for the possibility that one or more of the three leaders might be removed from the scene by death or political defeat. As it happened, he himself suffered the first of these fates and Churchill the second before the world struggle ended.

Roosevelt's death revealed the gap between his hopes and the realities of the situation, but it did not create that gap. This had been created already by his failure—and that of his Chiefs of Staff—to take account of post-war political factors in the determination of Allied strategy. That failure, the cause of so much of Europe's present suffering, had its origin partly in the immaturity of the Americans and partly in their history. At the risk of over-simplification, it may be said that the traditional attitude of the people of the United States to the recurrent conflicts of Europe is that war as a means of national policy is morally wrong. Consequently, the United States, if driven to war in self-defence or to uphold the right, should seek no national advantage or aggrandisement. Her sole purpose should be to bring about the defeat and punishment of the aggressor. Her aim should be Victory, nothing else. Since America fights for no political objective, except peace, no political directives should be given to American commanders in the field. They should be completely free to determine their strategy on military grounds alone, and the supreme military consideration is to bring hostilities to an end. To pursue a political aim is to practise Imperialism.

This was the doctrine applied by Marshall and his colleagues in the conduct of the war against Germany, although, with an ambivalence not uncharacteristic of the American people, it was not always applied in relation to the war against Japan. In the last eighteen months of the European conflict when Churchill became increasingly alarmed about Soviet policy, he sought to persuade the Americans that the military strength of the Western Allies should be employed in a manner calculated to achieve the double purpose of defeating Germany and preventing the Soviet Union from becoming too powerful. Only in Greece and Denmark was he successful, and in the former case his action provoked a public rebuke from Roosevelt's Secretary of State. Elsewhere he was repeatedly baulked by American policy which stood on the twin pillars of Roosevelt's belief that Stalin had no aggressive ambitions and Marshall's determination to concentrate on victory in the field.

The purely military attitude of the American Chiefs of Staff, combined with Marshall's predilection for the direct approach, resulted in the main Anglo-American effort being devoted to the assault on Germany from the West, and in the neglect of opportunities which developed in the Mediterranean and the Balkans. From the point of view of post-war Europe the most unfortunate manifestation of Marshall's non-political strategy was the curtailment of the offensive in Italy in the summer of 1944 in order to carry out the invasion of Southern France. Because of this, the Allied drive for Vienna was halted, and the Red Army was given a clear road into South-Eastern Europe. In the following year, when the fate of Central Europe was at issue, American forces which might have gone into both Berlin and Prague were held back and diverted to an objective of no political consequence—the National Redoubt. To the very end, Marshall maintained the view that " the single objective should be quick and complete victory."

The history of Europe reveals only too sharply the unhappy consequences of the policy which was pursued by the Americans and, until late in the war, by the British as well. Writing in 1941, Liddell Hart outlined these consequences in a statement which reads now like a prophecy:

> If you concentrate exclusively on victory, with no thought for the after-effect, you may be too exhausted to profit by the peace, while it is almost certain that the peace will be a bad one, containing the germs of another war. This is a lesson supported by abundant experience. The risks become greater still in any war that is waged by a coalition, for in such a case a too complete victory inevitably complicates the problem of making a just and wise peace settlement. Where there is no longer the counter-balance of an opposing force to control the appetites of the victors, there is no check on the conflict

of views and interests between the parties to the alliance. The divergence is then apt to become so acute as to turn the comradeship of common danger into the hostility of mutual dissatisfaction—so that the ally of one war becomes the enemy in the next.[1]

The two most serious miscalculations of the Second World War both concerned the Soviet Union: Hitler's miscalculation of Russia's military strength, and Roosevelt's miscalculation of Russia's political ambition. It was these two errors of judgment which gave Stalin the opportunity of establishing the Soviet Union as the dominant power in Europe. It is clear now that the Western democracies cannot afford to make another miscalculation about Russia's military power or political intentions. A third mistake might well be fatal to Western civilisation. It is equally clear that, even though Stalin may have no intention of precipitating another world war, there is not likely to be any lessening of the tension in Europe or Asia.

Nevertheless, the course of the wartime negotiations with the Soviet Union—whether conducted by the United States and Britain or by Germany—shows plainly that the present Russian rulers, while relentless in pursuit of what they believe to be Soviet interests, are respecters of strength. Concessions made as gestures of good-will were invariably interpreted by Stalin and Molotov as evidence of weakness and served only to encourage them to drive a harder bargain—witness the development of Stalin's demands during the discussions about his entry into the war against Japan, and his handling of the Polish problem. Over the last decade and more the only policy that has proved effective in dealings with the Kremlin has been firmness in diplomacy backed by military strength: a combination of patience and power. This, it seems, must be the policy of the countries now associated in the North Atlantic Alliance.

The necessary patience may be provided by Britain and her Continental neighbours, for they, being in the front line, are acutely aware of the danger of provoking a Third World War. The necessary power, however, must come from across the Atlantic. The balance of power in Europe having been destroyed, peace can be preserved only by the intervention of the United States to redress the balance. If the American people to-day are prepared to undertake that responsibility it is chiefly because Franklin Roosevelt led them out of Isolation into recognition of their international obligations and their new role of world leadership. It is Churchill's opinion—and few will wish to quarrel with his judgment[2]—that " in Roosevelt's life and by his actions he changed, he altered decisively and permanently the social axis, the moral axis, of

[1]Liddell Hart, *The Strategy of Indirect Approach*. p. 170.
[2]This tribute was paid at a dinner of The Pilgrim's Society on April 12th, 1948.

mankind by involving the New World inexorably and irrevocably in the fortunes of the Old. His life must therefore be regarded as one of the commanding events in human destiny."

The increasingly heavy international burdens which the American people have accepted since the war (involving the New World yet more closely in the fortunes of the Old) have devolved upon them largely as a result of the political and military mistakes of their wartime leaders, and especially Roosevelt, Marshall and Eisenhower, but these mistakes had to be made. The Americans had to find out for themselves that to strive for victory alone is not enough and that the balance of power must be the basis of peace. They had to learn from their own experience the difficulty of dealing with the Russians. They had to extend the hand of friendship and have it spurned. It is arguable that the Russians to-day would be difficult and dangerous no matter what policy had been adopted by the Western Powers during the war, but it is fortunate for the future of Europe that the policy which miscarried was American rather than British in origin. In the years following the war Truman's policy of firmness and preparedness—and of generous economic and military aid to Europe—would hardly have commanded such wide public support in the United States, if Roosevelt had not so diligently and sincerely sought to win the trust and co-operation of Stalin and the Soviet Union.

This was an essential stage in the emergence of the United States to her present world position, for during the decade between 1940 and 1950, when the American people became so deeply involved in the struggle for Europe, they discovered once again the truth of the words that Tom Paine had written on a drumhead by a camp fire in 1776:

*Tyranny, like hell, is not easily conquered.*

# A NOTE ON SOURCES

# A NOTE ON SOURCES

ONE OF the few favourable consequences of the Allied insistence upon the
' Unconditional Surrender ' of Germany was that a very substantial part of the
records of the German Government, and especially those of the High Command,
the Foreign Office and the Ministry of Armaments and War Production, fell into
Allied hands, and that the surviving political and military leaders of the Third
Reich became available for interrogation by Allied Intelligence officers and
historians, and, in certain cases, for trial before Allied courts. The Germans are
meticulous keepers of records, and during the Second World War they prepared
and preserved even the documentary evidence of their crimes against humanity.
The daily destruction of Nazi victims at the Mauthausen Concentration Camp
was recorded in seven volumes bound in red leather handsomely tooled. In these
volumes were recorded the name, sex, age, nationality, ' camp-number,' ' death-
number ' and cause of death of the 35,318 men, women and children who were
exterminated at Mauthausen in five years. The entries for March 19th, 1945
show that on this day 203 people were sent to death. " They were assigned,"
said one of the Allied Prosecutors at Nuremberg, " serial numbers from 8,390
to 8,593. The names of the dead are all carefully listed. . . . The victims are
all recorded as having died of the same ailment, heart failure. They died at brief
intervals. They died in alphabetical order."

The task of sorting, indexing and translating records preserved in such detail
might have been delayed for years but for the incentive provided by the necessity
of assembling evidence for the Trial of the Major German War Criminals which
began at Nuremberg in November 1945. During the next nine months a mass of
documentary material was examined in open court in conditions which gave the
defendants and their counsel the opportunity of challenging its validity. With
remarkably few exceptions, the documents presented at Nuremberg went unchallenged, at least so far as their intrinsic validity was concerned, with the
result that thousands of authenticated State Papers, which in normal circumstances would have remained secret for a generation or more, were made public
within fifteen months of the end of the war. Substantial extracts from the more
important Nuremberg Documents appear in the *Proceedings* of the Trial published
by His Majesty's Stationery Office and the full texts of these, and of certain other
documents assembled for but not submitted in evidence at this trial, have now

been released by the U.S. Government Printing Office in a series of volumes entitled *Nazi Conspiracy and Aggression*.

On behalf of the B.B.C. I covered the most important phases of the Nuremberg Trial and while there acquired my own collection of documents dealing with the strategic, diplomatic and economic aspects of the war. Where I have quoted from these I have identified each document by the serial number given to it by the Allied officials who classified and indexed the German records. In making use of these documents, however, I have not always relied on the translations made at the time, for many of these were hastily prepared and were not accurate. In some cases, therefore, the quotations I have given, having been checked with the original German, are different from the texts which appear in the official *Proceedings*.

Next to the Nuremberg Documents, the most valuable collection of German records so far made public are the minutes of the conferences between Hitler and his Naval Commanders-in-Chief, first Raeder and later Doenitz. These were found at Schloss Tambach, near Coburg, together with the German naval archives for the years 1868-1945, some 60,000 files in all. Edited by Anthony Martienssen and released by the Admiralty in 1947 under the title *Fuehrer Conferences on Naval Affairs*, these minutes, and other records published with them, provide an accurate and detailed account of the higher direction of the German Navy and throw valuable light on Hitler's general conduct of the war. (In footnotes, for the sake of brevity, I have referred to these records as the ' Führer Naval Conferences ' and have identified each extract by the date of the meeting in question.)

Of the other German naval archives captured, I have drawn upon the War Diaries of the Naval Staff and of Naval Group, West, the Operational Diary kept in great detail by Doenitz, and the daily record made by the German naval historian, Vice-Admiral Kurt Assmann. In working on these documents—and especially those dealing with Operation SEALION and the U-boat War—I have had considerable help from Anthony Martiennsen, from Commander H. G. Saunders of the Naval Intelligence Division at the Admiralty, and from Captain D. V. Peyton-Ward, who was Naval Liaison Officer at R.A.F. Coastal Command H.Q. during the war and later became a member of the Historical Section of the Air Ministry.

The economic aspects of the German war effort are as well documented as the naval, for Albert Speer brought with him into captivity an invaluable collection of records from the files of the Ministry of Armaments and War Production. I first saw these papers on May 23rd, 1945 at Flensburg, the last bolt-hole of the Doenitz Administration. That day I was present when the German Government and High Command were taken into custody by British troops. Speer was found shaving in a bedroom at Flensburg Castle and I then took delivery from him and duly handed over to British Counter-Intelligence officers a bulging brief-case which contained the essential statistical records of Speer's Ministry. Subsequently Speer and former members of his staff prepared more than sixty reports on various aspects of the German war economy with particular reference to the impact upon it of Allied bombing. These reports contain some special pleading, but for the most part they are both objective and authoritative, for they are based on the wartime records which Speer and others diligently preserved. Through the kindness of General Eisenhower I was given access to these reports at Frankfurt in October 1945. Since then a team of American investigators, known as the *United States Strategic Bombing Survey*, has made a more exhaustive examination of the German war economy and the effects of bombing, and has produced a series of admirable studies of which I have made liberal use. Their particular value lies in the fact that they were written in the light of a greater range of evidence than the Speer Reports and contain statistical tables which have been checked against other sources. In some cases, however, where ' production ' figures given by the *Survey* are higher than the ' acceptance ' figures found in the records of the High Command, I have preferred to take the total of actual deliveries as the truer index of the productive effort. This is particularly so with regard to aircraft, for it is believed that in their monthly output figures some manufacturers included aircraft which had been re-built at the factory and were not strictly ' new.' In addition to these sources, the minutes of Speer's regular conferences with Hitler on production questions provide further insight into the working of the German war economy and of the extent to which the Führer intervened in its direction.

So far as Hitler's overall conduct of the war is concerned, perhaps the best evidence of his methods of working and processes of reasoning is to be found in the shorthand transcriptions taken down at his staff conferences. These were held twice daily—usually at midday and midnight—and from September 1942 until April 1945 every word spoken was taken down by stenographers. In April 1945 Hitler's own typed copy and some of the shorthand notebooks were sent from Berlin to Berchtesgaden and there, just before the war ended, SS troops set fire to the file. About one per cent of the pages survived the burning and were salvaged by American Counter-Intelligence officers either in typescript or shorthand. Transcriptions dealing with 51 conferences were recovered, a few intact, some very nearly complete but the majority consisting of only a few snatches of conversation. The salvaged material was handed over to certain of the stenographers who had been present at the conferences and the collection of fragments which they prepared amounted to some 800 typed pages. A copy of this collection was made available to me by the United States Army and was translated by Mr. Otto Giles, the head of the German section of the B.B.C.'s Monitoring Service. The task of translating these fragments was very considerable, for there were many gaps in the transcript either because of damage to the source material or because the stenographers had missed what was said at the time.

I have called these documents the ' Führer Conferences ' and have identified each by the number of the fragment and the date of the relevant conference. (Incidentally, the fragments are not numbered in chronological sequence, but in the order in which they were retranscribed by the German stenographers.) In a note on these documents Mr. Giles says:

Their intrinsic value is very great, for they provide a record of the actual words spoken in Hitler's Supreme War Council at some of the most critical stages of the final campaigns. Inevitably, however, there were errors in the original text for the following reasons: some conferences lasted as long as four hours during which the two stenographers present were not relieved;

the subjects discussed were often highly technical, the speakers spoke quickly and not always clearly and Hitler himself used sarcasms which might be interpreted variously as orders, suggestions or comments. The two stenographers compared their notes before typing them out, but they were not allowed to correct what they had taken down, nor were they able to fill in anything they had missed.

The translation of these documents was especially difficult in the case of Hitler himself. What Professor Norman H. Baines says in his preface to *The Speeches of Adolf Hitler, August 1922—August 1939,* applies to the shorthand transcriptions even more strongly: " Colloquialism, diffuseness, sarcasm, not always recognisable as such in the absence of the visible or audible sneer, presented difficulties which could not be overcome in every case."

In spite of these difficulties Mr. Giles produced a translation which is both accurate and vivid, and I am most grateful to him for the great pains he took. Some of the more important passages in these fragments were published in New York in 1950 under the title *Hitler Directs His War.* This book, edited by Dr. Felix Gilbert, has a very useful introduction, but some passages of great historical interest are omitted from the translated text.

Further insight into Hitler's conduct of the war is provided by the diaries of Halder, Goebbels and Ciano, by the texts of 25 letters which passed between Hitler and Mussolini during the years 1940-1943, by the collection of German Foreign Office Documents published by the U.S. State Department and entitled *Nazi-Soviet Relations, 1939-1941,* and, of course, by the numerous directives, minutes of conferences, operational orders and diplomatic notes reproduced in the Nuremberg Documents. These provide a comprehensive and accurate record of the years 1939-1942. For the later years of the war the course of Hitler's policy is not as yet so fully documented, but the available evidence gives the broad pattern and the records kept by Speer and Doenitz fill in the essential details.

For the campaign in North-West Europe from June 1944 to May 1945 the historian is confronted with an almost overwhelming mass of German material in the form of contemporary documents and post-war interrogations. At the time a vast number of enemy orders, reports, strength-returns, signals and letters were captured and published in the Intelligence Summaries of the various Allied H.Q. Of the documentary evidence which became available then or later, the most important—for my purposes—was that concerning the Battle of Normandy. For this phase I have relied chiefly on the following:

(a) The ' Telephone Log ' of the H.Q. of the Seventh German Army, which took the shock of the Allied assault. This log, captured in the Falaise Pocket, records not only actual conversations between commanders at different levels, but also messages which reached this H.Q. from both higher and lower formations. On D-Day, for instance, it contains the hour-by-hour reports from the forward troops on the beaches and the orders which came from Hitler and Rommel.

(b) The ' Tempelhof Papers.' This is the title I have given to a file of reports and signals collected by Colonel Tempelhof, the Chief Operations Officer at Army Group B (Rommel's H.Q.). This file came into Allied hands by circuitous channels. In September 1944—following the attempt on Hitler's life—the German commands in the West were purged, and Tempelhof was ordered to the Eastern Front. On his way there, he stopped at his home and left with his English-born wife a bundle of papers which she was to hand over to British Intelligence after the war. This was done and, when the file had been translated, it was made available to me through the good offices of Field-Marshal Montgomery. The Tempelhof Papers contain the Weekly Reports sent by Army Group B to C.-in-C., West and to the Supreme Command throughout the Battle of France, as well as a number of teleprinter messages which passed between these H.Q. They contain also certain special appreciations prepared by Rommel, Model or von Kluge for Hitler's personal enlightenment. The information in this file has been supplemented by material extracted for me from Rommel's files by his son, Manfred, and by his former Chief of Staff, General Fritz Bayerlein.

Since I have had access to ample documentary sources, I have not been obliged to rely to any great extent on the testimony which so many German commanders have given in reply to Allied interrogators. Nearly all the German generals who were concerned in the Normandy campaign have been expertly interrogated by Captain Liddell Hart or by Major Milton Shulman, who was an Intelligence Officer in the Canadian Army. Both have published the results of their inquiries,[1] but I am fortunate in having been supplied by them with copies of their original notes or reports. These are more detailed than the extracts published. In addition, Liddell Hart has generously made available to me the files of his subsequent correspondence ' with the generals he interrogated. Valuable as this ' interrogatory evidence ' is, I have used it circumspectly unless I have been able to check the post-war testimony with the contemporary documents. Having done this, I have carried out further interrogations on my own account in cases of serious conflict, and have received valuable help, especially from Generals Halder, Blumentritt, Westphal and Bayerlein.

For the chapters which deal with Allied strategy and diplomacy on the highest level, I have relied primarily on American sources, at least for the last two years of the war, for the British official records have not yet been made public. In the first four volumes of *The Second World War*, Mr. Churchill (with the permission of His Majesty's Stationery Office) has published most of the relevant documents that he originated, but for the final phase, when decisions of the greatest importance to post-war Europe were made, very little first-hand evidence has yet been released except in the United States. The most valuable source of documents covering this period is, of course, Robert Sherwood's penetrating and comprehensive biography of Harry L. Hopkins, and I am indebted to him for having given me additional information drawn from his special knowledge of the Hopkins Papers.

The task of evaluating and interpreting the documents released in the United States was greatly facilitated by the advice and information generously given to me by those who worked closely with Mr. Churchill, and particularly by Marshal of the R.A.F. Lord Portal (Chief of the Air Staff from 1940 to 1945), General Lord Ismay (Chief of Staff to the Minister of Defence), Lord Beaverbrook, the

[1] See *The Other Side of the Hill*, by B. H. Liddell Hart, and *Defeat in the West*, by Milton Shulman.

late Field-Marshal Lord Wavell and Major-General Sir Ian Jacob (Military Assistant Secretary to the War Cabinet). To them I gladly express my appreciation.

So far as Allied operations are concerned I have relied very largely on documentary material which has not yet been published and on my own interrogations of the principal commanders and staff officers concerned. During the campaign from Normandy to the Baltic I was in the fortunate position, as a correspondent for the B.B.C., of being an eye-witness of many of the major operations, particularly on the British and Canadian fronts, and I kept a detailed day to day record, much of which could not be published at the time. After the war, in the winter of '45-'46, through the help of General Eisenhower and Field-Marshal Montgomery, I was able to travel freely throughout the American and British Zones of Occupation in Germany, examining the records and interviewing the officers of formations and units in their respective commands. The material gathered then was subsequently supplemented by the examination of official records and reports made available to me by the War Cabinet Historian's office in London, and the historical sections of the British Admiralty and Air Ministry, the Canadian Army and the U.S. Army and Navy. For this assistance I must record my great indebtedness to the following officers and officials: Brigadier H. B. Latham, Col. A. E. Warhurst, Lt.-Col. Graham Jackson and Mr. Brian Melland of the War Cabinet Historian's Office; Rear-Admiral R. M. Bellairs, Lieut.-Commander D. W. Waters, and Mr. G. H. Hurford at the Admiralty; Mr. J. C. Nerney, Squadron-Leader L. A. Jackets, Squadron-Leader J. C. R. Davies and Mr. C. L. James of the Air Ministry; Col. C. P. Stacey, the Chief Canadian War Historian and Lieut.-General G. G. Simonds, now Chief of the Canadian Army General Staff; General J. Lawton Collins, now Chief of Staff of the U.S. Army, and Rear-Admiral J. B. Heffernan, USN, Director of Naval History and Records.

The contemporary historian is in the happy position of being able in many cases to verify and amplify the documentary sources by interrogating the men who were directly or indirectly concerned in their origination. I have done so and I am most grateful to the many British and American officers who have answered my manifold questions or have made available to me personal records and other documents not available in the official archives. Almost every page of this book bears witness to the generous and considerable aid I have received, and although I cannot attempt to name them here, I am under a great obligation to those who have helped me and particularly to: Air Chief Marshall Lord Dowding; Marshal of the R.A.F. Lord Tedder; General W. Bedell Smith, Air Chief Marshal Sir James Robb, General Sir Frederick Morgan, Major-General K. W. D. Strong and Brigadier E. J. Foord (all of SHAEF); Major-General Sir Francis de Guingand, Major-General Sir Miles Graham, Brigadier R. F. K. Belchem, Brigadier E. T. Williams, and the late Col. J. O. Ewart (of 21st Army Group); Air Marshal Sir Philip Wigglesworth, who was Chief of Staff to the late Air Chief Marshal Sir Trafford Leigh-Mallory, and Admiral Sir George Creasy, who was Chief of Staff to the late Admiral Sir Bertram Ramsay; General Sir Miles Dempsey and Col. L. M. Murphy (of Second British Army); the late Lieut.-General George S. Patton, Lieut.-General W. H. Simpson, Major-General Clift Andrus, Major-General H. W. Blakeley, Major-General James M.

Gavin, Major-General C. H. Gerhardt, Major-General R. W. Grow, Brigadier-General E. L. Sibert, and Col. B. A. Dickson (of the U.S. Army); General Sir Evelyn Barker, Lieut.-General G. C. Bucknall, General Sir John Crocker, Lieut.-General Sir Brian Horrocks, General Sir Richard O'Connor (all of whom commanded corps in Second Army); Major-General C. M. Barber, Lieut.-General Sir George Erskine, Lieut.-General Sir Richard Gale, Major-General Sir Percy Hobart, Major-General G. P. B. Roberts, Major-General D. C. Spry, General Sir Ivor Thomas (all of whom commanded divisions in Second Army); Major-General G. W. Lathbury, Major-General J. H. N. Poett, Brigadier K. G. Blackader, Brigadier B. A. Coad, Brigadier J. W. Hackett, Brigadier C. B. C. Harvey, Brigadier S. J. L. Hill, Brigadier W. R. N. Hinde, Col. A. Jolly, Lt.-Col. R. M. P. Garver, Major A. D. Parsons, and Dr. J. M. Stagg.

Finally, I must express my gratitude to the many anonymous staff officers—British, Canadian and American—who prepared the operational studies, historical narratives, and After-Action Reports upon which I have drawn extensively in the preparation of this book.

# BIBLIOGRAPHY

ALLEN, Colonel Robert S. *Lucky Forward : the History of Patton's Third U.S. Army.* New York, Vanguard Press, 1947.

ARNOLD, General H. H. *Global Mission.* London, Hutchinson, 1951.

BADOGLIO, Marshal Pietro. *Italy in the Second World War.* London, Oxford University Press, 1948.

BALDWIN, Hanson W. *Great Mistakes of the War.* London, Redman, 1950.

BELOFF, Max. *The Foreign Policy of Soviet Russia : 1929-1941.* London, Oxford University Press, 1949.

BOLDT, Gerhard. *Die Letzten Tage der Reichskanzlei.* Wien, Rowohlt, 1947.

BRADLEY, General Omar. *A Soldier's Story.* New York, Holt, 1951.

BRERETON, Lieutenant-General Lewis H. *The Brereton Diaries.* New York, Morrow, 1946.

BULLITT, William C. *The Great Globe Itself.* London, Macmillan, 1947.

BUTCHER, Captain Harry C. *My Three Years with Eisenhower.* New York, Simon & Schuster, 1946.

*By Air to Battle : the Official Account of the British First and Sixth Airborne Divisions.* London, H.M.S.O., 1945.

BYRNES, James F. *Speaking Frankly.* London, Heinemann, 1947.

CARROLL, Wallace. *Persuade or Perish.* Boston, Houghton Mifflin, 1948.

*Chronology of the Second World War.* London, Royal Institute of International Affairs, 1947.

CHURCHILL, Winston S. *The Second World War.* London, Cassell, 1948-51. Vols. I-IV.

CIANO, Count Galeazzo. *Ciano's Diary.* London, Heinemann, 1946. (Ed. Malcolm Muggeridge.)

— *Diplomatic Papers.* London, Odhams Press, 1948. (Ed. Malcolm Muggeridge.)

CLARK, General Mark. *Calculated Risk.* London, Harrap, 1951.

CLAY, Major Ewart W. *The Path of the 50th : the Story of the 50th (Northumbrian) Division in the Second World War, 1939-1945.* Aldershot, Gale & Polden, 1950.

COLE, Colonel H. M. ' The Lorraine Campaign,' *United States Army in World War II : the European Theater of Operations.* Washington, Historical Division, Department of the Army, 1950.

COLVIN, Ian. *Chief of Intelligence.* London, Gollancz, 1951.

*Conquer, the Story of the Ninth Army.* Washington, Infantry Journal Press, 1947.

COOPER, R. W. *The Nuremberg Trial.* London, Penguin Books, 1947.

CUNNINGHAM, Admiral of the Fleet Viscount. *A Sailor's Odyssey.* London, Hutchinson, 1951.

DEANE, John R. *The Strange Alliance.* London, Murray, 1947.

EDWARDS, Commander Kenneth. *Operation Neptune.* London, Collins, 1946.

' Effects of Strategic Bombing on the German War Economy,' *The United States Strategic Bombing Survey* (Overall Economic Effects Division). October 31st, 1945.

EISENHOWER, General Dwight D. *Crusade in Europe.* New York, Doubleday, 1948.

— *Report by the Supreme Commander to the Combined Chiefs of Staff on the Operations in Europe of the Allied Expeditionary Force 6 June 1944 to 8 May 1945.* London, H.M.S.O., 1946.

FALLS, Cyril. *The Second World War.* London, Methuen, 1948.

FULLER, Major-General J. F. C. *The Second World War.* London, Eyre & Spottiswoode, 1948.

GAVIN, James M. *Airborne Warfare.* Washington, Combat Forces Press, 1946.

GILBERT, Felix (Ed.). *Hitler Directs his War.* New York, Oxford University Press, 1950.

GISEVIUS, Hans Bernd. *To the Bitter End.* London, Cape, 1948.

GOEBBELS, Dr. Joseph. *The Goebbels Diaries.* London, Hamish Hamilton, 1948.

GUINGAND, Major-General Sir Francis de. *Operation Victory.* London, Hodder & Stoughton, 1947.

HALDER, Franz. *Hitler as War Lord.* London, Putnam, 1950.

HANCOCK, W. K. and GOWING, M. M. *British War Economy.* London, H.M.S.O., 1949.

HARRIS, Marshal of the R.A.F. Sir Arthur. *Bomber Offensive.* London, Collins, 1947.

HASSELL, Ulrich von. *The von Hassell Diaries 1938-1944.* London, Hamish Hamilton, 1948.

*History of the 7th Armoured Division : June 1943-July 1945.* Germany, British Army of the Rhine, 1945.

HULL, Cordell. *Memoirs.* London, Hodder & Stoughton, 1948. 2 Vols.

INGERSOLL, Ralph. *Top Secret.* New York, Harcourt, Brace, 1946.

JACKSON, Lieutenant-Colonel G. S. *Operations of Eighth Corps.* London, St. Clements Press, 1948.

KING, Fleet Admiral Ernest J. *U.S. Navy at War, 1941-1945 : Official Reports to the Secretary of the Navy.* Washington, United States Navy Department, 1946.

LEAHY, Fleet Admiral William D. *I Was There.* London, Gollancz, 1950.

LEIGH-MALLORY, Air Chief Marshal Sir Trafford. ' Air Operations by the Allied Expeditionary Force in N.W. Europe from November 15th, 1943, to September 30th, 1944 ' (Dispatch of November 1944), Fourth Supplement to *The London Gazette*, December 31st, 1946.

*Lettres secrètes échangées par Hitler et Mussolini.* Paris, Éditions Pavois, 1946.

LIDDELL HART, Captain B. H. *The Other Side of the Hill.* London, Cassell, 1951.

MARSHALL, General George C. *The Winning of the War in Europe and the Pacific* (Biennial Report of the C. O. S. of the U.S. Army 1943 to 1945 to the Secretary of War). Published for the U.S. War Department, Simon & Schuster, n. d.

MARSHALL, Colonel S. L. A. *Bastogne : the Story of the First Eight Days.* Washington, Infantry Journal Press, 1946.

MARTIENSSEN, Anthony. *Hitler and his Admirals.* London, Secker & Warburg, 1948.

MARTIN, Lieutenant-General H. G. *The History of the Fifteenth Scottish Division : 1939-1945.* Edinburgh, Blackwood, 1948.

MAUND, Rear-Admiral L. E. H. *Assault from the Sea.* London, Methuen, 1949.

MERRIAM, Robert E. *Dark December.* Chicago, Ziff-Davis, 1947.

MIKOLAJCZYK, Stanislaw. *The Pattern of Soviet Domination.* London, Sampson Low, Marston, 1948.

MONTGOMERY, Field-Marshal Viscount. *El Alamein to the River Sangro.* Germany, British Army of the Rhine, 1946.

— *Normandy to the Baltic.* Germany, British Army of the Rhine, 1946.

— ' Operations in North-West Europe from 6th June 1944 to 5th May 1945 ' (Dispatch of June 1st, 1946), Supplement to *The London Gazette*, September 3rd, 1946.

MORGAN, Lieutenant-General Sir Frederick. *Overture to Overlord.* London, Hodder & Stoughton, 1950.

MORISON, Prof. S. E. *The Battle of the Atlantic.* Boston, Little, Brown, 1947.

MOUNTBATTEN, Vice-Admiral Earl. *Report to the Combined Chiefs of Staff by the Supreme Allied Commander South-East Asia 1943-1945.* London, H.M.S.O., 1951.

MOURIN, Maxime. *Les complots contre Hitler, 1938-1945.* Paris, Éditions Payot, 1948.

MUSSOLINI, Benito. *Memoirs : 1942-1943.* London, Weidenfeld & Nicolson, 1949. (Ed. R. Klibansky.)

*Nazi-Soviet Relations 1939-1941.* U.S. State Department, 1948.

*Nuremberg Trial Proceedings.* London, H.M.S.O., 1946-9. 21 Parts.

*Omaha Beachhead.* Historical Division, U.S. War Department, 1945.

PATTON, General George S. *War As I Knew It.* Boston, Houghton Mifflin, 1947.

PILE, General Sir Frederick. *Ack-Ack : Britain's Defence against Air Attack during the Second World War.* London, Harrap, 1949.

RAMSAY, Admiral Sir Bertram H. ' The Assault Phase of the Normandy Landings ' (Dispatch of October 16th, 1944), Supplement to *The London Gazette*, October 28th, 1947.

RANDEL, Major P. B. *A Short History of 30 Corps in the European Campaign : 1944-1945.* (Limited Edition, 1945.)

RAUSCHNING, Hermann. *Germany's Revolution of Destruction*. London, Heinemann, 1939.
— *Hitler Speaks*. London, Eyre & Spottiswoode, 1939.
ROOSEVELT, Elliott. *As He Saw It*. New York, Duell, Sloan & Pearce, 1946.
ROTHFELS, Hans. *The German Opposition to Hitler*. Hinsdale, Illinois, Regnery, 1948.
SAUNDERS, Hilary St. George. *The Red Beret : the Story of the Parachute Regiment at War, 1940-1945*. London, Joseph, 1950.
SCARFE, Norman. *Assault Division : a History of the 3rd Division*. London, Collins, 1947.
SCHACHT, Dr. Hjalmar. *Account Settled*. London, Weidenfeld & Nicolson, 1949.
SCHLABRENDORFF, Fabian von. *Revolt against Hitler*. London, Eyre & Spottiswoode, 1948. (Ed. Gero v. S. Gaevernitz.)
SCHMIDT, Dr. Paul. *Hitler's Interpreter.* London, Heinemann, 1951.
SEMMLER, Rudolf. *Goebbels—the Man next to Hitler*. London, Westhouse, 1947.
SHERWOOD, Robert E. *Roosevelt and Hopkins : an Intimate History*. New York, Harper, 1948.
SCHULMAN, Milton. *Defeat in the West*. London, Secker & Warburg, 1947.
*Spanish Government and the Axis, The*. U.S. State Department, 1946.
*Spearhead in the West :* Germany, the Third Armored Division, 1945.
SPEIDEL, Hans. *We Defended Normandy*. London, Jenkins, 1951.
STACEY, Colonel C. P. *The Canadian Army : 1939-1945*. Ottawa, King's Printer, 1948.
STETTINIUS, Edward R. *Roosevelt and the Russians : the Yalta Conference*. London, Cape, 1950.
STIMSON, Henry L. and BUNDY, McGeorge. *On Active Service in Peace and War*. New York, Harper, 1948.
*Taurus Pursuant : a History of the 11th Armoured Division*. Germany, British Army of the Rhine, 1945.
*Utah Beach to Cherbourg*. Historical Division, U.S. Department of the Army, 1947.
WHEELER-BENNETT, John W. *Munich*. London, Macmillan, 1948.
WILSON, Field-Marshal Lord. *Eight Years Overseas : 1939-1947*. London, Hutchinson, 1948.
WISKEMANN, Elizabeth. *The Rome-Berlin Axis*. London, Oxford University Press, 1949.

## BOOKS ON THE RUSSIAN CAMPAIGN PUBLISHED SINCE THE AUTHOR'S DEATH

CHUIKOV, V. I. *The Beginning of the Road*. MacGibbon and Kee, 1963.
ERICKSON, J. *The Soviet High Command 1918-1945*. Oxford University Press, 1962.
GOURE, L. *The Siege of Leningrad*. Oxford University Press, 1962.
WERTH, A. *Russia at War*. Barrie and Rockliff, 1964.

# THE HIGH COMMANDS

BRITISH COMMANDS

# THE ALLIED SUPREME COMMAND, 1944

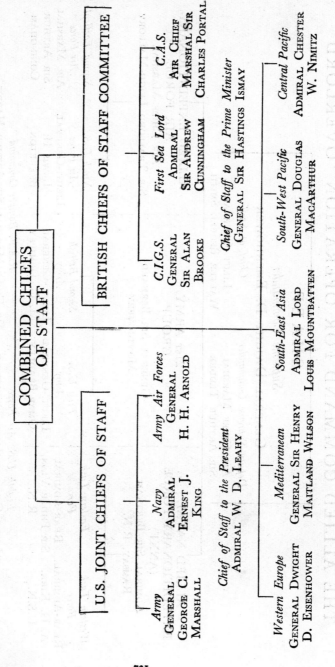

**COMBINED CHIEFS OF STAFF**

**U.S. JOINT CHIEFS OF STAFF**

*Army*
GENERAL GEORGE C. MARSHALL

*Navy*
ADMIRAL ERNEST J. KING

*Army Air Forces*
GENERAL H. H. ARNOLD

*Chief of Staff to the President*
ADMIRAL W. D. LEAHY

*Western Europe*
GENERAL DWIGHT D. EISENHOWER

*Mediterranean*
GENERAL SIR HENRY MAITLAND WILSON

*South-East Asia*
ADMIRAL LORD LOUIS MOUNTBATTEN

**BRITISH CHIEFS OF STAFF COMMITTEE**

*C.I.G.S.*
GENERAL SIR ALAN BROOKE

*First Sea Lord*
ADMIRAL SIR ANDREW CUNNINGHAM

*C.A.S.*
AIR CHIEF MARSHAL SIR CHARLES PORTAL

*Chief of Staff to the Prime Minister*
GENERAL SIR HASTINGS ISMAY

*South-West Pacific*
GENERAL DOUGLAS MACARTHUR

*Central Pacific*
ADMIRAL CHESTER W. NIMITZ

# THE ALLIED COMMAND FOR OPERATION 'OVERLORD'

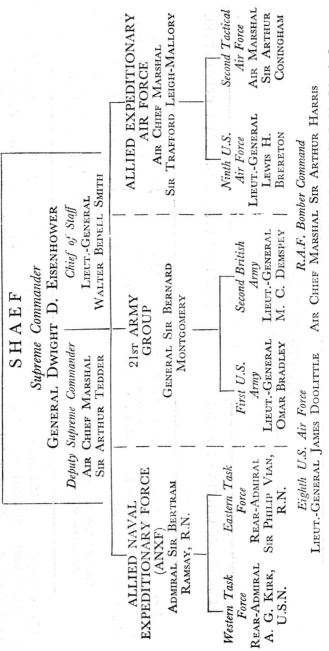

**SHAEF**

*Supreme Commander*
GENERAL DWIGHT D. EISENHOWER

*Deputy Supreme Commander*
AIR CHIEF MARSHAL
SIR ARTHUR TEDDER

*Chief of Staff*
LIEUT.-GENERAL
WALTER BEDELL SMITH

**ALLIED NAVAL EXPEDITIONARY FORCE (ANXF)**
ADMIRAL SIR BERTRAM RAMSAY, R.N.

*Eastern Task Force*
REAR-ADMIRAL SIR PHILIP VIAN, R.N.

*Western Task Force*
REAR-ADMIRAL A. G. KIRK, U.S.N.

**21st ARMY GROUP**
GENERAL SIR BERNARD MONTGOMERY

*Second British Army*
LIEUT.-GENERAL M. C. DEMPSEY

*First U.S. Army*
LIEUT.-GENERAL OMAR BRADLEY

**ALLIED EXPEDITIONARY AIR FORCE**
AIR CHIEF MARSHAL SIR TRAFFORD LEIGH-MALLORY

*Second Tactical Air Force*
AIR MARSHAL SIR ARTHUR CONINGHAM

*Ninth U.S. Air Force*
LIEUT.-GENERAL LEWIS H. BRERETON

*Eighth U.S. Air Force*
LIEUT.-GENERAL JAMES DOOLITTLE

*R.A.F. Bomber Command*
AIR CHIEF MARSHAL SIR ARTHUR HARRIS

*There was no single command for all the Air Forces. The strategic bombers were ultimately responsible to the Combined Chiefs of Staff, but for OVERLORD they were placed under Eisenhower's operational control. The co-ordination of the operations of all Air Forces, strategic and tactical, was entrusted by Eisenhower to Tedder. The U.S. Strategic Air Forces, operating against Germany from Britain and from the Mediterranean, were under the overall command of Lieut.-General Carl Spaatz.*

# THE ALLIED COMMAND IN NORTH-WEST EUROPE, AUTUMN 1944
## (Ground Forces Only)

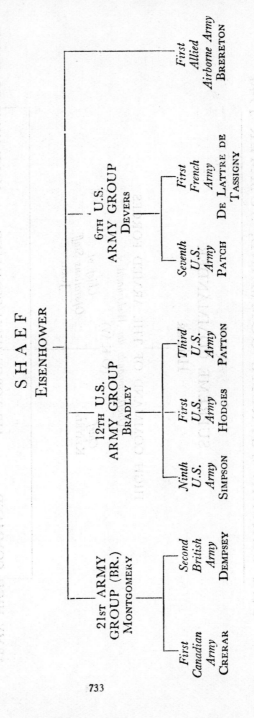

**SHAEF**
EISENHOWER

**21ST ARMY GROUP (BR.)**
MONTGOMERY

First Canadian Army
CRERAR

Second British Army
DEMPSEY

**12TH U.S. ARMY GROUP**
BRADLEY

Ninth U.S. Army
SIMPSON

First U.S. Army
HODGES

Third U.S. Army
PATTON

**6TH U.S. ARMY GROUP**
DEVERS

Seventh U.S. Army
PATCH

First French Army
DE LATTRE DE TASSIGNY

First Allied Airborne Army
BRERETON

# THE GERMAN SUPREME COMMAND, SUMMER 1940

## SUPREME COMMANDER
### HITLER

## HIGH COMMAND OF THE ARMED FORCES
*Oberkommando der Wehrmacht*
### (O K W)

*Chief*
KEITEL

*Chief of
Operations Staff*
JODL

## ARMY HIGH COMMAND
*Oberkommando des Heeres*
### (O K H)

*C.-in-C.*
VON BRAUCHITSCH

*Chief of Staff*
HALDER

## AIR FORCE HIGH COMMAND
*Oberkommando der Luftwaffe*
### (O K L)

*C.-in-C.*
GOERING

*Chief of Staff*
JESCHONNEK

## NAVY HIGH COMMAND
*Oberkommando der Kriegsmarine*
### (O K M)

*C.-in-C.*
RAEDER

*Chief of Staff*
SCHNIEWIND

# THE GERMAN HIGH COMMAND IN THE WEST, SUMMER 1944

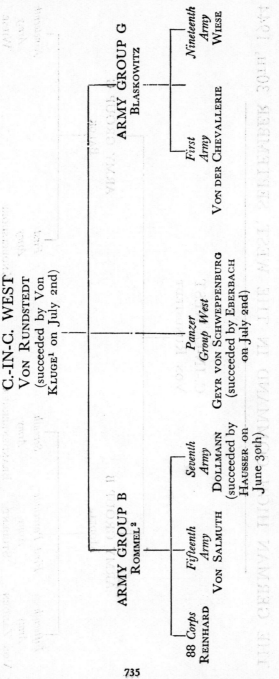

**C.-IN-C. WEST**
VON RUNDSTEDT
(succeeded by Von
KLUGE[1] on July 2nd)

**ARMY GROUP B**
ROMMEL[2]

88 Corps
REINHARD

*Fifteenth
Army*
VON SALMUTH

*Seventh
Army*
DOLLMANN
(succeeded by
HAUSSER on
June 30th)

*Panzer
Group West*
GEYR VON SCHWEPPENBURG
(succeeded by EBERBACH
on July 2nd)

**ARMY GROUP G**
BLASKOWITZ

*First
Army*
VON DER CHEVALLERIE

*Nineteenth
Army*
WIESE

[1]Von Kluge in turn was succeeded by Model on August 17th.
[2]No successor was appointed for Rommel when he was injured on July 17th. Command
of his Army Group was exercised direct by the C.-in-C. West.

735

# THE GERMAN HIGH COMMAND IN THE WEST, SEPTEMBER 30TH, 1944

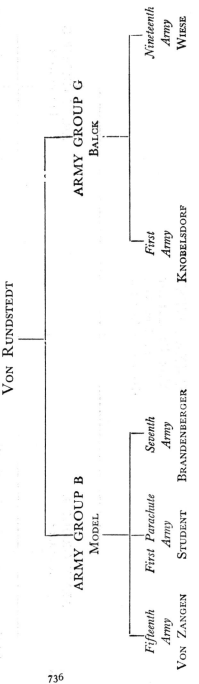

C.-IN-C. WEST
VON RUNDSTEDT

ARMY GROUP B
MODEL

Fifteenth Army
VON ZANGEN

First Parachute Army
STUDENT

Seventh Army
BRANDENBERGER

ARMY GROUP G
BALCK

First Army
KNOBELSDORF

Nineteenth Army
WIESE

# INDEX

# INDEX

Aachen, 459-60, 485-7, 508, 536, 560, 577-9, 587, 593, 596, 600, 608; assault on, 495-7, 531, 538, 540-1, 548, 561, 566-70, 576, 613; Gap, 491, 496, 562

Abbeville, 39, 281

Abwehr (German Counter-Intelligence Service), 167, 188, 217, 366

Adana, 127

Admiralty, British, 19, 33-4, 41-2, 65, 125-6, 175, 182, 223, 316

Africa, North, 60, 66, 69-72, 75, 178, 191, 208; Allied invasion of, 105-15, 124, 188, 227

Air Council, British, 36-7

AIR FORCE, AMERICAN: and bombing of Germany, 53, 155-8, 168, 207-8, 551-3; of Rumanian oilfields, 118, 135, 440; of V-weapon sites, 153-4; in support of Normandy landings, 207-12, 223, 228, 250, 277, 288-90; of Battle of Normandy, 305, 385-6, 390-2, 403, 411, 413, 422-3; of COBRA, 390-4; of TOTALIZE, 411-13; of Ardennes Offensive, 568; of Ardennes Campaign, 603-4
U.S. Strategic Air Forces, 207-8, 551-2
Eighth U.S. Air Force, 153, 156, 211, 355-8, 384, 413, 502, 556
Ninth U.S. Air Force, 212, 215, 250, 290

AIR FORCE, GERMAN, see LUFT-WAFFE

AIR FORCE, ROYAL: pre-war development of, 34-6; in Battle of Britain, 26, 31, 34-55; in support of Battle of Normandy, 303, 318, 340-1, 345, 350-1, 355-9, 361, 364, 385-6, 396, 398, 402-4, 422-3; of TOTALIZE, 411-12; of MARKET GARDEN, 501-2, 506-8, 517, 520, 526-7; of Walcheren Landings, 545-7; of Aachen Offensive, 568; of Ardennes Campaign, 603-4; of Reichswald Offensive, 672; of Rhine Crossing, 681, 683
Bomber Command, 37, 46, 50, 177, 350-1, 641; bombing of Germany, 68-

70, 155-8, 168, 384, 551-6, 699; of V-weapon sites, 153-4, 317-18; in support of Normandy landings, 207-12, 223, 228, 236, 238, 241, 247, 250, 269-70, 276, 288-90
Coastal Command, 46; in support of Normandy landings, 227, 276; attacks on U-boats, 125, 315
Fighter Command, 25, 317; in Battle of Britain, 31-55, 208
Desert Air Force, 340-1
Second Br. Tactical Air Force, 288-90, 340-1, 355-6, 527
No. 11 Group, 43, 45-6, 49-50
No. 83 Group, 506-8

Air Force, Russian, 146

Air Ministry, British, 35, 40, 153

Air Staff, British, 36-7

Airborne forces: plans to use in Normandy, 135, 175, 213, 220, 233-5; briefing of, 219-20; in Battle of Normandy, 233-49, 261-2, 277-80, 286-7, 292, 308; in MARKET GARDEN, 487-9, 498-528; Allied Airborne Army, 668

Aircraft factories, Bombing of: British, 32, 43; German, 135, 158, 441

Aircraft production: British, 34, 40, 42, 46, 54, 148; German, 54, 149, 156-9, 289, 385, 441-3, 551, 555, 615

Airfields: Allied (in Africa), 57; (in Normandy), 338-42, 352, 361, 385; (in Greece), 66; (in Italy), 118, 134-5, 140, 197; English (in Battle of Britain), 43-9, 53; German, 31, 40, 171, 289, 383-4, 443, 502

*Ajax*, H.M.S., 269

Alam Halfa, Battle of, 191, 596

Alamein, Battle of, 106, 111, 191, 279, 340, 535, 605

Albert Canal, 478, 480, 482, 486-8, 516, 545

Alençon, 135, 175, 337, 342, 348, 394, 400, 419; capture of, 415-17

Alexander, Gen. Sir Harold, 178, 449-52, 454, 457, 462, 666-8, 687, 704

737

PROPERTY
KETAB BAZAAR

DALLAS
COMPLETE RESALE & NEW BOOK
PERSIAN LIBRARY
1232 S. WELLS AVENUE, PLANO TEXAS
(972) 1233